Lawrence L Huntley

Substance Abuse
Clinical Problems and Perspectives

Substance Abuse
Clinical Problems and Perspectives

Edited by

Joyce H. Lowinson, M.D.

Clinical Professor of Psychiatry
Director, Division of Substance Abuse
Albert Einstein College of Medicine
Bronx, New York

Pedro Ruiz, M.D.

Professor of Psychiatry
Albert Einstein College of Medicine
Bronx, New York

WILLIAMS & WILKINS
Baltimore/London

Made in the United States of America

Library of Congress Cataloging in Publication Data

Main entry under title:

Substance abuse.

Includes index.
1. Drug abuse. 2. Drug abuse—Treatment. 3. Drug abuse—Social aspects. 4. Drug abuse—United States. I. Lowinson, Joyce H. II. Ruiz, Pedro, 1936–   [DNLM: 1. Drug abuse. 2. Drug abuse—Therapy. WM270 S941]
RC564.S83   362.2′93   80-15546
ISBN 0-683-05210-1

Composed and printed at the
Waverly Press, Inc.
Mt. Royal and Guilford Aves.
Baltimore, Md. 21202, U.S.A.

Foreword

This volume marks a real departure, for it lays out the groundwork of fundamental and applied knowledge for a new field which will rapidly develop in the 1980's. This is a practical and useful resource for medical specialists and medical students in providing a text and comprehensive view of "substance abuse," as well as of the substances abused—their pharmacology, clinical consequences, and treatments. I suspect, however, a decade from now the volume will be a Rosetta stone as historians try to account for the scientific origins which an exciting pace of progress will have eclipsed.

If the book is a template for the future, its uniqueness cannot be appreciated without a perspective on the extent to which knowledge has advanced in the past decade and a half when there was, initially, an epidemic of interest in "drug abuse." As such phenomena began to engage the institutions and children of the "culture-bearing elite," 1965 is a useful watershed against which to appreciate the progress marked by the present array of articles, as well as the paths of future progress that are limned.

How did this field appear 15 years ago? The answer is that the range of addictive behaviors and the popular lay use of drugs altering brain function had captured only fragmented and intermittent attention of the professions; the phenomena were at the periphery of the central foci of medicine and the preclinical sciences. For the clinician, the obtrusive psychiatric and medical complications of alcoholism had long been more or less unwelcome guests in the agenda of professional concerns. The clinical signs of physiological dependence to opiates, sedatives, or alcohol—even when finally perceived in the early 1950's as representing a fundamental biological process—were hardly conceptually related; delirium tremens—"rum fits"—required experimental clinical investigation to be established as a distinct phenomenon, and so too with other withdrawal syndromes. Pharmacological inquiry into these drugs and phenomena was largely aggregated at two select centers and, overall, engaged few clinical or basic science investigators. Only a handful of psychologists had conceived of central nervous system active substances either as tools to investigate the organization of behavior, or their effects as posing problems for basic biobehavioral investigation. Neurochemistry—since the 19th century thrust of Thudicum—was unrecognized as even a topic among leaders in biochemistry or in biochemical texts. Neurobiology was yet to be named. Social, psychological, epidemiological, and genetic studies into the disorders treated within this volume were classic, but rare. Classifications of different patterns of alcohol misuse began to gain focused attention of a few only in the early 1930's. Indeed the text of psychiatry (*The Theory and Practice of Psychiatry*), which Redlich and I issued in 1966, may have been the first to devote full chapters to alcoholism and narcotics addiction. The principles operative in self-help groups or inferred from the natural history of addictive behaviors had not been extrapolated for their possible application in different settings, for the treatment of different settings, or for the treatment of different "drug problems." The discovery of the "chemical brain,"—of the link of specific neurones to specific transmitters—was but a year old. The logic of these discoveries, of synaptic events and their link to brain subsystems relevant to behavior, is only now beginning to be discerned. We have a part of the alphabet, but the rules of syntax are only now beginning to be discerned.

Thus, in meeting the clinical and social problems which the decade of the 1960's posed, we had only a few "experts" in one or another cognate area, and knowledge possibly relevant to these problems was—where present—usually "segregated." Pharmacological expertise was not informed by clinical experience and vice versa; both areas were isolated from ethnology and epidemiology; and social policy, sustained by myth and the special lore of unexamined law enforcement experiences, was isolated from all those scattered sources of information.

The initial task of bridging these gaps was not—conceptually—unfamiliar to some for whom biobehavioral issues were central. But as a few psychiatrists, psychological, social, and biomedical scientists—many drawn from "neuropsychopharmacology"—began to meet the emerging problems and attempt, with others, to stabilize and rearticulate public policy, a sisyphean task was posed. Educating parents and policy makers and the professions as the cycles of denial, discovery, alarm, and blame recur, watching the rediscovery of "drug problems" as new generations of the young emerge, as new media, Congressional, and community leaders encounter the issues, those of us who met the "crises" of the 1960's may not yet grasp how far we have come.

Thus, while public support of the field is fickle, and while we cannot today truly implement all of what we are capable of delivering to patients, this volume documents the evidence that the neurobiology of habitual and entrenched behaviors may contain fundamental knowledge relevant to a wide span of "problems" in psychiatry and clinical medicine. The allure of a specific new molecule will distract others in years to come; public focus will oscillate between perceiving the misuse of substances as a "people problem," or focusing on a particular substance as the vehicle of human evil or frailty. Yet we can now assert that whatever this precise mode of action, it is the use we make of the *effects* of substances in order to implement our purposes that links biology and the social sciences around the topic of substance abuse. At bottom, the regulation of pain and pleasure, and the social and biological processes (and values) entailed in implementing these regulatory tasks, is the exciting fundamental topic underlying this volume. This basic and clinical science focus will, one trusts, be the momentum for advances in the decades ahead.

Daniel X. Freedman, M.D.

Preface

Psychoactive substances have been available for man's use throughout history, and they probably have been misused for an equally long time. However, since World War II, a variety of social forces coupled with the proliferation of psychoactive substances have converged producing a super problem the complexity of which has challenged the most resourceful and committed individuals who have sought solutions. The present generation has been faced with overpopulation, wars and the threat of nuclear world conflict, inflation, unemployment, pollution, the generation gap, and swiftly changing mores, values, and technology. Urbanization and industrial changes have weakened family ties; people have been uprooted from their native cultures. Those with ostensible tenure in the social system begin to question the value of their association. They have begun to lose a sense of confidence in their inner resources. Young people, particularly, have turned in increasing numbers to substances which appear to offer relief from boredom, acceptance by peers, and separation from parental and other authority. The tentativeness of their relationship to what is considered important in the world is increased through the existential character of risk-taking through drugs.

The field of substance abuse has changed markedly since the early 1960's when a handful of scientists, physicians, and others dedicated their lives to exploring ways to help the substance abuser. Some found themselves relegated to secondary roles in their own professions because they chose to work with a stigmatized population viewed as having little equity and no political power in society. Social and political attitudes have evolved since then toward a greater awareness that substance abuse has become an integral part of the American character. Like many chronic medical problems, subject to relapse and remissions, it is complex and intractable to easy solutions. Individuals working directly with victims of substance abuse have experienced a sense of self-deprecation in the face of society's general contempt. Many bemoan the fact that we have made too little progress in the solution of the drug abuse problem.

However, when we review the achievements that have occurred in the short period of two decades in our scientific understanding of substance abuse and the application of that understanding to treatment and rehabilitation, our progress might be seen as remarkable. And those who have remained committed should have a sense of pride that they persisted in working in an apparently hopeless area; indeed, they should be proud and hold their heads high. Our present achievements could not have happened without a changing social commitment on the part of the professions and a readiness of government to support that commitment. The substance abuse problem is now being attacked with skill and dedication by thousands of concerned specialists. While we know a great deal has been achieved, we know much more needs to be done. Where there have been limited successes in some areas in control of the abuse of some substances, the problem has grown out of control with other substances. Out of this constant struggle has come a great deal of understanding of the basic factors involved, and some of our newer techniques and programs for treatment and prevention which show promise. One point stands out: it is not the substances that are of primary importance; it is the individuals involved in their use whom we must seek to help.

The present volume has been forged out of our need for a consolidation of the best knowledge possible for approaching this old, yet new, problem. As we enter a new decade we appear to be on the threshold of making real inroads into the management of this problem, but there still exists in this field considerable confusion, discouragement, and a great many gaps in knowledge. A handicap has been the lack of a comprehensive manual which would bring together the best contemporary thinking on every aspect of this field. This book is, we think, such an instrument. It is intended to bring some order out of the confusion, and to offer hope in place of discouragement.

For this purpose, experts on significant current issues in the field and on each major substance of abuse were invited to share their knowledge and discuss areas of their particular expertise.

Topics examined and discussed include alternative treatment approaches and their applicability, and various approaches to prevention. There is an attempt to resolve some of the controversies currently encountered in the field.

The book consists of 11 parts, the first presenting the background of the problem including the epidemiology of substance abuse. The most recent trends in this area, such as the increase in polydrug abuse, the spread of narcotics to middle-class communities, and the substance abuse patterns in ghetto areas are discussed. Explanations for these phenomena are sought in the section on theories of substance abuse which in large part cuts across the specific substances abused.

The third part of the book consists of an examination of specific substances abused. Recent developments, such as the spreading use of cocaine and the abuse of phencyclidine are examined. Coping strategies are offered. Alcohol is, of course, included, as well as the use of tobacco and caffeine, the latter two of which have not generally been incorporated into the literature on substance abuse.

In Parts 4 and 5, a key focus is relating differential diagnosis and the matching of patient to the most appropriate form of treatment. Treatment programs and modalities and techniques of intervention are also covered in these sections. These include therapeutic communities, methadone maintenance treatment, transcendental meditation, and acupuncture. Religion as a treatment modality is also considered.

Special treatment problems as well as special problems in substance abuse are reviewed in Parts 6 and 7. Issues not frequently found in the literature which seriously interfere with the provision of treatment, such as community opposition to the establishment of treatment centers, are presented, and possible solutions are proposed. The recent concern with patients' rights and confidentiality also receives attention.

A basic premise of this book is that specific groups require specialized treatment. Among these groups are children, adolescents, the elderly, and substance abusers with severe underlying psychopathology. Specialists in the treatment of these groups as well as of various ethnic groups provide their insights.

An integral part of treatment is evaluation, which permits changes in treatment to be made to provide optimal and effective care. This is examined in Part 9. As part of the didactic nature of the book, training of service providers is addressed in Part 10.

Finally, in Part 11, an attempt is made to anticipate and predict some of the developments we can expect with regard to chemical alteration of mood and behavior and measures which might be taken to control the dangers inherent in this method of coping with reality.

The editors will be greatly satisfied if this book proves to be a comprehensive resource text for professionals in this field, and if it accomplishes the goal of integrating our understanding of the substance abuser not just in terms of the substance abused but as a whole person whose differing medical, psychological, and social facets are taken into account. Our hope is that it will be a useful guide to the entire field of substance abuse.

The Editors

Acknowledgments

We are especially grateful to our publisher for its part in the production of this book, and we would like to mention specifically James Sangston, who showed unusual patience, good judgment, and insight into the problem of substance abuse, and Carol Eckhart, who managed the details of production with great care and who was always ready with helpful advice when needed.

We wish to recognize John Langrod for his consistent staff support and his extensive knowledge of literature. The most important of the many individuals who contributed to the work that is this book is Lois Alksne. Mrs. Alksne has been involved in this effort from the beginning of its conceptualization by the editors to its final production as a complete text. Her skills as a behavioral scientist and editor have given endless support to the contributors and editors alike. Mrs. Alksne's extraordinary interpersonal ability and kind prodding helped the work along throughout its period of development.

The Drug Abuse Council, for many years under the guidance of Thomas Bryant, represented a significant force in the growth of an independent scientific approach to the problems of substance abuse in the United States. It was a rich resource for us. Many of the contributors have been consultants, fellows, or staff members of the Council.

Contributors

Harold Alksne, Ph.D.
Assistant Professor of Sociology
C.W. Post College
Greenvale, New York

Lois Alksne, M.A., M.S.
Director of Admissions and Evaluation
Albert Einstein College of Medicine
Substance Abuse Service
Bronx, New York

James B. Bakalar, J.D.
Lecturer in Law
Department of Psychiatry
Harvard Medical School
Boston, Massachusetts

Gene Barnett, Ph.D.
Research Chemist
Research Technology Branch
Division of Research
National Institute on Drug Abuse
Rockville, Maryland

Celia Benney, M.S.S.
Director of Rehabilitation Studies
Altro Institute for Rehabilitation
   Studies, Inc.
New York, New York

Peter B. Bensinger, Esq.
Administrator
Drug Enforcement Administration
Washington, D.C.

D. Vincent Biase, Ph.D.
Director, Research and Development
Daytop Village, Inc.
New York, New York

Bertram J. Black, M.S.W.
Deputy Director for Treatment Services
Director, Division of Rehabilitation
Rockland Research Institute
New York State Office of Mental Health
Professor of Psychiatry (Rehabilitation)
Albert Einstein College of Medicine
Bronx, New York

Jack D. Blaine, M.D.
Research Psychiatrist

Clinical Behavioral Branch
Division of Research
National Institute on Drug Abuse
Rockville, Maryland

Harvey Bluestone, M.D.
Director
Department of Psychiatry
Bronx Lebanon Hospital Center
Bronx, New York

Peter G. Bourne, M.D.
Assistant Secretary General
United Nations Development Programme
(Formerly Special Assistant to the
   President for Health Issues)
Washington, D.C.

Leon Brill, M.S.S.
Formerly Director of the Division of
   Drug Rehabilitation for the
   Commonwealth of Massachusetts
Winchester, Massachusetts

H. Daniel Carpenter
President
National Association on Drug Abuse
   Problems, Inc.
New York, New York

Frances E. Cheek, Ph.D.
Director of Behavioral Modification
Correction Officers Training Academy
New Jersey State Department
   of Corrections
Trenton, New Jersey

Sidney Cohen, M.D.
Clinical Professor of Psychiatry
Center for Health Sciences
University of California at Los Angeles
Los Angeles, California

Daniel R. Cook
Revson Fellow, Columbia University
Addiction Research and Treatment
   Corporation
Brooklyn, New York

Patrick R. Cowlishaw, J.D.
Staff Attorney

Legal Action Center
New York, New York

Paul Cushman, Jr., M.D.
Associate Professor of Pharmacology,
    Medicine and Psychiatry
Medical College of Wisconsin
DePaul Rehabilitation Hospital
Milwaukee, Wisconsin

G. G. De Angelis, Ph.D.
President
Health Care Delivery Services, Inc.
Los Angeles, California

David A. Deitch, Ph.D.
Chief, Substance Abuse Services
University of California
    at San Francisco
Department of Psychiatry
San Francisco General Hospital
Berkeley, California

Gerald A. Deneau, Ph.D.
Research Scientist
Toxicology and Research Laboratory
New York State Division of Substance
    Abuse Services
Brooklyn, New York

Judianne Densen-Gerber, M.D., J.D.
President
Odyssey Institute, Inc.
New York, New York

Sherry Deren, Ph.D.
Research Scientist
New York State Division of Substance
    Abuse Services
New York, New York

Don C. Des Jarlais, Ph.D.
Chief, Evaluation Research
New York State Division of Substance
    Abuse Services
New York, New York

Joan L. Donley, M.S.W.
Department of Psychiatry
Jewish Hospital of Cincinnati
Associate Professor of Psychiatry
University of Cincinnati College
    of Medicine
Cincinnati, Ohio

Joseph Drew, Ph.D.
Department of Political Science

University of the District of Columbia
Washington, D.C.

Loretta P. Finnegan, M.D.
Director of Nurseries; Director
    of Family Center Program
Associate Professor of Pediatrics
Associate Professor of Psychiatry
    and Human Behavior
Thomas Jefferson University
Philadelphia, Pennsylvania

Marc Galanter, M.D.
Associate Professor of Psychiatry
Department of Psychiatry
Albert Einstein College of Medicine
Bronx, New York

Frances R. Gearing, M.D., M.P.H.
Associate Professor of Epidemiology
School of Public Health and
    Administrative Medicine
Columbia University
New York, New York

Angel Gregorio Gómez, M.D.
Department of Addiction Services
Commonwealth of Puerto Rico
Luquillo, Puerto Rico

Efrain Gomez, M.D.
Associate Professor of Psychiatry
Department of Psychiatry
Baylor College of Medicine
Houston, Texas

Robert S. Graham, M.D.
Vice President and Director of Personal
    Concerns Program
Equitable Life Assurance Society of
    the United States
New York, New York

John F. Greden, M.D.
Associate Professor of Psychiatry
Medical Director, Clinical Studies
    Unit, Inpatient Program
Director, Neural and Behavioral
    Sciences
University of Michigan Medical Center
Ann Arbor, Michigan

Robert A. Greenstein, M.D.
Assistant Clinical Professor of
    Psychiatry
Department of Psychiatry
University of Pennsylvania

Medical School
Philadelphia Veterans Administration
   Medical Center
Philadelphia, Pennsylvania

Lester Grinspoon, M.D.
Associate Professor of Psychiatry
Department of Psychiatry
Harvard Medical School
Massachusetts Mental Health Center
Boston, Massachusetts

Gary B. Hirsch, M.S.
Director
Health and Social Systems Area
Pugh-Roberts Associates, Inc.
Cambridge, Massachusetts

Robin Import, J.D.
Washington, D.C.

Jerome H. Jaffe, M.D.
Professor of Clinical Psychiatry
Columbia University
College of Physicians and Surgeons
New York, New York
Associate Chief of Staff for Education
Veterans Administration Medical Center
Newington, Connecticut

Maureen Kanzler, Ph.D.
Assistant Professor of Clinical
   Psychology
Department of Psychiatry
Columbia University
College of Physicians and Surgeons
Research Scientist V
New York State Psychiatric Institute
New York, New York

Seymour R. Kaplan, M.D.
Professor of Psychiatry and
   Community Health
Department of Psychiatry
Director, Fellowship Teaching Program
   for Research and Evaluation of the Delivery of
   Mental Health Services
Albert Einstein College of Medicine
Bronx, New York

Harold M. Kase, Ed.D.
President
Altro Institute for Rehabilitation
   Studies, Inc.
Visiting Lecturer (Rehabilitation)
Albert Einstein College of Medicine
Bronx, New York

Edward Kaufman, M.D.
Associate Professor of
   Psychiatry and Family Medicine
Chief, Psychiatric Services
Director of Family Therapy Section
University of California, Irvine
California College of Medicine
Orange, California

Edward J. Khantzian, M.D.
Associate Professor of Psychiatry
Harvard Medical School
Associate Director, Department
   of Psychiatry
The Cambridge Hospital
Cambridge, Massachusetts

Elizabeth T. Khuri, M.D.
Clinical Assistant Professor of Public Health
Clinical Director of Adolescent
   Development Project
Cornell University Medical Center
New York, New York

Herbert D. Kleber, M.D.
Director, Substance Abuse Treatment Unit
Yale University School of Medicine
Department of Psychiatry
New Haven, Connecticut

Norman R. Klein, Ph.D.
Staff Psychologist
Bronx Lebanon Hospital Center
Bronx, New York

Maurice Korman, Ph.D.
Professor and Chairman
Division of Psychology
Department of Psychiatry
University of Texas Health Science
   Center at Dallas
Dallas, Texas

Alice B. Kornblith, Ph.D.
Research Fellow
Department of Psychiatry
Albert Einstein College of Medicine
Bronx, New York

Mary Jeanne Kreek, M.D.
Senior Research Associate and
   Physician
The Rockefeller University
New York, New York

John Kuehnle, M.D.
Clinical Director

Alcohol and Drug Abuse Research Center
The McLean Hospital
Belmont, Massachusetts

John Langrod, Ph.D.
Director of Clinical Services
Albert Einstein College of Medicine
Substance Abuse Service
Bronx, New York

Arnold Sterne Leff, M.D.
Health Services Director
The Contra Costa County Hospital
Martinez, California

Gilbert Levin, Ph.D.
Professor of Psychiatry
Department of Psychiatry
Albert Einstein College of Medicine
Bronx, New York

Alfred R. Lindesmith, Ph.D.
Professor of Sociology (Emeritus)
Indiana University
Bloomington, Indiana

Douglas Lipton, Ph.D.
Assistant Director of Research and
    Evaluation
New York State Division of Substance
    Abuse Services
New York, New York

Paul Lowinger, M.D.
Associate Clinical Professor of
    Psychiatry
University of California at
    San Francisco
San Francisco, California

Joyce H. Lowinson, M.D.
Clinical Professor of Psychiatry
Director, Division of Substance Abuse
Albert Einstein College of Medicine
Bronx, New York

Paul V. Luisada, M.D.
Chairman, Department of Psychiatry
The Mt. Vernon Hospital
Director, Mt. Vernon Center for
    Community Mental Health
Alexandria, Virginia
Staff Psychiatrist, Area D Community
    Mental Health Center
National Institute of Mental Health
Washington, D.C.

Peter K. Manning, Ph.D.
Professor of Sociology
Departments of Sociology and Psychiatry
Michigan State University
East Lansing, Michigan

Carl Leon McGahee, M.D.
Associate Director
Department of Psychiatry
Bronx Lebanon Hospital Center
Bronx, New York

Father John McVernon
Community Projects Director
National Association on Drug Abuse
    Problems, Inc.
New York, New York

Roger E. Meyer, M.D.
Professor and Chairman
Department of Psychiatry
University of Connecticut Health Center
Farmington, Connecticut

Donald E. Miller, J.D.
Chief Counsel
Drug Enforcement Administration
Washington, D.C.

Marie DiStefano Miller, M.A.
Correction Officers Training Academy
New Jersey State Department of
    Corrections
Trenton, New Jersey

Robert B. Millman, M.D.
Clinical Professor of Public Health
Cornell University Medical Center
New York, New York

Steven M. Mirin, M.D.
Assistant Professor
Harvard Medical School
The McLean Hospital
Belmont, Massachusetts

Lonnie E. Mitchell, Ph.D.
Chief, Manpower and Training
Division of Resource Development
National Institute on Drug Abuse
Rockville, Maryland

John P. Morgan, M.D.
Associate Professor
Sophie Davis School of Biomedical
    Education
College of the City of New York

Departments of Medicine and
  Pharmacology
Mt. Sinai School of Medicine
New York, New York

Salvatore J. Mulé, Ph.D.
Director
Toxicology and Research Laboratory
New York State Division of Substance-
  Abuse Services
Brooklyn, New York

David F. Musto, M.D.
Senior Research Scientist
Yale Child Study Center
Professor of Psychiatry and History
  of Medicine
Yale University
New Haven, Connecticut

Lorenz K. Y. Ng, M.D.
Chief, Pain Studies Program
Division of Research
National Institute on Drug Abuse
Rockville, Maryland

Charles P. O'Brien, M.D., Ph.D.
Professor of Psychiatry
Department of Psychiatry
University of Pennsylvania Medical
  School
Philadelphia Veterans Administration
  Medical Center
Philadelphia, Pennsylvania

Monsignor William B. O'Brien
President and Chief Executive Officer
Daytop Village, Inc.
New York, New York

Emil F. Pascarelli, M.D.
Chief, Department of Ambulatory Care
Beekman-Downtown Hospital
Adjunct Clinical Assistant Professor
School of Public Health
New York Hospital
Cornell Medical Center
New York, New York

Jane E. Prather, Ph.D.
Professor of Sociology
California State University
Northridge, California

Beny J. Primm, M.D.
Executive Director
Addiction Research and Treatment

Corporation
Brooklyn, New York

Pierre F. Renault, M.D.
Associate Director for Medical and
  Scientific Evaluation
National Center for Health Care Technology
Rockville, Maryland

Edward B. Roberts, Ph.D.
David Sarnoff Professor of the
  Management of Technology
Alfred P. Sloan School of Management
Massachusetts Institute of Technology
Cambridge, Massachusetts

Pedro Ruiz, M.D.
Professor of Psychiatry
Albert Einstein College of Medicine
Bronx, New York

Bernard Salzman, M.D.
Director
Drug Rehabilitation Program
Bellevue Hospital Center
Associate Clinical Professor of
  Psychiatry
New York University Medical School
Department of Psychiatry
New York, New York

Frank Seixas, M.D.
Medical Director
Norwood Hospital Comprehensive
  Alcoholism Program
Norwood, Massachusetts
Clinical Associate Professor of Public
  Health and
Clinical Assistant Professor of Medicine
Cornell University Medical School
  (on leave)
New York, New York

Saul B. Sells, Ph.D.
Research Professor and Director
Institute of Behavioral Research
Texas Christian University
Fort Worth, Texas

Edward C. Senay, M.D.
Professor of Psychiatry
Pritzker School of Medicine
University of Chicago
Chicago, Illinois

Howard Shaffer, Ph.D.
Clinical Instructor in Psychology

Harvard Medical School
Director, Drug Problems Resource
    Center
Department of Psychiatry
The Cambridge Hospital
Cambridge, Massachusetts

Charles W. Sharp, Ph.D.
Research Biochemist
Biochemical Research Branch
Division of Research
National Institute on Drug Abuse
Rockville, Maryland

Larry M. Siegel, M.S.W., M.P.H.
Director
Community Living Resource Center
Van Nuys Community Mental Health Center
Van Nuys, California

Eric J. Simon, Ph.D.
Professor
Departments of Psychiatry and
    Pharmacology
New York University Medical Center
New York, New York

David E. Smith, M.D., Ph.D.
Director
Haight-Ashbury Free Medical Clinic
San Francisco, California

Michael R. Sonnenreich, J.D.
Chayet and Sonnenreich, P.C.
Attorneys at Law
Washington, D.C.

Robert Spitzer, M.D.
Chief of Psychiatric Research
Biometrics Research Department
New York State Psychiatric Institute
New York, New York

David B. Thomas, D. Stat.
Research Scientist
Biometric Research Institute, Inc.
Washington, D.C.

J. Thomas Ungerleider, M.D.
Associate Professor of Psychiatry
University of California
    at Los Angeles Medical Center
Neuropsychiatric Institute
Los Angeles, California

Craig Van Dyke, M.D.
Associate Professor of Psychiatry

in Residence
School of Medicine, Department of
    Psychiatry
University of California
Veterans Administration Medical Center
San Francisco, California

Donald M. Vega, S.J., M.A.
Department of Addiction Services
Commonwealth of Puerto Rico
Luquillo, Puerto Rico

Andrew T. Weil, M.D.
Research Associate in Ethnopharmacology
Harvard University
Adjunct Professor of Addiction Studies
University of Arizona
Tucson, Arizona

Hsiang-Lai Wen, M.D.
Neurosurgical Unit
Kwong Wah Hospital
Tung Wah Group of Hospitals
Kowloon, Hong Kong

Donald R. Wesson, M.D.
Assistant Clinical Professor of Psychiatry
University of California Medical School
San Francisco, California

John A. Whysner, M.D., Ph.D.
President
Medical Research Applications, Inc.
McLean, Virginia

Charles Winick, Ph.D.
Professor of Sociology
City University of New York,
    Graduate Center
New York, New York

Leon Wurmser, M.D.
Director, Alcohol and Drug Abuse Program
Professor of Psychiatry
University of Maryland Medical School
Baltimore, Maryland

Norman E. Zinberg, M.D.
Clinical Professor of Psychiatry
Harvard Medical School
Cambridge, Massachusetts

Joan Ellen Zweben, Ph.D.
President
Pacific Institute for Clinical Training,
    Education and Consultation
Berkeley, California

Contents

PART 1

BACKGROUND

CHAPTER 1

REVIEW OF NARCOTIC CONTROL EFFORTS IN THE UNITED STATES[1]

David F. Musto, M.D.

The last three decades of the 19th century saw far-reaching transformations in American life. With immigration from all parts of Europe and from Asia, the population expanded greatly and became heterogeneous in speech, religion, and way of life. Many of the immigrants, unprepared to join the agricultural sector of the economy, crowded into the growing cities, which soon began to exhibit today's familiar urban problems. With the industrial revolution, large enterprises grew up that attained a new level of economic power; with the construction of the railroads, vast areas of the West were opened for settlement and exploitation of the timber and mineral resources. In social terms, the geographic dispersal of the population as many moved west spelled the end of the once close-knit family. In political terms, these changes terminated the hegemony of the Protestant, North European group that had controlled the affairs of the nation through the Civil War.

These rapid changes in all aspects of life were inevitably attended by a variety of ills that kept alive the spirit of reform. In actuality, the strains of reform that ran through

American culture from the mid-19th century to 1920 stemmed largely from the fear among middle- and upper-class citizens of growing disorder in society. The rapid transformations seemed to threaten the heart of American life. The reform movements that arose naturally responded to specific evils that seemed to result from the upheaval; however, some reforms, especially in the Progressive era of 1890–1910, were aimed at curing the disorder itself (4).

Limiting immigration would supposedly lessen the disruption caused by the constant influx of aliens, of those with strange ways who destabilized the culture and might even bring in ideas that were dangerous. Controlling or even busting runaway trusts would return control of the economy, especially economic opportunity, to the people. No longer able to restrain trade according to their own profit motive, companies would have to follow the good, wholesome, dominant American values made known to them through the marketplace. Not only would the new Big Government control the actual size of the corporations, but it also would regulate their use of resources to provide for public prosperity in future generations. In addition to the corporations, the groups that dominated the work force threatened stability; the push for unions posed the threat of labor violence. Although not conceding to labor's

[1] This investigation was supported in part by Research Scientist Development Award DA 0037 from the National Institute on Drug Abuse and a grant from the Ford Foundation.

demands themselves, the Progressive reformers hoped to appease the working classes somewhat by offering wider participation in the government. Rights of initiative, referendum, and recall, direct primaries, and ballot reform would theoretically afford the general populace more power.

The best known figure in the Progressive movement was, of course, Theodore Roosevelt. Others remembered for their efforts in this period include William Jennings Bryan, Robert LaFollette, and Woodrow Wilson in the sphere of government; jurist Oliver Wendell Holmes, Jr.; authors Jacob Riis, Henry Demarest Lloyd, Ida Tarbell, and Lincoln Steffens; social reformer Jane Addams; temperance leader Frances Willard; women's suffrage advocate Susan B. Anthony; conservationist Gifford Pinchot; and Harvey Washington Wiley, the backer of the Pure Food and Drugs Act of 1906.

In many ways the reform movements that characterized the Progressive era and the 1960's and 1970's have much in common. Many federal activities which seem modern—the battle against water and air pollution, legislation for pure foods and drugs, mine safety, meat inspection, etc.–came from the Progressive period, in which even the word *ecology* became a byword of conservationists and health reformers alike (16). The two eras also demonstrate the ways in which specific reforms can relate—or not relate—to one another. In the Progressive period, the reformers moved on all fronts simultaneously; no demonstated ill was omitted. In the 1960's and 1970's, however, the focus has been selective and the motivation different. Although the civil rights movement of the 1960's that led to the Civil Rights Act of 1963, the Voting Rights Act of 1964, and programs aimed at ameliorating the social, educational, and economic situation of the disadvantaged—the Great Society plans of Lyndon Johnson—resembled the Progressive era reforms in that they were designed to preserve the existing order, other movements of the 1960's and 1970's constituted rebellions against that order. The protest against the war in Vietnam is the clearest example, and its spirit pervaded such other movements as the environmental movement, the cause of women's rights, and experimentation with previously forbidden drugs. The Progressive era reformers would have immediately perceived the inconsistent stance of those today who are actively committed to environmental reform but who improve their leisure time with marihuana or cocaine.

ALCOHOL AND THE PROHIBITION MOVEMENT

In addition to consistency in their views, the Progressive era reformers viewed their political reforms as increasing the access of the underprivileged to government as well as uplifting them morally. This was also the goal of the Temperance movement, which would at least partially lift the burden of alcohol. Some sociologists in this period began to speculate that alcohol abuse was actually the result rather than the cause of poverty; however, alcohol seemed to exacerbate almost all the evils of a disorderly society. Even if it could not be wholly blamed for economic failure, it certainly did not help. Alcohol lowered efficiency and productivity and, in the eyes of the reformers, increased all the evils of the urban scene: prostitutes worked in and around saloons; alcohol apparently made men more susceptible to the influence of corrupt city bosses; it broke up families and incited violence. It reduced the chances for freedom, prosperity, and happiness and did not contribute to the virtue and enlightened character of an electorate needed by a democracy.

Furthermore, alcohol worsened the situation of Protestant Christianity. Not only was the saloon associated with Catholic immigrants, but also it seemed to make men incapable of responding to Evangelical Protestantism. If it made a man unconcerned about something as urgent as salvation, then surely it would make him oblivious to public concerns. Democratization, therefore, made it even more important that the saloon be abolished. Extending the powers of the landless class in itself posed quite a threat to stability; drunken masses would constitute an intolerable danger (32).

Indeed, alcohol had been the object of several prohibition crusades in the 19th century. With the final movement that led to the adoption in 1919 of the Eighteenth Amendment, the nation moved toward implementation of a prohibition justified on moral, religious, and scientific grounds (25). By 1919 it is quite likely that a majority of Americans believed that liquor prohibition would be a great benefit in reducing poverty, crime, broken families, lost work time, and immorality. Eventually every state except two, Rhode Island and Connecticut, ratified the amendment.

NARCOTIC DRUGS

By the end of the last century, the narcotics problem was also worrying reform-minded legislators, health professionals, and laymen. Opium in its crude form has been imported into North America from the time of the earliest European settlements. Various medicines were made from it. Alcohol extracts of crude opium included laudanum and paregoric, and opium was mixed with other drugs in patent medicines, among the most popular of which was Dover's Powder, originating in England in the 18th century. American statistics on opium imports were not kept until the 1840's, but from that time on domestic consumption rose rapidly until the mid-1890's when the annual importation of crude opium leveled off at about half a million pounds (31). After passage of federal laws in 1914 strictly limiting importation of opium, the import statistics are less helpful in estimating national consumption and smuggling became a greater problem. Yet statistics for the pre-World War I period provide good evidence that the rapid increase of opium use in the United States occurred in the last century, and that when the 20th century began there was already a substantial consumption of the drug for medical and nonmedicinal purposes. State laws regulating the availability of narcotics began to be enacted before the Civil War, and many states controlled the drugs by the 1890's. Yet by the turn of the century, state and local laws to control opium distribution, chiefly by putting it under the prescription of physicians and restricting quantities in over-the-counter remedies, were losing credibility as effective measures. The failure was usually ascribed to the patchwork-quilt character of laws below the federal level of government (54). Increasingly, crimes and immorality were blamed on easily obtained narcotics.

Several major technological and chemical advances made the most powerful ingredients in opium available in a pure, cheap form. In the first decade of the 18th century, morphine was isolated from opium, and by 1832

American pharmaceutical manufacturers were preparing morphine from imported crude opium. Codeine was isolated in 1832, and this less addicting substance became a common form of manufactured derivative, particularly after morphine and heroin were severely restricted in the United States after World War I (26, 27). Heroin, a trade name of the Bayer Company for diacetylmorphine, was commercially introduced in 1898 with the hope that acetylation of the morphine molecule would reduce its side effects while maintaining its effectiveness in suppressing the cough reflex. A similar hope was entertained the next year for acetylation of salicylic acid, a mild analgesic with undesirable side effects, which was then marketed as Aspirin, the Bayer trademark for sodium acetylsalicylic acid. Heroin, of course, proved to be at least as addicting as morphine and eventually ousted morphine as the drug of choice among American drug habitues (9). The increasing use of heroin in this period is an example of the effectiveness of three innovations adopted by large 19th-century enterprises, including pharmaceutical firms: large scale manufacturing, rapid distribution, and effective marketing techniques. It is these same innovations that made aniline dyes and vulcanized rubber cheap and available worldwide.

Coca leaves have been known in their indigenous growth areas in South America to have stimulant properties and had been used for centuries by natives. Coca's unusual properties were popularized in Europe and America in the mid-19th century, and an alcohol extract of the leaves, which contained some of the active stimulant cocaine, often went under the name of wine of coca. In the 1880's pure cocaine became more easily available due to advances in manufacturing technology, and it was immediately praised, especially in the United States. Its stimulant and euphoric properties were touted for athletes, workers, and students, and bottlers of popular soda drinks and easily obtained "tonics" added cocaine to obtain a stimulant effect. Medical uses were soon discovered, and world-wide experimentation established cocaine as an anesthetic for the surface of the eye and as a block to pain stimuli when injected near a nerve. The stimulant properties were bothersome side effects of cocaine when used as an anesthetic, but within a few decades satisfactory substitutes were developed that were considered less habituating, such as procaine in 1905. Cocaine was also convenient for shrinking nasal and sinus membranes, and it became one of the early effective remedies for "hay fever," allergies, and sinusitis. As an over-the-counter remedy for hay fever or "nasal catarrh," in powder form to be snuffed or as a spray, cocaine began to be criticized as misused or carelessly dispensed for mere pleasure or dissipation.

In the period from about 1895 to 1915, cocaine became associated in the popular and medical press with southern blacks' hostility to whites. Vicious crimes said to have been perpetrated by blacks were commonly attributed to the effects of cocaine. In efforts to pass antinarcotic legislation, this association was repeated by federal officials and spokesmen for the health professions, although direct evidence for such a close and specifically racial association was wanting or even contradictory (55). In an interesting contrast to present analyses of drug use, 60 years ago cocaine was considered a typically "Negro" drug, whereas opiates and specifically heroin were described as characteristically "white," illustrating the influence on interpretation of the narcotics problem of social tensions and racial stereotypes.

Cannabis or marihuana in the form of "reefers" or "joints" seems to have been unfamiliar in the United States until this century, yet there was a long-standing fear of hashish, a concentrated and powerful form of cannabis. Hashish was known as an esoteric and perilous drug popular in the Middle East and from description of its bizarre effects by literary figures who experimented with it in the mid-19th century (18).

PROGRESSIVE ERA REFORMS (1898 to 1917)

Leading up to the Progressive period was a growing belief that local and state governments could not correct national abuses. Reformers besought the federal government, so long aloof from many social problems because of the accepted sharp demarcation between federal and state powers, to step in, harmonize state legislation, and lead the way toward an effective fight against individual and group abuses. The many conflicting or weak state laws were inadequate. If one state

had strict laws, its neighbor had loose laws, and an easy supply of drugs was assured. Yet federal action was limited by the few constitutional bases for laws that would affect the abuses. The federal government was restricted mostly to regulating interstate commerce and levying taxes. Police and health powers, obviously the most appropriate for combating addiction and illicit drugs, were the province of the states. The United States Public Health Service and its antecedent agencies were, for example, limited to dealing with communicable diseases, gathering and disseminating such medical information as vital statistics and public health advice; they could not provide direct delivery of health services except to their legal wards, chiefly the Merchant Marine and American Indians (7). The armed services excepted, federal police agencies included alcohol tax agents, members of the Coast Guard, and customs and immigration officers. Therefore, there was little precedent for federal regulation of dangerous drugs, and no federal policing agency could easily add this burden to its current duties. Therefore, the gradual move into these problem areas was both an unusual journey for the government and a surprise for the affected citizens.

Prior to this era of ecological concern, the extent of activities that the federal government left to an individual's or company's sense of fair play was remarkably large. In the 19th century, federal law did not require the labeling of drugs on over-the-counter proprietaries. Thus, these patent medicines could contain any amount of, say, morphine without acknowledgment and could even aver that the potion contained no morphine. The percentage of alcohol in some popular remedies was higher than that in many cocktails today. Claims that a proprietary could cure cancer, tuberculosis, or any other ailment were legally unchallengable; no tests of efficacy, purity, or standardization were required. Newspapers, the primary source of information for most Americans, were chary of offending their advertisers, and many papers had contracts with proprietary manufacturers that would become invalid with the enactment of any state law requiring disclosure of contents or any infringement of advertising claims (57).

Thus, it is not surprising that no federal law requiring contents information and some accuracy of claims was enacted until 1906. This law, the Pure Food and Drugs Act, contained some of the first federal provisions affecting narcotics; if any over-the-counter remedy in interstate commerce contained an opiate, cannabis, cocaine, or chloral hydrate, the label was required to state its contents and percentage. The effect of this simple measure apparently reduced the amount of such drugs in popular remedies and also hurt their sales, although other proprietaries flourished. The Proprietary Association of America, dismayed at the accusation of being "dopers," favored strict limitation of dangerous drugs in their products and ostracized manufacturers who continued to put large amounts of such drugs as cocaine in "asthma cures."

Although a step had been taken to warn proprietary users of the amount of dangerous drugs in the remedies, still nothing had been done to bring under control another target of reform: "dope doctors" and pharmacists who purveyed opiates and cocaine to anyone who asked for them. The percentage of such deviants in each profession was not large, but they took advantage of the broad authority given to all licensed pharmacists and physicians to use their professional judgment in the delivery of medicines and services, and the dominance of the state in the licensing of the health professions seemed unassailable by the federal government. In addition to purchasing drugs from professional miscreants, one could order them from mailorder houses. How to rectify this promiscuous distribution of narcotics presented a difficult constitutional problem for federal action.

THE SHANGHAI COMMISSION AND THE SMOKING OPIUM ACT (1909)

Several national laws directed at the traffic in narcotics had been introduced into Congress before 1908, but only when President Theodore Roosevelt convened the Shanghai Opium Commission in 1909 was federal enactment of legislation accomplished. The Shanghai meeting was called to aid the Chinese Empire in its desire to stamp out opium addiction, particularly the smoking of opium (30). The first United States legislation was modest and limited, intended more as evidence of America's good faith in convening the commission than as an ade-

quate weapon against American narcotic abuse. The Smoking Opium Exclusion Act outlawed the importation of opium prepared for smoking into the United States (34). Its passage while the Shanghai Commission was in session under the chairmanship of an American, the Right Reverend Charles H. Brent, Episcopal bishop of the Philippine Islands, was designed to show the delegates of other nations that the United States was willing to take steps to aid control of world opium traffic. American delegates reported back to the State Department that the announcement of the act's passage was met with an impressive response from the other 12 nations represented.

REGULATION OF THE HEALTH PROFESSIONS

But the American delegates and indeed the departments most closely associated with narcotic policy planning—State, Treasury, and Agriculture—were aware that the legislation against smoking opium was but the first step in controlling a national problem described as serious and threatening to progress. The nation needed a law that more closely controlled sales of over-the-counter remedies, excessive or careless prescribing of narcotics, smuggling, and other avenues of easy access to narcotics. The question, of course, was how the federal government could accomplish this by constitutional means. After debating the wisdom of using its interstate commerce or taxing powers, the State Department, which coordinated domestic legislation and planning until 1915, opted for the latter. Through taxation, the department experts reasoned, all narcotics could be traced, not just drugs shipped from one state to another.

The first of the administration's proposed bills, drafted in 1909 and forming the basis of the Harrison Antinarcotic Law of 1914 (35), was extremely harsh in penalities and intricately detailed without any provision for the exemption of proprietaries that contained less than certain amounts of the narcotics (19). The intention of such bills would have been to make the handling of narcotic preparations so risky and complicated for retail outlets that the whole narcotic traffic would fall into the hands of physicians. The physicians would be limited only by their good judgment and restrictions placed by state legislatures on narcotics (for example, record keeping, prohibiting the refilling of narcotic prescriptions or maintaining addicts) (28).

Such tough state laws met with opposition from the rank and file of the drug trades, proprietary manufacturers, and some members of Congress, who feared that such a precedent might be extended to alcohol. Before the Webb-Kenyon Act was passed over President Taft's veto in 1913, it was legal to live in a dry state, purchase liquor from a wet state, and have it delivered via interstate commerce. President Taft believed an extension of federal control to prohibit this practice was unconstitutional, but passage of the Webb-Kenyon Act softened fear of an antinarcotic act as a dangerous precedent for liquor prohibition.

While domestic debate continued among the specific interests affected by the proposed narcotic tax legislation, the United States continued its campaign among the nations to regulate the international traffic in narcotics. The Shanghai Commission was not empowered to write a treaty; the delegates could only make recommendations. Building on the Shanghai Commission, the United States sought a second meeting for the preparation of an international treaty. After much persuasion and repeated setbacks, The Netherlands, at American request, convened the International Opium Conference at The Hague in December 1911. Again Bishop Brent, head of the American delegation, was chosen to preside, and, after weeks of debate and compromise, the delegates signed the Hague Opium Convention in January 1912 (31). The title is somewhat misleading; the treaty also sought to control coca and cocaine. An American and Italian suggestion that cannabis be included was not accepted.

THE HAGUE TREATY

The Hague Treaty emphasized enactment of legislation in each nation to control the production of crude substances, their manufacture into pharmaceuticals, and distribution within the nation and abroad (23). Within the State Department it was acknowledged that, if the nations that grew opium and coca enacted strict legislation in the spirit of the treaty, the American problem would be greatly reduced, perhaps vanish. The solution

to the American problem lay in persuading other nations to have a "correct" view of narcotic use and to enforce legislation in accord with this view. The United States government apparently believed that its people were extravagant consumers of opiates; federal publications reported that the country was by far the largest consumer of opium per capita among Western nations. In the words of the State Department's Opium Commissioner, Dr. Hamilton Wright, "Uncle Sam is the worst drug fiend in the world," consuming, he claimed, more opium per capita than the fabled opium-using Chinese (56).

Yet the stern international measures envisaged by such reformers as Dr. Wright were not adopted before the Great War. The Hague Treaty was not airtight; its vague phrases did not compel the ratifying nations to enact strict laws to reduce narcotic distribution to solely medical purposes. Moreover, American domestic legislation, now promoted as the American implementation of The Hague Treaty, was still hampered by doctrines of state's rights and constitutional interpretation. At the least, the federal government hoped that the Harrison Act would bring into the open the vast narcotic traffic so that the states could take appropriate health and police measures or step up enforcement of existing laws. At the optimum, Wright hoped the act would be recognized as the fulfillment of an international obligation, in accord with Article VI of the Constitution, and thus take precedence over the rights of states. In this instance the general phraseology of the Harrison Act, such as requiring the prescription of narcotics "in good faith," could be interpreted strictly and would allow prosecution of "dope doctors," other malpracticing professionals, and peddlers.

THE HARRISON ACT (1914)

The Harrison Act was passed in December 1914 and came into effect on the March 1, 1915 (35). Every dealer in narcotics had to register with the Bureau of Internal Revenue, pay a small fee, and receive a tax stamp. Detailed record keeping was required for most transactions, and legal possession by a consumer was made dependent upon a physician's or dentist's prescription. Individual consumers were forbidden to register (51). But when federal personnel sought to arrest the dope doctors for prescribing, they discovered that many judges of federal district courts thought the action was an infringement of state police powers. In a crucial Supreme Court interpretation, it was held to be beyond federal powers to prohibit narcotics possession by anyone to whom the Treasury Department had refused registration, such as a peddler or addict (19, 49).

Not until the height of the war effort—and in the midst of a zealous drive to purify the nation—was a successful campaign mounted to strengthen the Harrison Act to prohibit mere maintenance of addiction. If a physician could exercise his judgment as to when and whom to maintain in an opiate habit, it was certain that some physicians would be unscrupulous, thus spreading the habit and reaping a profit. Therefore, in addition to reforming leaders in the medical and pharmaceutical professions, the goal of the federal government was to restrict that breadth of medical judgment by law. The undertaking was hazardous, for such federal encroachment on medicine was unprecedented; the physician would be allowed to maintain an opiate addict only in cases of senility or intractable pain. The specter of state medical control was thus easily evoked among a segment of the profession.

ADOPTION OF A FEDERAL ANTIMAINTENANCE POLICY

Given the inadequacy and variety of state laws, there seemed no other way to control physicians and pharmacists—even though the unethical percentage was small—than by imposition of federal authority. One should keep in mind that physicians were thought to have created about half of the American opiate addicts. Partly to counteract the Jin Fuey Moy decision of 1916, the Treasury Department, which administered the Harrison Act, established in 1918 a Special Committee on the Narcotics Traffic. The committee helped persuade Congress to pass strengthening legislation in February 1919 (36). Then, aiding the government effort, the Supreme Court, in two fundamental interpretations of the act, rejected by five to four the argument that it was legal to maintain an addict by prescription if the addict had no illness except addiction (50). Whereas the Public Health Service in rather sober studies published in 1915 and

1924 argued that there were probably never more than a quarter million habitual users of opiates and cocaine in the nation, the Treasury committee, in its final report, assessed the number at slightly more than 1 million, who were described as moral wretches for the most part (13, 52, 53). New York City officials claimed that heroin addicts, who under state law could be legally maintained, were responsible for huge numbers of crimes and estimated by 1924 the remarkable figure of 75 per cent of all crimes (14). The mayor of New York City in 1919 linked heroin with anarchism and political bombings (15).

The federal agencies believed the narcotic problem was out of hand. In 1919 there was fear in the nation over several groups considered extreme domestic threats: socialists, members of The International Workers of the World, Bolsheviks, and addicts (17). And the image of the addicts as immoral and criminal, a belief dating back among respectable writers and observers well into the 19th century, made them a weak spot in American society. Their number at more than 1 million in a nation of 100 million justified stern action and uncompromising control.

THE NARCOTICS DIVISION

To carry out the strict Supreme Court ruling that maintenance be severely limited in the United States (after several decades of what one might call the "American system"), a Narcotic Division was established in December 1919 in the newly formed Prohibition Unit of the Internal Revenue Bureau, which had been created to enforce liquor prohibition. Its first head was Levi G. Nutt, a pharmacist from Ohio who had risen in the ranks of the tax unit. He now oversaw about 150 narcotic agents scattered across the nation. Unlike the liquor agents, the narcotic agents were not legally exempted from civil service requirements and were probably a step above their colleagues in quality (24).

In the enforcement of antimaintenance, which was backed by leading physicians and such reformers as Dr. Alexander Lambert, President of the American Medical Association in 1919, a curious regression occurred in the respectability of certain medical theories. This happened because reformers' and agents' fear of maintenance—and disgust with many subterfuges of some health professionals to justify a profitable trade—was extended to suspicion of any justification for maintenance. Supplying drugs to an addict was considered a form of medical malpractice that endangered society by perpetuating criminal and immoral persons in their esoteric pleasures. There was, however, a previously respectable scientific explanation of opiate addiction which would imply maintenance as a rational therapy response: the immunochemical theory of opiate addiction.

IMPACT OF FEDERAL POLICY ON MEDICAL OPINION

In the immunological reasoning, which was popular among many addiction experts prior to 1919, the argument ran that ingestion of, say, morphine stimulated the formation of antibodies like those produced against smallpox virus or of antitoxins like those produced against the toxins of the diphtheria bacterium. Such theories were popular explanations for illnesses in the late 19th and early 20th centuries and in many cases led to the saving of lives. With regard to addiction, and according to several competent and respected clinicians, the theory held that maintenance doses of an opiate would be required to bring an addict's physiology into balance with the level of antibodies or antitoxins present in his body. If too little opiate were administered, the body would begin to experience withdrawal symptoms by the action of unneutralized antibodies or antitoxins; if too much, the body would experience the physiological effects of opiates. According to Dr. Ernest Bishop of New York, the amount of opiate required to balance an individual's physiology could be determined with great precision, and the addict would remain a fully normal person only so long as this exact dose was maintained. Dr. Bishop, however, did not rule out "cure" in some instances by various popular medical regimens (2).

The intimate link between this scientific theory and its implications for public policy made its adherents suspect. If believers in these immunochemical theories practiced medicine according to what was then considered reasonable and was backed by a number of laboratory experiments, they could be indicted and convicted of violating the 1919 Supreme Court interpretations of what was

legitimate medical practice. The leading addiction expert of the United States Public Health Service had supported the immunological theory, and when Dr. A. G. DuMez of the Hygienic Laboratory (now the National Institutes of Health) published his endorsement of some of the immunological experiments in 1919, he was asked by the American Medical Association's Committee on Addiction to retract his statement, which he did partially, by qualifying his previous endorsement (1, 6). Within a year or two the question of the cause of addiction was so controversial that the Surgeon General of the Public Health Service wrote the president of the Louisiana State Board of Health to advise that the phrase "physiological balance" was too controversial to be included in a description of narcotic treatment and the enforcement problem (5).

It was soon demonstrated that immunological substances could not be found in the blood; the adherents of "addiction disease" caused by a simple and easily detectable immunological process were evidently in error. Yet the intense political nature of the addiction question and the fear of addicts, whose numbers were very likely overestimated, had an impact on the exchange of scientific information and medical practice. At the level of social planning, maintenance was judged poor public policy, and it was to be eliminated if at all possible. This decision might indeed have been the correct one, but the suddenness of implementation and the emotionally charged attitude toward addicts and their maintainers caused policy to collide dramatically with research and medical opinion.

This closure of the narcotic question came during a period of about a year. In 1918 New York State established a Narcotic Control Commission to create state-wide maintenance clinics that would treat on the theory of immunology. The action was taken by the legislature and the governor after 2 years of consideration and hearings (29). In 1919, the national antimaintenance policy was adopted, and by 1920 New York State had stopped addiction maintenance.

The rapidity with which controversial questions like addiction and narcotics can be dogmatically crystallized is one of the most interesting features of narcotic control in the

United States. To resist the closure of maintenance was difficult; the new policy ensued from the anger, scapegoating, fatigue, and frustration of the lawmakers because a simple answer to addiction was still not available. The burden for the next several decades would rest on law enforcement to prevent illegal access to narcotic supplies. The notion that there existed a simple medical cure had been dashed.

MAINTENANCE CLINICS

Forty-odd maintenance clinics were scattered across the country; these were closed because they seldom led to cure and merely perpetuated addiction. Indefinite maintenance was not only against the original policy of the Treasury in 1915, it had also been excluded by the Supreme Court decisions of 1919. A relatively small percentage of the nation's addicts were enrolled in these clinics, particularly if one accepted the extravagant estimate of more than a million addicts for the whole nation. It is likely that the number of addicts registered at any one time in maintenance clinics did not exceed 5,000 (8). The drug of maintenance was almost always morphine; heroin—which had a bad image—was popular mainly in New York City, and, if requested elsewhere, clinics substituted morphine. The average age of patrons was about 30, and they had usually been addicts for at least several years before joining the clinic. Some clinics were operated by the police department (e.g., New Haven) and others by health departments (e.g., Atlanta), and attitudes toward the clinics varied from one city to another. Some were clearly operated under political patronage and for a profit. In some instances cocaine was dispensed with morphine; Albany operated this kind of unjustified clinic. Yet clinics were now illegal even if records were carefully kept, and a physician examined every patient and tried to keep the drug down to a minimum. The violation was maintenance itself.

An exception to the policy of maintenance clinics was the one operated in 1919 to 1920 by the New York City Department of Health. Here heroin was used to entice addicts into a detoxification and rehabilitation program. After almost a year of operation, the city ended its experiment. It found that most ad-dicts, even if detoxified, returned to heroin after release from 6 weeks of hospital treatment. The Health Department concluded that restriction of availability by the police and federal agents was necessary if addiction was to be effectively diminished. About 7,500 persons registered at the clinic, and almost all received gradually decreasing doses of heroin; 10 per cent were under the age of 19 (11).

FEAR OF FEDERAL CONTROL ON THE PART OF HEALTH PROFESSIONS

By 1925 all the clinics known to the Narcotic Division had been closed. Court decisions continued to restrict a physician's right to maintain an addict. Procedures used by agents to get information led to hostility and suspicion, but the reason that enforcement personnel used such methods as informers was that they had repeatedly encountered determined profit-making physicians whose concern for the welfare of their patients and the community was nil. A further disagreement between the federal government and the medical profession arose from a question even more fundamental than maintenance: Did the federal government have the right to interfere with medical practice and exempt certain classes of patients from a doctor's judgment? The medical profession came out of the social agitation associated with World War I with a fear that the federal government would enter into "state medicine" or compulsory health insurance. After 1920 the American Medical Association (AMA) greatly resisted the various federal measures concerning health, for example the Sheppard-Towner Act for Maternal and Child Care, which was to be financed by matching grants to the states. The medical profession fought such federal intervention with great vigor and generally with success (3).

Yet the Harrison Act remained a thorn in the side of professional medicine. If it was constitutional for government to say who could be maintained or not, a precedent was set for further incursions into medical practice. A similar problem for the AMA was the Willis-Campbell Act of 1921, which limited a physician's prescriptions for alcohol to a fairly modest number and made other restrictions on the kind and amount of alcohol that could be prescribed. Thus physicians were in part outraged at the Harrison and Willis-Campbell Acts not because they wanted to maintain addicts or become saloonkeepers (although at times a few seemed quite willing to do just that), but because they were fearful of where this unprecedented use of federal power in the health fields might lead.

NARCOTIC DRUGS IMPORT AND EXPORT ACT (1922)

After the outlawing of addiction maintenance, a series of federal laws in the 1920's sought to fill gaps in the federal control of narcotics. The first, the Narcotic Drugs Import and Export Act of 1922, permitted only crude narcotics to enter the United States; manufacture into pure substances would be performed by American drug companies (37). Any foreign narcotic product in the United States, like Swiss morphine or German cocaine, was illegal. Intricate restrictions were made upon American export and transshipment of narcotics because it was feared that a great deal of morphine was arriving in China, via Japan, in this manner, or that it was being smuggled back into the United States after export to Canada or Mexico. Finally, the Federal Narcotic Control Board, composed of the Secretaries of Treasury, Commerce, and State, was established to authorize legitimate imports and exports.

RESTRICTIONS ON HEROIN (1924)

In the mid-1920's the United States attempted to obtain international sanctions against the manufacture of heroin, which was by then considered the most dangerous narcotic, particularly for adolescents. Most of the crime in New York City was blamed on heroin, including daring bank robberies, senseless violence, and murders. The danger of heroin was knowingly exaggerated by respectable antinarcotic reformers in order to inform the American people of its peril. One excellent example is the educational campaign of Captain Richmond Pearson Hobson, a hero of the Spanish-American War, former congressman, and ardent Prohibitionist, who directed his speaking and organizational talents against narcotics shortly after the Eighteenth Amendment began to be enforced.

Captain Hobson was wont to warn women who habitually used any particular face powder to have it checked for heroin, lest they become addicted. He claimed that one dose of heroin was addicting and that an ounce of heroin could addict 2,000 persons. He blamed a national crime wave on heroin, claiming that it was a stimulant to senseless violence. He desired that a compilation of such warnings be sent into every American home and requested Congress to print 50 million copies of his eight-page brochure, "The Peril of Narcotics" (48). The pamphlet was not printed, but a revised version of his message was printed in the *Congressional Record* and distributed by sympathetic congressmen (10). Hobson represents a popularizer of heroin dangers who disseminated grossly erroneous information on addiction that tended to alarm the public excessively and provided a convenient explanation for unrelated, serious social problems.

Partly to encourage other nations to regulate narcotics and partly to assist in the American fight against addiction, Congress prohibited in 1924 the importation of crude opium into the United States for the manufacture of heroin (38). The author of this legislation, Representative Stephen Porter of Pittsburgh, Chairman of the House Foreign Affairs Committee, took the leading congressional role in the international negotiations and planning for domestic control of narcotics in the 1920's.

FEDERAL NARCOTIC FARMS (1929)

Porter's second major effort was to provide for two "narcotic farms" where addicts could be treated as sick individuals and cured, and where they could perhaps assist investigators in the search for a cure (39). A factor in this legislation was that federal prisons were becoming jammed with Harrison Act violators, most of whom were also addicts. Congress either had to build two new prisons or two treatment centers. Thus came into being the Lexington and Fort Worth Narcotic Hospitals, operated by the United States Public Health Service. This legislation also provided for the Public Health Service Narcotics Division, which evolved into the present National Institute of Mental Health and National Institute on Drug Abuse.

THE FEDERAL BUREAU OF NARCOTICS (1930)

Finally, Representative Porter sought the establishment in the Treasury Department of an independent narcotics agency. The Narcotic Division had accompanied the Prohibition Unit when the latter was raised to the rank of bureau in 1927 and, although still subordinate and headed by an assistant commissioner, it was gradually expanding. In 1930, shortly before his death, Porter shepherded through Congress the act creating the Federal Bureau of Narcotics (FBN) (40). When the Prohibition Bureau moved from the Treasury to the Justice Department in mid-1930, the Narcotics Bureau remained behind, but its head, Levi G. Nutt, was not to become the first Commissioner of Narcotics. Nutt's son and son-in-law were implicated by a federal grand jury in "indiscreet" dealings with the recently slain New York narcotics czar Nathan Rothstein (47), and Nutt was transferred from his post a week after the filing of the grand jury's report, which also touched on his own activities and those of the New York District Office. Assistant Prohibition Commissioner Harry J. Anslinger was picked from the international control section of the Prohibition Bureau to take temporary charge of the Narcotic Division.

Anslinger had not been deeply involved with narcotics; his training was in the foreign service and in international negotiations to cut off rum running. To Representative Porter, however, he seemed the ideal man. Accustomed to foreign wiles and ulterior motives in areas of American moral concern, he could ably represent the United States in its struggle, dating back to 1906, to achieve international control of narcotics traffic. The medical aspect of the question seemed secondary, for if smuggling could be ended, the narcotic problem would take care of itself.

Thus began the 32-year tenure of Commissioner Anslinger. Most of the enforcement questions had been settled: maintenance was illegal; the image of the heroin addict was well publicized by such spokesmen as Captain Hobson; a national system of agents was established with fairly well defined styles of enforcement, although there was the eternal integrity problem in the agents' dealings with smugglers. The most

profound effect on narcotic enforcement in the immediate future was not new policies but rather the Depression, which drastically reduced the FBN's budget, led to detailed scrutiny of even its telephone bills by Congress, and probably helped explain the parsimony characteristic of the Anslinger tenure. Even in the 1960's the Bureau made a fetish of a low budget.

THE MARIHUANA PROBLEM

Commissioner Anslinger's first major issue appeared even as he took office—a quickly burgeoning fear centered in the Southwest about a plant grown and used by Mexicans who had poured into the region as farm laborers in the prosperous 1920's. This drug or plant was known as locoweed, marihuana, or, more scientifically, cannabis. As the fear of marihuana grew, it was accused of stimulating violence and being slyly sold to American school children. In the early 1930's the FBN tried to minimize these fears and suggested that state laws were the appropriate response. The Uniform State Narcotic Drug Act proposed in 1932 included marihuana regulations as an option for state legislation; "here was the solution," said the Bureau. The plant grew in the United States, so the best response was local, not by an agency that had its eyes on the smuggling of drugs from Turkey, France, Bolivia, China, and Siam.

Yet, recalled Anslinger, the Treasury Department decided to make marihuana use a federal offense, more as a gesture to the fearful Southwest than as a comprehensive and probably effective plan for marihuana control. The law was modeled on the National Firearms Act, which was declared constitutional by the Supreme Court in March 1937. In April, the Treasury representatives went before Congress to ask for a similar "transfer tax" and licensing system for marihuana. Congress passed the Marihuana Tax Act of 1937 without dissent, and by October it was in effect (41). Opposition to the act in committee came from an AMA representative, Dr. William C. Woodward, who stated that this was an area of state, not federal, concern and that it should not become one more example of federal encroachment on the medical profession.

In the enforcement of the act the Bureau

described marihuana as a fearful substance but played down any suggestion that it was a problem out of control. The apparent goal was to make the drug unattractive but not to create a panic over claims that it was widely disseminated to school children (18).

Control over the growth of opium poppies was secured in 1942 by the Opium Poppy Control Act (42). There was other legislation at this time to resolve technical problems, strengthen penalties, and include synthetic narcotics, such as meperidine, under federal regulations (33).

ADOPTION OF MANDATORY MINIMUM SENTENCES (1951 TO 1956)

World War II brought narcotic use, particularly opiates, to a low point. But at the close of hostilities the Bureau anticipated a resumption of illicit world narcotic trade. The Bureau looked back to World War I when, it was claimed, there was a postwar upsurge. And so when there was a rise in addiction among ghetto youth in Chicago and New York in the late 1940's and authorities noted a lower age among those sent to prisons or narcotic hospitals, the Bureau asked Congress for stronger penalties, particularly mandatory minimum sentences. The variability in judges' sentences and disposition of cases— a short sentence or probation for a trafficker the Bureau might have spent years trying to convict—led to the proposal to take sentencing of certain offenders out of the hands of judges. Also, a mandatory sentence might deter the potential trafficker or even the drug user.

Such legislation was introduced by Representative Hale Boggs and enacted in 1951 (43). In 1956, after Senate hearings chaired by Senator Price Daniel, the death penalty was allowed at the jury's discretion in some instances of heroin sales (44). This was the peak of punitive legislation against drug addiction in the United States. In a half century the federal response to dangerous drugs had advanced from requiring accurate labeling of narcotics in over-the-counter remedies (but with no limit on how much could be present) to the possibility of the death penalty, or at least a mandatory sentence, for conveying heroin to another person (regardless of the quantity of heroin).

Voices were raised against such harsh measures, but they were not very effective in modifying the course of events up to 1956. The American Bar Association (ABA) questioned the wisdom of mandatory minimum sentences, and a joint ABA-AMA committee began to examine the narcotics question with a philosophy far different from that embodied in the Boggs-Daniel Acts. Staff of the committee looked at the British experience, where legal heroin maintenance was available to the several hundred known addicts, and wondered whether some similar system would be suitable for the United States (12). Presidential and congressional confidence in various forms of psychological and chemical treatment flourished and was expressed in such national projects as the Community Mental Health Center program of 1963. Narcotic maintenance programs reappeared, using the synthetic narcotic methadone. The police effort to make narcotic supplies scarce—which seemed so reasonable to progressive medical leadership in 1919—began to seem crude, ineffective, and encouraging of gross malfeasance. A turning point in the national approach to narcotics was again at hand.

MEDICAL AND PSYCHOLOGICAL RESPONSE TO ADDICTION (1962 TO 1970)

When Anslinger retired in 1962—itself a sign of hope to those wanting to see some form of maintenance or at least less reliance on mandatory prison sentences—the President called the White House Conference on Narcotics and Drug Abuse (22). The conference participants represented the various conflicting points of view; after it was over, the President's Advisory Commission on Narcotics and Drug Abuse considered how to carry out the spirit of reexamination and made specific recommendations. The Commission's *Final Report*, published in 1963, marks a definite if small shift from the trend to see all "narcotics" as equal in the sight of the law. There was a suggestion that psychological treatment might be useful and that some variations in prison sentencing, such as civil commitment, might prove useful against addiction (20).

In the 1960's the appearance of psychedelic substances, such as lysergic acid diethylamide, and the quick rise in marihuana use drew attention to the varieties of drugs available and abusable. Further studies of marihuana suggested that it was less dangerous than had been assumed in the early 1930's, and the millions of individuals estimated to have used it in the 1960's also suggested that marihuana was not so very dangerous in moderate use. Other drugs, like amphetamines and barbiturates, became as popular in the streets as they had previously been common in middle-class homes. The number of heroin addicts began to rise, and the nation perceived itself under attack by a "drug culture" linked by many observers to a youth "counterculture." Congress responded in the 1960's to an increasing and threatening drug problem. Its legislation differentiated between the various drugs, provided alternatives to prison (as in the Narcotic Addict Rehabilitation Act of 1966), and dropped mandatory minimum sentences in favor of flexibility (45). The drug laws were brought together in the Comprehensive Drug Abuse and Prevention Act of 1970 (46). At long last, interstate commerce regulations were implemented as the constitutional basis for drug control, having greatly expanded in scope and power in the 70-odd years since they were first proposed for regulation of drug traffic.

The high hopes held for civil commitment of drug addicts in the early 1960's have not been realized. At first it seemed in keeping with advanced notions of psychological and milieu treatment, but it was modified to guarantee that the addict would remain for treatment. Yet the cost and length of treatment as well as the dismal success rate brought this apparently more sophisticated form of confinement under question. Civil commitment also conflicted with the legal rights of the individual: an addict could be confined for several years, not for a crime, but because he had a disease. These many difficulties with civil commitment caused a shift from optimism in the Advisory Commission's report of 1963 to a close questioning of the concept in the report of the President's Commission on Law Enforcement and the Administration of Justice.

In addition to changes in the criminal justice system and medical treatment, the 1960's also saw the reorganization of federal agencies to deal with drug abuse. In 1968, the Federal Bureau of Narcotics was joined with the Food and Drug Administration's Bureau of Drug Abuse Control (established in 1965) and placed in the Department of Justice. Thus, under strong political and social pressure, like the Prohibition Bureau in the late 1920's, the narcotics agency found its way out of Treasury to the main legal department of the government. The expenditure of the Bureau of Narcotics and Dangerous Drugs in fiscal year 1972 was more than $60 million, a remarkable amount when compared to the FBN expenditures in 1962 of about $4 million. The number of agents increased, and long range programs for combating crime syndicates and international smuggling were put into action.

The third great change in narcotics control in the 1960's, and perhaps the most fundamental, was the reintroduction of narcotic maintenance with methadone, a synthetic narcotic developed in Germany during World War II. It is given orally to lessen or even eliminate the desire for heroin, and this long acting narcotic has become a popular method of maintenance for addicts. Some of the similarities between the use and theoretical justification for methadone maintenance now and morphine maintenance in the World War I period are obvious, and both have encountered some of the same practical problems.

MAINTENANCE PROGRAMS

Some experts say that methadone is required by most hard core addicts indefinitely; that is, it does not end narcotic addiction but makes it more socially acceptable or feasible. This policy runs counter to an old theme in American attitudes, that addiction should be stopped, not catered to. As realized half a century ago, however, a maintenance system, if deployed across the nation, is difficult to regulate, and diversion of supplies to non-addicts can be a problem. One objection to the old maintenance clinics was the enormous profits garnered by some individuals who operated them; the implication was that profits stimulated the distribution of narcotics and the temptation to recruit new customers. Another problem was the failure of neat scientific explanations, such as Dr. Bishop's theory that a patient in precise opiate maintenance balance is quite normal. This did not work out so conveniently in practice. Maintenance, which was legal, for example, in New York State in 1918 and 1919, eventually led to abuses among health professionals and, in times of national fear, made the thousands of addicts scapegoats for social problems. Legal maintenance systems can thus become unpalatable or abhorred. They are sensitive to public pressure and political influences, and their existence is precarious, especially when the public believes that addiction itself is the cause of immorality, criminal behavior, and loss of productivity.

CONCLUSION

The great increase in American efforts to stop the smuggling of narcotics into the United States, which coincided with the establishment of the Bureau of Narcotics and Dangerous Drugs, now the Drug Enforcement Administration, represents the earlier trend in the history of narcotic control and, significantly, is the one finally adopted after a few intense years of concern after 1919. The curtailment of narcotic supplies mandates narcotic-free communities whether addiction-prone individuals want drugs or not. The more recent effort of the last 10 years, narcotic maintenance, contradicts the first. However, perhaps there will be some form of accommodation between them, especially because American belief in the ability of the law to prevent smuggling and bribery and to control sales of a desired product has been shaken by the excesses of the Prohibition era and by the continuing availability of some drugs, such as cocaine and marihuana, despite control efforts.

The rapidity with which the national attitude toward narcotics crystallized in the few years after World War I is a warning to present program planners. The effect of using addiction and drug abuse as a simplistic explanation for crime and social disorder is tempting, although the actual relationship seems much more complicated. Popular pressure for a "solution" can be intense and lead to the closing off of avenues of research and treatment, as after World War I. It is not just anger that leads to a rigid formulation for control of drug abuse; the equally powerful forces of fatigue with this chronic problem and frustration in the search for an effective answer play a role as well.

Narcotics abuse has been a political problem, and the legal response has been the result of political pressures rather than med-

ical or scientific principles. This political character is realistic and in itself does not bode ill for the approaches selected and implemented. The potential difficulty is that a political response may deal not with drug abuse but with the public perception and fear of drug abuse. Thus a massive campaign of isolating and confining drug addicts might result in some public emotional relief and a sense that the right thing is being done without actually aiding the drug users or affecting the social disorder and distortions for which drug abuse is blamed. The political nature of drug abuse, then, provides options in response which need not be directly relevant to drug abuse. The question must be: How can public concern be understood and relieved without adversely affecting the real problem of drug abuse, scientific research, and therapy? Many years may pass before a political solution is possible. In the interim, those formulating national strategy against narcotics abuse must strenuously resist the natural weariness of the long battle and try to put drug control into a realistic social and medical perspective.

In this battle, a possible ally may be waiting in the form of the mentioned recent concern for reform in other spheres of activity. Recall, once again, the two important periods of reform in American history, the Progressive era and the 1960's and 1970's.

Both periods have seen a concern for the environment and for public health. Actually, during the Progressive period, the effort toward improvement in public health, leading to the Pure Food and Drugs Act of 1906 and the Prohibition Amendment, was in large part based on the mentioned moralistic thinking unacceptable today. The very terms "Temperance" and "Prohibition" now have a bad name, suggesting overrighteousness and governmental interference in private life. Also, the Pure Food and Drugs Act was based on the principle that the average man would avoid risks if he was aware of them. The past decades have shown that such appeals to rationality often have little effect.

As mentioned in the introduction, the reform efforts of the Progressive period had a unity that is not present today. In the 1970's, there has been ongoing protest about environmental pollution and concern about apparently carcinogenic food additives, yet little has been heard about the ongoing problem of alcoholism. Ironically, there has been recent discussion of the presence of nitrosamines, a carcinogen, in beer but no accompanying alarm over the other well known, more dangerous drug in the same beverage.

When someone raises the point that both nitrosamines and alcohol are inherently dangerous, or when a consumer advocate voices concern not only about saccharin but also about cocaine, or when a lobbyist for environmental causes realizes that marihuana smoking is basically contradictory to his views on water pollution—and can express this thought without being ridiculed—then we may have in the mainstream of society a new unity in the ongoing reform movement and a consistency of views that will animate the struggle against drug abuse of all types.

References

1. American Medical Association, House of Delegates. Report of the committee on the narcotic drug situation in the United States. J.A.M.A. 74:1326, 1920.
2. Bishop, E. S. *The Narcotic Drug Problem*. New York, Macmillan, 1920.
3. Burrow, J. G. *AMA, Voice of American Medicine*. Baltimore, Johns Hopkins University Press, 1963.
4. Clark, N. *Deliver Us from Evil: An Interpretation of American Prohibition*, p. 29. New York, W. W. Norton, 1976.
5. Cumming, H. to Dowling, O. Letter dated February 12, 1921. Located in files of the United States Public Health Service, National Archives, Washington, D.C.
6. DuMez, A. G. Increased tolerance and withdrawal phenomena in chronic morphinism. J.A.M.A. 72: 1069, 1919.
7. Dupree, A. H. *Science in the Federal Government: A History of Policies and Activities to 1940*, pp. 267–270. Cambridge, Mass., Harvard University Press, 1957.
8. Federal Bureau of Narcotics. *Narcotic Clinics in the United States*. Washington, D.C., Government Printing Office, 1955.
9. Guggenheim, W. Z. Heroin: History and pharmacology. Int. J. Addict. 2:328, 1967.
10. Hobson, R. P. The peril of narcotic drugs. *Congressional Record*, 4088–4091. February 18, 1925.
11. Hubbard, S. D. New York City narcotic clinic and differing points of view on narcotic addiction. Monthly Bull. Department of Health, New York City, pp. 45–47. January, 1920.
12. Joint Committee of the American Bar Association and the American Medical Association on Narcotic Drugs, Interim and Final Reports. *Drug Addiction: Crime or Disease?* Bloomington, Ind., Indiana University Press, 1961.
13. Kolb, L., and DuMez, A. G. The prevalence and trend of drug addiction in the United States and factors influencing it. Public Health Rep. 39:1179, 1924.
14. Kuhne, G. Statement of Gerhard Kuhne, Head of Identification Bureau, New York City Department of Correction. In *Conference on Narcotic Education: Hearings before the Committee on Education of the House of Representatives, December 16, 1925*, p. 175. Washington, D.C., Government Printing Office, 1926.
15. Mayor appoints drug committee. The New York Times 8, May 27, 1919.
16. Mowry, G. E. *The Era of Theodore Roosevelt and the Birth of Modern America*. New York, Harper and Brothers, 1958.
17. Murray, R. K. *Red Scare: A Study of National Hysteria, 1919–1920*. Minneapolis, University of Minnesota, 1955.
18. Musto, D. The marihuana tax act of 1937. Arch. Gen. Psychiatry 26:101, 1972.
19. Musto, D. F. *The American Disease: Origins of Narcotic Control*, pp. 41–42. New Haven, Conn., Yale University Press, 1973.
20. President's Advisory Commission on Narcotics and Drug Abuse. *Final Report*. Washington, D.C., Government Printing Office, 1963.
21. President's Commission on Law Enforcement and the Administration of Justice. *The Challenge of Crime in a Free Society*, pp. 228–229. Washington, D.C., Government Printing Office, 1967.
22. *Proceedings of the White House Conference on Narcotic and Drug Abuse*. Washington, D.C., Government Printing Office, 1962.
23. Renborg, B. A. *International Drug Control: A Study of International Administration by and through the League of Nations*, pp. 15–17. Washington, D.C.. Carnegie Endowment for International Peace, 1947.
24. Schmeckebier, L. F. *The Bureau of Prohibition: Its History, Activities and Organization*. Washington, D.C., The Brookings Institution, 1929.
25. Sinclair, A. *Era of Excess: A Social History of the Prohibition Movement*, pp. 36–49. New York, Harper and Row, 1962.
26. Sonnedecker, G. Emergence of the concept of opiate addiction. 1. J. Mon. Pharm. 6:275, 1962.
27. Sonnedecker, G. Emergence of the concept of opiate addiction. 2. J. Mon. Pharm. 7:27, 1963.
28. State of Massachusetts, Acts of 1914, Chapter 694. An act to regulate the sale of opium, morphine and other narcotic drugs. Approved June 22, 1914.
29. State of New York, Laws of 1918, Chapter 639. An act to amend the public health law, so as to provide for the regulation and control of the sale, prescribing, dispensing, dealing in, and distribution of cocaine and opium and its derivatives, and making an appropriation therefor. Approved May 13, 1918.
30. Taylor, A. H. *American Diplomacy and the Narcotics Traffic, 1900–1939: A Study in International Humanitarian Reform*, pp. 47–81. Durham, N.C., Duke University Press, 1969.
31. Terry, C. E., and Pellens, M. *The Opium Problem*, pp. 50–51, 929–937. New York, Bureau of Social Hygiene, 1928.
32. Timberlake, J. H. *Prohibition and the Progressive Movement*. Cambridge, Mass., Harvard University Press, 1963.
33. Udell, G. G., compiler. *Opium and Narcotic Laws*. Washington, D.C., Government Printing Office, 1968.
34. United States 60th Congress, Public Law No. 221.

An act to prohibit the importation and use of opium for other than medicinal purposes. Approved February 9, 1909.

35. United States 63rd Congress, Public Law No. 233. To provide for the registration of, with collectors of internal revenue, and to impose a special tax upon all persons who produce, import, manufacture, compound, deal in, dispense, sell, distribute, or give away opium or coca leaves, their salts, derivatives or preparations. Approved December 17, 1914.

36. United States 65th Congress, Public Law No. 254, Sections 1006 to 1009. An act to provide revenue, by paying special taxes for every person who imports, manufactures, produces, compounds, sells, deals in, dispenses or gives away opium. Approved February 24, 1919.

37. United States 67th Congress, Public Law No. 227. To amend the act of February 9, 1909, as amended, to prohibit the importation and use of opium for other than medicinal purposes. Approved May 26, 1922.

38. United States 68th Congress, Public Law No. 274. Prohibiting the importation of crude opium for the purpose of manufacturing heroin. Approved June 7, 1924.

39. United States 70th Congress, Public Law No. 672. To establish two United States narcotic farms for the confinement and treatment of persons addicted to the use of habit-forming narcotic drugs who have been convicted of offenses against the United States. Approved January 19, 1929.

40. United States 71st Congress, Public Law No. 357. To create in the Treasury Department a Bureau of Narcotics. Approved June 14, 1930.

41. United States 75th Congress, Public Law No. 238. To impose an occupational excise tax upon certain dealers in marihuana, to impose a transfer tax upon certain dealings in marihuana. Approved August 2, 1937.

42. United States 77th Congress, Public Law No. 797. Opium poppy control act of 1942. Approved December 12, 1942.

43. United States 82nd Congress, Public Law No. 255. To amend the penalty provisions applicable to persons convicted of violating certain narcotic laws. Approved November 2, 1951.

44. United States 84th Congress, Public Law No. 728. Narcotic control act of 1956. Approved July 18, 1956.

45. United States 89th Congress, Public Law No. 793. Narcotic addict rehabilitation act of 1966. Approved November 8, 1966.

46. United States 91st Congress, Public Law No. 513. Comprehensive drug abuse prevention and control act of 1970. Approved October 27, 1970.

47. United States House of Representatives, Committee on Ways and Means. *Bureau of Narcotics: Presentment and Report by the Grand Jury on the Subject of the Narcotic Traffic*, pp. 73–77. Filed February 19, 1930.

48. United States Senate, Committee on Printing. *Use of Narcotics in the United States, June 3, 1924*. Washington, D.C., Government Printing Office, 1924.

49. United States Supreme Court. U.S. versus Jin Fuey Moy, 241 U.S. 394, 1916.

50. United States Supreme Court, Webb et al. versus U.S. 249 U.S. 96, 1919; U.S. versus Doremus 249 U.S. 86, 1919.

51. United States Treasury Department. Treasury Decision No. 2172, March 9, 1915.

52. United States Treasury Department. *Traffic in Narcotic Drugs*. Washington, D.C., Government Printing Office, 1919.

53. Wilbert, M. I. The number and kind of drug addicts. Public Health Rep. 30:3, 1915.

54. Wilbert, M. I., and Motter, M. G. *Digest of Laws and Regulations in Force in the United States Relating to the Possession, Use, Sale, and Manufacture of Poisons and Habit-forming Drugs*. Public Health Bulletin No. 56. Washington, D.C., Government Printing Office, 1912.

55. Wright, H. Report on the international opium commission and on the opium problem as seen within the United States and its possessions. In *Opium Problem: Message from the President of the United States*, p. 49. Senate Document No. 377, 61st Congress, 2nd Session, February 21, 1910.

56. Wright, H. Uncle Sam is the worst drug fiend in the world. New York Times, March 12, 1911.

57. Young, J. H. *The Toadstool Millionaires: A Social History of Patent Medicines in America before Federal Regulation*. Princeton, N.J., Princeton University Press, 1961.

CHAPTER 2

DSM-III CLASSIFICATION OF SUBSTANCE USE DISORDERS

John Kuehnle, M.D.

Robert Spitzer, M.D.

The following is a discussion of some of the issues, concepts, and controversies that went into the development of the section on Substance Use Disorders in the third edition of the American Psychiatric Association's *Diagnostic and Statistical Manual of Mental Disorders* (DSM-III). It is written from the perspective of one who played a major role in coordinating the work of the many outstanding contributors. As such, it reflects the views and opinions of the senior author.

One of the central concepts of DSM-III that sets it apart from its two predecessors, DSM-I and DSM-II, is the use of operational criteria, a phrase that has been changed in DSM-III to diagnostic criteria. The use of specific criteria was borrowed from work on Research Diagnostic Criteria (6), which in turn were derived from a modification and elaboration of some of the diagnostic criteria developed at the Washington University School of Medicine in St. Louis. These criteria are sometimes termed "the Feighner criteria," because Feighner is the senior author of the paper that described diagnostic criteria for 15 psychiatric conditions (5). This formed

the parentage and grandparentage of DSM-III in general. Although this is the lineage, in many cases the grandparents would not recognize their grandchildren. Nevertheless, use of diagnostic criteria represents a major advance in the state of the art of psychiatric nosology. By improving interrater reliability and test-retest reliability, diagnoses made by one psychiatrist using DSM-III criteria can be compared directly to diagnoses made by other psychiatrists. By use of the same specific criteria, clinicians using DSM-III will be able to arrive at the same diagnoses.

In research, as opposed to clinical practice, false positive diagnoses are a greater problem than false negatives. For example, inclusion of a patient who is falsely diagnosed as having a condition that he does not have will confound data obtained from a group with that diagnosis, whereas a false negative, a patient who has the condition but is not diagnosed, simply will be omitted from a study. In clinical practice, however, the danger of false negatives is much greater, insofar as a condition may remain untreated because the criteria are too narrow to make an appropriate diagnosis. Therefore, DSM-III has been modified from the Research Diagnostic Criteria to correct this imbalance. In general the criteria adopted for specific diagnoses are broader than those used in the Research Diagnostic Criteria.

If the use of diagnostic criteria represents the most significant technical advance in DSM-III, a shift in psychiatry's attitude toward drug abuse is the most significant philosophical shift in the Substance Use Disorders section of DSM-III. In the past, diagnostic categories of drug abuse have reflected prevailing theoretical biases of the times. Thus, one finds in DSM-I (1) that Alcoholism and Drug Addiction are listed under the general heading of Personality Disorders and under the subheading of Sociopathic Personality Disturbance, along with Sexual Deviation. This classification reflects the prevailing thought of that time—that addiction is directly related to personality development. In the description of Personality Disorders, DSM-I states: "Although the groupings are largely descriptive, the division has been made partially on the basis of the dynamics of personality development" (1).

Another emphasis in DSM-I is the diagnosis of alcoholism and drug addiction by exclusion. In other words, such diagnoses were to be made only in the absence of any other diagnosis. A diagnosis of alcoholism was to be made only if "there is well established addiction to alcohol without recognizable underlying disorder" (1). The same emphasis on diagnosis by exclusion was true of drug addiction, which was often considered secondary to some other psychiatric condition. Alcoholism and drug addiction in DSM-I were thus viewed as a subcategory of a subcategory, i.e., Addiction was subsumed under Sociopathic Personality Disturbance, which, in turn, was a subcategory under Personality Disorders. In addition there was a tendency to diagnose alcoholism by exclusion or as secondary to some other psychiatric condition.

By the time DSM-II was published, personality theories of alcoholism and drug abuse had loosened their hold on theoretical constructs to the extent that the classification of Alcoholism and Drug Dependence was shifted to the Certain Other Nonpsychotic Mental Disorders section of Personality Disorders and Certain Other Nonpsychotic Mental Disorders (2). The diagnoses of Al-

coholism and Drug Dependence moved up in level of categorization and were thus given almost equal categorization with Personality Disorders.

Another significant change in DSM-II was the relationship of alcoholism and drug dependence to other psychiatric conditions when they coexisted. In DSM-I the other psychiatric diagnosis was given preference over the diagnosis of alcoholism or drug dependence. The implication was that in most cases alcoholism or drug problems were secondary to the other psychiatric diagnoses. DSM-II permitted independent diagnosing of alcoholism and drug dependence from other psychiatric disorders. Independent diagnosing encouraged the observation of alcoholism and drug dependence as phenomena that could exist independent from other psychiatric conditions. Separate listing thus permitted clinicians to consider each condition independently and to treat accordingly.

Although DSM-II enhanced the diagnosis of alcoholism and drug dependence, nevertheless these diagnoses were relegated to the residual categories: Certain Other Nonpsychotic Mental Disorders and closely associated Personality Disorders (2). This theoretical bias has been eliminated in DSM-III. In this system a separate diagnostic category has been established under the title of Substance Use Disorders. Nine separate classes of substances are included under Substance Use Disorders, including alcohol, barbiturate or similarly acting sedatives or hypnotics, amphetamine or similarly acting sympathomimetics, opioids, cannabis, cocaine, phencyclidine (PCP) or similarly acting arycyclohexylamines, hallucinogens, and tobacco. Each class is then designated as producing either abuse or dependence or both. Specifically excluded from the diagnostic class of Substance Use Disorders are recreational or medical uses of any of these substances (3).

The diagnostic criteria for substance abuse include each of the following conditions: (1) pattern of pathological use; (2) impairment in social or occupational functioning due to substance use; (3) minimal duration of disturbance of 1 month.

The diagnostic criteria for substance dependence include: (1) tolerance or withdrawal; (2) for alcohol dependence and cannabis dependence an impairment in social or occupational functioning is also required. In general, substance dependence is a more severe form of substance use disorder than substance abuse, and the diagnosis requires the presence of physiological dependence.

As possible diagnostic categories, some classes of substances are associated with both abuse and dependence. These include alcohol, barbiturates or similarly acting sedatives or hypnotics, opioids, amphetamine or similarly acting sympathomimetics, and cannabis. Other classes of substances are associated only with abuse because physiological dependence has yet to be demonstrated. These include cocaine, phencyclidine (PCP) or similarly acting arylcyclohexylamines, and hallucinogens. One substance, tobacco, is associated only with dependence, because heavy use of tobacco is not associated with impairment in social or occupational functioning.

The Substance Use Disorders section of DSM-III also includes subtyping of the course of the illness (3). Arbitrarily designated courses are as follows:

Code	Course	Definition
1	Continuous	More or less regular maladaptive use for over six months.
2	Episodic	A fairly circumscribed period of maladaptive use, with one or more similar periods in the past.
3	In remission	Previously exhibited maladaptive use but currently is not. The differentiation of this from "no longer ill" requires consideration of the period of time since the last episode, the number of episodes, and the need for continued evaluation or prophylactic treatment.
0	Unspecified	Course unknown or first signs of illness with course uncertain.

The principal objective of DSM-III has been to develop a nosological system that is as theory free as possible, that has a high degree of reliability, and has sufficient validity to make sense and be used by clinicians. This task has not been an easy one, and there remain shortcomings. That is why there will be DSM-IV, DSM-V, ad infinitum. In the remainder of this chapter, we will share some

of the controversies that went into the Substance Use Disorders section. As stated earlier, these are personal observations.

It is indicative that one issue that arose early focused on the title proposed for this section. It had been called Drug Use Disorders in the early drafts, but this gave way to the broader Substance Use Disorders despite the fact that all the substances are drugs (including alcohol). Perhaps we are anticipating the inclusion of the substance "food" with the diagnosis of "obesity" as a substance disorder in DSM-IV. Furthermore, there were proponents who strongly advocated separating alcohol use disorder from other substance use disorders. This did not seem very logical, although historically treatment and theory of alcoholism have often been separated from drug abuse. Past differences, however, did not seem as compelling as the present similarities, and alcoholism was changed to alcohol dependence. Alcohol was listed under Substance Use Disorders along with the other substances.

Another area of great controversy concerned inclusion and exclusion of specific diagnoses. Here there were several problems. If a diagnosis is included that in fact does not exist, some clinicians will attribute drug effects to a condition on which drug effects may not be the major contributor. On the other hand, failure to note a potential diagnosis would prevent the reporting of that diagnosis and thus reinforce the erroneous assumption that the condition does not exist. One possible compromise was to provide for "write-in" diagnoses that would permit reporting if an unlisted clinical condition were detected. Unfortunately, write-ins in diagnoses are destined for the same fate as political write-ins. Another, more viable compromise was to include cannabis dependence but state that the diagnosis remains controversial. It was hoped that this caveat would encourage clinicians to be exceptionally critical of any evidence supporting the diagnosis. Although tolerance to cannabis has been demonstrated, its significance remains controversial. The existence of cannabis withdrawal also is questionable. Impairment of social or occupational function resulting from cannabis use had to be added to the diagnostic criteria in order to help distinguish cannabis dependence from heavy recreational use. The decision about cocaine dependence went the other way, and it was deleted. The exclusion of cocaine dependence from DSM-III may be more an artifact produced by the high cost of the drug than a lack of potential for dependence from the drug per se. Should cocaine become more available and less expensive in the future, DSM-IV may include the category Cocaine Dependence.

Two changes occurred that altered the format and, to some extent, changed an underlying concept in the Substance Use Disorders section of DSM-I. The underlying concept involved psychological dependence and a compelling desire to use a substance. The first change involved the deletion of the term "psychological dependence," and the second change involved the deletion of the phrase "a compelling desire to use a substance." The format that appeared in the DSM-III Draft of January 15, 1979, second printing, was as follows (3):

> *Diagnostic criteria for Substance X Abuse.* A, B, and C are required.
> *Diagnostic criteria for Substance X Dependence.* A, B, C, and D are required.
> A. Continuous or episodic use of Substance X for at least one month.
> B. Social complications of substance use: impairment in social or occupational functioning (e.g., fights, loss of friends, missed work) or legal difficulties (other than due to possession, purchase, or sale of an illegal substance).
> C. Either (1) or (2):
> (1) *Psychological dependence:* a compelling desire to use Substance X; inability to cut down or stop use; repeated efforts to control use through periods of temporary abstinence or restriction of use to certain times of the day.
> (2) *Pathological pattern of use:* remains intoxicated throughout the day; frequently uses excessive quantities of Substance X; has had two or more episodes of overdose with Substance X.
> D. Either (1) or (2):
> (1) *Tolerance:* increasing amounts of the substance required to achieve desired effect, or diminished effect with regular use of same dose.
> (2) *Withdrawal:* development of Substance X withdrawal after cessation or reduction of Substance X.

The term "psychological dependence" presented problems for two reasons. First, historically the term "psychological dependence" was often used in conjunction with the term "physical dependence." Because the term "physical dependence" per se is not used in DSM-III, there was some concern that the term "psychological dependence" might lead to confusion. In practice, however, the term "substance dependence," in requiring either tolerance or withdrawal as criteria, is a rough equivalent to physical dependence. Secondly, there was some concern that the term "psychological" might be interpreted as arising out of hypothesized developmental defects or conveying a nonbiological bias. In an attempt to keep the diagnostic categories as atheoretical and free from bias as possible, the term "psychological dependence" was deleted. Although the term "psychological dependence" was deleted, those conditions that had been subsumed under the term were thereafter subsumed under Pathological Pattern of Use. The one exception was the phrase "compelling desire to use a substance."

The reasons for deleting "a compelling desire to use a substance" were essentially the problems of measurement and reliability. How can one objectively measure someone else's desire to use a substance? Although pathological patterns of use can be objectively quantified, defining "a compelling desire" raises too many problems. The decision, therefore, was to delete the phrase. The senior author's preference would have been to change "psychological dependence" to "biological vulnerability" and to keep the phrase "a compelling desire to use a substance." Although it is clear that this would have violated the concept of keeping DSM-III as atheoretical as possible, it might have yielded significant benefits. The major benefit would have been to shift the focus of interest in the field of substance abuse from tolerance and withdrawal phenomena to what mechanisms might underly a compelling desire to use a specific substance. The tolerance and withdrawal phenomena are, to some degree, "red herrings" insofar as they reflect pharmacodynamic properties of a substance rather than the possible underlying biological vulnerabilities of an individual who becomes dependent. Physiological signs and symptoms of tolerance and withdrawal also fail to explain why many individuals who have been substance dependent in the past and who show neither signs nor symptoms of tolerance or withdrawal relapse into drug use. A biological vulnerability that is manifested by a compelling desire to use a substance would help explain relapses in drug use and refocus research into more productive areas.

The over-all plan for DSM-III thus emerged as (4):

The diagnostic criteria for Substance Abuse include each of the following conditions:
1. Pattern of pathological use;
2. Impairment in social or occupational functioning due to substance use;
3. Minimal duration of disturbance one month.
The diagnostic criteria for Substance Dependence include:
1. Tolerance or withdrawal;
2. For Alcohol Dependence and Cannabis Dependence an impairment in social or occupational functioning is also required.

The pattern of pathological use was further elaborated upon as follows:

Pattern of pathological use including inability to cut down or stop use; repeated efforts to control use through periods of temporary abstinence or restriction of use to certain times of the day; intoxication throughout the day; frequent uses of excessive quantities of Substance X; two or more episodes of overdose with Substance X.

In summary, the Substance Use Disorders section of DSM-III represents several major advances over previous nosologies. It permits independent diagnoses of drug use disorders and does not anchor diagnosis to any particular theory of drug use. In addition, the use of specific criteria will permit increased diagnostic reliability, thus increasing the value of data obtained from research or treatment in the field of drug abuse. Some of the controversies and some of the solutions have been cited. There is no doubt that the Substance Use Disorders section of DSM-III is imperfect, but then the state of the art in psychiatry also lacks perfection. This is why there will be future editions of DSM.

References

1. American Psychiatric Association, Committee on Nomenclature and Statistics. *Diagnostic and Statistical Manual, Mental Disorders*. Washington, D.C., American Psychiatric Association, 1952.
2. American Psychiatric Association. Committee on Nomenclature and Statistics. *Diagnostic and Statistical Manual of Mental Disorders*, ed. 2. Washington, D.C., American Psychiatric Association, 1968.
3. American Psychiatric Association, Task Force on Nomenclature and Statistics. *DSM-III Draft (1/15/78 First Printing)*. Washington, D.C., American Psychiatric Association, 1978.
4. American Psychiatric Association, Task Force on Nomenclature and Statistics. *Diagnostic and Statistical Manual of Mental Disorders*, ed. 3. Washington, D.C., American Psychiatric Association, 1980.
5. Feighner, J. P., Robins, E., Guze, S. B., et al. Diagnostic criteria for use in psychiatric research. Arch. Gen. Psychiatry 26:57, 1972.
6. Spitzer, R. L., Endicott, J., and Robins, E. Research diagnostic criteria. Arch. Gen. Psychiatry 35:773, 1978.

CHAPTER 3

EPIDEMIOLOGY OF SUBSTANCE ABUSE

Charles Winick, Ph.D.

Epidemiology of substance abuse has flourished in terms of funding and visibility in recent years. Administrators, during the last decade, realized that one way of facilitating legislators' interest in expansion of programs was to present information about substances in terms of the numbers and kinds of their users. "The numbers game" also provides material which is of interest to mass media, which can compare and contrast the number of users at some time in the past with the current number.

If the number of substance abusers has declined, program officials can take credit for the decrease. If the number has increased, the planners might request more money for the next year's budget and also suggest that the increase could have been much greater if the program had not been operating.

The appearance of new high risk groups of users can also be identified by epidemiological studies. In recent years, for example, more women have been reporting problems with alcohol and other substances of abuse. Most heroin addicts begin using the drug between the ages of 15 and 21. Such findings can help target a group for prevention efforts or suggest the nature and location of treatment facilities.

Public health officials have long used concepts from epidemiology in order to monitor the number and kinds of persons with a condition at a particular time, the number and kinds of persons who had acquired the condition in a specific period, patterns of spread of the condition, and its life cycle. The epidemiological approach could most directly be used in order to track contagious diseases and facilitated decisions about the nature and level of treatment facilities, comparative success of prevention campaigns, and similar matters.

During the last decade, the epidemiology of substance use, misuse, and abuse has begun to emerge as a significant specialty area, key concepts of which include incidence and prevalence. Incidence is generally used for the total of new cases in a given time period, such as a year. Prevalence refers to the total number of persons in the population who are affected by the condition.

Such concepts are relatively easy to apply in the case of a condition like diphtheria. Either a person has it or does not have it at any particular time, and the total number of cases can be identified. In the case of substance use, misuse, and abuse, determining incidence and prevalence is much more difficult, because of problems in definitions.

In the case of use of a substance, are we interested in one-time, occasional, frequent, or daily use? How about users in treatment? Drug abuse is often defined as the nontherapeutic use of a psychoactive substance in a manner that is harmful to the person and/or society. Such a nonoperational definition is lacking in precision. Although drug abuse, the subject of this book, is the focus of one of the National Institutes of Health, the term is not fully adequate because it includes a moral dimension and has more connotations than denotations. Similar objections could be made about the concept of drug misuse, which is often defined as the inappropriate use of drugs intended for therapeutic purposes.

In spite of such problems, valid data on epidemiology of drug use are necessary to guide decisions on legislative appropriations, treatment facilities, prevention, and control programs and to identify groups which are at risk.

There are at least three major dimensions of substance use: incidence of initial use, prevalence or total number of active users, and frequency and intensity of use (17). All of these dimensions are important, but few studies deal with all three.

The dimension of degree of use is significant as we increasingly have come to believe that only a minority of people who take substances of abuse advance to compulsive use, that drug use may be situational and/or episodic, and that a substantial proportion of even compulsive users can become abstinent without treatment.

A set of operational definitions of key epidemiological concepts has been developed and published (12). Among the concepts defined are: user, frequency/quantity, onset, recent use, interest in maintaining use, history of use, polydrug use, methods of use, conditions of use, reasons for use and nonuse, effects, pathology, and availability. Widespread employment of these definitions could lead to substantial upgrading of the quality of work in the field.

A very important change in epidemiology of substance abuse has been the recognition that there are many drugs other than heroin and marihuana that may be dysfunctional. We now know that many groups other than young male urban ghetto residents are using psychoactive substances in a maladaptational manner. Not only is this a recurrent survey finding but it has been dramatized by celebrities like actor Dick Van Dyke and moonwalking astronaut Buzz Aldrin, who publicly identified themselves as alcoholics; actor

Jerry Lewis, who has described his addiction to analgesics; and former First Lady Betty Ford, who has described her multiple addiction to alcohol, analgesics, and tranquilizers. In addition to such famous older persons, considerable media prominence has been given to celebrities' children who were involved in various kinds of substance abuse.

When methadone maintenance programs began in the 1960's, many older addicts who had been taking opiates for decades but were unknown to the authorities "came out of the closet" and confirmed the existence of substantial numbers of senior citizen users. Winick has followed, for two decades, a number of opiate addicts who have never been known to treatment or criminal justice authorities but maintained regular patterns of use (28).

TYPOLOGIES

Epidemiology of drug dependence has been enhanced by the promulgation of various kinds of typologies, which seek to clarify the different kinds of users. Such typologies often are based on interpretations of the functions served by drug use for their users. Thus, one typology identifies "heads," who try to achieve insight and expand the sensibility, and "freaks," who seek hedonistic satisfaction (9).

Another approach sees the "old-style junkie," who was using before 1964; the "transition junkie," who began in the psychedelic era, from 1964 through 1966; and the "new junkie," who started drug use after 1967, when there was disillusionment in the counterculture (13). Users' relationships to conventional or criminal life contribute to another typology: conformist (heavily involved in conventional life), hustler (deeply related to criminal life), two worlder (highly involved in both areas), and uninvolved (not significantly concerned with either area) (4).

Recent typological studies have turned away from either-or categories like addict or alcoholic. Instead, there is recognition of the existence of a continuum, ranging from none to very heavy use. Current typologies also recognize a continuum of functions of substance use, from experimentation to social recreational, committed, and dysfunctional use (6).

The newer approaches also focus on the life cycle of each substance's use (25). A number of the substances which are of interest could have their own cycle of use, and the epidemiologist is interested in knowing how many persons are at each step of the cycle. Marihuana, alcohol, and heroin, for example, each seem to have their own pattern of progression.

Our ability to identify the transitions between the various stages of substance abuse and the relative length of each stage is important. The relationship among several substances of abuse and the extent to which there is a progression from one to another are of concern to the epidemiologist. The stepping-stone theory, which held that one substance, e.g., marihuana, inevitably led to the use of another substance, e.g., heroin, has not been confirmed. Certain broad patterns of sequential tendencies have, however, emerged.

Policy makers and legislators are likely to ask researchers for "the" number of heroin addicts or marihuana smokers as a guide to program expenditures. The researcher, aware of the broad spectrum of relationships of use and the people moving in and out of the life cycle of use at any one time, is typically reluctant to provide "the" number.

THE EPIDEMIOLOGICAL MODEL

Because of the enormous impact of social, economic, and cultural factors, an epidemiological model cannot be completely predictive of the spread of drug abuse. The epidemic of drug abuse that seems to have occurred in this country from 1964 to 1971 surely reflected the Vietnam War, economic difficulties, intergenerational conflicts, the exceptionally high proportion of young people in the population, problems in gender identity, the women's movement, a generalized collapse in social control, the changing content of rock music, the existence of a drug subculture, a decline in the availability of risk-taking behavior, increases in law enforcement activity, a decline in opportunities for upward mobility, media highlighting of substance use, administration efforts to implement a war on crime by an antidrug crusade, the rapidity of social change, and similar factors (27).

In spite of the importance of such factors, the communicable disease model of epidemiology is still useful. The first investigator to apply the model of the spread of contagious disease to heroin addiction was de Alarcon (10). Working in a London suburb, he was able to trace the spread of heroin use from one individual to the next.

Applying the communicable disease model, we have learned that drug dependence is generally spread among peers. New users of heroin tend to occur in "generations" of about a year. One problem in application of the communicable disease model is that in drug dependence, the host is likely to seek out the disease agent, which is the reverse of what is found in large scale communicable disorders.

SURVEY METHODS

The probability sample survey method of a whole population has become perhaps the most important and certainly the most publicized method of determining the number of substance users, abusers, and misusers. It was originally developed in 1933 in order to meet an analogous need. When President Roosevelt took office in 1933, he wanted to know how many unemployed persons there were in America, so that he could deal appropriately with the problem. Because a full census of the population would have taken years, a probability sample was developed and its members were interviewed about their employment status. Their answers provided the President with findings that could be extrapolated to the whole adult population. This application of a probability sample was so successful that commercial organizations, like those of George Gallup and Elmo Roper, began systematic polling by 1935.

Similarly, when President Nixon identified drug abuse as one of the country's key problems in the late 1960's, he wanted to know how many people were involved in illegal drug use. His support made possible the availability of the substantial sums of money needed to conduct sophisticated national surveys. Among the representative national surveys that have been conducted are those involving psychotherapeutic drugs, all substances of abuse, a high risk group of young adult males, a panel study, and an investigation of alcohol.

There had been considerable concern about the extent of the use and misuse of licit psychoactive drugs, so that it was a real step forward in epidemiology when the Institute for Research in Social Behavior at Berkeley and the Social Research Group at George

Washington University combined forces to conduct the first national study of the use of psychotherapeutic drugs in 1970 to 1971 (20). The drugs were defined as those that have significant effects on mood, mental processes, and/or behavior and that should be obtained through a doctor's prescription. The most frequently prescribed psychotherapeutic drugs are minor tranquilizers, sedatives, hypnotics, stimulants, antidepressants, and major tranquilizers. There are also over-the-counter drugs such as stimulants, tranquilizers, and sedatives, which only contain small dosages of psychoactive chemical substances.

In the year preceding the interview, 22 per cent of the respondents had taken a prescription drug and 12 per cent had used over-the-counter substances. Relatively few of the respondents had employed the substances on a long term regular basis. Women were much more likely than men to have taken a prescription product, but both sexes used over-the-counter products at about the same level. Older persons were more likely than younger persons to use prescription substances. The researchers concluded that both physicians and their patients seem to have misgivings about the use of psychotherapeutic drugs except as a way of coping with impaired functioning.

The first large scale probability sample study, involving the whole range of substances of abuse by a sample of persons aged 12 or over, was conducted by the Commission on Marihuana and Drug Abuse in 1972 (1). This study set forth baseline data on American adults' use of a wide variety of substances, including marihuana, inhalants, hallucinogens, cocaine, opiates, stimulants, sedatives, tranquilizers, alcohol, and cigarettes. Since then, four such surveys have been conducted, most recently in 1977 with 4,594 respondents (7). Similar questions are asked in each survey in the series, so that trend information is available.

Young adults aged 18 to 25 are the heaviest users, with about one-fourth currently taking marihuana, one-fifth ingesting cocaine or hallucinogens, and one-tenth consuming opiates other than heroin. Older adults have relatively little experience with nonmedical drug use; 15 per cent have tried marihuana. Adolescents' drug experience rate is between the two older groups. Over the 5-year period, between the first and fifth survey, over-all drug use increased.

Another significant approach to epidemiology is to conduct a survey of a high risk population. Using Selective Service records, O'Donnell interviewed a national sample of 2,510 young men of 20 to 30, the age group most likely to be involved in drug abuse (22). The study was able to develop an over-all measure of drug use, which was called the Total Drug Index. High scores on this index were likely to be found among younger men, those with less education, not fully employed, living in a nonfamily situation, and engaging in deviant activity.

The only national panel study of high school students' drug use has been conducted by the University of Michigan Institute for Social Research (18). The patterns of drug use of young people, it was found, are largely established by the senior year of high school, and perhaps even earlier. In this study, it is possible to track the development of drug-abuse behavior during the respondents' years in high school and afterward, when young people move out into the world of work, college, marriage, the military, and other aspects of the larger society. Such a panel approach has the merit of enabling us to follow the same persons over time and see how their drug use may reflect situational, social, economic, and personal developments. It has also demonstrated the feasibility of obtaining data on a sensitive subject like illegal drug use via a mail questionnaire.

An advance in the epidemiology of alcohol use was made when Cahalan and his associates completed the first national study of drinking practices (5). They established how much of various alcoholic beverages was being consumed by the age, ethnic, socioeconomic, gender, geographic, and other subgroups in the population. By operationally defining concepts like heavy drinking and problem drinking, it was possible to establish empirical typologies of drinking. For example, heavy drinkers are likely to be men and women aged 45 to 49, of lower socioeconomic status, service workers, nonmarried, big city residents, Catholics and Prostestants, and American Indians. Such data have contributed substantially to better understanding of the problems posed by alcohol.

In spite of its obvious merits in obtaining access to a representative sample of the population, the survey method has a number of disadvantages. One problem is that in the case of a substance like heroin, which is used by relatively few people, but which is of great concern to the community, even a large probability sample may yield a small number of users. The National Commission on Marihuana and Drug Abuse found that well under 2 per cent of adults had ever used heroin (8). Even in the high risk group of males aged 20 to 30, only 2 per cent had used heroin in the year preceding the interview (22). Generalizations based on such a small number of actual heroin users would be somewhat risky. One way of getting a substantial number of serious heroin users in a probability sample survey is to oversample the high risk subgroup in the large sample and then weigh it back in (23).

Among the other problems of conducting surveys are high refusal rates, difficulties in sampling households, and assuring confidentiality of client records. In recent years, there has been an increasing proportion of subjects in sample surveys who will not consent to being interviewed. Some 25 per cent of the general population now refuses to be interviewed. This requires special sampling procedures for getting substitute respondents and increases survey costs.

The best probability samples are those of households, derived from census block tracts. However, street drug users may not be likely to live at a stable address. In efforts to follow samples of street users, as many as 30 per cent cannot be located after 6 months. Because street users are often not living in households likely to be sampled by survey procedures, a conventional household sampling procedure may be inadequate.

Maintaining confidentiality of client information and protecting respondents' anonymity are concerns of all survey researchers but must be of special urgency to drug researchers because of the dimension of illegality that surrounds much drug use. New sensitivity to the issue of informed consent and parental approval in the case of minors has emerged in the last few years.

Survey researchers often set up elaborate procedures to protect confidentiality, involving the replacement of names with code numbers, sending the only record of the respondents' names and code numbers to Canada, and similar techniques which insure the integrity of the records' confidentiality.

RATES FROM OTHER DISEASES RELATED TO DRUG ABUSE

Alcoholism and other drug abuse are conditions which are recognized by the courts and the American Medical Association as diseases. However, they are uniquely related to other diseases, and estimating how many people have the other diseases may permit an indirect approximation of the size of the population of abusers of various substances.

In the case of alcoholism, the death rate from cirrhosis of the liver has been used to estimate the number of alcoholics (19). How long a representative alcoholic takes to get cirrhosis is known, as is the course of cirrhosis itself. Alcoholism is the primary cause of cirrhosis. Working backward from the current death rate from cirrhosis of the liver, it is possible to estimate the total number of alcoholics.

Hepatitis has been used as an indicator of intravenous drug abuse because of the high proportion of abusers who contract hepatitis via infected needles. Although all physicians are required to report diagnosed hepatitis to public health authorities, few physicians actually do so. Hepatitis B, the kind likely to be associated with drug abuse, has an incubation period of 2 to 6 months, so that there is a substantial lag between infection and clinical signs of the disease. Another consideration is that serious hepatitis may be the result of so many things other than infected needles used in intravenous injection that it is probably an unreliable indicator of the latter.

Where there is a captive population of possible substance abusers, visual examination of their arms provides a reasonably valid test of intravenous drug use. Working in Sweden, Bejerot inspected the arms of 34,346 arrestees, looking for injection marks (3). Subsequently checking the validity of the identification, over 98 per cent of those examined had been correctly identified as drug abusers. Because of its speed, low cost, and validity, the method seems promising.

One method for indirect measurement of the number of drug abusers in a population is to make projections from the overdose death rate of narcotic addicts. It was believed, in the early 1970's, that addicts' overdose-related deaths occur at a fairly predictable rate of approximately 1 per cent per year. If the number who had overdosed were known, it should be possible to project the total population of addicts. However, questions about the constancy of the death rate have been raised.

When death rates are used to estimate the number of psychoactive drug users, among the resultant problems are the possible implication of suicidal and homicidal motivations, substantial intercity differences in the rate of such deaths, and errors resulting from inadequate quality control in toxicological laboratories (14).

RECAPTURE METHOD

An adaptation of a method used in biological research is represented by the recapture approach. In studies of wild animals, some are marked and when they reappear in captivity at some subsequent time, the number so recaptured is projected to the total population of the species.

In terms of an application to estimating the number of drug abusers, the recapture procedure was first used by Joseph Greenwood in 1971 (15). If an addict was listed by the Drug Enforcement Administration (DEA) and then reappeared on the DEA roster at a later date, he was said to have been recaptured. One problem with this technique is that a known criminal user has a much better chance of being arrested and reappearing on the DEA roster than a user who is not involved in criminal activity. The latter, of whom there are many, would thus be underrepresented in a recapture approach.

DRUG SEIZURES, BUYS, AND ARRESTS

Police activity in the form of drug seizures, buys, and arrests of persons violating the laws for drug possession and sales has provided indirect measures of the number of drug abusers.

Via a number of ways, police are continually seeking to seize illegal drugs and reduce their availability on the street. Customs officials are constantly attempting to block the importation of illegal psychoactive substances into this country. Such drug seizures represent an indirect measure of prevalence, because prevalence has a direct relation to availability of substances. If there are no illegal drugs available, people cannot use them.

Seizures depend on unpredictable market forces, but police and others can make buys of illegal substances on a systematic basis. Local and federal law enforcement personnel are continually using undercover agents to buy street drugs and then chemically evaluating their purity. Such buying activity provides information on the different substances available and their prices. Extrapolating to the number of users can then be accomplished.

Persons may be arrested for drug law violations or they may be arrested for other crimes. From a third to a half of arrests for drug offenses result from police investigation of other crimes. The Drug Enforcement Administration defines an active user as one who has been arrested in the last 5 years. Changes in the numbers and kinds of drug users arrested are often interpreted to reflect shifts in the numbers and kinds of persons who are using illegal drugs, based on various formulae that are used to estimate the amount of time that a typical user takes to be arrested from the time that he begins regular illegal drug use.

DRUG ABUSE WARNING NETWORK (DAWN)

Another approach to epidemiology is provided by the Drug Abuse Warning Network (DAWN), which was established in 1972 as a cooperating group of reporting sources. They include hospital inpatient centers and emergency rooms, medical examiners, crisis centers, coroners, and other facilities servicing drug abusers who have become ill. Crises and death related to drug use are reported and can be extrapolated to the nation (11).

In recent years, the racial composition of persons reported to DAWN is: whites 57 per cent, blacks 30 per cent, and other 5 per cent. The high proportion of whites makes this seem to be an unusual sample of drug users, inasmuch as approximately three-fourths of those in treatment are nonwhite.

Another problem with use of DAWN data is that users become increasingly sophisticated about dealing with emergencies and medical problems related to drugs. They probably become more likely to be able to handle such matters on their own, with the passage of time and the development of a word of mouth expertise on coping with drug emergencies, without having to go to a hospital or crisis center. DAWN data may, therefore, be less likely to reflect drug realities as time goes on.

LOCALIZED STUDIES

A localized survey can identify special qualities of the community that contribute to the area's rate or prevalence of substance abuse. Climate, life style, police activity, ethnicity, age patterns, proportion of transients, the economy, housing, and related factors can be important in understanding the meaning of local prevalence figures. A national survey, no matter how good, cannot adequately identify and interpret such factors for each community. For some purposes, community, state, or regional surveys are indispensable.

Cities and states increasingly are conducting their own epidemiological investigations. New York State, for example, has completed several substantial investigations of the prevalence of different kinds of substance abuse and fed the results of such studies directly into program plans and activities. Thirty-five other states have conducted surveys of drug abuse.

In addition to sample surveys of a community or region, less formal techniques are constructively employed in order to trace incidence and spread of drug abuse. In the copping area approach, an intensive count is conducted of a small geographic area in which an addict operates. Originally identified in Chicago, the copping area is a stable distribution site for heroin. By stationing a field team at these sites, it is possible to monitor prevalence by maintaining a simple census of the active addicts who regularly visit these locations (16).

Incidence, defined for this purpose as the date of first heroin use, occurs only once for each addict and is difficult to observe. When incidence of the spread of heroin in Chicago was studied via the copping area, it was found

to fluctuate sharply from periods of epidemic spread to times of quiescence. In specific areas, microepidemics and macroepidemics could be identified. Thus, between 1967 and 1971, 11 macroepidemics occurred.

Another approach to localized assessment of the number of drug users is the Delphi technique, in which a user in treatment is asked to name everyone he knows who is using drugs, whether or not they are in treatment. Each person so named is then interviewed and asked to name all the users whom he or she knows. This technique has the potential for providing an intensive view of the number of users in an area.

One way of estimating the number of users of illegal drugs in an area is to take a very small part of a community and interview every single person in residence. Thus, at one time in the 1970's, 100 Street between First and Second Avenue in New York City was believed to be typical of city areas with a very high rate of heroin use. A team of residents of the block interviewed every single person living there about their use of heroin, and the results were projected to the whole East Harlem area. In this type of work, as in copping area or other community studies, it is necessary to employ indigenous interviewers who are known to the interviewees and who may themselves be former drug users.

PRESCRIPTION AUDITS

An approach to the epidemiology of psychoactive drug use is via the several commercial services which provide syndicated audits of prescriptions by a sample of drugstores or physicians. Projecting from such sources, it has been estimated that some 214 million prescriptions for psychoactive drugs were filled in a typical year (1970), or roughly one per person (2). These prescriptions represented 17 per cent of all drug prescriptions. Both physicians and their patients seem to have a conservative attitude to the use of these substances. However, in 1977, 280 million prescriptions for psychoactive drugs, or 20 per cent of all prescriptions, were written.

It is also possible to compare the findings from prescription or store audits with data from manufacturers on how many pills or capsules they have shipped in a given time period. A comparison of the amount shipped with the amount prescribed and/or sold by a pharmacist can provide a measure of the number of pills or capsules being diverted to the illegal street market. In the case of psychoactive prescription drugs as well as methadone, the amount being diverted is substantial and provides clues to the number of illegal users.

ESTIMATES BASED ON TREATMENT POPULATIONS

Most people in treatment situations are, in one way or another, being financially assisted by a government agency, which may be concerned with treatment, welfare, or criminal justice. Because of this government presence, it is not difficult to obtain a census of treatment populations. Projections from the number of drug users in treatment to the total number in the whole country are relatively easy and have been frequently made.

Extrapolating from the number of people in treatment to total prevalence may, however, be hazardous, because there is little way of knowing how representative the treatment population is. In different communities, drug-using clients may enter treatment for a wide range of motivations in addition to the desire to get well. They may do so in order to reduce the size of their habits, avoid jail, drop out of the community, dodge a police sweep, or other reasons. Treatment availability may vary from one city to another, and criteria for admission may also differ. If a person comes once for treatment and never reappears, how should he or she be counted?

Another problem is that different programs attract different kinds of persons. Methadone maintenance programs, for example, tend to attract older users than do therapeutic communities. Generalizing about the age of the total number of heroin addicts from data deriving either from therapeutic communities or methadone programs would be difficult. Some programs may have particularly effective outreach and recruitment efforts that pull in substantial numbers of users, who may not be representative of the total population of users.

One source of epidemiological data is the Client Oriented Data Acquisition Process (CODAP), which is a national reporting system of information from clients entering federally funded treatment programs. CODAP information includes, for example, the primary and secondary or other drugs taken by newly enrolled patients. It also includes ethnicity and other background information.

Another major treatment source of epidemiological data is the Drug Abuse Reporting Program (DARP), which started in 1968 and was replaced in 1974 by CODAP. Based on analysis of the patients in treatment, street heroin addicts seem to come from urban ghetto high crime areas. They tend to be members of minority groups, to have ready access to heroin and other drugs, and to be tolerated with resignation in their communities. Although most use marihuana as their first illegal drug, many start on heroin (24).

Probably the country's largest collection of data from patients in treatment is at Texas Christian University's Drug Abuse Epidemiology Data Center (DAEDAC). In addition to DARP and CODAP files, it also has patient information from the United States Public Health Service Hospital in Lexington, Kentucky. Many different kinds of secondary analyses can be conducted with DAEDAC patient information.

ROSTERS AND REGISTERS

A roster or register is not a method of generating epidemiological information about drug abusers but is a repository for such information, which can come from a variety of sources. Courts, treatment agencies, and physicians are the usual sources of such data, which are recorded by name of the user.

Prevalence of narcotics use was determined, from 1933 through the 1960's, by reports to the Federal Bureau of Narcotics (FBN) from local police departments of persons whom they had arrested. The annual report of the bureau would integrate and summarize these arrest reports. A person would be carried on the FBN roster as an active addict for 5 years, after which he was considered to be inactive (26). The bureau rosters' estimates of the number of narcotic addicts had enormous influence and were widely accepted. Two major deficiencies of the estimates were that no effort was made to determine degree of use, and a person who was not arrested was not counted. The Drug Enforcement Administration has developed a much more sophisticated roster of drug users.

A few areas have experimented with establishment of a register, as in Maryland and New York City. Physicians, hospitals, police, and prisons were required to report each addict who came to their attention, for whatever reason. Absolute confidentiality was guaranteed to reporting agencies, so that a hospital turning in the name of an addict patient need not fear that the name would be given to law enforcement agencies. Courts have upheld the confidentiality of the records.

The New York City Narcotics Register staff estimated in 1972 that the city had 316,918 active heroin addicts. A former city health official has argued that this estimate is good enough for local planners (21). Up to recently, the register was kept current and was used in the many decisions being made about treatment and control programs. It also provided information on changes in the age, gender, ethnicity, and residence of the city's addicts. Unfortunately, adequate funding for the register became more difficult in the 1970's, with the city's fiscal difficulties.

EPIDEMIOLOGY OF ALCOHOL

Interest in patterns of alcohol use and in who is drinking what substance has been central for decades, long before other forms of drug abuse became matters of national concern.

One of the recurrent findings in the epidemiology of alcoholism is the difference in rates among ethnic groups (31). Jews and Italian-Americans, for example, have relatively low alcoholism rates, and Irish-Americans have comparatively high rates. The former groups tend to be exposed to alcohol early on, within the family, and in small quantities. The beverages are served in diluted form and tend to be taken with meals. Parents offer a model of moderate drinking, and drinking is not interpreted as a sign of manhood. The relatively high rates of alcoholism among the Irish have been attributed to their being raised in a situation involving permissiveness toward drinking and the importance of taverns, with alcohol's functions more convivial than religious.

Over-all drinking has been increasing, with annual per capita American adult alcohol consumption averaging 2.65 gallons. In recent years, the age of alcoholics has been declining, and the period of time over which the condition develops has decreased. Twenty-three per cent of teenagers are intoxicated four times a year or more, and 6 per cent of high school seniors take alcohol daily. Usually, problem drinking in youths is one dimension of a larger pattern of misbehavior.

Epidemiologists are especially aware of faddism in substance use patterns. Recently, phencyclidine has been a popular street drug. Light rum, gin, and vodka are among the popular "white goods" that have been superseding Scotch and bourbon as American drinking favorites. A few years ago, tequila was a favorite of young adults. Today, they are drinking more and more wines.

Demographic variables tend to make it more likely that a person will be growing up in an area in which there are available drugs, in which liberal attitudes toward their use will prevail, and where peers may be observed using them. Whether such variables are related to long term drug use is not clear (29).

One clear trend is the decreasing age at onset of substance use, which is true of most substances. Another development is the decline of the heroin addict who does not ingest other drugs and the emergence of the poly-dependent user who takes a wide range of substances. Street heroin is declining in purity, with 2 to 3 per cent strength not uncommon. Street methadone is widely used and is so easily available that fewer addicts are detoxifying in hospitals because they can buy street methadone and ease withdrawal symptoms. The hostility which used to exist between alcohol users and persons taking other drugs has diminished, and one common pattern involves a mixture of drinking and other drugs. Some people regularly take methadone and alcohol; others prefer opiates, pills, and alcohol.

SOME TRENDS IN EPIDEMIOLOGY OF SUBSTANCE ABUSE

Perhaps 550,000 persons in this country are dependent on heroin, of whom some 110,000 are in prison, 140,000 are in treatment, and 310,000 are neither in prison or treatment. From 2 to 3 per cent of adults have used barbiturates illegally, and some 280,000 barbiturate users are abusers. About 490,000 nonmedical users of tranquilizers are abusers. Some 10 million Americans have illegally used cocaine. Marihuana has about 3 million users daily and 13 million current users, many of whom take no other illegal drug. Eleven per cent of high school seniors use marihuana daily. About 7 per cent of junior and senior high school students have used solvents, like household cleaning chemicals, and inhalants, like toluene-containing model kit glue.

Certain occupational groups have long been overrepresented among persons dependent on opiates: physicians, nurses, and musicians (30). Each of these groups is likely to work in circumstances of easy access to the drugs and to have relatively liberal attitudes toward their use.

Bejerot has observed that the proportion of women who are regular users of a substance represents an important indicator of its penetration into society (3). Endemic use may be said to exist when the proportion of female users approaches 50 per cent.

THE OUTLOOK FOR EPIDEMIOLOGY OF DRUG ABUSE

In recent years, epidemiology of drug abuse has become a relatively precise area of investigation. It is much more likely than ever that the estimates from different sources will be compared, in the recognition that each source of information might be tapping different drug-using subpopulations.

Users who are in treatment, those in prison, those getting hepatitis or dying, and those identified in sample surveys may differ in terms of a number of characteristics (17). It is, therefore, difficult to extrapolate from any one of these groups to the total user population.

As epidemiologists become more precise in their estimates, their findings are more likely to be accepted by policy makers. The policy makers are less likely to misuse epidemiological data in order to alarm the public. Studies of high risk population and geographic groups will probably increase. Epidemiology gives every indication of continuing as a high priority part of the drug abuse field. However, our ability clearly to differentiate groups of abusers from nonabusers will probably decline. During the 1950's, when there was a relatively small endemic drug problem, the abusers were likely to be groups of people with clearly identifiable characteristics of personality, socioeconomic status, and comparable dimensions. More re-

cently, as the United States moved through an epidemic and perhaps even a pandemic of drug abuse, involving very large numbers of people, our ability to ascribe specific characteristics of background to the abusers has become less certain.

The large body of data now available has increased our ability to place epidemiological data in perspective and interpret such data with a sense of historical and social reality. Valid documentation will be necessary if there will be future alarm over pandemics or epidemics of drug abuse.

References

1. Abelson, H., et al. *Drug Experience, Attitudes, and Related Behavior among Adolescents and Adults.* Princeton, N.J., Response Analysis Corporation, 1972.
2. Balter, M. B., and Levine, J. Character and extent of psychotherapeutic drug usage in the United States. In *Proceedings of the Fifth World Congress of Psychiatry*, Mexico, 1971.
3. Bejerot, N. *Drug Abuse and Drug Policy.* Copenhagen, Munksgaard, 1975.
4. Brotman, R., and Freedman, A. M. *A Community Mental Health Approach to Addiction.* Washington, D.C., Government Printing Office, 1969.
5. Cahalan, D. *American Drinking Practices.* New Brunswick, N.J., Rutgers Center of Alcohol Studies, 1969.
6. Chambers, C. D. Speculations on a behavioral progression typology of pleasure seeking drug use. In *Sociological Aspects of Drug Dependence*, C. Winick, editor, pp. 127–131. Cleveland, CRC Press, 1974.
7. Cisin, I. H., et al. *Highlights from the National Survey on Drug Abuse.* Washington, D.C., George Washington University Social Research Group, 1978.
8. Commission on Marihuana and Drug Abuse. *Marihuana: A Signal of Misunderstanding*, vol. 1, pp. 434–439. Washington, D.C., Government Printing Office, 1972.
9. Davis, F., and Munoz, L. Heads and freaks. J. Health Soc. Behav., 9:156, 1968.
10. de Alarcon, R. The spread of heroin abuse in a community Bull. Narc. 21:17, 1969.
11. Drug Enforcement Administration. *Drug Abuse Warning Network*, Washington, D.C., Department of Justice, 1977.
12. Elinson, J., and Nurco, D. *Operational Definitions in Socio-Behavioral Drug Use Research.* Rockville, Md., National Institute on Drug Abuse, 1975.
13. Gay, G. R., et al. The Haight-Ashbury Free Medical Clinic. In *It's So Good, Don't Even Try It Once*, D. E. Smith and G. R. Gay, editors. Englewood Cliffs, N.J., Prentice Hall, 1972.
14. Gottschalk, L. A., and McGuire, F. L. Psychosocial and biomedical aspects of deaths associated with heroin and other narcotics. In *The Epidemiology of Heroin and Other Narcotics*, J. D. Rittenhouse, editor, pp. 122–129. Rockville, Md., National Institute on Drug Abuse, 1977.
15. Greenwood, J. A. *Estimating the Number of Narcot-*

ics Addicts. Washington, D.C., United States Bureau of Narcotics and Dangerous Drugs, 1971.

16. Hughes, P. H., and Crawford, G. A. Epidemiology of heroin addiction in the 1970s. In *Drug Use*, E. Josephson and E. E. Carroll, editors, pp. 89–104. New York, John Wiley, 1974.

17. Hunt, L. G. Prevalence of active heroin use in the United States. In *The Epidemiology of Heroin and Other Narcotics*, J. D. Rittenhouse, editor, pp. 61–86. Rockville, Md., National Institute on Drug Abuse, 1977.

18. Johnston, L. D. *Drug Use among American High School Students 1975–77.* Rockville, Md., National Institute on Drug Abuse, 1977.

19. Jolliffe, N., and Jellinek, E. M. Vitamin deficiencies and liver cirrhosis in alcoholics. Q. J. Studies Alcohol. 2:544, 1941.

20. Manheimer, D. Use of mood changing drugs among American adults. In *Sociological Aspects of Drug Dependence*, C. Winick, editor, pp. 103–110. Cleveland, CRC Press, 1974.

21. Newman, R. G., and Cates, M. S. The New York City Narcotics Register: A case study. Am. J. Public Health 64:24, 1974.

22. O'Donnell, J. A., et al. *Young Men and Drugs: A Nationwide Survey.* Rockville, Md., National Institute of Mental Health, 1976.

23. Robins, L. N. Surveys of target populations. In *Epidemiology of Drug Abuse*, L. R. Richards and L. B. Blevens, editors, pp. 39–45. Rockville, Md., National Institute on Drug Abuse, 1977.

24. Sells, S. B. Reflections on the epidemiology of heroin and narcotic addiction from the perspective of treatment data. In *The Epidemiology of Heroin and Other Narcotics*, J. D. Rittenhouse, editor, pp. 147–176. Rockville, Md., National Institute on Drug Abuse, 1977.

25. Winick, C. The life cycle of the narcotic addict and of addiction. U.N. Bull. Narc. 16:22, 1964.

26. Winick, C. The epidemiology of narcotics. In *Narcotics*, D. Wilner and G. G. Kassebaum, editors, pp. 3–18. New York, Blakiston, 1965.

27. Winick, C. Some reasons for the increase in drug dependence. In *Sociology of Youth*, H. Silverstein, editor, pp. 432–436. New York, Macmillan, 1973.

28. Winick, C. Some aspects of careers of chronic heroin users. In *Drug Use: Epidemiological and Sociological Approaches*, E. Josephson and E. E. Carroll, editors, pp. 105–128. New York, John Wiley, 1974.

29. Winick, C. Some consequences of chronic opiate use. In *the Epidemiology of Heroin and Other Narcotics*, pp. 232–238. Rockville, Md., National Institute on Drug Abuse, 1977.

30. Winick, C. The drug offender. In *Psychology of Crime and Criminal Justice*, pp. 373–404. editor, H. Toch, New York, Holt, Rinehart, and Winston, 1979.

31. Winick, C. The alcohol offender. In *Psychology of Crime and Criminal Justice*, H. Toch, editor, pp. 347–372. New York, Holt, Rinehart, and Winston, 1979.

CHAPTER 4

A 10-YEAR PERSPECTIVE ON THE ADDICTION PROBLEM

Peter G. Bourne, M.D.

Opiate addiction has historically been a cyclical phenomenon that has ebbed and flowed through time and geography. Although opiate use has remained endemic for generations in certain areas of the world, it has generally been in a constant state of flux with periodic epidemics developing in one place while at the same time receding elsewhere. Even within a single country the incidence of addiction has varied not only in its intensity, but also with regard to the different segments of society that it affected, at times being a monopoly of the rich and elite and at other times a scourge of the poor and underprivileged.

These vicissitudes of opiate addiction are influenced by many factors but most significantly by technological development. Originally limited to areas in the vicinity of cultivation, the spread of addiction has been dramatically enhanced by improvements in man's capacity to travel around the globe. Opium was introduced in China because the British and American clippers could make the trip from India fast enough to make the opium trade a highly profitable business. In our time jet travel has become a dominant feature in shaping the use of heroin in the modern world. International travel on an unprecedented scale between developed and developing areas of the world, with such speed that the period at risk for the trafficker

was reduced to a matter of hours, lured droves of amateurs into an informal worldwide distribution network.

The development of the hypodermic needle made it possible to use heroin effectively as a drug of addiction. It was no longer necessary to ship large, bulky quantities of opium that were easily detected both by their size and smell. Heroin not only caused a substantially greater effect but it was less bulky and much more easily concealed. Even in developing countries the availability of the hypodermic needle had an effect. Traditionally only the older man had smoked opium, and it was considered socially unacceptable for young men to do so. However, with the availability of injected heroin young men entered the drug-using market without feeling particular social opprobrium for doing something that had generally been restricted to their elders. The hypodermic needle made heroin addiction a universal threat to youth everywhere, a threat that opium itself never posed.

OPIATE USE IN THE UNITED STATES

Whereas opium was widely used in the United States during the 19th century, beginning around 1912 there was a dramatic change to the use of heroin and a concomitant decline in opium use. In the last 70 years opiate use in the United States has consisted, except for a modest number of smokers and sniffers, almost entirely of heroin injection. During that period of time there have been at least three major explosive and sudden increases in the use of drugs involving dramatic expansions in the population of users. The documentation of these epidemic episodes is generally inadequate, but there seem to have been three key peaks of use, one between 1915 and the early 1920's, the second from the late 1950's to the early 1960's, and the last from approximately 1965 to the early 1970's. The elements that triggered these episodes are both complex and in many ways poorly understood, being probably different in each instance. Why, one might ask, after many years of containment within the relatively stable subcultural group, should the use of the drug suddenly spread rapidly to involve tens of thousands of new users?

The epidemic of the 1960's is better understood than any of the others, partly because of the intense study it received and also because of its proximity to the present. However, although a number of factors were identified that were contributory, none can be considered a full explanation of the phenomenon. After a relative hiatus during the late 1950's and early part of the 1960's there was a youth population in the United States that had had little exposure to drug use. At the same time it was a period of major social change when many of the old prejudices and biases were being challenged. The civil rights movement of those years had set in motion a process where, not only was a whole value system being challenged, but young people were exerting their influence and finding that they had power to make dramatic changes in the structure of society. At the same time they began to question seriously the validity of any information they were given, particularly the old truisms that had been accepted for generations. With the advent of the Vietnam War the sense of alienation between youth in this country and the established order was considerably aggravated, and there was strong sentiment among many young people to protest not merely the war itself but what they perceived as an anachronistic system that had allowed the Vietnam War to occur at all. They wished to extend symbolically their protests to make them a confrontation not just with the specifics of the war but with the whole system itself.

Young people found that drugs, particularly marihuana, were not as dangerous as many of their elders believed, while at the same time the older generation, indoctrinated by years of misinformation, were convinced that drugs were not only alien to the American value system but that they were a heinous threat to society and highly medically dangerous. In terms of the symbolic confrontation between youth and the Establishment, it is hard to imagine a better vehicle for that protest than the widespread use of drugs. The fertile soil for the spreading use of drugs was amply cultivated by Timothy Leary and others who came as authority figures out of the Establishment yet who turned against it, giving credence to the notion that the established order was fallible. They could speak with authority in giving sanction to young people's use of drugs. In addition the widespread availability of lysergic acid diethylamide (LSD) and the peculiar mystique and aura that was created around its use made it a drug that was almost symbolic with membership in a new generation. Its supposed mind-expanding qualities fitted well with the belief of many young people that they were already going through a social mind expansion in which they were able to see a world changed from the way it had always been.

Ironically, the initial reaction of many parents, civic groups, and government organizations did much to help spread the use of drugs. So-called drug education programs launched throughout the country by well meaning individuals and organizations helped to publicize the availability, the use, and the excitment of drugs in every schoolroom, state legislature, and civic group in the country. We built an expectation and imposed it on young people that implied that the deviant was the child who had not at least tried marihuana.

Heroin addiction, which always lies lurking in the shadows of the ghetto, received a free ride into suburbia as a result of the new raging interest in drugs among America's middle-class youth. New and extraordinarily lucrative markets were opened up to which the traditional trafficking organizations were delighted to respond. Almost overnight unprecedented quantities of heroin were flooding into America and into every community on the coattails of marihuana and LSD. If you had tried everything else, the use of heroin was the ultimate test of manhood in the drug field. At the same time enterprising agents in Vietnam were making heroin widely available to American soldiers. In many locations the drug was cheaper than Coca-Cola, and there was a widespread belief that if one only smoked the drug sprinkled on a cigarette and inhaled one would not become addicted. The drug sold in Vietnam, however, was between 90 and 100 per cent pure as compared to 10 to 15 per cent for the best grade in the United States; even in the inhaled form it produced an even more rapid addiction than that being injected into the veins of addicts in the United States.

The spread of heroin addiction has been likened to the spread of an infectious disease. Indeed the involvement of new users is a geometrical progression, with one habituated user inducing one or more of his friends to become users, who then in turn proselytize other nonusers. During the mid-1960's there was a sense of daring and excitement associated with heroin use and a naive belief on the part of many young users that, although addiction could occur, it surely would not happen to them. This was particularly true among young blacks, many of whom now had money in their pockets and at the same time raised, but frustrated, expectations because of the social changes of the previous decade. As a result, by the early 1970's roughly one-half million young Americans were addicted to heroin.

THE GOVERNMENT'S RESPONSE

Two aspects of this problem dramatically influenced the manner in which the government responded and, as a result, the course of the epidemic spread of heroin addiction. First, there was associated with the heroin addiction a dramatic rise in urban crime. This was a matter of great consternation for the administration then in power and also created a sense of great urgency among citizens who were victims of the increasing crime wave. Second, the easy availability in Vietnam led to a shocking increase in addiction among soldiers to a point where, in some instances, as high as 100 per cent of the men in some units were addicted to the drug. These individuals began to return in increasing numbers to the United States in an addicted state. At the same time there was mounting concern about the combat readiness and effectiveness of individuals who were addicted. These two factors, mounting domestic crime rates and heavy addiction of soldiers in Vietnam, led the Nixon administration in 1971 to decide that drug, and particularly heroin, addiction should be made a major political issue and that some dramatic steps needed to be taken to respond to the mounting public pressure and outcry.

A multipronged attack was launched. First, in June of 1971 the Special Action Office for Drug Abuse Prevention was established under the direction of Dr. Jerome Jaffe to coordinate all federal drug abuse prevention activities out of the White House. At the same time the federal commitment to drug abuse treatment was increased approximately 10-fold. Prior to 1971 there were only 50 drug treatment facilities in the country, with in excess of $500 million being spent for treatment and prevention programs at the federal and state level.

A second major aspect of the strategy was to launch a world-wide program to begin to curtail the flow of heroin to the United States. The federal drug law enforcement effort was expanded and reorganized, resulting eventually in the creation of the Drug Enforcement Administration. At that time the predominant source of heroin was still through the diversion of opium from Turkey via the conversion laboratories in Marseilles, and then through New York into the domestic drug distribution network. A negotiated agreement was reached with the Turkish government whereby they would ban the cultivation of all opium in return for which the United States would pay them a subsidy of $35 million a year to replace the losses sustained by their withdrawal from the legitimate opium market. At the same time a coordinated law enforcement crackdown was initiated in conjunction with the French to close down the Marseilles conversion laboratories and to break up the trafficking networks that brought heroin to the United States. The strategy was successful, and the amount of heroin coming from France rapidly slowed to a trickle.

During that same period in 1972 and 1973, initial overtures were made to the Thai, Burmese, and Lao governments in order to get their cooperation in restricting the amount of heroin coming out of the so-called Golden Triangle. Although very little of this heroin reached the United States, it was the exclusive source of heroin being used by American soldiers in South Vietnam. Subsequently, as increasing numbers of addicted soldiers returned to the United States, connections were established, particularly out of Thailand, that led to an increasing role for the "Golden Triangle" as the major source of heroin reaching this country.

In addition to the effort to increase treatment capacity in the United States and the diplomatic initiatives to cut off heroin supplies from overseas, an important side effect of the increased intensity of interest in heroin addiction was a significant investment by the federal government in the field of research relating to addiction. A number of academic institutions that previously had little interest in the field established addiction research programs. The work they produced created a viable scientific base for addiction research as a discipline.

In addition the federal support allowed the building of an infrastructure at the state level to coordinate drug abuse treatment, education, and prevention activities. Among other things, each state was required to establish a so-called "single state agency" that had the over-all coordinating responsibility for dealing with drug problems in the state, and it was provided with a certain amount of federal money with which it was required to develop a state-wide plan year by year for coping with the drug problem. People were drawn into the drug abuse treatment field as a career. This was facilitated by a strong government investment in training programs, which resulted in an estimated 55,000 people working in drug abuse programs at the high point. These ranged from highly trained physicians to community health workers and ex-addict paraprofessionals.

In the private sector a number of foundations, most notable among them the Ford Foundation, combined their resources to create the Drug Abuse Council. This nonprofit private group provided sophisticated policy analysis independent of the federal government and, in addition, supported certain key areas of research. As an organization it gave additional stature and credibility to the field as a consequential discipline and as a major social issue to long term policy consideration.

TREATMENT

The most important aspect of the federal government's response to the drug abuse epidemic of the late 1960's and early 1970's was an acceptance at a policy level of drug abuse as an illness and the drug abuser as a sick person who was entitled to treatment. Furthermore, for the first time in a health area, the government accepted the responsibility for the direct provision of services, guaranteeing that "no addict who wants help can say there is no place I can go to get it." Treatment, apart from these humanitarian considerations, was seen as an integral part of the national strategy to reduce the magnitude of the drug problem and very specifically the crime rate. The sudden influx of money into the drug abuse treatment field was targeted not to support the traditional hospital-based inpatient programs but for the development of community-based outpatient programs, primarily those involving the use of methadone.

Methadone maintenance, developed in the early 1960's by Vincent Dole and Marie Nyswander, was achieving its peak of interest and support around 1970. Although it was subsequently to come under criticism on rather unfounded and irrational grounds, it had in their hands proven highly successful in enabling chronic recidivist addicts to return to functional productive existences. Methadone maintenance was increasingly seen as a highly cost-effective and successful way of drawing large numbers of people into treatment quickly, thereby getting them out of the addict pool on the street. There was also an apparent correlation between the ability of these programs to draw large numbers of individuals into treatment and a decline in the crime rate. Large scale addiction programs using outpatient methadone maintenance were started in most of the major cities in the country during the early 1970's. Some handled more than 10,000 patients on a daily basis. At the high point around 150,000 addicts were in methadone programs around the country.

With the massive expansion of methadone maintenance programs the quality of their operation diminished substantially and, as a result, the success rate declined. There were also many instances where private practitioners operated methadone programs purely for profit and did very little to ensure that the patients received the additional supportive treatment that was essential for their recovery and permanent abstinence from heroin. The federal government sought to establish certain required standards by issuing regulations that controlled the operation of methadone programs. However, inevitably, as an effort was made to move beyond the initial population of highly motivated addicts seeking treatment to those whose motivation was minimal at best, the failure rate increased. And methadone maintenance was subjected, fairly or unfairly, to increasing criticism.

In many ways methadone maintenance became a victim of its own success. Early on, eager to gain federal support and national acceptance, the operators of the major programs were happy to stress their successes, and the press, always eager to exaggerate, hailed methadone as a new panacea. When it in the long run turned out to have both benefits and shortcomings, the press criticized this treatment method because it had not lived up to the artificial expectations they had created for it.

The other major treatment modality that enjoyed a vogue during the 1970's was the therapeutic community approach. Ideologically at the opposite pole from methadone maintenance, the therapeutic communities derived from the Synanon programs started in California in the 1950's. This approach, based on group living in a state of total drug abstinence, resembled in some ways the Alcoholics Anonymous approach to the recovery from alcoholism. Addicts confronted each other in the group living situation and alternated psychological pressure and emotional support to help maintain their abstinence. Following on the heels of Synanon, such programs as Phoenix House, Odyssey House, and Daytop Village achieved early substantial success. The major failings of the program were not so much related to the percentage of their clients who eventually became permanently abstinent, which at least initially was very high, but had to do with the fact that as a modality the therapeutic community approach was extremely expensive and could accommodate only a relatively small number of addicts. Within the first 5 years of its operation, Daytop Village, one of the most successful programs, had taken only 700 addicts through their entire course out of a possible total addict population in New York City of something close to 300,000.

Although methadone maintenance and therapeutic community programs are fre-quently posed as quite different systems, they have in many ways a great deal in common. Both methadone maintenance and the therapeutic communities began to be less successful as they made an effort to reach out and involve much larger numbers of addicts and, inevitably, addicts who were not as highly motivated to be rehabilitated as those who initially entered the programs. The most successful therapeutic communities were those that were led by a strong, usually charismatic individual, whose own personality dominated the whole therapeutic process of the institution. Therefore, it was not possible to mass produce therapeutic communities and maintain the same recovery rate. At one point there were as many as 500 programs that one way or another could be described as drug-free or therapeutic communities. Most had a rather short life-span, and relatively few have survived more than 5 years.

A wide variety of other treatment approaches surfaced during the last decade. There were still those who adhered to the traditional approach of requiring hospitalization for addicts, even though it was generally felt these programs were good only for detoxification and could not help an individual to adjust to a drug-free existence on the outside. Acupuncture, hypnotism, biofeedback, transcendental meditation, "cold turkey," propoxyphene napsylate (Darvon-N), and propranolol were all hailed at different times by their advocates as major breakthroughs in the treatment of drug addiction. However, none achieved the widespread interest, enthusiasm, or success rate that therapeutic communities and methadone maintenance achieved. In fact, most proved to be interesting variations on the chemical detoxification process and had little bearing on whether an addict would subsequently remain drug free. What is much more important than the relative merits of individual therapeutic modalities is the fact that during the 1970's a very large percentage of the addict population was given access to treatment of one kind or another. The implied acceptance by government at the federal, state, and local levels and even by law enforcement agencies of the addict as a sick person constituted the most dramatic change in the attitude toward addiction in this country in 50 years. Not since the morphine maintenance clinics were closed around 1920 had there been such a government acceptance of addiction as a legitimate medical condition.

THE FIRST TURNAROUND

By the middle of 1973 it was apparent that the massive expansion of treatment programs as well as the international initiatives to cut off the supply of heroin were beginning to have some impact. There began to be a significant decline in heroin overdose deaths, the purity of heroin on the streets of America, and the number of people seeking treatment in the various therapeutic programs. For the first time since the beginning of the decade there were no longer waiting lists to get into these treatment programs. In retrospect, perhaps the most significant element in creating this improvement was the negotiated agreement with Turkey, whereby they agreed to stop the cultivation of opium, combined with the concerted law enforcement effort to close down the conversion labs in Marseilles. For a while the situation began to be so much better that the newly created Drug Enforcement Administration increasingly switched its attention to the problem of cocaine trafficking and attempted to stimulate public concern about this alternative drug lest, as the heroin problem was seen as coming under control, their perceived utility and hence Congressional appropriations diminished.

They need have had little fear, for beginning in 1974 the declining availability of heroin suddenly turned around and new waves of the drug began flooding the country. In our preoccupation with the heroin coming from Turkey and the Golden Triangle of Southeast Asia, we had paid very little attention to the increasing cultivation of opium in northern Mexico. Opium had grown there in small quantities since it was introduced by the Chinese in the 19th century. During World War II it had assumed quite significant proportions as a source of heroin on the West coast, but in the intervening 30 years this source had not contributed materially to the supply of the drug in the United States.

Suddenly, beginning in 1973 and 1974, substantial quantities of the drug were coming across the border from this new source, so that it rapidly exceeded the amount of heroin coming from any other location. By 1975 in excess of 80 per cent of all of the heroin coming into the United States was

from Mexico. Although there was perhaps never the sudden dramatic increase in new addicts that occurred in the early part of the 1970's, there was a depressing return to addiction, particularly by those who had been in treatment programs or had temporarily given up the use of heroin when supplies became short. Once again, treatment programs were faced with waiting lists, and it could no longer be said that any addict in the United States who wanted treatment could get it.

THE SECOND TURNING POINT

As a result of the development of opium cultivation in Mexico, a whole new international strategy was called for. Initial negotiations with the Mexican government were not very successful, as they were relatively disinterested in launching a massive program to crush the cultivation of opium. In part this was because of their feeling that the problem was primarily a problem of the United States, not of Mexico. Also, they did not want to anger the farmers in northern Mexico who were making large amounts of money out of the opium trafficking in a traditionally economically depressed area where there was also a tradition of political unrest. In addition, the immensely profitable opium trade had led to a high level of corruption in the Mexican law enforcement and judicial system. A serious crackdown was likely to cause considerable embarrassment. Over time, however, a high degree of cooperation between the United States and Mexican governments was achieved.

Initially supported by President Echeveria and then much more vigorously endorsed by President Lopez Portillo, opium eradication became a high priority for the Mexican government. In part this was out of the desire to improve relations with the United States, but also because heroin addiction was increasingly becoming a Mexican as well as an American problem. Providing helicopters, training, herbicide sprays, and various other forms of expertise and technical assistance, the United States government aided the Mexicans in developing what seemed to be a highly successful program during 1976 to 1977. The purity of heroin on the streets declined impressively to the lowest levels ever recorded—around 3 per cent. The overdose death rate from heroin dropped by 50 per cent, and the number of individuals seeking treatment similarly went down. By the end of 1977 the heroin supply coming into the United States had clearly been dramatically stemmed and the number of addicts seemed to have largely stabilized at a level perhaps 100,000 lower than it had been in 1975. It was the best the situation had been since the early 1960's.

The reduction in heroin availability and the diminution in the addict population in the United States were assisted by another interesting development that produced an interesting new balance in the world's opium supply. In the past, Europe had always been only a transit point for heroin as it passed through on its way to the United States, with the number of addicts in all of Europe amounting to only a few hundred. However, during the mid-1970's, with steadily increasing affluence in Europe and an acceptance by European young people of many elements of the American youth culture, drug use in general, and heroin use in particular, began to escalate significantly. With the money that they had never previously possessed and a new curiosity about drugs, the young people of Europe formed a market that provided a handsome profit for the traffickers. It was a profit that equalled or exceeded what had been made previously without the additional risk of bringing the drugs to the United States. During the latter half of the 1970's there was an extraordinary increase in the use of heroin in Western Europe. The most severely affected country was the Federal Republic of Germany, where in 1978 the number of heroin overdose deaths per capita was four times that for the United States. Although a major potential market remained for heroin in the United States because of the decline in supply from Mexico, the new European market essentially soaked up the available world supply from other sources.

America's effort to stem the flow of opium had become focused largely on Mexico and to a lesser extent on the Golden Triangle countries of Southeast Asia. In this latter region gradual progress had been made in Thailand, Burma, and Laos through a combination of crop substitution programs, the provision of helicopters for the interdiction of trafficking caravans, and the absorption of considerable quantities of heroin by addicts within those countries. Lesser attention had been focused on Afghanistan and Pakistan, which had always produced a certain quantity of illicit heroin but where the effort to achieve coordinated programs with the governments had been particularly unsuccessful. The national governments were not particularly effective, and certain areas, particularly the northwest frontier of Pakistan and the comparable land on the other side of the border in Afghanistan—the so-called "tribal areas"—were for all practical purposes outside the control of the central governments. They were, however, the areas where opium was most widely grown. The situation was further aggravated by the political turmoil in those two countries toward the end of the 1970's, which made international cooperation for the control of illicit opium cultivation a very low priority for these governments that were struggling for their own survival. By the end of 1978 the amount of heroin coming from Afghanistan and Pakistan exceeded substantially that coming from any other area of the world, including both the Golden Triangle and Mexico. The bulk of that heroin, however, was going to Europe rather than the United States. The problem in this region of the world was further aggravated by the change of government in Iran. There had always been a steady flow of opium from Afghanistan through Iran, where a certain amount remained for local use. After the fall of the Shah there was not only a marked decrease in the Iranian effort to interdict the drug flow, but also an increase in the domestic cultivation of opium, with little constraint from the authorities.

By the end of 1978 a relatively stable situation pertained. There had been some modest spillover effect from the flow of South Asian heroin to Europe into the United States, but by and large the low level of heroin purity on the street had been maintained. The number of addicts had continued to decline, as had the overdose death rate. Public concern about addiction was diminishing, and it became correspondingly more difficult to continue to get governmental support for treatment programs. There was, however, a recognition that constant vigilance was the price required to prevent a recurrence of the epidemic situation of the previous years, and a careful surveillance system was established within the State Department and the intelligence community in order to carefully monitor changes in heroin flow and opium cultivation around the world, particularly with a view to identify new sites of cultivation. However, it may well be that we are merely seeing a return to the state of relative quiescence that existed in this country in earlier decades between the epidemic bouts of widespread addiction. We will presumably stay in this state until a new and vulnerable generation of Americans comes along who are completely unfamiliar with the risks and dangers associated with heroin use. A strong argument has been made, however, that we can now keep the flow of heroin into this country low and thereby avoid a future epidemic.

Although persuasive, this line of reasoning has serious faults. Although there is a shortage of heroin in this country at the moment it is due to relatively transient events, the dramatic upsurge in heroin consumption in Europe and the success of the cooperative eradication program in Mexico. Once a surplus of heroin exists in Europe, there is little evidence that we would be any more successful in keeping it out of the United States than we have been in the past. In addition, the success of the Mexican program is fragile, and a change of government or policy could in a matter of months return us to the situation we had in 1975 when Mexico was our largest heroin supplier.

Improvements in the addiction problem in the United States are likely to be only transient until the problem of heroin supply can be dealt with on a world-wide basis. There were times during the last 10 years when it seemed we were moving in that direction, but it is clear that political instability in the major opium-growing regions of the world is likely to make global control unrealistic for the foreseeable future. During the early part of this century, in fact up until 1970, the United States strategy for dealing with our domestic addiction problem was based almost entirely upon an effort to keep heroin out of this country, with little regard for what was happening in the rest of the world. That approach is even less viable today than it was then, and we can only view the current drop in heroin availability here as a temporary respite.

The addiction problem of the last decade has, however, left an important legacy. It has been responsible for drawing large amounts of money and many talented people into the field of addiction treatment and research. A body of knowledge and skill now exists in the country that not only far exceeds anything that was previously available, but at the same time has advanced our fundamental knowledge of the addiction process by a quantum leap. For the first time since the 1920's, the study of addiction has achieved a degree of legitimacy as a scientific discipline. In addition, the studies that have been conducted on narcotic receptor sites and the role of the endorphins suggest that we may be on the verge of a dramatic scientific breakthrough in our understanding of the fundamental biochemical process that leads to addiction. There is also some suggestion that once fully delineated these biochemical pathways may prove a vital key to our understanding of brain function in mental illness in general.

Important developments have not been restricted to the biochemical area. Clinical and sociological studies have resulted in a highly sophisticated new appreciation of the many factors that interact to product the addictive state, moving us well beyond the concept of the "addictive personality" that had been accepted so readily in the past.

SUMMARY

The opiate epidemic of the last 10 years has irrevocably changed the relationship of the United States to drug use. The growth of addiction to involve all socioeconomic classes and the intensity of public focus on the issue of addiction has resulted in the dispelling of many old myths and prejudices and a relatively sophisticated and realistic understanding of the addiction problem. It has resulted in a redefining of America's addiction problem as not merely a question of how to keep heroin from crossing our borders, but as a global problem that in the long run can only be dealt with by recognizing our interdependence with other countries and by achieving a world-wide control of cultivation and trafficking. At the same time addiction has been redefined governmentally and in the public mind as a health problem rather than as a law enforcement problem, and the addict is now accepted as a sick person in need of help. Addiction as a discipline has come of age, and there is now a body of experts that gives the field a stature it has never before enjoyed.

PART 2

THEORIES OF SUBSTANCE ABUSE

CHAPTER 5

RECENT DEVELOPMENTS IN THE BIOLOGY OF OPIATES: POSSIBLE RELEVANCE TO ADDICTION

Eric J. Simon, Ph.D.

INTRODUCTION

Scientists have long been interested in elucidating the biochemical basis of the actions of drugs of abuse, in particular their tendency to produce addiction upon chronic use. For one group of addictive drugs, the opiates, there recently have been advances on the biochemical-pharmacological level that have created considerable excitement and have been widely hailed as breakthroughs that may lead to an understanding of opiate addiction as well as of analgesia and endogenous pain modulation.

In this chapter I will review these developments briefly in a chronological manner and will then discuss critically the evidence that has given rise to the claims that have been made, particularly those pertaining to narcotic addiction. I will finish by summarizing my views as to where the field may be going and what we may hope to learn that may ultimately benefit clinical medicine.

THE DISCOVERY OF OPIATE RECEPTORS

The hypothesis that narcotic analgesics must bind to highly specific sites or receptors in the central nervous system (CNS) in order to produce their many well known responses has been held by some investigators for several decades. There was, however, the question of why the human and animal brain should contain sites that can bind, with high specificity and affinity, substances derived from plants. Nevertheless, the evidence for such receptor sites was compelling. It consisted primarily of the remarkable stereospecificity and, for certain parts of the molecules, structural specificity displayed by many of the pharmacological actions of narcotic analgesic drugs.

As thousands of analogues of morphine were synthesized in search of the still mythical nonaddictive analgesic it became clear that one enantiomer of a racemic mixture (usually the levorotatory one) was generally much more active than the other. Moreover, whereas some parts of the molecule could be drastically altered with relatively little change in potency, tampering with certain regions had dramatic effects. The most interesting and best studied such region is the substituent on the tertiary nitrogen, one of the functional groups essential for narcotic analgesic activity. When the methyl group is substituted by a larger alkyl group, e.g., an allyl or cyclopropylmethyl group, analgesic potency is reduced, and the drug takes on the new pharmacological activity of a potent, specific antagonist against many of the actions of morphine and related narcotics. Some drugs have both agonist and antagonist properties, whereas others, such as naloxone (Narcan) and naltrexone (the N-allyl and N-cyclopropylmethyl analogues, respectively, of oxymorphone), are "pure" antagonists. The synthesis of mixed agonist-antagonist drugs as candidates for analgesics with low addiction liability has been a major enterprise in pharmaceutical company laboratories in recent years. Moreover, the pure antagonist naltrexone, longer acting than naloxone, has shown some promise for the treatment of heroin addicts.

The kinds of specificities described above are most easily explained by interaction with binding sites that exhibit complementary specificity. The search for such specific binding sites or opiate receptors began in the 1950's and bore fruit in the early 1970's. It was easy to show binding of opiates to cell constituents (66), but to distinguish specific from nonspecific binding proved difficult.

It was the measurement of stereospecific binding that led to success. Ingoglia and Dole (29) were the first to apply stereospecificity to the search for receptors by injecting *l*- and *d*-methadone into the lateral ventricle of rats, but they found no difference in the rate of diffusion of the enantiomers. Goldstein et al. (20) devised a method for measuring stereospecific binding of ^{3}H-levorphanol in mouse brain homogenates. They reported that only 2 per cent of the total binding was stereospecific, and the properties and distribution of this binding turned out to be quite different from those of the subsequently discovered "receptors."

In 1973 our laboratory (56) and those of Snyder (45) and Terenius (62), using modifications of the Goldstein procedure, independently and simultaneously reported the observation in animal brain homogenates of stereospecific binding of opiates that represented the major portion of the total binding. The modifications involved the use of very low concentrations of labeled drugs, made possible by high specific activity, and washing of homogenates pelleted or filtered, after incubation, to remove unbound or loosely bound contaminating radioactivity. Since that time stereospecific binding studies have been done in many laboratories, and much evidence has been accumulated suggesting that these stereospecific sites are indeed receptors that are responsible for many of the pharmacological actions of the opiates. They have been found in humans (23) and in all vertebrates so far studied. Very recently it has been reported that they also exist in some invertebrates (60a).

PROPERTIES AND DISTRIBUTION OF OPIATE RECEPTORS

The properties of the opiate-binding sites have been studied extensively, and their distribution in the brain and spinal cord has been mapped in considerable detail by dissection and in vitro binding measurement (23, 33), as well as by autoradiography (4–6, 44).

Stereospecific binding is saturable and binding, at saturation, amounts to 20 to 30 pmoles of opiate per gram of rat brain. Affinities range from K_D of 0.025 nM for a potent fentanyl analogue (60) to little or no affinity for drugs devoid of opiate activity. The pH optimum for binding is in the physiological range, with a fairly broad optimum between 6.5 and 8.0. The addition of salts to the incubation mixture tends to reduce binding. Sodium represents an interesting exception that will be discussed later.

The inhibition of stereospecific binding by proteolytic enzymes (42, 56) and a variety of protein reagents, including sulfhydryl reagents, suggests the involvement of protein moieties in opiate binding. The role of phospholipids is yet to be established. Binding is inhibited by some, but not all, phospholipase A preparations (42, 56) but not by phospholipases C or D. Moreover, we have recently shown (36) that inhibition by phospholipase A can be reversed by washing the membrane preparation with a solution of bovine serum albumin, suggesting that the nature of the phospholipid environment may be very important for the active conformation of the opiate receptor.

The extensive mapping studies can be summarized here only briefly. The highest levels of opiate receptors are found in areas of the limbic system and in the regions that have been implicated in the pathways involved in pain perception and modulation, such as the periventricular and periaqueductal gray areas, the medial thalamus, the nucleus raphe magnus, and the substantia gelatinosa of the spinal cord. It has been suggested that the limbic system receptors may be involved in opiate-induced euphoria (or dysphoria) and in the affective aspects of pain perception.

Perhaps the most convincing evidence suggesting that stereospecific binding has pharmacological relevance comes from a number of studies that show excellent correlation between pharmacological potencies and in vitro binding affinities for a large number of drugs, varying in analgesic potencies over five to six orders of magnitude (60, 69).

Recently, there has been considerable interest in whether multiple types of opiate receptors exist. Using classical pharmacological approaches, Martin and collaborators (17, 40) have suggested the existence of three types of receptors, named mu (for morphine), kappa (for ketocyclazocaine), and sigma for SKF 10,047. Results from Kosterlitz's laboratory also provide evidence for the heterogeneity of opiate receptors (38). Thus, the receptors present in the myenteric plexus of the guinea pig ileum seem to have properties distinct from those in the mouse vas deferens. These authors have also reported evidence that suggests that the brain may possess at least two families of receptors differing in their affinity for enkephalins and for exogenous opiates. Very convincing evidence in support of at least two different opiate receptors in rat brain has recently been obtained in Kosterlitz's laboratory (49) as well as in our own (59). These experiments involved a comparison of the ability of various ligands to protect opiate receptors from irreversible inactivation by alkylating agents.

CONFORMATIONAL CHANGES IN OPIATE RECEPTORS

I mentioned that sodium is an exception to the rule that increased salt concentrations present during incubation will inhibit binding. An apparent discrepancy between results in Snyder's laboratory (45) and in our laboratory (56) led to the realization that sodium can distinguish between agonists and antagonists (46, 57). Whereas agonist binding is inhibited by sodium salts, the binding of antagonists is either unaffected or, in many instances, augmented by the presence of sodium. This remarkable discrimination by a small ion between closely related molecules (e.g., morphine and nalorphine, oxymorphone and naloxone) is highly specific. It is exhibited, although less effectively, by lithium, but by none of the other alkali metals. In fact, no other inorganic or organic cations have been found that exhibit this effect (57). A study of the mechanism of this sodium effect has produced evidence that sodium is an allosteric effector, the binding of which produces a conformational change in the receptor. The sodium conformer has a higher affinity for antagonists and a markedly reduced affinity for agonists.

The best evidence for an alteration in receptor conformation by sodium ions came unexpectedly from a study of the kinetics of receptor inactivation by the sulfhydryl alkylating reagent, N-ethylmaleimide (NEM) in our laboratory (55). When a membrane fraction from rat brain was incubated with NEM for various periods, followed by inactivation or removal of unreacted NEM, there was a progressive decrease in the ability of the membranes to bind opiates stereospecifically. The rate of receptor inactivation followed pseudo-first-order kinetics consistent with the existence of one sulfhydryl (SH) group per receptor essential for binding. Protection against inactivation was achieved by the addition of low concentrations of opiates or antagonists during the preincubation with NEM, suggesting that the SH group is located near the opiate-binding site of the receptor.

Considerable protection was observed (half-time of inactivation was increased to 30 minutes from 8 minutes) when inactivation was carried out in the presence of 100 nM NaCl. Inasmuch as sodium salts were without effect on the alkylation of model SH compounds, such as cysteine or glutathione, this suggested that the SH groups were made less accessible to NEM by a conformational change in the receptor protein. The fact that this protection exhibited the same ion specificity (Na^+ protects, Li^+ protects partially, K^+, Rb^+, or Cs^+ not at all) and the same dose response to Na^+ as the differential changes in ligand affinities suggests that the conformational change that masks SH groups is the same as that which results in increased affinity of antagonists and decreased affinity of agonists.

These studies illustrate that the opiate receptor can alter its shape. The physiological function of this plasticity is not yet clear. A role in the coupling of opiate binding to subsequent physical or chemical events has been suggested, as has a role for Na^+ ions in the action of opiates.

The simple model for the allosteric effect of sodium ions on opiate receptors shown in Figure 5.1 encompasses the various changes in receptor properties discussed above. One additional property, the evidence for which was not discussed here, is positive cooperativity of opiate binding, which is the reason for representing the receptor as (at least) a dimer.

DISCOVERY OF ENDOGENOUS OPIOID PEPTIDES

The evidence that the brain of all vertebrates investigated, from the hagfish to humans, contains opiate receptors led investigators to raise the question why such receptors for plant-derived substances exist in the CNS and have survived eons of evolution. A physiological role for opiate receptors that confers a selective advantage on the organisms seemed probable. None of the known neurotransmitters or neurohormones was found to exhibit high affinity for opiate receptors, which encouraged a number of laboratories to search for new opiate-like substances in extracts of animal brain. This search was successful first in the laboratories of Hughes and Kosterlitz (26) and of Terenius and Wahlström (63). Goldstein and his collaborators (65), at about the same time, reported opioid activity in extracts of pituitary glands. Hughes utilized the in vitro bioassay for opiates, namely naloxone-reversible inhibition of electrically evoked contraction of the mouse vas deferens or the guinea pig ileum, and Terenius assayed endogenous opioid activity by measuring ability of brain extracts and fractions to compete with labeled opiates for receptor binding.

These studies culminated in the identification of the opioid substances in extracts of pig brain by Hughes et al. (28). They reported that the activity resided in two pentapeptides, Tyr-Gly-Gly-Phe-Met and Tyr-Gly-Gly-Phe-Leu, which they named methionine (Met) and leucine (Leu) enkephalin. Hughes et al. also reported the interesting observation that the sequence of Met-enkephalin was present as amino acid residues 61–65 in the pituitary hormone beta-lipotropin (beta-LPH). This hormone had been isolated in 1965 from pituitary glands by C. H. Li (35). It possessed weak lipolytic activity that was never seriously thought to be its real function. The report of Hughes et al., along with that of the Goldstein group, of the existence of opioid activity in the pituitary gland, led Guillemin to examine the extracts of pig hypothalami and pituitary glands (remaining in his freezer from his Nobel Prize-winning identification of hypothalamic-releasing factors). Two polypeptides with opioid activity were found and sequenced (37). They proved to have structures identical with amino acid sequences 61–76 and 61–77 of beta-LPH. Meanwhile, potent opioid activity was found in the C-terminal fragment of beta-LPH (LPH 61–91) in two laboratories (9, 11), although the intact beta-LPH molecule was inactive. The proliferation of endogenous peptides with opioid activity caused the author of this paper to suggest the term "endorphin" (a

Opiate Binding Sites

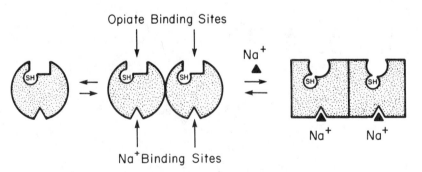

Na^+ Binding Sites

Figure 5.1. Model for the allosteric effect of sodium ions on the conformation of the opiate receptor.

contraction of "endogenous" and morphine"), which has been widely accepted. The C-terminal fragment was renamed beta-endorphin by Li, and LPH 61–76 and 61–77 were named alpha- and gamma-endorphin, respectively, by Guillemin.

All the opioid peptides exhibit opiate-like activity when injected intraventricularly. This activity includes analgesia, respiratory depression, and a variety of behavioral changes, including the production of a rigid catatonia. The pharmacological effects of the enkephalins are very fleeting, presumably due to their rapid destruction by peptidases. The longer chain endorphins are more stable and produce long lived effects. Thus, analgesia due to beta-endorphin (the most potent of all the endorphins so far found) can last 3 to 4 hours. All of the responses to endorphins are readily reversible by opiate antagonists, such as naloxone. There have been reports that certain analogues of enkephalin can produce analgesia after systemic injection or even oral ingestion (50).

Distribution of enkephalins has been studied by biochemical (52) as well as by bioassay (27) and immunohistochemical techniques (14, 53). The distribution of enkephalins in the CNS shows considerable, although not complete, correlation with the distribution of opiate receptors. Thus, the globus pallidus has a very high density of enkephalin (or at least enkephalin-like immunoreactive material), while it is low in opiate receptors. Certain cortical areas dense in opiate receptors have low levels of enkephalin.

In the earlier studies of Hökfelt and colleagues (14) the immunofluorescence was all found in nerve fibers and terminals but not in cell bodies. In a more recent paper this group (24) utilized colchicine, which is known to arrest axonal transport. After such treatment it was possible to find immunofluorescence in cell bodies after treatment with antiserum to Met-enkephalin. More than 20 cell groups containing enkephalin have so far been observed in the brain and spinal cord, a number somewhat larger than the 15 catecholamine cell groups known to exist in rat brain. The authors feel that their results indicate that these perikarya possess the machinery for enkephalin biosynthesis. This raises the interesting question of whether enkephalin is always derived from large endorphin precursors, inasmuch as levels of beta-lipotropin and beta-endorphin are very low in some of the areas that are found to have high enkephalin levels.

Studies on the distribution of beta-endorphin in the laboratories of Guillemin (51) and Watson (68) have provided convincing evidence for a distribution that is very different from that of the enkephalins. This has led to the suggestion that the CNS has separate enkephalinergic and endorphinergic neuronal systems. Beta-endorphin is present in the pituitary, where there is little or no enkephalin, as well as in certain regions of the brain. Brain beta-endorphin seems to originate in a single set of neurons located in the periarcuate region of the hypothalamus, with axons projecting throughout the brain stem. Figure 5.2 shows the distribution of the enkephalins and of beta-endorphin in rat brain.

PAIN AND ITS MODULATION

Inasmuch as it was work on the opiate analgesics that led to the discovery of the endorphins and their receptors, it was natural to postulate that they may be involved in pain modulation. The fact, mentioned earlier, that all CNS regions implicated in the conduction of pain impulses have high levels of opiate receptors supports this hypothesis, as does the finding that opiates seem to inhibit selectively the firing of nociceptive neurons in the substantia gelatinosa of the dorsal spinal cord (13). Moreover, as mentioned earlier, the intraventricular injection of all known opioid peptides produces analgesia. These findings did not prove that endogenous opioids are involved in the pain pathway but were sufficiently suggestive to encourage further testing of this hypothesis.

Attempts were made to demonstrate the role of the natural opioid system in pain perception by the use of the opiate antagonist naloxone. It was postulated that, if receptor occupancy by endorphins was involved in pain modulation, the administration of an opiate antagonist should lower the threshold or exacerbate perceived pain. Such an effect has been surprisingly difficult to demonstrate conclusively. Out of a great number of attempts in animals, only those of Jacob et al. (30) were successful in demonstrating a lowering of pain threshold by naloxone (decrease in latency period before rats or mice jumped off a hotplate). The results have recently been

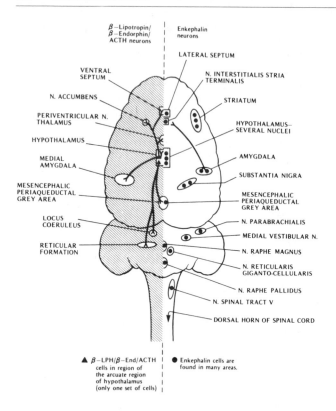

Figure 5.2. Localization of the enkephalins and of beta-endorphin in rat brain. (Reprinted by permission from Barchas, J. A., Akil, H., Elliott, G. R., Holman, R. B., and Watson, S. J. Behavioral neurochemistry: Neuroregulators and behavioral states. Science 200:964, 1978. Courtesy of A.A.A.S.)

replicated in other laboratories (16). Attempts to show exacerbation of experimental pain or lowering of pain threshold in human volunteers have been unsuccessful (15, 21).

Better success was achieved by studying the effect of naloxone on several types of analgesia that do not involve the use of drugs. Analgesia produced by electrical stimulation of the periaqueductal gray area of both animals (1) and humans (25) has been shown to be at least partially reversed by the administration of naloxone.

A more dramatic reversal by naloxone has been observed with analgesia resulting from electroacupuncture in mice (47) and from acupuncture in human subjects (41). The involvement of opiate receptors and endorphins in electroacupuncture has received additional support, not involving naloxone, by the finding that the CXBK strain of mice, which is deficient in opiate receptors, shows poor analgesia in response to electroacupuncture (43).

Recently there has been a report (34) indicating that analgesia due to "placebo effect" is also reversed by naloxone in patients with postoperative pain after extraction of impacted third molars. In this regard it is of interest that analgesia produced by hypnosis was found not to be affected by naloxone (19).

These results, although indirect, are supportive of the idea that the endorphin system may be involved in an endogenous pain modulation system. Such a system is likely to be of great survival value to the organism, because it will permit it to experience pain as an important warning of tissue damage without the suffering, except in pathological states, of unbearable, disabling pain. The importance of pain to the individual is best demonstrated by a disease called congenital insensitivity to pain. Individuals with this condition are unable to feel pain from either visceral or superficial tissue damage. This is a serious pathology that results in a significantly shortened life expectancy. A number of laboratories including our own are currently studying such patients to determine whether an abnormality in the opiate receptor-endorphin system may play a role in this inborn error.

There have indeed been two brief reports suggesting that naloxone may have an effect on these patients. Dehen et al. (12) report that the flexion-reflex threshold, which was 350 per cent higher in the patient than in controls, fell dramatically by 67 per cent within 10 minutes of naloxone administration. Yanagida (70) reported that tooth pulp-evoked potentials (TPEP) are absent in patients with congenital insensitivity to pain. However, 10 minutes after administration of naloxone (10 mg intravenously) some TPEP were observed, especially after stimuli of 15 mA (the highest used). The patient was able to recognize these stimuli as pressure sensations without apparent distress. These reports are still preliminary, and the effects observed are minimal. Nevertheless, they suggest that the endorphin system could play a role in this disease. The administration of large amounts of a long acting antagonist should be attempted as a possibly beneficial treatment of this serious pathology.

To prove conclusively the involvement of endorphins in endogenous pain regulation requires direct demonstration of changes in endorphin level or turnover during severe acute or chronic pain and during analgesia. Terenius and Wahlström (64) found decreases in opioid activity in the CSF of patients suffering chronic pain due to trigeminal neuralgia when compared to patients who were not in pain. More recently this group (58) also reported an increase in level of opioid activity after analgesia by electroacupuncture in patients with intractable pain. These reports have the drawback that the opioid activity in the CSF represents as yet poorly characterized chromatographic fractions that seem to differ from all of the known and well characterized endorphins.

Reports on the release of well characterized endorphins during analgesia have also appeared. Richardson and Akil (48) have reported good success in relieving intractable pain in patients by electrical stimulation with electrodes implanted in the periventricular gray region. The region found to be most effective and also the one at which the least side effects were seen was a site near the posterior commissure, adjacent to the ventricular wall at the level of the nucleus parafascicularis. This method is adaptable for pain relief by periodic self-stimulation by the patient over a period of months or even years. The analgesia so produced was found to be partially reversible by naloxone administration. More recently Akil et al. (3) have shown that stimulation analgesia is followed after 15 to 20 minutes by a small (less than 2-fold) but significant increase in release of Met-enkephalin into the ventricular CSF, measured by several techniques including bioassay, receptor binding, and radioimmunoassay. The same group (2) has reported a more dramatic release of beta-endorphin-like immunoreactive material under identical conditions of analgesia. Baseline release was undetectable (less than 25 fmoles per ml of CSF), whereas the level measured during stimulation-produced analgesia in five patients ranged from 319 to 481 fmoles per ml, an increase of at least 13 to 20-fold.

Thus, an impressive array of at least circumstantial evidence is accumulating suggesting the involvement of the enkephalins and probably also brain beta-endorphin in an endogenous analgesic system.

At this point it may be appropriate to say a word about stress. Guillemin et al. (22) have shown a parallel and equimolar secretion of adrenocorticotropic hormone (ACTH) and beta-endorphin into the blood of rats that have been severely stressed. The involvement of pituitary beta-endorphin in stress is further supported by the exciting discovery by Mains et al. (39) that ACTH and beta-endorphin are synthesized via a common large precursor peptide of molecular weight 31,000. The question of the relationship between pituitary endorphin, evidently involved in reaction to stress, and the brain enkephalins and beta-endorphin, which seem to play a role in pain modulation, is a very interesting and as yet unanswered one. The significance of the question is further enhanced by reports that certain types of stress can produce analgesia.

NARCOTIC ADDICTION

There were and continue to be great expectations that the discovery of opiate receptors and their endogenous ligands will result in major advances in our understanding of the mechanism of drug addiction. To date, progress in this area has been disappointing. In fact, evidence that the endogenous opioid system participates in aspects of the addictive process is, as can be seen from this brief review, still very indirect.

All opioid peptides will produce tolerance and physical dependence when injected repeatedly. Cross-tolerance with plant alkaloid opiates has also been shown. This does not prove that tolerance/dependence develop to endogenously produced and released endorphins nor that these peptides and their receptors are involved in the formation of tolerance and dependence to narcotics.

A theory that predated the discovery of the opiate receptors is one that suggests changes in either the number or binding characteristics of opiate receptors. A change in binding affinities similar to that seen when sodium concentration is increased during in vitro binding is especially attractive, because sensitivity to agonists decreases during tolerance formation while sensitivity to antagonists increases dramatically. Klee and Streaty (32) examined this question in whole rat brain and found no changes in the number or affinities of opiate-binding sites. Bonnet et al. (8) felt that this might be explicable by a "drowning out" of changes occurring in only a few brain regions. However, an examination of receptor number and binding affinities in the medial thalamus, periventricular gray region, and caudate nucleus gave equally negative results. Whereas these three areas have high levels of receptors and/or have been implicated in various aspects of opiate action, the possibility still remains that these were not the appropriate areas to examine. However, it is at least equally possible that detectable changes in receptors do not occur during chronic morphinization.

The possibility that a change in endorphin level might be observed during tolerance/dependence development has also received attention. A report by Simantov and Snyder (54) that enkephalin levels are elevated in brains of tolerant rats was recently refuted by experiments from the same laboratory (10). The earlier work which had been done using a radioreceptor assay was not supported when the much more specific radioimmunoassay was used.

Recently there has been a report (61) that the intravenous administration of 4 mg of human beta-endorphin to human addicts led to dramatic improvement in severe abstinence syndromes. There was no euphoria and little adverse effect. In a double-blind study it was found that subjects were able to distinguish morphine and beta-endorphin. After endorphin treatment they felt thirsty, dizzy, sleepy, warm, and had "a strange feeling throughout the body." However, all these symptoms disappeared in 20 minutes, whereas the beneficial effects of endorphin on the withdrawal syndrome lasted for several days. The long lasting suppression of especially the most severe symptoms of abstinence (vomiting, diarrhea, tremor, and restlessness) by a single dose of beta-endorphin suggested to the authors the possibility that this endogenous peptide may indeed have a role in the mechanism of tolerance/dependence development to opiates.

For completeness, I should like to mention two recent developments of considerable interest for which the relationship to the opiate receptor is still unknown.

Walter et al. (67) reported that it was possible to suppress the abstinence syndrome when rats were withdrawn from chronic morphine by administration of the dipeptide Z-Pro-D-Leu. There was no effect on the analgesic response to morphine. The mechanism of this phenomenon is not understood.

Based on the abundant literature which seems to implicate catecholamines in the actions of opiates, Gold et al. (18) treated human heroin addicts with clonidine (Catapres). In a double-blind, placebo-controlled study, clonidine eliminated objective signs and subjective symptoms of opiate withdrawal for 4 to 6 hours in all addicts. In an open pilot study, the same patients did well while taking clonidine for 1 week. All of the patients had been addicted to opiates for 6 to 10 years and had been on methadone for 6 to 60 months at the time of the study. The authors suggest that their success with clonidine indicates that abstinence may be produced by an interaction between opiate receptors and alpha-2-adrenergic receptors in the mediation of effects by endogenous opiates in noradrenergic areas such as the locus coeruleus.

DISCUSSION

It is quite a responsibility to write one of the few basic science chapters for a book on substance abuse. My prejudices about the importance of recent developments, in which my laboratory was fortunate to have a part, led me to ignore other important discoveries concerning the actions of opiates and of other abused substances. For this I apologize and cite space limitations as an excuse. Moreover, the editors clea ly selected me to write this chapter in the hope that I would emphasize the recent developments in the opiate field.

It is generally accepted that the discoveries of the opiate receptors and of the endogenous opioid peptides represent major advances in neuroscience. The influx of large numbers of distinguished investigators into this research area bears witness to the importance scientists attach to these discoveries and to the high expectations they entertain regarding the progress that will become possible in our understanding of brain function and behavior.

The way the opioid peptides in the nervous system function is not yet understood. There is evidence suggesting that they represent neurotransmitters or neuromodulators. The latter term implies that the release of enkephalins or endorphins regulates the release of other neurotransmitters. A model for such a neuromodulatory function is presented in Figure 5.3, where the transmitter regulated by enkephalin is substance P, a peptide thought to be the transmitter released by nociceptive neurons in the spinal cord.

At the present time the strongest and, at least to me, most convincing evidence for participation of the opiate receptor-opioid system exists for the pathways of pain perception and modulation. This evidence was summarized in some detail in an earlier section. Briefly, it consists of the ability of the opiate antagonist naloxone to reverse a variety of analgesic states produced without intervention by exogenous opiate analgesics. More recently, evidence has also been reported for the release of enkephalins and beta-endorphin into ventricular CSF during electrical stimulation analgesia in a patient with chronic pain. This is the most direct evidence for involvement of endogenous opioids and their receptors in the body's system of pain modulation. Definitive proof for or against such involvement should not be far away.

The situation is far more embryonic when it comes to attempts to establish a role for the endogenous opioid system in drug addiction. There is general conviction among scientists that knowledge of this system will aid in unravelling the mysteries of the biochemical basis of addiction, but the evidence for this is at present very meager.

To complicate matters, it must be pointed out that most biochemical studies, except for some work with human addicts, is not really

Figure 5.3. Schematic representation of a possible mechanism for opiate-induced suppression of substance P (*SP*) release. SP is shown localized within the terminal of a small diameter afferent fiber which forms an excitatory axodendritic synapse with the process of a spinal cord neuron originating in lamina IV or V and projecting rostrally. A local enkephalin-containing inhibitory interneuron (*ENK*), confined to laminae II and III, forms a presynaptic contact on the terminal of the primary afferent. Opiate receptor sites are depicted presynaptically. *Roman numerals* on the *right* refer to the laminae of Rexed. (Reprinted by permission from Jessel, T. M., and Iverson, L. L. Opiate analgesics inhibit substance P release from rat trigeminal nucleus. Nature 268:549, 1977. Courtesy of Macmillan Journals, Ltd.)

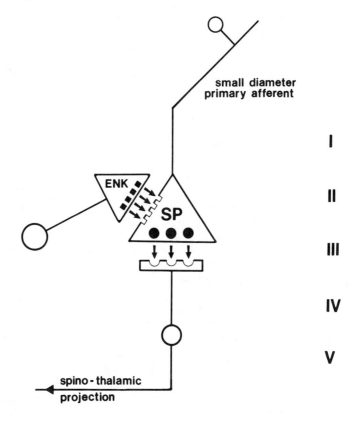

concerned with addiction as it is usually defined. The phenomena studied are tolerance and physical dependence (withdrawal), aspects of addiction that are amenable to pharmacological measurement in animals as well as humans. Psychic dependence, compulsive drug seeking, and abuse are much more difficult to study, and there is no agreement as to what constitutes a suitable animal model for studies of these phenomena that are central to drug addiction. However, even for tolerance and physical dependence, the role of enkephalins, endorphins, and opiate receptors is not established. No reproducible changes have been found in either number or properties of opiate receptors nor in the level of endogenous opioid peptides when animals are chronically treated with morphine. The suggestion of a role rests on such indirect evidence as the suppression of abstinence symptoms in addicts for several days after administration of a single, small dose of beta-endorphin and on large quantities of wishful thinking. It should be remembered that the enkephalinergic-endorphinergic system interacts with a number of other neurotransmitter systems in the CNS and elsewhere. Withdrawal symptoms may, therefore, result from changes in one or more of these other systems produced by chronic overloading of the endogenous opioid system by exogenous opiates.

I have presented the state of the art as realistically and honestly as possible and would now like to end up by speculating a bit about where I believe the field is going.

Within the next few years the neurotransmitter or neuromodulator function of the opioid peptides should be firmly established (or disproved). Methods for measuring their biosynthesis, release, and breakdown will become available, and this may facilitate the elucidation of their role in opiate addiction and in other behavior. In this connection I want to mention an exciting recent discovery in the laboratory of J. C. Schwartz in Paris, confirmed by several others. They have reported the existence of a membrane-bound peptidase enzyme that seems to be rather specific for the breakdown of enkephalins and could represent an "enkephalinase," equivalent to the acetylcholinesterase of the cholinergic system. Moreover, the level of this enzyme seems to change during chronic morphinization of animals. This finding clearly deserves watching.

Within the last year evidence has come to light that suggests the existence of several somewhat different types of opiate receptors. This finding is not only of considerable theoretical importance but could have great practical implications. Thus, preliminary evidence suggests that one of the receptors is primarily concerned with the analgesic function of opiates and opioid peptides, whereas another receptor may be responsible for their addiction liability. If this proves correct, molecules could be tailor-made to fit one but not the other receptor. Such an approach would provide a rational basis for the hitherto empirical search for analgesics of low addiction liability and for drugs useful in the treatment of addicts.

The day when drug addiction can be either prevented or treated in a rational manner may not yet be around the corner, but the enormous research activity that the recent discoveries have given rise to in the opiate field augurs well. If and when the molecular basis of the addictive process is understood for opiates, it may serve as a model for the elucidation of the mechanism of addiction to alcohol, nicotine, and other substances currently abused in this country and elsewhere.

References

1. Akil, H., Mayer, D. J., and Liebeskind, J. C. Antagonism of stimulation-produced analgesia by naloxone, a narcotic antagonist. Science 191:961, 1976.
2. Akil, H., Richardson, D. E., Barchas, J. D., and Li, C. H. Appearance of β-endorphin-like immunoreactivity in human ventricular cerebrospinal fluid upon analgesic electrical stimulation. Proc. Natl. Acad. Sci. USA 75:5170, 1978.
3. Akil, H., Richardson, D. E., Hughes, J., and Barchas, J. D. Enkephalin-like material elevated in ventricular cerebrospinal fluid of pain patients after analgestic focal stimulation. Science 201:463, 1978.
4. Atweh, S. F., and Kuhar, M. F. Autoradiographic localization of opiate receptors in rat brain. I. Spinal cord and lower medulla. Brain Res. 124:53, 1977.
5. Atweh, S. F., and Kuhar, M. J. Autoradiographic localization of opiate receptors in rat brain. II. The brainstem. Brain Res. 129:1, 1977.
6. Atweh, S. F., and Kuhar, M. J. Autoradiographic localization of opiate receptors in rat brain. III. The telencephalon. Brain Res. 134:393, 1977.
7. Barchas, J. A., Akil, H., Elliott, G. R., Holman, R. B., and Watson, S. J. Behavioral neurochemistry: Neuroregulators and behavioral states. Science 200:964, 1978.
8. Bonnet, K. A., Hiller, J. M., and Simon, E. J. The effects of chronic opiate treatment and social isolation on opiate receptors in rodent brain. In Opiates and Endogenous Opioid Peptides, Proceedings of the International Narcotic Research Conference Meeting, Aberdeen, U.K., pp. 335–343. Amsterdam, North Holland, 1976.

9. Bradbury, A. F., Smyth, D. G., Snell, C. R., Birdsall, N. J. M., and Hulme, E. C. C fragment of lipotropin has a high affinity for brain opiate receptors. Nature 260:793, 1976.

10. Childers, S. R., Simantov, R., and Snyder, S. H. Enkephalin: Radioimmunoassay and radioreceptor assay in morphine dependent rats. Eur. J. Pharmacol. 46:289, 1977.

11. Cox, B. M., Goldstein, A., and Li, C. H. Opioid activity of a peptide, β-lipotropin-(61-91), derived from β-lipotropin. Proc. Natl. Acad. Sci. USA 73:1821, 1976.

12. Dehen, H., Willer, J. C., Prier, S., Boureau, F., and Cambrier, J. Congenital insensitivity to pain and the "morphine-like" analgesic system. Pain 5:351, 1978.

13. Duggan, A. W., Hall, J. G., and Headley, P. M. Suppression of transmission of nociceptive impulses by morphine: Selective effects of morphine administered in the region of the substantia gelatinosa. Br. J. Pharmacol. 61:65, 1977.

14. Elde, R., Hökfelt, T., Johansson, O., and Terenius, L. Immunohistochemical studies using antibodies to leucine-enkephalin: Initial observations on the nervous system of the rat. Neuroscience 1:349, 1976.

15. El-Sobky, A., Dostrovsky, J. D., and Wall, P. D. Lack of effect of naloxone on pain perception in humans. Nature 263:783, 1976.

16. Frederickson, R. C. A., Burgis, V., and Edwards, J. D. Hyperalgesia induced by naloxone follows diurnal rhythm in responsivity to painful stimuli. Science 198:756, 1977.

17. Gilbert, P. E., and Martin, W. R. The effects of morphine and nalorphine-like drugs in the nondependent and cyclazocine-dependent chronic spinal dog. J. Pharmacol. Exp. Ther. 198:66, 1976.

18. Gold, M., Redmond, D. E., Jr., and Kleber, H. D. Clonidine blocks acute opiate-withdrawal symptoms. Lancet 2:599, 1978.

19. Goldstein, A., and Hilgard, E. R. Failure of the opiate antagonist naloxone to modify hypnotic analgesia. Proc. Natl. Acad. Sci. USA 72:2041, 1975.

20. Goldstein, A., Lowney, L. I., and Pal, B. K. Stereospecific and nonspecific interactions of the morphine congener levorphanol in subcellular fractions of mouse brain. Proc. Natl. Acad. Sci. USA 68:1742, 1971.

21. Grevert, P., and Goldstein, A. Endorphins: Naloxone fails to alter experimental pain or mood in humans. Science 199:1093, 1978.

22. Guillemin, R., Varga, T., Rossier, J., Minick, S., Ling, N., Rivier, C., Vale, W., and Bloom, F. β-Endorphin and adrenocorticotropin are secreted concomitantly by the pituitary gland. Science 197:1367, 1977.

23. Hiller, J. M., Pearson, J., and Simon, E. J. Distribution of stereospecific binding of the potent narcotic analgesic etorphine in the human brain: Predominance in the limbic system. Res. Commun. Chem. Pathol. Pharmacol. 6:1052, 1973.

24. Hökfelt, T., Elde, R., Johansson, O., Terenius, L., and Stein, L. The distribution of enkephalin-immunoreactive cell bodies in the rat central nervous system. Neurosci. Lett. 5:25, 1977.

25. Hosobuchi, Y., Adams, T. F., and Linchitz, R. Pain relief by electrical stimulation of the central gray matter in humans and its reversal by naloxone. Science 197:183, 1977.

26. Hughes, J. Isolation of an endogenous compound from the brain with properties similar to morphine. Brain Res. 88:295, 1975.

27. Hughes, J., Kosterlitz, H. W., and Smith, T. W. The distribution of methionine-enkephalin and leucine-enkephalin in the brain and peripheral tissues. Br. J. Pharmacol. 61:639, 1977.

28. Hughes, J., Smith, T. W., Kosterlitz, H., Fothergill, L. A., Morgan, B. A., and Morris, H. R. Identification of two related pentapeptides from the brain with potent opiate agonist activity. Nature 258:577, 1975.

29. Ingoglia, N. A., and Dole, V. P. Localization of d- and l-methadone after intraventricular injection into rat brains. J. Pharmacol. Exp. Ther. 175:84, 1970.

30. Jacob, J. J., Tremblay, E. C., and Colombel, M.-C. Facilitation de réactions nociceptives par la naloxone chez le souris et chez le rat. Psychopharmacologia 37:217, 1974.

31. Jessel, T. M., and Iversen, L. L. Opiate analgesics inhibit substance P release from rat trigeminal nucleus. Nature 268:549, 1977.

32. Klee, W. A., and Streaty, R. A. Narcotic receptor sites in morphine-dependent rats. Nature 248:61, 1974.

33. Kuhar, M. J., Pert, C. B., and Snyder, S. H. Regional distribution of opiate receptor binding in monkey and human brain. Nature 245:447, 1973.

34. Levine, J. D., Gordon, N. C., and Fields, H. L. The mechanism of placebo analgesia. Lancet, 2:654, 1978.

35. Li, C. H. Lipotropin: A new active peptide from pituitary glands. Nature 201:924, 1964.

36. Lin, H. K., and Simon, E. J. Phospholipase A inhibition of opiate receptor binding can be reversed by albumin. Nature 271:383, 1978.

37. Ling, N., Burgus, R., and Guillemin, R. Isolation, primary structure, and synthesis of α-endorphin and γ-endorphin, two peptides of hypothalamic-hypophysial origin with morphinomimetic activities. Proc. Natl. Acad. Sci. USA 73:3942, 1976.

38. Lord, J. A. H., Waterfield, A. A., Hughes, J., and Kosterlitz, H. W. Endogenous opioid peptides: Multiple agonists and receptors. Nature 267:495, 1977.

39. Mains, R., Eipper, E., and Ling, N. Common precursor to corticotropin and endorphins. Proc. Natl. Acad. Sci. USA 74:3014, 1977.

40. Martin, W. R., Eades, C. G., Thompson, J. A., Huppler, R. E., and Gilbert, P. E. The effects of morphine- and nalorphine-like drugs in the nondependent and morphine-dependent chronic spinal dog. J. Pharmacol. Exp. Ther. 197:517, 1976.

41. Mayer, D. J., Price, D. D., and Rafii, A. Antagonism of acupuncture analgesia in man by the narcotic antagonist naloxone. Brain Res. 121:368, 1977.

42. Pasternak, G. W., and Snyder, S. H. Opiate receptor binding: Effects of enzymatic treatment. Mol. Pharmacol. 10:183, 1973.

43. Peets, J. M., and Pomeranz, B. CXBK mice deficient in opiate receptors show poor electroacupuncture analgesia. Nature 273:675, 1978.

44. Pert, C. B., Kuhar, M. J., and Snyder, S. H. Autoradiographic localization of the opiate receptor in rat brain. Life Sci. 16:1849, 1975.

45. Pert, C. B., and Snyder, S. H. Opiate receptor: Demonstration in nervous tissue. Science 179:1011, 1973.

46. Pert, C. B., and Snyder, S. H. Opiate receptor binding of agonists and antagonists affected differentially by sodium. Mol. Pharmacol. 10:868, 1974.

47. Pomeranz, B., and Chiu, D. Naloxone blockade of acupuncture: Endorphin implicated. Life Sci. 19:1757, 1976.

48. Richardson, D. E., and Akil, H. Pain reduction by electrical brain stimulation in man. Part I. Acute administration in periaqueductal and periventricular sites. J. Neurosurg. 47:178, 1977.

49. Robson, L. E., and Kosterlitz, H. W. Specific protection of the binding sites of D-ala^2-D-leu^5 enkephalin (δ-receptors) and dihydromorphine (μ-receptors). Proc. R. Soc. Lond. B205:425, 1979.

50. Roemer, D., Buescher, H. H., Hill, R. C., Pless, J., Bauer, W., Cardinaux, A., Closse, A., Hauser, D., and Huguenin, R. A synthetic enkephalin analogue with prolonged parenteral and oral analgesic activity. Nature 268:547, 1977.

51. Rossier, J., Vargo, T. M., Minick, S., Ling, N., Bloom, F. E., and Guillemin, R. Regional dissociation of beta-endorphin and enkephalin contents in rat brain and pituitary. Proc. Natl. Acad. Sci. USA 74:5162, 1977.

52. Simantov, R., Kuhar, M. J., Pasternak, G. W., and Snyder, S. H. The regional distribution of a morphine-like factor enkephalin in monkey brain. Brain Res. 106:189, 1976.

53. Simantov, R., Kuhar, M. J., Uhl, G. R., and Snyder, S. H. Opioid peptide enkephalin: Immunohistochemical mapping in rat central nervous system. Proc. Natl. Acad. Sci. USA 74:2167, 1977.

54. Simantov, R., and Snyder, S. H. Elevated levels of enkephalin in morphine-dependent rats. Nature 262:505, 1976.

55. Simon, E. J., and Groth, J. Kinetics of opiate receptor inactivation by sulfhydryl reagents: Evidence for conformational change in presence of sodium ions. Proc. Natl. Acad. Sci. USA 72:2404, 1975.

56. Simon, E. J., Hiller, J. M., and Edelman, I. Stereospecific binding of the potent narcotic analgesic ^{3}H-etorphine to rat brain homogenate. Proc. Natl. Acad. Sci. USA 70:1947, 1973.

57. Simon, E. J., Hiller, J. M., Groth, J., and Edelman, I. Further properties of stereospecific opiate binding sites in rat brain: On the nature of the sodium effect. J. Pharmacol. Exp. Ther. 192:531, 1975.

58. Sjolund, B., Terenius, L., and Erikson, M. Increased cerebral spinal fluid levels of endorphins after electroacupuncture. Acta Physiol. Scand. 100:382, 1977.

59. Smith, J., and Simon, E. J. Selective protection by receptor ligands of stereospecific enkephalin and opiate binding from inactivation by N-ethylmaleimide: Evidence for two classes of opiate receptors.

Proc. Natl. Acad. Sci. USA 77:281, 1980.

60. Stahl, K. D., van Bever, W., Janssen, P., and Simon, E. J. Receptor affinity and pharmacological potency of a series of narcotic analgesic, antidiarrheal and neuroleptic drugs. Eur. J. Pharmacol. 46:199, 1977.

60a. Stefano, G. B., Kream, R. M., and Zukin, R. S. Demonstration of stereospecific opiate binding in the nervous tissue of the marine mollusc (*Mytilus edulis*). Brain Res. 181:440, 1980.

61. Su, C. Y., Lin, S. H., Wang, Y. T., Li, C. H., Hung, L. H., Lin, C. S., and Lin, B. C. Effects of β-endorphin on narcotic abstinence syndrome in man. J. Formosan Med. Assoc. 77:133, 1978.

62. Terenius, L. Stereospecific interaction between narcotic analgesics and a synaptic plasma membrane fraction of rat cerebral cortex. Acta Pharmacol. Toxicol. 32:317, 1973.

63. Terenius, L., and Wahlström, A. Inhibitor(s) of narcotic receptor binding in brain extracts and cerebrospinal fluid. Acta Pharmacol. Toxicol. 35 (Suppl. 1): 55, 1974.

64. Terenius, L., and Wahlström, A. Morphine-like ligand for opiate receptors in human CSF. Life Sci. 16:1759, 1975.

65. Teschemacher, H., Opheim, K. E., Cox, B. M., and Goldstein, A. A peptide-like substance from pituitary that acts like morphine. I. Isolation. Life Sci. 16: 1771, 1975.

66. Van Praag, D., and Simon, E. J. Studies on the intracellular distribution and tissue binding of dihydromorphine-7,8-^{3}H in the rat. Proc. Soc. Exp. Biol. Med. 122:6, 1966.

67. Walter, R., Ritzmann, R. F., Bhargava, H. N., Rainbow, T. C., Flexner, L. B., and Krivoy, W. A. Inhibition by Z-Pro-D-Leu of development of tolerance to and physical dependence on morphine in mice. Proc. Natl. Acad. Sci. USA 75:4573, 1978.

68. Watson, S. J., Barchas, J. D., and Li, C. H. β-Lipotropin: Localization of cells and axons in rat brain by immunocytochemistry. Proc. Natl. Acad. Sci. USA 74:5155, 1977.

69. Wilson, R. S., Rogers, M. E., Pert, C. B., and Snyder, S. H. Homologous N-alkylnorketobemidones: Correlation of receptor binding with analgesic potency. J. Med. Chem. 18:240, 1975.

70. Yanagida, H. Congenital insensitivity and naloxone. Lancet 2:520, 1978.

CHAPTER 6

A PSYCHOLOGY OF CRAVING: IMPLICATIONS OF BEHAVIORAL RESEARCH[1]

Roger E. Meyer, M.D.

Steven M. Mirin, M.D.

Clinicians working with heroin addicts and alcoholics generally take the view that drug use serves meliorative functions for the individual by binding or neutralizing negative affects (e.g., anxiety, aggressions, or depression). In this context relapse after a period of abstinence is generally comprehensible in psychodynamic terms wherein drug consumption results in the pharamcological reduction of neurotic conflict. It is somewhat surprising, therefore, that experimental studies of alcoholics (2, 19) and of heroin addicts (6, 9, 23) have consistently identified dysphoric mood states, increased psychopathology, and regressive and withdrawn behavior

[1] This research was supported, in part by the following: (1) Harvard-Boston University Center for Biobehavioral Studies in the Addictions, National Institute of Mental Health Grant 5P01 DA 00257; (2) Research Paradigm for the Study of Opiate Antagonists (McLean Hospital, Belmont, Massachusetts), National Institute of Mental Health Contract HSM 42-72-208; and (3) Alcohol and Drug Abuse Research Center (McLean Hospital, Belmont, Massachusetts), National Institute of Drug Abuse Grant DA4 RG010.

consequent to chronic alcohol and chronic opioid use in addicted individuals.

In the context of group and individual therapy, alcoholics and addicts seem to recall principally the pleasurable consequences of drug administration. In these settings, relapse is seen by the addict in terms of drug availability, and successful outcome is seen in terms of the individual's ability to "avoid" the drug. Alcohol and heroin are described in seductive terms; avoidance behavior is defined as a moral imperative. Heroin addicts and alcoholics sometimes engage in complex rituals around stimuli associated with the availability of their preferred drug. It is not uncommon for addicts leaving a residential therapeutic community after many months to visit old haunts in order to "test their mettle." Supporters of Alcoholics Anonymous fiercely oppose the notion of controlled drinking. This organization utilizes group and peer pressure and a belief in a higher power to help the recovered alcoholic to avoid alcohol. By taking disulfiram (Antabuse), the alcoholic is also engaging in behavior that makes alcohol unavailable.

The factors which were present at the outset of an addiction career that led to drug experimentation do not adequately explain the energy associated with the tendency to relapse. During the course of an addictive or alcoholic career, the individual accumulates a history of operant and classically conditioned responses that come to affect his cognitive understanding of his subjective and external environment. It is this history in each individual that is often ignored in our rush to explicate the "meaning" of drug use.

THE PHENOMENON OF "CRAVING"

For many heroin addicts (21) and alcoholics (15), the antecedent subjective state associated with drug consumption is "craving." The authors recently completed an experimental study involving 63 heroin addicts and observed that no other "mood" state was characteristically associated with actual drug self-administration (20). Actual heroin consumption was strongly correlated with self-reports of "craving." The latter seems to be the cognitive label applied by the addict to a predominantly dysphoric condition. Under conditions where the heroin addict does not expect to obtain heroin (e.g., in a residential therapeutic community), craving is markedly diminished or absent. Under conditions previously associated with drug procurement (e.g., interpersonal or intrapsychic stress, being in the presence of former drug-using peers, or passing drugstores or heroin "copping" sites), the subjective sense of craving increases to levels that make continued abstinence unlikely. Craving may include physiological concomitants (16) that contribute to a sense of powerlessness to resist the desire to take heroin. It is also associated with an approach-avoidance conflict about "getting high" and a feeling of inevitability ("if not this time, next time") regarding relapse. We believe that the subjective state, craving, is a learned response consequent to prior operant and classical conditioning of stimuli associated with episodes of heroin consumption. It is *the* subjective state associated with heroin availability. For the heroin addict, Wikler has specifically attributed relapse to conditioned abstinence in which the visceral concomitants of true pharmacological withdrawal are elicited in the presence of environmental and interoceptive stimuli previously associated with true pharmacological withdrawal (30).

Ludwig et al. postulated a similar mechanism to explain craving in alcoholics (17).

More recently, learning theorists have specified three stimulus properties associated with drugs of abuse that may have significant implications for the problem of relapse and addictive behavior (28). Opiate drugs and alcohol possess reinforcing stimulus properties, respondent stimulus properties, and discriminative stimulus properties (28). Recurrent heroin use defines the reinforcing stimulus properties of this opiate. Moreover, stimuli associated with the reinforcing event (e.g., the heroin injection) acquire reinforcing properties. For example, experimental animals receiving intravenous morphine injections will later "work for" saline injections, which merely provide the sound of the injection apparatus and other stimuli associated with intravenous administration (3). Some heroin addicts will also repeatedly self-administer saline or heroin in the presence of a narcotic-blocking drug, when in a double-blind clinical research design in which they could be receiving unblocked heroin (20). Cognitive factors can also diminish the "craving" response to alcohol and enhance the "craving" response to placebo in an alcoholic population (18). Thus, stimuli associated with the reinforcing event (alcohol or heroin administration) acquire reinforcing properties (1, 27). In the real world the environmental and internal stimuli (including affective states) that have been repeatedly associated with heroin or alcohol consumption also become positive reinforcers that come to shape individual behavior.

Animal studies have demonstrated that the agonistic autonomic effects of opioid injections can be conditioned (i.e., the respondent stimulus properties of opioid injections) (24). Heroin addicts who repeatedly challenged narcotic blockade (when a narcotic-blocking drug was administered on a double-blind basis versus placebo) experienced some respiratory depression, pupillary constriction, and subjective opioid-like effects that were extinguished over repeated administrations (20, Chapter 4). Individuals who did not experience heroin-like effects from the injections did not continue to challenge narcotic blockade. Those addicts who repeatedly challenged narcotic blockade maintained high levels of craving until the classically conditioned physiological and subjective effects were extinguished. At this point, heroin self-administration ceased. It was of heuristic interest that addicts who manifested conditioned opioid effects were not readily able to identify the absence of pharmacological effects—they could not easily differentiate the "heroin unavailable" condition. Later, when offered the opportunity to create the "heroin unavailable" condition by taking a narcotic antagonist (naltrexone) in the community, these individuals were much less likely to do so than peers who had easily identified narcotic blockade in the experimental situation (20, Chapter 4).

Finally, opioids and alcohol are potent discriminative stimuli signaling drug availability. We have observed that craving for heroin is highest when the addict is receiving heroin and (by history) during opiate withdrawal (20, Chapter 4). Karoly et al. at the University of Michigan have demonstrated high operant work output for alcohol in monkeys already receiving alcohol (11). Funderburk and Allen have experimentally demonstrated "loss of control" drinking in alcoholics utilizing a progressive ratio operant paradigm (7) in which an individual can earn a "bonus drink" after consuming two drinks. The period of delay that the subject experiences can be reduced by the operant work output performed to decrease the period of delay.

Ludwig et al. postulated that alcoholics who experience "loss of control" drinking suffer from a kind of feedback dysfunction that interferes with their ability to moderate their ethanol intake (17). Not all alcoholics suffer from "loss of control" drinking (17). Those individuals who do apparently experience "craving" for alcohol in the presence of alcohol.

In summary, "craving" is the cognitive label applied by the alcoholic (or the heroin addict) to a subjective state which he/she associates with alcohol (or heroin) availability. It is an intensely ambivalent state that is most intense in settings or situations in which drug procurement and consumption have previously occurred. Thus, under conditions of interpersonal or intrapsychic distress (such as loss of self-esteem), or in the presence of exteroceptive stimuli associated with substance use, the drug-free former heroin addict experiences high levels of craving. For the addict, craving results when he/she feels that heroin might be available. The returning

Vietnam veterans who had been addicted to heroin while in Southeast Asia have generally been able to avoid relapse in this country because the stimuli and subjective states associated with heroin consumption in Vietnam are not present in the United States (26).

Within therapeutic communities, individuals gradually experience a decrease in craving over the course of their stay in the drug-free environment. After discharge, they are again faced with familiar stimuli associated with their former heroin-associated life style. These heroin-associated stimuli ("the heroin stimulus") are seemingly ubiquitous in the addict's world, and the conditioned visceral feelings elicited by these stimuli tend to negate the system of values and beliefs learned in the therapeutic community. These conditioned discriminative stimuli (manifesting as the subjective state called craving) reinforce the addict's feelings of powerlessness, shame, despair, and lack of self-worth. The experience of craving marks him as a shameful person in his own eyes, and with its onset he sees no alternative to relapse. As a distinct subjective state, craving cannot be simply equated with other mood states such as sadness, anger, joy, etc. This may be consistent with the idea that addicts with preexisting narcissistic character pathology (14) do not readily differentiate affects. It is also consistent with the notion that craving is a specific subjective state serving as a conditioned discriminative stimulus in an individual expecting imminent and specific pharmacological reinforcement. Paradoxically, when the addict obtains reinforcement with consumption of heroin, craving remains elevated (20, Chapter 4). It is as though each heroin injection serves as a powerful cue for subsequent heroin use; the addict seems chained to a treadmill with the constant promise of light (and peace) at the end of the tunnel. The predominantly dysphoric state associated with chronic heroin (6) and alcohol (19) use is apparently a constant discriminative stimulus suggesting the availability of something unattainable: constant and sustained reinforcement. It is in this context that the unpleasant feeling states associated with heroin (6) and alcohol use (19) in clinical research settings may be understood. In his drug-free treatment setting, the addict or alcoholic apparently only recalls the "promise" of bliss associated with his addiction.

IMPLICATIONS FOR TREATMENT

Although craving as a distinct subjective state seems to be common to many heroin addicts in the context of those stimuli previously associated with opioid consumption, the "meaning" and "function" of the drug experience will vary with individual life experience and psychodynamics. For example, mood elevation, neutralization of aggression, feelings of fusion, and/or actual feelings of orgasm all may be associated with heroin use in different individuals or in the same individual at different times. Although the separate psychoanalytic formulations described by various authors (12, 29, 32, 33) seem to differ from each other, it is also likely that opiate or alcohol reinforcement (and its anticipation) may evoke different forms of symbolic expression in different individuals. In developing a relationship with addicted and alcoholic patients, treatment programs need to consider the "meaning" of the substance use to the individual. In assisting the patient who wishes to stop his addiction, the treatment program must help the individual cope with the problem of craving.

Established opiate addiction programs have developed a variety of approaches to the problem of craving. Dole and Nyswander observed, early in their work, that "drug hunger" was markedly reduced or absent in the presence of high maintenance doses of methadone (4). In addition, cross-tolerance to usual street dosages of heroin in these patients effectively "blocked" the pharmacological effects of injected heroin. In essence, even in settings previously associated with heroin use, heroin was "unavailable." In operant terminology, the methadone condition seemed to "satiate" the individual while serving also as the S_Δ for heroin (the discriminative stimulus indicating that heroin is unavailable). Alcohol treatment programs do not have a "methadone maintenance" alternative, although advocates of "controlled" drinking argue that individuals can be "taught" to drink without the problem of "loss of control." The problem with this approach stems from the fact that alcohol in the body serves as a powerful discriminative stimulus for "another drink" in a population of alcoholics. The stimulus conditions may be temporarily modified by the cues provided by, and in the person of, the behavior therapist. It is not clear that these cues can significantly and permanently modify past discrimination learning associated with alcohol in individuals who suffer from "loss of control drinking."

Alcohol and heroin addiction treatment programs also attempt to deal with the problem of craving by cognitive relabeling and by altering stimulus conditions in the patients' environment. Narcotic antagonist treatment of the heroin addict and disulfiram treatment of the alcoholic serve to create the S_Δ condition by the daily consumption of a drug that makes the addictive agent unavailable. Experimental data suggest that the effects of a narcotic antagonist (naltrexone) upon craving are the same as the effects of living in a drug-free setting (22). Data from ambulatory naltrexone treatment programs confirm that the addict who takes a narcotic antagonist every day does not take heroin (8, 13, 25). When the consumption of the narcotic-blocking drug stops, relapse is a risk (22).

In the early days of disulfiram treatment it was felt that the alcoholic needed to experience the aversive consequences of the alcohol/disulfiram reaction in order to avoid alcohol. More recent clinical experience suggests that this is not the case (5). The consumption of disulfiram serves as the discriminative stimulus for an alcohol-free environment.

Alcoholics Anonymous (AA) and residential therapeutic communities use peer and group support to maintain a drug-free state. For the individual attending AA regularly, alcohol is unavailable. In addition, the AA philosophy attempts to help the alcoholic avoid emotional responses that have been previously associated with alcohol consumption. Belief in a higher power outside the individual helps to override the power of environmental and subjective stimuli to elicit the autonomic concomitants of craving. In the case of the heroin addict, Wikler has demonstrated the importance of expectancy in modifying conditioned autonomic responses (31). When individuals leave a drug-free therapeutic community and return to their home environments, craving for opiates is often a problem. In many ways, AA takes a more realistic approach by insisting that the risk of relapse is ever present, requiring long term involvement with peer support and the structure offered by this organization.

A central problem facing substance abuse treatment programs concerns their ability to modify "craving." Work, human relationships, psychotherapy, and other interpersonal encounters do not by themselves provide sufficient alternative reinforcement to modify addictive behavior. On the other hand narcotic antagonists for the heroin addict and disulfiram for the alcoholic are more likely to be successful if the individual is motivated to use them. We have observed that the simple payment of $1 per day upon consumption of a narcotic antagonist at a local pharmacy significantly improved the rate of naltrexone consumption in the first month of ambulatory treatment (20, Chapter 11). We have heard reports of modest success with a program in San Francisco that paid addicts for drug-free urines (10). The advantage of daily naltrexone or disulfiram consumption is that the addicted individual need only decide once a day to create the stimulus conditions associated with the unavailability of the addicting substance. By this act the individual is able to diminish craving. The decision to discontinue treatment medication is an important issue in psychotherapy. We have heard of one psychoanalyst whose alcoholic patient consumes his disulfiram at the analyst's office just prior to the analytic hour. Failure to take any dose is an important issue during the treatment. It is our feeling that disulfiram and narcotic antagonist drugs are extremely important tools in the treatment of the addicted individual because of their power to diminish craving. Treatment programs that merely prescribe disulfiram without monitoring and reinforcing daily consumption should consider the potential advantages of contingent reinforcement and monitoring of disulfiram administration. In essence, disulfiram treatment of the alcoholic and naltrexone treatment of the heroin addict are examples of discrimination learning in which the individual appreciates that ingestion of his treatment medication initiates the S_Δ condition that persists for the duration of action of the drug. For all such patients, when the treatment medication is discontinued, the S_Δ condition is restored and alcohol or heroin is again "available." In the context of a total treatment program and adequate personal, emotional, and social resources, individuals may now be in a better position to deal with the S_Δ and its concomitant subjective state, craving. Under conditions of unusual and/or recurrent stress, patients should be able to resume their treatment medication in order to avoid relapse.

In summary, recent experimental studies in animal models and in clinical research settings have confirmed three stimulus properties of addictive drugs that have significant implications for an understanding of craving and of developing innovative approaches to addiction treatment. The authors believe that standard (e.g., disulfiram) and newer (e.g., naltrexone) pharmacological tools can be used in systematic ways to assist the alcohol or heroin addict to modify craving and to become engaged in programs of social and psychiatric treatment.

References

1. Carnathan, G., Meyer, R. E., and Cochin, J. Narcotic blockade, length of addiction and persistence of intravenous morphine self-administration in rats. Psychopharmacology 54:67, 1977.
2. Davis, D. Mood changes in alcoholic subjects with programmed and free choice drinking. In *Recent Advances in Studies of Alcoholism*, N. K. Mello and J. Mendelson, editors. United States Public Health Service Vol. #HSM 71 9045. United States Public Health Service, Bethesda, 1971.
3. Davis, W. M., and Smith, S. G. Naloxone use to eliminate opiate seeking behavior: Need for extinction of conditioned reinforcement. Biol. Psychiatry 9:181, 1974.
4. Dole, V. P., and Nyswander, M. E. A medical treatment for diacetylmorphine (heroin) addiction. J.A.M.A. 193:646, 1965.
5. Fox, R. Treatment of the problem drinker by the private practitioner. In *Alcoholism: Progress in Research and Treatment*, P. Bourne and R. Fox, editors, pp. 227–244. New York, Academic Press, 1973.
6. Fraser, H. F., Jones, B. E., Rosenberg, D. E., and Thompson, A. K. Effects of addiction to intravenous heroin on patterns of physical activity in man. Clin. Pharmacol. Ther. 4:188, 1963.
7. Funderburk, F. R., and Allen, R. P. Alcoholics' disposition to drink: Effects of abstinence and heavy drinking. Q. J. Stud. Alcohol, 38:410, 1977.
8. Goldstein, A. Naltrexone in the management of heroin addiction: Critique of the rationale. In *Narcotic Antagonists: Naltrexone Progress Report*, NIDA Research Monograph Series #9, pp. 158–161. Washington, D.C., United States Government Printing Office, 1976.
9. Haertzen, C. H., and Hooks, N. T. Changes in personality and subjective experience associated with the chronic administration and withdrawal of opiates. J. Nerv. Ment. Dis. 148:606, 1969.
10. Hargreaves, W. Personal communication.
11. Karoly, A. J., Winger, G., Ikomi, F., and Woods, J. H. The reinforcing properties of ethanol in the rhesus monkey. Psychopharmacology 58:19, 1978.
12. Khantzian, E. Opiate addiction: A critique of theory

and some implications for treatment. Am. J. Psychother. 28:59, 1974.

13. Kleber, H. Clinical experiences with narcotic antagonists. In *Opiate Addiction: Origins and Treatment*, S. Fisher and A. M. Freedman, editors, pp. 211–222. Washington D.C., Winston, 1974.

14. Kohut, H. Preface. In *Psychodynamics of Drug Dependence*, J. D. Blain and D. A. Julius, editors, NIDA Research Monograph #12, pp. vii–ix. Washington, D.C., United States Government Printing Office, 1977.

15. Ludwig, A. M. The irresistable urge and the unquenchable thirst for alcohol. In *Proceedings, 4th Annual Alcoholism Conference of the National Institute on Alcohol Abuse and Alcoholism: Research, Treatment and Prevention*, M. E. Chafetz, editor, DHEW Publication #76-284, pp. 3022. Washington, D.C., United States Government Printing Office, 1975.

16. Ludwig, A. M., and Stark, L. H. Arousal and alcoholism: Psychophysiological responses to alcohol. Adv. Exp. Med. Biol. 59:515, 1975.

17. Ludwig, A. M., Wikler, A., and Stark, L. H. The first drink: Psychobiological aspects of craving. Arch. Gen. Psychiatry 30:539, 1974.

18. Maisto, S. A., Lauerman, R., and Adesso, V. J. A comparison of two experimental studies of the role of cognitive factors in alcoholics drinking. J. Stud. Alcohol 38:145, 1977.

19. Mendelson, J. H., and Mello, N. K. Experimental analysis of drinking behavior of chronic alcoholics. Ann. N. Y. Acad. Sci. 133:828, 1966.

20. Meyer, R. E., and Mirin, S. M. *The Heroin Stimulus: Implication for a Theory of Addiction*. New York, Plenum Press, in press.

21. Meyer, R. E., Mirin, S. M., Altman, J. L., and McNamee, H. B. A behavioral paradigm for the evaluation of narcotic antagonists. Arch. Gen. Psychiatry 33:371, 1976.

22. Meyer, R. E., Randall, M. E., Barrington, C., Mirin, S. M., and Greenberg, I. In *Narcotic Antagonists: Naltrexone Progress Report*, NIDA Research Monograph Series #9, pp. 123–135. Washington, D.C., United States Government Printing Office, 1976.

23. Mirin, S. M., Meyer, R. E., and McNamee, H. B. Psychopathology and mood during heroin use: Acute vs. chronic effects. Arch. Gen. Psychiatry 33: 1503, 1976.

24. Perez-Cruet, J. Drug conditioning and drug effects on cardiovascular conditioned factors. In *Stimulus Properties of Drugs*, T. Thompson and R. Pickens, editors, pp. 15–38. New York, Appleton-Century-Crofts, 1971.

25. Rawlins, M., Randall, M., Meyer, R. E., et al. Aftercare on narcotic antagonists: Prospects and problems. Int. J. Addictions 11:501, 1976.

26. Robins, L. N., Davis, D. H., and Goodwin, D. W. Drug use by U.S. Army enlisted men in Vietnam: A follow-up on their return home. Am. J. Epidemiol. 99:235, 1974.

27. Smith, S. G., Werner, T. E., and Davis, W. M. Alcohol-associated conditioned reinforcement. Psychopharmacology 53:223, 1977.

28. Thompson, T., and Pickens, R. Interceptive stimulus control of behavior In *Stimulus Properties of Drugs*, T. Thompson and R. Pickens, editors, pp. 1–14. New York, Appleton-Century-Crofts, 1971.

29. Wieder, H., and Kaplan, E. H. Drug use in adolescents. Psychoanal. Study Child 24:399, 1969.

30. Wikler, A. Conditioning factors in opiate addiction and relapse. In *Narcotics*, D. M. Wilner and G. G. Kassebaum, editors, pp. 85–100. New York, McGraw-Hill, 1965.

31. Wikler, A. Dynamics of drug dependence: Implications of a conditioning theory for research and treatment. In *Opiate Addiction: Origins and Treatment*, S. Fisher and A. M. Freedman, editors, pp. 7–22. Washington, D.C., Winston, 1973.

32. Wikler, A. Psychodynamic study of a patient during experimental self-regulated readdiction to morphine. Psychiatr. Q. 26:270, 1952.

33. Wurmser, L. Psychoanalytic considerations of the etiology of compulsive drug use. J. Am. Psychoanal. Assoc. 22:820, 1974.

CHAPTER 7

PSYCHODYNAMICS OF SUBSTANCE ABUSE

Leon Wurmser, M.D.

THE FACTOR OF THE INNER NEED

The premise of psychoanalytic theory is that all mental processes are meaningful, no matter how bizarre they may seem, and that they follow an inner lawfulness of great complexity and one which is no less inescapable than the lawfulness of outer reality. The laws of this inner reality weave the many layers of personal and familial history into a web of meaningful connections. The richness of this tapestry does not tolerate arbitrariness, ("Everyone of us acts not only under external compulsion but also in accord with inner necessity" (11)), yet its patterns are so multiply interwoven and iridescent that in each individual they form an inexhaustible repertoire. Various observers, who have the privilege to gain access to this inner life, will see more or fewer and often quite different patterns emerge and again disappear, although the more skilled, experienced, and trained the therapists are, the more stable the observed configurations tend to become and the more understandably they can be communicated to patient and other observers.

No matter how substance abuse is defined (all use of psychoactive substances that contravenes common usage and legal and social practice, or all use that temporarily or continually interferes with mental functioning) it must be understood as part of this web of meanings; it cannot be an alien, shot-in element, no matter how disruptive it turns out to be. Dependent on such meaning we can discern great differences only loosely related to the behavioral pattern of substance abuse.

Case 1. In one case an 18-year-old boy tries out a few puffs of a marihuana cigarette and develops a serious depressive-paranoid reaction. The very transitory and light intoxication, combined with its illegality and fear of punishment, kindles a whole chain of conflicts around shame and guilt-laden transgressions and experiences—shame about his physical appearance, about some homosexual adventures, about masturbation, guilt about his wishes to break away from an overly protective family, and rebellion against his overly strict inner commands and ideals. Here we have an *experimental*, socially, but not legally sanctioned incident of abuse triggering an eventually life-threatening neurotic crisis. A few hours of focal analytically oriented psychotherapy break the fatal spell.

Case 2. A 30-year-old man several times a week uses barbiturates, heroin, cocaine, marihuana, and other drugs solicited from or given to him and his wife by his friends. It is *social, recreational* use which has led to his arrest for having served a few weeks as a middleman in trafficking and to serious menace to business, repute, and freedom. He needs the drugs to relax, to feel good, to enjoy life, but above all to dampen his very frequent anxiety attacks. The "feeling good" serves as a rationalization for his wish to undo unbearable anxiety—the reasons for which need to be uncovered in psychoanalysis, once this drug cover is resolutely removed. The suspicion is warranted that most, perhaps all, such social use really comes down to such symptomatic actions—attempts to cope from time to time with upsurging anxiety and other strongly unpleasant feelings. The voluntariness is more often feigned than real; the need to resort to such an euphoriant, often with friends, is more compelling than commonly admitted.

Case 3. A highly successful, sensitive social worker in her forties, caught in a sadomasochistic marriage with a hard-drinking, "hardnosed," taciturn, businessman, whose intense jealousy deepens her already marked emotional withdrawal still more and with whom communication is either shallow or acerbic, regularly gets moderately drunk when she joins him in social functions. She stifles her shame and self-doubt, her sense of debasement and pain, with alcohol, plays the somewhat frivolous, socially relaxed and outgoing companion, and thus maintains a mask of happiness and kindness while being deeply resentful that she feels neither fully acknowledged in her intellectual potential nor loved as a woman. She longs for creativity, imaginativeness, and human closeness, but disparages and destroys every such effort on her part and quickly returns to her habitual pattern of cold efficiency. Only temporarily she finds surcease from her feeling hurt, unworthy, inadequate, and unproductive, a brief respite from chronic self-criticism, self-blaming, and self-ridicule, not solely in these periodic intoxications, but also in an entire sham world of frantic but efficient activity, thrills, and political influence. On a deeper layer one may discern envy and anger at anyone felt to be superior to her, yet contempt and shame about her husband whom she sees, rather like Emma Bovary, as boorish and vastly inferior to herself, but to whom she is bound in guilt-laden loyalty and masochistic surrender. Occasionally and unexpectedly, expression of intense feelings of despair and rage, compassion or terror break through her stone mask of stoic self-control and cold, even haughty aloofness (43). Again this *circumstantial* abuse is part of an intricate

texture of meaning—first assuaging shame and pain, then redoubling them. More generally, they first smother her feelings, then suddenly they unleash them to her profound embarrassment and regret.

Case 4. An unmarried girl in her twenties, living with a violent, drug-abusing boyfriend, intoxicates herself quite regularly in the morning with diazepam (Valium) or barbiturates without becoming fully addicted in order to make it through the day at an unpleasant, boring, often frightening job. More and more often she has to stay home, because of having oversedated herself. Weekends are spent drugged, lying together with her boyfriend in bed, or drinking in dissolute company at a bar. She is not addicted; once drug free, her episodic depression and anxiety incapacitate her even more than her severe and *intensive* drug abuse prior to treatment.

Case 5. A very successful and self-made executive every day drinks more than a fifth of vodka and, in addition, "calms his nerves" with chlordiazepoxide (Librium) and diazepam. As soon as he tries to stop, he goes into "the shakes." His marriage has a mechanical, shallow quality; both spouses are engaged in frequent affairs. Their older daughter has entered adolescence in a chronic state of spite and emotional divorce from her parents. He refuses to enter psychotherapy, but goes to an out-of-state private hospital for withdrawal from his physical *addiction*. Upon return he immediately resumes his previous pattern.

These are five characteristic cases, all from my personal experience, and typifying diverse psychodynamic dimensions of the five patterns described for frequency of usage by the National Commission on Marijuana and Drug Abuse (61). In each case substance abuse fits into an inner constellation that has clinical significance. I hasten to add, though, that, particularly in the first two patterns (experimental and social-recreational), this does not always need to be so. The drug abuse or the alcohol intoxication may serve no particular inner need and thus may not recur again or only very rarely.

It is this *inner need* that is the crucial variable lending substance abuse pathological significance; it is not an "either-or," but a "more or less." In some of the instances described the need to use drugs becomes irresistibly intense; the drug effect is sought at all costs and at grave peril to social standing and emotional and physical well-being. In others (e.g., in Cases 1 and 3) the substance abuse is almost coincidental, an easily relinquished part of a larger constellation of deeper emotional and familial problems.

Dependent on the intensity of such inner need we speak of more or less *compulsive* substance abuse; this compulsiveness is directly proportional to the severity of underlying unsolved inner conflicts, usually of a largely unconscious nature.

What about physician-induced addiction? This is not as rare as we wish it to be; particularly, much abuse of tranquilizers today is iatrogenic. Although it is not difficult to bring about physical addiction in this way, the emotionally relatively healthy individual will, after properly conducted withdrawal, not feel again compelled to return to the drug of abuse. The precariously balanced person, however, will crave to reexperience the relief brought about and, at first signs of inner distress, may revert to what had "helped" him before. Again this compulsion reflects the deeper pathology; if the drug relief had not been shown to him, other symptoms or forms of expression for the conflicts would have prevailed—outbursts of anger, crying tantrums, chronic unhappiness, nagging anxiety, and worry.

In the following we will narrow our focus entirely to this issue of compulsiveness: What does it mean? What are its deeper determinants? How does the personality of a compulsive substance abuser present himself in the careful scrutiny possible in short or prolonged intensive psychotherapy or in psychoanalysis?

To answer the first question, we would call any form of substance abuse *compulsive* when there is substantial *subjective* psychological need to resort to or to continue using mind-altering drugs (including alcohol and nicotine), *regardless of the possible noxious consequences* such use entails socially, legally, somatically, or psychologically. In this view *physical* addiction is an irrelevant criterion for the definition, although it is often coextensive with compulsiveness and may be tightly intermeshed with it.

To respond to the other two questions, we have to resort to a much broader account. In the following, only compulsive drug use will be considered; all experimental and much social-recreational use, showing little compulsiveness, will be excluded.

INDIVIDUAL DYNAMICS

TRIPLE LAYERING

Chein and co-workers, in their seminal work *The Road to H* (9), state in regard to heroin: "Contrary to common belief, the drug does not contribute rich positive pleasures, it merely offers relief from misery." "Heroin is a tranquilizer—perhaps the most effective tranquilizer known—but it comes in expensive doses." It blunts "the perception of inner anxiety and outer strain." "In this sense, the drug itself is a diffuse pharmacological defense." Similarly, Krystal and Raskin (44) stress: "The drug is not the problem but is an attempt at a self-help that fails." Drug use is a "defense against affects"; it "is a selective 'numbing' and blocking," particularly of a global, undifferentiated, somatically experienced "affect combining depression and anxiety." These statements could be duplicated from most modern writers (6, 33, 35, 38, 69). This group of findings can be summarized thus: The drug use is the superficial layer, in itself fraught with all the problems of physical and mental damage, of self-perpetuating dependency (what Anthony says of Cleopatra: "She makes hungry, where most she satisfies"), and often illegality and derivative criminality. In that sense substance abuse, including alcoholism, is a disease, is *the* disease. Unless treated on this level, no further progress may be made.

Yet we have become accustomed to dialectical thinking in psychoanalysis and psychotherapy; that means that "a positive concept is always viewed in contrast with its opposite, in the hope that their joint consideration will yield a resolution through a more thorough and productive understanding" (8). What is indubitably *the* disease when we start working with the patient turns into a mere symptom once we look at him in the depth dimension ("the hidden dimension" alluded to in the title of my book (70)).

Thus, on the next deeper level, compulsive drug use has to be seen as a mere symptom. It uniformly functions as an *artificial affect defense*, as a relief from overwhelming feelings. Quite generally, the drugs combat a vague, diffuse, but pervasive mood of anxiousness, tension, uneasiness, and unhappiness. If probed more deeply, it becomes evident that there are quite specific affect states from which surcease is sought and, moreover, that not all drugs can be used indiscriminately for such pacification. The choice of drugs is pretty specifically correlated with the otherwise unmanageable affect. In a brief synopsis: Narcotics and hypnotics are arrayed against rage, shame, and jealousy, and the often panicky anxiety attacks derived from these partly repressed affects. Stimulants (including cocaine) are deployed against feelings of depression, weakness, inner emptiness, and helplessness. Psychedelics tend to be chosen to ward off boredom, disillusionment, apathy, a sense of meaninglessness, painful isolation, and detachment. Intense guilt and self-punishment, loneliness, and longing are said to yield to alcohol. Anxiety of an overwhelming nature and the emotional (not physical) experiences of pain, injury, woundedness, and vulnerability seem to me features common to all types of compulsive drug use. Much overlapping occurs, and hence these drugs are to some extent interchangeable, regardless of their pharmacological nature (i.e., alcohol or sedatives may very well substitute for narcotics, although there is no cross-tolerance).

Whatever triggers or threatens to trigger an intense affect of the nature just described precipitates a recurrence of drug use. The precipitant is most typically an intense disappointment in someone else or the self, a falling down from exaggerated expectations and hopes (in what I called a *"narcissistic crisis,"* because of the overvaluation preceding the disappointment). As Krystal in particular, in a number of outstanding studies (39–44), stresses, these affects quickly tend to become global, undifferentiated, resomatized (felt as if of somatic origin), and deverbalized (dissociated from words and other symbols); it is the process of *affect regression* (39, 40).

Very significantly also, affects of expectation and hope may be warded off as frightening: "When exposed to a potential good object, such patients panic and may have to ward off their yearnings for love and acceptance . . . they expect disappointment and rejection" (42).

Yet there is a third layer underneath, that of the *unconscious conflicts* underlying such radical and regressive (infantile) affect states. In other words, we encounter in every case a recrudescence of what Freud called "the infantile neurosis" (22), always of a serious and profound pathology. The conflicts of this infantile neurosis are very intense, usually of both an oedipal and preoedipal nature; the defenses are equally widespread and archaic. However, pathogenesis and etiology are not restricted to one phase of development but usually span all of childhood and continue into adolescence. Later damage perpetuates and deepens the infantile neurosis.

THE INFANTILE NEUROSIS

It is in vogue today to see in all more severely disturbed patients "borderline" pathology and to emphasize their fundamentally psychotic or near psychotic as well as their narcissistic features. This presupposes a continuum between psychosis and neurosis that, I believe, is still by no means assured; it may well be that too sloppy and too broad an application of the diagnosis "schizophrenia" or "cyclic depression" generates the faulty impression of such a continuum. Be that as it may, I suggest that we are better off to reserve the diagnosis "borderline" for those patients about whom we are not sure whether they had been at one time overtly psychotic or may become so again, in other words as a diagnosis of reservation, of embarrassment, not as a broad clinical category. Most of those severely disturbed patients that one calls nowadays "borderline" or "narcissistic" are more specifically related to the already well known and well described pictures of neuroses (symptom and character neuroses); they may be severely hysterical, phobic, obsessive-compulsive, impulse neuroses, etc. with their carefully studied pathology. If we critically read the leading psychoanalytic literature, most cases with their thoughtful differentiation of pathology would now be subsumed under the encompassing label "borderline" and thus their differentiae effaced. Moreover all severer pathology is eo ipso more "narcissistic." Inasmuch as specificity is the great virtue in our science, I think we lose more than we gain by the current extensive use of the "borderline" concept as essentially coextensive with serious, strongly preoedipally determined pathology (5).

With this polemic preamble, I have said nothing about the infantile neurosis itself. We cannot allow ourselves to be too exclusive about its definition; presumably there could be a great variety of it, probably even forms of circumscribed infantile psychoses. Still a rather consistent picture is emerging now: namely, that the infantile neurosis is in its core *phobic* and is surrounded by multiform conversion hysterical, paranoid, depressive, masochistic, impulsive, and depersonalizing features. The anxiety may be bound up in all kinds of objects and situations (as phobia is defined), but at least in quite a number of cases I have been struck by its specificity as *claustrophobia*, the fear of being closed in, trapped, captured. These patients feel stifled by limitations of any kind, confined by any closeness or commitment, and restlessly try to burst out of such constrictions and constraints. It makes sense, therefore, to study this phenomenon somewhat more in detail now (see also (71)).

In my experience Fenichel's explanation seems most apposite: " . . . *any state of anxiety is physiologically accompanied by feelings of being closed in*; and thus reversely, an *external closeness* (or idea of it) *facilitates the mobilization of the entire anxiety syndrome*" (13, italics added). This means that every intense affect (excitement, rage, etc.) has become equated with an undifferentiated global tension over which all control has been lost and which has left the person panicky, helpless, and overwhelmed, a tension reawakening an original truly and severely traumatic state (41–43).

Thus we are forced to assume that "the idea of a claustrum or of a claustrophobia" may be "behind all other phobias—and even behind all other symptomatic neuroses," as Leo Rangell (55) suggested. Even the word "anxiety" itself expresses a physical constriction and confinement: "angustiae" being a narrow, boxed-in place. Is not the basic experience of anxiety that of being entrapped, smothered, constricted, and quite physically so? Freud, in his relating anxiety back to the act of birth, equally states: "The name 'Angst'—'angustiae' 'Enge'—emphasizes the characteristic of restriction in breathing which was then present as a consequence of the real situation and is now almost invariably reinstated in the affect" (28). Leo Rangell added: "Behind all of the experiences is the physiological-psychological situation of the anxiety state itself being felt as a hemming-in from which one fears but also wants to burst out. Ultimate anxiety or four-plus anxiety in the decompensated state is felt as the danger of bursting asunder" (55).

This basic anxiety experience reaches from an all pervasive, generalized, internal one to a more localized one, where the body, particularly the chest, is felt to be a stifling enclosure, then to its projection to the surrounding structures, and thence to its displacement onto all forms of concrete and abstract limitations. On all levels this anxiety series is accompanied by a series of usually aggressive actions that would liberate the self from these various concentric bounds. Yet this liberation and bursting out itself raises many new specters: condemnation in form of guilt and shame, aloneness because of the separation from the protective, shielding claustrum, ultimately, as Rangell observed, the fear of the most radical bursting: that into small fragments of body and mind ("aphanisis") (34).

What the putative origin of this massive (traumatic) anxiety state may be will be studied later on. It is experienced as helpless confusion and loss of felt controls, a vague aimless tension. This leads now to the following paradox: On the one side we find that this severe anxiety, probably because of the physiological concomitants of somatically felt narrowness and stricture, becomes concretized in and attached to the general idea of confinement, entrapment, and enclosure and projected onto all external structures lending themselves to be viewed as claustra. On the other side, relief from such anxiety can only come from protection, yet this protection would have to be sought primarily again in external structures, in outside controls and limitations, in the hope that somebody else would take over, constrain him, and thus shield him against this dark overwhelming part within him. The tragic paradox, of course, is that all such protection against this devastating anxiety is bound to become once more just a new claustrum and, therefore, a renewed source of terror.

It is really quite surprising to find claustrophobia rarely mentioned in literature and clinic and to hear specifically from Anna Freud that "claustrophobia . . . is rare in children in whom, instead, situational phobias such as school phobia, phobia of the dentist, etc., play a prominent part" (15). I suspect that the reason for this comparative neglect may lie in that this symptom is often subsumed under less specific headings—like general anxiety, inhibition, hyperventilation—or hidden under other, more superficial forms of phobias.

At least as far as these very profoundly disturbed patients are concerned, it would make sense to see in claustrophobia the *primary phobia*. It can reach back into the deepest layers of experience, to the substrate of physiological experiences, but it does not have to have such archaic origins. Anxiety on all levels can give rise much later to the same phenomenon of being constricted (as the German word "zusammengeschnürt," "tied together," plastically expresses) and hence to the constitution of this symptom by defensive projection ab novo. Still I am convinced that the claustrophobia in our patients is of a very archaic nature, at least in its basic strata.

Now to the dialectic counterpoint: Wherever we have a phobic system we also find its antithesis, a *protective system* in the form of protective figures and protective fantasies. I use as prototype a well known vignette given by Anna Freud (14) of the boy who used the tamed lion as his protector. The phobically feared animal—the substitute for the hated and feared father—had become his protector: " . . . he simply denied a painful fact and in his lion fantasy turned it into its pleasurable opposite. He called the anxiety animal his friend, and its strength, instead of being a source of terror, was now at his service. The only indication that in the past the lion had been an anxiety object was the anxiety of the other people, as depicted in the imaginary episodes"; "he delighted in imagining how terrified the people would be if they guessed his secret." Once I became aware of this *"protective figure" fantasy* in the service of denial and repression I started discovering it in a number of otherwise refractory and nonunderstandable treatment cases as a very relevant element. Only by inserting the many and highly specific variants of such a protective figure between later symptoms and earlier anxieties was it possible to find access to the latter.

As dream analysis shows, displacement is a cardinally important defense in everybody. So much could be most parsimoniously ex-

plained by it. A case in point is the replacement of this "protective figure" by the "protective system" in the form of drug effect, drugs as substances, and drug culture.

The drug is part and parcel of such a protection system; *it is equally compulsively sought, as a phobic object may be compulsively avoided*. It is the photographic negative of a phobia just like the tamed lion is the negative of what Anna Freud called the "Angsttier," the phobically feared animal. There may be fascinating parallels to sexual perversions. Again, it seems that the perverse act is not primarily dictated by the goal of pleasure but by that of protection against otherwise overwhelming anxiety.

To be yet more exact, such a countervailing fantasy of a protective object, that has been split off from the hated and frightening anxiety object but shares in the power of the latter, is the direct counterpart to the phobia. It is in this novel sense that we may now correlate more convincingly the addictions to phobic neuroses.

Whereas the phobic neurotic compulsively *avoids* the condensed and projected symbol for his anxiety on the outside, the toxicomanic equally compulsively *seeks* the condensed and projected symbol of protection against uncontrollable, overwhelming affects, again on the outside. Its protective efficacy is proven by the introduction of the magically powerful means from the outside and the ensuing mobilization with its help of a transient and lastly spurious counterforce.

In both instances, addictions and phobias, the therapy can only succeed if this countervailing protective fantasy is reexperienced in the transference. This aspect of transference is in my experience much more resistant to recognition and working through than the negative transference.

The drug effect itself is a type of counterphobic fantasy that validates the attempted and hoped for protection against (denial of) the phobic fears, a protective, countervailing fantasy against the main anxieties, and with that also against the major phobias: "I am strong, not vulnerable" (with stimulants); "I am blissful, not enraged" (with narcotics and other sedative drugs); "I am trustful, not disillusioned" (with psychedelics); "I am accepted, approved, and belonging, not isolated and guilty" (with alcohol). (In a limited way this concept was presaged by Szasz (67).)

If we see in the therapist and, prior to him,

in the compulsive drug use a reincarnation, a transference manifestation, of this early and centrally important fantasy, the study of transference in both regards (onto drug and onto therapist) is very necessary and needs to be carried out continually from the beginning on, very tactfully and in very concrete and specific details. Only too often the patient bolts from therapy precisely when the transferring of his fantasies and feelings from drug use onto the therapist starts in earnest, when the claustrum becomes visible to the patient both as a sheltering and as a threatening reality. This transferring from addiction onto therapy is, however, crucial to bring about the desired deeper change—the therapist has to replace the drug as an object to depend upon, as Anna Freud proposed (15, 16)—but the intensity of anxiety and anger becomes so great that we lose very many patients precisely then. I have not yet found a generally applicable method to make this transition safer. But it seems to me that a consistent attention from the beginning to this problem of claustrophobia, as mobilized in the therapy and witnessed in countless situations of current and past life, may reduce the likelihood of flight from therapy.

In this context, it is good to remember that analysis is not predominantly an intellectual experience; "Today we observe that transference is sometimes useful as a 'corrective emotional experience'. . . . It is time we asked honestly whether transference is used only for the purpose of learning about the past. For example, some claim that 'borderline cases' respond more favorably to the use of transference as a corrective emotional experience" (18). In a concrete case: "During the treatment it becomes possible for him to reduce the addiction to alcohol because in the transference a new addiction, that to the analyst, took its place. He gave me the role of protecting him against his dangerous, masculine, destructive impulses, in short of 'holding him down'. . . . Where the relationship to the analyst takes the place of the satisfaction or reassurance gained from the symptom, the analysis turns into a battle between the two addictions, the addiction to the analyst holding the fort temporarily until the unconscious material appears and is analyzed" (16). I do not think such mutative protection and reassurance could or even should ever be analyzed away.

It is clear that the duality of phobic and protective systems is a nodal point of convergence from where we may reach a yet deeper understanding. As we know, the infantile neurosis is in itself only the outcome of complex conflicts and traumata. If we look at the components of this pair we find: (a) Closeness and dependency are feared as well as sought after as claustra or other phobic objects (e.g., devouring monsters and animals); i.e., we are referred back to very early object relationships and conflicts about them. (b) The phobic objects are seen as eminently menacing, i.e., aggressive; thus they obviously are projections of the subject's own aggression. The protective or reassurance system uses fire against fire, curing, so to speak, sadism with sadism (31); i.e., we have to look for very early vicissitudes of aggression and of oral and anal libido. (c) The anxiety has such a pronouncedly traumatic quality that we must be prepared to see massive early and ongoing traumatization as a probable causative agent, at least in a large number of such patients.

Here is not the place to enter into a detailed study of these features, but we can say that the conflicts underlying the infantile neurosis are predominantly preoedipal in nature. They apparently center around the triad of early separation anxiety and real object loss, castration anxiety and castration shame, and intensely anal-sadistic conflicts, as recently elucidated by Roiphe and Galenson (29, 30, 57–60). They speak for traumatization in the middle or late second year of life, in what is known from Mahler's research (49–51) as the "rapprochement phase." Such early damage would also explain the prevalence of untamed and largely self-directed aggression and of narcissistic expectations (grandiosity and haughtiness for the self, envious, oral demandingness and clinging dependency toward the overvalued other). Centrality and severity of anxiety allow two alternative explanations: Either the child was overstimulated, i.e., his aggressions and wishes for love and security were excited and encouraged to an extent completely unmanageable at his age, or the stress may be placed more on the massivity of outside violence or exposure to sexual actions and seductions. These two explanations probably address the same issue, first from an intrapsychic, then from an interpersonal point of view; they are complementary. Of course such traumatization would not be confined to the time mentioned.

On the contrary, it is part of an entire pathogenic family system exerting traumatic influences throughout childhood; special consideration will be given to this below.

An additional thought: Anna Freud distinguished two types of infantile psychopathology (which is then continued into that of adults): one based on *conflict*, the other based on trauma and leading to *developmental defects* in the personality structure (17).

We commonly see in our patients evidence of the dramatic intertwining of both. The severe ego and superego "defects" lead to archaic forms of defenses against poorly controlled affects and drives and hence to an exacerbation of inner and outer conflict.

Is it necessary to distinguish two types of addicts—those in whom the "defects" are most prominent versus those in whom intense anxiety as a mark of conflict prevails? Theoretically, yes; practically, I have not found this to be so. Again the "more or less" seems to be preferable to the "either-or."

STRUCTURE OF DEFENSES AND EGO SPLITS

Psychodynamics is the consistent understanding of psychic reality as being constituted by inner conflict. It is seen as an incessant dialectic of a wish being opposed by a contrary striving (a defense), which in itself may be modified again (defense against defense; secondary defense).

From his earliest writings on, Freud paid careful attention to the specific quality of defenses, distinguishing, e.g., in his two papers about the neuropsychoses of defense (26, 27), very carefully various syndromes by some of their specific defense mechanisms. Also, one of the hardly noticed requirements for a careful and competent interpretation of dreams is, as Freud describes (23), the observance of the about two dozen types of representations for logical relations—transformations by the dream work which by and large can be understood as finely detailed defenses. In each of his great cases (19–22, 24) he paid particular attention to defense formations, all of which did not find complete replication in the later systematizations (14, 25) and even today are only insufficiently integrated into our clinical technique and theoretical conceptualizations (32).

Much therapeutic effectiveness rests on the precise recognition of very *specific* connections and relevant details: of fantasies, feelings, memories, symptomatic actions, dreams, transference fears, and wishes. The same rule of specificity applies to the analysis of defenses (1–4). The great complexity as well as the much greater penetrance in understanding shown by skillful psychoanalysts rests on such detailed analysis of the many layers of defenses.

Turning now to the defense structure in compulsive drug users, we have to single out the defense mechanisms that are mainly at play: denial, externalization, and reversal.

Denial

Drug use is lastly only a pharmacologically reinforced denial, an attempt to get rid of feelings and thus of undesirable inner and outer reality. Denial can be defined as "a failure to fully appreciate the significance or implications of what is perceived" (68); it is a defense making the emotional significance of a perception (including that of a memory) unconscious.

Not only are the painful feelings quite generally denied, but so is the awareness of inner conflict. "There is really nothing wrong with me. I take drugs only to have some fun, to feel relaxed, and to enjoy the company of my friends," is a frequently encountered statement. Or in a case in my book (70): "I am calm while talking about and recognizing all these great worries. It is a detachment from myself." "I thought about myself as something else, as an object, as a character in a book, that I was creating the story about myself, a novel. I am not even actually aware of the pain anymore; it is not you, it is a character in a book you are creating."

What is currently so often described as "splitting" (36, 37, 49) is really the defense by denial combined with the *countervailing fantasy of idealization* (10, 14, 68, 70). All that which has been drawn into the phobic system is avoided as dangerous and bad, whereas all that which has become part of the reassurance system is sought out and idealized as all good and great. Such contradictory ("split") self and object images are very unstable and easily flipflop, as we shall shortly notice. These *countervailing idealizing, i.e., narcissistic, fantasies* serve denial much more frequently than is commonly brought out. "Clinical experience suggests that many of the so-called 'narcissistic moods' of high self-esteem and grandiosity may represent the affective concomitants of unconscious fantasies of omnipotence and omniscience, fantasies often structured around an identification with a specific person who represented an aggrandized archaic ego ideal (56). Reich demonstrated that frequently such fantasies originate as *defensive denials* of overwhelming anxiety, feelings of helplessness or rage stemming from narcissistic injury and humiliation" (4).

Also such extensive denial is always accompanied by much *displacement*, a spreading out and generalizing of what is avoided or sought. A typical example is the "withdrawal" reaction and craving in patients who are not physically addicted. Many addicts have noted that whenever they are anxious or angry, or when they return into the former drug-associated situation, they go into "acute withdrawal"; the absence of the drug (of the protector!) becomes equated with any acute anxiety. This occasionally occurs after many years of abstinence (e.g., return from jail to the home town). The longing for relief and the anxieties have been displaced from the original crisis to the city, the entire environment, and even to paraphernalia and injection rituals. The ensuing trembling and yawning are microconversions based on these displacements—all phenomena so thoroughly familiar to us from the psychopathology of everyday life and from dream analysis.

This is, of course, not the case with the real pharmacological withdrawal from true addiction. Displacement is necessary as such an auxiliary defense to cope with the acute sense of absence of the reassurance system (the drug and its effects).

One consequence of pervasive denial is *depersonalization* in its multiple variants. An entire side of the person (the dirty, the angry, the exhibitionistic self) may be detached, unreal, unfelt, not quite part of inner life. Feelings of tenderness and quiet or expressed caring are shunned as unbecoming, as shameful loss of control (equated with bed wetting or loss of bowel control), and are turned off and covered over by a stony mask of rigid, "manly" self-control, only to break through in sudden spells of weeping and overwhelming sadness or anxiety.

Quite often the patient feels "split" into the compliant, kind, yet false self, and the nasty, cruel, vengeful, spiteful self—an inner dissociation temporarily effaced with the help particularly of barbiturates and alcohol (in Cases 3 and 4 above).

Externalization

This defense is a counterpart to denial, just as projection is to repression. In it "the whole internal battle ground is changed into an external one" (15). Put in different words, externalization is the defensive effort *to resort to external action in order to support the denial of inner conflict*. That means an internal conflict is changed back into an external one. For example, ridicule, rejection, and punishment are provoked (not just suspected) from the outside world, a very frequent form, by no means restricted to compulsive drug users. Or limit setting is invited and demanded from the therapist, but then fought against. Or oral and narcissistic "supplies" are quite concretely requested and sought from spouses and friends; their limitation is responded to with envy and rage. Much of the "acting out," the "impulsiveness" is such a defensive use of action, an action with the aim of taking magical, omnipotent control over the uncontrollable, of risking the ultimate threats (separation, humiliation, castration, dismemberment) but—counterphobically—proving that these terrors are unfounded. It may be action by gambling, motorcycle jumping and racing; it may be by lying, manipulating, cheating; it may be by violence and revenge; it may be just by any exciting action. Or it may be by drugs: "I have the power, with help of this magical substance, to master the unbearable."

The all permeating tension and restlessness is broken by such externalization that, especially if forbidden and dangerous, is an attempt to get rid of the almost somatic uneasiness and pressure and is experienced as primitive "discharge," a breaking out of being trapped with this undifferentiated but deeply frightening tension within.

As a general characteristic of all defensive externalization, we discern its *dehumanizing quality*. With the defensive use of action, the action itself is relevant, not the needs, qualities, and properties of the persons "used," unless they happen to fit totally into this doing in the service of the denial. It is mainly this dehumanizing use of others that strikes us as so infuriating in all "sociopaths."

The development of symbolic activities, of the entire truly human suprastructure of manifold types of discursive (language, mathematics) and nondiscursive (music, literature, mythology, fantasy world) abstraction is based on the progress from concrete external action to internal representation occurring with increasing velocity during normal development after the middle of the second year of life. The rudimentary development of many important symbolic activities in our drug users (hyposymbolization) and the preponderance of action as defense (externalization) are both expressions of the traumatization suffered during the time of developing symbolization. So is the inclination to dehumanization and exploitation (7, 12, 49, 51, 70).

Reversal

A number of drive reversals are of greatest significance as defenses: turning active into passive, turning passive into active, and turning against the self. The latter is very important in depressions and the first in masochistic characters. It seems to me more and more persuasive, however, to see in the defense of *turning passive into active* a cardinal type of defenses in severe psychopathology—much as repression is in the more typical neurotics.

Just as the patient suffers and fears disappointment and helplessness as a main theme of life, he does everything in his power first to enlist help but then to turn the tables and to prove the therapist helpless and defeated.

This process is well illustrated by Case 4. In one of her first dreams in analysis, the patient saw her kitten scratching her and tearing up all her stockings. It got on her nerves and she began mistreating and scaring it badly as if to punish "her" (the kitten—she herself used the feminine). "Then she turned into a little girl. I asked her whether she was hungry. She said 'Yeah' and was crying because she was scared. I was laughing at her; she was not going to get anything to eat. I was a witch and she was scared. When I was little I always had that dream—about this witch chasing me down the street, and I would always fall down, and she was going to catch me, and then I would wake up. I put the two dreams together." Right—and how? "That I was hurt and scared—and that I tried to hurt someone else as she (the witch) had

scared me." Although I do not think we can usually interpret dreams without detailed associations, I can hardly think of a better illustration for what happens in this patient and, in many, perhaps most compulsive substance abusers, than by this dream. They want to defeat *us* because they feel defeated; they want to make *us* feel helpless, weak, and ashamed, because so do they; they try to scare *us*, because they are so scared. And they see *us* as confining and limiting authorities, break our rules and flee from us because of their own gnawing oppressive anxiety.

By these three mechanisms of denial, externalization, and turning passive into active, they try their hardest to provoke us into being just that which they fear most: to unmask us protectors as belittling and deceitful tyrants, to see us defeated by their own deceit, and "to spite the world"—just when they are most in dread of being abused, deceived, and helpless themselves. Much of their lying and arrogance is what Freud in the Dora case (19) called a "Retourkutsche," a repartee, a giving back in kind and with interest what they passively had suffered for so long.

Ego Splits

It is part of the archaic defenses, the equally primitive affects, and the traumatized ego core that there is a remarkable discontinuity of the sense of self (similar to what Pao (54) described in schizophrenia). They often resemble "split" or "multiple" personalities; what is characteristic is "the *sudden total flipflop*, a global lability with no mediation and no perspective. It is a picture of 'peripeteia,' of total turnabouts, which one might call the about-face syndrome" (70). It is the unreliability that is so infuriating for others, so humiliating and depressing for themselves. One moment they give honest pledges, make grand plans, engage in ambitious, often idealistic enterprises, show love and affection, considerateness, and caring—the next moment all promises are angrily broken, the plans forsaken, the commitments forgotten.

This is not a defense, but an "ego defect," a functional disparity and contradictoriness that affects not solely the ego, but no less the superego ("superego splits"). Ideals and loyalties are suddenly replaced by opposite ones; inner prohibitions are suddenly betrayed under the onslaught of desire and dread. The dread is partly again the one we already described: claustrophobia. All limitations, restrictions, and commitments are but confining encasements that have to be burst open.

A typical example for such rapid alternations is a patient I currently see in analysis (Case 2). He is a competent, basically decent, and kind craftsman and businessman who keeps using all types of illegal drugs to combat severe anxieties. Most of his dreams have a nightmarish quality with endless chases, arrests, physical attacks, castration, drowning, etc. His life is a series of counterphobic daredevil risks embedded in his solid work schedule. A number of particularly self-destructive and damaging parapraxias could suddenly be understood as a new link in a chain reaching back to his fifth year, when he took revenge on his mother for her getting involved with a lover after her divorce and for her leaving him alone for many desolate hours. A recurrent memory of a dream from that time is his being clutched and smothered by a giant rabbit. His screams for help are choked off in the embrace and go unheard; he remembers a desperate wish to burst the stifling enclosure. Most of these present acts of self-sabotage are set up to cause anguish to his mother. Their paradoxical meaning effectively is: "I punish her for having betrayed me; I punish myself at the same time for having betrayed her. And this shared suffering counteracts all the betrayals. All will eventually be forgiven." A similar multiple bond is repeated in the transference.

It is tempting to identify what has been described up to now with *"alexithymia,"* as used for these cases by Krystal (43) in an excellent study. Affectively, it is the impairment of recognition and utilization of emotions as signals to themselves, and it shows up in a multitude of phenomena, e.g., a stoneface expression and wooden stiffness. Cognitively, creativity, imagination, and use of symbols are restricted, ideas are monotonous and sterile, and thoughts are riveted to the tasks at hand in their trivialities and mundanities; but the patients are impoverished in their affective import, they are "superadjusted to reality." They treat themselves and others with cool detachment and almost as inanimate objects; "it is a form of numbness designed to block pain by becoming a 'lonely island'" (43).

I concur with Krystal's convincing descrip-

tion and see the picture painted perhaps even more largely than he as outcome of the assortment of archaic defenses: affect and drive regression, denial, externalization, and reversal, combined with some developmental defects as outlined. In particular, I am not persuaded that their aloofness and stoniness is not, at least often, profoundly defensive.

FAMILY DYNAMICS

No comprehensive study of the really *specific* features (dynamic, attentional, communicational) of the families of various types of compulsive drug users exists as yet, in contrast to what Lidz and co-workers (45–47) and Wynne and Singer (53, 62, 63, 72, 73) have done for schizophrenia. What we now know *does not seem specific enough*.

The best studies to date are those of Stanton and his group (64–66) based on the incisive work of Boszormenyi-Nagy (8). They see the drug addict's life in antithesis. On the overt side he breaks all the rules and commitments (described by me above as part of the claustrophobia) in order to show his independence and forceful breaking away from home; but whatever he does he ultimately attains the reverse: a cementing of his dependency on the family and a saving of the family cohesion. Were he to forsake his career of addiction, he would risk the dissolution of the family. Even his death may be a sacrificial move to keep the family together. In turn, the family needs him as the scapegoat, the attacking of which holds them together. "He is a loyal son who denies himself and rescues his family. He is a savior" (64). "Not only did the addict fear separation from the family, but the family felt likewise toward him ... this was an interdependent process in which his failure served a protective function of maintaining family closeness."

I have little question now that it is generally true—but perhaps too generally so—that all neurotics and psychotics show similar hidden loyalty conflicts in their family systems. It may be granted, though, that there is in these families a far excessive emphasis on such covert dependency and loyalty, while the front of the stage is ruled by treason and breach of faith.

It seems to me that we can discern four types of families, marked by massive traumatization, deception, intrusiveness, and inconsistency respectively.

1. Corresponding to the traumatic intensity of anxiety, including the phobic core, we should expect at least in many patients *severe and real external traumatization*. We find this in many, but not all, cases. I present a few examples.

Case 6. Danny, a case described by Dr. Anderson, is a polydrug user, alcoholic and homosexual, in his twenties: "The mother was extremely overprotective and intrusive with Danny, always interested in his every activity. She insisted on absolute obedience, and when he failed to do exactly as she wanted, she administered harsh physical punishment such as beatings with a belt and putting his head under water. Punishments were for such things as being a few minutes late for a meal or not practicing his piano lessons. Additionally, Danny was invited into his parents' bed when frightened at night, and he recalls they always slept in the nude."

Case 7. (70, Case 2). "My mother tried to kill herself when she was pregnant with me. I was always taught that sex is a bad thing. She now keeps me all the time at home and locks me up. . . . She said if I did not shape up—with sex or drugs—she would shoot me and herself. She slit up my clothes, so that I cannot leave the house. . . . " Her father tried to rape her. "My mother threatened to kill him. . . . They always yelled at each other. He used to whip us with a belt. If he tried again to sleep with me I'd kill him with a butcher knife. . . . The mother has already bought three burial plots." All this was confirmed to me by the mother. The girl, a barbiturates and narcotics addict, soon thereafter killed herself by overdose.

Case 8 (70, Case 16). "When I was 12 or 13, I stole some money from my father, then gave it to friends. When it was discovered, my father beat me up with a stick and made me eat a pack of cigarettes. My mother is just crazy. She steals and sells furniture and pictures of my stepfather. They scream all the time at each other. She is either raving about a person or feels persecuted." Again I found external corroboration for much of this.

Case 9 (70, Case 24). " . . . much physical abuse (and on a few occasions sexual abuse) by these older brothers. . . . When father would beat the children, mother would go to another room and cry. She never did anything!"

Case 10 (70, Case 23). " . . . many fist fights

between mother and father, grandfather and father. When I was about 5, my father tried to kill himself with iodine. He told me what he had done. . . . " Later, when the parents were separated, the mother had a coterie of boyfriends: "I slept in mother's bed and was often awakened by her intercourse (with a lover)—with me in the same bed. Often she left me alone in the 2nd story apartment to go out with one of her lovers. I remember how once they slammed the door and locked me in. I climbed out of the window and jumped onto the roof of the car, so they would not leave me alone. They brought me back, gave me a beating and left me at home anyway."

Let me stress again that this has not been the case in all instances of compulsive drug use. I see severe *parental violence* and *intense exposure to sexual activities* as a frequent, but not a regular, etiological family factor in compulsive drug use. Yet, I would at least like to single it out as one prominent group: that of traumatization by family violence, brutality, and overt, continued involvement of the child in sexual activities, including sexual abuse and incest.

Based on the extent of profound anxiety I would, however, postulate that other more subtle, more veiled forms of traumatization would have to have occurred in many other addicts—unmanageable *overstimulation of aggression and libido*. However, I do not know yet where exactly to look for it, without once again unduly stretching the concept of trauma. I am also quite certain that such traumatization would have originated in early childhood but would not have remained confined to it.

2. In a second group, *intrusiveness* is the prominent feature. It is quite similar to what has been described for families of schizophrenics and results in the same curious mixture of pseudoidentity and pervasive shame in the children. If anything, the abuse of the child for the parents' grandiose expectation and the disregard for his age-appropriate needs are often even more pronounced, more crass than in the families of schizophrenics. This includes the crossing of intergenerational boundaries, the parentification of the child, and the sexualization of the parent-child relationship. I am puzzled, though, as to the reason for this symptom choice and not schizophrenia. May it have a much lesser

impact on the cognitive and linguistic functions in the transactions? I hope further studies of shared focal attention and communication may give us some clues.

It needs to be emphasized how much such intrusive running of the lives of the children, this exploiting and "busybody" behavior, evokes both rage and shame in the child. The *intrusive family* breeds a child that is, although manifestly compliant, secretly then overtly rebellious and profoundly shame prone. There is nothing of which he feels proud and confident. Everywhere he senses impending putdowns and humiliation. Some neurotics with strong phobic and paranoid inclinations show milder forms of this correlation; severer versions are found among many compulsive drug users of various types. Why this prevalence of shame in the child? The steady intrusions into the emotional and physical intimacy leave him exposed, not in control over his most private concerns. He has to assume a mask-like pseudoidentity to shield the nucleus of something very much his own from the possessive, overbearing invasions—a *refuge of privacy protected by the walls of shame.* The "drug therapy" of shame is then a method of choice—as one form of affect defense. Not only does the drug dampen the shame anxiety, but it safeguards by yet an additional curtain the real self while simultaneously guarding the dependency on the parent.

3. The next group is almost a counterpart to the second one. Here it is not intrusiveness, but *secretiveness* and unavailability on the parent's part. It is *they* who live out their shame, hiding a family humiliation behind a sham existence. They live their "*life lie*" behind a facade of propriety and respectability—the false life described by Ibsen with the highest mastery in play after play, a life of masquerade and secret mongering. The barbiturate addict whom I quoted earlier (Case 4) was not informed, e.g., when her older brother had to get married; she was 9 years old at the time. She found out when the rest of the family came home from church in festive clothes. It was a screen memory for much else that had remained hidden from her, veiled by a thick muffling curtain of decorum and religious piety. Some of the demons hiding behind those curtains were cold self-centeredness of her mother, weakness and sexual seductiveness on the side of

her father, and the noticeable deep marital discord and mutual undermining. As the intrusive family, the secretive family promotes a profound depersonalization, a pervasive sense of unrealness and lack of authenticity; this estrangement is re-created or combatted by various drugs (barbiturates and narcotics deepening it, amphetamine and cocaine piercing the veil, psychedelics variably doing both).

4. A fourth type is represented by a family of utter *inconsistency and unreliability.* It is again any narcissistic whim that dictates what should be real, what should be right and proper. Today's sin is tomorrow's merit. Mother's reward is father's penalty. "Take but degree away, untune that string, and hark, what discord follows! Each thing meets in mere oppugnancy" (*Troilus and Cressida*). No law and no hierarchical structure holds: "the rude son should strike his father dead." In a number of the cases in my book this was nearly literally true. The *dissolution of hierarchy*, and with that of stable superego structures, is, to some extent, present in all compulsive drug users and may well be one of the most specific family hallmarks (48). However, we are probably entitled to single out a fourth group in which such a dissolution of boundaries and limitations is particularly remarkable, where just everything goes, where the law of the day is lawlessness. Much more study of this would be needed. Characteristically such patients do not stay in treatment and come perhaps, at best, to a first interview; therefore they have been quite insufficiently studied.

Looking back, I believe we can discern these four major types of families predisposing somewhat selectively to drug use without yet distinguishing more precisely what type of drug abuse may correspond to which kind of family. I do not think we can distinguish these types too sharply; much overlapping occurs. Still there may be some heuristic value in starting more systematic and controllable research with such clinical types.

In addition, these family types exemplify some of the central dynamic features of the individual patients: defective affect defense and externalization ("traumatizing families"); ego and superego splits; the flipflop syndrome ("inconsistent, antihierarchical, anarchical families"); denial and prevalence of shame ("deceptive and secretive families");

separation anxiety, clinging demandingness, and possessiveness ("intrusive families"). Because in most cases we see these types combined, it may be legitimate to talk about a *tetrad of family characteristics in compulsive drug use of aggressive and sexual overstimulation, inconsistency, deceptiveness and intrusiveness.*

Based on such in-depth understanding it should not be all that surprising that many of these patients become eminently treatable—not only with a slightly or more markedly modified psychoanalysis, but also with brief focal, psychoanalytically informed psychotherapy and related approaches. In all our work with them we need to respond to the plea of the barbiturate addict (Maggie) in Arthur Miller's great play "After the Fall" (52):

" . . . you should look at me, like I *existed* or something. Like you used to look—out of your *self.* . . . That's why I don't smile, I feel I'm fighting all the time to make you *see.* You're like a little boy, you don't see the knives people hide."

Acknowledgments. Gratitude is expressed for the help rendered in the preparation of this manuscript and its precursors above all by Drs. Hazen G. Kniffin, Richard H. Anderson, H. Krystal, Leo Rangell, and P. Gray.

References

1. Arlow, J. A. Unconscious fantasy and disturbances of conscious experience. Psychoanal. Q. 38:1, 1969.
2. Arlow, J. A. Fantasy, memory, and reality testing. Psychoanal. Q. 38:28, 1969.
3. Arlow, J. A. The only child. Psychoanal. Q. 41:507, 1972.
4. Arlow, J. A. Affects and the psychoanalytic situation. Int. J. Psychoanal. 58:157, 1977.
5. Beres, D. Character pathology and the "borderline" syndrome. Unpublished manuscript, 1974.
6. Berman, L. E. A. The role of amphetamine in a case of hysteria. J. Am. Psychoanal. Assoc. 20:325, 1972.
7. Blos, P. Adolescent concretization: A contribution to the theory of delinquency. In *Currents in Psychoanalysis*, I. M. Marcus, editor, pp. 66–88. New York, International Universities Press, 1971.
8. Boszormenyi-Nagy, I., and Spark, G. M. *Invisible Loyalties.* Harper & Row, Hagerstown, Md., 1974.
9. Chein, I., Gerard, D. L., Lee, R. S. and Rosenfeld, E. *The Road to H.* New York, Basic Books, 1964.
10. Dorpat, T. L. Is splitting a defense? Int. Rev. Psychoanal. 6:105, 1979.
11. Einstein, A. Quoted by D. E. Thomsen. Personality place and physics. Sci. News 115:213, 1979.
12. Eissler, K. R. Ego-psychological implications of the psychoanalytic treatment of delinquents. Psychoanal. Study Child 5:97, 1950.
13. Fenichel, O. Remarks on the common phobias (1944). In *Collected Papers*, vol. 2, pp. 278–287. New York, W. W. Norton, 1954.
14. Freud, A. The ego and the mechanisms of defense (1936). In *The Writings of Anna Freud*, vol 2. New York, International Universities Press, 1971.
15. Freud, A. Normality and pathology in childhood: Assessments of development (1965). In *The Writings of Anna Freud*, vol. 6. New York, International Universities Press, 1971.
16. Freud, A. Problems of technique in adult analysis (1954). J. Phila. Assoc. Psychoanal. 1:68, 1974.
17. Freud, A. A psychoanalytic view of developmental psychopathology. J. Phila. Assoc. Psychoanal. 1:7, 1974.
18. Freud, A. Panel: Advances in psychoanalytic technique. J. Phila. Assoc. Psychoanal. 1:43, 1974.
19. Freud, S. Fragment of an analysis of a case of hysteria (1905). In *Standard Edition of the Complete Psychological Works of Sigmund Freud*, vol. 7, pp. 3–122. London, Hogarth Press, 1953.
20. Freud, S. Analysis of a phobia in a five-year-old boy (1909). In *Standard Edition of the Complete Psychological Works of Sigmund Freud*, vol. 10, pp. 3–149. London, Hogarth Press, 1955.
21. Freud, S. Notes upon a case of obsessional neurosis (1909). In *Standard Edition of the Complete Psychological Works of Sigmund Freud*, vol. 10, pp. 153–318. London, Hogarth Press, 1955.
22. Freud, S. From the history of an infantile neurosis (1918). In *Standard Psychological Works of Sigmund Freud*, vol. 17, pp. 3–122. London, Hogarth Press, 1955.
23. Freud, S. The interpretation of dreams (1900). In *Standard Edition of the Complete Psychological Works of Sigmund Freud*, vols. 4 and 5. London, Hogarth Press, 1958.
24. Freud, S. Psycho-analytic notes on an autobiographical account of a case of paranoia (1911). In *Standard Edition of the Complete Psychological Works of Sigmund Freud*, vol. 12, pp. 3–82. London, Hogarth Press, 1958.
25. Freud, S. Inhibitions, symptoms and anxiety (1926). In *Standard Edition of the Complete Psychological Works of Sigmund Freud*, vol. 20, pp. 77–175. London, Hogarth Press, 1959.
26. Freud, S. The neuro-psychoses of defense (1894). In *Standard Edition of the Complete Psychological Works of Sigmund Freud*, vol. 3, pp. 43–61. London, Hogarth Press, 1962.
27. Freud, S. Further remarks on the neuro-psychoses of defense (1896). In *Standard Edition of the Complete Psychological Works of Sigmund Freud*, vol. 3, pp. 159–185. London, Hogarth Press, 1962.
28. Freud, S. Introductory lectures on psychoanalysis (1916–1917). In *Standard Edition of the Complete Psychological Works of Sigmund Freud*, vol. 16. London, Hogarth Press, 1963.
29. Galenson, E., and Roiphe, H. The impact of early sexual discovery on mood, defensive organization, and symbolization. Psychoanal. Study Child. 26:195, 1972.
30. Galenson, E., and Roiphe, H. Some suggested revisions concerning early female development. J. Am. Psychoanal. Assoc. 24:29, 1976.
31. Glover, E. On the etiology of drug addiction (1932). In *On the Early Development of Mind*, pp. 187–215. New York, International Universities Press, 1970.

32. Gray, P. On a "developmental lag" in the evolution of psychoanalytic technique. Unpublished manuscript, 1979.

33. Hartmann, D. A study of drug taking adolescents. Psychoanal. Study Child 24:384, 1969.

34. Jones, E. Fear, guilt and hate (1929). In *Papers on Psychoanalysis*, pp. 304–319. Boston, Beacon, 1967.

35. Kaplan, E. H., and Wieder, H. *Drugs Don't Take People, People Take Drugs*. Secaucus, N. J., Lyle Stuart, 1974.

36. Kernberg, O. *Borderline Conditions and Pathological Narcissism*. New York, Jason Aronson, 1975.

37. Kernberg, O. *Object Relations Theory and Clinical Psychoanalysis*. New York, Jason Aronson, 1976.

38. Khantzian, E. J. Opiate addiction: A critique of theory and some implications for treatment. Am. J. Psychother. 28:59, 1973.

39. Krystal, H. The genetic development of affects and affect regression. Annu. Psychoanal. 2:93, 1974.

40. Krystal, H. Affect tolerance. Annu. Psychoanal. 3:179, 1975.

41. Krystal, H. Trauma and affects. Psychoanal. Study Child 33:81, 1978.

42. Krystal, H. Self representation and the capacity for self care. Annu. Psychoanal. 6:209, 1979.

43. Krystal, H. Alexithymia and psychotherapy. Am. J. Psychother. 33:17, 1979.

44. Krystal, H., and Raskin, H. A. *Drug Dependence: Aspects of Ego Functions*. Detroit, Wayne State University Press, 1970.

45. Lidz, T. *The Origin and Treatment of Schizophrenic Disorders*. New York, Basic Books, 1973.

46. Lidz, T. Egocentric cognitive regression and the family setting of schizophrenic disorders. In *The Nature of Schizophrenia*, L. C. Wynne, R. L. Cromwell, and St. Matthysse, editors, pp. 526–533. New York, John Wiley, 1978.

47. Lidz, T., Fleck, S., and Cornelison, A. *Schizophrenia and the Family*. New York, International Universities Press, 1965.

48. Madanes, C., Dukes, J., and Harbin, H. Hierarchy and attachment in families of heroin addicts, schizophrenics and high achievers. Unpublished manuscript, 1978.

49. Mahler, M. S. *On Human Symbiosis and the Vicissitudes of Individuation*. New York, International Universities Press, 1968.

50. Mahler, M. S., Pine, F., and Bergman, A. *The Psychological Birth of the Human Infant*. New York, Basic Books, 1975.

51. McDevitt, J. B. Separation—individuation and object constancy. J. Am. Psychoanal. Assoc. 23:713, 1975.

52. Miller, A. *After the Fall*. New York, Bantam Books, 1967.

53. Morris, G. O., and Wynne, L. C. Schizophrenic offspring and parental styles of communication. Psychiatry 28:19, 1965.

54. Pao, P. N. On the formation of schizophrenic symptoms. Int. J. Psychoanal. 58:389, 1977.

55. Rangell, L. Personal communication.

56. Reich, A. Narcissistic object choice in women. J. Am. Psychoanal. Assoc. 1:22, 1953.

57. Roiphe, H. On an early genital phase. Psychoanal. Study Child 23:348, 1968.

58. Roiphe, H., and Galenson, E. Early genital activity and the castration complex. Psychoanal. Q. 41:334, 1972.

59. Roiphe, H., and Galenson, E. Object loss and early sexual development. Psychoanal. Q. 42:73, 1973.

60. Roiphe, H., and Galenson, E. Some observations on transitional object and infantile fetish. Psychoanal. Q. 44:206, 1975.

61. Shafer, R. P. *Drug Use In America: Problem in Perspective. Second Report of the National Commission on Marijuana and Drug Abuse*, R. P. Shafer, Chairman. Washington, D.C., United States Government Printing Office, 1973.

62. Singer, M. T. Attentional processes in verbal behavior. In *The Nature of Schizophrenia*, L. C. Wynne, R. L. Cromwell, and St. Matthysse, editors, pp. 329–336. New York, John Wiley, 1978.

63. Singer, M. T., Wynne, L. C., and Toohey, M. L. Communication disorders and the families of schizophrenics, L. C. Wynne et al., editors, pp. 449–511. New York, John Wiley, 1978.

64. Stanton, D. M. The addict as savior: Heroin, death, and the family. Family Process 16:191, 1977.

65. Stanton, D. M. Drug misuse and the family. Unpublished manuscript, 1977.

66. Stanton, D. M., Todd, T. C., et al. Heroin addiction as a family phenomenon: A new conceptual model. Am. J. Drug Alcohol Abuse 5:125, 1978.

67. Szasz, T. S. The role of the counterphobic mechanism in addiction. J. Am. Psychoanal. Assoc. 6:309, 1958.

68. Trunnell, E. E., and Holt, W. E. The concept of denial or disavowal. J. Am. Psychoanal. Assoc. 22:769, 1974.

69. Wieder, H., and Kaplan, E. H. Drug use in adolescents: Psychodynamic meaning and pharmacogenic effect. Psychoanal. Study Child 24:399, 1969.

70. Wurmser, L. *The Hidden Dimension*. New York, Jason Aronson, 1978.

71. Wurmser, L. Phobic core in the addictions and the paranoid process. Int. J. Psychoanal. Psychother., in press.

72. Wynne, L. C., and Singer, M. T. Thought disorder and family relations of schizophrenics. I and II. Arch. Gen. Psychiatry 9:191, 199, 1963.

73. Wynne, L. C., and Singer, M. T. Thought disorder and family relations of schizophrenics. III and IV. Arch. Gen. Psychiatry 12:187, 1965.

CHAPTER 8

THE SOCIAL BASES OF SUBSTANCE ABUSE

Harold Alksne, Ph.D.

It is the position of the sociologist that the addiction phenomenon—and its more general definitional descendant, substance abuse—is as much a social construct as it is a medical condition. This statement is made with the recognition that a better understanding of the function of an interrelated complex of physical, psychological, and biochemical processes within the human organism will probably present us with the most immediately negotiable solutions to the problem as it is now expressed in our society. Yet the dramatic growth of dependence on a variety of old and new substances suggests that the forces associated with the increase in prevalence of substance abuse are less likely to be found in our recognition of new physical and psychological processes than those that are social. Recent experience with social experimentation directed toward developing "The Great Society" has been disappointing. However, if we are eventually to come to a comprehensive approach to the changing problem of substance abuse, social factors will have to be involved.

Thousands of substances may be viewed as possible objects that may be "abused" (5). Whether or not they are so considered entails a social definition relating to the perceived negative consequences of the compulsive use of a particular substance at a point in time. The extent to which the consequence is considered negative is related to the degree to which it seems to threaten the norms and stability in the society. Should the behavior and its consequences be viewed as relatively mild violations of the norms or merely idiosyncratic, they will call up mild or no negative sanctions, depending on the role performed by the norm violator in the social system. Should the norm violation be seen as a serious threat to the welfare of the society, community, and violator, probably in that order, then it is likely that the mechanisms of social control will be brought into play to label the individual "deviant" (substance abuser) and return him to conformity. Thus our definition of what is deviant and in this case, substance abuse, depends on a perception that a problem exists and that in some way it negatively affects the social network that constitutes the fabric of society.

In the tradition of the simpler, "preliterate" society, the values that governed the life of the people were generally universally internalized. In such, now almost mythical, contexts the perception and control of offending behavior were readily accessible and effective. In our own social system—the networks of subgroups that make up the society at large, with their differing values, norms, and life styles—there is less consensus concerning the infallibility of universally applicable norms and the effect their violation may have on the stability of the society. Therefore, our definition of what is substance abuse is inevitably related to who is involved in the perceived substance abuse and who makes the judgment.

Any entry into scientific investigation must be preceded by a definition of the problem about which we want explanations. If the investigator begins with premises that are unclear and do not have the benefit of consensus, then developing a universally applicable theory or set of findings becomes less feasible. I would suggest that our movement from a relatively concrete physical definition of addiction to one that is more diffuse and all inclusive, substance abuse, has led to difficulties. The movement from the concept of addiction to that of substance abuse was, in part, based on the assumption that there is a commonality between various forms of compulsive behavior that, if studied together, could ultimately lead to a comprehensive, general theory explaining dependence on all substances. The concept is new and awaits exploration through cross-substance studies.

Unfortunately, we see no rush on the part of behavioral scientists to enter this broader area of scientific exploration. The reasons for this inertia are relatively obvious. Most of us are reluctant to give up the equity we have in developing the skills of specialization in a particular aspect of our work without new rewards. Those rewards, for most of us, come from the support of our work from institutional and governmental sources. There seems to be a time lag between institutional recognition of the potential values of the newer concept of substance abuse and readiness to support new research in this broader framework. Establishing priorities for research support is a political process depending on members of existing interest groups that, like the scientist, may see a threat in changing the framework within which they operate. Whether we are able to avoid the broader influences of social interest or not, we should acknowledge their probable influence on what social problems we investigate and how we investigate them.

Whatever the potential the concept of substance abuse holds for the future of this field, we still discover that the lack of precision that now prevails has led to a diffuseness in our theoretical orientation. This diffuseness has been based on the fact that individuals involved in scientific study of the social dimensions of substance abuse are left to respond to social priorities rather than clear scientific criteria. Unlike physical/medical observations concerning human behavior, there is considerable variability in our observations of social behavior.

In explaining the social bases of substance abuse, the sociologist has generated different classes of theory based on observations of different groups at different points in time. Much of the controversy and conflict among theorists is probably a consequence of the fact that many of our theories are temporally and spatially bound. If we appreciate the fact that our observations are the consequence of different settings and conditions, we may better be able to derive from them the commonalities. Thus, the fact that a theory of anomie is apparently not relevant in all settings and for all substances abused should not be viewed as a failure but rather the first step in developing a general understanding of the substance abuse phenomenon as a variable condition.

THE SUBSTANCE ABUSER AS AN OBJECT

The sociological perspective on drugs and drug use suggests that the meaning of drugs is affected by the social context within which they are used. Opiates provided in supervised medical settings take on different meanings from heroin or illicit methadone use on the street. Weil indicates that the effect of drugs on the user is dependent both on personal and social influences (45). Observers of substance use similarly focus their perceptions on the basis of the peculiar vantage points from which they look at the phenomenon.

One of the sources for the variability in explanations of substance abuse phenomena is that different categories of caretakers of the problem perceive it and its significant characteristics from the perspective of their functions in managing or controlling substance abuse and the substance abuser. How they perceive, manage, and exercise control of substance abuse and rationalize their professional activities through the use of theory are likely to be affected by the socially determined interests of the institutions they serve. In effect, the support of theory becomes political.

One of the perspectives on substance abuse that is supported by the medical community involves the idea that abuse is a consequence of the lack of medical supervision of the use of the drug. So long as a drug is prescribed and used in the context of a medical regime, it is generally viewed as appropriate, iatrogenic addiction notwithstanding. However, if the patient uses drugs outside the system of sanctions and controls of the physician, this is likely to be labeled as substance abuse. This observation is not made to void the substantial sophistication physicians bring to dealing with the problems in this area but rather to point out that physicians as well as other caretakers view their role in the context of medical and social control and territoriality.

Communities as aggregates of the public present a particularly difficult set of problems for those who seek to provide service to substance abusers. Increasing rejection of the substance abuser as a morally deficient, marginal individual has led to increasing difficulties in providing funding for treatment programs and, once funded, resistance to the location of programs in communities. In this context, substance abuse is keyed to the idea that those who suffer the problem may be instrumental in threatening the stability, security, and image of their community. Thus, the dominant reaction of communities to the substance abuser involves exercising techniques of control and, that failing, exclusion of the substance abuser from their life space.

The needs of government to exercise power and to develop public policy generally reflect or purport to reflect the attitudes of the community. As a consequence, government power is also focused toward the goal of control of the substance abuser through the myriad of bureaucracies that deliver services to the people. Out of the theoretical explanations that are rendered by the social scientist, those that suggest that structure, or "rational authority," needs to be provided for the substance abuser tend to be favored (9). Despite the questionable success of programs involving mandatory commitment of addicts to treatment, this approach continues to surface from time to time. The pervasiveness of the belief that addicts need external systems of control to return to conformity with community norms and values may be a factor in gaining greater support for the drug-free therapeutic community as compared with methadone maintenance approaches to treatment.

The role of the police as an instrument of social control needs no explanation. Once again sociological research is *used* to rationalize the community's concerns through police action. Social research which focuses on epidemiology is repeatedly employed to justify extension of the police role in control of substance abuse. Disease, its spread, and its control become the preferred framework for increased police action. The concept of contagion is highlighted to give scientific credibility to police crackdowns.

We recognize that different substances change in terms of their meaning to society during different periods of time. Tobacco, coffee, tea, ether, and a host of the other psychoactive substances available to humans have variously been viewed as symptomatic of evil, disease, mania, and a general threat to the system (5). Many have vacated their profane role because of changes in public attitude, but some, like the opiates, continue as objects which "justify" stigmatizing those who use them.

Dogma and theology have been used to justify the actions of governments in the past. Science and theory have taken over this function in formulating public policy today. In all of this, the rationalization that large scale intervention with substance abuse is based on humanitarian concerns for people suffering the problem, one cannot avoid the awareness that the systems we employ deal with the substance abuser as an object.

MAJOR THEORETICAL FRAMEWORKS FOR THE CONSIDERATION OF SUBSTANCE ABUSE

STRUCTURAL APPROACHES

Sociologists generally share a common framework in their analysis of social groups and the phenomena that emerge from them. In various ways, the character of the individual's social experience formulates the individual personality and all of the behaviors that make him a human animal able to function with varying degrees of competence in the life space allocated to him. However, different groups of sociologists tend to focus on specific areas of human experience with markedly different interpretations of their development and meaning.

American sociology continues to be dominated by the "structural-functional" orientation that finds its roots in the work of Weber (44), Durkheim (14), Radcliffe-Brown (32), Malinowski (26), Parsons (30) and, most recently, Merton (28). Although none of these formidable figures in the history of sociology had done any empirical work in substance abuse per se, their influence is felt in the research and writing of many of those who came after them.

Functionalism is based on the assumption that society—the social system—is built on commonly shared values, norms, role expectations and interactions that permit humans to relate in a mutually acceptable framework. In a stable, unchanging society there is a proper "fit" between all elements and institutions. Ideally, values, norms, expectations, and appropriate behaviors are commonly shared, with all elements having complementary functions. Deviance rarely emerges, and when and if it does it is dealt with with absolute certainty. In some instances, as is the case with the Plains Indians, there is an institutional incorporation of individuals' behavior for those who do not wish to comply with the requirements of the male role, the berdache (12). In other cases, the individual is ostracized or exiled. The model was built on observations of preliterate societies in which little external contact was present and little change occurred. It views society as a system.

Complex societies may also be viewed in this functionalist mode. For us to continue functioning as a group, be it the total society or an individual segment of it, some "rules of the game" must be developed and adhered to. Such "rules" permit us to get through each day without grievous harm to ourselves or others.

But complex societies have complex science and technologies that stimulate change, sometimes radically. Under such conditions the systems of norms and values that support social control become less pervasive and deviant behavior becomes more possible.

A key concept used by functionalists in examining deviance, and substance abuse in particular, is that of *anomie.* Originally developed by Durkheim in his classic study, *Suicide* (15), it describes a situation in which individuals detach from the values and norms of the society in which they live. Such a state of "normlessness" creates a condition of alienation of the individual from the major institutions in the system. Such alienation may become intolerable and lead one to suicide.

During the early part of the 20th century the paired concepts of anomie and alienation became favored explanations for a host of problems. Loneliness, the problems of immigrants, crime, mental illness, and, of course, substance abuse fitted nicely into the mold.

In the late 1930's, Robert K. Merton took his cue from this condition of anomie and moved it forward to develop an analytic system that explains its place in the development of various deviant behaviors. He created his famous paradigm on "modes of adaptation" that seeks to rationalize the emergence of various forms of deviant behavior in terms of a structural failure of the social system to meet the needs of groups within it. He points out that societies require certain appropriate institutionalized means for achievement of culturally supported goals (27). Merton suggested that a state of anomie emerges because the social system emphasizes goals but may not provide the means to achieve them for minorities, the poor, the newly arrived, and in some cases those who have not connected with what they feel are appropriate success tracks in the American system. This process is most likely to occur under conditions of social change.

Most people adapt or, in Merton's terms, respond to such change through *conformity,* accepting the means and goals of the institutional structure. Some, usually a small proportion, do not and move toward alternative approaches to adaptation that are often viewed as deviant.

The second form of adaptation is that of *innovation,* in which the goals of the system are accepted but the means are not. The third is *ritualism,* whereby the socially approved means are emphasized and the goals are given less emphasis. The fourth is *retreatism,* one that is most frequently associated with alcohol and drug abuse; in this case the individual rejects both the means and goals of the system. The final mode of adaptation is that of *rebellion,* in which the individual rejects both the means and goals of the system, as does the retreatist, but substitutes new means and goals as an effort to create a more acceptable system.

A direct theoretical descendant of the work of Durkheim and Merton is found in *Delin-*

quency and Opportunity by Cloward and Ohlin (11). These authors accepted Merton's contention that deviance is associated with lack of opportunities to achieve goals legitimately. They added, however, that not only do members of the lower class have a problem of differential legitimate opportunity and consequently experience anomie, but they also experience differential access to illegitimate goals. Their approach explains, in part, why the vast majority of persons in a disenfranchized group will not become involved in deviant activities. Only a proportion of the population develops an access to opportunities to become involved in a *criminal* subculture. Cloward and Ohlin suggested that most lower class youth are not integrated into a subculture of crime. They indicated further that a *conflict* subculture may provide goal achievement opportunities to some young people. The conflict subculture is represented in violent delinquent gang activity, where individuals may achieve status and a reputation by demonstrating willingness to fight and risk injury to themselves. Cloward and Ohlin finally postulated that a third subculture, the *retreatist* subculture, exists, where the only requirement is the willingness to use drugs. Young people who are unable to become engaged in the criminal or conflict subcultures are most likely to become involved in the retreatist subculture. Thus, those who are unable to achieve success in the conventional community or in either of the delinquent subcultures are likely to be candidates for the retreatist subculture. Cloward and Ohlin suggested that the candidates for this are "double-failures."

A series of criticisms has been directed at the anomie-oriented theories. Some suggest that concentration on adaptive responses and opportunities among those in the lower class of society places serious limitations on the use of these theories. It is difficult to apply them to those who are among the affluent. Further, one can raise questions concerning the applicability of a theory generated almost exclusively by observation of specific urban ghetto populations to a pluralistic American society varying by regional and cultural experiences.

In using the anomie approach, one could easily view the street addict's involvement in the life style of addiction as both retreat and rebellion. It requires little argument to justify the characterization of opiate use as move-

ment away from active engagement with the means and goals of the social system, i.e., a movement toward passivity. Yet if one is competently to carry out the "addict role," the individual must actively reject society's norms and values and seek new ways of managing his life space. Similarly, those who have worked extensively with street addicts will have little difficulty in recognizing the innovative and often aggressive approaches some addicts develop in order to support their habits. So Merton's various modes of adaptation thesis could separately be applied to various aspects of the addict's life style. But viewed together, the assumption that the drug-dependent person is primarily a retreatist is called to question.

Lindesmith and Gagnon (25) pointed out that those most at risk to addiction during the 19th century were not characteristically the disenfranchized who were cut off from the achievement system of their time. They were more likely to be white than black, women rather than men, and middle class as compared to lower class. Winick (47) suggested that the anomie-retreatist model does not apply to all contemporary high risk populations. His study of doctor-addicts found that physicians' use of drugs had an instrumental rather than retreatist function. They used them to reduce pain and fatigue and generally to continue doing their jobs. Similarly, our explanation of marihuana use through an alienation model is becoming less credible as it becomes more normative among achievement-oriented young people in higher education.

This set of theories has led to a number of action applications. Much of the work that has developed in delinquency prevention is based on the premise that opportunity systems must be changed to reduce the alienation that confronts people. The major efforts in drug and delinquency prevention programs, e.g., Mobilization for Youth and the Model Cities Programs, are direct derivatives of these functionalist models. They are based on the premise that the deviant can be influenced through modification of the system of means and goals to reenter the legitimate avenues of achievement. On a lesser scale community groups have supported efforts that propose "Reasonable Alternative Programs" (RAP) for those on the fringes of deviance. For whatever reason—insufficient funding, lack of community or political commitment, or weakness in the theoretical basis for these programs—they are yet to demonstrate a significant effect in preventing deviance and substance abuse.

Despite the theoretical weakness in the functionalist models and the disappointments in their application to action programs, they have had a great deal to do with how we view those who vary from the ideal norms of American society. Few behavioral scientists would deny the influence of the social structure on the generation of deviance and substance abuse.

PROCESS APPROACHES

At the turn of the century, Gabriel Tarde introduced learning theory to explanations of crime and deviant behavior. He observed that those who develop criminal careers were fostered in a "true seminary of crime" as unsupervised youngsters who "like bands of sparrows associate together, at first for marauding, and then for theft, because of lack of education and food in their homes" (41). He felt that criminal behavior was learned through a process of imitation of others whom the novice viewed as superior to himself and who in effect became role models (41). The idea that "bad" associates support the movement toward norm violation is part of folk wisdom. What Tarde and others have done is to isolate the elements that go into that social learning process. This approach adapts handily to substance abuse problems, especially those involving "the street addict."

Sutherland's theory of "differential association," first published as part of a textbook in 1939, focuses as does the work of Tarde, on the genesis of crime and delinquency. He indicated that delinquency and crime were likely to emerge at times of social disorganization, when normative controls cease to have a dominating influence on the individual's behavior. Under such conditions some groups are likely to respond positively to deviant attitudes and values present in the community. First, Sutherland suggested that criminal behavior (substitute substance abuse) is learned in interaction with others through communications occurring in intimate groups. The learning that is involved in such groups focuses on the technology of initiating and maintaining the deviant behavior. For the drug abuser this involves learning

how to use the drug for its maximum effect (the ritual of use) and learning how to maintain that use. Purchase, dealing drugs, theft, prostitution, avoidance of arrest, the development of an argot to facilitate communication, and the use of hospital detoxification and other services to manage their habit and avoid, if only temporarily, street pressures represent some aspects of that technology (40). Learning also involves the acquisition of motives, drives, rationalizations, and attitudes that facilitate the addict's role. Finestone summarized some of these attributes in his article describing the ideology of the "cool cat" (17).

A critical phase in Sutherland's process of becoming a delinquent or drug addict occurs when the individual internalizes an excess of definition favorable to the violation of law (or norms) over definitions unfavorable to violation. For the substance abuser, and here we can readily see the process in operation with the street addict, alcoholic, and compulsive overeater, the central life interest of the individual focuses on maintaining and rationalizing continuance of the compulsive use of the substance without concern for the mechanism of social control and the negative sanctions imposed by the community, friends, and family. The entire process of differential association moves the individual toward the development of an addict self-image. But it is at this point, when there is an excess of definitions favorable to the violation of law or norms, that that image becomes crystallized.

In his own statement of the theory, Sutherland suggested some cautions in viewing this as an absolute, unidirectional process. He pointed out that differential associations may vary in frequency, duration, priority, and intensity. Street addicts use terms that reflect relative degrees of involvement with addict life styles: the drug abuser (irregular use, "chipping"), the drug addict (regular use), the "junkie" (deep involvement with addiction), and the "dope fiend" (involvement to the extent that the maintenance of the addiction is virtually the only life interest). Addicts also point out that they may move between these different degrees of involvement on the basis of intensity of drug dependence and social conditions in their environment that support or negate full involvement.

Critics attack the Sutherland differential

association approach on a number of fronts. Sutherland and Cressey (40) themselves provide a convenient summary of some of these statements. Critics argue that it is defective because it omits consideration of free will, is based on a psychology of rational deliberation, ignores the role of the victim, does not take account of "biological factors," is not interdisciplinary, is too comprehensive because it is applied to deviants and nondeviants as well, and on and on. The extensive critical attention given the theory is some testimony to the interest behavioral scientists continue to have in it.

Despite the vigorous controversy concerning the validity of the differential association approach within the community of sociologists, it has found a following among those involved in the rehabilitation of substance abusers. If the substance abuser must engage in a process of learning or secondary socialization in order to effectively take a deviant or substance abuse role, it would follow that such individuals must also engage in a different process of secondary socialization in order to develop the capability of taking on the roles required to return to conventional community involvement. Although little deference is given by the advocates of the therapeutic community approach to the early work of Sutherland, the relationship is unmistakable.

RADICAL SOCIOLOGY

Radical sociologists, or conflict theorists, share a common assumption with functionalist theorists—that something in the society, not the individuals themselves, is responsible for the generation of deviant behavior. In addition, they agree that deviance is a rational response to the institutional structure of society that slights those without equity and power. But here the advocates of the two positions vigorously part. The conflict theorists charge that the functionalists are fundamentally not concerned with making the society responsive to the needs of those who do not have equity and power in it and that on a de facto basis they are in support of the status quo in seeking ways of developing approaches to encourage or force the deviant to fit in. Their position is that people in society are more in conflict than in consensus

and that the only way that problems can be reconciled is to give to the "have nots" what they need through equalizing the distribution of the resources available in the society (31).

The conflict theorists suggest that the legal system in the United States is controlled by those who have power and that the system functions to focus its control on the lower class as compared with the more privileged middle and upper class groups. Blumberg (7) pointed out that it is the powerless who are inevitably viewed as threats to the society and are targets of control. Historically, when we examine addiction in the 19th century, we find relatively little social concern with controlling this condition. During this period those who were recognized as drug dependent were not in the disenfranchised class. When we enter into the 20th century we find that, by accident or design, increased controls are associated with the shift from middle class to lower class drug abuse. Despite our awareness that drug abuse exists in the upper class, little attention has been directed toward its control.

A case history of this process may be seen in our social policy concerning marihuana use over the last 40 years. When it was perceived as a lower class problem, there was substantial pressure to bring it under control through the use of punitive legislation. As the use of marihuana began significantly to enter into the life activities of middle and upper class students, we note a turn toward liberalization of control legislation. This may be pointed out despite the recent trend toward reestablishment of controls in some jurisdictions.

Cocaine use is another case in point. It was first declared a narcotic in 1914 under the provisions of the Harrison Tax Act and is currently classified as a Schedule II controlled substance (i.e., having a high abuse potential and little value in medical treatment). Reports of negative consequences concerning its use have appeared in the literature for over 100 years (38), yet government policy has given it scant attention. Several reasons may be responsible for this. First, there had been a sense that its prevalence relative to use of other controlled substances was relatively low. In addition, the users were found to be male, young adults who had a higher level of education and income than the general population (38). The drug was the "champagne" drug of the jet set. Its high cost and relatively brief period of effect were viewed as providing a built-in, self-limiting control to its growth and popularity. Fashions of drug use and changes in distribution systems that now favor more widespread use of cocaine have increased its risk potential for all classes. We have seen and should continue to see increasing government attention addressed to the problem as it leaves the closed habitat of the rich and increasingly moves onto the streets of the poor.

Musto (29), in his penetrating analysis of the history of the opium problem in the United States, pointed out that the American Pharmaceutical Association supported the licensing and control provisions concerning distribution of drugs as much to rid themselves of the competition of street drug hawkers and door-to-door peddlers as to improve the quality of their service to the public. The role of the pharmaceutical community in the development of control legislation is of interest from the conflict theory approach. National legislation controlling the rules of distribution of drugs was repeatedly opposed by the drug lobbies during the early 19th century (29), because it was viewed as a force limiting a free market and possibly inhibiting profits.

Unlike the functionalists the conflict theorists feel that sufficient information is available for us to make judgments concerning more effective policy that would reduce the need for drug abuse. They are more interested in moving directly toward political action that would change the economic and legal structure of the society that they view as supporting the social basis for drug abuse and other deviant behaviors. It should be no surprise that they have received no support to test their orientation.

LABELING AND SUBSTANCE ABUSE

The labeling perspective has become both a popular and controversial explanation for the development of substance abuse. As such, the approach does not constitute a theory in itself; it does not possess the comprehensive integrity required for that designation. Rather, it represents a development out of several theoretical positions that have been clustered together to represent an "interactionist perspective." The approach is closely

linked with conflict theory, although not a direct derivative of it. These two frameworks share the premise that the individual achieves the status of substance abuser as a consequence of having been defined as such by those who control society.

Becker (6) held that: "Social groups create deviants by making the rules whose infraction constitutes deviance, and by applying the rules to particular people and labeling them as 'outsiders.'" The position draws our attention to the social process that designates deviance through group definitions and reactions. Advocates of the labeling perspective suggest that the phenomenon of labeling generates several problems for the deviant. Once the substance abuser is labeled and separated from assumedly conforming individuals in the society, several processes seem to be activated. First, the label itself tends to develop a structural separateness of the individual from significant community groups. The consequence of that separation may lead to stigmatization of the individual. Second, the separation and negative group pressures are likely to affect the individual's perception of himself, his self-image (46). This process is, in part, supported by an observation concerning the subjective quality of reality by W. I. Thomas (43) when he states that: "If men define things as real, they are real in their consequences." Merton (28) elaborated this notion in his development of the conception of "the self-fulfilling prophecy." He observed that: "The self-fulfilling prophecy is, in the beginning, a *false* definition of the situation evoking a new behavior which makes the originally false conception come *true*."

Duncan (13) argued that, if the label and stigmatization by the social system are accepted by the individual: "This stigma acts to foster delinquent role enactment, isolates the youth from effective social control, cuts him off from many legitimate opportunities, and opens up illegitimate opportunities for him."

Lemert (22) suggested that a distinction should be drawn between primary and secondary deviance on the basis of the effect of the labeling of the individual on the individual's behavior after the labeling process has taken effect.

There is a growing recognition that labeling through the process involving people in the criminal justice system may have significant negative effect that may outweigh the value of the rehabilitation efforts within that system. The observation that prisons and detoxification facilities constitute "schools for crime" is not unique. Young addicts report that the principal benefits they received from institutionalization involved learning more about the technology associated with maintaining a habit. In effect, they learned to "professionalize" their status as addicts. The national policy expressed by the Law Enforcement Assistance Administration of the Justice Department seems to be based on the recognition that labeling can have a deleterious effect on the rehabilitation of the offender. The primary thrust of innovation dealing with offenders, and this includes those arrested for substance abuse, has been toward court diversion of all but the most serious offenders. Where the possibility of treatment outside of the criminal justice system exists, this option is preferred by most judicial systems.

Critics of this orientation suggest that the labeling perspective errs in overstating this process as a foundation for a growing problem in substance abuse. They indicate that the labeling theory does not expand our understanding of the "causes" of drug-dependent behavior in the individual, i.e., the initial drug dependence is not seen as having been created by the labeling process. Others suggest that labeling may deter further deviance for a segment of the labeled population in instituting a process of social control on their subsequent behavior. Relatively little empirical testing has been carried out to assess these criticisms, and those that have been conducted provide inconclusive evidence concerning the validity of the approach.

Despite this we find the labeling perspective can enrich our understanding of the interactive process that sustains deviant identity and behavior. Originally, the concept of differential association was not associated with the labeling perspective. But the use of the concept of labeling helps us to better appreciate the process Sutherland pointed out as essential in moving toward a criminal identity, i.e., the internalization of a deviant self-image. Labeling and change of self-image clearly support the development of values and norms that separate the individual from the rest of society and reinforce his deviant role.

ADDICT CAREERS

Social investigation has been addressed to understanding the process of becoming delinquent for over three-quarters of a century. Hapgood (20) examined the process of becoming a thief in *Autobiography of a Thief*, published in 1903. Anderson (3) reported on the lives and histories of hoboes in 1923. The Gluecks (18) summarized 500 criminal careers in 1930. Shaw (35) presented a natural history of a delinquent career in his presentation of the life of a "jack roller" in 1931. And Sutherland (34) looked at the process of learning to become a professional thief in his classic study in 1937. Anthropologists have long used a case history approach focused through the experiences of expert informants to understand cultural processes and change (37). In general, few sociologists turned their attention to substance abusers until the 1940's. Prior to that time the literature was dominated by clinicians whose attention was directed toward identifying the psychiatric and physiological processes associated with addiction (42).

In 1947 Lindesmith (24) published his work on *Opiate Addiction* in which he observed that the drug user was not to become addicted, even after physiological dependence had set in, until the individual made an association in his mind between the absence of opiates and the presence of withdrawal distress. At this point of psychological awareness, a focused drug craving would ensue. He also suggested that linguistic symbols and cultural habits are associated with the development of the awareness. In effect, he anticipated some of the concerns that emerge out of the life style and subcultural analysis of the substance abuser that came after that time.

In the 1950's the substance abuse field was divided by two opposing perceptions concerning the outcome of those who were treated for narcotics addiction. Those involved in psychiatric, hospital-based treatment assumed, without benefit of patient follow-up studies, that psychiatric treatment and support could in most cases arrest the addiction process. Those involved with the criminal justice system, who repeatedly saw those under their jurisdiction return to drug use and deviant systems of supporting their drug habits, took a dim view of the outcome of drug dependence among their clientele.

The reality of the chronicity of return to drug abuse was demonstrated by two studies reported by Alksne et al. (2) on adolescent addicts treated at Riverside Hospital in 1959 and by Duvall et al. (16) in 1963 on adults treated at the Public Health Hospital in Lexington. Both indicated an incredibly high relapse rate for treated addicts. The Alksne study indicated that over 90 per cent of the patients returned to drug use within periods of 1 day to over 3 months after treatment. Despite the dismal picture presented by these studies, they in effect called for a reevaluation of the most popular treatment approaches to substance abuse of that period. These studies suggest that treatment goals might better be developed in a framework of expecting relative abstinence and success rather than absolute success.

Somewhat prior to the studies of Riverside and Lexington treatment outcomes, Winick (48) postulated that addicts may in effect experience their drug dependence in the framework of a "life cycle of addiction." In a study of 7,000 cases in the files of the Federal Bureau of Narcotics, Winick found that addicts disappeared from the files as they grew older. He suggested that this was due to a process of "maturing out" of addiction. Ray (33) observed that degrees of involvement with the addiction process were supported by shared interpersonal and institutional experiences that lead to the development of addict values and self-image.

Alksne et al. (1) amplified the concept of life cycle in suggesting that individuals enter addiction through a series of stages, each of which had to have social supports in order for the novice addict to move to subsequent stages. These authors indicated that, before the individual can enter into the "life cycle of addiction," an "addiction set" of predisposing social and psychological factors is necessary. The addiction set predisposes the individual to enter an experimental stage of irregular drug use. The next stage is the adaptation stage in which regular use begins. It is followed by a stage in which physiological addiction occurs. This model suggests that involvement with addiction is based on a system of roles that must be learned, internalized, and acted out. These authors indi-

cated that the potential addict may drop out of the addiction system, even after physiological addiction has taken place, if he is unable to accept the role requirements of performance within that system. Once the user has become physiologically addicted he may seek to avoid further involvement and commitment to the addiction system. Such addicts may use institutional aid in ridding themselves of their addiction through an "avoidance detoxification." Those who become more deeply involved with the addiction system may ostensibly go through the same process but with a different purpose. They may use this form of detoxification to maintain their way of life as addicts—hence the term "maintenance detoxification" is coined. Addicts have used hospitalization to avoid street pressures, "kick" habits down to more manageable levels, correct health problems, meet "crime partners," and generally return to a condition that would facilitate execution of their roles as competent street addicts. The life cycle and addiction system concepts assume that the entry into and movement out of drug addiction get much support from social conditions present in the individual's social environment. In this framework the notion of "tolerance of addiction" involves social as well as physiological dimensions. According to the authors this approach has treatment implications. If addicts must develop a "tolerance of addiction" they may also have to develop a "tolerance of abstinence" that requires the learning of conventional roles and values and the establishment of conventional associations. The concepts of the life cycle of addiction and the addiction system were later used by Brill (8) as the basis for elaborating a model of a deaddiction process.

Robins (34) and Winick (50) have summarized the current state of our knowledge concerning careers of heroin users. Among the factors that seem to be involved in structuring addict or substance abuse careers are methods of initiation of drug use, age of onset, social setting involved in initiating drug use and continuing subsequent use, work experience, requirements of criminal involvement, family relationships, psychological basis, and subsequent supports of use and treatment experience.

The factors of greatest importance in determining career patterns are the type of substance used and the degree of negative social sanction involved in the use.

Most of the research using the careers perspective has been conducted in connection with users of opiates. It has focused our attention on the fact that a wide variety of types of heroin users exists, having different life experiences and different potentials for success in treatment-rehabilitation settings. The application of a careers analysis approach to other types of substance abusers may well expand our knowledge of the commonalities of social patterns that move people into dependency on certain substances, support that dependency, and conceivably might be used to move the individual away from dependence on these substances.

PEER GROUP INFLUENCE AND ATTITUDES

Considerable attention has been paid over the years to the interaction effect between peer group influence, attitudes, and deviant behavior. Generally, investigators find a strong relationship among these factors.

Attitudes toward the deviant behavior and its acceptability to the individual allegedly predispose the individual to move toward its acceptance and involvement. Chein et al. suggested that there is a tendency for young adolescent heroin users selectively to perceive elements of the addict life as positive while screening out the negative elements (10). The persistent problem in these studies in addiction is that the measure of attitudes is usually taken after individuals have become involved with drugs.

Peer influence represents a companion factor to that of attitudes and appears in studies of drug abuse (21). Involvement with marihuana, heroin, and alcohol begins in adolescence when the individual is searching for identity and purpose. For many, the young person's peer associations are a significant force in helping the individual define his present and future roles in the social system. Where there is no major conflict between the role performances of the adolescent and the adult, the peer relationships may reinforce the early socialization experiences to conformity. Where there are conflicts between the role and value systems of adolescent and parents or where the parents are themselves

not in consonance with the existing system, the peer group is likely to take on greater prominence as a systems-producing and -maintaining mechanism for the young person. In the latter situations the reliance on deviance is likely to be greater, and the peer relationship is likely to be more predominant.

Andrews and Kandel (4) pointed out the importance of the interaction between parental, peer, and attitudinal influences on the initiation and continuation of marihuana use among adolescents. Kandel's earlier work indicated that peer norms are important correlates of marihuana use and strong predictors of initiation to marihuana.

Andrews and Kandel sought to amplify their understanding of the relationship between attitudes held by the novice marihuana user and confirmed user and the marihuana use itself. They hypothesized (4): "That a person will not necessarily behave in a certain way either when holding an attitude or when experiencing social pressure favorable to the behavior, but generally will do so when individual attitudes and group norms are mutually reinforcing." They indicated that group differences are expressed in interaction terms. Using a cross-sectional sample of ongoing versus new using adolescents, they sought to untangle the relative effects of parental role, peer relationships, attitudes to marihuana use, and involvement of marihuana use itself. Using two time periods involving degree of use by young people, the investigators analyzed the interaction effects of these factors through a multiple regression process. They found that the effect of the number of friends using marihuana was three to five times as large as attitudes. Marihuana use, when other variables are held constant, seems to be even less important when individuals are moving rapidly through the range of participation in the behavior. The fact that the interactions were found to occur at this particular developmental phase suggests that strong social norms, together with appropriate attitudes, favor extensive involvement in the behavior.

The study by Robins (34) of heroin addiction in Vietnam may be of interest in this context. In Vietnam half of those who tried heroin did not become addicted to it. Of those who used it at least five times, 73 per cent became addicted. However, of those who were addicted in Vietnam and returned to use in the United States, only 28 per cent of those who continued some use here became readdicted within the first 10 months after return. Of all of the soldiers who had been addicted in Vietnam, only 7 per cent became readdicted at any time since their return. Winick (49) suggested that Vietnam veterans developed a high incidence of drug dependence because there was (a) easy access to dependence-producing substances, (b) disengagement from negative proscriptions about their use, and (c) role strain and/or role deprivation. In interpreting the low readdiction rate of Vietnam veterans, he believes that the factors which encouraged high use and high rates of addiction were reversed. Therefore, the mechanisms that supported the original drug use and addiction were not present in the lives of those returning to their home community.

There exists a need for studies that follow the lead of Kandel, who views the interpersonal context that supports drug abuse, and Winick, who examines the broader network of availability, norms, and conditions of role performance associated with such use. Although there are a great many studies identifying factors leading to the use or reuse, few seek to examine the conditions and supports for abstinence.

The preceding material represents a sample of some of the theory and findings concerning the social bases of substance abuse. Factors involving social change, social class, ethnic identity, the role of the family, intergeneration transfer of deviance, past dependency history, work, and other issues could not be explored in this chapter. Each affects the etiology and development of substance abuse. What does seem to be clear is that an appreciation of factors of this character is essential if we are to evaluate and deal effectively with substance abuse as a social problem.

References

1. Alksne, H., Lieberman, L., and Brill, L. A conceptual model of the life cycle of addiction. Int. J. Addict. 2: 221, 1967.
2. Alksne, H., Trussell, R. E., and Elinson, J. *A Follow-up Study of Hospital Treated Adolescent Narcotic Users, 1959.* Report distributed by the Columbia University School of Public Health and Administrative Medicine.
3. Anderson, N. *The Hobo.* Chicago, University of Chicago Press, 1923.
4. Andrews, K. H., and Kandel, D. Attitudes and behavior: A specification of the contingent consistency hypothesis. Am. Soc. Rev. 44:298, 1979.
5. Austin, G. A. *Perspectives on the History of Psychoactive Substances Use.* NIDA Report #017-024-00879-6. Washington, D.C., United States Government Printing Office, 1978.
6. Becker, H. S. *Outsiders: Studies in the Sociology of Deviance.* New York, Free Press, 1963.
7. Blumberg, A. S. Drug control: Agenda for repression. In *Drug Abuse Control, Administration and Politics,* R. Lirachin and E. H. Czajkoxski, editors. Lexington, Mass., Lexington Books, 1975.
8. Brill, L. *The De-Addiction Process: Studies in the De-Addiction of Confirmed Heroin Addicts.* Springfield, Ill., Charles C Thomas, 1972.
9. Brill, L., and Lieberman, L. *Authority and Addiction.* Boston, Little, Brown and Company, 1969.
10. Chein, I., Gerard, D. L., Lee, R. S., and Rosenfeld, E. *The Road to H: Narcotics, Delinquency and Social Policy.* New York, Basic Books, 1964.
11. Cloward, R. A., and Ohlin, L. E. *Delinquency and Opportunity: A Theory of Delinquent Gangs.* Glencoe, Ill., Free Press, 1960.
12. Driver, H. E. *The Indians of North America.* Chicago. University of Chicago Press, 1961.
13. Duncan, D. F. Stigma and delinquency. Cornell J. Soc. Relations 4:41, 1969.
14. Durkheim, E. *The Division of Labor in Society* (1893). New York, MacMillan, 1933.
15. Durkheim, E. *Suicide.* London, Routledge and Kegan Paul, 1952.
16. Duvall, H. J., Locke, B. Z., and Brill, L. Follow-up study of narcotics addicts: Five years after hospitalization. Public Health Rep. 78:185, 1963.
17. Finestone, H. Cats, kicks and color. Soc. Probl. 5:3, 1957.
18. Glueck, S., and Glueck, E. T. *500 Criminal Careers.* New York, Alfred A. Knopf, 1930.
19. Gold, M., and Williams, J. R. The effect of 'getting caught': Apprehension of the juvenile offender as a cause of subsequent delinquencies. Perspectus 3:1, 1969.
20. Hapgood, H. *Autobiography of a Thief* (1903). New York, Fox, Duffield, reprinted 1930.
21. Kandel, D. Interpersonal influences on adolescent illegal drug use. In *Drug Use: Epidemiological and Sociological Approaches,* E. Josephson and E. E. Carroll, editors, pp. 207–239. New York, John Wiley and Sons, 1974.
22. Lemert, E. M. *Human Deviance, Social Problems and Social Control.* Englewood Cliffs, N. J., Prentice-Hall, 1967.
23. Lewis, O. *La Vida: A Puerto Rican Family in the Culture of Poverty—San Juan and New York.* New York, Random House, 1965.
24. Lindesmith, A. *Opiate Addiction.* Evanston, Ill., Principia Press, 1947.
25. Lindesmith, A., and Gagnon, J. H. Anomie and drug addiction. In *Anomie and Deviant Behavior,* M. B. Clinard, editor, pp. 164–165. New York, Free Press, 1964.
26. Malinowski, B. *A Scientific Theory of Culture and Other Essays.* London, Oxford University Press, 1964.
27. Merton, R. K. Social structure and anomie. Am. Soc. Rev. 3:672, 1938.
28. Merton, R. K. *Social Theory and Social Structure.*

New York, Free Press, 1949.

29. Musto, D. F. *The American Disease: Origins of Narcotics Control.* New Haven, Conn., Yale University Press, 1973.

30. Parsons, T. *The Structure of Social Action.* New York, Free Press, 1968.

31. Quinney, R. *The Social Reality of Crime.* Boston, Little, Brown and Company, 1970.

32. Radcliffe-Brown, A. R. On the concept of function in the social sciences. Am. Anthropol. 37:395, 1935.

33. Ray, M. B. The cycle of abstinence and relapse among heroin addicts. Soc. Probl. 9:132, 1961.

34. Robins, L. N. Addict careers. In *Handbook on Drug Abuse,* R. Dupont, A. Goldstein, and J. O'Donnell, editors. Washington, D.C., National Institute on Drug Abuse, 1979.

35. Shaw, C. *The Jack Roller: The Natural History of a Delinquent Career.* Chicago, University of Chicago Press, 1931.

36. Short, J. F., Jr. Differential association as a hypothesis: Problems of empirical testing. Soc. Probl. 8:14, 1960.

37. Simmons, L. W., editor. *Sun Chief: The Autobiography of a Hopi Indian.* New Haven, Conn., Yale University Press, 1942.

38. Spotts, J. V., and Shontz, F. C. *The Life Styles of Nine American Cocaine Users.* Washington, D.C., United States Government Printing Office, 1976.

39. Sutherland, E. H. *The Professional Thief.* Chicago,

University of Chicago Press, 1937.

40. Sutherland, E. H., and Cressey, D. R. *Criminology,* ed. 10. Philadelphia, J. B. Lippincott, 1978.

41. Tarde, G. Penal philosophy. In *Heritage of Modern Criminology,* F. S. Sawyer, Jr., editor. Cambridge, Mass., Schenkman, 1972.

42. Terry, C. E., and Pellens, M. *The Opium Problem.* Montclair, N. J., Patterson Smith, 1970.

43. Thomas, W. I., and Thomas, D. S. *The Child in America.* New York, Alfred A. Knopf. 1928.

44. Weber, M. *Theory of Social and Economic Organization.* London, William Hodge and Company, 1947.

45. Weil, A. *The Natural Mind: A New Way of Looking at Drugs and the Higher Consciousness.* Boston, Houghton Mifflin, 1972.

46. Williams, J. R. *The Effects of Labeling the "Drug Abuser": An Inquiry.* NIDA Research Monograph 6. Washington, D.C., United States Government Printing Office, 1976.

47. Winick, C. Physician narcotic addicts. Soc. Probl. 9: 174, 1961.

48. Winick, C. Maturing out of narcotics addiction. Bull. Narc. 14:1, 1962.

49. Winick, C. *Sociological Aspects of Drug Dependence.* Cleveland, CRC Press, 1974.

50. Winick, C. Some aspects of careers of chronic heroin users. In *Drug Use: Epidemiological and Sociological Approaches,* E. Josephson and E. E. Carroll, editors, pp. 105–128. New York, John Wiley and Sons, 1974.

CHAPTER 9

SOCIAL INTERACTIONS, DRUG USE, AND DRUG RESEARCH

Norman E. Zinberg, M.D.

Three factors or variables in drug use—the pharmaceutical properties of the intoxicant, the attitudes and personality of the user (the set), and the physical and social setting in which use takes place—interact with one another to affect an individual's decision to use an intoxicant, the acute effects it has, and the ongoing social and psychological reactions to use (16, 50, 67). Despite apparent acceptance of this theoretical position, which stresses the importance of all three variables, the influence of setting on intoxicant use and the user and the way in which setting interacts with the other two variables has been little understood (60, 66).

The role of the setting continues to be minimized because of greater preoccupation either with the pharmaceutical properties or personal health hazards of the drug itself or with the personality deterioration of those who have not been able to control their use (58, 63). These preoccupations obscure from the scientific community, as well as the public, the precise ways in which setting influences both use itself and the effects of use, acting either in a positive way to help regulate use or in a negative way to weaken control.

Even those who make use of this 3-fold theoretical construct in analyzing the patterns of drug use and treating users fail to realize the important role played by the setting (including both physical and social setting) as an independent variable in determining the impact of use. When a drug is administered in a hospital setting, for example, the effect is very different from that experienced by a few people sitting around in a living room listening to records. Not only is there a vast difference between the actual physical locations, but different social attitudes are involved. In the hospital the administration of opiates subsumes the concept of the institutional structure of therapy and of licitness. In the living room there is a flavor of dangerous adventure, antisocial activity, and illicit pleasure, as well as the considerable anxiety that accompanies all three. It is not surprising that few patients in hospital settings experience continued drug involvement after the necessity for therapy has passed (38, 57), whereas many living room users express an intense and continuing interest in the drug experience.

In this chapter I will consider first the controlled use of drugs and the three variables—drug, set, and setting—that interact to influence use. In the second section I will define the mechanisms or controls developed within the social setting, which I call social sanctions and rituals, and describe the theory behind their operation. Third, I will illustrate the process of social learning by which these mechanisms become active in controlling use. And finally I will discuss briefly the ethical problems associated with research in this area and the policy implications of such research.

NEW PERSPECTIVES ON CONTROL

Basically it is the enormous and continuing growth of marihuana use that is responsible for the new interest in the comparative study of drug use and drug abuse. Although the number of marihuana users is vast—51 million have used since 1964, according to government estimates (37)—few, if any, widespread debilitating health effects have appeared. Also, most marihuana use has been occasional and moderate rather than intensive and chronic (18, 29, 30). As a result of this widespread pattern of consumption of a drug that only a few years ago was regarded as extremely dangerous, the public and professionals alike have begun to consider the possibility that substances viewed as dangerously dependency producing can be used in a controlled fashion. At the same time the marihuana debate has provoked many comparisons with the use of alcohol. Attention is now being given to the fact that most drinkers moderate their consumption of this powerful intoxicant (23). The further question of how control operates at various levels of alcohol consumption has also begun to receive attention and some research support.

Probably the most influential work has been that of Lee N. Robins, whose research on drug use among Vietnam veterans (to be discussed in detail later) indicated that consumption of the illicit drug that the public considers the most dangerous, heroin, did not always lead to addiction or dysfunctional use, and that even when addiction occurred it was far more reversible than was popularly believed (43, 44). Her work paralleled my study, begun in 1973, on moderate, occasional ("controlled") users of marihuana, psychedelics, and opiates (17, 55). By means of in-depth interviews conducted for several years with self-selected subjects, my research team accumulated sufficient evidence to demonstrate that long term, controlled use of these drugs was possible. In 1976, we secured

new funding from the National Institute on Drug Abuse (NIDA) to pursue a study of controlled users of opiates, particularly heroin, with the broader goal of identifying factors associated with this pattern of use (59).

While recruiting new subjects who met the strict criteria for controlled use, my team unintentionally interviewed a small number of subjects with compulsive using patterns. Study of these users not only underscored how controlled our subjects were, but it also revealed that even compulsive users exercise some degree of control (64). Although it seems obvious now, the research team was struck at that time by the fact that compulsives did not use as much of the drug as they could have. Clearly they were using too much, but a variety of internal and external factors still kept use down. About the same time a substantial subgroup (42 per cent) of controlled subjects were identified who had been previously addicted to opiates but whose use had since been controlled for 2 or more years (13). These findings suggested that it was necessary to consider the commonalities as well as the differences among various patterns of opiate use, and they also indicated the importance of understanding how one using pattern evolved into another (64). Accordingly, this research was redefined as a study of control across various using patterns rather than as a study of controlled users. The sample was reconstituted so as to include subjects ranging from controlled, that is, occasional and moderate, users at one extremity, through a middle group of "marginal" users (those whose patterns of use vary and at times are neither controlled nor compulsive), to compulsive users at the other extreme.

During the period from the beginning of the Drug Abuse Council (DAC) study to the development of the present, on-going NIDA-sponsored project, that is, from 1973 to 1977, our findings, which initially were received with considerable doubt, began to be borne out by similar projects pursued by other researchers, as evidenced by a recent collection of such work (62). At the close of the DAC project there was still considerable resistance to accepting the existence of moderate users; today such resistance is rare in the scientific community. At the outset of our DAC research, only one published study focused on occasional use of any illicit drug, whereas now there are a few dozen studies dealing substantively with this kind of use (64).

The detailed findings of our NIDA research on controlled use will be published elsewhere, but misunderstandings occur so frequently when this work is discussed that specific comment on our perspective toward control is needed. Because many of our subjects have tried a variety of substances in addition to their favorite intoxicant, they have given us considerable information about the drug variable and have suggested answers to the constant question, "Why do they use it?"

The obvious reply, "Because they like it," is misleading. First, the question of what constitutes pleasure is extremely hard to answer, and even in a general sense the notion of personal gratification is misunderstood. It is most often used as a pejorative indicating a dangerous relationship with a substance that could lead to dependency or addiction. By implication, this definition suggests that controlled users do not get personal or personality gratification from their use. Although there unquestionably are people who use a small amount of a substance merely to be sociable, such as the guest who nurses one drink throughout a cocktail party, most users find their use gratifying. In fact, even those who obviously are in careful control of their use respond "Yes" to the question, "Would you like to use more than you do?" Besides citing their fear that they might get addicted—a fear expressed most strongly, of course, by those with the least to fear—our subjects state that they use moderately in order to preserve the pleasure obtained from the substance.

The issue, therefore, is not one of obtaining gratification from substance use, for most users do. The issue is the degree to which an individual can balance and hence control those wishes for substance gratification with other factors, such as moral revulsion, the desire to enhance gratification in the long run, automatic acceptance of peer group standards, or unconscious utilization of available social sanctions and rituals. In other words, the gratification aspect of drug use may not be very different from that aspect of the consumption of everyday things such as food. Some people who gratify themselves thoroughly and overeat one evening find that the next day food does not appeal to them. Others after a debauch can exercise a balancing

control by keeping busy, getting distraught by seeing the numbers on the scale, beginning a careful regimen of exercise, or consciously being where the food is less appetizing or low in calories. Still others try these same mechanisms but they succeed only intermittently or partially. They gain weight or, in psychodynamic terms, suffer from inhibitions against control. But the difficulty, in the case of both food and intoxicants, lies not in the pleasure factor but in the inhibition of existing controls.

As to how one fixes on a substance that is pleasurable, I am not sure that the food analogy holds. With drugs there is far less choice, and that choice is determined by what is socially available. Today respectable, middle class professionals can easily find marihuana as well as alcohol, but they probably would have to go to some unacceptable lengths to obtain heroin.

Much has been made of the possibility of drug specificity (26), the view that an individual is so enamoured of a particular drug that the pleasure from it overwhelms all other substances and nothing else would have the same appeal. Every once in a while a story emerges, usually from a patient under drug treatment, that tells of multiple and dysfunctional drug use until the user discovered the drug, which makes giving up all else easy, and despite its own problems is an over-all stabilizing experience. In my clinical experience the drug has always been heroin. But this kind of story goes beyond the question of extent of pleasure. One patient, for example, had been using "ups" (usually amphetamines), "downs" (usually barbiturates or diazepam (Valium)), some alcohol, and some marihuana. The combination kept her social, psychological, and physiological systems in a chaotic state. Periods of little sleep, food, personal interaction, or euphoria alternated, in no particular sequence, with periods of being constantly on the nod, gregarious, or high. When she finally found a drug with a strong, consistent, regular, and flexible action, it was a great relief. It is strange to think of heroin as being an integrating drug, but in this case it seemed to be just that.

If the idea of a particular drug for a particular person is less generally true than the popular myth implies, then could the reverse of that myth be true? Will any drug do as long as it gets one high? Probably not. There is no doubt that some people like one drug or some drugs better than others. And the converse is even more likely to be the case. Some who very much like to get high are quite negative about one drug or another. Although the split of the 1960's between heads and juicers has long since faded out, there still are regular marihuana users who express a distaste for alcohol, and few heroin users show much appreciation for marihuana. If they use it at all, they use it so heavily that it acts more as a "down" than as an experience enhancer.

Our interviews suggest that there are two large classes of drugs. One class, for want of a better term, may be called "bread and butter" drugs. Within it alcohol, cannabis, and the opiates can be depended upon to give a consistent but relatively flexible effect that can, thus, be adapted to the situation as desired. A small number of respondents would also include the minor tranquilizers in this class, but so far most clinical experience has not borne this out. The pleasurable effect of the bread and butter drugs can generally be depended upon, although alcohol, cannabis, and the opiates have quite different subjective qualities and, as already noted, liking one does not necessarily mean liking the others. Despite books with titles such as *It's So Good, Don't Even Try It Once* (46), I would guess that many people find the opiates dysphoric.

The other class of drugs I call the exotics. People try them either because they are pleasurable or because they are faddish. The fad factor is of great importance. Since the "drug revolution" of the 1960's, many people have discovered that they like to get high. If they hear that something new—remember the banana skin craze of 1967—will get them high, a mini drug explosion may occur. But among the exotics, even the pleasurable drugs have a limited application. The psychedelics, for example, are long lasting and have an extremely high impact. Although the content of trips may range widely from euphoria to depression to chaos, and even to an indication of a higher sensibility, the changed state of consciousness is invariant and repetitious (56). Despite the frequent reports of immense delight and discovery upon initial use, our subjects usually got bored with the experience after a time. Our DAC controlled use study and confirmatory report from the

Haight Ashbury Free Medical Clinic found not a single user who continued to use psychedelics frequently after a year or two (45).

Generally speaking, the amphetamines belong in the exotic class, as far as their pleasure-seeking use is concerned. Again the initial sense of enormous stimulation from these high impact, disorganizing drugs seems extremely pleasurable to some, but after a period of regular use the disorganizing qualities become uppermost and the difficulty of maintaining interpersonal relationships either creates serious troubles for the user or makes him give up the drug. In the late 1960's when there was a faddish outbreak of amphetamine use all over the country, even the most prodrug underground newspapers ran headlines reading, "Speed Kills" (3). Obviously, drug users of either exotics or bread and butter drugs can find that their use and interest in use can change over time, particularly after a period of heavy use.

The dependency-inducing potential of the amphetamines (and the barbiturates) can create a serious problem for another sort of user. Many a woman, and not a few men, who have been given a low dose of amphetamines for mild depression or as a diet aid have found that they could not get through the day without them. When there was a general crackdown on the overprescribing of amphetamines, many of these people became desperate and protested strongly that they were not taking the drugs for fun. In the words of one woman, "I have four children and a house to clean. I can't get through the day without Dexedrine" (67). To their knowledge, these people never got high from the drug and did not want to. Much of the heavy use of a variety of tranquilizers may fall into the same category rather than into that of pleasure seeking. It is often argued, of course, that this is to some extent true of all chronic substance use, but the research interviews of our control study support the contention of McAuliffe and Gordon that even the most chronic users continue to report a pleasurable response (24).

The difficulty of defining pleasure makes it very hard to discuss two other exotic drugs, phencyclidine (PCP) and amyl nitrate. There is no doubt that PCP, which has been readily available on the street for more than 10 years (47), produces some sort of high state. Nevertheless, interviews with many users rarely specify particularly pleasurable experiences. As is the case with any other drug, users learn how to use it so as to avoid the most dysphoric effects; these subjects have reported little of the violence and few of the toxic symptoms that have been emphasized in the recent flurry of frightening reports about PCP (39). They do, however, report considerable psychological and physiological disorientation as well as the heavy feelings in the limbs and body that are characteristic of this drug. Almost without exception they have understood why PCP, which can be sniffed, smoked, or eaten, generally is passed off as another substance, such as delta-9-tetrahydrocannabinol (THC), mescaline, psilocibin, or even LSD. Users of amyl nitrate, too, although mentioning the excitement of the pop in the head that comes with ingestion and repeating the traditional story of popping at orgasm, do not sound so interested in or pleased with the drug experience as when they are discussing the bread and butter drugs.

In the current climate it is possible for any of the exotic drugs to catch on for a time, but it is hard to imagine them in continuous usage for pleasure. Great media attention, if fueled by the "scare" reports from professional sources that always make a drug sound much more attractive than it actually is to those hungry for a high, can push usage beyond that which the drug would warrant on a simple pleasure scale. Even the constant discovery of one more drug menace probably cannot ensure continued popularity of a substance that is not intrinsically pleasurable (whatever that means), except among a relatively small group with highly specialized and possibly peculiar tastes.

The existence of a small group whose interest in a substance experience may be perverse raises again the familiar question of the set or personality variable. Set and personality are not identical; set subsumes personality but in a basic sense goes beyond personality. For example, as attitudes toward marihuana have changed, many people who had been negative or fearful about it, and whose personality did not polarize toward either adventurousness or righteousness, now find it easy to accept marihuana use or to try it themselves. Here, set has been affected by the interaction with the social setting, while personality has remained constant.

At no point should it be assumed that the social setting is the only active factor at work. Just as the actions of the small group mentioned above and of other groups who find some special attraction in an otherwise not pleasant experience are dominated by personality factors, there are those whose antipathy on personality grounds to specific intoxicants or intoxicants in general is so great that they would not use under most circumstances.

In the majority of instances, even the very extreme, it is the interaction of the three variables (drug, set, and setting) that is crucial. This can vary at different times, of course, and the powerful influence of one variable may even obscure the effect of another. The example of heroin use in Vietnam, which will be discussed later to illustrate the power of the social setting, also shows how easy it is to miss the influence of one of the other variables. Because so many servicemen used heroin in Vietnam, the social setting variable seemed predominant. But what of the group that continued to use the drug after returning to the United States? It is likely that their problems antedated Vietnam and may well have sprung predominantly from personality. My cohort of 12 addicts who began use in Vietnam are clinical examples of the influence of the set variable.

Even the existence of this group, however, poses serious questions about the nature of addiction and the interaction of the three variables. Did these men really have the sort of addictive personality structure that would have led them to some sort of addiction whether they had gone to Vietnam or not? Perhaps in the United States they might have become alcoholics. But might not some of them, despite their underlying personality disorders, have managed in a more regular social situation where they would not have had easy access to heroin and might, therefore, have avoided addiction, even though they would have had other psychological problems? Unfortunately, it is not possible to devise controlled experiments that can easily answer these questions.

Enough information is available, however, on one popular theory about addiction (20, 22, 52), which assumes that the addict suffers from an actual ego defect, to permit comment. Psychoanalytic theorists, of course, are keenly aware that no one has ever seen an "ego" (48). It is only a concept, a coherent series of functions, used to explain the consistent, regular responses of the psyche. By the term "defect" these theorists mean that either genetically or, more likely, as a result of early, unresolved developmental conflicts the addict's conceptualized psychic structure has not developed the specific capacities or controls needed to cope effectively with certain powerful primitive drives or wishes. Hence the structure of the ego, or a specialized part of it, the superego, is defective. Generally speaking, the wish of the individual with a psychic defect is described as an overpowering desire for personal gratification.

When I spoke of personal gratification earlier, rather than saying that the individual whose wishes for the drug's effects got out of hand was suffering from a lack of capacity to control these wishes, that is, from an ego defect, I said that he was inhibited against the use of controls that were available. In Vietnam many people wanted to escape from their conscious situation to such an extent that they were willing to put aside controls they would ordinarily have used, that is, to inhibit them—not because the controls were not there, but because the motivation to use them was cancelled out by other motives. Few, if any, Vietnam heroin users or, for that matter, any heroin users or alcoholics in the United States use as much of their desired substance as they could (23). They make distinctions and differentiations as to when they will use and when they will not. Obviously, the addict has a different standard for determining when he will allow a control to function—a standard different from that considered reasonable by the reigning cultural outlook—but still he makes distinctions. I have seen junkies shoot up, almost publicly, in the restroom of a public place who would never shoot up in front of their children. I have seen alcoholics literally get up out of the gutter and pull themselves together in order to collect a Social Security check.

Because the operative ego controls are available to them, the question is: "Under what circumstances will they choose to use them?" The circumstances are clearly socially determined, which again emphasizes the interrelationship between social setting and set. Iranians in villages where opium has been smoked for centuries feel no need to conceal what they do from their children, and alcoholic South American shamen, who often do not find the prospect of a fee, even if it promises future gratification, sufficient reason to exercise control, will do so for the performance of certain treasured rituals.

Those soldiers who became addicted to heroin in Vietnam but did not become readdicted in the United States demonstrate clearly the inhibition of controls under certain social circumstances. That those who became readdicted in the United States chose not to exercise the available controls, which must have existed inasmuch as they had not been addicts before going to Vietnam, is little evidence of an intrinsic defect. Many of the theorists who point to ego defects attempt to explain such phenomena through the notion of ego atrophy or vulnerability. Ego atrophy means that ego functions or controls that once were available go soft when not used, rather like unexercised muscles. That is a hard concept to sustain. It is true, of course, that in certain social circumstances specific ways of coping or adapting to those circumstances become more evident. A young person going to school and trying to pass exams must attempt to extend his or her capacity to use the defense mechanism of isolation, concentrating on one thing (the study subject) while pushing other interests out of consciousness. I have observed that when the goal of this process of realigning the psychic homeostasis, in this case by use of isolation, is socially acceptable, the theorists do not conclude that other ego functions atrophy. Because the student during the peak study years exercises fewer controls over the difficulties in tolerating intimacy, these theorists do not assume that that capacity has atrophied. Later, perhaps, if inhibitions against closeness continue after the reasonable period, questions may be raised, but then they would be stated in the way I have suggested, "How and for what unconscious motives is this person inhibited against intimacy?," rather than "Does he suffer from an ego defect or atrophy in his intimacy ego muscles?"

The concept of ego defect simply does not match clinical experience except for those few addicts whose life histories are unusually abysmal. In addition, the suggestion of some ego defect theorists that the use of heroin may be adaptive, so that, for example, it can help control aggression, seems paradoxical. In that case, the defects would aid users in dealing with aggression instead of making them unable to cope with frustration.

Although some theorists stretch the ego defect theory to include both ego atrophy and adaptation (21, 52), many more adhere strenuously to an internal conflict theory about most problems, only resorting to the defect theory when it comes to drug problems. True, the bizarre idea that a person chooses, albeit unconsciously, to put himself in an addicted position, with all that means in this culture, is hard to defend without positing serious emotional illness. It is not difficult to understand why theorists look to some powerful, destructive internal force to explain the syndrome. But as a result they overlook the subtle interactions between personality structure and the dynamic social forces that attempt, and sometimes fail, to regulate how the psychological interest in intoxicants functions. In the next section, I will consider some of the social structures devised for that regulation.

SOCIAL CONTROLS—SANCTIONS AND RITUALS

The use of any drug involves values and rules of conduct, called social sanctions, and patterns of behavior, called social rituals, which together are known as social controls. Social sanctions define whether and how a particular drug should be used. They may be informal and shared by a group—as in the maxims applied to alcohol use, "Know your limit" and "Don't drive when you're drunk"—or formal—as in laws and policies aimed at regulating drug use (23, 65). Social rituals are the stylized, prescribed behavior patterns surrounding the use of a drug and may apply to the methods of procuring and administering the drug, the selection of the physical and social setting for use, the activities undertaken after the drug has been administered, and the ways of preventing untoward drug effects. Rituals thus serve to buttress, reinforce, and symbolize the sanctions. In the case of alcohol, for example, the statement, "Let's have a drink," automatically exerts control by using the singular term "a drink."

Social controls (rituals and sanctions) apply to all drugs, not just to alcohol, and operate in a variety of social contexts, ranging all the way from very large social groups, representative of the culture as a whole, down to small, discrete groups (12). Certain types of special-occasion use involving large groups of people—beer at ball games, drugs at rock concerts, wine with meals, cocktails at 6:00—despite their cultural diversity, have become so generally accepted that few if any legal strictures are applied even if such uses technically break the law. For example, a policeman will usually tell young people with beer cans at an open-air concert to "Knock it off," but he will rarely arrest them; and in many states the police reaction would be the same even if the drug were marihuana (34). If the culture as a whole thoroughly inculcates a widespread social ritual, it may eventually be written into law, just as the socially developed mechanism of the morning coffee break has been legally incorporated into union contracts. The T.G.I.F. (Thank God It's Friday) drink may not be far from acquiring a similar status. But small group sanctions and rituals tend to be more diverse and more closely related to circumstances. Nonetheless, some caveats may be just as firmly upheld, such as: "Never smoke marihuana until after the children are asleep," "Only drink on weekends," "Don't shoot up until the last person has arrived and the doors are locked."

The existence of social sanctions or rituals does not necessarily mean that they will be effective, nor does it mean that all sanctions or rituals were devised as mechanisms to aid control. "Booting" (the drawing of blood into and out of a syringe) by heroin addicts seemingly lends enchantment to the use of the needle and, therefore, opposes control. But it may once have served as a control mechanism that gradually became perverted or debased. Some old-time users, at least, have claimed that booting originated in the (erroneous) belief that by drawing blood in and out of the syringe, the user could tell the strength of the drug that was being injected.

More important than the question of whether the sanction or ritual was originally intended as a control mechanism is the way in which the user handles conflicts between sanctions. With illicit drugs the most obvious conflict is that between formal and informal social controls, that is, between the law against use and the social group's condoning of use. The teenager attending a rock concert is often pressured into trying marihuana by his peers, who insist that smoking is acceptable at that particular time and place and will enhance his musical enjoyment. The push to use may include a control device, such as, "Since Joey won't smoke because he has a cold, he can drive," thereby honoring the "Don't drive after smoking" sanction. Nevertheless, the decision to use, so rationally presented, conflicts with the law and may make the user anxious as to whether the police will be benign in this instance. Such anxiety interferes with control. In order to deal with the conflict the user will probably come forth with more bravado, exhibitionism, paranoia, or antisocial feeling than would be the case if he or she had patronized one of the little bars set up alongside the concert hall for the selling of alcohol during intermission. It is this kind of mental conflict that makes control of illicit drugs more complex and difficult than the control of licit drugs.

The existence and application of social controls, particularly in the case of illicit drugs, does not always lead to moderate, decorous use, and yet it is the reigning cultural belief that controlled use is or should be always moderate and decorous. This requirement of decorum is perhaps the chief reason why the power of the social setting to regulate intoxicant use has not been more fully recognized and exploited. The cultural view that the users of intoxicants should always behave properly stems from the moralistic attitudes toward such behavior that pervade our culture, attitudes that are almost as marked in the case of licit drugs as in the case of illicit drugs. Yet on some occasions—at a wedding celebration or during an adolescent's first experiment with drunkenness—less decorous behavior is culturally acceptable. Although we should never condone the excessive use of any intoxicant, it has to be recognized that when such boundary-breaking occurs it does not necessarily signify a breakdown of over-all control. Unfortunately, these occasions of impropriety, particularly after the use of illicit drugs, are often taken by the advocate of abstinence to prove what he or she sees as the ultimate truth: that in the area of drug use there are only two possible types of behavior—abstinence or unchecked excess leading to addiction. Despite massive evidence to the contrary, many people remain unshaken in this belief.

Such a stolid stance inhibits the development of rational understanding of controlled use. As mentioned earlier, the fact is overlooked that the most severe alcoholics and addicts who cluster at one end of the spectrum of drug use exhibit some control in not using as much of the intoxicating substance as they could. Next, and of great importance, at the other end of the spectrum of drug use, as the careful interviewing of ordinary citizens has shown, highly controlled users and even abstainers express much more interest in and preoccupation with the use of intoxicants than is generally acknowledged. Whether to use, when, with whom, how much, how to explain why one does not use—these questions occupy an important place in the emotional life of almost every citizen. Yet hidden in the American culture lies a deep-seated aversion to acknowledging this preoccupation. As a result, our culture plays down the importance of the many social mores—sanctions and rituals—that enhance our capacity to control use. Thus the whole issue becomes muddied. Both the existence of control on the part of the most compulsive users and the interest in drugs and the quality of drug use (the questions of with whom, when, and how much to use) on the part of the most controlled users are ignored. We are left with longings for the utopian society where no one would need drugs either for their pleasant or their unpleasant effects, either for relaxation and good fellowship or for escape and torpor.

But, because such idealized abstinence is socially unacceptable and impossible, the reigning culture's model of extreme decorum overemphasizes the pharmaceutical powers of the drug or the personality of the user. It inculcates the view that only a disordered person would not live up to the cultural standard, or that the quantity or power of the drug is so great that the standard cannot be upheld. To think this way and thus to ignore the social setting requires considerable psychological legerdemain, for, as in most other areas of living, people can rarely remain indefinitely on so decorous a course. Intoxicant use tends to vary with one's time of life, status, and even geographical location. Many adolescents who have made heavy use of intoxicants slow down appreciably as they reach adulthood and change their social setting (their friends and circumstances); whereas some adults, as they become more successful, may increase their intoxicant use. A man born and bred in a dry part of Kansas may change his use significantly after moving to New York City. The effects on intoxicant use of such variations in social circumstances have certainly been perceived, but they are not usually incorporated into a sound theoretical understanding of how the social setting influences the use and control of intoxicants.

The history of the use of alcohol in America provides a striking example of the variability of intoxicant use and its control (2, 4). First, it illustrates the social prescriptions that define the social concept of control, and, second, it shows that the time span of these control variations can be as long as a major historical epoch.

Five social prescriptions that define controlled or moderate use of alcohol—and these may apply to other intoxicants as well—have been derived from a study of alcohol use in many different cultures. All five of these conditions encourage moderation and discourage excess (61).

1. Group drinking is clearly differentiated from drunkenness and is associated with ritualistic or religious celebrations.

2. Drinking is associated with eating or ritualistic feasting.

3. Both of the sexes, as well as different generations, are included in the drinking situation, whether they drink or not.

4. Drinking is divorced from the individual effort to escape personal anxiety or difficult (even intolerable) social situations. Furthermore, alcohol is not considered medicinally valuable.

5. Inappropriate behavior when drinking (violence, aggression, overt sexuality) is absolutely disapproved, and protection against such behavior is exercised by the sober or the less intoxicated. This general acceptance of a concept of restraint usually indicates that drinking is only one of many activities and thus carries a low level of emotionalism. It also shows that drinking is not associated with a male or female "rite de passage" or sense of superiority.

The enormous variations in alcohol use that have taken place during three major epochs of American history (the 1600's to the 1770's, the 1770's to about 1890, and 1890 to today) illustrate the importance of these social prescriptions in controlling the use of alcohol.

During the first period, the American colonies, although veritably steeped in alcohol, strongly and effectively prohibited drunkenness. Families drank and ate together in taverns, and drinking was associated with celebrations and rituals. Tavern keepers were people of status; keeping the peace and preventing excesses stemming from drunkenness were grave duties. Manliness or strength was measured neither by the extent of consumption nor by violent acts resulting from it. Pre-Revolutionary society, however, did not abide by all the prescriptions, for certain alcoholic beverages were viewed as medicines: "groaning beer," for example, was consumed in large quantities by pregnant and lactating women.

The second period, which included the Revolutionary War, the Industrial Revolution, and the expansion of the frontier, was marked by excess. Men were separated from their families and began to drink together and with prostitutes. Alcohol was served without food and was not limited to special occasions, and violence resulting from drunkenness grew. In the face of increasing drunkenness and alcoholism, people began to believe (as is the case with some illicit drugs today) that it was the powerful, harmful pharmaceutical properties of the intoxicant itself that made controlled use remote or impossible.

Although by the beginning of the third period moderation in the use of alcohol had begun to increase, this trend was suddenly interrupted in the early 1900's by the Volstead Act, which ushered in another era of excess. We are still recovering from the speakeasy ambience of Prohibition in which men again drank together and with prostitutes, food was replaced by alcohol, and the drinking experience was colored with illicitness and potential violence. Although repeal provided relief from excessive and unpopular legal control, the society was left floundering without an inherited set of social sanctions and rituals to control use.

SOCIAL LEARNING

Today this vacuum of social learning about alcohol has been largely filled. In most sectors of our society informal alcohol education is readily available. Few children grow up without an awareness of a wide range of behaviors associated with the use of alcohol, learned from that most pervasive medium, television. They see cocktail parties, wine at meals, beer at ball games, homes broken by drink, drunks whose lives are wrecked, along with all the advertisements that present alcohol as lending glamour to every occasion.

Buttressed by movies, the print media, observation of families and family friends, and often by a sip or watered-down taste of the grownups' potion, young people gain an early familiarity with alcohol. When, in a peer group, they begin to drink and even, as a rite de passage, to overdo it, they know what they are about and what the sanctions are. The process of finding a "limit" is a direct expression of "Know your limit." Once that sanction has been experientially internalized— and our culture provides mores of greater latitude for adolescents than for adults—they can move on to such sanctions as "It is unseemly to be drunk" and "It is O.K. to have a drink at the end of the day or a few beers on the way home from work, or in front of the television, but don't drink on the job" (65).

This general description of the learning or internalization of social sanctions, although neat and precise, does not take account of the variations from individual to individual that result from differences in personality, cultural background, and group affinity. Specific sanctions and rituals are developed and integrated in varying degrees with different groups (11). Certainly a New York child from a rich, sophisticated family, brought up on Saturday lunch with a divorced parent at The 21 Club, will have a different attitude toward drinking from the small town child who vividly remembers accompanying a parent to a sporting event where alcohol intake acted as fuel for the excitement of unambivalent partisanship. Yet one common denominator shared by young people from these very different social backgrounds is the sense that alcohol is used at special events and belongs to special places.

This kind of education about drug use is social learning, absorbed inchoately and unconsciously as part of the living experience (56). The learning process is impelled by an unstated and often unconscious recognition by young people that this is an area of emotional importance in American society and, therefore, knowledge about it may be quite important in future social and personal de-

velopment. Attempts made in the late 1960's and early 1970's to translate this informal process into formal drug education courses, chiefly intended to discourage any use, have failed (8). Formal drug education, paradoxically, has stimulated drug use on the part of many young people who were previously undecided, and at the same time has confirmed the fears of those who were already excessively concerned. Is it possible, one might ask, for formal education to codify social sanctions and rituals in a reasonable way for those who have somehow been bypassed by the informal process? Or does the reigning cultural moralism, which has pervaded all such courses, preclude the possibility of discussing reasonable informal social controls that may, of course, condone use? So far, these questions remain unanswered. It will be impossible even to guess at the answers until our culture has accepted the use not only of alcohol but of other intoxicants sufficiently to allow teachers to explain how they can be used safely and well. Teaching safety is not intended to encourage use; its main focus is the prevention of abuse. Similarly, the primary purpose of the few good sex education courses in existence today is to teach the avoidance of unwanted pregnancy and venereal disease, not the encouragement or the avoidance of sexual activity per se.

Whatever happens to formal education in these areas, the natural process of social learning will inevitably go on, for better or worse. The power of this process is illustrated by two recent and extremely important social events: the use of psychedelics in the United States in the 1960's and the use of heroin during the Vietnam War.

Following the Timothy Leary "Tune In, Turn On, and Drop Out" slogan of 1963, the use of psychedelics became a subject of national hysteria—the "drug revolution." These drugs, known then as psychotomimetics (imitators of psychosis), were widely believed to lead to psychosis, suicide, or even murder (27, 41). Equally well publicized were the contentions that they could bring about spiritual rebirth, mystical oneness with the universe, and the like (16, 50). Certainly there were numerous cases of not merely transient but prolonged psychoses after the use of psychedelics. In the mid-1960's psychiatric hospitals like the Massachusetts Mental

Health Center and Bellevue were reporting as many as one-third of their admissions as resulting from the ingestion of these drugs (41). By the late 1960's, however, the rate of such admissions had declined dramatically. At first, many observers concluded that this decline was due to fear tactics—the warning about the various health hazards, the chromosome breaks and birth defects, which were reported in the newspapers. These stories were later proved to be false. In time, although psychedelic use continued to be the fastest growing drug use in America through 1973, the dysfunctional sequelae virtually disappeared (29). What then had changed?

It has been found that neither the drugs themselves nor the personalities of the users were the most prominent factors in those painful cases of the 1960's. The retrospective McGlothlin and Arnold study of the use of such drugs before the early 1960's has revealed that, although responses to the drugs varied widely, they included none of the horrible, highly publicized consequences of the mid-1960's (25). Another book, entitled "LSD: Personality and Experience" (5), describes a study of the influence of personality on psychedelic drug experience that was made before the drug revolution. It found typologies of response to the drugs but no one-to-one relationship between untoward reaction and emotional disturbance. And Howard S. Becker, in his prophetic article of 1967, compared the then current anxiety about psychedelics to anxiety about marihuana in the late 1920's, when several psychoses were reported (7). Becker hypothesized that the psychoses came not from the drug reactions themselves but from the secondary anxiety generated by unfamiliarity with the drug's effects and ballooned by media publicity. He suggested that such unpleasant reactions had disappeared when the effects of marihuana became more widely known, and he correctly predicted that the same thing would happen with the psychedelics.

The power of social learning also brought about a change in the reactions of those who expected to gain insight and enlightenment from the use of psychedelics. Interviews have shown that the user of the early 1960's, with his great hopes or fears of heaven or hell and his lack of any sense of what to expect, had a far more extreme experience than the user

of the 1970's, who had been exposed to a decade of interest in psychedelic colors, music, and sensations. The later user, who might remark, "Oh, so that is what a psychedelic color looks like," had been thoroughly prepared, albeit unconsciously, for the experience and responded accordingly, within a middle range.

The second example of the enormous influence of the social setting and of social learning in determining the consequences of drug use comes from Vietnam. Current estimates indicate that at least 35 per cent of enlisted men used heroin, and 54 per cent of these became addicted to it (44). Statistics from the United States Public Health Service hospitals active in detoxifying and treating addicts showed a recidivism rate of 97 per cent, and some observers thought it was even higher. Once the extent of the use of heroin in Vietnam became apparent, the great fear of Army and government officials was that the maxim "once an addict, always an addict" would operate, and most of the experts agreed that this fear was entirely justified. Treatment and rehabilitation centers were set up in Vietnam, and the Army's slogan that heroin addiction stopped "at the shore of the South China Sea" was heard everywhere. As virtually all observers agree, however, those programs were total failures. Often people in the rehabilitation programs used more heroin than when they were on active duty (54).

Nevertheless, as the study by Robins et al. has shown (44), most addiction did indeed stop at the South China Sea. For addicts who left Vietnam, recidivism was approximately 10 per cent after they got back home to the United States—virtually the reverse of the previous United States Public Health Service figures. Apparently it was the abhorrent social setting of Vietnam that led men who ordinarily would not have considered using heroin to use it and often to become addicted to it. But evidently they associated its use with Vietnam, much as hospital patients who are receiving large amounts of opiates for a painful medical condition associate the drug with the condition. The returnees were like those patients (mentioned earlier) who, having taken opiates to relieve a physiological disturbance, usually do not crave the drug after the condition has been alleviated and they have left the hospital.

Returning to the first example—psychedelic drug use in the 1960's—it is my contention that control over use of these drugs was established by the development in the counterculture of social sanctions and rituals very like those surrounding alcohol use in the culture at large. "Only use the first time with a guru" was a sanction or rule that told neophytes to use the drug the first time with an experienced user who could reduce their secondary anxiety about what was happening by interpreting it as a drug effect. "Only use at a good time, in a good place, with good people" was a sanction that gave sound advice to those taking a drug that would sensitize them intensely to their inner and outer surroundings. In addition, it conveyed the message that the drug experience could be simply a pleasant consciousness change, a good experience, instead of either heaven or hell. The specific rituals that developed to express these sanctions—just when it was best to take the drug, how, with whom, what was the best way to come down, and so on—varied from group to group, though some rituals spread from one group to another.

It is harder to document the development of social sanctions and rituals in Vietnam. Most of the early evidence indicated that the drug was used heavily in order to obscure the actualities of the war, with little thought of control. Yet later studies showed that many enlisted men used heroin in Vietnam without becoming addicted (42). More important, although 95 per cent of heroin-addicted Vietnam returnees did not become readdicted in the United States, 88 per cent did take heroin occasionally, indicating that they had developed some capacity to use the drug in a controlled way (44). Some rudimentary rituals, however, do seem to have been followed by the men who used heroin in Vietnam. The act of gently rolling the tobacco out of an ordinary cigarette, tamping the fine white powder into the opening, and then replacing a little tobacco to hold the powder in before lighting up the O.J. (opium joint) seemed to be followed all over the country, even though the units in the North and in the Highlands had no direct contact with those in the Delta (53). To what extent this ritual aided control is, of course, impossible to determine. Having observed it many times, however, I can say that it was almost always done in a group and thus formed part of the social experience of heroin use. While one person was performing the ritual, the others sat quietly and watched in anticipation. It would be my guess that the degree of socialization achieved through this ritual could have had important implications for control.

Still, the development of social sanctions and rituals probably occurs more slowly in the secretive world of illicit drug use than with the use of a licit drug like alcohol, and it is hard to imagine that any coherent social development occurred in the incredible pressure cooker of Vietnam. Today the whole experience has receded so far into history that it is impossible to nail down what specific social learning might have taken place. But certainly Vietnam illustrates the power of the social setting to induce large numbers of apparently ordinary people to engage in drug activity that was viewed as extremely deviant and to limit the activity to that setting. Vietnam also showed that heroin, despite its tremendous pharmaceutically addictive potential, is not universally or inevitably addictive.

Further study of various patterns of heroin use, including controlled use, in the United States confirms the lessons taught by the history of alcohol use in America, the use of psychedelics in the 1960's, and the use of heroin during the Vietnam War. The social setting, with its formal and informal controls, its capacity to develop new informal social sanctions and rituals, and its transmission of information in numerous informal ways, is a crucial factor in the controlled use of any intoxicant. This does not mean, however, that the pharmaceutical properties of the drug or the attitudes and personality of the user count for little or nothing. As I stated at the beginning of this chapter, all three variables—drug, set, and setting—must be included in any valid theory of drug use. In every case of use it is necessary to understand how the specific characteristics of the drug and the personality of the user interact and are modified by the social setting and its controls.

ETHICAL AND SOCIAL POLICY ISSUES IN DRUG RESEARCH

Doing research on intoxicants, particularly illicit drugs, invariably raises the question as to whether the findings will act to increase use. As our current formal social policy is aimed unabashedly at attempting to decrease use of illicit substances (28), the question also arises whether research efforts, if they are to be judged ethical, must adhere to this social policy. Then, if research is so judged, and there is little doubt that to a large extent it is, what effect does that have on which research projects get funded, how the research is done, and how the findings are treated by the public, as represented by both professionals and the media?

Almost everyone doing drug research would agree that it is extremely difficult in this field to have one's work perceived as objective and relatively neutral. Not only do the popular radio and television shows try to "balance" their presentations by including someone considered "antidrug" on a program that negates the specific harmfulness of drug use, but scientific programs have often felt obliged to follow a similar procedure. In this climate almost any work or worker is quickly classified as for or against use, and halfway positions are not acknowledged. It is virtually equivalent to the old Marxist political litmus test. To a diehard advocate of the National Organization for the Reform of Marihuana Laws (NORML), any indication that marihuana can be disruptive is disputed, just as any claim that Communists were inhumane was disputed in the 1930's. When it was suggested at a recent scientific meeting that marihuana users should not drive when intoxicated, floor discussants were quick to point out that some experienced users claim to drive better while intoxicated. Conversely, at the same meeting the statement that there had been no deaths attributed to marihuana during the last 15 years, when over 51 million people had used the drug, was greeted by a retort from the floor that marihuana was not water-soluble and, therefore, was retained in the body. This non sequitur was not intended to counter the original statement but merely to show that no one could get away with saying something about marihuana that did not stress its dangers.

Although it is easy to ridicule the extremes of this litmus testing, the ethical issues themselves are serious, and the implications of publicizing and exploiting drug effects so as to make drug use glamorous, as in Timothy Leary's case, have given rise to grave concerns. There is little doubt that the explosion of LSD use in the 1960's was propelled by the wide publicity given such use. It certainly

could be argued that this explosion around Timothy Leary was not principally the result of the presentation of actual drug research. But the drug hysteria aroused by that drug use very quickly spread to research, so that one previously objective inquirer apparently saw little wrong in stating that he was setting out to prove the drug's potential for harm (10). Once that sort of attitude appeared, which was intended to support formal social policy and was more or less legitimized—and there have been numerous examples of it since, even on the part of the National Institute on Drug Abuse (31–33), the official research funding body—every researcher has had to take into account whether his work would meet a standard more concerned with discouraging use than looking for truth.

In a basic sense, truth is obviously not the issue because one man's truth is in another's view a gross misconception. I doubt if anyone in the field, no matter how misguided I may consider him or her to be, has set out to falsify the facts. Rather, within a certain frame of values—the outlook that any illicit drug is so bad that efforts to prove it so are legitimate and for the greater good—the search for truth can become deductive rather than inductive. And, indeed, because to a certain extent all scientific inquiry begins with an operating hypothesis, what we are worrying about in relation to the aims of research is hardly a 100 per cent or nothing matter. The issue is rather the subtle one of feeling sufficiently righteous about the culture's current policy or value of reducing illicit drug use to allow that to outweigh objectivity. Researchers who treasure objectivity and neutrality and present the data, whatever they are, may end up carrying on work that contravenes dearly held cultural beliefs. These beliefs are not only dearly held in their own right but are believed to be sacrosanct in that they help to prevent a bad thing, that is, more illicit drug use.

In 1968, when Andrew Weil and I began the first controlled experiments in giving marihuana to naive subjects in order to study the effects of acute intoxication (51), we were much criticized. If marihuana was as dangerous as many people thought at that time, we ran the risk of addicting or otherwise damaging our innocent volunteer subjects. If it should prove that marihuana was not so deadly as was assumed, then, we were told by many (but most amazingly by a senior partner in the law firm representing Harvard Medical School), our findings could be morally damaging to the country by removing the barrier of fear that was assumed to prevent drug use. It is, of course, impossible to say whether these experiments and others that replicated the findings were significant in increasing the popularity of drug use. Even by 1968 it was becoming clear that marihuana was not the devil drug of "Reefer Madness." During that period of criticism and ever since, I have believed that supplying credible and responsible information about the drug was essential as long as I was sufficiently objective to provide that information whether or not it supported my biases.

That last statement sounds rational and it is. In this field, however, there is great disagreement as to whether one is simply advocating free speech or is shouting fire in a crowded theatre. Because the issue is so polarized, withholding or distorting information so as to support the current social policy of use reduction runs the great risk of causing possible users whose experience with and information about the substance in question is different and more experiential to disbelieve any reports of potential harmfulness (19, 67). This situation makes it extremely difficult to separate use from misuse and to help people avoid the destructive and dysfunctional consequences of misuse. On the other hand, in this same climate the presenting of information indicating that all use need not be misuse, thus contravening formal social policy, runs the equally grave risk that the work will be interpreted and publicized as condoning use.

It is a frightening dilemma for a researcher, particularly for one who cannot believe that "the truth will set you free" in some mystical, philosophical sense. Of course, neither can one believe that hiding facts, hiding the truth, will make everything come out all right. And what makes it considerably harder when thinking about research on powerful intoxicating substances is that general principles about truth and objectivity are not all that is involved; human lives are at stake. It was relatively easy to bear the criticism of marihuana research. The growing popularity of the drug was evident; there were no fatalities reported from its use; the need for more precise information about its effects in order

to differentiate myth from fact was pressing. For example, at that time police officers and doctors believed that marihuana dilated the pupils. This misconception, which affected both arrests and medical treatment, needed to be cleared up. But when it became evident that the understanding of controlled use required looking at drugs whose physical properties, unlike those of marihuana, demanded control or there would be serious trouble, the ethical problem became more serious. Studying heroin meant studying a powerful addicting drug whose potential to kill through a misjudgment on dosage is very great. Informing the professional community and also the public (by way of the omnipresent media, which seize on anything in the drug area as good copy) that the belief that any use is inevitably addicting and destructive was not true ran the risk of reducing the barrier of fear that might have kept someone from using, and this possibility has been and is a tormenting concern. Whatever the devotion to research and the importance of knowledge may be, the work cannot be countenanced if the subjects are not protected from the harm caused by the research, either directly or by withholding information, as, for example, in the unfortunate United States Public Health Service research on syphilis that held back a treatment long after it had been proved effective.

Nevertheless, even my preliminary investigations of heroin and other opiate use confirmed what had been found in every investigation of drug use. The reality was far more complex than the simple pharmacological presentation that I had received in medical school. Certainly, heroin is a powerfully addicting drug with great potential for deadly overdose. But there were those who managed to use it in a controlled way, and even those who got into trouble with the drug displayed various patterns of response very different from that of the stereotypical junkie. And, because the truth, although it will not set you free, usually will out, other investigators such as Leon Hunt and Peter Bourne were beginning to report similar phenomena (1, 9, 15). Once it became clear that these phenomena were extensive and significant, it was also clear that any attempt to remove from the scientific purview such behavior patterns, or any behavior pattern, because they were morally reprehensible or disapproved would reduce the credibility of all scientific enterprise. In addition, in the process of controlling their use, these users might have developed a system of control that could be extremely valuable, not just as a principle to condone, but as a possible method of treatment for addiction (59).

That such research has a potentially positive application and is not for information alone does not figure in the principle of what makes work scientifically acceptable. Basic research needs no defense here. But, as I pointed out earlier, the way the work is received and treated, particularly by the media, can raise extremely serious problems. To what extent researchers who report findings have a responsibility for what is done with them publicly is a moot point. In a basic sense, although these researchers are as accurate and careful in their statements as possible, they cannot control what others say or do with the work. But in the present climate of emotionalism about drug research, they would be naive indeed if they did not realize that certain findings might be picked up by the press. Unfortunately, several researchers have called press conferences before publication in order to herald their findings (35, 36), and they have been willing to speculate there about far-reaching implications of the work that go beyond the actual published data.

Thus, it is not enough to avoid carelessness in one's actual work and the reporting of it. A researcher must also consider carefully whether the work might cause some people who would not otherwise use drugs to do so. In this context the potentially positive application of the work as a therapeutic aid may help shift attention away from the overwhelming preoccupation with illicit use. Although discussing the work from the viewpoint of possible therapeutic applications can lend itself to another brand of sensationalism and overstatement, this danger may be easier to avoid.

The difficulty of knowing what objectivity is and the problem of questioning the ethics of doing certain research and imparting its results are by no means confined to research on illicit drugs. Few people today, in this era of recognition of the overwhelming number of choices faced by each individual, are able to preserve the image of the disinterested scientist burdened by few if any values except

dedication to the purity of science. A searching article by a prominent jurist in *Science* (6) points out that even when scientists have been able to agree on what is scientific fact, such as that a certain amount of saccharine can give white mice cancer, they could not, because of the different value systems influencing their interpretation of those facts, agree on whether this risk was low or moderate for humans.

In his article (6) David L. Bazelon goes on to comment upon matters pertinent to this discussion of illicit drug use, although he did not have that particular subject in mind.

In reaction to the public's often emotional response to risk, scientists are tempted to disguise controversial value decisions in the cloak of scientific objectivity, obscuring those decisions from political accountability.

At its most extreme, I have heard scientists say that they would consider not disclosing risks which in their view are insignificant, but which might alarm the public if taken out of context. This problem is not mere speculation. Consider the recently released tapes of the NRC's deliberation over the accident at Three Mile Island. They illustrate dramatically how concern for minimizing public reaction can overwhelm scientific candor.

This attitude is doubly dangerous. First, it arrogates to the scientists the final say over which risks are important enough to merit public discussion. More important, it leads to the suppression of information that may be critical to developing new knowledge about risks or even to developing ways of avoiding those risks.

Who today is willing to assume the risk of deciding to limit our knowledge? The consequences of such limitation are awesome. I do not mean to equate the social issues of opening up areas of research on heroin use with the potentially frightening consequences of failing to disclose problems with nuclear reactions, but the principles are similar. It is understandable that government agencies, already overwhelmed by the number of factors that must be considered before reaching a decision, and buttressed by a sense of righteousness that what they are trying to do is for the public good, would want to minimize the confusion and uncertainty that might be engendered by facing the public with more controversial and conflicting information. Such bureaucracies, in principle, want all the information possible; but, once they are settled on a course or a value position that they can unabashedly support, they believe that anything which raises further doubts will raise greater risks. Also, as our cultural belief in the disinterested scientist wanes and our disillusion with the omnipotent court decision as a righter of wrongs grows, the bureaucracies' paternalism seems to be both necessary and unavoidable. Once "the buck stops here" mentality shifts from the acceptance of responsibility for a decision to a conviction that what must be presented most directly is what supports that decision, there is bound to be extreme difficulty in even imagining a genuinely flexible social policy. And that is exactly what has happened to the policy about illicit drugs.

Bazelon makes another point that supports my argument and those of John Kaplan (19) and other researchers (14, 23, 49). Regulations that attempt to limit risks have their own social cost. This does not mean that we should not have regulations. Of course we should, but even at the cost of increasing the uncertainty, the choices, and the number of factors to be considered, there must be a keen assessment of the risk cost of the regulations themselves. In few areas is this as true as it is in the drug area. Certainly much of the damage now resulting from marihuana and heroin use occurs because of the illicit status of these drugs and not from their pharmacology. Whether this would continue to be true under a different regulatory situation no one knows. Reasoning from the basis of historical precedents and from psychological and social attitudes as well as pharmacology, I believe that the use of drugs such as alcohol, marihuana, and heroin might well be regulated differently. But in each case we should not assume, as we now assume automatically, that the regulations will not be socially, psychologically, and clinically costly.

The research on controlled use of illicit drugs has one basic policy implication. If, as this work suggests, the problem is not the simple use of these drugs but rather how they are used—when, with whom, under what conditions, and how much—then a formal social policy is needed that separates use from misuse (40). It is obvious that misuse, like pregnancy, is avoided under conditions of total abstinence, but with both drugs and sex it is doubtful whether total continence is possible. As it now stands, in the case of illicit drugs anyone who is not abstinent is considered a criminal and a social deviant.

Under these conditions it is extremely difficult to develop viable social sanctions and rituals that will prevent the dysfunctional consequences of use. Even when such controls are developed by small social groups, it is not easy for knowledge about them to be transmitted through social learning.

The framers of current formal social policy, by attempting to restrict drug supplies and punish any use, hope to reduce the number of users, arguing that if there are fewer users there will automatically be fewer cases of dysfunctional use (28). This argument implies a straight-line arithmetical relationship between use and misuse. If there are 1,000 users, for example, and 10 per cent of them get into trouble, there will be 100 cases of misuse; with 10,000 users there will be 1,000 cases of misuse, and so on. To pursue this type of argument and policy in relation to alcohol use leads to the highly debatable decision to raise prices in order to discourage use.

But what if current social policy is discouraging only those who use drugs moderately? Certainly regular users, to whom the substance is more vital, would be less easily discouraged. Then, inasmuch as the socially derived sanctions and rituals that help maintain control are developed and embodied most definitively by moderate, occasional users, the conditions conducive to controlled use would gradually give way to conditions conducive to dysfunctional use. Thus, the formal social policy whose goal it is to minimize the number of dysfunctional users may actually be making more and more users dysfunctional.

By following the same simplistic mathematical argument, advocates of current social policy claim that preventing any use is crucial because of the high percentage of users who are indeed misusing. This circular reasoning leads to the view that what is needed is not a reassessment of policy but more of the same policy, that is, better law enforcement and stricter penalties on trafficking and using. My research on controlled use suggests that greater attention should be paid to conditions of use than to the prevention of use. What are the conditions under which dysfunctional use occurs, and how can these be modified? Conversely, what conditions maintain control in the nonmisusers, and how can they be promulgated?

Firm advocates of current policy fear that

use will increase if attention is shifted from the fact of use to the conditions of use. That is an understandable fear if one gives credence to the circular argument. But if that argument is challenged, then, on the basis of my research and the theory underlying it, what is needed is a reassessment of current social policy, with a new focus on preventing the dysfunctional problems of use rather than use itself. This new focus does not mean that all substances should be treated alike. Careful studies of the use of different substances and of the varying conditions of use may well result in a call for different policy strategies. Clearly, this question cannot be settled until drug use is separated from misuse. By means of competent psychosocial research the myths inherent in the emotionally laden subject of illicit drug use must be exposed, the realities of such use brought to light, and a theoretical framework constructed through which the research results may be understood and perhaps even employed to prevent or treat addiction.

References

1. Abt Associates. *Drug Use in the State of Ohio: A Study Based upon the Ohio Drug Survey.* Cambridge, Mass., Abt Associates, 1975.
2. Ade, G. *The Old Time Saloon: Not Wet-Not Dry, Just History.* Detroit: Gale Research Corporation, 1931.
3. *Avatar,* August 1968, p. 3.
4. Bacon, S. Introduction. In *American Drinking Practices: A National Survey of Behavior and Attitudes,* D. Cahalan, I. H. Cisin, and H. M. Crossley, editors. Rutgers Center for Alcohol Studies, No. 6. New Brunswick, N. J., Rutgers University, 1969.
5. Barr, H. L., Langs, R. J., Holt, R. R., Goldberger, L., and Klein, G. S. *LSD: Personality and Experience.* New York, Wiley-Interscience, 1972.
6. Bazelon, D. L. Risk and regulation. Science 205:277, 1979.
7. Becker, H. S. History, culture, and subjective experience: An exploration of the social bases of drug-induced experiences. J. Health Soc. Behav. 8:163, 1967.
8. Boris, H. N., Zinberg, N. E., and Boris, M. Social education for adolescents. Psychiatr. Opin. 15:32, 1978.
9. Bourne, P. G., Hunt, L. G., and Vogt, J. *A Study of Heroin Use in the State of Wyoming.* Report Prepared for Department of Health and Social Services, State of Wyoming. Washington, D.C., Foundation for International Resources, 1975.
10. Cohen, M. M., Marinello, M., and Bach, N. Chromosomal damage in human leukocytes induced by lysergic acid diethylamide. Science 155:1417, 1967.
11. Edwards, G. Drugs, drug dependence and the concept of plasticity, Q. J. Studies Alcohol 35:176, 1974.
12. Harding, W. M., and Zinberg, N. E. The effectiveness of the subculture in developing rituals and social sanctions for controlled drug use. In *Drugs, Rituals, and Altered States of Consciousness,* B. du Toit, editor. Rotterdam, Netherlands, A. A. Balkema, 1977.
13. Harding, W. M., Zinberg, N. E., Stelmack, S. M., and Barry, M. D. Formerly-addicted-now-controlled heroin users. Int. J. Addictions 15:47, 1980.
14. Herman, C. P., and Kozlowski, L. T. Indulgence, excess, and restraint: Perspectives on consummatory behavior in everyday life. J. Drug Issues 9:185, 1979.
15. Hunt, L. G., and Chambers, C. D. *The Heroin Epidemics: A Study of Heroin Use in the United States, 1965–1975.* New York, Spectrum, 1976.
16. Huxley, A. *The Doors of Perception.* New York, Harper and Row, 1954.
17. Jacobson, R., and Zinberg, N. E. *The Social Basis of Drug Abuse Prevention.* Drug Abuse Council Publication #SS-5. Washington, D.C., The Drug Abuse Council, 1975.
18. Josephson, E. Trends in adolescent marihuana use. In *Drug Use: Epidemiological and Sociological Approaches,* E. Josephson and E. E. Carroll, editors. Washington, D.C., Hemisphere Publishing Corporation, 1974.
19. Kaplan, J. *Marijuana: The New Prohibition.* New York, World Publishing Company, 1970.
20. Khantzian, E. J. The ego, the self and opiate addiction: Theoretical and treatment considerations. Int. Rev. Psychoanal. 5:189, 1978.
21. Khantzian, E. J., Harb, J., and Schatzberg, A. F. Heroin use as an attempt to cope. Am. J. Psychiatry 131:160, 1974.
22. Krystal, H., and Raskin, H. A. *Drug Dependence: Aspects of Ego Function.* Detroit, Wayne State University Press, 1970.
23. Maloff, D., Becker, H. S., Fonaroff, A., and Rodin, J. Informal social controls and their influence on substance use. J. Drug Issues 9:161, 1979.
24. McAuliffe, W. E., and Gordon, R. A. A test of Lindesmith's theory of addiction: The frequency of euphoria among long-term addicts. Am. J. Sociol. 79:795, 1975.
25. McGlothlin, W. H., and Arnold, D. O. LSD revisited: A ten-year followup of medical LSD use. Arch. Gen. Psychiatry 24:35, 1971.
26. Milkman, H., and Frosch, W. A. The drug of choice. J. Psychedelic Drugs 9:11, 1977.
27. Mogar, R. E., and Savage, C. Personality change associated with psychedelic (LSD) therapy: A preliminary report. Psychother. Theory Res. Pract. 1:154, 1954.
28. Moore, M. H. Limiting supplies of drugs to illicit markets. J. Drug Issues 9:291, 1979.
29. National Commission on Marihuana and Drug Abuse. *Drug Use in America: Problem in Perspective.* Washington, D.C., United States Government Printing Office, 1973.
30. National Institute on Drug Abuse. *Marihuana and Health: Sixth Annual Report to the United States Congress from the Secretary of Health, Education, and Welfare.* Washington, D.C., United States Government Printing Office, 1976.
31. National Institute on Drug Abuse. *Cocaine-1977.* Research Monograph #13. Washington, D.C., United States Government Printing Office, 1977.
32. National Institute on Drug Abuse. *The Epidemiology of Heroin and Other Narcotics.* Research Monograph #16. Washington, D.C., United States Gov-

ernment Printing Office, 1977.

33. National Institute on Drug Abuse. *Drug Use in Industry.* Washington, D.C., United States Government Printing Office, 1978.

34. Newmeyer, J., and Johnson, G. Drug emergencies in crowds: An analysis of "rock medicine," 1973–1977. J. Drug Issues 9:235, 1979.

35. *New York Times*, February 4, 1974. Interview with G. G. Nahas.

36. *New York Times*, April 9, 1974. Interview with R. C. Kolodny.

37. *New York Times*, June 23, 1979.

38. O'Brien, C. Personal communication, 1978.

39. Petersen, R. C., and Stillman, R. C., editors. *Phencyclidine (PCP) Abuse: An Appraisal.* National Institute on Drug Abuse, Research Monograph #21. Washington, D.C., United States Government Printing Office, 1978.

40. President's Commission on Mental Health. Report of the liaison task panel on psychoactive drug use/misuse. In *Volume IV, Appendix: Task Panel Reports Submitted to The President's Commission on Mental Health.* Washington, D.C., United States Government Printing Office, 1978.

41. Robbins, E. S., Frosch, W. A., and Stern, M. Further observations on untoward reactions to LSD. Am. J. Psychiatry 124:393, 1967.

42. Robins, L. N., and Helzer, J. E. Drug use among Vietnam veterans: Three years later. Med. World News October 27, 1975.

43. Robins, L. N., Helzer, J. E., and Davis, D. H. Narcotic use in Southeast Asia and afterwards. Arch. Gen. Psychiatry 32:955, 1975.

44. Robins, L. N., Helzer, J. E., Hesselbrock, M., and Wish, E. D. Vietnam veterans three years after Vietnam: How our study changed our view of heroin. In *Problems of Drug Dependence.* L. Harris, editor. Proceedings of the Committee on Problems of Drug Dependence. Richmond, Va., Committee on Problems of Drug Dependence, 1977.

45. Smith, D. E. Personal communication, 1975.

46. Smith, D. E., and Gay, G. R., editors. *It's So Good, Don't Even Try It Once: Heroin in Perspective.* Englewood Cliffs, N. J., Prentice-Hall, 1972.

47. Stickgold, A. The metamorphosis of PCP. Grassroots (October Supplement), 1, 1977.

48. Waelder, R. The principle of multiple function (1930). Psychoanal. Q. 5:45, 1936.

49. Waldorf, D., and Biernacki, P. Natural recovery from heroin addiction: A review of the incidence literature. J. Drug Issues 9:281, 1979.

50. Weil, A. T. *The Natural Mind.* Boston, Houghton Mifflin, 1972.

51. Weil, A. T., Zinberg, N. E., and Nelsen, J. Clinical and psychological effects of marihuana in man. Science 162:1234, 1969.

52. Wurmser, L. Psychoanalytic considerations of the etiology of compulsive drug use. J. Am. Psychoanal. Assoc. 22:820, 1974.

53. Zinberg, N. E. GI's and OJ's in Vietnam. *The New York Times Magazine Section*, December 5, 1971.

54. Zinberg, N. E. Heroin use in Vietnam and the United States: A contrast and a critique. Arch. Gen. Psychiatry 26:486, 1972.

55. Zinberg, N. E., principal investigator. *Controlled Nonmedical Drug Use.* Grant received from Drug Abuse Council, Washington, D.C., 1973–1976.

56. Zinberg, N. E. *"High" States: A Beginning Study.* Drug Abuse Council Publication #SS-3. Washington, D.C., Drug Abuse Council, 1974.

57. Zinberg, N. E. The search for rational approaches to heroin use. In *Addiction: A Comprehensive Treatise*, P. G. Bourne, editor. New York, Academic Press, 1974.

58. Zinberg, N. E. Addiction and ego function. Psychoanal. Study Child 30:567, 1975.

59. Zinberg, N. E., principal investigator. *Processes of Control among Different Heroin-Using Styles*, National Institute on Drug Abuse Grant #1-R01-DA-01360-01A1-A3, 1976–1980.

60. Zinberg, N. E., and DeLong, J. V. Research and the drug issue. Contemp. Drug Probl. 3:71, 1974.

61. Zinberg, N. E., and Fraser, K. M. The role of the social setting in the prevention and treatment of alcoholism. In *The Diagnosis and Treatment of Alcoholism*, J. H. Mendelson and N. K. Mello, editors. New York, McGraw-Hill, 1979.

62. Zinberg, N. E., and Harding, W. M., editors. Control over intoxicant use: Pharmacological, psychological and social considerations. J. Drug Issues 9:121, 1979.

63. Zinberg, N. E., and Harding, W. M. Introduction, control and intoxicant use: A theoretical and practical overview. J. Drug Issues 9:121, 1979.

64. Zinberg, N. E., Harding, W. M., Stelmack, S. M., and Marblestone, R. A. Patterns of heroin use. Ann. N. Y. Acad. Sci. 311:10, 1978.

65. Zinberg, N. E., Harding, W. M., and Winkeller, M. A study of social regulatory mechanisms in controlled illicit drug users. J. Drug Issues 7:117, 1977.

66. Zinberg, N. E., Jacobson, R. C., and Harding, W. M. Social sanctions and rituals as a basis for drug abuse prevention. Am. J. Drug Alcohol Abuse 2:165, 1975.

67. Zinberg, N. E., and Robertson, J. A. *Drugs and the Public.* New York, Simon and Schuster, 1972.

CHAPTER 10

A SYSTEM DYNAMIC VIEW OF SUBSTANCE ABUSE[1]

Gilbert Levin, Ph.D.

Edward B. Roberts, Ph.D.

Gary B. Hirsch, M.S.

Substance abuse has been anything but a static problem over the last 20 years. Many communities have been forced suddenly to confront growing rates of substance abuse by their young people. Often communities were taken by surprise and typically responded initially with the most readily available resource, police and legal sanctions. After a painful learning process, some communities expanded their response, combining preventive and rehabilitative components with law enforcement activities. In most cases, this multimodal approach seems to lead to somewhat better results. A failure to understand the dynamic nature of substance abuse problems and the factors responsible for their often rapid development has stood in the way of communities mounting an effective response in a timely manner.

This chapter presents a system dynamics model of substance abuse that provides a framework for understanding how communities develop and cope with substance abuse problems and why some approaches to coping are more effective than others. The chapter first presents a diagrammatic model that arrays the many variables and causal relationships needed to explain substance abuse patterns that develop in particular communities. The model is generic in nature and covers a wide range of different substances and communities. The remainder of the chapter is devoted to demonstrating how the diagrammatic model can be computerized and used to explore alternative policies for dealing with a specific substance abuse problem in a particular community. The application that is described is a heroin model developed by the authors to evaluate alternative strategies for a community in New York City during the early 1970's.

This chapter brings to substance abuse the outlook and methods of computer-based systems analysis, and in particular the system dynamics perspective. The development of

---

[1] This chapter draws upon the authors' previous work reported in Levin, G., Roberts, E. B., and Hirsch, G. B. *The Persistent Poppy: A Computer-Aided Search for Heroin Policy.* Cambridge, Mass., Ballinger, 1975. Portions of that work are reproduced in this chapter.

this philosophy and associated methodology has been progressing at the Massachusetts Institute of Technology under Jay W. Forrester and his colleagues since 1957. System dynamics was created as an integration of: (a) developments in computer technology and simulation; (b) new recognitions about decision-making processes; and (c) insights gained from the application of feedback-control principles to complex systems. The initial 10 years of work in this field emphasized the dynamic behavior of industrial systems, whereas the period since then has seen a shift primarily to the problems of complex social and economic systems.

The system dynamics approach begins with an effort to understand the system of forces that has created a problem and continues to sustain it. Relevant data are gathered from a variety of sources, including literature, informed persons (experts, practitioners, victims, perpetrators), and specific quantitative studies. As soon as a rudimentary measure of understanding has been achieved, a formal model is developed. This model is initially in the format of a set of logical diagrams showing cause and effect relationships. As soon as feasible, the visual model is translated into a mathematical version. The model is exposed to criticism, revised, exposed again, and so on in an iterative process that continues as long as it proves to be useful. Just as the model is improved as a result of successive exposures to critics, a successively better understanding of the problem is achieved by the people who participate in the process. Their intuition about the probable consequences of proposed policies frequently proves to be less reliable than the model's meticulous mathematical approach.

This is not as surprising as it may first seem. Socioeconomic systems contain as many as 100 or more variables that are known to be relevant and believed to be related to one another in various nonlinear fashions. The behavior of such a system is complex far beyond the capacity of intuition. Computer simulation is one of the most effective means available for supplementing and correcting human intuition.

A computer simulation model of the kind described here is a powerful conceptual device that can increase the role of reason at the expense of rhetoric in the determination of policy. A model is not, as is sometimes supposed, a perfectly accurate representation of reality that can be trusted to make better decisions than people. It is a flexible tool that forces the people who use it to think harder and to confront one another, their common problems, and themselves directly and factually.

A computer model differs principally in complexity, precision, and explicitness from the informal subjective explanation or "mental model" that people ordinarily construct to guide their actions toward a goal. It is an account of the total set of forces that are believed to have caused and to sustain some problematic state of affairs. Like the informal mental model, it is derived from a variety of data sources including facts, theories, and educated guesses. Unlike the mental model, it is comprehensive, unambiguous, flexible, and subject to rigorous logical manipulation and testing.

The flexibility of a model is its least understood virtue. If you and I disagree about some aspect of the causal structure of a problem, we can usually in a matter of minutes run the model twice and observe its behavior under each set of assumptions. I may, on the basis of its behavior, be forced to admit that you were correct. Very often, however, we will both discover that our argument was trifling, because the phenomenon of interest to us may be unchanged by a change in assumptions.

A computer model constructed and used by a policy-making group has the following advantages:

1. It requires policy makers to improve and complete fully the rough mental sketch of the causes of the problem that they inevitably have in their heads.

2. In the process of formal model building, the builders discover and resolve self-contradictions and ambiguities among their implicit assumptions about the problem.

3. Once the model is running, even in a rudimentary fashion, logical "bootstrapping" becomes possible. The consequences of promising but tentative formulations are tested in the model. Observation of model behavior gives rise to new hypotheses about structure.

4. Once an acceptable standard of validity has been achieved, formal policy experiments reveal quickly the probable outcomes of many policy alternatives; novel policies may be discovered.

5. An operating model is always complete,

although in a sense never completed. Unlike many planning aids, which tend to be episodic and terminal (they provide assistance only at the moment the "report" is presented, not before or after), a model is organic and iterative. At any moment, the model contains in readily accessed form the present best understanding of the problem.

6. Sensitivity analysis of the model reveals the areas in which genuine debate (rather than caviling) is needed and guides empirical investigation to important questions. If the true values of many parameters are unknown (which is generally the case in social planning), the ones that most affect model behavior need to be investigated first.

7. An operating model can be used to communicate with people who were not involved in building the model. By experimenting with changes in policies and model parameters and observing the effects of these changes on behavior, these people can be helped better to understand the dynamic forces at work in the real-world system.

THE SUBSTANCE ABUSE SYSTEM

This section presents a system dynamics model of substance abuse. The variables contained in the model will vary in importance for different substances of abuse. Fear of arrest, for example, may serve as a deterrent to the use of such illicit substances as heroin but have no effect in deterring people from using alcohol, tobacco, and other legal substances. The model is intended to be as general as possible in order to apply to the broadest range of substances of abuse and thereby provide a common framework within which substance abuse problems relating to different substances can be analyzed and contrasted with each other.

Figure 10.1 shows the stages through which people can move in developing and coping with substance abuse problems and the paths through which they may move among those stages. Numbers of people at each stage in the substance abuse process determine both the number of people available to move into the next stage in the process during future time periods as well as the impact of a substance abuse problem on the community (e.g., crimes committed by habitual users). Rates of movement of people among these statuses or stages determine how rapidly a substance abuse problem will develop in a

community, how readily it can be brought under control, the level at which its prevalence in a community will stabilize, and what impact the problem will have on the community over time.

Those least involved in the abuse of a given substance are nonusers, the group shown on the extreme *left-hand side* of Figure 10.1. Nonusers may include almost all residents of the community in the case of heroin in a middle-class community or a much smaller fraction as in the case of alcohol and other legal substances. Nonusers may remain nonusers indefinitely or may become occasional users at some point. Even if they do not become occasional users, nonusers are very much a "part of the problem" through their participation in the community's response to the abuse of a particular substance.

Occasional users use particular substances at varying frequencies. Unlike habitual users, they are presumed to be able to stop or significantly reduce their usage when they wish without difficulty. They are assumed to suffer no impairment as a result of their use and are able to carry out daily work, social, and family activities without impediment. Although their usage may have some adverse impact on the community (e.g., automobile accidents caused by occasional users of alcohol while intoxicated), the problems they cause are generally less severe than those caused by habitual users.

Habitual users, as the name implies, are assumed to be dependent upon a particular substance and unable to stop voluntarily or reduce their intake without a therapeutic intervention or externally imposed elimination of the substance. Some habitual users (e.g., cigarette smokers) may carry out their daily activities with few limitations, whereas others, such as chronic alcoholics and heroin addicts, may be substantially impaired. Habitual users in the community typically represent the most visible component of a substance abuse problem and are responsible for the largest fraction of society's costs in dealing with the problem.

Habitual users may be subjected to incarceration or lesser limitation in their freedom (e.g., suspension of their driver's licences) as a result of being apprehended in possession of or selling an illicit substance, committing a crime to raise funds to buy an illicit substance, or committing a crime while or simply being under the influence of a particular

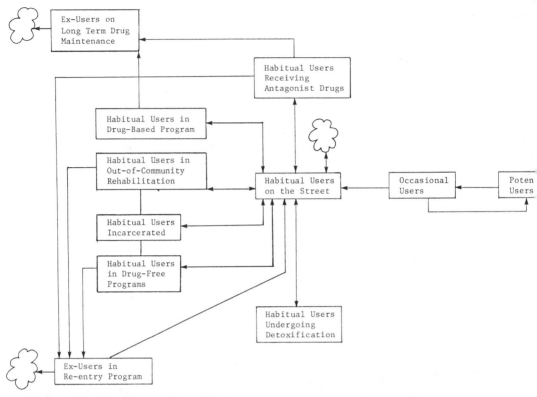

Figure 10.1. Total person flow. (Reprinted with permission from Levin, G., Roberts, E. B., and Hirsch, G. B. *The Persistent Poppy.* Copyright 1975, Ballinger Publishing Company.)

substance. In many states, being under the influence or in possession of certain substances has been "decriminalized," and incarceration, when it occurs, is deemed to serve a protective rather than punitive purpose. In a number of these states, compulsory treatment has replaced physical incarceration altogether for users of certain substances. Incarceration or other limitation in freedom generally constrains the impact a substance abuser can have on the community but, in itself, generally has little effect in stopping a pattern of abuse. Fear of arrest and the resultant incarceration or other criminal sanctions may help to dissuade occasional users from using a drug in certain situations (e.g., getting too drunk at a party to drive home safely, smoking marihuana in a public place where apprehension is more likely) but is unlikely to alter the behavior of a habitual user.

One can move from being a habitual user in the community or a habitual or occasional user who has been arrested into any one of a number of different rehabilitation pro-

grams. The intent of some of these "rehabilitation" programs, detoxification for example, is not a permanent alteration in behavior. Instead, it may involve keeping people under the influence of a drug from harming themselves or others or helping a person temporarily reduce consumption of a substance (e.g., heroin) in order to make the habit more manageable. This will also help to reduce such adverse impacts on the community as crime. Other programs involve institutional treatment outside of the community. These programs benefit by removing habitual users from the environment in which their pattern of abuse developed but incur the costs of treatment failure when clients are suddenly thrust back into that environment without adequate support.

Different forms of rehabilitation may be available in the community. These include "drug-free" programs in which there is total abstinence from the substance of abuse together with behavior modification attempted through some form of group therapy. Drug-free programs may be residential or involve participation for varying amounts of time during a week by people living at home. Other programs may involve the administration of substitute drugs such as methadone or of the substance of abuse itself (e.g., heroin) under controlled circumstances. Still another type of program may involve the administration of antagonists such as naloxone (Narcan) or disulfiram (Antabuse) that discourage former users from reverting to patterns of abuse. All of these programs may be employed in combination or in sequence with each other.

The effectiveness of any program or combination of programs will depend on such factors as the appropriateness of the program(s) for particular individuals; e.g., drug-free programs may be more effective with younger addicts, whereas methadone can work better with older addicts. Another determinant of effectiveness is the presence of support services such as job training that help to create viable alternatives for the ex-abuser. Those who fail to complete rehabilitation programs generally return to the habitual user group in the community, although their pattern of abuse may be somewhat altered (e.g., the cigarette smoker who cuts down although not being able to stop completely). Those who succeed go through a period of reentry during which they may be especially vulnerable to resuming their pattern of abuse. Success at reentry depends on the extent to which rehabilitation was able to deal with the behavioral problems underlying the original pattern of abuse and provide attractive alternatives such as satisfying employment and social activities. Those who successfully reenter go back to being members of the nonuser group. Graduates of certain types of programs may have to maintain their participation over extended time periods (e.g., continue to receive methadone) even though they have reentered the mainstream in terms of their employment and family and social ties.

Figure 10.2 indicates some of the causal forces responsible for the rate at which nonusers in a community become occasional users. Drug-associated cultures, manifested principally in social activities that revolve around consumption of a particular drug, are a major component of the appeal of drugs that contribute to higher use rates. Certain forms of music, styles of dress, and other cultural trappings add to this appeal. Poverty and ethnic status are factors in determining the appeal of drugs, because they often affect whether there are nondrug-oriented social and cultural alternatives to drug use. Peer pressures embodied in the cultural appeal of drug use would seem to hold true across a wide range of substances, from tobacco and alcohol to casual experimentation with heroin, and from the richest to poorest communities.

Factors that act as deterrents, on the other hand, vary greatly in strength depending upon substance and community characteristics. Fear of arrest is obviously dependent on whether consumption of a given substance is legal or illegal and the vigor of enforcement against certain categories of use (e.g., by minors, driving while intoxicated). Restricted substance availability can serve as a deterrent as well, especially if it is achieved through vigorous police activity. This applies as readily to drug availability as to access to alcohol or tobacco by those under the local legal age to purchase these substances. Dissuasive education can serve as a deterrent if it is credibly delivered. Its effectiveness, however, is also dependent on the prevalence of a particular substance's use in the community and the apparent consequences of its use. It is easier to dissuade middle-class youths from using heroin than from using the alcohol and cigarettes their parents are very likely using. In a lower income community in which the use of heroin and other "hard" drugs is prevalent, it is difficult to deliver any sort of credible drug education program. The number of people who become occasional users affects the supply of particular drugs and the strength of drug-associated culture, especially in the case of illicit drugs.

A similar set of factors, shown in Figure 10.3, affects the rate of movement from occasional to habitual use. The number of occasional users is one determinant of that rate, because occasional users form the "pool" from which habitual users are drawn. This is definitely not to say that occasional use must inexorably lead to habitual use (that "pot smokers become heroin addicts"), but rather that it is unlikely one will become a habitual user without first going through a period of occasional use. Psychopathology may be a factor in the development of habitual abuse. Drug-associated culture may also contribute to the appeal of habitual use in that it gives

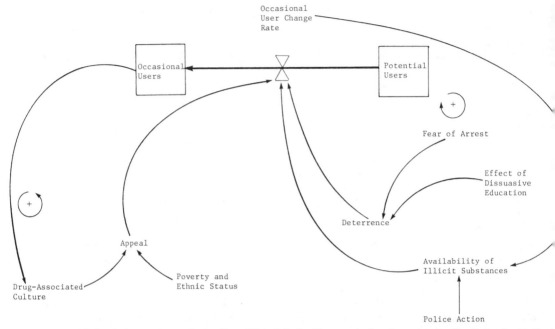

Figure 10.2. Substance use induction. (Reprinted with permission from Levin, G., Roberts, E. B., and Hirsch, G. B. *The Persistent Poppy*. Copyright 1975, Ballinger Publishing Company.)

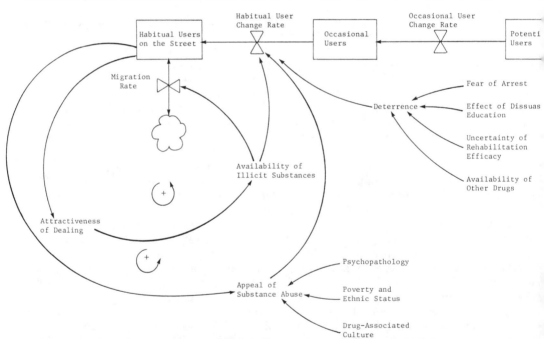

Figure 10.3. Habitual use. (Reprinted with permission from Levin, G., Roberts, E. B., and Hirsch, G. B. *The Persistent Poppy*. Copyright 1975, Ballinger Publishing Company.)

the impression of a particular life style with which to identify. Poverty and ethnic status are likely to be factors through their effect on the presence of positive alternatives. The number of habitual users itself will affect the rate at which new ones develop, both in terms of the extent to which habitual use seems to be "OK" and the likelihood that an occasional user will be induced by habitual users to join their ranks. In the case of illicit drugs, the number of habitual users will also affect the availability of a given drug and, through availability, its price. Growth in the number of habitual users will, all other things held equal, result in further growth over time.

The deterrents to habitual use are also many of the same ones that play a part in discouraging occasional use. Availability of "other" drugs may serve as a deterrent to drugs more likely to be used habitually. (For example, having marihuana readily available may provide an alternative to heroin use.) Another possible deterrent is uncertainty of rehabilitation efficacy, a factor that reflects the perceived difficulty of being rehabilitated once one becomes a habitual user. Paradoxically, the publicity given to rehabilitation successes may undermine the effectiveness of this deterrent. The director of a service program or partisan of a particular treatment method decreases the benefits of the favored program or method in the very act of advocating it.

The balance of these appeals and deterrents will determine and also change with the patterns of abuse of various substances in a community. If the use of a certain substance, for example, reaches some "threshold" level, those using the substance who might have been regarded as deviants or pariahs before may now be seen as conforming faithfully to the vows of this reference group. The balance of appeals and deterrents would then shift as prevalence of use and drug-associated culture overwhelm effects of fear of arrest and dissuasive education. Occasional use and later habitual use would grow rapidly in prevalence for a while and eventually stabilize at some level that is characteristic of both the community and the substance. This steady-state level is likely to be lower for drugs that are more clearly illicit and/or have more harmful side effects and lower for communities with higher socioeconomic levels. Price-prestigious abuse such as cocaine use may, in contrast, be higher in high socioeconomic level communities.

A community's initial response to a substance abuse problem is likely to focus on its law enforcement agencies. Figure 10.4 displays some of the mechanisms of this response. The community may respond to simply the prevalence of use of a given substance, a crime rate associated with that substance (e.g., drunk driving arrests, burglaries

committed by addicts), evidence of trafficking in the substance, or some combination of these facets of the problem. As alarm at the problem grows, a more vigorous police response is brought to bear on users and suppliers. The result is that some people are arrested and incarcerated, fear of arrest becomes a more formidable deterrent, and the supply of the substance is less than it would have been. Rarely, if ever, is this short term police-oriented response able to solve a substance abuse problem by itself.

More fundamental changes in community attitude are usually required before the problem can be dealt with effectively. Figure 10.5 shows several factors that have a role in changing the community's definition of a problem from one that focuses largely on the criminal aspects of substance abuse to one that stresses the medical and social aspects. Without this change, it is difficult for the various rehabilitation programs to gain the support they need in the community and for ex-abusers to gain the acceptance they need to successfully reenter the mainstream. Prevalence of substance abuse is a direct contributor to change in the community's view of a substance abuse problem. Prevalence also contributes indirectly through its effect on the likelihood that each person in the community will know someone who is a habitual user or who has been arrested for a crime related to substance abuse. Persistence of the problem and its criminal manifestations in the presence of a strong police response will lead to a frustration with a police-dominated approach and a search for better balanced approaches that include important medical and social components. Community education programs can also purposefully affect the rate at which a shift in the community's definition of the problem takes place.

Changes in community attitude followed by successful implementation of various rehabilitation programs may not "solve" the problem in terms of eliminating it completely but will generally cause the problem to stabilize at a level the community finds tolerable. The change in attitudes may also produce an environment conducive to mounting credible education programs that are balanced in their approach, do not resort to scare tactics, and are, therefore, more effective in deterring some fraction of the substance abuse that would otherwise take place.

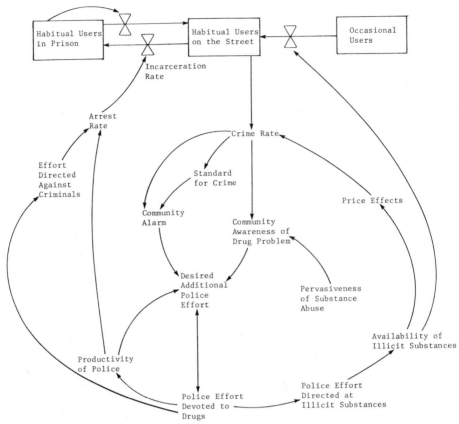

Figure 10.4. Police response. (Reprinted with permission from Levin, G., Roberts, E. B., and Hirsch, G. B. *The Persistent Poppy.* Copyright 1975, Ballinger Publishing Company.)

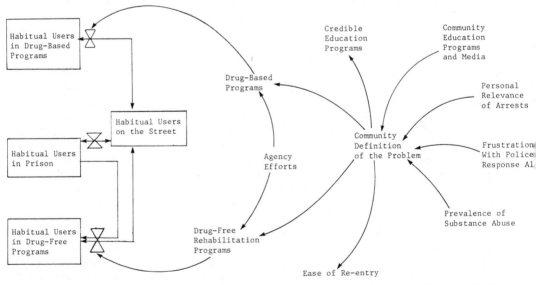

Figure 10.5. Community attitude. (Reprinted with permission from Levin, G., Roberts, E. B., and Hirsch, G. B. *The Persistent Poppy.* Copyright 1975, Ballinger Publishing Company.)

The next section describes how this framework was used to evaluate policies for controlling the heroin problem in a specific community.

POLICY ANALYSIS WITH A COMPUTER MODEL OF HEROIN ABUSE

The focus of the work being described was on the dynamics of growth of heroin addiction in an urban community, its consequences, and the attempts to cope with it. The investigatory field work that accompanied the analysis of the problem drew substantially from consideration of a specific ethnically and economically heterogeneous geographic region in New York City, an area of 8 square miles with a population of 180,000 persons. But the data were extended to include considerations of experiences with drug addiction in a wider array of urban and suburban environments. Confidence in the generation of the analysis was gained from careful study of the research literature, interviews, and consultation with numerous social scientists and medical and enforcement experts, and widespread public presentations of the analytical framework and tentative conclusions.

The authors' thinking was dominated by active work in a mixed income, but mostly blue-collar/middle-class, neighborhood undergoing transition. Lower income blacks and Puerto Ricans at that time constituted 20 to 30 per cent of the local population of the area, with this percentage steadily increasing. But we believe that what we have found about the underlying processes of heroin addiction applies to all large cities in the United States, nearly all medium-sized cities, and many smaller communities as well, excluding only the extremes of exceptional wealth or exceptional poverty.

The model deviates from the generic model presented in the previous section to better represent some of the unique characteristics of heroin abuse. The occasional user category, for example, contains all users of "soft" drugs in addition to occasional users of heroin, inasmuch as it is the combination of these two groups from which new addicts are drawn. The model also contains a more elaborate market sector and price mechanism than would be necessary for representing legal substances of abuse. The heroin model includes a set of equations that calculates burglary rates based on assumptions about the number of crimes per month required to maintain the average habit. Special considerations regarding treatment programs, such as the effect of "leakage" from methadone and hypothesized heroin maintenance programs in augmenting street heroin supplies, are also included.

The computer model developed in this setting was used to project the consequences of many different policy and programmatic options. The relative impacts of the different options were gauged by comparing their projected outcomes with the outcomes of other options and with a "baseline" scenario generated by the model. The baseline case assumed only that police budgets would rise in response to increases in crime rates in the simulated community. This baseline provided a neutral backdrop against which various other programmatic intervention could be evaluated. Figure 10.6 displays the results of this baseline, police-only simulation.

The simulation begins in 1965 with an initial addict group of 150 in a community with a population of 180,000, including a youth population of 51,000. As the run begins, the number of addicts on the street (the letter A in the graphic output) is rising at a steady rate. The number of total addicts on the street and in jail (T on the graph) is at about the same level as addicts on the street (A), because police effort is not yet great enough to arrest many addicts. The system structures of greatest importance during the first 100 months are the positive feedback loops that create the growth of addicts and the increasing availability of heroin. During this period, the community definition of the problem (plotted as U) stays near its initial assumption that addiction is a solely criminal problem. Police have not yet responded sufficiently to produce frustration with that viewpoint. Nor have enough addicts been arrested who are personally known to a large segment of the community. The relatively low crime incidence (represented as C in the figure) reflects the small addict population and the moderate socioeconomic level of the area. Total monthly program costs ($\$$ on the graph) remain low due to the small initial

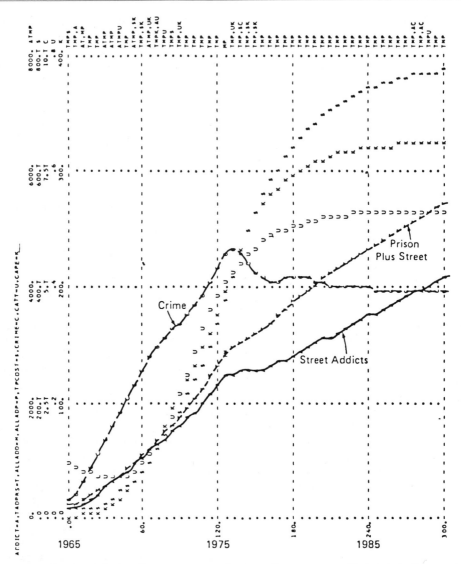

Figure 10.6. Heroin addiction: Base case—moderate police response. (Reprinted with permission from Levin, G., Roberts, E. B., and Hirsch, G. B. *The Persistent Poppy.* Copyright 1975, Ballinger Publishing Company.)

number of police, the only program element operating during this simulation run.

But, as the addict population continues to grow, crime grows with it. The size of the police force recruited due to the addiction situation grows, too, as crime escalates and as the community becomes increasingly aware of and concerned with the addict-criminal problem. Note that these police are not the "narcotics squad" alone; usually relatively few of the police brought on by the community due to the drug problem are allocated exclusively to going after either drug supply, or pushers, or even after addicts for

possession of drugs. Most of the new police are deployed to combat the increased robbery, breaking and entering, and other similar crimes—the crimes typically committed · by addict-criminals.

The increasing pervasiveness of addicts in the community leads to a heightened tendency to attribute the community's crimes to addicts. More police are allocated, increasingly pressured by the community to attempt to arrest addict-criminals. The rapid growth of police and their increasingly heavy arrest activity gradually produce some convictions. An addict prisoner population begins to build, drawing some addicts from the street. Not only does this tend to slacken the growth rate of street addict-criminals, but it also slightly slackens street demand for heroin, thereby easing price pressures on heroin. Fewer addicts and relaxed prices contribute to a turnaround in the growth of addict crime, leading to a period of decline of several years' duration.

But the lower price and the large addict population serve to encourage further entries into the addict pool. The increased police force is less effective relatively, increasing the number of arrests but not sufficiently to keep the street addict population from continuing steady growth. By directing attention more at addicts than at drug supply, the police action does lead to lower heroin prices. Thus, the higher number of addicts only maintains but does not further increase the crime rate.

The increased arrest rate brings more addicts to prison, thereby only transferring a growing part of the addiction problem to jail (as reflected in the T curve). The large and growing police force and prison population lead to rapidly rising total program costs. They also produce a reaction in community attitude, generated by the growing frustration with the results of the police efforts and the increasing number of arrests perceived as relevant by the community.

Addicts on the street and total addicts both continue to grow near the end of the 25-year computer-generated future. This marks the ultimate inability of police effort alone to solve the problem. Here, the positive feedback loops producing the growth of the problem have gained dominance and overpower even strong police effort. Crime increases with the number of addicts, and the community problem definition shifts more toward a sociomedical view as the residents become more frustrated with the failure of police effort. Program costs continue to rise as more police are hired and more addicts are imprisoned. In all, the narcotics problem has gotten out of control.

By 1990, the end of 25 years, the number of addicts on the street has reached 4,160 with an additional 1,280 in prison, and the total is still climbing. The crime rate persists at 4,900 incidents per month. Program costs are running at $780,000 per month, of which more than 60 per cent supports the direct and overhead costs of 325 policemen, the other 40 per cent supporting the addict-prisoners.

This computer projection is the "base" case against which most alternative simulations were evaluated. It represents a probably minimum reaction that can be expected from a community that encounters a growing incidence of addiction and its consequences.

We first explore the possibility that a community may elect to make a greater investment in police effort than was assumed in the "base" case. Some communities can be expected to follow this course, which is, after all, only a logical extension of the basic strategy of attempting to force the problem out of existence. To examine the implications of a more vigorous police approach, a future was generated based on a police effort twice as great for any given degree of provocation as that which the base case would have provided.

This approach leads to a community history that starts in the same manner as the base case.[2] But, as the community begins to see a need for a punitive response to its increasing addiction-crime problem, it acts more forcefully. As a result, police more actively attack the street addict population, attaining a higher arrest frequency at all levels of street population. The added police harassment makes drug selling less attractive, somewhat lessening the drug supply, thereby leading to higher heroin prices and less easy entry of new prospects into addiction.

By the end of 25 years, the street addict population is 2,720, apparently saturating at about that figure. But this 35 per cent reduction (from the base run's end point) in street addicts is not matched by comparable reduction in other aspects of the problem. The prison-addict population is 2,080, two-thirds greater than in the base case. The tradeoff that has been made, of one-third less on the street for two-thirds more in prison, is not

---

[2] It is worth noting that the scenarios we report are generated by modifying the structural components or policies of our base model before the run begins, not by simulating an active intervention at a specific time point in the model run. In the present case, therefore, we do not stop the run in a particular year and from that point onward double the allocation of police. Instead, we assume from the outset of the run that the community is doubly supportive of this type of program. Although runs using time point interventions have been made, their results are not materially different in policy implications and are, therefore, not reported.

desirable. The total addict pool in 1990, including both addicts on the street and in prison, of 4,800 is 12 per cent less than in the base case, hardly a dramatic change for so vigorous a police approach. And, although the street population is down 35 per cent, its crime has been reduced by only 25 per cent, to 3,600 crimes per month. The added police efforts have had sufficient restraining effect on heroin supply to increase price somewhat, causing a higher rate of crimes per addict. Thus, we have the disconcerting consequence that the by-product of increased police action partially offsets its initial impact on criminal head count. In addition, the community's direct costs have almost doubled from the base case, running at the end of the simulated period at $1.38 million per month, about two-thirds of it going to support the huge force of 608 police devoted to heroin-related problems.

An inspection of Table 10.1 indicates that varying the degree of intensity of police programs produces a continuum of effects. These results suggest that the strengthening of police programs is desirable in general.

However, in addition to the problems noted above, more intense police efforts generate other dysfunctional consequences. For example, the large number of police involved in the strong program—one for every 4.5 street addicts at the end of 25 years (compared with one per 12.5 addicts in the base case)—raises serious questions about other possible effects not explicitly treated in the system model. The quality of life in such a community would undoubtedly be diminished by the increased police presence. The consequences for civil liberties are also a matter for concern.

The next programmatic option examined

is the large scale use of methadone as a heroin substitute. The reasons for the methadone substitution approach differ among communities. In some communities, the primary motivation is providing a free heroin substitute so the addict will no longer need to commit crimes to support his habit. Other communities hope to use methadone to attract the addict into counseling and rehabilitation programs aimed at bringing him back into a constructive role in society. Mixtures of these motives are common.

In the anticipated futures generated using methadone programs in the simulated community, the primary assumptions are that those receiving methadone are not engaged in addict-crime while in the program. Some are rehabilitated without further drug support, and others are maintained in a long term methadone-supported environment. These assumptions say little about the specific manner within which the local community methadone program is conducted.

To the base-simulated situation, we now add the possibility of a methadone program to be developed by the community and implemented as it senses the need and as its over-all attitude permits definition of the problem in a sociomedical manner. This simulated case is shown in Figure 10.7 along with contrasting base curves. Note the key features of this methadone scenario. First the rate of growth of the street population is curtailed after month 120, once some addicts begin entering the methadone program. This leads over-all to a marked decrease in street addicts (2,320 at the end of 25 years in contrast with 4,160 in the base case) and an even more noticeable change in the imprisoned addict population (640 rather than 1,280). However, the enhanced drug supply creates 13 per cent

Table 10.1
Effect of Varying Police Program Intensity (End Conditions)[a]

	Street Addicts	Addicts in Prison	Total Addicts	Crime Rate	Program Costs
				(000/mo.)	($000/mo.)
No police	8,300	0	8,300	10.0	0
Weak police program	6,240	880	7,120	7.7	540
Typical police program	4,160	1,280	5,440	4.9	780
Strong police program	2,720	2,080	4,800	3.6	1,380

[a] Reprinted with permission from Levin, G., Roberts, E. B., and Hirsch, G. B. *The Persistent Poppy.* Copyright 1975, Ballinger Publishing Company.

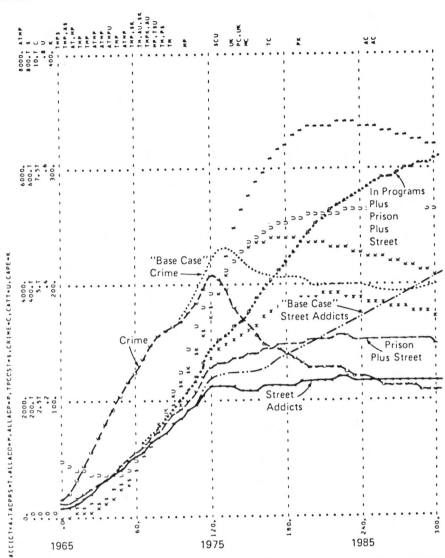

Figure 10.7. Heroin addiction: Methadone program added to moderate police response. (Reprinted with permission from Levin, G., Roberts, E. B., and Hirsch, G. B. *The Persistent Poppy.* Copyright 1975, Ballinger Publishing Company.)

more total narcotic addicts, however disposed (6,160 instead of 5,440). Offsetting this, the methadone program has attracted into short term and longer maintenance relationships 3,200 addicts, many drawn from what would have been alternative dispositions in the street or in prison.

During this process, crime decreases by a substantial amount, the 25 year-end figure of 2,700 crimes per month being only about 55 per cent of the base run's 4,900 monthly crimes. Finally, in contrast with the base case, the methadone program ends up costing less money in direct program outlays, the

$640,000 per month being about 20 per cent less than the base case. This is due primarily to the substitution of lower cost outpatient methadone care for more expensive inpatient prison.

The comparative benefits and costs of methadone maintenance are fewer addicts on the street, fewer in prison, less crime, lower dollar costs—but more total population induced into addiction and more ending up with a long term commitment to an addicted life, albeit addicted to methadone instead of heroin. But, if useful, is methadone by itself a sufficient response? This alternative future was simulated with dramatic results. In the base case, using police but no methadone, 4,160 street addicts resulted. In the present alternative attempt, using methadone but no police, 5,360 street addicts are generated. In the base case, an additional 1,280 addicts are in prison, making a total of 5,440. In the methadone-only case, no addicts are in prison (no arrests are being made), but about 5,000 more addicts are undergoing methadone treatment, producing more than 10,000 addicts in all. Crime is down about 10 per cent from the base case, despite the 30 per cent growth in street addicts, due to the heroin price-depressing effect of the enlarged methadone drug supply. But this slight benefit is insufficient compensation for the increased street and total addict populations.

When the methadone-only alternative is contrasted to the "do nothing" case—no police, no programs—we again see the relative impacts of methadone. As an attractive substitute, it does bring a significant number of addicts from the street into program control: 8,300 on the street in the no-police, no-programs case versus 5,360 in the no-police but methadone instead situation. But it adds to the total number of persons involved in narcotic addiction by attracting many into the methadone program itself—4,640 in this case. Thus supplementing the large street heroin supply that is available under the no-police situation with a supply of methadone adds to total drug availability. More youths are induced into heroin addiction, and from the street many of them are attracted into methadone programs.

If no police, in combination with methadone rehabilitation, is harmful, will strong police be helpful? The anticipated future for such a combination looks promising. The introduction of a methadone program with normal police support has been estimated above as reducing the end point street addict population to 2,320 addicts. Strengthening the police support further reduces street addicts to 1,600, now but 40 per cent of the street addict population encountered in the base case. Some of those who are no longer on the street as addicts can be found as addicts in prison instead. The stronger police approach has caused a higher arrest rate of street addicts, contributing to the lesser street population and to the greater prison population of 1,040 addicts at the simulation's end,

up from 640 in the methadone situation with fewer police. The over-all depressing effect on additional growth that is achieved by strengthened police shows up as well in methadone program enrollments. Whereas 3,200 were entered in the prior methadone setting, only 2,640 are enrolled in the stronger police scenario. An additional accompanying benefit is the lower crime rate of 2,100 incidents per month, reflecting proportionately the lower number of street addicts. Other than the increased number of addict prisoners, the only other negative aspect of this situation is the directly related increased cost—$980,000 per month—up 50 per cent from $640,000 in the earlier methadone simulation.

Once a number of single-program alternatives had been evaluated with the model, a set of multimodality approaches was simulated. In general, the results indicate dramatic, although by no means immediate, reduction in addict-related crime. Fewer untreated and unimprisoned addicts eventually are at large to steal. Vigorous multimodality action, however, tends to increase appreciably the total number of persons using narcotics.

In one multimodality scenario, we added drug-free rehabilitation, methadone and heroin maintenance, dissuasive education, and community education to the normal police response included in the base case assumption. In this run, as Figure 10.8 indicates, only 1,350 street addicts remain after 25 years, about one-third of the base case's end point of 4,160. The imprisoned population is proportionally reduced from 1,280 to 480. An even more dramatic benefit is effected in addict-related crime, which is reduced by a factor of eight to only 600 crimes per month versus 4,900 per month in the base case. However, the grand total of persons involved with narcotics is 6,860, as against the lesser number of 5,440 in the base case. These over-all improvements are achieved at approximately double the dollar cost. Monthly expenditures are running at about $780,000 at the end of the base run versus $1.27 million in this simulation.

Beyond this level of comprehensiveness, adding additional program components creates very small changes in the same general direction. For example, adding a narcotic antagonist program takes an additional 160 ad-

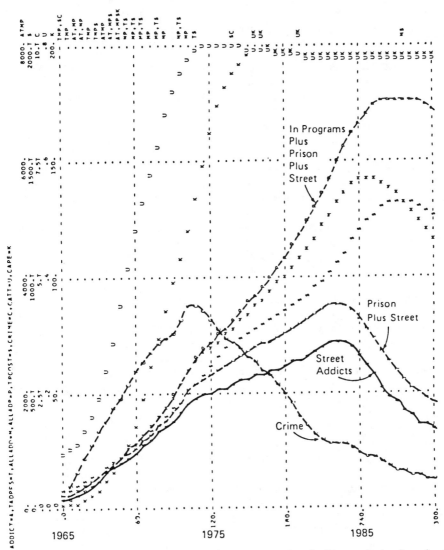

Figure 10.8. Heroin addiction: Multimodality response. (Reprinted with permission from Levin, G., Roberts, E. B., and Hirsch, G. B. *The Persistent Poppy*. Copyright 1975, Ballinger Publishing Company.)

dicts out of the street population and 80 out of prison. It is somewhat disappointing that these gains are not reflected in a lower total number of persons involved with narcotics, which remains at 6,880. All of the movement from the street and prison is into programs.

When still another modality, readily available detoxification, is added to the program mix, the results are similar. Some 80 more addicts are removed from the street and 160 from prison. However, most of these persons add to the total population of those involved with narcotics, which is now increased to about 7,200. Again, adding programs adds to

costs. For this all-modalities run, $1.44 million are being spent each month at the end of the run. The crime picture continues to improve further, but only marginally so, to a rate of about 400 incidents per month at the end of the simulated period.

Having established both the efficacy and the limits of comprehensive programming, what might less ambitious multimodal combinations achieve? We examined a far more modest combination of programs in a simulation that added to the normal police response only drug-free rehabilitation, dissuasive education, and community education.

This run shows an improvement over the base case, reducing street addicts by about one-third, with a similar reduction in prison addicts. Crime is also reduced by 25 per cent. Some additional 320 addicts are brought into drug-free rehabilitation, but the total number of people involved in the street, prison, and programs is decreased from the base by one-third, from 5,440 to 4,040. Monthly program costs rise by about 15 per cent by the end of the run.

Should methadone be added to this combination? In the single-modality methadone simulations, the answer seemed clear enough. But what occurs under multimodal circumstances? This simulated future further supports the usefulness of methadone as part of an over-all community strategy, as indicated in Table 10.2. More persons are involved in narcotics (in or out of treatment) when methadone is added to the other combined programs, but many are drawn into methadone from reductions in the street and prison populations. Crime is decreased markedly, and even total costs are down slightly, the cost of the methadone program being borne primarily by reduced prison and police expenses.

Several generalizations may be extracted from the total set of multimodality runs. These runs tend to be similar to one another and, in their gross characteristics, to the majority of single-program runs described earlier, in that all project an early rapid growth in the number of street addicts and in addict-related crime rates. However, in the multimodality simulations, aided in large part by a program-created rapid shift in community problem definition, program capacity achieves significant levels quite early in the scenario. By about the fifth year (approxi-

mately 1970) in all such runs, programs are drawing in considerable numbers of clients from the street addict status. Combined program growth that takes place past this point in time gives rise to several phenomena of interest.

First, the rate of growth of the street addict population slackens. This gives rise to the set of forces that eventually brings crime under control. Crime peaks around the tenth year (1975) and then recedes slightly in most futures. The causes of this eventual slackening in crime are the reduction in number of street addicts and a greatly reduced heroin street price.

At around the twentieth year, the number of persons active in most of the programs peaks. The final 5 years are characterized by saturation or by a modest decline. The one exception to this generalization is in the number of persons in long term narcotic maintenance. Although the total number in all programs tends to level off, the proportion of that group in long term maintenance continues to grow.

At the end of the 25-year period of multimodality programming, this is the general picture:

1. Addict-related crime is a mere fraction of its prior peak and is running as low as one-fifth its value during the 1974 peak period.

2. The population of street addicts has returned from its peak, which was two to three times higher than in the 1972 period. The final end point simulated values are in the neighborhood of 30 per cent worse than the situation in 1974, and the sum of street addicts plus prison populations is as much as 80 per cent worse.

Table 10.2
Incremental Effect of Methadone in Multimodal Program[a]

Multimodal Programs	Street Addicts	Addicts in Prison	Addicts on Methadone	Addicts in Drug-free Program	Total Involved	Crime Rate	Program Costs
						(000/mo.)	($000/mo.)
Base run	4,160	1,280			5,440	4.9	780
Drug-free rehabilitation plus dissuasive and community education	2,760	860		320	4,040	3.8	890
The above plus methadone	2,220	640	1,350	270	4,560	2.7	830

[a] Reprinted with permission from Levin, G., Roberts, E. B., and Hirsch, G. B. *The Persistent Poppy.* Copyright 1975, Ballinger Publishing Company.

3. A very large number of persons are involved with narcotics, the largest portion being in long term maintenance. The grand total of addicts on the street, in prison, in active programs, and in maintenance of indefinite duration is at or near its peak value, which is about twice as great as in the 1974 period.

4. Depending upon the specific combination of modalities chosen, total program costs run at a rate between two to three times their 1974 values.

CONCLUSIONS

This chapter has described a system dynamic model of substance abuse. A generic model was first presented, followed by an application of this type of model to heroin addiction. The application suggested several benefits that could be derived from a system dynamics model of substance abuse. One important benefit is the model's usefulness as a framework for clearly representing the complex set of causal factors responsible for the development of a substance abuse problem in a community. Another important benefit is the model's flexibility as a tool for projecting the impact of various sets of programs on a substance abuse problem. Results of these projections can then be compared and an advantageous set of programs selected. The heroin addiction simulations, for example, demonstrated the advantages of multimodality approaches over heavy investments in programs that involve only a single modality. The model also allowed various multimodality approaches to be compared for their effect on numbers of addicts, crime, and costs borne by the community.

PART 3

SUBSTANCES OF ABUSE

CHAPTER 11

PHARMACOLOGY OF THE OPIATES

Gerald A. Deneau, Ph.D.

Salvatore J. Mulé, Ph.D.

The medicinal use of opium probably dates as far back as 7000 B.C. The Ebers Papyri refer to its use in the treatment of colic in children. Homer referred to it as " . . . a drug to lull all pain and anger and bring forgetfulness to every sorrow. . . . " Celsus, Discordes, and Pliny recommended it for the relief of pain due to many causes, the relief of difficult breathing, and the induction of sleep. They also warned of deadly overdosage.

Opium is the sun-dried milky exudate from the capsule of the poppy, *Papaver somniferum*, of which 25 per cent is a mixture of 20 or more alkaloids. These alkaloids fall into two groups—the phenanthrene group and the benzoisoquinoline group. We are concerned here only with one group, the phenanthrene alkaloids, of which morphine is the major constituent and is almost entirely responsible for the pharmacological actions of opium.

The use of opium spread east and west along the trade routes from the Mediterranean, but its use was somewhat limited by its meager availability, its unpredictable potency, and the Galenical tradition of prescribing complicated polypharmaceutical preparations. The highly variable potency of different batches of opium prompted a young German pharmacist, Sertürner, to attempt to isolate an active ingredient. He succeeded in isolating morphine in 1803. It was the first medicinal alkaloid to be isolated in pure form. The availability of pure morphine facilitated the rapid and widespread proliferation of its use in medical practice for its unparalleled capacity to relieve pain. Morphine's other prominent and useful properties include the control of cough through the suppression of the cough reflex, the control of diarrhea by contraction of the intestinal musculature, thereby "splinting" the gut, and the relief of pulmonary distress due to cardiac insufficiency. Against this impressive array of medical indications for the use of morphine are two very serious toxic outcomes resulting from acute overdosage and chronic unsupervised use.

The acute toxicity from overdosage is death due to respiratory arrest that results from depression of the respiratory center so profound that carbon dioxide no longer serves as a stimulus of respiration. The chronic toxicity is compulsive drug abuse (chemical dependence, addiction), which results from morphine's remarkable ability to relieve psychological pain or the distress of anxiety arising from whatever cause. Opium smoking, which began in China, was brought to this country by immigrant laborers. Other factors that led to the unsupervised use of opium were the flood of patent medicines and nostrums containing opium and liberal amounts of alcohol, which were taken for every conceivable ailment. Morphine was also used extensively by the wounded of the Civil War, a use that was facilitated by the recent development of the hypodermic syringe.

Codeine and thebaine occur naturally in opium. Codeine is less depressant and more convulsant than morphine, whereas thebaine is almost purely convulsant. Chemical modification of morphine was found to yield a variety of semisynthetic alkaloids such as heroin, dionine, dilaudid, etc., of greater or lesser potency than morphine and with somewhat modified spectra of activity. With the hope of separating the desirable properties of morphine (analgesic, antitussive, antidiarrhea) from the serious toxic property of dependence induction, a large collaborative program was initiated by the National Research Council in 1929. In this program, over 400 new derivatives of morphine were synthesized under the direction of Lyndon F. Small and then evaluated pharmacologically under the direction of Nathan B. Eddy. The more promising of these compounds were evaluated for addiction liability under the direction of C. K. Himmelsbach (25). This program was interrupted during World War II. After the war, interest in this approach was stimulated by the discovery that Germany had developed two potent synthetic analgesics, meperidine (Demerol) and methadone, which did not have the phenanthrene nucleus. Thus, two new avenues were opened for chemical exploration, and many compounds in these series have been synthesized and evaluated. In addition, by simplifying the phenanthrene nucleus, drugs of the morphinan and benzomorphan series have been developed. Other narcotic analgesics, the thiambutenes and the nitrobenzimidazoles have also been discovered but not developed commercially.

Pohl reported that N-allyl-norcodeine prevented or abolished the respiratory depressant actions of morphine and heroin (20). This finding went unheeded until Unna (23)

and Hart and McCawley (7) reported the more potent antagonistic effects of N-allyl-normorphine (nalorphine). Echenhoff et al. (5) described the efficacy of nalorphine in the treatment of narcotic overdosage. Wikler et. al. (26) reported that nalorphine produced dysphoria in normal subjects and that it precipitated abstinence syndromes in subjects dependent upon a variety of narcotic analgesics. Subsequently, Lasagna and Beecher (15) reported that, although nalorphine antagonized the analgesic effect of morphine, adequate doses produced analgesia by itself. Dysphoric side effects precluded patient acceptance of nalorphine as an analgesic, however, but this finding encouraged the search for a nonaddicting antagonist that might be a suitable analgesic devoid of unacceptable side effects. Although this goal has not been achieved, a group of drugs with mixed agonist-antagonist properties has emerged. Some of these have acquired clinical status.

CHEMISTRY

The natural alkaloids of opium and the semisynthetics that are derived from them occur only in the levorotatory form. It is with these isomers that the typical narcotic activity is associated. The synthetic drugs, especially of the morphinan and methadone series, are also stereospecific.

Any alteration of the morphine molecule will alter its biological activity quantitatively. Substitutions on the N site may yield compounds of different qualitative properties, such as antagonists or mixed agonist-antagonists. N-allyl or N-cyclopropylmethyl substitutions in the morphine, morphinan, and benzomorphan series are most likely to yield antagonists. This is less likely to occur in the other series of narcotic analgesics.

Figure 11.1 depicts representatives of each of the known chemical classes of drugs that produce morphine-like agonistic effects. In addition, drugs that produce specific antagonist and mixed agonist-antagonist effects are also illustrated.

PHARMACOLOGICAL ACTIONS

The opiates produce a complex mixture of effects on the central nervous system and on smooth muscle. To some extent these effects,

AGONISTS:

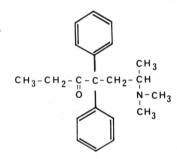

Morphine

Levorphanol

Meperidine

Phenazocine

Methadone

1-(Diethylaminoethyl)-2-
(para Ethoxybenzyl)-5-
Nitrobenzimidazole

Ethylmethylthiambutene

ANTAGONIST:

N-CH₂-CH=CH₂

Naloxone

AGONIST-ANTAGONIST:

N-CH₂-CH=C<CH₃ / CH₃

Pentazocine

Figure 11.1. Representative members of the various chemical classes of drugs possessing opiate agonist, antagonist, and mixed agonist-antagonist properties.

some depressant and some stimulant, partially counteract each other. The net effect of a given dose to any subject depends upon several factors including the drug, the species, the individual, and the setting.

The Drug. Morphine is primarily a depressant in man. Increasing doses lead to greater diminution in response to the environment and to depression of respiration so that death occurs after a state of coma and respiratory arrest has been reached. Codeine is less depressant, and increased dosages may produce a state of agitation and anxiety and, occasionally, convulsions. Thebaine is essentially a pure stimulant. In this respect it might be noted that the drugs that produce significant analgesia also cloud consciousness, so that those which have become useful clinical analgesics also depress anxiety and responsiveness to the environment in general. The stimulants that produce anxiety and agitation are not accepted clinically nor do they pose a public health problem of addiction.

The Species. The net effects of morphine are primarily depressant in man, monkey, dog, and rat. Horses, swine, and mice show marked psychomotor stimulation in response to morphine. Cats exhibit a syndrome referred to as morphine mania in which they are in a state of frenzied agitation mixed with unresponsiveness to normal stimuli. They usually die in convulsions.

Morphine-like drugs all show a typical spectrum of effects in laboratory species, including "hyenoid-gait" in dogs or depressed motor function, primarily of the hind limbs; "mania" in cats that is accompanied by profuse salivation and marked mydriasis; profound uninterrupted hyperactivity in mice as well as the Straub tail reaction (an S-shaped arching of the tail over the mouse's back— this reaction is not specific for the narcotic analgesics; it occurs with a wide variety of central nervous system stimulants); plastic catatonia in rats. In humans, toxic responses to opiates are characterized by loss of consciousness, severe respiratory depression, and pinpoint pupils.

The Individual. Some individuals show an idiosyncratic response, especially to the less effective agents such as codeine and propoxyphene. This is characterized by anxiety, agitation, and insomnia. In other words, the stimulant effects of the milder opiates override the depressant actions in these patients.

The Setting. It is not uncommon for normal subjects to experience dysphoria in response to opiates in experimental situations in which they are not experiencing pain. These same subjects do not experience dysphoria in clinical settings when pain and anxiety are present.

ANALGESIA

Pain is the outstanding indication for the use of opiates. They suppress the perception of pain without completely clouding the consciousness. Morphine is the standard to which all others are compared, and no other drug has been found that is sufficiently superior to replace it in the treatment of severe pain. Not only is the actual threshold of pain perception elevated, but the subjective response to pain is also reduced. Upon questioning, patients will often respond that the pain is still present but that it no longer "bothers" them.

Each opiate relieves pain in a dose-related manner up to its individual plateau, beyond which further increments in dosage do not produce better analgesia, only greater side effects. Morphine, dilaudid, methadone, and levorphanol are more effective than meperidine, which in turn is more effective than codeine. Because addiction liability is correlated with analgesic effectiveness, it is common practice to employ the drug with the least addiction potential that will control pain in the individual situation. The opiates' ability to allay anxiety, or mental pain, may contribute as much as elevation of the pain threshold to a patient's comfort. It is, no doubt, this anxiolytic effect that makes the opiates so attractive to the drug abuser.

Morphine is somewhat erratically absorbed when taken by mouth, and, because of the unpredictable result, this route of administration is not recommended. Levorphanol and methadone are more dependably absorbed after oral administration. Meperidine is extensively hydrolyzed and demethylated in its passage through the portal circulation, and its effectiveness is thus greatly reduced after oral administration. Codeine is reliably absorbed from the gastrointestinal tract, however, and because it is used primarily for less severe types of pain, often in ambulatory patients, the oral route is the preferred form of administration.

ANTITUSSIVE

The opiates possess pronounced antitussive activity and were formerly used extensively for this purpose, particularly in tuberculous patients. As the danger of opiate dependence became more widely recognized, there was a shift away from the more potent opiates, e.g., heroin, to codeine for the therapy of chronic cough. Although codeine is an effective antitussive, it is still not entirely free from abuse potential. Its use in cough preparations has been partially replaced by other antitussives. One such substitute is noscapine, one of the papaveraceous alkaloids of opium that, aside from its antitussive activity, shares none of the other common properties of morphine. Another commonly used codeine substitute in cough preparations is *d*-3-methoxymorphinan, the codeine analogue of the otherwise nonnarcotic dextrorotatory isomer of the morphinan series.

RESPIRATION

Morphine is a potent respiratory depressant. Respiratory arrest is the cause of death in man from acute overdosage with opiates. Other species are less sensitive to this effect. Rhesus monkeys die from respiratory arrest with doses of 70 to 100 mg/kg of morphine, but massive overdoses (250 mg/kg or greater) produce fatal convulsions. The respiration of dogs is depressed by morphine, but not to a fatal degree. The opiates produce their effect on respiration by depressing the sensitivity of the respiratory center to CO_2. Proprioceptive stimulation produced by enforced walking or painful stimulation from pinching, etc., partially counteracts opiate-induced respiratory depression. The opiate antagonists provide dramatic complete reversal of the respiratory depression.

EMESIS

The opiates often initially produce nausea and emesis through stimulation of the chemoreceptor trigger zone. After this initial phase has passed, patients become refractory to agents that produce vomiting by direct stimulation of the vomiting center, indicating that the vomiting center per se has become depressed.

GASTROINTESTINAL

The opiates produce pronounced effects on the intestines. Both the longitudinal and the circular muscle layers of the intestine are contracted simultaneously, thus "splinting" the gut and markedly reducing peristaltic activity. By inhibiting peristalsis in patients with dysentery, excessive losses of water and electrolytes are minimized. In patients who are receiving opiates for the treatment of pain, this same effect on the intestinal musculature often leads to the undesirable side effect of constipation.

The sphincters of the gastrointestinal tract are also contracted, and this effect further impedes the propulsion of gastrointestinal contents. Stimulation of the biliary tract and the sphincter of Oddi by the opiates leads to increased intraductal pressure. This effect may be so prominent in some patients that the pain of biliary colic is increased, rather than relieved, by the opiates. The gastrointestinal effects of the opiates are somewhat reduced by atropine. They are completely blocked by the narcotic antagonists, but so too is the analgesic effect.

Some smooth muscle beds are stimulated by the opiates, whereas others are depressed. Thus, on the basis of different responses to morphine and different sensitivities to the antagonists, one can postulate the existence of two or more different opiate receptors in smooth muscle, just as there are two or more receptors associated with the nervous system.

VASCULAR SMOOTH MUSCLE

The opiates dilate peripheral blood vessels through at least two different mechanisms. They release histamine, which results in reddening of the skin over the blush area as well as itching, particularly of the face. There is also a nonhistaminergic dilatation of peripheral blood vessels and an inhibition of normal reflex vasoconstriction. Thus, although there may be minimal cardiovascular changes in the recumbent patient, orthostatic hypotension and even fainting frequently occur when the subject becomes erect. Tolerance develops readily to this response.

OTHER SMOOTH MUSCLE

Opiates stimulate the sphincter as well as the detrussor muscle of the urinary bladder.

This can occasionally cause the troublesome side effect of a constant severe sense of urgency that necessitates catherization. In most patients, however, there is a decreased central perception of this irksome sensation.

The uterus is not profoundly affected by the opiates, but labor is usually prolonged. This may be due to less vigorous voluntary effort by the mother as a result of the analgesic action. The opiates cross the placental barrier, however, and produce undesirable respiratory depression of the newborn.

ENDOCRINE EFFECTS

The opiates affect the release of pituitary factors which in turn modify the activity of their respective target organs. Thus, the decreased release of adrenocorticotropic hormone results in reduced output of adrenal steroids. The decreased release of gonadotropins likewise causes decreased output of gonadosteroids and hence lessened sexual desire in both men and women. Thyroid activity is likewise somewhat reduced.

TOLERANCE AND PHYSIOLOGICAL DEPENDENCE

Upon repeated administration the opiates induce the phenomena of tolerance and physiological dependence. Tolerance is the condition that develops after repeated administration of an opiate. Its first manifestation is usually a decrease in the duration of effective pain relief so that either an increase in the dose or a reduction of the dosage interval, or both, are required to maintain analgesia. Tolerance does not develop at a uniform rate to the various effects produced by the opiates. It occurs most readily to those actions in which central nervous system functions are depressed (analgesia, respiratory depression, clouding of consciousness, etc.), less readily to depression of smooth muscle (orthostatic hypotension), and hardly at all to smooth muscle stimulation (constipation, miosis, etc.). Tolerance develops most readily when there is continuous tissue exposure to the drug and less readily if drug-free intervals are allowed to occur.

Tolerance is never absolute in the sense that a subject becomes immune or completely insensitive to the opiates. Williams and Oberst (27) reported a case of an individual who

self-administered over 500 times the recommended daily clinical analgesic dosage of morphine and still performed his daily routine satisfactorily. Monkeys will self-administer up to 100 mg/kg/day without exhibiting any profound behavioral deficits. Although some differences in the disposition of opiates between tolerant and nontolerant subjects have been demonstrated, they are not nearly of a magnitude sufficient to explain the degree of tolerance that is observed with the opiates (29).

Tolerance to some of the effects of the opiates is lost within a matter of days from the last dose administered, but tolerance to the antinociceptive and decreased swimming performance have been shown to persist for more than a year in rats (2). This leads to speculation concerning the nature of the biological mechanisms underlying tolerance development. How many types of adaptations are involved? Are these adaptations reversible or permanent? Is tolerance the result of changes in neurotransmission or modulation, or are there changes in the intrinsic responsiveness of cells, etc? Much effort has been expended in addressing these questions, but to date no simple explanation has emerged.

Tolerance to any opiate confers cross-tolerance to all other morphine-like narcotic analgesics but not to other classes of central nervous system depressants.

One of the difficulties involved with assessing the degree of tolerance that is present at any time is the necessity of reintroducing an opiate in sufficient dosage to elicit a measurable response. This procedure, in itself, increases or prolongs the preexisting state of tolerance. No biological response or chemical marker has yet been found that indicates the degree of tolerance development without reintroducing an opiate.

PHYSIOLOGICAL DEPENDENCE

Physiological dependence is a state of adaptation of the central nervous system to prolonged exposure to an opiate. Its existence is not apparent as long as adequate amounts of an opiate are present. When drug administration is discontinued, however, or when a specific opiate antagonist is administered, a characteristic set of signs of physiological dysfunction appears. This constellation of signs and symptoms is known as the abstinence or withdrawal syndrome. In a general way the abstinence syndrome is qualitatively opposite in character to the state induced by the opiates. The abstinence syndrome consists of signs of hyperactivity relating to behavior, involuntary somatic functions, and of both branches of the autonomic nervous system. These signs are: Behavioral—apprehension, anxiety, quarrelsomeness, restlessness, sleepiness in the early phase, insomnia in later stages; involuntary somatic—dyspnea, hyperalgesia (tenderness), muscular rigidity, muscular weakness, intention tremor, strabismus, convulsions (rare), dehydration, weight loss, hyperpyrexia; sympathetic—yawning, perspiration, piloerection (gooseflesh), pallor, hypertension, hyperglycemia, mydriasis; parasympathetic—rhinorrhea, lacrimation, cough, abdominal cramps, anorexia, nausea, salivation, retching, vomiting, diarrhea.

The abstinence syndrome from morphine (or heroin) begins to appear 6 to 8 hours after the last dose and gradually intensifies to peak severity at about 48 hours (earlier with shorter acting drugs) and then diminishes in severity until no overt signs remain 7 to 10 days after the last dose. Himmelsbach demonstrated that, even after the major abstinence syndrome had subsided, abnormal autonomic reflexes persisted for 6 months or more (10). Martin and Jasinski have confirmed and extended these observations (16).

As with tolerance, there are no known biological markers that indicate the presence or extent of the development of physiological dependence. It is necessary to interrupt the phenomenon to measure it. This is done by measuring the severity of the abstinence syndrome that develops upon removal of the drug from the opiate receptors. This is achieved either by the abrupt discontinuance of chronic dosage, thus allowing the opiate to be removed by normal biological processes of elimination, or by the administration of a specific opiate antagonist that in effect almost immediately blocks the opiate receptors from occupancy by the agonist. With the abrupt withdrawal procedure the abstinence syndrome intensifies gradually over the course of hours or days. With the antagonist-precipitated technique, the onset of the syndrome is rapid and explosive, reaching peak intensity in a matter of minutes. The opiate antagonist may be inactivated before the opiate has been entirely eliminated. If this occurs the opiate reoccupies the receptors, thus terminating the abstinence syndrome, even before another dose of the opiate has been administered.

The extent of development of physiological dependence depends upon the maximum daily dosage of opiate attained and the duration of chronic administration. The exposure to the opiate must also be continuous—one dose of morphine every third day will not induce dependence. Dependence to a fixed dose of morphine at 6-hour intervals in the monkey becomes maximal in 3 months but is nearly complete after 1 month of chronic administration. Dependence severity increases to a point as the daily dose is increased (tolerance development facilitates rapid increases in dosage) but reaches a maximum plateau for each drug, beyond which further increments in dosage have little effect on the severity of dependence development. Each drug has its inherent maximum capacity to induce physiological dependence. Codeine and d-propoxyphene, in any dosage, cannot induce dependence to a degree comparable with morphine or heroin.

Himmelsbach's "point score system" for grading the intensity of the opiate abstinence syndrome is a landmark in clinical pharmacology (8). He assigned point values to each of the signs of the syndrome relative to that sign's contribution to the over-all clinical significance. This system provides an objective measurement of the intensity of physiological dependence (withdrawal) and has been the standard of comparison for over four decades. Fraser et al. introduced questionnaires for rating subjective responses to the over-all assessment of abuse liability (6). These questionnaires also distinguish the various other pharmacological classes of drugs of abuse. Refinements in the methodology for determining abuse potential continue to be made. One of them is the subject's estimate of the dollar value of a given "fix." This may be a valuable benchmark at a given time in a given setting, but, because of the highly fluctuating purity of street drugs and the ever diminishing value of the dollar, it is incumbent upon the investigators to express such estimates in standard dosage units.

Opiate drugs that can induce physiological dependence will more or less substitute for each other in maintaining a subject in an abstinence-free condition. By establishing the dosage requirement of a test drug to maintain a given level of dependence, say to morphine, quantitative comparisons of physiological dependence capacity can be made. Himmelsbach used this 24-hour substitution technique in place of the longer, arduous primary induction or direct addiction technique (8). A further refinement in methodology, the single-dose suppression technique, was also developed by Himmelsbach (11). It, too, is based on the interchangeability of drugs that share common pharmacological properties. By this procedure one can determine the dose of a drug which is equieffective to a standard dose of morphine in suppressing or relieving the abstinence signs in subjects who are dependent on a stabilized dose of morphine. Similar quantitative procedures have been developed for the preclinical assay of opiate-like physiological dependence capacity in rhesus monkeys (21).

These shortened procedures of substitution or suppression require access to a group of subjects who are physiologically dependent on a primary drug, usually morphine. When he began these studies, Himmelsbach found that subjects presenting at the United States Public Health Service Addiction Research Center in Lexington, Kentucky, required about 400 mg of morphine per day to support their habits. In the late 1950's and 1960's this requirement fell to 240 mg/day, and since then it has fallen even lower. This progressive decrease in the daily maintenance dosage of "hooked" addicts is a reflection of the ever decreasing purity and increasing cost of street drugs.

A wide variety of other pharmacological classes of drugs will relieve some of the milder early signs of opiate abstinence and are useful in detoxification procedures. Unless a drug is capable of maintaining the state of opiate dependence or of uniformly suppressing the entire opiate abstinence syndrome without producing marked side effects, it should not be classified as an opiate.

PSYCHOLOGICAL DEPENDENCE

It is axiomatic that very few people would abuse drugs to the extent that they become physiologically dependent unless the drug produces some underlying effect that the subject wants to experience repeatedly. Behaviorists use the term "reinforcing property" to describe such an effect. There are many individual reasons why a subject might find the effects of certain drugs to be reinforcing, but once these reinforcing properties are discovered, and if they are strong enough that the subject clearly prefers the drug-induced condition to the drug-free state and his primary motivation becomes to seek more drug, psychological dependence has developed. This is the first and essential stage of all forms of chronic drug abuse. It occurs also with such drugs as cocaine and the amphetamines that do not induce physiological dependence. No drug that is not reinforcing and does not induce psychological dependence is ever likely to be abused, even if it has a high capacity to induce physiological dependence.

The importance of psychological dependence was clearly recognized by the investigators at the United States Public Health Service Addiction Research Center when they developed a series of subjective questionnaires and rating scales (6). With these instruments, drug-experienced subjects can identify drugs as being morphine-like or cocaine-like, etc. They can also give evaluations such as less than, equal to, or better than standard doses of drugs of comparison.

Comparable techniques for studying psychological dependence have been developed in the laboratory. Most of these procedures use monkeys, but some also utilize rats. The earliest was Spragg's study with chimpanzees (22). In some of these studies the experimental animal indicates a preference to put itself in a situation that is associated with previous drug experience. In other procedures the experimental animal is free to choose to self-administer a drug or not.

There are two basic types of self-administration studies. In one, naive animals are placed in a situation where they can self-administer drugs (4). If they find that the drug is reinforcing, they can continue to self-administer unlimited quantities of the drug. Using this technique, some, but not all, monkeys develop a predictable pattern of self-administration to all classes of drugs abused by humans except the psychotomimetics. They develop full blown syndromes of morphinism, cocainism, alcoholism, etc., and clearly exhibit tolerance, physiological dependence, behavioral toxicity, and pathological changes characteristic of each class of drugs.

Other techniques address the investigation of reinforcing properties of the drug. In these studies, susceptible monkeys are selected that initially show psychological dependence to a reference drug such as a short acting barbiturate or an amphetamine (28). These monkeys are then allowed limited access, e.g., 30 minutes every 6 hours, to very small doses of a drug on certain days. Under these conditions drug-seeking behavior (psychological dependence) is maintained, but the dosage schedule is such that tolerance development is minimal and physiological dependence does not develop. These subjects are used to assay new drugs for reinforcing properties. The situation is analogous to the use of former addicts for the evaluation of limited amounts of new drugs.

BIOLOGICAL DISPOSITION

All but a very few drugs, when introduced into an animal, undergo one or more of a variety of metabolic changes before they are eliminated from the organism. The opiates, which include several molecular species (Fig. 11.1), are no exception. Most metabolic transformations of drugs, whether by degradation or by synthesis, result in products that are more water soluble and, therefore, more readily excreted than the parent drug. Drug metabolites are often, but by no means always, less active than the parent drugs, but this is by no means always the case. There are important examples among the opiates where the metabolic products are more active biologically than the parent drug. In some cases the metabolic products produce qualitatively different biological effects. Once a drug has been absorbed from its site of administration, its duration of action depends mainly upon the time required for its metabolic inactivation and/or its elimination from the system. Other factors, such as redistribution into fat stores, can delay elimination and thus prolong the duration of action of some drugs. Other factors, which in some instances prolong the action of drugs, are the hydrolysis of conjugates that have been excreted in the bile and the subsequent reabsorption of the active drug from the intestine and pH-dependent renal reabsorption.

Meperidine is rapidly metabolized, by both demethylation and hydrolysis, and consequently has a much shorter duration of action than morphine, which is more slowly inactivated, primarily by conjugation. One of meperidine's metabolites is the demethylated product, normeperidine. Normeperidine has significant thebaine-like stimulant properties. Meperidine users who, because of tolerance development, self-administer large quantities of the drug may accumulate sufficient concentrations of normeperidine that its stimulant actions become manifest as severe anxiety, psychotic symptoms, tremors, and convulsions. Himmelsbach described such a case in his first study of meperidine's addiction potential (9).

In laboratory animals the duration of action of methadone is about the same as that of morphine. In humans, however, the duration of action of methadone is approximately 24 hours, and this is the basis of methadone's usefulness in maintenance therapy of heroin dependence. Methadone's prolonged action in humans is probably due to its intestinal and renal reabsorption (12).

l-Alpha-acetylmethadol (LAAM) has an even longer duration of action in humans than methadone and is currently being evaluated as an alternate agent in maintenance therapy. The biological disposition of LAAM is complex. It is preferentially distributed in adipose tissue from which it is slowly released, and two of its demethylated metabolites, nor-LAAM and dinor-LAAM, are more potent than it is itself (18).

The detailed treatments of the biological disposition of the opiates by Way and Adler (24), Mule' (19), and Misra (17) are recommended for those who have a particular interest in this aspect of drug abuse.

MECHANISM OF ACTION

The mechanism of action of the opiates has long been a fascinating challenge to pharmacologists. From the earliest recognition of the therapeutic usefulness of opium, it has been clear that opiates produce many biological responses. Bernard clearly demonstrated that some of these responses are more prominent with one opiate than with another or that, even with a single alkaloid, some effects were more prominent in some species than in others (1). As the concepts of "receptors" and "chemical transmission" became basic elements in pharmacological theory, investigators have tried to demonstrate that the actions of morphine are mediated through interaction with some chemical transmitter at some receptor site. Besides the difficulties encountered in explaining the diverse actions of a single dose of an opiate, there were also the problems of explaining the mechanisms of tolerance and of physiological dependence. Many hypotheses have been put forth over the years and later revised as additional experimental evidence accumulated to explain the mechanisms of action of the opiates. One fact became certain, however. Because the opiate antagonists do not block all of the actions of the opiates, there must be more than one type of opiate receptor. This line of thinking was encouraged by the demonstration of two types of adrenergic receptors.

With each major advance in biochemistry or in technology there has been a spate of reports of studies, usually negative, attempting to elucidate the mechanism of action of opiates. Thus we have passed through eras of attempts to explain morphine's actions in terms of mechanisms involving immune responses, toxic metabolites, thyroid function, cholinergic mechanisms, the cytochrome system, adrenal steroids, histamine, indole and catecholamines, the prostaglandins, etc.

During the past decade two outstanding developments have occurred that are basic to the action of the opiates. Specific opiate receptors have been identified and extensively mapped in several species. In addition, endogenous polypeptides that possess opiate-like activity have been isolated and identified. The larger of these have been termed the endorphins, and the smaller pentapeptides are known as enkephalins. These substances produce analgesia, respiratory depression, and other effects similar to morphine. They interact with the specific opiate receptors, and their actions are blocked by the specific narcotic antagonists. Many laboratories are engaged in elucidating the physiological role of these modulators. It is of interest that in a series of experiments Kornetsky and Kiplinger (14), Kiplinger and Clift (13), and Cochin and Kornetsky (3) studied factors from the serum of morphine-tolerant animals that on some occasions potentiated and at other times attenuated the action of morphine, depending upon the time of serum collection. These serum factors did not interact with barbitu-

rates, were heat labile, were nondialyzable, and lost activity when stored in the nonfrozen state. Although these authors did not isolate and identify these factors, it is possible that they were not only dealing with the endorphins or enkephalins but that there are also other polypeptides that mediate the stimulant-convulsant actions of morphine and that are not blocked by the antagonists.

The present status of research on opiate receptors and endogenous opiate mediators is discussed in detail by Simon in Chapter 5.

References

1. Bernard, C. Recherches expérimentales sur l'opium et ses alkaloides. C. R. Acad. Sci. (Paris) 59:406, 1864.
2. Cochin, J., and Kornetsky, C. Development and loss of tolerance to morphine in the rat after single and multiple injections. J. Pharmacol. Exp. Ther. 145:1, 1964.
3. Cochin, J., and Kornetsky, C. Factors in blood of morphine-tolerant animals that attenuate or enhance effects of morphine in nontolerant animals. In *The Addictive States*, A. Wikler, editor, Association for Research in Nervous and Mental Disease vol. LXVI, pp. 268–279. Baltimore, Williams & Wilkins, 1968.
4. Deneau, G., Yanagita, T., and Seevers, M. H. Self-administration of psychoactive substances by the monkey. Psychopharmacologia 16:30, 1969.
5. Eckenhoff, J. E., Elder, J. D., Jr., and King, D. B. N-allylnormorphine in the treatment of morphine or Demerol narcosis. Am. J. Med. Sci. 223:191, 1952.
6. Fraser, H. F., Van Horn, G. D., Martin, W. R., Wolbach, A. B., and Isbell, H. Methods for evaluating addiction liability. A. "Attitude" of opiate addicts towards opiate-like drugs. B. A short-term "direct" addiction test. J. Pharmacol. Exp. Ther. 133:371, 1961.
7. Hart, E. R., and McCawley, E. L. The pharmacology of N-allylnormorphine as compared with morphine. J. Pharmacol. Exp. Ther. 82:339, 1944.
8. Himmelsbach, C. K. Studies of certain addiction characteristics of (a) dehydromorphine ("paramorphan"), (b) dehydrodesoxymorphine-D ("desomorphine"), (c) dihydrodesoxycodeine-D ("desocodeine") and (d) methyldihydromorphinone ("metopon"). J. Pharmacol. Exp. Ther. 67:239, 1939.
9. Himmelsbach, C. K. Studies of the addiction liability of "Demerol" (D-140). J. Pharmacol. Exp. Ther. 75:64, 1942.
10. Himmelsbach, C. K. Studies on the relation of drug addiction to the autonomic nervous system: Results of tests of peripheral blood flow. J. Pharmacol. Exp. Ther. 80:343, 1944.
11. Himmelsbach, C. K., and Andrews, H. L. Studies on the modification of the morphine abstinence syndrome by drugs. J. Pharmacol. Exp. Ther. 77:17, 1943.
12. Inturrisi, C. E., and Verebey, K. The levels of methadone in the plasma in methadone maintenance. Clin. Pharmacol. Ther. 13:633, 1972.
13. Kiplinger, G. F., and Clift, J. W. Pharmacological

properties of morphine-potentiating serum obtained from morphine-tolerant dogs and men. J. Pharmacol. Exp. Ther. 146:139, 1964.

14. Kornetsky, C., and Kiplinger, G. F. Potentiation of an effect of morphine in the rat by sera from morphine tolerant and abstinent dogs and monkeys. Psychopharmacologia 4:66, 1963.

15. Lasagna, L., and Beecher, H. K. The analgesic effectiveness of nalorphine and nalorphine-morphine combinations in man. J. Pharmacol. Exp. Ther. 112: 356, 1954.

16 Martin, W. R., and Jasinski, D. R. Physiological parameters of morphine dependence in man: Tolerance, early abstinence, protracted abstinence. J. Psychiatr. Res. 7:19, 1969.

17. Misra, A. L. Metabolism of opiates. In *Factors Affecting the Action of Narcotics*, M. L. Adler, L. Manara, and R. Samanin, editors, pp. 299–343. New York, Raven Press, 1978.

18. Misra, A. L., Mulé, S. J., Bloch, R., and Bates, T. R. Physiological disposition of l-α-$[2$-^{3}H]-acetylmethadol (LAAM) in acutely and chronically treated monkeys. J. Pharmacol. Exp. Ther. 206:475, 1978.

19. Mulé, S. J. Physiological disposition of narcotic agonists and antagonists. In *Narcotic Drugs: Biochemical Pharmacology*, D. H. Clouet, editor. New York, Plenum Press, 1971.

20. Pohl, J. Ueber das N-allylnorcodeine, einen antagonisten des morphins. Z. Exp. Pathol. Ther. 17:370, 1914.

21. Seevers, M. H., and Deneau, G. A. Physiological aspects of tolerance and physical dependence. In *Physiological Pharmacology*, W. S. Root and F. G. Hofmann, editors, vol. I, pp. 565–640. New York, Academic Press, 1963.

22. Spragg, S. D. S. Morphine addiction in chimpanzees. Comp. Psychol. Monogr. 15:1, 1940.

23. Unna, K. Antagonistic effect of N-allylnormorphine upon morphine. J. Pharmacol. Exp. Ther. 79:27, 1943.

24. Way, E. L., and Adler, T. K. *The Biological Disposition of Morphine and Its Surrogates*. Geneva, World Health Organization, 1962.

25. White, W. C. *National Research Council Report of Committee on Drug Addiction 1929–1941 and Collected Reprints*. Washington, D.C., National Research Council, 1941.

26. Wikler, A., Fraser, H. F., and Isbell, H. N-allylnormorphine: Effects of single doses and precipitation of acute abstinence syndromes during addiction to morphine, methadone and heroin in man (post-addicts). J. Pharmacol. Exp. Ther. 109:8, 1953.

27. Williams, E. G., and Oberst, F. W. A cycle of morphine addiction: Biological and psychological studies. I. Biological investigations. Public Health Rep. 61:1, 1946.

28. Woods, J. H., and Schuster, C. R. Reinforcement properties of morphine, cocaine and SPA as a function of unit dose. Int. J. Addict. 3:231, 1968.

29. Woods, L. A. Distribution and fate of morphine in non-tolerant and tolerant dogs and rats. J. Pharmacol. Exp. Ther. 112:158, 1954.

CHAPTER 12

MARIHUANA

Lester Grinspoon, M.D.

James B. Bakalar, J.D.

The earliest record of man's use of cannabis is a description of the drug in a Chinese compendium of medicines, the *Herbal* of Emperor Shen Nung, dated 2737 B.C. according to some sources and 400 to 500 B.C. according to others. Marihuana was a subject of controversy even in ancient times. There were those who warned that the hemp plant lined the road to Hades and those who thought it led to paradise. Although its intoxicating properties were known to Europe during the 19th century, and for a much longer time in South and Central America, and although thousands of tons of Indian hemp (the common name of the *Cannabis sativa* plant from which the drug is obtained) were produced for its commercially useful long bast fiber—beginning in Jamestown, Virginia, in 1611—during its early American history, nothing was known of its intoxicating properties.

It was not until 1857—when Fitz Hugh Ludlow (13), largely influenced by those members of the French romantic literary movement who belonged to "Le Club des Haschischins," published *The Hasheesh Eater: Being Passages from the Life of a Pythagorean*—that a number of American literati became aware of cannabis' euphoriant properties. Unlike his European counterparts, Ludlow did not use hashish but, rather, Til-

den's Solution, one of a number of proprietary preparations of *Cannabis indica* (an alcoholic extract of cannabis), which he could obtain from his local apothecary. It was Ludlow, then, who established a link in the public mind, albeit a very narrow segment of it, between cannabis the medicine and cannabis the intoxicating drug. However, over the course of the half-century from the publication of his book to the appearance, across the southern border, of what we now commonly call marihuana, grass, pot, or dope (all names for the dried and chopped up flowering pistillate and staminate tops and leaves of the hemp plant), this awareness, to the limited extent to which it existed, all but completely vanished.

The history of cannabis as a Western medicine begins in 1839 with a publication by W. B. O'Shaughnessy, a British physician working in Calcutta (17). He reported on the analgesic, anticonvulsant, and muscle-relaxant properties of the drug. His paper generated a good deal of interest, and there are about 100 papers in the Western medical literature from 1840 to the turn of the century. In the 19th century the drug was widely prescribed in the Western world for various ailments and discomforts, such as coughing, fatigue, rheumatism, asthma, delirium tremens, migraine headache, and painful menstruation. Although its use was already declining somewhat because of the introduction of synthetic hypnotics and analgesics, it remained in the United States *Pharmacopoeia* until 1941. The difficulties imposed on its use by the Tax Act of 1937 completed its medical demise, and, from that time on, physicians allowed themselves to become ignorant about the drug.

In any case, throughout history the principal interest in the hemp plant has been in its properties as an agent for achieving euphoria. In this country, it is almost invariably smoked—usually as a cigarette called a reefer, a joint, or a number—but elsewhere the drug is often taken in the form of a drink or in foods such as sweetmeats.

Drug preparations from the hemp plant vary widely in quality and potency, depending on the type (there are possibly three species or, alternatively, various ecotypes), climate, soil, cultivation, and method of preparation. When the cultivated plant is fully ripe, a sticky, golden yellow resin with a minty fragrance covers its flower clusters and top leaves. The plant's resin contains the active substances. Preparations of the drug come in three grades, identified by Indian names. The cheapest and least potent, called bhang, is derived from the cut tops of uncultivated plants and has a low resin content. Much of the marihuana smoked in the United States is of this grade. Ganja is obtained from the flowering tops and leaves of carefully selected cultivated plants, and it has a higher quality and quantity of resin. The third and highest grade of the drug, called charas in India, is largely made from the resin itself, obtained from the tops of mature plants; only this version of the drug is properly called hashish. Hashish is roughly five to eight times more potent than most of the marihuana regularly available in the United States. Recently however, more potent and more expensive marihuana from Thailand, Hawaii, and California has become available in this country. Some northern California growers have been successful in cultivating an unpollinated plant by the early weeding out of male plants; the product is the much sought after Sinsemilla. Clandestine laboratories have developed, through a refluxing method, a product which is variously referred to as hashish oil, liquid hashish, and "the one." It is considerably more potent than hashish; in fact, samples have been found that contain more than 60 per cent tetrahydrocannabinol.

The chemistry of the cannabis drugs is extremely complex and not completely understood. In the 1940's, it was determined that the active constituents are various isomers of tetrahydrocannabinol. The delta-1 form has been synthesized and is believed to be the primary active component of marihuana. The drug's effects, however, probably also involve other components and the form in which it is taken. About 80 derivatives of cannabinol have been prepared, and some of these have been tested for effects in animals or in human volunteers.

The psychic effects of the drug have been described in a very extensive literature. Hashish long ago acquired a lurid reputation through the writings of literary figures, notably the group of French writers—Baudelaire, Gautier, Dumas père, and others—who formed "Le Club des Haschischins" in Paris in the 1850's. Their reports, written under the influence of large amounts of hashish, must be largely discounted as exaggerations that do not apply to moderate use of the drug. Hashish is supposed to have been responsible for Baudelaire's psychosis and death, but the story overlooks the fact that he probably had relatively little experience with hashish, was in all probability actually writing about his experience with laudanum, and, moreover, had been an alcoholic and suffered from tertiary syphilis.

Bayard Taylor—the American writer, lecturer, and traveler best known for his translation of Goethe's *Faust*—wrote one of the first accounts of a cannabis experience in terms that began to approach a clinical description. He tried the drug in a spirit of inquiry during a visit to Egypt in 1854. His narrative of the effects follows (8):

The sensations it then produced were . . . physically of exquisite lightness and airiness—mentally of a wonderfully keen perception of the ludicrous in the most simple and familiar objects. During the half hour in which it lasted, I was at no time so far under its control that I could not, with the clearest perception, study the changes through which I passed. I noted with careful attention the fine sensations which spread throughout the whole tissue of my nervous fibers, each thrill helping to divest my frame of its earthly and material nature, till my substance appeared to me no grosser than the vapours of the atmosphere, and while sitting in the calm of the Egyptian twilight I expected to be lifted up and carried away by the first breeze that should ruffle the Nile. While this process was going on, the objects by which I was surrounded assumed a strange and whimsical expression.... I was provoked into a long fit of laughter ... [the effect] died away as gradually as it came, leaving me overcome with a soft and pleasant drowsiness, from which I sank into a deep, refreshing sleep.

Perhaps a better clinical account is that of Walter Bromberg, a psychiatrist, who described the psychic effects on the basis of his own experience and many observations and talks with people while they were under the influence of marihuana (5):

The intoxication is initiated by a period of anxiety within 10 to 30 minutes after smoking, in which the user sometimes ... develops fears of death and anxieties of vague nature associated with restlessness and hyper-activity. Within a few minutes he begins to feel more calm and soon develops definite euphoria; he becomes talkative ... is elated, exhilarated ... begins to have ... an astounding feeling of lightness of the limbs and body ... laughs uncontrollably and explosively ... without at times the slightest provocation ... has the impression that his conversation is witty, brilliant ... The rapid flow of ideas gives the impression of brilliance of thought and observation ... [but] confusion appears on trying to remember what was thought ... he may begin to see visual hallucinations ... flashes of light or amorphous forms of vivid color which evolve and develop into geometric figures, shapes, human faces, and pictures of great complexity.... After a longer or shorter time, lasting up to two hours, the smoker becomes drowsy, falls into a dreamless sleep and awakens with no physiologic after-effects and with a clear memory of what happened during the intoxication.

Most observers confirm Bromberg's account as a composite and overinclusive description of marihuana highs. They find that the effects from smoking last for 2 to 4 hours, the effects from ingestion 5 to 12 hours. For a new user, the initial anxiety that sometimes occurs is alleviated if supportive friends are present. It is contended that the intoxication heightens sensitivity to external stimuli, reveals details that would ordinarily be overlooked, makes colors seem brighter and richer, brings out values in works of art that previously had little or no meaning to the viewer, and enhances the appreciation of music. Many jazz and rock musicians have said they perform better under the influence of marihuana, but this effect has not been objectively confirmed.

The sense of time is distorted: 10 minutes may seem like an hour. Curiously, there is often a splitting of consciousness, so that the smoker, while experiencing the high, is at the same time an objective observer of his own intoxication. He may, for example, be afflicted with paranoid thoughts yet at the same time be reasonably objective about them and even laugh or scoff at them and in a sense enjoy them. The ability to retain a degree of objectivity may explain the fact that many experienced users of marihuana manage to behave in a perfectly sober fashion in public even when they are highly intoxicated.

Marihuana is commonly referred to as a hallucinogen. Many of the phenomena associated with lysergic acid diethylamide (LSD) and LSD-type substances can be produced by cannabis. As with LSD, the wave-like aspect of the experience is often reported, as is the distorted perception of various parts of the body, spatial and temporal distortion, and depersonalization. Other phenomena commonly associated with both types of drugs are increased sensitivity to sound, synesthesia, heightened suggestibility, and a sense of thinking more clearly and having deeper awareness of the meaning of things. Anxiety and paranoid reactions are also sometimes seen as consequences of either drug. However, the agonizingly nightmarish reactions that even the experienced LSD user may endure are quite rare to the experienced marihuana smoker, not simply because he is using a far less potent drug but also because he has much closer and continuing control over the extent and type of reaction he wishes to induce. Furthermore, cannabis has a tendency to produce sedation, whereas LSD and LSD-type drugs may induce long periods of wakefulness and even restlessness. Unlike LSD, marihuana does not dilate the pupils or materially heighten blood pressure, reflexes, and body temperature. On the other hand, it does increase the pulse rate. However, it is questionable whether marihuana in doses ordinarily used in this country can produce true hallucinations. An important difference is the fact that tolerance rapidly develops with the LSD-type drugs but little if at all with cannabis. Finally, marihuana lacks the potent consciousness-altering qualities of LSD, peyote, mescaline, psilocybin, and so on. These differences, particularly the last, cast considerable doubt on marihuana's credentials for inclusion in this group.

There is now an abundance of evidence that marihuana is not a drug that produces physical dependence; cessation of its use produces no withdrawal symptoms, nor does a user feel any need to increase the dosage as he becomes accustomed to the drug. Furthermore, its capacity to lead to psychological dependence is not as strong as that of either tobacco or alcohol.

Only the unsophisticated continue to believe that cannabis leads to violence and crime. Indeed, instead of inciting criminal behavior, cannabis may tend to suppress it. The intoxication induces a lethargy that is not conducive to any physical activity, let alone committing of crimes. The release of inhibitions results in fantasy and verbal rather than behavioral expression. During the high, the marihuana user may say and think things he would not ordinarily, but he generally does not do things that are foreign to his nature. If he is not normally a criminal, he will not commit a crime under the influence of the drug.

Does marihuana induce sexual debauchery? This popular impression may owe its origin partly to the fantasies of dissolute writers and partly to the fact that in times past users in the Middle East laced the drug with what they thought were aphrodisiacs. However, there is little evidence that cannabis stimulates sexual desire or power. There are those, on the other hand, who contend that marihuana weakens sexual desire—with equally little substantiation. Many marihuana users report that the high enhances the enjoyment of sexual intercourse. This may be true in the same sense that the enjoyment of art and music is apparently enhanced. It is questionable, however, that the intoxication breaks down moral barriers that are not already broken.

Does marihuana lead to physical and mental degeneracy? Reports from many investigators, particularly in Egypt and parts of the Orient, indicate that long term users of the potent versions of cannabis are, indeed, typically passive, nonproductive, slothful, and totally lacking in ambition. This suggests that chronic use of the drug in its stronger forms may have debilitating effects, as prolonged heavy drinking does. There is a far more likely explanation, however. Many of those who take up cannabis in these countries are poverty stricken, hungry, sick, hopeless, or defeated, seeking through this inexpensive drug to soften the impact of an otherwise unbearable reality. This also applies to many of the potheads in the United States. In most situations one cannot be certain which came first: the drug, on the one hand, or the depression, anxiety, feelings of inadequacy, or seemingly intolerable life situation on the other.

There is a substantial body of evidence that moderate use of marihuana does not produce physical or mental deterioration. One of the earliest and most extensive studies of this question was an investigation conducted by the British Government in India in the 1890's. The investigating agency, called the Indian Hemp Drugs Commission, interviewed some 800 persons—including cannabis users and dealers, physicians, superintendents of insane asylums, religious leaders, and a variety of other authorities—and in 1894 published a report of more than 3,000 pages. It concluded that there was no evidence that moderate use of the cannabis drugs produced any disease or mental or moral damage or that it tended to lead to excess any more than the moderate use of whiskey (18, 20).

In the La Guardia study in New York City, an examination of chronic users who had averaged about seven marihuana cigarettes a day (a comparatively high dosage) over a long period (the mean was 8 years) showed that they had suffered no demonstrable mental or physical decline as a result of their use of the drug (14). The 1972 report of the National Commission on Marihuana and Drug Abuse (16), although it did much to demythologize cannabis, cautioned that, of people in the United States who used marihuana, 2 per cent became heavy users and that these abusers were at risk, but it did not make clear exactly what risk was involved. The claim is often made that heavy use of marihuana leads to the so-called amotivational syndrome, but there is no credible evidence that what is meant by this syndrome is related to any inherent properties of the drug rather than to different sociocultural adaptations on the part of the users. Furthermore, since the publication of this report, several controlled studies of chronic heavy use have been completed that have failed to establish any pharmacologically induced harmfulness, including personality deterioration or the development of the so-called amotivational syndrome (2, 4, 7, 11, 19).

A common assertion made about cannabis is that it may lead to psychosis. There is a vast literature on this subject, and it divides into all shades of opinion. Many psychiatrists in India, Egypt, Morocco, and Nigeria have declared emphatically that the drug can produce insanity; others insist that it does not. One of the authorities most often quoted in support of the indictment is A. Benabud of Morocco. He believes that the drug produces a specific syndrome, called "cannabis psychosis." His description of the identifying symptoms is far from clear, however, and other investigators dispute the existence of such a psychosis. The symptoms said to be characteristic of this syndrome are also common to other acute toxic states, including, particularly in Morocco, those associated with malnutrition and endemic infections. Benabud estimates that the number of kif (marihuana) smokers suffering from all types of psychosis is not more than five in 1,000 (3); this rate, however, is lower than the estimated total prevalence of all psychoses in populations of other countries. One would have to assume either (a) that there is a much lower prevalence of psychoses other than cannabis psychosis among kif smokers in Morocco or (b) that there is no such thing as a cannabis psychosis and that the drug is contributing little or nothing to the prevalence rate for psychoses.

The American psychiatrist Bromberg, in a report of one of his studies, listed 31 patients whose psychoses he attributed to the toxic effects of marihuana. Of these 31, however, seven patients were already predisposed to functional psychoses that were only precipitated by the drug, seven others were later found to be schizophrenics, and one was later diagnosed as a manic-depressive (6). The Chopras in India, in examinations of 1,238

cannabis users, found only 13 to be psychotic, which is about the usual prevalence of psychosis in the total population in Western countries (15). In the La Guardia study, nine of 77 persons who were studied intensively had a history of psychosis; this high rate could be attributed, however, to the fact that all those studied were patients in hospitals or institutions. Allentuck and Bowman, the psychiatrists who examined this group, concluded that "marihuana will not produce psychosis *de novo* in a well-integrated, stable person" (1).

An article by V. R. Thacore and S. R. P. Shukla in 1976 revived the concept of the cannabis psychosis (21). The authors compared 25 cases of what they call a paranoid psychosis precipitated by cannabis with an equal number of paranoid schizophrenics. The cannabis psychotics are described as patients in whom there has been a clear temporal relation between prolonged abuse of cannabis and the development of a psychosis on more than two occasions. All had used cannabis heavily for at least 3 years, mainly in the form of bhang, the weakest of the three preparations common in India (it is usually drunk as a tea or eaten in doughy pellets). In comparison with the schizophrenics, the cannabis psychotics are described as more panicky, elated, boisterous, and communicative; their behavior is said to be more often violent and bizarre and their mental processes characterized by rapidity of thought and flight of ideas without schizophrenic thought disorder. The prognosis is said to be good; the symptoms are easily relieved by phenothiazines, and recurrence is prevented by a decision not to use cannabis again. The syndrome is distinguished from an acute toxic reaction by the absence of clouded sensorium, confusion, and disorientation. Thacore and Shukla did not provide enough information to justify either the identification of their 25 patients' conditions as a single clinical syndrome or the asserted relation to cannabis use. They had little to say about the amount of cannabis used, except that relatives of the patients regarded it as abnormally large; they did not discuss the question of why the psychosis is associated with bhang rather than the stronger cannabis preparations ganja and charas. The meaning of "prolonged abuse on more than two occasions" in the case of men who are constant heavy cannabis users is not clarified, and the temporal relation between this situation and psychosis is not specified. Moreover, the cannabis-taking habits of the control group of schizophrenics are not discussed—a serious omission where use of bhang is so common. The patients described as cannabis psychotics are probably a heterogeneous mixture, with acute schizophrenic breaks, acute manic episodes, severe borderline conditions, and a few symptoms actually related to acute cannabis intoxication: mainly anxiety-panic reactions and a few psychoses of the kind that can be precipitated in unstable people by many different experiences of stress or consciousness change (21).

The explanation for such psychoses is that a person maintaining a delicate balance of ego functioning—so that, for instance, the ego is threatened by a severe loss or a surgical assault or even an alcoholic debauch—may also be overwhelmed or precipitated into a schizophrenic reaction by a drug that alters, however mildly, his state of consciousness. This concatenation of factors—a person whose ego is already overburdened in its attempts to manage a great deal of anxiety and to prevent distortion of perception and body image, plus the taking of a drug that, in some persons, promotes just these effects—may, indeed, be the last straw in precipitating a schizophrenic break. Of 41 first-break acute schizophrenic patients studied by Dr. Grinspoon at the Massachusetts Mental Health Center, it was possible to elicit a history of marihuana use in six. In four of the six it seemed quite improbable that the drug could have had any relation to the development of the acute psychosis, because the psychosis was so remote in time from the drug experience. Careful history taking and attention to details of the drug experiences and changing mental status in the remaining two patients failed either to implicate or exonerate marihuana as a precipitant in their psychoses.

Our own clinical experience and that of others (22) suggests that cannabis may precipitate exacerbations in the psychotic processes of some schizophrenic patients at a time when their illnesses are otherwise reasonably well controlled with antipsychotic drugs. In these patients it is often difficult to determine whether the use of cannabis is simply a precipitant of the psychosis or whether it is an attempt to treat symptomat-

ically the earliest perceptions of decompensation; needless to say, the two possibilities are not mutually exclusive.

Although there is little evidence for the existence of a cannabis psychosis, it seems clear that the drug may precipitate in susceptible people one of several types of mental dysfunction. The most serious and disturbing of these is the toxic psychosis. This is an acute state that resembles the delirium of a high fever and is caused by the presence in the brain of toxic substances that interfere with a variety of cerebral functions. Generally speaking, as the toxins disappear, so do the symptoms of toxic psychosis. This type of reaction may be caused by any number of substances taken either as intended or inadvertent overdoses. The syndrome often includes clouding of consciousness, restlessness, confusion, bewilderment, disorientation, dream-like thinking, apprehension, fear, illusions, and hallucinations. It generally requires a rather large ingested dose of cannabis to induce a toxic psychosis. Such a reaction is apparently much less likely to occur when cannabis is smoked, perhaps because not enough of the active substances can be absorbed sufficiently rapidly, or possibly because in the process of smoking those cannabinol derivatives that are most likely to precipitate this syndrome are modified in some way as yet unknown.

There are people who may suffer what are usually short lived, acute anxiety states, sometimes with and sometimes without accompanying paranoid thoughts. The anxiety may reach such proportions as properly to be called panic. Such panic reactions, although uncommon, probably constitute the most frequent adverse reaction to the moderate use of smoked marihuana. During this reaction, the sufferer may believe that the various distortions of his perception of his body mean that he is dying or that he is undergoing some great physical catastrophe, and similarly he may interpret the psychological distortions induced by the drug as an indication that he is losing his sanity. Panic states may, albeit rarely, be so severe as to incapacitate, usually for a relatively short period of time. The anxiety that characterizes the acute panic reaction resembles an attenuated version of the frightening parts of an LSD or other psychedelic experience—the so-called bad trip. Some proponents of the use of LSD in psychotherapy have asserted that the induced altered state of consciousness involves a lifting of repression. Although the occurrence of a global undermining of repression is questionable, many effects of LSD do suggest important alterations in ego defenses. These alterations presumably make new percepts and insights available to the ego; some, particularly those most directly derived from primary process, may be quite threatening, especially if there is no comfortable and supportive setting to facilitate the integration of the new awareness into the ego organization. So psychedelic experiences may be accompanied by a great deal of anxiety, particularly when the drugs are taken under poor conditions of set and setting; to a much lesser extent, the same can be said of cannabis.

These reactions are self-limiting, and simple reassurance is the best method of treatment. Perhaps the main danger to the user is that he will be diagnosed as having a toxic psychosis, an unfortunately common mistake. Users with this kind of reaction may be quite distressed, but they are not psychotic, inasmuch as the sine qua non of sanity, the ability to test reality, remains intact, and the panicked user is invariably able to relate his discomfort to the drug. There is no disorientation, nor are there true hallucinations. Sometimes this panic reaction is accompanied by paranoid ideation. The user may, for example, believe that the others in the room, especially if they are not well known to him, have some hostile intentions toward him or that someone is going to inform on him, often to the police, for smoking marihuana. Generally speaking, these paranoid ideas are not strongly held, and simple reassurance dispels them. Anxiety reactions and paranoid thoughts are much more likely in someone who is taking the drug for the first time or in an unpleasant or unfamiliar setting than in an experienced user who is comfortable with his surroundings and companions; the reaction is very rare where marihuana is a casually accepted part of the social scene. The likelihood varies directly with the dose and inversely with the user's experience; thus the most vulnerable person is the inexperienced user who inadvertently (often precisely because he lacks familiarity with the drug) takes a large dose that produces perceptual and somatic changes for which he is unprepared.

One rather rare reaction to cannabis is the flashback, or spontaneous recurrence of drug symptoms while not intoxicated. Although several reports suggest that this may occur in marihuana users even without prior use of any other drug (9), in general it seems to arise only in those who have used more powerful hallucinogenic or psychedelic drugs. There are also some people who have flashback experiences of psychedelic drug trips while smoking marihuana; this is sometimes regarded as an extreme version of a more general heightening of the marihuana high that occurs after the use of hallucinogens. Many people find flashbacks enjoyable, but to others they are distressing. They usually fade with the passage of time. It is possible that flashbacks are attempts to deal with primary process derivatives and other unconscious material that have breached the ego defenses during the psychedelic or cannabis experience.

Rarely, but especially among new users of marihuana, there occurs an acute depressive reaction that resembles the reactive or neurotic type. It is generally rather mild and transient but may sometimes require psychiatric intervention. This type of reaction is most likely to occur in a user who has some degree of underlying depression; it is as though the drug allows the depression to be felt and experienced as such. Again, set and setting play an important part.

References

1. Allentuck, S., and Bowman, K. M. The psychiatric aspects of marihuana intoxication. Am. J. Psychiatry 99:248, 1942.
2. Beaubrun, M. H., and Knight, F. Psychiatric assessment of 30 chronic users of cannabis and 30 matched controls. Am. J. Psychiatry 130:309, 1973.
3. Benabud, A. Psychopathological aspects of the cannabis situation in Morocco: Statistical data for 1956. Bull. Narc. 9:2, 1957.
4. Braude, M. C., and Szara, S., editors. *Pharmacology of Marihuana*, 2 vols. New York, Raven Press, 1976.
5. Bromberg, W. Marihuana intoxication: A clinical study of *Cannabis sativa* intoxication. Am. J. Psychiatry 91:303, 1934.
6. Bromberg, W. Marihuana: A psychiatric study. J.A.M.A. 113:4, 1939.
7. Dornbush, R. L., Freedman, A. M., and Fink, M., editors. *Chronic Cannabis Use*, vol. 282. New York, Annals of New York Academy of Sciences, 1976.
8. Ebin, D., editor. *The Drug Experience*. New York, Grove Press, 1961.
9. Ganz, V. P., and Volkman, F. Adverse reactions to marijuana use among college students. J. Am. Coll. Health Assoc. 25:93, 1976.
10. Grinspoon, L. *Marihuana Reconsidered*, ed. 2. Cambridge, Mass., Harvard University Press, 1977.

11. Hochman, J. S., and Brill, N. Q. Chronic marijuana use and psychosocial adaptation. Am. J. Psychiatry 130:132, 1973.

12. Keeler, M. H. Adverse reaction to marijuana. Am. J. Psychiatry 124:674, 1967.

13. Ludlow, F. H. *The Hasheesh Eater: Being Passages from the Life of a Pythagorean.* New York, Harper and Bros., 1857.

14. Mayor's Committee on Marihuana. *The Marihuana Problem in the City of New York.* Lancaster, Pa., Jaques Cattell Press, 1944.

15. Murphy, H. B. M. The cannabis habit: A review of the recent psychiatric literature. Addictions 13:3, 1966.

16. National Commission on Marihuana and Drug Abuse. *Marihuana: A Signal of Misunderstanding: First Report of the National Commission on Marihuana and Drug Abuse.* Washington, D.C., United States Government Printing Office, 1972.

17. O'Shaughnessy, W. B. On the preparation of the Indian hemp, or gunjah (*Cannabis indica*): The effects on the animal system in health, and their utility in the treatment of tetanus and other convulsive diseases. Trans. Med. Phys. Soc. Bombay 8:421, 1842.

18. *Report of the Indian Hemp Drugs Commission, 1893–94,* 7 vols. Simla, Government Central Printing Office, 1894.

19. Rubin, V., and Comitas, L. *Ganja in Jamaica.* The Hague, Mouton, 1975.

20. Solomon, D., editor. *The Marihuana Papers.* Indianapolis, Bobbs-Merrill, 1966.

21. Thacore, V. R., and Shukla, S. R. P. Cannabis psychosis and paranoid schizophrenia. Arch. Gen. Psychiatry 33:383, 1976.

22. Treffert, D. A. Marihuana use in schizophrenia: A clear hazard. Am. J. Psychiatry 135:10, 1978.

23. Walton, R. P. *Marihuana: America's New Drug Problem.* Philadelphia, J. B. Lippincott, 1938.

CHAPTER 13

HALLUCINOGENS

J. Thomas Ungerleider, M.D.

G. G. De Angelis, Ph.D.

In this chapter we will focus on the proto-type hallucinogen lysergic acid diethylamide (LSD). We will also cover the atypical but much publicized drug phencyclidine (PCP). Marihuana (THC), which some classify as a mild psychedelic (although others feel sedative-hypnotic properties are primary), will not be covered because much has recently been written about this much researched, publicized, and most controversial (morally and philosophically) of substances. Some hallucinogens are found in plants; all of these are organic compounds. No inorganic plant constituents, like minerals, have hallucinogenic properties. Most hallucinogens contain nitrogen in their structure; some do not. Those which do are alkaloids, and most biological activity of hallucinogenic plants is related to the alkaloids. The indole nucleus of the alkaloids often appears in the form of tryptamine derivatives (34).

Actually, much of the revolution in the drug abuse field that began in the United States in the mid-1960's came from the concern about the use of LSD. Timothy Leary and his "turn-on, tune-in, drop-out" followers proseletyzed that this most powerful drug known to man would provide instant happiness in a pill, instant creativity in art and music, and instant problem-solving ability in school and at work. Many, particularly the young, began to experiment with this drug. Up until this time, drug abuse was largely characterized by heroin in the ghettoes, jazz musicians and Mexican immigrants smoking marihuana, housewives using amphetamines, and businessmen taking tranquilizers; most also used alcohol. Then, as LSD experimentation increased, various adverse reactions began to be recorded from medical centers in the country, and the populace reacted with anxiety and fear.

Actually, the earlier users of LSD were older and organized their life style around the drug. They would never give it to anyone without their knowledge and would not take other kinds of drugs. They would not smoke tobacco or use amphetamines, barbiturates, or drink alcohol. In our original studies the average age of persons in difficulty was 21. The street quality of LSD (Owsley's Acid or Stanley's Stuff) was as good as that made by Sandoz Laboratories. As publicity about drug use increased, concern rose until drug abuse was perceived as the nation's number 2 or number 3 most pressing problem behind the economy and Vietnam (surveys for the National Commission on Marijuana and Drug Abuse) (26). The nation geared up to "declare war on drug abuse," and the national anti-drug abuse effort expanded from a relatively small research-oriented program under the

National Institute of Mental Health to the newly created National Institutes of Drug Abuse (NIDA) and Alcoholism and Alcohol Abuse (NIAAA). Massive funds were allocated, and one result was the creation of a new drug abuse industrial complex that supported more than 200,000 treatment slots and more than 35,000 treatment worker positions (mostly for ex-addicts).

Rapid enactment of new legislation essentially banned all human LSD research. Today LSD, along with heroin and marihuana, remains classified as a Schedule 1 drug (Controlled Substance Act). LSD was thus regarded as having no medical usefulness and a high abuse potential and to be unsafe. None of these conditions is necessarily true, however.

DEFINITIONS

The term hallucinogen means producer of hallucinations. Many drugs, when taken in sufficient quantity, can cause hallucinations, either auditory or visual. The hallucinations may be present as part of a delirium, accompanied by disturbances in judgment, orientation, intellect, memory, and emotion (an organic brain syndrome). Delirium may result from ingestion of a variety of substances, in sufficient amount, or by withdrawal from the drug state (e.g., delirium tremens in alcohol or sedative-hypnotic withdrawal).

The use of the term hallucinogen generally refers to a group of drugs that alter consciousness without delirium, sedation, or stimulation as prominent effects. This label is actually an inaccurate one, as true hallucinations are rare. What are commonly seen are illusory phenomena. An illusion is a perceptual distortion of an actual stimulus in the environment. To see someone's face seem to be melting is an illusion; to see a melting face when no one is present is a hallucination. Consequently, some have called this class of drugs illusionogenic, particularly in Canada.

There are a variety of more widely accepted synonyms for the hallucinogens. These include the term "psychedelic" or "mind-manifesting," which was coined in 1957 by Osmond in the hope of finding a nonjudgmental term (30). Unfortunately, those who use the term psychedelic have been criticized as being "prodrug" much as those who use the term hallucinogen have

been of being "antidrug." The term psychotomimetic, or producer of psychosis, has also been widely used. This nomenclature originally referred to the "model psychosis" produced by LSD, the prototype drug in this class. It was hoped that induction of this model psychosis would replicate schizophrenia and thus be used to study, and hopefully find a cure for, the major illness confronting psychiatry. These hopes have never materialized, as fundamental differences between this drug-induced model psychosis and the schizophrenic state have been perceived.

Other less widely used terms have included "pseudohallucinations" to emphasize the intactness of the observing ego, which recognizes at the time that the hallucination is imaginary, and "mysticomimetic" to call attention to the induced accompanying mystical states. Other suggested names include "phantastica, psychotaraxic, psycholeptic, psychotomystic" (6, 34).

Phencyclidine (PCP) is classified as an atypical hallucinogenic agent. The terms "dissociative anesthetic" and "cataleptoid or sympathomimetic analgesic" have also been used to refer to PCP (12). Siegel has discussed the excitory, sedative, hallucinogenic, and catatonic properties of PCP (38). Winters et al., in studying dose-related responses to PCP, showed that more LSD-like reactions than anesthetic reactions occur with increasing doses (48).

Perhaps it is the case that no single classification is adequate for PCP. Clinically administered doses of the drug give rise to analgesia with dissociative side effects. On the other hand "street" doses," which may include impurities and contaminants, give rise to hallucinatory and psychotic-like states.

HISTORICAL DEVELOPMENT

The search for ways to alter consciousness is almost as old as man. The means employed often included use of chemicals from herbs, potions, and vapors. For instance, in order to produce an altered state of consciousness, the Oracle of Delphi supposedly inhaled carbon dioxide fumes that emanated from a rock fissure.

Hashish (marihuana) is the best known of the ancient drugs. A variety of mushrooms have hallucinogenic properties, the most publicized being the Mexican or magic mushroom that contains psilocybin and psilocin. The peyote cactus in Mexico, worshiped by the Native American Church, contains the hallucinogen mescaline. Morning glory seeds contain lysergic acid derivatives, and in the Congo the Bantu chew a root containing ibogaine. These, along with nutmeg, are but a few of the naturally occurring hallucinogens. Lysergic acid is one of the constituents of the ergot fungus growing on rye. It has inadvertantly been baked into bread, with widespread mental changes recorded as a result (17). Because the diethylamide is a prerequisite for lysergic acid derivative hallucinogenic activity, it is not clear whether these reported epidemics were actually due to ergot in the bread or to some other substances or phenomena.

It was not until 1938 that Hofmann added the diethylamide group to lysergic acid. In 1943 he accidentally ingested some of the LSD and had a psychedelic experience. This he later repeated in a larger dose. He described the resultant "trip" in a number of ways, including a discussion of a most unusual bicycle ride home with a colleague (41).

CLASSIFICATIONS (7)

A. Substituted indolalkylamines
  1. LSD and related compounds, lysergic acid amide and isolysergic acid amide
  2. Dimethyltryptamine (DMT) (named the "businessman's LSD" for its rapid onset and short duration of action) and related compounds
  3. Bufotenine
  4. Psilocybin and psilocin, in the Mexican or magic mushroom
  5. Harmine and harmaline
  6. Ibogaine
B. Substituted phenylakylamines
  1. Mescaline and related alkaloids
  2. 2,5-Dimethoxy-4-methylamphetamine (DOM) (STP and related substituted amphetamines)
C. 3-N-Substituted piperidyl benzilates
  1. Ditran and related central anticholinergic agents like atropine and scopolamine
D. Phencyclohexylpiperidines
  1. Sernyl, phencyclidine (PCP), a dissociative anesthetic used in veterinary medicine
E. Myristicin, analogue of an amphetamine-like compound found in nutmeg and spices
F. Tetrahydrocannabinols, particularly Δ9-THC, the active ingredient in marihuana.

CHEMICAL STRUCTURE OF COMMON HALLUCINOGENS

Figure 13.1 (5) shows the chemical structures of common hallucinogens.

ETIOLOGY AND CLINICAL DESCRIPTION

GENERAL CONSIDERATIONS

It is important to emphasize the distinction between substance use and abuse. The behavior of taking a drug (whether legal or not) for recreational reasons versus medical prescription may be functional or dysfunctional. As more and more observers have noted, only behavior that interferes with functioning at work or school and with interpersonal relationships is dysfunctional and should be regarded as drug abuse. This means that much dysfunctional behavior in our culture, particularly surrounding alcohol, is also substance abuse, although legal and even socially encouraged. Likewise, not all hallucinogenic use is drug abuse. Drug *use* patterns include experimental, recreational, and circumstantial-situational versus the intensified and compulsive drug *abuse* patterns (22, 27). These patterns have been differentiated for a variety of drugs including marihuana, cocaine, and PCP (27, 37, 38).

Interest in mind-altering drugs has increased in Western countries in the past two decades. To some extent this increased interest is a result of changing psychosocial attitudes that have resulted in a youth culture for which the norms and values of an achievement-oriented society may have less relevance (32). Therefore, the use of LSD (and other hallucinogens) may, in some cases, be more related to the wish to belong to a society that expects its members to "turn-on," rather than to deeply rooted feelings of isolation, alienation, or the variety of psychological reasons that have also been posited as explanations for LSD usage (28). Most likely there are some LSD users who do so because of social norms and pressures and others who

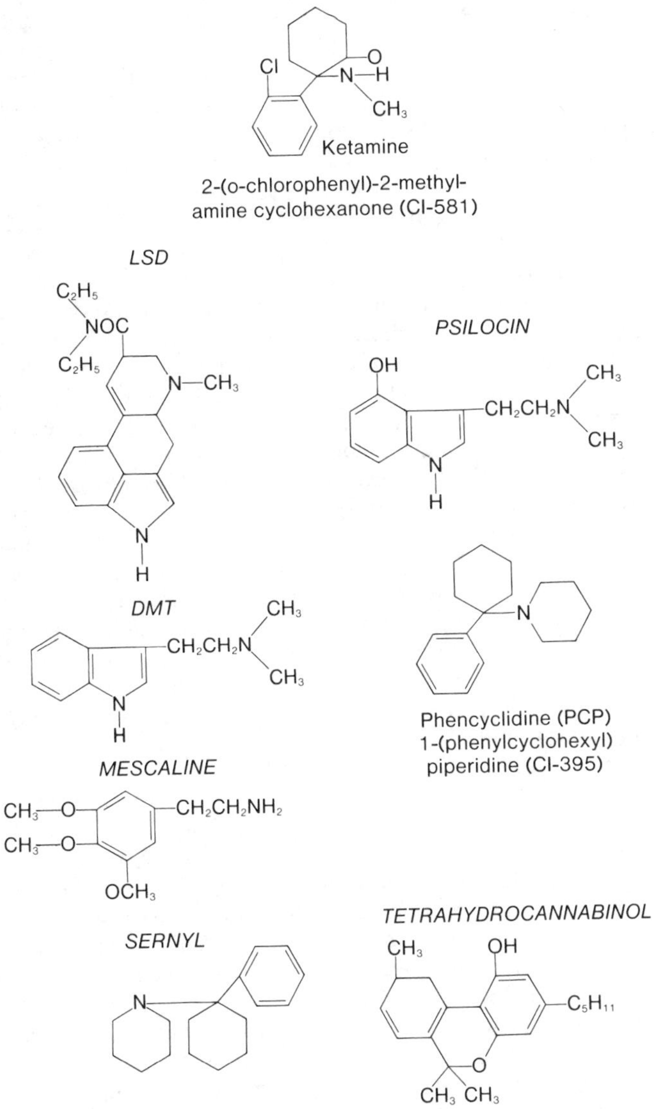

Ketamine

2-(o-chlorophenyl)-2-methyl-
amine cyclohexanone (CI-581)

LSD

PSILOCIN

DMT

Phencyclidine (PCP)
1-(phenylcyclohexyl)
piperidine (CI-395)

MESCALINE

TETRAHYDROCANNABINOL

SERNYL

Figure 13.1. The common hallucinogens.

do so as a form of self-medication aimed at maintaining what may be a tenuous but at least acceptable (to the user) psychological homeostasis.

LYSERGIC ACID DIETHYLAMIDE (LSD)

LSD is the most powerful of the hallucinogens with effects recorded after 20 to 30 μg. Psychological and behavioral effects are seen at 2 to 4 hours, with a gradual return to the predrug state in 6 to 8 hours (19). Gastrointestinal tract and other mucous membrane absorption occurs readily with drug diffusion to all tissues, including brain. Tolerance to repeated doses both develops and is lost rap-

idly. Thus, LSD users usually limit themselves to once or twice weekly (46). Cross-tolerance develops to mescaline and psilocybin, but not to amphetamines, PCP, or THC (tetrahydrocannabinol). There is no LSD withdrawal syndrome, nor is LSD drug-seeking behavior observed in humans or animals. Most LSD is excreted within 24 hours and found in the feces; some is also found in the urine. The lethal dose in humans has not been determined; fatalities reported have been due to perceptual distortions with resultant accidental death (i.e., "flying" off a roof, merging with an oncoming automobile on the freeway) (45). An elephant died from

0.1 mg/kg or approximately 300,000 μg of LSD.

Recent History

The original manufacturer of LSD, Sandoz Laboratories, stopped distributing the drug more than 10 years ago due to the adverse reactions and resulting public outcry and hysteria. All existing supplies were turned over to the government, which (theoretically) makes the drug available for legitimate research. Nonetheless, black-market LSD is plentiful, and, according to the "Analysis Anonymous" laboratories, street supplies are not usually contaminated. However, street dosages vary widely, and occasionally someone will try to purchase THC and receive LSD (or PCP or something else entirely). Before LSD became illegal and research stopped, over 1,000 articles on LSD had appeared in the medical literature (by the mid-1960's), but few publications now appear. The therapeutic potential of LSD as an adjunct to psychotherapy, in the treatment of the dying patient, and in the treatment of alcoholism remains unresolved.

Mechanism of Action

The mechanism of action for LSD remains unclear. The antagonism of this drug to serotonin (5HT) does not explain its effects in any simple fashion. It has been reported that LSD slows down serotonin metabolism and causes binding of serotonin in nerve endings (16). Concomitantly, brain levels of norepinephrine are decreased. Drugs that deplete serotonin in the brain, either by blocking its synthesis or impairing its storage, markedly enhance and prolong the LSD effect. This finding tends to corroborate the notion that high LSD activity correlates with a decrease in available serotonin in nerve endings. However, pretreatment with monamine oxidase inhibitors or serotonin precursors for several days or weeks decreases the effects of LSD.

Apparently LSD acts either to block the serotonin receptor sites or to imitate its effects. LSD has been shown to mimic serotonin in its several effects on isolated glands and thus to function as a serotonin agonist (4). The anatomical sites of action of LSD in the brain are not known at this time. Arguments have also been advanced that LSD does not work by antagonizing serotonin. It has been found that certain lysergic acid derivatives that have high antiserotonin potency do not possess hallucinogenic properties, even though they readily cross the blood-brain barrier. However, it has been shown that LSD is a more potent serotonin inhibitor on some (rather than all) central nervous system serotoninergic neurons. It may be that it is these specific neurons that are responsible for the drug's hallucinogenic activity (33).

LSD also possesses central activity that explains the marked pupillary dilatation (versus THC), tachycardia, and increased body temperature. Set and setting are crucial determinants of the LSD experience. Adverse reactions have occurred from as little as 40 μ, and no effects have been reported from 2,000 μ, although the drug's effects are usually proportional to dosage levels. Once commonly reported by medical facilities (47), adverse LSD reactions are rarely seen today, yet the drug remains in widespread use. Social factors, media presentations, and public hysteria are all determinants of the drug's effects. Prediction of who will have an adverse reaction is notoriously unreliable (44).

Effects

The subjective effects of LSD are dramatic. Visual alterations are marked and sounds are intensified. Synesthesias ("seeing" smells, "hearing" colors) are commonly reported. Touch is magnified and time is markedly distorted. Feelings of attainment of true insights and experiencing of delusional ideation are also common. Performance on tests involving attention, concentration, and motivation is impaired. There is no generally accepted evidence of brain damage, chromosomal abnormalities, or teratogenic effects.

The chronic effects of LSD must be differentiated from the effects due to personality disorders, particularly in those who use a variety of drugs in polydrug abuse-type patterns. Personality changes that result from LSD use may occur after a single experience, unlike that with other classes of drugs (PCP, perhaps, excepted). In some individuals with well integrated personalities and with no previous psychiatric history, chronic personality changes have also resulted from repeated LSD use. The suggestibility that may come from many experiences with LSD may be reinforced by the social values of any particular subculture in which the drug is used. For instance, if some of these subcultures embrace withdrawal from society (a noncompetitive approach toward life), the person who withdraws after the LSD experience(s) may be suffering from a side effect that is really more of a social value than a drug effect.

Adverse Reactions

Adverse reactions to LSD have been divided into acute and chronic. A person's reaction to the effects of the drug may be felt by the person either to be a pleasant or an unpleasant experience. Thus a perceptual distortion or illusion may provide intense anxiety in one person and be a pleasant interlude for another.

Acute anxiety reactions occur and usually wear off before medical intervention is sought. Paranoid ideation, depression, "hallucinations," and occasionally a confusional state (organic brain syndrome) are the more commonly reported acute side effects (43). Persons who place a premium on self-control, advance planning, and impulse restriction may do particularly poorly on LSD. The occurrence of multiple previous good LSD experiences renders no immunity from an adverse reaction (i.e., being arrested and read one's rights in the middle of a pleasant experience may precipitate an anxiety reaction).

Chronic adverse reactions include psychoses, depressive reactions, acting out, paranoid states, and flashbacks (15, 35). Chronic personality changes with a shift in attitudes and evidences of magical thinking also occur. An atypical schizophrenic-like state may persist, but whether predisposition to this condition is necessary is uncertain. There is always the associated risk that self-destructive behavior may occur during the acute or chronic reaction. In addition, these drugs interact in a variety of nonspecific ways with the personality, which may particularly impair the developing adolescent (25). Many chronic LSD users eventually use a variety of drugs, particularly the sedative-hypnotics and stimulants. This is a marked departure from the LSD users seen in the 1960's whose entire life style was organized in a psychedelic fashion.

Some small proportion of LSD and other hallucinogenic users have experienced flashbacks (36). These may occur spontaneously a number of weeks or months after the original drug experience. There may or may not be a precipitant in the form of stress, subsequent use of marihuana, etc. The original drug experience is re-created complete with (perceptual) time and reality distortion. Even a previously pleasant drug experience may be accompanied by anxiety when the person realizes he has no control over its recurrence. In time, these flashbacks decrease in intensity, frequency, and duration (although initially they usually last only a few seconds) whether treated (with tranquilizers and reassurance) or not. The exact mechanism of action of the flashback remains obscure.

Treatment of Adverse LSD Reactions

Treatment of the acute LSD reaction must be directed to preventing the patient from physically harming himself or others. Anxiety can be handled by warm support and reassurance, but the minor tranquilizers like diazepam may be effective. The oral route is usually sufficient for administering such medication. Some have pointed out that chlorpromazine is effective and can end an LSD trip, as will the barbiturates (6, 25). Severely agitated patients who fail to respond to diazepam may respond to 50 to 100 mg of chlorpromazine given orally or intramuscularly every hour (28). Chlorpromazine has also been found effective in treating LSD-induced psychosis (10). These same authors suggest that chlorpromazine in combination with electric shock therapy is the treatment of choice for PCP-induced psychosis. Prior to the use of chlorpromazine in treating an LSD reaction it is important to ensure that adequate liver function is present.

Psychotherapy consists of reassurance in the acute phase and avoidance of physical intrusion when the LSD user begins to calm down. Psychotherapy on a long term basis, of course, should be directed to finding out what needs are being fulfilled by the use of the drug for this particular person. Flashbacks can usually be handled with psychotherapy. A major tranquilizer may be indicated, but that probably is as much for the reassurance of the therapist as for the patient.

PHENCYCLIDINE (PCP)

Phencyclidine hydrochloride is a water-soluble powder that may be ingested or smoked (often on parsley or other leaves).

Some street names include angel dust, elephant or horse tranquilizer, *PeaCe Pill*, and rocket fuel. There are over 30 similar chemical analgesics, including the anesthetic ketamine. PCP is often classified as an atypical hallucinogen; it has stimulant, depressant, and analgesic properties as well. Tolerance develops, but unlike other hallucinogens, monkeys will self-administer PCP (9, 18).

Phencyclidine is a drug with many neuropsychiatric effects. It can produce anesthesia, analgesia, delirium, schizophreniform psychosis, disinhibition, euphoria, violent behavior, intense depersonalization, and postphencyclidine depression. In addition, neurological symptoms and signs may also be present, including ataxia, dysarthria, vertical and horizontal nystagmus, and convulsions. Depending upon the dosage and the individual consuming it, a pleasant disinhibition or a serious overdose resulting in death may occur. In between are a variety of undulating, unpredictable states that may be quite difficult to treat.

A reported cause of deaths resulting from PCP intoxication has been drowning. In one series of 19 PCP-related deaths in two California counties, 11 of the deaths were from drowning.

Effects and Adverse Reactions

PCP abuse may be differentiated from abuse of other drugs by consideration of some of its characteristic features. The initial experience is usually reported as a pleasurable "high" or numbness. This is usually seen with low dosages of the drug. With larger amounts of the drug dysphoric experiences occur, including feelings of isolation, inability to move, and more intense numbness. Episodes of cramps, nausea, and emesis have been reported, as well as bad trips that consist of confused and/or transient psychotic behavior, hallucinations, and coma or stupor. These are particularly common with periodic use of very large amounts of PCP. A chronic organic brain syndrome often develops with memory loss that also may be chronic. Longer lasting psychotic reactions may include bizarre behavior with confusion and agitation. Often a patient is mute, staring, and unresponsive to painful stimuli. There is often evidence of cerebellar dysfunction, including ataxia and dysarthria. Violence and aggressiveness are often seen as well as excessive

amounts of fearfulness. Chronic depression, lasting as long as 3 to 4 months after PCP ingestion, has been observed (40). A resumption of PCP use often follows bouts of depression as the individual self-medicates in an attempt to escape from his or her dysphoric state.

Treatment of Adverse PCP Reactions

Treatment of PCP overdose in the initial phase requires vigorous medical management. The most acute physical effects of the drug are evident at this time: respiratory depression, convulsions, coma, and combativeness. Treatment during this stage includes good life support systems in an emergency room or an intensive care unit. This emergency stage of PCP overdose requires staff familiar with PCP intoxication and overdose who are able to differentiate PCP's effects from other emergency situations, e.g., nontoxic psychosis.

Acidification of the urine and gastric lavage (1) are recommended. As the excretion time of PCP is variable, prolonged acidification of the urine for as long as 2 weeks is recommended. Cranberry juice in combination with ascorbic acid is often used for such acidification (2).

Treatment of PCP reactions after the stage of acute toxicity is directed at managing the various phases of psychosis and psychotic behavior that can follow the overdose. The initial phase of violent psychosis is handled as a psychiatric emergency by secluding the patient. Often chlorpromazine is administered both to ameliorate the psychosis and to provide sedation (24). However, the use of phenothiazines is not recommended because of the anticholinergic potentiation with PCP. Phenothiazines are contraindicated where a confusional state is associated with hypotension, ataxia, nystagmus, and tachycardia. There is no evidence that phenothiazines either shorten the intoxication stage or antagonize the behavioral effects of PCP. In fact, behavioral effects of PCP may be intensified by chlorpromazine (3, 11). Prolonged severe hypotension has been recorded after the administration of phenothiazines (21). Haldoperidol has been used, as has been diazepam. Intravenous diphenylhydantoin (Dilantin) and diazepam have been effective in control of seizures. Treatment of the hypertension that often accompanies acute phencyclidine intoxication is important. Diazoxide (Hyperstat) is one recommended drug.

The second phase of PCP psychosis, which is a mixed phase of restlessness and unpredictability, is treated by continuous monitoring of the patient and continuation of tranquilizer medication. During the third phase, which is characterized by rapid resolution of symptoms and rapid personality integration, the patient is best handled by brief psychotherapy. Unfortunately, many of these patients return to the drug, relapse into psychosis, and return for help again. A description of the depressive symptomtology as well as more detailed explanations of the various phases of PCP intoxication have been described in detail elsewhere (40). Treatment of adolescent PCP abuse in a residential setting has been described (8). Of note is the fact that these young PCP abusers remained in residential treatment longer than non-PCP-abusing youthful drug abusers. This finding is important, because long term therapy can only be initiated if the client remains within the treatment environment.

DIFFERENTIAL DIAGNOSIS

LSD

It is important to rule out paranoid schizophrenia, particularly as patients who in fact are paranoid often now complain of being poisoned with LSD, much as they once felt they were being talked about on all the television programs. A history of prior mental illness, a psychiatric examination that reveals the absence of an intact or observing ego, auditory (rather than visual) hallucinations, and the lack of development of drug tolerance all speak for schizophrenia. Other drug psychoses, including those from amphetamines and PCP, must be ruled out. An organic syndrome in general speaks against LSD, especially when obtunded consciousness is present. Toxicological analysis of body fluids may be helpful in making the ultimate diagnosis, but supportive treatment must not be withheld. Atropine poisoning can be differentiated by the dry mouth, blurred vision, and disturbances in swallowing, gait, and speech. Belladonna preparations cause cycloplegia.

Patients with amphetamine psychosis often fail to differentiate their perceptual distortions from reality, whereas LSD users have intact apperception. The effects of LSD, mescaline, and phencyclidine have been compared (49, 50).

PCP

PCP intoxication and/or overdose may be misdiagnosed as an acute schizophrenic episode, thereby resulting in therapeutic interventions often appropriate for schizophrenia but not so for phencyclidine intoxication (13). Luisada defines the PCP psychosis as (23):

... a schizophreniform psychosis which occurs in some individuals after phencyclidine use and persists for more than a day ... The PCP psychosis is characterized by the appearance of the cardinal signs of schizophrenia and unpredictable, aggressive behavior. Characteristically there is autistic and delusional thinking, commonly including global paranoia ....

Variations in response to PCP, probably dose dependent, have been reported (14). A summary of dose-dependent reactions most likely to be encountered in an emergency room situation or elsewhere is provided in Table 13.1 (1).

A number of psychological symptoms from PCP may be present that can also assist in the diagnosis. These include changes in body image, estrangement, disorientation of thought, feelings of inebriation, drowsiness, and apathy. The patient may show a marked degree of hostility, negativism, and bizarre behavior.

When persons present acutely confused or delirious, with no focal neurological findings, one can suspect that the symptoms are indicative of drug use. Phencyclidine users often display a "blank stare" appearance as well as catalepsy and catatonic behavior, which are characteristics of use of this drug (21).

An acutely excited, confused, and ataxic patient who presents with nystagmus but no mydriasis should be suspected of PCP intoxication rather than being under the influence of LSD and/or central nervous system stimulants. If patients are comatose with or without respiratory depression, PCP intoxication may be differentiated from a sedative-hypnotic overdose by the presence of hypertension and hyperreflexia.

Phencyclidine intoxication caused by ingestion of large doses of the drug may be

Table 13.1
Common Dose-dependent Reactions to PCP

Dose	Symptoms
5 mg (20–30 ng/ml in serum)	Agitation and excitement, gross incoordination, blank stare appearance, catatonic rigidity, catalepsy, inability to speak, horizontal or vertical nystagmus, loss of pinprick response, flushing, diaphoresis, hyperacusis
5–10 mg (30–100 ng/ml in serum)	Coma or stupor, eyes remain open, pupils in midposition or reactive, nystagmus, vomiting, hypersalivation, repetitive motor movements, myoclonus (shivering), muscle rigidity on stimulation, flushing, diaphoresis, fever, decreased peripheral sensations
10 mg (100 ng/ml and higher in serum)	Prolonged coma (12 hours to many days), eyes closed, variable pupil size but reactive, hypertension, opisthotonic posturing, decerebrate positioning, repetitive motor movements, convulsions (at doses of 0.5 to 1 mg/kg), muscular rigidity, absent peripheral sensation, decreased or absent gag and corneal reflexes, diaphoresis, hypersalivation, flushing, fever

accompanied by prolonged coma (several hours or days). Confusional states lasting up to 2 weeks are characteristic of PCP intoxication. Persistent paranoid or depressive psychosis after recovery from drug overdose often indicates PCP as the causal drug.

EPIDEMIOLOGY

About 5 per cent of youth aged 12 to 17 have had experience with LSD and other hallucinogens and 6 per cent with PCP. One of five (20 per cent) 18- to 25-year-olds has tried hallucinogens (the highest prevalence group), and one of seven (14 per cent) has tried PCP. DAWN (Drug Abuse Warning Network) data from November 1974 to October 1976 indicate that the rate of PCP *emergencies* doubled during that period. PCP *deaths* nearly doubled from April 1976 to March 1977. By April 1976 PCP had risen in rank from the twenty-third most abused drug in March 1973 to the sixteenth most abused drug (31).

Data from the various parts of the country support these survey data. Rapid escalation of PCP use and an increase in the number of PCP-related deaths in Los Angeles County and extensive use in New York and Connecticut have been reported as well (20, 29, 39, 42).

SUMMARY

We have discussed the psychotropic drugs called hallucinogens, particularly emphasizing the prototype hallucinogen LSD and the atypical hallucinogen PCP, from several aspects. These have included their pharmacology, epidemiology, and the clinical picture of positive and adverse reactions. Differential diagnosis and treatment of the latter have been described.

References

1. Aronow, R., and Done, A. K. Phencyclidine overdose: Emergency concepts of treatment. J. Am. Coll. Emerg. Phys. 7:56, 1978.
2. Aronow, R., Micelli, J. N., and Done, A. K. Clinical observations during phencyclidine intoxication and treatment based on ion trapping. In *PCP—Phencyclidine Abuse: An Appraisal*, R. C. Peterson and R. C. Stillman, editors, NIDA Research Monograph #21, chap. 12. Washington, D.C., United States Government Printing Office, 1978.
3. Balster, R., and Chait, L. The behavioral pharmacology of phencyclidine. Clin. Toxicol. 9:513, 1976.
4. Berridge, M. T., and Prince, W. T. The nature of the binding between LSD and 5-HT receptor: A possible explanation for hallucinogenic activity. Br. J. Pharmacol. 51:269, 1974.
5. Cohen, S. A quarter century of research with LSD. In *The Problems and Prospects of LSD*, J. T. Ungerleider, editor, chap. 3. Springfield, Ill., Charles C Thomas, 1972.
6. Cohen, S. *The Beyond Within*. New York, Athenum Press, 1972.
7. Cohen, S. Psychotomimetic (hallucinogens) and cannabis. In *Principles of Psychopharmacology*, W. G. Clark, and J. del Gudice, editors. New York, Academic Press, 1978.
8. De Angelis, G. G., and Goldstein, E. Treatment of adolescent phencyclidine (PCP) abusers. Am. J. Drug Alcohol Abuse 5:399, 1979.
9. Deneau, G., Varageta, T., and Seevers, M. H. Self administration of psychiatric substances by the rhesus monkey. Psychopharmacologia 16:30, 1969.
10. Dewhurst, K., and Hatrick, J. A. Differential diagnosis and treatment of lysergic acid diethylamide induced psychosis. Practitioner 209:327, 1972.
11. Domino, E. F. Neurobiology of phencyclidine (Sernyl), a drug with an unusual spectrum of pharmacological activity. Int. Rev. Neurobiol. 6:303, 1967.
12. Domino, E. F., Chodoff, P., and Corssen, G. Pharmacologic effects of CI-581, a new dissociative anesthetic, in man. Clin. Pharmacol. Ther. 6:279, 1965.

13. Fauman, B. T., Baker, F. B., Coppelson, L. W., Rosen, P., and Segal, M. S. Psychoses induced by phencyclidine. J. Am. Coll. Emerg. Phys. 4:223, 1975.

14. Fauman, M. A., and Fauman, B. J. The psychiatric aspects of chronic phencyclidine use: A study of chronic PCP users. In *PCP—Phencyclidine Abuse: An Appraisal*, R. C. Peterson and R. C. Stillman, editors, NIDA Research Monograph #21, chap. 9. Washington, D.C., United States Government Printing Office, 1978.

15. Fisher, D. D. The chronic side effects from LSD. In *The Problems and Prospects of LSD*, J. T. Ungerleider, editor, chap. 5. Springfield, Ill., Charles C Thomas, 1972.

16. Freedman, D. X. The psychopharmacology of hallucinogenic agents. Am. Rev. Med. 20:409, 1969.

17. Fuller, J. G. *The Day of St. Anthony's Fire.* New York, Macmillan, 1968.

18. Hoffmeister, F., and Wuttke, W. Psychotropic drugs as negative reinforcers. Pharmacol. Rev. 27:419, 1975.

19. Jones, R. The hallucinogens. In *Psychopharmacology in the Practice of Medicine*, M. E. Jarvik, editor. New York, Appleton-Century-Crofts, 1977.

20. Kleber, H. Personal communication to Dr. De Angelis, 1978.

21. Lerner, S. E., and Burns, S. R. Phencyclidine use among youth: History. epidemiology and acute and chronic interaction. In *PCP—Phencyclidine Abuse: An Appraisal*, R. C. Peterson and R. C. Stillman, editors, NIDA Research Monograph #21, Washington, D.C., United States Government Printing Office, 1978.

22. Liaison Task Panel on Psychoactive Drug Use/Misuse. *Report to President's Commission on Mental Health.* Washington, D.C., United States Government Printing Office, 1978.

23. Luisada, P. The phencyclidine psychoses: Phenomenology and treatment. In *PCP—Phencyclidine Abuse: An Appraisal*, R. C. Peterson and R. C. Stillman, editors, NIDA Research Monograph #21, chap. 14. Washington, D.C., United States Government Printing Office, 1978.

24. Luisada, P., and Brown, B. I. Clinical Management of the phencyclidine psychosis. Clin. Toxicol. 9:539, 1976.

25. Miller, D. The drug dependent adolescent. In *Adolescent Psychiatry* S. C. Feinstein, and P. Giovacchini, editors, chap. 6. New York, Basic Books, 1973.

26. National Commission on Marijuana and Drug Abuse. Appendices to *Marijuana: Signal of Misunderstanding* and *Drug Abuse: Problem in Perspective.* Washington, D.C., United States Government Printing Office, 1972, 1973.

27. National Commission on Marijuana and Drug Abuse. *Drug Use in America: Problem in Perspective: Second Report.* Washington, D.C., United States Government Printing Office, 1973.

28. Neff, L. Chemicals and their effects on the adolescent ego. In *Adolescent Psychiatry*, S. Feinstein, P. Giovacchini, and A. Miller, editors. New York, Basic Books, 1971.

29. Noguchi, T. T., and Nakamura, G. R. Phencyclidine related deaths in Los Angeles County. J. Forensic Sci. 23:503, 1978.

30. Osmond, H. A review of the clinical effects of psychotomimetic agents. Ann. N. Y. Acad. Sci. 66: 418, 1957.

31. Petersen, R. C., and Stillman, R. C., editors. *PCP—Phencyclidine Abuse: An Appraisal*, NIDA Research Monograph #21, pp. 1–17. Washington, D.C., United States Government Printing Office, 1978.

32. Pradhan, S. N., and Dutta, S. *Drug Abuse: Clinical and Basic Aspects*, St. Louis, C. V. Mosby, 1977.

33. Ray, O. S. The major hallucinogens. In *Drugs, Society and Human Behavior*, chap. 14. St. Louis, C. V. Mosby, 1972.

34. Schultes, R. E. *Hallucinogenic Plants.* New York, Golden Press, 1976.

35. Shick, J. F. E., and Freedman, D. X. Research in nonnarcotic drug abuse. In *American Handbook of Psychiatry*, S. Arieti, editor, vol. 6, chap. 25. New York, Basic Books, 1975.

36. Shick, J. F. E., and Smith, D. E. An analysis of the LSD flashback. J. Psychedelic Drugs 3:13, 1970.

37. Siegel, R. K. Cocaine: Recreational uses and intoxication. In *Cocaine 1977*, R. C. Peterson and R. C. Stillman, editors, NIDA Research Monograph #13, pp. 119–136. Washington, D.C., United States Government Printing Office, 1978.

38. Siegel, R. K. Phencyclidine and ketamine intoxication: A study of four populations of recreational users. In *PCP—Phencyclidine Abuse: An Appraisal*, R. C. Peterson and R. C. Stillman, editors, NIDA Research Monograph #21, pp. 119–148. Washington, D.C., United States Government Printing Office, 1978.

39. Sixsmith, D. Personal communication to Dr. De Angelis, 1978.

40. Smith, D. E., Wesson, D. R., Buxton, E., Seymour, R., and Kramer, H. M. The diagnosis and treatment of the PCP abuse syndrome. In *PCP—Phencyclidine Abuse: An Appraisal*, R. C. Peterson and R. C. Stillman, editors, NIDA Research Monograph #21, chap. 13. Washington, D.C., United States Government Printing Office, 1978.

41. Stoll, W. A. LSD[25]: A hallucinatory agent of the ergot group. Swiss Arch. Neurol. 60:279, 1947.

42. Strantz, I. *Overview of PCP Abuse in Los Angeles County.* Los Angeles, Los Angeles Department of Health Services, 1978.

43. Ungerleider, J. T. The acute side effects from LSD. In *The Problems and Prospects of LSD*, J. T. Ungerleider, editor, chap. 4. Springfield, Ill., Charles C Thomas, 1972.

44. Ungerleider, J. T., et al. The bad trip: The etiology of the adverse LSD reaction. Am. J. Psychiatry 124: 1483, 1968.

45. Ungerleider, J. T., et al. The dangers of LSD. J.A.M.A. 197:389, 1966.

46. Ungerleider, J. T., and Fisher, D. D. The problems of LSD[25] and emotional disorders. Calif. Med. 106: 55, 1967.

47. Ungerleider, J. T., et al. A statistical survey of adverse reactions to LSD in Los Angeles County. Am. J. Psychiatry 125:352, 1968.

48. Winters, W. D., Mori, K., Spoonter, C. E., and Bauer, R. O. The neurophysiology of anesthesia. Anesthesiology 28:65, 1967.

49. Wolbach, A. B., Isbell, H., and Miner, E. J. Cross tolerance between mescaline and LSD-25 with comparison of the mescaline and LSD reactions. Psychopharmacologia 3:1, 1962.

50. Wolbach, A. B., Miner, E. J., and Isbell, H. Comparison of psilocin with psilocybin D, mescaline and LSD-25. Psychopharmacologia 3:219, 1962.

CHAPTER 14

COCAINE

Craig Van Dyke, M.D.

For the past century, cocaine has been used clinically as a local anesthetic and socially as a drug of abuse. Its history, however, goes back for well over a millenium to the beginning of man's use of the coca plant (*Erythroxylon coca*) in South America. How and when the practice of chewing coca leaves actually began is lost in antiquity, but there is evidence from Indian burial sites that the practice commenced before the 6th century A.D. During the time of the Incas, coca leaves were considered to be precious and were usually reserved for nobility and religious ceremonies. Because of their energizing property, coca leaves were occasionally used by soldiers during military campaigns or by messengers who were traveling long distances in the mountains. When the Incan empire began to crumble in the 15th century, many of the restrictions on the use of coca leaves were lifted. This process was completed by the time of the Spanish Conquest, so that when Francisco Pizarro captured Cuzco in 1536 the chewing of coca leaves no longer occupied an exclusive or special status in the Indian culture.

The Spanish viewed this custom with considerable ambivalence (33). From one perspective they thought it represented an obstacle in the way of the Indian's religious conversion. It became clear, however, that coca leaves could be used to get the Indians to work long hours in the gold and silver mines under very difficult conditions. These practical issues soon overcame religious con-

siderations, and, in fact, the Indians were often paid part of their wages in the form of coca leaves. It was under the Spanish that coca plants were systematically cultivated and that the custom of chewing coca leaves or drinking coca tea was widely adopted as part of the Indian's daily life.

Today, it is estimated that over 4 million Indians in Peru and Bolivia use coca leaves on a regular basis. The coca leaves are mixed with an alkaline material (i.e., "tocra," "illipta," or "mambe") and placed in the mouth and chewed sufficiently to moisten the leaves and to form them into a quid (10). This quid is then placed between the cheek and gum for approximately 1 to 2 hours and the juice and saliva swallowed. The custom is usually viewed as helping the Indians cope with their arduous life at high altitude. Whether chewing coca leaves actually helps counteract the effects of hypoxia, cold, and a poor diet remains to be determined. It may be that this custom is nothing more than an ingrained part of their culture, just as chewing tobacco is a custom in certain occupations in the United States.

The fact that chewing coca leaves could produce euphoria and intoxication was not lost on the Spaniards. Although this constituted *Joyfull Newes out of the Newe Founde Worlde* (27), the use of coca leaves did not immediately take hold in Europe, as did the use of coffee, tea, and tobacco. The reason for this is unclear, but it may be related to the deterioration of the leaves on the long voyage to Europe (28). It was not until 1855 that Gardeke was first able to extract the active ingredient of coca leaves, which he called *erythroxylon*. Five years later Niemann isolated the alkaloid, naming it *cocaine* (7).

Once cocaine could be isolated from the leaves, there was a flourish of human experimentation with this compound in the late 1800's and the early 1900's. One of the first to sing its praises as a euphoriant was P. Mantegazza, an Italian neurologist. At about the same time (1884), Sigmund Freud became interested in the drug and wrote "Uber Coca," which for many years was the definitive description of the effects of cocaine in humans (14). One of the uses for cocaine that Freud noted was its ability to relieve the pain of peripheral lesions. This led to a priority fight over the discovery of local anesthesia with Karl Koller, a colleague of Freud, who some months later discovered that cocaine could produce sufficient topical anesthesia to permit painless surgery of the eye. History has settled this dispute in favor of Koller, and he is now generally credited with the discovery of local anesthesia (7).

Cocaine's effects on the central nervous system were also becoming more widely known. Freud, in fact, had called attention to the drug's pleasant effects on mood and its ability to reduce fatigue. As a result the drug was incorporated into a number of tonics and patent medicines. One of these was a coca-containing wine marketed as "Vin Mariani." So successful was this wine that its originator, Angelo Mariani, had testimonials from popes, monarchs, and presidents of the United States, not to mention Jules Verne, Thomas Edison, and Anatole France (2). Another coca-containing beverage that gained popularity somewhat more slowly was "Coca-Cola." In 1903 cocaine was eliminated from Coca-Cola, but to this day it continues to be flavored by decocainized coca leaves (29).

As already indicated, the major route of administration for cocaine through most of history was by oral ingestion. Why cocaine was first used intranasally is not certain; however, it may have originated with cocaine's use as a treatment for nasal congestion associated with seasonal allergies. Because the drug is a potent vasoconstrictor, it was actually the first successful treatment for this condition. For unknown reasons, snorting cocaine became the predominant route of administration of the drug over the past 70 years. The mythology even reached the point where it was presumed for all these years that the intranasal route was the only effective means of taking cocaine and that the drug was totally ineffective when taken orally because it was hydrolyzed by the acidity of the stomach (3, 6, 39).

Despite cocaine's popularity at the turn of this century, there was growing alarm over its addictive potential. For instance, Freud had briefly advocated cocaine as a cure for morphine addiction. However, he quickly abandoned this idea when his friend Fleischl stopped his dependence on morphine and began using cocaine excessively. William Halsted, the father of American surgery, pioneered the use of cocaine as a nerve block anesthetic. One of the unfortunate by-products of his research was that he became habituated to cocaine. Even an extended sea voyage did not cure this dependence. In addition to its addictive potential, cocaine was noted occasionally to produce a toxic psychosis (25) and rarely to cause death (26, 45).

Part of the growing concern about cocaine was over the drug's mythical effects on human behavior, especially on the reputed aggressive and sexual behavior of certain minority groups. Because of this, state governments began to restrict the use of cocaine in the early 1900's. By 1914 the Federal Harrison Narcotics Act prohibited the use of cocaine in patent medicines and effectively outlawed the recreational use of cocaine by other means. Under this law cocaine was classified as a narcotic, a misapprehension that persists to the present time (29).

Although synthetic local anesthetics, such as procaine, were developed in a successful attempt to find a local anesthetic that was free of cocaine's abuse potential, cocaine has continued to be used widely in clinical medicine as a local and regional anesthetic (5). Cocaine is particularly useful in otolaryngology, where its other property as a potent vasoconstrictor is helpful in allowing surgeons to operate in highly vascular areas, such as the nose. Cocaine is also used extensively in pharmacological investigations because of its ability to block the reuptake of endogenous amines in the sympathetic nervous system and to potentiate the effects of exogenous amines (15). This sympathomimetic action is usually presumed to be responsible for cocaine's effects as a central nervous system stimulant (39).

Although cocaine continued to be used as a drug of abuse after 1914 by a small segment of the population (e.g., musicians who snorted the drug or heroin addicts who combined cocaine with heroin to form a "speedball"), it was not until the 1960's that there was a major resurgence in its popularity. Cocaine gained the reputation as being the "champagne of drugs," and it became quite fashionable to snort cocaine. Adding to its mystique were inhalation rituals with paraphernalia such as golden spoons and rolled currency. Why cocaine suddenly had a recrudescence of popularity is not totally understood. Obviously its rediscovery by a large segment of the population occurred at a time when all forms of drug abuse were on the increase. Its rarity, high price, and exotic background probably appealed to the affluent members of our society, who in turn made the drug fashionable and alluring. The fact that the drug was reputed to produce an instant euphoria of relatively short duration made it an ideal drug for recreational use. At parties, it seemed to enhance social interactions without the risk of serious adverse reactions.

The latest chapter in the evolving story of cocaine use by humans involves the smoking of cocaine paste. This practice originated a few years ago in the urban centers of South America where young men began smoking a crude extract of coca leaves called "pasta" (i.e., paste) that is mixed with either tobacco or marihuana. It is now quite evident that this practice represents a severe form of cocaine abuse in Peru, Colombia, and Ecuador (23). This problem seems to be spreading beyond South America, and there are now reports of a small number of people in the United States who are smoking the free base of cocaine (42).

CURRENT KNOWLEDGE

Judging the effects of cocaine from street reports can be quite misleading. It is not difficult to understand that cocaine's longstanding mythology, high price, and exotic rituals can strongly influence the effects of taking the drug. Add to this the individual's frame of mind and the social setting when he takes the drug and it becomes almost impos-

sible to sort out the effects of cocaine. Finally, cocaine is often "cut" with adulterants such as mannitol, lactose, amphetamine, or other local anesthetics. At the very least these compounds reduce the dosage of cocaine being administered and in addition may have effects of their own.

Over the past 6 years a number of independent laboratories have begun to define the acute effects of cocaine in humans.[1] This work has defined the dose effects of cocaine after different routes of administration, and there is also new information about the metabolism of the drug. One of the major developments that has made much of this work possible was the recent ability to measure sensitively and reliably the concentrations of cocaine in the plasma (20).

ROUTES OF ADMINISTRATION

Intranasal Route. Snorting crystalline cocaine hydrochloride represents the most common method of using the drug. After intranasal administration of 1.5 mg/kg of cocaine (mean dose 110 mg) to 13 surgical patients, we demonstrated that plasma levels reached peak concentrations of 120 to 474 ng/ml at 15 to 60 minutes after administration (44). The time to peak concentration was subsequently confirmed in healthy volunteers for doses ranging from 16 to 96 mg (22). In our study, cocaine was detected in the plasma within 3 minutes, but, contrary to popular notion that it was an evanescent drug, cocaine persisted in the plasma for a total of 4 to 6 hours. Because we were able to detect cocaine on the nasal mucosa for as long as 3 hours after administration, we suggested that prolonged absorption of the drug was responsible for its persistence in the plasma. Presumably the drug's vasoconstrictive action was limiting its own absorption.

In a dose effect study of intranasal cocaine (.2, .75, and 1.5 mg/kg), we found that higher doses produced higher peak plasma levels and more intense psychological effects. The peak psychological effects occurred within 15 to 30 minutes after the drug was administered. In all our subjects, cocaine produced a "high" and pleasant feeling without any dysphoric effects. In another study, 10 mg of

---

[1] For a summary of what is known about the effects of cocaine in animals, please refer to the reviews by Van Dyke and Byck (45), Byck and Van Dyke (9), and Woods (52).

cocaine could not be differentiated from placebo, but doses of 25 mg and 100 mg produced euphoria (38). However, two of Resnick et al.'s subjects experienced dysphoria 45 to 60 minutes after the 100-mg dose. The dysphoria was characterized by anxiety, depression, fatigue, and a desire for more cocaine.

These same investigators (38) found that 10 mg of intranasal cocaine produced similar physiological effects as placebo. Doses of 25 and 100 mg produced increases in heart rate of 10 to 15 beats per minute and in systolic and diastolic blood pressures of 10 to 20 mm Hg. These effects peaked 15 to 20 minutes after drug administration. This is quite similar to the findings of other investigators (8, 22), who found that peak physiological changes occurred at approximately the same time as peak plasma levels of cocaine. No cardiac arrhythmias were reported in these studies.

Oral Route. Less is known about this route of administration. As stated previously, it is widely assumed in the United States that cocaine is inactive when given orally. In fact, textbooks of pharmacology consistently state that cocaine is hydrolyzed by the acidity of the stomach and is rendered ineffective (30, 39). In part, this may account for the almost total disinterest in this route by recreational users of the drug. Despite the conventional wisdom that cocaine is not effective orally, there is now overwhelming evidence to the contrary.

Even though the chewing of coca leaves has been a part of certain Indian cultures in South America for well over 1,000 years, it was not known to what extent the effects of coca chewing could be attributed to the cocaine present in the leaves. The argument was that the leaves contained only a small amount of cocaine (approximately 0.6 per cent) and, if cocaine was poorly absorbed by the gastrointestinal tract, then cocaine could not be responsible for the effects of coca leaves. It was further argued that perhaps the other alkaloids in the leaves were responsible for any physiological or psychological effects. This issue was settled only recently.

In a series of studies with native coca chewers, we determined that cocaine was well absorbed from chewing coca leaves (31). In one experiment, eight soldiers of relatively pure Indian ancestry each chewed 12 g of coca leaves for 90 minutes. The leaves contained 0.5 per cent cocaine for a total cocaine dose of 60 mg. At the cessation of chewing, the subjects achieved a mean peak plasma level of 95 ng/ml. In another experiment, 13 subjects chewed 50 g of leaves over the course of 3 hours. The total dose of cocaine was estimated at 325 mg. In this study, the mean plasma level was 249 ng/ml. One subject, who purposely swallowed the entire 50 g of leaves, achieved a plasma level of 859 ng/ml.

These plasma levels are of the same order of magnitude as those observed after similar doses of cocaine administered by the intranasal route and can certainly account for any psychological or physiological effects of chewing coca leaves. Our results were consistent with the report of Holmstedt and co-workers (18), who examined cocaine levels in the plasma of nonnative coca chewers. Absorption of cocaine probably occurs through both the oral mucous membrane and, because the saliva is swallowed, through the lower gastrointestinal tract mucosa. Chewing the leaves with the alkaline material "tocra" may either enhance extraction of cocaine from the leaves or improve the absorption of cocaine by the mucosal membranes.

In a series of experiments to investigate more systematically the oral absorption of cocaine, we administered 2.0 mg/kg of cocaine hydrochloride (dose range 115 to 246 mg) to four male subjects (47). The cocaine was administered in a gelatin capsule to eliminate the possibility of absorption from the oropharynx. Cocaine was not detected in the plasma until 30 minutes after ingestion, but it was then rapidly absorbed and reached a mean peak concentration of 210 ng/ml at 50 to 90 minutes after administration. Peak plasma concentrations and psychological effects were very similar to those observed after the same dose of cocaine was given to these same subjects intranasally. The reason for the delay in absorption was not clear but may reflect that cocaine (pKa = 8.6) was ionized in the acid medium of the stomach and was not absorbed until it reached the small intestine, where there was an alkaline environment.

Intravenous Route. A number of independent investigators have examined the effects of intravenous cocaine in the dosage range of 4 to 32 mg (11, 22, 38). Doses above 10 mg produced "high" and pleasant feelings that persisted for approximately 30 to 40 minutes. There was a clear-cut increase in physiological and subjective changes as the dose of cocaine increased. Onset of these effects occurred within a couple of minutes after injection and peaked within 5 to 10 minutes. These doses were well tolerated except for an occasional subject who experienced dysphoria 20 to 30 minutes after drug administration (38). Fischman and co-workers (11) found that 8 to 16 mg of intravenous cocaine produced subjective effects that were similar to 10 mg of intravenous dextroamphetamine in nine volunteers who were experienced with the use of intravenous cocaine. In fact, their subjects often had difficulty discriminating between these two drugs. At the 32-mg dose level, there was a 20 to 40 per cent increase in blood pressure and heart rate but no abnormalities in the electrocardiogram (11, 22). In the one study that measured plasma levels (22) the 32-mg dose produced a mean peak plasma level of 308 ng/ml that occurred in the first blood sample 5 minutes after injection.

Pulmonary Route. During the past few years, urban youth in Peru, Colombia, and Equador have begun to smoke a crude derivative of coca leaves called "pasta" (i.e., cocaine paste) (23). This paste contains 40 to 85 per cent cocaine sulfate, as well as other coca alkaloids and organic solvents from the extraction process. The paste is usually mixed with tobacco or marihuana and smoked rapidly. It is not uncommon for 10 to 25 g of the paste to be smoked by one individual in a single session.

Experienced "pastaleros" (i.e., paste smokers) report that the drug produces an intense euphoria almost immediately, followed shortly thereafter by dysphoria and a strong desire to smoke another "joint." This can quickly lead to very large quantities of the drug being consumed, and, in practice, smoking sessions are limited only by the amount of drug available or the onset of serious toxicity that effectively prevents the smoking of more paste. Individuals may drink alcohol while smoking in an effort to control the anxiety and insomnia that result from consuming large amounts of the drug. Other common effects include tremulousness, agitation, tachycardia, hypertension, and mydriasis.

What is even more worrisome was the recent report (23) that excessive smoking of cocaine paste produced personality changes,

depression, hallucinations (visual, auditory, and tactile), and paranoid psychosis. In fact, many individuals required psychiatric hospitalization for these adverse effects. Jeri et al. (23) reported that the anxiety, insomnia, and hallucinations usually resolved within a few days after cessation of smoking; however, the paranoid delusions took much longer to resolve and often required antipsychotic medication. Even with treatment, there was a very high recidivism rate, with many of these individuals quickly returning to use of the drug.

Understandably, chronic use of the drug is quite common and leads to many of the social problems associated with other forms of compulsive drug abuse. These individuals become isolated from their families and are unable to attend school or hold a job. To support their drug use, they usually resort to criminal behavior. They also suffer from chronic insomnia, anorexia with weight loss, and other forms of personal neglect. It is of note that many of the descriptions of this syndrome are reminiscent of the "bull horrors" that were observed in cocaine addicts at the turn of this century and the paranoid psychoses that were witnessed more recently in amphetamine addicts.

In conjunction with our Peruvian colleagues, we conducted the first scientific investigation of paste smoking at the Peruvian Museum of Health Sciences in Lima (32). Experienced male paste smokers between the ages of 20 and 25 smoked a known quantity of high grade "pasta lavada" (i.e., washed paste) mixed with tobacco. Subjects were allowed to smoke at their own pace.

The first observation of note was that at the slightest anticipation of smoking the drug the subjects became anxious and tremulous. After smoking the drug, they all experienced euphoria followed by dysphoria and a strong desire to smoke more paste. Behaviorally the most experienced user had relatively little effect, whereas one subject became withdrawn and two others became active and garrulous. All subjects developed tachycardia and dilated pupils. They also expressed a strong desire to consume alcohol halfway through the session, which they felt was necessary to calm themselves.

Plasma levels rose very rapidly and achieved concentrations as high as 975 ng/ml within 5 minutes after smoking 0.5 g of paste.

What is extremely important was the observation that plasma levels were still quite high (i.e., in the range of 200 to 300 ng/ml) when the subjects experienced dysphoria approximately 15 minutes after cessation of smoking. From this it is evident that the subjective effects of cocaine are not solely dependent on the absolute value of the drug plasma level but are also strongly influenced by the direction and rate of change of the drug levels. Euphoria seems to be a function of rapidly increasing plasma levels, whereas dysphoria seems to depend on decreasing plasma levels.

What is also apparent from these data is that smoking cocaine paste is a very effective route of administration that closely simulates intravenous injection of cocaine. It also offers an explanation for the virulent effects of smoking the drug. Smoking seems particularly hazardous, because it has none of the practical or psychological barriers that limit the use of intravenous cocaine. Because of this, it is quite likely that this practice will continue in popularity. For instance, there are now reports from the United States of individuals beginning to smoke the free base of cocaine (42). In addition, paraphernalia dealers are now marketing kits to convert cocaine hydrochloride to its free base.

CHRONIC EFFECTS

We do know that in animals, cocaine is a very potent reinforcer, with animals readily self-administering the drug, often to the point of serious toxicity and even death (52). At the turn of this century, cocaine addicts were not uncommon, with many of them suffering serious psychological toxicity in the form of hallucinations or paranoid psychosis (25, 34, 41). However, this is about all we know about the effects of cocaine after repeated administration. For instance, it is not known whether chronic use leads to tolerance or whether there is a withdrawal syndrome when the drug is stopped. Experiments with the chronic administration of cocaine in animals have not demonstrated any tolerance, and, in fact, there is some evidence of increasing sensitivity to the effects of cocaine. This was characterized by hyperactivity, hyperthermia, and a decrease in the minimal convulsive and lethal dosages (16, 43). The doses used, however, were much higher than those

used by humans. Other investigators (36) have likened this process to electrical kindling, in which repetitive and intermittent subthreshold stimulation of the limbic system leads eventually to generalized convulsions. Such phenomena, however, have not been observed in humans.

In contrast to the toxic effects observed in animals, Bolivian and Peruvian Indians have chewed coca leaves chronically without any dramatic evidence of toxicity. In addition, a withdrawal syndrome has not been described when these chronic users stop the practice of chewing coca leaves. Similarly, Jeri and his co-workers (23) did not observe a withdrawal syndrome in those paste smokers who required psychiatric hospitalization.

To my knowledge, there is only one experimental study of the effects of daily administration of cocaine (35). Post et al. administered oral cocaine for 6 consecutive days to depressed, middle-aged patients who had no prior cocaine experience. The doses started at 30 to 60 mg/day and gradually increased to a final dosage of 65 to 200 mg/day. Their results showed reduced total sleep and rapid eye movement (REM) sleep as well as REM rebound on discontinuation of the drug. There were no serious adverse effects reported, although most patients did not find it an emotionally pleasant experience (37).

METABOLISM

For many years it was assumed that cocaine was primarily metabolized by the liver (39). However, there is now considerable evidence challenging this position. We first reported that cocaine was hydrolyzed rapidly when added to human plasma and that this in vitro process could be prevented by sodium flouride or physostigmine (44). The implication of our study was that serum cholinesterase hydrolyzed cocaine. In an extension of this investigation, we demonstrated that cocaine was stable (i.e., was not hydrolyzed) when incubated in plasma from patients with succinylcholine sensitivity and low dibucaine numbers (i.e., patients who were homozygous for the atypical serum cholinesterase) (21). Inaba and co-workers (19) have now reported data from an in vivo study suggesting that serum cholinesterase may play a major role in the metabolism of cocaine in humans.

These new observations may have clinical significance. Individuals who are homozygous for the atypical serum cholinesterase may be unable to metabolize cocaine rapidly and hence may develop unusually high concentrations of cocaine in their plasma when they take the drug recreationally or are administered it clinically. These very high plasma levels could easily lead to serious toxicity.

PHARMACOKINETICS

As a potent vasoconstrictor, cocaine limits its own rate of absorption when administered intranasally and orally. For both these routes absorption follows first-order pharmacokinetics. The only real difference in the two routes is the approximately 30-minute delay in the onset of absorption after ingestion of the drug. The relative bioavailability of the drug after intranasal and oral administration is quite similar, and there does not seem to be a hepatic first pass effect, perhaps because serum cholinesterase represents a major site for cocaine metabolism (51).

When injected intravenously or smoked in the form of cocaine paste, the drug readily enters the blood stream and achieves high plasma levels within a couple of minutes after administration. Although information on these two routes of administration is still quite scanty, there are a few tentative conclusions that can be put forward. The first is that smoking cocaine paste closely simulates injecting the drug intravenously. The second conclusion is that the intravenous and pulmonary routes seem to be more efficient, with greater bioavailability of the drug, than when it is administered intranasally or orally. It may be that the latter two routes allow the drug into the systemic circulation at a slow enough rate to allow more efficient plasma metabolism of the drug. The final conclusion is that, regardless of the route of administration, cocaine is eliminated following first-order pharmacokinetics, with a half-life of approximately 1 hour.

DIAGNOSIS AND TREATMENT

Despite the widespread use of cocaine in the United States, adverse reactions are rare and usually self-limited. Cocaine intoxication is mild, with individuals experiencing euphoria, tachycardia, and elevated blood pressure. More serious intoxications may produce agitation, grandiosity, and hallucinations (visual, tactile, and auditory). The more serious symptoms may occasionally require brief psychiatric hospitalization and treatment with diazepam (Valium) (23, 50). Chronic use of the drug can lead to a paranoid psychosis with a frank delusional system that may require prolonged hospitalization and treatment with antipsychotic medication (23, 25, 34). Adverse physiological reactions do occur, and their treatment has been described in detail by Barash (4).

The differential diagnosis of cocaine intoxication includes anxiety disorders, affective disorders (e.g., hypomania), paranoid schizophrenia, and amphetamine intoxication. The key to the diagnosis is a history of recent cocaine use and the presence of cocaine metabolites in the urine. We have recently demonstrated that after intranasal cocaine in doses ranging from 13 to 130 mg, the metabolite benzoylecgonine was found in the urine for 18 to 27 hours after drug administration (46). The method used for detecting benzoylecgonine was the enzyme immunoassay technique (EMIT),[2] which is the most common method for large scale screening of urine for cocaine.

The treatment of cocaine dependence is a problem for which psychiatry has few effective answers at the present time. In the United States, many chronic abusers of cocaine are individuals who are enrolled in methadone maintenance programs. In some of these programs, the threat of dismissal may be an effective deterrant to the repeated use of cocaine.

FUTURE OUTLOOK

In the past 6 years a solid body of knowledge has formed about the acute effects of cocaine in man. We now have information on different routes of administration of the drug and new information about its metabolism and pharmacokinetics. Nevertheless, there is much about the drug and its effects that remains unknown.

For instance, we know that, after typical doses in euthymic individuals, the drug produces euphoria. This represents a confirmation of street knowledge but offers no particular insight into the subtler aspects of the subjective experience or what makes this

---

[2] "EMIT" (Enzyme Multiplied Immunoassay Technique) is a registered trademark of Syva, Palo Alto, California 94304.

drug unique. Post et al. (37) reported that, when cocaine was administered to depressed patients, it produced tearfulness and worsening of the depressed affect. This may reflect a mood-amplifying effect of cocaine similar to the enhancement of different emotional states by epinephrine (40). In addition, we have little understanding of whether cocaine's sympathomimetic action or local anesthetic action is responsible for cocaine's central nervous system effects. It has always been presumed that its sympathomimetic action was responsible, but there is now preliminary evidence in animals and humans that local anesthetics may also be psychoactive (13, 17, 48).

Although we now know that cocaine is absorbed in significant amounts when Peruvian Indians chew coca leaves, we do not know what psychological or physiological effects this practice produces. Undertaking the necessary experiments to resolve these issues is an extremely complex task. For example, these Indians often do not speak Spanish, and understanding the nuances of their subjective experience when they chew coca leaves is almost impossible. Experiments also need to be conducted to define the effects of coca on appetite and exercise tolerance at high altitude. More importantly, there has been a great deal of debate over the impact of coca on the Indian's health. Long term studies are clearly indicated to determine whether this custom represents a serious health hazard for these people.

Other issues need to be resolved. For instance, we do not know whether chronic cocaine use leads to tolerance, alterations in the metabolism of the drug, or a withdrawal syndrome when it is discontinued. The effects of smoking cocaine paste need to be more closely investigated. Finally, we have no effective method for treating cocaine dependence. In theory, chronic cocaine use could be treated by eliminating or modifying the euphoria produced by the drug.

Although there is almost no work on this with cocaine, there are now a number of studies investigating this issue with another central nervous system stimulant, amphetamine. Flemenbaum (12) reported three cases of lithium carbonate blocking amphetamine euphoria. In an experimental setting, Van Kammen and Murphy (49) administered 30 mg of amphetamine orally to nine patients. Seven of these patients experienced euphoria

and increased activity after both *d*- and *l*-amphetamine. When these patients were pretreated with lithium carbonate, there was a 60 per cent decrease in the euphoria and activation produced by *d*-amphetamine and almost a 100 per cent decrease after *l*-amphetamine. Angrist and co-workers (1) demonstrated that haloperidol was effective in blocking the central nervous system stimulation produced by oral amphetamine (dose range 70 to 190 mg) in three patients. In a more dramatic study, Jönsson et al. (24) reduced or blocked the euphoria produced by 200 mg of intravenous *d*-, *l*-amphetamine by pretreatment with alpha-methyl-para-tyrosine, an inhibitor of tyrosine hydroxylase.

References

1. Angrist, B., Lee, H. K., and Gershon, S. The antagonism of amphetamine-induced symptomatology by a neuroleptic. Am. J. Psychiatry 131:817, 1974.
2. Anonymous. Contemporary Celebrities from the Album Mariani. New York, Mariani & Co., 1901.
3. Ashley, R. *Cocaine: Its History, Uses and Effects.* New York, St. Martin's Press, 1975.
4. Barash, P. G. Cocaine in clinical medicine. In *Cocaine 1977*, R. C. Petersen and R. C. Stillman, editors, NIDA Research Monograph #13 pp. 193–200. Washington, D.C., United States Government Printing Office, 1977.
5. Barash, P. G., Kopriva, C. J., Langou, R., Van Dyke, C., Jatlow, P., Stahl, A., and Byck, R. Is cocaine a sympathetic stimulant during general anesthesia? J.A.M.A., 243:1437, 1980.
6. Brecher, E. M. *Consumer Reports: Licit and Illicit Drugs.* Boston, Little, Brown and Company, 1972.
7. Byck, R., editor. *Cocaine Papers: Sigmund Freud.* New York, Stonehill, 1975.
8. Byck, R., Jatlow, P., Barash, P., and Van Dyke, C. Cocaine: Blood levels, excretion, and physiological effects after intranasal application in man. In *Cocaine and Other Stimulants*, E. H. Ellinwood and M. Kilbey, editors, pp. 629–645. New York, Plenum Press, 1976.
9. Byck, R., and Van Dyke, C. What are the effects of cocaine in man? In *Cocaine 1977*, R. C. Petersen and R. C. Stillman, editors, NIDA Research Monograph #13, pp. 97–117. Washington, D.C., United States Government Printing Office, 1977.
10. Carroll, E. Coca: The plant and its uses. In *Cocaine 1977*, R. C. Petersen and R. C. Stillman, editors, NIDA Research Monograph #13, pp. 35–45. Washington, D.C., United States Government Printing Office, 1977.
11. Fischman, M. W., Schuster, C. R., Resnekov, L., Shick, J. F. E., Krasnegor, N. A., Fennel, W., and Freedman, D. X. Cardiovascular and subjective effects of intravenous cocaine administration in humans. Arch. Gen. Psychiatry 33:983, 1976.
12. Flemenbaum, A. Does lithium block the effects of amphetamine? A report of three cases. Am. J. Psychiatry 131:820, 1974.
13. Ford, R. F., and Balster, R. L. Reinforcing properties of intravenous procaine in rhesus monkeys. Phar-

macol. Biochem. Behav. 6:289, 1977.

14. Freud, S. Uber coca. Zentralbl. Ther. 2:289, 1884.
15. Frölich, A., and Loewi, O. Über eine Steigerung der Adrenalinempfindlichkeit durch Cocaine. Arch. Exp. Pathol. Pharmakol. 62:159, 1910.
16. Gutierrez-Noriega, C., and Ortiz, V. Z. Cocainismo experimental. I. Toxicologia general, acostumbramiento y sensibilizacion. Rev. Med. Exp. 3:279, 1944.
17. Hammerbeck, D. M., and Mitchell, C. L. The reinforcing properties of procaine and d-amphetamine compared in rhesus monkeys. J. Pharmacol. Exp. Ther. 204:558, 1978.
18. Holmstedt, B., Lindgren, J. E., Rivier, L., and Plowman, T. Cocaine in blood of coca chewers. Botanical Museum Leaflets 26:199, 1978.
19. Inaba, T., Stewart, J., and Kalow, W. Metabolism of cocaine in man. Clin. Pharmacol. Ther. 23:547, 1978.
20. Jatlow, P., and Bailey, D. Gas chromatographic analysis for cocaine in human plasma with use of a nitrogen detector. Clin. Chem. 21:1918, 1975.
21. Jatlow, P., Barash, P. G., Van Dyke, C., Radding, J., and Byck, R. Cocaine and succinylcholine sensitivity: A new caution. Anesth. Analg. 58:235, 1979.
22. Javaid, J. I., Fischman, M. W., Schuster, C. R., Dekirmenjiian, H., and Davis, J. M. Cocaine plasma concentrations: Relation to physiological and subjective effects in humans. Science 200:227, 1978.
23. Jeri, F. R., Sanches, C., Del Pozo, L., and Fernandez, M. El sindrome de la pasta de coca: Observaciones en un grupo de 158 pacientes del area del Lima. Rev. Sanid. Ministerio Interior 39:1, 1978.
24. Jönsson, L. E., Änggard, E., and Gunne, L. M. Blockade of intravenous amphetamine euphoria in man. Clin. Pharmacol. Ther. 12:889, 1971.
25. Lewin, L. *Phantastics, Narcotic and Stimulating Drugs: Their Use and Abuse.* New York, E. P. Dutton, 1931.
26. Mayer, E. The toxic effects following the use of local anesthetics. J.A.M.A. 82:876, 1924.
27. Monardes, N. *Joyfull Newes out of the Newe Founde World* (1569). New York, Alfred A. Knopf, 1925.
28. Mortimer, W. G. *History of Coca the Divine Plant of the Incas* (1901). San Francisco, And/Or Press, 1974.
29. Musto, D. F. *The American Disease: Origins of Narcotic Control,* New Haven, Conn., Yale University Press, 1973.
30. Osol, A., and Pratt, R. *The United States Dispensatory.* Philadelphia, J. B. Lippincott, 1973.
31. Paly, D., Jatlow, P., Van Dyke, C., Cabieses, F., and Byck, R. Plasma levels of cocaine in native Peruvian coca chewers. In *Cocaine 1980: Proceedings of the Interamerican Seminar on Coca and Cocaine,* F. R. Jeri editor, pp. 86-89. Lima, Peru, Pacific Press, 1980.
32. Paly, D., Van Dyke, C., Jatlow, P., Jeri, F. R., and Byck, R. Cocaine: Plasma levels after cocaine paste smoking. In *Cocaine 1980: Proceedings of the Interamerican Seminar on Coca and Cocaine,* F. R. Jeri editor, pp. 106-110. Lima, Peru, Pacific Press, 1980.
33. Petersen, R. C. History of cocaine. In *Cocaine 1977,* R. C. Petersen and R. C. Stillman editors, NIDA Research Monograph #13, pp. 17-34. Washington, D.C., United States Government Printing Office, 1977.
34. Post, R. M. Cocaine psychosis: A continuum model. Am. J. Psychiatry 132:225, 1975.
35. Post, R. M., Gillin, J. C., Wyatt, R. J., and Goodwin,

F. K. The effect of orally administered cocaine on sleep of depressed patients. Psychopharmacologia 37:59, 1974.
36. Post, R. M., Kopanda, R. T., and Black, K. E. Progressive effects of cocaine on behavior and central amine metabolism in rhesus monkeys: Relationship to kindling and psychosis. Biol. Psychiatry 11:403, 1976.
37. Post, R. M., Kotin, J., and Goodwin, F. K. The effects of cocaine on depressed patients. Am. J. Psychiatry 131:511, 1974.
38. Resnick, R. B., Kestenbaum, R. S., and Schwartz, L. K. Acute systematic effects of cocaine in man: A controlled study by intranasal and intravenous routes. Science 195:696, 1977.
39. Ritchie, J. M., and Cohen, P. J. Cocaine, procaine and other synthetic local anesthetics. In *The Pharmacological Basis of Therapeutics,* L. S. Goodman and A. Gilman, editors, ed. 5, pp. 379-403. New York, Macmillan, 1975.
40. Schacter, S., and Singer, J. E. Cognitive, social, and physiological determinants of emotional state. Psychol. Rev. 69:379, 1962.
41. Siegel, R. K. Cocaine hallucinations. Am. J. Psychiatry 135:309, 1978.
42. Siegel, R. K. Cocaine smoking. N. Engl. J. Med. 300: 373, 1979.
43. Tatum, A. L., and Seevers, M. H. Experimental cocaine addiction. J. Pharmacol. Exp. Ther. 36:401, 1929.
44. Van Dyke, C., Barash, P. G., Jatlow, P., and Byck, R. Cocaine: Plasma concentrations after intranasal application in man. Science 191:859, 1976.
45. Van Dyke, C., and Byck, R. Cocaine 1884-1974. In *Cocaine and Other Stimulants,* E. H. Ellinwood and M. Kilbey, editors, pp. 1-30. New York, Plenum Press, 1976.
46. Van Dyke, C., Byck, R., Barash, P. G., and Jatlow, P. Urinary excretion of immunologically reactive metabolite(s) after intranasal administration of cocaine, as followed by enzyme immunoassay. Clin. Chem. 23:241, 1977.
47. Van Dyke, C., Jatlow, P., Barash, P. G., and Byck, R. Oral cocaine: Plasma concentrations and central effects. Science 200:211, 1978.
48. Van Dyke, C., Jatlow, P., Ungerer, J., Barash, P., and Byck, R. Cocaine and lidocaine have similar psychological effects after intranasal application. Life Sci. 24:271, 1979.
49. Van Kammen, D. P., and Murphy, D. L. Attenuation of the euphoriant and activating effects of d- and l-amphetamine by lithium carbonate treatment. Psychopharmacologia 44:215, 1975.
50. Wesson, D. R., and Smith, D. E. Cocaine: Its use for central nervous system stimulation including recreational and medical uses. In *Cocaine 1977,* R. C. Petersen and R. C. Stillman, editors, NIDA Research Monograph #13, pp. 137-152. Washington, D.C., United States Government Printing Office, 1977.
51. Wilkinson, P., Van Dyke, C., Jatlow, P., Barash, P., and Byck, R. Intranasal and oral cocaine kinetics. Clin. Pharmacol. Ther. 27:386, 1980.
52. Woods, J. Behavioral effects of cocaine in animals. In *Cocaine 1977,* R. C. Petersen and R. C. Stillman, editors, NIDA Research Monograph #13, pp. 63-95. Washington, D.C., United States Government Printing Office, 1977.

CHAPTER 15

AMPHETAMINE

John P. Morgan, M.D.

DEFINITIONS AND TERMINOLOGY

Amphetamine refers to a unique chemical, which is precisely methylphenethylamine or phenylisopropylamine or 2-amino-1-phenylpropane. Intense interest in this compound plus frequent description and conversation has led to the careless use of the term "amphetamines" (38). There is no basis for the continuing use of the plural term, and this chapter will concentrate on amphetamine, a number of amphetamine salts and preparations, and a few amphetamine-like compounds that share some psychostimulant properties of amphetamine.

PREPARATIONS

A mixture of racemic d,l-amphetamine was first marketed in the United States as Benzedrine in 1931. The isolated d-isomer (dextroamphetamine) soon followed as Dexedrine. An n-methylated form (methamphetamine) achieved widespread use both orally and by injection (both in licit and illicit markets). A nearly unbridled growth in popularity over 35 years led to the marketing of many amphetamine salts and resins and a number of amphetamine combinations with other agents by the 1960's. Medicinal chemistry also produced many related amphetamine-like compounds that were (and are) sold in the United States as appetite-suppressing agents. Table 15.1 lists most currently available amphetamine and metham-

phetamine salts and preparations. Figure 15.1 depicts a number of amphetamine-like psychostimulants and anorexiants that have been introduced into clinical medicine in comparison to amphetamine.

HISTORY OF AMPHETAMINE USE

INTRODUCTION AND EARLY HISTORY

Amphetamine was first synthesized in 1887 by Edeleano (12). Its biological potential was at first not at all appreciated. Gordon Alles first described the psychostimulant, autonomic, and other pharmacological effects of amphetamine in 1928 (1). His work provoked a widespread interest that led to its first marketing as a medicinal agent.

In 1931, Smith, Kline and French (SKF) marketed a nasal inhaler that relieved the nasal congestion of coryza and other forms of rhinitis. The inhaler contained 250 mg of d,l-amphetamine impregnated in a paper wick. The product utilized the SKF trademark of Benzedrine. Users soon (or immediately) commented on an effect additive to nasal decongestion—sleeplessless. Tablets were marketed in 1935 to exploit this effect to treat narcolepsy. After these introductions, in a fashion that now seems naive, almost boundless claims for legitimate therapeutic uses of amphetamine emerged. If useful in combating narcolepsy why not the slightly less dramatic listlessness or drowiness and

Table 15.1
Principal Amphetamine Compounds Available in the United States

Generic Name	Trade Name (not all-inclusive)
Racemic amphetamine sulfate	Benzedrine
Dextroamphetamine sulfate	Dexedrine, Ferndex
Dextroamphetamine hydrochloride	Daro
Dextroamphetamine tannate	Obotan
Methamphetamine hydrochloride (desoxyephedrine hydrochloride)	Desoxyn, Methampex
Amphetamine complex (amphetamine and *d*-amphetamine resin)	Biphetamine
Amphetamine combined[a]	Obetrol, Delcobese
d-Amphetamine plus amobarbital	Dexamyl
d-Amphetamine plus prochlorperazine	Eskatrol

[a] Other mixtures of *d*-amphetamine, amphetamine in various salts.

exhaustion? The pills marketed for the treatment of narcolepsy were noted to depress appetite, and the available preparations and a host of others to follow were used as anorexiants. In a short period of time amphetamine was additionally applied to depression, alcoholism, epilepsy, barbiturate poisoning, and a variety of behaviors in problem children. To quote Jackson (23): "Even by the opening years of World War II many physicians and laymen viewed amphetamine as a virtual wonder drug." A harbinger of the future emerged at the University of Minnesota in 1936 (24). A research project was underway at the university and some students heard rumors of the drug's powerful stimulant effects. They obtained amphetamine and used it to combat sleepiness during "crash" study sessions. Soon, similar reports emerged from many Middle-Western universities. Reports of the utility of the stimulant to combat fatigue and enhance performance by athletes, truck drivers, and race horses followed. The parallel growth of legitimate and illegitimate use continued until the war, which provoked wider use for various operational purposes.

WORLD WAR II AND AMPHETAMINE

Extensive wartime use occurred domestically, but military use paralleled and perhaps exceeded domestic use. American military authorities have generally denied routine use among combat troops, admitting only to its use in bomber crews on long missions and its presence in the first aid kits of jungle fighters. It was believed that routine use occurred in German ranks. *Time* magazine reported this with the title "Nazi Pep-Pills" in 1942 (3). American military use was much

higher than the deceptive statements above indicate. One estimate states that as many as 180 million tablets were supplied to United States troops (18). A large number of American soldiers returned home with amphetamine experience. The wartime use by Americans was so obvious that Harry Gibson issued in 1944 a phonograph record entitled "Who Put the Benzedrine in Mrs. Murphy's Ovaltine?"[1]

An unusual outgrowth of the World War II experience was the methamphetamine epidemic in Japan. Japanese military troops had utilized amphetamine similarly to German and Allied fighters. Immediately after the war large stocks of methamphetamine were dumped on the Japanese market. The epidemic grew steadily to a peak in 1954, when users were estimated to number as many as 1.5 million. The government in Japan, by adopting stringent suppressive maneuvers, apparently eliminated nearly all use before 1960 (35).

THE BENZEDRINE INHALER

The story of this peculiar item, which first documents the resourcefulness of the recreational drug user, deserves a section of its own. The first marketed amphetamine product was the mixture of *d,l*-amphetamine issued as Benzedrine in 1931. The vasoconstrictive effect of the amphetamine was exploited by packaging the material in a cylindrical inhaler designed to permit the sniffing of amphetamine vapor to relieve nasal congestion. The inhaler sold for less than $1. It contained 250 mg of amphetamine that

---

[1] Harry "the Hipster" Gibson. Musicraft 346, 1944 Reissued Stash Records ST-100, 1976.

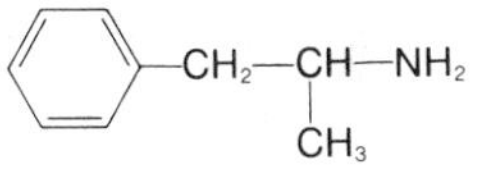
amphetamine (dextroamphetamine)

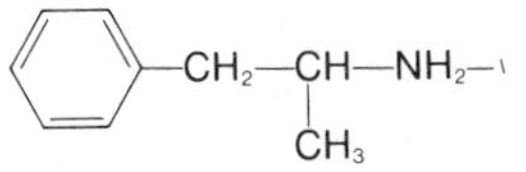
methamphetamine

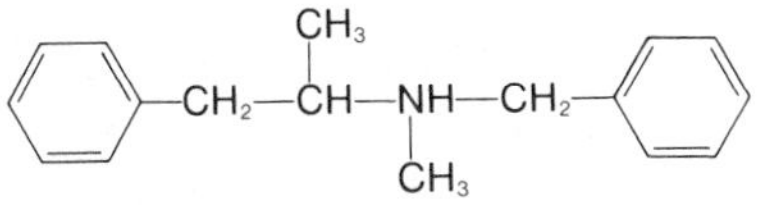
benzphetamine (Didrex)

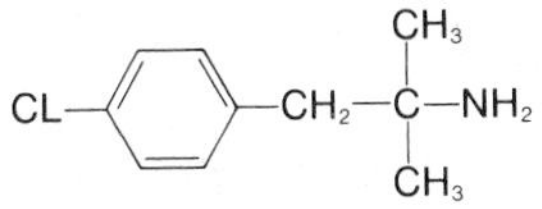
chlorphentermine (Pre-Sate)

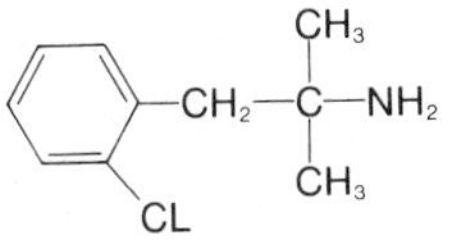
Clortermine (Voranil)

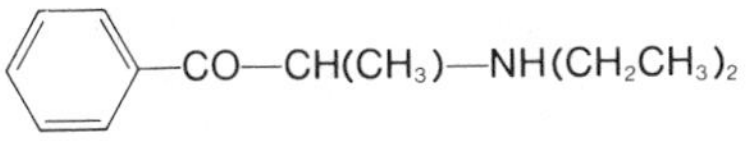
diethylpropion (Tenuate)

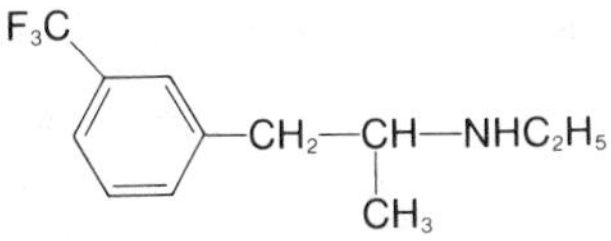
fenfluramine (Pondimin)

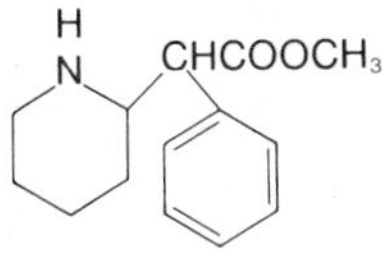
methylphenidate (Ritalin)

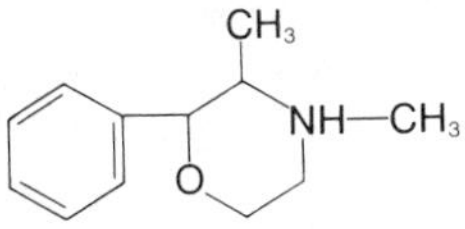
phendimetrazine (Plegine)

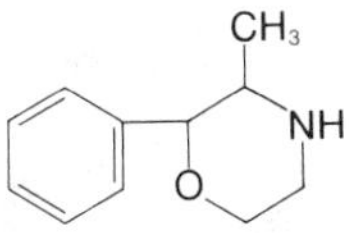
phenmetrazine (Preludin)

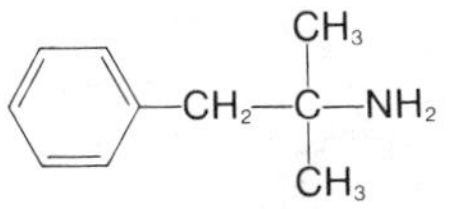
phentermine (Ionamin)

Figure 15.1. Amphetamine-related psychostimulants.

were applied to eight folded-paper sections. The paper also contained the message "Unfit for Internal Use—Dangerous if Swallowed"—a message read, of course, only by those who had broken open the container to experience said danger.

Multiple methods of ingestion were tried. One could simply chew and swallow a few strips at a time. Pieces of the wick were sometimes placed in chewing gum. Often the wicks were incorporated in beverages, particularly by brewing in coffee: "The greatest jazz trombonist of his time, which in his case meant all time, stared bleakly at the cup of black coffee before him while he tore apart the Benzedrine inhaler. He got the cardboard shell off, dumped the drug-soaked filler into the coffee, swished it around and then removed it with the handle of the spoon. He took a tentative sip of the steaming brew and told himself that he felt better" (43).

Before 1938, various states had recognized the abuse potential of amphetamine in tablet form and had limited sale to prescription only. In 1938, a reorganization of the Food and Drug Administration (FDA) and the Food, Drug and Cosmetic Act had granted to the agency new power. Various interpretations of this law promulgated the concept that amphetamine tablets could be safely taken only under the supervision of a physician and all over-the-counter sales of amphetamine tablets ceased. These regulations were not interpreted as applicable to the inhaler. It was safe when used as directed and dangerous only when employed in a method counter to the manufacturer's directives. There was no legal cause for action against a product merely because it was being misused and misapplied. A druggist might be prosecuted for sale of unprescribed amphetamine, but there was no legal deterrent to continued over-the-counter sale of the inhaler. Therefore, its abuse actually grew as federal regulatory activity decreased traffic in amphetamine tablets (22).

Continued reports of inhaler abuse emerged in the postwar years. Use was reportedly widespread in prison populations. Inhalers were smuggled to prisoners, or the impregnated strips were simply mailed in envelopes (31). There were frequent scandals involving sale to prisoners by their guardians and keepers. All this publicity led to several failed attempts to control the traffic. SKF experimented with an unbreakable iron container. In states where reports of misuse were common, inhalers were shipped in which denatured picric acid was added to the paper wick to promote vomiting on ingestion. Apparently, many users were willing to endure such nauseant effects because the pleasureable effects were still achieved.

In 1949, SKF simply gave up under pressure (and some desire to do right) and ceased marketing the product. They continued to market a "Benzedrex" inhaler to retain some of the brand name market but removed all amphetamine from the item.

In 1952, SKF's original patents expired, and by 1953 the abuse of a new generation of amphetamine inhalers had begun. Pfeiffer's "Valo" inhaler, Wyeth's "Wyamine" inhaler,

and Rexall's "Naso-Ato" inhaler reprecipitated the problem, and the whole story (including an attempt to use croton oil as denaturant) was repeated. In 1959, by utilizing the Drug Control Amendments of 1951 and by publicizing an extensive catalogue of reports of abuse, the FDA announced that the amphetamine inhaler was forever more a prescription item (22). The decision withstood legal attack, and the inhaler story came to an end nearly as strange as its beginning.

ABUSE IN THE 1950'S

The use and abuse of amphetamine tablets continued on an upward spiral throughout the 1950's as the federal agencies struggled with the inhaler and pill problems.

As previously stated, the return of amphetamine-experienced soldiers after World War II made some contribution. The continued use by college students grew apace in the 1950's and a distributional market based on long distance truck drivers and their refueling stations emerged. In the late 1940's and early 1950's those mentioned groups—students, prisoners, a few athletes, truck drivers, and race horses—were joined by upper class urban sophisticates (Earl Wilson had labeled these the "Benzedrine Set") and teenagers in various American settings. This constitutes a familiar drug use pattern; egalitarian spread of use from an early avant-garde to multiple layers of society.

Abuse became truly national in the 1950's. Amphetamine production by pharmaceutical houses grew at an astonishing rate. By 1958, uncertain estimates stated that the industry was producing 165,000 kg of amphetamine and methamphetamine. Part of this growth is directly related to the SKF patent expiration. Many major firms produced amphetamine products and sold them under trade names. Some firms and some chemical manufacturers also sold bulk amphetamine to smaller firms and repackagers so that there were many nonbranded (generic) sellers of amphetamine products as well. The literature of the explosive growth in the 1950's seems on first reading to be very naive. Few writers saw any link between the impressive medical sales for indications previously cited (obesity, narcolepsy, hyperkinesis, depression) and the use for fun, recreation, and performance enhancement. It is likely that few users of indicated amphetamine failed to note that the side effects included increased energy, decreased sleepiness, and mood enhancement. Users then (and their physicians) found various reasons to continue legal traffic. Other users with less self-deception obtained the drug simply to have fun and to decrease sleepiness. Such honest abusers might obtain the drug through illicit channels, although as we shall see the ultimate source for nearly all amphetamine tablets sold between 1932 and 1972 was the pharmaceutical industry.

A few more important points in the history of abuse between 1932 and 1960 are necessary. It is accurate to describe that abuse as low level. Almost all users took the material by mouth, and many described as abusers were in fact episodic misusers. In a strict definitional sense I believe there were relatively few amphetamine addicts during these three decades. Relatively few users progressed to the point where all life energies and resources were directed to obtaining, dealing with, and consuming the drug.[2]

THE 1960'S AND INTRAVENOUS AMPHETAMINE ABUSE

From 1960 to 1962, a localized epidemic of intravenous amphetamine use in San Francisco became manifest that was clearly a harbinger of serious troubles. Injectable forms of amphetamine and methamphetamine had been marketed in the 1930's for an unfocused utility in abetting psychotherapy and the diagnosis of some psychiatric conditions (21). Several Bay area physicians began using injectable methamphetamine as a substitute for heroin in addicts. Whether this idea actually originated with them or the heroin user is uncertain. Some of these physicians showed some care; others flagrantly sold the ampules for profit. Smith (40) quotes an ex-methedrine user who described the process of obtaining the ampules, obliterating the labels, and selling them to other users. Lenny Bruce, who later died of heroin overdose, had at least one arrest for his use of methamphetamine by injection. (He produced a letter from his prescribing doctor attesting that his

use was legitimate (15).) The expansion of intravenous methamphetamine abuse was so rapid that a request from law enforcement officials in California led to a voluntary withdrawal from the market of the licit methamphetamine ampules. Injectable methamphetamine remained available in some states until 1969 to 1970. These events signaled the emergence of a much more pervasive and destructive pattern of amphetamine abuse both orally and by injection. Users frequently began careers by oral ingestion followed by dosage escalation. They easily graduated to intravenous use. After 1963, this market was largely supplied by illicitly synthesized methamphetamine produced by "speed" labs, usually located in California. Such intravenous users were usually referred to as "speed freaks" and often went on "speed runs" where grams of the drug might be injected intravenously in a 24-hour period. This life style (obviously one of amphetamine addiction) blossomed in the San Francisco area and was much discussed after 1967 (39). The coexisting patterns of large dose amphetamine abuse (orally and parenterally), coupled with a continued growth in amphetamine sales and diversion from the licit market, led to important legislative events in the early 1970's that have changed the pattern cited. I shall return to that in detail. At this point in the narrative I would like to turn to some issues of the clinical pharmacology and abuse of amphetamine before again picking up the thread of the amphetamine culture.

CLINICAL PHARMACOLOGY OF AMPHETAMINE (32)

Amphetamine is packaged in various salts, resins, isomers, and methamphetamine-amphetamine mixtures. It is occasionally compounded with other drugs, such as amobarbital and prochlorperazine. Most of those preparations were marketed for the treatment of obesity. There are a great many related sympathomimetic phenethylamines that were marketed principally as anorexiants and that have also become to some degree subject to abuse, for example, phenmetrazine, diethylpropion, phendimetrazine, phentermine, etc. Methylphenidate, a piperidine derivative, is also abused, although it is seldom prescribed as an anorexiant. One amphetamine-related compound, fenfluramine, is

---

[2] There was some intravenous use of amphetamine before the 1960's. Injectable preparations of racemic amphetamine phosphate and methamphetamine were used, and tablets could be solubilized. Most of this use apparently occurred in heroin addicts.

used as an anorexiant but seems to have little stimulant effect.

ABSORPTION, METABOLISM, DISTRIBUTION, AND EXCRETION

Amphetamine and methamphetamine, in contrast to the catecholamines, whose effects they mimic, are effective when given orally, and they tend to act for prolonged periods. After oral administration, the effects generally appear within 30 minutes. Also, in contrast to catecholamines, they are found in high concentration in the central nervous system.

Because they lack the catechol structure, they are resistant to metabolic degradation by catechol O-methyltransferase. Additionally, they resist the action of monoamine oxidase (MAO) and in fact inhibit the action of MAO on other substrates.

There are several hepatic pathways available for amphetamine degradation (p-hydroxylation, N-demethylation, deamination), and a general metabolic scheme is presented in Figure 15.2.

The percentages in Figure 15.2 approximate the percentage of administered dose which appears as that metabolite in a 24-hour urine sample (10). These metabolic pathways produce compounds with distinct actions. 4-Hydroxyamphetamine is a presser agent significantly more potent than amphetamine. It has less central stimulant activity. 4-Hydroxynorephedrine, which bears a close structural resemblance to norepinephrine, is produced by beta-hydroxylation. The activity of dopamine beta-hydroxylase is unusual, because this enzyme is not usually involved in the biotransformation of drugs.

Significant amounts of unchanged amphetamine ordinarily appear in the urine. Excretion of unchanged compound is considerably enhanced in acid urine, and the half-life of amphetamine in the body is shortened considerably. At urine pH 8.0 only 2 to 3 per cent of unchanged amphetamine is excreted, and the metabolite secretion rate is high. If urine is acid, the proportion of unchanged compound approaches 80 per cent. Thus, urine acidification is a logical treatment for amphetamine poisoning.

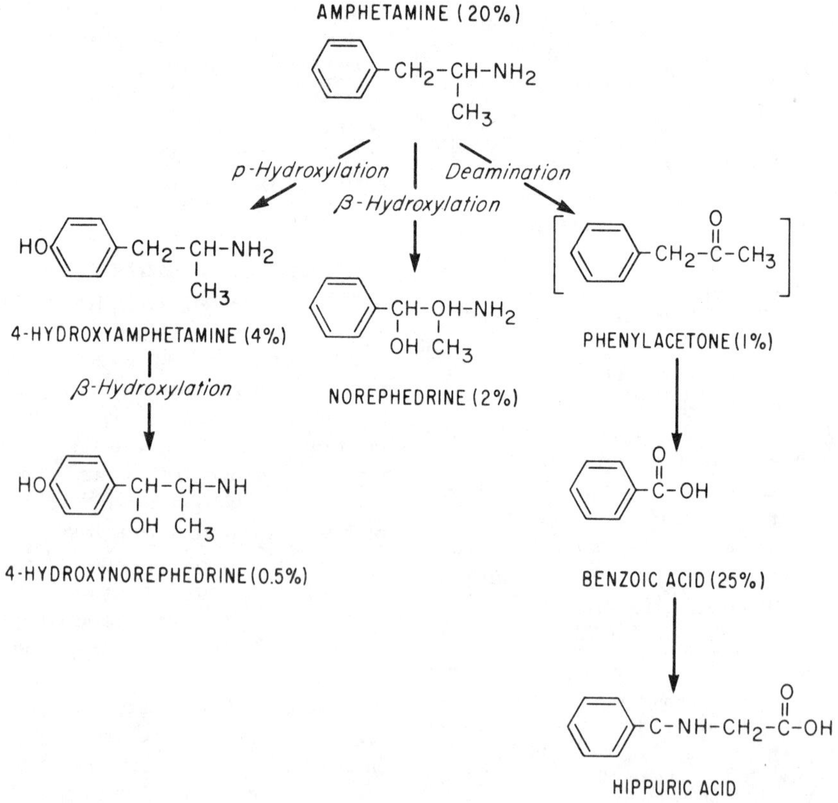

Figure 15.2. Hepatic pathways available for amphetamine degradation.

STRUCTURE-ACTIVITY RELATIONSHIPS

Alkylation of either the side chain or the amino group diminishes the biological activity of amphetamine. Ring hydroxylation essentially abolishes amphetamine stimulation of the central nervous system (CNS) and markedly diminishes related anorectic effects. Side chain hydroxylation, which yields ephedrine-like drugs, also decreases CNS stimulation and anorectic effects. Methoxy substitution in the ring may render the resultant molecule hallucinogenic; an example is mescaline. Some reduction of CNS stimulation is also effected by methylation of the side chain carbon that bears the amino group, and this methylation yields the phentermine series of related anorectic compounds. Other manipulation of the molecule with retention of anorectic properties, such as halogen substitution in the phenyl ring, yields fenfluramine and chlorphentermine (6).

SOME GENERAL PHYSIOLOGICAL EFFECTS

Some effects of amphetamine relate to its peripheral stimulation of alpha and beta receptors. In addition, and more importantly, amphetamine has pronounced effects in the CNS whose exact mediation is uncertain.

Amphetamine raises systolic and diastolic blood pressure and generally increases pulse pressure. Although beta activity exists, the heart rate in humans is often reflexively slowed. With large doses however, tachycardias and tachyarrythmias may occur. Cardiac output is not enhanced by usual doses. In contrast to the CNS, the cardiovascular system is more affected by the *l*-isomer than by the *d*-isomer. Bronchial muscles are relaxed, although amphetamine has not been useful therapeutically for asthma. The urinary sphincter is stimulated, and painful urination may occur. Amphetamine usually slows the movement of intestinal contents, causing constipation. By slowing gastric emptying, amphetamine slows delivery of some other drugs to the intestinal surface and interferes with absorption. Evidence indicates that absorption of amphetamine from the gastrointestinal tract is not entirely a first-order process. This may relate to the drug's own effect on gastrointestinal motility. An amphetamine preparation combined with aspirin (Daprisal) was once widely used for the treatment of menstrual cramps; however, data regarding amphetamine's impact on uterine contraction are conflicting.

METABOLIC EFFECTS

Amphetamine increases the metabolic rate and oxygen consumption slightly in humans, and users occasionally show a slight increase in body temperature. There is a regular increase in plasma free fatty acid concentration but no apparent modification of carbohydrate utilization or blood glucose concentration (19).

CENTRAL NERVOUS SYSTEM EFFECTS

Amphetamine markedly stimulates the CNS in humans. The *d*-isomer is three to four times as potent in this regard as the *l*-isomer. The results of a single dose in the 10- to 30-mg range include increased wakefulness and alertness and a decreased sense of fatigue. Mood is elevated, accompanied by increased initiative and confidence, even elation. There is a general increase in psychomotor activity. Performance of repetitive, simple tasks improves, and physical performance in other spheres may improve as well (45). A decrease in total sleep is accompanied by a marked decrease in rapid eye movement (REM) sleep, and withdrawal after repeated use provokes a rebound in REM sleep. Despite this, individuals stopping "speed runs" may sleep, apparently soundly, for prolonged periods of time. Amphetamine has some analgesic effect and may be used with narcotics for this effect and to counter drowsiness (14). Amphetamine augments spinal cord transmission and stimulates the respiratory center, although this use has no apparent clinical utility. Injectable amphetamine and methamphetamine, in addition to other claims, were marketed for utility in treating patients with sedative overdose. They were of no use.

Amphetamine and its congeners have been widely used to suppress appetite in the treatment of obesity. Subsequent weight loss is caused by decreased food intake and not by increased metabolism. In most studies initial weight loss is tangible but ceases after a variable period. This cessation or slowing of weight loss is often cited as evidence of human tolerance to the anorectic effect of amphetamine. This interpretation is supported by many studies of rats that show diminishing inhibition of food intake while the animals consume amphetamine (27, 44). In humans, subjective measures of appetite inhibition also decline during use of amphetamine (41). Despite these studies, the idea that humans develop tolerance to usual dosage is controversial. Stunkard (42) pointed out that a slowing of weight loss in humans (or rats) is by itself insufficient evidence for tolerance, because such slowing may relate to a variety of other factors. He also pointed out that humans gain weight when amphetamine use stops. If humans were tolerant, why would stopping the drug be accompanied by increased appetite and weight gain? In summary, the drug may be helpful in some individuals at the outset of a weight loss program, but extended use of any anorexiant is not likely to be helpful.

Various theories have been postulated to explain the central and peripheral effects of amphetamine. Four theories are currently espoused:

1. Amphetamine may inhibit MAO and augment the effects of endogenous catecholamines.

2. Similarly, they apparently augment catecholamine effects by displacing these agents from neuronal binding sites.

3. Amphetamine in some experiments shows properties similar to tricyclic antidepressants and cocaine in that it interferes with reuptake of secreted catecholamines into the nerve terminals, slowing catecholamine degradation and enhancing its effect.

4. Some of all of the above mechanisms may add to a direct effect of amphetamine on the adrenergic receptor.

The fact that amphetamine psychosis (see below) responds well to antipsychotic dopaminergic blocking agents has focused attention on dopamine as an important central transmitter in some amphetamine effects. All of the mechanisms cited that augment catecholamine effect can, of course, augment a particular catecholamine (37). The similarity of amphetamine psychosis to paranoid schizophrenia and the hypothetical linking of dopamine to both is a comforting and potentially valuable hypothesis (7).

CURRENT THERAPEUTIC USES

Therapeutic use of amphetamine has been attended by growing controversy because of widely publicized, abusive self-medication. In general, the use of amphetamine is now accepted in the treatment of obesity, narcolepsy, and hyperkinetic behavior in children with organic brain damage. These three indications are listed in current official package inserts. Clinicians have found it useful in treating certain psychotic patients and in withdrawing amphetamine users from high doses. Amphetamine use in narcotic mixtures to treat severe pain and occasional use to treat disabling menstrual cramps is defended by some clinicians.

Amphetamine was once widely used in the treatment of depressive disorders before tricyclic antidepressants were developed. Most such use has stopped because of an irregularity of response and because of the abuse potential. Despite the minimal utility, there have been reports of patients refractory to other antidepressant drugs who do respond to amphetamine. Careful documentation of this failure to respond should be a part of such a treatment plan. Several reports have also claimed that amphetamine-caused brightening of mood is a predictor of positive response to tricyclic treatment of depression.

ISSUES OF DEPENDENCE ABUSE AND MISUSE OF AMPHETAMINE

Controversy over definitions constitutes a major problem in the discussion of stimulant use and misuse. Prior to the large scale abuse of amphetamine in the late 1960's, most use and misuse was oral. We may assume that many patients taking the drug for an approved indication (obesity, narcolepsy, depression) noted that the CNS stimulant effects were pleasant and reinforcing. Such users may well have sought the drug for this effect, regardless of their initial reason for using the drug. Fortunately for those needing to justify their behavior and unable to think of themselves as drug misusers, most remained overweight and could continue obtaining prescriptions for that purpose. In a similar fashion, some pre-1965 misusers may have not used the drug for any approved purpose but found it helped facilitate studying, doing boring tasks, driving trucks, fighting battles, or running the end-around play. These users, as well, may have found the drug effect reinforcing and have been tempted to take it when not engaged in the tasks listed. In both instances misusers had choices. They could continue having drug fun episodically or even regularly by obtaining the drug from a prescriber without inordinate difficulty. The nonobese user might have resorted to illegal purchase more readily. Both groups described above could continue such misuse without obvious physical complications if dose escalation did not ensue.

ACUTE AMPHETAMINE TOXICITY

Overdose with amphetamine is analogous to overdose with heroin. It does not often occur in the experienced chronic user who has acquired a significant degree of tolerance. Wesson and Smith have discussed acute amphetamine toxicity (46). They pointed out that the diagnosis is most difficult when the examiner is unaware of the drug history. The picture logically is one of adrenergic excess with dilated pupils, tachycardia and hypertension, profound anxiety, and hyperreflexia. A few patients with massive doses consumed in suicide attempts (or accidental overdosage in children) have presented with seizures, hypertensive crises, or cerebrovascular accidents.

If the drug history is unknown, the diagnosis may be confused with other intoxications, (cocaine, phencyclidine) acute (nondrug) anxiety states, hyperthyroidism, mania, or other functional psychoses.

In most patients a benzodiazepine or phenothiazine sedative may sufficiently calm the amphetamine user who has "overamped."

Gastric lavage may be helpful, particularly because amphetamine decreases effective gastrointestinal motility. Administration of acidifying solutions (ascorbic acid, ammonium chloride) will ionize the weak base in the urine and in the gastric contents. At both sites the ionic trapping will decrease the body burden of the drug. The hypertensive episodes have been most often treated with the alpha-adrenergic blocking drug phentolamine. However, newer vasodilating agents such as nitroprusside or diazoxide should work as well, and clinicians are more likely to be familiar with their use. More serious behavioral aberrations have been treated with antipsychotic, antidopaminergic drugs such as chlorpromazine or haloperidol.

TOLERANCE

Tolerance develops to stimulant drugs. At relatively low dosage (episodic or continuous), tolerance is slow to develop and even the degree is uncertain. Users who begin to escalate the dose in hopes of recapturing or multiplying pleasures can develop significant tolerance to the euphoric effects and to the cardiovascular effects previously cited. High dose users face the difficulties of behavioral toxicity even in the face of tolerance, (see below). Such users may show evidence of social, economic, and emotional deterioration. There is evidence that some tolerance may be related to replacement of normal neurotransmitter stores by an amphetamine metabolite, 4-hydroxynorephedrine. This mechanism does not suffice to explain the central tolerance (27).

WITHDRAWAL

Psychostimulant drugs do not produce stereotyped abstinence syndromes. In fact, it is difficult to accept that humans become physically dependent on amphetamine. Despite this, the abrupt discontinuance of amphetamine is not devoid of complications. Individuals may "crash"—become lethargic, withdrawn, or depressed. Schizophrenic episodes have apparently been precipitated by withdrawal, but this phenomenon is not easily viewed separately from a consequence of active amphetamine use. Many authors have discussed the frequency of depressive syndromes after amphetamine withdrawal, but pharmacotherapy with tricyclic antidepressants or alternatives has not generally been helpful and most of the depressive states seem to disappear after 1 to 3 weeks off amphetamine.

ADDICTION

Addiction certainly may occur to this drug or some of its congeners, particularly phenmetrazine and methylphenidate. The absence of physical dependence and the absence of a withdrawal syndrome might seem to remove an important stimulus to continued drug use. However, individuals do certainly give over their strength, resources, and social lives to stimulant drugs, and amphetamine is one such example.

INTRAVENOUS AMPHETAMINE USE

Kramer's 1969 review is still extremely valuable to an understanding of intravenous use (25). High dose oral use may be attended by significant toxicity, including psychosis and compulsive use, but these complications are hallmarks of the intravenous user. The oral abuser may discover that intravenous injection gratifyingly multiplies all the desired effects of the drug. In the early 1960's the prototypical intravenous (IV) amphetamine user used pharmaceutical methamphetamine, but since that time the source for intravenous methamphetamine has been illegal synthesis.[3] Early IV use may be intermittent, with days or weeks intervening between injections. The "speed freak" who came to national attention in the 1960's progressed to a final pattern of injecting the drug multiple times per day, with total doses into the 1- to 2-g range or more over 24 hours. This consumption pattern leads to "runs" of 3 to 6 days of repeated drug injection without eating or sleeping. Such a user then stops ("crashes") and may sleep profoundly for a day or two. This pattern may be repeated again and again, dependent upon availability of drug and the consequences of such near terminal self-indulgence.

The effects of the drug, which are profound (even with the obvious tolerance), are complicated by insomnia and anorexia, which are invariably present. Adding to the uncertainty of attributing effects to amphetamine is the near certain use of other drugs (particularly sedatives and alcohol) and the other ingredients used to dilute the illicit speed (ether and monosodium glutamate were frequent ingredients in the 1960's). Users early in a run may overdose. Hepatitis is often experienced, and malnutrition (even with binges of food consumption) may lead to deterioration.

The behavioral impacts of this style of use are dramatic and disabling. Varying degrees of paranoia or a paranoid psychosis occur in many such users. There is reason to believe that all such users, with or without a psychotic predisposition, will become psychotic with prolonged use (see below). The paranoia is not rapid in onset and may be mild when it emerges. If the user repeats runs, it often becomes florid. Some users reportedly ceased using IV amphetamine when they realized that delusions and hallucinations were emerging. The folklore of speed use carries the belief that most users become violent.

The character of street dealing of illicit and impure drug, mixed with user tendencies to become paranoid and suspicious, lends some credance to this folklore.

AMPHETAMINE PSYCHOSIS

Prior to the clinical issues of amphetamine psychosis, it was known that small IV doses of amphetamine and related compounds could intensify a wide variety of preexisting psychotic symptoms. In fact, methamphetamine was available in the ampules chiefly at the request of psychiatrists who injected the drug with the intent of facilitating abreaction and communication and clarifying diagnoses of psychotic patients. This phenomenon of psychosis activation was seen with d,l-amphetamine, although methylphenidate was also causative. To confuse the picture, some schizophrenic patients showed improvement when treated with low dosage amphetamine. Interestingly, these low dose experiments, which led to psychotic activation, were not blocked by preadministration of antipsychotic drugs (37).

High doses of virtually all amphetamine-like drugs, including cocaine, can induce psychotic symptoms in nonschizophrenic individuals. The cardinal work here was done by Griffith and his associates, who prospectively produced paranoid psychoses in individuals who had previously abused amphetamine (17). Interestingly, some of Griffith's patients succumbed to relatively low doses. These and other studies supported the clinical reports cited, in that the paranoid psychoses emerged gradually and were often indistinguishable from nondrug-related paranoid schizophrenia (2).

The issue of tolerance and its interpretation have been aided by some experimental studies as well. Behavioral stimulation and euphoria may well diminish with repeated administration of amphetamine, but the psychotogenic tendency may progressively increase. A user on a run may then develop tolerance to some deleterious effects, but the likelihood of psychosis looms larger and larger.

CURRENT AMPHETAMINE USE

I have heavily emphasized the past history of amphetamine use in the United States, but I had good cause. There is convincing evi-

---

[3] Some IV users solubilized methamphetamine tablets for injection.

dence that the patterns cited and referred to have changed dramatically in the last decade. There is convincing evidence that amphetamine abuse has decreased, particularly IV amphetamine use; that amphetamine availability in the illegal market has precipitously diminished; and that physician prescribing of pharmaceutical amphetamine has fallen steadily. Some of these events are clearly interrelated, whereas others are not so. The remainder of this chapter will deal with these recent changes.

EPIDEMIOLOGY

Newmeyer recently reviewed the epidemiology of amphetamine in the 1970's (36). He cited the "common belief" that amphetamine use had declined sharply since the methamphetamine epidemic of the late 1960's. He cited at least three epidemiological surveys and came to these conclusions. Amphetamine in its various forms (and other psychostimulants) have been widely used in the urban youthful population. Fully 25 per cent of the population so characterized had used some psychostimulant, but the usage was light ("experimental" or "quasi-medical"). Fewer than 10 per cent of users could be characterized as current regular users, and much use was within a polypharmacy context. The data cited indicated that morbidity was low and that few people being treated for acute or chronic drug problems cited amphetamine as important. Revealing data had been gathered by Blackford in an ongoing (1968 to 1977) survey of young people in Mateo County California (8). The prevalence of use had peaked in this population in 1972 and had dropped sharply since that year. Furthermore, the 1972 to 1977 diminution was greater for the heavier use categories. Newmeyer also cited the data gathered by Greene and DuPont (16) and Kozel and DuPont (26), who assayed urines of arrestees admitted to the Washington, D.C., Superior Court jail for amphetamine. Amphetamine-positive urines were found in 5.1 per cent of all arrestees in the third quarter of 1972. This declined to a 0.3 per cent positive rate in the first quarter of 1975. This decline was attributed to a number of factors, particularly a decrease in the prescribing of licit amphetamine. I shall return to that issue but most importantly point out that this study is alone in the epidemiological literature in

that a survey of amphetamine use was confirmed by analysis for the drug. All of the other data cited by Newmeyer rely on self-reports of amphetamine or other stimulant usage by the user. Newmeyer discussed briefly the data obtained from "crisis contact sources," the Drug Abuse Warning Network (DAWN). This project gathers drug "mentions" from three sources: emergency rooms, drug treatment centers, and medical examiner offices (11). This project is funded by the Federal Government through a private contractor, IMS America, who has developed drug-monitoring plans chiefly on contract for the drug industry. Those in the federal apparatus interested in drug regulation, the Drug Enforcement Agency (DEA) and the Food and Drug Administration (FDA) rely heavily on DAWN as an informational source regarding trends in American drug abuse. DAWN data tend to confirm the epidemiology suggested by Newmeyer; that is, amphetamine mentions from crisis contact reporters have decreased. In recent years however, the DAWN data have been heavily manipulated and interpreted to show that amphetamine and stimulant abuse are still serious problems in America. These decisions rely heavily on DAWN and merit thorough discussion. Repetitively, I will mention that DAWN data, like other epidemiological data cited, are not confirmed by assay of biological fluids or drug samples. The acceptance of a report from a crisis center of amphetamine or Dexedrine or Obetrol or "crossroads" constitutes a nonconfirmed acceptance of the drug user's probity.

DIVERSION OF PHARMACEUTICAL AMPHETAMINE

McGlothlin (28) has, along with Jackson (22–24) and Grinspoon and Hedblom (18), written of the history of amphetamine use in the United States. Much of the following remarks rely on their work. As early as 1962, it had been noted in congressional hearings that legitimate manufacture of amphetamine was very large and that substantial proportions of this material were diverted to illegal sale. The FDA estimated that 8 billion 10-mg amphetamine tablets had been manufactured in 1962. This constituted enough 10-mg units to provide 40 for each resident of the United States. These estimates of overproduction were increasingly cited between 1962 and

1970, and numerous articles in the same period criticized the widespread prescribing of the drug, even though that prescribing could not alone have fully supplied the street market. It is apparently true then that the street market, which grew to supply illicit users of amphetamine, relied increasingly on diversion of material produced and/or repackaged by pharmaceutical firms. There were occasional other sources. Domestic clandestine laboratories existed, but their numbers and output were relatively small. Material manufactured outside the United States could be smuggled in, and at one point this became extremely important (see below). However, before 1970 there was little work for the illicit chemist (except for methamphetamine for injection) and smuggling because diversion supplied the market. It is important to mention that smuggling of amphetamine into the United States also represented diversion. After 1970, significant numbers of small amphetamine tablets containing from 2 to 8 mg of d-amphetamine were smuggled into Southern California from Mexico. The bulk material had been obtained from a European pharmaceutical manufacturer who ostensibly was shipping it to a legitimate purchaser.

The diversion of licit amphetamine before 1970 took place at all levels from bulk manufacturers to thefts from the medicine cabinet. McGlothlin lists three important categories: (a) intentional sales to unauthorized persons; (b) unintentional sales to unauthorized persons; (c) thefts.

These three methods in combination diverted approximately 50 per cent of licitly manufactured amphetamine to the illicit market. Thefts and intentional sales to unauthorized persons were documented but apparently never made up a large percentage of diverted drug. Prescription forgery using stolen or bogus prescription pads was also of some importance, although the volume was simply not known. The mechanism of sale to an individual or firm who clearly intended resale through illicit channels was most important. Drug suppliers (manufacturers or repackagers) carelessly sold amphetamine to the most questionable of sources. Sales to Mexican pharmacies from United States manufacturers provided one avenue, and sales to Mexican "wholesale druggists" provided a larger source. Fifteen million dosage units over a period of 10 years were shipped

by Bates Laboratories of Chicago to a fictitious address that corresponded most closely to the eleventh hole of the Tijuana Country Club golf course (9). Apparently the pills were usually held by a border customs agent to be picked up by the company. The setting up of a fraudulent mail drop purporting to be a drug wholesaler was also a profitable ploy. In 1964 a reporter, Jay McMullen, established McMullen Services at 35 West 45th Street in New York City. He contacted 51 drug firms, placed orders with 19 of them, and received large shipments of amphetamine and barbiturates. One manufacturer asked the New York State Board of Pharmacy whether a license had been issued for McMullen Services and inspection of the "firm" followed, but not before material from many other sources had been received (4).

In summary, the illicit market for oral amphetamine was supplied not by illicit synthesis in clandestine laboratories but by pharmaceutical synthesis and diversion. There are some other characteristics of the pre-1970 market that contributed to the events described above. The popularity of amphetamine and related drugs meant that many drug companies produced and/or packaged some version of amphetamine. After SKF patents expired, companies could package racemic amphetamine sulfate (and SKF continued to sell its original brand, Benzedrine) or dextroamphetamine sulfate (and SKF continued to sell Dexedrine). Competing companies could, of course, make other salts (dextroamphetamine tannate, dextroamphetamine saccharate, amphetamine aspartate, dextroamphetamine adipate, and amphetamine adipate). Methamphetamine was and is still available as an oral preparation, and variants on this theme appeared as well. All these could be marketed in tablets or capsules of varying size, color, dosage, and shapes. One could, as the R. J. Strasenburg (later Pennwalt) corporation did, put together dextroamphetamine and amphetamine and market it as Biphetamine. The largest Biphetamine black capsules contained 10 mg of each drug and were sold on the street as "black beauties," a "trade" name still commonly used by street drug dealers. Some companies, Palmedico, Obetrol, and Delco put together four salt-cong ner mixtures for no obvious reasons. Often the drug was marketed with other drugs in combination (e.g. Amytal, prochlorperazine, meprobamate, aspirin-phen-acetin, etc.). This plethora of psychostimulant medication was, of course, increased by a variety of phenethylamine derivatives marketed as anorexiants. A partial listing includes benzphetamine, phenmetrazine, phentermine, chlorphentermine, clortermine, phendimetrazine, and diethylproprion.

Some amphetamine products (particularly those of SKF) were distinctively marked and were popular on the street. They even acquired street names (hearts, peaches, greenies), and such names acquired cachet. A street dealer could claim to have "pharmaceutical" for sale (Dexedrine, Dexamyl, Benzedrine etc.). These products and others, including "black beauties," were counterfeited even before 1970. Some "generic" drug houses would package amphetamine (or even other drugs) so as to resemble these popular formats. Whether this increased sales in the legitimate market is not known. It surely helped sales that would later result in street diversion of these products. Such look-alikes were not in and of themselves illegal. Occasionally SKF would go to court and claim trademark infringement if the resemblance was too close. However, the most popular street format was the "cartwheel" or "crossroad." As stated, once amphetamine patents were exhausted many drug firms both major and minor began to market the drug. Occasionally firms marketed under their own brand names (Delcobese, Obotan, Obetrol, Methampex), but the most common dosage formulation was the relatively nondescript, double-convex, cross-hatched white tablet. These were available in the 1960's from more than 50 drug companies. In most instances these firms did not synthesize amphetamine sulphate (the most common salt) but brought the bulk powder from a larger drug company or even from a chemical firm that did not market drugs. They would then punch the tablets into the form noted above. These became the ubiquitous "whites," "crossroads," and "cartwheels" of street lore and song.[4] Although exact documentation is impossible, probably the majority of diverted pharmaceutical amphetamine came from these sources. Most materials shipped to McMullen Services were from repackagers or generic drug houses (36).

LEGISLATIVE EFFORTS

I have not comprehensively reviewed the multiple attempts by state and federal legislatures to exert some control on this strange illicit market. However, some legislation of the 1960's and a most important bill of 1970 need comment. The 1959 ban on amphetamine inhalers has been noted. The FDA obtained significant information on truck stop dealing in 1963 and the growing story of abuse of licitly manufactured material led to the introduction of several bills in Congress. Jay McMullen made an impressive statement before a House Commerce Committee in 1964 (30). The first post-1960 legislation was passed in 1965 as the Drug Abuse Control Amendments. This important bill did require the registration of manufacturers, formulators, and wholesalers of amphetamine and barbiturates, but retail pharmacies and physicians were exempt. This bill was further amended in 1968 to increase penalties for sale and to impose criminal sanction for use. These legislative attempts were inspired by the increasing visability of legal material and the already described diversion. Legislators had come to realize that pharmacists, physicians, and clandestine laboratories constituted only a part, and probably a small part, of the amphetamine supply problem.

The 1970 Controlled Substance Act (CSA) represents the most telling attack on the problem and, as we shall see, completely changed the amphetamine market. The CSA places abusable drugs in a number of schedules relative to their abuse potential. Schedule II contains the drugs that have therapeutic utility but are highly subject to abuse. Initially amphetamine was placed in Schedule III, but administrative procedures to reschedule drugs were included in the legislation and amphetamine was moved to Schedule II in 1971. This scheduling adds significantly to control. Manufacturers of Schedule II drugs must use special secure manufacture and storage areas. Purchasers must use preprinted federal order forms containing their names and registration numbers for each transaction. Import and export shipments require prior approval. In fact, today, no import or

---

[4] Lowell George wrote "Gimme weed, whites and wine" in a song entitled "Willin'," and Dave Dudley's truck driver's anthem Six Days On The Road included "I'm takin' little white pills and my eyes are open wide."

export quotas are approved for amphetamine for any manufacturer or purchaser. However, despite all this restriction, Schedule II imposes a much more significant control, that of manufacturing quotas. Any manufacturer must obtain permission from the FDA and DEA for synthesis, sale, and bulk resale to repackagers of amphetamine. Similarly, the repackagers have fixed quotas for wholesale volume. The DEA actually sets the quotas, and these are based on estimated medical needs. At this time, there are only two approved manufacturers of amphetamine in the United States—SKF, who does not sell to formulators, and Arenol Laboratories, who supplies the drug to approximately 30 formulators.

Production, import, and export data of amphetamine in the 1960's were remarkably imprecise. I have previously cited the 1962 estimate of 80,000 kg (this includes methamphetamine). Data for the rest of the decade are suspect, but the 1969 figures prior to the imposition of quotas are reasonably exact. Total production was near 38,000 kg. To support previous contentions, only some 12,000 kg could be easily accounted for by assessing legal sales data.

In 1972, the quotas set by the federal drug apparatus took effect. These were set at drastically low levels, approximately 10 per cent of the 1969 to 1970 figures, or approximately 3,500 kg. The intent of the federal government was clear. Not only was the drastic decrease designed to reduce the large amount of diversion, but the level "needed" for medical usage was drastically reduced as well. In 1969 to 1970, legal prescribing accounted for some 12,000 kg, but by 1972 only 3,500 kg were available. Physician prescribing of amphetamine obviously fell rapidly. The annual figure of between 3,000 and 4,000 kg has been maintained, and legal prescribing accounts for nearly all of this volume. Diversion has not stopped—the DEA has stated but not documented that 10 per cent of licit material may still be diverted—but licit manufacture and formulation no longer supply a lush illicit market.

STREET DRUG QUALITY AND THE 1970 CSA

The sudden curtailment of a readily available supply of a treasured drug changed the market. Additionally, there is ample evidence to believe that physicians were now much less likely to be easy marks for prescriptions. By law, Schedule II drugs cannot be prescribed by telephone (except in severe emergencies) and refills cannot be authorized. In New York State physicians must prescribe Schedule II drugs via a special triplicate prescription that results in monitoring of individuals prescribing and consuming these agents. A number of predictions were made. Most of these contained the belief that illicit synthesis and smuggling would make up the difference. The story is exactly the opposite.

My associate, D. Kagan, and I have studied the street quality of amphetamine before and after the imposition of the 1972 quotas. Some of these results have been previously reported (33, 34). We utilized a number of methods to study street drug quality. A number of laboratories surveying street drugs grew up in response to the explosion of illicit drug abuse in the late 1960's. These facilities, some governmental, some proprietary, some not for profit, were generally referred to as Street Drug Analytical Laboratories (SDA's). Their quality and surveillance areas varied. Some accepted anonymous samples and some did not. They were all prevented from reporting quantitative data. They could identify active ingredients in a sample but they could not report the amounts of active ingredients. Prior to 1974, there were many such labs, but more stringent regulation of their behavior and standards were imposed by the DEA in 1974 (5). Many went out of operation at that time. Our survey in 1979 located only 15 SDA's who could share data with us. Fortunately, a much more comprehensive survey had been carried out in 1974 by J. Bing Hart. This survey was not published, but Dr. Hart shared his results with us (20).

The composite data indicated a drastic change in street purity of amphetamine and methamphetamine after 1972. Our initial survey of 7,000 samples submitted as "speed," amphetamine, or methamphetamine showed the following. Drug consumers or others submitting samples in 1971 to 1972 submitted material that contained amphetamine or methamphetamine in approximately 65 per cent of instances. A decline in quality began in 1973 that has never reversed. The percentage of samples that actually contain amphetamine had fallen to approximately 10 per cent by 1976. Recent data from functioning SDA's (Pharm Chem Laboratories, the Street Pharmacologist) indicate a continuing downward trend. In 1979, the percentage of purported amphetamine samples that actually contained amphetamine fluctuated near 5 per cent. The street market has become one of near complete counterfeiting and deception. A large variety of drugs are sold on the street as amphetamine. By far the most common is caffeine. Entrepreneurs buy over-the-counter caffeine preparations and sell them or even formulate bulk caffeine into tablets. Ephedrine-caffeine mixtures are very common, as are proprietary (nonprescription) anorexiants that contain the nonstimulant phenethylamine, phenylpropanolamine. Occasionally non-Schedule II anorexiants such as phendimetrazine, diethylproprion, and phentermine are sold deceptively as amphetamine.

The issue of counterfeiting remains important. No great skill is needed to sell an over-the-counter preparation as speed or to utilize a cartwheel format. However, on file at the DEA laboratory concerned with identifying capsules and tablets and tracing them to manufacturers, are black beauties, pink hearts, and other popular forms that did not originate with SKF or Pennwalt and that contain caffeine or phendimetrazine. This phenomenon of the preservation of old amphetamine appearance on the street in the absence of amphetamine quality is important.

I have previously referred to DAWN. This system continues to record mentions at crisis center contact of amphetamine use. DAWN recorded an over-all decline in amphetamine mentions from 1972 to 1975, and this decline in their medical examiner reporting has continued. However, emergency room mentions held steady from 1975 to 1977 and have shown no trend either up or down in that period. This persistence of amphetamine mentions in DAWN, particularly in emergency departments, led to an intriguing interpretation by the DEA and the FDA that amphetamine abuse remains a problem of sufficient magnitude to warrant further action.

THE OBESITY INDICATION AND THE FDA

On July 17, 1979, the director of the Bureau of Drugs of the FDA proposed the removal of obesity from the official package insert as an indication for prescribing amphetamine (13). Inasmuch as 80 to 85 per cent of amphetamine is prescribed for anorexiant effect, this move will have some impact. Because a medical usage will be curtailed, the DEA-FDA mechanism for setting manufacturing quotas will operate, and, theoretically at least, the amount of manufactured amphetamine will fall to approximately 450 kg, enough to supply the small amounts needed for the treatment of narcolepsy and hyperkinesis.[5] The FDA notice spends some time in discussion of the fact that amphetamine has limited utility as an anorexiant, and other (non-Schedule II) anorexiants could be utilized with less abuse hazard. This issue has been discussed briefly in the section on clinical pharmacology and I shall not refer to it further. The bulk of the FDA notice is taken up by the official opinion that amphetamine is still importantly abused.

The notice focuses on the continued use of DAWN reports to promote a certain reality that amphetamine abuse, amphetamine diversion, and physician prescribing of amphetamine are all important and linked—as they were before 1972. Much statistical manipulation of the DAWN data is carried out to support these beliefs. The DAWN data utilized by the notice are based chiefly on emergency room reports. Much of the previous data from drug treatment centers (a variety of drug abuse treatment facilities) have been dropped from current reports because of evidence that drug mentions from some of these facilities were clearly inflated.[6] As I have noted, these mentions are almost never confirmed by analyses of body fluids

---

[5] The removal of an indication has practical import. Drug companies cannot advertise for a nonapproved indication, although most amphetamine advertising has ceased. SKF has not advertised any of its amphetamine products in medical journals or by direct mail for over a decade. Physicians may, of course, prescribe drugs for nonapproved indications and often do. In this controversial area, the removal of the indication will have significant impact, and most physicians who continue to use the drug will probably fear to do so in the future.

[6] DAWN only asks the centers to record drug mentions. These do not distinguish between pleasant and unpleasant reactions. I am aware of anecdotal reports that some crisis centers at filing time have interviewed clients and individuals in proximity to the clinics to increase their mention rate. These mentions have frequently inflated marihuana statistics.

or samples of drugs. This simply means that all these mentions are "generic." An individual recorded by DAWN may have said amphetamine, speed, diet pills, bennies, or Eskatrol, because these words are current and have a certain cachet. The street drug analyses I have reviewed were often submitted under such names. There is no reason to accept such mentions as authentic, and the use of mentions, although perhaps exploitable for certain goals, is misleading in this context. DAWN was constructed as a warning network, and guesses are acceptable in the setting. To use it as a policy or legislative tool is clearly inappropriate. An attempt to rehabilitate DAWN was signaled by certain sections of the FDA notice. In recent reporting some "jargon" was eliminated (what was considered jargon was not specified). The term amphetamine was considered to reflect a pharmacological reality, as were certain other pharmaceutical terms. This simply is not true. Street users use the term "amphetamine" just as they use "speed" or "uppers," without focus on pharmacological reality. "Amphetamine" is jargon on the streets. In the Hart data (1971 to 1974), when purity was significantly higher than it is now, the term amphetamine on submission signaled the presence of amphetamine alone approximately 40 per cent of the time. The Hart data also showed the following accuracy for pharmaceuticals between 1971 and 1974:

Benzedrine stated, as alleged	18 per cent
Dexamyl stated, as alleged	2 per cent
Dexedrine stated, as alleged	16 per cent
Methadrine stated, as alleged	3 per cent
Obedrine stated, as alleged	0 per cent

"As alleged" means the submittal material contained amphetamine. It does not necessarily mean that even then the brand name or pharmaceutical term used was correct. Recall that these samples reflected better days for the street amphetamine buyer and the numbers today would be surely lower. The DAWN sample would be improved according to the Hart data if the term "crossroads" was included as pharmacological, because it had a better record of containing amphetamine alone than any of those listed above. The combing of language for pharmaceutical terms, jargon, or other speculative labels provides DAWN and those of us who read it with no help as to the real contents of any

medication by users who appear at a DAWN survey center. Sellers, users, and DAWN reports seem engaged in the same conspiracy to prove that amphetamine abuse is real and potent, whereas, in reality, most street abuse seems to be that of caffeine or ephedrine.

DEA DATA

I obtained a significant volume of DEA amphetamine seizure data for the years 1971 to 1978. This extra window on the street drug market was valuable because I feared that SDA's disproportionately reflect bad drug. Users might send for analysis drug that does not look right or has unexpected effects (or lack of effects). DEA seizures may not be systematic either, but they too reflect to some degree the street market and add a piece to the solving of the amphetamine puzzle. The DEA supplied information on (a) the number of seizures made per year; (b) the volume of tablets or capsules taken per seizure; and (c) the amphetamine content of constituent tablets or capsules seized.

These over-all data support the contention that amphetamine abuse is steadily declining. The total number of seizures has declined every year since 1974. Concurrent with that decrease, the absolute number of pills seized has decreased. In 1977, illicit amphetamine seizures totaled 115, but 64 of these were in batches of 500 pills or less. Of more interest, a significant number of the seizures contained tablets that seemed to be amphetamine but were not. As early as 1973, the first year after manufacturing quotas were imposed, nearly 50 per cent of DEA seizures made were counterfeit and contained no amphetamine. In 1978, of the 89 illicit batches seized, 37 contained no amphetamine. In 1971, before the quotas took full effect, only 22 per cent of seized batches were counterfeit. DEA agents have the same difficulty and lack of success as do recreational users, because amphetamine availability is remarkably decreased.

LOOK ALIKES AND LICIT MATERIAL

DEA data are subdivided. They are filed as reflecting illicit or licit amphetamine. Tablets are examined by DEA laboratories for trademarks, logos, colors, and tableting machine impressions that reflect their origins, illicit labs, or some known manufacturer or formulator. Amazingly, the same low purity described for illicit samples is seen in licit samples. This means that the DEA seized drug samples that appeared to be (or were sold as) pharmaceutical amphetamine. These dosage units had originated from known manufacturer or formulators. One assumes that they resembled popular branded amphetamine products or the well known generic cross-hatched white tablet (the cartwheel or cross-road) that once characterized much diverted amphetamine. On analysis, these licit samples of "amphetamine" contained caffeine, ephedrine, phenylpropanolamine, phendimetrazine, phentermine, and others.

CONCLUSIONS

The story of amphetamine abuse in America has evolved to an unlikely point. The effective curtailment of supply after nearly 40 years of easy trafficking in the drug has nearly destroyed the street market. This has been coupled with evidence of a diminishing interest in amphetamine on the part of youthful Americans. The surprise is that the architects of this policy refuse for many reasons to accept the evidence of their success and seem now to be engaged in overkill to curtail nearly completely physicians' ability to prescribe a drug that some wish to continue to use.

Perhaps the above is not surprising. It took decades to convince American physicians to not casually prescribe the drug and American patients to not casually consume it. Now that these goals are accomplished, the task of convincing anyone that the drug probably has some utility and can be used safely seems insurmountable.

References

1. Alles, G. A. The comparative physiological action of phenylethanolamine. J. Pharmacol. Exp. Ther. 32: 121, 1928.
2. Angrist, B. M., and Gershon, S. The phenomenology of experimentally induced amphetamine psychosis. Biol. Psychiatry 2:95, 1970.
3. Anonymous. Nazi pep pills. Time 66, September 14, 1942.
4. Anonymous. Pep pills bought by carton in test. New York Times, September 3, 1964.
5. Anonymous. DEA Issues Street Drug Lab Guideline. J. Am. Pharm. Assoc. 13:675, 1973.
6. Becket, A. H., and Brookes, L. G. The effect of chain and ring substitution on the metabolism, distribution and biological action of amphetamines. In International Symposium on Amphetamines and Related Compounds, E. Costa and S. Garattini, editors, pp. 109–120. New York, Raven Press, 1970.
7. Berger, P. A., Elliott, G. R., and Barchas, J. D. Neuroregulators and schizophrenia. In Psychopharmacology: A Generation of Progress, M. A. Lipton, A. DiMascio, and K. F. Killam, editors, pp. 1071–1081. New York, Raven Press, 1978.
8. Blackford, L. Summary Report: Surveys of Student Drug Use, San Mateo County, California. San Mateo County California Research and Statistics Section, Department of Health and Welfare, 1977.
9. Caldwell, E. Maker sent drugs to dummy outfit. New York Times, October 26, 1969.
10. Caldwell, J., and Sever, P. A. The biochemical pharmacology of abused drugs. I. Amphetamines, cocaine and LSD. Clin. Pharmacol. Ther. 16:625, 1974.
11. Carabillo, E. A., Jr. U.S.A. Drug Abuse Warning Network. In Central Mechanisms of Anorectic Drugs, S. Garattini and R. Samanin, editors. New York, Raven Press, 1978.
12. Edeleano, L. Uber Einige Derivate der Phenylmethocrylsure wid der Phenylisobuttersaure. Ber Dtsch. Chem. Ges. 20:616, 1887.
13. Federal Register. Notice 44 Federal Register 41552, July 17, 1979.
14. Forrest, W. H., Brown, B. W., Brown, C. R., et al. Dextroamphetamine with morphine for the treatment of postoperative pain. N. Engl. J. Med. 296: 712, 1977.
15. Goldman, A. Ladies and Gentlemen, Lennie Bruce, p. 12. New York, Ballantine Books, 1975.
16. Greene, M. H., and DuPont, R. L. Amphetamines in the District of Columbia. I. Identification and resolution of an abuse epidemic. J. A. M. A. 226:1437, 1973.
17. Griffith, J. Schizophreniform psychosis induced by large administration of amphetamine. J. Psychedelic Drugs 2:42, 1969.
18. Grinspoon, L., and Hedblom, P. The Speed Culture: Amphetamine Use and Abuse in America, p. 18. Cambridge, Mass., Harvard University Press, 1975.
19. Haefely, W., Bartholini, G., and Pletscher, A. Monoaminergic drugs: General pharmacology. Pharmacol. Ther. (B) 2:185, 1976.
20. Hart, J. B. Personal communication, 1978.
21. Hope, J. M., Calloway, E., and Sands, S. L. Intravenous pervitin and psychopathology of schizophrenia. Dis. Nerv. Syst. 12:67, 1951.
22. Jackson, C. O. The amphetamine inhaler: A case study of medical abuse. J. Hist. Med. 26:187, 1971.
23. Jackson, C. O. The amphetamine democracy: Medicinal abuse in the popular culture. South Atlantic Q. 74:308, 1975.
24. Jackson, C. O. Before the drug culture, barbiturate/amphetamine abuse in American society. Clin. Med. 11:47, 1976.
25. Kramer, J. C. Introduction to amphetamine abuse. J. Psychedelic Drugs 2:1, 1969.
26. Kozel, N. J., and Dupont, R. Criminal Charges and Drug Use Patterns of Arrestees in the District of Columbia, Publication No. (ADM) 72-27. Rockville, Md., United States Department of Health, Education and Welfare, 1977.
27. Lewander, T. Experimental studies on anorexigenic drugs: Tolerance, cross-tolerance and dependence. In Central Mechanisms of Anorectic Drugs, S. Garattini and R. Saminin, editors, pp. 343–356. New York, Raven Press, 1978.
28. Lu, T. C., Claghorn, J. L., and Schoolar, J. C. Chronic

administration of *d*-amphetamine and chlorproma-zine in rats. Eur. J. Clin. Pharmacol. 21:61, 1973.

29. McGlothlin, W. H. *Amphetamines, Barbiturates and Hallucinogens: An Analysis of Use, Distribution and Control.* Prepared for Department of Justice, Bureau of Narcotics and Dangerous Drugs, Contract No. J-70-33. Los Angeles, Department of Psychology, University of California at Los Angeles, 1973.

30. McMullen, J. Photocopy of testimony before House Commerce Committee, 1964.

31. Monroe, R. R., and Drell, H. J. Oral use of stimulants obtained from inhalers. J. A. M. A. 135:909, 1947.

32. Morgan, J. P. The clinical pharmacology of amphet-amine. In *Amphetamine Use, Misuse, and Abuse*, D. E. Smith, editor. Boston, G. K. Hall, 1979.

33. Morgan, J. P., and Kagan, D. Street amphetamine quality and the Controlled Substances Act of 1970. J. Psychedelic Drugs 10:303, 1978.

34. Morgan, J. P., and Kagan, D. Street amphetamine quality and the Controlled Substances Act of 1970. In *Amphetamine Use, Misuse, and Abuse*, D. E. Smith, editor. Boston, G. K. Hall, 1979.

35. Nagahama, M. A review of drug abuse and counter measures in Japan since World War II. U. N. Bull. Narc. 20:19, 1968.

36. Newmeyer, J. A. The epidemiology of amphetamine use. In *Amphetamine Use, Misuse, and Abuse*, D. E. Smith, editor. Boston, G. K. Hall, 1979.

37. Segal, D. S., and Janowsky, D. S. Psychostimulant-induced behavioral effects: Possible models of schizophrenia. In *Psychopharmacology: A Genera-tion of Progress*, M. A. Lipton, A. Dimascio, and K.

F. Killam, editors, pp. 1113–1123. New York, Raven Press, 1978.

38. Shulgin, A. T. Abuse of the term "amphetamines." Clin. Toxicol. 9:351, 1976.

39. Smith, D. E., and Fircher, C. M. An analysis of 310 cases of acute high-dose methamphetamine toxicity in Haight-Ashbury. Clin. Toxicol. 3:117, 1970.

40. Smith, R. Traffic in amphetamine: Patterns of illegal manufacture and distribution. J. Psychedelic Drugs 2:30, 1969.

41. Strata, A., and Zuliani, U. Amphetamines in the treatment of obesity. In *Central Mechanisms of An-orectic Drugs*, S. Garattini and R. Samanin, editors, pp. 405–418. New York, Raven Press, 1978.

42. Stunkard, A. J. The development of tolerance to appetite suppressant medication: New theory, new hope. In *Amphetamine Use, Misuse, and Abuse*, D. E. Smith, editor. Boston, G. K. Hall, 1979.

43. Sylvester, R. *The Lost Chords: Eddie Condon's Treasury of Jazz*, E. Condon and R. Gehman, editors. New York, Dial, 1956.

44. Tormey, J., and Lasagna, L. Relation of thyroid func-tion to acute and chronic effects of amphetamine in the rat. J. Pharmacol. Exp. Ther. 128:201, 1960.

45. Weiss, B., and Laties, V. G. Enhancement of human performance by caffeine and the amphetamines. Pharmacol. Rev. 14:1, 1962.

46. Wesson, D. R., and Smith, D. E. A clinical approach to diagnosis and treatment of amphetamine abuse. In *Amphetamine Use, Misuse, and Abuse*, D. E. Smith, editor. Boston, G. K. Hall, 1979.

CHAPTER 16

ABUSE OF SEDATIVE-HYPNOTICS

Donald R. Wesson, M.D.

David E. Smith, M.D., Ph.D.

Abuse of sedative-hypnotics has attracted considerable public attention and has been the topic of legislative hearings and many professional papers and conferences. Given the number of papers published and words spoken about sedative-hynotic abuse, one might be tempted to conclude that abuse of sedative-hypnotics represented a well defined and commonly agreed upon concept. Like most concepts in drug abuse, impassioned concern, conviction, and efforts to combat the problem precede scientific scrutiny by decades, and massive mobilization cannot spare the time or effort for academic exercises of definition, nosology, and acquiring concensus. *Abuse of sedative-hypnotics* can be viewed as a richly endowed type of word salad with vaguely defined ingredients of pharmacological Calvinism, overprescribing, unacceptable or self-destructive behavior, and addiction, along with more precise concepts of physical dependence and tolerance. The exact ingredients and blending are highly idiosyncratic among authors, depending upon their world view and placement with the drug abuse treatment industrial complex.

After the introduction of barbiturates in 1903 until the introduction of meprobamate in the mid-1950's, the various barbiturates drew the most attention. The pharmaceutical industry has not remained static however, and we now have a plethora of drugs to consider, with diazepam (Valium) currently occupying center stage.

There is no dearth of statistics related to sedative-hypnotics and their abuse. Because these drugs are all manufactured by pharmaceutical industries that are subject to many levels of government control and reporting requirements, one approach involves tallying production and trying to divine the amount that is ultimately diverted out of medical channels and thus abused.

National data bases like Drug Abuse Warning Network (DAWN) provide a stratified measure of episodes of adverse consequences coming to medical attention that include suicidal attempts, accidental poisoning, and adverse medical circumstances occurring in chronic sedative-hypnotic users. The relationship between sedative-hypnotic abuse, therapeutic misadventure, and suicidal use is not precisely known, but DAWN does provide, in spite of inherent limitations that its detractors are fond of recounting, an estimate of the prevalence with which sedative-hypnotic use becomes problematic—a consideration of public health importance.

The Client Oriented Data Acquisition Program (CODAP) used in federally supported drug abuse treatment programs provides another estimate of the number of "abusers" who are in treatment. This system is likely to identify the seriously involved individual, is not geographically stratified, and, therefore, probably provides a conservative estimate of abuse.

Unless one is comfortable accepting a high degree of uncertainty and a highly ambiguous definition of sedative-hypnotic abuse, there is little reason to believe that the incidence and prevalence of sedative-hypnotic abuse is, at present, known.

Our definition of sedative-hypnotic abuse is idiosyncratic, but it has the merit of being clinically quantifiable: sedative-hypnotic abuse is the self-administration of a sedative-hypnotic-type drug—excluding alcohol—in such a manner as to produce significant impairment of health or economic or social functioning, except in a deliberate suicidal attempt by an individual who would not otherwise qualify.

There is no pharmacological reason to exclude alcohol from our definition, and our decision to do so is mediated by social-cultural considerations. Our definition includes episodic use leading to impairment, daily use, and social-recreational use, as well as self-medication to the point of detriment. We exclude therapeutic misadventure in which an individual may experience an adverse reaction to drugs when taken as prescribed by a physican. However, the individual who sequentially visits different physicians to obtain a supply or who obtains sedative-hypnotics from a physician and takes them in variance from the instructions would be included.

RELATIONSHIP OF MEDICINE TO SEDATIVE-HYPNOTIC ABUSE

Physicians are frequently cited as being the major cause of sedative-hypnotic abuse through overprescribing, misprescribing, or misbehavior. Inasmuch as physicians are the usual gatekeepers to pharmaceutically produced drugs and because sedative-hypnotics are produced by the pharmaceutical industry, it is not unreasonable to suspect a relationship between the availability of sedative-hypnotics and physicians' suppliers. It is, however, not very thoughtful to suspect that the relationship would be unitary or simple.

The conditions for which sedative-hypnotics are most commonly prescribed are anxiety and insomnia. Although both conditions are extremely common and are not unknown to most individuals on occasion, their definitions, particularly that of anxiety, are ambiguous and are viewed differently by individuals of various persuasions.

Within the medical model and that of some behavioral theorists, anxiety is viewed as a symptom that, if adequately treated, results in a "cure." The commonness with which anxiety is experienced leads some individuals to espouse the viewpoint that anxiety is a normal experience of everyday life and that to treat anxiety with drugs is tantamount to using pharmacological solutions to everyday problems of living. Physicians retort, however, that they distinguish between incapacitating or morbid anxiety and "normal" anxiety and would not advocate that all anxiety be ameliorated with psychotropic drugs.

A psychodynamic orientation would view anxiety as symptomatic of underlying psychopathology and requiring treatment directed toward understanding and resolving the underlying reasons for anxiety rather than the anxiety symptom itself. Because anxiety is often the symptom bringing the person to psychotherapy, many psychodynamically oriented psychotherapists regard tranquilizing medications as antithetical to psychodynamic resolution.

There is a moral perspective, shared by many individuals, that views individuals who resort to tranquilizers as being either weak willed or intolerant of stresses of everyday life who have become victims of physicians who, themselves, are victims of pharmaceutical companies' advertising that has promoted a pharmaceutical pill for all ills. Although few individuals would attest to the moral value of declining penicillin for a bout of pneumoccocal pneumonia, emotional distress is viewed from a quite different perspective.

Physicians are accused of having developed a position of defining all human misery and suffering as *illness* that should be treated primarily through the use of medication. A benign interpretation of physicians' behavior views the physician as a victim of training and/or the pharmaceutical industry's advertising. A more malevolent interpretation describes the physician (as well as the pharmaceutical company) as motivated by purely economical gain considerations without regard for the welfare of the patient.

Having accepted a not completely undeserved faith in 20th-century technology, to include medical therapeutics, patients look to their physicians to treat their diseases and to alleviate their pain and suffering. After exhausting the potential of over-the-counter drugs, many individuals go to their physician requesting some form of relief. Even if the distress is due to family discord, grief, or an intolerable life situation, some individuals will look to their physicians for at least temporary amelioration of their suffering. If relief is not sufficient or forthcoming from the first physician, they may consult a second or third. Some individuals are firmly convinced that their physician does not understand the severity of their distress and believe that only by sequentially visiting several physicians can they acquire sufficient quantities of drugs to allow themselves to be adequately medicated.

In their transactions with patients, physicians fall into one of the following categories:

1. A miniscule number of physicians who, knowingly and for profit motive, initiate or maintain a patient's dependence upon sedative-hypnotics without substantial regard for the welfare of the patient. The physicians may be aware of the strictly economic motive or may rationalize to themselves that they are performing a dispensing function, similar to over-the-counter medications, and that if they did not supply the individuals with the requested drugs, then they would obtain them elsewhere. The physicians may rationalize that obtaining medications via medical prescription is less hazardous than obtaining them from "street sources" and, in that sense, may actually believe that they provide a service.

2. Some physicians who are simply misinformed and are not very knowledgable concerning the prescription of psychoactive drugs.

3. Physicians who find themselves the victim of manipulations on the part of the patients and end up prescribing in ways the physicians may realize are not optimal. There are few active clinicians who have not had this happen on occasion, and those of us who work with large numbers of drug-dependent individuals probably find it of even more frequent occurrence.

4. Physicians who unknowingly contribute to their patients' drug dependency through well intentioned and appropriately prescribed medications for patients who are sequentially, and unknown to the physician, obtaining medications from several different physicians. It is unlikely that most practicing physicians have completely avoided finding themselves in this situation.

5. Physicians who underprescribe to the detriment of patients by withholding useful drugs. Although these physicians do not attract attention from drug enforcement personnel and, in fact, may be seen as model physicians from the enforcement perspective, their withholding of appropriate medications may produce a detriment to the patient's health, perhaps exposing the individual to unwise physiological stresses or even death through suicide.

A number of physicians claim that when their patients request antianxiety medications that they prescribe phenothiazines and rarely have their patients ask a second time, if they return to the office at all. Phenothiazines are not the first drug of choice for psychopharmacological intervention in anxiety and, in that sense, such prescription does not constitute optimal medical practice.

From a psychological perspective, the prescription of psychotropic drugs are malevolent in one of two circumstances. Psychotropic drugs may rob the patient of the opportunity to develop a more satisfactory, nonpharmacological solution or the patient may develop a pathological dependency or adverse side effects that are more severe or disabling than the condition being treated.

The benzodiazepines are currently the drugs of choice for the pharmacological treatment of anxiety. This is not because the other sedative-hypnotics lack effectiveness, but rather because the benzodiazepines possess certain advantages: (a) Benzodiazepines have low lethality, even when taken in massive overdose. (b) Benzodiazepines do not activate liver microsomal enzymes and, therefore, do not alter the rate of metabolism of other drugs. (c) Benzodiazepines have a lower abuse potential.

For insomnia, flurazepam (Dalmane), also a benzodiazepine, is considered the first drug of choice. This is a result of the above listed advantages of benzodiazepines in addition to all-night studies in sleep laboratories that suggest that barbiturates and other hypnotics lose effectiveness after a few nights. This is, of course, quite contrary to the claims of many patients.

ABUSE POTENTIAL OF SEDATIVE-HYPNOTICS

Although the barbiturates and other sedative-hypnotics are widely abused, there is a differential rate of abuse between the various sedative-hypnotics, and abuse is associated with differing risks. For example, the large number of overdose deaths that occur each year with the barbiturates attests to their lethality. However, the benzodiazepines are rarely associated with overdose death when used alone. Although abuse of benzodiazepines seems less common than the other sedatives and abuse in the form of massive overdose is less likely to result in death, one should not conclude that benzodiazepine abuse is benign. Diazepam (Valium) has become a "street drug." The publicity that diazepam has received and the subsequent reluctance of physicians to prescribe the drug as freely as before have raised the cost of black-market diazepam. Current cost on the west coast ranges from 50¢ per 10-mg tablet when purchased in bulk to $3.00 per 10-mg tablet when purchased singly.

Intoxication with sedative-hypnotics is qualitatively similar to intoxication with alcohol and, like alcohol intoxication, the effects may vary from time to time, even with the same individual, depending upon the "set" and "setting." The desired effect of intoxication is generally "disinhibition euphoria," in which mood is elevated, self-criticism, anxiety, and guilt are reduced, and energy and self-confidence are increased. Although euphoria may occur with sedative-hypnotic intoxication, the mood may be quite labile and the individual may also experience sadness, rapidly fluctuating mood shifts, irritability, hypochondriacal concerns, increased anxiety, and agitation.

Individuals intoxicated with sedative-hypnotics commonly show unsteady gait, slurred speech, sustained vertical and horizontal nystagmus, and poor judgment. The perception of a drug effect as pleasurable is partly a learned response and partly the pharmacology of the drug, but it is always influenced greatly by expectation and environmental stimuli.

Sedative-hypnotics can produce psychological dependence, physical dependence, and tolerance. Psychological dependence refers to a strong need to experience the drug effect repeatedly, even in the absence of physical dependence. Physical dependence refers to the establishment of objective signs of withdrawal that occur after the drug is abruptly stopped, and tolerance refers to the adaptation of the body to the drug in such a manner that larger doses are required to produce the original effects. Drug disposition tolerance develops from activation of drug-metabolizing enzyme systems in the liver capable of more rapidly destroying barbiturates (9). Pharmacodynamic tolerance is due to the adaptation of the central nervous system to the presence of the drug. As the individual increases the dose to maintain the same level of intoxication, the margin between the intoxicating dose and the lethal dose becomes smaller.

The medical aspects of barbiturate withdrawal are well described in an excellent monograph, *The Barbiturate Withdrawal Syndrome: A Clinical and Electroencephalographic Study* (16). The barbiturate withdrawal syndrome was experimentally studied in humans by Isbell et al. (7). Hollister et al. (6) reported an experimental study of chlordiazepoxide (Librium), and Hollister et al. (5) reported an experimental study of diazepam (Valium). Clinical case reports include Swartzburg et al. (14), methaqualone; Flemenbaum and Gumby (2), ethchlorvynol (Placidyl); and Swanson and Okada (13), meprobamate.

The sedative-hypnotic withdrawal syndrome can be conceptualized as a spectrum of signs and symptoms occurring after stopping or markedly reducing the daily intake of the sedative. Symptoms do not follow a specific sequence and can include anxiety, tremors, nightmares, insomnia, anorexia, nausea, vomiting, postural hypotension, seizures, delirium, and hyperpyrexia. The syndrome is similar for all sedative-hypnotics, however the time course depends upon the particular drug involved. With pentobarbital, secobarbital, meprobamate, and methaqualone, withdrawal symptoms typically begin 12 to 24 hours after the last dose and peak in intensity between 24 and 72 hours. The symptoms may develop more slowly in individuals with liver disease or in the elderly. The withdrawal reactions to phenobarbital, diazepam, and chlordiazepoxide develop more slowly and peak on the fifth to eighth day.

During untreated sedative-hypnotic withdrawal, the electroencephalogram may show paroxysmal bursts of high voltage, slow frequency activity that precedes the development of seizures. The withdrawal delirium may include disorientation to time, place, and situation as well as visual and/or auditory hallucinations. The delirium generally follows a period of insomnia. Some individuals may have only delirium, others only seizures, and some may have both delirium and convulsions.

TREATMENT OF PHYSICAL DEPENDENCY UPON SEDATIVE-HYPNOTICS

There are two major methods of detoxifying the barbiturate-dependent patient: gradual withdrawal of the addicting agent on a short acting barbiturate (7) or the substitution of long acting phenobarbital or other long acting barbiturate for the addicting agent and gradual withdrawal of the substitute drug (10–12). Either method is acceptable practice and uses the principle of stepwise withdrawal. Abruptly discontinuing sedative-hypnotics in an individual who is physically dependent upon them is poor medical practice and has resulted in death (3) and malpractice suits (1).

The pharmacological rationale for phenobarbital substitution technique is similar to the rationale for substituting methadone for heroin withdrawal. The longer acting drug permits a withdrawal characterized by fewer fluctuations in blood levels of the drug throughout the day and thus enables the safe use of a smaller daily dose. The safety factor for phenobarbital is greater than that for the shorter acting barbiturates; lethal doses of phenobarbital are several times greater than toxic doses, and the signs of toxicity (e.g., sustained nystagmus, slurred speech, and ataxia) are easy to observe. And finally, because phenobarbital intoxication usually does not produce disinhibition euphoria, the behavioral problems commonly associated with the short acting barbiturates seldom occur.

The phenobarbital substitution technique can also be used with short acting sedative-hypnotics other than barbiturates. With-

drawal from glutethimide using phenobarbital was reported by Vestal and Rumack (15). Table 16.1 shows the equivalent of phenobarbital used to withdraw patients from the barbiturates and a variety of other sedative-hypnotics.

In using the phenobarbital substitution and withdrawal technique, one may, if the patient is in acute withdrawal and in danger of having seizures, administer the initial dose of phenobarbital by injection, using 200 mg intramuscularly for stabilization. If nystagmus and other signs of intoxication develop after the intramuscular dosage, it is doubtful that the individual is in immediate danger from barbiturate withdrawal. Based on the phenobarbital dosage calculated using the withdrawal equivalence, the patient is maintained on the oral dose schedule for 2 days and then withdrawn with a graded reduction not to exceed 30 mg per day.

The beginning daily dosage of phenobarbital is calculated by substituting one *sedative dose* (30 mg) of phenobarbital for each *hypnotic dose* (100 mg) of the short acting barbiturate the patient reports using, up to a maximum phenobarbital dosage of 500 mg

Table 16.1
Phenobarbital Withdrawal Equivalents for Common Sedative-Hypnotics Equal to 30 mg. of Phenobarbital[a]

Drug	Daily Dosages of Common Sedative-Hypnotics Equivalent to 30 mg. of Phenobarbital in Management of Withdrawal
Amobarbital	100
Butabarbital	60
Pentobarbital	100
Secobarbital	100
Chloral hydrate	500
Ethchlorvynol (Placidyl)	350
Glutethimide (Doriden)	250
Meprobamate (Equanil, Miltown)	400
Methaqualone (Quaalude, Sopor, etc.)	300
Methyprylon (Noludar)	100
Chlordiazepoxide (Librium)	100
Clorazepate (Tranxene)	50
Diazepam (Valium)	50
Flurazepam (Dalmane)	30
Oxazepam (Serax)	100

[a] Withdrawal equivalence is not the same as therapeutic equivalency.

per day. For example, a daily dosage of 500 mg of amobarbital suggests that 5 × 30 mg of phenobarbital should be used initially in managing withdrawal. In spite of the fact that many addicts exaggerate the magnitude of their addiction, the patient's history is the best *guide* to initiating withdrawal. If the extent of the addiction has been grossly overstated, toxic symptoms will occur during the first day or so of treatment. This problem is easily managed by omitting one or more doses of phenobarbital and recalculating the daily dose.

Detoxification from barbiturates and other sedative-hypnotic dependence should be generally done in a hospital setting. Outpatient barbiturate detoxification has been reported (4), but should only be attempted by experienced staff with patients with a low level of tissue tolerance for whom hospitalization is not possible.

The treatment of physical dependence on barbiturates at the clinical level is usually successful when the patient will cooperate, but postdetoxification treatment is still unsuccessful in many cases. Teaching abusers to cope with everyday anxieties without resorting to pharmacological oblivion, through such treatment modalities as biofeedback and acupuncture, shows promise, but these modalities need more clinical research to ascertain their optimal utility in the postdetoxification treatment of sedative-hypnotic dependency.

References

1. American Medical Association. Failure to diagnose barbiturate intoxication. Citation 24:22, 1971.
2. Flemenbaum, A., and Gumby, B. Ethchlorvynol (Placidyl) abuse and withdrawal. Dis. Nerv. Syst. 32:188, 1971.
3. Fraser, H. F., Shaver, M. R., Maxwell, E. S., Isbell, H., and Wikler, A. Fatal termination of barbiturate abstinance syndrome in man. J. Pharmacol. Exp. Ther. 106:387, 1952.
4. Gay, G. R., Wesson, D. R., Smith, D. E., and Sheppard, C. W. Outpatient barbiturate withdrawal using phenobarbital. Int. J. Addict. 7:17, 1972.
5. Hollister, L. E., Bennett, L. L., Kimbell, I., Savage, C., and Overall, J. E. Diazepam in newly admitted schizophrenics. Dis. Nerv. Syst. 24:246, 1963.
6. Hollister, L. E., Motzenbecker, F. P., and Degan, R. O. Withdrawal reactions from chlordiazepoxide. Psychopharmacologia 2:63, 1961.
7. Isbell, H. Addiction to barbiturates and the barbiturate abstinence syndrome. Ann. Intern. Med. 33:108, 1950.
8. Isbell, H., Altschul, S., Kornetsky, C. H., Eisenman, A. J., Flanery, H. G., and Fraser, H. F. Chronic barbiturate intoxication: An experimental study. A.M.A. Arch. Neurol. Psychiatry 64:8, 1950.
9. Remmer, H. Tolerance to barbiturates by increased breakdown. In *Scientific Basis of Drug Dependence*, H. Steinberg, editor. New York, Grune and Stratton, 1969.
10. Smith, D. E., and Wesson, D. R. A new method for treatment of barbiturate dependence. J. A. M. A. 213:294, 1970.
11. Smith, D. E., and Wesson, D. R. A phenobarbital technique for withdrawal of barbiturate abuse. Arch. Gen. Psychiatry 24:56, 1971.
12. Smith, D. E., Wesson, D. R., and Dammon, G. Treatment of the polydrug abuser. In *Proceedings of the National Drug Abuse Conference*. New York, Marcel Dekker, 1978.
13. Swanson, L. A., and Okada, T. Death after withdrawal of meprobamate. J. A. M. A. 184:780, 1963.
14. Swartzburg, M., Lieb, J., and Schwartz, A. H. Methaqualone withdrawal. Arch. Gen. Psychiatry 29:46, 1973.
15. Vestal, R., and Rumack, B. Glutethimide dependence: Phenobarbital treatment. Ann. Intern. Med. 80:670. 1974.
16. Wolff, M. H. The barbiturate withdrawal syndrome: A clinical and electroencephalographic study. Electroencephalog. Clin. Neurophysiol. 14 (Suppl.), 1959.

CHAPTER 17

ALCOHOL

Frank A. Seixas, M.D.

The United States is a country marked by extreme historical, cultural, racial-biological, and economo-class heterogeneity. I must make my modifiers complex, as there is over all these disparate ties to different heritages and prospects in the United States a cultural and national patina of uniformity, perhaps more than a thin veneer, which can be said to approach a national uniformity of philosophies and goals based on the astounding technological success of the combination of democracy, capitalism, and a very large and fertile land. The incongruity of America's divergences is perhaps best captured in the statement of the father in the movie "Breaking Away": "I don't want any of the Eyetalian foreign food. I want something American—like French fries!"

To describe alcoholism in the United States, then, is to examine a disease that is so affected by cultural mores as to delude some sociologists into thinking it is not a disease at all, so characterized by emotional vicissitudes as to encourage many of its victims into pointless psychotherapy, and so productive of physical symptoms as to drive many scientists to their laboratory to determine a still elusive chemical solution to its depradations.

And I am asked to sandwich this disease into a volume in which the main focus is other "substances of abuse"—that is, many illegal or semilegal psychoactive chemicals—the seventh of 11 contributions in Part 3, perhaps as buried in the middle of a text as it could be. One will need large powers of concentration to reach these pages, unless the binding of the book is such that it opens automatically here, although, for sure, any reader will peek a bit into the first pages (opiates) or, while hunting in the index, will find the last one (caffeine). Of course, he will be again confused, because caffeine is legal and generally considered harmless. It has taken so long after Prohibition to learn again what harm alcohol does that it seems a shame to muddy the new understanding with comparative obscurities, by insisting we know about all psychoactive materials and their similarities and differences. And yet that is what life is like and what the United States is like, a jumble of disparate people to which we ascribe a uniformity. And we see in many cases that is what patients are like, one individual with a combination of incompatible chemicals mixing in him. So we must accept the complexities in our search for the nature of alcoholism and bid the reader, who has by chance landed at this chapter first, to read and digest it thoroughly and then go on and look at the others cautiously at first, because insights into other psychoactive chemicals illuminate our understanding of alcohol and alcoholism.

The United States, it must be said, has had a special relationship to alcoholic beverages throughout its history. It is true that Sir John Smith did introduce tobacco as well as Pocohontas to the English court, and caffeine was the treat that prompted the Boston Tea Party, but that was before we were free from England.

When the Revolution was done, there *was*

the Whiskey Rebellion testing the new government's power to tax the farmers' booze, and also there was the man who can perhaps be called the Father of American Medicine, Dr. Benjamin Rush (66), who proclaimed alcoholism a disease and cited the case of a man who testified that a fusillade of cannonballs through the middle of a room would not be enough to stop him from going across to whiskey on the other side. The triangular trade not only supplied rum to the new nation and fortunes to New England shipowners but a legacy of slavery that saddled our country throughout its history. We were not long into the 19th century before a temperance crusade was started, a crusade that swelled its voice and its ranks through 100 years, waxing throughout until the Anti Saloon League was formed. In the most effective political action campaign mounted up to that time, Dry's were elected and Wet's were defeated, until the 19th Amendment was passed in 1920, and the sin (and disease) of drinking was made illegal (29). The vigor and success of this campaign can be attributed to many factors, one being the dramatic evidence of the effects of alcohol on lawlessness, disease, and disability that was apparent, perhaps as in other cultures, in the struggle between the settled agrarian and commercial life, with its more restrained and steady drinking habits, and the hunter and trapper, forester and cowhand-type of life fostered by the frontier that encouraged binge-type drinking. Perhaps Prohibition was the salute to the end of the frontier. It was also a writing into law of the beliefs of the Fundamentalist sects that had written their own rules of morality in the wake of the sturdy pioneers of the Massachusetts Bay Colony.

The curious thing about Repeal was that, at the same time that it took away the sin of drinking, it seemed to repeal the disease of alcoholism. Alcohol became an innocuous drug (82). Not only were popular accounts derisive of the harm of alcohol, but serious research into, for instance, cirrhosis of the liver, found that it was not alcohol but malnutrition that caused cirrhosis of the liver (60). Meanwhile, hands that had not lost their skill promoted whiskey, beer, and wine with ever-increasing success and volume of business, encouraged by advertising that showed it to be the most fashionable and success-laden attribute to drink the fanciest Scotch and the most virile and manly to drink it all.

It is striking that household survey data (11) showed that fully one-third of the adults in the United States are either abstinent or drink less than once a month. The greatest concentration of such people is in the rural South and Midwest—the places that select themselves as "The Buckle of the Bible Belt" and include rural Caucasions and blacks. It is interesting that, even in the cities, heavier drinkers seem more transient. They also had higher divorce rates, maintained less contact with relatives, and were more likely, when married, to have no children or very large families (52).

In all, over 100 million people in the United States drink (25). Alcohol produces more federal tax revenue than anything else except for income taxes. Yet alcoholic beverages are felt by economists to be relatively underpriced in relationship to other unessential commodities. The alcohol consumption of women seems to be rising (34). Beer seems to have increased its share of the alcohol beverage sales, particularly among young men, and wine is beginning to make a larger and larger share of the alcohol beverage dollar (70).

Bootlegging of home brew has steadily declined since Prohibition, the risk and inconvenience seeming at present to be greater than the cost of buying taxed beverages.

The question of who among the drinkers is an alcoholic is a difficult one. The late E. M. Jellinek proposed a formula based on the number of deaths from cirrhosis (64), a complication of long standing heavy drinking, that has been found fairly accurate when checked against interviews and reports from other sources in small communities. The development of the constants used in this formula, however, bespeak a knowledge that is not always present in communities. Other assays made to produce ways of detecting alcoholism use combinations of long range hazards, i.e., suicides, homicides, etc., and come up with scarcely more accurate results. The most usual figure now used is about 10 million suffering from "alcoholism or alcohol abuse" (71).

Each one of this huge number of victims complicates the lives of at least four or five others in the circle of his or her life. They do this by their own loss of efficiency at work, job loss, emotional insecurity for their dependents, and highway carnage of themselves and of innocent victims (half the fatal accidents are alcohol related—about 23,000—

and, of these, 19,000 involve people with alcoholism). Fatalities of pedestrians, too, are related to high blood alcohol levels. 85 per cent of adult drownings are alcohol related, 60 per cent of murders, and 80 per cent of murder victims have measurable blood alcohol levels. The list is long—over one-third of home accidents, as well as fatal fires, snowmobile injuries and deaths, and private airplane fatalities (16 per cent or more). The number of child abuse and neglect cases that are alcohol related has not yet been sought. Suicides have been estimated among alcoholics to be between 11 and 30 times the number of suicides among others (71).

But to these violent sudden deaths must be added the manifold disease causes of death that are alcohol related (76). We have already mentioned cirrhosis of the liver—the sixth most common cause of death in the United States. Although there are other causes of cirrhosis—carbon tetrachloride poisoning, schistosomiasis, and posthepatitic cirrhosis—unquestionably the largest contribution comes from alcohol-related or Laennec's cirrhosis. Alcoholic pancreatitis (50 per cent of the cancer of pancreatitis) and alcoholic heart disease, including cardiomyopathy, arrhythmias, and beri beri heart, must be added to causes of morbidity and mortality. Perhaps closely related is the large incidence of sudden death in individuals with no pathology except fatty liver. Chronic disability and death also plague those with alcoholic brain disease (77), including the rare Marchiafava-Bignami disease and central pontine myelinolysis. The estimate of 250,000 deaths from alcoholism and related causes per year is certainly conservative (71). The tendency has been to scatter reports of these deaths, but the time has come to collect them so we can measure the cost to society in life. In industry, the cost of alcoholism has been estimated at $46 billion per year, and that estimate was before inflation had attained its present height (71).

Tragic as is the waste of people and life due to addiction, it cannot be said for any of the other drugs at this time that they even begin to approach the striking toll of alcohol (with the possible exception of cigarette deaths that finally exert their effect without the previous social and emotional dislocations that disrupt the alcoholic and his surround). The numbers are not the whole story, however, for the alcoholic is more likely to be a "square" individual, a family man or woman who wants to get along and whose trouble entangles others in the family who depend on him for physical or emotional support (4). This contrasts to the lone agent drug addict, whose youth, although it seems to make the tragedy more poignant, contains that tragedy often to a single individual and his or her unrecognized prospects. This, of course, is a limited view of drug addiction; as it is more studied, a wider and wider circle of people seems involved.

PHARMACOLOGY OF ETHANOL

Ethanol is the second in a class of "alcohols," organic aliphatic hydrocarbons containing a hydroxyl group. Unlike methyl alcohol, the first in the series, it is not permanently toxic in small quantities (methyl alcohol causes optic neuritis). Other alcohols—butanol, octanol, etc.—of higher molecular weights are found in small quantities in naturally fermented beverages but are insignificant contributors to the effects of these drinks. Ethanol (and I will hereafter use alcohol interchangeably with this term) is the principal product of the fermenting of such organic compounds as grapes, wheat, barley, corn, potatoes, or honey with yeast. Natural fermentation stops at about 14 per cent, the concentration that is lethal to the yeast. This is the concentration of wine, which gets its color from the fermentation with or without the skin of the grape and its bubbles (in those wines that are "sparkling") from carbon dioxide, the other product of fermentation of sugars, when the wine is bottled immediately. Beer also is bottled before the carbon dioxide escapes from the "mash" of malt, hops, and yeast, and it attains an alcohol percentage of about 5 per cent. Distillation of wines produces higher alcohol content brandies. The products of fermentation of grains are whiskeys, of potatoes, vodka (23).

Ethanol, the active ingredient, is a clear, colorless liquid at room temperature and has an acrid taste and odor. The color and flavor of alcoholic beverages come from congeners, or additive substances, dissolved in the process of manufacture. Such things as higher alcohols, fusel oil, and such materials as can be found on the interior of a charred oak cask will be discovered here. Recently nitrosamines have been found in some (31) Scotch whiskeys, leading to the speculation that chronic ingestion will lead to cancer. If, from two molecules of ethanol, one of water was taken away (a process that does not happen in the body), ethyl ether would be formed. This may influence our thinking about another of its actions. Ethanol being a hydrocarbon, yields calories, about 7 calories per gram as opposed to the 4 calories per gram of carbohydrates and protein and the 9 calories per gram of fats. This is the only quality it has as a food; there are no essential minerals, amino acids, or vitamins delivered by ethanol. Thus, it is the worst of foods (63).

ABSORPTION

Ethanol is absorbed through mucus membranes in the mouth (which may be a factor in the oropharyngeal cancers related to alcohol ingestion), through the stomach, and very rapidly and completely through the walls of the duodenum. Absorption is so complete in the small intestine that none reaches the fecal matter. Because of the partial absorption in the stomach, taking food with alcohol, which slows the passage through the stomach, is associated with a lower and more delayed peak blood alcohol level. This demonstrates the desirability of eating while drinking and also explains one reason the alcoholic tends to avoid eating—so that he will get a greater effect from what he drinks.

ELIMINATION

Once absorbed, ethanol reaches the blood stream and circulates throughout the body. Its action on reaching the brain is of most interest. But before discussing that, we can look at how alcohol is eliminated. Only 5 per cent of alcohol is excreted–and that is the combination of ethanol excreted in the urine, in perspiration, in insensible loss, and through the breath. The alcohol excreted through the breath is of interest because it is the source of the breath test for alcohol. The proportion—about 1/2300 of that in the blood—is used to recalculate (39) the blood level. Breath tests are fairly accurate if there has been no alcohol left in the oral cavity (it is standard procedure to rinse out the mouth and wait 15 minutes before testing) and if there is not a significant amount of emphysema. If a positive result is found, it is advisable to check it with a blood test.

METABOLISM

All the ethanol not excreted is metabolized or oxidized in the body, primarily in the liver, where there are large stores of the primary enzyme associated with its metabolism. Alcohol is oxidized through the catalyzation of alcohol dehydrogenase (ADH), a zinc-containing enzyme that was one of the first to be purified and thoroughly analyzed. The co-factor nicotinamide adenine dinucleotide (NAD) is reduced in the process:

$$\text{Alcohol} \not{+} \text{NAD} \text{-----} \text{Acetaldehyde} \not{+} \text{NADH}$$
$$\text{C2H5OH} \qquad \text{ADH} \quad \text{CH3CHO}$$

and acetaldehyde goes through a similar process:

$$\text{Acetaldehyde}$$
$$\text{CH3CHO}$$
$$\text{CH3COO—}$$
$$\not{+} \text{NAD} \text{-----} \text{Acetate} \not{+} \text{NADH}$$
$$\text{Acetaldehyde dehydrogenase}$$

The problem for the liver is handling the large overload of hydrogen ions. The adjustments made to do this include the production of fat from fatty acids, of lactate from pyruvate (leading to the retention of uric acid in the blood stream), and perhaps the metabolism of biogenic amines by abnormal reductive rather than oxidative pathways (18).

There are several matters of clinical importance more understandable because of our knowledge of this phase of alcohol metabolism. The first matter is the relative lack of adaptability of alcohol dehydrogenase. ADH is said to have a zero order of kinetics. In other words, it will not increase the velocity of the reaction with a higher load. No matter how much alcohol is presented, AHD will only catalyze about ¾ ounce of whiskey per hour. A limiting factor in this reaction speed may be the availability of NAD, nevertheless it is this way. Any alcohol taken in excess of ¾ ounce per hour will merely contribute to increasing the blood alcohol level (and thus intoxication). The person may, by exceeding his capacity to metabolize alcohol, imperceptibly increase his inebriation.

The second insight we get from this is by examining the second step, in which acetaldehyde is destroyed. In contrast to the first step, acetaldehyde is rapidly, almost immediately, destroyed in the body. This is fortunate, bacause acetaldehyde is much more immediately toxic than ethanol. A series of chance observations led to the discovery of a drug that could inhibit the destruction of acetaldehyde. This drug, a chemical used to cure synthetic rubber and that was also under investigation as an antihelminthic agent, was disulfiram (Antabuse). Disulfiram (35) blocks the conversion of acetaldehyde to acetate. When alcohol is ingested, it produces a dramatic reaction due to the accumulation of acetaldehyde, including facial flushing, tachycardia, nausea, vomiting, and shock. With sufficient amounts of both drugs, death can and has ensued. However, in the dosage prescribed, such a reaction has not been reported in recent years. Disulfiram is used as a deterrent for someone who wants to give up drinking but who can be trapped by the impulse to drink on the many social occasions afforded daily in modern life. Taking one pill a day is the reminder and the insurance against taking the first drink.

Disulfiram has some hazards, in addition to the disulfiram-alcohol reaction itself. Some people find it has an unpleasant metallic taste and a slight odor (CS_2, the malodorous gas produced by rotten eggs, is a metabolic product), but others are not bothered by this. More serious are reports of toxic hepatitis as an idiosyncratic reaction; however, this is very rare and not totally documented in such a way as to prove that disulfiram was the culprit. Some men complain of impotence when disulfiram is started. In many of them, the impotence disappears on a smaller dose. More serious, particularly in former days when larger doses were given, is the occurrence of a toxic depression or psychosis. Dr. John Ewing has proposed that people with congenitally low quantities of dopamine beta-carboxylase (which is also inhibited by disulfiram) may be particularly susceptible to this (22). Even more serious is the recent report of women who were taking disulfiram during pregnancy and delivered babies with phocomelia (arm "buds" or "flippers" similar to those in the thalidomide babies) (56). Although these birth defects have not been definitively assigned to disulfiram, there is insufficient research to contradict this striking clinical report, and pregnant women should not be given the drug.

When considering disulfiram therapy, the physician must weigh the hazards of unchecked, recurrent, or recrudescent alcoholism against the dangers of the drug when self-administered by an intelligent and informed patient who has the option of desisting from taking it. In order to avoid a reaction, one must desist for 4 days before drinking, which gives a chance to reconsider the abandonment of sobriety. Using these guidelines, thousands of people have commenced or continued their sobriety with the use of disulfiram. Dr. Ruth Fox had a patient who took the drug for 17 years until his death from other causes (27). Disulfiram definitely has a place in the treatment of alcoholism because of the way in which it manipulates the toxicity of acetaldehyde for the patient's good.

ACETALDEHYDE

Acetaldehyde has become a focal point for several other interests (89). For many years, it has been observed that there is a very low incidence of drunkenness and alcoholism among the Chinese. Recently, this has been investigated on a basis other than cultural. It is striking the frequency with which Orientals will complain that even the first glass of an alcoholic beverage causes an unpleasant reaction of flushing. Investigations on a chemical basis have suggested that this may be due to an excess of acetaldehyde, with the same reaction that develops with the alcohol-disulfiram combination. Studies performed on Japanese have found that an isoenzyme of alcohol dehydrogenase, which makes up only 10 per cent of the chemical (84) in a sample of people in London, is present to the extent of 88 per cent (61) in a sample of Japanese. This different isoenzyme could be the cause of the racial difference in metabolism and symptoms of drinking. Whether it then can explain the small number of alcoholics among the Chinese (but not seemingly today among the Japanese) is another story. It has been suggested that American Native (Indian) populations (44) have a flushing effect similar to that of the Chinese on their first drink, but American Natives suffer from an intense problem with alcoholism. Whether the sociocultural stresses to which they are put encourage the drinking of alcohol despite the unpleasant symptoms, or perhaps even to induce the unpleasant symptom, has not been elucidated. But much in this ongoing story may tell us more about the nature of alcohol's relation to the body and about biological variation and may finally help us offer new ways to help those who are addicted.

A third exciting new story has developed from the measurement of acetaldehyde after an alcohol load. Korsten et al. (44), who have studied this, find that people who have taken large doses of alcohol over periods of time have a significantly higher than usual level of acetaldehyde. This striking change with P values in some measurements showing the possibility of it being accounted for by chance in only 1 in 1,000 times, raised the question of adaptation to alcohol causing chemical changes in its metabolism. Then, in January 1979 (69), it was reported that a small number of people who were nonalcoholic brothers and sisters of alcoholics were also given an alcohol load and acetaldehyde was measured. Here, also (although the people were Caucasian), a significant increase in acetaldehyde was found. This could be (if replicated) the first easily measurable way in which potential alcoholics could be recognized before alcoholism develops.

In still one more way, acetaldehyde has assumed importance in alcoholism research. Chemists have noticed that the simple acetaldehyde molecule, if attached to the molecules of some of the biogenic amines which act as neurotransmitters in the central nervous system, would produce alkaloids strikingly like morphine (53). The products—isoquinoline alkaloids, terahydropapaveroline, and salsolinol—have not been detectable in vivo in sufficient quantities to seem active after ethanol ingestion by any animal, but the injection of tetrahydropapaveroline in minute quantities into specialized location on the wall of the third ventricle in rats has caused a 20-fold increase in those animals' ingestion of alcohol (53). In addition, once this reaction was started, the animal would continue to choose large amounts of ethanol long after the injections had stopped (once an alcoholic, always an alcoholic). These experiments were replicated in another laboratory, so it is possible that we have come to the day when we will have either an endorphin theory or an endorphin-like theory of alcoholism by virtue of the actions of the simple compound acetaldehyde on some already existing chemicals in the brain.

ANOTHER PATHWAY OF ALCOHOL METABOLISM

In the early 1970's, evidence was accumulated to show that, although alcohol dehydrogenase was resistant to handling more alcohol than its optimal quantity, after a large amount of alcohol was taken on repeated occasions, there was an acceleration of the disappearance of alcohol (87). This kind of so-called *metabolic tolerance* or adaptation by the body to larger doses seemed only to affect a small amount of alcohol—not more than 25 per cent of the dose (although Lieber cites some studies showing up to 50 per cent (48). There are two theories about how this came about—via the use of catalase and hydrogen peroxide or via a microsomal ethanol-oxidizing system. The evidence is now favoring the microsomal system (47).

Should it be that the microsomal system is in fact the second pathway of ethanol oxidation, it will explain many other mysteries about ethanol and its interactions with other drugs.

INTERACTIONS OF ETHANOL AND OTHER DRUGS

Ethanol is a depressant of the central nervous system. In large enough quantities (sufficient to produce blood levels over 500 mg/100 ml in the naive animal), it is lethal by itself. There is, however, a synergistic action with other central nervous system depressants. In humans, a blood level of only 100 mg/100 ml in combination with only 0.5 mg/100 of phenobarbital has proven fatal (63). (Phenobarbital alone is lethal at 10 to 29 mg/100 ml.) Although this synergism exists on the "down" side, people who have become accustomed to alcohol and/or phenobarbital and are not taking these drugs require a far higher dose of the medication to produce anesthesia. The idea of the microsomal ethanol-oxidizing system helps explain this.

This is true because, in those that have taken large quantities of ethanol before, the microsomal ethanol-oxidizing system, which is equivalent to the mixed function-oxidizing system, has been "induced." Therefore, it can help metabolize the other anesthetic faster than usual, thus necessitating more anesthetic to achieve the required effect. On the other hand, if ethanol were present, engaging the available mixed function or microsomal system, there would be less material free to

:liminate by metabolism the other sedative hat had been introduced.

In the case of carbon tetrachloride, whose :oxic mainfestations are due to metabolites produced by the mixed function-oxidizing system, chronic alcohol use, by inducing that system, enhances carbon tetrachloride's toxcity (86).

In the case of other drugs using the mixed function-oxidizing system—warfarin, dilantin, tolbutamide, and isoniazid—their half-life is diminished 50 per cent in dry alcoholic subjects (73) who have induced that system. This makes essential a knowledge of past or present alcoholism in patients in whom such materials are to be used.

ACTION OF ALCOHOL ON THE BRAIN

Alcohol is taken for its action on the brain, and that action is as a depressant of brain function. In the naive drinker, there is a simple dose relationship of its action. However, in those that drink heavily, tolerance to the drug appears. This tissue or cell tolerance is different from the small amount of metabolic tolerance offered by the microsomal ethanol-oxidizing system. Cell tolerance is an adaptation of the brain cells to doses of alcohol so that they react less to a given dose of alcohol, and larger doses are needed to provide equivalent degrees of effect. With alcohol, unlike morphine, the lethal dose does not change. However, the acclimatization of the brain tissues to ethanol is great between a small and a lethal dose. This means that a person who ordinarily would seem intoxicated does not, even though the blood levels are high. This tolerance does not come without its price, however, and the price includes a decrease in judgment or higher brain function at the high level and the appearance of blackout periods. Blackout periods are periods of time for which the person loses all memory, although he seems to others to be acting perfectly normal and not intoxicated. These are times when there is a high level of alcohol in the blood stream, about 280 mg/100 ml according to one experimenter (32).

The phenomenon of tolerance is under intense investigation at this time to give clues to the management of alcoholism. The possibility that alcohol acts only on a small number of specific receptor cells in a small region of the brain (like opiates) has been enter-

tained but has been discarded by most, although a condensation product might do exactly this. Rather, it has seemed to many that alcohol acts like the general anesthetics on the membranes of cells throughout the brain and specifically acts on the lipid-protein interface in those membranes. On the basis of experiments in physical chemistry, then, alcohol could change the reaction of the cell by making the membrane more fluid or more stiff, changing the pathway for other chemicals—such as sodium, potassium, and particularly calcium—in their ability to move in or out of the cell and produce functional changes (91).

Elegant methods, such as electron spin resonance and flourescent probes (chemicals that penetrate specific cell regions then are made to flouresce), are being used to explore the effect of ethanol on the fluidization of the membrane, and what happens when large quantities are given over long periods of time, that differs from other states. One interesting general theory of anesthesia, which relates the anesthesia-producing potential of a chemical to the length of the molecule, has correlated with the relationship of ethanol to the other alcohols (Richardson's law) (63).

It has also been found that the mechanisms that produce withdrawal symptoms from alcohol are not identical to those that produce tolerance. However, it is inescapable that they are related (85).

The alcohol withdrawal syndrome (the basis for calling the alcoholic "pharmacologically dependent") is a specific series of symptoms that occur when alcohol has been taken in large quantities for a long period of time and then the amount is decreased or stopped. Symptoms include nausea, vomiting, dizziness, anxiety, wakefulness, profuse perspiration, and sometimes elevated temperature. There are four neurological signs that are more characteristic and specific: tremor, grand mal seizures, hallucinosis, and delirium tremens. Of these, delirium tremens is the most serious (with a 15 per cent or more mortality) and the most dramatic (because there is confusion for time, place, and person and because the hallucinations are present with no insight into their unreality). Delirium tremens have a delayed time of onset after alcohol intake stops, and this makes it important to observe a withdrawing alcoholic beyond the time that alcohol has been eliminated from his body (72).

DISEASE CONSEQUENCES OF ALCOHOLISM

For many reasons, alcohol is distinct from other psychoactive materials, but perhaps the most dramatic of these is that it is associated with many alcohol-related diseases (80). It was originally thought that these diseases were to be attributed not to the alcohol but to the malnutrition inevitably associated with alcoholism. But recent research has suggested that alcohol itself, acting as a toxin, is also and perhaps more specifically and directly involved.

The most striking of these experiments have been those of Dr. Charles Lieber, who, by giving a fully nutritious diet with alcohol substituted for 50 per cent of the calories, produced fully developed alcoholic fatty liver, hepatitis, and cirrhosis in baboons. Lieber had been unable to produce these lesions with 30 per cent of the calories as alcohol, and the results suggest that tolerance would be a necessary phenomenon if an individual were to drink a quantity sufficient over a long period of time to develop this lesion. Other lesions, such as alcoholic pancreatitis and alcoholic cardiomyopathy, likewise require such quantities over such periods of time, to suggest the key role that tolerance plays in making possible the eventual organ damage of alcohol. In addition to tolerance, however, bringing the noxious chemical to the cells, there must, in some cases at least, be a hereditary susceptibility of the organ to damage. Recently, Blass and Gibson discovered a hereditary anomaly (7) of thiamin co-carboxylase that may predispose certain alcoholic individuals to Wernicke-Korsakoff's psychosis. This awaits confirmation.

In reminding ourselves of biochemical variability, we come to the question of the hereditary predisposition to alcoholism. Family pedigree studies and clinical studies have for a long time shown a striking tendency for family involvement (over 50 per cent) in alcoholism. This has been thought to be due to cultural influences. However, twin studies by Partanen and by Kaij and later studies by Loehlin of twins taking National Merit scholarship exams suggested strongly that a hereditary predisposition to alcoholism might exist (79). Goodwin et al. (33) have demonstrated this possibility more definitively. They showed a 4-fold or more greater diagnosis of alcoholism in children with an alcoholic parent, from whom they had been separated at birth, than was present in matched controls. This adds to the group assembled by Schuckit (67), in whom, among half siblings, a similar preponderance of the alcoholic individuals had blood relative parents who were alcoholic, without regard to family of upbringing.

FETAL ALCOHOL SYNDROME

Between the time of germ cell maturation and fertilization and the appearance of the formed individual at birth are 9 months of nurturing in the special environment of the womb, in which the individual is acted upon by forces over which he or she has no control. Under these circumstances, alcohol ingestion by the mother can have profound effects on her offspring.

Alcohol freely passes the placental barrier. In 1968 in France (46) and independently in 1972 in the United States (40), a syndrome of birth defects was described in children of alcoholic women, confirming observations made since antiquity, now named the fetal alcohol syndrome. Confirmatory studies of many kinds—case reports in widely scattered locations, epidemiological studies, experiments in 11 species of animals—have reaffirmed the reality of this syndrome and its relationship to alcohol. It consists of a group of major abnormalities, found in most of the cases, and the sporadic appearance of others. The main characteristics are a low birth weight and length with failure of "catch up growth," small head circumference, midfacial anomalies resulting in microophthalmia, an epicanthal fold, poor development of the bridge of the nose, hypoplastic philtrum, a short up-turned nose, micrognathia, and brain maldevelopment with mild to moderate mental retardation (14). Other features found in some but not all cases include skeletal and joint abnormalities (including the Klippel-Feil syndrome), an abnormal "simian crease" in the hand, cardiac abnormalities (including atrial and ventricular septal defects, with individual case reports of patent ductus arteriosus, tetralogy of Fallot, and pulmonary atresia), abnormalities of sexual organs and of the ears, hemangiomas, and kidney abnormalities (74). On the few specimens which have presented at autopsy, abnormal migration of nerve cells has been found with heterotopias consisting of a feltwork of cells of every neurological type, in sheets and masses in unusual locations in the brain. Anencephaly, meningomyelocele, and lumbosacral lipoma have been described. Exencephaly has been produced in alcohol-exposed mice (13).

Experience with the fetal alcohol syndrome has brought out several clinical conclusions: (a) Although the degree of severity, incidence, and extent of the lesions seem to be directly related to the amount of alcohol consumed, no threshold dose has been found which can be definitively said to exist, under which no defect will occur. Luckily, most women seem to lose their taste or desire for alcohol when pregnant. (b) Stopping the alcohol ingestion seems to have a positive benefit in decreasing the number or severity of the lesions, even during the second trimester of pregnancy (65). (c) Recent experiments in beagle dogs suggest that very early in pregnancy (the first 2 weeks for the dogs) large doses of alcohol do not seem to be followed by abnormalities in the offspring (20). This would be fortunate if it also applied to women, because it would suggest that a woman who drinks socially would be spared anxiety in the very early stages—before she knew about her pregnancy—about fetal damage. Of course, it is hazardous to assume that a phenomenon occurring in dogs would necessarily apply also to humans.

TREATMENT

The appropriate place to treat alcoholism was suggested by Benjamin Rush to be an asylum or inpatient facility. The Washingtonian movement, starting in the 1830's, concentrated mostly on comrades escorting people to meetings where, by hearing of another's success, they were encouraged to take the "pledge." However, they also started "homes" for the inebriates, the last of which just recently closed in Boston, as an appropriate place to treat alcoholism (29).

In 1870, the first declaration of principles of the American Association for the Cure of Inebriates stated (9):

All methods hitherto employed having proved insufficient for the cure of inebriates the establishment of asylums for the purpose is the great demand of the age. Every large city should have

its local or temporary home for the treatment and care of such persons. The law should recognize intemperance as a disease and provide other means for its treatment than fines, station houses and jails.

However, treatment for alcoholism remained for the most part a matter of arrest during the century that followed. Of course, there were some institutions. However, most were psychiatric institutions that admitted alcoholics during acute deliria. But when the delirium was over, the alcoholic seemed definitely out of place among the chronically psychotic patients that surrounded him.

Other kinds of institutions arose. The Keeley Cure—a regimen based on hot baths and inspirational lectures that seemed, because of its long financial success, to be doing something for somebody—had its centenary in the 1970's. Private psychiatric hospitals would admit chronic alcoholics of the carriage trade. It was perhaps the founding and the growth of Alcoholics Anonymous (AA) that encouraged the development of alcoholism facilities that made the greatest alteration in treatment, although it had the echoes of the old Washingtonian Fellowship and biography idea. Bill W., the co-founder of AA, began to get the idea when a blinding flash of heavenly light descended on him as he attempted to get over a hangover in New York's Towns Hospital, a place where drunks could "dry out" (88). After this revelation, he repaired to a house in Akron, Ohio, where he helped Dr. Bob, and they gathered around them the first others to whom they had carried the message. The AA program was a live-in program from the beginning. And then, in many places around the country, other recovered alcoholics founded farms and homes and retreats and hospitals that did the job of indoctrinating people into the AA way of life. Such places were Chit Chat Farm and Livengrin in Pennsylvania, Melrose Farm in Washington, D.C., Willingway Hospital and Peachford in Georgia, Hazeldon and St. Mary's Hospital in Minnesota. As time has gone by, these places have developed sophistication. Some have developed special detoxification facilities with physicians and nurses. Some have employed psychologists and psychiatrists. And more and more general hospitals and specialized psychiatric hospitals have altered their alcoholism treatment toward this model.

More recently enterprising management groups have developed programs and staffs that can put an alcoholism team into any hospital[1] that will contract with them for this service.

The treatment program that has developed under this rubric includes several elements:

1. Pretreatment or motivation to treatment by:
   A. Labor management employment programs (55)
   B. Traffic courts that remand highway offenders to educational programs leading to treatment (37)
   C. Family intervention that is guided by a method of confrontation designed by the Johnson Institute (38)
   D. Certain hospitals and clinics that intercede with alcoholic pregnant women threatened with producing a fetal alcohol syndrome baby (65)
   E. Physicians who are able to translate their patient's alcohol-related disease into a reason for alcoholism treatment.
2. Detoxification
   Getting the alcohol out of the patient and having the patient go safely through the alcohol withdrawal syndrome is the first treatment step. This can be accomplished most safely in the hospital, but under certain circumstances it is possible on an outpatient basis or in a "sobering up station" or "social model detoxification" facility (75).
   The important thing is to see that treatment does not end at this point, but goes on to rehabilitation.
3. Rehabilitation—at first intensively, and often best done in an inpatient setting such as described above. Most such treatment programs ask the patient to remain in the setting for 4 to 6 weeks. A structured program is set up that includes individual counseling, group therapy of varying types, and educational programs and movies about the disease of alcoholism. AA meetings are held on the premises and sometimes visits to local AA meetings are offered

during the later weeks. Psychiatric evaluation and psychometric testing may be performed initially. Family involvement is usually sought, and couples, groups, or family groups may meet. Discharge planning includes vocational assessment. No alcohol is allowed, and penalties for drinking on or off the premises are severe, including discharge (12, 42).

4. Discharge from the facility is and should be accompanied by a long range life plan that includes abstinence. Follow-up outpatient appointments are possible. Many facilities have annual reunions of former patients, which aid in giving feedback about success rates and provide group cohesion. A long standing commitment to "working the program" of AA is the obvious choice for many.

OTHER TREATMENT

DETERRENT MEDICATION

Disulfiram, discovered in Denmark, was introduced to the United States by Dr. Ruth Fox. This medication (27), reasonably innocuous when taken by itself, produces an intense unpleasant reaction when even a small amount of an alcohol-containing beverage is taken. The reaction, primarily due to interference with the degradation of acetaldehyde (the first metabolite of ethanol) has been described above. The reaction generally lasts about ½ hour and is followed by sleep, from which the patient awakens refreshed and not drinking. Because deaths have occurred when large quantities of disulfiram are taken with large quantities of alcohol, the prescription of disulfiram must be made with the patient's full understanding of the reaction. Prescription should be undertaken only when the risk of drinking is more serious than taking the drug. With this provision, thousands of people have had disulfiram treatment. Some have taken it for as long as 17 years, with positive effect in giving them "insurance" that they will not succumb to invitation or impulse in their program of not drinking in a drinking society. Implantation of long acting, absorbable disulfiram pellets for long duration effect is not effective and is not permitted by the FDA in the United States (49).

[1] For instance, Raleigh Hills Hospital, 881 Dover Drive, Newport Beach, California; Comprehensive Care, 600 Newport Center Drive, Newport Beach, California, 92660.

CONDITIONED REFLEX THERAPY

Many attempts to associate drinking with a noxious stimulus have been made in order to induce a conditioned reflex against the idea of taking an alcoholic beverage (90). These have varied from posthypnotic suggestion to covert self-suggestion, electric shock, succinyl choline-induced apnea (a hazardous and totally abandoned procedure), and emetine-induced vomiting. The last of these has been the most actively used, initially by the Shadel Sanatorium in Seattle (and later other locations) and in other programs. Claims of the proponents of very high success rates have been disputed by other observers, but the programs continue and have their strong adherents. Even in the Shadel Program at this time, Alcoholics Anonymous is advocated as an assist in dealing with sobriety.

In recent years, it has been noted that on follow-up a small number of patients claim or are said to have not maintained abstinence but have been able to engage in moderate controlled drinking after treatment for alcoholism. The first well publicized report of this sort was published by Dr. D. L. Davies of the Maudsley Hospital in London, which showed seven of 43 patients who had undergone treatment intended to lead to abstinence who on long term follow-up were drinking in this manner (17). This discovery—tied to the supposed "normalcy" of drinking, the embarrassment some people might undergo in having to refuse an offered drink, and an attack on the proposition that some magical chemical trigger set off by a drop of alcohol could lead to disastrous binges—led some investigators, particularly among experimental psychologists, to attempt the feat of getting alcoholic patients to moderate but not eliminate their drinking. These experiments, greeted with dismay by alcoholics who found a new life in abstinence and sobriety, still go on and are hotly debated (51). Whereas the theory has been considered persuasive, the trial in practice has not shown sufficient success to persuade most practitioners to make the more complicated attempt to cut the intake down but not out. In the first place, there have been no guidelines arrived at to distinguish which candidates should be treated in this way. Even the most ardent supporters of the controlled drinking goal say that anyone with physical complications of alcoholism should stop altogether. And there are few dependent alcoholics who have not already had some physical complications. There have been those who have attempted to induce social drinking and found all the patients (of a small series) relapsed or elected to become abstinent during a 5-year follow-up period (23).

A large impetus was given to the search for a controlled drinking goal by follow-up studies that tended to show small success rates for the "classical" treatment. The initial pragmatic way in which treatment programs began and the small number of studies of outcome that could be said to be scientifically adequate added to the possibility of presenting a case against such treatment. Three careful reviews of outcome studies were made—by Baekeland et al. (2), Emrich (21), and Costello et al. (16). The conclusions in general were dismal. It seemed there was no great advantage for any kind of treatment, except that Costello found that in programs with careful screening of applicants for those most likely to benefit from treatment, and where the treatment program included the enthusiastic use of disulfiram, outcome was improved. In general, however, the conclusions of the reviewers were that (a) the better the people were when they entered treatment, the more probability of a successful outcome; (b) the type of treatment was not important; and (c) therefore, the cheapest treatment was best.

It was at this stage of the art that the federal government gave a contract to the Rand Corporation to assess the success of the 44 alcoholism treatment centers it had funded throughout the United States (1). Rand was given not a mandate to design and carry out a study, but rather data collected over a period of 18 months from these centers, on a form designed by the National Institute of Alcohol Abuse and Alcoholism, which had been the subject of a 6-month evaluation by the Stanford Research Institute. Rand then participated in the collection of 18-month follow-up data and in the analysis of the whole. The study already had some unfortunate gaps. Of the 44 treatment centers, only those that volunteered to be part of the study were included. This totaled eight centers, not selected from any considerations of population served, etc. The data had been (and continued to be) collected by interviewers in the regular employ of the treatment center itself (not considered to be scientifically optimum for independent results). The 18-month follow-up came primarily from three of the centers and contained data on people not in the 6-month sample (there was an overlap). The study produced some useful statistics. However, an attempt was made to use the analysis of data for some very sophisticated conclusions, and the most tenuous of those conclusions was utilized as the basis for a press conference initiated by the Rand Corporation. At this conference, these conclusions were presented as the definite results of the "largest scientific study ever carried out on the follow-up of alcoholism." The results were inflammatory and produced a sharp reaction from alcohologists and many other scientists throughout the country.

What Rand had said was that on the basis of this largest scientific follow-up study, it had been proved that controlled drinking was an equally sound goal for alcoholism treatment as was abstinence. The basis for their claim was, as they said: "relapses from controlled drinking were the same volume between 6 and 18 months as were relapses from abstinence" (74). The evidence for this came from a table in which the outcome at 6 and 18 months was compared for 163 clients who were "really alcoholic" at entry into the study and whose outcome was known 18 months later. And it is true that the same percentage (17 per cent) relapsed from the "controlled drinking" as the "abstinent" column between 6 and 18 months. Calculating from the number in the sample, it turns out that they are talking about *three* alcoholics and *five* controlled drinkers. This is scarcely to be called a firm conclusion in a study purporting to get information from 30,000 treatment entries to 44 treatment centers. More than 100 clients died in the over-all sample during the year of follow-up, but the results on them are not analyzed at all! Results might have been useful if random or even representative sampling had occurred—perhaps a small number in a crucial relationship could have been a guide to the whole—but this was not the case. This logic suggested that certain conclusions of the Rand research would not hold up under further scrutiny. There are two types of such scrutiny: (a) the immediate criticism of the document based on inspection and (b) the replication of parts of the type of research

involved. On inspection, criticisms from Doctors Sheila Blume, John Wallace, David Pittman, and many others on clinical and scientific grounds have been presented (15). In the book, *Alcohol and Treatment*, the authors of the Rand report state: "The relapse sample is too small to establish definitively the relapse rates for normal drinkers." Yet in the reprinting of their original work, they have not altered the text in which it says "We cannot over-emphasize the significance of these findings. *Based on relapse rates* of a small subsample of clients . . . it appears that some alcoholics do return to normal drinking with no greater likelihood of relapse than alcoholics who choose permanent abstention."

Using the figures in the same table, one can calculate the chances of an individual who was in one condition at 6 months remaining in that condition at 18 months. An individual who had any period of abstinence at 6 months would have a better than even chance of being abstinent at 18 months. He would have an even chance of being abstinent at 18 months even if he were in one of the drinking categories at 6 months (including "normal drinking." The outcome of the "normal drinker" category was less stable, because a normal drinker at 6 months would have only a one in three chance of remaining a normal drinker at 18 months. A nonnormal drinker at 6 months would have a six to one chance of not being a normal drinker at 18 months (74).[2]

Paredes et al. have taken a different method of examining the conclusions of the Rand report. They made a relapse analysis of another sample of clients of which 342 met inclusion criteria (59). Their conclusion was:

The clients in our "normal drinker category" at 6 months follow-up had the highest relapse rate of all remitted groups when assessed at the 18 month follow-up. The data of our study suggest that those alcoholics who chose to reduce their drinking as an option, experienced a substantial risk of relapse.

In a 4 year follow-up study of the same sample, the Rand authors did analyze death

---

[2] The 4-year follow-up of the Rand report, although not retracting its original interpretation, makes points both about the instability of controlled drinking outcome and the over-all mortality of the sample.

rates (finding them higher for drinkers than abstinents), and found a stronger tendency for "normal" drinkers to relapse.

But the Rand report has not been the only examination of outcome requiring a hard look to avoid making inaccurate goals of treatment. In another careful scientific study, Orford and Edwards (57) treated 50 men applying for alcoholism treatment with "advice" and follow-up only and gave a matched sample of similar clients the full "treatment." Their analysis of the results concluded that the advice patients did quite as well as the treatment patients. This conclusion, too, was examined in an international conference. There reexamination of the figures suggested that there *were*, in fact, some inadvertently hidden differences between the two groups of clients, and it supported the conclusions of others that treatment indeed had more effect than nontreatment.

As we pass into a time of serious and severe examination of the efforts being made, we must not discount the importance of critical studies that examine carefully what is being done with the aim of improving our idea of "what works." Neither can we be hasty in scrapping treatment approaches that seem to work for some of the people some of the time until we have something better to offer. We also must examine programs that claim effectiveness. Such a program is that of the United States Navy that, like the industrial (or labor-management) programs it resembles, claims a very high percentage of success among its clients (10). Between 70 and 85 per cent success in these abstinence-oriented programs has been reported. Admittedly, they take clients who are starting from a higher base than many public programs. It may be also that such people could succeed in a nonabstinence program. However, experience such as that of Paredes and Ewing would suggest that this is not the case, and people interested in abstinence programs see no logical reason to make drinking a health goal—or at least no more reason than there would be to make "social smoking" a health goal.

One of the frequently mentioned criticisms of outcome studies such as the Rand report is the difficulty in incorporating into the study design the many variables that our disparate population in the United States may bring to the picture. For even if we see the end result, alcoholism, as a unitary phenomenon, certainly social and psychological factors must enter into the development of alcoholism. A good Moslem or even a Mormon whose religion forbids drinking would never have the chance of testing whether he might become alcoholic, and if they do nevertheless, the alcoholism might be more difficult to overcome. Similarly women, from the societal pattern of many years' in which drunkenness appeared unladylike, until recently would hide their alcoholism; when it was discovered, it would often be intractable. With the continual pattern of liberation of women, some people postulate an increase in the numbers of them who appear for treatment of alcoholism (92). Cultural norms may have a relationship. The Irish are said to be culturally predisposed to drink by their life in the Old Country where primogeniture, the Catholic Church, and poverty conspired to put the younger sons in the tavern (5); whereas Jews, drinking only at the family Seder service, considered drinking fine but drunkenness a permanent shame or 'shanda.' But now, becoming acculturated, numbers of Jewish people are also found requiring AA and alcoholism treatment (83). Blacks, relatively understudied according to Harper, have major patterns of alcoholism in the urban getto, less so in the rural South. Whereas some have suggested that AA will not help them, the installation of Alcoholics Anoymous in Trinidad, through the efforts of Dr. Michael Beaubrun, is a model of success (6).

EFFORTS OF ASSESSING ALCOHOLISM AND ALCOHOL PROBLEMS AMONG THE YOUNG

We have varying estimates that either there is a huge increase in drinking and alcohol abuse among the young or that it has changed very little (68). There does seem to be a decrease in the age of commencing drinking from 14 to perhaps 12. Whereas a case has been reported of delirium tremens in a 9-year-old boy, it turns out he was a Native American living with his alcoholic uncle, and so more an exception than the rule (81). Mark Keller has pointed out that we probably owe merely to compulsory education and child labor laws the lack of outright alcoholism among our youth. In the late 19th century, working children with the money and the time to drink were masters at entering the ranks of the physically dependent alcoholic (41).

Today, our problems about alcohol and youth are tied to our problems with road traffic. The young and the alcoholic are our two worst offenders on the American highway. Half the fatal highway crashes are alcohol related. Young people who crash are less likely to be alcohol dependent than adults, even when the crash is alcohol related. Because of the increase, over 100 per cent in some jurisdictions, of alcohol-related crashes of youths between 18 and 21, many states are attempting to reverse legislation enacted during the Vietnam War that allowed the purchase of alcoholic beverages to 18-year-olds, who had suddenly been deemed adult enough to vote and to die for their country. Whether this retrogressive legislation will succeed and will cut down the highway fatalities is now a moot point.

ALCOHOL AND THE AGED

The old, like the young ignored for their alcohol problems, can be treated like a special population (19). It is widely believed (without definitive testing) that tolerance decreases with age without regard to drinking history. It is often stated in addition that alcoholism is more often secondary to changed life situations among the old, for instance, that alcoholic drinking will happen after a man has been widowed. Many times, however, in this case, it will turn out that the drinking before the spouse's death was on inspection in reality alcoholic but protected from the patient and the world by the social situation.

Some therapists, however, find that in the elderly, often a change in the social situation by increased social supports ameliorates the alcoholism problem without the great dislocations necessary in dealing with addictive alcoholism among the middle-aged (78).

PSYCHIATRIC DIAGNOSIS

As differences in culture and age modify treatment needs and possibilities, so also do variations in psychiatric structure and diagnosis alter treatment needs.

Many authors attempt to present people with different psychiatric disorders as different types of alcoholics. The National Council on Alcohol Criteria Committee considered this but felt that more flexibility and a greater accuracy of diagnosis could be attained if the diagnosis of alcoholism was made separately from a purely psychiatric diagnosis (54). This scheme has been useful for those who have adopted it, although the percentage of alcoholics with schizophrenia is fairly low (about 4 per cent) in studies made thus far, and the percentage of alcoholics with manic-depressive disease is also not significantly different from its occurrence in the general population (26). These findings are of importance, however. Schizophrenic alcoholics require, in addition to treatment for their alcoholism, some treatment for the schizophrenia—such as phenothiazine tranquilizers.

Manic-depressive alcoholics must also have lithium treatment to ensure a good result. Kline et al. have offered lithium treatment for all primary alcoholics (43). Reynolds et al. (62) think this would be ineffective except for the alcoholics in whom manic-depressive disease is also found. This controversy has not been settled as yet.

OTHER DRUGS

One major modifier of alcoholism treatment is the use of other drugs. There is no question that larger and larger percentages of clients for alcoholism treatment also take other depressants and sedatives and often stimulants (28). These patterns complicate withdrawal (which must be longer) and treatment, which involves a more intensive pursuit of changing patterns of procurement that involve deceiving prescribing physicians or illegal street procurement of the drugs.

For most of these people, however, treatment for alcoholism, the primary addiction, is apparently sufficient (if instruction about the other drugs is given) to deal with the problem. Iatrogenic interference by lax prescribing methods can be mischievous.

Opiate addiction combined with alcoholism is not at all uncommon; frequently alcoholism precedes the trial of opiates (28). In methadone programs, alcoholism can achieve rates of 50 per cent. The alcoholism, when it is a new phenomenon, is very rapid in onset, is severe, and is disruptive of methadone regimens.

Research is now going on to explore any cross-reactions of disulfiram with methadone (30). Barring harmful cross-reactions, a combined methadone-disulfiram program is possible and seems helpful. Alcoholics Anonymous groups do not in general welcome methadone maintenance patients, who are considered as taking ongoing drugs and thus not available for the program of AA. However, some independent groups of combined users, having a similar—although adapted—scheme as AA, have grown up.

Combined treatment settings where alcoholism and drug abuse are attacked together have been advocated by a number of authors. At Eagleville Hospital in Pennsylvania, this has been carried on for many years. People who have dealt with alcoholism primarily have been reluctant to abandon too readily and without good cause a scheme and a method of treatment that have achieved a good or great degree of success (45).

The Veterans Administration has, in a cooperative study, explored the use of combined settings (10 in number) as opposed to separate alcoholism (seven in number) and drug abuse facilities (also seven) (58). Reporting on only a 6-month outcome study, there were no large differences between the combined and separate settings. However, there were small differences or trends, that favoring the alcoholics particularly but also other drug abusers somewhat, that the separate setting was superior. Experience with other 6-month follow-up studies suggests that the differences would become larger with more time.

Another similar but different population is that of the active armed forces. In the late 1960's, faced with a problem of drug abuse in Vietnam and elsewhere, the Army and the Air Force instituted programs of combined alcohol and drug abuse efforts. Meanwhile, the Navy, which had already instituted an alcoholism program, kept it separate from the drug abuse program (3).

Ten years later, the outstanding success of the Navy program has been acknowledged by the other services; the Air Force is beginning to adopt a program similar to that of the Navy and is sending its physicians through the Navy program for instruction. A President's wife and a President's brother have been treated in the Navy program, a tacit acknowledgment that it is a preeminent one in the country today.

Meanwhile, the theoretical basis of "addiction proneness," a concept much bruited about but little studied, has been shaken by a careful look at it (10). Hill et al. (36) studied the clustering of alcoholism and opiate addicts in families. Interviews conducted with 32 alcoholics, 72 opiate addicts, and 42 alcohol-opiate addicts determined the practice of their families. Using the Weinberg proband method for concordance between relatives and a tetrachoric correlation to measure family clustering, it was determined that, although alcoholism tended to cluster in families significantly, alcoholism and opiate abuse did not occur in the same families significantly more or less often than expected by chance. The authors concluded that doubt is clearly cast on any unitary concept of addiction proneness.

CONCLUSIONS

Students of alcoholism can make a strong case for the uniqueness of the condition among conditions caused by psychoactive drugs and drugs of pharmacological dependency. I have suggested four things that make alcoholism unique among conditions entailing "substance" abuse:

1. The well defined cultural patterns of use of alcohol in those parts of the world that have contributed most to the background of the United States

2. The caloric value of alcohol which makes for specific physical difficulties

3. The growing evidence of a specific toxic effect of alcohol itself affecting the liver, heart, brain, pancreas, and other tissues and, in particular, damaging the fetus in the "fetal alcohol syndrome"

4. Alcohol attacks the "square" members of society who want to get along rather than to be deviant (in this it resembles cigarette and caffeine dependence).

Arguments, however, that reify "social drinking" as a norm are not persuasive to those who weigh the balance of harm that alcohol does to that of good, the possibility of alternate sources of the desired effects of alcohol, and the unsuccessful course of at least a strong majority of those who try to achieve "social drinking" when alcoholism is present.

A careful examination of the evidence strengthens the position of those who would continue individual programs for research, prevention, and treatment of alcoholism, and comparative analyses may well also provide illumination on new fields to explore and new directions to take.

References

1. Armor, D., Polich, J. M., and Stambul, H. G. *Alcoholism and Treatment*. New York, John Wiley, 1978.
2. Baekeland, F., Lundwall, L., and Kissin, B. Methods for the treatment of alcoholism: A critical appraisal. In *Alcohol and Drug Problems*, R. J. Gibbins, Y. Israel, H. Kalant, R. E. Popham, W. Schmidt and R. G. Smart, editors, vol. 2. New York, John Wiley, 1975.
3. Baker, S. L., Lorei, T., and McKnight, H. A. Jr. The V.A. comparison study: Alcoholism and drug abuse combined and traditional treatment settings. Alcohol Clin. Exp. Res. 4:285, 1977.
4. Bailey, M. B. *Alcoholism and Family Case Work*. New York, Community Council, 1968.
5. Bales, R. F. Attitudes towards drinking in Irish culture. In *Alcoholism*, D. Pittman, editor. Springfield, Ill., Charles C Thomas, 1959.
6. Beaubrun, M. The treatment of alcoholism in Trinidad and Tobago, 1955–65. Br. J. Psychiatry 113:499, 643, 1967.
7. Blass, J. P., and Gibson, G. E. Genetic factors in Wernicke Korsakoff syndrome. Alcohol Clin. Exp. Res. 3:126, 1979.
8. Blum, K., editor. *Alcohol and Opiates*. New York, Academic Press, 1977.
9. Blumberg, L. The American Association for the Study and Cure of Inebriety. Alcohol Clin. Exp. Res. 2:235, 1978.
10. Brownell, S. M. The Navy Alcoholism Prevention Program—Worldwide. Alcohol Clin. Exp. Res. 2: 362, 1978.
11. Cahalan, D., Cisin, I., and Crossley, H. M. *American Drinking Practices*. New Brunswick, N. J., Rutgers Center of Alcohol Studies, 1969.
12. Catanzaro, R. *Alcoholism*. Springfield, Ill., Charles C Thomas.
13. Clarren, S. K., Alvord, E. C., Jr., Sumi, B. M., Streissguth, A. P., and Smith, D. W. Brain malformations related to prenatal exposure to ethanol J. Pediatr. 92: 64, 1978.
14. Clarren, S. K., and Smith, D. W. The fetal alcohol syndrome. N. Engl. J. Med. 298:1063, 1978.
15. Comments—The Rand Report. J. Stud. Alcohol, 38: 152, 1977.
16. Costello, R. M., Brevier, P., and Baillargeon, J. G. Alcoholism treatment programming: Historical trends and modern approaches. Alcohol Clin. Exp. Res. 1:311, 1974.
17. Davies, D. L. Normal drinking in recovered alcoholics Q. J. Stud. Alcohol 23:94, 1962.
18. Davis, V. E., Huff, J. A., and Brown, H. A. Alcohol and biogenic amines. In *Biochemical and Clinical Aspects of Alcohol Metabolism*, V. M. Sardesai, editor, pp. 95–104. Springfield, Ill., Charles C Thomas, 1969.
19. Douglass, R. L., and Freedman, J. A. *Alcohol Related Casualties and Alcohol Beverage Market Response to Beverage Alcohol Availability in Michigan: Final Report*, vol. 1. (Rep. No. UM HSR 1 77-37-1.) Ann Arbor, Mich., University of Michigan, Highway Safety Research Insitute, 1977.
20. Ellis, F. University of North Carolina, personal communication.
21. Emrick, C. D. A review of psychologically oriented treatment of alcoholism. Q. J. Stud. Alcohol 35:523, 1974; II. Q. J. Stud. Alcohol 36:88, 1975.
22. Ewing, J. Can dopamine beta-hydroxylase levels predict adverse reactions to Disulfiram? Alcohol Clin. Exp. Res. 2:93, 1978.
23. Ewing, J., and Rouse, B. *Drinking*. Chicago, Nelson Hall, 1978.
24. Ewing, J. A., and Rouse, B. A. Failure of an experimental treatment program to inculcate controlled drinking in alcoholics. Br. J. Addict. 71:123, 1976.
25. Faris, D. The prevention of alcoholism and economic alcoholism. Prev. Med. 3:39, 1974.
26. Fowler, R. C., Liskow, B. L., Tanna, V. L., and Van Valhenberg, C. Psychiatric illness and alcoholism. Alcohol Clin. Exp. Res. 1:125, 1977.
27. Fox, R. Antabuse as an adjunct in the treatment of alcoholism. N. Y. State J. Med. 58:9, 1958.
28. Freed, E. X. Drug abuse by alcoholics. Int. J. Addict. 8:461, 1973.
29. Furnas, J. C. *The Life and Times of the Great Demon Rum*. New York, G. P. Putnam's Sons, 1965.
30. Gerard, D. L. Intoxication and addiction: Psychiatric observations in alcoholism and opiate drug addiction. Q. J. Stud. Alcohol 16:681.
31. Goff, E. V., and Fine, D. H. Analysis of volatile N-nitrosamines in alcoholic beverages. Food Cosmet. Toxicol. 17:569, 1979.
32. Goodwin, D. Two species of alcoholic blackout. Am. J. Psychiatry 127:1665, 1971.
33. Goodwin, D. W., Schulsinger, F., Hermansen, L., Guze, S. B., and Winokur, G. Alcohol problems in adoptees raised apart from alcoholic biological parents. Arch. Gen. Psychiatry 28:238, 1973.
34. Greenblatt, M., and Schuckit, M. A., editors. *Alcohol Problems in Women and Children*. New York, Grune and Stratton, 1976.
35. Hald, S., and Jacobsen, E. The formation of acetaldehyde in the organism after the ingestion of Antabuse and alcohol. Acta Pharmacol. Toxicol. (Kbh) 4: 305, 1948.
36. Hill, S., Cloninger, C. R., and Ayre, F. R. Independent familial transmission of alcoholism and opiate abuse. Alcohol Clin. Exp. Res. 1:335, 1977.
37. Israelstam, S., and Lambert, S. *Alcohol, Drugs and Traffic Safety*. Toronto, Canada, Addiction Research Foundation, 1975.
38. Johnson, V. E. *I'll Quit Tomorrow*. New York, Harper and Row, 1973.
39. Jones, A. W., Wright, B. M., and Jones, T. P. A historical and experimental study of the breath/blood alcohol ratio. In *Alcohol, Drugs and Traffic Safety*, pp. 509–526. Toronto, Canada, Addiction Research Foundation, 1975.
40. Jones, K. L., Smith, D. W., Ulleland, C. W., and Streissguth, A. P. Pattern of malformation in offspring of alcoholic women. Lancet 1:1267, 1973.
41. Keller, M. Alcohol and Youth. Address at Conference of Alcohol and Youth, Institute of Psychiatry, Northwestern University Memorial Hospital, Chicago, June 1–2, 1978.
42. Kissin, B., and Begleiter, H. Treatment and rehabilitation of the alcoholic. In *Biology of Alcoholism*, vol. V. New York, Plenum Press, 1976.
43. Kline, N. S., Wren, J. C., Cooper, T. B., et al.

Evaluation of lithium therapy in chronic and periodic alcoholism. Am. J. Med. Sci. 268:15, 1974.

44. Korsten, M. A., Matsozaki, S., and Feinman, L. High blood acetaldehyde levels after ethanol administration: Difference between alcoholic and non-alcoholic subjects. N. Engl. J. Med. 292:386, 1975.

45. Kreek, M. J. Rockefeller University, personal communication.

46. Lemoine, P., Harousseau, H., Borteyru, J. P., and Menuet, J. C. Les enfants de parents alcoholiques: Anomalies observee, A prosos de 127 cas. Ouest Med. 25:477, 1968.

47. Lieber, C. S. Summary of the discussion. Alcohol Clin. Exp. Res. 1:49, 1977.

48. Lieber, C. S., editor. *Metabolism of Alcohol.* London, University Park Press, 1978.

49. Malcolm, M. T., and Madden, J. S. Use of disulfiram implantation in alcoholism. Br. J. Psychiatry 123:41, 1973.

50. Mayer, J., Lewis, D. C., and Zubey, N. E. Treatment of drug addiction and alcoholism in the same facility: Experience and issues. In *Critical Concerns in the Field of Drug Abuse,* A. Schecter, H. Alksne, and E. Kaufman, editors, pp. 889-893. New York, Marcel Dekker, 1976.

51. Mills, K. C., Sobell, M. B., and Schaefer, H. H. Training social drinking as an alternative to abstinence for alcoholics. Behav. Ther. 2:18, 1971.

52. Mowrer, H. R., and Mowrer, E. R. Ecological and family factors associated with inebriety. Q. J. Stud. Alcohol 6:36, 1943.

53. Myers, R. D. Tetrahydroisoquinolines in the brain: The basis of a rat model of alcoholism. Alcohol Clin. Exp. Res. 2:145, 1978.

54. National Council on Alcoholism. Criteria for diagnosis of alcoholism. Am. J. Psychiatry 129:127, 1972.

55. National Council on Alcoholism. Labor Management Journal, New York.

56. Nora, A. H., Nora, J. J., and Blu, J. Limb reduction anomalies in infants born to disulfiram-treated alcoholic mothers (letter). Lancet 2:664, 1977.

57. Orford, J., and Edwards, G. *Alcoholism.* Oxford, Oxford University Press, 1977.

58. Ottenberg, D. S. Combined treatment of alcoholics and drug addicts: A program report from Eagleville. Contemp. Drug Prob. 1, Spring 1975.

59. Paredes, A., Gregory, D., Rundell, O. H., and Williams, H. L. Drinking behavior, remission and relapse: The Rand Report revisited. Alcohol Clin. Exp. Res. 3:310, 1979.

60. Patek, A. J., Post, J., Ratnoff, O. D., Mankin, H., and Hillman, R. W. Dietary treatment of cirrhosis of the liver. J.A.M.A. 138:543, 1948.

61. Reed, T. B., Kalant, H., and Gibbins, R. J. Alcohol and acetaldehyde metabolism in Caucasians, Chinese and Americans. Can. Med. Assoc. J. 115:851, 1976.

62. Reynolds, C. M., Merry, J., and Coppen, A. Prophylactic treatment of alcoholism by lithium carbonate: An initial report. Alcohol Clin. Exp. Res. 1:109, 1977.

63. Ritchie, J. M. Alcohol. In *The Pharmacological Basis of Medical Practice,* L. S. Goodman, and A. Gilman, editors, ed. 3. New York, 1965.

64. Robinson, D. *From Drinking to Alcoholism: A Sociological Commentary.* London, John Wiley, 1976.

65. Rosett, H., Oulette, E., Weiner, L., and Owens, E. The prenatal clinic: A site for alcoholism prevention and treatment. In *Currents in Alcoholism,* F. A. Seixas, editor, vol. 1, pp. 419-430. New York, Grune and Stratton, 1977.

66. Rush, B. *An Inquiry into the Effects of Ardent Spirits.* Philadelphia, 1785.

67. Schuckit, M. Family history and sibling research in alcoholism. Ann. N. Y. Acad. Sci. 197:121, 1972.

68. Schuckit, M., and Greenblatt, M. *Alcoholism in Women and Children.* New York, Grune and Stratton, 1978.

69. Schuckit, M., and Rayses, N. Ethanol ingestion: Differences in blood acetaldehyde concentrations in relatives and controls. Science 203:54, 1979.

70. Secretary, Department of Health, Education and Welfare. *First Special Report to the U.S. Congress,* (DHEW Publ. (HSM) 72-9099). Washington, D.C., United States Government Printing Office, 1971.

71. Secretary, Department of Health, Education and Welfare. *Third Special Report to the U.S. Congress.* Washington, D.C., United States Government Printing Office, 1978.

72. Seixas, F. A., editor. *Treatment of the Alcohol Withdrawal Syndrome.* New York, National Council on Alcoholism, 1971.

73. Seixas, F. A. Alcohol and its drug interactions. Ann. Intern. Med., 83:86, 1975.

74. Seixas, F. A. Assessing Emerging Concepts (editorial), Alcohol Clin. Exp. Res. 1:281, 1977.

75. Seixas, F. A. The Fetal Alcohol Syndrome in the Year of the Child, Plenary Session, ICAA Meeting, Tours, France, 1979. Lausanne, Switz., 1979, in press.

76. Seixas, F. A., Cadoret, R., and Eggleston, S. The person with alcoholism. Ann. N. Y. Acad. Sci. 233:1974.

77. Seixas, F. A., and Eggleston, S. Alcoholism and the central nervous system. Ann. N. Y. Acad. Sci. 215:1975.

78. Seixas, F. A., et al. Alcohol in the elderly: A seminar. Alcohol Clin. Exp. Res. 2:15, 1978.

79. Seixas, F. A., Omenn, G. S., Burke, E. D., and Eggleston, S. Nature and nurture in alcoholism. Ann. N. Y. Acad. Sci. 197: 1972.

80. Seixas, F. A., Williams, K., and Eggleston, S., editors. Medical consequences of alcoholism. Ann. N. Y. Acad. Sci. 252:399, 1975.

81. Sherwin, D., and Mead, B. Delirium tremens in a nine year old child. Am. J. Psychiatry 132:1210, 1975.

82. Smith, W. H., and Helwig, F. C. *Liquor, the Servant of Man.* Boston, Little, Brown and company, 1939.

83. Snyder, C. *Drinking among the Jews.* Glencoe, Ill., Free Press, 1958.

84. Stamatoyannopoulos, G., Chen, S-H., and Fukui, M. Liver alcohol dehydrogenase in Japanese: High population frequency of atypical form and its possible role in alcohol sensitivity. Am. J. Hum. Genet. 27: 789, 1975.

85. Tabakoff, B., and Ritzmann, R. F. Acute tolerance in inbred and selected lines of mice. Int. J. Drug Alcohol Depend. 4:87, 1979.

86. Teschke, R., Hasumuraand, Y., and Lieber, C. S. Increased carbon tetrachloride toxicity and its mechanism after chronic alcohol consumption. Gastroenterology 66:415, 1974.

87. Teschke, R., Matsuzaki, S., Ohnishi, K., DeCarli, L., and Lieber, C. S. Microsomal ethanol oxidizing system (MEOS): Current status of its characterization and role. Alcohol Clin. Exp. Res. 1:7, 1977.

88. Thomsen, R. *Bill W.* New York, Harper and Row, 1975.

89. Truitt, E. B., and Walsh, M. J. The role of acetaldehyde in the actions of alcohol. In *The Biology of Alcoholism*, B. Kissin and Begleiter, editors. New York, Plenum Press, 1971.

90. Voegtlin, W. L., and Broz, W. R. The conditioned reflex treatment of chronic alcoholism; an analysis of 3123 admissions over 10½ years. Ann. Intern. Med. 30:580, 1949.

91. Von Wartburg, J. P., and Seminzar, A. Effects of alcohol on membrane structure and function. Alcohol Clin. Exp. Res. 3:46, 1979.

92. Youcha, G. *A Dangerous Pleasure: Alcohol and Women.* New York, Hawthorn Books, 1978.

CHAPTER 18

PHENCYCLIDINE

Paul V. Luisada, M.D.

Phencyclidine (PCP, 1-(1-phenylcyclo-hexyl)piperidine monohydrochloride) is unique among psychoactive substances which are presently in general use in the United States: It is a recently discovered, synthetic drug which is unrelated to and not derived from any naturally occurring alkaloid. It can be manufactured relatively easily in large quantities in relatively unsophisticated laboratories from relatively simple and available raw materials. It defies simple classification under traditional systems on the basis of its unique array of pharmacological effects, and it has required the creation of a new category: dissociative or cataleptoid anesthetics. Its spectrum of effects is so polymorphous, pernicious, and persistent that phencyclidine might be termed the syphilis of abused substances. Although many users find some of its effects disagreeable and a majority of users have experienced adverse reactions, it has become one of the most widely abused psychoactive drugs in the United States less than 20 years after its discovery and within 7 years of its emergence as a street drug. Where did this fascinating but contradictory substance come from?

HISTORY AND BEHAVIORAL PHARMACOLOGY

Phencyclidine was first discovered in the late 1950's by Parke Davis Laboratories (25). It was found to have an extremely broad variety of species-dependent behavioral and physiological effects in experimental animals (24). In rats and mice PCP was found to have stimulant effects like those of amphetamines (15). In general, the drug produces agitated, repetitive stereotyped behavior in these species. By contrast, PCP has calming and tranquilizing effects in nonhuman primates: Aggressive monkeys become docile to the point of immobility.

Despite these behavioral differences at lower dosages, administration of the drug at higher doses resulted in very high levels of general anesthesia in these animals while they were in a cataleptic state (15). Research on PCP's therapeutic uses, therefore, followed two pathways: its potential as a general anesthetic for use during surgery in humans and its potential as a veterinary tranquilizer for use in primates. PCP was the first of a new class of general anesthetics known as "cataleptoid anesthetics" or "dissociative anesthetics" (23).

Initial trials with humans were taken with the expectation that PCP would have great promise for surgical anesthesia. As an anesthetic it fulfilled all expectations during surgery. However, as the patients emerged from anaesthesia, one-sixth of the original group were severely psychotic and remained so for several hours. These patients' behavior was described as extremely agitated and bizarre, with echolalia and logorrhea as prominent symptoms (42). It was noted that this agitated psychotic emergence reaction was most commonly seen in young or middle-aged male patients.

These severe postoperative psychotic reactions ended PCP's promising career as a surgical anesthetic and caused it to follow a path that eventually lead to its status today as one of the most widely abused and most widely available psychoactive drugs in our society. The focus of research on the effects of PCP in humans shifted from the drug's possible use as an anesthetic to its utility for producing model psychoses. A number of research studies were undertaken in the early 1960's, during which PCP was given to "normal volunteers" in low to moderate doses. The resulting psychoses were studied carefully and were documented in a number of papers that appeared through 1965, when Parke Davis withdrew PCP from experimental use in humans (71).

The major finding of the studies of PCP was that it had no equal in its ability to produce brief dissociative psychotic reactions that were nearly indistinguishable from schizophrenic psychoses (74). Generally, the psychoses began immediately after infusion of the drug (20), lasted approximately 2 hours, and were characterized by changes in body image, thought disorders, feelings of estrangement, dissociation, autism, and occasional catatonia (54). At higher doses, subjects reported feeling numb from the drug's anesthetic effects, and they had great difficulty in differentiating between themselves and their surroundings. They often complained afterward of feeling extremely isolated and apathetic (5).

A smaller proportion of these volunteer experimental subjects was found to become suspicious, hostile, and paranoid, occasionally to the point of violence, while they were under the influence of PCP.

Some of these studies compared the effects of PCP to those of mescaline and lysergic acid diethylamide (LSD) and noted that the psychotic reactions produced by PCP were rather ego alien (9). It was noted that preoccupation with death and fear of death was a common subjective experience while under the influence of PCP, and other workers noted that the drug had an impressive ability to "loosen up" the experimental subject's unconscious conflicts.

These studies generally agreed that PCP could produce the signs and symptoms of schizophrenia on demand in most humans to whom it was administered. In most subjects, the psychotic reactions lasted for a maximum of several hours and were generally described as rather unpleasant. The finding that PCP was the first drug to produce shifts in the psychological test patterns of normal subjects that were essentially similar to those previously observed in schizophrenics led Luby to administer the drug to four hospitalized chronic schizophrenics. The effect of PCP in those patients was far more severe and prolonged than what had been seen when the drug was given to normal volunteers: "It was as though in these patients, the acute phase of their illness had been reinstated." They became nearly unmanageable in an inpatient setting and remained so not for several hours, but for up to 6 weeks (54).

Because of these severe adverse reactions, PCP never achieved status as a legitimate therapeutic drug, and its use as an experimental drug was discontinued in 1965. PCP was marketed as a legitimate veterinary tranquilizer under the trade name Sernylan (23). Its usefulness for this purpose and its acceptance became so high that efforts to outlaw its manufacture for any purpose in 1978 were initially met by considerable resistance from veterinary circles. However, a structural analogue 2-(o-chlorophenyl)-2-(methylamino)-cyclohexanone (ketamine) was found to have similar anesthetic properties with few of phencylidine's psychoactive effects in humans. Ketamine is currently in use as a general anesthetic, although significant quantities of this drug are now being diverted from legitimate channels (by theft) to the underground drug markets (23).

PCP first appeared as an abused street drug in 1967 in the Haight-Ashbury district of California (81). At that time it became available through illicit channels under the name "PeaCePill." Early users of the drug in tablet form experienced a very high number of adverse reactions. In retrospect, many of these early adverse reactions can be traced to the fact that the drug was taken orally. The oral route of administration introduces a significant delay between the time phencyclidine is taken and the time its effects become apparent. An impatient user may take a second dose during the interval before the effects of the first dose have become noticeable. This problem is compounded and exacerbated by the notorious variability of dosages of drugs sold through illicit channels. Because of these severe adverse reactions, PCP quickly earned a poor reputation in the California drug culture, and the oral preparation of PCP was a marketing failure as a street drug.

Rather than disappearing into obscurity as a result of this setback, PCP reappeared within several years under an assumed name and in disguise. Parsley or marihuana was impregnated with a solution of PCP, and the resulting preparation was smoked after the solvent had evaporated. To aid the disguise produced by this radically different form, PCP began traveling under an ever expanding array of assumed names: "Hog," "Angel Dust," "Embalming Fluid," "Super Grass," "LSD," "THC," and "Crystal." The evolution of assumed names for PCP continues to this day, and some recent examples include: "K," "KW," "Killer Weed," "Wacky Weed," "Whack," "Window Pane," and "Mr. Lovely" (23). This panoply of assumed names has generated a rule of thumb among those treating PCP abusers: a new drug with a bizarre name that is smoked or snorted can be assumed to be PCP unless proven otherwise; and its corollary: the more bizarre sounding the name, the higher the probability that the drug in question is PCP, all other factors being equal.

That PCP's transformation from tablet to leaf 10 years ago was a stroke of marketing genius is attested to by the drug's present popularity and ubiquity. The drug's new appearance as a leafy herb capitalized on the movement away from "chemicals" and toward "natural" and "organic" foods and herbs. The rather pungent odor produced when the "natural herb" was smoked clearly did not deter potential users, perhaps because potent forms of marihuana also tend to have an acrid odor. Also, the change in route of administration dictated by PCP's new form resolved many of the earlier problems of dosage. When PCP is smoked, its effects are almost immediate, and the user can titrate his drug intake against the effects that are produced, thereby avoiding the problem of accidental overdosage. This greatly enhanced

consumer acceptance of PCP as a recreational drug. Finally, the appearance of the drug as a leafy vegetable product somewhat resembling marihuana gave PCP access to the middle-class "gray market" in marihuana and the widespread underground distribution network that serves that market. Marihauna dealers and users, who routinely avoided drugs in the forms of pills or injectable powders because of underworld connotations and the implications of entering the world of "junkies" and "dope addicts" but who nevertheless sought a more potent "natural high," found little reason to resist PCP in its innocent looking leafy disguise.

CHARACTERISTICS OF PHENCYCLIDINE USERS

Several studies of phencyclidine users have been undertaken in an attempt to define their characteristics and to determine whether phencyclidine users, as a group, show characteristics which differentiate them from users of other drugs. Although these studies have been conducted as much as 4 years apart in time and at widely different geographical locations, their findings have generally been consistent and will be summarized here.

PCP users are primarily young adults who use a variety of psychoactive substances for recreational purposes (41, 49, 78, 81). Studies of adolescent and juvenile PCP users generally find the age of first use to be between age 13 and 15 (49, 81). Studies of adult users generally report the age of first use to be considerably later, but this is understandable in view of the fact that PCP was not available until the subjects of these studies were beyond their adolescence. In these samples, the heaviest incidence of PCP use generally clusters around the late teen years or early twenties.

These studies show the PCP users are nearly always also users of other psychoactive substances (49, 78, 81). Between 90 and 100 per cent of PCP users are also users of marihuana and alcohol, and about 75 per cent use "psychedelics." Roughly 50 per cent use amphetamine or sedatives other than alcohol, but only 5 to 40 per cent have used heroin or cocaine at least once (36, 49, 78, 81).

Shick (78) sampled drug users at two regional congregation sites in the Chicago area. He found that PCP use was a relatively recent phenomenon in the sample studied, having begun within 3 to 4 years prior to the survey. Most PCP users had been users of alcohol, marihuana, sedatives, amphetamine, and psychedelics prior to their first PCP use but had not been exposed to and were not users of cocaine or opiates. Shick also noted that the demographics of his sample differed widely from those of heroin users. Siegel's (81) study of 20 juvenile users of PCP found that 40 per cent used marihuana or alcohol, but only 15 per cent had used barbiturates and only 5 per cent had used heroin at least once. Thus, the majority of PCP users were recreational users of marihuana or alcohol before experimenting with PCP, a minority had been exposed to sedatives or amphetamine, and a very few had experienced heroin or cocaine.

Regular or occasional users of PCP tend to alternate their use of these other substances at approximately the same relative frequencies while they use PCP, and they often combine the use of PCP with one of these other substances, the favorite being alcohol.

Several attitudinal surveys indicate that PCP is the favorite drug much less commonly than one might expect in regular or intermittent users of phencyclidine. The Faumans' (36) Chicago study of PCP and multiple drug users in a treatment center found that phencyclidine was the drug of choice for 56 per cent of the sample, whereas Graeven's (41) Oakland survey of PCP users found it to be the drug of choice for only 8 per cent, with marihuana and alcohol the preference drugs.

The Faumans' (36) study found that 68 per cent of their sample were first introduced to PCP by their friends, and that 96 per cent of the users believed PCP was dangerous at the time they used it. Despite these opinions, and despite the fact that 12 per cent of these opinions were reached on the basis of personal experience, 72 per cent of those sampled continued to use the drug regularly.

Most studies agree that between 70 and 80 per cent of PCP users have experienced at least one "bad trip," and the Faumans' (36) study found that 48 per cent of the users had experienced multiple "bad trips." Other adverse reactions that have been reported by a majority of PCP users in this and other studies include (in relative order of frequency) memory loss, paranoia, perceptual distortions, disorientation, and restlessness (36, 49, 81). Adverse effects that are reportedly experienced by a minority of users include hyperexcitability, irritability, confusion, single or multiple accidental overdoses, and life-threatening, dangerous stiuations (36, 49, 81).

Despite the high frequencies of adverse and unpleasant reactions, the majority of users continue to take PCP. The most common reasons cited in explanation of this include the intensity or character of the intoxication, the economy or relative cheapness of the drug, its relatively high availability, and the rapid onset of its effects (36, 49, 81).

Lerner and Burns (49) produced a profile of a PCP user based on their analysis of the National Youth Polydrug Study (NYPS) that studied 2,750 subjects under 19 years of age, of whom 31 per cent had used PCP. They found several consistent patterns including an overrepresentation of Caucasians among PCP users, with males more likely to be regular or chronic users.

Characteristics of PCP users that differentiated them from other drug users included a tendency to use a greater number of different drugs regularly, the use of a number of drugs in combination, more frequent episodes of drunkenness, more arrests for substance-related or other criminal offenses, more overdoses, and more arrests for violent or weapons-related offenses. They concluded that PCP users are more likely to be white, to be frequently drunk, to frequently experience overdoses, to have more extensive criminal justice involvement than other drug users, to have greater educational dysfunction, and to have a much lower level of heroin use than other drug users. The mean age of first PCP use was approximately 14 years. Additional factors that differentiated those who use phencyclidine from other drug users at statistically significant levels included surburban residence, higher educational level, higher socioeconomic status, and greater age at admission for treatment.

The significance of these studies is that they profile the PCP user as one who does not restrict his drug use to PCP. He is most likely to be a better-educated adolescent or young adult male who lives in a suburb and has a higher socioeconomic level. He primarily uses PCP, marihuana, and alcohol for recreational purposes, occasionally uses barbiturates or sedatives, and infrequently uses or has been exposed to heroin or cocaine. Despite at least one adverse experience and several adverse reactions to the drug, he occasionally or regularly uses PCP because of the intensity of its psychic effects, its relative availability, and the fact that it is relatively inexpensive. The following pages describe the clinical syndromes that result from PCP use.

CLINICAL SYNDROMES RESULTING FROM PHENCYCLIDINE USE

Four distinct clinical syndromes resulting from the use of PCP have been identified to date: (a) acute phencyclidine intoxication, (b) phencyclidine overdose, (c) phencyclidine psychosis, and (d) chronic phencyclidine use.

Of these, the first three usually present as acute clinical problems requiring prompt and immediate intervention, and the treatment of these three syndromes will be explored in this chapter. The phenomenology of chronic phencyclidine use is unique and will also be presented. However, there is little evidence to indicate that the chronic, compulsive, or repetitive use of phencyclidine is intrinsically different from the chronic, repetitive, or compulsive use of other psychoactive substances for which pharmacological tolerance and withdrawal have not been demonstrated.

ACUTE PHENCYCLIDINE INTOXICATION

Diagnosis

Acute PCP intoxication is an altered state of consciousness induced by the administration of phencyclidine. It is the clinical state commonly desired by the PCP user, and it is generally produced by serum PCP levels of less than 100 ng per ml. The acute intoxication is self-limiting and rarely exceeds 6 to 8 hours in duration. Phencyclidine intoxication may be distinguished clinically from phencyclidine overdose (poisoning) by the absence of severe sedation, stupor, or coma; it is distinguished clinically from the phencyclidine psychosis by the absence of neurological signs and symptoms and other stigmata of phencyclidine intoxication in patients presenting with the persistent psychotic reaction.

Those who present with acute phencyclidine intoxication do so at emergency treatment facilities most commonly after their behavior brings them to the attention of others. The presenting picture has been described as a confusional state (49) or as a delirium (34) characterized by either agitation or hyperexcitable catatonic immobility. These patients are disoriented and apprehensive and often present with a "blank stare" appearance.

These patients seem awake but preoccupied. Their responses to verbal stimulation are generally monosyllabic or by means of head nodding. In general, in a patient who is not agitated, there is no spontaneous speech.

Behavior may be agitated and hyperactive or catatonic and withdrawn, depending upon the level of stimulation in the patient's environment. Aside from shouting, which may occur during periods of agitation, speech is generally slurred and perseveration is occasionally observed.

On examination, these patients are disoriented to time and place and are often amnesic for the circumstances immediately preceding their arrival. Responses to questions will indicate the presence of confusion and often fearfulness. Vital signs may show slight increases of temperature, pulse, and respiration, but systolic blood pressure is usually at least 20 mm Hg above normal. Diastolic blood pressure is not consistently elevated more than 5 or 10 mm Hg (12).

The patient's gait is ataxic on the basis of impaired proprioceptive and tactile input. Muscle tone is hypertonic with rigidity, and catatonic-like waxy flexibility is often reported. The deep tendon reflexes will be increased, and the patient will be restless and prone to repetitive stereotyped movements and occasional facial grimacing.

The patient's eyes are fixed in a stare with very little spontaneous eye movement. Horizontal nystagmus is always present, although vertical nystagmus may be absent at lower levels of intoxication. The corneal reflex may be decreased or absent. Increased lacrimation, salivation to the point of drooling, and occasional diaphoresis will be observed (49).

Management

Patients who are intoxicated with PCP lack sufficient judgment to care for or to protect themselves from harmful situations. The anesthesia produced by the drug makes them feel invulnerable to pain or serious injury and this is complicated by delusions of great strength. At the same time, they are unable to perceive their environment accurately and may feel threatened by innocuous objects or persons or may deliberately place themselves in positions of great physical danger. Therefore, patients intoxicated with PCP require protective supervision in a nonstimulating environment while the immediate effects of the drug wear off.

The goals of management of suspected acute phencyclidine intoxication are: (a) avoidance of injury to the patient, and (b) establishing the diagnosis. The first goal of management may be met primarily by isolation in an empty, featureless room that allows for the close but unobtrusive monitoring of behavior and vital signs. Blood pressure, respiration rate, and behavior should be continuously monitored, preferably by mechanical means such as video cameras and physiological monitoring equipment rather than direct personal contact. Depending upon the patient's level of agitation and the facilities available, restraints may be necessary. If restraints are used, they should be applied as tightly as possible without compromising circulation, in order to ensure total immobility of the patient. If the patient is unrestrained, he should not be approached unless there are adequate staff available so that immobilization and restraint can be accomplished promptly and without a struggle during which either the patient or staff members might be injured.

Despite these precautions, sedation may be necessary to manage an acutely agitated patient. Major tranquilizers should not be used for this purpose, as their use in acute phencyclidine intoxication has not been adequately tested and remains controversial at the present time. If sedation for the purpose of reducing the patient's agitation is necessary, diazepam (Valium), 10 to 20 mg intramuscularly or orally, may be used. Diazepam should not be used routinely or prophylactically, because the sedation produced by this drug may mask signs of an undetected phencyclidine or sedative overdose or of occult cerebral trauma.

The diagnosis of phencyclidine intoxication may presumptively be made in a patient with the above symptomatology if there is a history of recent (within the past 6 to 8 hours) phencyclidine use. However, the amnesia produced by phencyclidine, the uncommunicativeness of these patients, and their presenting circumstances may make obtaining a reliable history extremely difficult. The patient's belongings should be carefully searched for any leafy, powdery, or liquid matter as well as for capsules, tablets, or "joints." Test kits for phencyclidine preparations are now available through law enforcement agencies, and these should be applied to any materials found with the patient.

Although prompt and reliable tests for PCP in body fluids are not generally available, toxicological studies should be performed on blood and urine samples to rule out intoxication with other substances. The pupils should always be examined for myosis, mydriasis, and equality.

Isolated patients should be closely monitored for improvement in level of confusion, return of orientation, and reduction in agitation. These signs of improvement should be evident within 2 to 4 hours in most cases of uncomplicated phencyclidine intoxication. Patients should be kept under observation until their thought processes are rational, they are no longer disoriented, and they no longer show agitated or aggressive behavior.

After recovery, patients should be cautioned against resuming their normal activity level for 24 to 48 hours. They should remain in the company of a responsible friend or relative for this period, and both should be warned of the possible occurrence of feelings of depression, nihilism, irritability, nervousness, and isolation. Both should also be warned of the possibility of suicidal ideation or attempt or the onset of a PCP psychosis, either of which are indications for further observation or treatment.

Complications

The complications of PCP intoxication include (a) undetected PCP overdose, (b) seizures, (c) hypertensive crisis, and (d) phencyclidine psychosis.

The possibility of phencyclidine overdose should always be kept in mind when treating patients who present with PCP intoxication. Overdoses nearly always result when the drug has been taken orally, as the slower absorption of the drug through this route may result in considerable delay in the appearance of the signs and symptoms of phencyclidine overdose. The possibility of oral phencyclidine overdose should always be kept in mind in young children, in patients from whom an adequate history is unobtainable, and in those who are taken into police custody while intoxicated, as well as in those who become more intoxicated after having been taken into police custody; it is common for suspects to ingest their supply of PCP in an attempt to hide it from law enforcement authroities. Overdose should also be considered in patients who either fail to improve after 3 hours of observation or in those whose level of confusion seems to increase rather than decrease with time, especially if there is concomitant reduction in level of consciousness and continuing disorientation.

Close monitoring during the observation period is essential to detect the appearance of seizures and to prevent the occurrence of status epilepticus. Seizures are treated symptomatically with 10 to 20 mg of intravenous diazepam and intravenous phenytoin (Dilantin). If hypertension becomes severe, it should be reduced with diazoxide (Hyperstat) or hydralazine (Apresoline).

The onset of a phencyclidine psychosis is indicated by the appearance of delusions, auditory hallucinations, increased agitation, and unpredictability, as well as paranoid ideation during the period in which the patient's level of confusion lessens, his orientation returns, and his level of alertness increases. It should be noted that the absence of these signs of a phencyclidine psychosis at the time of recovery from acute phencyclidine intoxication does not rule out the possibility of their appearance within 1 or 2 weeks after the intoxication.

PHENCYCLIDINE OVERDOSE

Diagnosis

Phencyclidine overdose is clinically distinguished from phencyclidine intoxication on the basis of level of consciousness and activity: Patients with phencyclidine overdose are stuporous or comatose, whereas patients with phencyclidine intoxication at levels below overdose are cataleptoid but conscious. The most characteristic feature of phencyclidine overdose is prolonged coma that may be due to effects on the neocortex and limbic system rather than brain stem depression (85). Coma and other signs of overdose seem to result

from phencyclidine doses in excess of 20 mg (12, 51).

Although the eyes may remain open, the patient may respond only to deep pain, if at all. Hypertension is present to at least the degree observed in phencylidine intoxication but is usually more severe and is nearly always more prolonged. Respiration may be affected, depending upon the size of the overdose.

The patient is rigid, may emit occasional grunts or groans, and may show repetitive stereotyped movements. Increased oral and bronchial secretions and profuse sweating will be observed (12).

Horizontal and vertical nystagmus is always present and may appear at rest, depending upon the level of intoxication. Deep tendon reflexes are hyperactive, except in cases of massive overdose, when they are diminished. Muscles are hypertonic, but there may be repetitive, purposeless movements. Vomiting may occur but is thought to reflect by-product contamination (80).

Because of limited availability of laboratory resources for the prompt identification of phencylidine in blood and urine samples, identification of phencyclidine as the cause of the coma rests heavily upon the methods suggested in diagnosing phencyclidine overdose. Additionally, electroencephalography may be of assistance in establishing the diagnosis. Stockare and Chiappa (85) described the appearance of rhythmic theta activity sometimes interrupted by periodic slow or sharp wave complexes. Similar phenomena have been observed by Fariello and Black (32).

Pharmacokinetics

The treatment of phencyclidine overdose and of the phencyclidine psychosis has been revolutionized by Domino (who helped develop phencyclidine originally), Aronow, and Done's work on the pharmacokinetics of phencyclidine and its manipulation by pH (3, 28, 29). These studies demonstrated that the relative concentration of phencyclidine in the bodily fluids and tissues of an intoxicated person is profoundly influenced by the pH of those fluids: Absorbed phencyclidine is a lipophilic, acidophilic, and hydrophobic substance at physiological pH ranges. The serum concentration of absorbed phencyclidine rapidly reaches low serum levels not only because of hepatic metabolization, but also because it is sequestered in fatty tissue and brain tissue where it escapes hepatic metabolization. Furthermore, the drug has a half-life in these tissues that approaches 3 days at higher levels of intoxication. This accounts for the prolonged coma observed in phencyclidine overdose and may account for the persistence of the phencyclidine psychosis.

Because phencyclidine is a weak base with a pK$_a$ of about 8.5, its solubility in aqueous solution at physiological pH can be vastly increased by relatively small reductions in pH. Aronow and Done's studies indicated that PCP concentrations in the acid gastric secretions were 20 times serum levels at pH's greater than 2.5 and an average of 42 times serum levels at a gastric pH of less than 2.5. Thus, PCP in the patient's serum is secreted into his stomach at a high rate as a result of the normal production of stomach acid. Phencyclidine in the gastric contents is primarily in its ionized form and is not significantly reabsorbed there. Unfortunately, when the gastric contents are passed on into the alkaline small intestine, the PCP becomes unionized and is promptly reabsorbed into the serum. Done has termed this process the gastroentric recirculation of PCP. This same process accounts for the delayed absorption of PCP when it is taken orally, because significant absorption does not take place until the oral dose has reached the small intestine. Aronow and Done's technique takes advantage of ion trapping in the kidneys by artificially inducing urine with a pH of 5 or less. This ensures the ionization of a much higher percentage of phencyclidine in the glomerulous, minimizing reabsorption in the tubule. Diuresis is then induced to further increase glomerular filtration and excretion. Smaller proportions of PCP are retrieved through gastric suction.

Small shifts in serum pH can also have major effects on the concentration of PCP in other body fluids. Representative data from Done's study indicates that decreasing the serum pH from 7.4 to 7.2 alters the relative concentration of PCP in cerebrospinal fluid from roughly 2.5 to 1 in favor of cerebrospinal fluid to roughly 6 to 1 in favor of serum. Finally, Done's observations in the same patient showed that a reduction in urinary pH from 7.5 to 5.0 increased the urinary concentration of PCP (and therefore its rate of excretion at the same glomerular filtration rate) by roughly 100-fold.

These studies allow some additional inferences to be drawn about the dynamics of the absorption of PCP. The rapid reduction observed in serum PCP levels after PCP administration may as much be a result of rapid absorption and sequestration of PCP in fatty tissue and nervous tissue as it is a result of metabolism and excretion of the drug. Furthermore, the serum concentration of PCP is clearly a much less accurate indicator of a given patient's level of intoxication than had previously been supposed based upon experience with other psychoactive drugs. A much closer approximation of the true level of systemic intoxication may be obtained by the use of a fat biopsy (4).

Treatment

The duration of comas following phencyclidine overdose may be several hours, but a case has been reported in which the coma lasted 10 days (28). The patient should be observed for signs of respiratory depression and examined for laryngeal stridor, which indicate the need for prompt intubation and maintenance of respiration.

Aside from supportive measures, such as maintenance of respiration and electrolyte balance, the principal strategy for the treatment of phencyclidine overdose rests upon the rapid removal of the drug from the patient's system by means of ion trapping in the acidic gastric contents and by means of acidifying the urine to induce ion trapping (4).

The goals of treatment are the removal of phencyclidine-enriched gastric secretions from the patient's stomach and the enhancement of urinary excretion of phencyclidine. The first goal is accomplished by continuous gastric suction and the second by first reducing the urinary pH to 5 or lower and then promoting diuresis.

In order to accomplish removal of phencyclidine secreted into the stomach contents, a nasogastric tube should be inserted and gastric lavage performed with a liter or more of half-normal saline. The patient should then be placed on continuous gastric suction. Vital signs should be monitored every 15 minutes and electrolytes, blood gasses, and serum pH closely followed (4).

Urine pH is lowered by the administration

of ammonium chloride 2.75 mEq/kg dissolved in 60 ml of saline through the nasogastric tube every 6 hours until the urine pH is 5 or less. The patient should be catheterized and urine pH and serum carbon dioxide monitored closely so that ammonium chloride dosage can be titrated against the desired urine pH, with avoidance of CO_2 levels below 18 mEq/liter. Additionally, ascorbic acid is administered with intravenous fluids at the rate of 2,000 mg in 500 ml every 6 hours. Aronow and Done (4) advise that two doses of ammonium chloride in conjunction with intravenous ascorbic acid suffice to achieve a minor pH of 5 or less, and they recommend discontinuing gastric suction for 1 hour after the administration of ammonium chloride.

When a urine pH of 5 or less has been reached, 20 to 40 mg of furosemide (Lasix) are administered intravenously. Improvement is usually observed after the first diuresis, but a second diuresis may be necessary when the patient's fluid and electrolyte balance permits. Electroencephalographic improvement will be observed before consciousness returns.

Gastric suctioning should continue for 3 days after the patient becomes conscious, and ascorbic acid administration should continue orally until the end of hospitalization. Cranberry juice may be given liberally to help maintain acid urine. Urine acidification should continue for a week after consciousness returns. Conscious patients will show signs of phencyclidine intoxication for a time and should be managed according to the principles previously described.

Complications

The complications of phencyclidine overdose include hypertensive crisis, which may occur as long as 3 or more days postingestion, status epilepticus, opisthotonos, acute dystonia, cerebrovascular symptoms, cardiac arrhythmia, and acute renal failure (18, 23, 42, 51, 82). Acute renal failure is secondary to hypotension and myoglobinuria. Although most often these complications occur at higher levels of overdose, patients should be monitored for the occurrence of phencyclidine psychosis and other psychiatric complications of phencyclidine intoxication during the recovery phase, and psychiatric consultation and hospitalization may be necessary.

(See sections of this chapter on phencyclidine intoxication and phencyclidine psychosis).

PHENCYCLIDINE PSYCHOSIS

Diagnosis

The PCP psychosis is an acute schizophreniform psychosis that occurs in susceptible individuals after phencyclidine use and that persists for more than 24 hours. The psychosis may continue for days or weeks despite subsequent abstinence from the drug, and it characteristically becomes increasingly severe during the first few hours and days of its course. The psychosis is most commonly seen after a given individual's first or second exposure to the drug, although it may also occur in a regular daily user after a period of prolonged exposure at moderate to high doses (84).

Prodromal symptoms usually make their appearance at the time the drug is used or within the next 24 hours but may be delayed as much as a week. In some individuals, the psychosis seems to begin during the initial intoxication with PCP and to develop from that point. In other individuals, there is a latent period of several hours or several days with a relatively gradual onset of prodromal symptoms before the full blown psychosis appears. The reasons for this difference in pattern of onset are not clear, and psychoses that begin after a latent period do not seem to be qualitatively or quantitatively different from the psychoses that develop as outgrowths of the initial intoxication (55, 56, 60).

Prodromal symptoms include insomnia, restless, purposeless, or hyperactive behavior of gradually increasing intensity; bizarre, aggressive, and agitated behavior with insomnia and auditory hallucinations; and the development of persecutory and/or grandiose delusions. Additionally, there may be feelings of depersonalization and the formation of somatic delusions. Although the foregoing symptoms are most common, nearly all the symptoms and signs that have been seen in schizophrenia have also been seen in cases of PCP psychosis. Additionally, these patients may misperceive their friends, relatives, or associates as monsters or demons (55, 56, 58, 61).

These symptoms generally worsen over the course of several hours or several days until the patient presents for treatment. The presenting picture closely resembles that of an acute schizophrenic episode. A history of phencyclidine use may not be reliably obtainable on admission, either because of the confusion and florid psychotic state of the patient or because of his amnesia. Patients with prior histories of schizophrenic psychoses are exquisitely sensitive to PCP and often experience reactivations of their acute psychotic episodes after exposure to the drug even if they are on maintenance antipsychotic therapy.

Management

Based upon behavioral differences and treatment approaches, the treated PCP psychosis can be divided into three phases of approximately equal length (55, 56, 58, 61):

1. **Agitated Phase:** Agitated or cataleptic psychotic behavior; unpredictable assaultiveness; high susceptibility to environmental stimulation; anorexia and insomnia; often severe paranoia and paranoid delusions.

2. **Mixed Phase:** Alternating agitated and quiet periods; episodic waxing and waning of judgment and reality testing; gradual increase in "lucid" periods; intermittent sensitivity to environmental stimulation; psychosis may be aggravated by exercise.

3. **Resolution Phase:** Rapid disappearance of psychotic signs and reemergence of premorbid personality; reestablishment of normal sleep and eating patterns; return of normal thought processes; apparent recovery that may revert to psychosis if treatment is discontinued prematurely.

Although these phases are of approximately equal length in a given individual, the duration of the psychosis and, therefore, of each phase varies widely from patient to patient. Factors that influence the duration of the psychosis seem to include individual susceptibility to phencyclidine, degree of exposure to the drug, relative dosage of antipsychotic medications used, and whether or not urine acidification has been employed to accelerate phencyclidine excretion. The average patient spends approximately 5 days in each phase when seclusion and antipsychotic agents are employed exclusively. Urine acidification seems to reduce the length of each phase by 1 or 2 days and may also reduce the patient's requirement for antipsychotic medication. Some individuals may proceed through all three phases in as little as 24 hours or as much as 4 weeks.

The phencyclidine psychosis in its initial agitated phase constitutes a psychiatric emergency. These patients are an immediate danger to others merely on the basis of their misperceptions, paranoia, and hostility; this threat is compounded by their confusion, tendency toward violence, and the extreme unpredictability of their behavior. They also constitute a danger to themselves, not only on the basis of impaired judgment and inability to care for themselves, but also because their violent, threatening behavior may provoke lethal countermeasures by those around them.

Patients in the agitated phase of the PCP psychosis almost invariably require inpatient psychiatric treatment. Furthermore, these patients are poor candidates for voluntary treatment, first because their paranoia makes them unlikely to sign in on admission, and second because their restlessness, ambivalence, confusion, and unpredictability at this stage of the psychosis leads to a high percentage of premature discharges against medical advice. A factor that further militates against successfully continuing treatment on a voluntary basis is admission under pressure from family or friends. Patients admitted under such circumstances usually demand to leave as soon as their relatives or friends leave the hospital and cannot be dissuaded from doing so on the basis of rational discussion during this phase of their illness.

The immediate goals of treatment at this stage are: (a) prevention of injury to the patient and others, (b) assurance of continuing treatment, (c) reduction of stimuli, (d) amelioration of the psychosis, (e) reduction of agitation, and (f) detoxification.

Treatment that meets the first three of these goals includes immediate hospitalization, preferably on a voluntary basis. Isolation in a bare, locked seclusion room with frequent but unobtrusive observation is the treatment of choice. Seclusion not only safeguards other patients and staff, but also calms the patient through the reduction of stimuli that he can misperceive as threatening. As this applies particularly to the sight of other people, the patient's behavior in seclusion should be monitored through the use of concealed television cameras rather than direct personal observation if such facilities are available.

Both chlorpromazine (Thorazine) and haloperidol (Haldol) have been found to be effective toward the goals of amelioration of the psychosis and reduction of agitation. Clinical judgment and the patient's response to seclusion will indicate which antipsychotic agent is preferable in each case. The strong sedative qualities of chlorpromazine make it preferable for patients who remain hyperactive and agitated despite the absence of further stimuli in a locked seclusion room; haloperidol may be used in patients whose agitation responds to the stimulus reduction of seclusion. However, if urine acidification cannot be promptly initiated because of the patient's resistance or agitation, the patient's stay in seclusion may be prolonged if haloperidol is used instead of chlorpromazine because of the lower degree of sedation produced.

Although the use of antipsychotic agents in the treatment of PCP intoxication remains controversial, there is considerable experience with the use of these medications in the PCP psychosis, because this condition was initially routinely misdiagnosed as schizophrenia, rather than as a drug-induced psychotic reaction. Therefore, it is important to examine the patient's eye movement for the presence of horizontal or vertical nystagmus, ataxia, or slurred speech. These signs indicate PCP intoxication rather than PCP psychosis, and the patient should be treated for that condition as outlined previously rather than for the PCP psychosis as follows.

Although diazepam has been found useful for the management of agitation in phencyclidine intoxication, it has been our experience that this drug is relatively ineffective in the management of the phencyclidine psychosis at anything less than anesthetic doses. Furthermore, there is some evidence that administration of diazepam to a patient with the PCP psychosis may further aggravate the patient's agitation (25). We have treated several patients whose level of agitation became increasingly severe in emergency treatment facilities despite the administration of diazepam in dosages of up to 75 mg. Although environmental stimulation cannot be ruled out as an exacerbating factor in the agitation of these patients, it is also possible that the administration of diazepam may have further aggravated their agitation.

Because of the anticholinergic properties of antipsychotic medications, anticholinergic drug intoxication must be ruled out before initiating treatment with these agents. If chlorpromazine is utilized, the daily dose may be increased by 400 to 600 mg per day from a starting dose of 400 mg per day in divided doses. The starting dose of haloperidol for less agitated patients is 30 mg per day in divided doses, with daily increases of 20 mg per day until control of psychotic symptoms has been achieved. On the average, a daily dose of 1,600 mg per day of chlorpromazine or 80 mg per day of haloperidol has been reached by the end of the initial phase of the psychosis if the detoxification procedure that follows has not been initiated; if urine acidification is employed, improvement in psychotic symptoms may be observed at approximately two-thirds of these dose levels. It is of interest that hypotensive reactions to these medications seem to be rare in patients with the phencyclidine psychosis.

The third major treatment strategy, in addition to seclusion and the use of major antipsychotic agents, consists of the accelerated elimination of residual phencyclidine from the patient's system. Detoxification is accomplished through the administration of urine-acidifying agents, adequate hydration, and the promotion of diuresis. Although detoxification by means of urine acidification is potentially the definitive treatment for the PCP psychosis, its major drawbacks are that it requires some degree of consistent cooperation from the patient, as well as a higher frequency of staff-patient interaction. Patient compliance or cooperation is required for the frequent oral administration of acidifying agents and diuretics, as well as for the acquisition of blood specimens for electrolyte levels and urine specimens for pH testing. Similarly, these procedures require a much higher level of staff-patient interaction than may be tolerated by some extremely agitated patients. Because of these constraints, and because urine acidification is a major metabolic challenge to the patient's acid-base metabolism and, therefore, a potentially hazardous procedure, it should not be initiated unless the patient is capable of some degree of cooperation, and it should be terminated if consistent administration of acidifying agents or consistent monitoring of electrolyte levels is not possible. Urine acidification may be deferred in patients who fail to meet these criteria until seclusion and antipsychotic agents ameliorate their psychoses to a level where urine acidification is feasible.

Urine acidification is accomplished in ambulatory, agitated patients through the administration of ammonium chloride, cranberry juice, and ascorbic acid (vitamin C). Ammonium chloride is administered as a liquid solution, 500 mg/5 ml. The liquid may be made more palatable by using cherry syrup or aromatic syrup as a vehicle. Although ammonium chloride tablets may be used for this purpose, the syrup is often easier to administer to marginally cooperative patients.

Urine specimens should be obtained for pH measurements at least four times daily during the initiation of acidification. An initial loading dose of 15 to 20 ml of ammonium chloride (depending upon body weight), followed by 10 to 15 ml four times daily should produce a lowering of urine pH to 5.5 or less within 12 hours. Subsequent ammonium chloride dosage of 10 to 15 ml four times daily should be titrated according to the urine pH that is observed. pH testing may be accomplished directly in the seclusion room from specimens on the floor using commercially available Labstix.

Once a urine pH of 5.5 or less has been achieved, diuresis may be encouraged by the administration of furosemide (Lasix), 40 mg twice daily. The patient should be given 8 to 16 ounces of cranberry juice at least four times daily, and he should be encouraged to drink liberally from full juice glasses left in the seclusion room for that purpose. Oral potassium supplements will be necessary during the administration of furosemide in order to avoid potassium depletion. Serum electrolytes should be monitored daily. The administration of ascorbic acid at the rate of about 4,000 mg per day is also helpful in reducing urine pH.

Most patients will show clear signs of improvement within 6 to 48 hours after an ample diuresis has been achieved at pH of 5.5 or less. Some patients respond to urine acidification with a dramatic remission of the psychosis within 12 hours. In most patients who show a response to urine acidification, further increases in dosage of antipsychotic medication will not be necessary.

Urine acidification should continue for at least 3 days after all evidence of the psychosis has disappeared to ensure complete excretion of the residual phencyclidine. Patients should be monitored for signs of gastric irritation,

and ammonium chloride should be discontinued if epigastric pain becomes severe. Alkalinizing agents such as Maalox or Mylanta should not be administered concurrently with ammonium chloride as these agents will simply nullify each other. Gastric symptoms resulting from ammonium chloride usually remit spontaneously with discontinuation of the acidifying agent.

Most patients will require a 3- to 10-day course of urine acidification, depending upon their response to this procedure and the total amount of phencyclidine in their fatty tissues. Treatment should be discontinued in patients who fail to respond within 5 days of acidification unless there is a history of prolonged exposure to PCP through chronic use.

The transition from the *agitated phase* to the *mixed phase* is characterized by several gradual changes that become prominent in the patient around the fifth day of treatment or by the third day if urine acidification has been successfully initiated. Although restless, the patient is no longer hyperactive; he is less threatened by or overtly hostile to the presence of others in the seclusion room. He is cooperative to the extent of following simple concrete suggestions, and he accepts medication without suspicious vacillation. He can agree to seclude himself if he becomes upset.

Thus, although the patient is still confused and still demonstrates a thought disorder, hallucinations, blocking, and paranoid ideation, he is relatively calm and reasonable a good portion of the time and can accept some degree of responsibility for control of his behavior.

Despite these signs of progress, there are still intermittent periods of gross paranoia, agitation, terror, and hyperactivity alternating with quiet paranoid watchfulness. Affect remains quite constricted, and inappropriate demands that are not met immediately may cause the patient to explode in an unexpected flurry of violence. Thus, patients in the second (mixed) phase are psychotic, paranoid, unpredictable, and intermittently dangerous, although they are no longer as sensitive to stimuli as they were on admission.

The goals of treatment in this stage are (a) prevention of injury, (b) amelioration of the psychosis, (c) reduction of paranoia, and (d) detoxification.

The first goal may be met by close and continuous monitoring of behavior and a flexible seclusion policy aimed at helping the patient voluntarily to seek seclusion at the first sign that he is losing control. Operationally, a patient who sits near other patients shows stability, whereas a patient who isolates himself in a corner with his back to the wall, watching others suspiciously, requires further isolation.

Clinical judgment will indicate whether further increases in antipsychotic medication are necessary at this point. Reestablishment of sleep pattern may be aided by switching the entire dosage of antipsychotic medication to bedtime. Participation in group and milieu therapy is helpful in restoring the patient's confidence in his perceptions and in establishing rapport.

If urine acidification has been withheld because of patient noncompliance, it can usually be started successfully during the mixed phase. Urine acidification that is initiated during the mixed phase will reduce the duration of this phase from approximately 5 days to approximately 3 days or less.

The *resolution phase* begins, on the average, during the tenth day of hospitalization in patients who have not been subjected to acidification and several days earlier in patients who have had their urine acidified. The third phase is characterized by rapid reintegration of the premorbid personality and the development of insight into the events leading into the hospitalization. There is often some amnesia for the early events of the psychosis, but a history of the use of phencyclidine prior to the onset of the psychosis is usually obtained during this period. Patients may be converted to voluntary status during this stage and the groundwork for outpatient follow-up laid.

Antipsychotic medication should be tapered off and carefully discontinued during the week after remission of psychotic symptoms. Clinical judgment will indicate whether this is best done on an outpatient basis or while the patient remains hospitalized. Adequate monitoring is essential, as premature reduction or discontinuation of antipsychotic treatment will precipitate an acute reactivation of the psychosis within a few days in patients whose recovery seemed to have been complete. Therefore, it is advisable to examine the patient daily for the first 4 days after antipsychotic medication has been discontinued. Patients who have not been detoxified or whose detoxification has been terminated prematurely seem to require higher dosages of antipsychotic agents for longer periods of time in order to prevent recurrence of psychotic symptoms, as their bodies may still contain sufficient phencyclidine to cause psychotic reactivation in the absence of antipsychotic medication.

Complications

It has been our experience that at least half the patients we have treated for initial PCP psychoses use the drug again, commonly within 2 weeks of discharge. This has occurred despite repeated warnings that these patients are especially sensitive to this drug and that further exposure will precipitate another psychotic episode.

The clinical signs and symptoms of the first episode will usually be recapitulated in the second one. Consequently, patients and their family members should be thoroughly educated to be alert for recurrence of the earliest prodromal signs identified in that particular patient. Patients generally rationalize these second episodes on the basis of feeling quite well and thinking they were "strong enough" to handle the drug. Recidivism in this form has occurred despite education that the occurrence of a phencyclidine psychosis in an individual indicates hypersensitivity to the drug and that reexposure to the drug will result in another psychosis.

Approximately one-fourth of patients who experience a phencyclidine psychosis will undergo a schizophrenic psychosis within 2 years. The onset of these schizophrenic psychoses is usually gradual, follows a prodromal period, and occurs despite abstinence from PCP. Patients at risk for developing subsequent schizophrenic illness seem to be those whose response to antipsychotic agents and urine acidification is slower and more prolonged than the norm for the treated phencyclidine psychosis.

We have used urine acidification routinely for treatment of the PCP psychosis for approximately 2 years. The procedure produces dramatic improvement with some patients and more gradual, sometimes equivocal, improvement in others. The reasons for this variability are not clear, and there have been no systematic studies of the use of this method for treating PCP psychosis. However, it should be noted that systematic studies of the phencyclidine psychosis treated with antipsychotic agents alone also shows a high degree of individual variability with respect to duration and degree of the psychosis (56, 61).

A number of factors seem to influence the length and severity of the psychosis and may account for the observed variability in course: individual sensitivity to phencyclidine, dosage of phencyclidine, duration of exposure, amount of residual phencyclidine in brain and other fatty tissues, concomitant use of other psychotogenic drugs, and environmental factors.

Of these, it seems that individual sensitivity to phencyclidine is the most important factor contributing to the occurrence of the psychosis in an individual as well as its subsequent duration. Inasmuch as the vast majority of occasional phencyclidine users do not develop a phencyclidine psychosis, and because most of those who develop the psychosis do so after their first or second exposure to the drug, the PCP psychosis more closely resembles an idiosyncratic hypersensitivity reaction than a direct drug effect. Moreover, the tendency for those patients who have longer and more severe phencyclidine psychoses subsequently to develop schizophrenia points to a susceptibility to that illness as the most likely source for an individual's hypersensitivity to phencyclidine. This relationship is more fully explored in the portion of this chapter entitled "Phencyclidine and Schizophrenia."

CHRONIC PHENCYCLIDINE USE

There have been relatively few systematic studies of chronic phencyclidine use; therefore, little is known about the effect of chronic use of the substance. Lerner and Burns (49) conducted a study of 15 male and five female chronic phencyclidine users to describe chronic use patterns and to determine evidence of chronic toxicity. Selection criteria for the study required that reported use occur at a frequency of at least 3 or more days per week for a duration of at least 6 months without concurrent heavy use of other drugs. The cumulative period of regular use from first exposure to the time of study ranged from 6 months to 5½ years, with a mean duration of use of 27½ months. The users were found sporadically to increase

their phencyclidine use in 2- to 3-day bursts of continuous and uninterrupted drug taking without sleep.

Ninety per cent of those studied used phencyclidine in the form of cigarettes, and the remainder administered it by nasal insufflation. The average estimated daily intake for the smokers was approximately 216 mg, with maximum daily usage reported to be 1 g. These users reported that the subjective effects of the drug began within 1 to 5 minutes of smoking and reached a peak or plateau within 5 to 30 minutes after the drug had been used, with the average intoxication lasting 4 to 6 hours.

The majority of these phencyclidine users had their first exposure to the drug in a social setting and found the experience pleasant. The intoxication was reported as being very intense, with profound effects on the user's thinking, time perception, sense of reality, and mood. A prominent effect was described as "no more reality." Users reported perceiving situations as being complete and making more sense. There were frequent reports of floating sensations, as well as feelings of enhanced strength and endurance. They described feeling powerful, superior, and arrogant, with bursts of energy. Mood states were reported to be intensified with a predominance of euphoric or happy feelings. On the other hand, all the users had experienced severe depressions or other adverse reactions and recognized the drug's potential for "bringing one to either the heights or the depths of being." Sensory modalities were intermingled: music was absorbed, light was felt, and depth became two dimensional. Visual hallucinations were extremely rare.

Most of these chronic phencyclidine users took the drug in a social setting and did so because they liked the "high." Groups of phencyclidine users were identified who shared in the use of their common supply and remained stable over long periods of regular use. They tended to isolate themselves from others and to continue their phencyclidine use around the clock from time to time.

Tolerance was reported by this group of chronic users in the sense that they had to increase their drug intake in order to achieve the same psychic effects. Psychological dependence, which was described as a craving for the drug, was also reported, although none of the users experienced any withdrawal effects upon discontinuation of use.

Reported physiological effects of regular use included insomnia, anorexia, constipation, and urinary hesitancy. Regular users were found to eat less than one meal per day and to lose between 10 and 35 pounds during periods of intensified use. They reported persistent problems with memory and speech and difficulty with thinking after long periods of regular drug use. Memory impairment was limited to recent events and was manifested by frequent episodes of disorientation. Speech problems consisted of stuttering, blocking, and impaired articulation. These last effects were noted to persist for 6 months to 1 year after daily use of large doses of phencyclidine.

Other psychological effects found in this sample included anxiety, nervousness, severe depressions, suicide attempts, personality changes, social withdrawal, and isolation, as well as occasional bursts of violent behavior. Lerner and Burns also found that some episodes of chronic phencyclidine use were terminated by psychotic episodes characterized by violent, aggressive behavior with paranoid delusions and auditory hallucinations in patients with no prior psychiatric histories. These patients had typically used phencyclidine for several months or several years with the same group of friends prior to the onset of the psychotic episodes.

The principal effects of chronic phencyclidine use, therefore, seem to be psychological and neurological. Chronic users associate with each other, isolate themselves from nonusers, and spend their time experiencing the drug's effects. During periods of peak drug use, they eat and sleep very little and may lose a great deal of weight, a pattern reminiscent of that seen in amphetamine users. The chronic use of phencyclidine for several months may result in the appearance of a phencyclidine psychosis. Those users who do not experience psychotic reactions have persistent difficulty with recent memory, blocking, and persistent slurring of speech and disarticulation for several months after abstinence begins. However, horizontal and vertical nystagmus is the only neurological sign that persists for more than 48 hours after abstinence begins. Although some degree of psychological tolerance seems to occur with repeated use of the drug, no consistent withdrawal syndrome has been identified. It is particularly noteworthy that hepatotoxicity has not been reported with frequent and chronic use of this drug.

PHENCYCLIDINE AND SCHIZOPHRENIA

Just as phencyclidine has been difficult to classify as a drug using traditional categories, the phencyclidine psychosis poses classification problems as a mental disorder. Since it was first identified in 1974, the phencyclidine psychosis has been unusual in that it is a drug-induced psychosis with symptomatology that more closely resembles that of a functional psychosis than had been true of previously described drug-induced psychotic states. Additional characteristics that distinguish it from most other toxic psychoses include its prolonged duration and the tendency for some of those who apparently recover from the phencyclidine psychosis subsequently to develop schizophrenia. Finally, phencyclidine itself is unusual because of the peculiar hypersensitivity shown by schizophrenics to its effects. Nevertheless, the phencyclidine psychosis' curious amalgam of organic and functional aspects provides a link of unusual theoretical interest between these two major categories of psychiatric illness.

The disorganizing and psychotogenic effects of PCP on schizophrenics are remarkable in that chronic schizophrenics tend to be highly resistant to such other drugs as LSD and mescaline and can subjectively distinguish the effects of these drugs from their psychosis (53).

Among normals as well as schizophrenics, LSD, amphetamine, mescaline, etc., tend to mimic the secondary or restitutional signs of schizophrenia, as well as produce symptoms rarely seen among schizophrenics, such as kaleidoscopic visual hallucinatory phenomena. In contrast, PCP's effects are impressively similar (if not identical) to the primary signs of schizophrenia, including formal thought disorder and social withdrawal (34, 53).

Model psychosis studies have provided confirmation of these clinical impressions. Groups of chronic schizophrenics were compared with normals who had been administered either PCP, LSD, or amobarbital (Amytal). PCP was the only one of the three drugs producing in normals the deficit level of schizophrenics in tests of attention, motor function, proprioception, and capacity for appropriate abstract thinking (54, 74, 75).

Some authors have postulated that the distinctive effects of PCP in contrast to other psychoactive drugs may be based on PCP's function as an inhibitor of sensory input. Domino's (24) neurological investigations provide evidence that phencyclidine impairs the responses of the central nervous system to all sensory inputs, particularly proprioceptive, in contrast to other psychotomimetic drugs, which often enhance sensations. He reported that "the psychic state crudely resembles sensory isolation, except that sensory impulses, if tested electrophysiologically, reach the neocortex, but the neuronal signals are grossly distorted" (25).

Luby et al. (53) speculated that the impaired transmission or central integration of proprioceptive feedback constitutes a necessary condition for the schizophrenomimetic effects of PCP. They suggested that the same mechanism may underlie transient psychoses due to sleep deprivation and sensory isolation. Following Federn, they proposed that depersonalization may be the core of schizophrenia and the PCP intoxication psychosis and that disturbed body input transmission may be its basis. Later research has shown evidence for a proprioceptive deficit in schizophrenia that is due to inadequate sensory input and not to insufficient proprioceptive memory (72).

A competing (although by no means incompatible) theory of PCP's schizophrenomimetic effects involves the effects of the drug on general neurotransmission. PCP selectively enhances the sensitivity of adrenergic and serotonergic neurons to their neurotransmitters, and this enhancement persists long after the drug has been fully metabolized. (25). Luisada and Brown (58) speculated that this prolonged enhancement of sensitivity could account not only for PCP's psychotogenic effects in normals and its prolonged exacerbation of psychoses in schizophrenics, but also for the longer psychoses seen in susceptible nonschizophrenics. Meltzer and Stahl (64) suggested that the dopaminergic or anticholinergic properties of PCP, or some combination thereof, may be responsible for the psychotomimetic effects of the drug. Levy et al. (50) found that the psychotomimetic

effects of PCP intoxication were antagonized by chlorpromazine, and Helrich and Atwood (43) reported similar observations with haloperidol. Levy et al. (50) speculated that there is a common physiological mechanism linking PCP intoxication with acute paranoid and schizophrenic reactions. Although the evidence for PCP-induced alterations of neurotransmitter function is impressive, it should be noted that there is no neurotransmitter explanation at this point for the superiority of PCP over other psychotomimetic drugs in reproducing the schizophrenic psychosis.

Until 1974, only two forms of psychotic reaction to PCP were recognized: (a) a schizophrenic syndrome lasting several hours in "normals" and (b) an extreme exacerbation of their original psychoses lasting up to 6 weeks in chronic schizophrenics. Basing their findings on a review of a recent epidemic of what seemed to be unusually long, severe, and treatment-resistant acute schizophrenic psychoses, Luisada and Reddick (60) reported the existence of a PCP-induced psychosis that lasted an average of 2 weeks in patients with no previous history of psychotic episodes and often no previous psychiatric history at all. This study found that, out of 11 patients meeting strict criteria for PCP psychosis (a history of exclusive PCP use during the 2 months prior to admission), six were readmitted after smoking the drug again. However, two patients returned later with briefer psychoses in the absence of drug use and showed evidence of chronicity upon remission of the spontaneous psychosis.

Luisada and Reddick noted that the PCP psychosis was extremely difficult to differentiate clinically from an acute schizophrenic episode, but they suggested that PCP psychoses would be partially distinguished by the following features: (a) lack of an extended prodrome in the history; (b) the high incidence of violent, aggressive, or threatening behavior; (c) marked tension and anxiety bordering on panic, including terror of their own delusions; and (d) occasionally gross perceptual distortions in the visual sphere. Luisada (56) also noted that these patients tend to be more independent of their families than schizophrenics.

The extent to which PCP psychosis depends on preexisting psychopathological or biochemical factors continues to be an unanswered question, although the contribution of these individual predispositions has been thought to be substantial. Luisada and Reddick (61) suggested that PCP psychosis falls between the brief psychosis experienced by normal volunteers and the exacerbation of symptoms observed in chronic schizophrenics. They speculated that, because sensitivity varies with the individual and this sensitivity varies between extreme for schizophrenics and mild for "normals," the patients they studied may fall on a graded continuum between those who are most "schizophrenic" in terms of their neurophysiology and those who are least so.

Fauman et al. (33) argued that PCP psychosis is rare considering the extent of PCP use and suggested that the individuals who develop such psychoses may have premorbid personalities similar to those of LSD and marihuana users who experienced prolonged psychiatric difficulty. However, they concluded that the PCP psychosis is a drug effect rather than a brief functional psychosis precipitated by the disorganizing PCP experience, but that the drug effect works in combination with a vulnerable, pathological personality (see also 36).

Smith et al. (84) also considered the PCP-precipitated psychotic episode to be a functional psychosis that may occur after a single-dose administration and that the majority of patients with PCP-precipitated psychoses have had prepsychotic or psychotic personalities. They considered the distinction between PCP toxic psychosis and PCP-precipitated psychotic episodes to be vital, in that they believed that PCP-precipitated psychoses require long term antipsychotic drug maintenance.

A closely related question concerns whether and to what extent PCP may precipitate the development of chronic schizophrenia. Luisada and Reddick (61) reported that two of their 11 patients returned with briefer psychoses in the absence of any drug use, followed by "typical postpsychotic schizophrenic personality changes." Although this finding is often cited in the literature as evidence for long term psychiatric sequelae of PCP psychosis (33, 56), it has yet to be replicated. Moreover, we have no way of determining whether those two patients would have developed a chronic schizophrenic picture regardless of whether they had used PCP.

Therefore, the phencyclidine psychosis may constitute: (a) an unusually persistent version of the toxic psychosis observed by Greifenstein et al. (42), Luby et al. (53), Davies and Beech (20), and other researchers who worked with normal volunteers; (b) a true acute schizophrenic episode precipitated by the transient depersonalization and other disorganizing effects of the drug, disrupting unstable defenses and unmasking hidden psychopathology; (c) a combination of (a) and (b) such that it is a toxic psychosis to which those with "borderline" or "prepsychotic personalities" are particularly vulnerable; (d) a true schizophrenic episode that is initiated by a special biochemical sensitivity to the drug; (e) one of a class of psychoses with similar phenomenology involving different underlying processes with different patients. A final, more radical alternative is (f) the PCP psychosis and schizophrenia are different labels for the same organic psychosis, which is called PCP psychosis when its etiology is PCP use and schizophrenia when its etiology is unknown.

Which of these alternatives best explains the pathophysiology of the PCP psychosis remains a matter of speculation. The question has a number of important implications. If PCP psychosis is a sui generis disorder, special care must be taken to distinguish it from schizophrenia in terms of its epidemiology, diagnosis, course, treatment, and prognosis. If it represents a drug-induced exacerbation of underlying prepsychotic psychopathology, clinicians should be made aware of the special danger PCP poses for their drug-abusing borderline patients and should consider the use of maintenance antipsychotics after the episode. If PCP is a true schizophrenogenic drug through some biological action on physiologically vulnerable individuals, the nature of this mechanism and the vulnerability should be of paramount interest for both clinicians and researchers studying the biochemistry of schizophrenia.

Erard et al.'s recently reported study attempted to answer these questions (31). A sample of 35 cases of phencyclidine psychosis was compared to 11 cases of acute schizophrenia on the basis of 57 demographic or treatment variables and 54 symptom variables. The patients were all treated at the Area D Community Mental Health Center during the 4-year period 1973 to 1977, although none of the phencyclidine-related cases had been treated with urine acidification.

This study was able to find remarkably few statistically significant differences between these two groups in terms of presenting symptomatology or course in treatment. Demographic variables that were found to differentiate those patients with phencyclidine psychoses from the schizophrenics included a six to one preponderance of males in the phencyclidine sample, versus an even sex distribution in the schizophrenics, and a significantly higher incidence of school problems and non-drug-related brushes with the law in the phencyclidine group.

However, PCP psychotics were no more likely to have displayed threatening, violent, or assaultive behavior prior to hospitalization or during treatment; they were no more likely than schizophrenics to be admitted voluntarily; there were no significant differences in "resistance to treatment" as measured by length of stay, highest per diem dosage of antipsychotic medication, total time spent in seclusion, and number of discharges against medical advice. Moreover, significantly more PCP psychotics than schizophrenics become extremely anxious or panicky. Other symptoms that failed to differentiate PCP psychosis from schizophrenia at statistically significant levels included elation, insomnia, suspiciousness, nudism, negativism, body image disturbances, preoccupation with death, disorientation, confusion, and memory problems. There were also no significant differences in improvement category or number of readmissions.

The few symptom variables that were found to be significantly more common in PCP psychotics included elevated serum glutamic-oxaloacetic transaminase levels, poor judgment, and visual hallucinations. Symptoms that occurred more frequently in schizophrenics included extreme anxiety/panic, religious preoccupation, persecutory and grandiose delusions, depression, disheveled appearance, and poor judgment.

Forty-six per cent of the phencyclidine group were readmitted after their index admission, and 17 per cent of the phencyclidine group were diagnosed as having acute schizophrenia on their most recent admission in the absence of further drug use. Finally, 5 per cent of the phencyclidine group were later diagnosed as chronic schizophrenics.

What seems most striking about these findings is a lack of statistically significant differences between the PCP psychotics and acute schizophrenics. Comparisons of the two groups on data concerning demographic characteristics, status prior to hospitalization, hospital course, physiological measures, and outcome provide little evidence to differentiate these patients beyond what one would intuitively suspect on the basis of the fact that one group abuses drugs and the other does not. Thus, as is true of PCP users generally when compared to the rest of the population, they were more likely to be male, to have had more trouble with the law, to have poor judgment, to have visual hallucinations, and to have liver pathology.

On the other hand, the various suggestions in the literature for differentiating PCP psychosis from an acute schizophrenic episode were not confirmed. PCP psychotics were not found to be more violent, panicky, resistant to treatment, or "organic" (e.g., disoriented, confused, or ataxic) than acute schizophrenics. However, it is possible that the measures used in this study, which was retrospective and based entirely on chart data, may have been too gross or that the size of the schizophrenic sample may have been too small to reveal some of the subtler differences that may exist.

Breakey et al. (10) studied 40 hospitalized schizophrenics, 26 of whom had taken hallucinogenic drugs prior to the onset of their illness ("users") and 14 of whom had not used drugs. They found significant differences in age of onset, age of admission, and premorbid personality between the two groups. The mean age of admission for schizophrenics who used drugs prior to onset was 21; for nonusers it was 25. This closely approximates the age difference observed in Erard et al.'s (31) study: 22 for PCP psychotics and 25 for nonuser acute schizophrenics. They found that premorbid personality scores for "users" were slightly lower than the scores for nonusers, suggesting that the users had healthier premorbid personalities.

The fact that Breakey et al.'s "user" patients had better premorbid functioning but were hospitalized earlier than the nonusers, taken together with the fact that users and nonusers alike met strict Research Diagnostic Criteria for the diagnosis of schizophrenia, furnishes presumptive evidence that the taking of drugs in general (e.g., amphetamine, marihuana, hashish, or mescaline) "may play a precipitating role in the onset of schizophrenia, bringing this disorder on more quickly, and to patients who seem somewhat less constitutionally vulnerable" (10).

These findings raise the question of whether we are perhaps looking at the same phenomenon under different labels. Are the PCP psychotics merely a subclass of Breakey et al.'s "acute schizophrenics with pre-onset drug histories"—people who were perhaps functioning a little better over-all than the nonabusing preschizophrenics but whose inevitable psychosis was touched off by the PCP experience?

Given Erard et al.'s (31) findings, it seems reasonable to regard PCP psychosis tentatively as a special form of acute schizophrenic episode precipitated and exacerbated by ingestion of the drug in certain susceptible individuals. Further research will be necessary to confirm this view and to establish the particular clinical and prognostic significance of drug-precipitated schizophrenic episodes. More systematic investigation of the premorbid and postmorbid personalities of patients with PCP-precipitated psychotic episodes, including personal and family interviews, psychological testing, and periodic follow-ups, would be particularly desirable.

Another central question for further research has to do with the nature of susceptibility to PCP, particularly the mechanism of action by which the drug precipitates a schizophrenic reaction. Does phencyclidine's alteration of neurotransmitter levels (25) produce a pathogenic imbalance in physiologically susceptible individuals? Is the effect mediated by the depersonalization and distortion of body image resulting from the reduction of proprioceptive cues (53), or is the effect caused by some combination of neural biochemicals and psychological mechanisms?

Answers to these questions may have significant implications regarding the nature of vulnerability to schizophrenia and perhaps even its physiological and psychological bases. Neurological and psychological study of individuals in remission from PCP-precipitated psychoses—in comparison with nonabusing schizophrenics, amphetamine psychotics, and PCP abusers in general—would be helpful in exploring these issues.

A final question raised by Erard et al.'s (31) findings relates to what effects the use of urine acidification might have on these results. None of the patients in that study were subjected to urine acidification, as the procedure was not in general use at the time they were hospitalized. Although urine acidification is now in general use, the evidence of its effectiveness remains at an anecdotal level. A decline in new cases of PCP psychosis continues to hamper efforts to assemble for study a sample of patients treated with urine acidification that can meet the necessary selection criteria in sufficient numbers to be statistically meaningful.

In conclusion, the use of phencyclidine poses special hazards to schizophrenics and to other susceptible individuals in that it can precipitate schizophrenic psychosis in these groups. Additionally, our results support the notion that the phencyclidine psychosis is an acute schizophrenic psychosis initiated by phencyclidine intoxication. However, the question of whether the phencyclidine psychosis has an organic or functional cause remains unanswered.

The study of drug-induced "model psychoses" as such has been repeatedly disappointing. As this study shows, the phenomenology of the PCP psychosis resembles what has been called schizophrenia even more closely than had previously been supposed. The notion that a specific drug may produce specific psychiatric sequelae that are distinguishable from both the direct effects of drug intoxication and from the naturally occurring disorder it mimics continues to be highly questionable. The most fruitful path for future theory and research in this field may be to try to understand the interface between the drug effect and the naturally occurring syndrome (schizophrenia), rather than treating the drug effect as an analogue of the syndrome. Hopefully, such research will shed light on both components—how the drug works, and how the natural syndrome may be precipitated.

IMPLICATIONS OF PHENCYCLIDINE FOR DRUG ABUSE PREVENTION

PCP may be a harbinger of future trends and problems in the field of drug abuse and drug abuse prevention. It is a completely synthetic drug that can be made from basic chemicals. Its manufacture is relatively simple and has been reduced to the level of cookbook formulas that are in active circulation and have reached a wide distribution. It can be manufactured under relatively primitive conditions, does not require the installation of sophisticated or complex laboratory equipment, and does not require the purchase or importation of exotic substances or the cultivation of specific botanicals. For the first time it has been possible for an individual entrepreneur to manufacture an extremely potent psychoactive substance without recourse to the legitimate pharmaceutical or the illicit drug markets for raw materials, equipment, or supplies.

A second aspect of this problem results from the existence of an operational nationwide network for the distribution of illicit psychoactive substances. The growing social acceptance and increased recreational use of marihuana by the American middle class over the past 15 years has nurtured the growth of an extralegal distribution system for illicit substances, because to a large extent it consists of middle-class individuals with no other criminal activity who sell primarily to each other. The system provides a ready market for any person with any psychoactive substance to sell in large or small quantities and a ready medium for word-of-mouth advertising. Thus, an entrepreneur who was interested in establishing himself as a manufacturer of phencyclidine prior to the control of piperidine could do so without recourse to the more traditional illicit drug distribution channels, not only for supply of raw materials or production, but also for marketing.

The consequences of these developments imply a major shift in the pattern of domestic illicit drug distribution. Rather than a high centralized supply system, with a few importers shipping and distributing larger proportions of the total drug supply from foreign sources, phencyclidine permits a decentralized supply system, with a multiplicity of small domestic manufacturers feeding the distribution system at multiple points and in relatively small quantities. This vastly complicates the task of law enforcement agencies charged with the responsibility of drug abuse control.

The control of piperidine may result in a significant reduction in phencyclidine production. However, the circumstances that made it possible for a new synthetic psychoactive substance with phencyclidine's propensity for adverse reactions to assume nation-wide acceptance, production, and usage in less than 7 years still remain. Moreover, because phencyclidine was a relatively unknown drug to law enforcement, drug abuse prevention, drug abuse detection, and drug treatment authorities, there was a lag of several years between the time it first appeared in general use and the time it was generally recognized as a major drug problem. These circumstances are also essentially unchanged. Paradoxically, restrictions in the availability of piperidine may stimulate underemployed phencyclidine producers to search for other, as yet uncontrolled, psychoactive substances and to convert their facilities to the production of such substances, inasmuch as the financial incentives for such activities remain enormous.

An appreciation of the significance of phencyclidine's ascent to nation-wide distribution in such a short time may be gained by considering the efforts legitimate manufacturers make to achieve this goal with such consumer products as a new brand of margarine, whiskey, or soap. Even established firms with national distribution of familiar consumer products plan the marketing strategy for the introduction of a product with great care. After the investment of painstaking design of the product and its container in all its aspects, a period of test marketing begins. The product is introduced with announcements in all appropriate media. Representatives provide stores with special displays, barter for prime space, and provide free samples. Consumer reactions to product, packaging, and advertisements are monitored, and each of these may be redesigned to maximize sales.

PCP achieved its current level of distribution and consumer acceptance largely without the benefit of such marketing techniques. To some degree, this success is a reflection of the ever-rising level of social acceptance of the use of drugs for recreational purposes in contemporary America. PCP's success is also a measure of the level of demand which currently exists for psychoactive substances. Finally, PCP's success is a measure of the underground distribution system's ability to deliver new psychoactive substances to consumers.

Therefore, it seems extremely likely that the next major drug of abuse in the United States will involve another, as yet unnamed, synthetic psychoactive substance with unknown adverse effects that can be readily produced from commonly available materials and that is presently uncontrolled and generally unknown to drug abuse enforcement, prevention, or treatment agencies. If it follows the pattern of phencyclidine, it will first appear in some part of the United States. Next, formulas for its production will circulate, and small entrepreneurs in a number of cities will begin its manufacture. Its initial distribution will then follow the same channels as PCP, namely the undergound marihuana distribution network in multiple states. Depending upon the nature and severity of its clinical symptoms, the drug will remain undetected and unrecognized by law enforcement or drug abuse treatment agencies for an unknown latent period. Once it has been recognized as a major problem, there will be a delay of at least another year before legislative efforts toward its control are completed.

If there is a lesson to be learned from phencyclidine, it is that the current situation strongly favors the development, production, and swift widespread use of new psychoactive substances, whether or not their side effects or symptoms are clinically toxic or severe.

What can be done about the current situation to prevent or curtail the appearance of successive generations of increasingly hazardous synthetic psychoactive substances in the United States? There are several possible strategies: control of raw materials, control of manufacturers, control of distributors, control of the distribution network, and early detection of new drugs of abuse.

Control of raw materials has been the traditional approach to the regulation of the use of psychoactive substances in the United States. In the case of the opiates, cocaine, and marihuana, recent control efforts have focused on the countries where the plants harvested for the production of these substances are grown. Other efforts have focused on the detection of illegal importation and the detection of major transshipping centers. These efforts are, of course, futile with respect to substances that can be synthesized domestically from commonly available raw materials that do not require importation.

Efforts to control phencyclidine have focused on the raw material piperidine, a previously uncontrolled chemical with wide application in the plastics and rubber industry.

However, it is impractical to control all potential raw materials for psychoactive substances that are currently available in the United States. Therefore, control of the raw materials for the production of illicit psychoactive substances rests upon the swift identification of those raw materials that are being diverted for this purpose, and this will inevitably introduce a time lag. This approach has the additional disadvantage of requiring a new psychoactive substance to appear in general use in order for its precursors to be controlled.

It was possible to exert some degree of control on manufacturers of illicit psychoactive substances as long as these drugs were produced primarily from raw materials that were derived from foreign vegetable sources. This approach is significantly less effective in the case of a domestically produced synthetic drug. Furthermore, as can be seen from the case of phencyclidine, the detection and effective control of hundreds of thousands of small, independent, individual manufacturers requires law enforcement resources far exceeding those that have been available to date. The effective control of small scale, local manufacturers does not currently seem to be feasible.

As with the case of manufacturers, effective control of an illicit drug distribution system requires that it be relatively centralized. Again, this has not been the case with phencyclidine and will probably not be the case with the next synthetic psychoactive substance that appears in the United States.

Control of the current marihuana distribution network in the United States would seem to be an effective means of reducing the probability that a new synthetic psychoactive substance could readily reach a broad market. However, the current extralegal marihuana distribution system is so pervasive and infiltrates so many classes and strata of society within the United States that its interdiction would require the arrest and incarceration of a significant proportion of the national population. As was the case during national Prohibition, significant numbers of otherwise law-abiding citizens flagrantly break the law and provide the necessary cash flow to sustain the importation and distribution of vast quantities of a single psychoactive substance.

The control of the next synthetic psychoactive substance to appear in the United States will, therefore, rest heavily upon early detection, not only for purposes of alerting the public to the identified dangers of this substance, but also for purposes of promptly studying it, developing treatment strategies, and, lastly, controlling its raw materials. Another lesson of the phencyclidine experience has been that current systems for the detection of the abuse of new drugs are inadequate. Because of phencylidine's propensity for appearing under assumed names, because it was initially misclassified as a hallucinogen, because it was a drug of a completely new class, and because it was distributed through new channels, drug abuse authorities at the national level were unaware of its existence as a major drug abuse problem until phencyclidine abuse had reached epidemic proportions. Our present system for the early detection of drug abuse patterns is clearly not up to detecting hitherto unclassified or unknown drugs of abuse. An improved capability for detecting the abuse of drugs that do not fall within currently recognized categories must be developed. At the same time, a system for promptly alerting legislators about the identity and effects of new drugs of abuse must be developed.

In conclusion, the outlook for drug abuse prevention in the United States is not good and is likely to become worse. The factors that enabled phencyclidine to achieve nationwide distribution and use in less than a decade remain essentially unchanged and do not seem to be easily amenable to change. As LSD was the drug of the 1960's and as PCP became the drug of the 1970's, "drug X" may well become the drug of the 1980's. Although such comparisons are imprecise, PCP overshadows LSD in its overdose toxicity and behavioral toxicity, in its adverse effects on schizophrenics, and in its psychotogenic potential. If "drug X" continues the trend in this decade, one can anticipate even greater problems to come.

Acknowledgments. The author gratefully acknowledges the helpful assistance of Mary Lou O'Brien of The Mount Vernon Hospital and Sally Feldner of The Mount Vernon Community Mental Health Center in the preparation of the manuscript and the references.

This chapter presents the views of the author and should not be construed as representing those of the National Institute of Mental Health, the Area D Community Mental Health Center, The Mount Vernon Center for Community Mental Health, or The Mount Vernon Hospital.

References

1. Allen, R. M., and Young, S. J. Phencyclidine-induced psychosis. Am. J. Psychiatry 135:1081, 1978.
2. Anonymous. Congress considers bill to control angel dust. Science 200:1463, 1978.
3. Aronow, R., et al. Clinical observation during phencyclidine intoxication and treatment based on iontrapping. In *PCP Abuse: An Appraisal*. NIDA Research Monograph #21. Washington, D.C., United States Government Printing Office, 1978.
4. Aronow, R., and Done, A. K. Phencyclidine overdose: An emerging concept of management. J. Am. Coll. Emerg. Phys. 7:56, 1978.
5. Bakker, C. B., and Amini, F. B. Observations on the psychotomimetic effects of Sernyl. Compr. Psychiatry 2:269, 1961.
6. Balster, R., and Chait, L. The behavioral pharmacology of phencyclidine. Clin. Toxicol. 9:513, 1976.
7. Balster, R. L., and Chait, L. D. The behavioral effects of phencyclidine in animals. In *PCP Abuse: An Appraisal*. NIDA Research Monograph #21. Washington, D.C., United States Government Printing Office, 1978.
8. Balster, R. L., and Chait, L. D. The effects of phencyclidine on amphetamine stereotypy in rats. Eur. J. Pharmacol. 48:445, 1978.
9. Ban, T. A., Lohrenz, J. J., and Lehamann, H. E. Observations on the action of Sernyl—a new psychotropic drug. Can. Psychiatr. Assoc. J. 6:150, 1961.
10. Breakey, W. R., Goodell, H., Lohrenz, P. E., and McHugh, P. R. Hallucinogenic drugs as precipitants of schizophrenia. Psychol. Med. 4:225, 1974.
11. Burns, R., Lerner, S., and Corrado, R. Phencyclidine: States of acute intoxication and fatalities. West. J. Med. 123:345, 1975.
12. Burns, R. S., and Lerner, S. E. Perspectives: Acute phencyclidine intoxication. Clin. Toxicol. 9:477, 1976.
13. Burns, R. S., and Lerner, S. E. Causes of phencyclidine-related deaths. Clin. Toxicol. 12:463, 1978.
14. Burns, R. S., and Lerner, S. E. Phencyclidine deaths. J. Am. Coll. Emerg. Phys. 7:135, 1978.
15. Chen, G., Ensor, C. R., Russell, D., and Bohner, B. The pharmacology of 1-(1-phenylcyclohexyl)piperidine HCl. J. Pharmacol. Exp. Ther. 127:241, 1959.
16. Cohen, S. Angel dust. J.A.M.A. 238:515, 1977.
17. Cohen, S. M. The "angel dust" states: Phencyclidine toxicity. Pediatrics 64:17, 1979.
18. Crossley, C., and Binet, E. Cerebrovascular complications in phencyclidine intoxication. J. Pediatr. 94:316, 1979.
19. Davies, B. M. Phencyclidine: Its use in psychiatry. In *The Proceedings of the Quarterly Meeting of the Royal Medico-Psychological Association*, R. Crocket, R. A. Sandison, and A. Walk, editors. London, H. K. Lewis, 1963.
20. Davies, B. M., and Beech, H. R. The effect of l-arylcyclohexylamine (Sernyl) on twelve normal volunteers. J. Ment. Sci. 106:912, 1960.
21. Delgado, J. M. *Physical Control of the Mind: Toward*

a *Psychocivilized Society.* New York, Harper and Row, 1971.

22. Doherty, J. D. Reserpine and PCP psychosis (letter). Am. J. Psychiatry 136:1618, 1979.

23. Dolan, M. PCP: A plague whose time has come. Am. Pharm. 18:23, 1978.

24. Domino, E. F. Neurobiology of phencyclidine (Sernyl), a drug with an unusual spectrum of pharmacological activity. Int. Rev. Neurobiol. 6:303, 1964.

25. Domino, E. F. Neurobiology of phencyclidine—An update. In *PCP Abuse: An Appraisal.* NIDA Research Monograph #21. Washington, D.C., United States Government Printing Office, 1978.

26. Domino, E. F. Treatment of phencyclidine intoxication (letter). J.A.M.A. 241:2505, 1979.

27. Domino, E. F., Chodoff, P., and Corssen, G. Pharmacologic effects of CI-581, a new dissociative anesthetic in man. Clin. Pharmacol. Ther. 6:279, 1965.

28. Domino, E. F., and Wilson, A. E. Effects of urine acidification on plasma and urine phencyclidine levels in overdosage. Clin. Pharmacol. Ther. 22:421, 1977.

29. Done, A. K., Aronow, R., and Micelli, J. N. The pharmacokinetics of phencyclidine in overdosage and its treatment. In *PCP Abuse: An Appraisal.* NIDA Research Monograph #21. Washington, D.C., Government Printing Office, 1978.

30. Ease of production, high profits, tied to widespread PCP abuse. U.S. Med. 29: July 15, 1978.

31. Erard, R., Luisada, P., and Peele, R. PCP psychosis and schizophrenia: A controlled study. Paper presented at the 133rd meeting of American Psychiatric Association, San Francisco, May 3–9, 1980.

32. Fariello, R., and Black, J. Pseudoperiodic bilateral EEG paroxysms. J. Clin. Psychiatry 40:154, 1979.

33. Fauman, B., Aldinger, G., Fauman, M., and Rosen, P. Psychiatric sequelae of phencyclidine abuse. Clin. Toxicol. 9:429, 1976.

34. Fauman, B., Baker, F., Coppleson, L. W., Rosen, P., and Segal, M. B. Psychosis induced by phencyclidine. J. Am. Coll. Emerg. Phys. 4:223, 1975.

35. Fauman, B. J. PCP abuse (editorial). J. Am. Coll. Emerg. Phys. 7:255, 1978.

36. Fauman, M. A., and Fauman, B. J. The psychiatric aspects of chronic phencyclidine (PCP) use: A study of chronic phencyclidine users. In *PCP Abuse: An Appraisal.* NIDA Research Monograph #21. Washington, D.C., United States Government Printing Office, 1978.

37. Fauman, M. A., and Fauman, B. J. Violence associated with phencyclidine abuse. Am. J. Psychiatry 136:1584, 1979.

38. Forester, D. PCP treatment . . . continued. Clin. Toxicol. 14:209, 1979.

39. Fox, S. M. Haloperidol in the treatment of phencyclidine intoxication. Am. J. Hosp. Pharm. 36:448, 1978.

40. Garfield, S. L. Research problems in clinical diagnosis. J. Consult. Clin. Psychol. 46:496, 1978.

41. Graeven, D. B. Patterns of phencyclidine use. In *PCP Abuse: An Appraisal.* NIDA Research Monograph #21. Washington, D.C., United States Government Printing Office, 1978.

42. Greifenstein, F. E., DeVant, M., Yoshitake, J., and Gajewske, J. E. A study of a cyclohexylamine for anesthesia. Anesth. Analg. 37:283, 1958.

43. Helrich, M., and Atwood, J. M. Modification of Sernyl anesthesia with haloperidol. Anesth. Analg. 43:471, 1964.

44. Herskowitz, J., and Oppenheimer, E. More about poisoning by phencyclidine. N. Engl. J. Med. 297: 1405, 1977.

45. Hoogwerf, B., et al. Phencyclidine-induced rhabdomyolysis and acute renal failure. Clin. Toxicol. 14:47, 1979.

46. Ital, T., et al. Effect of phencyclidine in chronic schizophrenia. Can. Psychiatr. Assoc. J. 12:209, 1967.

47. Johnson, K. M. Neurochemical pharmacology of phencyclidine. In *PCP Abuse: An Appraisal.* NIDA Research Monograph #21. Washington, D.C., United States Government Printing Office, 1978.

48. Johnstone, M. The use of Sernyl in clinical anaesthesia. Anaesthesist 9:114, 1960.

49. Lerner, S. E., and Burns, R. S. Phencyclidine use among youth: History, epidemiology, and acute and chronic intoxication. In *PCP Abuse: An Appraisal.* NIDA Research Monograph #21. Washington, D.C. United States Government Printing Office, 1978.

50. Levy, L., Cameron, D. E., and Aitken, R. C. B. Observations of two psychotomimetic drugs of piperdine derivation—CI 395 (Sernyl) and CI 400. Am. J. Psychiatry 116:843, 1970.

51. Linden, C., et al. Phencyclidine: Nine cases of poisoning. J.A.M.A. 234:513, 1975.

52. Lohr, L. PCP: White House caution vs. Senatorial ire. Am. Pharm. 18:32, 1978.

53. Luby, E. D., Cohen, B. D., Rosenbaum, G., Gottlieb, J. S., and Kelley, R. Study of a new schizophrenomimetic drug—Sernyl. A.M.A. Arch. Neurol. Psychiatry 81:363, 1958.

54. Luby, E. D., and Gottlieb, J. S. Model psychoses. In *The Lafayette Clinic Studies on Schizophrenia.* Detroit, Wayne State University Press, 1971.

55. Luisada, P. The PCP psychosis: A hidden epidemic. Presented at the VI World Congress of Psychiatry, Honolulu, August 29, 1977.

56. Luisada, P. The phencyclidine psychosis: Phenomenology and treatment. In *PCP Abuse: An Appraisal.* NIDA Research Monograph #21. Washington, D.C., United States Government Printing Office, 1978.

57. Luisada, P. Testimony before the House Select Committee on Narcotics Abuse and Control, August 8, 1978.

58. Luisada, P., and Brown, B. I. Clinical management of the phencyclidine psychosis. Clin. Toxicol. 9:539, 1976.

59. Luisada, P., et al. The hysterical personality: Myth and reality. Presented at the Annual Meeting of the American Psychiatric Association, Toronto, 1977.

60. Luisada, P., and Reddick, C. Angel dust and an epidemic of "schizophrenia." Presented at the annual meeting of the Medical Society of St. Elizabeths Hospital, Washington, D.C., April 1974.

61. Luisada, P., and Reddick, C. An epidemic of drug-induced "schizophrenia." Presented at the 128th annual meeting of the American Psychiatric Association, Anaheim, May 5, 1975.

62. Lundberg, G. D., Gupta, R. D., and Montgomery, S. H. Phencyclidine: Patterns seen in street drug analysis. Clin. Toxicol. 9:503, 1976.

63. McMahon, B., Ambre, J., and Ellis, J. Hypertension during recovery from phencyclidine intoxication. Clin. Toxicol. 12:37, 1978.

64. Meltzer, H. Y., and Stahl, S. M. The dopamine

hypothesis of schizophrenia. Schiz. Bull. 2:19, 1976.
65. Meltzer, H., et al. PCP: Neurochemistry, treatment and more. Am. J. Psychiatry 136:235, 1979.
66. Petersen, R. C., and Stillman, R. D. *Phencyclidine: A Review*. National Institute on Drug Abuse pamphlet. Washington, D.C., United States Government Printing Office, 1978.
67. Petersen, R. C., and Stillman, R. C. Phencyclidine: An overview. In *PCP Abuse: An Appraisal*. NIDA Research Monograph #21. Washington, D.C., United States Government Printing Office, 1978.
68. Picchioni, A., and Consroe, P. Activated charcoal—a phencyclidine antidote, or hog in dogs (letter). N. Engl. J. Med. 300:202, 1979.
69. Raifman, M. A., and Berant, M. Flying high with angel dust (letter). Am. J. Dis. Child. 132:432, 1978.
70. Rainey, J. M., and Crowder, M. K. Prolonged psychosis attributed to phencyclidine: Report of three cases. Am. J. Psychiatry 132:1076, 1975.
71. Reed, A., and Kane, A. W. Phencyclidine (PCP): Another illicit psychedelic drug. J. Psychedelic Drugs 5:8, 1972.
72. Ritzler, B., and Rosenbaum, G. Proprioception in schizophrenics and normals. J. Abnorm. Psychol. 83:106, 1974.
73. Rosen, A. Case report: Symptomatic mania and phencyclidine abuse. Am. J. Psychiatry 136:118, 1979.
74. Rosenbaum, G. Feedback mechanisms in schizophrenia. In *The Lafayette Clinic Studies on Schizophrenia*. Detroit, Wayne State University Press, 1971.
75. Rosenbaum, G., Cohen, B. D., Luby, E., Gottlieb, J., and Yelen, D. Comparison of Sernyl with other drugs. Arch. Gen. Psychiatry 1:651, 1959.
76. Schuckit, M. A., and Morrissey, E. R. Propoxyphene and phencyclidine (PCP) use in adolescents. J. Clin. Psychiatry 39:7, 1978.
77. Shaffer, C. B. Treating phencyclidine intoxication (letter). Am. J. Psychiatry 135:388, 1978.
78. Shick, J. F. E. Epidemiology of multiple drug use

with special reference to phencyclidine. In *PCP Abuse: An Appraisal*. NIDA Research Monograph #21, Washington, D.C., United States Government Printing Office, 1978.
79. Showalter, C. V., and Thornton, W. E. Clinical pharmacology of phencyclidine toxicity. Am. J. Psychiatry 134:1234, 1977.
80. Shulgin, A. T., and MacLean, D. Illicit synthesis of phencyclidine (PCP) and several of its analogs. Clin. Toxicol. 9:553, 1976.
81. Siegel, R. K. Phencyclidine and ketamine intoxication: A study of four populations of recreational users. In *PCP Abuse: An Appraisal*. NIDA Research Monograph #21. Washington, D.C., United States Government Printing Office, 1978.
82. Sioris, L., and Krenzelok, E. Phencyclidine intoxication: A literature review. Am. J. Hosp. Pharm. 35:1362, 1978.
83. Slavney, P. R., Rich, G. B., Pearlson, G. S., and McHugh, P. R. Phencyclidine abuse and symptomatic mania. Biol. Psychiatry 12:697, 1977.
84. Smith, D. E., Wesson, D. R., Seymour, R. B., and Buxton, M. E. The diagnosis and treatment of the PCP abuse syndrome. In *PCP Abuse: An Appraisal*. NIDA Research Monograph #21. Washington, D.C., United States Government Printing Office, 1978.
85. Stockard, J. J., and Chiappa, K. H. Pseudoperiodic bilateral EEG paroxysms. J. Clin. Psychiatry 40:154, 1979.
86. Thompson, T. N. Malignant hyperthermia from PCP. J. Clin. Psychiatry 40:327, 1979.
87. Tong, T. G., Benowitz, N. L., Becker, C. E., Formia, P. J., and Boerner, U. Phencyclidine poisoning. J.A.M.A. 234:512, 1975.
88. Wright, H., and Green, G. Clinical manifestations of phencyclidine intoxication. J. S. C. Med. Assoc. 73:401, 1978.
89. Yesavage, J., and Freman, A. Acute phencyclidine intoxication: Psychopathology and prognosis. J. Clin. Psychiatry 39:664, 1978.

CHAPTER 19

VOLATILE SUBSTANCES

Charles W. Sharp, Ph.D.

Maurice Korman, Ph.D.

Everyone likes to sniff pleasant odors; some inhale more deeply trying to derive an altered state of consciousness, which varies from person to person and drug to drug. Smoking and breathing of mystical fumes have been used in various cultures for centuries. More recently, organic chemists have widened the horizon of potential substances. Thus, in the 18th and 19th centuries, various anesthetics—such as nitrous oxide, ether, and chloroform—became widely used for parties or just for feeling good. It is, therefore, not surprising to find today that adults, and especially children, are inhaling aerosol paints, gasoline, various glues, nitrous oxides, alkyl nitrites, and many other "solvents."

This chapter will concentrate on some of the recently gained knowledge regarding the use of these volatile materials and the known hazards. For a review of the area, the reader is referred to two recent volumes on the subject (157, 158). Thus we will concentrate our discussion on details of the prevalence of the abuse situation, identify groups of substances abused, and correlate known and recognized human toxicities where possible. We will also discuss in some detail social and psychological manifestations of this problem.

PREVALENCE OF INHALANT USE

Many surveys are conducted by states, regional offices, and national organizations. None of these, however, gives us a very suitable overview of such a diverse group of drugs as inhalants. For most drug abuse subjects, the surveys only touch upon those who utilize drugs excessively; therefore, the knowledge to be gained form these surveys is often based on a small sample size of drug users for any one drug class. Realizing these and other limits (33, 34), we will, however, strive to reach some conclusions from an analysis of two different nation-wide surveys. One of these is a household survey conducted every 1 to 2 years; the other is an annual survey of high school seniors in a sample of 125 schools. Data on inhalant use from these recent surveys are combined in Table 19.1 for easy reference, although one must examine the methodologies of each before the data can be compared. The prevalence of inhalant abuse in the two surveys is very similar, even though the high school survey includes only part of the age range included in the household survey. These values are generally supported by other state and regional surveys (33) and give a general view of inhalant use, although they tell us nothing about the use of specific inhalants.

Many reviewers speak of the maturing out of inhalant use. If one examines some of these recent values, one might question such a conclusion. When one compares the use of inhalants with other drugs there seems to be a higher use of other drugs indicated in the "senior" age group as compared to use reported in the nation-wide household survey,

Table 19.1
Drug Use Prevalence in Nation-wide Surveys

Substance	Survey[a]	Year of Study	% Ever Used	% Used in Past Year but Not in Past Month	% Used in Past Month
Inhalants	Household, age 12–17	1977	9	1.5	0.7
		1976	8.1	2.0	0.9
	High school seniors	1978	12	2.6	1.5
		1977	11.1	2.4	1.3
		1976	10.3	2.1	0.9
Hallucinogens	Household, age 12–17	1977	4.6	1.5	1.6
		1976	5.1	1.9	0.9
	High school seniors	1978	14.3	5.7	3.9
		1977	13.9	4.7	4.1
		1976	15.1	6.0	3.4
Cocaine	Household, age 12–17	1977	4.0	1.8	0.8
		1976	3.4	1.3	1.0
	High school seniors	1978	12.9	5.1	3.9
		1977	10.8	4.3	2.9
		1976	9.7	4.0	2.0
Sedatives	Household, age 12–17	1977	3.1	1.2	0.8
		1976	2.8	0.8	0.5
	High school seniors	1978	16.0	5.7	4.2
		1977	17.4	5.7	5.1
		1976	17.7	6.2	4.5
Stimulants	Household, age 12–17	1977	5.2	2.4	1.3
		1976	4.4	1.0	1.2
	High school seniors	1978	22.9	8.4	8.7
		1977	23.0	7.5	8.8
		1976	22.6	8.1	7.7

[a] House survey values were obtained from Abelson, H. I., Fishburne, P. M., and Cisin, I. *National Survey on Drug Abuse: 1977*, vol. 1. National Institute on Drug Abuse, DHEW Publication ADM 78-618, 1977. High school seniors values were obtained from Johnston, L. D., Bachman, J. G., and O'Malley, P. M. *Drugs and the Class of '78: Behaviors, Attitudes and Recent National Trends.* National Institute on Drug Abuse, DHEW publication ADM 79-878, 1979.

whereas the use of inhalants is similar in both (Table 19.1). This indicates that the use of all drug categories except inhalants has increased in the older age (seniors) group. This is most evident when grades 7 and 8 are compared to grades 11 and 12 in the one study (Table 19.2). There is some decline in the use of inhalants, but there is a greater increase in the use of other drugs. These studies of the New York area are generally in agreement with the nation-wide school survey (Table 19.2). Therefore, one might speculate that with increasing age, the drug users phase in other drug use but only partially diminish their use of inhalants.

There has been no significant change noted in the percentage of inhalant use (lifetime, recent, or current) over the past few years indicated in the nation-wide household survey. However, all categories of inhalant use have increased, although not significantly

each year, in the nation-wide school survey. More dramatically, the New York survey shows a doubling over the past 5 years to 16 per cent (lifetime prevalence) and 4.7 per cent (current use) in 1978. The lifetime prevalence of inhalant use in the New York survey, although at 7 per cent in 1972, was down to about 5 per cent in 1975. These latter surveys cover a more recent period (1978) than the nation-wide household survey and may include an increased use of more widely advertised volatile substances, such as the alkyl nitrites and nitrous oxide. With the ease of administration and the lack of federal control of most "volatile drugs," one might suspect that their popularity could increase even more with appropriate marketing of desirable materials. Inhalant abuse seems to be more widespread and not primarily limited to the indigent. However, it is still the only monitored group of drugs whose use is more

Table 19.2
Drug Use Prevalence in Students

Substance	% Lifetime or Ever Used[a]			% Used in Last 30 Days[a]		
	New York Grades 11–12	Nation-wide Seniors	New York Grades 7–8	New York Grades 11–12	Nation-wide Seniors	New York Grades 7–8
Marihuana	71	59	32	50	37	19
Stimulants	23	23	7.2	9.7	8.7	3.3
PCP	22		7.6	5.5		3
Hallucinogens	15	14	3.5	5.2	3.9	1.7
Cocaine	16	13	5.6	5.2	3.9	2.1
Sedatives	16	16	4.8	5.2	4.2	1.8
Tranquilizers	18	17	6.3	6.9	3.4	3.2
Inhalants	12	12	18	2.7	1.5	6.8

[a] All numbers are rounded off to two significant figures. Values for nation-wide seniors are from Johnston, L. D., Bachman, J. G., and O'Malley, P. M. *Drugs and the Class of '78: Behaviors, Attitudes and Recent National Trends.* National Institute on Drug Abuse, DHEW publication ADM 79-878, 1979. PCP was not a separate drug category in this survey. Values for New York Grades 11–12 and Grades 7–8 are from *Substance Use among New York State Public and Parochial School Students in Grades 7 through 12.* New York State Division of Substance Abuse Services, Albany, 1978.

prevalent in rural than in urban school districts (93).

The nation-wide school survey also denotes that the use of inhalants still predominates in the male population by a two to one ratio. Previous reports have observed a male to female ratio of inhalant use as high as 10 to one.

INCIDENCE OF INHALANT USE

Another type of data input that has been used to identify trends in drug use comes from health delivery systems, crisis centers, hospital emergency rooms, and medical examiners' offices. Most of the subjects included herein have had health problems, although not necessarily linked to any of the drugs mentioned. Two major systems, DAWN (Drug Abuse Warning Network) and CODAP (Client Oriented Data Acquisition Program) collect data on numbers and types of drugs mentioned in the medical histories of admitted subjects. Data are also collected on all toxicity episodes reported to the Consumer Product Safety Commission by the National Electronic Injury Surveillance System (NEISS).

These data bases have sometimes been used by others to indicate the magnitude of the problem. Although some of these data have been used to estimate heroin use, it is a very poor indicator of inhalant use. Inhalant abuse subjects seldom need or attempt to

receive any direct medical treatment for relief of inhalant-associated problems or for life support. They usually enter treatment for other reasons. Thus, only 1 per cent of the clients reported by CODAP systems are primary inhalant users (37). This is less than an average of two per clinic for 1978. This would not seem to represent very many of the inhalant abusers. However, it may be worth noting that almost two-thirds of these subjects use inhalants once a week or more and a third once or more daily.

Many substances are mentioned by drug abusers and included in the inhalant category of DAWN. In a recent printout of the medical examiners' reports, 40 per cent of the deaths are associated with cyanide and carbon monoxide. These deaths were probably not a result of euphoric use but were more likely suicides. In contrast, there are very few mentions of PAM- or other aerosol-related deaths in DAWN. However, several deaths are listed under freon. Also the number of PAM or nitrous oxide-related deaths reported in one Texas county (Dallas 57) are almost as high as those recorded for all the United States in DAWN. From their death certificate files, the Consumer Product Safety Commission has recorded about 150 deaths due to PAM in the 1970's. Of all aerosol deaths reported in the NEISS data analyzed for the year 1955, PAM accounts for about 20 to 25 per cent of the total aerosol-related deaths. Almost 100 "aerosol deaths" were reported for 1975. This report is an "underreport," as it is missing some United States health jurisdictions and also accepts only those where products are "most likely" identified. Based on these and other values of aerosol-related incidents in NEISS reports, it can be estimated that the number of aerosol deaths may have exceeded 700 in the 1970's. Based on all information to date, lethality must be considered to be one of the most serious problems related to inhalant abuse. An estimated 6,000 injuries, mostly minor, related to aerosols are reported and treated annually (1978). This number comprises about 5 per cent of the total number of reported injuries. Although most of these are accident-related incidents, most of the deaths described above seem to be attributable to inhalant abuse.

The extent of the over-all problem of aerosol abuse is unclear, even after careful examination of the NEISS and other data. Other values in DAWN reports have also not assisted in defining the inhalant abuse problem. For example, the high number of mentions of transmission fluid would indicate more of a problem than has any other study. In addition, probably because of coding, aerosol paint sniffing was not identified through DAWN but was uncovered by a field survey (190). The popularity of paint spray inhalation has also been confirmed by a study of inhalant abusers in Dallas. It is interesting to note that certain inhalants have a greater "density" for a particular ethnic group (i.e., have a greater frequency of usage than for the group considered as a whole). Spray paints seem to be preferred by Mexican-Americans; gasoline, shoe polish, and amyl nitrites by Anglos; Liquid Paper thinner and glues or cements by blacks (Table 19.3).

One of the oldest known inhalants, nitrous oxide, may be increasingly used on our campuses today. Although anesthetic tanks are often stolen, nitrous oxide cartridges (whippets) are now available in grocery stores and other outlets. As with any inhalant, this points out the need for more systemized, in-depth accounting of inhalant use, perhaps through small ethnographic studies in select regions.

More recently, use of alkyl nitrites has also become more widespread. Although amyl nitrite (poppers or snappers) was widely used in the gay community in the 1960's a change of Food and Drug Administration (FDA) reg-

Table 19.3
Density by Drug Category[a]

Substance	Anglo (N = 92)	Mexican-American (N = 60)	Black (N = 36)
Gasoline	52.2	33.3	33.3
Lacquer thinner	17.4	20.0	13.9
Glues or cement	50.0	36.7	63.9
Other aerosols	4.3		
Spray paint	77.2	125.0	66.7
Lighter fluid	28.3	26.7	11.1
Deodorant	10.9	1.7	2.8
Pam	8.7		5.6
Toluol	9.8	5.0	2.8
Fingernail polish remover	16.3	6.7	8.3
Amyl nitrite	21.7	6.7	2.8
Shoe polish	26.1		2.8
Paint brush cleaner	8.7	6.7	
Hair spray	2.2	1.7	
Liquid Paper thinner	2.2	1.7	19.4

[a] Density is based upon the number of times each drug category appears in the particular ethnic group, not necessarily on a one-to-one correspondence with the number of subjects. The number of mentions is divided by the number of subjects in that group, e.g., N ÷ 92 for Anglo subjects. The density value may exceed 100 per cent, as it does in the case of spray paint for Mexican-American inhalant users.

ulations to make this a prescription drug (in the Unites States, but not in Canada) promoted production and sales of a substitute, (iso) butyl nitrites. The extent of recreational use may be derived from estimated sales figures by one of the leading manufacturers, that 4,000,000 vials (10 to 15 ml) were sold in 1977 and 2.5 million in the first half of 1978. In the most recent high school survey, as many as one of nine seniors have used an alkyl nitrite (personal communication, L. D. Johnston).

Alkyl nitrite use also appears very seldom in DAWN mentions (about 64 in the last 5 years). The lack of mentions of various volatile substances in DAWN may be related to very few toxic episodes associated with this type of drug use or more likely to the difficulty of associating health problems and even deaths to substances that are volatile and readily eliminated. Toxicities related to the various substances will be discussed in a succeeding section.

PSYCHOSOCIAL CONTEXT OF USE

Inhalation of solvents typically results in a relatively brief period of intoxication with characteristic short term symptomatology, including emotional, behavioral, and cognitive disinhibition. Together with marihuana, smoking tobacco, and alcohol, inhalants are among the earliest drugs of use among teenagers.

The reasons for sniffing's popularity are outlined in recent papers by Cohen (47, 48). Solvents are attractive because they are widely available to all strata of the community; they are inexpensive or, if need be, can be easily appropriated; they are legal—particularly aerosols and paint solvents; their packaging can be quite compact; their effect is quickly felt, and their impact dissipates rapidly, permitting many "highs;" hangovers are relatively mild.

Normally, solvent users are aware that inhalants are not a group of individual drugs. This concern results, for example, in a significantly greater tendency to worry than exhibited by matched noninhalant controls who used other drugs.

Similarly, earlier reports had posited a modal sniffer to be poor and frequently Hispanic. Vargas has voiced concern (190) over this stereotype. In three samples, a Phoenix school sample (123), a Dallas neighborhood Youth Corps sample (181), and a Dallas county hospital emergency room sample (99), the deviations between the compositions of the sample of sniffers and the base rates from which they sprang were as follows: Black: −11 per cent, −7 per cent, −6 per cent; Mexican-American: +2 per cent, +10 per cent, 5 per cent; Anglos: +9 per cent, −3 per cent, 0 per cent. It appears that Mexican-Americans are slightly overrepresented among sniffers, blacks are slightly underrepresented, and Anglos are close to their base rate. The distribution of sniffers in a given community seems to depart from demographic expectations in a consistent but clearly limited manner.

As far as socioeconomic status is concerned, it has been noted that drug use is, to a large extent, a middle-class phenomenon (23). Because of its low cost and wide accessibility, inhalants may clearly have unusual appeals for the poor. Visual inspection of plotted addresses of large samples of sniffers corroborates the finding in the early 1970's (75) that inhalant use seems to be spread fairly heterogeneously across socioeconomic lines.

Environmental Pressures. A number of studies have reported that school adjustment has represented one of the most frequently reported troublesome areas for the sniffer. Typically, sniffers receive lower grades, experience more suspensions in school, are absent more frequently from school, and exhibit negative school-related attitudes. Furthermore, teachers are perceived by sniffers as being significantly stricter and controlling. It is, of course, possible that schools and teachers may react to the obvious signs of sniffing at least as much as they set the stage for alienation and disaffection. They would, thus, become involved in the etiology and the consequences of inhalant use. Such a dual role for schools, frequently noted clinically, needs to be confirmed experimentally, particularly in Mexican-American communities where increased inhalant use and unsatisfactory educational situations coexist.

Problems in acculturation and social alienation have sometimes been implicated as important factors in the initiation of inhalant use. Such a hypothesis would in part explain the slight preponderance of sniffers among Mexican-American children that has been widely reported (46). In a recent study which focused on Mexican-American youngsters, Bonnheim and Korman (24) found no differences in levels of acculturation between sniffers and youths using other drugs.

Boredom and idleness represent other environmental conditions apparently reported with some frequency among inhalant users (124, 129, 181). It has been concluded that community programs emphasizing recreation might be initiated with some success, particularly for groups of sniffers.

Peer use represents a significant environmental pressure directed toward inhalant use, and reference is persistently made to the role that peers play in introducing youths to sniffing (1, 100). Inasmuch as inhalant use is among the earliest experimental drugs appearing in the behavioral repertoire of children—at a time when they are most susceptible to peer modeling—this is not an unexpected finding.

Finally, a recent study by Gotway (77) dealt

with stressful life events as possible catalysts for the initiation of inhalant use. Such a hypothesis was not borne out, although it was clear that inhalant users experienced levels of negative life events subsequent to the beginning of sniffing. As one would expect, many of the events recorded by the inhaling subjects were events that were largely self-induced, such as school suspensions.

Familial Disorganization. Early research in this area focused on the level of intactness of the family and over-all judgment of family effectiveness and functioning (1, 89, 121, 143). Families of inhalant users were reported as being "multiple problem families" that had gone through considerable periods of turmoil and discord. Seldom were such children found to be living with both parents at the time of admission to treatment centers. Often one or both parents were alcoholic. Although most of these studies lacked control groups, such investigations as those of Barker and Adams (16) concluded that sniffers' families showed a greater level of clinical deterioration than control groups, even though family pathology was present across the board.

Bonnheim and Korman (24) videotaped structured interactions among family members of sniffers and other-drug controls. Blind readings of the tapes by professionals reflected a significantly more conflictual, anxious atmosphere in sniffer families with particular problems in communication and organization. A replication of this study by Gotway (77), which focused on Anglo families, likewise reported that families of inhalant users were less psychologically adjusted than controls. Furthermore, this was corroborated by self-report measures (the Family Environments Scale).

As with environmental pressures that might be implicated in inhalant use, it is not possible to evaluate the extent to which lack of parental support and control antecedes the use of inhalants, because no longitudinal studies are available in this area.

Personality Factors. Although it has been difficult to distinguish predisposing personality factors from the psychological reactions secondary to being known as a sniffer, a number of studies have posited roughly similar sets of personality variables as impacting on the psychological life space of inhalant users.

Nylander (135) described an "emotionally disturbed background" in many of the 20 intensively studied youngsters in Stockholm. In an investigation of inhalant users in a remote part of Australia, Nurcombe et al. (134) hypothesized the greater than average need for discharge of tension associated with sexual, aggressive, and acquisitive drives. Inhalant-promoted disinhibited behavior thus aids in establishment and assertion of masculinity. Some confirmation of this hypothesis was obtained through a technique based on teacher ratings (presumably not on a blind basis) that resulted in higher tension discharge scores and higher anxiety index scores for inhalant users in contrast to the control group.

Massengale et al. (121) conjectured that inhalants were helpful in controlling anxiety that would otherwise have accompanied strong sexual and aggressive impulses. Press and Done (143) inferred from their study of 60 inhalant users that the principal personality factors at work in inhalant use included a sense of inadequacy, bashfulness, and feelings of frustration over inability to reach high standards set by parents.

Meloff (125) reported on intergroup differences on the California Psychological Inventory. Inhalant users scored lower on scales reflecting poise, ascendancy, self-assurance, socialization, maturity, and responsibility. Control groups, however, were not fully adequate and it is unclear, as it is in most of the research he reported, whether these differences reflect drug use in general or inhalant use specifically.

In a study of inhalant users' coping behavior, Korman et al. (99) administered an experimental test in which the subject could elect one of five coping strategies (direct aggression, indirect aggression, denial, self-aggression, and substitution) as a reaction to an anger-arousing situation. Three groups participated: an inhalant group (I), a light other-drug (L-OD) group, and a heavy other-drug (H-OD) group. Generally, inhalant and H-OD groups performed similarly. They were both clearly differentiated from the L-OD groups on their heightened use of direct aggression and substitution. Inhalant users, however, were differentiated from heavy other-drug users to a significant extent in their propensity to utilize self-directed aggression and in their greater tendency to opt for substitutive mechanisms.

MENTAL STATUS OF USERS

Cognitive Difficulties. Early experience with inhalants gave rise to a number of anecdotal reports of a possible relationship between inhalant use and signs of acute brain damage. Many of these studies found abnormal electroencephalograms and occasionally reported on psychological test results suggesting impaired memory and concentration, perceptual motor difficulties, and disorientation (27, 35, 66, 107).

In a number of studies, care was taken to compare inhalant users with appropriately controlled subjects, using objective behavioral measures of brain involvement. Dodd and Santostefano (58) gave 12 glue sniffers a series of tests of concentration, continuous performance in the face of distraction, and visual motor coordination some 14 hours postinhalation. The authors concluded that their "performances were strikingly similar to those of controls."

In a carefully designed study, Berry et al. (21) evaluated 46 inhalant users with lengthy histories of solvent inhalation. The Halstead-Reitan Neuropsychology (NP) Battery was used with subjects who were primarily inhalers of metallic spray paints, and results were contrasted with a very closely matched control gorup. On nearly half of the tests making up the NP battery, inhalant users scored significantly lower than controls, with approximately 40 per cent of the inhalant subjects scoring in the brain damaged range on impairment indices. Corroboration for these results was obtained by Korman et al. (99) reporting on similar psychological evaluations of mild to moderate inhalant users. Approximately 30 per cent of the measures used were found to differentiate experimental from control subjects at the 0.05 level or better. Decrements in language-perceptual and abstractive skills seemed to be related to inhalant abuse, as was rapid information processing; in addition, there were scattered indications of sensory perceptual decrements (Table 19.4). Although none of these studies are in a position to establish causal relationships, the relatively tight statistical controls applied make the picture a suggestive one.

Danger to Self and Others. Sniffers have frequently come to the attention of authorities because of their involvement with some form of antisocial behavior. Many clinical studies have stressed the sniffer's sense of

Table 19.4
Comparison of Inhalant and Other-drug Groups on Halstead-Reitan Neuropsychology Measures[a]

Inhalant group scores more poorly on:	p
Wechsler Verbal IQ	< .001
Wechsler Full Scale IQ	< .001
Total Wechsler Verbal Scaled Score	< .001
Total Wechsler Scaled Score (VSS + PSS)	< .001
Comprehension	< .001
Wechsler Performance IQ	< .01
Similarities	< .01
Arithmetic	< .01
Wide Range Achievement Test—Reading	< .01
Wide Range Achievement Test—Spelling	< .01

[a] Inhalant group, N = 68; other-drug group, N = 41.
Effect of other drugs eliminated by analysis of co-variance.

grandiosity and invulnerability (195). This seems frequently to lead to self-directed destructive behavior. Others (47) have pointed out that inhalants may, like alcohol, diminish behavioral control capabilities long before motor activity is diminished. A representative clinical study (143) detected sniffing behavior to be "a precursor to criminality" in about a third of the subjects. These individuals were seen as suffering from serious deficits in their judgment and reality perception that led them to be accident prone and to indulge in antisocial and self-destructive acts. It is interesting to note that in Kalogerakis' (94) report on a series of patient assaults at Bellevue Hospital in New York, only one incident was due to an intoxicant, and that was glue.

Tinklenberg and Woodrow (186) contrasted groups of youthful assaultive and nonassaultive incarcerated offenders with reference to their history of drug use. Although inhalants were used with low frequency by both groups, their increased prevalence in the assaultive group was of suggestive proportions in contrast to the control group.

Friedman and Friedman's (69) large sample studies on drug use and delinquency yielded self-reports of greater violence and aggression on the part of drug users in contrast to non-drug-using controls. Within-drug-group analyses suggested that "users of inhalants reported the greatest overall amount of violence, both in order to obtain drugs and while under the influence of drugs." They also noted that, among boys with police records, some 40 per cent attributed to drug use their loss of control leading to violence. Official records implicated solvents more frequently than any other drug.

In a psychiatry emergency room study, Korman et al. (100) found that their sample of 162 inhalant users differed significantly from matched other-drug users in that they displayed significantly more self-directed destructive behavior, as well as some degree of recent suicidal and homicidal behavior (Table 19.5). Mean differences in clinical ratings, however, were small. Some interactive effects were suggested: The non-Hispanic, post-adolescent inhalant user is particularly at risk. Another aspect of this study investigated the question, what combination of drugs best predicts self-directed destructive behavior? An inhalant, and no other drug with it, seemed to be the significant predictive drug variable.

The relationship between inhalants and aggressive behavior represents an important current research issue: What psychological mechanisms are involved? Is the problem primarily a predisposition to aggress or is it a failure of internal controls? What role do inhalant-produced internal states play? These are some of the important, unresolved questions.

Diagnosis and Prognosis. The modal prognostic picture that any group of professionally evaluated patients presents is primarily a function of the selection (or self-selection) process with reference to a particular health setting. Not surprisingly, the literature reveals such variability on this issue. For example, Brozovsky and Winkler (27) found that three-quarters of a small sample of sniffers were schizophrenics. By contrast, Alapin (4) evaluated sniffers in Britain and Poland and reported about a third of them to be schizophrenic. Comstock (50), describing a sample of sniffers hospitalized in a polydrug treatment center, reports a diagnostic breakdown as follows:

Sociopathic personality	23 per cent
Adolescent adjustment reaction	45 per cent
Depressive neurosis	23 per cent
Schizophrenia	9 per cent

In a setting that accommodates a wide range of patients, the prevailing base rates for both "drug" and "nondrug" patients are fundamental to an assessment of the diagnostic picture of inhalant users. The diagnostic structure of inhalant (I), other drug (O.D.) and nondrug groups (N.D.) is taken from a recently completed study by Korman et al (100) (Table 19.6). Interestingly, the three groups do not differ in the incidence of psychosis. The inhalant group seems to include a relatively large number of persons noted for their lifelong pattern of maladaptive behavior. Does the difference in drug dependence diagnoses reflect a more committed drug orientation on the part of the inhalant users than nonsniffing polydrug users?

Prognosis seems to be poorer for inhalant users than for users of other drugs. In Comstock's (50) study, for instance, sniffers responded to a total hospital therapeutic program with "an apparent mobilization of agitation, impulsiveness, and of antisocial manifestations as well." As seen in the emergency room (100), inhalant users differed from other-drug users in that the duration of their illnesses was significantly longer, as was the index episode's duration (Table 19.7). Furthermore, the typical disposition was more frequently to hospitalize the patient and less frequently to use outpatient treatment or no further treatment (Table 19.8).

Long Term Effects. The development of an apparent tolerance for inhalants, particularly toluene-based compounds, has been noted by a number of investigations (27, 72, 142, 143). Brozovsky and Winkler, for instance, noted an increase of up to 25 tubes per day in one child. A more typical progres-

Table 19.5

Danger to Self and Other Variables Differentiating Inhalant from Other-drug Users

	Recent	Last 6 Months	6 Months to 2 Years	2 Years +
Thoughts of suicide			< .05	< .001
Suicidal behavior				< .001
Other self-destructive behavior	< .02	< .05		

Table 19.6
Admission Diagnosis of Inhalant (I), Other-drug (O.D), and Nondrug (N.D.) Users

Diagnosis[a]	I	O.D.	N.D.
	%	%	%
Psychotic organic brain syndrome (OBS)	7	6	1
Nonpsychotic OBS	4	2	2
Affective psychosis	4	4	4
Nonaffective psychosis	23	19	26
Neurosis	15	15	15
Personality disorder	20[b]	0	0
Sexual deviation	2	1	1
Alcoholism	8	7	1
Drug dependence	35[b]	17	1
Psychophysiological disorder	0	0	2
Transient situational disturbance	10	15	19
Behavior disorder of childhood or adolescence	15	10	7
Mental retardation	1	6	8
No diagnosis made	2	5	15

[a] Based on N = 162 psychiatric emergency room patients per group; percentages include primary and secondary diagnosis.
[b] Significantly different from O.D. group.

Table 19.7
Duration of Illness for Study Groups

	0 to 6 Months	6 Months to 2 Years	2 Years +
	%	%	%
Inhalants (n = 124)	15	19	66
Polydrugs (n = 137)	30	17	53
Nondrugs (n = 111)	37	16	47

$Chi^2 = 16.22$, $p < .01$

sion is that "over a one or two year period the user may experience less effect with eight to ten tubes of plastic cement, for example, than was noted initially with one or two" (59).

Not enough is reliably known concerning the antecedents of increased tolerance for the major classes of inhalants. There are indications (60) that the sniffing of gasoline, for instance, may likewise involve eventual tolerance build-up. As increasing numbers of adults are reported to be returning to occasional or compulsive inhalant use (65), prospective and retrospective research on tolerance needs to be undertaken.

Table 19.8
Postemergency Room Disposition for Three Study Groups

	Home or Outpatient Treatment	Hospital Treatment	Left Prior to Treatment
	%	%	%
Inhalants	27	64	9
Polydrugs	43	49	8
Nondrugs	39	45	16

$Chi^2 = 16.43$, $p < .002$.

A number of investigators have commented anecdotally on sniffers' symptoms of psychological dependency primarily in terms of the persistence with which the goal of inhaling is pursued (1, 41). There have also been reports of a negative psychological state induced in confirmed inhalers when prevented from sniffing. Some investigators (1, 56, 142) have reported increases in irritability, restlessness, excitability, and anxiety under such conditions. Frequently, it has been difficult to establish the causal relationship between the inaccessibility of the drug and such psychological states. This is particularly true when the sniffer comes to the attention of professionals because he is apprehended or needs medical care. Further research is also needed that will chart the extent to which the deprived inhaler departs from an optimal state of well-being as a result of the nonavailability of inhalants, and under what conditions the urge to use or fantasies about use are most frequently experienced.

There has been disagreement in the literature over the existence of a withdrawal syndrome upon abrupt cessation of long and frequent inhalant use. Some authors specifically point to its absence (59), although there have been reported observations of a syndrome resembling delirium tremens under conditions of abrupt cessation (111, 127, 135).

In an interesting study, de la Garza et al. (56) described an abstinence syndrome in 22 per cent of a group of sniffers characterized not only by dysphoric symptoms but by physical signs as well: abdominal pain, general paresthesias, leg cramps, headaches, and other discomforts. Furthermore, a small group (9 per cent) kept some plastic cement to inhale early the next day to counteract deprivation symptoms. Because this is an unusual finding, its replication and further explication are highly desirable, particularly in populations other than the one investigated.

TOXICOLOGY

Inhalant abuse subsumes a variety of different solvents and volatile mixtures comprised of a variety of substances of different proportions. This section will concentrate on the different substances identified by chemical class and correlated as much as possible with the different products used. In this way, toxicities related to certain substances can be described, and an attempt can be made to correlate certain pathological changes such as might occur after exposure to the products. This very tenuous step is being taken in order to steer our thoughts one step away from generalizing that all inhalants produce any one syndrome, as though there is a commonality to the toxicology of this diverse group of agents. Although many, if not all, can be generally classified as belonging to the sedative or to the anesthetic class of substances, toxicities resulting from their use range from relatively nontoxic to carcinogenic in nature. It is hoped that the perspective given here will aid clinicians and others in dealing with this problem from a more realistic approach.

In reading the following overview of the toxicology of these various substances, the reader should keep in mind that this is an oversimplification of the problem. Many other constituents than those discussed are often present in products and may contribute markedly or little at all to the general toxicity of a compound. This review takes into account only the most volatile components, because most products are not ingested during recreational inhalation. However, paints are often sprayed so that pigments and metals coat the nasal and buccal mucosa, and other products are spilled on other epidermal tissue. This results in absorption to varying degrees of nonvolatile resins, heavy metals, and other toxic materials, the effects of which are presently unclear. It might also be noted that knowledge of major toxicities has not usually come from studies of inhalant abusers but from accidents or ailments occurring in the general workplace or occupational settings. Several incidents related to recreational use are listed in a recent review (51).

Because there is no specific treatment for any of the disabilities brought about by volatile substances other than symptomatic relief (51, 144), this section will concentrate on what potential idiosyncrasies develop from solvent exposure and their potential consequences. Although numerous toxicities have been identified, there is little evidence to date of withdrawal symptoms in animals or humans that would indicate that physical dependence develops with these substances. One group is attempting to critically evaluate physical dependence in an unusual clinical setting and may provide some answers to this question. Tolerance to different volatile substances, however, has been ascertained through animal studies (148).

Toluene and Toluene Mixtures. Toluene is one of the most ubiquitous substances associated with inhalant abuse. Its use became prominent in the 1950's when this behavior was referred to as "glue sniffing." Yet there is little direct evidence, either clinical or preclinical, that indicates that any serious problems are associated with the inhalation of pure toluene (28). Usually other more toxic substances have been present, such as benzene or hexane, in the materials associated with clinical reports of toxicities identified with the inhalation of toluene (28). However, deaths have resulted from acute overdoses where anoxia is a major contributing factor or from mishaps related to the intoxicated state (28, 113, 132).

Toluene is available in large drums at industrial sites and may contain varying but low concentrations of xylenes, benzene, and other related aromatics. Toluene is still a major ingredient in airplane glues with or without added allyl-isothiocyanate to prevent excessive inhalation. Although animal studies to date have not indicated major toxicities occurring as the result of several weeks of intensive, high level, intermittent exposure to pure toluene (139), future studies could yet reveal that toluene potentiates toxicities of some other substances. However, no such potentiation has been demonstrated, even though metabolic interactions between toluene and other solvents are known (86, 154). This leaves us unable to explain reports identifying some clinical neuropathies (2, 9, 96, 136, 147, 184) and other toxicities. Although they cannot be explained based on our present knowledge of solvent toxicology, the symptoms may have resulted in part due to the inhalation of toluene.

It becomes even more complex when one considers paints, substances that often contain moderate to high concentrations of toluene. Other solvents and propellants, also present in paint sprays (e.g., propane, isobutane, methylene chloride, ketones, ethyl or butyl acetate, and short chain alcohols), are more volatile than toluene. Thus they (especially methylene chloride) will be the major contributors to the intoxication state of the individual. Again, animal studies have not revealed any toxicities resulting from several weeks of repeated, high level, intermittent exposure to mixtures of toluene, methylene chloride, xylene, heptanes, and methanol. Although these animal studies did not measure any persistent central nervous system effects, cognitive and sensory deficits have been measured in subjects such as painters (78, 81, 128, 133, 155) and recreational users (51) who inhale paint over prolonged periods. The components responsible for these physiological insults are unknown, especially the role of toluene. Although we cannot at this juncture rule out any contribution due to toluene, one should be very cautious in attributing any neurological or other deficit to this chemical alone. It may be a much safer substance than some studies have led us to believe. Additional critical and extensive psychological and clinical studies of painters, especially those who work in a closed environment, might aid in our search for an understanding of this complex problem (81, 82, 182). The chemical compositon of the products used should be carefully documented. However, only careful animal studies will identify the substances responsible for those physiological insults suggested by studies of workers.

Benzene and Substances Containing Benzene. The toxicity of benzene is more striking in contrast with toluene. The absence of the methyl side chain present in toluene alters the chemistry as well as the biochemistry of this aromatic compound. Although chemists, factory workers, and others have in the past carelessly exposed themselves to benzene fumes, there is now increased concern about the possibility that leukemia and pancytopenia might result from benzene exposure (3, 73, 87). Animal studies have demonstrated a reduction in lymphocytes and conditions of aplastic anemia after weeks of exposure to benzene, although no indications of leukemia were evident (169). Although it seems that benzene is hematotoxic, it is unclear at this point whether benzene is the only factor contributing to leukemogenic changes in humans (194). In any event, there is a worldwide recognition of the problem, and there are attempts to reduce the levels of benzene in the environment (95); it will not be an easy or clear-cut task. First, it is costly to remove all benzene from toluene or xylene preparations such that recreational users can avoid exposure to benzene when inhaling toluene from commercial drums or from glues, paints, or other products containing toluene. Another substance where benzene content is highest (up to 7 per cent) is gasoline. With energy costs already high, the likelihood of removing benzene from gasoline is minimal. Therefore, continual exposure to this substance, intentionally or as a result of being a gasoline attendant, may very likely promote hematotoxic changes in many individuals. Good clinical surveys of gas station attendants could aid in the clarification of the hazards associated with the frequent inhalation of gasoline, especially because the aroma of gasoline is generally euphoric.

Nonsolvent Additives. Neurotoxic effects related to the intoxication or prolonged exposure to gasoline may also be correlated to other constituents such as tetraethyl lead, other metal additives, and triorthocresyl phosphate (TCP) (110). Chronic gasoline inhalers show symptoms of dysmetria and dysarthria (152, 156, 189) with motor as well as cerebral involvement. Inhalation of gasoline may cause death, even though the patient is hospitalized and treated including the use of dialysis and lead chelating agents (152, 189). Serious neurological problems or death are associated with blood lead levels greater than 50 μg/dl, especially over 100 μg/dl. Delta-aminolevulinic acid dehydratase (ALAD) levels have also been used to determine the severity of the problem (156). Pulmonary alveolitis is another symptom associated with the frequent administration of gasoline vapors (118). Although lead levels of gasoline may decrease, other additives, including different metal chelates, may pose yet different problems for those who inhale gasoline excessively.

Another commonly abused substance, spray paint, also contains heavy metals—copper, zinc, aluminum, and sometimes lead to mention a few. One study examined the levels of these metals in heavy users. Little increase above a high normal level was noted in plasma or urine except that a few had urine zinc levels two to three times the average level (192). Therefore, whether metals are likely to contribute to any toxic response as a result of paint inhalation is questioned and awaits further exploration.

Hexane. Another hydrocarbon, hexane, is present in low concentrations in gasoline and also in some glues, especially glass and other spray adhesives, rubber cements, and solvents. Presently, this has been one of the most carefully and well studied solvents. It was recognized in the early 1960's after studies of workers in Japan and elsewhere that showed hexane might be the cause of sensorimotor neuropathies in these subjects (173). Since then similar lesions have been observed in inhalant abuse cases (7, 74, 76, 101, 187). Subsequent animal studies have clearly correlated hexane-produced central and peripheral lesions in rats with similar changes in humans (173). An onset of numbness occurs after weeks to months of exposure, followed by loss of touch and pain sensation, especially in the feet. With more prolonged exposure, limb weakness, numbness, and ataxia set in, along with anorexia and abdominal discomfort. More extreme neurological deficits have been noted in several human cases and in animals. These reveal paranodal giant axonal swelling and myelin degeneration similar to the Guillain-Barre syndrome. Cerebral involvement has also been noted (173). One of the troublesome aspects of the disease is its continuing progression after hospitalization, a finding characteristic of either industrial or recreational exposure of individuals to hexane and related ketones.

Animal studies have aided in the clarification of the neuronal involvements described above. They have also enabled us to obtain a better perspective of recreational as compared to continuous low level exposure. In animals, decrements in the brain stem auditory evoked response, peripheral nerve conduction velocities, and grip strength have occurred by the fourth week of 5 days of continuous exposure to 1,000 ppm of hexanes. These effects occur after several weeks of intermittent 10-minute exposures of 48,000 ppm twice hourly for 8 hours but not at reduced levels or periods of exposure (148).

Although the basis of these differences is known, it heightens the importance of the continuity of exposure and the time of nonexposure as of equal or greater importance than is concentration in determining the toxicity of hexane (and maybe other solvents). The type of exposure may also be critical in determining the nature of any retrogression of the disease, a condition that seems to be dependent on the severity of the axonal degeneration. It is not yet clear whether any animal experiments will elicit those cortical interferences noted in human inhalant abusers described earlier.

These neurological changes have been correlated to a specific swelling of the paranodal giant axons after the metabolism of hexane to 2,5-hexanedione (173). It has been postulated that inhibiton of the glycolytic enzyme glycerophosphate dehydrogenase may be the primary site of action of these chemicals. This theory fits in with the knowledge that polyneuropathies have been associated with diabetes mellitus, renal malfunction, and alcohol use (173). Thus, subjects suffering from the latter conditions will be even more susceptible to hexane-induced neurotoxicities. Although increasing efforts are being made to eliminate this substance from the general living environment, trace amounts often present in products may contribute to the hazard of such products (146).

Ketones. Another solvent, 2-hexanone or methyl-n-butyl ketone (MBK), which may be a constituent in rubber cements, printing ink, and paints, has been observed to cause similar neuropathies (5, 120, 172) through formation of the same 2,5-hexanedione metabolite (171). This toxicity was again indicated by afflicted workers in an industrial setting (126). Neuropathies have also been observed in subjects inhaling products containing MBK for recreational purposes (137). The onset of the neurotoxicity is more rapid with MBK as compared to hexane. This is not surprising, because the ketone is more polar and a probable intermediate in the metabolism of hexane to the postulated neurotoxin 2,5-hexanedione.

In many products, MBK has been replaced by an isomer, methyl isobutyl ketone (MIK) or by a homologue, methyl isopentyl ketone, both of which apparently do not form a similar metabolite. Methyl-n-pentyl ketone does not produce neuropathies in monkeys

(92); 2,5-heptanedione, a possible metabolite is, however, neurotoxic (173). Here again, when one uses the close isomer MIK, there will likely be present some neurotoxic MBK. The incidence of toxicity should be greatly reduced, but many factors could alter the safety factor introduced by substituting MIK for MBK.

Although ketone metabolites may be readily identified in the urine after MBK administration (173), no corresponding metabolites could be detected in afflicted persons exposed to hexane. However, alveolar concentrations have been correlated with the environmental levels (29) and may be suitable for measuring exposure. It has been suggested that electromyography may be used to detect early abnormalities after MBK exposure (173). Whether this will suffice for hexane-exposed individuals is unknown.

The toxicity of methyl ethyl ketone (MEK) has been reviewed (196). Pure MEK may not be a neurotoxin, yet it potentiates the neurotoxicity of MBK or hexane in animals. For example, subjects had not reported any severe symptoms from sniffing a glue thinner containing hexane until the formulation was changed to include MEK, whereupon they developed pronounced motor neuropathies (6, 7, 173). Other reports, especially in animals, corroborate that hexacarbon neuropathies are enhanced by the presence of MEK (8, 53, 173). Neuropathies have also been detected in industrial plants where high levels of MEK and many other solvents were also present (19, 64). The nature of this interaction is unknown, but it may signify still other substances that produce or enhance the development of neuropathies.

Acetone, another ketone, is readily soluble in blood and tissues, is retained for long periods, and its effects are slowly reversible (139). Although it seems to be nontoxic (53), it has not been adequately studied in regard to its interaction with other volatile substances (e.g., in paint thinners).

Other Hydrocarbons. Other higher molecular weight aliphatic hydrocarbons are also present in gasoline and may cause similar neurological changes (173). Tremors were noted in rats after 63 days of administration of 1,500 ppm of nonane on 5 days of each week (32). Also, seizures have been observed in rats after inhalation of 150 mg/l (33,000 ppm) of heptanes for 10 minutes (148). How-

ever, in the presence of 20 per cent toluene, these seizures were prevented during single or repeated exposures. This is one example where a toxic effect may be reduced by the presence of another volatile substance.

Short chained hydrocarbons (propane, isobutane) have not been known to be used for recreation purposes. However, they are chief propellants of spray paints, which are widely abused, and are now replacing fluorocarbons in hair and deodorant sprays. Minimal toxic reactions have been observed for these substances (12), even after repeated, low level exposures in humans (179, 180). However, they are very combustible (used as cooking gas). Any potentiation of toxicity by these small hydrocarbons of other oxy-, chloro-, and unsubstituted hydrocarbons, which are present in paint sprays or other products, is unknown.

General Mixtures. One of the most heterogenous and variable group of products known to be inhaled for recreational purposes is the class of substances contained in lacquer or paint thinners or solvents. Although these substances are used in the United States, use of paint thinners seems to be a larger problem in Mexico (131). These mixtures contain acetone, toluene, methanol, acetates, and methylene chloride ($MeCl_2$), to list some of the more volatile solvents. Not only are there variations in the types of substances present but also in the quantities and purities of one mixture to another. Thus, some of the previously mentioned neurotoxins (hexane, MBK) may not be listed but may be present as impurities along with other noted materials.

Only a few studies have been conducted to determine toxicities related to mixtures of some of the above. After several weeks of exposure of rats to a mixture containing $MeCl_2$, toluene, methanol, and heptane, no toxicity related to this mixture was observed by the termination of exposure (148), even though methanol did accumulate. The experiment was not designed to study the well known neurotoxicities of methanol (53, 83, 141), because the occurrence of such changes are not clearly documented for rats. Any problem that may occur as a result of the administration of methanol may be minimal, inasmuch as no reports have clearly identified this substance in products that are inhaled and have resulted in serious physiological impairments as a result of inhalation abuse.

Chlorohydrocarbons. Much of the previous discussion has centered on hydrocarbons (some of which are oxygenated derivatives). There is another much different class of solvents, the halogenated hydrocarbons (halocarbons). One of the more volatile is methylene chloride ($MeCl_2$) which is becoming more widely used as a solvent in spray paints, thinners, and other inhalable products (138). It is widely known for its conversion to CO in the body and in the formation of carboxyhemoglobin (COHb). The quantity of COHb is dependent on the environment. Although few toxic episodes of COHb occur in properly ventilated areas, high levels have been reported (17). Not only do patients with certain heart ailments need to be concerned about overexposure to $MeCl_2$ (11), increased levels of COHb from cigarette-produced CO may be further elevated by $MeCl_2$ exposure (177). Neurological problems have been associated with the lower halocarbon homologue, methyl chloride (79), but no such hazards have yet been noted for methylene chloride.

Other halogenated hydrocarbons are also inhaled for recreational purposes. Many of these substances are used as anesthetics. The most common ones include trichloroethylene, halothane, chloroform, and methylchloroform. Trichloroethylene is also a major constituent of a very common dry cleaning solvent (sometimes referred to as PERC) and Liquid Paper, a typing correction liquid paste. These, like most chlorohydrocarbons, have been known for a long time to be hepatorenal toxic (11, 19, 40, 44, 62, 140, 149, 150, 175, 176). More recently several halocarbons have been associated with carcinogenesis, abortion, and other developmental effects (13, 44, 67, 71, 84,). Although anesthetics can produce anomalies in the developing animal, the hazards these substances produce at lower concentrations in the anesthetic environment on working personnel are unclear (44, 63, 67, 80, 98). As in most oncogenic studies, the dose is important in determining the outcome. Thus, chloroform, trichloroethylene, and halothane apparently all have a carcinogenic potential when repeatedly used for recreational purposes.

Numerous incidents have been associated with dry cleaning operators who have intentionally or unintentionally overexposed themselves to a cleaning fluid (4, 54, 90, 117, 188, 197). A most interesting phenomenon was observed for these operators when they stopped for a beer on the way home from work. These subjects become flushed after several drinks (178). This alcohol-trichloroethylene interaction is now widely known as "degreasers flush." It also demonstrates the additive-type action this group of depressants can cause when administered during the same period (193). Studies on the effects of several other solvents on animal behavior have shown them to be additive; there are exceptions such as methyl isobutyl ketone and toluene (148).

Besides trichloroethylene, Liquid Paper and household cleaning fluids contain the saturated chlorohydrocarbon trichloroethane (methylchloroform). Death and other problems have been associated with exposure to this mixture (15, 31, 40, 112, 188). Recently, an investigator has observed that nystagmus occurs at low levels (75 ppm) of methylchloroform (105). Whether other more pronounced and maybe irreversible changes occur after repeated administration of trichloroethane alone or in combination with trichloroethylene should be rigorously investigated using suitable paradigms to evaluate any chronic effects.

One of the more common anesthetics, halothane, is also abused, often by hospital personnel because of easy access (38, 170). As characteristic of all halocarbons, hepatic effects comprise the majority of toxicities arising from acute or subchronic administration (174–176). However, recently, a delayed onset of behavioral and other changes has been associated with perinatal exposure (25, 42, 168). As previously mentioned, halothane has been considered to be potentially carcinogenic, yet exposure of animals to concentrations exceeding that in the anesthetic theatre have not been oncogenic (14, 43). Short term behavioral effects, as well as changes resulting from frequently repeated aministration of anesthetics, are only beginning to be investigated (61, 102, 183).

Fluorocarbons. Aerosols in the past (including hair sprays, deodorants, and PAM) used another group of halocarbons, the fluorocarbons, as propellants. It was noted as early as 1960 that many youths were dying from cardiac sensitization after breathing the vapors of these substances from bags (18, 116, 185). A recent study of one region revealed that most of the inhalant deaths could be attributed to fluorocarbon-containing substances (70). Several hundred such deaths have now been recorded by NEISS. Of particular concern regarding this type of exposure is that, even when subjects were still alive when hospitalized, they could not be saved (70, 91). Due to the concern about our atmosphere, these fluorocarbons are no longer used as propellants in United States products but have been replaced by short chain hydrocarbons such as propane and isobutane. These latter substances may be more of a fire hazard than they are toxic to the individual as a result of inhalation.

Nitrous Oxide. Another anesthetic, ether, was enjoyed in the 19th and early 20th centuries in parties. Nitrous oxide was also used during this period. Little use of ether occurs today, whereas N_2O use is apparently on the increase. Nitrous oxide has been known to be dangerous when administered under anesthetic conditions where insufficient (20 per cent) oxygen can be delivered to prevent anoxia. It also can cause seizures (174). Deaths have occurred most likely as a result of anoxia (57). Also myelotoxicities have been associated with N_2O administration (10, 103). However, only recently have several reports appeared correlating the use of N_2O with neuropathies marked by distal paresis, numbness, Lhermitte's sign, and related symptoms (108, 109, 153). These same signs have been reported by dentists and their technicians who frequently use N_2O gas for their patients (45). Although no toxicity has been observed after chronic administration, tolerance and physical dependence have been recently observed after repeated administration of N_2O (165–167). Therefore, the toxicities of this common anesthetic should be carefully reexamined with special emphasis on chronic administration. Presently, it should be considered potentially neurotoxic when used extensively over long periods, even when sufficient oxygen is being administered.

One interesting approach to the study of N_2O action concerns the use of naloxone to block its action. Although there seems to be some antagonism of N_2O-induced analgesia in the presence of naloxone in animals or human subjects (20, 36), there does not seem to be any effect on the anesthetic state (164).

One other group of volatile substances, from a chemical as well as a pharmacological point of view, is the alkyl nitrites. Amyl (nitrite) was the original "popper" and was available for a short time over the counter but is now available only by prescription. Therefore n-butyl and isobutyl nitrites are now manufactured and are widely sold and distributed (e.g., Rush, Locker Room) (88, 114, 115, 160). These substances act as smooth muscle relaxants and thereby dilate blood vessels. This is completely different from most of the inhalants, which are believed to act on neuronal membranes to reduce excitatory impulses, possibly after an initial enhanced excitation.

Methemoglobin is formed immediately after inhalation of these nitrites and can reach levels as high as 20 per cent (85). Although it is easy to kill rats by excessive exposure to these nitrites, fainting is a general safeguard that prevents self-exposure much beyond 20 per cent methemoglobin levels. However, oral administration of organic nitrites may lead to death (159, 191). Treatment with methylene blue is recommended for overdose victims with high methemoglobin levels (163). Although hemoglobin is reformed from methemoglobin at a rate with a half-life ($t_{1/2}$) of about 1 hour, there are subjects with a deficiency in this enzyme system that increases the $t_{1/2}$ to 2 hours (85). Inhalation of nitrites would also be contraindicated in subjects with certain heart conditions (49). From studies in rats, there does not seem to be a build-up of methemoglobin after 10 days of repeated high exposure. However, the total nitrite level in plasma was observed to rise. That is, after one dose it was 0.9 mg/ml, whereas after 11 days of dosing the level of total nitrites had increased to 1.8 to 2.1 mg/ml 16 hours after the last exposure (148). Although the effects in humans are unknown, these results would contraindicate prolonged or frequent use of these organic nitrites.

The preceeding paragraphs have enumerated many enduring or long lasting effects of volatile substances. The acute effects, even though usually reversible, should not be ignored. Just as one should not drive while intoxicated with alcohol or other drugs, the same is true after exposure to solvents. Therefore, more attention is being given to determining those concentrations of volatile substances that affect the worker (52, 80, 102, 183).

Because many solvent abusers are young, it would also be useful to know more about the affects of these different substances on their coping and learning abilities after having a "sniff" in the morning, at lunch time, or even over the weekend. We are only beginning to comprehend the specific hazards and the limiting parameters associated with high intermittent inhalation for recreational purposes.

TREATMENT AND PREVENTION

General Treatment. It has already been stated that no clearly defined physical dependence has been observed. As most of these substances are anesthetic in nature, any overdosed subject would be revived and treated symptomatically as would a subject who has been over anesthetized. Cardiac arrythmias may occur with several of the substances although more frequently with the fluorocarbons. However, few life-threatening cases of inhalant abuse are presented for medical service care.

Inhalant abusers may be admitted to different treatment programs for related problems. It is, therefore, appropriate for the admitting physician to be alert for signs of solvent abuse such as unusual breath odors, irritated mucosa, lightheadedness, conjunctivitis, and other signs of intoxication. Conventional medical exams seldom uncover any unusual symptomatology in these abusers (51, 144), however Prockop (145) has discussed the importance of a good neurological exam to determine whether the subject may have cerebral or peripheral neurological dysfunction. These disorders may often be mistaken for laziness, retardation, or inattentiveness. It would also be important for the physician who determines that a subject has been exposed to volatile substances to determine which substances were involved and to define the length and frequency of exposure.

Recently, however, evidence correlating kidney dysfunction with the intentional inhalation of transmission fluid, paint spray, or glue has been published (68, 104, 130, 151). In contrast with most inhalant abuse subjects, these had identifiable and treatable clinical symptoms of metabolic acidosis, electrolyte imbalance, and often associated vomiting and/or muscle weakness or paraparesis. In all cases, subjects responded well to intravenous fluids of bicarbonate and potassium

chloride. These symptoms have been correlated with toluene and other hydrocarbons present in products that have not yet been quantitatively analyzed.

Treatment and/or prevention of neurological or associated dysfunctions associated with inhalant abuse may depend more on the level of solvent present during intermittent periods. In other words, a subject exposed continuously to moderate levels of solvent (an artist in a nonventilated basement) may be at greater risk than a sniffer in an open cornfield. Thus, only those who sniff in closed, unventilated rooms where the solvents cannot escape when the rag, bag, or can is no longer near the mouth or nose may be at high risk.

Psychological Treatment. Anecdotal accounts abound regarding the difficulties in modifying sniffing behavior (1, 39, 41). Comstock (50) reports fewer favorable pre-post changes on psychometric instruments for a sample of inhalant users in contrast to groups of other-drug users after a period of hospitalization during which psychotherapy, social work, and vocational rehabilitation were available.

Laury (106) described his experience with a sample of 30 sniffers, 10 of whom were seen in outpatient psychotherapy. He stressed the need for careful diagnostic evaluation and pointed out that removal of the sources of glue is insufficient. He emphasized the importance of helping the child secure new peer relationships, of investigating community resources in order to find alternative "square" activities, and particularly of changing the family interaction with the aim of increasing communication and heightening reinforcement for appropriate behavior. Unfortunately, no outcome information is provided.

Chevaili (39) found inhalant users to be unreachable by traditional therapeutic methods because of the lack of verbal ability and the unavailability of basic support systems usually provided by family, school, and work institutions. Like Laury, he stressed the need to work with the family, the school, and the work setting while providing for an integration of verbal therapy and corporal exercises. Campuzano (30) focused on the utilization of psychodrama and the inclusion of paramedical personnel in alternating group therapy sessions. A somewhat similar attempt to avoid the pitfalls of the verbal therapies through a very active "reality therapy-confrontation" approach is outlined by Bratter (26).

A series of studies have been reported that are based on conditioning principles and other learning paradigms. Although most of these efforts are based on a very small sample, they reflect increasing interest in a specific delineation of the therapeutic procedures and a concern with information regarding outcome.

Mecir (122) reported on an attempt to pair inhalation of a cleaning liquid containing trichloroethylene with discomfort produced by an injection of apomorphine. Twenty such trials were given to a 17-year-old boy in the space of a month, followed by five booster shots. The author reported success over a 7-year follow-up. Skoricova and Molcan (162) treated 22 adolescents and 10 adults with aversive therapy after a period of detoxification and symptomatic treatment. They reported therapy as being successful in 50 per cent of their treated cases, using resumption of sniffing as the criterion.

Kolvin (97) reported on the treatment of a 15-year-old gasoline sniffer by the use of relaxation and aversive imagery techniques. Self-report information during a 17-month follow-up period showed no resumption of sniffing. Blanchard et al. (22) treated a patient with a 7-year history of spray paint inhalation with a combination of covert sensitization and apneic aversion, with apnea induced by an injection of succinylcholine chloride (Anectine). Dependent variables included two types of free access measures. Follow-up for a year indicated a discontinuation of sniffing and an appreciable degree of social rehabilitation.

Maletsky (119) treated 10 Army drug abusers, one of whom was a spray paint user, with covert sensitization assisted by the inhalation of a foul but safe odor. Behavioral measures included self-report information (incidence of drug abuse and urges to abuse drugs), reports from the authorities, and randomly scheduled urinalysis. The experimental group improved more than a control group receiving counseling on all three sets of criteria; follow-up lasted 6 months.

Other Control Techniques and Prevention. A number of authors reporting on psychological treatment have indicated the importance of adjunctive methods involving school, home, and work (26, 39, 106).

Additional reports deal with the effectiveness of such other approaches in the absence of psychological treatment. Unfortunately, these are largely anecdotal accounts that do not report outcome evaluation data.

Silberberg and Silberberg (161) focused on the role of the school and pointed out that a spurt of arrests for glue use sometimes follows on the heels of a school drug education program, a fact that seems to be in keeping with difficulties occasionally encountered with drug information programs. They emphasized the need to initiate programs that develop self-worth within the context of the schools. They concluded that the typical sniffer can succeed most easily in an alternative school setting of the type where traditional skills are not the only aptitudes necessary for success.

De Hoyos (55) organized youth groups designed to develop positive status on the basis of attainable achievements in sports and the arts, particularly in relationship to peers. Simultaneously, workers facilitated the formation of formal neighborhood groups of parents (consilios) who interacted with youth groups in drug abuse seminars. The community group also developed audiovisual and written materials (e.g., comic books) as a preventative measure.

A number of attempts at prevention have been reported (16) stressing the need to appeal to merchants to control in some fashion the sale of the more popular inhalants in a particular community. Such efforts, complicated by the patchwork of local laws regulating the sale of various inhalants, seem not to have markedly altered inhalant-related behavior. Success may depend on clear, uniform laws regulating such sales, as well as on a total community committed to compliance. Rather than list products, one area has restricted sales of items containing solvents (e.g., hexane, benzene, toluene, methyl butyl ketone, trichloroethylene, nitrous oxide, butyl nitrite, etc.) to minors.

Another effort to control inhalant use through the addition of unpleasant additives (e.g., oil of mustard to glue) has been thwarted by sniffers' discoveries of other intoxicating solvents (46). The pros and cons of additives have been previously discussed (156). If other additives could be found that were miscible with the product and their effectiveness established, this might be one possible approach. Not only would the substance reduce inhalant abuse, it would serve to warn a person during normal use of the product that improper ventilation has created excessive levels of solvent in the atmosphere.

References

1. Ackerly, W., and Gibson, G. Lighter fluid sniffing. Am. J. Psychiatry 9:1056, 1964.
2. Akiguchi, I., Fujiwara, T., Iwai, N., and Kawai, C. A case of chronic thinner (toluene) intoxication with myeloneuropathy and EEG abnormality. Rinsho Shinkeigaku 17:586, 1977.
3. Aksoy, M., and Erdem, S. Followup study on the mortality and the development of leukemia in 44 pancytopenic patients with chronic exposure to benzene. Blood 52:285, 1978.
4. Alapin, B. Trichloroethylene addiction and its effects. Br. J. Addict. 68:331, 1973.
5. Allen, N., Mendell, J. R., Billmaier, D. J., Fontaine, R. E., and O'Neill, J. Toxic polyneuropathy due to methyl n-butyl ketone. Arch. Neurol. 32:209, 1975.
6. Altenkirch, H. Sniffing addiction: Chronic solvent abuse with neurotoxic effects in children and juveniles. Dtsch. Med. Wochensch. 104:935, 1979.
7. Altenkirch, H., Mager, J., Stoltenburg, G., and Helmbrecht, J. Toxic polyneuropathies after sniffing a glue thinner. J. Neurol. 214:137, 1977.
8. Altenkirch, H., Stoltenburg, G., and Wagner, H. M. Experimental studies on hydrocarbon neuropathies induced by methyl-ethyl-ketone (MEK). J. Neurol. 219:159, 1978.
9. Amaducci, L., Arfaioli, C., Inzitari, D., and Martinetti, M. G. Another possible precipitating factor in multiple sclerosis: The exposure to organic solvents. Boll. Inst. Sieroter. (Milan) 56:613, 1978.
10. Amess, J. A. L., Burman, J. F., Rees, G. M., Nancekievill, D. G., and Mollin, D. L. Megaloblastic haemopoiesis in patients receiving nitrous oxide. Lancet 2:339, 1978.
11. Aviado, D. M. Preclinical pharmacology and toxicology of halogenated solvents and propellants. In Review of Inhalants: Euphoria to Dysfunction, C. W. Sharp and M. L. Brehm, editors. National Institute on Drug Abuse Research Monograph # 15, pp. 164–184. Washington, D.C., United States Government Printing Office, 1977.
12. Aviado, D. M., Zakhari, S., and Watanabe, T. Non-Flourinated Propellants and Solvents for Aerosols. Cleveland, CRC Press, 1977.
13. Axelson, O., Andersson, K., Hogstedt, C., Holmberg, B., Molina, G., and deVerdier, A. A cohort study on trichloroethylene exposure and cancer mortality. Occup. Med. 20: 194, 1978.
14. Baden, J. M., Mazze, R. I., Wharton, R. S., Rice, S. A., and Kosek, J. C. Carcinogenicity of halothane in Swiss/ICR mice. Anesthesiology 51:20, 1979.
15. Baerg, R. D., and Kimberg, D. V. Centrilobular hepatic necrosis and acute renal failure in "solvent sniffers." Ann. Intern. Med. 73:713, 1970.
16. Barker, G., and Adams, W. Glue sniffers. Sociol. Res. 47:289, 1973.
17. Barrowcliff, D. F. Chronic carbon monoxide poisoning caused by methylene chloride paintstripper. Med. Sci. Law 18:238, 1978.
18. Bass, M. Sudden sniffing death. J. A. M. A. 212: 2075, 1970.
19. Berg, E. F. Retrobulbar neuritis. Ann. Ophthalmol. 3:1351, 1971.
20. Berkowitz, B. A., Finck, A. D., and Ngai, S. H. Nitrous oxide analgesia: Reversal by naloxone and development of tolerance. J. Pharmacol. Exp. Ther. 203:539, 1977.
21. Berry, G., Heaton, R. K., and Kirby, M. W. Neuropsychological assessment of solvent inhalers: Final report to the National Institute on Drug Abuse, 1977; and neuropsychological assessment of chronic inhalant abusers: A preliminary report. In Voluntary Inhalation of Industrial Solvents, C. W. Sharp and L. T. Carroll, editors, pp. 111–136. Rockville, Md., National Institute on Drug Abuse, 1978.
22. Blanchard, E., Libet, J., and Young, L. Apneic aversion and covert sensitization in the treatment of hydrocarbon inhalation addiction: A case study. J. Behav. Ther. Exp. Psychol. 4:383, 1973.
23. Block, J., Goodman, N., Ambellan, F., and Revenson, J. A Self Administered High School Study of Drugs. New York, Institute for Research and Evaluation, 1974.
24. Bonnheim, M., and Korman, M. Family Interaction and Inhalant Use. Dallas, University of Texas Health Science Center, 1977.
25. Bowman, R. E. Preclinical behavioral toxicology of inhalant solvents. In Review of Inhalants: Euphoria to Dysfunction, C. W. Sharp and M. L. Brehm, editors, National Institute on Drug Abuse Research Monograph # 15, p. 200–223. Washington, D.C., United States Government Printing Office, 1977.
26. Bratter, T. Treating alienated, unmotivated drug abusing adolescents. Am. J. Psychother. 27:585, 1973.
27. Brozovsky, M., and Winkler, E. Glue sniffing in children and adolescents. N. Y. State J. Med. 65: 1984, 1965.
28. Bruckner, J. V., and Peterson, R. G. Review of the aliphatic and aromatic hydrocarbons. In Review of Inhalants: Euphoria to Dysfunction, C. W. Sharp and M. L. Brehm, editors, National Institute on Drug Abuse Research Monograph # 15, p. 124–163. Washington, D.C., United States Government Printing Office, 1977.
29. Brugnone, F., Perbellini, L., Grigolini, L., and Apostoli, P. Solvent exposure in a shoe upper factory. Int. Arch. Occup. Environ. Health 42:51, 1978.
30. Campuzano, M. A group psychotherapy model for drug dependent adolescents. In Voluntary Inhalation of Industrial Solvents, C. W. Sharp and L. T. Carroll, editors, pp. 389–396, Rockville, Md., National Institute on Drug Abuse, 1978.
31. Caplan, Y. H., Backer, R. C., and Whitaker, J. Q. 1,1,1-Trichloroethane: Report of a fatal intoxication. Clin. Toxicol. 9:69, 1976.
32. Carpenter, C. P., Geary, D. L., Myers, R. C., Nachreiner, D. J., Sullivan, L. J., and King, J. M. Petroleum hydrocarbon toxicity studies. XVII. Animal response to n-nonane vapor. Toxicol. Appl.

Pharmacol. 44:53, 1978.

33. Carroll, E. Notes on the epidemiology of inhalants. In *Review of Inhalants: Euphoria to Dysfunction*, C. W. Sharp and M. L. Brehm, editors, National Institute on Drug Abuse Research Monograph # 15, pp. 14–24. Washington, D.C., United States Government Printing Office, 1977.

34. Carroll, E. Inhalant use. In *Voluntary Inhalation of Industrial Solvents*, C. W. Sharp and L. T. Carroll, editors, pp. 1–8. Rockville, Md., National Institute on Drug Abuse, 1978.

35. Chapel, J., and Taylor, D. Glue sniffing. Mo. Med. 65:288, 1968.

36. Chapman, C. R., and Benedetti, C. Nitrous oxide effects on cerebral evoked potential to pain: Partial reversal with a narcotic antagonist. Anesthesiology 51:135, 1979.

37. *Characteristics of Clients Reported to CODAP in 1978 with a Primary Drug Problem of Inhalants*, Rockville, Md., National Institute on Drug Abuse, 1979.

38. Chenoweth, M. B. Abuse of inhalation anesthetics. In *Review of Inhalants: Euphoria to Dysfunction*, C. W. Sharp and M. L. Brehm, editors, National Institute on Drug Abuse Research Monograph # 15, pp. 102–111, Washington, D.C., United States Government Printing Office, 1977.

39. Chevaili Arroyo, A. Is the inhalant user incurable? In *Voluntary Inhalation of Industrial Solvents*, C. W. Sharp and L. T. Carroll, editors, pp. 379–388. Rockville, Md., National Institute on Drug Abuse, 1978.

40. Clearfield, H. R. Hepatorenal toxicity from sniffing spot-remover (trichloroethylene). Dig. Dis. 15:851, 1970.

41. Clinger, O., and Johnson, N. Purposeful inhalation of gasoline vapors. Psychiatr. Q. 25:555, 1951.

42. Coate, W. B., Kapp, R. W., and Lewis, T. R. Chronic exposure to low concentrations of halothane-nitrous oxide: Reproductive and cytogenetic effects in the rat. Anesthesiology 50:310, 1979.

43. Coate, W. B., Ulland, B. M., and Lewis, T. R. Chronic exposure to low concentrations of halothane-nitrous oxide: Lack of carcinogenic effect in the rat. Anesthesiology 50:306, 1979.

44. Cohen, E. N. Toxicity of inhalation anaesthetic agents. Br. J. Anaesth. 50:665, 1978.

45. Cohen, E. N., Brown, B. W., Wu, M. L., Whitcher, C. E., Brodsky, J. B., Gift, H. C., Greenfield, W., Jones, T. W., and Driscoll, E. J. Occupational disease in dentistry and exposure to anesthetic gases. J. Am. Dent. Assoc. 101:21, 1980.

46. Cohen, S. The volatile solvents. Public Health Rev. 2:185, 1973.

47. Cohen, S. Inhalant abuse. Drug Abuse Alcohol Newsletter 4:3, October 1975.

48. Cohen, S. Inhalant abuse: An overview of the problem. In *Review of Inhalants: Euphoria to Dysfunction*, C. W. Sharp and M. L. Brehm, National Institute on Drug Abuse Research Monograph #15, pp. 2–11. Washington, D.C., United States Government Printing Office, 1977.

49. Cohen, S. Amyl nitrite rediscovered. Drug Abuse Alcohol Newsletter 7: January 1978.

50. Comstock, B. Psychological measurements in long term inhalant abusers. In *Voluntary Inhalation of Industrial Solvents*, C. W. Sharp and L. T. Carroll, editors, pp. 159–168. Rockville, Md., National Institute on Drug Abuse, 1978.

51. Comstock, E. G., and Comstock, B. S. Medical evaluation of inhalant abusers. In *Review of Inhalants: Euphoria to Dysfunction*, C. W. Sharp and M. L. Brehm, editors, National Institute on Drug Abuse Research Monograph # 15, pp. 54–80. Washington, D.C., United States Government Printing Office, 1977.

52. Cook, T. L., Smith, M., Winter, P. M., Starkweather, J. A., and Eger, E. I., II. Effect of subanesthetic concentration of enflurane and halothane on human behavior. Anesth. Analg. 57:434, 1978.

53. Couri, D., and Nachtman, J. P. Toxicology of alcohols, ketones, and esters—inhalation. In *Review of Inhalants: Euphoria to Dysfunction*, C. W. Sharp and M. L. Brehm, editors, National Institute on Drug Abuse Research Monograph # 15, pp. 112–123. Washington, D.C., United States Government Printing Office, 1977.

54. Cragg, J., Castledine, S. A. A fatality associated with trichloroethylene inhalation. Med. Sci. Law 10:112, 1970.

55. de Hoyos, L. *The Manco/Spoda Tri-City Chicano Alliance Project*. San Antonio, Mexican American Neighborhood Civic Organization, 1975.

56. de la Garza, F., Mendiola, I., and Rabago, S. Psychological, familial and social study of 32 patients using inhalants. In *Voluntary Inhalation of Industrial Solvents*, C. W. Sharp and L. T. Carroll, editors, pp. 75–89. Rockville, Md., National Institute on Drug Abuse, 1978.

57. DiMaio, V. J. M., and Garriott, J. C. Four deaths resulting from abuse of nitrous oxide. J. Foren. Sci. 23:169, 1978.

58. Dodd, J., and Santostefano, S. A comparison of the cognitive functioning of glue-sniffers and non-sniffers. J. Pediatr. 64:565, 1964.

59. Done, A. Inhalants. In *The Technical Papers of the Second Report of the National Commission on Marijuana and Drug Abuse*, vol. 1, pp. 107–115. Washington, D. C., United States Government Printing Office, 1973.

60. Easson, W. Gasoline addiction in children. Pediatrics 29:250, 1962.

61. Eger, E. I., II, White, A. E., Brown, C. L., Biava, C. G., Corbett, T. H., and Stevens, W. C. A test of the carcinogenicity of enflurane, isoflurane, halothane, methoxyflurane, and nitrous oxide in mice. Anesth. Analg. 57:678, 1978.

62. Ehrenreich, T., Yunis, S. L., and Churg, J. Membranous nephropathy following exposure to volatile hydrocarbons. Environ. Res. 14:35, 1977.

63. Ericson, A., and Kallen, B. Survey of infants born in 1973 or 1975 to Swedish women working in operating rooms during their pregnancies. Anesth. Analg. 58:302, 1979.

64. Fagius, J., and Grönqvist, B. Function of peripheral nerves and signs of polyneuropathy in solvent-exposed workers at a Swedish steelworks. Acta Neurol. Scand. 57:305, 1978.

65. Faillace, L., and Guynn, R. Abuse of organic solvents. Psychosomatics 17:18, 1976.

66. Faucett, R., and Jenson, R. Addiction to the inhalant of gasoline fumes in a child. J. Pediatr. 41:364, 1952.

67. Ferstandig, L. L. Trace concentrations of anesthetic gases: A critical review of their disease potential.

Anesth. Analg. 57:328, 1978.

68. Fischman, C. M., and Oster, J. R. Toxic effects of toluene: A new cause of high anion gap metabolic acidosis. J. A. M. A. 241:1713, 1979.

69. Friedman, C., and Friedman, A. Drug abuse and delinquency. In *The Technical Papers of the Second Report of the National Commission on Marijuana and Drug Abuse*, vol. 1, pp. 398–484. Washington, D. C., United States Government Printing Office, 1973.

70. Garriott, J., and Petty, C. S. Death from inhalant abuse. Toxicological and pathological evaluation of 34 cases. Clin. Toxicol. 16:305, 1980.

71. Garro, A. J., and Phillips, R. A. Mutagenicity of the halogenated olefin, 2-bromo-2-chloro-1, 1-difluoroethylene, a presumed metabolite of the inhalation anesthetic halothane. Mutat. Res. 54:17, 1978.

72. Glaser H., and Massengale, O. Glue sniffing in children. J. A. M. A. 181:300, 1962.

73. Goldstein, B. D. Hematotoxicity in humans. J. Toxicol. Environ. Health (Suppl.) 2:69, 1977.

74. Gonzalez, E. G., and Downey, J. A. Polyneuropathy in a glue sniffer. Arch. Phys. Med. Rehab. 53:333, 1972.

75. Gossett, J. T., Lewis, J. M., and Phillips, V. A. Extent and prevalence of illicit drug use as reported by 56,745 students. J. A. M. A. 216:1464, 1971.

76. Goto, I., Matsumura, M., Inoue, N., Murai, Y., Shida, K., Santa, T., and Kuroiwa, Y. Toxic polyneuropathy due to glue sniffing. J. Neurol. Neurosurg. Psychiatry 37:848, 1974.

77. Gotway, B. Family characteristics and stressful life events among male adolescent inhalant users. Dissertation, University of Texas, Health Science Center, Dallas, Texas, 1979.

78. Gregersen, P., Mikkelsen, S., Klausen, H., Dossing, M., Nielsen, H., and Thygesen, P. A chronic cerebral syndrome in painters: Dementia due to inhalation of cryptogenic origin? Ugeskr. Laeger. 140:1638, 1978.

79. Gudmundsson, G. Methyl chloride poisoning 13 years later. Arch. Environ. Health 32:236, 1977.

80. Gun, R. T., Grygorcewicz, C., and Nettelbeck, T. J. Choice reaction time in workers using trichloroethylene. Med. J. Aust. 1:535, 1978.

81. Hane, M., Axelson, O., Blume, J., Hogstedt, C., Sundell, L., and Yareborg, B. Psychological function changes among house painters. Scand. J. Work Environ. Health 3:91, 1977.

82. Hanninen, H. Psychological test methods: Sensitivity to long term chemical exposure at work. Neurobehav. Toxicol. (Suppl. 1) 1:157, 1979.

83. Hayreh, M. S., Hayreh, S. S., Baumbach, G. L., Cancilla, P., Martin-Amat, G., Tephly, R., McMartin, K. E., and Makar, A. B. Methyl alcohol poisoning. Arch. Ophthalmol. 95:1851, 1977.

84. Henschler, D., Eder, E., Neudecker, T., and Metzler, M.. Carcinogenicity of trichloroethylene: Fact or artifact? Arch. Toxicol. 37:233, 1977.

85. Horne, M. K., III, Waterman, M. R., Simon, L. M., Garriott, J. C., and Foerster, E. H. Methemoglobinemia from sniffing butyl nitrite. Ann. Intern. Med. 91:417, 1979.

86. Ikeda, M. Mutual suppression of oxidation involved in the metabolism of thinner constituents. In *Voluntary Inhalation of Industrial Solvents*, C. W. Sharp and L. T. Carroll, editors, pp. 322–332.

Rockville, Md., National Institute on Drug Abuse, 1978.

87. Infante, P. F., Rinsky, R. A., Wagoner, J. K., and Young, R. J. Leukaemia in benzene workers. Lancet 2:76, 1977.

88. Israelst, A. M. S., Lambert, S., and Oki, G. Poppers, a new recreational drug craze. Can. Psychiatr. Assoc. J. 23:493, 1978.

89. Jackson, R., Thornhill, E., and Gonzalez, R. Glue sniffing—brief flight from reality. J. La. State Med. Soc. 119:451, 1967.

90. James, W. R. L. Fatal addiction to trichloroethylene. Br. J. Ind. Med. 20:47, 1963.

91. Jefferson, I. G. Accidental death of child playing with deodorant aerosol. Lancet 1:779, 1978.

92. Johnson, B. L., Anger, W. K., Setzer, J. V., Lynch, D. W., and Lewis, T. R. Neurobehavioral effects of methyl n-butyl ketone and methyl n-amyl ketone in rats and monkeys: A summary of NIOSH investigations. J. Environ. Pathol. Toxicol. 2:113, 1978.

93. Johnston, L. D., Bachman, J. G., and O'Malley, P. M. *Drugs and the Class of '78: Behaviors, Attitudes and Recent National Trends.* Rockville, Md., National Institute on Drug Abuse, 1979.

94. Kalogerakis, M. The assaultive psychiatric patient. Psychiatr. Q. 45:372, 1971.

95. Kaye, S. Insidious benzene poisoning. Bol. Assoc. Med. P. R. 70:42, 1978.

96. Knox, J. W., and Nelson, J. R. Permanent encephalopathy from toluene inhalation. N. Engl. J. Med. 275:1494, 1966.

97. Kolvin, I. Aversive imagery treatment in adolescents. Behav. Res. Ther. 5:245, 1967.

98. Konietzko, H., Haberlandt, W., Heilbronner, H., Reill, G., and Weichardt, H. Cytogenetische untersuchungen an trichlorathylen-arbeitern. Arch. Toxicol. 40:201, 1978.

99. Korman, M., Price, G., Weis, C., Semler, I., and North, A. *A Psychosocial and Neuropsychological Study of Young Inhalant Users: Preliminary Findings.* Dallas, University of Texas Health Science Center, 1979.

100. Korman, M., Semler, I., and Trimboli, F. A psychiatric emergency room study of 162 inhalant users. Addict. Behav. 5:143, 1980.

101. Korobkin, R., Asbury, A. K., Sumner, A. J., and Nielsen, S. L. Glue-sniffing neuropathy. Arch. Neurol. 32:158, 1975.

102. Korttila, K., Pfäffli, P., Linnoila, M., Blomgren, E., Hänninen, H., and Hakkinen, S. Operating room nurses' psychomotor and driving skills after occupational exposure to halothane and nitrous oxide. Acta Anaesth. Scand. 22:33, 1978.

103. Kripke, B. J., Talarico, L., Shah, N. K., and Kelman, A. D. Hematologic reaction to prolonged exposure to nitrous oxide. Anesthesiology 47:342, 1977.

104. Kroeger, R. M., Moore, R. J., Lehman, T. H., Giesy, J. D., and Skeeters, C. E. Recurrent urinary calculi associated with toluene sniffing. J. Urol. 123:89, 1980.

105. Larsby, B., Tham, R., Odkvist, L. M., Norlander, B., Hyden, D., Aschan, G., and Rubin, A. Exposure of rabbits to methylchloroform: Vestibular disturbances correlated to blood and cerebrospinal fluid levels. Int. Arch. Occup. Environ. Health 41:7, 1978.

106. Laury, G. Psychotherapy with glue sniffers. Int. J. Child. Psychother. 1:98, 1972.

107. Lawton, J., and Malmquist, C. Gasoline addiction in children. Psychiatr. Q. 35:551, 1961.
108. Layzer, R. B. Myeloneuropathy after prolonged exposure to nitrous oxide. Lancet 2:1227, 1978.
109. Layzer, R. B., Fishman, R. A., and Schafer, J. A. Neuropathy following abuse of nitrous oxide. Neurology 28:504, 1978.
110. LeQuesne, P. M. Clinical expression of neurotoxic injury and diagnostic use of electromyography. Environ. Health Perspect. 26:89, 1978.
111. Lindstrom, K. Psychological performances of workers exposed to various solvents. Work Environ. Health 10:151, 1973.
112. Litt, I. F., and Cohen, M. I. "Danger...vapor harmful": Spot-remover sniffing. N. Engl. J. Med. 281: 543, 1969.
113. Longley, E. O., Jones, A. T., Welch, R., and Lomaev, O. Two acute toluene episodes in merchant ships. Arch. Environ. Health 14:481, 1967.
114. Lowry, T. P. Amyl nitrite: A toxicological survey. In Isobutyl Nitrite and Related Compounds, M. Nickerson, J. O. Parker, T. P. Lowry, and E. W. Swenson, editors, pp. 89-91. San Francisco, Pharmex, 1979.
114a. Lowry, T. P. The volatile nitrites as sexual drugs: A user survey. J. Sex Educ. Ther. 1:8, 1979.
115. Lowry, T. P. Amyl nitrite: An old high comes back to visit. Behav. Med. 6:19, 1979.
116. Luckstead, E. F., Jordan, F. B., and Prouty, R. W. Sudden death following fluorohydrocarbon aerosol "sniffing." J. Okla. State Med. Assoc. 71:117, 1978.
117. Lüpke, H., Gerchow, J., and Schmidt, K. On two cases of lethal trichloroethylene intoxication. Z. Rechtsmed. 81:237, 1978.
118. Lykke, A. W. J., and Stewart, B. W. Fibrosing alveolitis (pulmonary interstitial fibrosis) evoked by experimental inhalation of gasoline vapours. Experientia 34:498, 1978.
119. Maletzky, B. Assisted covert sensitization for drug abuse. Int. J. Addict. 9:411, 1974.
120. Mallov, J. S. MBK neuropathy among spray painters. J. A. M. A. 235:1455, 1976.
121. Massengale, O., Glaser, H., and LeLievre, R. Physical and psychologic factors in glue sniffing. N. Engl. J. Med. 269:1340, 1963.
122. Mecir, J. Therapeutic measures in addiction of minors to inhalation of volatile substances affecting the activity of CNS. Cesk. Psychiatr. 67:224, 1971.
123. Medida, M., and Cruz, A. A Survey of Paint and Glue Inhalation among Phoenix Inner City Youth. Phoenix, Az., Valle Del Sol, Inc., 1972.
124. Medina-Mora, I. M. E., Schnaas, A. A. L., Terroba, G. G., Isoard, V. Y., and Suarez, U. C. Epidemiology of inhalant use in Mexico. In Voluntary Inhalation of Industrial Solvents, C. W. Sharp and L. T. Carroll, editors, pp. 15-22. Rockville, Md., National Institute on Drug Abuse, 1978.
125. Meloff, W. An exploratory study of adolescent glue sniffers. Dissertation Abstr. Int. 31:1391, 1970.
126. Mendell, J. R., Saida, K., Ganansia, M. F., Jackson, D. B., Weiss, H., Gardier, R. W., Chrisman, C., Allen, N., Couri, D., O'Neill, J., Marks, B., and Hetland, L. Toxic polyneuropathy produced by methyl n-butyl ketone. Science 185:787, 1974.
127. Merry, J., and Zachariadis, N. Addiction to glue sniffing. Br. Med. J. 2:1448, 1962.
128. Mikkelsen, S., Gregersen, P., Klausen, H., Dossing, M., and Nielsen, H. Presenile dementia as an occupational disease following industrial exposure to organic solvents: A review of the literature. Ugeskr. Laeger. 140:1633, 1978.
129. Montiel, M. Paint inhalation research in the context of a Chicano barrio. Valle Del Sol, Inc., Phoenix, Arizona. Presented at the First International Symposium on the Voluntary Inhalation of Industrial Solvents, Mexico City, June 1976.
130. Moss, A. H., Gabow, P. A., Kaehny, W. D., Goodman, S. I., and Haut, L. L. Fanconi's syndrome and distal renal tubular acidosis after glue sniffing. Ann. Intern. Med. 92:69, 1980.
131. Natera, G. Study on the incidence of use of volatile solvents in 27 centers in Mexico. In Voluntary Inhalation of Industrial Solvents, C. W. Sharp and L. T. Carroll, editors, pp. 41-57. Rockville, Md., National Institute on Drug Abuse, 1978.
132. Nomiyama, K., and Nomiyama, H. Three fatal cases of thinner-sniffing, and experimental exposure to toluene in human and animals. Int. Arch. Occup. Environ. Health 41:55, 1978.
133. Nomura, N., Mitani, K., Terao, A., and Shirabe, T. A case of myeloneuropathy induced by chronic exposure to organic solvents. Rinsho Shinkeigaku 18:259, 1978.
134. Nurcombe, B., Bianchi, G., Money, J., and Cawte, J. A hunger for stimuli: The psychosocial background of petrol inhalation. Br. J. Med. Psychol. 43: 367, 1970.
135. Nylander, I. Thinner addiction in children and adolescents. Acta Paedopsychiatr. 29:273, 1962.
136. O'Brien, E. T., Yeoman, W. B., and Hobby, J. A. E. Hepatorenal damage from toluene in a "glue sniffer." Br. Med. J. 2:29, 1971.
137. Oh, S. J., and Kim, J. M. Giant axonal swelling in "Huffer's" neuropathy. Arch. Neurol. 33:583, 1976.
138. Perbellini, L., Brugnone, F., Grigolini, L., Cunegatti, P., and Tacconi, A. Alveolar air and blood dichloromethane concentration in shoe sole factory workers. Int. Arch. Occup. Environ. Health 40:241, 1977.
139. Peterson, R. G., and Bruckner, J. V. Animal model for studying the toxicological and pharmacological effects resulting from exposure to volatile substances. Final Report on Contract 271-75-3067, National Institute on Drug Abuse, April 1978.
140. Pinkhas, J., Cohen, I., Kruglak, J., and deVries, A. Hobby-induced factor VII deficiency. Haemostasis 1:52, 1972.
141. Posner, H. S. Biohazards of methanol in proposed new uses. J. Toxicol. Environ. Health 1:153, 1975.
142. Preble, E., and Laury, G. Plastic cement: The ten cent hallucinogen. Int. J. Addict. 2:271, 1967.
143. Press, E., and Done, A. Solvent sniffing: Physiologic effects and community control measures for intoxication from the intentional inhalation of organic solvents. Pediatrics 39:451, 1967.
144. Prockop, L. Specific neurological evaluation of inhalant abusers: Clinical and laboratory. In Review of Inhalants: Euphoria to Dysfunction, C. W. Sharp and M. L. Brehm, editors, National Institute on Drug Abuse Research Monograph #15, pp. 81-96. Washington, D.C., United States Government Printing Office, 1977.
145. Prockop, L. Neurotoxic volatile substance. Neurology 29:862, 1979.
146. Prockop, L., and Couri, D.: Nervous system damage

from mixed organic solvents. In *Review of Inhalants: Euphoria to Dysfunction*, C. W. Sharp and M. L. Brehm, editors, National Institute on Drug Abuse Research Monograph # 15, pp. 185–198. Washington, D.C., United States Government Printing Office, 1977.

147. Prockop, L. D., Alt, M., and Tison, J. "Huffer's" neuropathy. J. A. M. A. 229:1083, 1974.

148. Pryor, G. T., Howd, R. A., Bingham, L. R., and Robert, C. S. Biomedical studies on the effects of abused inhalant mixtures. Reports on Contract 271-77-3402, National Institute on Drug Abuse, 1978, 1979.

149. Ranek, L. Halothane hepatitis. Arch. Toxicol. (Suppl.) 1:137, 1978.

150. Ravnskov, U. Exposure to organic solvents—a missing link in poststreptococcal glomerulonephritis? Acta Med. Scand. 203: 35, 1978.

151. Ravnskov, U. Acute glomerulonephritis and exposure to organic solvents in father and daughter. Acta Med. Scand. 205:581, 1979.

152. Robinson, R. O. Tetraethyl lead poisoning from gasoline sniffing. J. A. M. A. 240:1373, 1978.

153. Sahenk, Z., Mendell, J. R., Couri, D., and Nachtman, J. Polyneuropathy from inhalation of N₂O cartridges through a whipped-cream dispenser. Neurology 28:485, 1978.

154. Sato, A., and Nakajima, T. Dose-dependent metabolic interaction between benzene and toluene in vivo and in vitro. Toxicol. Appl. Pharmacol. 48:249, 1979.

155. Seppäläinen, A. M., Husman, K., and Märtenson, C. Neurophysiological effects of long-term exposure to a mixture of organic solvents. Scand. J. Work Environ. Health 4:304, 1978.

156. Seshia, S. S., Rajani, K. R., Boeckx, R. L., and Chow, P. N. The neurological manifestations of chronic inhalation of leaded gasoline. Dev. Med. Child Neurol. 20:323, 1978.

157. Sharp, C. W., and Brehm, M. L. *Review of Inhalants: Euphoria to Dysfunction*, National Institute on Drug Abuse, Research Monograph # 15, Washington, D.C., United States Government Printing Office, 1977.

158. Sharp, C. W., and Carroll, L. T. *Voluntary Inhalation of Industrial Solvents*. Rockville, Md., National Institute on Drug Abuse, 1978.

159. Sharp, C. W., and Stillman, R. C. Blush not with nitrites. Ann. Intern. Med. 92:700, 1980.

160. Sigell, L. T., Kapp, F. T., Fusaro, G. A., Nelson, E. D., and Falck, R. S. Popping and snorting volatile nitrites: A current fad for getting high. Am. J. Psychiatry 135:1216, 1978.

161. Silberberg, N., and Silberberg, M. Glue sniffing in children. A position paper. J. Drug Educ. 4:301, 1974.

162. Skoricova, M., and Molcan, J. Catamnestic study on volatile solvent addiction. Act. Nerv. Super. (Praha) 14:116, 1972.

163. Smith, M., Stair, T., and Rolnick, M. A. Butyl nitrite and a suicide attempt. Ann. Intern. Med. 92:719, 1980.

164. Smith, R. A., Wilson, M., and Miller, K. Naloxone has no effect on nitrous oxide anesthesia. Anesthesiology 49:6, 1978.

165. Smith, R. A., Winter, P. M., Smith, M., and Eger, E. I., II. Rapidly developing tolerance to acute exposures to anesthetic agents. Anesthesiology 50:496, 1979.

166. Smith, R. A., Winter, P. M., Smith, M., and Eger, E. I., II. Convulsions in mice after anesthesia. Anesthesiology 50:501, 1979.

167. Smith, R. A., Winter, P. M., Smith, M., and Eger, E. I., II. Tolerance to and dependence on inhalation anesthetics. Anesthesiology 50:505, 1979

168. Smith, R. F., Bowman, R. E., and Katz, J. Behavioral effects of exposure to halothane during early development in the rat: Sensitive period during pregnancy. Anesthesiology 49:319, 1978.

169. Snyder, C. A., Goldstein, B. D., Sellakumar, A., Wolman, S. R., Bromberg, I., Erlichman, M. N., and Laskin, S. Hematotoxicity of inhaled benzene to Sprague-Dawley rats and AKR mice at 300 ppm. J. Toxicol. Environ. Health 4:605, 1978.

170. Spencer, J. D., Raasch, F. O., and Trefny, F. A. Halothane abuse in hospital personnel. J. A. M. A. 235:1034, 1976.

171. Spencer, P. S., Bischoff, M. C., and Schaumburg, H. H. On the specific molecular configuration of neurotoxic aliphatic hexacarbon compounds causing central—peripheral distal axonopathy. Toxicol. Appl. Pharmacol. 44:17, 1978.

172. Spencer, P. S., Schaumburg, H. H., Raleigh, R. L., and Terhaar, C. J. Nervous system degeneration produced by the industrial solvent methyl n-butyl ketone. Arch. Neurol. 32:219, 1975.

173. Spencer, P. S., Schaumburg, H. H., Sabri, M. I., and Veronesi, B. *The Enlarging View of Hexacarbon Neurotoxicity*, CRC Critical Reviews in Toxicology. Boca Raton, Fla., CRC Press, In press.

174. Steen, P. A., and Michenfelder, J. D. Neurotoxicity of anesthetics. Anesthesiology 50:437, 1979.

175. Stevens, W. C., Eger, E. I., II, White, A., Biava, C. G., Gibbons, R. D., and Shargel, R. Comparative toxicities of enflurane, fluroxene and nitrous oxide at subanaesthetic concentrations in laboratory animals. Can. Anaesth. Soc. J. 24:479, 1977.

176. Stevens, W. C., Eger, E. I., II, White, A., Halsey, M. J., Munger, W., Gibbons, R. D., Dolan, W., and Shargel, R. Comparative toxicities of halothane, isoflurane, and diethyl ether at subanesthetic concentrations in laboratory animals. Anesthesiology 42:408, 1975.

177. Stevenson, M. F., Chenoweth, M. B., and Cooper, G. L. Effect on carboxyhemoglobin of exposure to aerosol spray paints with methylene chloride. Clin. Toxicol. 12:551, 1978.

178. Stewart, R. D., Hake, C. L., and Peterson, J. E. "Degreasers' flush." Arch. Environ. Health 29:1, 1974.

179. Stewart, R. D., Herrmann, A. A., Baretta, E. D., Forster, H. V., Sikora, J. J., Newton, P. E., and Soto, R. J. Acute and repetitive human exposure to isobutane. Scand. J. Work Environ. Health 3:234, 1977.

180. Stewart, R. D., Newton, P. E., Baretta, E. D., Herrmann, A. A., Forster, H. V., and Soto, R. J. Physiological response to aerosol propellants. Environ. Health Perspect. 26:275, 1978.

181. Stybel, J., Allen, P., and Lewis, F. Deliberate hydrocarbon inhalation among low-socioeconomic adolescents not necessarily apprehended by the police. Int. J. Addict. 11:345, 1976.

182. Sundell, L., Axelsson, O., Blume, J., Hane, M., Hogstedt, C., and Ydreborg, B. Investigation on

housepainters exposed to different paints and solvents. Bull. Inst. Marit. Trop. Med. Gdynia. 28:67, 1977.

183. Snyder, B. D., Thomas, R. S., and Gyorky, Z. Behavioral toxicity of anesthetic gases. Ann. Neurol. 3:67, 1978.

184. Taher, S. M., Anderson, R. J., McCartney, R., Popovtzer, M. M., and Schrier, R. W. Renal tubular acidosis associated with toluene "sniffing." N. Engl. J. Med. 290:765, 1974.

185. Taylor, G., IV, and Harris, W. Cardiac toxicity of aerosol propellants. J. A. M. A. 214:81, 1970.

186. Tinklenberg, J., and Woodrow, K. Drug use among youthful assaultive and sexual offenders. In *Aggression*, C. Frazier, editor. Baltimore, Williams & Wilkins, 1974.

187. Towfighi, J., Gonatas, N. K., Pleasure, D., Cooper, H. S., and McCree, L. Glue sniffer's neuropathy. Neurology 26:238, 1976.

188. Travers, H. Death from 1,1,1-trichloroethane abuse: Case report. Milit. Med. 139:889, 1974.

189. Valpey, R., Sumi, S. M., Copass, M. K., and Goble, G. J. Acute and chronic progressive encephalopathy due to gasoline sniffing. Neurology 28:507, 1978.

190. Vargas, P. A preliminary assessment of NIDA programs and activities regarding the inhalation of toxic substances as a drug abuse problem. Special Report to the Director of the National Institute on Drug Abuse, 1975.

191. Wason, S., Detsky, A. S., Platt, O. S., and Lovejoy, F. H., Jr. Isobutyl nitrite toxicity by ingestion. Ann. Intern. Med. 92:637, 1980.

192. Wilde, C. Aerosol metallic paint intoxication. Final Report on Grant DA 01308, National Institute on Drug Abuse, 1977.

193. Windemuller, F. J. B., and Ettema, J. H. Effects of combined exposure to trichloroethylene and alcohol on mental capacity. Int. Arch. Occup. Environ. Health 41:77, 1978.

194. Wolman, S. R., Cytologic and cytogenetic effects of benzene. J. Toxicol. Environ. Health (Suppl.) 2: 63, 1977.

195. Wyse, D. Deliberate inhalation of volatile hydrocarbons: A review. Can. Med. Assoc. 108:714, 1973.

196. Zakhari, S., Leibowitz, M., Levy, P., and Aviado, D. M., editors. *Isopropanol and Ketones in the Environment.* Cleveland, CRC Press, 1977.

197. Zaninovic, M., Trichloroethylene poisoning in a dry cleaning establishment. Arh. Hig. Rada Toksikol. 28:171, 1977.

CHAPTER 20

NICOTINE: TOBACCO USE, ABUSE, AND DEPENDENCE

Jerome H. Jaffe, M.D.

Maureen Kanzler, Ph.D.

There are several broad issues that can be considered under the heading of tobacco smoking as a form of drug abuse. First, to what extent does smoking of tobacco resemble other forms of drug-using behaviors? Second, what are the practical and social implications of including heavy tobacco use along with alcoholism and opioid addiction as a form of drug dependence? Third, ignoring the semantic issues, what are the factors—psychological, biological, sociological, and pharmacological—that contribute to the perpetuation of tobacco use and the relapse after a period of abstinence? Fourth, what is the status of our current capacity to modify (treat) smoking behavior? This chapter is intended as an overview rather than as a detailed presentation of any one of these important questions.

HISTORY

The resemblance between tobacco use and consumption of other substances that produce dependence has been debated throughout history. In 1604, James I, in his *Counterblaste to Tobacco* (12), condemned the use of tobacco and drew an analogy between smoking habituation and the process by which a drinker of alcohol became a drunkard. Among some segments of society, tobacco use continued to be seen as a behavior quite comparable to alcohol use well into the 20th century. The Temperance movement in the United States, which was eventually successful in enacting a national prohibition of alcohol use, had, by the 1920's, also succeeded in fostering the prohibition of tobacco use in 14 states (10). Although many medical authorities in the 19th century viewed tobacco use as a form of drug dependence and some believed that such use was linked to cancer, by the beginning of the 20th century the preponderant view of the medical establishment had become considerably more tolerant. Undoubtedly, the changed attitude was related to the rapid rate at which tobacco smoking was becoming "normal behavior." This rapid increase, in turn, was undoubtedly related to four technological changes that occurred in the latter half of the 19th century: the introduction of new and milder varieties of tobacco, the use of flue curing, the development of machinery for mass manufacture of cigarettes, and the advent of modern advertising techniques. All these combined to facilitate the spread of a new product—the cigarette—which was neater than pipes and cheaper than cigars and so mild that the smoke could be inhaled. In the space of a few decades in the United States, the consumption of cigarettes rose from millions per year to billions per year (10).

By 1922, A. A. Brill, one of the pioneers of the psychoanalytic movement, could say (80):

... one is justified in looking with suspicion on the abstainer; most of the fanatical opponents of tobacco that I have known were all bad neurotics.

The German pharmacologist, Louis Lewin (sometimes called the father of psychopharmacology), wrote of tobacco in 1924 (49):

It must be pointed out that the attraction of tobacco is not exercised with that vigour and inexorable constraint which we have remarked in the case of the narcotic substances . . . . If the use of tobacco has to be stopped for medical or other reasons, no suffering of the body or morbid desire for the drug appears. The consumption of tobacco is an enjoyment which man is free to renounce, and when he indulges in it he experiences its benevolent effects on his spiritual life . . . . Smoking does not call forth an exaltation of internal well being as does the use of wine, but it adjusts the working condition of the mind and the disposition of many mentally active persons to a kind of serenity or "quietism" during which the activity of thought is in no way disturbed . . . .
. . . It is, moreover, common knowledge that the use of tobacco for smoking and chewing does not necessitate a progressive increase of the dose as in the case in other toxic substances and that the symptoms due to withdrawal of tobacco, if they occur at all, are easily overcome. These latter consist of an extreme feeling of discomfort and eventually bad humour and dejection. It is very exceptionally that graver symptoms occur.

Sir Humphrey Rolleston, whose committee recommendations in 1926 set the tone for the British response to opiate dependence, when asked whether tobacco smoking was not properly viewed as an addiction, replied (61):

This question turns on the meaning attached to the word "addiction," and may therefore be a verbal problem . . . . That smoking produces a craving for more when an attempt is made to give it up . . . is undoubted, but it can seldom be accurately described as overpowering, and the effects of its withdrawal, though there may be definite restlessness and instability, cannot be compared with the physical distress caused by withdrawal in morphine addicts. To regard tobacco as a drug of addiction may be all very well in a humorous sense, but it is hardly accurate.

As Rolleston noted, the issue is a semantic one. And when semantic problems rise, there is always a possibility that the arguments about whether tobacco smoking is properly grouped with other forms of nonmedical drug use will divert energy from more pragmatic questions.

Not all dependence on drugs results in problems for society and/or the individual. Caffeine consumption is viewed by many as appropriately classed with other forms of dependence, and caffeine dependence can be found in the eighth edition of the *International Classification of Diseases* (ICD-8). There is a caffeine withdrawal syndrome, and caffeine can be abused to the point where it causes problems and disrupts behavior (21). But no one is proposing that advertising coffee be banned, caffeine content be taxed, or that coffee drinkers should sit in the rear of airplanes. The personal and social costs of caffeine dependence seem to be relatively low; tobacco dependence, on the other hand, has enormous cost to the individuals who develop smoking-related diseases. These diseases in turn affect the economic well-being of society. Thus, we can conclude that what we choose to be concerned about is not determined by any one criterion—i.e., a drug that produces physical dependence—but by a complex of concerns about social and individual well-being.

TOBACCO DEPENDENCE: GROPING FOR CRITERIA

It is obvious that, just as not everyone who uses alcohol is an alcohol abuser, problem drinker, or alcoholic, not everyone who uses tobacco is an abuser or is tobacco dependent. Although there were difficulties in developing criteria to separate alcohol or opiate *use* from alcohol or opiate *dependence,* and it was difficult for experts to reach concensus, the difficulties in achieving agreement on criteria for tobacco dependence were even more troublesome. In the case of alcoholism, it was possible to include physical dependence and social and physical disability as elements in a definition.

Mark Keller has defended the disease concept of alcoholism against both opponents of psychiatry and those who would demedicalize all problems, pointing out that the disease concept is not a recent "gimmick" designed to exculpate the excessive drinker from responsibility for his own behavior. He emphasized that at the center of the disease concept was "disablement" and that as long as disablement is "a prime criterion for identifying disease, then the present conceptualization of alcoholism as a disease will hold up" (45). But what are the implications of Keller's argument for tobacco dependence? To what degree is the tobacco user disabled? If we think solely about his/her ability to function, we might reasonably conclude that, unlike alcohol use by the alcoholic, there is little direct disablement associated with the use of tobacco. In the absence of tobacco-induced medical problems, the behavior of the tobacco user would be more analogous to that of the coffee drinker—technically a form of dependence, but practically of little concern to medicine or psychiatry. Certainly, no one has suggested that pipes, cigars, and cigarettes used by millions of productive citizens make them less mentally able. Thus, the significance of the syndrome is intimately intertwined with the medical problems it causes. It is necessary, therefore, to review briefly a few salient points.

First, not all forms of tobacco use are equally implicated in causing medical dis-ease. Pipe and cigar smoking are considerably less hazardous than smoking cigarettes. Indeed, according to the recent Surgeon General's report (78), the chewing of tobacco is not associated with any *demonstrable* increase in over-all mortality or in the incidence of any specific medical disorder in the United States. (It is associated with precancerous lesions of the mouth in other parts of the world.) In short, tobacco dependence may or may not be of medical significance, depending on the specific pattern of use. Furthermore, even in the case of cigarettes, there is a clear-cut dose-response gradient for all the known tobacco-induced disorders (84). For some disorders there is a much steeper gradient as the dose is increased (Fig. 20.1). What does all this have to do with the behavior? In one sense, very little. But in another sense it may determine to a large degree how we view the behavior, how we respond to it, and even what we call it.

We can probably agree that at the extreme some smokers could be called addicts without distorting the term. Department of Health, Education, and Welfare Secretary Califano described cigarette smoking as "slow-motion suicide" (78). Surely he had in mind the heavy cigarette smoker. Should we

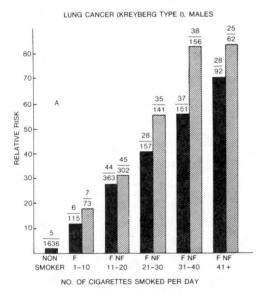
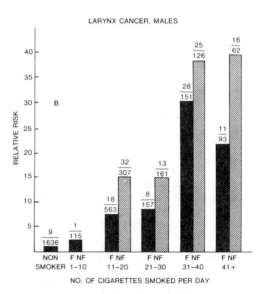

Figure 20.1. Age-adjusted relative risk of (A) lung or (B) larynx cancer for filter (F) and nonfilter (NF) smokers by quantity smoked. Fraction = number of cases/number of controls. A, Lung cancer, males; number of cases = 143 filter smokers, 150 nonfilter smokers. B, Larynx cancer, males; number of cases = 66 filter smokers, 86 nonfilter smokers. (From Wynder, E. L. and Stellman, S. D. Impact of long-term filter cigarette usage on lung and larynx cancer risk: A case–control study. J. Natl. Cancer Inst. 62:471, 1979.)

view the smoker of two cigars in the same night? And what if there were no adverse consequences to cigarette use? Would the smoker of even several packs be viewed as having an addiction? These were some of the questions that arose when a subcommittee of the American Psychiatric Association's Task Force on Nomenclature gathered to try to define the point at which smoking becomes a psychiatric disorder and to draft criteria for inclusion in the third edition of the American Psychiatric Association's *Diagnostic and Statistical Manual of Mental Disorders* (DSM-III). Some of those who participated in the preparation of DMS-III said that it would depend solely on how difficult it was for the smoker to stop and that the issue of consequences was irrelevant. Still others pointed out that with a definition restricted to difficulty in smoking cessation we would be hard pressed to know what to do with the smoker who claimed that he never tried to stop and that he/she continues smoking because of the "pleasure" he/she gets from it. Others said it should be possible to infer a loss of flexibility from the pattern of use and the amount smoked.

After much soul searching and debate, DMS-III (2) now includes two headings: "Tobacco Dependence" and "Tobacco Withdrawal." In earlier drafts (1) the term "Tobacco Use Disorder" was used in order to emphasize the special status of tobacco as a drug of dependence. In those early versions, the diagnosis did not apply to smokers, even heavy smokers, if they had no medical disorders, experienced no distress at their continued use, and were not seeking help in stopping. The concept of tobacco dependence was viewed as relevant for two major groups: (a) Those who considered themselves dependent and were seeking help in stopping, and (b) those who, although denying an interest in stopping, were obviously suffering from smoking-related disorders. This was an attempt at compromise, but it lead to a situation in which a heavy smoker without a medical illness would have tobacco use disorder whenever he was seeking help but would cease to have it when he quit trying to stop. This effort to avoid labeling approximately 30 million heavy smokers as having a "mental disorder" proved too awkward conceptually. In the final version of DMS-III (2), the headings and criteria are as follows:

1. *Tobacco Withdrawal*
    A. Use of tobacco for at least several weeks at a level equivalent to more than ten cigarettes per day, with each cigarette containing at least 0.5 mg of nicotine.
    B. Abrupt cessation of or reduction in tobacco use, followed within 24 hours by at least four of the following:
        (1) craving for tobacco
        (2) irritability
        (3) anxiety
        (4) difficulty concentrating
        (5) restlessness
        (6) headache
        (7) drowsiness
        (8) gastrointestinal disturbances
(These quantities and these times are arbitrary or close to it. They represent "best guesses." But the committee felt that the quantitative issues required emphasis.)
2. *Tobacco Dependence* (which replaces Tobacco Use Disorder)
    A. Continuous use of tobacco for at least one month.
    B. At least one of the following:
        (1) serious attempts to stop or significantly reduce the amount of tobacco use on a permanent basis have been unsuccessful
        (2) attempts to stop smoking have led to the development of Tobacco Withdrawal
        (3) the individual continues to use tobacco despite a serious physical disorder (e.g., respiratory or cardiovascular disease) that he or she knows is exacerbated by tobacco use.

But note this interesting statement that precedes the criteria: "In practice, this diagnosis will be given only when either the individual is seeking professional help to stop smoking or, in the judgment of the diagnostician, the individual's use of tobacco is seriously affecting his or her physical health" (2).

While criteria now committed to print have a stamp of official approval, they do not automatically make tobacco dependence a precise analogue of other forms of dependence. We need to be aware of both the similarities and the differences.

SOME PSYCHOLOGICAL PARALLELS

Although there is great overlap between the psychological characteristics of smokers and nonsmokers, in study after study, cigarette smokers on average tend to be more extroverted (77), more intolerant of rules, more adventuresome and risk taking, and, in some studies, more angry (81) than appropriately matched nonsmokers (47, 48, 78). Some of these differences may be a result of smoking, but they are observed even among young people just beginning to smoke (76) and they seem to persist when the smoker becomes abstinent (81). Eysenck (17) has postulated that the smoker is an extrovert who is usually at less than his or her optimal level of arousal and, therefore, uses nicotine to raise the level of arousal. Such a view leads to a "normalizing" hypothesis to account for the maintenance of the habit in at least some smokers. Yet many of these same personality characteristics seem to be associated with experimentation with other drugs—e.g., lysergic acid diethylamide, opiates, and alcohol (29, 35)—that are not commonly viewed as inducing arousal, an observation that is difficult to reconcile with Eysenck's hypothesis.

If tobacco were an illicit drug, its spread would be described as "epidemic." The initial experimentation and regular use of tobacco begin in youth. In the present climate, which is considerably less approving of cigarette use than it once was, the behavior often is seen more commonly among the less well adjusted (77), the less scholastically successful (7, 75), and especially among those who have friends who smoke (48).

Most of those who begin to smoke cigarettes believe that they will some day give them up (50). Very few cigarette smokers at present start out to become dependent. We must infer from their behavior that gradually the capacity to choose is eroded and, although the user may want to believe she/he can stop at any time, the behavior indicates that this is not the case. The attitudes and beliefs about the likelihood of becoming dependent are not very different among those who begin to use opiates and alcohol.

There are numerous theories that attempt to account for the transition from experimentation to continued use. Even with the opiates and alcohol, researchers recognize that, in certain social settings, the act of using the drug (rather than its pharmacological effects) may continue to provide some of the reinforcement. So it is with cigarettes—it is a matter of degree. Russell et al. (65) investigated motives for smoking in two groups—

one composed of "normal" smokers, the other an addicted group of heavy smokers attending a withdrawal clinic. A factor analysis of their responses to a questionnaire separated a "pharmacological addiction" dimension from the sensorimotor, indulgent, and psychosocial factors. However, the mere presence of nonpharmacological factors in the maintenance of smoking does not serve to distinguish cigarette smoking from other drug-using behaviors. Social reinforcers and symbolic aspects of the drug-taking behavior are also postulated to play a major role in the development of a variety of drug-using behaviors and, indeed, of deviant behaviors in general (42).

PHARMACOLOGICAL FACTORS IN CONTINUED USE

Researchers have assumed that, although smoking is initiated through psychosocial factors, the behavior becomes habitual because the pharmacological effects of nicotine are reinforcing (16, 36, 39, 47, 48). Russell (62, 63) and Russell and Feyerabend (64) have emphasized that a small "bolus" of nicotine reaches the brain within seconds after a puff from a tobacco cigarette is inhaled, so that, if nicotine is a reinforcer, then the hundreds of puffs inhaled each day produce a well established puff-inhalation habit. Indeed, nicotine is probably the major reinforcing component in cigarette smoking (although it may not be the only reinforcer). People show definite preferences for certain tastes independent of their caloric values; it is not unreasonable to assume that smokers "like" the "taste" of tobacco. However, when nicotine and tar content are varied independently, it is the nicotine content that is correlated with ratings of strength and satisfaction (22). When provided with low or nonnicotine cigarettes, most smokers complain bitterly or refuse to continue smoking them (39). Nevertheless, reliable laboratory evidence that nicotine is a reinforcer of drug-taking behavior was relatively difficult to develop. In contrast to drugs like morphine, amphetamine, or cocaine, which animals will self-administer over a wide range of doses, animal self-administration of nicotine has been more difficult to induce. When it does occur, it seems to be a less powerful reinforcer of behavior than drugs such as cocaine and amphetamine, at

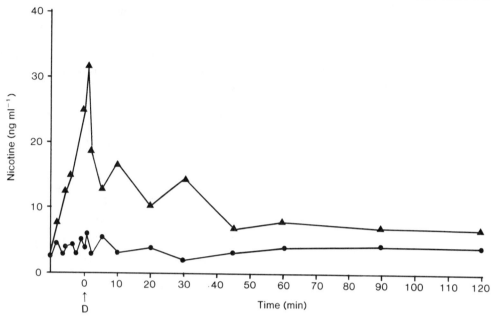

Figure 20.2. Plasma nicotine concentrations in an inhaling smoker (▲) and a noninhaling smoker (●) during and after smoking one cigarette, which was discarded at *point D*. (From Feyerabend, C., Levitt, T., and Russell, M. A. H. A. rapid gas-liquid chromatographic estimation of nicotine in biological fluids. J. Pharm. Pharmacol. 27:434, 1975.)

least as judged by the number of lever presses that the animal will make for a single dose of nicotine (88). Recently, McGill et al. (52) described the inhalation of cigarette smoke by baboons. Inhalation was inferred from increases in their blood carboxyhemoglobin levels, which would not occur unless the smoke were inhaled.

Of all the substances that are self-administered by man, nicotine is one of the most rapidly metabolized; it has a half-life of about 40 to 80 minutes. This very brief period of action makes it necessary to smoke many times each day to continue to get the effect, thus ensuring that the behavior will be repeatedly reinforced. The short half-life of nicotine is illustrated in Figure 20.2.

POSSIBLE MECHANISMS OF REINFORCEMENT

Nicotine has both peripheral and central effects. The peripheral effects—such as inhibition of stomach contractions, acceleration of heart rate, release of epinephrine from the adrenal gland, and effects mediated by peripheral release of noradrenaline—do not seem to be of major importance in reinforcing

smoking. Most of these can be blocked without altering the psychological effects in humans (11). The central effects are obviously more relevant. But which one? Nicotine seems to produce multiple effects—and in this respect the problem of identifying the site of the reinforcing effects of nicotine is not unlike the problem of determining which of the multiple effects produced by the opioids or alcohol are responsible for their reinforcing properties. In man, nicotine produces an alerting pattern in the electroencephalogram (EEG) and behavioral arousal (14, 48). It also stimulates release of a number of hormonal substances from the central nervous system (13, 34, 85). Smoking-related increases in plasma norepinephrine, epinephrine, growth hormone, and cortisol are illustrated in Figures 20.3 and 20.4. Vasopressin is also released by cigarette smoking. Animal studies indicate that nicotine releases norepinephrine and dopamine from brain tissue (23, 48, 63). Depending on the dose, it may increase or decrease the release of acetylcholine (4, 63). The increase in plasma cortisol produced by smoking is due to increased release of adrenocorticotropic hormone (ACTH). Recent findings that ACTH and

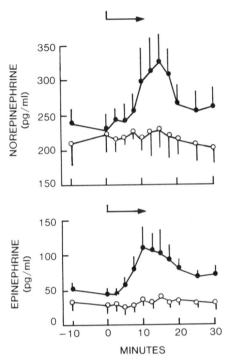

Figure 20.3. Mean (± S.E.) plasma norepineph-rine and epinephrine concentrations in associ-ation with smoking (*closed symbols*) and with sham smoking (*open symbols*). The *arrows* in-dicate the period of smoking (or sham smoking). (From Cryer, P. E., Haymond, M. W., Santiago, J. V., and Shah, S. D. Norepinephrine and epi-nephrine release and adrenergic mediation of smoking associated hemodynamic and meta-bolic events. N. Engl. J. Med. 295:573, 1976.)

beta-lipotropin and/or beta-endorphin are released in parallel fashion suggest that smoking produces increased plasma levels of the latter peptides as well. Since ACTH and vasopressin may have direct effects on mem-ory and behavior, and considering the wide ranging effects of the endogenous opioid peptides, there would seem to be numerous ways in which nicotine could act as a rein-forcer.

BIOLOGICAL FACTORS IN CONTINUED AND DEPENDENT USE

Many people drink alcohol; a relatively small proportion become dependent. Not all of those who use opiates become dependent. With the latter drugs, those who become dependent tend to come from disturbed fam-ilies where alcoholism and, often, a history

of sociopathy or other psychiatric illness is prominent (35). One at first suspects that it is the stress of growing up in such a family that leads to the later tendency to overuse alcohol or illicit drugs. However, for males, a genetically transmitted biological vulnera-bility to alcoholism that may be independent of disturbed family background seems to be fairly well established (24). Some opioid users maintain that they use opioids not to get high but to feel normal, not to alleviate withdrawal symptoms but to experience a state of normality that the nonuser enjoys without the benefit of exogenous substances. The existence of a biological vulnerability to tobacco dependence is even more specula-tive, but the possibility of such a biological substrate cannot be excluded. We might also note that alcoholics and opiate users are not only more likely to be smokers but they smoke much more heavily (15) and often find it easier to give up opiates or alcohol than cigarettes.

We need to know more about the where and the how of tobacco's effect on the brain and the rest of the central nervous system. We also need to know whether there are people who function better when smoking and experience impairment only over the long term. The studies that have been carried out on heavy smokers acutely deprived of nicotine do not answer this question. Most smokers, even those who were heavy smok-ers for a long time, if they are able to stop smoking state that they feel much better and note no decline in function.

PHYSICAL DEPENDENCE AND WITHDRAWAL

The withdrawal syndrome following smoking cessation is not as well studied as other forms of withdrawal, but few who are knowledgeable doubt that it exists. It differs in time course and character from that follow-ing alcohol or opiate deprivation. The onset of smoking withdrawal symptoms may occur within hours of the last cigarette or may be delayed for days. The symptoms may last from days to months. Like the other with-drawal syndromes, there are associated phys-iological changes, e.g., decreased heart rate, EEG slowing. In addition to craving for to-bacco, other symptoms have been reported following the cessation of smoking, such as

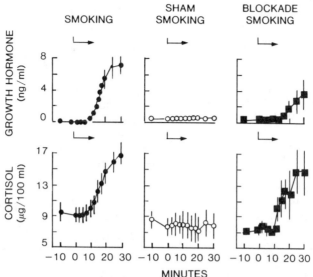

Figure 20.4. Mean (± S.E.) plasma growth hormone and cortisol concentrations during smoking (*left, closed circles*), sham smoking (*center, open circles*), and smoking during adrenergic blockade (*right, closed squares*). The *arrows* indicate the periods of smoking (or sham smoking). (From Cryer, P. E., Haymond, M. W., Santiago, J. V., and Shah, S. D. Norepinephrine and epinephrine release and adrenergic mediation of smoking associated hemodynamic and metabolic events. N. Engl. J. Med. 295:573, 1976.)

restlessness, dullness, sleep disturbances, gastrointestinal disturbances, drowsiness, headache, irritability and impairment of memory concentration, judgment and psychomotor performance (27, 36, 48, 62, 73, 74, 78). As little as 90 minutes of deprivation may increase irritability (70).

There are areas of smoking withdrawal that are virtually unexplored, including the factors that determine the severity of the syndrome, the time course of its development and decay, the degree to which it can be conditioned to internal and external (environmental) stimuli, and the relation of the type and severity of the withdrawal phenomena to subjective craving, to successful cessation, and to relapse after cessation.

With other drugs, the problem of tolerance is usually discussed in relation to physical dependence. It is apparent that tolerance to nicotine can develop quickly and that tolerance levels can be influenced by environmental factors (40, 41). There are now hundreds of thousands of smokers who every day purchase cigarettes delivering only 0.1 mg of nicotine. Many smokers who at first find such cigarettes to be totally unsatisfying can become accustomed to them. We still know

very little about the nature of tolerance to nicotine and the factors regulating its development.

TITRATION

The nature of nicotine tolerance and physical dependence has some very immediate and practical implications. If smoking leads to physical dependence and if the withdrawal syndrome is an aversive state, then one might expect to find that smokers would try to avoid withdrawal by maintaining their tobacco (or nicotine) intake. Indeed, it has been proposed that heavy smokers may not get any significant positive effects from nicotine, but smoke primarily to avoid withdrawal (69). This general proposition has provided the basis for a number of experiments that ask the related questions: Do smokers smoke tobacco primarily to get nicotine? (i.e., Is nicotine the reinforcer in tobacco smoking?) Do smokers adjust (titrate) their level of smoking to maintain a given level of nicotine in the body? The experiments have included: (a) administration of nicotine (orally, subcutaneously, and intravenously) coupled with observations of the number of cigarettes smoked (or number of puffs taken or the total puff volume) and/or degree of satisfaction (39, 46, 63); (b) changing the nicotine content of the tobacco, diluting the smoke, or shortening the length of the cigarette and measuring the smoking patterns (39) and sometimes the plasma levels of nicotine (68, 79); and (c) administering various drugs that alter the pharmacological effects of nicotine (39) or its metabolic disposition (69) and then observing smoking behavior and the psychological effects of smoking. The evidence from most of these studies strongly supports the view that, within limits, some heavy smokers attempt to regulate their plasma nicotine levels by adjusting the rate and amount of tobacco smoked. Heavy smokers seem to be more consistent in reducing intake of high nicotine cigarettes to avoid unusually high plasma levels of nicotine than in increasing the number of low nicotine cigarettes to avoid unusually low levels (68).

When subjects smoke cigarettes delivering different amounts of nicotine, changes in their short run puffing behavior do not compensate perfectly so as to maintain a constant nicotine intake or plasma nicotine level (68), but this imperfect titration does not mean that tobacco smoking is a distinct form of substance-using behavior. Perfect titration of plasma levels of drug is not found in the classic addictive disorders. Alcoholics titrate alcohol levels imperfectly. Depending on environmental circumstances and schedules of reinforcement, such individuals may tolerate major decreases in plasma levels. Similarly, some opiate-dependent subjects may continue to work for intravenous opiate when maintained on high cross-tolerance inducing doses of methadone (51). Many opiate users, given adequate motivation, will voluntarily accept withdrawal from chronically administered opiates. In addition, addicts may continue to inject themselves and experience opiate-like effects while on blocking doses of narcotic antagonists (53, 55). It is likely that with nicotine, as with other drugs, not only does the act of drug use itself acquire secondary reinforcing properties, but also, despite the development of tolerance, the acute effects of each dose of nicotine may continue to produce effects that are distinct from relief of withdrawal. We should not expect a perfect correlation between nicotine levels and smoking behavior any more than we expect

such correlations among the "classic" addictive disorders.

CESSATION, TREATMENT, AND RELAPSE

The treatment of tobacco dependence, like that of other dependence disorders, has been approached from several perspectives, none of which is entirely satisfactory. Increasingly, tobacco dependence, particularly chronic cigarette smoking, has been recognized as a multidetermined complex behavior, which in its extreme form is very difficult to change.

Description and assessment of progress in smoking cessation have been reviewed periodically since the late 1960's by Schwartz (72). During the 1970's, additional reviews were published by Bradshaw (8), Bernstein and McAlister (6), Hunt and Bespalec (33), and Raw (59). The most recent Surgeon General's report has a chapter on modification of smoking behavior (57). Schwartz (72) listed eight categories of major cessation methods: education, medication, individual counseling, group counseling, hypnosis, behavior modification, self-control, and miscellaneous. We have further collapsed these categories in the following summaries.

SELF-STOPPING

The National Clearing House on Smoking and Health estimated that, in 1975, over 32,000,000 Americans were former smokers (60). Most of these people must have stopped on their own without treatment in a formal program, because such programs could handle only a small fraction of the smoking population and the average long term success rate of those programs that were operating was only a modest proportion of those who participated (33, 72). *Why* this vast number of former smokers quit smoking is a matter of conjecture. We can guess that some drew their motivation from the health warnings of the 1964 Surgeon General's report or from the subsequent television commercials. It is probable that some were told by their doctors that they had better quit. Some may have been worried by shortness of breath, hoarseness, or sore throat. *How* these "self-stoppers" managed their cessation experience is largely unknown. Self-help devices exist, such as instruction books with tips on behavior modification of the habit aspects of smoking, or a series of filters that progressively reduce the smoker's nicotine and tar intake (assuming that the smoker does not increase either the number of cigarettes per day or change his/her inhalation patterns). Also, there have been a number of radio and television programs to educate the public regarding hazards of smoking and to offer specific advice on quitting, sometimes involving specific steps and scheduled over a period of days. The impact of such programs is difficult to estimate. But for all we know, millions of Americans have said to themselves simply, "I'm stopping smoking," and did so.

HYPNOSIS

Hypnosis has been used for many years by ethical therapists and serious researchers, and more recently by commercially oriented behavior control enterprises. Used ethically, the process requires a judgment regarding the smoker's psychological health and ability to use the trance state to imprint suggestions regarding the negative aspects of smoking or the positive effects of mastery over the habit. The trance state is first induced by the therapist, who may then teach the patient self-hypnosis to repeat the process of suggestion at his/her convenience. Hypnosis may be of some benefit for some smokers, and most reports (72) indicate that on average the short and long term results are comparable to those achieved by other approaches. However, there are few direct comparisons and it is difficult to know how results may have been affected by subject selection.

OTHER DRUGS

The use of other drugs to reduce craving or to make smoking unpleasant has a long history. Lobeline, once thought to act as a nicotine substitute, is ineffective, and it is now clear that its actions do not mimic those of nicotine. Tranquilizers to reduce anxiety and amphetamine to combat hunger and fatigue have been of negligible value. Nicotine itself, in the form of injections, has been used in Europe with some claimed benefit (16), and more recently a buffered nicotine-containing chewing gum has been developed and evaluated (9, 67). It seems to have some value and is available on prescription in Canada and in some European countries. A still more recent approach is suggested by the use of

sodium bicarbonate to raise the urinary pH and thereby reduce the excretion of unchanged nicotine (69). This is said to help maintain blood levels of nicotine and to minimize withdrawal discomfort. In general, pharmacological approaches to cigarette smoking cessation have been of minimal value.

BEHAVIOR THERAPY

Prominent among the behavioral modification approaches are aversion techniques that associate the act of smoking with immediate and unpleasant consequences, such as electric shock or warm, stale smoke puffed in the smoker's face. Other ways of making smoking itself aversive are rapid smoking (in which the smoker is required to inhale every 6 seconds) and smoking to satiation. Theoretically, the high dose of nicotine produces the adverse effects. These approaches, although reported to be quite effective by several different groups, have been criticized as presenting serious health hazards to subjects who are exposed to high levels of both CO and nicotine (32, 54).

In a study of 24 healthy males, in which the electrocardiogram and blood gases were monitored during rapid smoking (a puff every 6 seconds until the subjects felt unable to continue), no myocardial rhythm abnormalities were observed, although carboxyhemoglobin (COHgb) and pulse rate were substantially elevated as compared to values obtained during normal smoking. There was also a decrease in arterial oxygen saturation and decreases in pCO_2 and serum K+. Because hypokalemia, decreased pO_2, and increased COHgb can also sensitize the myocardium to abnormal rhythms, the authors cautioned that, although rapid smoking seems to be safe for the normal myocardium, it could lead to serious problems for individuals with cardiac disease (28). Russell and co-workers (66) examined plasma nicotine and COHgb levels after rapid smoking and found that they both were much higher than the levels produced by ordinary smoking. Interestingly, this study found that there was little relationship between the levels of plasma nicotine and COHgb achieved and any subsequent lowering of desire to smoke.

"Covert desensitization" uses the smoker's imagination to form a mental bond between smoking and a noxious stimulus and to associate pleasant feelings with imagined not smoking. There are also a variety of behaviorally oriented approaches to self-control that involve record keeping, timing of intercigarette intervals, and numerous other procedures designed to break the link between environmental stimuli and cigarettes and to make the behavior less automatic.

MULTIFACETED PROGRAMS

Multifaceted programs have been offered by various benevolent organizations, research projects, and by private profit-oriented organizations. Because of space limitations, only a few examples of such programs can be given here. Perhaps the best known is the "5-Day Plan" of the Seventh Day Adventist Church. This plan incorporates education regarding the health consequences of smoking, emphasis on general physical fitness, exercise, deep breathing, and hydrotherapy. A "buddy system" provides mutual support to participants. In general, the "5-Day Plan" is more exhortational and educational than behaviorally oriented.

The Multiple Risk Factor Intervention Trial (MRFIT) is a large prospective research project (56) designed to test the efficacy of intervention in preventing coronary heart disease in males who are at greater than average risk because of cigarette smoking and/or hypercholesterolemia and/or hypertension. Participants are randomly assigned to Special Intervention and Usual Care groups. The Special Intervention groups meet for 10 sessions of education about the consequences of smoking, information about nutrition and blood pressure, and group discussion in which both smokers and nonsmokers participate. The Usual Care groups are, in effect, controls who have the usual care of their own physicians.

SmokEnders (43) is a proprietary program operating through franchise arrangements. It consists of an 8-week program (nine sessions involving large groups) utilizing self-monitoring of time and occasion of smoking, planned postponement of smoking for increasing intervals of time, cigarette brand changes, compilation and recitation of a personal list of reasons for not smoking, a buddy system, group interactions, and accent of a "positive thinking" approach to freedom from enslavement to cigarette bondage.

Other large scale commercial enterprises have been built around various combinations of behavioral modification and aversive conditioning and/or acupuncture.

Evaluation of the efficacy of cessation methods arouses controversy. It is important to note that definitions of "success" vary. Some programs count only those who complete the entire treatment and some use percentage reduction rather than total cessation as a measure of effectiveness. Schwartz (72) measured both immediate and long term success in terms of all participants who begin a given program and are completely abstinent at the time of follow-up. Reviewing 160 smoking cessation programs Schwartz (72) found success rates (across all methods) which ranged from 0 per cent to 88 per cent with a median success rate of 25 per cent when all dropouts are counted as failures. One-year follow-up rates were available for 89 programs; these reported a mean long term success rate of 29 per cent. For many multifaceted programs using behavioral principles, short term success rates at completion of treatment are higher, with 60 per cent to 70 per cent abstinence as a representative figure. It would seem, therefore, that relapse rather than initial success is a major problem in current smoking cessation techniques.

An even more significant problem is motivating the smoker to try to stop. Many smokers will say they want to quit but they do not respond in large numbers when offered smoking cessation help. In one hospital, for example, a survey of employees yielded 204 smokers; 51 per cent said they wanted to stop smoking, but only 4 per cent enrolled in a cessation program when it was offered (44). Switching to cigarettes with lower tar and nicotine delivery rather than quitting smoking entirely may be a more acceptable alternative, but, as noted below, the nature of the behavior may minimize the apparent benefits.

SOME POTENTIALLY IMPORTANT DIFFERENCES BETWEEN TOBACCO USE AND OTHER FORMS OF DRUG DEPENDENCE

Despite the parallels that may be drawn between tobacco use and the use of other dependence-producing substances, there are some important differences. Perhaps the most important is that tobacco does not induce the acute behavioral toxicity that is seen with alcohol, opiates, amphetamine, cocaine, and hallucinogens. The serious adverse effects of tobacco are almost exclusively remote and stem from chronic use rather than from occasional indulgence. Furthermore, the likelihood that regular users of tobacco will suffer a medical illness seems to be directly related to the total dose of certain tobacco constituents over time (78). This relationship between dose and adverse effects raises the possibility that there may be some level and some patterns of regular use that are less hazardous (25). This situation is in contrast to other recreational drug use, where we have thus far been unsuccessful in finding ways to control the acute adverse effects of such drugs on physiology or behavior (i.e., preventing acute overdose deaths, intoxications requiring medical care, accidents and violence related to drug use).

LESS HAZARDOUS CIGARETTES?

The changing attitudes toward smoking are now beginning to produce changes in the population of smokers. The heaviest smokers and those with the most emotional difficulties are the least likely to give up smoking successfully (15, 58). However, there is some question about the kinds of help that smokers of tomorrow will require. Tobacco manufacturers are racing against time to produce a product that is less toxic than those used in the past.

Over the past decade, both nicotine and tar levels have been reduced by all major cigarette companies. The mean tar level of the average cigarette is substantially lower than it was only 5 years ago (78). This trend is likely to continue until all the cigarette manufacturers have at least one entry to compete with the very low tar-nicotine brands that deliver only 0.1 to 0.3 mg of nicotine and 1 to 3 mg of tar per cigarette. If the degree of dependence is a function of the daily intake of nicotine, this trend toward lower nicotine delivery may tend to offset the effects of the self-selection process induced by the changing social climate. The smoker of tomorrow may be less pharmacologically dependent. Much depends on the degree to which tolerance develops to the effects of nicotine, to which effects, and the degree to which smokers attempt to compensate for reduced nicotine delivery.

Gori (25) reviewed a number of studies which showed that health hazards of smoking were dose related over time. He computed critical values for intake of tar, nicotine, and several other cigarette components below which there did not seem to be a statistically significant increased risk of morbidity. Gori and Lynch (26) then examined the machine-rated deliveries of several toxic components in low tar-low nicotine cigarettes that have come to the marketplace. In general, they found a positive correlation between tar and nicotine content and amount of carbon monoxide delivered when the cigarettes are smoked on a machine. A positive correlation existed also for hydrogen cyanide. However, the correlations were not perfect and there was considerable variability in CO and HCN delivery among brands with similar tar delivery. In general, Gori and Lynch (26) have concluded that some cigarettes now on the market are "less hazardous" than others.

The above conclusion was based on machine-rated deliveries of toxic substances. It must be emphasized, however, that what a cigarette delivers depends not only on its composition but also on how it is smoked. At its burning tip, a cigarette converts the tobacco leaf into a stream of smoke carrying more than 4,000 chemical compounds, many of which are known to be toxic. Furthermore, the various substances seem to have major adverse effects on different organ systems. Some are believed to be carcinogenic, others ciliotoxic, and others exert their toxic effects on the cardiovascular system (Tables 20.1 and 20.2). The exact composition of the stream of smoke delivered to the smoker can be substantially altered not only by the composition, weight, and packing of the tobacco, but also by the structure of the filter, the porosity of the paper, and the rate and intensity of puffing. Changes in puffing rate and depth affect not only the temperature at the burning tip (which, in turn, affects the kinds and size of particles generated) but also the efficiency of combustion and the amount of air that is mixed with the mainstream smoke and thereby the amount of carbon monoxide.

The figures for tar and nicotine delivery presented to the public and printed on the carton represent the amounts of material obtained when a machine smoked the cigarette by taking 2-second, 35-ml puffs once each minute until the cigarette was smoked to a

Table 20.1
Major Toxic Agents in the Gas Phase of Cigarette Smoke (Unaged)[a,b]

Agent	Biological Activity[c]	Concentration/Cigarette	
		Range Reported	United States Cigarettes[d]
Dimethylnitrosamine	C	1–200 ng	13 ng
Ethylmethylnitrosamine	C	0.1–10 ng	1.8 ng
Diethylnitrosamine	C	0–10 ng	1.5 ng
Nitrosopyrrolidine	C	2–42 ng	11 ng
Other nitrosamines (4 compounds)	C	0–20 ng	?
Hydrazine	C	24–43 ng	32 ng
Vinyl chloride	C	1–16 ng	12 ng
Urethane	TI	10–35 ng	30 ng
Formaldehyde	CT, CoC	20–90 μg	30 μg
Hydrogen cyanide	CT,T	30–200 μg	110 μg
Acrolein	CT	25–140 μg	70 μg
Acetaldehyde	CT	18–1,400 μg	800 μg
Nitrogen oxides (NO$_x$)[e]	T	10–600 μg	350 μg
Ammonia	T[f]	10–150 μg	60 μg
Pyridine	T[f]	9–93 μg	10 μg
Carbon monoxide	T	2–20 mg	17 mg

[a] From Wynder, E. L., and Hoffman, D. Tobacco and health: A societal challenge. N. Engl. J. Med. 300:894, 1979.
[b] Cigarettes may also contain such carcinogens as arsine, nickel carbonyl and possibly volatile chlorinated olefins and nitro-olefins.
[c] C, carcinogen; BC, bladder carcinogen; TI, tumor initiator; CoC, cocarcinogen; CT, cilia toxic agent; T, toxic agent.
[d] 85-mm cigarettes without filter tips bought on the open market 1973–1976.
[e] NO$_x$ > 95 per cent NO; rest NO$_2$.
[f] Not toxic in smoke of blended United States cigarettes because pH < 6.5, and therefore, ammonia and pyridines are present only in protonated form.

predetermined length. For 58 seconds out of 60, the smoke simply curls upward into the atmosphere. The smoker who takes a 3-second puff, assuming that the puff intensity does not change, might increase the tar and nicotine delivery of the cigarette by 50 per cent. Because the change may alter the temperature, what happens to the CO delivery is far less certain.

Because of the tendency to "titrate" or compensate for reductions in nicotine, there is considerable controversy about just how much benefit we can expect from this effort to produce "less hazardous" cigarettes. Some researchers believe that the tendency of smokers to "titrate" will largely offset the reductions produced by the manufacturers.

Unlike nicotine and "tar," CO and some other gases produced by cigarettes are not selectively removed by filters. If smokers change their smoking patterns to compensate for decreased nicotine, they could be exposed to increased levels of CO and other gaseous elements. Since cardiovascular disease may be related to carboxyhemoglobin levels as well as to nicotine intake (3, 20), it is important to know what happens to the COHgb of the smoker as tar and nicotine are reduced. Vogt (83) reported that CO in air expired by his subjects exhibited a dose-response relationship with the number of cigarettes per day the subjects said they smoked. Working with men who volunteered for the Multiple Risk Factor Intervention Trial program, Vogt (83) found no correlation between the amount of tar and nicotine delivered by the cigarette and the expired CO level, but he did not indicate the brands his subjects smoked or the proportion of subjects smoking the very low tar-nicotine brands. He did find, as have others, that CO in expired air correlated closely with the number of cigarettes smoked per day. In our own work, in which a substantial proportion of smokers were selected because they were smoking very low tar-low nicotine brands, we also

Table 20.2
Major Toxic Agents in the Particulate Matter of Cigarette Smoke (Unaged)[a,b]

Agent	Biological Activity[†]	Concentration/Cigarette	
		Range Reported	United States Cigarettes[‡]
Benzo(a)pyrene	TI	8–50 ng	20 ng
5-Methylchrysene	TI	0.5–2 ng	0.6 ng
Benzo(j)fluoranthene	TI	5–40 ng	10 ng
Benz(a)anthracene	TI	5–80 ng	40 ng
Other polynuclear aromatic hydrocarbons (>20 compounds)	TI	?	?
Dibenz(a,j)acridine	TI	3–10 ng	8 ng
Dibenz(a,h)acridine	TI	?	?
Dibenzo(c,g)carbazole	TI	0.7 ng	0.7 ng
Pyrene	CoC	50–200 ng	150 ng
Fluoranthene	CoC	50–250 ng	170 ng
Benzo(g,h,i)perylene	CoC	10–60 ng	30 ng
Other polynuclear aromatic hydrocarbons (> 10 compounds)	CoC	?	?
Naphthalenes	CoC	1–10 μg	6 μg
1-Methylindoles	CoC	0.3–0.9 μg	0.8 μg
9-Methylcarbazoles	CoC	0.005–0.2 μg	0.1 μg
Other neutral compounds	CoC	?	?
Catechol	CoC	40–460 μg	270 μg
3- and 4-Methylcatechols	CoC	30–40 μg	32 μg
Other catechols (> four compounds)	CoC	?	?
Unknown phenols and acids	CoC	?	?
N'-Nitrosonornicotine	C	100–250 ng	250 ng
Other nonvolatile nitrosamines	C	?	?
Beta-naphthylamine	BC	0–25 ng	20 ng
Other aromatic amines	BC	?	?
Unknown nitro compounds	BC	?	?
Polonium-210	C	0.03–1.3 pCi	?
Nickel compounds	C	10–600 ng	?
Cadmium compounds	C	9–70 ng	?
Arsenic	C	1–25 μg	?
Nicotine	T	0.1–2.0 mg	1.5 mg
Minor tobacco alkaloids	T	0.01–0.2 mg	0.1 mg
Phenol	CT	10–200 μg	85 μg
Cresols (three compounds)	CT	10–150 μg	70 μg

[a] From Wynder, E. L., and Hoffman, D. Tobacco and health: A societal challenge. N. Engl. J. Med. 300:894, 1979.
[b] Incomplete list.

have found that carbon monoxide in expired air correlates substantially and positively with the number of cigarettes smoked per day (r = .52) in a group of 34 female smokers. The correlation with CO is increased (r = .62) if the total weight of the tobacco smoked is used in the calculations (37).

There is a growing body of observations to the effect that, although taste, odor, and the rituals of handling smoking implements may be important, people who smoke heavily do not smoke cigarettes because of "oral fixations" but because the cigarettes deliver nicotine. When the nicotine content is abruptly decreased, as when they switch to lower tar brands or use ventilated cigarette holders, they change the way they smoke, presumably to increase the amounts of nicotine delivered

(68, 69, 79). The compensation involves all the parameters of smoking to some degree: puff duration, puff volume, extent to which the cigarette is consumed, and the number of cigarettes per day. Because the latter may be the least important mechanism for compensation, it is scant reassurance that smokers who switch to low nicotine-low tar cigarettes may not substantially increase the number of cigarettes smoked per day (30, 38).

The prospects for less hazardous smoking are not as bright as might appear from the paper by Gori and Lynch (26), which did not emphasize the importance of compensatory mechanisms, or as bleak as the picture painted by Schacter (69), who laid great stress on titration and withdrawal and who believed that switching results in either a significant increase in the number of cigarettes smoked per day or a state of chronic partial nicotine withdrawal.

There are several papers that suggest that when the cigarette smoke is diluted by use of a ventilated cigarette filter or the cigarette itself is very low in tar and nicotine, the net result is a modest decrease in intake of tar-nicotine (19, 79) and of CO (79, 82), despite the substantial compensatory changes observed in inhalation patterns. Figure 20.5 shows the way smokers compensate for the dilution of smoke that occurs when they use

a specially ventilated cigarette holder. Although there is compensation, there is also a net decrease in nicotine levels and in COHgb. In addition, there are papers suggesting that lower tar-nicotine cigarettes are associated with a lower mortality among smokers (30) and a lower prevalence of respiratory symptoms in both sexes (31) and that substantial reductions over the past decade of the tar-nicotine content of the average cigarette sold are associated with a very sharp decline in the likelihood of seeing precancerous pathology in sections taken from the respiratory tract of male smokers dying from causes other than lung cancer (5).

Despite these findings suggesting that the tendency toward lower tar and nicotine levels may have some beneficial effects, we need to recognize that cigarettes deliver many different substances that are toxic to different body systems. A cigarette that is safer in terms of inducing lung cancer (because of a net reduction in carcinogens) might be no less, or even more, hazardous with respect to cardiovascular disease or bronchitis (because "titrating" may result in no reduction or even higher levels of CO or gaseous elements that are ciliotoxic). At present the smoker who "switches" buys, at best, a modest reduction in risk.

We are left, then, with a drug-using behav-

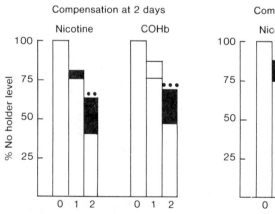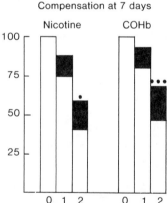

0 = No holder   1 = Holder 1   2 = Holder 2

Figure 20.5. Amount of compensation after using MD4 holders (holders with increasing size of air hole) for 2 days and 7 days. The observed and "expected" levels on the holders are expressed as a per cent of the mean no-holder plasma nicotine and CoHb levels (means of 18 subjects). The *shaded areas* represent the difference between the observed and "expected" levels, which is a measure of the amount of compensation. The *lined area* indicates a negative 0 - E difference, i.e., observed levels were lower than the "expected" levels. Thus, although there was significant compensation on Holder 2 at 2 days, there was clearly none on Holder 1. (From Sutton, S. R., Feyerabend, C., Cole, P. V., and Russell, M. A. H. Adjustment of smokers to dilution of tobacco smoke by ventilated cigarette holders. Clin. Pharmacol. Ther. 24:395, 1978.)

ior that, in terms of its association with disability, is much more like alcohol, opiates, and amphetamine than it is like coffee. Finding better ways to help smokers change their behavior so as to reduce their risks remains a challenge for the future.

References

1. American Psychiatric Association. Task Force on Nomenclature and Statistics. *DSM-III Draft*, Third Printing. Washington, D.C., American Psychiatric Association, 1978.
2. American Psychiatric Association. *Diagnostic and Statistical Manual of Mental Disorders* ed. 3. Washington, D.C., American Psychiatric Association, 1980.
3. Aranow, W. S. Carbon monoxide and cardiovascular disease. In *Modifying the Risk for the Smoker*, E. L. Wynder, D. Hoffman, and G. B. Gori, editors, vol. I, pp. 321-328. (DHEW Pub. No. (NIH)76-1221). Washington, D.C., United States Government Printing Office, 1976.
4. Armitage, A. K., Hall, G. H., and Sellers, C. M. Effects of nicotine on electrocortical activity and acetylcholine release from cat cerebral cortex. Br. J. Pharmacol. 35:152, 1969.
5. Auerbach, O., Hammond, E. C., and Garfinkel, L. Changes in bronchial epithelium in relation to cigarette smoking, 1955-1960 vs. 1970-1977. N. Engl. J. Med. 300:381, 1979.
6. Bernstein, D. A., and Mc Alister, A. The modification of smoking behavior: Progress and problems. Addict. Behav. 1:89, 1976.
7. Borland, B. R., and Rudolph, J. P. Relative effects of low socioeconomic status, parental smoking and poor scholastic performance on smoking among high school students. Soc. Sci. Med. 9:27, 1975.
8. Bradshaw, P. W. The problem of cigarette smoking and its control. Int. J. Addict. 8:353, 1973.
9. Brantmark, B., Ohlin, P., and Westling, H. Nicotine-containing chewing gum as an anti-smoking aid. Psychopharmacologia 31:191, 1973.
10. Brecher, E. M. *Licit and Illicit Drugs*. Mt. Vernon, N. Y., Consumers Union of United States, 1972.
11. Carruthers, M. Modification of the noradrenaline related effects of smoking by beta-blockade. Psychol. Med. 6:251, 1976.
12. Corti, C. *A History of Smoking*. New York, Harcourt Brace, 1932.
13. Cryer, P. E., Haymond, M. W., Santiago, J. V., and Shah, S. D. Norepinephrine and epinephrine release and adrenergic mediation of smoking associated hemodynamic and metabolic events. N. Engl. J. Med. 295:573, 1976.
14. Domino, E. F. Neuropsychopharmacology of nicotine and tobacco smoking. In *Smoking Behavior: Motives and Incentives*, W. L. Dunn, Jr., editor, pp. 5-31. Washington, D. C., Winston and Sons, 1973.
15. Dreher, K. F., and Fraser, J. G. Smoking habits of alcoholic outpatients. Int. J. Addict. 3:65, 1968.
16. Ejrup, B. The role of nicotine in smoking pleasure, nicotinism, and treatment. In *Tobacco Alkaloids and Related Compounds*, V. S. Von Euler, editor, pp. 333-346. Oxford, Pergamon, 1965.
17. Eysenck, H. J. Personality and the maintenance of the smoking habit. In *Smoking Behavior: Motives and Incentives*, by W. L. Dunn, Jr., editor, pp. 113-146. Washington, D. C., Winston and Sons, 1973.
18. Feyerabend, C., Levitt, T., and Russell, M. A. H. A rapid gas-liquid chromatographic estimation of nicotine in biological fluids. J. Pharm. Pharmacol. 27: 434, 1975.
19. Forbes, W. F., Robinson, J. C., Hanley, J. A., and Colburn, H. N. Studies on the nicotine exposure of individual smokers. I. Changes in mouth-level exposure to nicotine on switching to lower nicotine cigarettes. Int. J. Addict. 11:933, 1976.
20. Frederiksen, L. W., and Martin, J. E. Carbon monoxide and smoking behavior. Addict. Behav. 4:21, 1979.
21. Gilbert, R. M. Caffeine as a drug of abuse. In *Research Advances in Alcohol and Drug Problems*, R. J. Gibbons, Y. Israel, H. Kalant, R. E. Popham, W. Schmidt, and R. G. Smart, editors, vol. 3, pp. 49-176. New York, John Wiley, 1976.
22. Goldfarb, T., Gritz, E. R., Jarvik, M. E., and Stolerman, I. P. Reactions to cigarettes as a function of nicotine and "tar." Clin. Pharmacol. Ther. 19:767, 1976.
23. Goodman, F. R. Effects of nicotine on distribution and release of ^{14}C-norepinephrine and ^{14}C-dopamine in rat brain striatum and hypothalamus slices. Neuropharmacology 13:1025, 1974.
24. Goodwin, D. W. Alcoholism and heredity. Arch. Gen. Psychiatry 36:57, 1979.
25. Gori, G. B. Low-risk cigarettes: A prescription. Science 194:1243, 1976.
26. Gori, G. B., and Lynch, C. J. Toward less hazardous cigarettes: Current advances. J.A.M.A. 240:1255, 1978.
27. Guilford, J. S. *Factors Related to Successful Abstinence from Smoking*. Pittsburgh, American Institute for Research, 1966.
28. Hall, R. G., Sachs, D. P., and Hall, S. M. Medical risk and therapeutic effectiveness of rapid smoking. Behav. Ther. 10:249, 1979.
29. Hamburg, B. A., Kraemer, H. C., and Jahnke, W. A hierarchy of drug use in adolescence: Behavioral and attitudinal correlates of substantial drug use. Am. J. Psychiatry 132:1155, 1975.
30. Hammond, E. C., Garfinkel, L., Seidman, H., and Lew, E. A. Some recent findings concerning cigarette smoking. In *Origins of Human Cancer*, Cold Spring Harbor, N. Y., Cold Spring Harbor Laboratory, 1977.
31. Hawthorne, V. M., and Fry, J. S. Smoking and health: The association between smoking behaviour, total mortality, and cardiorespiratory disease in West Central Scotland. J. Epidemiol. Community Health 32:001, 1978.
32. Horan, J. J., Hackett, G., Nicholas, W. D., Linberg, S. E., Stone, C. I., and Lukaski, H. S. Rapid smoking: A cautionary note. J. Consult. Clin. Psychol. 45:341, 1977.
33. Hunt, W. A., and Bespalec, D. A. An evaluation of current methods of modifying smoking behavior. J. Clin. Psychol. 30:431, 1974.
34. Husain, M. K., Frantz, A. G., Ciarochi, F., and Robinson, A. G. Nicotine-stimulated release of neurophysin and vasopressin in humans. J. Clin. Endocrinol. Metab. 41:1113, 1975.
35. Jaffe, J. H. Factors in the etiology of drug use and drug dependence—two models: Opiate use and tobacco use. In *Rehabilitation and Treatment Aspects of Drug Dependence*, A. Schecter, editor, pp. 23-68.

Cleveland, CRC Press, 1977.

36. Jaffe, J. H., and Jarvik, M. E. Tobacco use and tobacco use disorder. In *Psychopharmacology: A Generation of Progress,* M. A. Lipton, A. Di Mascio, and K. F. Killam, editors, pp. 1665–1676. New York, Raven Press, 1978.

37. Jaffe, J. H., and Kanzler, M. Unpublished data.

38. Jaffe, J. H., Kanzler, M., Cohen, M., and Kaplan, T. Inducing low tar-nicotine cigarette smoking in women. Br. J. Addict. 73:271, 1978.

39. Jarvik, M. E. Further observations on nicotine as the reinforcing agent in smoking. In *Smoking Behavior: Motives and Incentives,* W. L. Dunn, Jr., editor, pp. 33–49. Washington, D. C., Winston and Sons, 1973.

40. Jarvik, M. E. Biological factors underlying the smoking habit. In *Research on Smoking Behavior,* M. E. Jarvik, J. W. Cullen, E. R. Gritz, T. M. Vogt, and L. J. West, editors, National Institute on Drug Abuse Research Monograph 17, pp. 122–148. (DHEW Pub. No. (ADM)78-581). Washington, D.C., United States Government Printing Office, 1977.

41. Jarvik, M. E. Tolerance to the effects of tobacco. In *Cigarette Smoking as a Dependence Process,* N. A. Krasnegor, editor, National Institute on Drug Abuse Research Monograph 23, pp. 150–157. (DHEW Pub. No. (ADM)79-800), Washington, D. C., United States Government Printing Office, 1979.

42. Jessor, R., and Jessor, S. L. *Problem Behavior and Psychosocial Development: A Longitudinal Study of Youth.* New York, Academic Press, 1977.

43. Kanzler, M., Jaffe, J. H., and Zeidenberg, P. Long- and short-term effectiveness of a large-scale proprietary smoking cessation program: A 4-year follow-up of Smokenders participants. J. Clin. Psychol. 32:661, 1976.

44. Kanzler, M., Zeidenberg, P., and Jaffe, J. H. Response of medical personnel to an on-site smoking cessation program. J. Clin. Psychol. 32:670, 1976.

45. Keller, M. The disease concept of alcoholism revisited. J. Stud. Alcohol 37:1694, 1976.

46. Kumar, R., Cooke, E. C., Lader, M. H., and Russell, M. A. H. Is nicotine important in tobacco smoking? Clin. Pharmacol. Ther. 21:520, 1977.

47. Larson, P. S., and Silvette, H. *Tobacco: Experimental and Clinical Studies,* Supplement 2. Baltimore, Williams & Wilkins, 1971.

48. Larson, P. S., and Silvette, H. *Tobacco: Experimental and Clinical Studies,* Supplement 3. Baltimore, Williams & Wilkins, 1975.

49. Lewin, L. *Phantastica: Narcotic and Stimulating Drugs.* New York, E. P. Dutton, 1964.

50. Lieberman Research, Inc. *The Teenager Looks at Cigarette Smoking.* New York, American Cancer Society, 1969.

51. Martin, W. R., Jasinski, D. R., Haertzen, C. A., Kay, D. C., Jones, B. E., Mansky, P. A., and Carpenter, R. W. Methadone: A reevaluation. Arch. Gen. Psychiatry 28:286, 1973.

52. Mc Gill, H. C., Jr., Rogers, W. R., Wilbur, R. L., and Johnson, D. E. Cigarette smoking baboon model: Demonstration of feasibility. Proc. Soc. Exp. Biol. Med. 157:672, 1978.

53. Meyer, R. W., and Mirin, S. M. *The Heroin Stimulus: Implication for a Theory of Addiction.* New York, Plenum Press, 1979.

54. Miller, L. C., Schilling, A. F., Logan, D. L., and Johnson, R. L. Potential hazards of rapid smoking as a technique for the modification of smoking behavior. N. Eng. J. Med. 297:590, 1977.

55. O'Brien, C. P. Experimental analysis of conditioning factors in human narcotic addiction. Pharmacol. Rev. 27:533, 1976.

56. Ockene, J. Multiple Risk Factor Intervention Trial (MRFIT): Smoking cessation procedures and cessation and recidivism patterns for a large cohort of MRFIT participants. In *Progress in Smoking Cessation,* J. L. Schwartz, editor, pp. 183–198. New York, American Cancer Society, 1978.

57. Pechacek, T. F. Modification of smoking behavior. In *Smoking and Health: A Report of the Surgeon General,* Office on Smoking and Health, editors, chapter 19. (DHEW Pub. No. (PHS)79-50066). Washington, D.C., United States Government Printing Office, 1979.

58. Pomerleau, O., Adkins, D., and Pertschuk, M. Predictors of outcome and recidivism in smoking cessation treatment. Addict. Behav. 3:65, 1978.

59. Raw, M. Treatment of cigarette dependence (summary). WHO Chronicle 33:98, 1979.

60. Reeder, L. G. Sociocultural factors in the etiology of smoking behavior: An assessment. In *Research on Smoking Behavior,* M. E. Jarvik, J. C. Cullen, E. R. Gritz, T. M. Vogt, and L. J. West, editors, National Institute on Drug Abuse Research Monograph #17, pp. 186–201. (DHEW Pub. No. (ADM)78-581). Washington, D. C., United States Government Printing Office, 1977.

61. Rolleston, H. Medical aspects of tobacco. Lancet 1: 961, 1926.

62. Russell, M. A. H. Cigarette smoking: Natural history of a dependence disorder. Br. J. Med. Psychol. 44:1, 1971.

63. Russell, M. A. H. Smoking and nicotine dependence. In *Research Advances in Alcohol and Drug Problems,* R. J. Gibbins, Y. Israel, H. Kalant, R. I. Popham, W. Schmidt and R. G. Smart, editors, vol. 3, pp. 1–48. New York, John Wiley, 1976.

64. Russell, M. A. H., and Feyerabend, C. Cigarette smoking: A dependence on high-nicotine boli. Drug Metab. Rev. 8:29, 1978.

65. Russell, M. A. H., Peto, J., and Patel, U. A. The classification of smoking by factorial structure of motives. J. R. Statist. Soc. 137:313, 1974.

66. Russell, M. A. H., Raw, M., Taylor, C., Feyerabend, C., and Saloojee, Y. Blood nicotine and carboxyhemoglobin levels after rapid smoking aversion therapy. J. Consult. Clin. Psychol. 46:1423, 1978.

67. Russell, M. A. H., Wilson, D., Feyerabend, D., and Cole, P. V. Effect of nicotine chewing gum on smoking behavior and as an aid to cigarette withdrawal. Br. Med. J. 2:391, 1976.

68. Russell, M. A. H., Wilson, C., Patel, U. A., Feyerabend, C., and Cole, P. V. Plasma nicotine levels after smoking cigarettes with high, medium and low nicotine yields. Br. Med. J. 2:414, 1975.

69. Schachter, S. Pharmacological and psychological determinants of smoking. Ann. Intern. Med. 88:104, 1978.

70. Schechter, M. D., and Rand, M. J. Effect of acute deprivation of smoking on aggression and hostility. Psychopharmacologia 35:19, 1974.

71. Schuckit, M., Goodwin, D., and Winokur, G. A

study of alcoholism in half siblings. Am. J. Psychiatry 128:1132, 1972.

72. Schwartz, J. L. Helping smokers quit: State of the art. In *Progress in Smoking Cessation*, J. L. Schwartz, editor, pp. 32–65. New York, American Cancer Society, 1978.

73. Shiffman, S. M. The tobacco withdrawal syndrome. In *Cigarette Smoking as a Dependence Process*, N. A. Krasnegor, editor, National Institute on Drug Abuse Research Monograph #23, pp. 158–184. (DHEW Pub. No. (ADM)79-800). Washington, D.C., United States Government Printing Office, 1979.

74. Shiffman, S. M., and Jarvik, M. E. Smoking withdrawal symptoms in two weeks of abstinence. Psychopharmacologia 50:35, 1976.

75. Simon, W. E., and Primavera, L. H. The personality of the cigarette smoker: Some empirical data. Int. J. Addict. 11:81, 1976.

76. Smith, G. M. Relations between personality and smoking behavior in preadult subjects. J. Consult. Clin. Psychol. 33:710, 1969.

77. Smith, G. M. Personality and smoking: A review of the empirical literature. In *Learning Mechanisms in Smoking*, W. A. Hunt, editor, pp. 42–61. Chicago, Aldine, 1970.

78. Surgeon General. *Smoking and Health*, Office on Smoking and Health, editors. (DHEW Pub. No. (PHS)79-50066). Washington, D.C., United States Government Printing Office, 1979.

79. Sutton, S. R., Feyerabend, C., Cole, P. V., and Russell, M. A. H. Adjustment of smokers to dilution of tobacco smoke by ventilated cigarette holders. Clin. Pharmacol. Ther. 24:395, 1978.

80. Tamarin, J. S., and Eisinger, R. A. Cigarette smoking and the psychiatrist. Am. J. Psychiatry 128:1224, 1972.

81. Thomas, C. B. The relationship of smoking and habits of nervous tension. In *Smoking Behavior: Motives and Incentives*, W. L. Dunn, Jr., editor, pp. 157–170. Washington, D.C., Winston and Sons, 1973.

82. Turner, J. A. McM., Sillett, R. S., and Ball, K. P. Some effects of changing to tar and low-nicotine cigarettes. Lancet 2:737, 1974.

83. Vogt, T. M. Smoking behavioral factors as predictors of risks. In *Research on Smoking Behavior*, M. E. Jarvik, J. W. Cullen, E. R. Gritz, T. M. Vogt, and L. J. West, editors, National Institute on Drug Abuse Research Monograph #17, pp. 98–111. (DHEW Pub. No. (ADM)78-581). Washington, D.C., United States Government Printing Office, 1977.

84. Wilson, R. W. Morbidity. In *Smoking and Health: A Report of the Surgeon General*, Office on Smoking and Health, editors, chapter 3 (DHEW Pub. No. (PHS)79-50066), Washington, D.C., United States Government Printing Office, 1979.

85. Winternitz, W. W., and Quillen, D. Acute hormonal response to cigarette smoking. J. Clin. Pharmacol. 17:389, 1977.

86. Wynder, E. L., and Hoffman, D. Tobacco and health: A societal challenge. N. Engl. J. Med. 300:894, 1979.

87. Wynder, E. L., and Stellman, S.D. Impact of long-term filter cigarette usage on lung and larynx cancer risk: A case-control study. J. Natl. Cancer Inst. 62:471, 1979.

88. Yanagita, T. Brief review on the use of self-administration techniques for predicting drug dependence potential. In *Predicting Dependence Liability of Stimulant and Depressant Drugs*, T. Thompson and K. R. Unna, editors, pp. 231–242. Baltimore, University Park Press, 1977.

CHAPTER 21

CAFFEINISM AND CAFFEINE WITHDRAWAL[1]

John F. Greden, M.D.

INTRODUCTION AND DEFINITIONS

CAFFEINE

Caffeine, a widely ingested member of the chemical class of alkaloids, is a xanthine derivative (1-, 3-, 7-trimethylxanthine), pharmacologically categorized as a central nervous system (CNS) stimulant (40, 50, 51, 68). In addition to renown as a CNS stimulant, the drug has many less well publicized pharmacological actions (41). Caffeine is available in the forms of tea, coffee, cocoa, soft drinks, chocolate, and many brands of analgesic tablets, stimulants, diet preparations, and cold tablets (5, 16, 34). It is also prescribable—but infrequently used—in several medicinal forms, including caffeine and sodium benzoate, and citrated caffeine. Caffeine has intermittently been considered a drug of abuse throughout history (25, 39, 56, 61, 65). Recent investigations confirm traditional claims that this remarkably domesticated agent can be overused. Chronic use is often associated with habituation and tolerance. Excessive use frequently induces a characteristic toxicity syndrome. Discontinuation may produce withdrawal manifestations. Based upon these

factors, consideration of caffeine in a comprehensive textbook of drug abuse seems both appropriate and indicated.

CAFFEINISM

Caffeinism is a recently introduced clinical term (34, 55), operationally defined as a multifaceted syndrome produced by acute or chronic overuse of caffeine, with resultant pharmacological toxicity. The syndrome is predominantly characterized by anxiety symptoms, mood changes, sleep disturbances, and psychophysiological complaints. In most cases, symptoms are dose-related extensions of caffeine's expected pharmacological actions.

CAFFEINE WITHDRAWAL

Caffeine withdrawal is a physiological state induced by sudden discontinuation of caffeine intake among chronic users of that drug (17, 38). Prior development of pharmacological tolerance is necessary for withdrawal to occur (13). Principal manifestations include headaches, irritability, changes in mood state, lethargy, sleep disturbance, and mild physiological arousal.

HISTORY

The word caffeine interestingly derives from the Arabic term gawah designating a

---

[1] Adapted from Greden, J. F. Caffeine and tobacco dependence. In *Comprehensive Textbook of Psychiatry*, ed. 3, H. I. Kaplan, A. M. Freedman, and B. J. Sadock editors. Baltimore, Williams & Wilkins, 1980.

type of wine (25). Now paradoxically—and inaccurately (27, 48)—considered an "antidote" to wines and other liquors, caffeine has become one of the most widely used psychoactive substances in the world. Despite current enthusiastic use of caffeine-containing substances, however, they have not always been readily accepted. In fact, their history is riddled with controversy (35, 61).

Ingestion of both tea and coffee began approximately 1,000 years ago (18, 56, 65). Tea was reportedly introduced to Europe by way of China in the 16th century. Earliest legends always seemed to fuse religion and pharmacology, such as the poignant story about tea's origin. A Buddhist saint was said to have fallen asleep during a 9-year meditation. Upon awakening—filled with shame—he cut off his eyelids to ensure no repetition of his unacceptable behavior. His eyelids sprung into tea plants, promptly used by mortal man to produce a beverage that overcame sleepiness. Legends about coffee similarly blended the drug's stimulant qualities with religious responses to these effects. Specifically, a goatherd named Kaldi reportedly noted sprightly behavior among his goats after they ate red berries from a local shrub. He tried the berries himself, with similar results. Soon, some religious leaders consumed Kaldi's berries in a hot drink and promoted such ingestion as assisting lengthy prayer. Others attacked the practice, however, insisting that such users were not "true followers" (18).

These early religious arguments were accompanied by medical debates about whether caffeine should be considered a chemical of abuse. Historical claims of abuse potential were often strongly worded. As early as 1601, Parry suggested that "a certain liquor which they call caffeine. . .will soon intoxicate the brain" (25). Others concurred, insisting that tea and coffee caused palsies, sterility, nervousness, leanness, and impotence. Claims were made that Colonial American women were "such slaves to it that they would rather go without their dinners than without a dish of tea" (39). Pharmacological withdrawal and tolerance were described in a report from Victorian England, in which the habitual coffee drinker was characterized as "a sufferer" who is (61):

tremulous and loses his self-command; he is subject to fits of agitation and depression; he loses color and has a haggard appearance. The appetite falls off, and symptoms of gastric catarrh may be manifested. The heart also suffers; it palpitates, or it intermits. As with other such agents, a renewed dose of the poison gives temporary relief, but at the cost of future misery.

A 19th-century physician even claimed that tea and coffee consumption promoted later use of tobacco, alcohol, opium, and other stimulants. This "domino effect" would, of course, be suggested for marihuana 100 years later.

Proponents of caffeine always countered these claims of abuse potential with contentions that the drug was medicinally important (18, 56, 65). Coinciding with the first public sale of tea to British subjects at Garway's Coffee House in London, the brew was promoted as "That Excellent *and by all Physitians approved* China drink" (emphasis added). Tea was said to (65):

removeth lassitude, vanquisheth heavy dreams, easeth the frame, and strengtheneth the memory. It overcometh superfluous sleep, and prevents sleepiness in general, so that without trouble whole nights may be passed in study. It is of great avail to men of corpulent bodies and to such as eat much flesh. It clears a dull head, and maketh the frame active and lusty.

In addition to these stirring endorsements, tea's perceived psychological effects were always stated in graphic terms, such as when a Chinese mystic of the Tang dynasty wrote (56):

The first cup of tea moistens my lips and throat. The second shatters my loneliness. The third causes the wrongs of life to fade gently from my recollection. The fourth purifies my soul. The fifth lifts me to the realms of the unwinking gods.

A glamorous drug or a drug of abuse? In milder forms, the question is still debated today.

Tea and coffee have historically provoked strong political reactions wherever they appeared. In most parts of the world, at one time or another both drugs were banned. The evolution of such bans was always similar. Following introduction, coffee or tea would promptly become popular. Such popularity was soon followed by criticism, often orchestrated by alarmed moralists and usually culminating is restrictive legislation. Restrictions were always defied, however, gradually requiring legal reacceptance. The following narration of a typical 16th-century conflict illustrates such reacceptance (18):

the (coffee) habit had become so strong, and the use of it so generally agreeable, that the people continued, notwithstanding all prohibitions, to drink it in their own houses. The officers of the police, seeing they could not suppress the use of it allowed of the selling it, on paying a tax; and the drinking it provided it was not done openly; so that it was drunk in particular places, with the doors shut, or in the back room of some of the shopkeepers houses. . ...

The most recent of these cycles occurred in England, when Charles II briefly closed coffee houses but was forced to rescind his stance; in Germany, when Bach protested a governmental ban by writing his *Coffee Cantata*; and in America, when revolutionary colonists fervently and violently boycotted tea because it symbolized domination by the British Empire (35).

Because of these controversies, a realistic perspective of caffeine abuse was often difficult to formulate. Medical reports that did strive to detach themselves from political, economic, and religious issues, however, always carried a consistent theme: A distinct clinical profile—"caffeinism"—could be identified among excess users (44, 53).

As recent as the 1960's and 1970's, caffeinism and caffeine withdrawal were not official diagnoses within the second edition of the American Psychiatric Association's *Diagnostic and Statistical Manual of Mental Disorders* (DSM-II). Following clinical reports of caffeinism, they were added to early drafts of the third edition (DSM-III) but then predictably debated. These fluctuations confirm continued uncertainty among members of the medical profession about whether caffeine should be categorized as a drug of abuse.

EPIDEMIOLOGY

Caffeine develops naturally in a multitude of botanical products (25, 41). These include kola nuts, coffee seeds ("beans"), tea leaves, cocoa trees, mate' or ilex plants, and cassina. Total world-wide production of caffeine is virtually impossible to determine accurately. Consumption of caffeine—ubiquitous virtually everywhere—must be measured in billions of kilograms (41). More than 1 billion kilograms of coffee alone are consumed an-

nually in the United States. Tea intake is perhaps one-quarter of that, but this still constitutes more than 40 billion servings a year. Our synthetic caffeine use also exceeds 1 million kilograms annually. In summary, millions of individuals in the United States join hundreds of millions elsewhere in their daily ingestion of the drug. Along with tobacco and alcohol, caffeine certainly ranks with the most widely used psychoactive substances in America.

Common commercial and medicinal preparations that contain caffeine are listed in Tables 21.1 and 21.2. In the United States, the majority of caffeine is ingested through coffee. Elsewhere in the world, other vehicles may be more widely used. Although not a primary topic for this chapter, caffeine-containing vehicles themselves—e.g., coffee versus tea versus medicinal agents—also contain other pharmacologically active ingredients (5, 41, 42), and these substances may alter the clinical syndrome or induce important manifestations in their own right.

Most consumers of caffeine do not seem to overuse or abuse caffeine (2, 26, 34). Accurate incidence and prevalence for caffeine abuse, although virtually unknown, can be indirectly estimated by coupling two factors, namely dose-effect relationships and pharmacokinetics of the drug with findings from caffeine surveys (2, 4, 26, 36). To illustrate, pharmacokinetic studies reveal that an acute

Table 21.1
Some Common Sources of Caffeine (5, 16, 34)

Source	Approximate Amounts of Caffeine per Unit[a]
Beverages	
Brewed coffee	80–140 mg per cup
Instant tea	66–100 mg per cup
Tea (leaf)	30–75 mg per cup
Tea (bagged)	42–100 mg per cup
Decaffeinated coffee	2–4 mg per cup
Cola drinks	25–55 mg per glass
Cocoa	5–50 mg per cup
Many over-the-counter cold preparations	30 mg per tablet
Many over-the-counter stimulants	100–200 mg per tablet
Small chocolate bar	25 mg per bar

[a] Cup = 5 to 6 ounces; cola drink = 8 to 12 ounces.

Table 21.2
Caffeine Content of Selected Analgesics (5, 16, 34, 45)

Analgesics	Caffeine per Unit
	mg
Anacin	32.5
A.P.C's (aspirin, phenacetin, caffeine)	32
B C Tablet	16
Bromo-Seltzer	32.5
Cafergot	100
Capron	32
Comeback	100
Cope	32
Darvon Compound	32
Dolor	30
Easy-Mens	32
Empirin Compound	32
Excedrin	64.8
Fiorinal	40
Goody's Headache Powder	32.5
Medache	32
Maranox	15
Midol	32
Migral	50
Nilain	32
P A C	32
Pre-Mens	66
Stanback Tablets	16
Stanback Powder	32
Trigesic	30
Vanquish	32

dose of caffeine that reaches 250 mg is pharmacologically potent for most nontolerant individuals. When consumed chronically, tolerance usually develops to such dosages. Although the careful clinician can identify some clinical effects from even low doses, higher doses are tolerated well, but only to a certain level. This "cut-off" level, after which clinical signs and symptoms more commonly develop, differs among individuals, presumably depending upon their unique pharmacokinetics and innate sensitivity. It is the author's impression that the point at which most consumers clinically exceed tolerance occurs at approximately 500 mg per day (36). Above this, symptoms of caffeinism rise sharply. Five hundred milligrams per day, then, may be epidemiologically employed to designate a high risk group. Because various North American surveys have documented that 20 to 30 per cent of adults consume more than 500 mg per day, a substantial percentage of our population seems to be at high risk for caffeinism. Gilbert (26, 28) estimated that 10 per cent of North Americans actually func-

tion with this condition. Only a few substance abuse conditions have higher prevalences.

Most subjects with caffeinism have daily intakes from all sources that approximate 1,000 mg. It is not rare, however, for patients to report using 2,000 mg per day or even up to 5,000 mg per day (38, 46). Among these individuals, the clinician can conclude with a high degree of certainty that the syndrome of caffeinism is present, whether the patient is aware of causal associations or not. Epidemiological assessments of caffeinism have been conducted among several hospitalized samples. Greden observed that among psychiatric patients in a university hospital, when caffeine intake from all sources was summed, approximately 23 per cent reported ingesting more than 750 mg per day (36). Winstead noted that 25 per cent of hospitalized psychiatric patients in a military hospital were "high users," defined as consuming more than five cups of coffee daily (70). When nonpsychiatric patients were studied, Greden observed that 16 per cent consumed more than 750 mg per day. These figures reflect the potential magnitude of caffeine intake among individuals requiring hospital treatment. Similar studies among outpatients have not been conducted.

Researchers should note that high caffeine users ingest the drug in multiple forms. Thus, for accurate studies, *total* caffeine intake must be calculated, rather than utilizing simpler tallies of coffee or tea.

PHARMACOLOGY OF CAFFEINE

The etiology, clinical manifestations, and treatment of caffeinism must be considered within a pharmacological context. Thus, a brief review of the drug's pharmacology is essential before dealing with these facets.

Caffeine is actually a safe drug, probably because it is generally consumed in diluted form (4, 11, 13, 41, 68). Few deaths have been documented from overdose. The lowest fatal oral dose for an adult is probably in the order of 5 to 10 g, grossly equivalent to short term consumption of 50 to 100 cups of commercial coffee. After oral ingestion, caffeine appears in tissues within minutes. Peak plasma levels usually occur 30 to 45 minutes later. Approximately 15 per cent of the drug is metabolized per hour. It is debatable whether day to day accumulation occurs (26).

The impact of caffeine upon human performance has been elaborately evaluated and reviewed (68). Although somewhat conflicting, most results conclude that certain parameters of human performance and alertness are mildly enhanced, but fine motor movements may be impaired. It is important to note that caffeine has biphasic psychomotor effects; small doses stimulate activity, but large doses depress it. As with other pharmacological effects, tolerance develops to the psychomotor stimulation (66).

The majority of the clinical manifestations observed in individuals with caffeinism depend upon well documented pharmacological effects on the central nervous system, the cardiovascular system, the gastrointestinal system, and the renal system. Caffeine's effect upon each will be briefly reviewed, as well as several known miscellaneous actions.

CENTRAL NERVOUS SYSTEM

Caffeine possesses potent CNS stimulation capacity (11, 36, 41). Such stimulation apparently underlies claims that the drug promotes rapid clear thinking, improved intellectual effort, enhanced mental acuity, decreased drowsiness, less fatigue, and decreased reaction time. Similar to psychomotor effects, these factors have a dose relationship, and there is some evidence for a bimodal effect with stimulation at low and moderate doses but slowed functioning at high doses. Although not all actions are fully understood, caffeine has diffuse neuropharmacological consequences (6–10, 14, 24, 40, 41, 51, 52, 66, 67). All parts of the cortex are affected. Vasomotor, vagal, and respiratory centers of the medulla are modified by caffeine. The spinal cord is directly impacted. Whether these effects result from direct stimulation of the drug itself or are produced by caffeine's effects on other neuropharmacological systems must be reconsidered as new developments occur. The known CNS effects of caffeine are summarized in Table 21.3. Certainly, future research will have to focus upon the respective importance of each of these, including how they interact with each other.

CARDIOVASCULAR SYSTEM

Caffeine promptly produces changes in systemic, coronary, and cerebral circulation patterns (11, 36, 41). Coronary, pulmonary,

Table 21.3
Neuropharmacological Changes following Caffeine Toxicity (6–10, 14, 24, 40, 51, 52, 66, 67)

   I. Significant increase in norepinephrine secretion
  II. Inhibition of phosphodiesterase breakdown of cyclic 3′,5′-adenosine monophosphate (cyclic AMP)
 III. Sensitization of central catecholamine postsynaptic receptors
  IV. Antagonism of CNS adenosine and related nucleotides
   V. Enhancement of cyclic guanosine 3′,5′-monophosphate (cyclic GMP)
  VI. Possible modulation of acetylcholine and serotonin activity
 VII. Modification of calcium metabolism

and general systemic vessels become dilated after ingestion. Heart rate and force of contraction also increase. Although some individuals are markedly affected and describe cardiovascular effects as the most prominent consequences of caffeine ingestion, among others these effects tend to be masked by central stimulating effects upon the medulla. At moderate doses, an individual may, therefore, notice no change in heart rate, a tachycardia, a slight bradycardia, or an arrhythmia (thus explaining the previously noted historical observation that the heart "palpitates or intermits") (61).

GASTROINTESTINAL SYSTEM

Perhaps the most prominent gastrointestinal consequence of caffeine is a significant increase in gastric secretion (34, 36). Both volume and acidity are augmented. Other components of caffeine-containing vehicles may be important in producing or modifying these gastrointestinal effects, such as the tannin contained in tea, the oils in coffee, or the acetylsalicylic acid in analgesic tablets.

RENAL SYSTEM

Caffeine has prompt diuretic effects (11, 36). This well known action is probably the result of the methylation on the 3-position of the xanthine nucleus.

MISCELLANEOUS

In addition to these above mentioned effects, caffeine relaxes smooth muscles (especially of the pulmonary bronchi), enhances the contraction of skeletal muscles, and increases the basal metabolic rate a reported average of 10 per cent.

ETIOLOGY

The etiology of caffeinism must be considered from three perspectives. First, why do consumers initiate intake? Second, why do they continue and even increase their dosage? Third, what are the mechanisms by which the drug exerts its effects?

Only partial information is available for determining why individuals launch a cycle of caffeine consumption. The appeal is presumably not simply due to excellent taste, because the drug is described by some as tasteless and by others as having a bitter taste. As Levenson and Bick (41) noted, many individuals may be insensitive to the bitterness of caffeine, and this may have a genetic basis. If not solely taste, what other factors might be involved? Some genetic investigators (1, 49) suggested coffee drinking showed significant heritability when the amount consumed was considered and that there may be genetically transmitted variations in sleep alterations from caffeine. No firm documentation for genetic patterns for caffeinism currently exists, however. If genetic influence is unproven, clinical interviewing suggests that peer example, media advertising, familial patterns, and cultural and ethnic traditions are all important. Usually, the drug's stimulant qualities seem to be most highly sought by previous nonusers. Young students, for example, begin consuming while studying at late hours. Interestingly, many consumers report initially disliking, or at least not liking, caffeine-containing beverages on first exposure.

Once begun, various factors seem to explain partially why intake tends to continue. Consumption is often accompanied by friendly social interactions ("Let's go have a cup of coffee."). "Coffee shops" and "coffee breaks" are major components of our social system. Classical Pavlovian conditioning also seems to help perpetuate the pattern (69). Caffeine consumption commonly coincides with other activities that are perceived as pleasurable, such as eating and smoking. There is a pleasant aroma and often a soothing warm temperature. Even paraphernalia used may reinforce ingestion (favorite coffee or tea cups, favorite brand, grinding machines, etc.).

These social and "learned conditioning" factors seem inadequate in explaining chronic caffeine consumption, however. Indeed, it is reasonable to hypothesize these aspects are less important than neuropharmacological effects of caffeine upon the reward system ("pleasure centers") of the brain. These centers are involved with the median forebrain bundle and consist predominantly of dopamine and norepinephrine fibers. Because caffeine is known to sensitize dopamine receptors (24, 67) and increase norepinephrine functional activity (12, 40), and because stimulants that have similar actions (such as amphetamine) are known to potentiate reward-seeking behavior, it is not unreasonable to speculate that chronic high caffeine users seek repetitive consumption predominantly because the drug stimulates the brain's diffuse "reward centers." Documentation of this hypothesis is unfortunately not available at this time.

Recent findings also suggest various neuropharmacological interactions may be more complex than once thought. To illustrate, caffeine is a potent antagonist of the action of adenosine (51, 52). Because adenosine and related nucleotides themselves depress the spontaneous firing of CNS neurons, caffeine's antagonism of adenosine may be the mechanism underlying its central stimulant actions, rather than a direct effect of the drug itself. Once chronic ingestion develops, the drug's known pharmacological effects probably explain most of the manifestations associated with caffeinism. As stated previously, the common signs and symptoms are dose-related extensions of expected actions rather than "side effects" per se.

No precise findings are available to document how long caffeine use must be continued before a persistent caffeine-seeking behavior develops. What is apparent is that individuals with operationally defined caffeinism generally are older and report having started caffeine consumption many years previously (36). This suggests that chronic use with gradual build-up is necessary in order to develop a persistent syndrome of caffeinism.

A final etiological factor that perpetuates chronic caffeine use may be related to tolerance (13). Among most high consumers, the syndrome of caffeinism develops insidiously. The "abuse pattern" is thus established without the individual even being aware of it. Then, if dosage is too sharply curtailed, unpleasant withdrawal symptoms develop. Similar to many other drugs, the user promptly seeks renewed administration of the agent to lessen these aversive symptoms. Thus, both reward seeking and pain avoidance may be implicated.

Further research will be required to clarify many nagging etiological questions that have never been answered, new ones that have recently emerged, and important ones that have yet to be formulated.

CLINICAL DESCRIPTION

The onset of caffeinism tends to be inconsistent and difficult to pinpoint (34, 36). Various reasons account for this. First, many users only infrequently exceed tolerance levels and only intermittently develop symptoms. Second, among those who chronically exceed pharmacological tolerance levels, this usually does not occur until after years or decades of intake, and clinical symptoms tend to develop insidiously. Third, most patients with caffeinism do not cognitively associate their clinical complaints with their caffeine intake, and clinical history of an association is hard to obtain.

Demographically, caffeinism may occur at any age (5, 23, 25, 34, 36). Most patients with this condition are older than 35. Because age is clearly confounded with marital status, most are also married. There is a statistically significant inverse correlation between religious activity and caffeine consumption.

A consistent clinical observation by the author was that significantly fewer high caffeine users—those whose intake exceeds 750 mg per day—report that their physical health is excellent or good (36). In fact, a majority consider their health only fair or poor. Presumably, this global health rating correlated at least partially to the presence of various symptoms associated with caffeinism.

A number of symptom constellations seem to occur most frequently among subjects with caffeinism (34, 37). These include anxiety manifestations, sleep disorders, somatic complaints, and affective disturbances. These will be considered sequentially, followed by a discussion of how caffeinism might also affect other aspects of medical practice.

ANXIETY MANIFESTATIONS

The most frequently reported anxiety features of caffeinism include nervousness, tension, irritability, tremulousness, feeling upset, jittery, "high-strung," and tired (34). On rating scales, some caffeinism patients report feeling beleaguered by the belief that "difficulties are piling up" (34, 70). When evaluated with the State-Trait Anxiety Index (STAI) (63), patients with highest caffeine intakes reported significantly greater levels of state anxiety (how one feels at the moment). This existed among both psychiatric and nonpsychiatric subjects. Trait anxiety scores (how one generally feels) were also significantly elevated. These elevations in anxiety scores are fully compatible with nonhospital subjective surveys conducted by Goldstein et al. (29–33) among housewives and medical students.

In addition to psychological anxiety symptoms, numerous psychophysiological symptoms also contribute to the anxiety state described by patients. These include disturbed cardiac function, loose stools or diarrhea, epigastric pains, sensory disturbances, hyperesthesia, ocular dyskinesias, muscular twitching, dry mouth, and quivering voice (34).

Whether the increased anxiety symptoms among high caffeine users predate caffeine abuse or develop from it cannot be answered with finality. Clinically, many patients with caffeinism report "they were not always so anxious." For them, caffeine abuse may have been the predominant etiology of anxiety. Others report lengthy premorbid histories of hyperactivity, restlessness, and chronic anxiety that clearly preceded caffeine use. A few even believe high caffeine intake calms them down. Regardless of whether caffeinism is causal, contributory, or simply associated, highest users consistently reported frequent use of anxiolytic agents, such as the benzodiazepines and meprobamate. When compared with low or moderate users, their use of these agents was significantly greater (36). Whether they are treating caffeinism or a preceding anxiety state again can only be answered with prospective studies. Meanwhile, therapists must be aware that the composite clinical state of the patient with caffeinism is often confounded by polydrug use.

Anxiety features associated with caffeinism probably depend upon the interaction of the drug's pharmacological actions and other psychosocial stresses. Cobb (12), for example, noted that unemployed auto workers who consumed coffee under stress (after losing their jobs) had greater increases in norepinephrine output than when they ingested coffee at nonstressful times and greater than that of controls. In addition to the possible synergistic effect of these stressors, other factors such as diet, fatigue, physical conditioning, and the presence of concurrent illnesses may partially determine the effects of the drug on any given day.

SLEEP DISORDERS

The majority of nontolerant users report that caffeine impairs sleep if consumed before bedtime (21, 23, 25, 29, 47, 62). This action is paradoxically responsible for much of the drug's popularity, but obviously it can also become a clinical problem. Chronic high users with clinical tolerance deny that caffeine's antisoporific effect is dramatic. Specifically, in one study (36), 53 per cent of low consumers (<250 mg per day) reported that caffeine before bedtime prevented sleep, compared to 43 per cent of moderate consumers (250 to 749 mg per day) and only 22 per cent of high consumers (750 mg or more per day). Caffeine has been documented in laboratory settings to produce delayed sleep onset and more frequent nighttime awakenings. A relevant observation by Goldstein et al. (29–33) was that traditional caffeine consumers claimed that caffeine at bedtime did not disrupt their sleep, even though objective assessment documented that it did. Clinical reports from the patient, therefore, cannot always be taken at face value. If intake above 1,000 mg per day is present, the clinican can reasonably conclude that some objective interference with sleep is likely, but that subjective tolerance may have developed and the patient may not describe being aware of sleep impairment. These observations at least partially explain why highest caffeine users report statistically significantly greater use of sedative-hypnotics, similar to their greater consumption of antianxiety agents (36). As further documentation of caffeine's clinical interference with sleep, in a hospital setting the drug was noted to counteract the sedative-hypnotic effect of barbiturates (21). This interference suggests that spiraling requests for increased intake of sedative-hypnotics would follow. Sleep disruptions, such as re-

duced rapid eye movement (REM) sleep have been associated with various psychiatric conditions. Caffeine's effects upon REM sleep and other sleep stages are still not completely documented, but the drug's interference with sleep could be one of the causal mechanisms for inducing the clinical symptoms of caffeinism. With the recent development of sleep laboratories, sleep dysfunctions associated with caffeinism will hopefully be better elucidated in future years.

SOMATIC MANIFESTATIONS

The most common somatic symptoms that users associate with caffeine use, in descending order of frequency, include diuresis, headache, tachypnea, tachycardia, tremulousness, diarrhea, and lightheadedness (25, 34, 36, 41). Other symptoms—reported by fewer than 10 per cent of caffeinism subjects—include seeing "spots" in front of the eyes, stomach pains, "ringing" in the ears, cardiac palpitations, a feeling of being unable to breathe, "tingling" in the hands and feet, and excessive perspiration. An intriguing finding among nonpsychiatric patients was that, when compared with low and high users, significantly fewer moderate consumers associated somatic symptoms with caffeine intake. This unexpected dose-effect relationship might be explained by the fact that low users have not developed tolerance (and the drug produced noticeable somatic symptoms), whereas high users have exceeded tolerance (and the somatic symptoms are again noticeable), and only moderate consumers consider the somatic effects insignificant. Other explanations are also possible.

Numerous patients present to clinicians with a number of somatic symptoms. Considering the somatic profile that characterizes caffeinism and the drug's widespread intake, such patients must be evaluated as "high risk" for caffeinism.

AFFECTIVE DISORDERS

Affective disturbances associated with caffeinism are less well defined than anxiety or somatic features. Although several historical case reports described "depression" or hyperactive agitation, these conditions have not been commonly associated with the syndrome (44, 53). Recent studies conducted by the author (36), however, documented that highest caffeine consumers—among both psychiatric and nonpsychiatric samples—attained the highest scores on the Beck Depression Scale. Among psychiatric patients, one-half of those who consumed greater than 750 mg per day had Beck scores of 23 or above, suggesting severe depression. Although clinical diagnoses of depression cannot be made from scores on rating scales, and no study has yet shown that subjects with caffeinism have more diagnoses of depression, these rating scale scores strongly suggest that patients with caffeinism need to be screened for depressed mood. Winstead (70), in his study of military subjects, actually noted a lower prevalence of the diagnosis of depression among highest caffeine consumers, but this finding must be considered in conjunction with a simultaneous finding that significantly more high consumers were taking antidepressant medications. Other data suggesting that clinicians need to consider caffeinism among patients presenting with depression and/or mania include the facts that 22 per cent of highest consumers reported that caffeine made them feel "less depressed" (36) and that Neil et al. (47) linked caffeinism with affective states by documenting that both depressed and bipolar patients with mixed states consumed significantly greater amounts of caffeine than other affective subgroups.

Considering caffeine's stimulant actions on the adrenergic system (7, 12, 40), hypomanic or manic symptomatology is a conceivable consequence of chronic caffeinism. Little information is currently available to confirm any causality, however.

MISCELLANEOUS CLINICAL FEATURES

In addition to the predominant syndrome constellations described above, several other clinical aspects merit mention.

First, drug users tend to be drug users. Highest caffeine consumers also report greater use of sedative-hypnotics, minor tranquilizers, alcohol, and cigarettes (22, 26, 36, 38). Certainly, the use of these other psychoactive substances must affect clinical presentations, and detailed polydrug histories should be obtained.

Another clinical feature awaiting verification by controlled studies is that caffeine

abuse might induce or exacerbate psychosis among certain individuals. Milliksen (45) sugested that schizophrenic relapses were associated with caffeinism among several cases. Considering caffeine's effects upon dopamine function and the documented linkage of dopamine function to schizophrenia and other psychoses, such clinical observations may be potentially sound.

A third clinical feature is that acute caffeine toxicity might actually produce a classical CNS delirium, with disorientation, cognitive disruption, and marked perceptual disturbances (64). A dog sled racer recently ingested more than 1,000 mg of caffeine in 3 hours and was noted to develop a flagrant delirium syndrome.

Undiagnosed or untreated caffeinism may also interfere with various treatments prescribed by physicians (9, 37). Several reports have suggested adverse interactions with monoamine oxidase inhibitors, synergistically resulting in excessive irritability, increased jitteriness, and even greater than usual insomnia. Caffeine excess has been said to mimic hyperactivity among children (15, 34, 58). Not surprisingly, inasmuch as stimulants are an accepted treatment for accurately diagnosed hyperkinesis, the drug was also tested as a treatment for hyperactivity (3, 58). Although some reports found it beneficial, caffeine is less effective than other stimulants commonly used (3).

Finally, caffeinism has been implicated as a possible cause of persistent low grade fever (55), fluid retention (57), and impaired fetal development if consumed by pregnant women (43).

CAFFEINE WITHDRAWAL

If caffeine use is discontinued among tolerant, chronic high consumers—or presumably even if plasma levels fall precipitously because of a drastic reduction in intake—a characteristic caffeine withdrawal syndrome generally appears within 18 to 24 hours (17, 30–33, 38). Most people who experience withdrawal are consuming at least 600 mg per day, and may ingest 1 to 2 g daily. Key features of the syndrome include headache, irritability, inability to work effectively, nervousness, restlessness, mild nausea, and lethargy. Many withdrawal subjects also note excessive yawning, the etiology of which is unexplained. Because yawning occurs with use of apomorphine, a dopamine agonist, another suggestive link-up to dopamine activity can be hypothesized. Caffeine withdrawal is more likely to occur on weekends (38). Intake is most often decreased on Saturdays and Sundays, probably because employment stresses change. Subsequent neuropharmacological balances might also be altered on weekends.

The caffeine withdrawal headache may be an especially common syndrome (17, 38). In one study by Greden et al. (38), 20 per cent of a hospitalized patient population reported previous caffeine withdrawal headache. These headaches start with "cerebral fullness," followed by throbbing, diffuse pain. Movement accentuates the pain. Relief tends to occur promptly with renewed caffeine intake. This "analgesic" relief may perpetuate the problem cycle, because those who develop the headache tend to drift toward use of combination analgesics that contain caffeine (Table 21.2). The caffeine itself may be the effective pain-relieving agent, simply because it terminates the withdrawal process. Unfortunately, while doing so, the renewed caffeine intake also continues the cycle, and other withdrawal episodes are likely to occur on subsequent days.

DIFFERENTIAL DIAGNOSIS

The differential diagnosis of caffeinism is complex, because the syndrome itself can mimic a number of other entities. The most common entities to consider are anxiety disorders, hyperthyroidism, affective disorders (including depression, hypomania, or mania), electrolyte disturbances (causing muscle twitching, for example), pheochromocytoma (with its four p's—head *pain*, *palpitations*, *pallor*, and *perspiration*), sleep disorders stemming from other causes, or other types of drug abuse, especially from amphetamine, cocaine, or other sympathomimetic agents. Most of these conditions can be ruled out by thorough evaluations.

To diagnose caffeinism, the history *must* include an assessment of all common caffeine sources. Plasma levels of caffeine can be conducted but are expensive and not routinely available.

Self-rating survey forms (36) can be utilized to assist busy clinicians in compiling total caffeine intake but cannot replace the clinical history. If high consumption (e.g., 500 to 600 mg per day or more) is found and the user has a clinical profile compatible with caffeinism, the diagnostician ought to assume that a direct correlation between drug intake and symptoms is likely. Such a presumption is necessary in order to increase the sensitivity of diagnosis for an otherwise neglected syndrome.

A presumptive diagnosis of caffeinism can be tested by a withdrawal program. A list of target symptoms is compiled and monitored for 1 to 2 weeks. Predictably, if due to caffeine, they will dramatically lessen after clinical withdrawal. If further causal association is needed, a caffeine challenge should be employed; with reinstitution of intake, the return of symptoms would be likely. This "A-B-A" design not only provides clinical validity to diagnosis, but it assists patients in making causal associations between caffeine intake and troublesome symptoms.

Diagnosticians have recently recognized the importance of compiling explicit descriptions for clinical entities. This emphasis upon descriptive phenomenology not only enhances accurate diagnosis and treatment for individual patients, but it also enables clinicians and researchers to identify homogeneous populations for future study. Such explicit criteria have never been compiled for caffeinism, but, because the new diagnostic nomenclature being adopted by the American Psychiatric Association (DSM-III) will utilize this approach, Table 21.4 provides a preliminary listing of essential and associated features for diagnosis.

TREATMENT

Subjects with caffeinism often respond cynically to clinicians who suggest their symptoms stem from excessive use of the drug. Comments like "I've *always* been a coffee drinker and no one ever before suggested this was a problem" are not uncommon. If such skepticism (which might be enhanced by a subliminal fear that the drug's reinforcing qualities will be taken away from them) is to be overcome, an imaginative educational program is necessary. The clinician should briefly explain the pharmacology of caffeine, describing how the drug produces symptoms of caffeinism if used in excess.

Table 21.4
Caffeinism

Essential Features

1. Confirmed history of recent caffeine consumption, usually exceeding 250 mg and more commonly exceeding 500 mg per day
2. The presence of at least five of the following signs and symptoms at a time when caffeine is being consumed:
   a. Restlessness, nervousness, irritability, agitation, tremulousness, muscle twitching, or fasciculation
   b. Insomnia or sleep disruption
   c. Headache
   d. Sensory disturbances (hyperesthesia, ringing in ears, lightheadedness, flashing of light, ocular dyskinesias)
   e. Diuresis
   f. Cardiovascular symptoms (palpitations, extrasystoles, arrhythmias, flushing, tachycardia, increased cardiac awareness)
   g. Gastrointestinal complaints (epigastric pain, nausea, vomiting, diarrhea)
   h. Rambling flow of thoughts and speech, periods of inexhaustibility
3. Persistence of symptoms daily or sporadically for at least 2 weeks in conjunction with caffeine consumption, or consistent development of such symptomatology each time higher caffeine consumption occurs
4. The absence of any disorder that otherwise accounts for the symptoms of caffeinism, such as anxiety, hyperthyroidism, pheochromocytoma, mania, hypomania, electrolyte disturbances. Caffeinism may contribute to and aggravate these conditions.

Associated Features

1. The onset of caffeine withdrawal symptoms following cessation of caffeine consumption after a prolonged period with at least three for probable, or four for definite, of the following signs and symptoms present:
   a. Headache, being relieved by further caffeine intake
   b. Irritability
   c. Inability to work effectively
   d. Nervousness
   e. Lethargy

Reading materials may be helpful. Then, as early as possible, a discontinuation program should be launched. The clinician should list all products containing caffeine and give it to the patient. Caffeine-containing products at home, in the medicine chest, or even in automobile glove compartments should be discarded during this discontinuation phase. The patient should be instructed to observe for withdrawal symptoms. If dysphoric symptoms develop, they can be treated symptomatically, including the temporary use of caffeine-containing analgesics when needed (but only under the *doctor's* prescription). If total abrupt cessation seems unworkable, a staged reduction or a switch to decaffeinated drinks are alternative approaches.

Patients may need practical hints to divert them from returning to their previous pattern. Examples include drinking water when thirsty, sucking sugarless mints, consuming decaffeinated soft drinks or coffee or lightly brewed tea, limiting their consumption to several specified times of the day (caffeinism is much less likely if consumption occurs *only* during "coffee breaks."), and removing easy sources of caffeine (such as coffee pots on the desk). Patients going through discontinuation will predictably have a temporary increase in anxiety symptoms. The clinician should ideally see these symptoms within the context of the pharmacological withdrawal and should avoid whenever possible the use of antianxiety agents. Continued evaluation of the patient's anxiety state should be conducted throughout an adequate drug-free period, ideally at least 2 to 3 weeks. If severe anxiety symptoms are still present, appropriate treatment programs can then be considered.

A recent popular appeal to caffeine consumers was recommending a switch to other herbal preparations. Although many of these may be quite harmless, a number have been reported to produce their own patterns of toxicity (42, 59, 60). As with many other drugs, drug "substitution" for caffeinism is likely to be riddled with pitfalls.

Caffeinism is often a remitting condition. After withdrawal, many afflicted subjects ingest only low doses for awhile. In the author's experience, however, there is a gradual return to previous dosage levels and often a gradual return of symptomatology. Understanding this pattern may be necessary if clinicians are to avoid a therapeutic nihilism.

FUTURE OUTLOOK

Because of its intriguing history, its almost complete domestication, and its many recently discovered neuropharmacological effects, caffeine is a fascinating drug. It will continue to be widely used in America. Safe use is certainly possible. Indeed, uncomplicated use is the norm. This does not imply, however, that caffeinism and caffeine withdrawal are uncommon. These conditions are probably underdiagnosed. Future research is needed to place them in proper perspective with other psychoactive drug syndromes. Meanwhile, clinicians who search for caffeinism will be surprised to discover a significant number of afflicted subjects, most of whom will benefit from treatment and education.

References

1. Abe, K. Reactions to coffee and alcohol in monozygotic twins. J. Psychosom. Res. 12:199, 1968.
2. Abelson, H. I., and Fishburne, P. M. *Nonmedical Use of Psychoactive Substances: 1975–76 Nationwide Study among Youth and Adults.* Conducted by Social Research Group, The George Washington University, for the National Institute on Drug Abuse. Princeton, N. J., Response Analysis Corporation, 1976.
3. Arnold, L. E., Christopher, J., Huestis, R., et al. Methylphenidate vs dextroamphetamine vs caffeine in minimal brain dysfunction. Arch. Gen. Psychiatry 35:463, 1978.
4. Axelrod, J., and Reichenthal, J. The fate of caffeine in man and a method for its estimation in biological material. J. Pharmacol. Exp. Ther. 107:519, 1953.
5. Barr, W. H., and Penna, R. P. Over-the-counter internal analgesics. In *Handbook of Non-Prescription Drugs, 1969*, G. B. Griffenhagen, editor, pp. 26–37. Washington, D.C., American Pharmaceutical Association, 1969.
6. Beer, B., Chasin, M., Clody, D. E., et al. Cyclic adenosine monophosphate phosphodiesterase in brain: Effect on anxiety. Science 176:428, 1972.
7. Bellet, S., Roman, L., DeCastro, O., Kim, K. D., and Kershbaum, A. Effect of coffee ingestion on catecholamine release. Metabolism 18:288, 1969.
8. Berkowitz, B. A., et al. Effect of caffeine and theophylline on peripheral catecholamines. Eur. J. Pharmacol. 16:193, 1971.
9. Berkowitz, B. A., Spector, S., and Pool, W. the interaction of caffeine, theophylline and theobromine with monoamine oxidase inhibitors. Eur. J. Pharmacol. 16:315, 1971.
10. Berkowitz, B. A., Tarver, J. H., and Spector, S. Release of norepinephrine in the central nervous system by theophylline and caffeine. Eur. J. Pharmacol. 10:64, 1970.
11. Boyd, E. M., Dolman, M., Knight, L. M., et al. The chronic oral toxicity of caffeine. Can. J. Physiol Pharmacol. 43:995, 1965.
12. Cobb, S. Physiologic changes in men whose jobs were abolished. J. Psychosom. Res. 18:245, 1974.
13. Colton, T., Gosselin, R. E., and Smith, R. P. The tolerance of coffee drinkers to caffeine. Clin. Pharmacol. Ther. 9:31, 1968.
14. Corrodi, H., Fuxe, K., and Jonsson-G. Effects of caffeine on central monoamine neurons. J. Pharm. Pharmacol. 24:155, 1972.
15. Damrau, F., and Damrau, A. M. Use of soft drinks by children and adolescents. Rocky Mountain Med. J. 60:37, 1963.
16. Day, R. L. Over-the-counter medications for menstrual problems. In Handbook of Non-Prescription Drugs, G. B. Griffenhagen, editor, pp. 52–57. Washington, D.C., American Phamaceutical Association, 1969.
17. Dreisbach, R. H., and Pfeiffer, C. Caffeine-withdrawal headache. J. Lab. Clin. Med. 28:1212, 1943.
18. Ellis, J. *An Historical Account of Coffee.* London, Edward and Charles Dilly, 1774.
19. Erhardt, E. Psychic disturbances in caffeine intoxication. Acta Med. Scand. 71:94, 1929.
20. Flynn J. T. Arrhythmias related to coffee and tea (letter to the editor). J.A.M.A. 211:633, 1970.
21. Forrest, W. H., Bellville, J. W., and Brown, B. W. The interaction of caffeine with pentobarbital as a nighttime hypnotic. Anesthesiology 36:37, 1972.
22. Friedman, G. D., Siegelaub, A. B., and Seltzer, C. C. Cigarettes, alcohol, coffee, and peptic ulcer. N. Engl. J. Med. 290:469, 1974.
23. Furlong, F. W. Possible psychiatric significance of excessive coffee consumption. Can. Psychiatr. Assoc. J. 20:577, 1975.
24. Fuxe, K., and Ungerstedt, U. Action of caffeine and theophylline on supersensitive dopamine receptors: Considerable enhancement of receptor response to treatment with DOPA and dopamine receptor agonists. Med. Biol. 52:48, 1974.
25. Gilbert, R. M. Caffeine beverages and their effects. Addictions 21:68, 1974.
26. Gilbert, R. M. Caffeine as a drug of abuse. In *Research Addresses in Alcohol and Drug Problems*, R. G. Gibbin, Y. Israel Hiklart, R. E. Pophom, W. Schmidt and R. G. Smart, editors, vol. 3. New York, John Wiley, 1976.
27. Gilbert, R. M. Dietary caffeine and alcohol consumption by rats. J. Stud. Alcohol 37:11, 1976.
28. Gilbert, R. M. Letter to the editor: Toxicity. J.A.M.A. 236:1452, 1976.
29. Goldstein, A. Wakefulness caused by caffeine. Exp. Pathol. Pharmacol. 248:269, 1964.
30. Goldstein, A., and Kaizer, S. Psychotropic effects of caffeine in man. II. Alertness, psychomotor coordi-

nation and mood. J. Pharmacol. Exp. Ther. 150:146, 1965.

31. Goldstein, A., and Kaizer, S. Psychotropic effects of caffeine in man. III. A questionnaire survey of coffee drinkers and its effects in a group of housewives. Clin. Pharmacol. Ther. 10:477, 1969.

32. Goldstein, A., Kaizer, S., and Whitby, O. Psychotropic effects of caffeine in man. IV. Quantitiative and qualitative differences associated with habituation to caffeine. Clin. Pharmacol. Ther. 10:489, 1969.

33. Goldstein, A., Warren, R., and Kaizer, S. Psychotropic effects of caffeine in man. I. Individual differences and sensitivity to caffeine-induced wakefulness. J. Pharmacol. Exp. Ther. 49:156, 1965.

34. Greden, J. F. Anxiety or caffeinism: A diagnostic dilemma. Am. J. Psychiatry 131:1089, 1974.

35. Greden, J. F. The tea controversy in Colonial America. J.A.M.A. 236:63, 1976.

36. Greden, J. F. Anxiety and depression associated with caffeinism among psychiatric inpatients. Am. J. Psychiatry 135:963, 1978.

37. Greden, J. F. Coffee, tea and you. Sciences 19:6, 1979.

38. Greden, J. F., Victor, B., Fontaine, P., and Lubetsky, M. Caffeine-withdrawal headache: A neglected syndrome. In *Scientific Proceedings of the 132nd Annual Meeting, American Psychiatric Association*, p. 389. Chicago, American Psychiatric Association, 1979.

39. Kalm, P. *Travels into North America*, vol. 1, p. 372. Warrington, Pa., William Eyres, 1770.

40. Levi, L. Effect of coffee on the function of the sympatho-adrenomedullary system in man. Acta Med. Scand. 181:431, 1967.

41. Levinson, H. C., and Bick, E. C. Psychopharmacology of caffeine. In *Psychopharmacology in the Practice of Medicine*, M. D., Jarvik, editor, pp. 451–463. New York, Appleton-Century-Crofts, 1977.

42. Lightfoot, C. J., Blair, H. J., and Cohen, J. R. Lead intoxication in an adult caused by Chinese herbal medication. J.A.M.A. 238:1539, 1977.

43. Mau, G., and Netter, P. Kaffee-und Alkoholkonsum-Riskofaktoren in der Schwangerschaft? Geburtshilfe Frauenheilkd. 34:1018, 1974.

44. McManamy, M. C., and Schube, P. G. Caffeine intoxication: Report of a case the symptoms of which amounted to a psychosis. N. Engl. J. Med. 215:616, 1936.

45. Milliksen, E. J. Caffeine and schizophrenia. J. Clin. Psychiatry 1:732, 1978.

46. Molde, D. A. Diagnosing caffeinism. Am. J. Psychiatry 132:202, 1975.

47. Neil, J. F., Himmelhoch, J. M., Mallinger, A. G., Mallinger, J., and Hanin, I. Caffeinism complicating hypersomnic depressive episodes. Compr. Psychiatry 19:377, 1978.

48. Newman, H. W., and Newman E. J. Failure of Dexedrine and caffeine as practical antagonists of the depressant effect of ethyl alcohol in man. Q. J. Stud. Alcohol 17:406, 1956.

49. Perry, A. The effect of heredity on attitudes toward alcohol, cigarettes and coffee. J. Appl. Psychol. 58:275, 1973.

50. Peters, J. M. Factors affecting caffeine toxicity: A review of the literature. J. Clin. Pharmacol 7:131, 1967.

51. Phillis, J. W., Kostopoulos, G. K., and Limacher, J. J. Depression of corticospinal cells by various purines and pyrimidines. Can. J. Physiol. Pharmacol. 52:1226, 1974.

52. Phillis, J. W., Kostopoulos, G. K., and Limacher, J. J. A potent depressant action of adenosine derivatives on cerebral cortical neurons. Eur. J. Pharmacol. 30:125, 1975.

53. Powers, H. The syndrome of coffee. Med. J. Record 121:745, 1925.

54. Primavera, L. H., Simon, W., and Camiza, J. An investigation of personality and caffeine use. Br. J. Addict. 70:213, 1975.

55. Reimann, H. A. Caffeinism: A cause of long-continued, low-grade fever. J.A.M.A. 202:1105, 1967.

56. Repplier, A. *To Think of Tea!* Boston, Houghton Mifflin, 1932.

57. Ross, B. D. Caffeine and fluid retention (letter to the editor). J.A.M.A. 218:596, 1971.

58. Schnackenberg, R. D. Caffeine as a substitute for schedule II stimulants in hyperkinetic children. Am. J. Psychiatry 130:796, 1973.

59. Segelman, A. B., Segelman, F. P., Karliner, J., et al. Sassafras and herb tea: Potential health hazards. J.A.M.A. 236:477, 1976.

60. Siegel, R. K. Herbal intoxication: Psychoactive effects from herbal cigarettes, tea, and capsules. J.A.M.A. 236:475, 1976.

61. Siegerist, H. E. Literary controversy over tea in 18th-century England. Bull. Hist. Med. 13:185, 1943.

62. Silver, W. Insomnia, tachycardia and cola drinks. Pediatrics 47:635, 1971.

63. Speilberger, C. O., Gorsuch, R. L., and Lushene, R. E. *State-Trait Anxiety Inventory Manual*. Palo Alto, Calif., Consulting Psychologists Press, 1970.

64. Stillner, V., Popkin, M. K., and Pierce, C. M. Caffeine-induced delirium during prolonged competitive stress. Am. J. Psychiatry 135:855, 1978.

65. Ukers, W. H. *The Romance of Coffee*. New York, The Tea and Coffee Trade Journal Company, 1948.

66. Waldeck, B. Modification of a caffeine-induced locomotor stimulation by a cholinergic mechanism. J. Neurol. Transm. 35:195, 1974.

67. Waldeck, B. Effect of caffeine on locomotor activity and central catecholamine mechanisms: A study with special reference to drug interaction. Acta Pharmacol. Toxicol. (Suppl. IV) 36:1, 1975.

68. Weiss, B., and Laties, V. G. Enhancement of human performance by caffeine and the amphetamines. Pharmacol. Rev. 14:1, 1962.

69. Wikler, A. Dynamics of drug dependence: Implications of a conditioning theory for research and treatment. Arch. Gen. Psychiatry 28:611, 1973.

70. Winstead, D. K. Coffee consumption among psychiatric inpatients. Am. J. Psychiatry 133:1447, 1976.

PART 4

TREATMENT APPROACHES

CHAPTER 22

SYNANON: A PIONEERING RESPONSE IN DRUG ABUSE TREATMENT AND A SIGNAL FOR CAUTION

David A. Deitch, Ph.D.

Joan Ellen Zweben, Ph.D.

In 1979 many drug treatment therapeutic communities in the United States were seriously considering changing their descriptive brochures—and some were wishing that they could rewrite history. Why? Simply because all were influenced by an organization referred to as Synanon. Once therapeutic communities were only too glad to claim a Synanon origin; by 1979 this claim had the potential of a negative press.

For in this year, the term "cult" began to have devastating significance. In 1979 one such group was said to have successfully panhandled millions of dollars; another recruited thousands of youths; a third group sadly was responsible for the greatest mass suicide/murder of faith system members ever recorded in Western history; and a fourth group was accused of storing of weapons, beating defectors, and attempting to murder a proclaimed enemy.

The final activities above were attributed to Synanon. In 1962 Senator Thomas Dodd had referred to Synanon as a " . . . man-made miracle that I feel can benefit thousands of drug addicts" (28). Yet in December 1977, 15 years later, *Time* magazine (27) subtitled an article about Synanon: "A once respected drug program turns into a kooky cult." Many have speculated that this single article was the catalyst to even more bizarre behavior in Synanon. Without question, both the article and Synanon's subsequent actions made what have been a major source of effective treatment of drug addiction—the therapeutic communities in the United States—quite anxious about being identified with their real progenitor: Synanon.

And yet, despite the recent irrational and personally tragic stories of and about Synanon to be found everywhere in the field, very few can deny the genius and the broad positive social-psychological contributions made by this young (just 22 years old) organization in the fields of drug treatment, mental health, education, corrections, and even industry.

There are psychiatrists, sociologists, psychologists, lawyers, educators, and presidents of industry who were positively influenced by Synanon and others who, of course, had their feelings hurt. But paramount is the legion of people who say (regardless of their personal disappointment and treatment) "thank God for Synanon." A recent example of this came to our attention. It was a formal letter sent to the Attorney General of the State of California by a former Synanon resident who simply offers

Let me do any "time" you consider giving to the "old man." Regardless of what he has done wrong, he saved my life and thousands of others like me.

Here is a perfect example of what could be considered cult-like membership behavior, and yet the author of that letter has had no direct contact with Synanon in 11 years. From a psychological point of view the letter could be called an example of unresolved transference. Or it simply could be the letter of someone who feels a debt of immense magnitude. Certainly there is important material to discuss regarding the development of Synanon—the phases it has gone through and lessons to be learned from its most recent activities. Within this brief chapter we hope in some small way to provide the beginnings of a constructive and instructive discussion. Synanon certainly deserves this.

Synanon is a rather well known word (especially in the mental health field), which triggers a variety of reactions in most people, including such stereotypes as attack therapy, head shaving, ruthless honesty, a revolutionary social experiment, a life saver, the most efficient business enterprise in the United States, and on and on. Yet curiously the word Synanon did not exist before September 1958. Synonymous with Synanon and always highlighted in *all* articles written about it is the name Charles E. Dederich, the founder. Until recently he was always described as a tough, dynamic, and charismatic leader. It has been mentioned repeatedly that, regardless of his title in the organization, he insisted on absolute authority. In 1962, while the senior author was a young member of the organization, an often repeated topic in the seminars was the concept: "Power corrupts and absolute power corrupts absolutely." Yet

many remember hearing directly from the "old man" (as he was fondly referred to in the 1960's), "I would rather lose everything—all the people, all the buildings—everything—and retreat to the beach with just a few people rather than lose control over any and everything."

There is no question that this man guided and built an organization from a small storefront in Ocean Park, California in 1958, with a mix of down-and-out alcoholics and narcotic addicts with no money and no resources, to a nationally recognized organization with real estate and other equity valued at $33 million in 1978, and which at one time had as many as 1,000 residents and over 2,000 "game" club members (1967).

Naturally, there is curiosity over what imprints and circumstances influenced this individual toward these great achievements and, of course, what went on when the primary tenets of the organization's philosophical system were turned upside down, and all who were familiar with the organization got "dizzy."

This chapter is based on personal experiences, theoretical analyses, and conjecture. Verifiable information on what is currently occurring in Synanon is difficult to come by, so some of our material on Synanon's development over time is necessarily speculative.

In this chapter, we will first look at the crucial therapeutic elements in Synanon as they relate to the treatment of drug abusers. We will comment briefly on some of their current applications and the state of the art in the existing therapeutic community modality. We will then explore the evolution of Synanon over time and offer the reader an analysis of the critical themes at work in Synanon that contributed to its most recent notariety. Finally, we will conclude with major issues to be considered by the drug abuse treatment community in its own system approaches.

CRUCIAL THERAPEUTIC ELEMENTS IN SYNANON

We will examine the key elements in Synanon's therapeutic system and discuss how they were transformed as they were applied to other settings. Therapeutic communities today still utilize Synanon concepts and techniques as part of their core program, although frequently with considerable modification. Factors that influence these modifications are quite varied: changing cultural values; changing client profiles and, hence, needs; a funding base with radically different demands; improved sophistication in therapeutic techniques. But however great the alteration, much of what is unique about therapeutic communities in the field of substance abuse can still be traced to Synanon influence.

A SUBSTITUTE FAMILY

Much of the powerful attraction of Synanon lies in its ability to provide an extended family to a population whose previous experiences with family life often have been unsatisfactory. In exchange for compliance with the Synanon code of behavior, the member was provided with food, shelter, a clearly defined role, and the concern and support of other family members. Dederich himself conceptualized the process as one in which the addict is reborn and goes through an accelerated maturation, and he took the position that the autocratic family structure was necessary initially to buy time for the recovering addict (2). Although in the early days of Synanon there were suggestions of its intention to produce strong, independent personalities, as time went on the qualities of loyalty and obedience grew increasingly more important.

Despite the drawbacks of the autocratic model, there is no question that the family atmosphere, with intense expressions of loyalty and support, was a crucial context in which the confrontations and attacks could result in a positive outcome. This 24-hour support system made possible the stripping of maladaptive defenses and their replacement by more positive coping patterns. It is controversial to what extent positive behaviors, vigorously shaped by the Synanon "family," can be seen as providing an ego so long as the member remains in Synanon.

Most therapeutic communities today have retained the concept of a family model (4), although they generally espouse the view that it is desirable to be less autocratic than Synanon. Although the trend toward increased use of professionals and nonex-addicts has eliminated one equalizing force, those who work in therapeutic communities frequently are attracted because their status hierarchies are differently constituted than those of traditional mental health settings. Abysmally low salaries for front line staff also means these are likely to be persons under 30 and often without families to support; hence, the appeal of the family concept is likely to be greater for them than for those who work in traditional settings.

A major distinction between the Synanon family concept and those of subsequent programs is that by 1968 Dederich had decided to make Synanon a "birth to death" experience in order to cope with the recidivism problem (1), whereas other therapeutic communities have continued to view some form of reentry process as an appropriate and achievable goal. Dederich, by contrast, had concluded that the greater world was unsalvable and continuing participation in the alternative society created by Synanon was the only hope for successful recovery.

THE CHARISMATIC LEADER

The Synanon family structure had as its patriarch the remarkably charismatic figure of Chuck Dederich. His passion, brilliance, and poetic streak made him a source of inspiration from Synanon's inception until his arrest in November 1978. For many years, his quotable quotes made him the darling of the media, and even those who left Synanon with great pain and bitterness subsequently spoke of the "old man" with unmistakable fondness. His value to the recovering addict in Synanon was incalculable. He cheerfully volunteered to fill any need for an omnipotent father figure who could dictate the terms of redemption; and, although his content might be contradictory, his sense of conviction never wavered. Hence, devotion to him personally was a crucial element in the rehabilitation of the members. The term "transference cure" seems hardly adequate to summarize what his personal touch was able to accomplish.

BEHAVIOR SHAPING: REWARD SYSTEMS

A gifted, charismatic leader is by no means sufficient to account for Synanon's effectiveness; it was the total environment he created that gave Synanon its unique stamp. Two key ingredients were a powerful reward system that provided actual jobs conferring status and recognition (4) and a series of behavior-shaping techniques that have become widely applied and, hence, need to be examined in some detail.

The addict entering Synanon was offered a step-by-step achievable status system with rewards analogous to those in the larger culture. The initiate would likely work in the house or offices doing relatively routine maintenance activities, such as food preparation or housekeeping chores. As the member demonstrated responsibility, he or she ascended the status hierarchy with tasks commensurate with skills and talents. Although members were not paid directly, all the other rewards were there: potential for mobility, recognition, privileges, and material comforts. Thus, the entering addict was surrounded by examples of those who started like himself but who very visibly had "made it." This provided a very important balance for the severe sanctions that were also utilized.

Other therapeutic communities also utilized this reward system, but they operated under constraints that did not affect Synanon. From the outset, Dederich refused to take any money that came with stipulations and, hence, never became dependent on the tax dollar for funds. In principle he was also capable of any level of expansion. The drug programs that followed were committed to facilitating reentry and not to creating unlimited opportunities within. Hence, they frequently employed ex-addicts with relevant interests and talents, but the number of available positions were far more limited. Thus, one of the most powerful motivating forces was severely reduced, as the recovering addict could not be assured that there was a place for everyone who behaved as prescribed. One consequence of this is that punishments became more immediate and tangible than rewards. To this date, one of the outstanding clinical challenges for therapeutic communities is to develop a reward system as powerful as the punishments (6).

BEHAVIOR SHAPING: THE DISSONANCE MODEL

A basic strategy that distinguishes Synanon from Alcoholics Anonymous (AA) as well as from conventional mental health approaches is its use of confrontation, frustration, and attack as an integral part of the rehabilitation. With his characteristic intuitiveness, Dederich understood that addicts primarily were people with character disorders who needed to have their complacency shattered before they would be genuinely receptive to treatment. He also recognized that the confession used in AA as an initiation ritual was insufficient as a test of motivation. Hence, from the time the prospective member made that initial contact, liberal doses of challenge and provocation were included with the promise of total support. The member was continually subjected to criticism, frustration, sudden demotions in rank, and various provocations as part of the price of belonging. The process of creating continual dissonance in the members helped keep them vulnerable to Synanon's shaping influence.

BEHAVIOR SHAPING: SPECIFIC TECHNIQUES

Certainly Synanon's best known contribution to therapeutic techniques is "The Game" (3, 7, 23, 29). To most people who are familiar with Synanon, the very name conjures up images of a vicious and relentless attack; but surprisingly little exploration is done of its conceptual underpinnings.

The games as usually played have only two rules: no chemicals and no violence or threats of violence. This latter injunction was, of course, modified when Dederich reversed his position on violence around 1973, but his original intention was to create an atmosphere where it was safe to say anything without editing. Generally, the group was leaderless but included members seasoned in the use of the game. The group engaged in aggressive and provocative interchanges, centering on one person at a time for about 20 minutes and then moving on. The norm was to support the probe, i.e., not to defend the person on the hotseat, and to break all "contracts," i.e., tacit or deliberate collusions with someone to conceal material during the game. Composition of the groups for the game was continually shifted to maximize variety of input.

The basic philosophy behind the game is the same as AA's fourth step: to take a fearless and searching look at oneself. Self-examination is fostered by considering *all* feedback, no matter how seemingly farfetched; hence, all members are encouraged to project freely onto the one on the hotseat. This license to project also allows the members to externalize the negative in themselves and thereby reinforce their own redeemed behavior.

Although the games are the best known of the group techniques, other kinds of confrontation are part of the members' daily life, with the effect that members are constantly under scrutiny by peers. "Haircuts" are given in small groups composed of those who know the member well, either for specific transgressions or when it is felt the member needs to "tighten up." Such sessions usually include specific prescriptions for future behavior. Morning meetings provide a forum for the community (or subcommunity) to meet as a whole and deal with issues that may be generating friction. Less confrontational are the seminars, in which members meet to discuss philosophical topics often pertaining to issues of freedom and responsibility and try to integrate these ideas with personal experiences. Such sessions help dissolve social isolation, provide practice at verbal interchange, and offer an opportunity to grapple with ideas they have never been exposed to because of the narrowness of their lifestyle (2).

Other ingenious group techniques include the perpetual stew, in which constantly changing composition is used to develop and maintain a high level of momentum. A group of about 18 members met 24 hours a day, 7 days a week. Two members would enter and two others would leave every few hours, so that the group would always have "warmed-up" members to quickly bring the others to their level of intensity. And most intense of all the group techniques was "the trip," a structured 48-hour session with the same members present throughout. This was the group in which the most extreme pressure was exerted, and it was generally a one-time experience.

The sum total effect of such techniques, with the continuing feedback they provided, was to heighten the members' self-awareness and foster the consolidation of an identity. In other words, the environment permitted the stripping of the character defenses as first presented and drastic reduction of the addict's impulsivity. Concurrent with this stripping was a clear presentation of acceptable modes of behavior, with the total environment designed to reinforce the same kinds of behavior. There is little question that Synanon supplied a firm ego structure for those who remained within. The major clinical questions focus on how much of this identity is truly internalized, how much the ego controls are maintained if the individual leaves the environment. Assessment is hampered by Synanon's taking the position that members cannot possibly survive outside and by the fact that no attempt is made to foster reentry (12).

RELIGIOUS ZEAL

Within a short time after its inception, Synanon evolved from what outsiders called a cult to an open acknowledgement that it was a religion. Lest we be guilty of professional myopia, we must recognize that religious zeal has proven to be a potent healing force throughout history, and the clinical questions revolve not around its efficacy but around its price. For the membership, the conviction that they, the "scum of the earth," were in fact creating a utopian community was a powerful motivating and rehabilitative force. The clinical issue to be examined is the relative efficacy of the faith system elements as compared to how much the techniques stand on their own.

Unfortunately, a number of therapeutic communities have inadvertently or otherwise attempted to emulate Dederich's example, without possessing either his giftedness or vision. This results in programs in which the rigid and arbitrary impulsivity of management is rationalized by the "need to keep the clients in line." Inane cruelties, such as having clients wear self-denigrating signs for days on end, are rationalized by a staff that has insulated itself from critical feedback from peers. Such programs are often characterized by the absence of accountability mechanisms for the leadership, as reflected in a board of directors composed largely of paid staff of the program itself.

Clinically, such programs seem to have little appreciation for differentiation in the use of behavior-shaping tools (6). There is abnormal emphasis on extinguishers (such as signs, bald heads, attacking) and an overemphasis on screaming as the only acceptable form of affect expression. Reward systems are much less well developed, as the need for them is only dimly understood. Such programs would seem to be a caricature of the negative elements of Synanon, without its redeeming qualities.

We will now examine how certain negative forces became runaway in Synanon itself.

FACTORS INFLUENCING DEVELOPMENT AND CRITICAL CHANGES

For purposes of a book dealing with substance abuse, one could select for discussion only those phases of Synanon's history in which it dealt primarily with substance abusers. However, an examination of Synanon's development to date has much that is constructive for therapeutic community practitioners. There are many who currently discuss Synanon in terms of its rise and fall, but such terminal language may be quite premature. We are mindful of the developmental struggles all humans go through as they attempt to try out various roles and behaviors in their attempt to establish an identity. We have often erred by considering as final the regressive mistakes of a formerly highly talented youth. We often condemned people to living hopeless lives by attaching final and negative definitions to them, for example, "Once a dope fiend, always a dope fiend." Use of that definition provided little that was instructive or helpful to anyone. Hence, it is our position that the final chapter has yet to be written, and Synanon may yet turn in new and surprising directions.

In looking at Synanon's development to date, we will consider the following factors: containment, in which the system grew increasingly closed; the amplification of the use of projection and guilt; the unbalanced development of repertoires for emotional expression; the shifting population; the acquisition of great wealth; the reversal of the philosophical stance on violence; and, finally, the growing disorganization of the founder. We have selected to explore the above aspects of Synanon, fully aware that one could easily have discussed Lifton's ingredients of a brainwashing community.[1] However, many

organizations possess these: current therapeutic communities, religious schools, military boot camps, and countless others. The question is, To what degree do these coercive principles operate? We do not consider the following categories as exhaustive, but ones that are worthy of consideration by the substance abuse community.

CONTAINMENT: THE CLOSING OF THE SYSTEM

In Synanon's formative years there were three stages of member involvement. Although these were not identified explicitly with stages of treatment, they certainly implied such and were especially useful to the organization from the point of view of garnering national media coverage. *Life*, *Look*, *Time*, and countless other periodicals from 1961 to 1965 spoke of Synanon and "cures" for narcotic addicts. The three stages referred to were: (a) full 24-hour involvement for lengthy periods of time, (b) living in Synanon and working outside the organization, and (c) living and working outside Synanon but remaining affiliated. However, by 1964 two factors were at work to change this: increased need for trained personnel due to rapidly expanding organizational facilities, and the struggle with successful (i.e., drug-abstinent) reentry in the third stage.

---

[1] The following are Lifton's themes, next to which we have added a brief explanation. (From Lifton, R. J. *Thought Reform and the Psychology of Totalism: A Study of "Brainwashing" in China*, chapter 22. New York, W. W. Norton, 1961.)

Eight psychological themes:

1. *Milieu control*—the control of human communication.
2. *Mystical manipulation*—the mystique of doing it for a higher purpose, regardless of what we do.
3. *The demand for purity*—black and white, right and wrong, good and evil. The good and pure are, of course, everything that is part of policy—and, of course, for your own good.
4. *The cult of confession*—confess to crimes; create crimes for people to confess to.
5. *The "sacred science"*—sacredness around its basic dogma. Reverence demanded for the organization of the words, the concepts. Do not question basic assumptions.
6. *Loading the language*—cliches; reduce complex thoughts and human problems into brief definitive sounding phrases that all can remember and repeat on cue.
7. *Doctrine over person*—change history; discredit former members. Sincerity judged by compliance to doctrine.
8. *The dispensing of existence*—outsiders are non people, i.e., not deserving of human-caring considerations, etc.

By 1964, as a result of an influx of large numbers of New York addicts and the support of key citizens in San Diego, San Francisco, and New York, Dederich's prophecy of a national movement generating Synanon facilities throughout the country seemed to be coming true. As more and more newcomers flocked to Synanon, those wellschooled in the norms of the community became increasingly more valuable, as they could facilitate the socialization of the initiates. The expansion was also mandated by increased client retention. Those who stayed were given a seductive social definition: "helper," with the rewards of status, privilege, and power. Thus, the struggle with successful (drug-abstinent) reentry was totally avoided. After all, not only did this serve the organization's needs for expansion, but it gave people the opportunity for roles, status, and privilege that were much more difficult to acquire in the greater world. Synanon thus commanded greater loyalty and conformity to its every inclination and could also boast of great numbers of addicts being helped. In short, those steps (Stages 2 and 3) leading out of Synanon into the greater world were abandoned.

By the end of 1964 a series of money-generating businesses were underway, including gas stations and advertising specialties that ultimately, in the 1970's, generated millions of dollars. Simultaneously, more sponsors were contributing ever growing amounts of critical goods and services, all of which helped the organization acquire its first exclusively owned land in Marin County, California, which was destined to be a complete and totally contained community.

As increasing emphasis was placed on the total commitment to the Synanon "social movement," there was a concomitant effort to engage "squares" in playing the game, and by 1967 2,000 game club members existed. This provided a source of support and interaction with members of the greater community. However, networks once formed were frequently broken up, and the appointment to leadership of game clubs or tribes became a means of seducing influential or wealthy people further into Synanon lifestyles (13). More money was generated, and large holdings of real estate were acquired, which provided more exclusively Synanon activities.

By the mid-1970's a large membership was able to enjoy new and growing amounts of affluence: its own schools, planes, fleets of autos and trucks, and choice real estate holdings. Perhaps even more important was the thrill of winning some major legal battles against the Hearst newspaper, the *San Francisco Examiner.* This resulted in more money and, of course, greater motivation to comply with whatever direction the leadership chose.

"We have to contain ourselves so we feel like one strong group" (20). In the latter 1970's it became increasingly important to "squeeze out" (14, 20) members of the early core group, especially those who had influence over the dwindling addict population. These were the ones most likely to create dissension over the direction Synanon was taking, as they were witnesses to the early philosophical tenets. These were called "splits": "We have to close the gap and move on when we have someone split" (21).

For many years Synanon had made use of the common enemy outside as a way of fostering internal cohesion and strengthening containment. Consequently, any questioning of new directions—violence, weapons, militance (the Syn-Do, for example, a version of the martial arts)—was viewed as aiding the enemy by weakening the group. One tool of this containment was "the wire," the electrical audio device which permitted anyone, anywhere, to hear what the leadership viewed as important, whether that be a game or a message from "the Founder."

For example, whenever Dederich spoke on the wire, all children in the Synanon school were to discontinue any activity and immediately write what the Founder had to say (22). In short, the more removed members became from normal stimuli, social interaction, diverse media, multiple ideas, and varying opinions, the more dependent each became on accepting the available stimuli. Combine this with great rewards for repeating the words and doing the steps, and the result is greater danger for conformity to a faith system, without differentiation and healthy autonomy.

AMPLIFICATION OF THE USE OF PROJECTION AND GUILT

The evil I dimly perceive in myself I try to stamp out in others.[2]

---

[2] This was a common Synanon seminar topic in the early 1960's.

To indict a person, to find another guilty of something, is the opening tactic in the central and dominant force in Synanon—the game. Without the license to indict over an issue, regardless of importance, the major force generating anxiety, self-doubt and self-questioning, would be lost. If a team member did his job poorly, then the team leader was naturally guilty of poor management. The leadership became committed to fostering guilt and dependency as a way of achieving group conformity, rather than encouraging the ability to trust and rely on one another. Projection was used increasingly: "If I fail to be on time, I'll question you about time."

All of this has merit in producing lively group interactions and rigorous attention to acceptable behavior in a given environment; however, as years passed Synanon's leadership became the ever increasing authority about the members' limitations, by defining what they were and by manipulating the environment in unexpected ways. Enright describes an example of this: "I once watched Dederich take a leisurely three hours to parlay the location of the toilet paper holder in the men's room into a detailed analysis of exactly *what was wrong with everyone* (emphasis ours) in the management of that particular Synanon house" (12). These stories are legion, and variations exist in every therapeutic drug treatment community.

However, of concern here is how these processes get amplified. In Synanon, examples of increasing totalitarianism grew more evident. In the 1970's Dederich attempted to change his own smoking habits by projecting that struggle onto the entire community. To the awed delight of many, all Synanon members stopped smoking.

Then came weight reduction, the emphasis on exercise, and the increasingly symbolic and *violent* forms of control such as coercion applied for vasectomies, abortions, and marital separation. Members grappled with their own difficulties regarding these decisions by focusing on others' limitations. Naturally, those who were reluctant to have abortions or vasectomies were made to feel guilty for that reluctance, and they had to relieve their dissonance by one of two means. One way was to consent to the vasectomy or abortion and then to convert the disturbed feelings into an exaggerated hatred of the outer world, the outer world being less concerned than they, for example, about the problems of overpopulation.

The second effort to reduce this dissonance was to recruit others into the same act. The alternative was to leave the wonderful Synanon environment. In short, with the amplification of projection and guilt by increasingly totalitarian leadership, the movement had to find ever greater reasons to condemn others. Hence, members handled their own psychological turbulence by focusing on the heretics within—systematically removing former core group members—and the enemies without, particularly the media (15, 21).

INCREASINGLY IMBALANCED EMOTIONAL REPERTOIRE

Throughout its history Synanon emphasized the toughening up, especially of the "too" vulnerable, sensitive individuals who were too readily injured by life events. After all, the organization did begin with acting-out, devious, manipulative and often criminal addicts. A hard and tough line had to be maintained to get these individuals to try out new behaviors. However, even when Synanon's population changed and lifestylers without these histories became a major force, the leadership still created frantic and pressured environments (13) with demands for efficiency in functioning, regardless of personal or situational circumstances.

The emphasis on the pragmatic and materialistic did not overshadow morals, but valued above all was the ability to function no matter how one felt. In addition, the search for insight was greeted with total suspicion. If a member was continuously setting himself up for rejection as a way of avoiding fear of intimacy, the rejection was discussed in terms of coping. Furthermore, if this same individual functioned efficiently and held a leadership position, the new direction would, of course, be that organizational functioning is of greater value than a sustained relationship.

Repeatedly, emotionally complex or diverse issues were reduced to single themes. Verbal expression of pain was viewed as self-indulgence, tears or signs of anguish as self-pity, grieving over the loss of someone (or something) as self-destructive indulgence, warmth with others as a seduction into compromise, feeling nurturant or protective toward others as building contracts. The leaders were unable to deal with the more tender, caring, vulnerable aspects of themselves and compensated with a drive for toughness: to bare one's soul without flinching. A perfect example occurred when a significant member died; all of Synanon was asked to play the game (21). Simple grieving was considered self-indulgence.

Certain feelings were never explored or dealt with; rather, the usual thrust was to convert them into activity. Ultimately all the membership developed imbalanced emotional repertoires that set the scene for violence, as some form of aggression was all that was acceptable.

THE IMPACT OF CHANGING POPULATIONS

By the end of 1978 there were four distinct populations in Synanon: the ex-addicts, the squares, the children of both groups, and the "punks." These waves of migration each stimulated a new dynamic, and their mixture created unexpected tensions that resulted in some startling positions.

Throughout the history of Synanon, efforts were made to recruit "squares." From the original Sponsors of Synanon (SOS) organization and game club memberships, individuals who were not down and out and who were not addicts were invited to move in. The lure was the chance to give their life meaning and become an integral part instead of being on the sidelines of a great social movement (7):

Squares have a more difficult time understanding why they are here. They do not realize that it is because they want to become ex-squares and get away from the kind of life that produces the world we live in, the world of wars and riots and mass poverty cheek by jowl with vast wealth.

With every recruit, a nonaddict member to share the lifestyle, the entire community felt more confident that it had the right answers, especially if these individuals were wealthy or successful in their regular life. For those nonaddicts who joined, their need to confirm their choice resulted in further zealous recruitment of others like them.

Over time, more nonaddicts were making the choice to live the Synanon life style. The primary recruitment zone was the game clubs, which had developed around each Synanon installation. One must examine some of what attracted these people and their means of entry.

Synanon was an exciting place, doing the unusual; it was superbly efficient, and members' energy levels were always high. The game was attractive because it was exciting, different, and filled with the unexpected. Here people were addressed as equals regardless of their social position and were often talked to like idiots regardless of their achievements (8–11). For many in a state of personal anomie or situational crisis, Synanon offered structure, direction, and a unique opportunity to have impact on a group. Within Synanon, one could possess power not available elsewhere, regardless of wealth or position. Furthermore, the route of entry was generally at Synanon's invitation to take a meaningful role in the organization. Unlike the entry of the addict, who had to "fight" his way in despite massive personal dissonance created during intake, the square member was generally seduced in with the offer of status, an important job role, and privilege: "Why are you living a life of many parts, none of them satisfying, when you could join us in the most exciting social experiment there is, live more comfortably than you ever have, have servants, efficient workers, a chance to do your experiments without the debilitating consequences of feeling fragmented?—Jesus Christ, we could use you— here you would be important—why not come in and head up our school—or sales—or research—or game clubs?"

Subsequent to such entry, once involvement had occurred and the rewards of community, status, privilege, and power had been realized, there would inevitably be a confrontation creating dissonance. Often it was the loss of the original job and transfer to another role. The massive guilt for not wanting the new assignment was submerged by exhortations on the need to expand to one's total potential, the importance of functioning without props, etc. The square member generally complied rather than face the loss of community, structure, child care, romance, and, of course, the opportunity to regain power.

It is important to consider the psychodynamic relationship between the street addicts and the squares as potentially one in which the addict previously acted out the forbidden impulses of the square. The street addict had a history of violence, jail, street fights, games of cops and robbers, and numerous other peak experiences. The squares were attracted in part by these revelations and by the atmosphere of "up-frontness" that the addicts contributed to Synanon. So, in addition to other rewards, the squares could talk and act tough with little fear of physical retaliation. This was an intoxicating experience for a middle-class group with inadequate outlets for aggressive fantasies. Perhaps it paved the way for them to condone Dederich's subsequent endorsement of violence.

With more children, the opportunity for new experiments began: separation of parents and children and the development of special education models. Children were given "full knowledge" of how members outside the Synanon world were "dishonest, stupid, and irresponsible." Now at last children would learn the truth (20): "Chuck is one step ahead of the world . . . Synanon gives its members money and riches." Of course, the children's assumptions of their world were a constant delight and reinforcement for the adults. Long before adulthood, the Synanon children were willing to demonstrate their commitments by having vasectomies. These and other stances were a true confrontation to their hesitant elders.

Spurred by its many successes, Synanon began to look toward new frontiers. The down-and-out addicts stayed clean in Synanon. They were prosperous as a result of organizational and intellectual contribution of the life stylers. Their children were almost always ready to comply without question to any direction they took, regardless of how unexpected. Synanon leadership naturally felt they could handle anyone or anything; thus, they advertised their willingness to handle problem youths, who became known as "punks" (24, 25).

The emergence of the punk squad brought unanticipated difficulties to Synanon. Here were youngsters from various youth authorities and the courts, who were viewed by their parents or the correctional system as having good potential, while being currently unmanageable. This group had not bottomed out, were not interested in reducing anomie or existential despair, viewed prison sentences as a kind of status, and, like most acting-out youth, had magical notions of their invulnerability. Suddenly Synanon was confronted with groups who did not readily comply and who viewed their environment not as an opportunity for renewal but as a restricting impediment.

Even the most zealous and vehement of both the older Synanon children and the ex-addict toughs experienced frustration with these "punks." We can safely speculate that it was not Dederich's throwing the root beer can (1) that marked the first use of real violence in Synanon. In the face of their first disconcerting inability to gain compliance, Synanon experienced the frustration that parents and workers in the juvenile justice system had known for years. Like some of these same parents and workers, Synanon retreated into a violation of its own philosophical tenets of nonviolence. Now violence was rationalized as a way to penetrate the youths' resistant defenses and provide learning on a deep level. It became policy (15) to have permission to knock a punk down and then offer the reason for it: ". . . and corporal punishment is used fully to keep the punk squad in line" (17). In addition, with this new population, another long standing tenet of Synanon was reversed, namely the open-door policy (18).

Now a variety of people who never before had so much opportunity to exercise power over others were granted the additional right to use physical force. The combination of the new tensions, new behaviors, and the moral righteousness inflamed by their victories in lawsuits with the media led to more and more overt physical violence. Now this violence was directed not only toward the punks, but also toward "intruders" (for example, neighbors), members who left, and others who spoke out against Synanon. It was the so-called intruders who provoked the acquisition of weapons, but the weapons requirements kept growing. After all, here was a chance for many formerly middle-class people to at last play their own games of cops and robbers, and, regretfully, it was sanctioned by the founder.

THE GROWING DISORGANIZATION OF THE FOUNDER

There are three books (2, 7, 29) that describe in some detail aspects of Dederich's early and pre-Synanon life. For those with psychological curiosity and a penchant for interpretive activity, we would most recommend Casriel's *So Fair a House* (2). Regardless, we are all vulnerable to categorizing or at least bringing to the forefront that which seems significant to us. We have elsewhere in this paper and in other publications (4) described the many influences at work in the evolution of the drug-related therapeutic community in America. We will comment briefly on some of the significant events in Dederich's life that left their imprint on his work.

Dederich was born in the Midwest, the oldest of three children. He lost his father when he was 4 and became, in his own words, "the man in the family" (2). He felt great attachment to his mother and serious loss when she remarried, years after his father's death. He spent time at Notre Dame, and its Jesuit influence was most strongly felt whenever he engaged in intellectual inquiry. He was seriously involved with Western transcendentalist literature, particularly Emerson and Thoreau, and was also intrigued with Lao-Tse. A significant experience with lysergic acid diethylamide also preceded the beginnings of Synanon.

Dederich was already drinking heavily at the age of 18. Groomed in Gulf Oil industry for a management role, he suffered a major illness (meningitis) and then the loss of his first wife through his alcoholism. He then moved to the West Coast, went to work for the aviation industry, and immersed himself in Santa Monica beach life. He continued drinking, married again, lost that wife too due to his alcohol abuse. His exposure and renewal through Alcoholics Anonymous led to a protracted involvement with them. These are some of the major influences that helped shape the Synanon movement into a highly acclaimed treatment model for narcotic addicts and allowed it to generate many other rehabilitative innovations.

Elsewhere in this chapter we have described the imbalanced emotional repertoire at work in Synanon and have pointed out how the compensating dynamics of the leadership set the tone for what could be modeled and explored. It seems that the founder had a great need to be in control and to turn himself into a winner even if it looked like a loss. A perfect example of this occurred during a zoning struggle of Synanon's early days. After spending 25 days in jail, he managed to get himself proclaimed a hero.

Dederich was fond of yelling and threatening all types of physical violence on erring Synanon members, but all know of his commitment to nonviolence. Nonetheless, there was always great hilarity whenever he wove a particularly imaginative fantasy of how a member could be punished. Here was a man capable of taking great risks for his convictions, capable of genius and great good, brilliant at pulling others out of self-indulgent moods. However, he could not disclose his own pain, his own fears of inadequacy, his vulnerabilities, and instead found it necessary to ridicule softness.

As Synanon grew more wealthy, it began to seem as if Dederich's every direction would be blessed with success and victory. He was enjoying the autocratic control of a totalitarian community. His early 1958 prediction that someday Synanon would be as famous as Coca Cola (7) was coming true. Even his jokes began to have the ring of divinity.

However, if he was dependent on continuous winning to take care of some very unresolved fears, the mid-1970's began to erode this string of victories. First there were the punks, who remained resistant to what usually worked. Despite the great rewards available in Synanon—cars, planes, motorcycles, sexual liaisons, status, etc.—they still kept trying to get away and even stole the cars to do so (18). Such minor disconfirmation was easily dismissed by Synanon, which was now becoming a religion. But by 1975, violence was increasing (neighbor Alvin Gambioni was attacked and then sued them) (1), and Synanon became more openly militant, with the Syn-Do and weapons purchases.

Certainly one does not win over aging and death. It is quite easy to consider the push for abortions and vasectomies of all the males except himself as a way of handling his own aging crisis. Not only was he the sole leader but the only male capable of procreation. In addition, by 1977 he and Synanon were under fire from the California Department of Health as a result of complaints about their handling of youths in the punk squad. Many people in Marin County were alarmed at their growing store of weapons. And then came the most terrible loss, the death of his wife Betty in 1977. In her own words (7): "I became his bouncing board and he listens to what I have to say."

How does a person handle the loss of this

kind of mate, a wife of 14 years? Dederich had not built a mechanism for grieving into this Eden. To cry, to mourn, was not Dederich's way or Synanon's way. All felt the loss of Betty Dederich, who was much beloved, and many cried. "But the way we were told to express our pain for Betty was to get to work and do more for Synanon." And indeed, once again, Dederich used projection of his own unresolved issues. Within 6 months he directed all members to separate from their mates and, as he did, to take new ones promptly (27).

It was at this point that many conversant with the organization, and, importantly, now outside of it, consider the beginning of Dederich's decline and disorganization. There is no question that the December 1977 *Time* magazine article critical of Synanon further exacerbated this decline. Now all-out war was declared (22): "Our holy war with *Time* magazine." Dederich's language became further filled with threats of violence (22): "We are going to hurt the people who tried to hurt our cause." Then came another defeat, the NBC television documentary critical of Synanon. This time the threats by Synanon members to the television crews were made known on national television. Dederich was now under siege. Yet his capacity for denial is demonstrated by the move to Washington, D.C., and the purchase of an apartment building there to set up an "embassy" in the capital. Dederich threatened a tenant who did not move out as quickly as Synanon wanted, and in a subsequent confrontation with the press about this he allegedly hit a news photographer. The use of threats and violence then escalated throughout the Synanon movement. Dederich was asked personally to leave Washington and to remove the organization, in return for nonprosecution (16).

Now the themes in Synanon were to separate the religion of Synanon and move it to another country (21). No one in the organization appeared at this time to either console or confront Dederich about his increasingly unpredictable and often bizarre behavior. On the contrary, it was applauded and emulated elsewhere, with further attacks on defectors. Dederich moved to Italy and began to experiment with the use of alcohol, despite what he knew about his own vulnerability due to his history of alcoholism. He encouraged those who were with him to reverse yet another philosophical tenet, this one prohibiting the use of intoxicating chemicals.

It is not at all unusual for people to attempt to reduce their own dissonance over new or otherwise dangerous behavior by engaging others in doing the same. And, of course, the core group joined him in drinking. Their subsequent behavior as a result of this experiment with chemicals caused the departure of a leading core member and head of the entire legal division. Yet no one questioned; the remaining members justified their behavior as yet another example of Dederich doing the unusual relevant to Synanon's growth.

Then came another singularly significant defeat. In 1978 a major child custody and damage suit was awarded to an attorney regarded by Synanon as an enemy. Soon after came the snake attack on Paul Morantz and the indictment of Dederich for conspiracy to commit murder. Dederich's denial of his own decompensation is equaled by the organization's fear of confronting the flaw in the divinity of their system. No one stopped this agonized man from slipping into a chronic drunk. Never had Dederich or other members of the Synanon core group learned how to handle the feelings of defeat or painful loss of loved ones without the action of victory.

Now Synanon must, we all hope, deal with their humanness and develop a more balanced repertoire of emotional expression. It is hoped that Synanon will engage in the struggle to reclaim its virtues and maintain its unquestionable skills, while reopening itself to the principles upon which it was built:

The Synanon Prayer

Please let me first and always examine myself.
Let me be honest and truthful.
Let me seek and assume responsibility.
Let me have trust and faith in myself and my fellow men.
Let me love rather than be loved.
Let me give rather than receive.
Let me understand another rather than be understood.

CONCLUSION

The wonderful gifts of Dederich, combined with the energy and talents of hundreds, built an organization that was the prototype of the American drug-related therapeutic community movement. From Synanon grew Daytop, Phoenix, Gaudenzia, Marathon, Gateway, The Family, Awareness House, Walden House, Safari, Tinley Park, and countless other therapeutic communities. Its other achievements are similarly impressive. Synanon confronted racism in every community in which it opened its doors. It created wings of model prisoners among gambling tables in one of the roughest penitentiaries in the Southwest. It cared enough about energy conservation that by 1962 there was a policy prohibiting anyone driving Synanon vehicles from exceeding 55 miles per hour. It cared enough about ecology that it built water recycling plants in its Marin County facilities as early as 1970. It created industries to help fund its operations and set examples in self-reliance. It introduced extended work days so that there could be extended time off, as well as many other treatment and social innovations.

Admittedly, Synanon accomplished most of the above long before it acquired wealth and converted itself into a religion. Much of its innovativeness was facilitated by its highly vertical structure, which did not have delays imposed by accountability demands such as an external board. Much was possible because the leader could point his finger and marshall the entire resources of Synanon in any direction he wished (7):

You'll see . . . one of these fine days your Chuck will turn out to have stashed away loads of real estate, several millions of dollars in cash, and there will be one hell of a tax scandal . . . . You'll see, because it happens to all the founders of new religions. And it will happen to Synanon too. Bound to happen if the followers keep making a God out of him.

This quote of a former Synanon member showed there was anxiety years ago regarding the direction of Synanon should too much unequivocable power be given to the founder. That, of course, did take place. Serious problems have occurred in Synanon. Some of their contributions to the world of drug treatment have been specifically pointed out. However, after much national applause for these efforts, other factors, some of which have been described, began to occur. The outcome has resulted in a crisis for Synanon. Regardless of the outcome of Dederich's murder conspiracy trial, the question is

whether Synanon will, as it so often has, make use of recent events as another learning experience to promote renewed growth, or will they still feel it necessary to emulate every aspect of the founder?

Certainly for the drug treatment therapeutic community world there are lessons to be learned. The fact that Synanon made a unique and special contribution to the treatment of impulse and character disorders cannot be overlooked. Admittedly, much of this contribution has been refined, and important innovations have been added by other leaders in the current therapeutic community movement. However, there remains a great need for practitioners to develop their conceptual understanding of the rationale behind the techniques. It may be that once the therapeutic communities chose to interact with the great community and chose to attempt to "treat" addicts rather than to become a social movement, the dangers inherent in the Synanon model were reduced. There are certainly two factors here worth highlighting.

Most American drug treatment therapeutic communities that receive public funding have had to have a board of directors. Funding agencies have been careful to insist that board membership include people not organizationally affiliated. Synanon is accountable only to itself. This made for rapid growth, great development of skills, unusual innovation, and worthy risk taking; on the other hand, it also made for insulation that regrettably led to containment. Boards of directors, even those totally enchanted by talented program executives, at least bring diversity of opinion, values, and experiences outside of the faith system and, ideally, some rigorous questions. Although many an executive may feel frustrated at delay (5) and may wish the board were more understanding and compliant, this accountability structure is a strong factor to mitigate against impulsive behavior and to prevent too much concentration of power.

A second factor relevant to drug treatment and the current difficulty of Synanon is the need for members to reenter the world, with all of its shortcomings and ambiguities, and participate in that reality regardless of one's personal faith system. The struggle to achieve a healthy reentry for therapeutic community members has forced "the movement" to expand its original techniques of behavior shaping and individual-centered approaches into greater consideration of the family and social networks. This struggle has forced the treatment system to open its doors to multiple input from practitioners separate from the faith system, who have different opinions and attitudes. Reentry forces therapeutic communities to interact with less arrogance with the many agencies that can be of help, whether for housing, job placement or training, or continuing education. Finally, and quite importantly, reentry demands have provided a variety of models for members of therapeutic communities to look at, a variety of life styles to try out, and a variety of social definitions that at least have the potential of relative autonomy.

Do these two factors mean the loss of spirit, the inability to imbue members with values that they will live by? Not at all. They do mean, however, that without calling the world your common enemy you cannot create synthetic cohesion among your membership. Therapeutic communities must grapple with the often discouraging and complicated questions of why and how—but then again, that is what they are there for.

References

1. Anson, R. S. The Synanon Horrors. New Times, November 1978.
2. Casriel, D. So Fair a House. Englewood Cliffs, N. J., Prentice-Hall, 1963.
3. Dederich, C. E. The Synanon Game. Marshall, Ca., Synanon Foundation, 1973.
4. Deitch, D. A. Treatment of drug abuse in the therapeutic community: Historical influences, current considerations and future outlook. In National Commission on Marijuana and Drug Abuse: Report to Congress and the President, vol. 5. Washington, D.C., United States Government Printing Office, 1973.
5. Deitch, D. Program management: Magical expectations and harsh realities. In Handbook of Drug Abuse, A. Goldstein, J. O'Donnell, and R. Dupont, editors. National Institute on Drug Abuse and Office of Drug Abuse Policy, The White House. Washington, D.C., United States Government Printing Office, 1979.
6. Deitch, D., and Zweben, J. The impact of social change or treating adolescents in therapeutic communities. J. Psychedelic Drugs 8:3, 1976.
7. Endore, G. Synanon. New York, Doubleday, 1968.
8. Endore, G. #1 The Human Spirit. Synanon pamphlet. Marshall, Ca., Synanon Foundation, 1976.
9. Endore, G. #2 Outrageous Impudence. Synanon pamphlet. Marshall, Ca., Synanon Foundation, 1976.
10. Endore, G. #3 The Perpetual Stew. Synanon pamphlet. Marshall, Ca., Synanon Foundation, 1976.
11. Endore, G. #4 Synanon: The Learning Environment. Synanon pamphlet. Marshall, Ca., Synanon Foundation, 1976.
12. Enright, J. On the Playing Fields of Synanon Confrontation: Encounters in Self and Interpersonal Awareness, Blank, Gottsegen, and Gottsegen, editors. New York, Macmillan, 1970.
13. Enright, J. Synanon: A challenge to middle class views of mental health. In Community Psychology and Mental Health, D. Adelson and B. Kalis, editors. Scranton, Pa., Chandler, 1970.
14. Former Synanon member #1. Personal communication, Los Angeles, 1977.
15. Former Synanon member #2. Personal communication, 1978–1979.
16. Former Synanon member #3. Personal communication, 1978.
17. Grand Jury of Marin County. Interim Report #6: Synanon. Marin County Superior Court, March 1978.
18. Health Department. Taped transcript—press conference. Marshall, Ca., October 5, 1977.
19. Lifton, R. J. Thought Reform and the Psychology of Totalism: A Study of "Brainwashing" in China, chapter 22, pp. 419–437. New York, W. W. Norton, 1961.
20. Synanon child #1. Student lessons and homework. Synanon School, 1977.
21. Synanon child #2. Student lessons and homework. Synanon School, 1978.
22. Synanon child #3. Student lessons and homework. Synanon School, 1978.
23. Synanon Foundation. Fact Sheet: Synanon Basic Training. Marshall, Ca., Synanon Foundation, 1975.
24. Synanon Foundation. Synanon Fact Sheet. Marshall, Ca., Synanon Foundation, 1976.
25. Synanon Foundation. Synanon Punk Squad Fact Sheet. Marshall, Ca., Synanon Foundation, 1976.
26. Synanon Foundation. Nature of Activities: Synanon Articles of Incorporation. Marshall, Ca., Synanon Foundation, 1976.
27. Time, December 1977.
28. United States Congressional Record, 1963.
29. Yablonsky, L. The Tunnel Back: Synanon. New York, Macmillan, 1965.
30. Zweben, J., and Deitch, D. The emergence of primadonnahood in prominent psychotherapist. Voices 12:75, 1976.

CHAPTER 23

THE THERAPEUTIC COMMUNITY: THE FAMILY - MILIEU APPROACH TO RECOVERY

William B. O'Brien

D. Vincent Biase, Ph.D.

THERAPEUTIC COMMUNITY—THE MOVEMENT!

Youth is the first victim of war; the first fruit of peace! It takes 20 years or more of peace to make a man; it takes only 20 seconds of war to destroy him!

We often think of these observations of Belgium's King Baudoin I. They sprung, you can be sure, from the horror of viewing the unspeakable misery of two wars that converted his own beautiful homeland into a wall-to-wall graveyard of young bodies with scarcely a shaving growth on their radiant faces.

Beyond the sectionalized forays of Korea and Vietnam, ghastly as they were, the great gunpowder conflagrations have given way to a perduring ideological struggle on the blackboards of America, spilling out across the television and cinema colorboards. It takes the form of a bombardment of issues, confrontations, accusations, and oftentimes contradictions. It begs questions that are deeply rooted in philosophy, psychology, theology, and epistemology. What is life about? What is man's purpose? His destiny? The young are screaming for answers—basic answers to basic questions. Adlai Stevenson sensed it some years ago when he queried: "What is more difficult: to think of an encampment on the moon or of Harlem rebuilt? Both are now within reach of our resources. Both now depend upon human decision and human will."

To carry this thinking along a few steps down the road, let us walk by the side of the young man we are building during a relative period of peace (1969 to 1979). Young America of 1969 awoke to the excitement of man's first footprints on the moon (they were Neil Armstrong's). There was a recognizable surge of national pride in this phenomenal achievement. Heads were spinning with double messages, however. Timothy Leary for 6 years now had been exporting (from the mid-Hudson Village of Millbrook where Daytop, with design, subsequently positioned a treatment center) the message of "getting high and dropping out" of all this hassle, but 1969 saw Woodstock and its symbol of ambivalence.

Heroin continued to be the drug of choice through the 1960's and into the 1970's, although the clientele was changing drastically. From Daytop's outset (1963) and through its first 5 years, the name of the game was hard core, ghetto heroin addiction. Middle-class involvement centered upon Doridens, Tuinals, Seconals mostly—all barbiturates. By 1969, however, the shift was underway and heroin was emerging as the middle-class "in thing" on Westchester Avenue and Morris Park in the Bronx, in Brooklyn's Bay Ridge and Bensonhurst, at the Ferry Slip at Port Richmond.

In 1970, young people fell at the end of National Guard rifles at Kent State University. Expanding the American troop presence from Vietnam into Cambodia that year connoted a widening of the prospects of carrying a gun in a questionable war. Haight-Ashbury, Washington Square, the Village Gate, the Sheep Meadow of New York's Central Park swayed to the peace ballads of Janis Joplin and Jimi Hendrix, idolized by millions of the young. Both would be found dead from drug overdoses within 5 weeks of each other the next fall.

By 1971, there was a glimmer of hope with the opening to Peking and the great land mass of China. The bloody outrage of the Munich Olympic games was seen in 1972, and in 1973 there was Watergate. All these had a telling effect upon the young and in an unforeseen way helped shape the course of the copping-out pattern via drugs among the young. The geometric growth of drug addiction and abuse in the Bronx, Brooklyn, and even Scarsdale had some revealing fallout. One could no longer hold that it was "those people" from the ghetto who fed the plague. It was the children of our own neighbors, our friends, and our own kids. And among them, the median age began dropping and dropping. Marihuana was as common as Coca-Cola and Yoo-Hoos at the high school basketball game. Arrests were noted in screaming headlines in the local newspaper.

Then something happened that never occurred in the past (especially in the 1950's and early 1960's when 61 per cent of Harlem's youth were using drugs and no one cared). Important people from affluent communities began to feel the embarrassment of a son arrested for drugs. Instead of taking a hard look at the youngster, his problems, and the family unit itself, parents began to submit to the specious rationales of their own kids; i.e., drugs should be legal; it is nothing more than the highball in your hand; cops should stop arresting; in the interim, I will give him the money to make "a buy" rather than have him arrested for burglary and stain the family name.

Presidential elections were rolling around in 1972, and, in preparation, a vast campaign was undertaken many months before to roll back the drug plague afflicting our young people. There were three White House conferences on drug abuse alone. But, the hidden agenda was crime on the streets and its swift reduction, which could ring bells at the ballot box. The massive Rockefeller Program had been locking up junkies since 1966 in nothing more than carpeted prisons, totally devoid of any true treatment construct. Parallel to that, New York was treated to the most outrageous brand of methadone maintenance in the nation. It is difficult to comprehend, for example, that while Chicago under Doctor Senay was fielding a promising methadone effort (as were some eminent, private New York treatment professionals in places like Beth Israel and Bronx State) with low dosage (40 mg average) and goaled toward a drug-free state, New York City methadone was scaled for high dosage only (beginning at 80 mg) and without any drug-free goal setting. Compounding the problem were many proprietary clinics that took some while to close down as methadone profiteers. Clients soon discovered that heroin was effectively blockaded on minimum dosages of methadone and sold the excess. By the end of 1972, methadone flowed like water on the streets, matching heroin in popularity. At this time, Daytop admissions revealed that 68 per cent had street methadone as the primary drug of abuse.

There was a silver lining to all of this. Treatment people in New York by late 1973 developed an awareness that we were in this together and that we should close ranks if we were to help this town's kids. Drug-free centers became increasingly conscious of the high dropout rate during the early phase of treatment (initial 90 days) and of the imperative to adapt professional standards of operations in both clinical and administrative zones. Methadone maintenance directors recognized the problems of client shifting to methadone-plus (whether pills, alcohol, cocaine) and saw the need for 24-hour treatment settings for more than a few clients. Out of this mutual need discovery came shortly thereafter the city-wide Greater New York Coalition of Drug Treatment Directors (inspired and headed by our own good friend and colleague, Doctor Harold Trigg at Beth Israel) as well as the Association of Voluntary Agencies on Narcotic Treatment (under Reality House's Sydney Moshette) and Therapeutic Communities of America, Inc./New York Regional Chapter (under Samaritan's Don Russakoff). This phenomenon is unique in the nation. Such consortia have reaped dividends in a sophisticated referral construct allowing for the client to be serviced by the agency responsive to his or her needs.

Parallel to these developments, a revolution in treatment was underway locally. Drug-free, self-help therapeutic communities across the city and state took root, offering more and more young people the hope of rehabilitation. New York (with California) developed the heaviest concentration of drug-free alternatives. We speak of a host of Daytop's colleagues, structured for the wide range of socioeconomic and ethnic needs: Phoenix House, Odyssey, Project Return, Samaritan, Veritas, Renaissance, Reality, J-Cap, Promesa, and a host of others.

In 1974 a President resigned his office; in 1975 came the emergency evacuation of the Embassy in Saigon, and in 1976 we celebrated the Bicentennial. The growing vitality and diversity of the drug-free treatment network in New York over these years represented a fortuitous development. The nature of drug abuse had continued to evolve by the mid-1970's from the hard core heroin addict with a criminal background of the 1960's and a median age of 22 years, to polydrug abuse (phencyclidine, butyl nitrate, sedatives, cocaine, chronic marihuana, illegal methadone) with a median age of 24, but with an alarming drop in the age of exploration from 16 years to 10 years. This trend continues to the present. By focusing in on the symptom (heroin) rather than on the person behind the drug, how much of a role the governmental planners played in spreading the problem laterally to other substances we will leave to subsequent research.

And on the precise subject, may we intrude upon this narrative in favor of an abstract

from a message from White House Advisor/Deputy Director of Domestic Policy Staff Lee I. Dogoloff (7):

For the past ten years, you, as members of Therapeutic Communities across the country, have been telling the Federal government that we have to focus on the behavior of the individual who turns to drugs rather than on a specific substance. Well ahead of the times, you have been able to bring about this "new" and sensible approach to the drug abuse problem.

The 1979 Federal Strategy for Drug Abuse and Drug Traffic Prevention presented to the President on April 2nd clearly enunciates what therapeutic communities have said for years—"To have a lasting effect and to reach those in need of assistance, domestic treatment, rehabilitation and prevention should focus primarily on compulsive drug-taking behavior rather than on the drugs themselves.

There is no question that the period described above witnessed a war of sorts for the minds and souls of America's young. In a unique and fortuitous way, the hunger for values and authenticity on the part of the young in a shifting, plastic society positioned the therapeutic community as a safe harbor in the swirling storm. The revolutionary strides made by the American therapeutic community movement over two decades now and reaching into 577 communities represents one of the brightest developments in health service delivery in the latter half of the 20th century anywhere in the world.

Yet, it bears a fascinating etiology!

Although Maxwell Jones a decade earlier than Synanon was experimenting in humanizing institutional treatment settings both at Dingleton Hospital in Scotland and Henderson Hospital in London via "open therapeutic milieu therapy," those of us in the movement profoundly acknowledge an acreage of beachfront in Santa Monica, the year 1958, and the "Ole Man at Tomalis Bay" as our historic first beginnings. Shortly thereafter, on the floor of the United States Senate, Senator Thomas J. Dodd sounded what was not unlike a clarion call (6): "Mr. President, there is indeed a miracle on the beach at Santa Monica, a man-made miracle that I feel can benefit thousands of drugs addicts."

New York psychiatrist Daniel Casriel and Monsignor O'Brien travelled different trails to Synanon. For Dan it began with a newspaper interview centered about New York's vexing addiction problem. "Put him away," he proposed, in his soon to be regretted, professionally doctrinaire pronunciamento, "either in hospitals or jails for the rest of his life—or give him all the heroin he wants" (4). (The latter strikes a very familiar note, incidentally.) His later study-residence at Santa Monica and subsequent preachings and writings on Synanon ran parallel to my own stumbling course through the bureaucratic labyrinth that was the New York community health establishment in search for an answer to an alarming increase in drug overdose and abuse in the nation's largest city. The twin journeys converged on the front porch of a new Synanon House in Westport, Connecticut in the summer of 1961. We had been working in our separate spheres to advance the cause of Synanon and therapeutic community treatment for many months before. The third and important "catalyst" in this front porch conspiracy was the Co-Director of that House, David Deitch.

In 1963, Synanon's fifth anniversary year, we found ourselves in grave difficulties with Dederich's radically changed Synanon policy and emphases. The issues were essentially 5-fold and were confronted—or rather failed to be confronted—at a high level meeting at Dan's apartment on 72nd Street in New York with Dederich's Deputy, the late Reid Kimball, dispatched to respond to the dissidents. The five prominent issues were:

1. *Reentry was abolished.* Society was recognized as irreversibly corrupted and Synanon as singularly utopian. Ergo, no one goes home anymore.

2. *Entrance fee leveled at $1,000.* This requirement foreclosed upon most New York admissions. It required either the "dope fiend" stealing a few weeks more before entering treatment or his family further mortgaging their lives.

3. *Government funding was "evil money"* and would be accepted only as a donation. The principle of responsible partnership with government was rejected a priori. We felt that such a relationship represented a sine qua non for eliminating the $1,000 prohibitive entrance fee, as well as for fielding any meaningful treatment response to a massive drug epidemic.

4. *Professionals as well as the cross-fertilization process with same were rejected in the most hostile terms.* We felt that professional and para professional expertise in this

zone was imperative and that one needed the other in order to field an effective mental health delivery system in the field of drug abuse.

5. *Research was rejected out of hand* as "outside meddling." We recognized Synanon as the historic breakthrough in the treatment of addiction and felt that a sharing of data on this succcessful effort would redound to the saving of lives across America as well as to Synanon's prestigious position.

The meeting on 72nd Street accomplished nothing in resolving the aforementioned major difficulties. Casriel, Deitch, and O'Brien embarked immediately with the blessing of New York's Mayor Wagner to field a Synanon-style therapeutic community that incorporated the resolution of the five problem matters. Within 30 days, a second generation of therapeutic communities was born—on another beachfront—this time on Staten Island's Raritan Bay at the gateway to New York's Harbor. David Deitch took command of a fledgling project, called "Daytop Lodge," and 22 drug addict probationers. With all the skills of an accomplished surgeon, he excised the glaring malignancies in the environment, nurturing a vibrantly healthy treatment milieu that was destined to be the breeding ground for third and subsequent generations of therapeutic communities both here and abroad. Dr. Alexander Bassin, a Research Psychologist with the Brooklyn Supreme Court Probation Department (now Professor of Criminology, Florida State University), was largely instrumental in navigating this nonconventional project through the vagaries of Court restrictions. He remained over the years a key mentor of Daytop.

The path to Daytop Lodge—soon after Daytop Village (which absorbed the former)—was beaten by a growing army of visitors from the governmental, health professional, political, and media sectors, both locally and abroad. One distinguished visitor, Doctor Abraham H. Maslow, best summarized the outcome of these inspection visits in his own reaction to his hours at Daytop in the summer of 1965 (11):

The process here basically poses the question of what people need universally. It seems to me that there is a fair amount of evidence that the things that people need as basic human beings are few in number. It is not very complicated. They need a feeling of protection and safety, to be taken care of when they are young so that they feel safe. Second, they need a feeling of belongingness, some kind of a family, clan or group, or something that they feel that they are in and belong to by right. Third, they have to have the feeling that people have affection for them, that they are worth being loved. And fourth, they must experience respect and esteem. And that's about it . . . . Could it be that Daytop is effective because it provides an environment where these feelings are possible? . . . Isn't it a pity we're not all addicts; because if we were, we could come to this wonderful place!

Beginning in 1966, with increased confidence on the part of the public sector (although the *Journal of the American Psychiatric Association* consistently soft pedalled the movement and berated the "lay approach"), new therapeutic communities began to spring up across New York City, the Midwest, and the West. After a long period of competitiveness and uneasiness that had all the characteristics of "sibling rivalry," moves were made to bring the therapeutic community field together. Although Mike Sach out of Wisconsin had pioneered such an effort, represented by the North American Association of Therapeutic Communities, it was Harry Sholl out of Chicago and Gateway House that sparked the thriving national alliance of therapeutic communities 5 years ago, from which was fashioned the unified spokesman for the American therapeutic community movement, viz., Therapeutic Communities of America, Inc. (TCA). Presently, a 120-member consortium, TCA represents over 12,601 treatment slots from New England to Seattle and Alaska, from Florida to California and Hawaii. An average of 10 new therapeutic community members are added to the roster at each quarterly meeting. Five years ago, under the sponsorship of the National Institute on Drug Abuse and with Bob Dupont's encouragement, a monumental step forward was achieved by a specialized Washington Conference on Therapeutic Communities.

Internationally, under the aegis of the International Council on Alcohol and Addictions (ICAA) based in Lausanne, Switzerland, therapeutic communities and the self-help, drug-free approach have received increasing recognition at international meetings and conferences. Both the World Health Organization and the Council of Europe based in Strasbourg have paid increasing attention to our movement. We are extremely proud of our achievement on the international scene represented by the World Conference of Therapeutic Communities beginning in 1976 in Sweden; followed by increasingly successful conferences in Montreal (1977), Rome (1978), and New York (1979), with Amsterdam and Manila scheduled for 1980 and 1981, respectively. Not the least of the benefits of the world-wide interaction of therapeutic communities is the training and exchange programs that have been operative. Currently, we number among our colleagues around the globe therapeutic communities in Canada, the Philippines, Malaysia, Great Britain, the Netherlands, Belgium, France, Sweden, Norway, Federal German Republic, Italy, Thailand, Iceland, Ireland, Brazil, Panama, Venezuela, Algeria, Scotland, Puerto Rico, and South Africa, among others. Although we encourage indigenous leadership to adapt the therapeutic community model to their own culture and needs and to select their own banner/name, we do have a Phoenix House in London and 12 Daytops in the Federal German Republic.

Toward further increased focus on the therapeutic community approach, the International Congress on Rehabilitation in Psychiatry, a world-wide group of mental health professionals, staged a therapeutic community symposium in Geneva in 1976 and a second one in Orebro, Sweden, in the fall of 1978. We have official liaison with this group via the Therapeutic Community Section of ICAA.

Responding both to the eternal verity "Publish or Perish!," as well as to the imperative to create national and international communication vehicles, *The Addiction Therapist*, a journal published by our colleagues at Portage in Montreal, has been deputed as the official organ of the international movement (Therapeutic Section of ICAA) as well as of national TCA in America. In addition, TCA publishes a quarterly *Newsletter* out of Spectrum House in Massachusetts.

The thrust of the times has been, as indicated previously, toward regional, national, and international associations with two major goals: (a) to engender the growth of the movement by fielding both logistical as well as training resources, mostly from the seasoned

(American) therapeutic communities; and (b) to enhance treatment impact by sophistication in skill training in both clinical and administrative zones.

The net result of national TCA's formation has been the sharing of treatment data, the sharpening of target goals, the increase in specialization as well as the movement toward standards and norms for therapeutic community operations. This promises to maximize treatment effectiveness, while reducing the potential for abuse and corruption inherent in the mental health delivery field, especially in the therapeutic community where power corrupts sooner and with graver consequences. The name of the game is accountability.

A by-product of the national association has been the chartering of regional (state) chapters, enabling the therapeutic communities to deal with specialized area needs. The New York Regional Chapter has in its brief life forged an enviable position in both city and state. Funding restoration for the past 4 years has been the direct outcome of New York Regional's reputation as well as its public information efforts. Pennsylvania, California, Massachusetts and Wisconsin have moved in the same direction, and other states are considering such moves. Interestingly, similar movements abroad have been inspired by our ICAA world federation. In early 1977, under our colleague Doctor Christian Brule in Versailles, an inaugural conference of European therapeutic community delegates was staged south of Paris in the chateau countryside of the Loire, resulting in the beginnings of a European counterpart of America's national TCA. The European effort is currently directed by Don Mario Picchi of Rome's Il Centro.

In the final half of the 1970's, the American therapeutic community movement has mobilized its resources to improve its skills, enhance its treatment impact, and develop close and responsible relationships with our colleagues beyond the borders of drug-free treatment, across the health field in general.

We have problems—huge ones—that we are struggling with currently, including:

1. Power becomes a major risk zone in therapeutic communities. Add "charisma" to the figure of the executive or house director and you have maximized the opportunity for abuse of clients and corruption of program.

The "master-serf syndrome" has not been an uncommon phenomenon troubling us, with residents in some instances serving as lackeys for staff. We are well down the road toward developing professional pride and insights on the part of staff as insurance against such abuses. Accountability mechanisms and staff "codes of ethics" have been installed in many of our constituent programs. National TCA is currently coming to grips with this area of concern. A nationwide Code of Ethics and Code of Client Rights have been put in place.

2. The professional-paraprofessional impasse has been resolved in most of our agencies. TCA stresses the imperative of widening the horizons of professional staff roles, especially in the training area and in induction screening, as a vital complement to our native ex-addict skills.

3. Across the therapeutic community scene, women in treatment are, more often than not, brutalized (in want of a better word) in a prevailing male-oriented, male-dominated environment. The fact that the male to female addict street ratio is adequately reflected in therapeutic community population rosters is often accepted as a rationale for angling treatment toward men. However, many of us are developing currently innovative female treatment components that will reduce the risk of female hardship in therapeutic communities and will more meaningfully respond to the specialized needs of women in treatment by a radically new program design, along with proportionate female staffing and awareness training for male staff. In a 1975 paper, New Jersey Psychologist Stephen J. Levy, Ph.D., examined this question and concluded that (10): " . . . empirical and anecdotal evidence is mounting rapidly which points towards sexist attitudes and practices which directly cripple the attempts to effectively rehabilitate female clients and indirectly distort quality treatment of males as well."

4. Sophistication in treatment models is an imperative for American therapeutic communities. Most of us long ago recognized the validity of an ambulatory therapeutic community track to respond to the younger, less disoriented drug abuser in daylong, 6-day-a-week centers. (Almost one-half of Daytop's 950 clients are in the ambulatory component currently.) An important companion to ambulatory treatment, in particular, is the

weekly family therapy session in the evening in which we attempt to reconstruct healthy parent-child relationships. When the damage is discovered to be irreversible in the family unit, the youngster is transferred into the residential component. However, there must be distinctive residential treatment models for this younger (adolescent) resident in the therapeutic community, inasmuch as most of the current residential population is 24 years of age or older.

A second area demanding sophistication surrounds women with children. It is not sufficient to rest with a therapeutic community decision to include or exclude the children. It is vital to the mother's successful response to treatment that the continuity of contact with the children be preserved and that her treatment include her relationship with her children (and husband, if he is still around).

A third area of sophistication rests with early educational and vocational evaluation of the client in order to build in companion educational achievement programming and/or employment training workshops as he or she progresses through treatment. Daytop, with Brooklyn College, in 1979 fields a full, intramural university program.

5. The socially accepted and quasiaccepted substances (alcohol, marihuana) as they impact upon the therapeutic community's drug-free graduate represent a central concern. Alcohol remains the number one problem zone both for staff and graduates. In addition, there is increasing pressure for a shift in the therapeutic community philosophy in favor of pot smoking. We continue to resist, especially in the light of current research findings.

6. Aftercare becomes an increasingly important area of therapeutic community focus. Because we teach our residents/graduates never to flee stress but to deal responsibly with same, they are reluctant to return to the therapeutic community family because it connotes an admission of failure. A separate and distinct, heavily professional aftercare component should be established by therapeutic communities. There is little question about the urgency of this move.

7. The split rate in the high risk zone, i.e., the first 90 days of treatment, continues to haunt every therapeutic community. Whether this can be relieved by a more meaningful interface with the criminal justice

sector or by an interim "marriage" with pharmacology (methadone toward a drug-free state), we have been remiss on not moving more swiftly to address this problem area.

This catalogue of major problem zones confronting therapeutic communities currently provides some insight into the on-going emphasis of TCA to serve as a catalyst for program growth as a fitting companion to our emphasis in treatment on personal growth.

The international movement is confronted with its own set of hurdles currently, mostly arising from societal-cultural adaptation of the therapeutic community model in respective national situations. In addition, we would be less than candid if we failed to note that the philosophical conflict between the Maxwell Jones' adherents and the traditional American therapeutic community of Mowrer/Glasser/Daytop is central to the turbulence. Europeans, especially the Swedes and Danes, find a 2-fold problem with the American model:

1. Admission to the therapeutic community must be a purely voluntary act by the client, free from any semblance of coercion, such as a rejection by wife/parent/family or via a criminal justice hold. American therapeutic communities look upon external intervention in the life of the addict, such as described above, as very therapeutic and encourage such interventions.

2. The therapeutic community must be totally democratic from the onset, governed by the members and not by staff who should assume the role of family members in a better position to assist brothers and sisters. On the other hand, American therapeutic communities generally teach that the addict, rather than a prisoner of his own biochemistry, is merely an emotional infant in an adult's body. His problem surrounds the stress factor thrust upon him by virtue of his chronological-physiological age and his consequent inability to cope with same due to his infantile emotional attainment level. Thus, therapeutic communities target in on the process of maturation that broke down during the first trip through the natural family, i.e., the transference from parental-imposed controls on an increasing scale via the mechanism of challenge toward self-imposed controls. However, one must first install "parental-imposed controls" (therapeutic community family-im-

posed controls) for the new client in the therapeutic community; thus commencing the actual transferal process down the road, often by the sixth month in treatment. The Swedes and Danes, following the Maxwell Jones school, with some reason, object to the imposition of "parental-imposed controls" in the therapeutic community and characterize this early phase of American treatment as "totalitarian."

Our view from here as to where the future will find the therapeutic community movement is perforce apocalyptic in tone:

1. An increasing professionalization in both clinical and administrative zones of operations for the therapeutic community, away from the haphazardry of the past with all its messianic potential for exploitation. A caution: we do not see shingled psychiatrists, psychologists, sociologists, etc. displacing paraprofessional ex-addict staff in the therapeutic community. God forbid! I do see a more dynamic partnership between both within the therapeutic community. In this prospect, to my mind, rests the ultimate viability of the therapeutic community. I do see, also, ex-addict movement in great numbers toward the helping professions.

2. More diversification in treatment techniques for a shifting drug abuse population.

3. Major development of self-sufficient therapeutic communities, with monastic-style self-reliance and with only partial reliance on government funding at best.

4. Widening of the therapeutic community horizons for inclusion of other segments of the acting-out disorder spectrum, e.g., adolescent and young adult alcoholics, unemployables, first-time servers in penal institutions, prescription drug abusers.

5. Firming up of international bridges around the world via a distinct World Federation of Therapeutic Communities and via our international conferences. Cross-fertilization and closer working relationships between national groups within the therapeutic community world will assist measurably on the demand side of the addiction equation to ease world-wide youth concerns.

6. Concerted movement on the part of psychiatry in general as well as criminology in acknowledging their failure in the character disorder-sociopath zone and toward a meaningful utilization of alternate "lay models of treatment."

We are reminded of an incident that speaks to this last prognostication and with which we shall close this section of our treatise. In the fall of 1974, we were gathered by invitation of the Skandia Insurance Group at a select international symposium in Stockholm. I (Monsignor O'Brien) had been selected as the international spokesman for the therapeutic community approach among a faculty of "home-run hitters" in our field drawn from around the world, e.g., Evang, Higichi, Vaillant, Rettersol, Teigen, Connell, Bewley, Wikler, Ball, and Bejerot, among others.

Having meekly presented my case in a presentation entitled: "The Daytop Model for Addiction Treatment," I was swiftly assaulted, verbally that is, by our British cousin and a good friend (subsequently), Phil Connell of Maudsley in London. He hastened to challenge my "major," dismiss my "minors," and characterize the general conclusions of my work with characteristic British aplomb: "Rubbish." Suddenly, I was transported to the year 1690 and to the Boyne where we sons of James II took our lumps from the forces of William of Orange. But his name was "Connell," I consoled myself blandly. And just as suddenly, before I had completely regained my equilibrium, a calm voice from the far end of the rostrum cast a spell over the room. It was Harvard's George Vaillant (12):

I just wanted to comment on Dr. Connell's feeling that the patients he dealt with were too fragile for an encounter. I've been studying the defenses that underlie character disorder. I spent two years at Lexington, Kentucky, among addicts with character disorder in a pure culture as it were. I've also been following a group of 100 men selected 30 years ago and studying the character disorder which occurs in a healthy population and at least qualitatively I don't think there's any difference. I don't think that character disorders are special to just drug addicts or prisoners. But one of the things that characterizes character disorder, as Msgr. O'Brien suggests, is that the person doesn't feel pain. The paranoid doesn't realize his prejudice, the hypochondriac never goes to the psychiatrist about the fact that he imagines complaints, delinquents don't go to see a psychiatrist. The most effective way of breaching these defenses is not by sending them to a psychiatrist but by confrontation.

The encounter model of Daytop and Synanon is really no different from the gentler model in

Alcoholics Anonymous, in Weight Watchers, in the effort by the Germans after the First World War to cure hypochondriasis by confrontation groups. But one of the characteristics is that confrontation or encounters have to be done by people who are in the same boat. People are too fragile—Dr. Connell's patients are too fragile—for their defenses to be breached by doctors, social workers, ministers, parents, etc. These defenses can be breached and I don't think anybody is too fragile to have them breached, by relatively loving confrontation, by people who are in the same boat.

Certainly my experiences with AA in observing half-way houses in watching how relatively healthy people find ways of breaching the defensive detachment that Msgr. O'Brien refers to indicate that nobody is too fragile to have his defenses breached, if he is given enough social support and the encounter is done by peers and not by some deus ex machina psychiatrist.

THERAPEUTIC COMMUNITY: THE PROCESS

THE TREATMENT CONCEPT

Rejecting a prevailing premise that the addict-abuser's problem is solely physiologically based and, hence, his or her treatment must be pharmacological, the therapeutic community treatment concept contends that addiction/abuse is a psychosocial and complex problem. The solution is also complex. It requires dealing with the total human person and etiological factors that are at once social, ethical, psychological, physiological, cultural, and existential. There are just no simple answers.

It proceeds from the premise that man benefits from honest confrontation and human challenges to grow into maturity and responsibility. This is achieved via a caring but demanding "family group," a peer group therapeutic community. Further, the therapeutic community impresses upon the young drug abuser that "only you can do it but you cannot do it alone." It does not dismiss the potential of physiological influences, but rather selects to emphasize a behavioral-social thrust as the primary therapeutic route to altering addictive and related self-destructive abuse behaviors.

The phenomenon of polydrug abuse, as cited above in this chapter, has been evident to therapeutic community researchers and clinical workers for the last decade as the most frequently presented profile. However, this phenomenon has only in the last few years been recognized nationally. Recent Client Oriented Data Acquisition Process (CODAP) admissions data indicate that only 40 per cent of clients seeking treatment report heroin as the primary drug problem. Similarly, in comparing the drug problem profile in 1978 and 1979 of more than 1,000 admissions to Daytop during that period, we find only 40 per cent report heroin as the primary drug problem as compared to 88 per cent in 1969. Moreover, more than 98 per cent report secondary and tertiary drug problems, often indicating severe abuse rather than addiction patterns. The presenting client profiles are also indicative of employment and criminal justice problems, educational, family, and social relationships and mental health needs. With such a presenting pattern the therapeutic community represents the kind of robust, intensive milieu that can successfully supervise and enhance positive social growth and development.

In 1978, National Drug Abuse Treatment Utilization Survey (NDATUS) results reported that 8 per cent of all clients sought treatment in drug-free residential settings and 48 per cent were placed in drug-free outpatient settings. Although each modality has its role in drug treatment, it is increasingly apparent that the goals of the therapeutic community are certainly of particular importance with the increasing numbers of nonaddicted polydrug abusers, the younger addict/abuser, and those maintenance clients who seek an alternative to methadone.

CLINICAL APPROACH

The specific goals of the therapeutic community program are to (a) eliminate the addict's or abuser's drug-taking behavior, (b) rehabilitate him in modifying his personality to deal with personal and environmental stress, and (c) assist in readjusting and returning the resident to the outside community as a functioning, independent individual.

The theory underlying the traditional therapeutic community approach views drug addiction and abuse as being largely symptomatic of a psychological character disorder and/or social privation and alienation. Abuse behavior resulting primarily from the former is assumed to stem from or be exacerbated by faulty sociopsychological development.

The individual manifesting this kind of disorder typically reacts to personal stress by compulsively utilizing the psychophysiological reinforcing properties of mood-altering substances, using drugs chronically, to avoid dealing with conflict and withdrawing into a protective shell. Such compulsive and destructive behavior is viewed as stunted and immature in the context of psychosocial development. It reflects felt inadequacy or incompetence in dealing with stress. In response to these real or imagined personal shortcomings, the abuser, while using drugs as a defensive cover, tends often to deny and overtly to compensate by developing an inflated self-image and a false sense of superiority. As a consequence, he does not relate openly and honestly about himself, frequently attempts to manipulate others through a portrayal of urgent dependency, and is unable to express real concern for others.

For those individuals whose drug dependency seems to emanate mainly from social privation and alienation, the theory assumes a lesser degree of personal immaturity and more of a given debilitating social environment as the etiological issue. The abusers who would fall into this diagnostic category often include individuals of minority ethnic groups who are subjected to racial, social, and economic discrimination and frustration. These individuals seem to see their existential condition as bleak and, in response, tend to seek a temporary respite, alleviation, or oblivion from social reality through the use of drugs.

The above formulation is based on clinical experience within the therapeutic community program. It is not a formal theory nor does it claim a full understanding of the abuser dynamics. Its principal use has been in providing a conceptual framework out of which the therapeutic techniques are derived, tested, and used. Based on this formulation of drug abuse, the clinical theory of the program suggests specific methods. In most cases, the severe abuser is aided by being removed from his/her immediate natural environment and the sociopsychological environment which contributes to continued abuse behavior. The alternative is for the new resident to reside within a controlled therapeutic setting that has the capability of removing negative environmental influences and stimuli. These are the stimuli that foster the compulsive drug behavior—drug accessibility, drug-abusing peers, and recurring stress factors that trigger drug-seeking behavior.

The therapeutic environment provides a family milieu in which the process of self-realization is the major focus. In this structured setting, the ex-addict or ex-abuser is provided the opportunity to explore his/her own self, clarify life goals, and move toward a greater sense of moral responsibility and values clarification. Through the forces of group dynamics, his/her own behavioral motivations and interpersonal relationships are revealed. The new resident's involvement in the program is strongly motivated as a result of identification with older residents who act as role models.

During the residential period, personality and interpersonal dynamics that underlie abuse can be improved through a regimen of varied therapeutic activities and social-peer supervision, thereby lessening and eventually modifying destructive drug-taking behaviors. Although mood, attitude, and behavioral consistency tend to oscillate during treatment phases, there is an accompanying increase in self-awareness, unearthing major and more subtle personal motivations and learning of new social-interpersonal skills—factors that were previously being disguised by a chemical shroud. When these positive experiences occur in the drug-free therapeutic community, the result is enhanced self-esteem and reduction in pathological thinking and feeling states. Also emerging are the beginnings of goal-oriented, more purposive behavior and improved psychological integration.

After this period and as a means of testing the individual's growth derived from the residential experience, the individual gradually reenters the outside community. During this latter period the resident is provided increasingly with direct assistance in social and economic survival skills.

The operation of the therapeutic community or ambulatory treatment unit plays a significant role in the learning experiences of the client. The individual takes responsibility for the operation of the facility within a hierarchical system of increased responsibility and earned status. Starting off, the new client would be serving on one of several operational crews under continuous supervision. Based upon whether his performance warranted it, the client assumes increasing responsibilities of planning, coordinating, and supervising a crew or department. The significance of this hierarchical system is that it internally motivates the individual toward responsibility and earning status based on observable and deserving behaviors. In this context, negative reinforcement is applied as part of the over-all learning process rather than as a strictly punitive measure. This is accompanied by expressions of personal concern, which facilitate the learning process. A system of social reward and punishment is operative based on clinical evaluation and review. Rewards include increasing responsibility, group approval of positive behavior, and upward mobility; punishments include verbal reprimand, temporary status/role demotions, and increased work assignments directed toward achieving a positive behavior change.

The resident is confronted daily about aspects of his/her behavior as part of the over-all therapeutic process. To accomplish treatment goals effectively, a wide variety of clinical techniques is utilized, including behavioral modification, individual psychotherapy, intensive counseling, varied group therapy and encounter formats, cognitive and informational input.

This multifaceted approach of the therapeutic community has stimulated an increasing dialogue among workers internationally, to grapple with the process issues of psychological change and resocialization. There exists for them an intrigue to better explain the myriad dynamics of the peer group, self-help human process that fosters positive behavior and attitudinal change, the understanding of which holds promise for new directions in psychosocial growth and development, family life, and education.

The result of measuring the impact of therapeutic community modalities can now be based on empirical follow-up studies with local and nation-wide samples. Although these various follow-up studies may have their particular methodological limitations— such as limited at risk time frame, select client sampling, significant client postprogram life experiences, self-report data—the findings are revealing. The follow-up efforts are impressive for a modality so recently developed. The researchers have studied the former client follow-up adjustment and drug behavior and have not relied upon assessment of client satisfaction and attitudes as the measures for program effectiveness. The results of these data, particularly the Sells' Drug Abuse Reporting Program (DARP) follow-up studies, certainly attest to the treatment effectiveness and positive impact of the therapeutic community in influencing the client's positive behavior changes. The National Institute on Drug Abuse states that post-DARP outcomes were generally quite favorable for the treatment modalities of methadone maintenance and therapeutic community. However, "using the most rigid criteria, including drug abstinence and no return to drug treatment, the therapeutic community group would probably be selected as having the most successful outcomes" (9). The interested reader is also referred to a range of additional outcome studies on therapeutic community and other modalities that have been previously cited (8).

RESEARCH INQUIRIES

The therapeutic community provides a fertile opportunity to explore facets of the resident population within the context of this innovative modality. Such inquiry provides insights on drug abuse-addiction behaviors, the impact of the therapeutic community on altering these behaviors, and the therapeutic community program elements that may require a program modification to respond more effectively to new client populations.

Ethnography

Public awareness of the therapeutic community is critical for those in need of drug treatment. The Research Department at Daytop undertook an ethnographic street survey with several objectives. One of these was to determine "product recognition" of therapeutic communities. The survey, conducted over a 6-month period in 1978, indicated an over-all recognition rate of therapeutic communities at 41 per cent. A sample of 675 persons was conducted in 33 New York City sites. These sites represented a purposive sample that was derived from Drug Enforcement Administration and New York Police Department sources that were identified as high street drug-dealing areas. A subsample of this survey was conducted in areas immediately adjacent to each established Methadone Maintenance Treatment Service unit in the city, including both public and private agencies.

Results were focused on the target population of using street addicts and abusers. Each subject when interviewed was either engaged in drug sales, purchase, or observable use at time of contact. There was an overall 41 per cent recognition rate of either Daytop or other drug-free therapeutic communities as treatment programs. The results indicated that these programs were more recognized and identified by older active methadone clients between 29 and 50 years of age. Only about 10 per cent of the 18- to 25-year-olds knew about either Daytop or other therapeutic communities. The study poignantly indicated that, recognition is highest amongst older addicts and abusers and those who are currently part of the drug treatment system in the methadone track, the therapeutic community is significantly less well known by those who are in a currently high risk population and out of treatment. Those persons most visibly abusing drugs on the street regularly are unemployed and under 25 years of age. There also is, unfortunately, an image distortion of the therapeutic community concept—older individuals tended to view therapeutic communities as programs designed only for young persons and would frequently emphasize the perceived restrictions of the program environment. These perceptions need to be altered by more intensive programs of information dissemination for the general public and the high risk abuser population in need of treatment.

A second objective of the ethnography study, which used an indigenous field team, was to pilot test a follow-up technique. It sought to locate and identify the rate of former Daytop residents who frequented active drug-dealing locales. The approach proved feasible, and the results yielded a significantly low rate of 6 per cent. These data suggest a notable nonparticipation in the street drug scene by former residents and a change from their more typical preprogram patterns.

READMISSIONS

Another recent phenomenon in therapeutic communities is the increasing number of former clients who return to program. Over-

all readmission rates at Daytop and other therapeutic communities are ranging between 25 and 35 per cent. These are the base rates of clients admitted within a given year who have had some prior therapeutic community experience.

In order to better understand this readmission group, we undertook an empirical study of 103 therapeutic community readmits and a control-comparison group of 50 new admits who shared similar drug abuse, criminal history, social and demographic characteristics. Both groups were studied for a minimum of 1 year post-Daytop. The readmissions after their second treatment episode had a significantly greater tendency to become involved in a methadone maintenance program: 23 per cent as compared to 8 per cent of the controls. Also readmits had a greater tendency to be incarcerated after leaving the program than did the control-comparison group. Over-all the readmits were a higher risk group with regard to drug, criminal behavior, and psychological problems postprogram (3).

A most interesting finding was that on their return to treatment many of the readmits tended to use the therapeutic community as an alternative health care agency. They returned with significant physical problems and sought services that required periods of hospitalization and/or intensive medical or dental care during their second therapeutic community treatment episode.

PHENCYCLIDINE

Other ongoing work includes the effect of preprogram low and high phencyclidine (PCP) abuse levels and response to therapeutic community treatment. Results to date do not substantiate any differential between high and low PCP abusers in either their clinical response to therapeutic community treatment or their length of participation in the program. This study will continue to monitor these results.

EMPLOYMENT

Concern with the issue of postprogram work force participation has stimulated a current study at Daytop of the relationship between time in the treatment program and subsequent active employment. The study of 250 former residents has produced data indicating a reliable relationship between pre-program and postprogram levels of employment. Current data gathering will pursue the critical issue of partial employment of former residents. The data are being used to plan for career-job training and development efforts within the therapeutic community.

PROMISING PROJECTS

The role of the therapeutic community modality has been demonstrated effective in impacting upon the treatment of substance abusers and has thus created opportunities to respond to a broader range of drug-related problems. Consequently, there is current demand to study how extension and transferability of the therapeutic community concept can respond to the areas of prevention, criminal justice, higher education, and self-evaluation. Through basic demonstration grant funding, several such projects have been realized and are showing notable results.

HIGHER EDUCATION

The Daytop Miniversity is a new and notable development in utilizing the therapeutic community as a clinical-academic learning environment. Currently underway as a successful project in conjunction with the Brooklyn College School of Sciences, it seeks to identify and establish the inherent benefits of the therapeutic community for initiating higher education for residents in treatment 3 or more months. Currently more than 80 therapeutic community residents have earned in excess of 1,302 rigorous college credits while simultaneously participating in their clinical treatment program. A sample of courses includes Finite Math, Computer Science, Statistics, Geology, Human Sexuality, Comparative Literature, and Constitutional Law. Formal evaluation data are supporting the fact that the therapeutic community provides an ideal setting to actualize academic-career goals. They are documenting positive changes in self-concept and continuation of academic pursuit. Over-all the Daytop Miniversity Project is highlighting the expanding potential of the therapeutic community to support the future achievements of former addicts and substance abusers in treatment. A comprehensive follow-up study is currently ongoing to determine the impact on social adjustment, drug behavior, and educational and work achievement (2).

CRIMINAL JUSTICE

In a joint effort of the New York State Division of Substance Abuse Services, New York Therapeutic Communities, Inc., New York State Department of Correctional Services, and the New York State Division of Parole, the innovative "Prison Project" therapeutic community for substance abusers has been launched. Inmates identified as substance abusers are recruited from state correctional facilities and reassigned to a special prison therapeutic community unit that is staffed and directed by ex-addict and ex-offender paraprofessionals. Although a programmatic evaluation on longer term outcome is planned, current findings are demonstrating the striking therapeutic contrast between this unit and the prison environment. The Prison Project has duplicated the environment of a therapeutic community and prisoner-residents have been shown by objective measurement to be interpersonally more open, trusting, and sharing. The program is carefully planned and provides for an orderly process from the prison therapeutic community to a community-based therapeutic community for a period of 6 months and a scheduled reentry process (13).

PREVENTION

The Youth Alternative Learning Project proved to be a most effective prevention program for high risk, preadolescent, inner-city youths. This 2-year demonstration project funded by the National Institute on Drug Abuse utilized a therapeutic community as a parent agency. The prevention program relied heavily on the positive identity of the therapeutic community within the local community. The programmatic design emphasized the principle of peer responsibilities, role models, modified encounters and work-school learning performance. The project provided senior therapeutic community residents an opportunity to serve as positive change agents with youths, particularly in group interaction and with social and organizational activities. An empirical evaluation of the project demonstrated success in reducing the amount of physical aggression and fostering greater affective social communications; stabilizing levels of drug use and experimentation; improving school performance and development of leadership qualities. What is particularly noteworthy is that this project functioned most effectively in an area that was designated as having the highest levels of street addicts and drug trafficking in Washington, D.C.

The program was fully endorsed by the parents and public school teachers of the youth participants. This successful model supports the notion that the concept of the therapeutic community can be modified and effectively applied to youth in need of positive social learning experiences and prevention strategies (1).

SELF-EVALUATION

Although there is an expressed need for research and evaluation within the therapeutic community, the stark reality is that often program resources do not provide for these activities. Moreover, evaluations conducted by external agencies rarely, if ever, are designed to build such a capability. In an initial attempt to address this problem and study the varieties of substance abusers participating in therapeutic community treatment, a multiagency, self-evaluation project has been launched under the auspices of TCA. Results to date show a uniformity of clinical therapeutic community environments among the participating programs, regardless of size and geographical region. Staff perceptions of their therapeutic community environment and treatment goals show a high degree of concordance. This pattern suggests that, although treatment methods may differ, the therapeutic effect can be realized among similar programs, supporting an empirically based treatment network (5).

The therapeutic community movement and its clinical process share the fairly recent life-span of other drug treatment modalities. Although each of the modalities plays particular roles in responding to the needs of addicts and substance abusers, the therapeutic community modality is generic in its applicability. This is of particular moment with the increased concern focused on nonaddicted polydrug abusers, younger abusers, and those persons who camouflage their chronic psychosocial distress by compulsive drug taking. The therapeutic community, moreover, is beginning to show its heuristic potential in helping persons find solutions to living prior to the onset of destructive and compulsive drug abuse behaviors.

References

1. Biase, D. V. A non residential TC model for pre and early adolescents: A prevention demonstration project within a TC agency. Addict. Ther. (Special Ed.) 2:20, 1978.
2. Biase, D. V., and Devlin, C. Daytop Miniversity (NIDA Project #1H81DA 01911-01AI). Presented at the Fifth World Conference of Therapeutic Communities, The Hague, Holland, September 1980.
3. Biase, D. V., and Isaac, M. Readmissions to the TC. Presented at the National Drug Abuse Conference, Seattle, Washington, April, 1978.
4. Casriel, D. So Fair a House, p. 3. Englewood Cliffs, N. J., Prentice-Hall, 1963.
5. DeLeon, G. Therapeutic Communities: Self Evaluation of 7 Programs (NIDA Project #1-H81 DA 01976-01). First year Progress Report May 1979. New York, New York, 1979.
6. Dodd, T. J. Statement of Senator Thomas J. Dodd concerning the Synanon Foundation on the floor of the United States Senate, September 6, 1962.
7. Dogoloff, L. I. Message to the therapeutic communities of America. Ther. Communities Am. Newsletter June, 1970.
8. Dupont, R., et al. Handbook on Drug Abuse. Rockville, Md., National Institute on Drug Abuse, 1979.
9. Follow-up Evaluation of Drug Abuse Treatment Services, NIDA Services Research Report (DHEW Publication No. ADM 79-765). Washington, D.C., United States Government Printing Office, 1978.
10. Levy, S. J., and Broudy, M. Sex role differences in the therapeutic community: Moving from sexism to androgyny. Presented at The Training for Living Institute, New York City, April 4-7, 1975.
11. Maslow, A. H. The Farther Reaches of Human Nature, p. 228. New York, Viking Press, 1971.
12. Vaillant, G. E. Drug dependence: Treatment and treatment evaluation. In Proceedings of Skandia International Symposia, pp. 54-55. Stockholm, Skandia Group, 1975.
13. Wexler, H. "Stay'n out" prison therapeutic community evaluation: Design and Variables. Presented at Fourth International Conference of Therapeutic Communities, New York City, September 1979.

CHAPTER 24

DETOXIFICATION FROM NARCOTICS

Herbert D. Kleber, M.D.

The treatment of physical addiction is so easy and yet so difficult and discouraging . . . (34).

There is a well known expression in relationship to heroin addiction: "it is easy to get off, but hard to stay off." This delightfully ambiguous statement, the modern version of Kolb and Himmelsbach's lament above, points out the ease of obtaining heroin and the relative ease of kicking the habit, as compared to the very real problems that lie ahead for someone who is trying to stay off the drug for the long term. Prior to the use of maintenance approaches to addiction, detoxification, with or without follow-up therapy, was usually the only treatment available for the heroin addict. It is still the necessary pretreatment route to the therapeutic community, narcotic antagonist maintenance, or drug-free treatment on either an outpatient or inpatient basis. However, many individuals who start a detoxification program do not complete it, and most neither go on to longer term treatment nor stay off drugs on their own (7, 16, 26, 40, 45, 48, 55, 56, 68).

Of course, many addicts enter such a program just to reduce their habits and obtain a momentary respite from the arduous task of supporting an expensive way of life. They fully intend to resume their drug use and get high at lower dosage and cost than when they began withdrawal.

This chapter will examine the historical approaches to narcotic withdrawal, current methods, and new ideas that have been put forth to improve the outcome.

DEFINITION

Detoxification refers to the process whereby an individual who is physically dependent upon a drug—in the case of this chapter, narcotics—is taken off that drug. This can occur abruptly or gradually; the agent the individual is dependent upon can be used, or other drugs that produce cross-tolerance can be employed; or symptomatic treatment can be given to ameliorate discomfort; or drugs that affect the mechanisms by which withdrawal is expressed can be utilized. Detoxification can take place in an inpatient, residential, or outpatient setting.

The method chosen is to a great extent dependent upon what is available rather than what would be ideal, and availability is often a complex situation relating to federal and state laws, physician or patient preference or bias, community opinion, and other non-scientific issues. In general, the purposes of detoxification could be stated as follows:

1. Ridding the body of the acute physiological dependence associated with the chronic daily use of narcotics.

2. The relieving of the pain and discomfort

that can occur during withdrawal, especially if it is abrupt.

3. The providing of a safe and humane treatment that can help the individual over the initial hurdle of stopping narcotic use.

4. Providing an environment that encourages a more long range commitment to treatment and making appropriate referrals to such other modalities.

WHEN IS DETOXIFICATION SUCCESSFUL?

Because the narcotic addicts who are able to stop using drugs after detoxification alone are felt to make up only a small minority, there is, therefore, agreement among most clinicians that detoxification should be considered pretreatment or, at best, the first stage in the treatment process. Whereas many years back the outcome of narcotic addiction treatment was considered successful if the patient refrained from using narcotics and did not switch to other illicit drugs or excessive use of licit ones like alcohol, today success has taken on a more complicated meaning. It is defined now in terms of the total picture having to do with a variety of outcome measures, including employment, criminal activity, dependence on public assistance, interpersonal relationships, and general physical and mental well-being.

If detoxification is considered as pretreatment or the first step in treatment, it is unrealistic to apply at this early stage the goals applicable to long term treatment. Instead, it should be asked whether the client is able to do two things—successfully complete the detoxification process itself and get into longer term treatment. In looking at any particular detoxification method, therefore, criteria such as the ability of the method to withdraw the individual safely and with minimal discomfort are of major importance, closely followed by the percentage of clients who successfully complete the treatment, and finally by the percentage going on to longer term treatment. Some authors disagree with this and argue that detoxification should be viewed (42):

as an independent modality . . . pursuing its own limited, but clearly defined objectives. . . . the elimination of acute physical dependence on narcotics must be accepted as a sufficient, if not necessarily optimal, goal of treatment. In addition, detoxification programs can and should be viewed as a referral source. . . . Eligibility for admission must not be made contingent upon an avowed commitment to accept long-term treatment. . . . Quite the contrary: detoxification programs exist primarily to attract those addicts who do *not* accept long-term treatment. . . .

HISTORICAL OVERVIEW

The history of the treatment of narcotic withdrawal is one, with a few exceptions, of finding treatments that are even more addictive or difficult to break than the one being treated, or else treatments that are far more dangerous for the individual undergoing withdrawal than the untreated withdrawal itself. An early example of this in recent medical history was the introduction in the late 1800's of injectable morphine to treat the habit of opium eating. Injectable morphine did not come into widespread use until the invention of the hypodermic syringe around the time of the Civil War. There were complaints in 1870 by physicians about the greater difficulty of getting rid of the morphine habit than of the opium-eating habit (1). The lack of deterrence of this example is illustrated by the introduction at the turn of the century of the drug that has remained to plague us for the past 75 years, namely, the use of heroin to treat the morphine addiction that had treated opium eating. Nonaddicting heroin was clearly a superior choice to addicting morphine and was so touted. In 1938, looking back on the preceding 40 years of mostly futile attempts to treat narcotic withdrawal, Kolb and Himmelsbach, in a masterful review, noted the uselessness or dangerousness of the treatments that had been introduced (34). Some lessons of the heroin fiasco had obviously sunk in, however, so that the majority of these treatments, although dangerous in their own way, did not introduce the patient to more addicting agents and instead used nonnarcotic drugs to treat withdrawal.

TREATMENT FROM 1900 TO 1940

Belladonna Treatments

Although drugs of this category had been used for a long period of time to treat narcotic addiction, it was not until the early part of this century that they came into widespread use and then dominated withdrawal treatment for about 30 years. In 1901, both Lott and Petty published articles on the use of scopolamine, a member of the belladonna group of drugs, in the treatment of addiction. Lott gave his patients scopolamine every 30 to 60 minutes for 24 to 48 hours until scopolamine intoxication occurred. Kolb and Himmelsbach described it with characteristic understatement (34): "According to Lott, patients have diarrhea but do not suffer during this period. Nevertheless, they may see and imagine things that do not exist and grow quite wild and . . . should be taken care of in a downstairs room by a strong nurse constantly at the bedside so as to prevent self-injury or injury from falls as the patients are 'incoordinate and unable to stand.'" Strychnine, nitroglycerine, or digitalis were also sometimes given during this period for the heart. "At the end of this first delerious period, 'the patient no longer craves the drug and would not take it.'" The second stage consists of giving pilcarpine every hour "until the drugs that have been stored in the cord and body are eliminated." Even after 10 days, "pain, nervousness, restlessness and insomnia continue and are controlled by hot and cold baths, bromides, chloral, pilcarpine, atropine, hyoscine, strychnine and electricity." The theory behind this belladonna treatment was that morphine was stored in the cord and other tissues and needed to be eliminated in order to be able to effect a cure.

The most famous variant of the hyoscine treatment was called the Towns-Lambert treatment. It was a rapid withdrawal method in which potent purgatives and a variety of belladonna derivatives were given orally. The end point of the successful treatment was a mild belladonna intoxication accompanied by liquid green stools following a dose of castor oil roughly 2 to 3 days after treatment had started. In addition, Lambert used a variety of other drugs, including at one time or another, oxgall, phenacetin, pyramidon, caffeine, salicylates, sodium nitrate, sodium bromide, sodium bicarbonate, codeine, and chloral. The problem with this whole approach is explained concisely by Kolb and Himmelsbach (34). They note that, "It is true that small doses of morphine and hyoscine antidote each other, but in morphine withdrawal we are not laboring to antidote the physiological effect of morphine but of abstinence from it." Use of these drugs "illus-

trates again that patients from whom morphine is taken get well in spite of the treatment." As far as why these treatments were considered successful for so long in spite of the extreme distress they caused patients, Kolb and Himmelsbach noted, "the knock-out feature of these treatments . . . doubtless had the effect of holding until cured many patients who would have discontinued a withdrawal treatment before being cured, and the psychological effect of doing something for patients practically all the time has a tendency, by allaying apprehension, to hold them even though what is done is harmful." To give some idea of the potential harmfulness of these treatments, the authors noted that in 1 year in a hospital where 130 patients were given the hyoscine treatment, there were six deaths.

Peptization and Water Balance Treatments

Bancroft et al. believed that "protein colloids of the nervous system are coagulated by the morphine in chronic morphinism and these colloids may be dispersed again by a peptizing agent, the best of which . . . is sodium thiocyanate. . . . Upon withdrawal morphine leaves the tissues slowly and peptization takes place gradually, . . . more water is bound, giving rise to excitement which is manifested by withdrawal symptoms" (34). Kolb and Himmelsbach conclude that if Bancroft "had used controls, he would have found that those receiving sodium thiocyanate suffered more than the controls." In this form of treatment, patients often became "wildly delerious and psychotic," with the psychosis lasting as long as 2 months.

Bromide Sleep Treatment

Bromide sleep treatment—consisting of 120 grains of sodium bromide every 2 hours with the patient ultimately being revived by use of oxygen, strychnine, etc.—was also used to treat narcotic withdrawal. To illustrate its danger, Kolb and Himmelsbach noted that one patient, for example, lost 18½ pounds in 20 days and that in 10 patients so treated there were two deaths. In spite of these risks and deaths, its proponents continued to advocate its use "in well selected cases."

Lipoid Treatments

Inasmuch as opium was noted to act on the nervous tissues and because these tissues contain lipoids, withdrawal treatments were devised to remedy what was seen as a lack of adequate lipoids in the nervous system produced by chronic use of narcotics. The most famous of these treatments was called Narcosan, a solution of lipoids together with protein and water-soluble vitamins. It was claimed that patients who took it "would soon become normal and develop a contempt for the opiates which was most pronounced" (34). Although greeted enthusiastically at the time, it was later found to be not only useless but in fact to increase the severity of withdrawal symptoms and to be "positively dangerous to life."

Endocrine Treatments

A variety of endocrine systems were implicated at one time or another as being the primary cause of narcotic withdrawal. As a result, various hormone treatments were attempted, including thyroid hormone, epinephrine, and ovarian extracts. The most famous endocrine treatment was put forth by Sakel, the developer of insulin shock therapy, who felt the "withdrawal symptoms are caused by oversaturation of the nerves with epinephrine and a disturbance in the equilibrium of the vegatative nervous system. Insulin . . . eliminates signs of abstinence by reestablishing the equilibrium . . . " (34). The insulin was given for 6 to 8 days in doses of up to 80 units in 24 hours. Unlike his use of insulin in schizophrenia, he did not attempt to bring about insulin shock. In later controlled studies it was found that insulin had little or no effect on withdrawal symptoms.

Immunity Treatments

A number of authors tried to explain tolerance and withdrawal along the general theory that morphine acted as an antigen leading to antibody production and later withdrawal symptoms when the morphine was withdrawn. There were two principle immunity treatments used in narcotic withdrawal. The first was Modinos' autogenous serum therapy. He produced artificial blisters and after 12 to 14 hours withdrew serum from these blisters and injected it under the skin of the addicts. A different approach, based on the theory of immunity, was autohemotherapy, injection of blood previously drawn from the patient. Both treatments eventually were

shown to be worthless in treating narcotic addicts, but at least they had the advantage compared to the earlier approaches of only increasing discomfort and not significantly increasing the dangers of withdrawal.

Kolb and Himmelsbach noted (34):

We have found this psychological factor to be very important in the treatment of drug addicts. Any form of treatment, even though it increases the severity of the objective symptoms as so many treatments do, gives the patients a subjective sense of relief through allaying the fear so many of them have that nothing will be done for them. Intensely apprehensive patients complain bitterly about any kind of withdrawal if it is started as soon as they enter the hospital, while the same type of patients, if stabilized on morphine for a few days until they can get used to the environment and find that some interest is being taken in them, may be taken off the drug without exhibition of fear and without showing undue subjective phenomenon. We have not found it necessary, however, to subject a suffering patient to the added discomfort of several blisters in order to ease his mind.

Abrupt and Rapid Withdrawal Methods

After reviewing these various treatments, Kolb and Himmelsbach concluded that the best treatment methods that produced the least discomfort and the best results were either abrupt or rapid withdrawal of the narcotic. Abrupt withdrawal consisting of withdrawing the narcotic in 24 to 36 hours was used in individuals who were in good physical health and seemed to have very mild habits. The majority of patients were given rapid withdrawal that consisted of gradually decreasing doses of codeine and morphine in 4 to 10 days. A typical schedule was 15 mg of morphine four times a day for 2 days, then 7.5 mg of morphine were substituted for two of the daily doses for 1 day then for all the doses the next 2 days. Next codeine, 60 mg, was substituted for two of the morphine doses and then for all the doses, and then it was reduced to 30 mg per dose. The final step was gradually substituting thiamine for the codeine until the patient was getting four shots of thiamine a day; then all shots were stopped. Abrupt withdrawal for addicts with strong habits, they felt, was "cruel, dangerous and unnecessary. Such treatment is often given in prisons and sometimes in hospitals because of the feeling that the addict does not deserve anything better. This, of course, goes along with the generally hostile attitude toward the addict that is bad psychologically and lays the ground work for relapse." Along with the rapid withdrawal, patients were given warm baths for restlessness, bismuth subcarbonate for diarrhea, and paraldehyde or sodium bromide for trouble sleeping.

The major contribution of Kolb and Himmelsbach was not so much in discounting the previous theories and therapies of withdrawal, but in objectively studying withdrawal, its course under controlled conditions, and laying out the symptoms in such a way that future treatments could be objectively evaluated. Too many of the previous so-called treatments for narcotic withdrawal were based on faulty observations of the course of withdrawal and what was to be expected during that period of time.

The "rapid withdrawal" method using morphine and codeine remained in use well into the 1950's, being gradually superceded by methadone substitution and withdrawal (43).

TREATMENT FROM 1940 TO 1970

Convulsive Therapy

A variety of methods that involve shock therapy have been used to treat the narcotic withdrawal syndrome. These include Metrazol (3), 70 per cent carbon dioxide inhalation (3), insulin-induced hypoglycemia (61), and electroconvulsive therapy (ECT). ECT was reported on as early as 1946 (32), but, after a series of 35 patients described by Thigpen et al. in 1953 (60), there were no more reports for more than 10 years. This was in spite of the fact that these authors claimed the narcotic withdrawal syndrome was totally suppressed by the use of ECT. In 1964 (33) an additional paper on ECT appeared describing only one case but again stating that narcotic withdrawal symptoms were totally suppressed. The author stated (33) that ECT was better than the methadone withdrawal method because of the latter's "length, its inability to entirely suppress withdrawal syndrome and often the failure of the patient to complete the treatment because of the discomfort he suffers." The confusion caused by ECT treatment was seen as desirable, and one of its best features was that the patient was sufficiently confused from the potent

effects on the brain so as not to leave prematurely. It was suggested that ECT may work by producing a temporary functional frontal lobectomy that prevented the autonomic hyperactivity that characterizes narcotic withdrawal.

Hibernation Therapy

Newman and Berris in 1941 (41) reported on treatment of three addicts with "artificial hibernation." The treatment consisted of 30 to 72 hours of narcosis produced by sodium pentothal supplemented with rectal or stomach instillations of paraldehyde. The patients' body temperatures were maintained at 85° to 88° F. During the hibernation state, the patients displayed "tremors and restlessness"; they then "awaken with sore muscles, diarrhea, abdominal cramps and nervousness, but well satisfied not to have to continue the drug."

Methadone

The most common method of treating the withdrawal syndrome of opiate addiction is to substitute methadone, a synthetic narcotic developed by the Germans during World War II, for the opiate in question and then gradually withdraw the methadone over 5 to 12 days, the length depending on a variety of factors discussed later. This technique has been known in this country since the work of Isbell and Vogel in 1948 (30). With the possible exception of one or more of the experimental approaches discussed at the end of this chapter, it is the most effective, safest, and most humane of the methods described in this chapter. Methadone is orally effective and long acting. Because of cross-tolerance, it can substitute for any other narcotic. Its own withdrawal pattern is less intense but longer lasting than drugs like heroin or morphine. After the patient is stabilized on methadone for a few days, it apparently becomes the drug the body is dependent upon rather than the original narcotic. At the end of the gradual tapering period, the patient, in essence, is experiencing the tail end of methadone withdrawal, a much less painful and intense experience than heroin or morphine withdrawal. The methadone withdrawal period has been described as similar to "a mild case of the flu," although many patients describe much less discomfort than this.

Phenothiazines

It is not surprising, given the earlier history of trying practically everything, that as soon as the phenothiazine drugs became available for treatment of various psychiatric disorders, they began to be used in the treatment of narcotic withdrawal as well. It is also not surprising that, just like all the treatments described by Kolb and Himmelsbach, this too was first found to be remarkably effective and only later to be not of much use. The first authors, Friedgood and Ripstein (15), to use chlorpromazine for narcotic withdrawal reported that it effectively relieved these symptoms and hypothesized that it was due to a "lobotomylike effect in that patients are relaxed, emotionally indifferent, quiet and immobile." In reviewing the paper it turns out that the patients slept for most of the first 72 hours because they received 100 mg chlorpromazine intramuscularly every 4 hours during that time. Because this is the peak of withdrawal, it is not surprising that it was felt that the drug relieved withdrawal symptoms. A later study by Fraser and Isbell (13) concluded that chlorpromazine was not of significant help in narcotic withdrawal and that reserpine aggravated the withdrawal syndrome.

This did not prevent others from trying the new phenothiazines as they came along and being enthusiastic about the findings. For example, Rolo (52) described giving promazine to 45 patients and stated that "withdrawal was effected easily and without major complications in all cases. All patients seemed relatively comfortable and were accessible to psychotherapy during the withdrawal period. . . . " Because of this enthusiasm about phenothiazines, many hospitals today that do not wish to use narcotics in withdrawal use members of this family. Major side effects that have occurred tend to be the drowsiness and fatigue induced in the patients at the high doses necessary to suppress withdrawal symptoms and the observation that often the withdrawal symptoms are not so much suppressed as is the patient's ability or lack of interest in complaining about them. In Rolo's series, 37 of the 45 patients had their narcotic stopped abruptly and the promazine substituted, and in eight cases the narcotics were gradually withdrawn simultaneously with the giving of the phenothiazine. The former is the most common way to use these agents in withdrawal.

Diphenoxylate

In an attempt to find a withdrawal agent that is as safe and effective as methadone and yet has less addictive potential, other drugs continue to be tried for detoxification. One of these is diphenoxylate, a mild narcotic principally used in combination with atropine (Lomotil) as a treatment for diarrhea. In this form it is unsuitable for injection and will "greatly diminish the intensity of the autonomous symptoms, but seemed to do little to reduce the mental symptoms of the withdrawal phase, such as fears, anxiety, tension, etc. We, therefore, combined Lomotil with Chlormethiazole—a sedative-hypnotic . . . " (17, 18). Another author (24) who used diphenoxylate recommended it may at times be necessary to combine it with a barbiturate—obviously a risky practice in an addict.

CLINICAL DESCRIPTION

FACTORS INFLUENCING SYMPTOM SEVERITY

The nature and severity of withdrawal symptoms that appear when opiate-type drugs are abruptly halted are related to a variety of factors that include the following:

1. **Which Narcotic Drug the Person Is Dependent upon.** In general, the longer the duration of the drug, the less intense but longer lasting the withdrawal symptoms. Thus, the short acting drug heroin has a more intense but shorter withdrawal period than the long acting drug methadone.

2. **Total Daily Amount Usually Taken.** In general with any given narcotic, the larger the daily dose, the more severe the withdrawal from that particular narcotic.

3. **Duration of Use.** This holds only up to a certain point. In general, once the individual has been taking narcotics for 2 to 3 months, there is not a great difference in severity for periods beyond that.

4. **General Physical Health of the Patient.** The more weakened the patient is by his physical illnesses, the less able he or she is to tolerate the stress of withdrawal and the more severe the symptoms will seem.

5. **Psychological Factors.** The personality of the patient, his state of mind at the time of

withdrawal, the setting in which withdrawal takes place, his expectations as to the severity of the symptoms, and the possibility of obtaining relief for them all have a marked effect on the severity of withdrawal, and the cumulative effect of these factors can be as great as any of the pharmacological factors noted above. Experienced clinicians have long noted that, other factors being approximately equal, the greater the expectation of the patient that suffering will be relieved by available medication, the more severe the withdrawal symptoms. If an individual is in a setting where there is little hope of obtaining any relief from the symptoms, and if the patient is aware of this, there seems to be a marked decrease in the intensity of the pain experienced. Settings such as certain therapeutic communities where patients are expected to kick the habit without medication and where the magnitude of the individual's habit and severity of symptoms tend to be down-played by other residents and staff, all of whom have gone through it themselves, tend to lead to a situation with minimal overt withdrawal symptoms. As one article points out (2), the withdrawal syndrome can be divided into

"purposive symptoms" which are goal-oriented, highly dependent on the observer and environment, and directed at getting more drugs; and "non-purposive symptoms" which are not goal-oriented, are relatively independent of the observer, and of the patient's will and the environment. The purposive phenomena, including complaints, pleas, demands and manipulations, and symptom mimicking are as varied as the psychodynamics, psychopathology and imagination of the drug dependent person. In a hospital setting, these phenomena are considerably less pronounced when the patient becomes aware that this behavior will not affect the decision to give him a drug.

SIGNS AND SYMPTOMS OF OPIATE WITHDRAWAL

Grade 0

Drug craving
Anxiety
Drug-seeking behavior

Grade 1

Yawning
Perspiration

Lacrimation
Rhinorrhea
"Yen" (restless, broken sleep)

Grade 2

Mydriasis (with progressive decreased reaction to light; at peak of withdrawal, pupils are dilated and fixed)
Gooseflesh (piloerection)—from whence comes the term kicking "cold turkey"
Muscle twitches—from whence comes the term "kicking" the habit
Hot and cold flashes and chills
Aching bones and muscles
Anorexia
Irritability

Grade 3

Insomnia
Fever (usually low grade, less than 100°)
Increased respiratory rate
Increased pulse rate
Increased blood pressure
Restlessness
Abdominal cramps
Nausea
Vomiting
Diarrhea
Weakness
Weight loss

The grades as outlined above are to some extent arbitrary, and not all signs are necessary to diagnose each grade. Individually, signs overlap the grades to some degree. The grading system is used simply for clinical convenience, with mydriasis and gooseflesh perhaps the most objective to evaluate. An untreated addict in withdrawal may be noted to lie in the fetal position (to ease the abdominal cramps) and to be covered with a blanket even on warm days (because of the hot and cold flashes and chills).

The meperidine withdrawal pattern (Table 24.1) is one in which "craving may be intense but the non-purposive autonomic signs, while present, are not so prominent; the pupils may not be widely dilated and there is usually little nausea, vomiting or diarrhea. However, at peak intensity the muscle twitching, restlessness, and nervousness are worse than during morphine withdrawal" (31).

Table 24.1
Usual Frequency of Use in Established Habits and First Appearance of Withdrawal

Drug	Usual Frequency of Use	Appearance of Nonpurposive Withdrawal Symptoms	Peak
Meperidine	2–3 hours	4–6 hours	8–12 hours
Dilaudid	3 hours	4–5 hours	
Heroin	4 hours	8–12 hours	48–72 hours
Morphine	5–6 hours	14–20 hours	
Codeine	3 hours	24 hours	
Methadone	8–12 hours	36–72 hours	72–96 hours

	Majority of symptoms over
Heroin	5–10 days
Methadone	14–21 days

THE PROTRACTED ABSTINENCE SYNDROME

In 1963, Martin et al. (37) noted that in rats the morphine abstinence syndrome was biphasic, with the second phase persisting for 6 months or more after withdrawal. These findings suggested that morphine dependence could bring about changes in the central nervous system that persisted for months after withdrawal and could give rise to altered physiological functioning and drug-seeking behavior. In additional studies, Martin and Jasinski (36) looked at the relevance of these observations in humans. Their findings were as follows. During the initial withdrawal phase and lasting up until the tenth week after complete withdrawal, there were increases in systolic and diastolic blood pressure, pulse rate, pupillary diameter, temperature, and respiratory rate. The respiratory rate remained slightly elevated for 7 weeks, but the respiratory center was hyposensitive to CO_2 from the eleventh through the thirtieth week of abstinence. During the initial withdrawal period there was a marked decrease of caloric intake and a fall in body weight. At 5 weeks postwithdrawal, body weight had returned to the preaddiction level, but caloric intake, although increasing, did not return to the level of the preaddiction state. Between the sixth and ninth week, the systolic and diastolic blood pressure, body temperature, and pulse rate were below mean preaddiction values. Pupillary diameter, which had been greater than the control value, became significantly less than this value. Urinary excretion of epinephrine was elevated above the level of the preaddiction stage for at least 17 weeks postmorphine withdrawal. The clinical significance of these persisting changes and their relationship to drug craving and to narcotic relapse is still not known, although more than 10 years have passed since Martin and Jasinski published their findings.

Behavioral manifestations that accompany the above findings may include weakness, irritability, decreased stress tolerance, anxiety, and increased tiredness. The magnitude of these symptoms is usually not great, and they often go unmentioned unless specifically asked about.

EVALUATION AND DIAGNOSIS

The Interview

Drug History. A review of current and past drug and alcohol use/abuse is a prerequisite to any evaluative effort for these patients. For each current substance or group of substances, the following information should be obtained:

Name of drug used
Length of time used
Frequency of use
Date or time of last use
Route
Amount
Cost
Purpose (to get high, relieve depression, relieve boredom, to sleep, for energy, etc.)
For drugs previously used:
Name
Age started
Length of time used
Adverse effects
Previous treatment experiences: where, what kind, outcome

Prescription drugs currently used: name, reason for use, amount, frequency and duration of use, last dose

Other Medical History. This includes serious illnesses, accidents, hospitalizations.

Existence of Current Symptoms in the Various Body Systems. It is important to look for both illnesses that may complicate withdrawal and those that the addict may have ignored getting treatment for because of his chaotic life style.

In obtaining the above information, especially the drug history, it is important to maintain a nonjudgmental attitude and not by words or facial expression indicate disdain toward the individual and his habits. Such behavior is likely to create on-going difficulties in the relationship, complicate the detoxification process, produce false information, and even lead to the driving away of the patient.

Social Functioning. Material should be elicited on the following: (a) living arrangements (alone, with family, etc.); (b) marital status; (c) sexual orientation and functioning; (d) employment and/or educational status; (e) family members' (parents, siblings, spouse, other key members) occupation, education, psychological state, history of drug or alcohol problems; (f) friends (particularly, are there non-drug-using ones); (g) recreational and leisure time activities; (h) current and past legal status.

The interviewer should try to get a feel of the emotional as well as factual aspects of the above areas, e.g., the patient's attitude toward his job as well as the type of job, the quality of his marital or family relations as well as the type. How does he cope with spare time nights and weekends when relapse is most likely to occur. Such gentle questioning should reveal the nature and degree of the patient's social supports and aid in planning for postdetoxification treatment. Prior attempts at withdrawal and what was associated with relapse should be especially explored.

Psychological Status. Psychological evaluation has a number of purposes. When carried out by a nonpsychiatrist, it may single out patients who need early psychiatric referral around the possibility of psychosis, organic brain syndrome, serious depression, suicide, or being violence prone. The psychiatrist, in addition to evaluating the above

factors that could complicate withdrawal, can look for conditions for which special treatments exist, e.g., lithium for mania. It is helpful to try to ascertain whether detectable psychiatric conditions predate or postdate the drug abuse. Certain patients take drugs on a self-medicating basis to try to cope with dysphoric states of loneliness, depression, or anxiety or to control unacceptable aggressive or sexual drives. Conversely, continued use of certain drugs may lead to or exaggerate psychiatric states not evident before (69). It should be kept in mind that opiates seem to have an ameliorating effect on psychosis, and, in such patients, withdrawal can lead to exacerbation or sudden appearance of psychotic symptoms (9, 20).

As part of evaluating the psychological state, a mental status review should be carried out to include orientation for place, person, and date; presence or absence of hallucinations, delusions, or suicidal ideation; memory; intelligence, mood, and affect; thought processes; preoccupations and behavior during interview; judgment; insight.

The Physical Examination

Although there is no special physical examination for narcotic addicts, it is useful to keep in mind certain conditions that can be either direct or indirect sequelae of drug abuse. Although many of them can be found in nonaddicts and many addicts may have few or none of them, their presence helps in the diagnostic process.

Cutaneous Signs. These may be directly or indirectly associated with drug abuse.

1. Needle puncture marks—usually found over veins especially in the antecubital area, dorsum of the hands, and forearms but can be found anywhere on the body where a vein is reachable, including the neck, tongue, and dorsal vein of the penis.

2. "Tracks"—one of the most common and readily recognizable signs of chronic injectable drug abuse. They are scars located along veins and are usually hyperpigmented and linear. They result both from frequent unsterile injections and from the deposit of carbon black from attempts to sterilize the needle with a match. Tracks tend to lighten over time but may never totally disappear.

3. Tatoos—because "tracks" are a such well known indication of drug abuse, addicts may try to hide them by having a tatoo over

the area. Tatoos not over veins are also not uncommon among certain groups of drug abusers.

4. Hand edema—when addicts run out of antecubital and forearm veins they often turn to finger and dorsum of the hand veins, which can then lead to hand edema. Such edema can persist for months.

5. Thrombophlebitis—commonly found in addicts on arms and legs both because of the unsterile nature of the injections and the irritating quality of some of the adulterants used with the active drug.

6. Abscesses and ulcers—particularly common among individuals who inject barbiturates because of the irritating quality of these chemicals. These abscesses are often secondary to narcotic injection and are more likely to be septic and around veins.

7. Ulceration or perforation of the nasal septum—frequent inhalation, "snorting," of heroin can lead to ulceration of the septum whereas similar chronic use of cocaine can cause perforation secondary to the vasoconstriction and loss of blood supply.

8. Cigarette burns or scars from old burns—can occur due to drug-induced drowsiness. Fresh burns are usually seen between the fingers, and old scars are often seen on the chest as a result of the cigarette falling out of the user's mouth. It has been estimated that over 90 per cent of addicts and alcoholics smoke.

9. Piloerection ("gooseflesh")—an opiate withdrawal sign, usually found on the arms and trunk.

10. Cheiloses (cracking of skin at corners of mouth)—especially seen in chronic amphetamine users and in opiate addicts prior to or during detoxification.

11. Contact dermatitis—in solvent abusers, seen around the nose, mouth, and hands and sometimes called "glue-sniffer's rash." In other abusers it may occur around areas of injection secondary to use of chemicals to cleanse the skin.

12. Jaundice—due to hepatitis in these patients usually secondary to use of unsterilized shared needles and syringes.

Medical Complications Associated with Drug Abuse.

1. Cardiovascular—endocarditis, myocarditis, cardiac arrhythmias, thrombophlebitis, arteritis, necrotizing angiitis, hypertension and hypotension.

2. Pulmonary—multiple microinfarcts, chronic pulmonary fibrosis, foreign body granulomas, pulmonary edema, bacterial pneumonia, aspiration pneumonia, tuberculosis.

3. Hepatic—serum hepatitis, cirrhosis.

4. Reproductive system—menstrual irregularities.

5. Neurological—seizures, usually grand mal but can also have focal seizures and status epilepticus; acute delerium; blindness; acute transverse myelitis; peripheral nerve lesions; acute rhabdomyolysis; chronic fibrosing myopathies; bacterial meningitis; central nervous system, abscess; tetanus.

6. Hematopoietic—bacteremia; bone marrow depression, rarely aplastic anemia.

7. Genitourinary—nephrotic syndrome.

8. Skeletal—septic arthritis, osteomyelitis.

9. Gastrointestinal—chronic constipation or diarrhea, Pancreatitis.

Laboratory Tests.

1. Urine screen for drugs, including narcotics, barbiturates, amphetamine, cocaine, benzodiazapines, tricyclic antidepressants, and phencyclidine (PCP).

2. Complete blood count and differential—leukocytosis is common and white blood cell counts above 14,000 are not unusual

3. Urinalysis

4. Liver function profile (e.g., SMA 12/60)

5. Chest x-ray if not done in past year

6. Electrocardiogram in patients over 40.

7. Australian antigen

8. Venereal Disease Research Laboratory Test

9. Pregnancy test

10. Pap smear

11. Tuberculin skin test

12. Any other test suggested by the history or physical examination, e.g., failure to take in adequate food and fluids plus vomiting, sweating, and diarrhea can lead to weight loss, dehydration, ketosis, and disturbed acid-base balance.

Specific Diagnosis of Opiate Dependence Requiring Treatment for Withdrawal. The information gathered above during the interview, physical examination, and laboratory tests does not usually *prove* the diagnosis of narcotic dependence sufficient to need withdrawal treatment *unless* one has found present the actual signs and symptoms of opiate withdrawal. The *history* of drug taking, regardless of the description of its length, amount, and recent use, is not always reliable and could be altered either by exaggeration to increase the amount of narcotic obtained during withdrawal or by minimizing to conceal a habit, as is often done by physician and nurse addicts. It may be wrong even when the patient is trying to be honest because of the variable nature of illicitly obtained drugs. *Physical* signs such as tracks tell of past drug use, not necessarily current use. Even fresh needle marks say nothing about the frequency, nature, or amount of what was injected. *Urine* findings of drugs testify to recent use but not necessarily to a duration long enough to require detoxification. Heroin, which is found as morphine in the urine, can be detected up to about 48 hours after last use, whereas quinine, a common dilutant, can last up to a week or more.

If definitive evidence of physical dependence is needed, there are only two methods by which to obtain it—wait until the patient develops withdrawal signs and symptoms or do a Naloxone Provocative Test. It has been shown in humans that parenteral naloxone (Narcan) can distinguish opiate abusers from nonabusers and that the severity of withdrawal is related to the dose of naloxone. One way of doing the test is to inject 0.2 mg of naloxone to be followed by 0.4 mg in 30 to 60 minutes if the results are inconclusive from the smaller dose. Because the validity of the test can be affected if the patient feigns withdrawal or is only minimally tolerant, one author recommends using a placebo (5), and another group has worked out a method that enables quantification of the precipitated withdrawal syndrome (70). This latter paper found that hand tremor, trapezius electromyogram, and heart rate were the most sensitive signs of withdrawal and could be used in combination to form an assessment test. Because of the possibility of fetal injury or induced abortion, the naloxone test should not be done if the patient is pregnant.

Program philosophy, whether the program is inpatient or outpatient, and availability of trained medical personnel will determine whether programs will prefer to wait for withdrawal signs and symptoms to develop, use a naloxone challenge, or use the combined evidence of the history, physical, and urine screen, as interpreted by experienced personnel, to form a presumptive diagnosis.

If the latter method is chosen, as is probably more often the case today, the program should still be prepared in questionable situations to use one of the first two approaches.

At the conclusion of the data-gathering process used for evaluation, the clinician needs to make decisions on the following: the presence of narcotic abuse sufficient to require detoxification; where such detoxification should take place (if there are choices available in a community; often, only one of the three possible environments is available); the initial starting dose; the presence of concurrent physical illness or emotional problems that may require separate treatment during withdrawal or a modification of the withdrawal method or even the choice of method. When there are serious physical or emotional problems present, one may choose to delay withdrawal by temporarily maintaining the individual on methadone, attending to the specific problem, and then beginning withdrawal once some stability has been achieved in the other areas. Even with gradual methadone withdrawal, the process of detoxification produces mental and physical stress, and the organism at any given moment may not be able to tolerate additional stress.

TECHNIQUE OF WITHDRAWAL

CHOICE OF AN AGENT

Excluding some of the newer withdrawal approaches discussed later in the chapter, the best method of withdrawal currently is that of methadone substitution and withdrawal. Methadone is a long acting, orally effective, synthetic narcotic. The cross-tolerance and cross-dependence between the various synthetic and natural narcotics mean that in theory one could use any of them to prevent withdrawal and gradually detoxify any individual dependent on any of the others. In such a situation the choice of agent is related to the following factors:

1. Orally Effective. To avoid continuing an individual on his "needle habit" and avoid the risks associated with injection, it is preferable to have an orally effective agent.

2. Long Acting. A general pharmacological principle is that narcotics with shorter durations of action tend to have shorter but more intense withdrawal patterns, whereas longer acting drugs have withdrawal syndromes that are milder but last longer. A longer acting agent also needs to be given less often and can produce a smoother withdrawal with fewer ups and downs.

3. Safety. Although narcotic withdrawal can be painful when unaided, it is usually not dangerous unless the individual has other medical problems. The withdrawal technique or agent should not present undue safety risks.

4. Addictive Potential. In general, a more addictive drug should not be used to detoxify a patient from a less addicting one. In practice this means that methadone can be used to withdraw from narcotics such as heroin, morphine, Dilaudid, and meperidine but should be avoided for drugs such as propoxyphene (Darvon) or pentazocine (Talwin). Withdrawal from these drugs is best handled by gradual decrements in dosage of the agent dependent upon. Codeine and oxycodanone (Percodan) are in between these two groups, and clinicians differ as to whether to use methadone or the other drugs themselves during their withdrawal. Methadone, however, is the only narcotic drug approved by the Food and Drug Administration (FDA) for use in opiate withdrawal.

WHERE SHOULD DETOXIFICATION TAKE PLACE?

Currently detoxification occurs in outpatient, residential, and inpatient settings. There are advantages and disadvantages to each of these, and no one approach will be suitable for either all narcotic addicts or even the same addict at different stages of his drug-using career. Outpatient detoxification is clearly the cheapest approach but also the most problemmatic. Craving, as we understand it today, increases with the perceived psychological availability of the drug. In outpatient detoxification, almost independent of the method used, there is bound to be some degree of discomfort, no matter how slight. In an inpatient or residential program, such discomfort would be passed off without great to-do. On an outpatient basis, it can be the source for additional withdrawal phenomena that lead to even more symptoms, because the individual knows that he can obtain drugs without too much trouble and that the drugs would take away the discomfort. Outpatient detoxification is more likely to be successful, therefore, in the context of social support that

helps the addict deal with the craving as well as in those individuals that have very strong reasons for needing to withdraw. Otherwise it is very much a revolving door. It should also be mentioned that under federal rules, methadone for detoxification is not permitted to be taken out. Such programs must, therefore, be open 7 days a week.

Residential detoxification is a relatively new program and involves the client being off the street but not in an inpatient hospital unit. Residential detoxification may take place in therapeutic communities or in special residential centers set up for detoxification. Staffing is usually paraprofessional with some medical coverage, usually limited to a physician making rounds once or twice a day and being on call, and a nurse being present at least during the day and usually during the evening and night shifts as well. Staff are trained to deal with the usual physiological and psychological symptoms of detoxification, and it is possible to give medication. The staff are also trained to be alert to symptoms suggesting serious complications that would require that the person be transferred to a hospital. Because of the decreased medical input and the lack of the facilities available in hospitals, the cost is much cheaper than a hospital slot although more expensive than an outpatient program. It could be suitable for addicts who are addicted only to narcotics, who are not polydrug users, and who have no serious medical or psychiatric illness.

Inpatient detoxification is the most expensive approach, and there are no good studies that indicate its results surpass the other two loci. This may reflect the way it is carried out rather than the lack of inherent advantages. Too often, inpatient detoxification occurs in a setting devoid of sophisticated psychiatric input where there are too many patients and too few staff—such as in state psychiatric hospitals—or else it takes place in general hospital medical units where there is a total lack of emphasis on the psychosocial aspects of rehabilitation and almost exclusive focus on the medical problems. In either of these settings it would not be surprising if success rates are no better than the outpatient approach. It is possible, however, to develop inpatient detoxification programs that combine psychiatric input, a psychosocial framework, and good medical care, and there are some of these units scattered across the country. In general, however, because of the cost, inpatient detoxification should be reserved for sedative-hypnotic detoxification; narcotic addicts whose problems are compounded by serious polydrug abuse, concurrent medical illness, or serious psychiatric problems; and detoxification from alcohol or similar drugs in methadone-maintained patients.

INITIATION OF DETOXIFICATION

If the patient is receiving narcotics for medical purposes and the physician is reasonably sure about the amount the patient is taking, Table 24.2 can be used to convert the dose into milligrams of methadone.

In the situation of illicit drug use, it is less likely that the patient will be able to give an accurate picture of the amount used because, even with the best of intentions and lack of any desire to deceive, the amount of narcotics in an illegal "bag" varies from dealer to dealer and week to week, if not day to day. Under these circumstances, the physician must guess at the initial dose. Usually 10 to 20 mg of oral methadone are a sufficient starting dose. This dose is large enough to control the majority of illicit habits and small enough not to be very dangerous, unless the individual has little or no tolerance. The patient should be kept under observation so as to judge the effect of the dose. If withdrawal symptoms are present initially, the dose should suppress them within 30 to 60 minutes. If not, an additional 5 to 10 mg of methadone can be given. If withdrawal symptoms are not present, the patient should be observed for drowsiness or depressed respiration. Except in those cases referred to earlier where there is documented evidence of

Table 24.2
Drug Relationships for Withdrawal

Methadone—1 mg is equivalent to:	
Heroin	1–2 mg
Morphine	3–4 mg
Dilaudid	½ mg
Codeine	30 mg
Meperidine	20 mg
Paregoric	7–8 ml
Laudanum	3 ml
Dromoran	1 mg
Levo-dromoran	½ mg
Pantopon	4 mg
Leritive	8 mg

use of narcotics in excess of 40 mg of methadone equivalent a day, the initial dose should never exceed 30 mg and the total 24-hour dose should never exceed 40 mg. Where 10 to 20 mg were given as the first dose, a similar amount may be given 12 hours later if deemed necessary. This is usually not practical in outpatient detoxification but is not uncommon in inpatient or residential settings.

There is disagreement as to whether to start the withdrawal regime without the actual presence of withdrawal signs and symptoms. As noted in the section on diagnosis, it is usually difficult to know with certainty that an individual is currently physically addicted. With the exception of either waiting for symptoms to develop or doing a Naloxone Provocative Test, all other indicators point to use rather than tolerance and addiction. In order to prevent nonaddicts from being given narcotics, some clinicians insist on the presence of symptoms, either naturally occurring or precipitated. A good case for the opposite position has been made by Newman (42):

Generally, however, there is no need to go to such lengths if the history is credible and consistent with the findings on physical examination . . . certainly, there is no justification for insisting on observing objective signs of withdrawal as a prerequisite to admission. The withdrawal syndrome, after all, is what the treatment regime is designed to *prevent.* Heroic measures to preclude admission of an application who is not physiologically dependent imply that there is an incentive for nonaddicts to seek such admission. There is no evidence to suggest that this is the case, and intuitively the possibility seems remote indeed. . . . The notion that non-addicts would submit to the comprehensive intake evaluation (interview, medical history, physical examination, and laboratory testing) which is part of any approved program, merely in order to obtain "free" methadone for a few weeks, is highly implausible. . . .

LENGTH OF WITHDRAWAL

The total dose necessary to stabilize the patient for the first 24 hours should be repeated on day 2 either in one dose (for outpatients) or two (for inpatients), and corrections should be made up or down if the dose either excessively sedates the patient or fails to sufficiently suppress the abstinence syndrome. After the patient is stabilized, the dose can then be gradually withdrawn. One common pattern is to decrease by 5 mg per day. A second is to decrease by 5 mg a day until a dose of 10 to 15 mg is reached and then decrease more slowly.

Typical daily patterns may then look like this:

Day   1 2 3 4 5 678
30–30–25–20–15–10–5–0

Day   1 2 3 4 5 6 7 8 9 10 11
30–30–25–20–15–12–10–8–5– 3– 0

In general, inpatient residential withdrawal takes place over 5 to 10 days, and outpatient withdrawal may be stretched out longer in order to minimize any symptoms. (Withdrawal from methadone maintenance is a separate issue and is discussed in Chapter 29.) The role of the patient in helping to regulate the duration and speed of his withdrawal should continue to be explored. However, methadone cannot be given for longer than 21 days and still be considered detoxification. Under FDA regulations, beyond 21 days is considered maintenance, and a unit would need to have appropriate governmental approval for such a program.

USE OF OTHER DRUGS AND SUPPORTIVE MEASURES

Even with gradual withdrawal all symptoms may not be totally suppressed; after withdrawal is completed certain symptoms may persist, albeit in a rather mild form (4). There is no consensus as to the use of other drugs during these periods. The American Medical Association Council on Mental Health (2) noted: "the use of tranquilizers and/or bedtime sedation can help allay the patient's anxiety and minimize his craving for morphine-like drugs. . . . " On the other hand, Dole (10) has asserted that "non-narcotic medications are ineffective in relieving the specific symptoms of narcotics abstinence. They add stupor and depression but do not bring restful sleep. If insomnia and other withdrawal symptoms are unusually severe, especially in older patients, relief can be provided by an increment in the next dose of methadone and, therefore, a slower withdrawal schedule."

Dufficy (12) tried a variety of drugs in combination with methadone-aided with-

drawal and noted that "chlorpromazine, for example, caused our patients to complain of feeling 'spaced out' and did not relieve their severe depression, cramps, nausea and fear. On the other hand, doxepin proved extremely effective . . . and made our patients less restless and more amenable to group therapy."

Insomnia is one of the more debilitating withdrawal symptoms, inasmuch as it is not only difficult to tolerate in and of itself, but it also weakens the addict's ability to deal with other withdrawal problems. There is general agreement that barbiturates, because of their addicting nature, should not be used to treat this. Drugs that have been advocated included chloral hydrate, flurazepam, diphenhydramine, and such tricyclic antidepressants as amitriptyline and doxepin. This author has used all of them in withdrawal and, although objective comparisons are difficult as far as actual efficacy, flurazepam seemed most preferred by the patients, and its continuation was more often requested than the others. Because of its cumulative nature, it should not be continued for longer than 3 weeks.

Nonpharmaceutical supports can also play an important and useful role during the detoxification period. Most helpful is a warm, kind, and reassuring attitude of treatment staff. As noted elsewhere in the chapter, patients' involvement in their own detoxification schedule has usually been found to be of positive value and not abused. It is, therefore, not necessary most of the time to have an adversary role develop around medication dose. Staff do need to take a firm stand around visitors, however, because it is not uncommon to have them smuggle in drugs. Visitors should be limited to only immediate family (parents, spouse) who are not known to be drug abusers themselves. Even parents, though, have been known to smuggle in drugs under the pressure of entreaties from sons who claim staff do not understand their needs and distress. A watchful presence may be necessary, therefore, for all visitors. Such attempts are less likely to occur if there are family meetings and patient involvement in dose.

Other measures that have been advocated include warm baths, exercise when the patient feels up to it, and various diets. Unless there are specific deficiencies, there is no evidence of the usefulness of one or another dietary regime. However, because addicts are often malnourished, general vitamin-mineral supplements should be given.

SPECIAL PROBLEMS

Seizures

Convulsions are not characteristic of opiate-type withdrawal or intoxication with the exception of meperidine or propoxyphene intoxication when they may occur. Therefore, if a patient has a seizure, it usually signifies an undiagnosed barbiturate-sedative withdrawal or another medical condition (such as epilepsy), or they may be faked or hysterical. Because there are many instances of mixed addictions, the possibility of abuse of sedative-type drugs (including alcohol, barbiturates, and benzodiazepines) should be kept in mind when dealing with any addict. This can be quickly checked out by giving 200 mg of pentobarbital. A nontolerant individual on this dose will either be asleep in an hour or show coarse nystagmus, gross ataxia, positive Romberg's sign, and dysarthria. If these are lacking, addiction to these drugs should be presumed and correspondingly treated.

Mixed Addictions

Unrecognized sedative dependence can produce serious hazards. Not only seizures, as noted above, can occur, but in addition toxic psychosis, hyperthermia, and even death can take place. Abrupt withdrawal from stimulant-type drugs is much less of a physical hazard but can be associated with severe depression and even suicide. If sedative dependence is present, it is often useful, unless the physician is very experienced in withdrawal, to maintain the patient on methadone, withdraw the sedative gradually, and then withdraw the methadone.

Vomiting

Strong efforts should be made to give all medication by mouth. Patients sometimes resist this and purposefully vomit to get repeat medication or intramuscular doses. Observation for 30 minutes after a dose usually eliminates this. Although vomiting can be a symptom of withdrawal, some patients vomit with no relation to the degree of physical abstinence and in spite of all kinds of supporting measures, including reintoxication

with opiates. This kind of vomiting may be associated with fantasies of getting the poison out of the system. It can usually be handled by intramuscular injections of a drug such as trimethobenzamide (Tigan) or perphenazine (Compazine).

Intoxication

Intoxicated patients should be kept in low beds, permitted to smoke only when accompanied, and assisted when ambulatory to avoid injury. Because intoxication is not necessary to prevent withdrawal and complicates the safety and adequacy of care, it should be avoided if possible and a sufficient dose cut made to prevent it at the next medication period.

Repetitive Withdrawal

Most addicts have a repetitive characteristic withdrawal syndrome that they repeat each time they withdraw. Thus, one addict will focus on the gastrointestinal system, and vomiting or abdominal cramps will be a usual symptom. Another will focus on the muscular system, and aching in his bones will be typical of him each time. In general, a firm, supportive, reassuring but authoritarian approach is most successful for physicians treating withdrawal. In the absence of psychosis, phenothiazine or other tranquilizing drugs are usually unnecessary.

Other Medical Conditions

When there are concurrent medical problems present, two general principles should be kept in mind (2). The first is that acute febrile illnesses may temporarily increase opiate tolerance and the severity of withdrawal symptoms, thus requiring more methadone. The second is that withdrawal can be quite stressful to the body and, when serious medical or surgical problems are present, should be very gradual to minimize the degree of stress. The patient should be brought to the point of tolerance, kept there for several days, and then slowly withdrawn. In certain circumstances (e.g., acute myocardial infarction, renal colic, etc.), withdrawal should be postponed and the patient maintained on methadone until circumstances are stabilized enough to permit withdrawal. Patients should be evaluated carefully to see whether longer term maintenance is indicated. When withdrawal does take place, giving methadone three or four times a day instead of once or twice can also minimize discomfort.

Pregnancy

Pregnancy in a heroin addict presents the patient and her physician with the choice of which of several undesirable alternatives is the least undesirable (11). From the standpoint of the fetus, it is clear that the best circumstance would be for the woman to abstain totally from drugs, licit or illicit, during the pregnancy. This is also, unfortunately, not very likely to occur. On an outpatient drug-free regime, past experience suggests the patient will go in and out of heroin use, subjecting the fetus to periods of intoxication and withdrawal and a risk of spontaneous abortion, stillbirth, prematurity, and anomalies. The drug effects are compounded by the life style, poor prenatal care, inadequate diet and drug adulterants. Residential placement during pregnancy to ensure the drug-free status is usually totally resisted, especially if there are other children at home. Narcotic antagonists are still considered experimental and cannot be used for maintenance during pregnancy. This leaves methadone maintenance at the lowest dose possible as the least undesirable available option. The infant will be born addicted and need to be withdrawn but should otherwise not have problems if there has been adequate obstetrical care during the pregnancy.

If withdrawal from methadone maintenance does have to take place, certain considerations should be kept in mind. Withdrawal should be very slow, no greater than 5 mg reduction per week. The best time for withdrawal is during the middle trimester. During the first trimester, withdrawal may be especially deleterious to fetal development; during the third trimester, withdrawal may trigger premature labor.

RECENT AND EXPERIMENTAL APPROACHES

SELF-REGULATION OF DETOXIFICATION

In an attempt to improve the retention rate of addicts during detoxification, a number of authors have tried to involve the patients more in the process. Raynes and Patch (46)

tried self-determined versus physician-determined reduction schedules using methadone in ambulatory withdrawal. They found that twice as many of the self-regulated group completed detoxification, regardless of the initial dose level. The mean time taken for the self-regulation group was 22 days. They felt the technique created a situation of shared responsibility for detoxification, helping to overcome the barrier of addicts' problems with authority figures. The addicts in the self-regulated group stated they felt more involved with their treatment and felt less as though they were victims. Razani et al. (47) tried a similar approach in an inpatient setting. Their method allowed the addict to receive methadone on an "as needed" basis within specified guidelines. Of the 30 heroin addicts beginning the described detoxification program, 28 completed it, 22 reported their experience to be satisfactory or very satisfactory, and 26 of the subjects at least began a follow-up program. The mean length of stay in the hospital was 9 days, with all of the patients having completed withdrawal by the eighth day. The total amount of methadone used during the hospital stay was far less than would have been prescribed by the physician on the basis of the clinical history. They also required a shorter period of time to complete the detoxification than those on schedules determined solely by physicians' clinical judgment. The authors stressed, as the earlier work had done, the importance of placing the addicts in a position to create a working alliance between patient and physician to enhance their self-esteem and feeling of mastery in controlling their habit. Given the small number of patients and the fact that this was an open study, one should be careful not to generalize too extensively from it. As Senay (53) pointed out in reviewing this article:

clinical experience suggests that self-regulation is not desirable for every patient undergoing detoxification. Many prefer standard approaches, in which the patient appears to feel less anxiety with the physician in control. Thus, self-regulation is properly viewed as one possible approach to detoxification. The wise clinician will choose the approach most appropriate for each patient. In a field so dominated by stereotypical thinking, it is encouraging to see the development of flexible approaches to the difficult problem of opiate detoxification.

Stern et al. (57), in an open study of 11 heroin addicts also on an inpatient basis, found similar findings. They noted that the addicts did not abuse the program, that they used less methadone than would otherwise have been prescribed, and that staff-staff and staff-patient interaction improved markedly.

PROLONGED DETOXIFICATION

Because the outcome of short term detoxification has not been good, one approach has been to markedly lengthen the period of time during which methadone is tapered. Because under FDA regulations, giving methadone longer than 21 days converts the procedure from withdrawal into maintenance, it may be more legally correct to call these programs short term maintenance rather than extended withdrawal. From the medical point of view, however, because the dose is being gradually tapered, withdrawal is the more accurate description. Regardless of name, there is no agreement as to efficacy. Wilson et al. (67) studied three groups of 10 patients each. All the patients were tapered down to 10 mg of methadone in 10 days on either an inpatient or outpatient basis. Then with a double-blind procedure, Group 1 patients received 10 mg of methadone daily for 30 days, 5 mg daily for 30 days, and 2 mg daily for the remainder of the 90-day period; Group 2 received 5 mg daily for 30 days and 2 mg daily for the remainder of the 90 days; Group 3 received placebo throughout the program after being brought to the 10-mg dose. Only two of the 30 patients completed the 90-day study and, although there was a tendency for the first two groups to stay in treatment slightly longer than Group 3, the difference was not statistically significant and there was no real difference in the groups as far as becoming or remaining drug free.

Senay and Dorus (54) studied 21-day versus 84-day detoxification in heroin addicts. Seventy-two patients were assigned on a double-blind, random-assignment basis to either a 21-day gradual detoxification followed by 69 days of placebo or 84 days of detoxification followed by 6 days of placebo. None of the 21-day group completed the study, and their mean participation was 23 days. Four patients in the 84-day group finished, and the mean for the total group was 43 days. Withdrawal symptoms were judged to be more severe for the 21-day group, and 6.5 per cent of this group were judged to have had a favorable treatment experience compared to 22 per cent of the 84-day group. The authors conclude that "the 21 day detoxification schedule is not an effective treatment approach for helping addicts become drug-free.... A review of the current policies on detoxification is in order."

CONTINGENCY MANAGEMENT

In an attempt to improve the number of patients completing outpatient detoxification and to decrease their use of heroin during detoxification, Hall et al. (27) used a contingency management and feedback system in a random-assignment protocol. The experimental group received money for negative urines and rapid feedback as to the urine results. They found that this produced a significant decrease in illegal drug use and longer sequences of drug-free days. However, there was no significant difference in the percentage of patients dropping out of the detoxification program before completion.

PROPRANOLOL

Propranolol, a beta-adrenergic blocking agent, has been tried in the treatment of narcotic withdrawal (25, 28). It was found that patients treated with the drug required a somewhat smaller methadone dose for detoxification and that the patients who responded favorably had milder withdrawal symptoms. The over-all conclusion, however, was that "the small benefit from the drug hardly merits its consideration as an adjunct to the treatment of withdrawal from opiates" (25).

The attempt to use propranolol in narcotic withdrawal was suggested by the work of Grosz (25) who noted that propranolol given to heroin addicts abolished the euphoric effect of the narcotic as well as the compulsive craving for the opiate that followed heroin withdrawal. Although he did not feel that the drug helped in the management of the acute physical withdrawal syndrome, Hollister and Prusmack (28) decided to try it anyway because Grosz had noted that it possessed narcotic antagonist potential.

PROPOXYPHENE

Propoxyphene, a mild analgesic derived from methadone but having less addictive and analgesic potential, has been tried to relieve the symptoms of narcotic withdrawal, and particularly its napsylate form has received a good deal of attention in this regard (29, 59, 59). The napsylate form is only slightly soluble in water, whereas propoxyphene hydrochloride is very water soluble. This lowered water solubility leads to slower absorption in the gastrointestinal tract and lower peak plasma levels; therefore, it is believed to have a much lower overdose potential. Because of the similarities to methadone and because, at times, it has been difficult to use methadone in many places on an outpatient basis for withdrawal, programs have tried the propoxyphene napsylate for withdrawal. The results to date suggest that, although this drug is not as good an agent as methadone in suppressing the full spectrum of narcotic withdrawal, it can partially block the development of withdrawal symptoms with the notable exception of insomnia. Because it is addicting itself and because, especially mixed with alcohol, the addictive effects on respiratory depression can be fatal, it is important that, if the drug is used, the amounts given the patient to take by prescription are not excessive. The studies seemed to indicate that 800 to 1,000 mg a day, given in two or three divided doses, are sufficient. It should also be pointed out that this use of propoxyphene in either the hydrochloride or napsylate form is not an approved indication for the drugs and that, if research is to be done, a status of "investigational new drug" (IND) would be required from the Food and Drug Administration.

NALOXONE-PRECIPITATED WITHDRAWAL ("THE FLUSH")

Although the usual methods of withdrawal tend toward the slow gradual approach and the new Senay method is slower than most, some authors have tried to markedly *compress* the abstinence syndrome on the theory that *total* discomfort may be less in such an approach even though the peak may be higher (6). Both Blachly et al. (6) and Resnick et al. (49) have used naloxone-precipitated withdrawal to bring about this shortened detoxification syndrome. The technique consists, primarily of giving intramuscular or intravenous naloxone repeatedly at frequent intervals for 1 or 2 days until further injections produce no withdrawal symptoms. Blachly used dioperidol, propranolol, and ketamine to handle the symptoms produced, but these agents had minimal ameliorating effect. Resnick initially used amobarbital, atropine, and chlorpromazine but later gave nothing except nighttime sedation and found the acute symptoms subsided about an hour after each dose. More recently he has premedicated with diazepam and atropine (50).

A recent modification of this technique may markedly increase its usefulness and acceptability to patients. Riordan and Kleber (51) found that if the patients are pretreated with clonidine and then continued on this while the naloxone is given, withdrawal takes place without the drastic symptoms reported earlier. The technique used so far is as follows:

Day 1: clonidine, 0.1 mg three times a day
Day 2: clonidine, 0.2 to 0.3 mg three times a day; naloxone 0.2 mg i.m., then 0.3 mg i.m., then 0.4 i.m. for 3 doses. (the doses are given 2 hours apart)
Day 3: same clonidine dose. Increase naloxone to 0.8 mg intramuscularly every 2 hours for five doses
Day 4: naloxone 0.4 mg intramuscular test dose. If no withdrawal response, repeat 0.8-mg dose 1 hour later. If still no response, can now begin naltrexone maintenance. If not going on the naltrexone, day 4 can be omitted.

ACUPUNCTURE

The use of acupuncture to manage pain goes back thousands of years in Chinese medicine. Its use to treat narcotic withdrawal is a relatively recent phenomenon, however, with the first paper reporting results in 1973 by Wen and Cheung (64). They reported on 40 patients using acupuncture with electrical stimulation. This paper and others were critically reviewed by Whitehead (65), who concluded that, "the use of acupuncture in the management of withdrawal symptoms is insufficiently reported as to constitute an adequate clinical trial. No control subjects and no control conditions have been employed. Those results that have been reported are incomplete and inadequate and these same results have been misinterpreted by others in the direction of 'gilding the lily'. . . . " In later papers, Chen (8) suggested that acupuncture may work by stimulating enkephalin release, and Wen (63) reported that, if patients were treated with naloxone at the same time as receiving acupuncture, the whole procedure was markedly shortened.

Although a controlled trial would add considerably to evaluation of the technique, there is debate over the possibility of a double-blind trial (65). Even without this, it seems that acupuncture with electrical stimulation (AES) has some effect on withdrawal symptoms but is cumbersome, has to be given frequently, and takes 7 to 8 days to detoxify patients. The new procedure using naloxone may improve the usefulness of the technique, but better designed studies need to be done to prove this.

VITAMIN C

Because high doses of ascorbid acid (vitamin C) have been used to treat or prevent a number of conditions as varied as the common cold, heart disease, leprosy, and viral hepatitis, it is not surprising that it would be tried with narcotic withdrawal. Libby and Stone (35) reported 100 cases of heroin addicts they had detoxified using doses of ascorbic acid in the 25 to 85 g per day range. The patients were treated for 1 to 2 weeks in a residential setting and then discharged on holding doses of 10 g per day. The patients reported a loss of craving for narcotics while taking the megadoses of vitamin C. Free and Sanders (14) reported an outpatient trial of the ascorbic acid regime. Patients volunteered for one of three groups—ascorbic acid only; symptomatic medications (e.g., propoxyphene, librium, chloral hydrate); and symptomatic medications for 3 days followed by megadose ascorbic acid. Group 1 had 30 clients, Group 2 had 186 clients, and Group 3 had 11 clients. The combined group reported fewer withdrawal symptoms and a shorter withdrawal period. In addition, many subjects in either Group 1 or 3 using ascorbic acid reported increased energy, loss of drug craving, and some block of narcotic effect if they used narcotics while they were taking the vitamin C. Doses of vitamin C in Group 1 were 24 to 48 g per day for 5 to 7 days, tapering to 8 to 12 g per day for 14 days. In

addition to the vitamin C, patients were given multivitamin and mineral preparations, calcium and magnesium tablets, and liquid protein.

Although no side effects other than nausea in one subject and a rash in a second one were reported, megadoses of vitamin C have been suggested to cause kidney stones, destruction of vitamin B_{12}, pentosuria, and possible increased chance of infertility and abortion. Given these possible complications, the fact that the two trials to date were uncontrolled studies and that the improvement noted was not very large, megadose ascorbic acid treatment should be considered experimental and risky.

CLONIDINE

Gold et al. (21, 22) first reported in 1978 that clonidine, an alpha-adrenergic agonist used to treat hypertension, could suppress or reverse the symptoms of opiate withdrawal. They have since published a number of papers (19, 20, 23) on this extending the original findings, and their results have been confirmed by Washton et al. (62). The major withdrawal symptom not totally blocked is difficulty in falling asleep. Clonidine has been used to treat both heroin and methadone withdrawal. The usual regime for methadone withdrawal is:

Day 1: 6 μg/kg twice a day

Day 2 to 10: 7 μg/kg at 8 a.m.; 3 μg/kg at 4 p.m.; 7 μg/kg at 11 p.m.

Day 11: 3 μg/kg at 8 a.m.; 2 μg/kg at 4 p.m.; 4 μg/kg at 11 p.m.

Day 12: 2 μg/kg at 8 a.m.; 1 μg/kg at 4 p.m.; 2 μg/kg at 11 p.m.

Day 13: 1 μg/kg twice a day

For heroin withdrawal, the length of the clonidine treatment can usually be reduced to 4 days and lower doses can be used. To check for completeness of detoxification, a naloxone test dose (0.8 mg) can be given the next day to determine whether any symptoms are precipitated.

The major side effect of clonidine is lowered blood pressure, so patients should be checked for this up to 2 hours after each dose. If blood pressure is less than 90/60 at the time to receive the next clonidine dose, it should be postponed until the pressure has risen. There have also been instances of acute psychiatric problems after clonidine detoxification is over, so patients with a prior history of schizophrenia or major affective disorder should probably be excluded from this technique (20). It is important to keep in mind that, although clonidine increases the chance of an individual completing detoxification, it does nothing to keep addicts off, and the relapse rate remains at 50 per cent or higher (19).

The discovery of clonidine's acting on opiate withdrawal has suggested the following model of how withdrawal takes place in the brain (19)

... opiate withdrawal may be due, in part, to increased noradrenergic neural activity in areas such as the locus coeruleus which are regulated by both opiates through opiate receptors and clonidine through alpha-2 adrenertic receptors.... Opiates administered systemically turn off the locus coeruleus by stimulation of inhibitory opiate receptor sites with reversal of this effect by the opiate antagonist, naloxone. Clonidine also inhibits the locus coeruleus but by stimulation of a different receptor, this effect being reversed by specific alpha-2 adrenergic antagonists....

CONCLUSION

Narcotic addiction remains an inadequately understood phenomenon. In spite of the advances in recent years in the area of opiate receptors and endogenous opiate-like hormones and neurotransmitters, we still do not understand why some individuals become opiate addicts in the first place compared to others in their environment, and why some relapse after treatment and others remain abstinent. The complex interplay of pharmacology and psychology in these decisions has not yet been unraveled. Those who are quick to stress the role of endorphins or protracted abstinence in affecting relapse would do well to recall the pioneer work of Wikler (66) and the recent studies of O'Brien et al. (44) on the conditioned abstinence phenomenon and of Meyer and associates on craving (38, 39). Individuals can develop a full blown withdrawal syndrome years after their last narcotic dose in the presence of certain stimuli. In this state of uncertainty, there are only two things that can be stated with surety about treating the opiate withdrawal syndrome: (a) new approaches to it will be tried, and, if history is any guide, a number of them will do more harm than

good; and (b) regardless of this, a substantial number of addicts will continue to seek detoxification as either pretreatment or definitive treatment. The treatment approaches already available are able to detoxify individuals with minimal discomfort compared to 50 years ago, and such new methods as clonidine may both shorten the necessary time and decrease further the discomfort. There is no evidence, however, that, as yet, any of this has any effect on the relapse rate, and this is where future research must concentrate.

References

1. Allbutt, C. On the abuse of hypodermic injections of morphine. Practitioner 3:327, 1870.
2. American Medical Association Council on Mental Health and Committee on Alcoholism and Drug Dependence. Treatment of morphine type dependence by withdrawal methods. J.A.M.A. 219: 1611, 1972.
3. Avery, L. W., and Campbell, L. K. Shock therapy as an aid to the withdrawal of morphine in addiction. Dis. Nerv. Syst. 2:333, 1941.
4. Babor, T. F., Meyer, R. E., Mirin, S. M., et al. Behavioral and social effects of heroin self-administration and withdrawal. Arch. Gen. Psychiatry 33: 363, 1976.
5. Blachly, P. H. Naloxone for diagnosis in methadone programs. J.A.M.A. 224:334, 1973.
6. Blachly, P. H., Casey, D., Marcel, L., and Denney, D. D. Rapid detoxification from heroin and methadone maintenance using naloxone: A model for study of the treatment of the opiate abstinence syndrome. In *Developments in the Field of Drug Abuse*, E. Senay, V. Shorty, and H. Alksne, editors, pp. 327–335. Cambridge, Mass., Schenkman, 1975.
7. Canada, A. T. Methadone in a thirty-day detoxification program for narcotic addicts: A critical review. Int. J. Addict. 7:613, 1972.
8. Chen, G. S. Enkephalin, drug addiction and acupuncture. Am. J. Chinese Med. 5:25, 1977.
9. Comfort, A. Morphine as an antipsychotic: Relevance of a 19-century therapeutic fashion. Lancet 2: 448, 1977.
10. Dole, V. P. Management of the opiate abstinence syndrome. In *A Treatment Manual for Acute Drug Abuse Emergencies*, P. G. Bourne, editor, pp. 34–37. Rockville, Md., National Institute on Drug Abuse, 1974.
11. *Drug Dependence in Pregnancy: Clinical Management of Mother and Child*, Services Research Monograph Series, Chapter III, pp. 29–49. Rockville, Md., National Institute on Drug Abuse, 1979.
12. Dufficy, R. G. Use of psychotherapeutic drugs in the acute detoxification of heroin addicts. Milit. Med. 138:748, 1973.
13. Fraser, H. F., and Isbell, H. Chlorpromazine and reserpine. (a) Effects of each and of combinations of each with morphine. (b) Failure of each in treatment of abstinence from morphine. AMA Arch. Neurol. Psychiatry 76:257, 1956.
14. Free, V., and Sanders, P. The use of ascorbic acid and mineral supplements in the detoxificationof nar-

cotic addicts. J. Orthomolecular Psychiatry 7:264, 1978

15. Friedgood, C. E., and Ripstein, C. B. Use of chlorpromazine in the withdrawal of addicting drugs. N. Eng. J. Med. 252:230, 1955.

16. Gay, G. R., Metzger, A. D., Bathurst, W., and Smith, D. C. Short-term detoxification on an outpatient basis. Int. J. Addict. 6:241, 1971.

17. Glatt, M. M. The treatment of the withdrawal stage in narcotic addicts by diphenoxylate and chlormethiazole. Int. J. Addict. 7:593, 1972.

18. Glatt, M. M., Lewis, D. M., and Wilson, D. T. An oral method of the withdrawal treatment of heroin dependence: A 5 years' study of a combination of diphenoxylate (Lomotil) and chlormethiazole (Heminevrin). Br. J. Addict. 65:237, 1970.

19. Gold, M. S., Pottash, A. L. C., Sweeney, D. R., and Kleber, H. D. Clonidine: A safe, effective and rapid nonopiate treatment for opiate withdrawal. J.A.M.A. 243:343, 1980.

20. Gold, M. S., Pottash, M. D., Sweeney, D. R., et al. Rapid opiate detoxication: Clinical evidence of antidepressant and antipanic effects of opiates. Am. J. Psychiatry 136:982, 1979.

21. Gold, M. S., Redmond, D. E., and Kleber, H. D. Clonidine blocks acute opiate withdrawal symptoms. Lancet 2:599, 1978.

22. Gold, M. S., Redmond, D. E., and Kleber, H. D. Clonidine in opiate withdrawal. Lancet 1:929, 1978.

23. Gold, M. S., Redmond, D. E., and Kleber, H. D. Noradrenergic hyperactivity in opiate withdrawal supported by clonidine reversal of opiate withdrawal. Am. J. Psychiatry 136:100, 1979.

24. Goodman, A. Diphenoxylate hydrochloride in the withdrawal of narcotic addiction. South. Med. J. 61: 313, 1968.

25. Grosz, H. J. Narcotic withdrawal symptoms in heroin users treated with propranolol. Lancet 2:564, 1972.

26. Gudeman, J. E., Shader, R. F., and Hemenway, T. S. Methadone withdrawal in the treatment of heroin addiction. Dis. Nerv. Syst. 33:297, 1972.

27. Hall, S. M., Bass, A., Hargreaves, W. A., and Loeb, P. Contingency management and information feedback in outpatient heroin detoxification. Behav. Ther. 10:443, 1979.

28. Hollister, L. E., and Prusmack, J. J. Propranolol in withdrawal from opiates. Arch. Gen. Psychiatry 31: 695, 1974.

29. Inaba, D. S., Newmeyer, J. A., Gay, G. R., and Whitehead, C. A. "I got a yen for that Darvon N": A pilot study on the use of propoxyphene napsylate in the treatment of heroin addiction. Am. J. Drug Alcohol Use 1:67, 1974.

30. Isbell, H., and Vogel, V. H. The addiction liability of methadone and its use in the treatment of the morphine abstinent syndrome. Am. J. Psychiatry 105: 909, 1948.

31. Jaffe, J. H., and Martin, W. R. Narcotic analgesics and antagonists (Chapter 15). Drug addiction and drug abuse (Chapter 16). In The Pharmacological Basis of Therapeutics, L. S. Goodman and A. Gilman, editors, ed. 5, pp. 245–324. New York, Macmillan, 1975.

32. Kalinowsky, L. B., and Hoch, P. H. Shock Treatments and Other Somatic Procedures in Psychiatry. New York, Grune and Stratton, 1946.

33. Kelman, H. Narcotic withdrawal syndrome: Sup-

pression of by means of electric convulsive therapy. Minn. Med. 47:525, 1964.

34. Kolb, L., and Himmelsbach, C. K. Clinical studies of drug addiction. III. A critical review of the withdrawal treatments with method of evaluating abstinence syndromes. Public Health Rep. 128:1, 1938.

35. Libby, A., and Stone, I. The hypoascorbemia-kwashiorkor approach to drug addiction therapy: A pilot study. J. Orthomolecular Psychiatry 6:300, 1977.

36. Martin, W. R., and Jasinski, D. R. Physiological parameters of morphine dependence in man: Tolerance, early abstinence, protracted abstinence. J. Psychiatr. Res. 7:9, 1969.

37. Martin, W. R., Wikler, A., Eades, C. G., and Pescor, F. T. Tolerance to and physical dependence on morphine in rats. Psychopharmacologia 4:247, 1963.

38. Meyer, R. E., McNamee, H. B., Mirin, S. M., and Altman, J. L. Analysis and modification of opiate reinforcement. Int. J. Addict. 11:467, 1976.

39. Mirin, S. M., Meyer, R. F., McNamee, H. B., and McDougle, M. Psychopathology, craving and mood during heroin acquisition: An experimental study. Int. J. Addict. 11:525, 1976.

40. Moffett, A. D., Soloway, I. H., and Glick, M. X. Posttreatment behavior following ambulatory detoxification. In Methadone—Experience and Issues, C. D. Chambers, and L. Brill, editors, pp. 215–227. New York, Behavioral Publications, 1973.

41. Newman, M. K., and Berris, J. M. Artificial hibernation therapy. Arch. Phys. Ther. 22:161, 1941.

42. Newman, R. G. Detoxification treatment of narcotic addicts. In Handbook on Drug Abuse, R. I. DuPont, A. Goldstein, and J. O'Donnell, editors, pp. 21–29. Rockville, Md., National Institute on Drug Abuse, 1979.

43. Nyswander, M. The Drug Addict as a Patient. New York, Grune and Stratton, 1956.

44. O'Brien, C. P., Testa, T., O'Brien, T. J., Brady, J. P., and Wells, B. Conditioned narcotic withdrawal in humans. Science 195:1000, 1977.

45. O'Malley, J. E., Anderson, W. A., and Lazare, A. Failure of outpatient treatment of drug abuse. I. Heroin. Am. J. Psychiatry 128:865, 1972.

46. Raynes, A. E., and Patch, V. D. An improved detoxification technique for heroin addicts. Arch. Gen. Psychiatry 29:417, 1973.

47. Razani, J., Chisholm, D., Glasser, M., and Kappeler, T. Self-regulated methadone detoxification of heroin addicts: An improved technique in an inpatient setting. Arch. Gen. Psychiatry 32:909, 1975.

48. Renner, J. A., and Rubin, M. L. Engaging heroin addicts in treatment. Am. J. Psychiatry 130:976, 1973.

49. Resnick, R., Kestenbaum, R., Gaztanaga, P., Volavka, J., and Freedman, A. M. Experimental techniques for rapid withdrawal from methadone maintenance: Results of pilot trials. In Developments in the Field of Drug Abuse, E. Senay, V. Shorty, and H. Alksne, editors, pp. 321–326. Cambridge, Mass., Schenkman, 1975.

50. Resnick, R. B., Kestenbaum, R. S., Washton, A., and Poole, D. Naloxone-precipitated withdrawal: A method for rapid induction onto naltrexone. Clin. Pharmacol. Ther. 21:409, 1977.

51. Riordan, C. E., and Kleber, H. D. Rapid opiate detoxification with clonidine and naloxone. Lancet 1: 1079, 1980.

52. Rolo, A. Drug withdrawal with promazine hydro-

chloride. N. Y. State J. Med. 62: 1429, 1962.

53. Senay, E. C. Detoxification of heroin addicts. J.A.M.A. 233: 356, 1975.

54. Senay, E. C., and Dorus, W. Short versus long term detoxification with methadone. Presented at National Association for Drug Abuse Prevention Conference on Research Developments in Drug and Alcohol Use, New York, December 4–5, 1979.

55. Sheffet, A., Quinones, M., Lavenhar, M. A., Doyle, K., and Prager, H. An evaluation of detoxification as an initial step in the treatment of heroin addiction. Am. J. Psychiatry 133:337, 1976.

56. Silsby, H., and Tennant, F. S. Short-term, ambulatory detoxification of opiate addicts using methadone. Int. J. Addict. 9:167, 1974.

57. Stern, R., Edwards, N. B., and Lerro, F. A. Methadone on demand as a heroin detoxification procedure. Int. J. Addict. 9:863, 1974.

58. Tennant, F. S. Propoxyphene napsylate for heroin addiction. J.A.M.A. 226:1212, 1974.

59. Tennant, F. S., Russell, B. A., Casas, S. K., and Bleich, R. N. Heroin detoxification: A comparison of propoxyphene and methadone. J.A.M.A. 232:1019, 1975.

60. Thigpen, F. B., Thigpen, C. H., and Cleckley, H. M. Use of electric-convulsive therapy in morphine, meperidine, and related alkaloid addictions. AMA Arch. Neurol. Psychiatry 70:452, 1953.

61. Tillim, S. J. Opiate withdrawal treated with induced hypoglycemic reactions. Am. J. Psychiatry 99:84, 1942.

62. Washton, A. M., Resnick, R. B., and Rossen, A.

Clonidine hydrochloride: A non-opiate treatment for opiate withdrawal. In *Proceedings of the 41st Annual Scientific Meeting of the Committee on Problems of Drug Dependence*, National Institute on Drug Abuse Research Monograph Series #27, L. S. Harris, editor, pp. 233–239. Rockville, Md., National Institute on Drug Abuse, 1979.

63. Wen H. L. Fast detoxification of heroin addicts by acupuncture and electrical stimulation (AES) in combination with naloxone. Comp. Med. East West 5: 257, 1977.

64. Wen, H. L., and Cheung, S. Y. C. Treatment of drug addiction by acupuncture and electrical stimulation. Am. J. Acupuncture 1:71, 1973.

65. Whitehead, P. C. Acupuncture in the treatment of addiction: A review and analysis. Int. J. Addict. 13:1, 1978.

66. Wikler, A. Dynamics of drug dependence: Implications of a conditioning theory for research and treatment. Arch. Gen. Psychiatry 28:611, 1973.

67. Wilson, B. K., Elms, R. R., and Thompson, C. P. Low dosage use of methadone in extended detoxification. Arch. Gen. Psychiatry 31:233, 1974.

68. Wilson, B. K., Elms, R. R., and Thompson, C. P. Outpatient vs hospital methadone detoxification: An experimental comparison. Int. J. Addict. 10:13, 1975.

69. Woody, G. E., and O'Brien, C. P. Development of psychiatric illness in drug abusers: Possible role of drug preference. N. Engl. J. Med. 301:1310, 1979.

70. Zilm, D. H., and Sellers, F. M. The quantitative assessment of physical dependence on opiate. Drug Alcohol Depend. 3:419, 1978.

CHAPTER 25

THE CASE FOR HEROIN MAINTENANCE

Alfred R. Lindesmith, Ph.D.

The case for heroin maintenance may be most simply and emphatically made by noting that past experience in the effort to control popular personal vices like the abuse of drugs has almost always indicated that the most effective and, in the long run, the most socially acceptable way of minimizing such "evils" is to control by regulation rather than by prohibition and punishment. This was the case with alcohol and tobacco abuse, which are in many respects two of the most serious problems of this sort. There is virtually no popular sentiment for placing either of these substances under prohibition controls. It is well known that control of popular vices by prohibition virtually inevitably creates an illicit traffic that perpetuates the problem and drives it underground, more or less out of sight and out of control. In the case of heroin and other opiate drugs, this tactic has had the effect of creating an enforcement bureaucracy that is dependent on the illicit traffic for its existence. Indeed, the traffic and the bureaucracy are mutually interdependent; without one the other could not exist. A comprehensive heroin maintenance program would be a serious or fatal blow to both.

The discussion that follows will be within the framework created by the current program in the United States, one that might be characterized as a mixture or confusion of control by regulation and by prohibition. Rel-ative to the magnitude of the opiate problem in the United States, there is a relatively small maintenance program here that is rigidly confined to the use of methadone only. Heroin, still the drug of choice of many American addicts, has long been outlawed in medical practice and is commonly viewed as an unmitigated evil, a kind of devil drug, that should be totally suppressed at all costs. Proposed experimentation with heroin maintenance has so far not been authorized, although demands for such a trial have increased. As part of an orientation to resistance to maintenance programs, methadone programs are so encumbered with multiple sets of rules and regulations that they are threatened by death from strangulation with red tape. Consequently, their coverage of the addicted population is not enough to threaten the economic health of the black market in heroin. It is this illicit market that plays a dominant role in supporting the system that develops and spreads dependence on drugs. That system has existed unchanged and has entrapped addicts for the last six decades.

The methadone movement seems to have changed its focus from that of becoming a functional replacement of the bankrupt prohibition scheme to that of "curing" and rehabilitating addicts. Unfortunately, these two goals are incompatible within the same program. This point may be made by imagining what would have happened in this country if, instead of repealing the Volstead Act, we had sought to remedy the evils of the Prohibition era by resolving the problem by curing and rehabilitating our alcoholics. Suppose that we had then set up a network of government-financed and -operated facilities for this purpose and then waited for the evils of alcoholism and of Prohibition to come to an end—would we still be waiting?

Concerning heroin in medicine, it is my judgment that this drug should again be given respectable status, because it was outlawed for political reasons rather than on sound medical judgment in the first place. In England positive medical experience with heroin led physicians to resist and defeat their government's attempt to ban heroin as has been done in the United States. Heroin, in fact, is much like morphine in its effects, and even experienced users may mistake one drug for the other when they do not know which is being given to them (2). Although most American and British physicians probably used morphine in preference to heroin when both were available, some doctors in both countries regarded heroin as having advantages in certain medical situations. Under these circumstances, they asserted, it was indefensible to ban it. It should also be observed that heroin has long been used in the British maintenance program and continues to be used, along with methadone and other drugs. It is of interest that under these circumstances some practitioners in England do not agree that methadone is superior to heroin as a maintenance drug. One should observe as well that the British experience with opiate maintenance exceeds our own by several decades. Such experience deserves a candid evaluation.

It must be admitted that finding a universally satisfactory method of dealing with heroin addiction throughout the world has at best been difficult and unsatisfying. In the United States, this is particularly true because of the slow and extended build-up of the problem, which, despite the effort to use punitive controls, has continued to spread and become more complex.

Instead of learning from foreign experience, we have attempted to export our prohibition system abroad where it is equally ineffective. We must recognize that any efforts to modify our present attitude toward addiction in the United States are made more difficult by the fact that if a new system were to go into effect it would take a period of years before its positive consequences would become noticeable through such indicators as the increased average age of known addicts, diminished rates for drug-related crime, and diminished numbers of new recruits. Thus, the process of bringing about changes in the fundamental attitudes that support the punitive approach to addicts and addiction is made difficult. Defeat will be foretold before the experience is completed.

"PROHIBITION" OR MAINTENANCE?

One might ask whether the traditional American "program," i.e., the street heroin traffic, is not in reality a kind of do-it-yourself heroin maintenance operation run by private enterprise and supported by the bureaucracy that ensures the underworld monopoly. It is true, of course, that the heroin trade is illegal and that the prohibition goal was to make the drug unavailable, thereby causing addicts to quit their habits when supplies were cut off or when they were threatened by negative social sanctions and imprisonment. Inasmuch as no one, even those within enforcement, any longer expects these goals to be fulfilled after many years of failure, there is, in terms of reality, nothing much left of the prohibition system except its rhetoric. We can no longer expect the supplies of heroin to stop flowing into this country, nor should we expect heroin users to quit their habits because of threats or punishment. We also know that even if the poppy were to become an extinct plant, synthetic equivalents could quickly be produced and distributed. The illicit trade is now virtually accepted as a fact of life, and the relevant question has become that of organizing a better maintenance system than that now run by gangsters for profit. Our choice is not one between abstinence and addiction. It is a choice between a legal system of distribution designed to minimize the negative consequences of addiction and to prevent its spread and an illegal one that funnels the profits to the underworld at the expense of the American economy.

We have already noted that the enforcement organization and the illicit heroin industry are in some respects interdependent and achieve some of the same goals. High price levels are cited by the police as evidence of police efficiency in the war on dope, but the same high prices mean high profits in the trade. If the number of addicts increases this means increased demand on an expanded black market, and for the police it may mean enlarged narcotic squads and more generous budgets. Increases in the numbers of addicts have usually been attributed to courts that are too lenient or to foreign plotters—rarely to inadequate enforcement.

Another anomaly of enforcement is that some of its practices constitute direct subsidies and price support programs for the illicit heroin business. For example, public funds amounting to untold millions of dollars are constantly being fed into the illicit trade when supplies are purchased by the police and other governmental agencies, and little of it is recovered. Some years ago, the payment of $35 million to Turkey to ban poppy cultivation surely functioned as a price support program that tended to encourage increased production elsewhere. Similar programs have frequently been utilized by the Department of Agriculture to maintain the prices of essential farm products in this country. The purchase and burning in the northern Thai city of Cheng Mai some years ago of around 20 tons of opium is another case in point. Subsequent to this incident it was reported that Shan operators in the Golden Triangle offered to sell the United States 400 tons of opium for $20 million. The most remarkable feature of this incident was not that the offer was rejected but that it was made at all and that it seems to have been seriously discussed by authorities in the United States.

MAINTENANCE FOR PRIVILEGED ADDICTS

Throughout the history of the American effort to deal with opiate addiction, some addicts have been exempted from the penalties prescribed by criminal law and allowed to maintain their habits with legal drugs obtained through legal channels. Two outstanding examples of this have been supplied by none other than Harry J. Anslinger, who was for about 30 years the head of what was then the Federal Bureau of Narcotics (FBN) and which lives on as the Drug Enforcement Ad-

ministration (DEA). In one of these cases Mr. Anslinger became aware that a personal acquaintance of his, a woman prominent in Washington society, had become addicted to meperidine (Demerol). He made arrangements, without her knowledge, to have her supplies delivered to her with progressively smaller doses of the drug in the containers so that after a time she was consuming something that she thought was Demerol but that, in fact, did not contain any opiate or equivalent drug. After this point had been reached, Mr. Anslinger was among those who saw this lady off on a trip abroad. He drew her aside before she boarded the ship and told her that she was "cured" and might as well throw overboard her supplies of the Demerol that he assumed she was taking along. He reported that she "wept tears of joy" (1).

The other instance involved an important member of Congress who was known to be addicted. Mr. Anslinger explained that he did not wish to prosecute this man because to have done so would have created a scandal that could have been exploited by the Communists. In an interview with this man, he proposed to him that if he would promise never to buy illicit drugs, it would be arranged that he secure prescriptions from a specific physician and obtain his supplies regularly from a particular pharmacy in the Washington area. The latter naturally agreed to this, as any addict would have, and continued to use drugs from this source until he died some years later. When a well known columnist got wind of this deal, Anslinger prevented him from publishing the story by threatening him with prosecution if he did so on the grounds that he would be violating laws relating to the confidentiality of pharmacy records (1).

Both of these cases involved procedures that were forbidden to physicians by Mr. Anslinger's bureau and for which they could have been criminally prosecuted. Nevertheless, physicians have long practiced a subrosa program of maintenance, usually using morphine, for certain addicted patients. Sometimes, as in the two cases described, this has been done with the approval or even at the suggestion of narcotics agents. At other times it was done without such approval. The addicts accorded such privileges include nurses, doctors, elderly addicts with long records of addiction, prominent persons (often from the entertainment field), chronically ill persons, and others. An important feature of this practice is that it has been relatively successfully controlled by the principles and ethics of medicine without the enormous apparatus of bureaucratic controls and the threats of criminal prosecution or withdrawal of funds that now burden government-controlled methadone maintenance programs.

In the two illustrative examples cited, for instance, there were no urine analyses required, no physical examinations were conducted, there was no institutional treatment, and in both cases self-administration of the drug was permitted. In the case of the Congressman, he was not required to undergo detoxification and an attempted cure. Most important, there was no harassment.

This program obviously raises a serious question of equal justice under law, especially when one considers how the disproportionate numbers of heroin addicts from minority groups, such as blacks and Puerto Ricans, are handled in the criminal justice system. The main point that we wish to stress here, however, is that this system, although limited in scope, seems to have been remarkably successful where it has been permitted. It has never become a significant public issue or been regarded as a significant social problem; even narcotics agents have sometimes collaborated with it. In a detailed study of 45 former patients from the Lexington institution who were handled in this manner, O'Donnell found that only five, or about 11 per cent, had ever been sentenced in a court of law after they became addicted. All of these 45 had consistently secured their supplies from only one doctor at a time. Most of them evidently lived in smaller communities removed from urban centers where the illicit traffic flourishes (5).

A HYPOTHETICAL COMPREHENSIVE SUBSTITUTE FOR PROHIBITION

A basic assumption of what follows is that private practitioners will have their right to utilize heroin restored to them in the future. Other assumptions are that the support and cooperation of addicts are essential and that those elements of the population from which most heroin addicts come will have more to say about what is done to or for them than they now have. It is also assumed that a heroin maintenance program will be simplified in design, primarily by reducing the intrusion of governmental control to give those who use heroin the chance to be law-abiding persons even though they are addicts, and that the very difficult and costly attempt to "cure" and rehabilitate them socially will be dealt with in separate nonmedical programs should such rehabilitation programs be seen as necessary. It is further assumed that coercive means should be used sparingly if at all, except in the case of those addicts who refuse to enter the maintenance program.

In view of the apparent success of the practice of allowing doctors to provide privileged addicts with their drug, selected private practitioners throughout the nation might be authorized to provide maintenance drugs for addicts under their care. A monitoring function over this scheme could be exercised by the public health network. Certainly, it should not be done by the police. Physicians involved should have available to them, besides heroin, a spectrum of opioids and other drugs that may be proven to be useful. These doctors would be permitted and even encouraged to attempt cures and, should institutionalization be indicated, facilities that they could utilize should be made available. Such cures should be undertaken voluntarily by the addict.

Advantages of this portion of the projected scheme would be that the opportunity to become a law-abiding citizen could be extended to all parts of the nation where physicians are available and where there are any heroin addicts. The current methadone programs are located largely in urban centers where addicts are numerous and where the drug subculture and the illicit market make it especially difficult to deal with them and where the addict who wants to quit or to get out of the rat race finds the difficulty of doing so at a maximum. With private practitioners available as maintenance sources, some of these urban addicts might even wish to migrate to smaller communities as some of them do even now in what has been called the "geographic cure." Some of the stigma of addiction might also be removed for those under the care of physicians and, more than now, addicts would be able to work for a living. The advantages noted here have also been noted in Britain, where this system had long been in existence. Unfortunately in recent years, and probably because of the intervention of American experts, the role of control of treatment by private physicians has eroded in favor of congregate treatment in government-controlled clinics.

Concerning on-going methadone programs, heroin, morphine, and other opiates and equivalents should be added to the drugs that might be used in maintenance. Because heroin remains the drug of choice of most addicts, they might initially be offered heroin maintenance and self-administration. To reduce the problems of congregate treatment, the practice of sending batches of prescriptions to a particular pharmacy might be adopted so that the addict could pick them up each time that he visited the pharmacy to renew his supply without going to a clinic. With the passing of time, addicts receiving heroin might be instructed in the advantages of using morphine, methadone, or perhaps the new, long acting methadone variant, LAAM (levo-alpha-acetylmethadol), which is still in a testing stage (3). Heroin, in short, might be used as bait to attract addicts and as a steppingstone to more effective maintenance. As has been observed, the maintenance program, if it is to be relatively comprehensive, probably ought to make maintenance, not cure—as represented in total abstinence—its top priority. However, when the addict wishes to try for abstinence, facilities to which he could resort should be made available.

As a final note, I should like to add that, in my opinion, the simultaneous discussion of all the so-called problems of drug abuse tends to introduce confusion into the consideration of appropriate control measures by obscuring the differences between types of drugs. The arguments and suggestions in this paper are, therefore, intended to apply only to the control of opiate drugs. They arise, as I have tried to indicate, from the observation of aspects of our traditional prohibition approach and from some of the anomalous discriminatory practices that have been virtually a part of it. They are also related to practices in a number of European nations from which much of value could be learned and which we have largely ignored.

References

1. Anslinger, H. J., and Oursler, W. *The Murderers: The Story of the Narcotic Gangs.* New York, Farrar, Straus and Cudahy, 1962.
2. Beecher, H. K. *Measurements of Subjective Responses.* New York, Oxford University Press, 1959.
3. Du Pont, R. L., Goldstein, A., and O'Donnell, J., editors. *Handbook on Drug Abuse.* Rockville, Md., National Institute on Drug Abuse, Department of Health, Education and Welfare and Office of Drug Abuse Policy, Executive Office of the President, 1979.
4. (The) Knapp Commission. *The Knapp Commission Report on Police Corruption.* New York, George Braziller, 1972.
5. O'Donnell, J. A. *Narcotic Addicts in Kentucky.* Public Health Service Publication No. 1881. Washington, D.C., Department of Health, Education and Welfare, 1969.

CHAPTER 26

METHADONE MAINTENANCE IN PERSPECTIVE

Joyce H. Lowinson, M.D.

INTRODUCTION

In the fields of medicine and psychiatry neither methadone maintenance treatment nor the therapeutic community represents a radical departure from previous approaches used to help troubled people.

The protocol developed by Dole and Nyswander in 1964 for using methadone to treat opiate addicts had precedence in the United States in a medically managed system of opium maintenance clinics that existed from the year 1918 until the mid-1920's, when the last of these was closed as a result of political and social pressure. Well before this period those suffering addiction could be maintained on opiates either with or without the assistance of medical management without facing the sting of public rebuke. Within Great Britain a noncontroversial system of opium maintenance has existed to treat the addict within the framework of private medical practice for a great many years. It is only recently in Britain that control of the addiction problem has moved from the primary jurisdiction of medical practice to a system guided by governmental control.

The landmark year for the emergence of a prototype for the treatment of opiate users through the use of therapeutic communities was 1958, when Charles Dederich began the first Synanon in California. Today, (see Chapter 23) over 12,601 clients are in residential treatment programs for drug abuse guided by the principles of treatment originally formulated by Dederich and later developed by David Deitch, among others. But the therapeutic community concept also had its roots in a series of precedent programs. The self-help concept, focused through a "total institution" approach to managing behavioral change through resocialization of the individual, had its origins in Alcoholics Anonymous (AA), which was begun in the United States in 1934. AA had its roots in the Oxford Movement. One could make the case that one of the earliest therapeutic communities existed in Gheel in the 13th century (20) when this small town in Belgium first began to accept the mentally ill into their homes and communities as part of an early system of rehabilitation. Though we must give credit to those who have worked toward scientific and medical innovations, few are remarkably new.

Why, then, is it that the two major approaches currently in vogue in the United States are viewed as being radically different from what preceded them? Part of the reason for this is that for somewhat over 60 years Americans had been exposed to a carefully orchestrated program of government policies that turned the image of the addict from a sometimes benign and dependent individual to that of one that is threatening and often predatory.

The development of such a public image interacted with efforts to manage those who suffer it. We moved from a position that viewed addicts as patients who properly deserved concern and treatment to one that increasingly relied on criminal sanctions and a punitive approach. The development of methadone maintenance treatment and therapeutic communities some 15 years ago represented a radical departure from the approaches of recent history rather than the earlier, pre-Harrison Act, evolution of treatment of addiction in the United States.

Why should such considerations be presented in an explication of any treatment modality for drug dependence? We must recognize that the social forces that now support or negate programs for the treatment of those who become drug dependent swing from an early 19th-century approach of humanistic, "moral treatment" (5) to that demanding punitive incarceration for human failings.

All addicts either in or out of treatment confront this ambivalence—sorrow and sympathy for their plight on the one hand and disdain on the other. The insistence of therapeutic communities that their residents not only abstain from mind-altering (or psychotropic) medications (with the exception in some cases of alcohol) creates the illusion of being "stronger" than methadone patients, where medication is part of the treatment. Therefore, those who enter therapeutic communities fare better in changing their image in the eyes of the public when compared with those in methadone treatment. According to the Protestant ethic, abstinence is viewed as the first step in the return of the sinner to the fold of those deserving respect by society. Certainly it is not suggested here that those responsible for management of therapeutic communities hold such a position but rather that segments of the public responsible for supporting such programs and receiving the products of their work, recovered drug addicts, back into the community may be motivated to accept or reject the recovered addict on the basis of abstinence.

The patient who enters methadone treatment does not benefit from such a clearly visible change in public image after treatment. Simplistically, the public views the fact of the original use of illicit drugs as the root of the evil that is followed by subsequent probable norm violation. The fact that methadone treatment does not clearly embody what we may loosely refer to as a "salvation phenomenon" places programs and their patients in a disadvantageous social position that affects program funding, community and political support, and acceptance of the patients who become rehabilitated through this approach.

Dole and Nyswander had set rehabilitation rather than abstinence as the primary goal of treatment. In view of the high rate of recidivism for all other previous treatment attempts, they hypothesized that, if narcotic craving, the apparent cause of relapse, could be controlled, the possibility of rehabilitation would be enhanced. In fact, this has proven to be so. At the time of this writing methadone maintenance treatment has succeeded in restoring thousands of hard core addicts to responsible citizenship, and very possibly has saved the lives of thousands more. The initial success of methadone maintenance as a tool in rehabilitating heroin addicts led many people to presume that patients on methadone would soon be cured of dependency on any narcotic drug, including methadone. Nevertheless, this modality has not gained the support it seems to merit. Those who are philosophically committed to the concept of abstinence as the primary goal of treatment attack the use of a substitute drug, even though abstinence itself has not allowed a significant number of confirmed hard core heroin addicts to reenter the community at large. Legislators, disappointed that methadone maintenance did not fulfill their expectation of markedly reducing crime—a promise never made by Dole and Nyswander—react by denying this modality adequate funds that would provide the special services required to treat that small percentage of emotionally disturbed patients who manifest their pathology by loitering, engaging in secondary drug abuse, and occasionally even diverting methadone. The disappointments have grown to the point where the very future of this very effective treatment approach remains in jeopardy. This happens at a time in history when needs of a heterogeneous group of addicts require a wide range of treatment modalities—including drug-free, methadone maintenance, and others—that are both appropriate for and acceptable to the individuals affected.

The first attempt of organized medicine to advocate medical research and treatment for drug addicts (outside of federal hospitals) came in 1955, when the New York Academy of Medicine strongly objected to federal regulations that "prohibited physicians from prescribing a narcotic drug to keep comfortable a confirmed addict who refuses withdrawal, but who might under regulated dosage lead a useful life and later might agree to withdrawal" (47). The Academy report observed that the early morphine maintenance clinics were closed—not because they had failed but because their goals did not accord with the prevailing philosophy of a punitive approach to a so-called "criminal problem." (For a history of the early maintenance clinics and their relationship to federal legislation and public attitudes, see Chapter 1.)

In 1957, however, the American Medical Association, via its Council on Mental Health, once again took an ambivalent position on the subject of maintenance. The Council concluded that lack of objective data (including the operations of the narcotic dispensaries between 1919 and 1923) left the matter to individual opinion. And opinions differed (13). Disagreement among medical experts and an increasing number of proposals favoring maintenance led to a report of the Joint Committee of the American Bar Association and the American Medical Association in 1959 that called for a softening of penalties and the establishment of an experimental outpatient clinic for the treatment of drug addicts (45). In 1962 the Ad Hoc Panel at the White House Conference on Narcotics and Drug Abuse took a tentative first step toward maintenance by recommending research to determine the validity of the arguments pro and con.

In February, 1962, the Medical Society of the County of New York recognized the need for systematic clinical investigation of medical maintenance treatment and ruled that "physicians who participate in a properly controlled and supervised clinical research project for addicts on a non-institutional basis would be deemed to be practicing ethical medicine" (43). Lindesmith and Gagnon speculated that, inasmuch as prior to 1914 the addict was primarily white and upper middle class, the subsequent legislative trend toward criminalization of addiction had led to its predominance in urban poverty cultures (36).

In any case, the assumption that the prescription of a narcotic medication would do no more than "gratify a bad habit" had led to the neglect of maintenance research for 40 years (37). And "the Federal philosophy of curability . . . continued, until the emergence of methadone and the general acceptance of maintenance as a legitimate treatment modality" (45).

DEVELOPMENT OF METHADONE

Methadone is a synthetic analgesic compound developed in Germany during World War II as a substitute for morphine, which was in short supply. The compound was seemingly unrelated structurally to the opiates, but its acute pharmacological effects were almost indistinguishable. It has since become clear that its structure is closer to that of the opiates than had been realized by the chemists who developed it (26).

The advantage of methadone as a detoxifying agent had been recognized at the United States Public Health Service Hospital in Lexington, Kentucky. Attempts to modify the acute narcotic withdrawal syndrome using tranquilizers and sedative-hypnotics afforded only symptomatic relief; more effective in attenuating the withdrawal syndrome was the use of other narcotics in diminishing doses. In 1948 Isbell (30), using the Himmelsbach scale (28) for calibrating the intensity of withdrawal from different drugs, demonstrated that, whereas the course of withdrawal was almost the same for morphine and heroin, it was different for methadone. Withdrawal from morphine produces intense discomfort of comparatively brief duration. The intensity of withdrawal from methadone is less severe although of longer duration.

Isbell and Vogel (31) stated that, although withdrawal symptoms could be attenuated by using methadone, detoxification is only the first step in the treatment of narcotic addiction. Others inferred that associated rehabilitative efforts were needed to enable a recovered addict to reenter society.

In the 1950's New York City saw a rise of heroin addiction among adolescents. As a response to this problem, the city turned over Riverside Hospital for the exclusive treatment of adolescent addicts. Staffed with psychiatrists, psychologists, and counselors trained in rehabilitation, the hospital provided psychotherapy (individual and group), occupational therapy, remedial teaching, and social services. Initially, admissions were voluntary; later, patients were remanded by the courts. In 1959, after 7 years of operation, an extensive follow-up (1) revealed that, of the 247 adolescent patients who were admitted in 1955 for treatment of addiction, 86 per cent of the group were rehospitalized for treatment of drug abuse or arrested by the police or both. Six per cent of the remaining patients had died or continued to have difficulties that suggested both narcotic and nonnarcotic abuse; 4 per cent were lost to follow-up contact; and 4 per cent (nine patients) were found to be abstinent and without other negative information available on them. This last group of nine patients is of special interest, because both hospital records and follow-up interviews established that eight of the nine patients had never been addicted to heroin prior to hospitalization. The study further found that for any 6-month period of the follow-up, one-half of the patients spent some time in an institution. After the initial release from the hospital, patients spent 25 per cent of their time during this follow-up period in hospital treatment, jail, or a combination of both. Using the then popular criterion of treatment success as complete abstinence, the hospital was deemed a failure. As a result of this evaluation, it was decided to close Riverside Hospital.

The next year the city contracted with Manhattan General Hospital (now known as the Morris J. Bernstein Institute of the Beth Israel Medical Center) to open a detoxification program using methadone. The detoxification service had 9,000 admissions a year. "It's a form of social first aid and we've never had any illusions that it was anything else," said Dr. Ray Trussell, New York City Commissioner of Hospitals (57).

The New York City Health Research Council, which had recommended the closing of Riverside Hospital and the opening of a detoxification center, also recommended research in the area of narcotic addiction, which they viewed as a chronic disease. Rockefeller Institute (now Rockefeller University) accepted the challenge and asked Dr. Vincent Dole, a widely respected internist and biochemist, to undertake research in this area. Dr. Marie Nyswander, a psychiatrist with extensive experience in the treatment of heroin addiction, joined him in this research. Based on her experience at Lexington and in East Harlem, as well as in private practice in New York City, Dr. Nyswander was convinced that psychiatry alone could not effect the needed change. In fact, it was observed that "a careful search of the literature has failed to disclose a single report in which withdrawal of drug and psychotherapy has enabled a significant fraction of the patients to return to the community and live as normal individuals" (18). Dole and Nyswander observed that relapse in most cases was related to persistent or recurring narcotic craving. They theorized that control of this craving would be an important first step. To test this theory, two patients were admitted to the hospital of Rockefeller Institute to be stabilized on a narcotic. Initially Dole and Nyswander tried morphine maintenance, but the patients remained sedated and apathetic. Methadone, which had the benefit of being longer acting (24 to 36 hours) and orally effective, eliminated the mood swings and allowed patients to function normally. As a result, it released the patient for normal pursuits after one daily oral dose. Four additional "hard core" heroin addicts were admitted, and the same benefits were repeated.

These six patients were studied clinically for the next 15 months in a research program at Rockefeller Institute. For Dole and Nyswander, the question at issue was "whether a narcotic medicine, prescribed by physicians as part of a treatment program, could help in the return of addict patients to normal society" (13). The successful outcome of this in-depth study of six patients justified expansion to include a larger number of addicts with simultaneous outside evaluation. The Dole-Nyswander protocol for the expanded program was developed with infinite care in order to replicate the findings of the research project. It may be useful to review the original Dole-Nyswander treatment model as a starting point for a critical analysis of the controversial dilemmas that surfaced as the program expanded and was implemented by others.

DOLE-NYSWANDER RESEARCH PROTOCOL FOR METHADONE MAINTENANCE TREATMENT

Heroin addicts were accepted for treatment in the order in which they applied, subject to criteria established to eliminate all but the "hard core" heroin addicts. The established criteria called for a 4-year history of heroin addiction with repeated attempts at detoxification followed by relapse. It also limited patients to the age group between 20 and 39 years of age. (The age requirement was set to eliminate younger addicts who might prove amenable to other treatment as well as to eliminate older patients because of the prevailing belief that addicts mature out of their addiction.)

Treatment was divided into three phases. During Phase One (a 6-week period of hospitalization), patients were started on small doses of oral methadone (10 to 20 mg per day); the dose was increased gradually to a blocking level (80 to 120 mg per day) as tolerance permitted. During this phase patients received a thorough medical work-up and were evaluated to determine the kind of services they would require after discharge from the hospital.

Phase Two began when, as outpatients, they returned to the clinic each weekday for medication and to leave a urine specimen. As a safeguard against intravenous misuse, methadone was dispensed in fruit juice. Phase Two was a period of major transition for the patient; support, encouragement, and guidance from professional staff and from older patients serving as research assistants were considered essential. However, there were no formal psychotherapy or group sessions. Family adjustment and job placement took priority, with the view that real needs should be addressed first to give the patients an improved self-image. Once the patient had successfully made the transition from addict to patient and was productively engaged in normal outside activities, he entered Phase Three. The maintenance dosage was continued, with periodic review by a physician. After careful review and evaluation the program allowed well adjusted patients to visit the clinic once a week and to take home six bottles. In 1967, after a 2-year trial of the research program involving 120 patients admitted, Dole and Nyswander reported: "To date, we have seen no indication to remove the blockade from any patient in the treatment program, since all of them are still in the process of rehabilitation, and no patient has been limited by intolerance to the medication" (14). Although 13 patients "failed" (discharged for sociopathic behavior or intractable nonnarcotic drug abuse, primarily

alcohol), the program retained 107 patients, previously street addicts. Seventy one per cent were employed in a steady job, going to school, or both. Results were promising, but the sample was still small; the time for admitting additional patients was at hand.

INDEPENDENT EVALUATION

As the Dole-Nyswander program expanded, the New York City Interdepartmental Health Council allocated a separate budget for independent evaluation of this modality. With Dr. Frances Gearing of the Columbia University School of Public Health serving as chairman, the committee consisted of impartial judges, including Drs. Henry Brill and Donald Louria; thus, "the cards were stacked against over optimism" (3).

Criteria established to evaluate treatment outcome emphasized the social function and rehabilitation of drug-dependent persons. Evaluation was based on: (a) a decrease in antisocial behavior measured by arrest and/or incarceration; (b) an increase in social productivity measured by employment and/or schooling or vocational training; (c) clinical impression of freedom from heroin "hunger" confirmed by negative urine specimens after stabilization on methadone; (d) a recognition of, and willingness to accept help for, psychiatric and other problems, including those related to excessive use of alcohol or other drugs. Over a 3-year period, the evaluation committee reported consistent success and, in 1969, recommended expansion of the methadone maintenance treatment program.

METHADONE MAINTENANCE

By 1967 research programs in Philadelphia (59) and Washington, D.C. (19) demonstrated that most addicts could be stabilized on an ambulatory basis, vastly reducing the cost of treatment.

By 1969 there were 2,000 patients enrolled in methadone maintenance programs in New York City and several thousand applicants were awaiting admission (49). The New York Academy of Medicine termed the situation a crisis. Although they recognized that treatment of heroin addiction with methadone substituted one addiction for another and might be a lifelong affair, they felt that "no other regimen currently available offers as much to the chronic addict" (48). Legislators in New York State responded by appropriating $15 million for the establishment of additional methadone maintenance programs.

In 1970 the Bureau of Narcotics and Dangerous Drugs, in a joint statement with the Food and Drug Administration, approved the use of methadone as an investigational drug for "experimental" maintenance programs and interdicted further research except in accordance with guidelines to be promulgated by regulations (21). Emphasis continued to be on eventual abstinence.

INTERFACE OF PROGRAMS AND GOVERNMENT REGULATION

Evidence of the effectiveness of methadone maintenance established it as the treatment of choice, and legal barriers to maintenance went down in most parts of the country. Methadone maintenance clinics proliferated rapidly, perhaps too rapidly to acquire enough qualified and properly trained staff. Counseling and rehabilitation services were too often inadequate. Loitering in the vicinity of clinics, polydrug and alcohol abuse, and illicit diversion of methadone all came to be defined as "problems of methadone treatment, but were in fact the problems of inadequately funded clinics" (33). In a 1970 speech Dr. Ray Trussell addressed this issue: "Our (Beth Israel) patients do not get high, but there are patients in other programs who sometimes do, because doctors are playing with methadone who have not had any training in how to use it. They may indeed discredit methadone because they are not following the Dole-Nyswander technique, or if they're using other techniques they're not following them with careful, scientific evaluation" (57). Evaluation became a problem, because different programs set up different criteria for success, and many of them set eventual abstinence as an objective, despite the lack of evidence demonstrating that maintenance led to abstinence. Varying criteria for admission and discharge made it difficult to compare treatment outcome or even retention rates. The farther programs moved philosophically from the Dole-Nyswander model, the more important became the goal of eventual detoxification from methadone.

Some controversy centered around the question of dosage. Where eventual detoxification was seen as the goal of maintenance, low dosage was favored. It was found also that "blocking" doses were not necessary for some patients who sought only relief from narcotic hunger. In general it was found that the best approach was to determine dosage in terms of each individual patient's needs; it should be one that makes the patient feel comfortable and that prevents further use of heroin.

Diversion of methadone for illicit use was also a concern. By 1972, over 50,000 patients were being treated in "research investigations" across the country (4). The status of methadone was officially changed from IND (investigational new drug) to NDA (new drug application) by the Food and Drug Administration (FDA). With this move, the FDA issued regulations setting treatment standards with minimum staff to patient ratio, specific criteria for eligibility for methadone maintenance, and a basic minimum level of supportive rehabilitative services (22). Interestingly, many of these criteria echoed those of the original pilot project and failed to consider subsequent evidence that these restrictions were no longer necessary. Individual states added their own regulatory procedures, and individual programs were allowed to develop even more restrictive criteria.

Although the Food and Drug Administration attempted to maintain or improve standards in methadone maintenance clinics, its regulations were interpreted by many as a means of controlling diversion and of collecting data to assess the safety and efficacy of methadone (45). New regulations, proposed in 1978 by a joint FDA-National Institute on Drug Abuse committee provide for flexibility, but at this writing (1980), these governmental regulations have yet to be promulgated. Staff of maintenance programs feel pressure to maintain patients on low doses and to detoxify patients after an arbitrary period of treatment. There is little provision for the rehabilitated former addict who needs continued maintenance or follow-up treatment after detoxification. The regulations assume, wrongly and unfairly (17) that a patient has no need for medication if he is rehabilitated (17). What the regulations do not take into account is the heterogeneity of the addict population. Heroin addicts vary in age, personality, constitution, environmental background, culture, their mode of becoming addicts, and the duration of their addiction, to name only a few points of difference. What they have in common is their addiction (47). Numerous studies (2, 24, 50, 51) of personality variables have failed to identify predisposing characteristics or an "addictive personality." Although there is ample evidence of psychological deviance among ex-heroin addicts in treatment programs, these deviances are not sufficient to define the majority of heroin addicts as dysfunctionally psychotic or neurotic (29, 46, 58). Finally, the old adage that "heroin addiction burns itself out with time" (61) has been seriously challenged. When upper age limits were removed, large numbers of older addicts applied for methadone maintenance treatment. According to one investigator (33): "After many years of hard-core heroin addiction, addicts find themselves either incapable of supporting their habits without being arrested, or incarcerated for life, or dead."

TARGET POPULATIONS

There are special treatment populations with special needs. Community-based programs should be flexible enough to adapt their services to accommodate the needs of adolescents, pregnant women, and the medically or mentally ill, among others. For those whose development has been seriously handicapped by poverty, lack of education, or minority status, "habilitation" must come before rehabilitation.

Adolescent drug abuse is a most difficult challenge to rehabilitation programs, and there is a pressing need for careful study of this problem that is on the increase, with drug abuse occurring in preadolescent young people to an alarming extent. (Adolescent drug abuse is treated in greater detail in Chapter 59.) In their initial research, Dole and Nyswander excluded addicts under the age of 20 because they felt these youngsters might be amenable to other approaches. Other investigators have used methadone in low dose, long term (6 months to 1 year) ambulatory detoxification as an adjunct to rehabilitation of the addict under age 18 (44, 54). Lehman and DeAngelis reported some success using low dose methadone with psychotherapy treatment and antidepressants (35).

Although the majority opinion seems to be in the direction of long term ambulatory

detoxification for adolescent addicts, investigators treating adolescents at Boston City Hospital concluded that adolescents should receive the same treatment that older addicts receive so that they can return to school rather than spend their time "hustling" (52). The authors believed that careful individual evaluation of each adolescent should be made to ascertain which treatment modality, or which combination, is indicated for each young person. Careful evaluation and consideration are necessary for long term ambulatory detoxification for those under the age of 16 who have been using narcotics for at least 2 years and who have not responded to other treatment approaches (37).

The most common chronic medical problems presented at admission to methadone maintenance treatment programs, aside from generally poor nutritional and health status, are chronic liver disease, chronic pulmonary disease, tuberculosis, and venereal diseases (34). In most cases, however, patients with medical complications can be maintained on methadone by being treated concurrently for their medical problems (see Chapter 53). The physical work-up required for admission to a methadone program may uncover serious medical problems that need treatment. In many cases, intervention may result in avoiding serious complications that could develop if these problems had not been detected.

A large percentage of patients who enter methadone maintenance treatment exhibit little or no psychopathology, but patients who do have psychiatric problems may require a large amount of time and energy from the staff. Because psychiatric facilities and community mental health centers are often reluctant to treat patients with a history of drug use for a variety of reasons, methadone maintenance treatment programs should have staff psychiatrists and psychiatric social workers who can make reliable diagnoses and provide treatment where possible and referral where necessary. Some methadone-maintained patients respond to psychotropic medication coupled with counseling (9, 53, 60). A well supervised staff may be able to provide brief therapy in the clinic. For long term therapy, there should be referrals to psychiatric clinics or community mental health centers that are willing and capable of providing this service. Therapists who have worked with methadone-maintained patients individually, in dyads, in groups, and in family therapy confirm that methadone does not blunt or otherwise alter affect, anxiety level, perception, or mood. However, one should not expect that the resolution of a patient's psychiatric problems means that his narcotic hunger will not return if he is withdrawn from methadone (41).

The pregnant woman who abuses drugs must be designated as "high risk" (as is the unborn fetus and neonate). She requires support and psychosocial counseling. Treatment modalities should be capable of meeting the needs of the patient and providing treatment that is acceptable. The duration of narcotic addiction and the possibility of multidrug abuse must be considered. Acute detoxification of a pregnant patient with a long drug history might prove harmful. If the use of heroin is of relatively recent onset or infrequent, a drug-free existence should be considered (23). Good prenatal care and a warm, supportive staff can result in the birth of healthy infants to these mothers. Generally, the methadone dose can be reduced most safely during the second trimester. Maintaining a pregnant woman on methadone is done with the intention of preventing heroin injection with its attendant complications (56) or to prevent the substitution of alcohol or other drugs. All investigators agree that good prenatal care and counseling result in favorable outcomes. (Care of the pregnant addict is treated in greater detail in Chapter 44.)

What should be the approach to the methadone patient who is "rehabilitated," who does not take unprescribed drugs or excessive alcohol, who does not commit crimes, who is reintegrated in some fashion with the community—but whose conditioned life style and lack of education and vocational skills allow for only marginal adjustment to the "straight" world? For this special population there persists discrimination in the work place, in housing, and in the fundamental lack of social acceptance and legal protection. Vigorous social services must be made available if the inner-city addict is to move into a more productive, happier life. "Without such help the patient is likely to be trapped in his past, even if he stops using heroin" (10). From a public health point of view, this group may be satisfying criteria for "success" in methadone maintainence treatment programs; nevertheless, from his or her own individual perspective, countless impediments to the achievement of personal satisfaction and growth remain. Corman et al. (7) reported deep concern about the welfare of methadone-maintained patients who fall into this category. The degree of success of the early Dole-Nyswander programs, where maintenance was accompanied by rehabilitation efforts of a dedicated staff, has not been reached because most programs have set different goals and have failed to build in the services needed by their special populations.

DETOXIFICATION, RELAPSE, AND THE SECONDARY ABSTINENCE SYNDROME

Detoxification from methadone (treated at greater length in Chapter 29), long an issue with critics of maintenance, was also becoming a goal for some patients who felt they no longer needed medication to continue living normal lives. Dole's observation of physiological abnormalities after withdrawal of narcotic drugs had made him cautious. Experiments with animals and humans showed that narcotic drugs produced permanent changes, leaving an imprint on the central nervous system, and that abnormal drug-seeking behavior might well have a neurochemical cause (11). Until an answer was found, the Dole-Nyswander team would hold to their original goals. Other approaches, they commented, seek the goal of total abstinence, "even if it means confinement of subjects in an institution" (15). However, they believed that patients had the right to set their own goals—and those patients seeking detoxification would continue to receive support and assistance in reaching these goals.

The procedure for detoxification from methadone is relatively easy, even for patients who have been maintained on methadone for years. The difficulties come after detoxification (see Chapter 29). Generally, very small percentages of patients who detoxify, even when carefully selected and detoxified under the most favorable circumstances, are able to remain abstinent (12, 40). Dole and Nyswander reported particular concern for patients who came to them at Rockefeller University for help some months after having been detoxified at other clinics. "Usually too embarrassed to return to their former programs, they report break-up of marriages, alcoholism, loss of jobs, drug abuse (heroin, cocaine), and depression" (16).

All of these symptoms are in accord with

the "secondary abstinence" syndrome in a report published by Martin et al. (42) describing the primary abstinence syndrome: "Two salient characteristics appear to worsen during protracted abstinence: 1) A poor self-image and 2) An incapacity to tolerate stress and a proneness to over-react or be overly concerned about discomfort." The pattern of changes after withdrawal is likened to that after withdrawal from morphine. However, their findings provide additional support for the hypothesis that the "chronic administration of narcotic analgesics causes a long lasting disturbance in physiological functioning for many months after withdrawal" (42). In a pharmacological sense, there is, as yet, no proof of "cure" following prolonged addiction to narcotics. After many years of abstinence in jail or in a treatment center, one rapidly becomes readdicted when exposed again to narcotics (8). Animal studies show that adaptive changes induced by narcotics may persist indefinitely after withdrawal (6, 32).

PROGRESS IN BASIC RESEARCH RELEVANT TO DRUG ABUSE

That narcotic drugs (as well as other mood-altering drugs) are positively reinforcing is evidenced by the fact that they are self-administered by experimental animals in the laboratory, whereas drugs of other classes are not. The search to identify the mechanism of addiction has focused on identifying specific receptor sites in the nervous system (55) (see Chapter 5). In the early 1970's it was discovered that the vertebrate brain contains receptors for opiates and that the central nervous system itself produces endogenous morphine-like substances. The term "endorphin" was coined by Eric Simon at New York University to denote the morphomimetic action of these endogenous peptides.

In speculating about a possible role of the endorphins in opiate addiction, Goldstein (25) observed that, if a hormone is administered, the body tends to shut down production of that same hormone. Conceivably, when the opiate receptors are continuously exposed to exogenous opiates, the natural production of endorphins might be shut down, and the withdrawal syndrome could be due to an endorphin deficiency when the narcotic is removed. Return of normal endor-

phin production might take months or years. Long lasting mood disorders and other protracted abstinence phenomena could possibly reflect the endorphin deficiency. However, one must recognize that, despite extraordinary progress in the area of basic research, the final answers may lie in the distant future (see Chapter 5). Until we have a more satisfactory explanation for the alarming relapse of detoxified patients, we must rely on empirical evidence. This shows that patients on methadone should not be detoxified until they are rehabilitated, request detoxification, and plan it in consultation with program staff. Detoxified patients should be allowed to resume maintenance when and if they wish it. Even if this becomes a "revolving door" pattern, it is preferable for both the patient and the community that he or she be in treatment. Moreover, the continuation of maintenance therapy should not be conditioned on a patient's progress in rehabilitation. As in psychiatry and other medical specialties, limited goals may have to be accepted for some patients (37). Many blind alleys will doubtless have to be run down before this long sought goal is reached. We may find that the role of endorphins or other, still undiscovered, neurotransmitters in mental illness, pain, addiction, and homeostatic regulation will provide us with greater insight into the mechanisms involved in brain functioning (see Chapter 5).

CONCLUSION

It is clear that from its inception many accepted the methadone maintenance modality for the wrong reasons, seeing it as a means of lowering the social costs of addiction, such as crime, penal incarceration, and hospitalization. That promise is still being kept, if not at levels expected by early evaluations. What cannot be measured and is too often discounted is the individual experience of a patient stabilized on methadone, relieved of narcotic hunger, and once more able to enjoy normal living. Although law enforcement agencies, especially the Drug Enforcement Administration, have made progress in controlling the traffic in heroin, complete control is an unrealistic goal.

If the elusive cause of chronic narcotic addiction can be found in basic research, eventually a "cure" may be arrived at. Interest in narcotic addiction over the years has undoubtedly spurred recent scientific research. To the clinician this offers a glimmer of light at the end of the tunnel. Although methadone maintenance is not a panacea for narcotic addiction—and never promised to be—its contribution to successful treatment for thousands is undeniable. It remains a very useful tool in our treatment armamentarium.

References

1. Alksne, H., Trussell, R. E., and Elinson, J. *Follow-up Study of Treated Adolescent Narcotics Users.* New York, Columbia University School of Public Health and Administrative Medicine, 1959.
2. Berzins, J. I., Ross, W. F., and Monroe, J. J. Cross-validation of the Hill-Monroe Acceptability for Psychotherapy Scale for addict males. J. Clin. Psychol. 26:199, 1970.
3. Brecher, E. *Licit and Illicit Drugs.* Boston, Little, Brown and Company, 1972.
4. Bureau of Narcotics and Dangerous Drugs. *Fact Sheet on Methadone,* 3. Washington, D.C., United States Government Printing Office, 1972.
5. Caplan, R. B. *Psychiatry and the Community in Nineteenth Century America.* New York, Basic Books, 1969.
6. Cochin, J., and Kornetsky, C. Development and loss of tolerance to morphine in the rat after single and multiple injections. J. Pharmacol. Exp. 145:1, 1964.
7. Corman, A., Johnson, B., Khantzian, E., and Long, J. Rehabilitation of narcotic addicts with methadone: The public health approach vs. the individual perspective. Contemp. Drug Probl. 2: 576, Winter, 1973.
8. Cushman, P., and Dole, V. P. Detoxification of rehabilitated methadone-maintained patients. J. A. M. A. 226:747, 1973.
9. Demirjian, A., and Dowell, S. Resocialization: A treatment modality for heroin addicts with severe psychiatric disorders. In *Proceedings of the Fourth National Conference on Methadone Treatment,* San Francisco, 1972, pp. 521–524. New York, National Association for the Prevention of Addiction to Narcotics, 1972.
10. Dole, V. P. Blockade with methadone. In *Narcotic Drugs: Biochemical Pharmacology,* D. Clouet, editor, p. 480. New York, Plenum Press, 1971.
11. Dole, V. P. Pharmacological treatment of drug addiction. Mod. Med. (Minneap.) 40:19, 1972.
12. Dole, V. P., and Joseph, H. Long-term outcome of patients treated with methadone maintenance. Ann. N. Y. Acad. Sci. 311:181, 1978.
13. Dole, V. P., and Nyswander, M. A medical treatment for diacetylmorphine (heroin) addiction: A clinical trial with methadone hydrochloride. J. A. M. A. 193: 80, 1965.
14. Dole, V. P., and Nyswander, M. E. Rehabilitation of heroin addicts after blockade with methadone. N. Y. State J. Med. 66:2011, 1966.
15. Dole, V. P., and Nyswander, M. E. Heroin addiction: A metabolic disease. Arch. Intern. Med. 120:19, 1967.
16. Dole, V. P., and Nyswander, M. E. Rehabilitation of patients on methadone programs. In *Proceedings of the Fifth National Conference on Methadone Treat-*ment, pp. 1–7. New York, National Association for the Prevention of Addiction to Narcotics, 1973.
17. Dole, V. P., and Nyswander, M. E. Methadone maintenance treatment: A ten year perspective. J. A. M. A. 235:2117, 1976.
18. Dole, V. P., Nyswander, M. E., and Kreek, M. J. Narcotic blockade. Arch. Intern. Med. 118:301, 1966.
19. Dupont, R. L., and Piemme, T. E. Evolution of an urban drug treatment program. Clin. Res. 29:573, 1971.
20. Ellenberger, H. F. Psychiatry from ancient to modern times. In *American Handbook of Psychiatry,* S. Arieti, editor, ed. 2, vol. I, chapter I. New York, Basic Books, 1974.
21. Federal Register. 35. 9013. June 11, 1970.
22. Federal Register. 37. 16790. Dec. 15, 1972.
23. Finnegan, L. Women in treatment. In *Handbook on Drug Abuse,* R. Dupont, A. Goldstein, and J. O'Donnell, editors, pp. 121–131. Washington, D.C., National Institute on Drug Abuse, 1979.
24. Gendreau, P., and Gendreau, L. P. The "addiction-prone" personality: A study of Canadian heroin addicts. Can. J. Behav. Sci. 2:18, 1970.
25. Goldstein, A. Recent advances in basic research relevant to drug abuse. In *Handbook on Drug Abuse,* R. L. Dupont, A. Goldstein, and J. O'Donnell, editors, pp. 439–443. Washington, D.C., National Institute on Drug Abuse, 1979.
26. Goldstein, A., Aronow, L., and Kalman, S. *Principles of Drug Addiction: The Basis of Pharmacology,* ed. 2. New York, John Wiley & Sons, 1974.
27. Guillemin, R. Beta-lipotropin and endorphins: Implications of current knowledge. Hosp. Pract. 13:53, 1978.
28. Himmelsbach, C. K. Studies of certain addiction characteristics of (a) dihydromorphine (Paramorphan), (b) dehydrodesoxymorphine-D (Desomorphine), (c) dehydrodesoxy-codeine-D (Descodeine) and (d) methyldehydro-morphinone (Metopon). J. Pharmacol. Exp. Ther. 67:239, 1939.
29. Hunt, L. G., and Chambers, C. D. *The Heroin Epidemics. A Study of Heroin Use in 1965–75.* New York, Spectrum, 1976.
30. Isbell, H. Methods and results of studying experimental human addiction to the newer synthetic analgesics. Ann. N. Y. Acad. Sci. 51:108, 1948.
31. Isbell, H., and Vogel, V. The addiction liability of methadone (Amidone, Dolophine, 10820) and its use in the treatment of the morphine abstinence syndrome. Am. J. Psychiatry 105:909, 1949.
32. Khazan, N., and Colasapti, B. EEG correlates of morphine challenge in post addict rats. Psychopharmacologia 22:56, 1971.
33. Kreek, M. J. Pharmacologic modalities of therapy: Methadone maintenance and the use of narcotic antagonists. In *Heroin Dependency: Medical, Economic and Social Aspects,* B. Stimmel, editor, pp. 232–290. New York, Stratton Intercontinental Medical Book Corporation, 1975.
34. Kreek, M. J. Medical complications in methadone patients. Ann. N. Y. Acad. Sci. 311:110, 1978.
35. Lehman, W. X., and DeAngelis, G. G. Adolescents, methadone and psychotherapeutic agents. In *Proceedings of the Fourth National Conference on Methadone Treatment,* San Francisco, 1972, pp. 55–58. New York, National Association for the Prevention of Addiction to Narcotics, 1972.

36. Lindesmith, A. R., and Gagnon, J. H. Anomie and drug addiction. In *Anomie and Deviant Behavior*, M. Clinard, editor, pp. 158–188. New York, Free Press of Glencoe, 1964.

37. Lowinson, J. H. The methadone maintenance research program. In *Rehabilitating the Narcotic Addict*, Report of Institute on New Developments in the Rehabilitation of the Narcotic Addict, Fort Worth, Texas, February 16–18, 1966, pp. 271–284. Sponsored jointly by the Division of Hospitals of the United States Public Health Service, Vocational Rehabilitation Administration and Texas Christian University. Washington, D.C., United States Government Printing Office, 1967.

38. Lowinson, J. H. Commonly asked clinical questions about methadone maintenance. Int. J. Addict. 12: 821, 1977.

39. Lowinson, J. H., and Millman, R. B. Clinical aspects of methadone maintenance treatment. In *Handbook on Drug Abuse*, R. Dupont, A. Goldstein, and J. O'Donnell, editors, pp. 49–56. Washington, D.C., National Institute on Drug Abuse, 1979.

40. Lowinson, J. H., Ruiz, P., Alksne, L., and Langrod, J. Implications of detoxification from methadone and public policy. Presented at the Annual Meeting, American Psychiatric Association, May 1977, Toronto, Canada.

41. Lowinson, J. H., and Zwerling, I. Group therapy with narcotic addicts. In *Comprehensive Group Psychotherapy*, H. Kaplan and B. Sadock, editors, pp. 602–622. Baltimore, Williams & Wilkins, 1971.

42. Martin, W. R., Jasinski, D. R., Haertzen, C. A., Kay, D. C., Jones, B. E., Mansky, P., and Carpenter, R. W. Methadone: A reevaluation. Arch. Gen. Psychiatry vol. 28:286, 1973.

43. Medical Society of New York. Quoted in Hentoff, N. *A Doctor among the Addicts*, p. 44. New York, Grove Press, 1968.

44. Millman, R. B., and Nyswander, M. E. Slow detoxification of adolescent heroin addicts in New York City. In *Proceedings of the Third National Conference on Methadone Treatment*, pp. 88–89. Washington, D.C., United States Government Printing Office, 1971.

45. Morrell, M. X. Maintenance of opiate dependent persons in the United States: A legal medical history. In *Drug Use in America: Problem in Perspective*, The Technical Papers of the Second Report of the National Commission on Marihuana and Drug Abuse, March, 1973, vol. IV: *Treatment and Rehabilitation*, pp. 516–533. Washington, D.C., United States Government Printing Office, 1973.

46. Myerson, D. J., and Mayer, J. The drug addict. In *The Practice of Community Mental Health*, H. Grunebaum, editor, pp. 197–218. Boston, Little, Brown and Company, 1970.

47. (The) New York Academy of Medicine, Committee on Public Health, Subcommittee on Drug Addiction. Report on Drug Addiction. Bull. N. Y. Acad. Med., 31:592, 1955.

48. (The) New York Academy of Medicine, Committee on Public Health. *Methadone Management of Heroin Addiction*. Bull. N.Y. Acad. Med. 46:391, 1970.

49. Newman, R. G. *Methadone Treatment in Narcotic Addiction*. New York, Academic Press, 1977.

50. Ogborne, A. C. Two types of heroin reactions. Br. J. Addict. 69:237, 1974.

51. Platt, J. J. "Addiction-proneness" and personality in heroin addicts. J. Abnorm. Psychol. 84:303, 1975.

52. Rosenberg, C. M., and Patch, V. C. Twelve month follow-up of adolescent addicts treated with methadone. In *Proceedings of the Fourth National Conference on Methadone Treatment*, San Francisco, 1972, pp. 51–54. New York, National Association for the Prevention of Addiction to Narcotics, 1972.

53. Salzman, B., and Frosch, W. Methadone maintenance for the psychiatrically disturbed. In *Proceedings of the Fourth National Conference on Methadone Treatment*, San Francisco, 1972, pp. 117–118. New York, NAPAN, 1972.

54. Schooff, K. G., and Stanczak, S. A. A methadone withdrawal program for young heroin addicts. In *Proceedings of the Committee on Drug Dependence*, pp. 1904–1934. Washington, D.C., National Research Council, 1971.

55. Simon, E. J. In search of the opiate receptor. Am. J. Med. Sci. 266:161, 1973.

56. Stimmel, B. *Heroin Dependency; Medical, Economic and Social Aspects*, pp. 173–174. New York, Stratton Intercontinental Medical Book Corporation, 1975.

57. Trussell, R. E. Methadone maintenance and how it works. Presented at a program of The Greater New York Hospital Association, New York, January 21, 1970.

58. Vaillant, G. E. A twelve year follow-up of New York narcotic addicts. III. Some social and psychiatric characteristics. Arch. Gen. Psychiatry 123:599, 1966.

59. Weiland, W. F., and Chambers, C. D. A comparison of two stabilization techniques. Int. J. Addict. 5:4, 1970.

60. Weiland, W. F., and Tislow, R. F. Use of phenothiazines and antidepressants in the treatment of depression and schizophrenia in methadone-maintained patients. In *Proceedings of the Third National Conference on Methadone Treatment*, pp. 73–74. Washington, D.C., United States Government Printing Office, 1971.

61. Winick, C. Maturing out of narcotics addiction. Bull. Narc. 14:1, 1962.

CHAPTER 27

ORAL OPIUM MAINTENANCE FOR HEROIN ADDICTS: SOME CONSIDERATIONS

Andrew T. Weil, M.D.

Nonmedical use of drugs continues to be a powerful focus for projection of individual and collective anxiety within our society. Of all the unapproved drugs, heroin has drawn the most emotion. It has been for many years the "devil drug" among us, and its addicts have inspired the most extreme and curious attitudes.

Today, as part of a larger change in conceptions about drugs, some of the myths about heroin are beginning to lose their credibility. Many physicians now understand that heroin is no different fundamentally from other, accepted opiates and that it may have therapeutic value they have never had a chance to test. At least one public lobby is calling for the legalization of heroin for treatment of intractable pain, especially in terminal cancer patients.[1] Many students of drug abuse now admit that some people can use heroin in a controlled and stable fashion over time (2)—a notion that seemed incredible not long ago. And many social authorities are coming to realize that the worst aspects of the heroin problem are direct results of the

criminalization of the drug rather than of the drug itself.

All of these new attitudes are slowly changing the public conception of heroin. It is losing its status as the devil drug par excellence (perhaps phencyclidine will now assume that position of honor), and one hears restrained but growing clamor for its decriminalization.

Decriminalization is a fashionable term. Marihuana has been decriminalized in a number of states. There is mounting pressure to decriminalize cocaine. It is a shame that these battles are occurring over individual drugs, because what is wrong is the entire structure of criminal law that has been created to deal with drug abuse. The private use of all drugs, whether approved by medical authorities or not, must be decriminalized if we are to begin improving our relationships with these substances. It should not be a matter of arguing the merits or demerits of each one.

But, apparently, we are to have limited wars over specific drugs at this stage of things. Greater progress has occurred with marihuana so far just because more people use it than any other illegal psychoactive drug. Some progress has occurred with co-

---

[1] The National Committee on the Treatment of Intractable Pain, P.O. Box 34571, Washington, D.C. 20034. This organization publishes a monthly newsletter.

caine because its users, although fewer, tend to be affluent, articulate, and influential.

What is interesting about the growing demand for heroin decriminalization is that it does not come from the using lobby. Most heroin addicts are disenfranchised in our society. They are deviants and outcasts, in and out of trouble. And those who use the drug successfully and stay out of trouble usually do not want their use known. Instead, the heroin reform movement is an odd coalition of government officials, law enforcement agents, and drug abuse professionals. They ought to be more persuasive than users in arguing for change; consequently, we may expect significant change in policy on heroin before long.

If we decriminalize heroin, what can we do about it? How can we minimize abuse of that drug and render it as harmless as possible to society? One alternative, of course, is to provide it legally to those who want to use it.

Heroin maintenance programs for addicts were unthinkable only 10 years ago. (There is great collective amnesia in America about the morphine maintenance clinics of the 1920's (4).) Now heroin maintenance is discussed as a serious option (1, 5). This development should force us to talk about what is good and what is bad about using heroin as opposed to using something else.

What is good about heroin from the user's point of view is that it provides a reliable, intense high, marked by euphoria and insulation from unpleasant experience. If we are not going to give heroin addicts heroin, we are going to have to give them something they regard as good in the same way.

Methadone fails as an alternative in this respect. Oral methadone just does not give a good high to an addict. It may be useful and desirable from many other points of view, especially those of methadone program administrators, but it will never replace heroin or solve the problem of addiction.

Because heroin users take their drug to change their awareness and feel high, it is impossible to discuss this behavior without some understanding of altered states of consciousness.

We all spend time in other states of consciousness throughout the day. In fact, if we add up the scattered moments of daydreaming and other varieties of light trance, we may find that these experiences take up a majority of our clock time. Some of the most interesting of these states we call highs. There are many ways of achieving them: from athletics and lovemaking to music and dance to creative expression to meditation and religious ecstasy. High does not mean intoxicated, but, clearly, psychoactive drugs, including heroin, are one route to these experiences.

I am convinced that it is necessary to our mental and physical health to experience highs periodically, and I am not surprised that so much human effort goes into achieving them. One reason they may be good for us is that they help us integrate conscious and unconscious experience and balance the mind and body through the circuitry of the autonomic nervous system (7).

Although highs and other altered states are part of our experiential repertoire, we cannot always place ourselves in them at will. Perhaps, this difficulty arises from the involvement of unconscious or involuntary brain centers in their production. Common methods used to alter awareness seem to focus conscious attention (on intense or novel sensation, for example), to stimulate unconscious mental activity (such as internal imagery), or to produce unusual psychophysical states (as in fasting, long distance running, or drug experience).

Drugs work to elicit highs because they make people feel different temporarily. But a "drug high" is a learned association between the direct psychophysical effects of a chemical and an altered state of consciousness latent within the human nervous system. Drugs work only if set and setting encourage the development of this association. The same high can be had without the drug, and the same drug can be taken without giving a high. In other words, psychoactive drugs function as *active* placebos.

Many methods used to alter awareness can be dangerous acutely and can produce tolerance and dependence over time. In a society like ours that does not recognize the need for periodic alteration of consciousness and does not provide social support for it, people do not easily learn how to enter high states safely. The drug problem has its roots in our attitudes about altered states of consciousness.

There are multitudinous ways of achieving highs without drugs (6, 9). Drugs are popular because they seem to work powerfully and immediately. I reject the notion that some drugs are good and others bad. Drugs are drugs, and all have an ambivalent potential for constructive or destructive use. Good and bad are valid terms only in describing a particular individual's use of a particular drug.

I find it more interesting to talk about relationships with drugs than about drugs themselves. Some people can form good relationships with the most dangerous, most disapproved drugs. Some people form bad relationships with the mildest, most approved drugs.

What are the characteristics of a good relationship with a drug? First, the user should be aware that he is using a drug. With that awareness, there is, at least, a basis for caution, because it is the nature of drugs to get out of control and cause problems. Second, the user should get something positive out of the drug: a useful high, for example, and not just the relief of negative symptoms that are results of overuse. Third, the user should be able to separate himself from the drug easily. Fourth, his use should not lead to any adverse effects on health or social functioning.

Now, here are several key observations about drugs and highs: As people use any drug more and more frequently, they get less and less high on it; the earliest experiences with any drug are the strongest; people who use drugs most frequently and most compulsively get the least out of them.

Why should drugs become less effective at eliciting highs as they are used with greater frequency? The explanation lies in the indirect relationship between the pharmacological effects of drugs and the high state, which is a latent capacity of the human nervous system. Drugs can only continue to work for us as long as they make us feel unusual when we take them. The unusual feeling is strongest in our earliest experiences with the drug and becomes a learned cue for the desired altered state of consciousness. With increasing frequency of use, the novelty of the psychophysical change fades, and the drug no longer serves as well as an active placebo to bring on a high. This change can be very frustrating for the user who thinks the high is synonymous with the drug. Such a person will often pursue the disappearing high by using more frequently or by looking for "better" forms of the drug—actions that make the problem worse.

Paradoxically, the way to retrieve a lost drug high is to decrease frequency of use until the psychophysical effects of the drug become novel and noticeable again. In other words, less is more: the quality of drug use correlates inversely with frequency of use. Moreover, those users who take drugs most frequently take them the most compulsively, having difficulty separating themselves from the drugs, and sometimes suffering adverse effects of their overuse. Explanations of this basic principle of human interaction with drugs should be a cornerstone of drug education.

Let us now consider heroin in the light of the foregoing analysis. Are there any special disadvantages of heroin as a choice of psychoactive drug?

I have three complaints with heroin. First, it is too short acting. Second, it lends itself too easily to intravenous use. Third, it provokes tolerance and dependence of a difficult sort, and many users do not discover methods for containing these problems.

In calling drugs active placebos, I do not mean to imply that they do nothing. Clearly, drugs have direct actions that serve as cues for eliciting altered states of consciousness. The more powerful the drug, the more the experience is shaped by direct pharmacological action, and the less easy it is for the user to notice other sorts of highs, especially those not associated with drugs at all. This problem is very clear among heroin addicts. Heroin is a powerful derivative of opium. Its power correlates with its potency, its short duration of action, and the tendency of addicts to use it intravenously. These factors combine to provide a very intense, brief, psychophysical change that users call a "rush."

To hear a heroin addict talk about this rush is both fascinating and dismaying. Words cannot describe it. No other experience matches it. Other sorts of highs pale by comparison.

The spellbinding power of the mainline heroin rush is the essential difficulty with this drug. Heroin addicts have backed themselves into a pharmacological corner where it is hard or impossible to appreciate the virtues of other psychophysical changes that are less intense but much more manageable over time. Pursuit of the heroin rush leads many users into greater and worse involvement with the drug, often at serious cost to themselves and society. Hence, the much quoted admonition of one addict: "It's so good, don't even try it once."

I have a strong memory of interviewing a

17-year-old girl who was undergoing withdrawal from heroin in a psychiatric hospital. She was intelligent and articulate, the child of a well-to-do military family, who had grown up all over the world. She was interested in meditation and other drugless methods of changing her consciousness, and in our discussion she remembered getting high throughout childhood by rolling down hills. She saw clearly that her addictive use of heroin had created great problems for her. "But you can't imagine what that rush feels like," she told me. "It's just the most intense, wonderful feeling, and I worry that I will always be tempted to feel it again because nothing else I've tried comes close to it."

Now, it is clear that some people can experience this rush and learn to stabilize their use of heroin over time. They avoid the pattern of dependence by limiting frequency of consumption in some way, perhaps by developing rituals and sanctions around their use. As long as they do not use too frequently, they can avoid the trap of subjective tolerance. The effect of the drug remains novel for them, and they can continue to use it to trigger high states. Of course, it is important to find out what kinds of people become controlled users of heroin and how they do it. With that information, possibly, we could prevent some addiction and encourage some of those just starting to take heroin to do so in a nondependent fashion. In a society where the nonmedical use of heroin was not a criminal act, such persons would not be drug abusers, especially if they had access to heroin of reasonable price and consistent quality and the knowledge and equipment to inject themselves cleanly.

But what about people who cannot control their use of heroin and remain stable, nonabusive users over time? Can we offer them anything other than abstinence or methadone?

Heroin maintenance does not seem to me an attractive option for several reasons. First, we are not ready for it politically. Heroin still provokes too much fear and suspicion, and the idea of giving it to addicts is unacceptable to too many people. Secondly, the mechanics of heroin maintenance are unwieldy. The drug is too short acting. Addicts would have to come to treatment centers several times a day or reside in them to get their injections, inasmuch as it is unlikely that anyone would favor giving them take-home supplies.

Thirdly, heroin maintenance would not teach addicts to improve the quality of their drug use: to learn better controls or better ways of getting high.

I would like to suggest an alternative that has not been tried to my knowledge: oral opium maintenance.

Opium is an official, medically legitimate drug. Deodorized tincture of opium (DTO, laudanum) is an old remedy, still prescribed occasionally for the treatment of diarrhea and intestinal cramps. In moderate dosage (20 drops in a person with no tolerance to opiates), it gives a feeling of relaxation and well-being that may last 4 hours or more. I have interviewed several heroin addicts who have tried this preparation of opium (many have not), and they say they like it and would readily accept it in a treatment program designed to reduce or eliminate their intravenous use of heroin. In high dosage, oral opium causes significant nausea that all persons perceive as aversive. This effect is a natural deterrent to overuse.

I have written at length elsewhere about the many differences between complex, natural forms of drugs and purified, isolated derivatives (10). Opium and heroin show these differences clearly. In the first place, crude plant drugs, by their physical natures, do not lend themselves to parenteral use; they must be taken by mouth. Secondly, natural drugs are relatively dilute preparations, usually containing 1 to 10 per cent of the major active compound. Thirdly, natural drugs are mixtures of many active substances, and the minor compounds modify or synergize the dominant compound in ways that make the drug safer. Opium contains 22 alkaloids, one of which is morphine. The nausea caused by high doses of oral opium may be an effect of all these drugs acting in concert; certainly, it encourages moderate use. In view of the much greater safety of whole plant drugs, it seems a shame that contemporary pharmacology and medicine ignore these differences in drug forms and encourage the use of potent, isolated chemicals as more "scientific."[2]

---

[2] A good analogy holds between opium versus heroin and coca leaf versus cocaine. Coca contains a low dose of cocaine diluted by other alkaloids that modify its effect and by inert substances. It is used by mouth. Cocaine users who like the rush of intravenous or intranasal dosing often have trouble limiting their intake

In a program of oral opium maintenance, addicts could be given take-home supplies and could be taught to shift from intravenous use of a potent, short acting drug to oral use of a dilute, long acting drug. They would have to sacrifice the intensity of the rush for a more muted but much more manageable effect that is easier to stabilize over time. Heroin users who could learn to be satisfied with oral opium could also learn to experiment with other methods of getting high, including ones that do not require drugs at all.

Oral opium would lend itself much more readily to a maintenance program than smoked opium. Taken by inhalation, opium produces more immediate effects that are more easily titrated. That is, the user gets faster feedback from smoking and can regulate the dose. But smoked opium does not have the built-in deterrent to overuse that comes with oral opium; there is no strong nausea with too much. And opium smokers can easily fall into the habit of smoking all of the time instead of taking discrete doses. Besides, there is no official preparation of opium for smoking, whereas DTO is a standard, available medication.

I do not mean to suggest that oral opium maintenance will be any sort of miraculous solution to heroin addiction. It may only work for a small percentage of properly motivated addicts, and it may present difficulties of its own. As an example of a practical problem that might arise with oral opium maintenance, there is always the possibility that some clients would attempt to smoke their medication by evaporating the tincture and mixing it with tobacco or marihuana. Of course, there would have to be a rule against this practice and some way of enforcing it.

Even if oral opium maintenance will only work for some addicts, it seems to me to be worth trying. We have been enormously reluctant to experiment and innovate in this area. Heroin addiction is a vastly complicated problem, unlikely to be solved by any one technique. Why not, then, experiment with as many reasonable approaches as possible? We can certainly try out new ideas on a small scale to determine whether they work.

Public and professional attitudes about all psychoactive drugs, including heroin, are changing. In many cases the changes are painfully slow. But a kind of creeping enlightenment is discernible, as more and more of us come to see the folly of using the criminal justice system to try to modify patterns of drug use. Decriminalization of the private use of all drugs, including heroin, is an urgent priority. It is by no means synonymous with legalization. It is merely a way of undoing some of the worst complications we have made of the drug problem.

Our best hope is prevention of drug abuse in the first place: through real education about sensible ways to use drugs and about alternatives to drugs, and through the evolution of social sanctions and controls on drug use. Much of what we have done up to now has made such education impossible and has actively interfered with the development of social controls (3).

As for the treatment of those who have not learned how to control their use of drugs, all reasonable ideas should be tested to determine effectiveness. In that spirit I propose a trial of oral opium maintenance for heroin addicts.

References

1. Danaceau, P. *What's Happening with Heroin Maintenance?* Washington, D.C., Drug Abuse Council, 1977.
2. Hunt, L. G., and Zinberg, N. E. *Heroin Use: A New Look.* Washington, D.C., Drug Abuse Council, 1976.
3. Jacobson, R., and Zinberg, N. E. *Social Basis of Drug Abuse Prevention.* Washington, D.C., Drug Abuse Council, 1975.
4. *Morphine Maintenance: The Shreveport Clinic, 1919–1923.* Washington, D.C., Drug Abuse Council, 1974.
5. Olson, L. *Heroin Maintenance Policy Seminar: Summary of Proceedings.* Washington, D.C., National League of Cities, 1978.
6. Rosenfeld, E. *The Book of Highs.* New York, Quadrangle/The New York Times Book Company, 1973.
7. Weil, A. T. *The Natural Mind: A New Way of Looking at Drugs and the Higher Consciousness.* Boston, Houghton Mifflin, 1972.
8. Weil, A. T. The green and the white. In *The Coca Leaf and Cocaine Papers.* G. Andrews and D. Solomon, editors. New York, Harcourt, Brace, Jovanovich, 1975.
9. Weil, A. T. *The Marriage of the Sun and Moon: A Quest for Unity in Consciousness.* Boston, Houghton Mifflin, 1980.
10. Weil, A. T. Botanical vs. chemical drugs: Pros and cons. In *Herbal Medicine and Folk Medicine,* K. Blum and G. G. Meyer, editors. Austin, The University of Texas Press, in press.
11. Zinberg, N. E., Jacobson, R. C., and Harding, W. M. Social sanctions and rituals as a basis for drug abuse prevention. Am. J. Drug Alcohol Abuse 2:165, 1975.

of the concentrated drug when it is available to them in quantity. Coca leaf chewers do not have the same problem and easily learn to stabilize their consumption (8).

CHAPTER 28

LEVO-ALPHA ACETYLMETHADOL (LAAM): CLINICAL UTILITY AND PHARMACEUTICAL DEVELOPMENT

Jack D. Blaine, M.D.

David B. Thomas, D. Stat.

Gene Barnett, Ph.D.

John A. Whysner, M.D., Ph.D.

Pierre F. Renault, M.D.

CLINICAL UTILITY OF LAAM

Although opiates have been used by humans for centuries, only periodically do opiate abuse and addiction emerge as serious social phenomena, stimulating a societal response. The recent "heroin epidemic" of the 1960's was closely associated with other serious social phenomena of the 1960's, including the Vietnam War, the economic impact of street crime on the developing urban ghetto community and the more affluent suburban communities, and the alienation of a visible and vocal segment of the youthful generation. One societal response in the early 1970's was that the federal government allocated considerable resources to improving the treatments available for heroin addicts with the objective of reducing the social and economic costs (8).

For many years, heroin addicts were treated by abrupt or gradual discontinuation of heroin, leading to abstinence. Resulting withdrawal symptoms were often treated palliatively with nonopiate medication. However, the failure of medically controlled heroin detoxification alone to achieve the goal of long term continued abstinence had been voluminously documented in the United States. The reduction of human suffering and temporary freedom from the compulsive search for and use of heroin did have value as a first step in rehabilitation by permitting a shift to more constructive pursuits. Also, efforts at treatment by maintenance of opiate-dependent individuals on legally dispensed heroin seemed to be an inadequate and impractical treatment approach at the time.

Fortunately, an alternative pharmacological treatment agent, methadone, was available. Methadone, a synthetic opiate developed as an analgesic, has a pharmacological profile similar to morphine (40). However, methadone retains its activity when taken by mouth and is slowly inactivated. Thus, one oral daily dose of methadone can substitute for several intravenous doses of heroin interspersed throughout the day. Furthermore, methadone's action over the 24-hour period between doses was relatively smoother and more prolonged, producing more "normal" states of consciousness with less euphoric intoxication and less dysphoric withdrawal than commonly occurs with intravenous street heroin usage patterns.

Dole and Nyswander demonstrated during the mid-1960's that heroin addicts could be "stabilized" for extended time periods on a single daily dose of methadone (15). The dose is gradually increased as tolerance develops, starting from the dose that relieves the abstinence syndrome. As the dose is raised, a level is reached that relieves the individual's craving or "hunger" for heroin but is not intoxicating itself. As the dose level is increased further, sufficient tolerance is induced to block the euphoric effect of intravenous heroin. Thus, long term stabilization on methadone—called methadone maintenance—frees the individual from heroin-oriented hustling and allows participation in a comprehensive treatment and rehabilitation program, providing necessary support services such as vocational, employment, legal, medical, social, and psychological counseling. Data generated by several clinical researchers in the ensuing years supported the safety and effectiveness of this form of treatment under good medical supervision (24, 41).

The success of the initial few methadone maintenance treatment programs led to a rapid nation-wide expansion of variants of this approach stimulated by the availability of federal treatment funds. Although the basic methadone maintenance approach continued to be valid, more extensive clinical experience with methadone uncovered several problems (4, 42, 43). Daily clinic attendance for supervised medication ingestion was inconvenient and burdensome for patients. Some clinicians believed this focus compromised the primary goal of treatment—freeing the heroin addict from dependence on drug and the drug-oriented life style—by substituting dependence on methadone and clinic attendance to the point of disrupting school and work and attaining a non-drug-oriented life style.

Take-home methadone became one of the solutions to this problem. Thus, patients making satisfactory treatment progress were permitted to come to the clinic 3 days a week, and take-home methadone doses were dispensed for out-of-clinic ingestion the other 4 days if daily clinic attendance was viewed as hampering rehabilitation. Unfortunately, take-home methadone created additional problems in large part due to diversion of methadone by patients into illicit channels. These included methadone toxic reactions and overdose deaths in nontolerant individuals, especially children, and the development of an illicit methadone market. The new market supplemented street heroin for some heroin addicts. But illicit methadone also made readily available an oral opiate high for some nonaddict drug users previously avoiding the intravenous route, resulting in primary methadone addicts.

These problems led some clinicians to realize that a longer lasting maintenance medication would offer practical therapeutic advantages over methadone. Fortunately, chemical and pharmacological data already available suggested the potential clinical usefulness of methadyl acetate (levo-alpha acetylmethadol, LAAM), a methadone derivative developed two decades earlier by German chemists (11, 16, 17, 64, 71, 72).

In the late 1960's and early 1970's several teams of treatment researchers investigated the usefulness of LAAM in heroin addiction treatment programs (4, 27, 42, 43, 81). These researchers found that LAAM was a useful

opiate maintenance agent. Also, LAAM offered the patient, clinician, and treatment
program several important advantages over
methadone. Patients found participation in
treatment more acceptable and attended
more regularly when clinic attendance and
dosage schedule were reduced from daily to
three times weekly even for those just entering treatment (57). Many patients found
LAAM preferable to methadone and believed
it was a more efficacious drug (26, 74).
LAAM's smoother, sustained drug effect permitted them to feel healthier, more alert,
emotionally level or "normal." Even during
the induction period, escalating doses did not
produce excessive sedation or subjective euphoria. Patients did not experience nodding
and felt less "loaded," less anxious or nervous. They reported LAAM had less effect
on daily activities. Despite the absence of
these common opiate effects, patients reported that LAAM reduced heroin craving
more than methadone and that LAAM provided a better blockade of intravenous heroin. As a consequence, patients believed their
use of heroin was significantly less on LAAM
than on methadone.

Furthermore, researchers found that
LAAM was less likely than methadone to be
a reinforcer of daily drug-taking behavior
(27, 43, 69). The three times weekly dosing
schedule made the habitual pattern of daily
medication seeking and taking no longer necessary. The individual felt less psychologically dependent, which strengthened his
identification with the drug-free population.
Less treatment program emphasis was placed
on medication taking-related activities (e.g.,
dosage increases, take-home privileges), and
more emphasis could be placed on counseling, human relations, and alternative sources
of gratification (26).

Several psychopharmacological properties
made LAAM less reinforcing and prone to
abuse than methadone. LAAM itself is less
active than its metabolites that take several
hours after oral ingestion to build up adequately for psychoactivity. Drugs with rapid
onset of psychoactivity are more reinforcing
and desired by drug users. Also, LAAM is
more rapidly effective orally than intravenously (4, 21).

Goldstein described a major attitudinal
change of clinic staff and patients in a LAAM-
only clinic, primarily accounted for by an
absence of the take-home issue (26). Much of

the deceit, game playing, cheating, manipulation, argumentation, and corruption in the
staff-patient relationship occurred around the
issues of urine collection results and take-
home methadone. He found that in a LAAM
clinic much of the hassle and unpleasantness
common in methadone clinic operations dramatically improved. Freed from jeopardizing
take-home privilege, patients could be honest
with their counselors about drug use. Therefore, the time and energy of patients and staff
could be more effectively focused on counseling.

Based on the controlled pharmacological
studies and early clinical trials, LAAM was
shown to be a safe and effective opiate maintenance medication possessing several important advantages over methadone. Therefore, the pharmaceutical development of
LAAM became, in 1971, one of the high
priority projects of the Special Action Office
for Drug Abuse Prevention (SAODAP) of the
Executive Office of the President (8). Since
then, the resources of several federal government agencies, particularly the National Institute on Drug Abuse (NIDA), have focused
on LAAM's pharmaceutical development to
permit marketing for treatment of heroin addiction.

A New Drug Application (NDA) was submitted to the Food and Drug Administration
(FDA) in September 1979 requesting approval to market LAAM for treatment of
male heroin addicts; this is currently under
review. The many clinical studies supporting
the safety and effectiveness of LAAM will be
extensively reviewed in the following section
on the pharmaceutical new drug development of LAAM. The final section will summarize and discuss the safety and efficacy
findings and present areas for future research.

PHARMACEUTICAL NEW DRUG DEVELOPMENT OF LAAM

The pharmaceutical development of a new
drug product is a long and complex process.
Before a drug can be marketed under an
approved NDA, controlled testing in animals
and humans must provide the FDA with
substantial scientific evidence that the drug
is safe and effective for the intended use.
After extensive short and long term toxicity
studies in several animal species, three phases
of clinical investigation proceed sequentially

under a "Notice of Claimed Investigational Exemption for a New Drug" (IND) (8).

Unlike methadone, which was marketed as an analgesic prior to its use in narcotic addiction treatment, LAAM was not marketed for any approved medical use. Furthermore, LAAM had been in the public domain for many years and was not patentable. The pharmaceutical industry was not interested in developing a drug without exclusivity for a limited market and a controversial treatment population. Thus, SAODAP created and coordinated the federal government's effort for the pharmaceutical development of LAAM. In 1974 this role was transferred to the Division of Research, National Institute on Drug Abuse (NIDA), whose organizational predecessor, the Division of Narcotic Addiction and Drug Abuse, National Institute of Mental Health, had played an integral part in much of the previous animal and clinical studies on LAAM. NIDA coordinated and conducted under contract the IND studies necessary for the NDA submission from 1974 to 1979 (8).

PHASE I: CLINICAL PHARMACOLOGY—DRUG ACTION AND TOXICITY

GENERAL PHARMACOLOGY AND TOXICITY STUDIES

In the late 1940's and early 1950's, extensive investigations of the clinical pharmacology of LAAM were carried out at the Addiction Research Center, Lexington, Kentucky, using subjects formerly dependent on opiates and withdrawn (21, 22, 39, 40). Single doses of LAAM produced morphine-like physiological and subjective effects. However, Fraser and Isbell commented that "the results were very peculiar," based on the time-effect curves by the parenteral and oral routes of administration. When 10 to 30 mg of LAAM were given by the subcutaneous and intravenous route, no objective manifestations of opiate-like action were noted for 4 to 6 hours after injection, after which time the opiate-like effects slowly became apparent over 12 to 16 hours. The opiate effects after a single dose were extremely long lasting compared to other opiates. These effects were always detectable 24 hours postinjection, usually seen at 48 hours, and occasionally persisted for 72 hours. After oral administration of 30

to 40 mg of LAAM, definite, more intense, morphine-like effects were observed much more rapidly, within 90 minutes, reaching maximum effect in 4 hours, and had a similar persistent action to the parenteral route. Thus, LAAM's activity by mouth was greater than by the parenteral route of administration, and LAAM's delayed onset and prolonged duration of action were noted.

Fraser and Isbell further demonstrated that single oral doses of 30 to 60 mg of LAAM rapidly abolished all signs of abstinence in patients who had been stabilized on 400 mg of morphine daily and abruptly withdrawn 28 hours previously. Substitution of LAAM for morphine was completely adequate when 1 mg daily of oral LAAM was substituted for each 6 to 8 mg of parenteral morphine given four times a day. Thus, LAAM was found to be about as efficacious as 1-methadone in alleviating abstinence from morphine by the oral route, but the drug was inconsistent by the parenteral route of administration due to the slow onset but persistent activity. However, LAAM's complete substitution for morphine persisted over 72 hours, in contrast to methadone, which lasted for 24 hours.

Fraser and Isbell's multiple dose studies of LAAM also revealed interesting results. When sequential doses of LAAM were substituted for morphine dependence, no withdrawal signs appeared when the interval between LAAM doses was increased to 72 hours. When LAAM was given by mouth every 48 to 72 hours, no toxicity occurred, and complete tolerance to the opiate effects was noted. However, when subcutaneous doses of LAAM were given twice daily for several days, cumulative opiate toxicity or opiate overdosing resulted, including respiratory depression, mental confusion, altered consciousness approaching coma, and severe nausea and vomiting.

Patients treated subacutely with LAAM developed a definite but mild abstinence syndrome 84 hours after abrupt discontinuation of LAAM. The abstinence syndrome was quite similar in time course and intensity to methadone. Gradual reduction of LAAM dose over a period of 7 days did not seem to alter the course or intensity of abstinence after the last dose.

EVALUATION AS AN ANALGESIC

Fraser and Isbell suggested LAAM may possess advantages over methadone and other narcotic analgesics if the drug's analgesic effect has as long a duration as the physical dependence-supporting and miotic actions. They cautioned that "if the drug is used clinically, it should be given orally in small dose and at widely separated intervals in order to prevent cumulation of the toxic effects" (21).

Early clinical investigation did focus on the usefulness of LAAM as an analgesic for chronic pain. As predicted, LAAM was less effective than morphine when administered subcutaneously, and the onset of analgesic activity was delayed for about 90 minutes. Delayed cumulative toxic effects of opiate overdose were noted when larger doses of LAAM were given more than once daily to nontolerant chronic pain patients (1, 54). Effective analgesia with extended duration was noted with lower doses of orally administered racemic alpha acetylmethadol (13, 14). The LAAM metabolite, nor-LAAM, was shown to be a more potent analgesic than morphine or LAAM, and toxic side effects were less when taken by mouth (28). Analgesic effects were equivalent with a similar time course to morphine when nor-LAAM was given parenterally (30). However, the delayed onset of action, prolonged time course, and cumulative effect limited the clinical usefulness of LAAM and nor-LAAM for analgesia. Thus, its development was not undertaken by the pharmaceutical industry.

CLINICAL PSYCHOPHARMACOLOGY OF LAAM

Irwin, Blachly, and co-workers compared, in double-blind, randomly controlled studies, the psychopharmacological profiles of 0.1 to 0.2 mg per kg doses of oral methadone and LAAM in nontolerant subjects (6, 33, 35, 36). Peak effects occurred 3 to 4 hours after administration for both drugs. Durations of action were similar for both drugs at lower doses. At higher doses the action of methadone lasted less than 12 hours, whereas LAAM persisted over 24 hours. The higher dose of LAAM produced similar but somewhat less intense subjective effects than the lower dose of methadone.

Biphasic effects were noted for both drugs with early activation, elevation of mood, and liking for the drug, followed by a later depressant effect and dislike for the drug. The effects of LAAM were primarily activating, including slightly increased capacity for functioning, increased arousal, drives, energy, speed, and durations of movement and expressiveness; and slightly improved mood. In contrast, depressant effects predominated with methadone, including impaired arousal, focusing, and psychomotor activity; distorted perceptions; and worsened mood. Methadone and LAAM were quantitatively equipotent in many other effects characteristics of opiates, including causing ataxia, unusual body sensations, distortion of sensations, impaired memory, reduced impulse control, mild headaches, itching, nausea and vomiting, facial palor, slowed respiratory rate, and miosis.

Since then, several investigators have reported data that seem to support these subtle psychopharmacology differences between LAAM and methadone. Crowley et al. reported on a pilot study in which subjects' daily activity was meaured by a pedometer (12). Methadone maintenance patients were compared to LAAM maintenance patients. The LAAM group was more active on the day they ingested LAAM than on the nondrug day. The methadone group did not evidence a significant day to day activity difference. Trueblood et al.'s study discussed previously also confirms those psychopharmacological differences as perceived by patients treated with LAAM and methadone (74).

EVALUATION OF CROSS-TOLERANCE TO INTRAVENOUS OPIATES

Several investigators have studied the development of cross-tolerance by LAAM to the effects of intravenous opiates. Irwin and co-workers found that LAAM was usually effective in providing blockade to 30 mg of morphine sulfate in subjects stabilized on a variety of LAAM doses (35). Occasionally, a slight high was reported, usually within 8 hours or after 48 hours of LAAM consumption. Subjects could distinguish morphine from placebo and experienced a slight rush.

In studies by Zaks and Fink, LAAM provided complete blockade to 25 mg of intravenous heroin administered 24 hours after the LAAM dose in subjects maintained on low doses (30 to 40 mg twice weekly and 50 mg on Friday), whereas 50 mg of heroin produced mild, transient euphoria in these subjects (81). LAAM provided complete blockade to 50 mg of heroin in subjects maintained on an 80-mg dose on Monday, Wednesday, and Friday.

In another study, a dose-response curve was established for the dose of LAAM and blockade of 25 mg of intravenous heroin given 72 hours after the previous LAAM dose in maintenance patients (57). At maintenance dose levels of 30 mg of LAAM given Monday, Wednesday, and Friday, some effects of heroin were experienced. At 50-mg levels, no effect of heroin was perceived by the subjects, but slight pupillary constriction was detected. At dose levels of 70 mg and above, blockade was complete. Interestingly, this approximated the dose-response curve of LAAM to produce sustained maximum pupillary constriction (miosis): 20 mg for 24 hours; 30 to 50 mg for 48 hours; 80 to 90 mg for 72 hours.

METABOLISM IN HUMANS

The recent development of methodologies for identifying and quantitating levels of LAAM and its metabolites in human biofluids has stimulated interest in the metabolism of LAAM (48, 49). The delayed onset, long duration of action, differences by oral and parenteral routes of administration, and cumulative effects of LAAM have, in part, been attributed to the biotransformation to two active metabolites, nor-LAAM and dinor-LAAM, by the n-demethylating enzymes in the liver (2). Several studies indicate that the opiate-like effects of LAAM may be determined primarily by these metabolites rather than the parent compound (3, 25, 29, 50–52).

PHASE I: CLINICAL PHARMACOLOGY—EARLY DOSE RANGE STUDIES AND CLINICAL TRIALS FOR SAFETY AND EARLY EVIDENCE OF EFFECTIVENESS AS A MAINTENANCE DRUG FOR TREATMENT OF CHRONIC HEROIN DEPENDENCE

Jaffe and co-workers in Chicago in the late 1960's initiated the first clinical trials of acetylmethadol (42, 43). In a series of well controlled, double-blind studies, these researchers investigated the safety and efficacy of LAAM and racemic acetylmethadol compared to methadone in chronic heroin-dependent persons (44–46, 68). Subjects already stabilized on methadone or street heroin addicts entering treatment were randomly as-signed to LAAM or methadone. The experimental groups received LAAM on Monday, Wednesday, or Friday, and dextromethorphan placebo on alternate days, and the control group received methadone daily.

Generally, these controlled clinical trials revealed few differences between LAAM and methadone patients on outcome measures of use of heroin and other illicit drugs, illegal activity and arrests, employment, education, clinic attendance, patient acceptance, or dosage changes. They confirmed earlier findings that LAAM can be administered at 48- to 72-hour intervals without the development of an opiate abstinence syndrome.

Few reports of toxicity or side effects were noted. Those adverse reactions that did occur were usually associated with excessive dosage and were also reported with methadone; such events can be considered common to all opiates. Results of hematology, blood chemistry, urinalysis, and physical examinations revealed few differences between LAAM and methadone patients. Most results were within normal limits, and treatment commonly produced an improvement in some abnormal pretreatment laboratory values. The isolated deaths that occurred during the studies were not directly related to LAAM or methadone. Although there were several reports of anxiety and nervousness in an earlier study with racemic acetylmethadol, these were not present when using LAAM. No occurrences of confusion, unpleasant subjective states, or psychotic symptoms caused by LAAM were reported. Several instances of nightmares and anxiety and one report of a dissociative state with bizarre behavior were reported (69).

In the ensuing years after the reports of the initial pilot studies, several additional teams of investigators conducted clinical trials with LAAM (5, 27, 35, 56, 66, 69, 77, 80, 81). Generally, these studies confirmed the findings of comparable safety and effectiveness of LAAM and methadone as maintenance drugs for use in the treatment of chronic heroin-dependent persons. Approximately 750 patients were given LAAM in these studies. Dosages varied widely, with a mean LAAM dosage of 60 mg three times weekly and a range of 20 to 90 mg. Treatment period in these studies had a range of 7 weeks to 48 weeks, with a mean of about 20 weeks.

These investigators found that LAAM given Monday, Wednesday, and Friday prevented the occurrence of withdrawal symptoms equally to methadone given seven times a week (7). Some reported that increasing the dosage either at each administration or on Friday was necessary to completely prevent abstinence symptoms for 72 hours (56, 81). However, the results of a double-blind controlled study by Goldstein and Judson suggest that complaints of LAAM not holding the entire weekend were psychological rather than pharmacological in origin and arose out of the patient's attitude and concern that the medication would not prevent withdrawal for 72 hours (27).

Treatment outcome measures were generally found not to show significant differences between LAAM and methadone treatments. The main difference between LAAM and methadone treatment groups noted in all these studies was that a larger proportion of LAAM than methadone patients dropped out of the study, although the differences between groups were often not statistically significant. The dropouts tended to occur early in the studies, during the period of dose stabilization (7).

Results of these studies confirmed the absence of significant toxicity or adverse reactions for both LAAM and methadone. Laboratory tests and physical examinations were generally normal and unchanged by the drug. The few adverse experiences that did occur were general opiate effects attributable to excessive dosage of LAAM or administration more frequently than three times a week with resultant accumulation of active drug (7).

PHASE II: CLINICAL INVESTIGATION—CONTROLLED CLINICAL TRIALS OF THE EFFECTIVENESS AND SAFETY OF LAAM

PHASE III: CLINICAL TRIALS— EXPANDED CONTROLLED AND UNCONTROLLED TRIALS FOR ADDITIONAL EVIDENCE OF EFFECTIVENESS AND MORE PRECISE DEFINITION OF DRUG-RELATED ADVERSE EFFECTS IN PATIENTS REPRESENTATIVE OF THE INTENDED POPULATION

The encouraging results from these early clinical trials and evidence of long term safety

from concurrent animal toxicity studies (78) gave support for further pharmaceutical development of LAAM. Between 1973 and 1976, two large multiclinic controlled trials (referred to as Phase II studies in FDA jargon) were carried out (55, 60, 61, 76).

From 1976 to 1979, an even larger clinical trial was carried out to confirm LAAM's safety in a patient sample and clinical settings close to its intended application (Phase III study in the FDA schema) (9, 76).

STUDY DESIGNS

The purpose of the three large scale, multisite cooperative trials was to establish the safety and efficacy of LAAM, relative to methadone, in large numbers of patients followed under a common protocol (Table 28.1). The first of these, the Veterans Administration Cooperative Study, was a double-blind fixed-dose study with patients randomized to either LAAM (80 mg three times a week) (LAAM-80 group) or one or two doses of methadone, a high (100 mg) (methadone-100 group) or a low (50 mg) (methadone-50 group) daily dose. LAAM patients received a placebo on their nondrug-scheduled days. The protocol specified 40 weeks of treatment. Study patients were eligible for the trial if they met the existing criteria (1973) for admission to methadone maintenance programs as defined by the FDA and were males between the ages of 18 to 60. Patients were excluded for incapacitating or life-threatening conditions, disease requiring regular repeated medication, frankly psychotic states, epilepsy, current severe alcoholism, and pending criminal charges. Upon signing an informed consent, eligible patients were given a physical examination with psychiatric evaluation, chest x-ray, electrocardiogram, urinalysis, and blood studies.

In the 12 participating clinics, 430 men were inducted; 142 received LAAM, and 142 and 146 patients received methadone at 100 mg and 50 mg daily, respectively. The first dose in all three groups was 30 mg, which was incremented by 10 mg on each succeeding Monday until the patient achieved his target dose.

SAFETY

In order to evaluate safety problems or possible drug toxicity, laboratory data (he-

Table 26.1
Phase II and III LAAM/Methadone Comparative Studies

	Study Design		
	VA	SAODAP	Phase III
Sample size	430 (males)	772 (males)	3649 (males to date)
Population	Street (heroin) addicts	Crossover (methadone) patients	Crossover and street patients (see protocols below)
Design	Double-blinded/fixed dose	Open/randomized to drug/variable dose	Open for drug/randomization and blind for dosage regimen (varies with protocols)
Numer of clinics	12	16	89

Protocols

VA

No. 1—Randomized to:

Methadone 50 mg:	7 days a week	(N = 146)
Methadone 100 mg:	7 days a week	(N = 142)
LAAM 80 mg:	3 days a week	(N = 142)

SAODAP

No. 1 and No. 2—Randomized to:

Methadone:	7 days a week	(N = 308)
LAAM:	3 days a week	(N = 328)

No. 3—Randomized to:

Methadone:	7 days a week	(N = 71)
LAAM:	Methadone Monday thru Thursday, LAAM Friday	(N = 65)

No. (VANGARD)
Patients from initial study continued beyond 40 weeks on LAAM (N = 145) or Methadone (N = 129)

Phase III

No. 1
Crossover and street patients
Placed on LAAM 3 days a week (N = 2,308)

No. 2
Crossover and street patients
Randomized (open) to:

LAAM:	3 days a week	(N = 816)
or Methadone:	7 days a week	(N = 525)

Supplemental Induction Regimens:

No. 3
Crossover patients
Randomized to:
three open dosage regimens of LAAM (N = 178)

No. 4
Crossover and street patients
Placed on LAAM and blinded to one of three dosage regimens (N = 445)

No. 5
Crossover and street patients
Placed on LAAM and blinded to one of three dosage regimens (N = 120)
Control group open on Methadone (N = 78)

No. 6
Patients from initial 40-week study (Protocols 1 to 5) continued on in an open study on:
LAAM (N = 1,011); or Methadone (N = 234)

matology, blood chemistry, and urinalysis), vital signs, and weight were obtained before treatment, at 4-week intervals during treatment, and upon a patient's termination. To evaluate patient complaints, a symptom-sign list of difficulties commonly reported by maintenance patients was elicited weekly for the first 8 weeks and then every 4 weeks thereafter. The complete physical examination was repeated at the twelfth week and at the end of the study. Clinic physicians were obliged to report any adverse reactions to the medical monitor of the study coordinating committee and to follow the patients' course when possible. For all early patient terminations, clinics were required to determine a primary reason from a preestablished list and also provide a supporting narrative, detailing the circumstances of the termination.

Over the course of this study (and the preceding studies described below), various analyses were carried out to evaluate safety parameters. Statistically, comparisons of changes from baseline and between groups were carried out to detect subtle effects that might have been clinically important. Various algorithms to isolate individuals with outlying values were employed to identify cases for review by the medical monitor. Finally, cases of possible adverse reactions and terminations for reasons that might have been related to the study medication were reviewed by the medical monitor and the study's medical advisory panel.

EFFICACY

This study was not designed to establish absolute efficacy, inasmuch as no placebo or nontreatment group was included. However, previous work had established the ability of both methadone and LAAM to suppress opiate withdrawal and maintain individuals without the supplemental use of illicit narcotics. Thus, it was judged reasonable to assume that both drugs were effective (and also that the three dosing regimens used in this particular study were adequate substitutes for morphine).

Although none of the indices of efficacy was entirely unambiguous, they did provide, in aggregate, a fairly comprehensive picture of patient functioning over the course of the study. The succession of the use of illicit opiates was monitored by a weekly urine screen. The particular test of each patient's urine screen was scheduled according to a random sequence, which was supplied centrally. Specimens were sent to the clinical laboratory at the Sepulveda Veterans Administration (VA) Hospital, where they were tested for morphine, barbiturates, amphetamine, and a variety of other substances. Patient reports and staff assessment of illicit drug use were also recorded at 4-week intervals and upon termination. Retention of patients over the trial (40 weeks) was monitored, and reasons for early termination were categorized according to whether they were related to treatment with the drug.

A variety of indicators of a patient's psychosocial functioning were also collected. A global evaluation rating, based upon staff consensus at the time of a patient's termination from the study, was completed on several parameters. Finally, a variety of other kinds of information was gathered, either by patient or staff assessment, regarding events such as encounters with the law, employment, and patient mood.

The SAODAP Cooperative Study of LAAM compared with methadone differed from the VA protocol in that all patients entered into the study had already been stabilized on methadone for at least 3 months. Also, the study utilized an open, rather than double-blind, controlled design. Patients who were randomly assigned to LAAM were abruptly switched (crossed over) to LAAM on their first study day at a dose that was the same dose as that of methadone (1.0 crossover ratio). Later, clinicians were allowed to vary dosage in response to changing state of physical dependence or individual requirements. In this study, 636 patients were randomized to either LAAM (N = 328) or methadone (N = 308).

Of the two Phase II studies, the VA trial constituted the primary clinical investigation; the SAODAP study evaluated the feasibility of crossing patients from methadone to LAAM and also provided adjunct safety and efficacy data. The relative strengths and weaknesses of these two study designs have been discussed previously. It is clear that the open design of the SAODAP study increased the level of complaints by patients who were aware that they were assigned to LAAM, an experimental drug. Also, clinicians were more likely to terminate patients with difficulties if they knew they were receiving LAAM. Finally, a LAAM patient who tired of the considerable burden of completing forms, being interviewed, and giving urine and blood samples could drop from the study and return to methadone (a drug upon which he had been previously stabilized); no such option was available to the methadone patients. Thus, the interpretations of efficacy data generated in this study must be viewed with caution, although it does provide LAAM safety data on more than twice as many patients as had been exposed to the drug in the VA study.

The Phase III trial was intended to provide LAAM to a large number of maintenance patients, who would be representative of the future intended clinical population, and to provide nation-wide experience with LAAM. The focus of the study was on producing a large amount of safety-related data on low incidence phenomena sufficient to provide the FDA with information to approve an NDA for LAAM. Toward this end, most patients in the study were inducted into an uncontrolled trial (Protocol I). For previous methadone patients, crossover ratios of 1.2 to 1.3 were utilized. Here, data collection involved a complete physical examination, with laboratory studies done and vital signs taken before an initial dose of study medication was given and also upon a patient's termination. Efficacy data included a weekly urine screen for illicit drugs and the termination global evaluation by the clinic staff.

In order to make a comparison with methadone, a second protocol (II) provided for a 60:40 randomization of patients to either LAAM or methadone, on an open basis. In this protocol, 816 patients were assigned to LAAM and 525 to methadone. The symptom-sign checklist and the Profile of Moods Scale (POMS) were also collected at specified intervals. Finally, several other protocols (III, IV, and V) were developed to evaluate the effects of various schedules of induction and crossing over. These employed various regimens of supplementation with LAAM or methadone and/or gradual increases in LAAM dosage that paralleled decreases in methadone dosages. These protocols have been described in detail elsewhere.

Patient induction in the Phase III trial was closed in April 1979, and data collection ceased on September 15, 1979. A total of 3,649 patients in 89 clinics were inducted into the 40-week trial (3,124 on LAAM and 525 on methadone). Of these, about 20 per cent were street inductees and 80 per cent were crossed over from prior methadone maintenance. A total of 1,133 LAAM patients and 287 methadone patients completed the 40-week phase of the trial. In addition, a continuation phase of the trial produced data on 540 patients who had a minimum of 80 weeks' experience in the study and 134 patients who had been in the trial at least 120 weeks.

At this time, data have been fully analyzed on only the first 2,090 LAAM and 324 methadone patients during the initial 40 weeks of the study. This cohort was deemed adequate for an NDA submission. Induction into the study was left open and data were gathered to gain additional experience with LAAM and keep the drug generally available in treatment settings. In sum, over the three studies, a total of 4,715 patients have been followed; 3,594 of these were on LAAM, and 1,121 were assigned to methadone.

EFFICACY RESULTS

The concept of efficacy for an opiate maintenance agent should be viewed differently than most other medically prescribed pharmaceuticals. The currently accepted opinion is that an opiate maintenance drug cannot itself cure or ameliorate some specific somatic illness or aberrant physiological process. Rather, as explained in the introduction, an opiate maintenance agent is intended to replace intravenous heroin and thus achieve a more pharmacologically stable physiological state. Important characteristics of this state are the absence of craving for opiates and the absence of the opiate abstinence syndrome, as well as the presence of a blockage of the euphorogenic effects of intravenous heroin due to development of considerable opiate tolerance. These are the primary or direct effects of the maintenance drugs. When these primary or direct effects are achieved, use of intravenous heroin should be minimal. Once achieved, adequate pharmacological maintenance facilitates the individual's ability to participate in the rehabilitation and treatment components of the program. This participation represents a secondary or indirect effect. Through program participation the addict will be able to stabilize his life style and actively participate in a self-change-oriented program to gain education, vocational training, or employment and improve his interpersonal relationships. These later changes are contingent on tertiary effects of the maintenance drug and on an effective treatment and rehabilitation program complementing the pharmacological effects (76).

Because of the well designed, well controlled nature of the VA cooperative study, the findings permit meaningful comparisons between the three treatment groups regarding the relative efficacy of LAAM and methadone and will be discussed in more detail (60, 76). Complementary findings from the Phase III and SAODAP Phase II will then be presented (61, 76).

ILLICIT OPIATE USE

Use of heroin during maintenance treatment is the most important measure of drug effect as it indicates cessation or decrease of use of the addict's primary drug of dependence.

Generally, LAAM was superior to both methadone doses based on urine tests positive for morphine, an objective measure. In the VA study, sensitive statistical analysis indicated that the frequency of illicit opiate use between all three groups was signficantly different after the 8-week stabilization period. The LAAM-80 group had significantly less frequent occurrence of urines positive for morphine than both methadone groups. The methadone-100 group was statistically superior to the 50-mg group on this measure. No significant differences were found between groups during the 8-week stabilization period. When this stabilization period with the highest proportion of positive urines is included, the LAAM-80 and methadone-100 groups are still significantly superior to the methadone-50 group.

Interestingly, the pattern of positive urines seems to differ among groups (Fig. 28.1). All groups show similar initial drops in the proportion of positive urines during the 8-week stabilization period from a baseline of about 79 per cent to about 24 per cent. However, during the 9- to 40-week period a gradual increase in positive urines occurred in the methadone-50 groups, stabilizing at a rela-

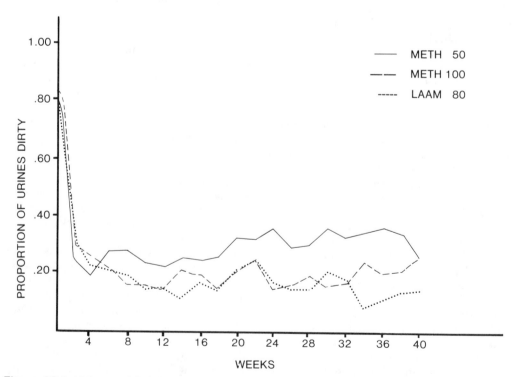

Figure 28.1. Veterans Administration study: proportion of urines positive for morphine by study week.

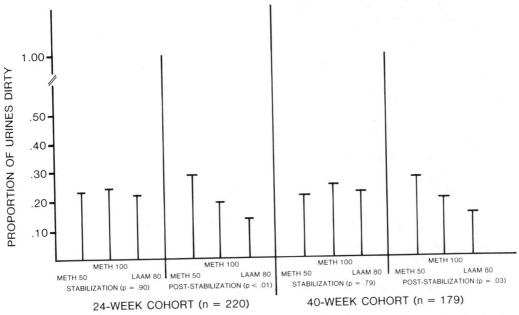

Figure 28.2. Veterans Administration study: proportion of urines positive for morphine for the 24- and 40-week cohorts during and after stabilization.

tively high rate (approximately low to mid thirties) by mid-study. The methadone-100 group and the LAAM-80 group stabilized at a slightly lower level (mid to high teens) for weeks 10 through 32. During the last 8 weeks of the study, the LAAM-80 group continued to maintain that level and slightly decline, whereas the methadone-100 group showed a moderate increase in the percentage of positive urines. The frequency of positive urines was significantly higher ($p \leq .05$) in the methadone-50 group from the sixth week on, whereas LAAM patients had significantly lower frequencies of positive urines than either methadone group after the thirty-second week. A particularly striking finding was the relatively small number of LAAM-80 group members compared to methadone-50 with high frequencies of urines positive for morphine, especially after stabilization.

This relationship is further explored by an analysis of the cohorts of patients who completed at least 24 weeks and 40 weeks in the study, respectively (Fig. 28.2). These groups were compared for frequency of positive urines during the initial 8 weeks, and examination of the proportions indicates that none of the groups in either cohort differed significantly during the first 8 weeks. However,

later in the study, methadone-50 patients apparently actually increased their use of illicit opiates, whereas the LAAM-80 group showed a pronounced drop. This finding reflects a true decrease in illicit opiate use over time rather than an apparent decrease due to possible differential termination of persistently positive LAAM subjects. All of the group differences reach statistical significance ($p < .05$) during the later period.

Evaluation by staff for illicit opiate use and subjects' self-reports of heroin use made blind to treatment group represent subjective measures of this primary maintenance drug effect. The staff evaluations show a marked tendency for improvement of the LAAM-80 patients. Both groups of methadone patients showed less improvement. The LAAM-80 and methadone-50 group differences reached statistical significance. Self-reported heroin use by the methadone-50 group was significantly higher than by the LAAM-80 or methadone-100 group after the first 8 weeks of treatment.

In summary, all of the above VA data support the finding that LAAM patients had less involvement with illicit opiates than methadone patients, especially the low dose methadone patients.

OCCURRENCE OF CHRONIC OPIATE ABSTINENCE SYNDROME

Evidence of the occurrence of a chronic opiate abstinence syndrome (59) is a crucial parameter in evaluating the relative efficacy of drug maintenance regimens. Objective direct evidence of opiate abstinence from inadequate opiate maintenance can be evaluated by elevating blood pressure, pulse, and temperature. Subjective supporting evidence are patient reports of underdosing-related symptoms or signs and early terminations related to the drug not holding.

The analysis of vital sign data revealed that both diastolic and systolic blood pressure were somewhat elevated in the methadone-50 group, whereas the methadone-100 and LAAM-80 groups showed a decrease in blood pressure over time. Patient temperatures also showed a mild elevation in the methadone-50 group over the first 24 weeks of study, whereas the methadone-100 and LAAM-80 groups evidenced a significant drop in temperature in the initial weeks of the study. Data on pulse rates did not differentiate drug groups and they all dropped slightly during the initial 8 weeks of treatment.

Patient complaints of underdosing revealed few clinically significant findings between drug groups on any one variable of underdosing, although more methadone-50 patients reported anxiety, tension, and nervousness during the course of the study. There was a persistent but slight pattern of overrepresentation of methadone-50 subjects with multiple complaints related to underdosing.

Review of reasons for early termination reveals that termination for "medication not holding" occurred primarily in the stabilization period for all groups. Although there were no significant differences among drug groups during later intervals of the study, early termination during the stabilization period for medication not holding occurred more frequently in the LAAM-80 and methadone-50 groups than in the methadone-100 group. However, the number of patients terminating during the first 16 weeks of the study for "drug not holding" was not large. Five subjects, representing 3.5 per cent of starters, terminated in the methadone-100 group compared to 11 and 12, respectively (about 8 per cent of starters), in the methadone-50 and LAAM-80 groups.

PROGRAM PARTICIPATION

Parameters of program participation provide indirect or secondary measures of efficacy. In this regard, active program participation implies adequate drug substitution. Both retention in the study and clinic attendance are objective measures of program participation. Staff judgment of treatment acceptance is a subjective measure.

SUBJECT RETENTION

Forty-two per cent of the starting sample of 430 completed the 40 weeks of treatment. As seen in the cumulative retention curve (Fig. 28.3), early termination occurred in 69 per cent of the LAAM-80 patients, 58 per cent of the methadone-50 patients, and 48 per cent of the methadone-100 patients. Methadone-100 had statistically significantly greater retention than methadone-50 and LAAM-80. Half of the patients who terminated early did so by the eighth week for all three treatment groups. There was no trend for these early terminations to occur earlier in any of the three treatment groups.

Upon closer examination of these retention curves, several interesting aspects emerge. Each curve seems to be comprised of three rather distinct phases (early, middle, and late phases) as characterized by both termination rate per week and also the proportion of subjects surviving through each 4-week interval. The early phase lasted 8 weeks for LAAM and methadone-100 but only 4 weeks for the methadone-50 group. This early phase closely approximated the induction periods for drug groups. During the early phase, the LAAM-80 and methadone-50 groups had essentially the same proportion of survival of the interval (82 per cent) and early termination rate (about six patients per week), whereas the methadone-100 group had moderately better proportion of survival (87½ per cent) and early termination rate (about four patients per week). These same trends continued in the middle phase, with methadone-100 having a lower weekly termination rate (94 per cent, one and one-half per week) than LAAM-80 mg (88 per cent, two and one-half per week) and methadone-50 mg (89 per cent, three per week). All groups are practically equal in the final phase (about 95 per cent, three-fourths per week) after about 20 weeks of treatment.

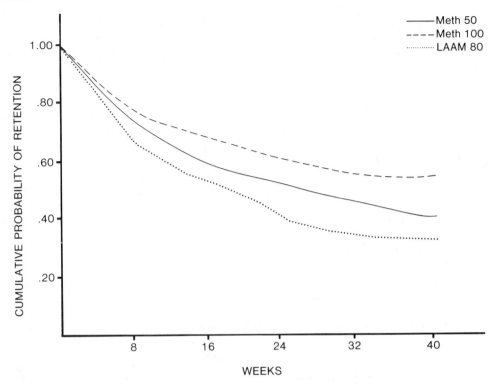

Figure 28.3. Veterans Administration study: cumulative probability of retention.

Examination of reasons given by the subjects for early termination from the study revealed that 38 per cent gave drug-related reasons (side effects, medication not holding, dose too high, did not like drug, psychiatric, miscellaneous, excessive drug use), and 62 per cent gave non-drug-related reasons (jail, no show for 7 days, moved from area, disciplinary discharge, did not like study, detoxification, could not attend clinic). Approximately 40 per cent of the early terminators in the LAAM-80 and methadone-100 groups, compared to about 30 per cent in the methadone-50 group, gave drug-related reasons for early termination. Viewed alternatively, 22 per cent of the subjects who entered the study terminated for drug-related reasons, and 39 per cent of the LAAM-80 subjects, 20 per cent of the methadone-100 subjects, and 17 per cent of the methadone-50 subjects listed drug-related reasons for early termination.

Few significant differences between treatment groups were reported for specific drug-related reasons for early termination. Terminations for side effects were more frequent in the LAAM group (5.5 per cent of starters) than the methadone-50 group (none), whereas the methadone-100 group had 2 per cent of terminators for this reason. Review of these LAAM terminators reveals the "side effects" were almost exclusively underdosing symptoms.

Of the LAAM starters, 11.5 per cent (or 40 per cent of the LAAM drug-related terminators) terminated for "medication not holding," compared to 7.5 per cent of methadone-50 starters (44 per cent of drug-related terminators) and 5.5 per cent of the methadone-100 starters (29 per cent of the drug-related terminators). Seven per cent of the methadone-100 subjects terminated early due to "dose too high," compared to about 3 per cent of the methadone-50 and LAAM-80 patients. As shown in Figure 28.4, when these terminators for early underdosing are removed, the retention curves among groups are much closer, and the group differences do not reach statistical significance.

CLINIC ATTENDANCE

The other objective measure of program participation is patient's clinic attendance,

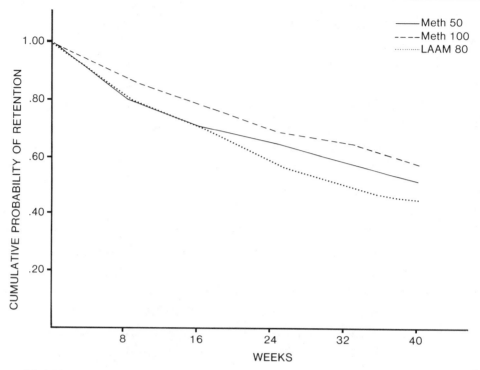

Figure 28.4. Veterans Administration study: cumulative probability of retention censoring subjects terminating for underdosing symptoms during stabilization.

which showed few differences between treatment groups. Attendance data indicated essential homogeneity between drug groups, with earlier terminators having poorer attendance records than subjects remaining in the study longer.

The only statistically significant differences (p = .05) in attendance was that, for all subjects who were in the study at least 7 days, the methadone-100 group averaged fewer missed clinic appointments (5 per cent) than the 50-methadone group (7 per cent) and LAAM group (9 per cent). Interestingly, these LAAM patients missed 7 per cent of the clinic appointments for active medication days (Monday, Wednesday, Friday).

Staff evaluation of a patient's treatment acceptance was a more subjective measure of program participation. The methadone-50 group was rated lowest, on the average, in treatment accceptance and the methadone-100 group the highest. Treatment acceptance by the LAAM subjects was intermediate for the 24-week cohort, comparable to methadone-100 for the 40-week cohort, and approached that of methadone-50 when all subjects including 1 to 23-week terminators are

considered. Overall, the methadone-50 group was rated lower, with the LAAM group judged slightly superior to the methadone-100 group.

CONTINGENT EFFECTS

Contingent effects are tertiary effects of the drug in that they are therapeutic outcomes representing psychological adjustment attributable to active participation in a self-change-oriented treatment and rehabilitation program. These are presumably not directly effected by the pharmacological properties of the maintenance drug.

Random weekly urine screen for barbiturates, amphetamine, cocaine, benzodiazepines, and methaqualone provides objective evidence of general drug use. Methadone-50 patients evidenced a statistically higher usage of barbiturates than the LAAM-80 subjects. Among methadone-100 patients, usage of amphetamine was higher. These findings may indicate attempts of the methadone-50 group to alleviate discomfort due to underdosing and of a few methadone-100 subjects to counteract symptoms of a too high maintenance dose.

Subjective measures of these contingent effects included staff and patient ratings of general psychosocial functioning. At study termination, judgments were made on patient's change from baseline and functioning compared to nonaddict peers. In the over-all global assessment of patient status, patients in the methadone-50 group were less likely (p < .05) to have shown over-all improvement compared to the LAAM and methadone-100 groups. These group differences in improvement are substantially greater for subjects continuing in the study for 40 weeks. In the area of difficulties with the criminal justice system reflected in arrests, time spent in jail, and persistent involvement in illegal activities, the methadone-50 group was significantly (p < .05) poorer than the methadone-100 and LAAM groups. No significant group differences were found for change in employment and educational status, alcohol problems, psychiatric problems, family/living arrangements, patient's mood, social relations, and functioning in major roles.

COMPLEMENTARY EFFICACY FINDINGS FROM THE SAODAP AND PHASE III STUDIES

In the SAODAP study, for frequencies of detected urine morphine, both groups showed improvement with time, although there were no statistically significant group differences. Abstinence indicators showed that methadone patients had a small increase in mean blood pressure. Sixty per cent of methadone patients and 39 per cent of LAAM patients completed the study protocol. As evidenced by the global evaluation ratings, clinic staff felt that LAAM patients tended to have made superior improvement in psychosocial adjustment. These group differences reached statistical significance (p ≤ .05) in four of the eight parameters examined: employment/education, drug abuse, psychiatric problems, and over-all adjustment.

In the Phase III study, although there were no significant differences between groups in the percentages of positive urines, *all* groups did show improvement in this parameter over the course of the study. As in the two Phase II studies, methadone crossover patients had slight mean increases in blood pressure, but in this study there were no changes in pulse or temperature and no symptom-signs indic-

ative of withdrawal. As in earlier studies, more LAAM patients terminated for "medication not holding." Over-all, study retention was lower for LAAM patients. In general, Protocols III, IV, and V showed no clear advantage in terms of subject retention over the less complex induction schedules.

Among socioeconomic variables, LAAM patients showed superior improvement in extent of criminal involvement, opiate abuse, psychiatric problems, and the over-all global rating.

SAFETY RESULTS (60, 61, 76)

LABORATORY VALUES, VITAL SIGNS, AND SYMPTOM-SIGN RECORD

Detailed statistical analyses were carried out on all of the quantitative safety data and involved cross-sectional tests among drug treatment groups, trend analysis of changes from the prestudy scores, and a variety of other models. Due to the large number of variables upon which data were collected and the extensiveness of the analysis plan, a large number of tests of significance were calculated, and several of these showed sporadic significant differences between drug treatment groups. From systematic monitoring of patients' hematology, blood chemistry (SMA-12), urinalysis, vital and symptom sign checklist, only a very small number of parameters showed any systematic changes. There was a persistent, but small, mean drop in red blood cell count, hematocrit, and hemoglobin levels in LAAM patients in most protocols across the trials. This change was not clinically meaningful ($\Delta \approx -2$ per cent), and no individuals were noted as having difficulties in this area. Likewise, in all trials there was a persistent slight mean elevation ($\Delta \approx +1$ per cent) in blood pressure, both systolic and diastolic, among methadone patients. Again, no individuals manifested clinically significant changes, nor were there any terminations for this reason.

The symptom-sign record manifested the usual complaints associated with patients taking opiates. Complaints of constipation, delayed ejaculation, and impotence were particularly common across all trials; of these, constipation was most likely to cause chronic problems for individuals. In the open trials, there was a tendency for a greater number of complaints by LAAM patients, although, in the double-blind VA trial, these differences among treatment groups were greatly reduced. LAAM patients had more complaints associated with the underdosing syndrome during the initial 8 weeks of the trials. These problems were transient: there were fewer complaints later in the studies and also few differences betweeen LAAM and methadone. However, in the VA study, the methadone-50 group experienced mild underdosing symptoms that did persist later into the trial.

Of the other symptoms reported, delayed ejaculation and sweating were the most common, with few individuals having multiple complaints. There were a few more individuals in the LAAM group with such persistent difficulties. However, the treatment group differences do not reach statistical significance. The reports of sweating are largely confined to the stabilization period and are probably manifestations of transitory undermedication.

POSSIBLE SAFETY-RELATED EARLY TERMINATIONS

In the VA study, no patient deaths or serious adverse reactions necessitating termination occurred among LAAM patients. One methadone-100 subject was terminated for possible bone marrow suppression not conclusively linked to methadone. Early terminations for side effects were more frequent in the LAAM group (5.5 per cent of starters) than the methadone-50 group (none) but not significantly different from the methadone-100 group (2 per cent of starters). Of the 11 LAAM patients who terminated early primarily due to drug side effects, four experienced inability to ejaculate; one noted swelling of joints, decreased sexual interest, heartburn, nodding, and constipation; another could not keep the medication down; one complained of being tired and dizzy with pains in the chest and both arms; and another subject experienced jerking of extremities at bedtime and nausea. Besides the termination for apparent bone marrow suppression mentioned above, two other high dose methadone subjects terminated for side effects; one for a pruritic maculopapular rash on the second treatment day, and another for abnormally high liver function values that were present at pretreatment but did not significantly improve after 85 days of treatment.

Terminations for psychiatric reasons (3.5 per cent of all starters) were equally distributed among treatment groups and were not believed to be related to the psychopharmacological effect of the drugs.

Termination for "dose too high" is possibly relevant for safety analysis. Nineteen subjects (4.5 per cent of all starters) terminated for this reason. Ten of these subjects (7 per cent of starters) were in the methadone-100 group, compared to four in the methadone-50 and five in the LAAM-80 groups (3 per cent of starters).

The finding that only 30 subjects out of the 430 in the sample (7 per cent) terminated the study early for these safety-related reasons further attests to the low toxicity of these two maintenance drugs. Patients terminating for medically related reasons tended to leave the study quite early. Over half of them terminated by the eighth week of treatment; the mean survival time was about 10 weeks. As discussed previously, careful review of the 10 case records of the LAAM patients terminating early for "side effects" revealed that all except one were accounted for by underdosing signs and symptoms, not truly a safety-related reason for termination.

The SAODAP study complemented the VA study of street addicts by obtaining information on the feasibility of safely switching patients already maintained on methadone to LAAM. However, the open design clouds interpretations of differences between methadone and LAAM safety-related early terminations. Methadone patients were continued on the same drug they had been taking for considerable time prior to the study, whereas LAAM patients knew they were assigned to a new "experimental" drug. Also, LAAM patients with a side effect or mild adverse reaction had an acceptable therapeutic choice available: return to methadone. Methadone patients could only discontinue maintenance treatment.

No LAAM or methadone patient deaths or serious adverse reactions necessitating termination occurred. Interestingly, about the same percentage of LAAM and methadone starters, 30 per cent to 40 per cent, terminated the study early (prior to 40 weeks) for nonstudy-drug-related reasons, e.g., jail, no show, moved, disciplinary, did not like study, detoxification, could not attend clinic, excessive alcohol or illicit drug use, unrelated death or medical illness. However, although no methadone subjects terminated early for study-drug-related reasons, an additional 30 per cent of LAAM starters did so. As in the VA study, almost all of these can be attributed to undermedication or anxiety over receiving a new "experimental" drug. Specifically, patient narrative reports of reasons for termination revealed: medication not holding, 19 per cent; psychiatric, 4 per cent; did not like drug, 2 per cent; and irritability, 2 per cent. Careful review of these case records indicated that none of these were toxic reactions to the study medication. An additional 11 patients, representing 3 per cent of the starters, terminated in the first 8 weeks after crossover for side effects. Complaints included constipation, nausea, headaches, "allergic reaction," headache with lower extremity edema, sexual problem, "amphetamine-like reaction" in two patients, hyperactivity, and an "LSD-like reaction" in two patients who had previously been heavy LSD users. Review of the case records of these "side effects" indicates that they are primarily underdosing or functional difficulties.

There were no safety-related terminators among the 29 methadone and 24 LAAM patients who left treatment during the vanguard long term safety study. Allergic rashes and pruritis occurred in all groups.

In the Phase III trial, a large number of LAAM patients (1,114 patients, or 53 per cent of starters) did not complete the 40-week treatment period. Terminations for medical reasons related to LAAM were minimal (217 patients, or 13 per cent of the LAAM starters). Patients crossed over from methadone terminated twice as frequently for medically related reasons as street-inducted patients (15 per cent and 8 per cent of starters, respectively). Terminations for "medication not holding" accounted for most of this difference. Among crossover starters, 9 per cent terminated due to undermedication, compared to 3.5 per cent of street patients. Other categories were about equal between street and crossover patients: side effects, 2 per cent; adverse reactions, 0.2 per cent; and overmedication, 2 per cent. As in the open SAODAP study, no methadone patients terminated for drug-related reasons, although about 20 per cent did so in the double-blind VA study. Almost two-thirds of these LAAM-related terminations occurred in the

first 8 weeks during the dosage stabilization period after crossover from the methadone or street heroin. Few of these early terminations are safety related; nearly all are related to inadequate dose adjustment.

A noteworthy finding is that the percentage of starters who terminated early among LAAM patients decreased dramatically—from 39 per cent in the VA study to 30 per cent in the SAODAP study to 13 per cent (8 per cent street, 15 per cent crossover) in the Phase III study. Several factors probably account for this finding, including improved flexible induction and crossover dosage schedules and increased physician, staff, and patient experience with, confidence in, and acceptance of LAAM.

As in the VA and SAODAP studies, there were large interclinic differences in the frequencies of the various reported reasons for termination. Apparently some clinics more readily than others attributed vague complaints to LAAM side effects and terminated patients from the study. There were also considerable differences among clinics in over-all termination rates for both drugs, suggesting that clinical management is an important factor in retaining maintenance patients, whatever the drug.

ADVERSE REACTIONS AND EXPERIENCES

In the VA study, there were few clinically significant findings that bear on the safety of LAAM or methadone. Besides routinely reported undermedication, overmedication, and generalized somatic symptoms, occasional moderate and severe headaches were reported by both LAAM and methadone patients. A range of psychiatric problems was reported, but these do not seem to be drug-related adverse reactions or side effects. Most of these psychiatric problems—including paranoid ideation, hallucinations, depression, and confusion—most likely represented the underlying psychopathology in these individuals.

Three LAAM patients suffered allergic reactions characterized by combinations of the following: chills, nausea or vomiting, pruritis, myalgia, skin rash, high or low temperature. Other isolated LAAM patients had memory loss and rash; vomiting, photophobia and weakness, diplopia, unexplained peripheral edema; and apparent precipitation of opiate abstinence when the first dose of LAAM was taken during acute alcoholic intoxication and recent heroin use. One methadone patient was reported to have cerebral vasculitis characterized by numbness and weakness.

There were no serious adverse reactions reported in the SAODAP study. One LAAM patient had unexplained leg edema associated with headaches, another had central nervous system stimulation, and another had unexplained pruritis.

Despite the large numbers of patients treated in the Phase III study (3,124 LAAM and 525 methadone), there were remarkably few adverse reactions and experiences. Nine LAAM patients died of mixed overdose during the dosage stabilization period (73). In only one of these was LAAM believed to have a primary role based on LAAM blood level determination, toxicological examination, and historical data. Contrary to protocol instructions, during induction this patient was dosed daily and was in addition given several increasingly larger doses of LAAM, despite an immediate history of minimal heroin dependence. In the other eight fatalities, other psychoactive depressant drugs—expecially alcohol, heroin, benzodiazepines, sedative-hypnotics, and other opioid analgesics—were prominently involved. LAAM patients do seem vulnerable to mixed overdoses during the dose stabilization period (early induction in street addicts and early crossover period from methadone maintenance) when tolerance to the depressant effects of the maintenance drug is not well established and undermedication is more frequently present.

DISCUSSION AND CONCLUSIONS

SUMMARY OF SAFETY RESULTS

The three large controlled clinical trials of LAAM provide a comprehensive and objective view of the safety of LAAM in the maintenance treatment of heroin addicts. The three studies have included the experience of 94 clinical investigators with over 3,500 LAAM patients and 1,150 methadone patients. This extensive clinical experience unquestionably indicates that LAAM and methadone are comparably safe medications over extended time periods (up to at least 120 weeks). Few adverse reactions or fatalities

directly related to either study medication occurred. There was no evidence of systematic, progressive, or clinically meaningful changes indicating toxicity in any laboratory parameter, vital sign, or symptom-sign complain. Adverse reactions were exceedingly rare, occurring at a rate of about two per 1,000 over-all. The various manifestations were idiosyncratic and did not reflect any specific organ system involvement.

The only patient-reported complaints were the usual ones associated with opiate dependence: undermedication, overmedication, or nonspecific symptoms (especially impotence, constipation, and delayed ejaculation). These opiate effects were generally minimal to mild in severity, transient, occurring more frequently during stabilization (induction or crossover period) and decreasing in frequency thereafter. No medical contraindications or problematic therapeutic drug-drug interactions were found.

A potentially hazardous interaction was observed during early dosage stabilization with other psychoactive drugs with depressant actions, especially alcohol, benzodiazepines, sedative-hypnotics, and other narcotic analgesics. Thus, patients (especially those with uncontrolled polydrug abuse) should be cautioned that the use of these other drugs during maintenance on LAAM or methadone can produce a lethal mixed overdose.

At first glance, LAAM patients seem more vulnerable to mixed overdose than methadone patients. However, this conclusion lacks certainty because of the absence of an adequate control group to estimate incidence of mixed overdose deaths during methadone induction (73). All 3,500 LAAM patients had stabilization periods (either street induction or cross over from prior methadone maintenance). However, only 288 VA methadone patients and about 100 Phase III methadone patients had induction periods, as the remainder were continued on their previously stabilized methadone dose.

Clinical reports indicate a notable psychotropic difference between LAAM and methadone prominent during dosage stabilization. Some LAAM patients feel less sedated or narcotized or experience less of a reduction in craving than methadone patients at comparable dosage levels. These LAAM patients may experience a decreased ability to accurately assess and adjust their psychophysiological state due to these differing psychoactive properties of LAAM and methadone (73). Due to the lack of previous experience with LAAM, they may believe that the drug is not working, which may lead to attempts to self-medicate with illicit drugs to correct this inaccurately perceived assessment of their physiological state. Alternatively, some LAAM patients may accurately perceive that they are experiencing less drug-induced euphoria than desired or accustomed to with methadone. They might take illicit drugs to alter this state of consciousness.

SUMMARY OF EFFICACY RESULTS

The over-all results of these studies indicate that in general LAAM and methadone are both effective maintenance medications. Both drugs produce dramatic decreases in heroin use in street heroin addicts, and these decreases persist throughout maintenance. The data across all studies indicate that LAAM is somewhat more effective in reducing heroin use than methadone. Furthermore, both drugs were found to permit successful rehabilitation. Global assessment of psychosocial improvement favored LAAM over methadone in the double-blind study.

The major clinical parameter in which methadone is consistently superior to LAAM is termination for symptoms of undermedication—"drug not holding" during the drug stabilization period. When the retention curves are censored for these terminations, LAAM and methadone retention are comparable. Again, it should be emphasized that the majority of terminations are for non-drug-related reasons.

Several factors, artifacts of the study design, seem to contribute to this occurrence (55). In the open SAODAP and Phase III studies, methadone patients had already been stabilized on the drug. Thus, there was no period of pharmacological instability in the methadone group. Also, knowledge of assignment to either the "experimental" drug, LAAM, or the familiar control drug, methadone, introduces the possibility of bias for the patients and staff. The methadone patients and staff knew methadone's effects and did not have reason to fear that it would not continue to control abstinence or would produce undesirable side effects. Furthermore, no alternative maintenance medication was available for methadone patients if they were dissatisfied with its effects; only detoxification was left. In the LAAM group, similar dissatisfaction with the drug effects or any other aspect of the patient's status was dealt with by termination from the study and switching back to methadone maintenance.

The fixed-dose protocol of the VA study did not permit individualized dose adjustment to alleviate undermedication (59). Patients in both groups seemed to attempt to compensate for undermedication during induction by self-medicating with heroin. However, the LAAM patients terminated more frequently during induction. This seems to be related to the longer length of induction and pharmacokinetic stabilization for LAAM (8 weeks) as opposed to low dose methadone (3 weeks).

On balance, it seems that a portion of the differences in study retention between the LAAM and methadone groups using the dosage schedules studied is the result of pharmacokinetic differences between the drugs, exacerbated by confounding factors in the study designs. The fact that a number of experienced clinicians were able to retain a high proportion of LAAM patients (at equal or higher rates than methadone patients) indicates that clinical management can override whatever limitations LAAM may have during the induction of patients. Several alternative dosage schedules were used in minor protocols. None of these dramatically improved over-all retention. However, complaints of undermedication did seem to be reduced by a few of the schedules. Possibly other induction and crossover schedules would further alleviate the problem of initial undermedication.

CLINICAL PHARMACOKINETICS OF LAAM

In order to study the pharmacokinetics of LAAM, Finkle and co-workers (20) hospitalized for 1 month 13 subjects maintained on methadone. Subjects were abruptly crossed over from methadone to LAAM. The dosage of LAAM was 1.0 to 1.3 times the prestudy methadone dose, or approximately 1.1 mg/kg. Ten doses of LAAM were administered to each subject at the same time of the day on a Monday-Wednesday-Friday schedule over a 21-day period. At the conclusion of the LAAM dosage period, the subjects were crossed back to their prior daily methadone dose and followed for 10 days. Samples of blood and urine were collected throughout the entire experimental period. Subsequently, Finkle and co-workers analyzed these samples to determine both plasma concentrations of LAAM, N-LAAM and DN-LAAM, and quantification in urine (18, 19).

Average plasma concentrations of LAAM and metabolites versus time are reported in Table 28.2 for seven subjects. These are the subjects from whom a sufficient number of plasma samples were collected to characterize fully the pharmacokinetic curve for the tenth (last) dose of LAAM, which was followed out to at least 10 days postadministration. For the metabolites N-LAAM and DN-LAAM, only the terminal portions of the respective plasma curves are reported here. The individual variability is reflected in the mean data by the magnitudes of the standard errors of the means, which are generally less than 20 per cent. The variability increased to well above 50 per cent for values beyond 10 days, which is more a reflection of the lower limits of sensitivity of the chemical assay (5 to 10 ng/ml) than individual variation.

PHARMACOKINETIC ANALYSIS

Figure 28.5 shows curves for the log plasma concentration of LAAM versus time for the data of Table 28.2, which are compared to the curve for the first LAAM dose. Both curves have three phases to account for the processes of absorption, distribution, and elimination. The maximum concentrations (C_{max}) occur at 4 hours, with values of 138 ng/ml and 349 ng/ml for the first and last dose, respectively. Pharmacokinetic analysis of the data for the last dose was carried out by performing a nonlinear regression of the experimental data to the function

$$C = Le^{-k_{ab}t} + Ae^{-\alpha t} + Be^{-\beta t}$$

where L, k_{ab}, A, α, B, β were obtained by computer fitting. The constants k_{ab}, α, and β were used to calculate the pharmacokinetic half-lives. The absorption half-life is estimated at $t_{1/2(ab)} = 1.6$ hours; the distribution half-life $t_{1/2(\alpha)} = 6.8$ hours; and the terminal plasma half-life is $t_{1/2(\beta)} = 92$ hours. For N-LAAM and DN-LAAM , a similar analysis was carried out on the terminal portions of the plasma curves with a monoexponential function $C = Be^{-\beta t}$. The estimates for the terminal plasma half-lives $t_{1/2(\beta)}$ are 71 hours for N-LAAM and 143 hours for DN-LAAM.

Because the data of Table 28.2 extend only to 2.4 $t_{1/2(\beta)}$ for LAAM, to 2.6 $t_{1/2(\beta)}$ for N-LAAM, and to 2.3 $t_{1/2(\beta)}$ for DN-LAAM, rather than four to five times $t_{1/2(\beta)}$, these pharmacokinetic parameters should be used

Table 28.2
Plasma Concentrations of LAAM and Metabolites[a]

Time (hr)	LAAM (tenth dose)			Nor-LAAM (tenth dose)[b]			DN-LAAM (tenth dose)[b]		
	ng/ml	SEM	N	Ng/ml	SEM	N	ng/ml	SEM	N
.25	119	32	5						
.5	133	19	7						
1	200	13	7						
1.5	236	24	7						
2	269	42	7						
4	349	66	6						
6	317	55	7						
12	221	34	7						
16	169	29	7						
24	143	29	7	237	50	7			
48	79	18	6	184	43	7	102	21	7
72	62	15	7	152	46	7	79	21	7
168	30	8	7	55	22	7	56	9	7
240	18	4	6	30	13	7	36	8	7
336							24	8	5

[a] Concentrations are average values for Subjects 4 to 10, with a standard error of the mean, SEM, and value of N. Dose = 1.1 mg/kg with SEM = 0.1.
[b] For metabolites, only the log-linear terminal portion of the curve is reported.

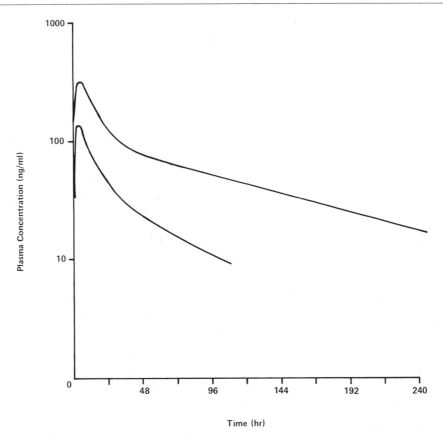

Figure 28.5. Plasma concentration versus time for LAAM on a log-linear scale. *Top curve* is average data for tenth (last) LAAM dose from Table 28.2. *Bottom curve* is for first LAAM dose for the same seven subjects.

with caution in drawing final conclusions as to the clinical disposition of LAAM. The assumption was made that the shortest half-life corresponds to absorption, but an intravenous study is required to verify this. The longest half-life of a concentration-time curve represents the slowest process. For metabolites, the slowest process may be the rate of formation rather than the rate of elimination. This is a possibility for DN-LAAM because the increasing slope of the DN-LAAM concentration-time curve for the first dose is similar in magnitude to the decreasing slope for the last dose in Table 28.2. To verify this would require intravenous administration of the metabolite itself. This was done in dog and showed the rate of formation of DN-LAAM to be slower than the terminal plasma half-life of intravenously administered DN-LAAM (75).

PLASMA LEVEL STABILIZATION

The time required to reach stabilized plasma levels depends upon the terminal half-life of the drug. Based on the model of first-order pharmacokinetics, dosing for a time interval of four times the half-life $(4\ t_{1/2(\beta)})$ will yield plasma concentrations within 10 per cent of the steady state values C_{ss}. Using the estimates of $t_{1/2(\beta)}$, the length of time required to reach steady state levels should be approximately 15 days for LAAM, 12 days for N-LAAM, and 24 days for DN-LAAM.

The plasma levels of LAAM and metabolites obtained at stabilization depend on both the amount of LAAM administered (dose in mg/kg) and the frequency of administration (dosing interval). The relative increase in plasma levels at stabilization is determined by the ratio of the dosing interval to the terminal plasma half-life. For example, when dosing is done on the $t_{1/2(\beta)}$, the steady state plasma level will be two times the level after the first dose (100 per cent accumulation). For more frequent dosing, accumulation is even greater. If dosing is done in the postabsorptive, postdistributive phase of the plasma curve, the extent of dose accumulation can be predicted by the accumulation factor R, which is expressed as

$$R = \frac{1}{1 - e^{-\beta\tau}}$$

where τ is the dosing interval and $\beta = 0.693/t_{1/2(\beta)}$ is the rate constant for the terminal phase of the plasma curve. For LAAM, $4_{1/2(ab)} + 4\ t_{1/2(\alpha)}$ is approximately 34 hours, therefore, with an average dosing frequency $\tau = 56$ hours, LAAM is dosed during the β-phase. Thus the accumulation factors for oral administration of 1.1 mg/kg of LAAM on a Monday-Wednesday-Friday schedule are 2.9 for LAAM, 2.4 for N-LAAM, and 4.2 for DN-LAAM. It can also be shown that $R = C_{min}^{ss}/C_{min}^1$, where C_{min}^1 is the minimum plasma concentration after the first dose and C_{min}^{ss} is the minimum concentration at the end of a dosing interval at steady state. Using experimental data from the first and tenth doses at 48 hours, the ratio C_{min}^{ss}/C_{min}^1 is 3.4 for LAAM, 3.1 for N-LAAM, and 5.4 for DN-LAAM. The ratios give reasonable agreement with the respective R values when one considers both the variability within the average data and the added variability of the metabolism process. Therefore, it is reasonable to assume that plasma levels reported in Table 28.2 for the tenth dose of LAAM approximate steady state concentrations for LAAM, N-LAAM, and DN-LAAM.

A graphical representation of a plasma concentration curve is presented in Figure 28.6 for the case of multiple dosing of methadone with an abrupt crossover to multiple dosing of LAAM. For methadone, with an approximate $t_{1/2(\beta)}$ of 24 hours, equal doses are administered daily for 8 days and the curve is followed for 4 additional days. On day 9 a change to LAAM is represented. LAAM is then administered in equal doses on a Monday-Wednesday-Friday protocol for 10 doses, and the curve is followed for 10 additional days. Also plotted are some experimental values for average concentrations of N-LAAM and DN-LAAM. From the concentration-time profile, it is clear that methadone approaches steady state concentrations in 4 to 5 days. For LAAM, six doses over a 2-

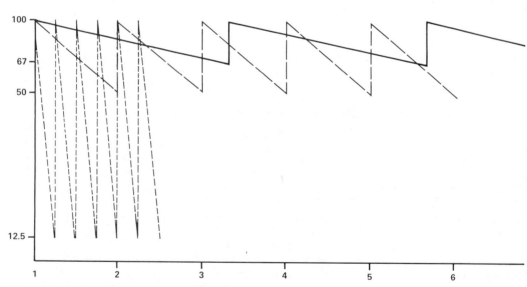

Figure 28.6. Percentage of maximum plasma concentration C_{max} versus time for multiple dose at steady state. *Solid line* (——) represents LAAM with dosing frequency $\tau = 56$ hours. *Long dashed line* (— —) represents methadone with dosing frequency $\tau = 24$ hours. *Short dashed line* (---) represents morphine with dosing frequency $\tau = 6$ hours.

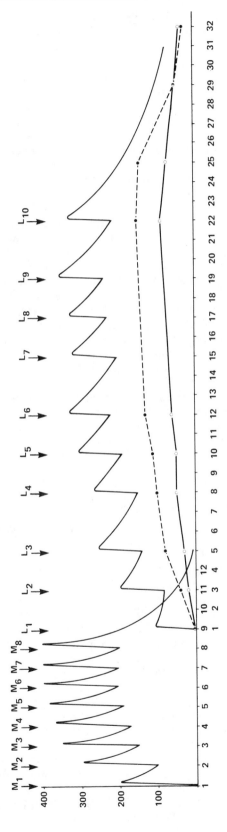

Figure 28.7. Comparison of plasma concentration versus time curves for methadone and LAAM. Eight daily doses of methadone and LAAM, are represented and the final dose is followed for 4 days postdose. Crossover to LAAM occurs on day 9 with frequency of dosing indicated by arrows, are represented and the final dose is followed for 4 days postdose. Crossover to LAAM occurs on day 9 with frequency of dosing a Monday-Wednesday-Friday protocol as indicated by arrows. Experimental average concentrations of N-LaAM (● connected by dashed curve) and DN-LAAM (○ connected by solid curve) are also shown.

week period are required to achieve plasma level stabilization. The relative fluctuation of plasma levels once stabilization has occurred are depicted graphically in Figure 28.7. For methadone, plasma levels will decrease to 50 per cent of maximum values at the end of the 24-hour dosing interval (32). For LAAM, with an average 56-hour dosing interval, plasma concentrations decrease to 67 per cent of maximum values. Comparison to morphine, with an approximate $t_{1/2(\beta)}$ of 2 hours, shows plasma concentrations decrease to 12 1/2 per cent of maximum values within a 6-hour interval.

IMPLICATIONS

These pharmacokinetic parameters detailed above may help account for several clinical observations reported in the clinical trials. The underdosing symptoms that resulted in greater termination of LAAM patients during the induction from street heroin and abrupt crossover from methadone maintenance can, in part, be understood pharmacokinetically, as Figure 28.6 graphically depicts. Thus, the time required to establish stabilized plasma levels after abrupt crossover from methadone is about 2 weeks for LAAM and N-LAAM and probably 3 weeks for DN-LAAM. The time course of improvement of the clinical parameters—e.g., physiological measures, complaints of and terminations for undermedication, and illicit heroin use—closely parallels the gradual increase in plasma levels of LAAM and its metabolites prior to steady state.

A similar but more prolonged profile would be obtained for a dosage schedule with weekly incremental increases in dose as occurs for induction of street heroin addicts. In such a case, stabilization would occur after each five daily doses of methadone. For LAAM, stabilization would not occur until 2 to 3 weeks after the last increase in dose. Thus, 8 to 9 weeks would be necessary to reach LAAM stabilization using the VA induction protocol.

The knowledge of these pharmacokinetic parameters can be used to design improved dosage schedules. Dosage schedules delivering early LAAM loading doses should achieve steady state plasma levels more rapidly and diminish undermedication. Judson and Goldstein utilized a faster induction schedule of sequential dose increases from 20 mg to 50 mg in four or five successive, three times weekly doses (47). Neither symptoms of overmedication nor difficulty with signs and symptoms of undermedication were reported. Definitive improvement in retention was not demonstrated in the several alternative dosage schedules in the Phase III study that investigated supplemental doses of methadone or LAAM and a gradual crossover schedule. However, reduction of undermedication complaints was seen in a few of these schedules.

These pharmacokinetic parameters and figures represent average data. Individual variability is present in metabolic capacity. Thus, considerable variability occurs in the individual terminal half-lives. Probably, some proportion of patients who terminated early due to undermedication were slow demethylators of LAAM and would require even longer to reach steady states. In these cases, physicians would have to individualize the dose schedule to adequately treat the complaints of undermedication.

Another clinical dosage management technique which seems to reduce complaints of undermedication on Sunday of the 72-hour period between doses is increasing the Friday dose an additional 10 to 15 mg (65). Examination of Figure 28.6 (Doses 6 to 10) shows that there is a slight decline in peak LAAM levels after stabilization between the Friday and Monday doses, with an incremental increase between Monday and Friday to the preceding Friday's level. The additional dose increment would probably alleviate this degree of decline over the weekend.

Figure 28.6 also depicts the accumulation at steady state of LAAM and its metabolites, as well as methadone, during induction. Experimental data available on comparable doses (1.0 mg/kg) of daily methadone (32) and three times weekly LAAM indicated that average plasma concentration of methadone 24 hours after the dose was 265 ng/ml, whereas average concentrations 48 hours after the LAAM dose were LAAM 79 ng/ml, N-LAAM 184 ng/ml, and DN-LAAM 102 ng/ml for a total concentration 365 ng/ml (18–20). Thus, the average levels of LAAM and metabolites achieved are considerably higher than methadone. Perhaps these higher LAAM levels result in more effective maintenance. A higher degree of cross-tolerance and blockade of injected opiates than are seen with methadone may result, which could account for the lower illicit opiate use in the clinical trials.

The last portion of the methadone and LAAM plasma concentration curves in Figure 28.6 shows the decline after the final dose. The rate of decline is considerably slower for LAAM (12.5 per cent per day; N-LAAM, 17 per cent per day, and DN-LAAM, 8 per cent per day) than for methadone (50 per cent per day). Possibly this accounts for the clinical impression that detoxification to abstinence is more comfortable from LAAM maintenance than methadone maintenance (26).

Plasma level variability during such dosing interval at steady state displayed in Figure 28.7 for methadone and LAAM indicates that LAAM levels remain relatively constant each day in comparison to methadone levels. Although not displayed, N-LAAM would be about the same as LAAM, whereas DN-LAAM would decline about 20 per cent over the dosing interval. Thus, the relatively larger increase in methadone plasma levels after the dose and smaller decline from LAAM during the dosing interval may account for the "rush" often experienced for a few hours after the methadone dose (53), the chronic abstinence noted in the methadone-50 group in the VA study (59), and the often noted stable emotional state called "feeling normal" by LAAM patients (26, 74).

Pharmacokinetic investigation of methadone has indicated that the terminal half-life is considerably shorter, approximately 14 hours, when single 15-mg doses were given to naive subjects (31, 32). Further research is needed to determine whether this difference is related to the lower dose level or the drug naivete. The decline during each dosing interval would be even greater at lower doses and during detoxification if the half-life is dose dependent.

FUTURE RESEARCH AREAS

Several areas emerge from this review as promising for future research. First, in terms of the pharmaceutical development of LAAM, a large body of data remains unanalyzed on comparative detoxification from LAAM and methadone maintenance. Pharmacokinetic differences between the drugs theoretically could lessen the severity of abstinence symptoms in the final phase of detoxification and the postdetoxification period with LAAM. Clinical vignettes lend support

to this possibility. Secondly, the analysis of the long-term safety and efficacy data generated in the Phase III trial should be completed. Finally, studies comparing the clinical psychopharmacology, safety, and efficacy of LAAM and methadone in women should be performed.

A scientifically interesting area deserving high priority clinical research is the elucidation of patient characteristics determining differential success with LAAM or methadone. Clinical experience has revealed that some patients do extremely well on one drug but not the other. Clinicians have the reported occurrence of dramatic turnabouts in some patients' rehabilitation when switched to LAAM from methadone, and these individuals are vehement in their desire to remain on this drug. Some patients seem to benefit more than others from the psychopharmacological effect of LAAM, an effect referred to by patients as "feeling normal." Others seem to prefer the different feeling state of methadone. Pharmacokinetic and metabolic differences among patients should be investigated further, as should the relationship between the psychotropic differences of LAAM and methadone and patients' expectations of the subjective state of maintenance (9).

Next, the possibility of interactions between LAAM and other psychoactive drugs should be explored, although animal studies do not reveal any differences between LAAM and methadone (10). Finally, strategies of treatment program management should be sought to optimize treatment outcome for both of these safe and effective medications.

CURRENT STATUS OF LAAM—WINTER 1980

The major clinical studies in males have been completed. The data have been extensively analyzed, and a New Drug Application (NDA) was submitted in September 1979 to the Food and Drug Administration (FDA) for review. Until an approved NDA is granted and the drug is marketed, LAAM will be available from NIDA to investigators for research conducted under an IND.

References

1. Beecher, H. K. Analgesic power and the question of "acute tolerance" to narcotics in man. J. Pharmacol. Exp. Ther. 108:158, 1953.
2. Billings, R. E., McMahon, R. E., and Blake, D. A. 1-

Acetylmethadol (LAAM) treatment of opiate dependence: Plasma and urine levels of two pharmacologically active metabolites. Life Sci. 14:1437, 1974.

3. Billings, R. E., McMahon, R. E., and Blake, D. A. 1-Acteylmethadol treatment of opiate dependence: The crucial role of active metabolites. Fed. Proc. 33: 473, 1974.

4. Blachly, P. H. L-Alpha acetylmethadol in the treatment of opiate addiction: Progress report, 1971. In *Methadone, 1971: Workshop Proceedings*, P. H. Blachly, editor, pp. 23-25. Corvallis, Or., ACEB Books, 1971.

5. Blachly, P. Recent developments in the therapy of addictions. Curr. Psychiatr. Ther. 12:98, 1972.

6. Blachly, P. H. David, N. A., and Irwin, S. Alpha-acetylmethadol (LAM): Comparison of laboratory finding, electroencephalograms, and Cornell Medical Index of patients stabilized on LAM with those on methadon. In *Proceedings of the Fourth National Conference on Methadone Treatment*, San Francisco, January 1972, pp. 203-205. New York, National Association for the Prevention of Addiction to Narcotics, 1972.

7. Blaine, J. D. Early clinical studies of levo-alpha-acetylmethadol (LAAM): An opiate agonist for use in the medical treatment of chronic heroin dependence. In *The International Challenge of Drug Abuse*, R. C. Peterson, editor, NIDA Research Monograph 19, pp. 249-259. Rockville, Md., Department of Health, Education and Welfare, 1978.

8. Blaine, J. D. and Renault, P. Introduction. In *Rx LAAM: 3x/week: LAAM Alternative to Methadone*, J. D. Blaine and P. F. Renault, editors, NIDA Research Monographs #8, pp. 1-7. Rockville, Md., Department of Health Education and Welfare, 1976.

9. Blaine, J. D. Renault, P. F., Levine, G. L., and Whysner, J. A. Clinical use of LAAM. Ann. N. Y. Acad. Sci. 311:214, 1978.

10. Braude, M. D. Personal communication regarding finding of NIDA contract with Parke, Davis & Company. #HSM-42-72-167, Detroit, Michigan. Principal Investigator S. Kurtz and D. Downs, entitled Preclinical Pharmacologic and Toxicologic Evaluation of Compounds Used in the Treatment of Narcotic Addiction, 1978.

11. Chen, K. K. Pharmacology of methadone and related compounds. Ann. N. Y. Acad. Sci. 51:83, 1948.

12. Crowley, T. J., Jones, R. H., Hydinger-MacDonald, M., Lingle, J. R., Wagner, J. E., and Egan, D. J. LAAM g.o.d. disturbs circadian cycles of human motility. Psychopharmacology 62:151, 1979.

13. David, N. A. and Semler, H. J. Clinical trial of alpha acetylmethadol (dl-6-dimethylamino-r, 4-diphenyl-3-acetoxy-heptane) as an analgesic. J. Pharmacol. Exp. Ther. 106:380, 1952.

14. David, N. A., Semler, H. J. and Burgner, P. R. Control of chronic pain by dl-alpha-acetylmethadol. J.A.M.A. 161:599, 1956.

15. Dole, U. P., and Nyswander, M. A. A medical treatment for diacetylmorphine (heroin) addiction. J.A.M.A. 193:646, 1965.

16. Eddy, N. B., May, E. L., and Mosettig, E. Chemistry and pharmacology of the methadols and acetylmethadols. J. Organ. Chem. 17:321, 1952.

17. Eddy, N. B., Touchberry, C. F., Lieberman, J. E., and Khazan, N. Synthetic analgesics: Methadone isomers and derivatives. J. Pharmacol. Exp. Ther. 98:121, 1950.

18. Finkle, B. S., Jennison, T. A., and Chinn, D. M. Technical Report to NIDA, Contract 271-76-3323, April 30, 1977.

19. Finkle, B. S., Jennison, T. A., Chinn, D. M., and Crouch, D. J. Technical Report to NIDA, Contract 271-76-3323, December 31, 1977.

20. Finkle, B. S., Jennison, T. A., Chinn, D. M., Ling, W., and Holmes, E. D., The plasma and urine disposition of 1-2-acetyl methadol and its principal metabolites in man. Clin. Pharmacol. Ther., Submitted, 1980.

21. Fraser, H. F., and Isbell, H. Actions and addiction liabilities of alpha-acetylmethadols in man. J. Pharmacol. Exp. Ther. 105:458, 1952.

22. Fraser, H. F., Nash, T. L., Vanhorn, G. D., and Isbell, H. Use of miotic effect in evaluating analgesic drugs in man. Arch. Int. Pharmacodyn. Ther., 98:443, 1954.

23. Goldstein, A. Blind controlled dosage comparisons in two hundred patients. In *Proceedings of the Third National Conference on Methadone Treatment*, p. 31, Washington, D.C., United States Government Printing Office, 1971.

24. Goldstein, A. Heroin addiction and the role of methadone in its treatment. Arch. Gen. Psychiatry 26: 291, 1972.

25. Goldstein, A. LAAM and LAAM metabolites: Plasma levels in patients: Summary progress report, 1975. Unpublished.

26. Goldstein, A. A clinical experience with LAAM. In *Rx LAAM: 3x/week: LAAM Alternative to Methadone*, J. D. Blaine and P. F. Renault, editors, NIDA Research Monograph #8, pp. 115-117. Rockville, Md., Department of Health, Education and Welfare, 1976.

27. Goldstein, A., and Judson, B. Three critical issues in the management of methadone programs: Critical issue 3: Can the community be protected against the hazards of take-home methadone? In *Addiction*, P. G. Bourne, editor, pp. 140-148. New York, Academic Press, 1974.

28. Gruber, C. M., Jr., and Babtisti, A., Jr. Estimating the acceptability of morphine of noracetylmethadol in postpartum patients. Clin. Pharmacol. Ther. 4:172, 1962.

29. Henderson, G. L. A two-year pharmacokinetic study of LAAM: Progress report, 1974-1975. Prepared under Contract HSM-42-73-211 at the University of California at Davis. Unpublished.

30. Houde, R. W., Murphy, T. W., and Wallenstein, S. L. Clinical studies of narcotics at Memorial Sloan-Kettering Cancer Center. A. Relative analgesic potencies of (1) noracymethadol (dl-a-3-acetoxy-6-methylamino-4, 4-diphenylheptane) and morphine; (2) dextropropoxyphene and pethidine; (3) RO-4-1778/1 (1-[p-chlorophenethyl]-6, 7-dimethoxy-2-methyl-1,2,3,4-tetrahydroisoquinoline) and codeine; (4) oral codeine and morphine. B. Relative respiratory depressant potencies of piminodine (ethyl 4-phenyl-1-[3-phenylamino-propyl]-4-piperidine carboxylate) and morphine. Committee on Drug Addiction and Narcotics and the Committee on Problems of Drug Dependence, National Research Council, Division of Medical Sciences. 24th Meeting, App. 14, p. 2852, 1962. Unpublished.

31. Inturrisi, C. E., and Verebely, M. A. Disposition of methadone in man after a single oral dose. Clin. Pharmacol. Ther. 13:923, 1972.

32. Inturrisi, C. E., and Verebely, K. The levels of meth-

adone in the plasma in methadone maintenance. Clin. Pharmacol. Ther. 13:633, 1972.

33. Irwin, S., Blachly, P. H., Marks, J., Carlson, E., Loewen, J., and Reade, N. Preliminary results of methadone and methadyl maintenance therapy. Proceedings of the Committee on Problems of Drug Dependence, 35th Meeting. National Academy of Sciences, National Research Council, 1973.

34. Irwin, S., et al. The behavioral, cognitive and physiologic effects of long term methadone and methadyl treatment, 1973. University of Oregon Medical School, Portland, Oregon. Unpublished.

35. Irwin, S., Blachly, P., Marks, J., and Carter, C. Preliminary observations with acute and chronic methadone and 1-alpha-acetylmethadol administration in humans. University of Oregon Medical School, Portland, Oregon. Unpublished.

36. Irwin, S., Kinohi, R., Cooler, P., and Bottomly, D. Acute time-dose-response effects of cyclazocine, methadone, and methadyl in man. Prepared under NIMH Contract ND-72-115 at University of Oregon Medical School, Portland, Oregon. Unpublished.

37. Isbell, H. Addiction liability of the acetylmethadols. Committee on Drug Addiction and Narcotics and the Committee on Problems of Drug Dependence, National Research Council, Division of Medical Sciences, 7th Meeting, App. C., p. 161, 1951. United States Public Health Service Hospital, Lexington, Kentucky. Unpublished.

38. Isbell, H., and Eiseman, A. J. The addiction liability of some drugs of the methadone series and 6-methyldihydromorphine. Committee on Drug Addiction and Narcotics and The Committee on Problems of Drug Dependence, National Research Council, Division of Medical Sciences, 2nd Meeting, App., p. 28, 1948. United States Public Health Service Hospital, Lexington, Kentucky. Unpublished.

39. Isbell, H., and Fraser, H. F. Addictive properties of methadone derivatives. J. Pharmacol. Exp. Ther. 13: 369, 1954.

40. Isbell, H., Wickler, A., Eisenman, A. J., Daingerfield, M., and Frank, E. Liability of addiction to 6-dimethlamino-4-4-diphenyl-3-hepatone in man. Arch. Intern. Med. 82:362, 1948.

41. Jaffe, J. H. The maintenance approach to the management of opioid dependence. In Drug Abuse: Proceedings of the International Conference, C. Zarafonelis, editor, pp. 161–170. Philadelphia, Lea and Febiger, 1972.

42. Jaffe, J. H., Schuster, C. R., Smith, B. B., and Blachly, P. Comparison of dl alpha-acetyl methadol and methadone in the treatment of narcotics addicts. Pharmacologist 11:256, 1969.

43. Jaffe, J. H., Schuster, C. R., Smith, B. B. and Blachly, P. H. Comparison of acetylmethadol and methadone in the treatment of long-term heroin users: A pilot study. J.A.M.A. 211:1834, 1970.

44. Jaffe, J. H., and Senay, E. C. Methadone and 1-methadyl acetate: Use in management of narcotics addicts. J.A.M.A. 216:1303, 1971.

45. Jaffe, J. H., Senay, E. C., and Renault, P. F. A six-month preliminary report of the rehabilitative efficacy of 1-methadyl acetate compared to methadone. In Proceedings of the Fourth National Conference on Methadone Treatment, San Francisco, January 1972, pp. 199–201. New York, National Association for the Prevention of Addiction to Narcotics, 1972.

46. Jaffe, J. H., Senay, E. C., Schuster, C. R., Renault, P.

F., Smith B., and diMenza, S. Methadyl acetate vs. methadone: A double-blind study in heroin users. J.A.M.A. 222:436, 1972.

47. Judson, B. A., and Goldstein, A. Rapid induction to stable dosages of levomethadyl acetate (LAAM). Drug Alcohol Depend. 4:461, 1979.

48. Kaiko, R. F., Chatterjie, N., and Inturrisi, C. E. Simultaneous determination of acetylmethadol and its active biotransformation products in human biofluids. J. Chromatogr. 109:847, 1975.

49. Kaiko, R. F., and Inturrisi, C. E. A gas-liquid chromatographic method for the quantitative determination of acetylmethadol and its metabolites in human urine. J. Chromatogr. 82:315, 1973.

50. Kaiko, R. F., and Inturrisi, C. E. Identification of some biotransformation products of acetylmethadol in human urine. Fed. Proc. 32:764Abs, 1973.

51. Kaiko, R. F., and Inturrisi, C. E. Time course of plasma levels of acetylmethadol and biotransformation products in relation to pharmacological activity in man. Fed. Proc. 33:473, 1974.

52. Kaiko, R. F., and Inturrisi, C. E. Disposition of acetylmethadol in relation to the pharmacological activity. Clin. Pharmacol. Ther. 18:96, 1975.

53. Karp-Gelernter, E., Wurmser, L., and Savage, C. Therapeutic effects of methadone and l-alpha acetylmethadol. Am. J. Psychiatry 133:955,1976.

54. Keats, A. S., and Beecher, H. K. Analgesic activity and toxic effects of acetylmethadol isomers in man. J. Pharmacol. Exp. Ther. 105:210, 1952.

55. Klett, C. J. The SAODAP cooperative studies of LAAM: Unblinded comparison with methadone. In The International Challenge of Drug Abuse, R. C. Petersen, editor, NIDA Research Monograph #19, pp. 271–276. Rockville, Md., Department of Health, Education and Welfare, 1978.

56. Lehmann, W. X. The use of l-alpha-acetylmethadol (LAAM) as compared to methadone in the maintenance and detoxification of young heroin addicts. Vitam Center, Norwalk, Connecticut, 1973. Unpublished.

57. Levine, R., Zaks, A., Fink, M., and Freedman, A. M. Levomethadyl acetate: Prolonged duration of opioid effects, including cross tolerance to heroin, in man. J.A.M.A. 226:316, 1973.

58. Ling, W., and Blaine, J. D. The use of LAAM in treatment. In Handbook on Drug Abuse, R. J. DuPont, A. Goldstein, J. O'Donnell, and B. Brown, editors, pp. 87–96. Rockville, Md., Department of Health, Education and Welfare, 1978.

59. Ling, W., Blakis, M., Holmes, E. D., Kleet, C. J., and Carter, W. E. Restabilization of methadone after methadyl acetate (LAAM) maintenance. Arch. Gen. Psychiatry 37:194, 1980.

60. Ling, W., Charuvastra, V. C., Kaim, S. C., and Kleet, C. J. Methadyl acetate and methadone as maintenance treatments for heroin addicts. Arch. Gen. Psychiatry 33:709, 1976.

61. Ling, W., Kleet, C. J., and Gillis, R. A cooperative clinical study of methadyl acetate. Arch. Gen. Psychiatry 35:345, 1978.

62. Moreton, J. E., Roehrs, R., and Khazan, N. Sleep-awake activity and self-injection pattern of rats dependent on morphine, methadone or L-alpha-acetylmethadol (LAAM). Fed. Proc. 33:516, 1974.

63. Nickander, P., Booher, R., and Miles, H. α-l-Acetylmethadol and its N-demethylated metabolites have potent opiate action in the guinea pig isolated ileum.

Life Sci. 14:2011, 1974.

64. Pohland, A., Marshall, F. J., and Carney, T. P. Optically active compounds related to methadon. J. Am. Chem. Soc. 71:460, 1949.

65. Resnick, R., Orlin, L., Geyer, G., Schyten, E., Kestenbaum, R., and Freedman, A. M. l-Alpha-acetylmethadol (LAAM): Prognostic considerations. Am. J. Psychiatry 133:814, 1976.

66. Savage, C., Karp, E., and Curran, S. A methadone/l-alpha-acetylmethadol (LAAM) maintenance study. Compr. Psychiatry 17:6415, 1976.

67. Senay, E. C., and diMenza, S. Methadyl acetate in the treatment of heroin addiction: A review. 34th Annual Scientific Meeting of the Committee on Problems of Drug Dependence, 1972, Ann Arbor, Michigan.

68. Senay, E C., Jaffe, J. H., diMenza, S., and Renault, P. F. A 48-week study of methadone, methadyl acetate, and minimal services. In *Opiate Addiction: Origins and Treatment*, S. Fisher and A. M. Freedman, editors, Washington, D.C. V. H. Winston & Sons, 1974.

69. Senay, E. C., Renault, P. F., diMenza, S., Collier, W. E., Daniels, S. J., and Dorus, W. Three times a week LAAM equal seven times a week methadone: A preliminary report of a control study. In *Developments in the Field of Drug Abuse*, E. Senay, V. Shorty and H. Alksne, editors. Cambridge, Mass., Schenkman, 1974.

70. Smits, S. E. The analgesic activity of α-l-acetylmethadol and two of its metabolites in mice. Res. Commun. Chem. Pathol. Pharmacol. 8:575, 1974.

71. Speeter, M. E., Byrd, W. M., Cheney, L. C., and Binkley, S. B. Analgesic carbinols and esters related to amidone (methadon). J. Am. Chem. Soc. 71:57, 1949.

72. Sung, C. Y., and Way, E. L. The fate of the optical isomers of alpha-acetylmethadol. J. Pharmacol. Exp. Ther. 110:260, 1954.

73. Thomas, D. B., Whysner, J. A., and Newmann, M.

C. *The Phase III Clinical Epidemiology of Mortality in LAAM and Methadone*. NIDA Research Monograph Series. In press, 1980.

74. Trueblood, B., Judson, B. A., and Goldstein, A. Acceptability of methadyl acetate (LAAM) as compared to methadone in a treatment program for heroin addicts. Drug Alcohol Depend. 3:125, 1978.

75. Tse, F. L. S., and Welling, P. G. The pharmacokinetics of the acetylmethadols. II. Plasma levels of dextro and levo acetylmethadol and major metabolites in the dog. J. Biopharmaceutics Drug Disposition. In press, 1980.

76. Whysner, J. A. Associates, Inc./Medical Research Applications, Inc., Washington, D.C./McLean, Va. Data from studies submitted to FDA in a New Drug Application, September, 1979.

77. Wilson, B. K. Research report of clinical effects of l-alpha-acetylmethadol on man observed during pharmacokinetic studies. Yolo County Mental Health Service, Broderick, California. Unpublished.

78. Wolven, A., and Archer, S. Toxicology of LAAM. In *Rx 3x/week LAAM: Alternative to Methadone*, J. D. Blaine and P. F. Renault, editors, NIDA Research Monograph Series #8, pp. 29–38. Rockville, Md., Department of Health, Education and Welfare, 1976.

79. Zaks, A., and Feldman, M. Private methadone maintenance: Analysis of a program after one year. J.A.M.A. 222:1279, 1972.

80. Zaks, A., Fink, M., and Freedman, A. M. 1-Alpha-acetylmethadol in maintenance treatment of opiate dependence. In *Proceedings of the Fourth National Conference on Methadone Treatment*, San Francisco, January 1972, pp. 207–210. New York, National Association for the Prevention of Addiction to Narcotics, 1972.

81. Zaks, A., Fink, M., and Freedman, A. M. Levomethadyl in maintenance treatment of opiate dependence. J.A.M.A. 220:811, 1972.

CHAPTER 29

DETOXIFICATION AFTER METHADONE TREATMENT

Paul Cushman, Jr., M.D.

For many years narcotic addiction has been seen as a complex cyclical disorder. Although psychological and environmental factors have been clearly implicated, recently speculation has arisen about greater susceptibility to narcotic addiction in some individuals, possibly related to their endorphins-enkephalins. Over the years, cycles of abstinence were all too frequently followed by return to opiate use amongst chronic opiate addicts. Although the causes of relapses were usually unknown, some have considered the availability of the drug, the psychological status of the user, environmental circumstances, and possibly operant conditioned learning (25). Others envisioned an unspecified metabolic disturbance remaining after opiate addiction, producing a subtle biochemical instability, which is rapidly and specifically corrected upon reuse of opioids (10). Accordingly, it was logical to use a treatment process with a relatively cheap, long acting oral opioid—like methadone—as a substitute for the costly and highly risky street narcotics. The efficacy of methadone maintenance treatment has been amply documented in terms of reduced mortality, lesser amounts of illicit drugs used, better social and economic adjustments, and lowered frequencies of illicit activities by treated patients compared to controls (11).

Methadone maintenance treatment was initially devised to last indefinitely, possibly the remainder of the patient's life. Subsequently, it has become increasingly evident that the majority of patients have rejected indefinite treatment in favor of detoxification. In New York City, which has the largest number of addicts and the greatest experiences with their management, about 27,000 individuals were receiving methadone maintenance treatment in mid-1979, whereas an additional 58,000 (or 68.2 per cent of all those ever enrolled in methadone maintenance treatment) were no longer there. Also episodes of treatment had become common because readmissions outnumbered new admissions about two to one (6).

This chapter examines the following questions regarding methadone treatment:

1. How often does spontaneous remission occur amongst narcotic addicts?

2. What happens to former methadone patients?

3. Should methadone maintenance be available primarily for management of relapses?

4. Should it be a "term" treatment with a definite duration, or should it continue indefinitely?

5. What factors can be identified with the ability to remain abstinent from narcotics amongst former methadone patients?

SPONTANEOUS RECOVERY AFTER OPIATE USE

Although many persons are exposed to opiates, the majority seem able to discontinue their use spontaneously (18). An important, longitudinal epidemiological study used United States soldiers who used heroin, even to the point of addiction, while in Vietnam. On follow-up 1½ years later, only a small fraction (4 to 12 per cent) had continued their use in an addicting manner after their return to the United States (19). This finding is supported by other data in drug abusers known to the Baltimore police, in whom current use of narcotics was reported in only 7 per cent of the 267 persons interviewed (14). Burt Associates interviewed a random sample of largely young addicts, formerly treated with methadone, therapeutic community, or outpatient drug-free modalities in both Washington, D.C., and New York City (4). They found most (59 per cent) did not admit to narcotics use within 2 months of the interview. Furthermore, neither the duration nor the specific type of treatment seemed to be associated with abstinence from narcotics. Their interview data were substantiated by urinary drug studies. Many of these persons in these follow-up studies seemed to be in the stage of drug experimentation or to have an opiate addiction of recent onset.

Methadone maintenance treatment is offered those who are beyond these experimentation stages, because a minimum period of 1 and most often 2 years of addiction is required before admission. This population is usually thought, on the basis of follow-up studies of the Riverside Hospital experiment in New York City in the 1950's and the clinical impressions at the major urban penal detoxification and treatment centers, to have a very high probability of returning to addiction after confinement or treatment (1, 24). On the other hand, some chronic addicts, perhaps 3 per cent a year, out of 100 addicted New Yorkers who had been treated in the 1950's at Lexington, Kentucky, and followed for 20 years, seem to achieve stable abstinence from narcotics. Similar findings (25 per cent apparently abstinent from narcotics) were reported by Richman and Bowles (16) in a 10-year follow-up of 100 randomly selected patients who were admitted to Bernstein Institute in New York City for narcotic detoxification. Therefore, chronic narcotic addicts also may spontaneously cease opiate use. Some have argued (2) that termination of opiate addiction after a mean term of about 8 to 9 years is common amongst chronic urban addicts. Winick has suggested that some addicts mature out of opiate use (26). Accordingly, it would be expected that many methadone maintenance patients would detoxify and also remain abstinent from narcotics. Whether these chronic addicts, who are currently not actively using narcotics, are in a period of remission or permanently abstinent cannot be known until their life-span is complete.

TECHNIQUES OF DETOXIFICATION

Although some patients will undergo detoxification in the streets or as a result of being confined to jail or other institutions, the methadone treatment providers should have available on request a regularized system of methadone detoxification. An often recommended regimen includes 5 mg/week dose reduction schedules while the dose is above 20 mg/day and then 2.5 mg/biweekly thereafter is tolerated. Patient discomfort may be managed by further slowing or reversing detoxification. A careful prospective study by Senay et al. (21) showed the superiority of decrements of 3 per cent of the starting dose weekly over 30 weeks to a 10-week more rapid detoxification schedule.

In contrast, the usual narcotic detoxification procedures in ambulatory or inpatient detoxification use 5 to 20 mg of methadone initially, and then decrease the daily dose over 7 to 10 days. Occasionally, longer periods of treatment and somewhat higher initial doses may be needed for completion of the detoxification, which must end by governmental fiat in 21 days.

Some have urged more rapid alternatives to the slow detoxification (5). One noteworthy variant of methadone detoxification was devised by Resnick et al. in New York Medical College (15), in which methadone patients en route to oral naltrexone received repeated injections of naloxone until their symptoms of narcotic withdrawal ceased. Although a surprisingly large number of their methadone patients have accepted a short but intensive narcotic withdrawal syndrome, this procedure has not had wide acceptance elsewhere. Also, the long term fate of those who undergo rapid detoxification remains unknown.

Methadone to abstinence is an 18- to 24-month term treatment concept, heterogenously applied, in which methadone initially is provided to encourage cessation of illicit narcotics as in the maintenance program. During the rest of the term, efforts are made to help the patient with his other drug and his social, economic, and psychological problems and to carry out a planned detoxification. Although the concept of term methadone treatment has broad political appeal, it only has attracted about 740 in New York City in mid-1979 (2.7 per cent of all chronic methadone-treated patients). Lacking are precise data regarding their activities while on methadone and long term outcome. Evidently, the time period may be rather short for many patients, not only to achieve their psychological and socioeconomic goals, but also to complete detoxification smoothly, because many are shifted to methadone maintenance at the end of the term treatment.

Another variant of detoxification uses propoxyphene, a weak orally effective opioid analogue of methadone. Although it will alleviate the opiate abstinence symptoms and is acceptable to some patients, its relatively narrow toxic therapeutic ratio limits its effectiveness as does its potential for abuse. Controlled studies of its use in ambulatory detoxification show propoxyphene to be less effective than methadone in keeping patients in treatment (42). Recently, clonidine, an alpha-sympathetic agonist, which is used in hypertension to reduce central nervous system sympathetic outflow, has been helpful in acute opioid detoxification. Although experience is limited, divided doses of oral clonidine seem to reduce the craving for opiates as well as the usual opiate withdrawal syndrome, even in patients addicted to methadone.

CATEGORIES OF DETOXIFIED PATIENTS

The immediate and long term outcomes of detoxification are greatly affected by the patients' reasons for seeking detoxification. Some detoxifications take place because of illness, rule violations that result in administrative discharges or in confinement, as in jail; others can be categorized as voluntary or patient initiated, without staff assent; others are categorized as initiated jointly by the patient and staff, who reach a decision that the rehabilitation may have reached the point where further methadone maintenance may not be necessary. The latter process can be called "therapeutic detoxification." Although criteria for inclusion in the category of therapeutic detoxification vary amongst different clinics, most centers consider many months of no recognized drug abuse, responsibility in handling appointments, stable home situation, and steady employment as important factors.

In addition to the myriad of reasons for the patients to seek detoxification, society, family, friends and other drug-abusing patients often exert pressures on the patient to discontinue methadone treatment. Also staff attitudes may add subtlely to the pressures for detoxification, inasmuch as Brown et al. (3) found that most methadone treatment staff believed methadone treatment to be less desirable than functioning without drugs. Furthermore, governmental regulations require that all patients be periodically reviewed for discontinuation of methadone treatment. As a result, many patients undergo detoxification in various stages of their rehabilitation, including many who detoxify prematurely.

It is important to make a clear distinction between detoxification from methadone, i.e., the cessation of the oral opioid, and the state of enduring abstinence. Many persons, both patients and others outside the treatment process, view detoxification as a desirable end point in itself. The highly optimistic wish that abstinence will continue indefinitely after detoxification is frequently a stronger force in patients' behavior than the careful consideration of the possible hazards that pharmacological relapse may introduce to the patient's survival, health, or psychological and economic levels of functioning.

FOLLOW-UP OF FORMER METHADONE-MAINTAINED PATIENTS

In fact, follow-up studies of former methadone patients show that they are much worse pharmacologically and in their functional state than those who remained in treatment. A stratified sample of 17,000 New

Yorkers who received methadone for the first time in 1972 was studied in 1977. Ninety-two per cent of the targeted group were traced (9). In Table 29.1 are presented the results. Of the discharged patients, 92 per cent were judged to be opiate users or to have other serious problems. Only 8 per cent were judged to be apparently well. In contrast, the group of patients who remained in treatment had small frequencies of opiate use and a modest amount of other problems. The large number of persons who had been detoxified but readmitted into methadone maintenance treatment attested to the relapse potential of many. Retreated patients showed only somewhat greater frequencies of opiate use or other problems than those who had never left treatment. These gloomy data raise doubts about the wisdom of encouraging detoxification from methadone maintenance in the majority of patients.

Some patients seem to have cycles of narcotic addiction, methadone maintenance treatment, detoxification, relapse to opioids, retreatment with methadone, and detoxification anew, etc. There is some evidence that secondary or tertiary cycles of methadone treatment may be shorter than the first one. Drug treatment centers should be alert to this cycle phenomenon and be prepared for the management of relapses. Treatment centers should maintain a continuing care relationship with former methadone recipients until 3 years have elapsed, after which the probability of relapse seems low.

In prospective studies of detoxification in methadone clinics (13, 17, 23), some patients fail to detoxify despite a verbal wish to do so (7). Usually they are unable to tolerate symptoms encountered during the detoxification. As the methadone dose is lowered below 30 to 40 mg/day, symptoms suggestive of the opiate abstinence syndrome may appear, i.e., insomnia, malaise, pain, fatigue, irritability, anxiety, restlessness, hyperactive gastrointestinal tract, and sexual problems. As detoxification proceeds, a variety of other symptoms may appear that are even less clearly related to opiate abstinence. Whether these symptoms are psychological or pharmacological, they are frequently associated with patient use of a variety of drugs and alcohol, sometimes to the point of abuse. Patients need increased supportive care during detoxification directed at improving their understanding of the pharmacological consequences of reduced opioid ingestion and symptoms management. Some centers use courses of hypnotics or benzodiazepines or other sedatives in some patients, but their routine use is not advised.

Relapse to opiates is most likely shortly after detoxification. However, relapse rates tend to vary according to the specific categories of detoxified patients. About 95 per cent of therapeutically detoxified patients at Mt. Sinai (23) are abstinent from narcotics after 1 year, whereas only 55 per cent of all the other detoxified patients were abstinent. The same group found that abstinence from

Table 29.1
Opiate Use and Other Problems in Former Methadone-maintained Patients, Compared to Other Patients Who Had Been Discharged and Readmitted and to Others Who Had Been Continuously Treated[a]

	Continuously Treated		Discharged and Readmitted		Discharged	
	Number	%	Number	%	Number	%
Opiate + +[b]	5	1	8	3	540	64
Opiate +[c]	12	2	16	7	50	6
Opiate O						
Other problems[d]	195	34	97	40	184	22
Apparently well	355	63	120	50	72	8
Total	567	100	241[e]	100	846	100

[a] Reprinted from Dole, V. P., and Joseph, H. Long term outcome of patients treated with methadone maintenance. Ann. N. Y. Acad. Sci. 311:181, 1978.
[b] Opiate + +, two or more times weekly use of opiates.
[c] Opiate +, less than twice weekly use of opiates.
[d] Other problems include alcoholism, use of nonopiate drugs, criminal activity with arrest, and nonopiate-caused death.
[e] The 241 discharged and readmitted are part of the 846 who were discharged.

Table 29.2
Follow-up of Therapeutic Detoxification (TD) in Former Methadone Patients

Author	Total in Study	Completing TD		Duration of TD (Mean)	Duration of Follow-up (Mean)	Narcotic Abstinent	Known Return to Narcotics
		Number	%				
				mos	yrs	%	%
Cushman (7)	646	89	14	14.5	1.9	46	30
Dole and Joseph (9)	846	167	20			33[a]	
Millman et al. (13)	153	41	39	36	2.8	69	5[b]
Stimmel et al. (23)	1,220	88	7.2	22	2.3	57	25

[a] Abstinent from narcotics, free of alcohol and other drug abuse, and not arrested.
[b] Includes alcohol abuse.

Table 29.3
Abstainers from Narcotics (NA) in Former Methadone-maintained Patients in Follow-up Studies

Author	Total in Series	Abstainers from Narcotics		All Discharged Patients	NA % of All Discharged Patients
		Number	%		
Cushman (7)	646	49	7.5	225	21.7
Dole and Joseph (9)	1,410	256	18.1	846	30.3
Millman et al. (13)	153	42	27.6	77	54
Stimmel et al. (23)	1,220	98	8	427	23
TOTAL	2,865	445	15.6	1,576	28.2

narcotics was much higher in the therapeutic detoxified group (56.8 per cent) than in those who were jailed (4.5 per cent) or the rule violators (13.2 per cent) or those who detoxified voluntarily without the staff's concordance (22.4 per cent). Similar data (Table 29.2), showing much better rates of apparent abstinence from narcotics in the therapeutic detoxified group than all other groups, have emerged from other clinics that tried to follow all patients leaving treatment.

Table 29.3 indicates the relatively low yield of abstainers from narcotics if all patients ever admitted into treatment are considered.

The detoxified patient has a greater mortality rate, perhaps twice that of the patient who remains in treatment. The excess mortality is due to trauma, violence, drug deaths, and alcoholism in addition to the usual perils. Alcoholism has emerged as a major problem in methadone treatment (22) and it is especially important in those who were detoxified. Alcohol abuse is very common amongst opiate addicts, frequently being abused before initiation of narcotics, and it is the second drug most frequently abused during addiction. It is often viewed as the major drug of abuse during methadone maintenance

treatment. Detoxification from methadone in the methadone-maintained, mixed opiate-alcohol addict is usually of little value in management of their alcoholism. On the contrary, detoxification may be associated with sizeable increases of alcohol use in both the alcoholic methadone patient (8) and in the patient without evident alcoholism during methadone treatment (20).

There are no systematic data on the use (or abuse) of drugs other than alcohol and opioids among former methadone patients after the detoxification is completed. Nor is it possible to determine rigorously whether employment, stability of residence, and criminal activities are changed by detoxification, although the trends suggest that they are adversely affected.

PREDICTORS OF ABSTINENCE

Predictors of abstinence from narcotics among those who have had a course of methadone maintenance treatment include:

1. High staff estimation of the patient's level of rehabilitation, which results in agreement for initiation of the therapeutic detoxification procedures.

2. Steady employment.

3. Social life primarily not in the drug world. This variable and the previous one overlap with the therapeutic detoxification criteria. Gender, marital status, alcoholism, ethnicity, and level of educational achievement were not associated with narcotic abstinence. Because age was not a predictor, it is uncertain how many methadone patients mature out of addiction.

4. Long duration of methadone treatment. Those in treatment for 3 or more years were more likely to be abstinent. Those in treatment for less than 1 year are much more likely to resume opioid use.

Methadone maintenance is a treatment process wherein the patients are administered methadone as a pharmacological substitute for other opioids. It keeps the patients coming to the clinic where the opportunity to assist the patient with his other problems is presented. Methadone centers vary widely in the quality of their supportive services from well run treatment centers to mere filling stations. Because the degree of rehabilitation, as reflected by the outcome of the therapeutically detoxified patient, is a major predictor of abstinence from narcotics, efficacy of treatment in terms of long term abstinence seems to relate both to the rehabilitation potential of the patient and the degree to which the supportive services are made available.

CONCLUSION

Detoxification after methadone treatment is possible for most who try. Those with steady employment and who, after many months of treatment, are considered to be in good standing in the clinic, which may have refined the process to select out the most favorable patients for mutually agreed detoxification, do reasonably well. The majority of detoxified patients relapse to opiates, develop or maintain alcoholism, and are exposed to higher mortality rates than those who do not detoxify. Only a small fraction of those entering methadone treatment, about 15 per cent, seem to maintain abstinence in followup studies.

The frequency with which abstinence from narcotics is attained by former methadone-treated patients is between 8 and 27 per cent in four series. Because these clinics have been operating for at least 8 years, the annual yield of abstinence from narcotics is 1 to 3 per cent or rather similar to the data obtained after detoxification or after treatment in Lexington in the 1950's. Therefore, to expect a term of methadone treatment to produce large numbers of abstainers from narcotics is unreasonable.

The data recommend that detoxification not be a goal for all, the discontinuing treatment is more hazardous than continuation in treatment, that a predetermined time period for a course of methadone treatment may not be an optimal policy for treatment providers, and that efforts of staff and patients are most rewarded when expended in fostering rehabilitation rather than in questions of duration of methadone treatment.

References

1. Brecher, E. M. *Licit and Illicit Drugs.* Mount Vernon, N. Y., Consumers Union, 1972.
2. Brill, L. *The De-Addiction Process.* Springfield, Ill., Charles C Thomas, 1972.
3. Brown, B. S., Jansen, D. R., and Bonn, G. J. Changes in attitudes toward methadone. Arch. Gen. Psychiatry 32:214, 1975.
4. Burt Associates. *Drug Treatment in Washington, D.C., and New York City: Followup Studies.* National Institutes of Drug Abuse Services Research Monograph Series (DHEW Publication No. 77-506). Washington, D. C., Department of Health, Education and Welfare, 1977.
5. Chappel, J. N., and Senay, E. C. A technique for the ambulatory withdrawal from methadone maintenance. In *Proceedings, Fourth National Conference on Methadone Treatment.* New York, National Association for the Prevention of Addiction to Narcotics, 1972.
6. Community Treatment Foundation records.
7. Cushman, P. Methadone maintenance: Long term followup of detoxified patients. Ann. N. Y. Acad. Sci. 311:165, 1978.
8. Cushman, P., and Dole, V. P. Detoxification of rehabilitated methadone maintained patients. J.A.M.A. 226:747, 1973.
9. Dole, V. P., and Joseph, H. Long term outcome of patients treated with methadone maintenance. Ann. N. Y. Acad. Sci. 311:181, 1978.
10. Dole, V. P., and Nyswander, M. E. Heroin addiction: A metabolic disease. Arch. Intern. Med. 120:19, 1967.
11. Gearing, F. G., and Schweitzer, M. D. An epidemiologic evaluation of long term methadone maintenance treatment for heroin addiction. Am. J. Epidemiol. 100:101, 1974.
12. Jasinski, D. R., Pevnick, J. S., Clark, S. C., et al. Therapeutic usefulness of propoxyphene napsylate in narcotic addiction. Arch. Gen. Psychiatry 34:227, 1977.
13. Millman, R. B., Khuri, E. T., and Nyswander, M. E., Therapeutic detoxification of adolescent heroin addicts. Ann. N. Y. Acad. Sci. 311:153, 1978.

14. Nurco, D. M., Bonito, A. J., and Lerner, M. Studying addicts over time: Methodology and preliminary findings. Am. J. Drug Alcohol Abuse 2:183, 1975.

15. Resnick, R. B., Kestenbaum, R. S., Washton, A., et al. Naloxone-precipitated withdrawal: A method for rapid induction onto naltrexone. Clin. Pharmacol. Ther. 21:409, 1977.

16. Richman, A., and Bowles, E. V. Recent status of New York City narcotic addicts detoxified 1961–3. In *Critical Concerns in the Field of Drug Abuse*, A. Schecter, H. Alksne, and E. Kaufman, editors. New York, Marcel Dekker, 1976.

17. Riordan, C. E., Mezritz, M., Slobetz, S., et al. Successful detoxification from methadone maintenance. J.A.M.A. 235:2604, 1976.

18. Robins, I. N. Addict careers. In *Handbook on Drug Abuse*, R. I. Dupont, A. Goldstein, and J. O'Donnell, editors. Washington, D. C., National Institute of Drug Abuse, Department of Health, Education and Welfare, 1979.

19. Robins, L. N., Heltzer, J. E., Hesselbrock, M., and Wish, E. D. Vietnam veterans three years after Vietnam. In *Problems of Drug Dependence*, L. Harris, editor, Proceedings of the Committee on Drug Dependence, Washington, D.C., 1977.

20. Schut, J., File, K., and Wohlmuth, T. Alcohol use by narcotic addicts in methadone maintenance treatment. Q. J. Stud. Alcohol 34:1356, 1973.

21. Senay, E. C., Dorus, W., Goldberg, F., et al. Withdrawal from methadone maintenance. Arch. Gen. Psychiatry 34:361, 1977.

22. Stimmel, B., Cohen, M., and Hanbury, R. Alcoholism and polydrug use in persons on methadone maintenance. Ann. N. Y. Acad. Sci. 311:99, 1978.

23. Stimmel, B., Goldberg, J., and Cohen, M. Detoxification from methadone maintenance: Factors associated with relapse to narcotic use. Ann. N. Y. Acad. Sci. 311:173, 1978.

24. Trussell, R. E. Treatment of narcotic addicts in New York City. In *Methadone Maintenance*, S. Einstein, editor. New York, Marcel Dekker, 1971.

25. Wikler, A. Conditioning factors in opiate addiction and relapse. In *Narcotics*, D. M. Wilner and G. G. Kassebaum, editors. New York, McGraw Hill, 1965.

26. Winick, C. Maturing out of narcotic addiction. Bull. Narc. 14:1, 1962.

CHAPTER 30

MULTIMODALITY PROGRAMMING IN ILLINOIS: EVOLUTION OF A PUBLIC HEALTH CONCEPT

Edward C. Senay, M.D.

The literature on multimodality programming is sparse and it alludes to more than it describes this concept (1–5). Given the fact that multimodality programming gave shape to many community responses to drug problems in the United States and in particular for those of many of the largest cities and states, it is surprising that there is so little written about it in a formal way. But the lack of explicit description probably is explainable by the apparent simplicity of the concept and by the facts that it is only 10 to 15 years old and that it became operational during the enormous expansion of drug treatment services in the past decade. Those involved in this expansion were too busy with other things. In this paper I will describe multimodality programming and how it became operational in Illinois, where the concept was born.

Multimodality programming was created in the late 1960's as a response to the factionalism that had grown up among different methods of treating heroin addicts. In the 1960's, therapeutic communities, principally Synanon, had had an experience with not

more than a few hundred addicts. And in the late 1960's experience with methadone maintenance similarly was limited to a few hundred or more patients. Each of these treatment modalities was exhibiting a historically unprecedented success in treating so-called hard core heroin addicts. Prior to that time, detoxification attempts and treatment in the federal centers in Fort Worth, Texas, and Lexington, Kentucky, had been singularly unsuccessful (8).

In the major cities of the United States there was a massive public health need for successful methods for treating heroin addicts. Both of the new methods, therefore, found fertile soil for expansion. But there was no unifying focus on federal, state, or municipal levels in drug treatment efforts. Each treatment method was isolated from the other, and each was struggling to survive.

Therapeutic communities were hostile to outside intervention of any kind. Charles Diderich, the creator of the therapeutic community movement, had steadfastly refused government evaluation and government funds (9). On the other hand, methadone units had not demonstrated on a scientifically sound basis that their efforts were effective because they had not employed control groups. As a consequence, there was suspicion in scientific quarters about this method. The result was a fragmentation of efforts with a concern for program survival to the exclusion of considering the service needs of addicts.

A heroin addict in a therapeutic community would not ordinarily be advised of the possibilities for treatment in a methadone maintenance program. Similarly, addicts in methadone maintenance programs would not be advised systematically about potentials for treatment in a therapeutic community. The notion in both camps was that heroin addicts were essentially homogenous, and proponents of narcotics substitution or of abstinence maintained, in pseudoreligious fashion, that their approach was the proper way. For example, a heroin addict who was married, had children, and was employed legitimately was often not a candidate to enter a therapeutic community. To give up his job and to leave his family was not economically or therapeutically indicated. Such an addict usually chose and usually benefitted from narcotic substitution. On the other hand, a young, highly mobile addict without a stable job and without stable family relationships might not benefit from narcotic substitution and might much more appropriately be involved in a therapeutic community.

In the 1960's, detoxification was also sought after and a frequently applied treatment method (7). Another treatment had been created by Martin and his co-workers at Lexington and involved narcotic blocking agents such as cyclazocine. Thus, there were a number of options for treatment but no systematic presentation of these options to street addicts.

In the middle of the 1960's, Illinois had formed a Narcotic Advisory Council; its members debated which kinds of treatment would be most appropriate for the state. They hired Dr. Jerome Jaffe as their chief consultant and he suggested that the state could create an innovative attempt to serve its addicts. He proposed the multimodality program. It would have as its primary value service to addicts rather than the promotion of any one particular treatment modality.

A second purpose in Dr. Jaffe's vision was services research. He recognized that, although methadone maintenance had much to offer some addicts and therapeutic communities had much to offer other addicts, these methods by no means exhausted the addict's needs for services. Some addicts, for example, would only accept detoxification, whereas other addicts sought treatment with the new narcotic blocking agents (2). It was clear to Dr. Jaffe that research was needed to create a typology of patients to see which treatments were most appropriate for the different types of patients.

At base the multimodality concept was administrative and not scientific, although it was an administrative arrangement that would facilitate research. There would be one administrative authority, an authority concerned not with keeping one or another program defended but with the job of providing services to heroin addicts as effectively as possible. As Jaffe envisioned the Illinois Drug Abuse Program (IDAP), an addict could receive a thorough review of each treatment option and then could elect to go to a therapeutic community, a methadone maintenance program or a detoxification program and, if desired, detoxification followed by treatment with narcotic-blocking agents. With many treatment options available, an addict could transfer easily from one modality to another if the addict and/or the staff found that the initial choice of a treatment was not correct or acceptable to the addict.

In line with the research objective of the multimodality concept, Jaffe's first thought was that he would assign addicts randomly to the various treatments. But he was not able to do this. Eighty per cent of the addicts coming for treatment wanted methadone maintenance and would not accept any other treatment. Another important factor militating against random assignment was pressure from the public health interests who funded the program. This pressure was for direct service and not for services research. Still another factor that prevented random assignment studies was the literally immense pressure for service. Jaffe began IDAP with no announcements of any kind. Word about the program spread "on the street" with such effect that within a few weeks hundreds were on the waiting list, and this was for a clinic with a capacity of 75 to 150. In the second year of operation, when the IDAP census was around 700 to 800, there were 2,000 addicts on the waiting list.

As the multimodality system began to form, many complex questions appeared. Should relatively scarce program funds be allocated for a predominantly professional and, therefore, more expensive staff? Or should program funds be allocated to a paraprofessional, less expensive staff? Jaffe decided to go the latter route. The effectiveness of paraprofessionals in relating to "street people" and in creating an "affiliation" model of drug treatment seemed self-evident. The recruitment from patient ranks of ex-addicts who then became ex-addict counselors provided a vital chain for the program that linked the program with the pool of addicts in the street in a manner that could never have been effected with professional programming.

The therapy model of programming—i.e., the model utilizing professional staff devoting itself to insight-oriented treatment—did not seem appropriate for the conditions of the time. Growth of the treatment effort would have been slower because of the time necessary to recruit professionals. The fact was that recruitment of professionals was problematic. Many were fearful of working with populations of people with whom the professions had not had major experience. Professionals were also hesitant about the potential for violence in the areas in which the clinics were located. And pay scales for professionals in public programs, in many instances, were not competitive with pay scales in the private sector.

Street addicts did not seek therapy in the sense in which therapy was offered in most mental health centers. They did seem to be seeking affiliation, that is, a sense of belongingness within an organization. Their motives for entering IDAP were frequently not traditionally therapeutic. In mental health centers many of them would have been regarded as "unmotivated." Some wanted to escape legal pressure, others wanted to reduce the size of their habit, others were responding to family pressure—but the commonest motivation was fatigue from "hustling." There were some who did have a desire to change and who seemed to want a sense of sharing in an attempt at trying to change their life style. Few sought self-examination and behavior change based upon an intellectual analysis and/or emotional catharsis of past behaviors.

The lack of interest in traditional therapy was expressed in the very high rate of refusal to enter group therapy. The groups that were accepted by the addicts were confrontational in nature and basically were aimed at creating a sense of affiliation with the program and not with one person or one group. There was rejection on the part of the addicts and on the part of the ex-addict staff of the notion that people had unconscious conflicts. The ideology of the addicts was that people knew what they were thinking and feeling and could report it if they chose to. If they did not choose to report what they were thinking and feeling, they were dishonest and defensive.

The motivation of the addicts was best responded to by having a number of different treatment options available to them rather than trying to fit them all into one or another modality.

The administrative problem in multimodality programming was simple to identify but difficult to implement: how to create conditions under which ideologues of abstinence or narcotic substitution could work together. Early experiences with combining the two were problem ridden. Each viewed the other with distrust, and the working coalition created by Jaffe was constantly in danger.

To improve working relations, Jaffe utilized a number of outside group consultants in sessions separate from regular business meetings. No one of these series of extraadministrative sessions seemed to be clearly successful. These extra sessions turned out to be very much like regular administrative sessions, and the same ground was covered. Ideologues of abstinence asked: How effective or desirable was it for people to be taking methadone? The reply was to look at social and family gains. Methadone maintenance advocates consistently pointed out the fact that therapeutic communities were not acceptable to many, if not most, addicts, and dropout rates from therapeutic communities were very high. But in turn they had to admit that a drug-free graduate of a therapeutic community was the ideal outcome for drug treatment. Although these groups did not lead to explicit acceptance of the multimodality concept on the part of the participants, the fact was that the coalition did not break up and as these extra group sessions continued surprising changes appeared. For example, the therapeutic community leadership accepted the use of methadone in the therapeutic community for a 5-day period when an addict was just coming off the street and needed some assistance with narcotic withdrawal.

In the formative years of IDAP, the use of methadone in the therapeutic community element of IDAP was the subject of heated debate in administrative and extraadminsitrative group sessions. But after a time, the friction ceased, and then for a period of years addicts were detoxified for 5 days with methadone in the therapeutic community element of IDAP without question or comment.

The philosophy that evolved from the collective experience of the IDAP group was something every faction came to accept—i.e., "Be concerned with the behavior of the client or patient. If he or she is making a serious attempt to pull himself or herself together that is what really counts—not the treatment modality he or she is in." In a few instances, people who were absolutely inflexible and remained that way had to be let go. There were only a small number of these. The experience was that most people, regardless of their prior experience and convictions, could accept, work with, and respect the most basic notion of multimodality programming—to wit, "Different strokes for different folks." That is, heroin addicts are not homogenous. They have different needs at different times in their careers.

Most workers in IDAP eventually came to see the fact that the different approaches were effective. This process was facilitated because of the broad utilization of ex-addict paraprofessionals at all levels of the program. In any debate in IDAP usually there were people around the table who had "made it" in a therapeutic community, there were people who had "made it" in methadone maintenance, and usually there were ex-addicts who had "made it" by self-imposed detoxification and/or by utilizing narcotic-blocking agents and some who had "made it" on medically supervised detoxification. The presence of such a variety of treatment experiences made it difficult for ideologues to insist that theirs was the only way.

Jaffe created the central intake concept to provide each addict with an unbiased description of the different treatment methods and to ensure that an accurate diagnosis was made. The addict applying for treatment in IDAP spent most of the day in the central intake. This facility also helped solve the problem of scarce medical services. In many parts of Illinois and particularly in Chicago there were only a handful of physicians for tens of thousands and in a few areas for hundreds of thousands of people. Having physicians available on a daily basis for many different units in a metropolitan area was not possible.

If there had been enough physicians, there was not enough money to support the size of medical effort that would have been necessary to have a daily on-call physician to serve every clinic. With full time physician coverage at central intake, many clinics could be served efficiently and economically. The training process was also facilitated. It did not take long for central intake physicians to learn about addicts when they were seeing 10 to 30 every day of the week. Uniform diagnostic procedures were employed, and there were many economies.

With a central intake facility, the logistics of urine testing were superior to what they would have been with a unit by unit testing system. One laboratory located in the same building as the central intake facility could test the urine and return the result in a few hours. Thus the examining physician would have the physical examination and the urine results available for final diagnosis and referral on the day of intake. The same economy of time and effort was achieved for the chest films. All applicants could be x-rayed, and the results could be read for rapid decision making.

The central intake facility also served well to meet the services research goals of the multimodality program. Research efforts and opportunities were described to the addicts in an atmosphere of straightforward discussion and professionalism. Many addicts were interested in narcotic-blocking agents and signed up for research protocols with fully informed consent. What was striking in this regard was the openness of most street addicts to listen to different options. Their openness was in contrast to the antiresearch bias of many ex-addict paraprofessionals. Their bias was difficult to understand, because they had frequently been involved successfully as research patients. But their newly won status as counselors and their perception that their jobs were threatened by research served to create an antiresearch bias that caused many difficulties in implementing the services research goal of multimodality programming.

The daily experience of the central intake staff created a strong impetus for the "different strokes for different folks" principle, inasmuch as the variety of needs in the hundreds of addicts who came through the facility was self-evident. This experience of central intake workers also reduced bias against research.

Thus, there were many administrative and clinical advantages in the central intake concept. But there were clinical disadvantages. The most serious was the problem of the discontinuity between the central intake experience of the patient and the patient's experience in the treatment unit receiving the patient. Those who diagnosed were not those who treated. The patient had to transfer feelings and get to know a second set of people.

On occasion there was not perfect agreement between the judgment of the clinical intake staff and the staff of the treatment unit. This created a problem for the patient-client caught in the middle of these two positions. In IDAP, the decision was made that the line treatment units had the right of refusal. If central intake, for example, judged that methadone maintenance was the treatment modality of choice, a given methadone maintenance treatment unit might disagree. The receiving unit could judge that it was not the appropriate unit on the grounds that methadone maintenance was not the proper treatment or more commonly that the methadone maintenance unit was not the appropriate treatment unit because of conditions concomitant with the addiction, such as alcoholism, severe mental illness, propensity for violence, or pregnancy.

Refusal by the receiving unit to accept a patient created a difficulty for the central intake staff. Where should they or could they send the patient? This problem reflected the fact that a drug addict with a mental illness was caught (and still is) in a football game between the mental health centers, not equipped to respond to the drug problem, and the drug treatment centers, not equipped to respond to the mental illness of the mentally ill drug addict. Because this kind of problem was quite frequent, Jaffe decided to create a special component of the multimodality system called the special treatment

unit. This unit had sections specifically designed to meet the needs of special groups. In the psychiatric section schizophrenic, manic, or violent addicts would have regular review by psychiatric consultants and would have more consultant time available than was available in "line" units. In the medical section, addicts with medical problems such as hypertension, diabetes, epilepsy, Hodgkin's disease, etc., could receive a degree of medical supervision that would have been inordinately expensive to achieve in every line unit. Similarly, the alcoholic section could respond to the addicts who were also alcoholics. Lastly, the pregnancy section could unify care for pregnant addicts.

Another substantial clinical advantage of multimodality programming was discovered when Jaffe and co-workers began to examine what was happening to "deviants" in the treatment system. Basic clinic rules made violence or the threat of violence, among other behaviors, grounds for termination from the program. Multimodality programming made it possible to transfer "deviants" rather than to exclude them completely from the entire program. Thus, the program as a whole was able to respond to the clinical needs of those who frequently had been socialized to respond to frustration with violence. The program as a whole could say to such an addict: "You cannot stay in that unit because you violated its rules, but you can be transferred to a different clinic if you will try to change the way you respond to frustration." The experience was that more than half such patients could be retained in treatment by administrative transfer rather than by absolute termination from treatment. It was not a new finding for the mental health professionals involved in building IDAP that staff conflicts were frequently important factors in patient "deviance." Creating special support units that serviced large numbers of "regular," "line" units became an integral part of the multimodality concept. The relatively simple "different strokes for different folks" concept was becoming the blueprint for a sophisticated system of services.

In discussing the concept of multimodality programming, DeLong pointed out that there were potential hazards (1): "Most of the benefits to be gained from eliminating accidental assignment, allowing rapid reassignment and experimenting with new programs may be achieved just as well by better administration and consideration of separate modalities. Faith is a very important part of every modality... mixing different modalities may undermine all of them by confusing the patient about the expectations and possibilities of the program."

Experience in IDAP and in other multimodality programs across the country did not seem to validate these possible hazards. Addicts seemed to benefit from the honest description of different treatment possibilities. Once the IDAP staff had been trained in the basic concepts of multimodality programming, they reflected this to the patients, and the patients' responses were to the program and not to any one of its elements.

When Jaffe began the program he had not come to terms with the questions of size but, as he began to make the concept of multimodality programming operational, he had to come to terms with this question.

As noted above, the pressure for services was intense. One of the facets of this pressure was that it was coming from communities. Jaffe, as director of a state-wide effort, was responding to requests for help with drug dependence problems from representatives of cities and counties with both urban and rural spheres of interest. The multimodality concept was a made to order response. It was at this point that the concept began to become important as a public health concept, as a way of thinking about a community's needs for addiction services. Multimodality programming consisted of an organized system of clinics with a central intake unit and special support units to serve the needs of "line" clinics; it functioned under one administrative authority and was in the best possible position, if a community desired, to evaluate what it was getting for its money. A funding body could relate to a single administrative line, and uniform accounting and personnel procedures could be carried out, thus making the system easily compatible with established county or municipal administrative systems.

If addiction services were to come of age, as they have, job descriptions and appropriate pay scales for workers in the field had to be established. Again, the multimodality programming concept lent itself well to such needs. Jaffe sought and obtained strong linkages with the State Department of Mental Health. A new series of job descriptions for

addiction counselors was established. Workers in one modality could have the option of transfer to a different modality, thus creating the highly desirable quality of job mobility for workers in the system. The multimodality concept also provided these workers with system-wide training.

Counselors in the multimodality programming regularly rotated through different modalities and acquired job skills more easily than was possible in most circumstances. As was the case with deviant patients, multimodality programming created a useful option for "deviant" staff members. Many were in the difficult transition period between street life and the middle-class world of regular work, meeting time deadlines, etc. Having administrative control over many units meant that staff members who relapsed to street behavior could be transferred rather than fired from the program. The experience was that staff "deviants" could continue to work effectively and to contribute both to themselves and to the program.

To date there has not been resolution of the problem of job mobility for addiction counselors outside the drug field. This author attempted unsuccessfully to create a flow from addiction services agencies (more than 50 were operating in IDAP) to other human services delivery systems in Illinois, such as mental health counselors, parole and probation counselors, children and family service agencies, etc. The opening of this path could have been important in improving services all around. The addiction workers could have provided a skill and perspective badly needed in mental health centers and vice versa. But political and bureaucratic events prevented this development.

One important question that arose repeatedly throughout the life of IDAP was that of linkage with other health delivery systems. Although the special treatment units could absorb some of the many health needs of addicts, daily clinical experience was teaching that they had many more such needs than could be managed in the addiction budget. The dental needs alone were formidable; once addicts were in treatment they began to present many medical needs for which they were unable and/or unwilling to present when they were addicted or incarcerated. But this placed a major stress on the system.

Referral to existing bureaucratic structures

was rarely effective. The addict knew this, and it did not take long for the professionals working in the system to realize it. Jaffe and co-workers were faced with yet another major question. Should the multimodality program attempt to offer comprehensive health services to addicts, or should its resources continue to be applied predominantly to the drug dependency program? The result in IDAP was a compromise. Some comprehensive services were offered. The most notable example was in the pregnancy section of the special treatment unit. This section treated more than 500 pregnant addicts and provided a resource to the state that was unique.

It would have been interesting to have explored implementing the multimodality concept entirely within the administrative line of the health department of a city or county. As it stands, at this writing, we have experience only in creating services for the drug dependent under administrative lines separate from those established for mental health services.

Multimodality programming lent itself well to services research and to the development and/or modification of existing programs, as well as to the development of creative programs. One of the major modifications of the therapeutic community concept developed in IDAP was the use of therapeutic communities for short term crisis resolution. If a methadone maintenance patient was unable to resist social pressures to continue to use heroin and was possibly under heavy stress levels, he could be admitted to a therapeutic community in IDAP for a period of a few weeks to remove him from street pressure and from stress. Frequently such an addict would be able to improve his functioning and could be transferred back to an outpatient line clinic within a short time.

As the character of the drug problem changed in the early 1970's to use of multiple substances, IDAP was able to respond. An example of this was in its development of programming for youth (6).

We have now acquired a substantial national experience with the multimodality concept. This development was a direct consequence of the fact that Dr. Jaffe became the first Director of the Special Action Office for Drug Abuse Prevention in the Executive Office of the White House and was, therefore, the chief architect of the federal expansion of drug treatment services in the early 1970's. But in historical terms this is a very recent development. Hopefully, our experience with this national public health concept will be documented in a growing literature.

References

1. DeLong, J. *Treatment and Rehabilitation: Dealing with Drug Abuse: A Report to the Ford Foundation Program.* New York, Praeger, 1972.
2. Fisher, S., and Freedman, A. M., editors. *Multimodality approaches to the treatment and prevention of opiate addiction.* In *Opiate Addiction: Origins and Treatment.* Washington, D. C., V. H. Winston, 1973.
3. Glasscote, R. M., Sussex, J. N., Jaffe, J., and Ball, J. *The Treatment of Drug Abuse: Programs, Problem, Prospects.* Washington, D. C., American Psychiatric Association, 1972.
4. Jaffe, J. H. Experience with the use of methadone in a multimodality program for the treatment of narcotic users. Int. J. Addict. 4:481, 1969.
5. Jaffe, J. H. Whatever turns you off. Psychol. Today 3:42, 60, 1970.
6. Kajdan, R. A., and Senay, E. C. Modified therapeutic communities for youth. J. Psychedelic Drugs 8:209, 1976.
7. Newman, R. G. *Methadone Treatment in Narcotic Addiction.* New York, Academic Press, 1977.
8. Senay, E. C. The treatment of drug abuse. In *American Handbook of Psychiatry,* S. Arieti, editor. New York, Basic Books, 1976.
9. Yablonsky, L. *The Tunnel Back.* New York, Macmillan, 1965.

CHAPTER 31

TREATMENT APPROACHES: OPIATE ANTAGONISTS

Charles P. O'Brien, M.D., Ph.D.

Robert A. Greenstein, M.D.

All treatment approaches for substance abuse have to contend with a high vulnerability for relapse after the individual leaves the protected treatment environment. This vulnerability may persist for months or years after stopping drug use, and it is most dramatic when the drug-free patient returns to the environment where he formerly obtained and self-administered the addicting substance. Although there are certainly physiological factors (protracted abstinence (12)) and social factors involved in this vulnerability, Wikler first called attention to its similarities to classically conditioned phenomena (24). Stimuli that have been repeatedly paired with drug effects (usually withdrawal) may eventually be able to elicit these effects in the absence of pharmacologically induced changes. In other words, former addicts may experience physical disturbances similar to withdrawal when exposed to environments and situations that they have previously associated with drug use. At times, these effects may be fairly strong and involve acute discomfort and vomiting. All too often the individual resumes drug use to relieve these feelings.

Whether or not the vulnerability to relapse is a conditioned phenomenon, it is a clinical reality. Maintenance treatment protects the patient but perhaps prolongs the physical dependence. One treatment option that protects the former opiate addict from relapse to opiate use is provided by a group of drugs known as opiate antagonists (17). These drugs are not addicting in themselves. However, if an individual maintained on an antagonist experiences craving or withdrawal and administers an opiate, the effects are effectively blocked. With this protection, the patient can be exposed to the conditions where relapse is probable without the danger of readdiction.

PHARMACOLOGY OF OPIATE ANTAGONISTS

Opiate antagonists are substances that bind opiate receptors but do not produce opiate effects. Thus they compete with opiate agonists, both exogenous opiates such as morphine and the endogenous opiates, known as endorphins. When a person has received an antagonist in sufficient quantity to occupy all or most of the opiate receptors, agonist drugs such as heroin are prevented from reaching the receptors. In this condition a heroin injection will have little or no effect. Because opiates are prevented from reaching the receptor sites, addiction (or readdiction) is prevented.

This effective neutralization of the agonist by an antagonist should be contrasted to the activity of a metabolic inhibitor such as disulfiram (Antabuse) used in the treatment of alcoholism. Disulfiram does not antagonize the effects of alcohol; rather it blocks an enzyme in the pathway of alcohol metabolism and leads to the accumulation of a noxious metabolite. The resulting unpleasant effects may deter alcohol use. In the case of narcotic antagonists, use of a narcotic after the individual has received the antagonist does not produce an unpleasant pharmacological reaction.

Narcotic antagonists can also displace agonists from receptor sites and thus reverse opiate effects. This is the basis for the use of antagonists in the treatment of opiate overdose, and it is one of the few cases of a clinically available specific antidote. This displacement effect can also be used diagnostically to precipitate withdrawal in chronic users who are physically dependent on opiates (1). The diagnostic value of this phenomenon must be tempered with caution, because precipitated withdrawal can be produced after acute opiate use under certain conditions (15). However, the failure to respond to an opiate antagonist can be regarded as good evidence against current opiate dependence.

There is increasing evidence that several types of opiate receptors exist (10, 11). This may explain how some drugs can act as opiate antagonists and agonists simultaneously. Their molecular configuration may enable them to activate some opiate receptors while fitting but not activating others. The earliest clinically useful antagonist was nalorphine (Nalline), which blocked morphine effects but produced separate agonist effects. It has been replaced by naloxone (Narcan), which has no agonist effects over reasonable dose ranges and is, therefore, considered to be a "pure" antagonist.

Another interesting mixed agonist/antagonist is pentazocine (Talwin). It has analgesic effects (agonist), but it can also block other opiate effects. Because it is a mixed agonist/antagonist, pentazocine was considered to have minimal addictive potential. In recent years, however, pentazocine abuse and dependence have become increasingly common. Although the level of physical dependence associated with its use is limited, its consistent agonist effect makes it highly desirable as a street drug.

Mixed agonist/antagonists may also have unpleasant agonist effects. This is the case with cyclazocine, a drug with antagonist effects lasting up to 24 hours. It was used successfully in several studies (8, 18) as a means of preventing readdiction in opiate addicts. Its agonist effects include paresthesias, hallucinations, and other perceptual distortions. Thus it was not practical to use on a large scale in clinics.

A "pure" antagonist such as naloxone would seem to be preferable in preventing readdiction. It blocks the effects of opiates but produces no direct effects of its own. Even with a pure antagonist, however, there is the potential for creating untoward effects by blocking tonic or phasic functions of the endorphin system. Volavka and colleagues (23) have reported acute rises in adrenocorticotropic hormone and cortisol after naloxone injections, and Mendelson and co-workers (14) reported increases in luteinizing hormone and delayed rises in testosterone after oral ingestion of another antagonist, naltrexone. There is also the possibility that opiate antagonists will interfere with normal central pain inhibitory systems, although experimental evidence of this effect is conflicting at present.

Naloxone has other attributes that also limit its use. It is poorly absorbed after oral administration, and its effective duration of action is several hours after an oral dose (after intravenous administration, half-life is 20 minutes). Naltrexone is an analogue of naloxone synthesized in 1963 (21). It, too, has a very high affinity for opiate receptors, but it is well absorbed by the gastrointestinal tract. Naltrexone has been shown to have antagonist activity in humans for intravenous injections of opiates up to 72 hours after oral ingestion (20). Weak agonist activity has been reported for naltrexone (22), but so far this has not been found to be clinically significant. Patients have been maintained on effective blocking doses of naltrexone for up to 18 months.

Phase II naltrexone studies, which included over 1,000 patients, failed to find evidence of naltrexone toxicity in humans after chronic administration. Although long term endocrine studies have not yet been undertaken, there was no evidence of clinical problems relating to the acute endocrine changes mentioned above. A large Phase III study of naltrexone is about to begin; however, it has been delayed pending the outcome of carcinogenesis studies in rodents. Preliminary analysis of the studies indicates a lack of carcinogenicity. Because naltrexone is the best available opiate antagonist, a description of its use in the clinic follows.

CLINICAL STUDIES OF NALTREXONE

The first human studies with naltrexone were conducted at the Addiction Research Center, Lexington, Kentucky, in the early 1970's. Martin and co-workers found that 30 to 50 mg of naltrexone administered orally blocked subjective effects of morphine for up to 24 hours (13). Later, investigators in New York (20) and in Philadelphia (16) demonstrated that 150 to 200 mg of naltrexone attenuated heroin or hydromorphone for 72 hours, although some subjects reported a rush or brief high. The National Academy of Sciences (NAS) and the National Institute on Drug Abuse (NIDA) sponsored cooperative safety and efficacy studies with naltrexone (3, 7). Five clinics and 192 subjects participated in the double-blind, placebo-controlled NAS study, and 12 clinics with 1,005 subjects took part in the NIDA study, which was generally nonblind and without control subjects. There were no serious medical complications attributable to naltrexone in either study, although several patients did experience allergic skin rashes that cleared after cessation of study medication.

Three groups of subjects were included in the clinical studies of naltrexone: recently detoxified street addicts, detoxified methadone maintenance patients, and "postaddicts" who were drug-free after incarceration or residence in a drug-free therapeutic program. Men over 18 years of age and a small number of women of nonchildbearing potential were considered for the studies. Patients with active medical disorders such as heart disease, ulcer, or liver disease could not be treated.

Most clinics required an opiate-free interval of at least 5 days preceding naltrexone induction in order to avoid precipitating withdrawal. If induction was begun less than 4 days after the last dose of opiate, the incidence of opiate withdrawal symptomatology was relatively high (6). An intravenous or subcutaneous naloxone challenge (0.8 to 1.2 mg) was predictive of difficulties during induction. If the challenge was negative, subjects were usually asymptomatic during naltrexone induction, but if it was positive (yawning, abdominal cramps, irritability, anxiety, chills), the first dose of naltrexone following it usually precipitated withdrawal. In the NAS study, recently detoxified subjects were kept opiate free for 7 to 14 days before random assignment to the naltrexone or placebo control group. Those assigned to naltrexone were given graduated doses of naltrexone during the first 7 days of treatment and were then given 50 mg Monday through Friday and 100 mg each Saturday. After 8 weeks of treatment, 100 mg of naltrexone were given each Monday and Wednesday and 150 mg each Friday.

Generally, "postaddicts" were most easily inducted onto naltrexone and remained in treatment for longer periods of time. "Street addicts" and methadone maintenance patients were less likely to begin study medication because of inability to complete detoxification or to remain opiate free prior to beginning naltrexone induction. Resnick reported that those patients who were involved in a meaningful relationship with a nonaddict mate, were employed full time or attended school, and were living with family members were most likely to benefit from treatment (19).

Of the 735 candidates who volunteered for the study, 543 (74 per cent) dropped out before receiving any study medication. The retention rate for the naltrexone and placebo groups was similar in that 40 per cent of both groups left treatment before completing the first month, but naltrexone retention was significantly better during the second to fifth months. However, both groups had very few subjects remaining by the eighth month, with seven in the naltrexone group and six in the placebo group. A follow-up of 54 naltrexone-treated subjects and 64 placebo controls showed only random differences with regard to employment status, contacts with law enforcement, opiate and nonopiate drug abuse, and over-all status.

Results of the larger NIDA study were

similar to those of the NAS study. Again the early dropout rate was very high, with 42 per cent of the subjects stopping study medication during the first month of treatment and only 12 per cent of the study population remaining in treatment beyond 6 months. Of the 1,005 naltrexone-medicated subjects, 18 per cent had more than one treatment episode with naltrexone (separated by at least 1 month without study medication). During treatment with naltrexone, 36 per cent of the subjects had at least one urine positive for opiates, 14 per cent had at least one urine positive for barbiturates, and 12 per cent had at least one urine positive for amphetamine. The over-all percentage of urines negative for opiates was 96.5 per cent, indicating a very low level of opiate use during treatment. Amphetamine and barbiturate use increased slightly over baseline,but the percentage of positive urines was relatively low.

In a follow-up of 281 patients, Resnick reported that 40 per cent of those treated for more than 3 months were opiate free 6 months after terminating treatment, whereas only 2 per cent of those treated for less than 6 months were opiate free (21). Greenstein et al. did not find significant differences between short term (7 days to 2 months) and long term naltrexone subjects (more than 3 months), although 30 per cent of both groups were opiate free 6 months posttreatment (51).

It is obvious from these results that a major problem with opiate antagonist treatment is the high initial dropout rate. Naltrexone has almost no reinforcing properties of its own. It is perceived as a subjectively "neutral" drug that prevents a former addict from getting "high." As a result many patients chose very early on to return or switch to methadone maintenance. Various external reinforcers, such as money (4), have been tried on various schedules to induce patients to remain longer on naltrexone. Although this has had some success, it presents practical problems of implementation.

Another approach has been to develop opiate antagonists that are partial agonists and thus have some intrinsic positive reinforcement. Naltrexone had been considered an ideal antagonist because it significantly lacked agonist properties. Experience with naltrexone suggests that it may be too "neutral" and restrictive to appeal to large numbers of patients. Perhaps an antagonist with

reinforcing properties would ease the transition from methadone maintenance to naltrexone.

A promising partial agonist/antagonist is buprenorphine (9). Although it is still in the early stages of development, it seems to have mild opiate effects (maximum euphoric activity equivalent to 20 to 30 mg of morphine parenterally) plus good antagonist properties. Higher doses do not increase the opiate effects. This new drug may induce more patients to try antagonist treatment, and the weak opiate effects may reduce the dropout problem.

CURRENT STATUS OF ANTAGONIST TREATMENT

The only opiate antagonist in clinical use as an option for addiction treatment at this time is naltrexone. It is an investigational drug about to enter Phase III clinical trials. In a large multimodal program, 5 to 10 per cent of opiate addicts show an interest in naltrexone, and 30 to 40 per cent of those who take it for 3 months have good outcomes (opiate free 6 months after stopping treatment). There is a high dropout rate, but even those who drop out early often show improvement. Double-blind comparisons of antagonist with placebo are difficult to implement and to interpret. Opiate antagonist treatment is unlikely ever to become a popular method when compared to methadone maintenance. It is too demanding and provides little or no intrinsic reinforcers. However, in our view antagonists are the most logical choice for patients who wish to remain opiate free, and clinicians who have used antagonists in treatment generally agree that they are an important option to have available.

References

1. Blachly, P. H. Naloxone for diagnosis in methadone programs. J.A.M.A. 224:334, 1973.
2. Blumberg, H., Dayton, H. B., and Wolf, P. S. Analgesic and narcotic antagonist properties of noroxymorphone derivatives. Toxicol. Appl. Pharmacol. 10: 406, 1967.
3. Bradford, H. A., and Kaim, S. National Institute on Drug Abuse studies evaluating the safety of the narcotic antagonist naltrexone. Washington, D.C., Biometric Research Institute, Inc., 1977.
4. Grabowski, J., O'Brien, C. P., Greenstein, R. A., Long, M., Steinberg-Donato, S., and Ternes, J. Effects of contingent payment on compliance with a naltrexone regimen. Am. J. Drug Alcohol Abuse 6: 355, 1979.

5. Greenstein, R. A., O'Brien, C. P., McLellan, A. T., Woody, G. E., and Long, M. Naltrexone: A six year appraisal. Manuscript submitted.

6. Greenstein, R., O'Brien, C., Mintz, J., Woody, G., and Hanna, N. Clinical experience with naltrexone in a behavioral research study: An interim report. In *Narcotic Antagonists: Naltrexone*, D. Julius and P. Renault, editors, National Institute on Drug Abuse Research Monograph #9, pp. 141–149. Rockville, Md., National Institute on Drug Abuse, 1976.

7. Hollister, L. Clinical evaluation of naltrexone treatment of opiate-dependent individuals: Report of the National Research Council Committee on Clinical Evaluation of Narcotic Antagonists. Arch. Gen. Psychiatry 35:335, 1978.

8. Jaffe, J. H., and Brill, L. Cyclazocine, a long-acting narcotic antagonist: Its voluntary acceptance as a treatment modality by narcotics abusers. Int. J. Addict. 1:99, 1966.

9. Jasinski, D. R., Pevnick, J. S., and Griffith, J. D. Human pharmacology and abuse potential of the analgesic buprenorphine. Arch. Gen. Psychiatry 35: 501, 1978.

10. Martin, W. R. Opioid antagonists. Pharmacol. Rev. 19:464, 1967.

11. Martin, W. R., Eades, C. G., Thompson, J. A., Huppler, R. E., and Gilberg, P. E. The effects of morphine- and nalorphine-like drugs in the nondependent and morphine-dependent chronic spinal dog. J. Pharmacol. Exp. Ther. 197:517, 1976.

12. Martin, W. R., and Jasinski, D. R. Physical parameters of morphine dependence in man: Tolerance, early abstinence, protracted abstinence, J. Psychiatr. Res. 7:9, 1969.

13. Martin, W. R., Jasinski, D., and Mansky, P. Naltrexone, an antagonist for the treatment of heroin dependence. Arch. Gen. Psychiatry 23:784, 1973.

14. Mendelson, J. H., Ellingboe, J., Kuehnle, J., and Mello, N. Heroin and naltrexone effects on pituitary-gonadal hormones in man: Tolerance and supersensitivity. In *Problems of Drug Dependence*, NIDA Research Monograph #27, pp. 302–308. Washington, D.C., United States Government Printing Office, 1979.

15. Nutt, J. G., and Jasinski, D. R. Methadone-naloxone mixtures for use in methadone maintenance programs. Clin. Pharmacol. Ther. 16:156, 1974.

16. O'Brien, C., Greenstein, R., Mintz, J., and Woody, G. Clinical experience with naltrexone. Am. J. Drug Alcohol Abuse 2:365, 1975.

17. O'Brien, C., Greenstein, R., Ternes, J., and Woody, G. Clinical pharmacology of narcotic antagonists. Ann. N.Y. Acad. Sci. 311:232, 1978.

18. Resnick, R., Fink, M., and Freedman, A. M. Cyclazocine treatment of opiate dependence: A progress report. Comp. Psychol. 12:491, 1971.

19. Resnick, R., Schuyler-Resnick, E., and Washton, A. Narcotic antagonists in the treatment of opioid dependence: Review and commentary. Comp. Psychol. 20:116, 1979.

20. Resnick, R., Volavka, J., Freedman, A. M., and Thomas, M. Studies of EN-1639A (naltrexone): A new narcotic antagonist. Am. J. Psychiatry 131:646, 1974.

21. Resnick, R. B., Washton, A. M., Thomas, M. A., and Kestenbaum, R. S. Naltrexone in the treatment of opiate dependence. In *The International Challenge of Drug Abuse*, R. C. Petersen, editor, National Institute on Drug Abuse Research Monograph #19, pp. 321–332. Rockville, Md., National Institute on Drug Abuse, 1978.

22. Verebey, K., Volavka, J., Mule, S. J., and Resnick, R. Naltrexone: Disposition, metabolism and effects after acute and chronic dosing. Clin. Pharmacol. Ther. 20:315, 1976.

23. Volavka, J., Cho, D., Mallya, A., and Bauman, J. Naloxone increases ACTH and cortisol in man. N. Engl. J. Med. 300:1056, 1979.

24. Wikler, A. Dynamics of drug dependence: Implication of a conditioning theory for research and treatment. Arch. Gen. Psychiatry 28:611, 1973.

CHAPTER 32

A RELIGIOUS APPROACH TO THE REHABILITATION OF ADDICTS

John Langrod, Ph.D.

Lois Alksne, M.A., M.S.

Efrain Gomez, M.D.

In the search for effective approaches to the treatment of drug addiction, methods used by religious programs should not be neglected. These methods seem to have some success, and by examining them we can come closer to an estimation of what the common denominators in successful treatment are. Some of these methods are unique to religious programs; others are shared with other modalities. Not every addict can find religious programs useful. On the other hand, for many this type of program can be of help where others cannot.

By examining and comparing two important religious drug treatment programs, we will attempt to isolate and describe some of the psychosocial factors that are involved in this kind of treatment and their relation to treatment outcome.

The programs that have been selected for this purpose are Teen Challenge and Way Out. These are two examples of the type of concern about narcotic addiction that began to be expressed by charismatic religious groups in the 1950's when addiction was a ghetto problem.

Most of the early church-related programs were Protestant. Although they all stressed religious values, only the Pentecostal programs, such as Teen Challenge and Way Out, used religious conversion as the primary tool in combatting addiction. It is generally believed by Pentecostals that there is no other way of completely overcoming heroin addiction, alcoholism, and other "deviant" behavior such as homosexuality or prostitution. It is essential, according to their beliefs, that the troubled person, having sinned, be "born again" by accepting Jesus Christ as "savior," which involves a change in personality and life style. The converted sinner is brought into the church as a brother or sister in a strong fellowship characterized by love and concern. He is taught to pray, depending on God to assist him with all problems. Ideally he is freed from the mistakes of his past life and has no desire to continue in his "evil" ways. His interests become largely spiritual rather than "worldly"; he relates to something bigger than himself.

THE NATURE OF RELIGION

For a perspective on ways in which religion can relate to rehabilitating drug abusers, some basic concepts in this field should be presented briefly. Sociologists of religion define the subject of their investigation as a "system of communally experienced beliefs and practices oriented toward some supernatural transcendent realm" (7). An anthropological view of religion based on Geertz (9) suggests that religion is a "system of transformation in which conceptions of order and the denial of chaos, along with a belief in justice and morality in the face of injustice and evil, are passionately affirmed as dominating reality in the face of contrary evidence" (13).

Religion, always comprising a system of beliefs and rituals, is a universal phenomenon that obviously answers some very fundamental human needs. The two factors to be stressed here are inherent in the definitions given. The first one refers to the communal nature of religion; the second emphasizes the belief in the dominance of good over evil.

Durkheim, one of the founders of modern sociology, attributed the origin and persistence of religion to the social condition of humans; its source is in the collective consciousness of society (6). This can be questioned, but perhaps the greatest value of Durkheim's contribution is his analysis of the religious group's power over its individual members.

Religion is not simply a method of answering questions that science cannot answer—i.e., man's place in the universe, what is good and what is evil. Religion is an aid to living. It adds to an individual's strength.

He feels within him more force, either to endure the trials of existence, or to conquer them. It is as though he were raised above the miseries of the world, because he is raised above his condition as a mere man; he believes he is saved from evil, under whatever form he may conceive this evil (6).

Durkheim pointed out that in every creed there is a belief in salvation by faith and asked how a mere idea could have this kind of efficacy, how, inasmuch as ideas are only part of ourselves, they can provide us with greater powers than our own natures provide. The believer would respond that it is the spiritual that is more powerful than man and that is the outside source of this strength. Durkheim's response, however, has meaning for both believer and nonbeliever. To Durkheim, the power of religion is the unity of the religious group in belief and in performing rituals that represent this belief. "Religion is something eminently social" (6). It is inseparable from the idea of a church (6). "Religious representations are collective representations which express collective realities; the rites are a manner of acting which take rise in the midst of the assembled groups and which are destined to excite, maintain or recreate certain mental states in these groups" (6).

Collective representations are the result of an immense cooperation, which stretches out not only into space but into time as well; to make them, a multitude of minds have associated, united and combined their ideas and sentiments; for them, long generations have accumulated their experience and their knowledge. A special intellectual activity is therefore concentrated in them which is infinitely richer and complexer than that of the individual . . . (6).

The religious group develops moral forces and awakens a sentiment of a "refuge, of a shield and of a guardian support which attaches the believer to his cult" (6). It is belonging to the cult that gives rise to emotions of joy, serenity, and enthusiasm, these being proof to the believer of his beliefs (6).

The unique characteristic of all religious thought is the division of all phenomena into the "sacred" and the "profane." These create a bipolar relationship. The sacred is concerned with an ideal conception of the world to which we attribute moral superiority; the profane is concerned with the external and material world. The soul is identified with the sacred; the body, with the profane. In most societies a rite of passage is necessary in order to pass from the profane life of the child into the spiritual life where one can be in touch with the sacred. As in all initiation rites, the young person is said to die only to be reborn; the Protestant concept of "conversion" also involves a transformation of the individual from a material, profane orientation to a sacred, spiritual orientation.

The concept of religion as a category separate from other aspects of social life is one that emerged with the Judeo-Christian tradition. Some small nonindustrialized societies do not recognize it as a separate category. There are many characeristics of Western religions that are not necessarily associated with religion in other societies: an anthropomorphic divinity, a sharp distinction between the natural and the supernatural, a set of ethical principles, and the relation of earthly behavior to an afterlife (7).

Although church attendance is declining elsewhere in modern, industrialized societies, this is not true in the United States, where churches are becoming to some extent secularized (7). Growth in this country has been especially noticeable in the Fundamentalist sects of Protestantism. These sects are particularly appealing to the disadvantaged, for example, low income migrants to urban centers.

PENTECOSTALISM

Pentecostalism had its origins in the early Christian movement when, according to the Book of Acts, the Holy Spirit manifested itself in the form of tongues of fire. Its modern revival began in the Middle Western United States in the beginning of this century. It is fundamentalist in theology; the Bible is accepted literally as the inspired word of God. It is believed that individuals who are "touched by the Holy Spirit" can speak "in tongues." They can also heal by "laying on of hands" or through prayer, and prophesy.

Holiness in personal life is stressed and worldly activities such as divorce, dancing, excessive ornamentation in dress, smoking and drinking are condemned. Singing, clapping and spontaneous participation of the congregation distinguish the Pentecostal services from those of other Protestant denominations such as the Episcopalian, the Presbyterian, and the Methodist (16).

Fellowship is strongly valued in Pentecostal churches. Sexton (19) described them as specializing in "togetherness, friendliness, activity, excitation, warmth." These are qualities valued by working-class members of most American ethnic groups. "While the middle class Protestant church treats strangers with polite cordiality, the Pentecos-

tal Church draws the stranger in and treats him as part of the snug family (19).

The largest Pentecostal group is the Assemblies of God, with headquarters in Springfield, Missouri. Teen Challenge is affiliated with this branch.

TEEN CHALLENGE

Teen Challenge is a religious residential program for drug abusers that originated in Brooklyn in 1961 through the work of one man, an Assemblies of God minister, David Wilkerson. Reverend Wilkerson came to New York from Phillipsburg, Pennsylvania, in 1958 in order to work with street gangs that had aroused his concern. As he developed rapport with young delinquents, he learned that they needed help with many problems such as addiction, homosexuality, and prostitution. More basically, he believed they needed "something to fill the void in their lives." He firmly believes that devotion to Christ can and should be the basis for the development of a healthy personality and satisfying life. A life devoted to Christ begins with conversion, which is a strong emotional experience associated with a subsequent dedication to Christian principles and spiritual, rather than worldly, matters.

After a time in the slums of East Harlem, narcotics addiction seemed to be the greatest challenge, and Reverend Wilkerson began to focus more specifically on that problem. He sensed that something more powerful, attractive, and rewarding than the needle was needed, and he believed that religious conversion was the answer. Most of the youth coming into the Teen Challenge Center were addicts seeking help. In 1964 Reverend Don Wilkerson, David's brother, took over the Directorship of the Center, which became the induction and detoxification center. The group established a Training Center on a 200-acre farm in Rehrersburg, Pennsylvania, away from the city's temptations.

The program has grown rapidly since then, through word of mouth referral, financial contributions from various churches and private individuals, and dynamic leadership. Today there is a Teen Challenge Induction Center in most large cities of the United States, and also in Canada, Europe, Puerto Rico, and Australia. There are now three Training Centers (in Missouri, California, and Pennsylvania) and several camps that serve as post-induction rehabilitation centers.

Teen Challenge will accept anyone who has been using drugs and is willing to follow the rules, except the mentally ill (12). It serves adolescents and some adults of all races and ethnic groups. The racial and ethnic make-up of the program depends on the locale. Two-thirds of the group in the New York area are Puerto Rican. This reflects, in part, Reverend Wilkerson's original involvement with young Puerto Rican gang members. The Los Angeles program is largely Chicano. There are very few blacks in the program, which Glasscote et al. (10) explained as probably due to the fact that black addicts stigmatize other black addicts who enter a predominantly nonblack program. Two-thirds of the members are from low income ghetto backgrounds; one-third are middle class (5). There are facilities for both sexes, but the majority are male.[1]

Only a small percentage of Teen Challenge's clients were originally Pentecostal. Most of them are Catholic, which may be associated with the high proportion of clients being Puerto Rican or Chicano. Puerto Ricans tend to be eclectic in religion, medical care, and other aspects of life (22). Their often nominal Catholicism is easily replaced or supplemented by a faith that encourages greater expressiveness and more tightly knit, family-like congregations.

Teen Challenge records on applicants to their program, in addition to demographic characteristics, indicate types of drugs used in the past. Table 32.1 lists drugs for 1969.

Most of the clients became addicted in their late teens and did not have heavy habits.

According to Teen Challenge philosophy, an individual on drugs cannot be helped until he reaches the stage of desperation. He must admit that he has a problem and must actively seek assistance (10). The Teen Challenge induction centers are crisis centers and accept people "off the street" for immediate help or counseling. They are accessible 24 hours a day. If the individual wishes to stay, he goes through an intake interview on the basis of which it is determined whether or not the program is suited to his needs.

Many admissions are self-referrals, but

Table 32.1
Teen Challenge Records of Applicants' Past Drug Use (N = 734)[a]

Drug	%[b]
Heroin	89
Barbiturate/sedatives	34
Amphetamine	20
Cocaine	32
LSD	11
Solvent (glue)	6
Alcohol	26

[a] From Langrod, J., Joseph, H., and Valdes, K. The role of religion in the treatment of opiate addiction. In *Major Modalities in the Treatment of Drug Abuse*, p. 180. New York, Behavioral Publications, 1972.
[b] In some cases individuals used more than one drug.

clients are sometimes referred by a judge, probation officer, minister, or counselor. Some enter through street evangelism efforts, others through the urging of ex-addict friends in the program or of relatives.

The initial phase of rehabilitation, which takes place at the Induction Center, involves detoxification from drugs, usually "cold turkey," with staff members staying with the new entrants, giving them emotional support, hot baths, and rubdowns to make them as comfortable as possible. Those who are addicted to barbiturates or alcohol are referred to a hospital to avoid medical complications. The individual remains in residence at the Induction Center for 2 to 3 weeks, or until he is deemed ready to move on to the second phase of rehabilitation at a camp or Training Center. It is at the Induction Center that the client is encouraged to embrace religion. Time is spent in prayer, Bible reading, chapel services, and recreational activity. The goal is to give the client a feeling of self-worth. The prevailing atmosphere is one of support, love, warmth, and firm discipline.

A set of rules must be adhered to. These are designed to lead to self-discipline and personal responsibility. They include the following (10):

No street talk. This includes swearing, talking about drugs, bragging about what you used to be or do.

No leaving the center for the first two weeks, except for any visit needed to a hospital. This does not apply to group activities in which staff members participate.

[1] For information on the Hoving House for Girls, see Benton's *Debs, Dolls and Dope* (2).

No visitors for the first two weeks.

No outgoing telephone calls for the first two weeks. Incoming calls must be cleared with the center supervisor. Calls must be limited to three minutes.

Attendance at chapel services and Bible studies is mandatory, except for those in withdrawal.

Visits home are not permitted during the first six weeks.

All residents must attend scheduled recreational activities and street witnessing.

No snacks or coffee are permitted between meals.

The goals of the initial induction period are instilling discipline, developing Christian character, and helping the resident gain insight about himself and his problems. Dependence on commitment to Christ as the solution to all problems is such that relatively little attention is paid to medical or psychological problems. No records are kept concerning medical or psychological adjustment (11).

The second phase of rehabilitation begins at a Training Center or Camp. At Rehrersburg, a minimum of 5 months, but as much as a year, is spent on "Bible study and fundamentals of Christian living ...., English or Spanish grammar (or later, literature), custodial, kitchen and limited farm chores (mainly dairy)" (5). The chores are designed to give the residents a sense of responsibility, good work attitudes, to help them accept authority and rules, and to develop a sense for helping others. Ministers and teachers help the residents with adjustment and other difficulties. Vocational training in automobile repair, woodworking, and printing is available at a later stage.

The living experience at the Training Center is seen as therapeutic in itself.

The pain that previously allowed drugs to be so satisfying is now used as motivation. The direction this motivation takes ... depends to a large extent upon those persons in the immediate environment and their interaction and relationship with the individual student who is going through this experience (23).

More than 140 students live together, four in a room, and a camaraderie develops that is influential on the student's character at this point.

There are various forms of therapy provided, in addition to the supportive, protective, ordered environment. First, there is work therapy. This "offers the opportunity for concrete results of physical output that can be viewed as accomplishments by the individual student" (23). Group and individual counseling are carried on regularly and when special problems arise. Each student is assigned an advisor when he enters the training phase of the program, and there are counselors available upon request. Music therapy is offered, and the cooperation and involvement required to "make a joyful noise" are also expected to be of great benefit to the students. There is a period of unstructured time each day during which students may participate in recreational activities such as baseball, weight lifting, basketball, and swimming. Besides the relaxation provided by these activities, "therapeutic benefits include physical release, team cooperation, coping with mistakes, self awareness and limited competition" (23).

The third phase of the program is "reentry," during which the resident prepares for life outside of Teen Challenge. The leaders of Teen Challenge attempt to develop autonomy in the students so that they will not substitute dependence on Teen Challenge for dependence on drugs. However, because employment outside of the program or the church is difficult to obtain for individuals who may have criminal records or lack education, most of the residents prepare for the ministry or other work in Teen Challenge centers or the church. This not only provides them with a livelihood (they must pay for room and board) but also provides a protective environment away from neighborhoods within which their drug use began.

Teen Challenge has a large staff. The leadership is composed of ministers, missionary workers, church officials, and their wives. Ex-addicts and other converts to the movement "fill administrative positions, serve as directors of the residences, as counselors, Bible teachers, field representatives and office workers" (5). There are also part time and volunteer workers. Teen Challenge does not employ psychologists, social workers, psychiatrists, or other professionals of this type, but it is not antiprofessional (10).

TREATMENT OUTCOME

What are the results of Teen Challenge's mission? Four outcome studies have been done; one by Calof in 1967 (5), an internal evaluation reported by Langrod et al. in 1972 (16), a study of the program in Northern California and Nevada by Glasscote et al. in 1972 (10), and one by Hess in 1975 (11). Catherine B. Hess, M.D., M.P.H., was formerly Assistant Commissioner of Health for New York City and served as a special consultant for Teen Challenge. Her 7-year follow-up study (12) was on selected individuals who entered the program in Brooklyn in 1968. She divided the eligible respondents into three groups. "P1" are those who dropped out during the induction period (N = 70), "P2" are those who dropped out at the Training Center level (N = 52), and "P3" are Training Center graduates (N = 64). The author did not give criteria for the selection procedure. Some of her findings follow:

Sixty applicants out of 186 (32 per cent)

dropped out of the program in the first 4 weeks. Reasons given were: could not relate to concept; violated rules; too sick; urge to use drugs too great; too much religion; family needs. Approximately 5 per cent of these dropouts were asked to leave the program; the remainder dropped out voluntarily.

The demographic characteristics of the three groups are presented in Table 32.2. There are a number of mistakes and obvious typographical errors in her data. However, it is being utilized because very few evaluations of this type of program are available. Where figures do not add up to 100 per cent, this is presumably due to rounding.

This table suggests that blacks tend to drop out of the program early. The high early dropout rate for Protestants seems to be an artifact of ethnicity. It is of interest that nearly three-fourths (73 per cent) of those who claim

Table 32.2
Demographic Characteristics (at Time of Admission) of Individuals Admitted to Teen Challenge[a]

Characteristic	Induction Center Dropouts (P1) (N = 70)	Training Center Dropouts (P2) (N = 52)	Training Center Grads (P3) (N = 64)	Total (N = 186)
Mean age	23	25	24	
Race				
Hispanic	49%	79%	69%	64%
Black	33%	8%	17%	20%
White	19%	13%	14%	15%
Religion				
Catholic	4%	50%	36%	44%
Protestant	39%	21%	23%	28%
Muslim	6%	2%	0%	23% (Sic)
Other	10%	4%	0%	5%
None	9%	23%	39%	23%
Religiosity				
Very	4%	4%	3%	4%
Somewhat	54%	27%	23%	36%
Not at all	41%	69%	73%	60%
Regular church attendance at age 12				
Yes	80%	56%	53%	64%
No	20%	44%	47%	36%
Arrests prior to Teen Challenge				
Yes	93%	90%	88%	90%
No	7%	10%	12%	10%
Did not finish high school	87%	87%	75%	83%
Drug use				
Heroin	90%	79%	89%	86%
Alcohol	33%	37%	62%	7%
Polydrugs	0%	6%	2%	2%
Cigarettes	91%	90%	83%	96%
Marihuana	44%	27%	38%	36%

[a] Modified from Hess, C. B. *Teen Challenge Training Center, Research Summation*, p. 34. Rehrersburg, Pa., Teen Challenge, 1975.

to be "not at all" religious stay in the program to graduate but that an overwhelming majority (80 per cent) of those who report having attended church regularly at age 12 drop out in the induction stage of the program. No interpretation for this is provided by the author of the study.

In terms of education, the percentage of high school dropouts is very high (83 per cent of the total group).

Ninety-six (52 per cent) of the 186 subjects (P1, P2 and P3) "pursued more education" after leaving Teen Challenge. Nineteen received their High School Equivalency Diplomas, two received college degrees, 48 attended Bible school, 25 completed their Bible school courses, and 14 became ministers (one

from P1, three from P2, and 10 from P3)" (11).

Employment is another parameter that attests to the efficacy of a drug treatment program. Employment status in 1975 is shown in Table 32.3.

In terms of drug use, 24 per cent of the population for which this information is available never used narcotics after their Teen Challenge experience (11). Seventy-six per cent did return to heroin, but some of these were drug free at the time of follow-up (5 per cent), having been treated in other programs or having detoxified on their own.

In terms of the patients' perception of their experience, Table 32.4 concerns aspects of Teen Challenge that residents disliked.

Table 32.3
Employment Status at Time of Teen Challenge Interview (1975)[a]

Status	P1 (N = 70)	P2 (N = 52)	P3 (N = 64)	Total (N = 186)
	%	%	%	%
Working	47	52	70	56
Temporary illness or vacation	7	3	6	5
Unemployed	23	21	14	19
Retired	0	0	2	.5
In school	4	6	0	3
Staying home	16	13	5	11
Institutionalized	4	3	5	4

[a] Modified from Hess, C. B. *Teen Challenge Training Center, Research Summation*, p. 44. Rehrersburg, Pa., Teen Challenge, 1975.

Table 32.4
Aspects Residents Disliked about Teen Challenge[a]

	P1 (N = 187)	P2 (N = 80)	P3 (N = 107)	Total (N = 374)
	%	%	%	%
Expected too much	3	1	8	4
Drugs easy to get	6	3	3	4
Detoxification without medication too hard	16	6	7	11
Forced to go to church	6	5	3	4
Program too religious	13	8	12	11
Too much discipline	4	11	4	6
Too far from home	2	5	4	3
No radio, TV, outside	7	11	15	10
Too hard to stop drugs and cigarettes at same time	17	11	10	14
Bible classes too heavy	6	3	1	4
Needed more than spiritual help	14	13	9	13
Other	4	6	5	5
Liked everything	1	18	21	10
Total[b]	50	21	29	100

[a] From Hess, C. B. *Teen Challenge Training Center, Research Summation*, p. 49. Rehrersburg, Pa., Teen Challenge, 1975.
[b] This figure represents the percentage of respondents; some respondents reported more than one "dislike."

Some of the dissatisfaction indicated may explain the limits to the acceptability of this type of treatment. Detoxification without medication and having to give up cigarettes and narcotics simultaneously are not required in most other programs, even some religious ones, and the necessity of this might be questioned. Patients must accept the religious nature of the program, and those who cannot will find it difficult to remain, but that 13 per cent felt they needed more than spiritual help raises questions about the desirability of adding social workers, physicians, psychiatrists, and other such professionals to the staff.

Hess' study (11) found Teen Challenge to have a graduation rate of 18.3 per cent, which is somewhat higher than that which Smart (21) reported in a review of outcome studies of therapeutic communities (no more than 15 per cent).

In conclusion, it can be said that Teen Challenge is successful in reorienting the lives of some young drug-abusers.[2]

The second program to be considered, Way Out, is similar to Teen Challenge in many ways, although it is smaller and limited to one geographic area. Its leadership is Puerto Rican, whereas that of Teen Challenge is white.

WAY OUT

The theme adopted by Way Out Home for Addicts, Inc., is II Corinthians 5:17: "Therefore, if any man be in Christ, he is a new creature; old things are passed away; behold, all things are become new" (14). The philosophy of the program, like that of Teen Challenge, is that conversion to Christianity, along with certain rehabilitative techniques, is necessary to cure addiction and other "sinful" conduct. Again, addiction is seen as a moral problem that requires the intervention of Christ. Other, nonreligious, programs may help for a time, but if an individual does not give his life to Christ, he will inevitably fall back into sinful ways.

Way Out is a drug-free residential community of ex-addicts living together in a therapeutic setting, "a family structure based on the philosophy of love, concern and responsible demands on each other to change former destructive attitudes and behavior." It incorporates aspects of secular therapeutic communities.

Contrary to Teen Challenge, there are no books or evaluations available on Way Out except for several descriptive flyers printed by the program. There have been no follow-up studies, and few records are kept. There are many testimonials on file, however.

Way Out accepts anyone in need of help; indeed, one of their flyers describes the program as "A residential center for addicts, alcoholics, delinquents and outcasts." In Way Out's locale, the poverty-stricken South Bronx, alcohol is a major problem. At present there are 15 heroin addicts and 38 alcoholics in residence. They live in two dilapidated but scrupulously clean houses in a very run-down area. The average number of residents is 75. Formerly, there existed a separate facility for women, but currently women seeking help are referred to other religious programs. The need for a female residence is recognized and the leaders of the program, Reverend Eddie Villafane and his wife, Anna, also a minister, are planning to open one in the near future.

The Villafanes have a great deal of energy, compassion, and charisma. They each have worked for many years with addicts and alcoholics. Eddie Villafane is an ex-addict who graduated from the Damascus Christian Church Program. In addition to these two minister-directors, there are eight staff members, all volunteers. Previously there were 20 staff members, including 12 ministers, a psychologist, a sociologist, a Certified Public Accountant who was a Muslim, and five teachers, one of whom was reportedly an agnostic. This staff was mandated when Way Out was supported by the New York City Addiction Services Agency. The Villafanes report that there was some conflict between the Christian staff members and the professional staff members.

Way Out has no steady source of income and struggles constantly to make ends meet. It has been located in the South Bronx for 8 years. Residents may "walk in" 24 hours a day, or they may be referred by the church, hospitals, probation officers, relatives, other programs, social agencies, and civil courts. Ninety-eight per cent of the residents are Puerto Rican, 1 per cent are white, and 1 per cent are black. The South Bronx is predomi-

---

[2] For further information on this program see David Wilkerson's *Beyond the Cross and the Switchblade* (25).

nantly Puerto Rican and black.

As in Teen Challenge, applicants wishing to come into Way Out are given a list of rules to follow. These rules are similar enough to those of Teen Challenge that they need not be repeated, the major difference being that smoking cigarettes, although discouraged, is permitted in restricted areas in Way Out. After signing the list of rules, a new resident is assigned a counselor. The counselor is seen for any problem the resident may have—making an appointment to see a doctor or dentist, getting permission to make a telephone call, discussing a personal problem, etc. Detoxification takes place either at Way Out (cold turkey) or at a local hospital or detoxification program.

During the initial phase, the new resident, after detoxification and attention to medical and other immediate problems, is initiated into Bible training and is expected to undergo a conversion experience. A great deal of time is spent in religious services, which, on Fridays, last through the night. The services are intense, consisting of testimonials; group singing with tambourines, an electric guitar, and drums; fervent preaching; and much praying. Although the service is mainly in Spanish, much of the congregation, including the residents, are bilingual.

During Phase II there is training for the High School Equivalency Diploma, tutoring in various subjects, occupational therapy, recreational activities, individual counseling, encounter sessions, and time for meditation and prayer. Christian values, self-discipline, and responsibility are stressed in all activities. The group resembles a family, headed by the Villafanes. Love is expressed, although behavior is under considerable scrutiny (as in searching and opening mail). Residents are encouraged toward honesty in encounter sessions. By sharing secrets, fears, and feelings with others, an individual is no longer alone. He develops a clear, realistic self-image and can "take root and grow." The Way Out form of the encounter is more supportive than it is in many therapeutic communities. Violence, of course, is not permitted, nor is profanity. The goal is change in attitude, emotions, behavior, and spirit through devotion to each other and to God.

Fellowship is a key concept at Way Out. Many of the residents have no family or other social ties, and the togetherness of Way Out

is extremely important. It can be active for the rest of the resident's life, because the group bond extends to all of "the community of Christ." As long as he belongs to the church, he is a brother.

The last phase of treatment is further education, job training, church membership, Baptism, encouraging healthy family and community relationships, and Bible College for those who wish to enter the ministry. The average stay is 7 months. Five of the current residents, who are old and sick, have remained for 3½ years. They have little reason to leave, and the Villafanes are content to have them stay. Way Out is their home.

Way Out seems to recognize and deal with psychological and social problems to a greater extent than Teen Challenge, which tends to see all problems as spiritual. Neither program, however, believes that a lasting cure for addiction can come about in any way other than through religious conversion. Both programs reinforce the religious experience by public testimonials, which also help to draw people into the programs.

COMPARISON OF TEEN CHALLENGE AND WAY OUT WITH SECULAR THERAPEUTIC COMMUNITIES

Some aspects of secular therapeutic communities are shared by Teen Challenge and Way Out. There are usually three phases of treatment—induction, rehabilitation, and reentry into the community. Type of treatment, thus, is geared toward special needs of residents at each stage of the deaddiction process. Treatment takes place within a primary group where peer pressure and authority are directed toward the development of a nonaddicted life style. The individual is surrounded by loving, concerned people with problems similar to his own. Time is structured. Skills are taught. Various forms of therapy are offered, among them work and recreation. In some cases the setting is isolated from the environment of addiction; in all there are limitations on contact with the outside, at least initially. Part of the therapeutic quality of these communities is the give and take of living together under close supervision. There are rules that are maintained by a system of punishments and rewards. Honesty and insight are encouraged. Healthy values are strengthened or, if absent, they are taught; destructive ones are discouraged. Drugs, of course, are forbidden. Finally, residents who manage to develop a new drug-free life style graduate. They may or may not leave this sometimes harsh but always protective environment. Many stay in the system as counselors or clerical workers or in some other capacity.

Unique to the religious programs is that the first requirement upon joining is to accept the definition of addiction as a sin and the notion that sin can be forgiven and overcome through spiritual help. Addiction is seen not simply as a product of one's environment, a psychological or physiological need; it is also morally wrong. Addiction is placed in the context of all "sinful" behavior, all of which must be abandoned if one is to follow Christ. The second requirement, or expectation, of the kind of religious program described here is to undergo a conversion experience. The third is to live a "Christian" life. This means joining the church, which can provide the member with a continued close relationship with an organization that is concerned with his welfare and behavior.

STRENGTHS OF THE RELIGIOUS DRUG TREATMENT PROGRAMS

The fact that many addicts are unable or unwilling to join a religious residential program restricts the usefulness of such programs. For those who can accept the dogma, rituals, and commitments of such programs, however, religious programs seem to offer certain advantages that secular therapeutic communities may not.

Being "born again," for example, provides the convert with a clean slate. He is free to substitute a new life style based on faith, hope, and love for one that was characterized by fear, despair, and hate. His central life interest is no longer drugs but serving Christ. In his new reference group he is surrounded by significant others who serve as role models for behavior appropriate to his new social identity. He is guided by newly acquired values and normative expectations, focused around religion, that are constantly reinforced through membership in the religious community.

The convert's values and new life style are supported not only by his identifying with the group but also by other powerful factors such as family-like bonds, peer pressure from others who love him and whom he loves, and his belief in God as the ultimate authority. His association with a church, once he completes the program, places him within a group that is socially approved. Hopefully, the program provides him with a set of skills with which he can develop other socially acceptable roles in the areas of work, home, and social life.

THE CHURCH AS A SUPPORT SYSTEM

It is impossible for any human being to live in total isolation, and individuals having social or psychiatric problems require even greater social support than others. A satisfactory support system may be essential to living in the general community. Social interaction with the potential for support may be with "spouse, children, parents, other kin, friends, work associates, formal or informal voluntary associations, and organized service organizations such as churches, the welfare department, physicians, and mental health services" (8). Once a client has left the therapeutic community, he may look to one or more of these individuals or agencies for financial help, assistance with household tasks, child care, or help when ill, and he may discuss problems with them and seek their help in times of distress (8). The network of individuals and agencies performing these services constitutes a support system for the individual.

Ties with the church can be strong and similar to ties with the family and can provide the believer with emotional satisfaction and security as well as concrete services. Members of Pentecostal churches call each other "brother" or "sister." Congregations are usually small and intimate, members numbering on the average 49 people (8). Members can count on each other for most types of assistance needed, including housing, employment, clothing, and moral support. Different congregations support the Pentecostal programs for addicts and others in need. The entire congregation may be asked to pray for a member who is ill or having difficulties. Thus, an ex-addict who is a member of a Pentecostal church is not alone in coping with problems that otherwise might overwhelm him.

THE CONCEPT OF CONVERSION

To return to the concept of conversion, it should be noted that this route to freedom from drugs has particular value for those young people who equate giving up certain attitudes and behavior with "selling out" or "giving in." Because the prevailing atmosphere in Teen Challenge and Way Out is that religious conversion can and should occur, and because one's status in the group is enhanced by conversion, the event is a strong motivating force for a commitment to a new way of life (10). According to Hess (11), this new way of life and its "benefits, pleasures, rewards, reinforcements and acceptable behavior make attainment more desirable than drugs."

James (15) differentiated between two types of conversion—the sudden and the gradual. Pentecostals tend to acknowledge only the former, "revival," type as being related to divine intervention. Gradual transformation into a recognized adherent of a faith is characteristic, for example, of the Catholic and Episcopalian churches, which, however, mark this recognition by the rite of confirmation. A sudden conversion often follows a crisis in which an individual, undergoing a developmental crisis and experiencing a sense of incompleteness and imperfection, feels the conviction of sins and anxiety about the hereafter. The "acceptance of salvation" in such an individual could lead to explosive emotions of hope, elation and resolve.

James (15) described religious conversion as follows: "To say that a man is 'converted' means ... that religious ideas, previously peripheral in his consciousness, now take a central place, and that religious aims form the habitual centre of his energy." This transformation is possible, in psychological rather than religious terms, because the individual's personality during a crisis is unstable and seeking a new state of equilibrium (18).

The sense of sin can be overwhelming and, if this is accentuated in revival-type religious services together with the proferred hope of release through acceptance of a set of religious tenets, the conversion experience can be an expected outcome.

The source of this transformation lies in forces outside of the individual's consciousness—either the supernatural or the unconscious, depending on one's point of view. Whichever is the case, the individual must abandon himself to these forces for "conversion" to take place. Some are unable to do this, hence limiting the usefulness of conversion in the rehabilitation of drug abusers.

THE RELIGIOUS "HIGH" IN COMPARISON WITH DRUG "HIGHS"

There is something to be said for religious emotional highs in comparison with drug highs. Religion has been called the opium of the masses. In this regard one can consider religion as a device for alleviating human misery such as painful anxiety and depression generated by feelings of utter helplessness and hopelessness. The presence of euphoria and even elation may be viewed as defenses against despair. The use of alcohol and drugs may serve the same purpose. The relief of unbearable tension in both instances, together with the illusory freedom from oppressive reality, can be described as a "high." In the case of drugs the results are usually temporary, and the situation gets worse. In the case of religion the results can be prolonged by the assurance that the believer is protected by a truly omnipotent and eternal parent in heaven and by the support of a group of believers on earth.

Weil (24) made the important point that "highs" come from the mind, not from a drug. This being the case, it is possible to "isolate the desired aspect of the chemically induced state ... " and obtain it through nonchemical means. Weil observed that, this being a superior high, "one sees a great many experienced drug takers give up drugs for meditation, but one does not see any meditators give up meditation for drugs" (24). This kind of high is not used "to drop out of the social process, to rebel against ... parents or teachers, or to hurt (oneself)" (24). The falling in love experience, sexual fulfillment, and the mystical religious experience are examples of highs (3). Highs may also be obtained from other "nonchemical routes to altered states of consciousness": Sensitivity training, encounter therapy, Zen Buddhism, Yoga, massage, hypnosis, skiing, and sky diving.

Religious ecstacy, then, can be an alternative to the high that drug takers seek. Apparently religion can fulfill some of the needs for which drugs are taken–to relieve anxiety, boredom, alienation, and depression, for example.

SHORTCOMINGS OF RELIGIOUS PROGRAMS

The foregoing observations concerning the power of religion to cure addiction must be qualified and limited to those cases in which the individual is able to accept religion as the most important force in his life. Even those who initially do well in this environment do, of course, sometimes lose faith and drop out, returning to drug use and/or other antisocial behavior.

It has been observed that the religious approach to "curing" drug addiction may have certain disadvantages (1). Adams and Fox referred to "mainlining Jesus" as "the new trip." They observed that religious conversion can indeed "cure" drug addiction, and that the attendant life style—not markedly different from the drug culture—can substitute for the drug addict's way of life. However, it may be argued that this kind of religion, as used by many young ex-drug addicts, becomes another addiction (17). As such it may harm the individual in ways similar to the harm that drug abuse does. Peel and Brodsky summarized the dangers (17):

...the denial of past and future, the release from anxiety and effort, the evasion of sexual maturity, the unassailable group ideology. A total commitment to a religious sect negates everything a person has been and done and suffered and learned, and reconstructs his or her thinking along the rigid lines of doctrinaire faith. Order is imposed by the strictures of the group, assurance and integration are found in faith in an all-powerful God, and the threatening responsibility of self-assertion is removed.

Adams and Fox believed that "religion as represented in (the Jesus movement) is a step backwards" (1):

The Jesus trip, like drugs, appears to be used in such a way as to avoid coming to terms with the anxieties related to the identity crisis . . . Instead of progressing toward adult ethics, the Jesus person clutches tenaciously to childhood morality, with its simplistic black-and-white, right-and-wrong judgments. Rather than developing behavior oriented towards reality, he flies into ideational, ideological abstractions to numb his awareness of his

newly arisen needs. Spurning a reality that begins with individual feelings, he subordinates himself to peer approval.

These quotations are not cited as a blanket indictment of religion; rather, they are observations that religion may be used in such a way as to limit personal growth. That religious fervor can result in violence was recently seen in the mass suicides of Jim Jones' followers. Another negative consequence is to be found in the Unification Church of Reverend Moon and other sects that alienate young people from their families through brainwashing techniques. A criticism directed specifically to the programs described here might be that the nonspiritual aspects of life tend to be neglected and that religion serves to perpetuate the status quo and is an obstacle to social change.

CONCLUSION

One conclusion that can be drawn from the foregoing description and analysis is that the religious approach to rehabilitation of drug abusers is not a panacea or a perfect approach to the solution of drug addiction. It has flaws as well as strengths. It should not be ruled out, however, as a viable modality and perhaps the most appropriate one for some individuals.

Further and more sophisticated research is needed to learn the psychosocial characteristics of those for whom this approach is most suitable.

References

1. Adams, R. L., and Fox, R. J. Mainlining Jesus: The new trip. Society 9:50, February 1972.
2. Benton, J. Deb, Dolls and Dope. Old Tappan, N. J., Fleming H. Revell and Company, 1968.
3. Brecher, E. M. Licit and Illicit Drugs. Boston, Little, Brown and Company, 1972.
4. Brill, L., and Lieberman, L. Major Modalities in the Treatment of Drug Abuse. New York, Behavioral Publications, 1972.
5. Calof, J. A Study of Four Voluntary Treatment and Rehabilitation Programs for New York City's Narcotic Addicts. New York, Community Service Society of New York, 1967.
6. Durkheim, E. The Elementary Forms of the Religious Life. New York, The Free Press, 1965.
7. Encyclopedia of Sociology. Guilford, Conn., Dushkin Publishing Group, 1974.
8. Garrison, V. Support systems of schizophrenic and non-schizophrenic Puerto Rican migrant women in New York City. Schizo. Bull. 4:561, 1978.
9. Geertz, C. Religion as a cultural system. In Reader in Comparative Religion, W. A. Lessa and E. Z. Vogt,

editors, ed.2. New York, Harper & Row, 1965.

10. Glasscote, R. Sussex, J. Jaffe, J., Ball, J., and Brill, L. *The Treatment of Drug Abuse: Programs, Problems, Prospects.* Washington, D.C., The Joint Information Service of the American Psychiatric Association and the National Association for Mental Health, 1972.

11. Hess, C. B. *Teen Challenge Training Center, Research Summation.* Rehrersburg, Pa., Teen Challenge, 1975.

12. Hess, C. B. A seven-year follow-up study of 186 males in a religious therapeutic community. In *Critical Concerns in the Field of Drug Abuse,* A. Schecker, H. Alksne, and E. Kaufman, editors, pp. 270–274. New York, Marcel Dekker, 1977.

13. Hoebel, E. A. *Anthropology: The Study of Man.* New York, McGraw-Hill, 1972.

14. *Holy Bible,* II Corinthians 5:17. Authorized King James Version. London, Oxford University Press.

15. James, W. *The Varieties of Religious Experience.* New York, Mentor Books, 1958.

16. Langrod, J. Joseph, H., and Valdes, K. The role of religion in the treatment of opiate addiction. In *Major Modalities in the Treatment of Drug Abuse,* L. Brill and L. Lieberman, editors, New York, Behav-ioral Publications, 1972.

17. Peele, S. and Brodsky, A. *Love and Addiction.* New York, New American Library, 1975.

18. Rapoport, L. The state of crisis: Some theoretical considerations In *Crisis Intervention,* H. J. Parad, editor, pp. 22–31. New York, Family Service Association of America, 1965.

19. Sexton, P. *Spanish Harlem.* New York, Harper and Row, 1965.

20. Schecter, A., Alksne, H., and Kaufman, E. *Critical Concerns in the Field of Drug Abuse.* New York, Marcell Dekker, 1977.

21. Smart, R. Outcome studies of therapeutic community and halfway house treatment for addicts. Int. J. Addict. 11:143, 1976.

22. Suchman, E., and Alksne, L. Communication across cultural barriers. Am. Catholic Sociol. Rev. 22:306, 1961.

23. Teen Challenge Center, Program Description.

24. Weil, A. Altered states of consciousness. In *Dealing with Drug Abuse,* pp. 329–344. New York, Praeger Publishers, 1973.

25. Wilkerson, D. *Beyond the Cross and the Switchblade.* Old Tappan, N. J., Chosen Books, 1974.

CHAPTER 33

RELIGIOUS EXPERIENCE AND THE REGULATION OF DRUG USE

Marc Galanter, M.D.

In this chapter we will consider religious experience in terms of its psychological functions and how it serves to regulate individuals' use of drugs. We will first develop an operational approach to the role of religion in regulating behavior. This will allow us to examine how religious practice relates to experiences of altered states of consciousness in a number of different settings.

This will lead to some of our own work on changes in drug use in two contemporary charismatic sects, the Divine Light Mission and the Unification Church ("Moonies"). In both groups, affiliation apparently serves as the basis for a marked decline in drug use. We will finally consider religious experience as a model for certain group treatment approaches to drug abuse.

Among other things, religion is a system of norms for attitude and belief. Even those who do not strongly espouse a particular religious creed are subject to a similar system of norms within their social world. These norms influence attitudes and behavior and ultimately affect the use of drugs, to the extent that they impinge on this issue. Any change in beliefs or norms can change attitudes toward the use of drugs. This issue may seem a bit academic but, in many respects, social interventions into the use of drugs and social treatments

for drug abuse must either bring about a change in the implicit beliefs of their target population or end up considerably limited in their effect.

RELIGION AND INFORMAL SOCIAL CONTROLS

We often consider specific religions as separate entities, each sustaining the affiliation of its own membership. This can lead to an emphasis on parochial aspects of religion, on specific rituals and beliefs of a given sect. An alternative perspective begins with observations that all societies have some organized religion (33). The universality of this phenomenon suggests that institutionalized religion may rest on universal social and psychological functions, rooted in man's innate social and psychological needs.

Some insights on this issue are derived from sociobiology, a discipline that attempts to explain behavior on the basis of the interaction between social adaptation and the principles of evolutionary biology (35). Behaviors as wide ranging as altruism and mating styles may be considered in light of the adaptive role they serve in the evolution of a given species.

Sociobiologists have become interested in

many aspects of behavior reflected in the communal function of large groups, and religion has been the focus of some attention. Analogous behaviors in other species can add to our understanding of the evolutionary basis of this phenomenon, just as they do to our understanding of the evolution of physical traits. Among the higher primates, for example, a morphological similarity between humans and apes (such as bipedal locomotion) and a similarity in social behavior (such as the style of parenting) reflect on a common evolutionary background.

Extensive evidence, in fact, has been found demonstrating the existence of rudimentary culture in higher primates. Van Lawick-Goodall (32) has suggested homologues of religious ritual among chimpanzees in the wild. Wilson (35) concluded that it is a "reasonable hypothesis" that magic and totemism constituted direct adaptations to the environment and were the antecedents of formal religion in man's social evolution.

Robin Fox (9) put the issue of innateness of culture in a rather intriguing manner. He conjectured that man's inclinations to certain cultural traits would result in the emergence of these traits in the absence of an antecedent cultural history; he surmised that if children reared in isolation were to survive in good health, they would, in time, develop their own language, laws, and "beliefs about the supernatural and practices relating to it."

Radcliffe-Brown, an anthropologist, did much to define our understanding of the role of religion in society. He reviewed Western knowledge of primitive religion in Polynesia, and he wrote in his classic *Taboo* (24) that magic and religion impart fear and anxiety that serve as a bulwark for the performance of group rituals. This latter view of the function of religion in its social context may serve as an introduction to the effects of membership in religious sects on diminished drug use, which we shall examine.

INTOXICATION AS NORMATIVE BEHAVIOR

We have just considered some possible antecedents of religious experience. Now let us adopt a similar approach to man's tendency to become intoxicated through drug use. We will consider two aspects of this issue. The first relates to the hypothesis that humans are innately inclined to alterations in consciousness and that these alterations play a role in normative social behavior. The second aspect is drug intoxication as one form of altered consciousness.

Nikolaas Tinbergen, one of the founders of modern ethology, outlined the relationships between what he termed "innate releasing mechanisms" and "social releasers" in his classic work, *The Study of Instinct* (30). The innate releasing mechanism, observed in different forms in many species, is a biologically grounded means of initiating a specific complex behavior. Such behavior is triggered by a specific signal in the environment. Among birds, for example, certain mating behaviors are consistently initiated upon the presentation of certain body parts by opposite-sex birds. Tinbergen and other ethologists inferred that the existence of such a phenomenon meant that underlying neurosensory mechanisms exist that release such reactions. The triggering stimuli are termed social releasers if they consist of a physical attribute or a particular behavior of another individual.

One complex example of this phenomenon is the "waggle-dance" of the bees. Unoccupied honeybees waiting in the hive can be activated by a specific movement pattern, or the "honeybee dance," delivered by a dancer bee that has located flowers. The direction that the bees follow in their subsequent flight is a function of the specific pattern of the dance. There are analogues between such complex social releasers and behaviors that initiate certain responses among humans. An interesting comparison might be made to certain human behaviors in groups, triggered by leaders who demonstrate certain behavioral configurations. Humans often manifest considerable changes in behavior and state of mind in large group settings. We might consider Freud's original writing on large group behavior at this juncture (in a context akin, perhaps, to "mob psychology"). In formulating his ideas on group psychology, he cited LeBon, as follows (10):

... contagion also intervenes to determine the manifestation in groups of their special characteristics, and at the same time the trend they are to take. Contagion is a phenomenon of which it is easy to establish the presence, but which is not easy to explain. It must be classed among those phenomena of a hypnotic order....

Freud surmised that the herd instinct (suggested by Trotter) might be a primary one, just as are those of self-preservation, nutrition, and sex.

Man's capacity to be drawn into a "herd" and to experience alterations of his normal attitudes and state of mind may be considered in light of the phenomenon of the innate releasing mechanism observed by the ethologists. It may well be that this inclination, so often a part of intense group religious experience, is more than an artifact of culture.

What type of altered state may be evinced by a group setting? Let us first turn to a definition for an altered state of consciousness, as given by Ludwig (21):

Any mental state(s), induced by various physiological, psychological or pharmacologic maneuvers or agents, which can be recognized subjectively by the individual himself, or by the objective observer of the individual as representing a sufficient deviation in subjective experience or psychological functioning from certain general norms for that individual during alert, waking consciousness.

One interesting consideration regarding the viability of this concept is the reliability and consistency with which an altered mental state can be defined by the individual who experiences it. At this point I would like to turn to a body of investigation in which I was engaged, which dealt with the interface between drug experiences and cues from the social context. In one of our studies of the marihuana intoxication state (16), we found certain remarkable consistencies in a smoker's assessment of his subjective experience. Self-assessments of this state were as reliable an indicator as physiological measures, such as pulse change and blood concentrations of labeled delta-9-tetrahydrocannabinol. In addition, subjects' total scores for items on a subjective symptom checklist correlated very highly with their global ratings for intoxication.

Interestingly, when subjects were given placebo marihuana they reproduced a mild subjective intoxication state. Here, too, there was a high rank order correlation between symptoms experienced in the placebo and active states. The subjective intoxication state, both drug induced and induced by contextual cues, seemed to be rather well defined, as if registered and held on file in the mind.

In a subsequent study (15), we examined the interaction between an intoxication state and social behavior. In this case, marihuana, placebo, and no-drug states were utilized in a small group setting. Significantly, the only consistent affective response observed across subjects for the three states was an increase in anxiety seen in subjects who were given placebo in a group where the other members were apparently intoxicated. This observation may relate to the anxiety that Radcliffe-Brown noted as inherent in the violation of group norms. It provides an interesting sidelight on the discomfort felt by individuals who perceive themselves as not in the same relation to an altered state as their peers in a group setting.

Altered consciousness achieved by means of intoxicants in a group setting may fit in well with man's innate sociobiological needs. Indeed, Roueche (25) pointed out that all but three of the numerous stone-age cultures that survived into modern times demonstrated an endogenous familiarity with alcohol. He observed that cereal agriculture itself received a powerful stimulus from the discovery of fermentation; in most parts of the Old and New Worlds, the produce of cereal agriculture was, from an early period, largely consumed in the manufacture of some species of beer. Indeed, wine may have accidentally become available prior to the evolution of agriculture merely from the storage of wild grapes (4).

Where do these observations lead? We may now have a clearer understanding of the roots of man's inclination to become involved in religious experience, associated with need to adhere to normative creed and ritual; humans may also have an innate inclination toward altered consciousness and, perhaps, may be drawn into alterations of consciousness by cues within the social context. Intoxicant use certainly has a long history as a vehicle for achieving such a state.

We may now move from the means by which drugs may trigger an altered social and mental state to consider what mechanisms allow the social context itself to feed back and regulate the use of drugs. Subsequent observations will be directed at the mechanism by which engagement into religious experience can lead to diminished drug use. As noted above, Radcliffe-Brown observed that the *violation* of ritual was associated with the experience of anxiety. We found (in the sects studied) that the inverse phenomenon existed among individuals who became *engaged* in religious belief and practice: they experienced relief of neurotic distress symptoms (11). Elsewhere we presented evidence for an innate relationship in man between affiliations with large groups who share a common creed and system of rituals and the enhancement of psychological well-being. In addition, we found that sect members who experience an increase in neurotic distress subsequent to conversion were likely to have been ones who experienced a decline in their religious belief during that period (14).

These observations, taken together, adumbrate some relevant aspects of religious experience. In the first place, as stated, they point to an apparent innate inclination in man to religious-like behavior. Although such behavior may be manifested in very different fashions, dependent on the context, it would seem that some such behavior would in some form be influential under any circumstances. Secondly, the observance of ritual and acceptance of creed may well be associated with the implicit danger of psychological distress experienced in the breach. We may now ask how this formulation might fit in with the alteration of a compulsive behavior, such as drug taking.

RELIGIOUS NORMS AND SOCIAL REGULATION OF DRUG USE

The mechanisms by which society exercises control over the use of drugs may be divided into two types: formal social controls, which reflect explicit social regulation and legal codes, and informal social controls, which operate by consensus and by the pressure inherent in social relations. In our own society, examples of formal controls include laws against heroin use, legal restraints on the licensing of taverns, and codes involving physicians' prescribing of addicting drugs. Informal controls include parental pressure on teenage children, disapproval by strangers of public drunkenness, and pressure from co-religionists to conform to codes for proper behavior. Significantly, the latter group are generally conceded to carry the principal weight of the regulation of drug use (2). In a setting where religion is influential, then religious norms may assume a primary role in the network of informal social controls.

One aspect of informal social controls is

observed in the nature of the drug experience itself. The social context and the rituals of drug use associated with it are potent determinants of the course that a given drug experience will take. One interesting example of this is the contrast observed between the psychotomimetic experiences, often with "bad trips," of many American young adults when they took mescaline in the late 1960's and the experiences of American Indians who were members of the Native American Church. The latter group had for generations used peyote, whose active agent is mescaline, in their religious rites. These religious rituals begin at sunset and end at the following sunrise, and they follow an order sequence in which the interpersonal cues and religious ritual are clearly defined. Bergman (3) reported interviewing Peyotists and finding that they seldom reported experiencing hallucinations, despite the fact that the doses of mescaline taken were quite large (45 to 450 mg). Unlike Caucasians taking psychotomimetics, Peyotists also experienced very few psychopathological sequelae or even anxiety reactions during the period of intoxication.

The social context also regulates the *patterns* of drug use. Harner (18), for example, accumulated reports on South American Indian tribes using a brew made from the plant Banisteriopis, whose active ingredient is the fast acting hallucinogen dimethyltryptamine. It is brewed in a variety of drinks, the best known of which is Yagé. Most striking is how hallucinogenic experiences are deeply integrated into the supernatural life and culture of the community. Harner examined the belief system underlying the use of Banisteriopis and outlined the mythological meaning imparted to the hallucinatory experiences. For example, hallucinations are interpreted by the Indians as visions of demons and deities. The drug experience is understood as the soul leaving the body and returning when the drug taker is no longer intoxicated.

Such a consensually held mythology serves to restrict the drug use to ritual purposes. Sometimes consensually supported delusion may contribute to the system of informal controls. The Mazatec Indians of Oaxaca Province (Mexico), for example, eat hallucinogenic mushrooms only at night, in absolute darkness; they believe that eating them in daylight will cause madness (22).

DeRios and Smith (6), based on their review of drug use in nonindustrial societies, in fact, concluded that drug use is generally a means to a socially approved end, such as contacting the supernatural. They observed that drugs are used to reconfirm the values of the culture. In most cases, drug use is controlled by rituals, rather than legal means.

In this regard, it is interesting to note that even when rigidly applied formal controls are the principal means of regulation, the components of an informal network are still important. An interesting example of this existed among the Pre-Columbian Aztecs, where multiple offenses of drunkenness were harshly punished (by death!). Concomitantly, the culture had a mythology that described alcohol as a potentially dangerous drug and had specific myths involving the difficulties experienced by Aztec gods in relation to excessive drinking (23).

Alcohol, because of its ubiquity, also offers the opportunity for study in a large number of cultures. Field was able to study the incidence of drunkenness in primitive societies and ascertained that it "is determined less by the level of fear in a society, than by the absence of corporate kin groups with stability, permanence, formal structure, and well-defined functions" (19).

Therefore, we find that the interplay between drug use and the informal social structure may have to be understood as an interaction between behavioral phenomena with complex sociobiological antecedents. Either one may affect the form that the other takes. We will now consider what may occur when individuals acquire over a short time a complex set of beliefs, which includes a different orientation to values associated with drug use.

THE EFFECT OF CHARISMATIC SECT MEMBERSHIP ON DRUG USE

One of the most notable social phenomena of the 1970's has been the appearance of a large but uncounted number of religious sects across the country. These sects range in size from a handful of people living together in a small apartment to national networks of thousands. Reaction to these sects has generally been one of alarm, because of some of the very attributes that contribute to their altering members' drug use patterns. These attributes can be divided into three categories: fervent belief in an alien creed, and often an alien leader; intense social cohesiveness to the exclusion of previous social ties; and adherence to behavioral norms of the group, which are typically at variance with those of the general population.

Before we consider these issues in greater detail, it will be useful to consider some background information on two groups that I studied with colleagues in some depth over the past 5 years, and from whom we have succeeded in obtaining a full body of data regarding changes in their psychological state and drug use (11–13). The first of these was the Divine Light Mission (DLM). This sect was initiated by the family of Guru Maharaj Ji, a young man who came to the United States from India in 1971. Guru Maharaj Ji was born in India in 1957; his father was acclaimed as a Satguru, the one living master who reveals divine knowledge. Maharaj Ji is said to have begun giving holy discourses at the age of 2 and soon joined his mother and elder brothers in public programs where his father was addressing disciples. His father singled out his youngest son for future leadership shortly before his death, when the boy was 8 years old. At the funeral, Maharaj Ji began to preach and was indeed soon given a leadership role.

The young Guru achieved rapid acceptance in the United States, and his followers numbered in thousands in a few years. In 1972, the DLM chartered seven Boeing 747's and many members flew to India for a religious festival. This was followed by another major event in the Houston Astrodome in which Rennie Davis (a convert from the Chicago Seven Vietnam protesters) played a principal role in organizing.

Like many of the sects of Indian origin, the DLM has relatively little formal theology. Central to their beliefs is the initiation experience of "receiving Knowledge," which is regarded as a direct experience of God. This occurs at a secret initiation ritual held for people who are considered by a Mahatma (a principal disciple of the Guru) to be spiritually prepared. Devotees listen to and give spiritual discourses or "Satsang" on a daily basis. Almost all meditate daily, and at such times they concentrate on four specific "techniques." Most important is the Divine Light, which is often perceived as an actual light by the meditator. Vision of this light is also a key aspect of the ceremony of "receiving Knowledge." The other techniques are music, divine harmony; nectar, a spiritual sense of taste; and the Word, said to represent a primordial vibration. Members are also required to participate at intervals in "Darshan," direct contact with the Guru.

The DLM study described here was conducted in late 1975 at a religious festival held in Orlando, Florida, drawing members from all parts of the country. Shortly thereafter, the majority of DLM members moved to the Denver area.

The second sect that was studied is the Unification Church (UC), whose members are colloquially known as the "Moonies." Reverend Sun Myung Moon, their leader, first came to the United States in 1972 from Korea, where the UC was already established. Reverend Moon's background was originally in business, and he is reported to have considerable manufacturing holdings in Korea. The UC theology and mythology are elaborated in *The Divine Principle*, a book written by the Reverend Moon and held sacred by members of the sect. The church considers itself a Christian sect and regards its seminary in Barrytown, New York (where Reverend Moon resides at the time of this writing), as a very important focus of its functions.

A fair portion of the membership in the United States (altogether 5,000) resides in the New York City area, which is not far from Barrytown and which is the location of the UC national headquarters. At any given time, many of the members circulate to different geographic areas, and many are on mobile fundraising teams that solicit donations and sales for the UC; other teams are active in recruitment. Our study on long standing members was conducted in UC residences in the New York area, where residents were drawn from all parts of the country. The study on potential recruits attending workshops was conducted in Southern California.

Given the context in which long standing members were studied, these samples were likely to be representative of the over-all membership of each of the sects. The long-standing members were typically in their mid-twenties (DLM: m = 25.2, UC: m = 24.7), single (82 percent, 91 percent), and white (97 per cent, 89 per cent). DLM respondents had been members for almost 2 years and UC members almost 3 years. Most

had had college experience (76 per cent, 78 per cent).

After extensive interviews with sect members, questionnaire instruments were pretested, revised, and finally administered. They consisted of a series of multiple-choice questions coded for computer analysis. Subjects were tested under the supervision of the experimental team and given a fixed set of instructions; test administration was preceded by an explanation from a sect official indicating the desire of both the collaborating team and the sect itself to obtain objective information about the members. Respondents were fully cooperative because of the official status accorded to the survey. Among long standing members, 119 DLM members were surveyed and 237 (American-born) UC members. In the UC workshops, 104 registrants were surveyed. The latter surveys were conducted among those attending 21-day induction workshops, at which only a small minority of the initial registrants chose to join (in this case, only nine of the 104).

I shall summarize some of the findings and discuss their relevance to the issue at hand. The first area to be considered is the effect of membership on psychological state. This bears on the points raised earlier regarding the role of neurotic distress in the maintenance of religious ritual and belief. The issue was addressed in a number of ways. In the first place, the longstanding members in both sects were asked to respond to cue sentences that assessed levels of neurotic distress, such as, "I felt nervous and tense" (for anxiety), and "I felt depressed and glum" (for depression). These items were rated in relation to the period immediately before joining, the one right after joining, and the present time. The difference in scores for the period immediately before and immediately after was ascertained for both groups, and it was found that there was a 37 per cent decline in symptom scores for DLM members and a 30 per cent decline for UC members, reflecting a considerable difference in psychological state. This was comparable to a shift on each of the neurotic distress items from "moderately" to "slightly" (i.e., from 3 to 2 on a five-point scale). The findings are compatible with our expectation, suggested earlier in this chapter by Radcliffe-Brown's observation of the reciprocal relationship between anxiety and adherence to religious rituals.

Further confirmation of this latter point

was obtained as follows. One scale on the tests included measurements of affiliativeness toward fellow sect members. By means of multiple regression analysis, we ascertained that a significant portion of the variance of both the decline in the neurotic distress and of the current levels of neurotic distress was accountable for by affiliativeness toward the sect (37 per cent and 32 per cent, respectively). Stated otherwise, this means that members' psychological state was dependent on the degree to which they felt affiliated with the group.

To clarify the role of religious creed in changes in neurotic distress, a series of questions associated with religious norms were applied to UC members. Here, too, adherence to religious norms was correlated with enhanced psychological well-being. Additional corroboration for the change in psychological state was obtained by recourse to the workshop members. It was found that they had significantly lower psychological well-being scores than members who had joined 3 years earlier. Indeed, the well-being scores of workshop members who ultimately joined the UC were the lowest of those attending the workshops.

With regard to altered consciousness per se during membership, some of the information provided by the study is most interesting. As indicated before, meditation is an integral part of membership in the DLM. Of members surveyed, 80 per cent meditated at least twice a day. UC members also devote a considerable amount of time to *prayer*, about ½ hour a day, according to the respondents. Although the UC members do not expressly place a high value on alterations of consciousness during prayer, we found that they, like the DLM members, experienced considerable alteration in their mental state at these times. For example, when asked if they "saw something special that no one else could see" at these times, about a third of each of the groups indicated that "I could almost see it in front of me," or "I could see it clearly with my eyes." More than half indicated that they could clearly feel "a special and unfamiliar feeling in my body" and that "time passed faster or slower in a very special way." Group-sanctioned alterations in mental state were apparently a prominent phenomenon.

Members of both sects had been extensively exposed to drugs before entering the group. In fact, about a quarter of the members

of both groups answered affirmatively when asked if they had had "serious problems wih drugs" at some point in the past (27 per cent, 23 per cent). For example, as compared to age- and sex-matched respondents in a national survey, about twice as many DLM members indicated that they had ever taken each of the groups of drugs of abuse, e.g., for marihuana, 92 per cent (versus 52 per cent) and for heroin 14 per cent (versus 6 per cent).

On the other hand, drug use declined sharply from the period immediately before joining to that immediately after. For example, the prevalence of daily marihuana use declined from 45 per cent to zero, and the use of any heroin at all fell from 7 per cent to 1 per cent. Here again, there was a significant correlation between the decline in drug use and variables associated with involvement with the sect, such as social cohesiveness, group activities and meditation. In addition, the diminished level of drug use was preserved up to the time of the survey.

The influence of the sects' ethos extended beyond the diminution of *illicit* drug use. DLM attitudes toward moderation and "natural living" were also reflected in a large decline in the prevalence of daily coffee use from the period immediately before to that after joining (43 per cent to 24 per cent). This is a good example of the implicit effect of informal social controls, because the group does not take an explicit stand on coffee use as it does on the major drugs of abuse.

The DLM and UC may also be contrasted, because the latter group is relatively more insistent on the value of abstinence. A comparison of the two groups on the actual decline in drug use reflects on this issue. Sect members' highest incidence of marihuana use was compared to their level of use at the time of the survey. UC members showed a decline of 96 per cent, whereas DLM members showed a decline of only 55 per cent. The differential change in alcohol use also reflected this difference (85 per cent versus 62 per cent).

WHAT CAN WE LEARN FROM OUR OBSERVATIONS ON THE RELIGIOUS SECTS?

In our studies, we observed that scores of long standing sect members on psychological well-being were below those of a matched comparison sample. Both UC and DLM members had apparently experienced greater neurotic distress and drug use than the general population. This is compatible with findings by Simmonds (29), who studied a commune of "Jesus Freaks."

Simmonds felt that these people were continuing a basic psychological pattern that existed prior to their joining the group and inferred that they might be described in terms of the "addictive personality." He felt that the sect members had, in relation to drugs, switched "from their former source of gratification (e.g., drugs) to another, 'the Lord.' " Such an observation, however, runs contrary to other observers of the "cult" scene. Among these are Ungerleider and Wellisch (31), who did not find major psychopathology among sect members whom they studied by formal testing.

Another perspective is offered by Westermeyer and Walzer (34). They remarked on the historical coincidence of drug use within the process of religious rituals seen in certain primitive cultures, although contemporary cultures demonstrate relatively little of this. They pointed out that for young people who withdraw from multigenerational traditions, such as religious activity and ritual, illicit drug use may come to provide an alternative focus for their ritualized social interactions. They prefer to consider such drug use as a basis for socialization, rather than as an evidence of psychopathology per se. Perhaps contemporary sects serve as a focus for socialization and thereby offer a substitute for some of the functions that antecedent drug use subsumed.

I have described elsewhere (11, 14) a model for psychological functions in a "large group," based on observations of these sects. The large group sustains intense affiliative feelings and a mutually supported ideology. This model can shed light on some of the phenomena associated with these sects. It was observed that relief from neurotic distress was apparently experienced by persons joining these large groups, and that this relief was proportional to the degree to which they experienced affiliative feelings toward the group. Acceptance of the sect's belief system also led to alleviation of distress. Both these factors were seen as a basis for generating further commitment to the large group. That is to say, the more one feels socially cohesive to the group and the more he accepts its

ideals, the better he feels (a "relief effect"). As a consequence, disaffiliation from the group becomes a potentially threatening option; a close and committed affiliation provides the opportunity for psychological well-being.

With regard to drug use, one may surmise that the acceptance of patterns of moderation or abstinence, as espoused by the sect, becomes a price of affiliation. As strong as a drug use habit might be, it comes to stand in opposition to the psychological benefits of membership. It is because of this that the balance may tip in favor of relinquishing drug use if the attraction of membership and enhanced psychological well-being is sufficiently strong.

It might be useful to consider some of the characteristics of a large group in relation to religious sects and other such groups. They are:

1. Large Membership. In the first place, these groups must have a membership at least in the dozens. Meetings may be conducted in small chapters or in a setting in which all members are present simultaneously. The group, however, must exceed in size the number where easy face-to-face communication is possible.

2. Consensual Belief System. Their mutually held beliefs generally have a messianic quality, such as the Pentecostalist religious groups, the "est" (Erhard Seminars Training) movement in the secular realm, and certain revolutionary movements.

3. Ritual. In addition, they generally develop a system of rituals and totemic objects, seen sometimes in the mental health movement, as with Fritz Perls' Gestalt Prayer ("I am I and you are you . . . "); also, in the near sanctity accorded to regressive experiences in R. D. Laing's Kingsley Hall.

4. Redefined Social Roles. Additionally, the social roles and identities of members tend to be defined by their relationship with the group, particularly as their affiliations outside the group are diminished. Thus there tends to be a redefinition of social roles, and the group itself tends to appoint helpers and healers within its own membership, often obviating the need to turn to outside professionals for assistance. This, for example, is inherent to Alcoholics Anonymous and Recover, Inc. (for the mentally ill).

5. Relief Effect. Cohesiveness and belief

engender psychological well-being, as described above. A *relief* of distress is experienced as one becomes closer to the group.

In relation to the issue at hand, such phenomena are also seen in the sphere of organized systems for drug abuse treatment. The therapeutic communities—such as Synanon, Odyssey House, and Phoenix House—all have much in common wih the model just described. They are large groups maintained by strong social ties, and they tend to have at least a bit of messianic zeal regarding their mission. They practice a number of rituals relevant to life in the "house," and these serve to tie members together. In addition, the social status and life roles of members tend to become increasingly involved in the structure of the therapeutic community, unless strong attempts are made to avert this. Whereas programs like Phoenix House make considerable effort to get their members involved in other social and occupational systems, Synanon has tended to maintain members within its own structure and thereby expand over time.

The therapeutic communities have also been shown to lead to enhanced psychological adaptation among their members, in ways probably similar to the religious sects. Objective changes have been observed in psychological traits (5, 26) in addition to alterations of drug use patterns. Difficulties have been observed in maintaining abstinence among members after they leave the therapeutic community: Disaffiliation through moving out of the therapeutic community is likely to make the person vulnerable to loss of norms that may never be fully internalized unless he stays within the group. This is reminiscent of the loss of faith among cult members isolated from the larger group, as described by Festinger (8).

The effectiveness of religious sects in altering deep rooted behaviors should, of course, be understood from a broad perspective, allowing for other considerations. For example, a fairly low key meditation-oriented program, Transcendental Meditation, may elicit a reduction of alcohol and marihuana use (27, 28). Among a psychiatric population, it may induce changes in psychiatric symptoms (17). The importance of meditation per se, apart from affiliation with the group and its ideology, should, therefore, be considered in its own right. In our studies, DLM offered both together, but Transcendental Meditation may well have given more expression to meditation in isolation.

Religious and meditative experiences have also been described with regard to relief of suicidal intent (20), and the potency of such experiences in altering other ominous pathology has been considered. Deutsch (7), for example, studied a small religious sect with an Indian orientation, whose members had been very heavily involved in psychedelic experience (each had taken about a dozen "trips"). In addition, they were adjudged to be limited by serious psychopathology. Nonetheless, the members tended to maintain a relatively stable existence within the group.

In another very different context, the issue of Peyotism may again be considered. In addition to having few observed psychopathological side effects, as noted above, peyote is used as a vehicle for the treatment of alcoholism among certain groups of Native American Indians (1). In this case, we see an experience of altered consciousness as a "treatment" utilizing "drugs of abuse." The drug serves as a *vehicle* for establishing informal social controls in order to discourage the abuse of alcohol.

In relation to religious experience, this last example demonstrates the very fine lines between drug use, drug abuse, and treatment; between social ritual and the demands for medical care. As a consequence, one thing we may certainly learn from the religious cults is the importance of sustaining a mutually accepted system of norms and beliefs for the treatment personnel and those who are treated. In recent years, for example, we have found that many of those who were successfully taken off illicit opiates by means of methadone maintenance again become addicted to a variety of other agents. These patients were alienated from the social establishment at the outset of treatment, and limited, if any, support was provided to engage them in the value system of the general population (which is generally achieved through regular employment). To treat the substance abusers in isolation from addressing their value systems is to wage a steep uphill battle.

Acknowledgments. Dr. L. Rotkin and L. Cohn assisted with the data analysis.

References

1. Albaugh, B. J., and Anderson, P. O. Peyote in the treatment of alcoholism among American Indians. Am. J. Psychiatry 131:1247, 1974.
2. Amar, A. M. Social control as a factor in non-medical drug use. In *Symposium of the World Health Organization, Toronto, Canada: 1977*, pp. 113–139, Geneva, World Health Organization.
3. Bergman, R. L. Navajo peyote use: Its apparent safety. Am. J. Psychiatry 128:695, 1971.
4. Chafetz, M. E., Demone, H. W., Jr., and Solomon, H. C. *Alcoholism and Society*, pp. 62–63. New York, Oxford University Press, 1962.
5. DeLeon, G., Skodol, A., and Rosenthal, M. S. Phoenix House: Changes in psychopathological signs of resident drug addicts. Arch. Gen. Psychiatry 28:131, 1973.
6. DeRios, M. D., and Smith, D. E. Drug use and abuse in cross cultural perspective. Hum. Organization 36: 14, 1977.
7. Deutsch, A. Observations on a sidewalk Ashram. Arch. Gen. Psychiatry 32:166, 1975.
8. Festinger, L. *A Theory of Cognitive Dissonance.* Stanford, Calif., Stanford University Press, 1957.
9. Fox, R. The cultural animal. In *Man and Beast: Comparative Social Behavior*, J. F. Eisenberg and W. S. Dillon, editors, pp. 263–296. Washington, D.C., Smithsonian Institution Press, 1971.
10. Freud, S. Group psychology and the analysis of the ego. In *The Standard Edition of the Complete Psychological Works of Sigmund Freud*, J. Strachey, editor, vol. 18, pp. 67–144. London, Hogarth Press, 1955.
11. Galanter, M. The "relief effect": A sociobiological model for neurotic distress and large-group therapy. Am. J. Psychiatry 135:588, 1978.
12. Galanter, M. Psychological induction into the large-group: Findings from a contemporary religious sect. Presented at the Annual Meeting of the American Psychiatric Association, Chicago, May 14, 1979.
13. Galanter, M., and Buckley, P. Evangelical religion and meditation: Psychotherapeutic effects. J. Nerv. Ment. Dis. 166:685, 1978.
14. Galanter, M., Rabkin, R., Rabkin, J., et al. The "Moonies": A psychological study of conversion and membership in a contemporary religious sect. Am. J. Psychiatry 136:165, 1979.
15. Galanter, M., Stillman, R., Wyatt, R. J., et al. Marihuana and social behavior: A controlled study. Arch. Gen. Psychiatry 30:518, 1974.
16. Galanter, M., Wyatt, R. J., Lemberger, L., et al. Effects on humans of Δ^9-tetrahydrocannabinol administered by smoking. Science 175:934, 1972.
17. Glueck, B. C., and Stroebel, C. F. Biofeedback and meditation and the treatment of psychiatric illness. Comp. Psychiatry 16:303, 1975.
18. Harner, M. J., editor. In the primitive world: The upper Amazon. In *Hallucinogens and Shamanism*, pp. 1–8. London, Oxford University Press, 1973.
19. Horton, D. J. The functions of alcohol in primitive societies: A cross-cultural study. Q. J. Stud. Alcohol 4:199, 1943, p 223.
20. Horton, P. C. The mystical experience as a suicide preventive. Am. J. Psychiatry 130:294, 1973.
21. Ludwig, A. M. Altered states of consciousness. Arch. Gen. Psychiatry 15:225, 1966.
22. Munn, H. The mushroom languages. In *Hallucinogens and Shamanism*, M. J. Harner, editor, pp. 86–122. London, Oxford University Press, 1973.
23. Paredes, A. Social control of drinking among the Aztec Indians of Mesoamerica. J. Stud. Alcohol 36: 1139, 1975.
24. Radcliffe-Brown, A. R. *Taboo.* Cambridge, Cambridge University Press, 1939.
25. Roueche, B. *The Neutral Spirit.* Boston, Little, Brown and Company, 1960.
26. Sacks, J. G., and Levy, N. M. Objective personality changes in residents of a therapeutic community. Am J. Psychiatry 136:796, 1979.
27. Shafii, M., Lavely, R., and Jaffe, R. Meditation and marijuana. Am. J. Psychiatry 131:60, 1974.
28. Shafii, M., Lavely, R., and Jaffe, R. Meditation and the prevention of alcohol abuse. Am. J. Psychiatry 132:942, 1975.
29. Simmonds, R. B. Conversion or addiction: Consequences of joining a Jesus movement group. Am. Behav. Sci. 20:909, 1977.
30. Tinbergen, N. *The Study of Instinct.* London, Oxford University Press, 1951.
31. Ungerleider, J. T., and Wellisch, D. K. Coercive persuasion (brainwashing), religious cults, and deprogramming. Am. J. Psychiatry 136:279, 1979.
32. van Lawick-Goodall, J. The chimpanzee. In *The Quest for Man*, V. Goodall, editor, p. 162. New York, Praeger, 1975.
33. Washburn, S. L., and McCown, E. R. Evolution of human behavior. Soc. Biol. 19:163, 1972.
34. Westermeyer, J., and Walzer, V. Drug usage: An alternative to religion? Dis. Nerv. Sys. 36:492, 1975.
35. Wilson, E. O. *Sociobiology: The New Synthesis.* Cambridge, Mass., Belknap Press (Harvard), 1975.

PART 5

TECHNIQUES OF INTERVENTION

CHAPTER 34

PREVENTION STRATEGIES IN THE FIELD OF SUBSTANCE ABUSE

Don C. Des Jarlais, Ph.D.

John Langrod, Ph.D.

Pedro Ruiz, M.D.

Joyce H. Lowinson, M.D.

The concept of prevention is used to justify a more diverse set of activities than any other concept in the drug abuse field. Some feel for this diversity can be obtained from the following partial list of activities—all undertaken with the rationale of preventing drug abuse:

1. Televising public service announcements that depict drug use as immature
2. Counseling youth who are experimenting with drugs but who have not yet become drug dependent
3. Showing films that dramatically portray possible dangers of drug abuse
4. Teaching yoga and meditation as means of relieving stress
5. Educating physicians about the dangers of overprescribing psychoactive medications
6. Outlawing "head shops" that sell paraphernalia for using drugs

7. Teaching values to youth through experiential exercises in values clarification
8. Putting warning labels on various products that contain drugs—currently done with cigarettes and advocated for alcoholic beverages
9. Distributing pamphlets and booklets that contain information about drugs that varies greatly in its scientific accuracy
10. Beverage industry advertisements that urge moderation in the use of alcohol
11. Providing alternative schools for students who are not faring well in conventional classrooms.

At present there is no satisfactory method of even classifying the great variety of prevention activities. The most commonly used classification system is borrowed from the field of mental health and divides activities into primary prevention—the prevention of drug abuse in persons who have not used drugs—and secondary prevention—prevention of drug abuse in persons who have used drugs but have not yet become drug dependent. Secondary prevention is also frequently called "intervention." Other classification schemes distinguish prevention programs by providing information only versus involving the feelings-values-emotions of the recipients, by whether the activity is specific to drug abuse prevention or also attempts to prevent other socially undesirable behavior, and whether or not the program includes "alternatives" to drug abuse.

The lack of an integrated classification scheme to describe prevention programs reflects the diversity of the persons involved in these programs and the variety of governmental and private agencies involved. It also reflects the fact that there is no consensus on what constitutes and causes "drug abuse." (See reference 11 for a discussion of the prevention implications for the different models of alcoholism and alcohol abuse.)

EMPIRICAL FINDINGS

Despite the lack of a governing paradigm for drug abuse prevention, there has been sufficient research to produce some generalizations with respect to the need for these programs and with respect to their effectiveness. Measured in terms of drug use rates among youth, the need for drug abuse prevention seems to have increased greatly during the 1970's.

In a national survey comparing the high school senior classes of 1975 through 1978, Johnston and colleagues (7) found an appreciable rise in self-reported marihuana use. Forty-seven per cent of the class of 1975 reported using marihuana at least once, whereas 59 per cent of the class of 1978 had done so. There has also been a marked increase in the proportion of high school seniors who use marihuana daily (6 per cent in 1975 and 10.7 per cent in 1978). Cocaine and inhalant use have become slightly more popular, whereas the popularity of sedatives seems to be declining, as is the lifetime prevalence of heroin. The prevalence of alcohol use has shown a "gradual but steady" upward shift since 1975 (90.4 per cent lifetime prevalence in 1975 compared with 93.1 per cent in 1978). Daily use, however, remained steady at 5.7 per cent for both years.

A study of high school students in New York State conducted in 1978 by the State Division of Substance Abuse Services (10) showed a dramatic increase in substance abuse over 1971 levels. The following trends were reported:

Lifetime use and current use of marijuana have more than doubled since 1971.

The use of cocaine among 9th through 12th graders has tripled. Lifetime use was reported by 12% of the 9th through 12th graders in 1978, compared to only 4% in 1971. Current cocaine use also increased, although not by the same magnitude.

A surprising increase has occurred in the use of inhalants. Lifetime use of these drugs increased from 5% in 1975 to 14% in 1978; current inhalant use also showed an increase, from 2% in 1975 to 3% in 1978. These findings are a reversal of earlier trends showing that both life time and current use had decreased from 1971 to 1975.

Use of hallucinogens has increased only slightly since 1971, while heroin use has remained virtually the same.

Among the pills, nonmedical use of tranquilizers shows the sharpest increase at both lifetime and current use levels. The percentage of students in grades 9 through 12 who ever used tranquilizers nearly doubled between 1971—8%—and 1978—15%. Current use also doubled during this period, from 3% to 7%.

The use of stimulants has only slightly increased since 1971. . .

Lifetime and current use of depressants has remained fairly uniform since 1971. . .

Both of these studies also indicated a lowering of the age of first use for illicit drugs. This is particularly troublesome in that early initiation into drug use has been consistently associated with greater difficulties in avoiding dysfunctional use (8).

In addition to general surveys of drugs use, there have been sufficient longitudinal studies to help identify persons who have the greatest risk of becoming dysfunctional drug users. Kandel (8) reviewed these studies and noted that: "The period for risk of initiation into illicit drug use is usually over by the mid-twenties; the dysfunctional attributes of drug users appear to precede rather than to derive from drug use; and personality factors indicative of maladjustment usually precede the use of marijuana and other illicit drugs."

Various indicators of adjustment problems, e.g., school performance, poor relationships with peers and/or authorities, can thus be used to target programming to those youth who are most likely to benefit from prevention efforts. (Blum and Richards (2), in a review of Kandel's analysis, point out that these adjustment problem indicators may not be as useful in group situations that have norms of high drug use.)

Given that there seems to be a growing need for drug prevention programs and that there are reliable methods of selecting clients who are most likely to be in need of prevention programming, the final empirical question is the extent to which prevention programming is successful in preventing drug abuse. Schaps et al. (12) reviewed 127 evaluations of prevention programs. In all of these studies, there was a specified group of clients for the programs, who could be assessed in terms of knowledge of drugs, drug use or intentions to use drugs, and/or correlates of drug use, such as poor school performance. This is by far the most extensive review of prevention programs that has been done to date.

Schaps and associates described their findings as "tentatively encouraging." Although there was great variation among the programs, the average effect was weakly positive. For a subsample of eight programs that provided intensive services and has rigorous evaluation, one program (an information only program) was counterproductive, another program had no effect, and six programs had positive effects. This review clearly indicates that a sound evaluation of an intensive, well implemented prevention program will likely show a positive effect.

To summarize the current empirical findings with respect to drug abuse prevention: There is strong evidence of a growing need for prevention, persons likely to receive the greatest benefits from intensive services can be identified, and programs can have positive effects. There are a number of areas in which greater knowledge is needed, however, before we are likely to be able to significantly improve upon the average of a weakly positive effect found in the large sample of evaluations reviewed by Schaps et al.

AREAS FOR ADDITIONAL RESEARCH

One area in which there is not sufficient current knowledge is how programs work. In the Schaps et al. review, they found that no one type of program was likely to be more successful than other types. The content of

the programs—e.g., values clarification, alternatives, counseling—was not strongly associated with effectiveness. It is unlikely that large numbers of effective programs can be established until we have a more thorough understanding of what makes programs work.

In the literature on psychotherapy research, where the particular content of the therapy is also not associated with effectiveness, the development of a collaborative relationship between the service provider and the client has been found to be strongly associated with effectiveness (7). We have not yet had enough studies that examined the relationship between the prevention program worker and clients to judge what types of relationships are formed in the typical prevention program. Given the importance of counselor-client relationships in most types of counseling and the importance of interpersonal relationships in initiating drug use (5), it is likely that specific research in this area would lead to a better understanding of the process in effective prevention programs.

A second area where greater knowledge is needed is in the implementation and management of prevention programs. Establishing and maintaining a drug prevention program is a complex undertaking, requiring considerable organizational and negotiating skills. Prevention programming does not have an institutionalized base throughout the country, and setting up a program often means creating an alliance among groups that can have conflicting interests. At present there has been little study of what strategies are likely to be effective in establishing drug prevention programs. One study that did examine the extent to which prevention programs were established in the school districts within a metropolitan area led to the disturbing finding that functioning programs were least likely to be established in lower socioeconomic areas (6).

An important prospect for improving the implementation of drug prevention programs is the increased use of formative evaluation research. Bry and George (3) described where the "same" drug prevention program was being implemented at two different school sites. A formative evaluation design was used, where the achievements of the programs were continuously monitored using data on various correlates and antecedents of drug abuse, e.g., attendance, grade averages.

The data indicated that the program was functioning well at one site but not at the other. Changes were made in the delivery of the program at the second site, and positive results were then obtained for both sites.

The great majority of the research that has been done in the evaluation of drug abuse prevention programs has used social psychological experimentation as a paradigm. The research has used the content of the program as an experimental treatment and attempted to determine the cognitive, affective, and behavioral effects of the "treatment" on the individual participants. "Information only" programs, particularly those presented over a short time period, seem to be limited in their effectiveness, and there does not seem to be any clearly superior type of program. Rather each type has been effective in some instances and not effective in others. It is time for a shift in the directions of research on drug prevention programming. Rather than continuing to try to find the "best" type of program, we need to learn more about the common processes in the various types of programs that have been effective, the various situational factors that affect the implementation of prevention programming, and formative evaluation to monitor the progress of programs.

A final area in which further research on drug prevention efforts is urgently needed is on the relationships between prevention efforts and social change. Prevention programs have been conceptualized as changing the knowledge, affects, and behavior of individuals. We do not yet have a formulation of how drug prevention programs might change social group factors. Presumably programs could change group norms with respect to drug use, the social status associated with different patterns of drug use/nonuse, and the relative power of peer versus parent groups. There have been individual reports of community-based efforts that have produced such group level changes (9), but we do not know what components are critical in the success or failure of these group level change efforts. It is possible that attempts to change the social environments that promote drug abuse may be much more effective than attempts to change the psyches of the various individuals who might be likely to abuse drugs. At present, however, we have essentially just begun developing the concepts needed for designing prevention programs aimed at communities rather than at individuals.

We can safely assume that pharmacological research will continue to produce a great variety of new drugs, many of which will have a serious abuse potential and be well suited to illicit manufacture. At present there is a modest resurgence of interest in drug abuse prevention, both at the national level and within many communities (4). This may be a rare opportunity to consolidate current knowledge of effective programming, conduct the needed research to improve the functioning of programs, and provide an institutionalized base for comprehensive prevention efforts. If we do not improve upon the "weakly positive" average effect of present prevention programs, we risk significant increases in our already high levels of substance abuse.

References

1. Bergin, A. E., and Lambert, M. J. Treatment outcomes. In *Handbook of Psychotherapy and Behavior Change: An Empirical Analysis*, S. L. Garfield and A. E. Bergin, editors, 2nd ed., pp. 139–190. New York, John Wiley & Sons, 1978.
2. Blum, R., and Richards, L. Youthful drug use. In *Handbook on Drug Abuse*, R. L. Dupont, A. Goldstein, and J. O'Donnell, editors, pp. 257–269. Washington, D.C., National Institute on Drug Abuse, 1979.
3. Bry, B. H., and George, F. E. Evaluating and improving prevention programs: A strategy from drug abuse. Eval. Program Planning 2:127, 1979.
4. Brynner, E. C. New parental push against marijuana. The New York Times Magazine, February 10, 1980.
5. Elinson, J., Josephson, E., Zanes, A., and Haberman, P. *A Study of Teenage Drug Behavior*, Final Report to NIDA, Grant DA 00043. New York, Columbia University School of Public Health, 1977.
6. Horst, L., and Des Jarlais, D. C. Socio-economic status and drug abuse prevention in a metropolitan area. J. Drug Educ. 9:359, 1979.
7. Johnston, L. D., Bachman, J. G. and O'Malley, P. *Drugs and the Class of '78: Behaviors, Attitudes and National Trends.* Washington, D. C., National Institute on Drug Abuse, 1979.
8. Kandel, D. *Longitudinal Research on Drug Use.* Washington, D.C., Hemisphere Publishing, 1978.
9. Manatt, M. *Parents, Peers and Pot.* Washington, D.C., National Institute on Drug Abuse, 1979.
10. New York State Division of Substance Abuse Services. *Substance Use among New York State Public and Parochial School Students in Grades 7 through 12.* Albany, Division of Substance Abuse Services, 1978.
11. Room, R. Governing images and the prevention of alcohol problems. Prev. Med. 3:11, 1974.
12. Schaps, E., DiBartolo, R., Palley, C., and Churgin, S. *Primary Prevention Evaluation Research: A Review of 127 Program Evaluations.* Walnut Creek, Calif., Pyramid Project, Pacific Institute for Research and Evaluation, 1978.

CHAPTER 35

FAMILY THERAPY: A TREATMENT APPROACH WITH SUBSTANCE ABUSERS

Edward Kaufman, M.D.

Family therapy is the most promising treatment approach for substance abusers to have evolved in the past decade. A recent survey of 2,012 agencies involved with treating substance abuse found that 93 per cent provided some type of family therapy (11). In drug abuse programs, the focus of family therapy historically has been on the family of origin; in alcoholism, it has been on the spouse system. More recently, these emphases have broadened so that both types of programs are viewing family therapy as involving three generational systems. Family therapists are also extending their sphere of intervention into the community network. In some cases, a new network may be provided through multiple family therapy (MFT) and other support groups for families of substance abusers. It is not suggested that all the problems of the substance abuser can be solved through family therapy. In many cases, family therapy alone is not enough. In most cases, it is a valuable or essential adjunct to other modalities. In all circumstances, observation of the total family is always a valuable part of the diagnostic process.

This presentation will focus on family therapy that includes the substance-abusing patient rather than treatment systems that exclude the client from direct participation in family intervention. Group family treatments will also be discussed.

FAMILY SYSTEMS AND STRUCTURES OF SUBSTANCE ABUSERS

DRUG ABUSERS

The first major step in the treatment of substance abusers is a diagnosis of the existing family systems and structures. This diagnosis is essential regardless of the therapist's approach. As Tolstoy said in *Anna Karenina*, "Happy families are all alike; every unhappy family is unhappy in its own way." The author's work with the families of substance abusers has attempted to define the various patterns in these unhappy families. The family structures of drug abusers were the subject of a 4-year study conducted at two therapeutic communities (22), Su Casa in

New York City and The Family in Los Angeles. This study included 75 families, each of whom was seen for about 6 months. Although all of the identified patients had been dependent on heroin, they were also, in the majority of cases, polydrug abusers. The patterns their families demonstrated were similar to those seen in other families treated by the author in other settings where the identified patients used drugs seriously but were not dependent.

The basic patterns of familial interaction were analyzed structurally using the concepts of Minuchin (30). Thus, parent-child relationships were designated as enmeshed, clear, or disengaged.

Enmeshment and disengagement refer to a preference for a type of transactional interaction. In enmeshed family systems, the heightened sense of belonging requires a major yielding of autonomy. Thus, stresses in one family member cross over to the other. Such systems tend to react with immediacy and intensity to stress. Disengaged systems tolerate a wide range of individual variations but lack a feeling of loyalty, belonging, and the ability to request support when needed (30). Narcotic addiction in a family member is such a strong stress on the family that secondary enmeshment or disengagement can be expected. However, the author's impressions are that these patterns, particularly mother-child enmeshment, antedate and indeed precipitate the abuse of and dependence on narcotics.

Fifty-six of 64 (88 per cent) mother-child relationships were considered enmeshed, as were 23 of 56 (41 per cent) father-child relationships. Two mothers (3 per cent) were disengaged, as were 24 fathers (43 per cent) (22).

Of the 17 mates of male addicts, 12 (70 per cent) were quite passive and submissive. Three were dominant, and two relationships were too egalitarian to be so classified. All three male mates who attended were former addicts on methadone treatment who were quite dominant. Addict males who dominate their mates frequently focus their domination around meeting the needs of their habit. The wife may pay for drugs through working or a welfare check, to the neglect of the family's basic material needs, or blatantly deny that her husband has a problem. When the female spouse is also an addict, she may depend on her mate for supply and injection of drugs. The male will reinforce this, even beating her when she obtains drugs elsewhere. The addict spouse pairs frequently duplicate roles with each other that they have developed in their own families of origin and that may require resolution within that family before successful work can be done with the addict pair (22).

Siblings Tended to Fall Equally into Two Basic Categories. The "bad" group was composed of fellow addicts whose drug dependence was inextricably fused with that of the resident. The other group was composed of "good" siblings. These were parental children who assumed an authoritarian role when the father was disengaged and/or were, themselves, highly successful. Some of these successful siblings had individuated from the family, but many were still enmeshed. A small group of "good" siblings was quite passive and not involved with substance abuse. Enmeshed addicted siblings buy drugs for and from each other, inject one another, set the other up to be arrested, or even pimp for one another. At times, a large family may show sibling relationships of all the above types. Many successful older siblings were quite prominent in their fields, and, in these cases, the addict sibling withdrew from any vocational achievement rather than compete. In a few cases addicts were themselves parental children who had no way of asking for relief of responsibility except through drugs. More commonly, they were the youngest child, and their addiction fulfilled the family's need to retain a baby in the family system.

Family Patterns of Drug-dependent Patients Vary in Different Ethnic Groups. Mothers tended to be enmeshed with addict children in all ethnic groups. Six of 10 Jewish and seven of 13 Italian father-child pairs were enmeshed. Puerto Rican and Protestant fathers tended to be disengaged or absent from the therapy. Most of the black families had strong, involved mothers and absent or passive fathers. The one Greek family consisted of three totally enmeshed generations (22).

The extent of pathological enmeshment varied quantitatively. In an extreme case, a mother who was frequently psychotic, with repeated psychiatric hospitalizations, was symbiotically tied to her addict son. Early in their family therapy, the addict left the residence. His mother was able to refuse to take him back. However, the pressure of doing this helped trigger another psychotic episode. After the mother emerged from her psychosis, she poignantly told her son, "I will not hold you to me anymore." Her ability to let go helped her son free himself from her and his addiction. Enmeshed mothers tend to think, act, and feel for their addict child. Several mothers regularly ingested prescribed minor tranquilizers or narcotics that were shared overtly or covertly with their sons. Many mothers suffered an agitated depression whenever their son or daughter "acted out" in destructive ways. Mothers who received prescription tranquilizers or abused alcohol frequently increased their intake whenever the addict "acted out." The mother's psychosomatic symptoms are frequently blamed on the addict. In a Puerto Rican family, his brothers told the family addict that if their mother died from asthma, it would be his fault and they would kill him. These mothers will do anything for their addict sons except leave them alone (15). In a comparison of mothers of drug addicts, schizophrenics, and normal adolescents, the mother's symbiotic need for the child was highest in the mothers of drug abusers (1).

The relationship between mothers and daughters tended to be extremely hostile, competitive, and, at times, chaotic. Half the mother-daughter relationships were severely enmeshed. When her mother suicided, a daughter also made a serious suicide attempt. Several other mothers threatened or attempted suicide. In intact, enmeshed families, daughters were fused with their fathers as well as their mothers. Rarely was the mother excluded by the father-daughter dyad. One father suicided after his wife ordered him out of the house for his brutality. A third of the fathers were alcoholic, but all except four of these had abandoned their families or died from alcoholism and were not a part of treatment. The one father who had himself been a heroin addict raised five of his six children as addicts. In the majority of Italian and Jewish families, the entire family was quite enmeshed. Frequently, both parents collaborated with the addict to keep him or her infantilized under the guise of protecting them from arrest or other dangers. The pattern of father-son brutality was quite common, although it was seen in fathers who were enmeshed as well as disengaged. With disengaged fathers, brutality was frequently their only contact with their children. However, enmeshed fathers also beat their children, which pushes the addict or potential addict into coalitions with the mother against the father. It is much easier for these fathers to hit a child once or twice than to enforce a discipline over hours and days.

Fort (15), in a group comprised mainly of ghetto addicts, noted the "frequent virtual absence of a father figure." Some studies of middle-class families have noted the presence of a "strong" father (2). However, more commonly, "the father's position as strong leader of the family seems to be a fiction . . . needed and nourished by the mother as the 'real head of the family.'"

Frequently dysfunctional systems cannot be understood or shifted until many members of the extended family are included. Grandparents, uncles, aunts, and cousins, as well as friends, have thus been found to be crucial in understanding and changing many family systems.

There may be an extended early period of familial difficulty during which the addict's abuse of drugs is denied by the entire family. Alternately, the addict is the scapegoat upon whom all intrafamilial problems are focused. Often, the family's basic interactional pattern is dull and lifeless and only becomes alive when mobilized to deal with the crises of drug abuse (31). Guilt is a frequent currency of manipulation and may be induced by the addict to coerce the family into supporting the maintenance of a habit or by parents to curb individuation. Many mothers had severe psychosomatic symptoms that were blamed on the addict, thereby reinforcing the pattern of guilt and mutual manipulation. Mothers' drug and alcohol abuse and suicide attempts were also blamed on the addicts.

Physical expressions of love and affection are either absent or used to deny and obliterate individuation or conflict. Anger about interpersonal conflicts is not expressed directly unless it erupts in explosive violence. Anger about drug use and denial of it is expressed quite frequently and is almost always counterproductive. All joy has disappeared in these families, as lives are totally taken up with the sufferings and entanglements of having an addict child. However, in many cases, the joylessness preceded the addiction. As Reilly noted, communication is most frequently negative, and there is no appropriate praise for good behavior. There is a lack of consistent limit setting by parents in which deviance may be punished or rewarded at different times (31).

These families frequently undergo "mock separations" through overdoses or institutionalizations that ultimately strengthen loyalty bonds. In a study of 85 addicts, Stanton (34) noted that, of addicts with living parents, 82 per cent saw their mothers and 58 per cent saw their fathers at least weekly; 66 per cent either lived with their parents or saw their mothers daily. In 1966, Vaillant (38) reported that 72 per cent of addicts still lived with their mother at age 22, and 47 per cent continued to live with a female blood relative after age 30. Interestingly, Vaillant also noted that, of the 30 abstinent addicts in his study, virtually all were living independently from their parents. This may be evidence of how strong an enemy the family members are if they are not made an ally through treatment.

Drug use is frequently essential to maintaining an interactional family equilibrium that resolves a disorganization of the family system that existed prior to drug taking. When drug use stops, that disorganization may return.

FAMILY STRUCTURES AND SYSTEMS OF ALCOHOLICS

The author's experience with younger alcoholics, particularly those involved with the abuse of multiple drugs, as younger alcoholics tend to be (22), is that their family dynamics are quite similar to those of primary drug abusers. Another argument for the similarity in the family structures of alcoholics and drug abusers is the high incidence of parental alcoholism in both groups. In an Eagleville study, 58 per cent of alcoholics and 46 per cent of drug abusers had an alcoholic parent (43). There are also significant differences between the two groups that may depend much more on age, ethnic, social, and cultural factors than on primary substance of abuse.

Alcoholics, like drug abusers, create a suction that draws everyone around them into their problematic orbit. This suction first draws in and may later repulse their family and intimate relationships and, if given the chance, their therapist. Drinking may be a direct expression of stress created by conflicts within the system or an integral part of maintaining a system, particularly distribution of power or role functioning. Excessive drinking occurs when family anxiety is high or when family affect is low and needs stimulation. Drinking stirs up higher anxiety in those dependent on the one who drinks. The anxiety causes everyone to do more of what they are already doing. Drinking to relieve anxiety and increased family anxiety in response to drinking can spiral into a crisis or establish a chronic pattern (8).

Triangulating family systems are prone to alcoholism. In such systems, conflict or distance between two parties is automatically displaced onto a third party (e.g., in-law, lover, therapist, child), issue, or substance (e.g., alcohol or drugs) (9). This is in contrast to a threesome where each member can move freely with the other two.

People tend to marry spouses with equal levels of ego strength and lack of knowing who they are but with opposite ways of dealing with stress (opposites attract). Each person sees him/herself as giving in to the other. The one who gives in the most becomes "deselfed" and is vulnerable to a drinking problem. If it is the wife, she begins drinking during the day to help her through her chores, hiding it from him to be ready for ideal togetherness when he returns—until she passes out several times and the problem is recognized. If it is the husband, he becomes more and more burdened by his responsibility at work and to his wife and children and increases his social drinking. He drinks excessively at home but manages to prolong his functioning at work until this too eventually falls apart (8).

The alcoholic's spouse has been labeled the "co-alcoholic." Many Alcoholics Anonymous-oriented programs use the concept of the "disease of co-alcoholism." In most cases, women with certain preexisting personalities tend to select alcoholics to satisfy unconscious needs of their own. In addition, women who undergo stress as a result of living with an alcoholic will show reaction disturbances. Whalen (40) has described women who may choose an alcoholic mate to make their lives miserable in order to punish themselves; to fill their need to dominate or punish someone; or, by choosing a weak husband, to fill their desperate need to be loved.

Fox (16) has suggested five categories of

the husbands of alcoholics—the long suffering martyr who spoils his child-wife; the unforgiving and self-righteous husband; the punishing, sadistic husband; the dependent husband disappointed at his formerly self-confident wife now dependent on him; and the normal man's dismay at finding himself married to an alcoholic.

The alcoholic leaves his spouse starved for attention and affection. He expresses love through sex and material possessions. Spouses withhold affection because it leads to sex, an act the alcoholic believes forgives all past transgressions, particularly drinking. The spouse and family build up defenses that create problems when and if the alcoholic gets sober (33). Males tend to be able to leave their alcoholic wives much more readily than females can leave their alcoholic husbands (19). Female alcoholics tend to marry male alcoholics, but male alcoholics rarely marry female alcoholics, particularly in upper social classes (19).

The alcoholic who is sober and does not want to be is still psychologically drunk and must punish everyone around him because he expects and does not receive exceptional rewards for giving up the most important thing in the world. The romance of sobriety wears off after a while, and the slightest stress will tip him off again. The grief work in giving up alcohol may last for months or years. During this period, the so-called "dry drunk" will trigger family crises unless the "dry drunk" changes his/her attitude and/or the family system is shifted in therapy. As evidence of the stress of diminished drinking on alcoholic family systems, 11 of 18 wives of alcoholics who required psychiatric hospitalization did so after a decrease in the husband's drinking (28).

Approximately 30 per cent of the children of alcoholic families marry alcoholics (33), mainly women marrying alcoholic men and repeating this pattern in multiple marriages. The rest go through life with a lot of problems that they will never resolve without assistance. The nonalcoholic wife may encourage the older son to take over responsibilities abdicated by the father, placing the son in overt competition with the father (19). Daughters in such families feel that the alcoholic father prefers them to the mother and that, if their mother were more loving, their father would not drink (5). Thus they believe the ills of weak men can be cured by love

and tend to marry alcoholics. As nonalcoholic members take over full management of the family, the alcoholic is relegated to child status, which perpetuates drinking. Children are terrified of the violence so commonly seen in alcoholic families. School phobia may result from the child's desire to stay home to protect the parent(s) from harm. Alcoholic fathers are prone to abuse their children through violence, sexual seduction, or assault. Alcoholic mothers are more prone to abuse their children through neglect (1). The nonalcoholic spouse may neglect children through directing their attention to the alcoholic. The emotional disturbance that characterizes alcoholic families leaves the children feeling rejected and unable to identify with either parent (27).

Certainly these observations emphasize the importance of family therapy for the ultimate benefit of progeny. What has frequently been neglected is the importance of involving the total family system, including children, parents, and in-laws, in order to ameliorate or stop the drinking of the alcoholic. A 6-year-old may encourage a parent to drink to quiet their violence or to loosen their controls to a point where affection is shown. An alcoholic mother drank herself into a stupor because her son would not cease daily pot smoking. A 15-year-old helped provoke a cycle of drinking and fighting in his parents so that they then became unable to set limits and enforce punishments. Most essential is identifying and eliminating the cross-generational coalitions between nonalcoholic parents and opposite-sex children that tend to alienate and infantilize the alcoholic.

The family dysfunctions I have described are the basis for structurally oriented family treatment, which I will now describe.

GENERAL PRINCIPLES OF FAMILY TREATMENT

If the substance abuser is habituated to drugs or is unable to attend sessions without being under the influence of a chemical, then the first priority is getting him/her off the substance, at least temporarily. It is difficult to initiate family therapy unless the regular use of chemicals or a pattern of habituation is interrupted. Generally, the first goal is to persuade the family to pull together to initiate detoxification. If, after detoxification, the chemical-free state is not maintained, then a drug-aided measure to keep the client from abusing chemicals can be initiated or detoxification can be repeated. Disulfiram (Antabuse), narcotic antagonists, or short term, low dose methadone maintenance can be used in this way. Disulfiram should not be given to a family member for daily distribution, as this reinforces the family's being locked into responsibility for the alcoholic's drinking. Some individuals will require a longer hospitalization, a day program, or a residential therapeutic community to ensure sufficient abstinence from chemicals to enable family therapy to occur. Therefore, the second step is to help the family initiate and support these modalities. Frequently, intensive treatment of substance abuse cannot begin unless the family and significant social network, particularly the employer, are involved. Several authors, notably Bowen (8) and Berenson (6), have suggested approaches that permit work with the family while the index patient is still drinking. There are no proponents of working with a family while the index patient is habituated to drugs. Extended treatment that takes place within the "wet" or drug-abusing system runs the risk of perpetuating that system by offering a pretense of help while no actual change occurs (25).

FAMILY THERAPY TECHNIQUES

This author's approach is basically an adaptation of S. Minuchin's structural theory to the specific family problems of substance abusers. However, other frames of reference—including systems (8), psychodynamic (7, 44), communication (4, 18, 32), behavioral (37, 42), and existential (41)—are incorporated. These varying systems are not so clearly delineated and have contributed much to each other.

The psychodynamic and systems approaches are the only ones that emphasize the importance of history to uncover past actions that are inappropriately applied to the present and to create change through insight. In the psychoanalytic approach, this insight is achieved by cognitive or affective reencounter with the past. In Bowen's systems approach (9), the cognitive is emphasized, and every attempt is made to eliminate the use of affect. Systems therapists such as Guerin and Pendagast (17) employ the genogram, which is an extremely helpful family

pictorial chart of the three generational systems that mark marriages.

Past history may be extremely helpful if it can be utilized without blaming, guilt induction, and dwelling on the hopelessness of long standing, fixed patterns. A family chronology of each individual in family treatment is thus extremely helpful in providing information that can be used to enhance change. A psychoanalytic interpretation can be used directively to accomplish immediate shifts in the family system. Two examples of this approach follow.

The 17-year-old son of a professional had lost his driver's license in an accident while intoxicated. Immediately after disciplining the son for driving in a car where beer was consumed, the mother embraced and kissed him. When she was given the task of disciplining him without embracing him, she was asked to remember that all discipline was not being held by the feet and dipped head first into a bucket of water as she had been disciplined as a child. Another mother who could not ask for support from her husband was reminded that she was not a Cossack army officer as her rigid father had been and had demanded that she be.

The goals of communication-centered therapy are to correct discrepancies in communication. This is done by having messages clearly stated, by clarifying meanings and assumptions, and by permitting feedback to clarify unclear messages. The therapist acts as an objective governor of communication, who teaches people to speak clearly and directly in a structured, protected experience.

Most family therapists who work with substance abusers are experiential in that they deal with the immediate moment of experience between themselves and the family. The therapist should be involved as a real human being who is not afraid to share his/her own feelings and experiences. The lack of self-disclosure on the part of previous professional therapists was given as the main reason their previous therapy had failed by a group of successfully recovering alcoholics.

Behavioral family techniques teach extinction of those responses on the part of significant others that trigger alcoholism as well as how to give positive reinforcement for deserved behavior.

Although I had used a variety of family therapy techniques for many years, it was only with the incorporation of structural treatment that I have felt the family treatment of substance abusers falling into place.

Minuchin's structural family therapy (30) divides therapeutic tactics into two major categories: joining, which consists of those tactics that are done to enhance the therapist's leverage within the family; and restructuring, which is composed of strategies designed to change dysfunctional relationships.

JOINING

The first joining maneuver takes place in the beginning of the first interview as the therapist functions as a host and provides a comfortable social setting. The therapist should shake hands with each member, introduce himself or herself individually, and remember everyone's name. The family should be given a flexible choice of seating arrangements so that they can have a full range of possibilities for seating. Seating choices are a strong initial key to family structure. Social interaction should take place between the therapist and each family member before the problem is presented. The therapist must be capable of joining each subsystem, including the siblings. He must enable each family member to feel his respect for them as individuals, as well as his firm commitment to healing. The therapist must make contact with each family member so that they are following him even when they sense he is unfair. The therapist should not be stationary but should feel comfortable in moving himself/herself, as well as the family, around the room.

Minuchin describes three types of joining techniques: maintenance, tracking, and mimesis. (a) *Maintenance* requires supporting the family structures and behaving according to the family's rules. Maintenance operations include talking through the "family switchboard," supporting areas of family strength, rewarding, affiliating with a family member, supporting a threatened member, including sitting next to or touching him or her. (b) *Tracking* begins with actively allowing and receiving the family's verbal and nonverbal communications. It involves adopting the content of family communications and using the family's own special language to offer the therapist's ideas. (c) *Mimesis* involves the therapist's adopting the family's style and

affect as reflected by the members' actions and needs. If a family uses humor, so should the therapist, but without double binds. If a family communicates through touching, then the therapist should also touch. Sharing food in multiple family therapy encourages a joining of all the families present, as well as uniting the therapist with each family. Joining with every member of the substance abuser's family is part of the art of therapy. The family therapist does not have to be tattooed and speak in four-letter words in order to relate to the drug abuser, yet a thorough knowledge of the vernacular is essential. With older alcoholics, a certain respect for the pristine language of sobriety, as well as a basic knowledge of the 12 steps of Alcoholics Anonymous (AA), is likewise important.

Most families will feel quite defensive, particularly in feeling that the fact they are being asked to come in implies that they are the problem rather than the identified or index patient. At these early joining stages the therapist should avoid premature sharing of information, as this would increase the inevitable defensiveness of the family (18).

Many joining maneuvers may also produce stress, as when alignment with one member of a family affects the over-all family system. Generally, the therapist avoids stressing the family until the therapeutic system has developed to a point where the therapist can support the family and its individual members under stress. These early joining maneuvers are supported and reinforced as the therapist demonstrates his/her understanding and helpfulness throughout the course of therapy.

RESTRUCTURING

Unlike joining, restructuring involves a challenge to the family's homeostasis and takes place through changes in the family's bonding and power alignments. In restructuring or changing, the therapist uses expertise in social manipulation, with the word "manipulation" being used in a positive, rather than a pejorative, sense. Techniques used for change production, as suggested by Minuchin (30), include the contract, probing, actualization, marking boundaries, assigning tasks, utilizing symptoms, manipulating mood, and, lastly, support, education, and guidance. Joining is necessary as a facilitator for change production, and the therapist frequently alternates between joining and restructuring.

The Therapeutic Contract. This deals with establishing the terms, duration, and cost of therapy. How the family should deal with continued substance abuse or dependence should be made a part of the contract. This would vary from detachment from the symptom to insistence on residential treatment. The contract is an agreement to work on mutually agreed upon, workable issues. The clearer the statement of the problem, the clearer will be the contract and the therapy. The contract should always promise help with the identified patient's problems before it is expanded to other issues. Goals should be mutual. If there is disagreement about them, then work on resolving disagreements should be part of the contract. The family's involvement in AA, Narcotics Anonymous, Al-Anon, and other support groups may also be a part of the contract, although such a commitment may be a later goal in therapy. The contract can be expanded to contingency contracting, in which each family member agrees to provide specific contributions to solving the problem. It is formulated at the end of the first session and can be continuously revised.

Assigning Tasks. Tasks may be assigned within the session or as homework. The best task is one that uses the presenting problem to make a structural change in the family (18). It is preferable for a task to be accomplished in the session before tasks are given to be performed at home. A couple might be asked to speak to each other in the session while facing each other directly and without a child sitting between them. If this is successful, then the couple can be assigned to eat dinner in a restaurant without their children or take a vacation by themselves. The tasks should be compatible with the therapist's goals for restructuring the family at each given point in the therapy (30). Therapeutic homework assignments permit the therapist and the therapeutic work to live with the family until the next session. Another way to give tasks is to assign the direction of a task: have the family choose the specifics and then reinforce their choice. A father who had neglected his medical and dental care because he was worried about his son's substance abuse was asked to make an appointment with a dentist. A wife who was overinvolved with the amounts of alcohol her husband was consuming on a daily basis was given the task of estimating how many drinks he had every day and writing it down without telling him. He was asked to write down the actual amounts, and they were compared in the next session. The discrepancies demonstrated the futility of her efforts and diminished her overinvolvement in his drinking (14). This task was also a paradoxical one, a concept that will be described below.

Utilizing the Symptom of the Index, or Identified, Patient. The symptom of the identified patient is in a very special position, and the first goal should be to influence the rest of the family to help the identified patient with the symptom. If the symptom of some other family member is focused on before the index patient's symptom is alleviated, the family may be unduly stressed and leave treatment.

The symptom may be exaggerated in order to emphasize the family's need to extrude it. An example of this is to encourage a family to continue the "glories" of overindulging and infantilizing the alcoholic. A symptom that is an externalized acting out of family conflicts can be prescribed to be performed within the family so that the family can deal with it, e.g., adolescent stealing, secret drinking.

The Paradoxical Nature of Symptoms Must Be Recognized, As Well As the Use of Paradoxical Directives to Achieve Change (39). Such tasks may seem absurd because they require families to do what they have been doing rather than to change because the latter is what everyone else has been demanding. If the family then follows the therapist and continues what they have been doing, then the therapist assumes power over the symptom. If the family continues to oppose the therapist, then they will reverse the symptom. If they comply with the therapist, then they can acknowledge their power over the symptom and have the power to change it (35). The paradox uses the principle of the double bind to change the symptom. It is an overt message that urges the family to obey the opposite, covert message. Paradoxes may seem weird, unexpected, or puzzling as they utilize extraordinary measures (39). When properly delivered, the paradox leaves the family chafing at the bit to make the desired changes.

Relabeling or reframing the symptom may

be very helpful, as when adolescent acting out is termed an attempt to bring disengaged or divorced parents together or to relieve parental child responsibilities.

Reenactment (Actualization). Patients usually direct their communications to the therapist. They should be required to talk to each other. They should be asked to enact transactional patterns rather than describe them. Role playing and family sculpture are helpful ways to facilitate actualization of patterns (as well as change them). Manipulating space (by changing seating or placing one member behind a one-way mirror) is a powerful tool for generating actualization. Working with the family when the identified patient is intoxicated creates a powerful reenactment of family interactions. The family should resolve still unresolved conflicts in the sessions rather than talk about old disagreements. When a therapist finds himself bored with a session, it is frequently because actualization (or change) has not occurred.

Marking Boundaries. This is done by delineating individual and subsystem boundaries. Individuals should not answer for or feel for others, should be talked to and not about, and should listen to and acknowledge the communication of others. Nonverbal checking and blocking of communications should also be observed and, when appropriate, pointed out and halted.

The parental subsystem should be protected from intrusion by children as well as other adults in and outside the family. Frequently, in order to strengthen the executive, parental system, sessions that exclude everyone else should be held. When individuals are deprived of a key role by a boundary that does not generally exist in the family, they should be provided with a substitute role. If a family member is placed behind a one-way mirror, that person should be given the role of expert observer and permitted to comment later.

Education and Teaching. Giving the family knowledge about alcoholism and drug abuse is almost always helpful. The support and nurturance that a family can appropriately offer its members should be taught, understood, and encouraged. The therapist may have to assume executive functions as a model and then step back so the family can assume them. Families may be taught how to handle schools or social agencies, parents taught how to confirm each other or react differently to their children. Children may be taught how to deal with their peers, including peers as co-therapists. Helpless family members can be taught to tap their potential in social and vocational areas.

Use of the Total Family or Network. Other significant family members and associates, including employers, housekeepers, siblings, aunts, and uncles, who did not attend the first session, should be invited to future meetings. Families who present as only two persons are very difficult to change. Couples' groups or multiple family therapy can provide some leverage by supplying other parental figures to such systems. Invariably there is another person—such as a boyfriend, sibling, aunt, or grandparent—who can be extremely helpful in changing such systems; e.g., triangulation, which led to the problem, is reversed by a threesome in order to achieve otherwise impossible structural changes. Other family members who are actively abusing chemicals present a problem. They should be invited to at least one session to understand their effect on the family and how the family deals with them. However, if their substance abuse is too disruptive to the family therapy, then they may be excluded from the treatment until their abuse subsides. Future sessions will have to deal with the family's efforts to enter that abuser into appropriate treatment. Once that person has achieved a drug-free state or a level of occasional substance abuse, then the former substance abuser must be included in the treatment, as he or she is invariably crucial to the abuse pattern of the identified patient. In the author's experience, drug-abusing siblings can be treated in the same residential setting if the total family is in therapy. Spouse systems where both have been dependent on drugs are more difficult unless work can also be done on that family of origin.

GROUP TECHNIQUES

Multiple family therapy (MFT) is particularly useful with families of substance abusers. The techniques of MFT have been described elsewhere (26). However, many of the steps of MFT emphasize and complement the tools of structural family therapy described above, and they will be summarized.

Generally, techniques that are most familiar to the treatment system are most readily used in MFT. Thus, in MFT's in a Phoenix

House or Daytop type of residence, confrontation and encounter are used in the service of structural changes. The therapist must join the treatment system, as well as each family. New techniques can be gradually introduced to MFT and thence to the over-all program or vice versa.

In the early phases of treatment, the families support each other by expressing the pain they have experienced through having a drug abuser in the family. The family's sense of loneliness and isolation in dealing with this major crisis is greatly attenuated by sharing the burden with other families. The means by which they have been manipulated are quite similar and are the beginning of a common bond. The addict son or daughter has lied to and stolen from the family. The alcoholic has broken many promises. Most families have given the addict money for his habit to keep him from stealing and resultant incarceration and have protected the alcoholic from responsibilities. The family learns to see the hostile aspects of this rather than its benevolence. Many patients who have difficulty with the demands of treatment will try to convince their families to take them back once again and protect them from the "evils" of therapy, just as they had protected them from jail and responsibility. Intervening in this system helps prevent many early "splitees" from leaving treatment. Many families are able to do this merely through group support. Others must learn to recognize and reduce the patterns of guilt, provocation, and enmeshment before they can close the door to the cycle of symbiotic reinvolvement. An initial period of ventilation of anger and resentment may be necessary before strategies for change can be introduced. An atmosphere is created in which all families are encouraged to be open and express everything about everyone. This does not give the family permission to hurt sadistically under the guise of honesty.

The giving of food may be utilized as an important family transaction. Food may also be limited to gifts to the entire group. This helps create a sense of the group as one family. It may also alleviate the family's guilt and permit them to gratify their need to give without infantilizing the identified patient.

As the therapy progresses, patterns of mutual manipulation, extraction, and coercion are identified and negated. The family's need to perpetuate the identified patient's abuse of drugs and dependent behavior through scapegoating, distancing, protection, or infantilization is identified, and new methods of relating are tried and encouraged. Families tend to feel guilty when confronted with their role in the addiction cycle. If the therapist does not intervene, the family will retaliate by inducing guilt or undermining growth and may ultimately pull the patient out of treatment.

Many families learn to express love and anger directly for the first time in these groups. Deep emotional pain is expressed when appropriate, and other family members are encouraged to give support to such expressions rather than nullify them or deny them. Frequently, this is done by the tears of the entire group or by appreciative applause. Kissing, hugging, and rocking are ways that families tend to obliterate pain under the guise of giving comfort. In situations where families are emotionally isolated, encouraging the mutual exchange of physical affection is helpful. MFT is particularly helpful in providing the emotional support necessary for enmeshed parents to separate themselves from the substance-abusing identified patient.

In the latter phases of MFT, families express intense repressed mourning responses that are essential to a healthy family adaptation. This is easiest with feelings about a child who has died from an overdose. In still later phases, a lost parent can be mourned. Family secrets and myths are also revealed in the later phases of MFT. When the anxiety stirred up by early shifts has been resolved, more advanced tasks can be assigned. In the final phases, the family and identified patient deal with their separation from the group. Some families may maintain contact after leaving the group and may replace the entire network of the substance abuser with a new therapeutic network.

Al-Anon and Alateen may provide the same type of emotional support for structural change as MFT (13). Inasmuch as the significant other is invariably enmeshed with the alcoholic personally as well as with his consumption of alcohol, the goals of Al-Anon and Alateen are compatible with structural theory. That is, they provide a mechanism for and support for emotional disengagement. With male spouses, it is important to find an Al-Anon group that includes men or is not intrinsically hostile to men. Narcotics Anonymous and Significant Others groups may accomplish the same goals of support and detachment. However, such groups are most effective when they do not occur in a vacuum but are accompanied by the type of family evaluation and therapy described in this presentation.

The evaluation of the effectiveness of family therapy techniques with substance abusers is far from complete. Reilly (31), Hirsch and Imhoff (20), and Stanton (35), utilizing structural techniques, cite encouraging results. P. Kaufmann of Phoenix House (26) has demonstrated that family therapy decreases the 12- to 18-month rate of recidivism to drugs from 50 per cent without family therapy to 20 per cent with it. Meeks and Kelly (29), Steinglass (36), Janzen (21), Cadogan (10), and Corder et al. (12) have demonstrated the effectiveness of family therapy with alcoholics.

In the author's experience, family therapy reduces the incidence of premature dropouts, acts as a preventive measure for other family members, acts as an extended "good family," and creates structural family changes that interdict the return of both drug and alcohol abuse.

Acknowledgments. The author wishes to acknowledge the input of Pauline Kaufmann and Judith Anderson in formulating the concepts in this chapter and of Leo Mailman, Helen Bray, and Catherine Spiewak in manuscript preparation.

References

1. Ablon, J. Family structure and behavior in alcoholism: A review of the literature. In *The Biology of Alcoholism*, B. Kissin and H. Begleiter, editors, vol. 4, pp. 205–242. New York, Plenum Press, 1976.
2. Alexander, B. K., and Dibb, G. S. Opiate addicts and their parents. Fam. Process 14:499, 1975.
3. Attardo, N. Psychodynamic factors in the mother-child relationship in adolescent drug addiction: A comparison of mothers of schizophrenics and mothers of normal adolescent sons. Psychother. Psychosom. 13:249, 1965.
4. Bateson, G., et al. Towards a theory of schizophrenia. Behav. Sci. 1:251, 1956.
5. Beckman, L. J. Women alcoholics. J. Stud. Alcohol 36:747, 1975.
6. Berenson, D. Alcohol and the family system. In *Family Therapy*, P. J. Guerin, editor, pp. 284–297. New York, Gardner Press, 1976.
7. Boszormenyi-Nagy, I., and Spark, G. *Invisible Loyalties*. New York, Harper and Row, 1973.
8. Bowen, M. Alcoholism as viewed through family systems therapy and family psychotherapy. Ann. N. Y. Acad. Sci. 233:115, 1974.
9. Bowen, M. Theory in the practice of psychotherapy. In *Family Therapy*, P. J. Guerin, editor, pp. 42–90. New York, Gardner Press, 1976.
10. Cadogan, D. A. Marital group therapy in the treatment of alcoholism. Q. J. Stud. Alcohol 34:1187, 1973.
11. Coleman, S. B., and Davis, D. I. Family therapy and drug abuse: A national survey. Fam. Process 17:21, 1978.
12. Corder, B. F., Corder, R. F., and Laidlaw, N. An intensive treatment program for alcoholics and their wives. Q. J. Stud. Alcohol 33:1144, 1972.
13. Davis, D. Alcoholics Anonymous and family therapy. Presented at the National Conference on Alcoholism, St. Louis, Missouri, April 30, 1978.
14. Fisch, R. Paradoxical techniques in family therapy. Presentation at Newport Beach, California, November 5, 1978.
15. Fort, J. P. Heroin addiction among young men. Psychiatry 17:251, 1954.
16. Fox, R. Children in the alcoholic family. In *Problems in Addiction: Alcohol and Drug Addiction*, W. C. Bier, editor, pp. 71–96. New York, Fordham University Press, 1962.
17. Guerin, P. J., and Pendagast, E. G. Evaluation of family system and genogram. In *Family Therapy*, P. J. Guerin, editor, pp. 450–464. New York, Gardner Press, 1976.
18. Haley, J. *Problem Solving Therapy*. San Francisco, Josey-Bass, 1977.
19. Hanson, K. J., and Estes, N. J. Dynamics of alcohol families. In *Alcohol: Development, Consequences, and Interventions*, N. J. Estes and E. Heineman, editors, pp. 67–75. St. Louis, C. V. Mosby, 1977.
20. Hirsch, R., and Imhoff, J. A family therapy approach to the treatment of drug abuse and addiction. J. Psychedelic Drugs 7:181, 1975.
21. Janzen, C. Families in the treatment of alcoholism. J. Stud. Alcohol 38:114, 1976.
22. Kaufman, E. The abuse of multiple drugs: Psychological hypotheses, treatment considerations. Am. J. Drug Alcohol Abuse 3:293, 1976.
23. Kaufman, E. Family structures of narcotic addicts. Int. J. Addictions, In press.
24. Kaufman, E., and Kaufmann, P. Multiple family therapy: A new direction in the treatment of drug abusers. Am. J. Drug Alcohol Abuse 4:467, 1977.
25. Kaufman, E., and Kaufmann, P. From a psychodynamic to a structural understanding of drug dependency. In *Family Therapy of Drug and Alcohol Abuse*, E. Kaufman and P. Kaufmann, editors. New York, Gardner Press, 1979.
26. Kaufman, E., and Kaufmann, P. Multiple family therapy with drug abusers. In *Family Therapy of Drug and Alcohol Abuse*, E. Kaufman and P. Kaufmann, editors, New York, Gardner Press, 1979.
27. Kern, J. C., et al. A treatment approach for children of alcoholics. J. Drug Educ. 7:207, 1977–1978.
28. MacDonald, S. E. Mental disorders in wives of alcoholics. Q. J. Stud. Alcohol 17:282, 1956.
29. Meeks, E. D., and Kelly, C. Family therapy with the families of recovering alcoholics. Q. J. Stud. Alcohol 31:399, 1970.

30. Minuchin, S. *Families and Family Therapy.* Cambridge, Mass., Harvard University Press, 1975.

31. Reilly, D. M. Family factors in the etiology and treatment of youthful drug abuse and addiction. Fam. Ther. 2:149, 1976.

32. Satir, V. *People Making.* Palo Alto, Calif., Science and Behavior Books, 1972.

33. Sauer, J. *The Neglected Majority.* National Council on Alcoholism, Milwaukee, Wisc., May 1, 1975. Milwaukee, DePaul Publications, January 1976.

34. Stanton, M. D. Some outcome results and aspects of structural family therapy with drug addicts. Presented at National Drug Abuse Conference, San Francisco, Calif., May 5–9, 1977.

35. Stanton, M. D. Family therapy: Systems approaches. In *Treatment of Emotional Disorders in Children and Adolescents,* E. P. Sholevar, R. M. Benson, and B. J. Blinder, editors. New York, Spectrum Publications, In press.

36. Steinglass, P. Experimenting with family treatment approaches to alcoholism, 1950–1975: A review. Fam. Process 15:97, 1976.

37. Stuart, R. B. Behavioral contracting within the families of delinquents. J. Behav. Ther. Exp. Psychiatry 2:1, 1971.

38. Vaillant, G. A 12-year follow-up of New York narcotic addicts. Arch. Gen. Psychiatry 15:599, 1966.

39. Watzlawick, P., Weakland, J. H., and Fish, R. *Change: Principles of Problem Formulation and Problem Resolution.* New York, W. W. Norton, 1974.

40. Whalen, T. Wives of alcoholics: Four types observed in a family service agency. Q. J. Stud. Alcohol 14: 632, 1953.

41. Whitaker, C. A family is a four-dimensional relationship. In *Family Therapy,* P. J. Guerin, editor, pp. 182–192. New York, Gardner Press, 1976.

42. Wood, P., and Schwartz, B. *How to Get Your Children to Do What You Want Them to Do.* Englewood Cliffs, N.J., Prentice Hall, 1977.

43. Ziegler-Driscoll, G. The similarities in families of drug dependents and alcoholics. In *Family Therapy of Drug and Alcohol Abuse,* E. Kaufman and P. Kaufmann, editors. New York, Gardner Press, 1979.

44. Zuk, G. H., and Boszormenyi-Nagy, I., editors. *Family Therapy and Disturbed Families.* Palo Alto, Calif., Science and Behavior Books, 1967.

CHAPTER 36

GROUP APPROACHES IN DRUG TREATMENT PROGRAMS

Alice B. Kornblith, Ph.D.

Seymour R. Kaplan, M.D.

The group approaches in residential drug treatment programs utilize both the small group and the larger group settings. The former is exemplified by the encounter group and the larger group by the therapeutic community. Although each of the two settings has a separate historical development and each has distinct structural and process properties, there is a significant interrelationship between the small and the larger group settings when they are conducted within the same institutional context. The major use of group approaches in ambulatory drug treatment programs is in the context of methadone maintenance programs. We will discuss group approaches according to the context within which they are conducted.

GENERAL BACKGROUND

The forerunner of the encounter group was the organized use of small group process as an experiential learning method, developed in 1946 at the National Training Laboratories (NTL) under Kurt Lewin's leadership. Originally referred to as the "human relations

training group", it was later called the "T-group" ("T" for training) or the "sensitivity training group." The more recent use of the term "encounter group" for this small group method is attributed to Carl Rogers. The first extensive use of the encounter group in a drug addiction program was at the Synanon program, which was founded by Charles Dederich in 1958.

The term "therapeutic community" was popularized in the mental health field in the early 1950's by Maxwell Jones (24). However, there were similar program efforts developed in psychiatric institutions during the 1940's (i.e., milieu therapy) that were directed toward turning the influence of the internal environment of the institution (custodial staff and facilities) into a constructive therapeutic influence.

Viewed from a historical perspective, the underlying element of the therapeutic community in this country was an effort to regain the humanistic principles that characterized private and state mental hospitals during the past century. Many of these hospitals during the 1800's had explicit regulations to limit the number of residential patients to 200 and were conducted under the humanistic principles referred to as "moral treatment" (4). Since the 1900's, most of the state mental hospitals have become excessively large and impersonal "total institutions" (20), which can only provide custodial functions.

SIMILARITIES IN GROUP APPROACHES

A common thread in the background of both the small group human relations movement and the therapeutic community movement was an effort to foster a "sense of community" in their respective fields. The NTL program evolved from Lewin's successful work with local community leaders, representing polarized constituencies in Connecticut, to reduce racial tensions and to improve human relations through small group methods. Jones similarly fostered group interactions between patients and staff in a shared "community" effort to improve the quality of human relationships in the milieu of psychiatric institutions.

Maxmen et al. (36) defined the therapeutic community as follows:

A therapeutic community is defined as a type of psychiatric hospital unit which attempts not only to maximally utilize the therapeutic potential of the entire staff, but more importantly to place the major responsibility upon the patients themselves to serve as primary change agents. The therapeutic program is designed to facilitate patients having a significant role in the rehabilitation of themselves and other patients. A vehicle must be provided by which all staff and patients can participate in decision-making processes about patient care and the implementation of these plans. Although historical data are utilized in arriving at a treatment plan, a necessary ingredient of a therapeutic community is that the in-hospital behavior of the patient is an important source of information for the treatment . . . . In order to assure that this occurs, a therapeutic community needs a well-defined coordinated, and structured program, so that almost any interpersonal situation in the hospital helps to transform the "patient" to "change agent."

The following is a description of the characteristics of encounter groups, by an American Psychiatric Association Task Force Report (1):

Despite widely varying formats, most of the groups share some common features: they attempt to provide an intensive group experience; they are generally small enough (six to twenty members) to permit considerable face-to-face interaction; they focus on the here-and-now (the behavior of the members as it unfolds in the group); they encourage openness, honesty, interpersonal confrontation and total self-disclosure; they encourage strong emotional expression; the participants are not labeled patients; the experience is not labeled "therapy," but nonetheless the groups strive to increase inner awareness and to change behavior. The goals of the groups vary: occasionally they are explicitly entertainment—to "turn on," to experience joy, etc.—but generally the goals involve some type of change—a change of behavior, a change of values, a change of being in the world.

SIZE OF GROUPS—NUMBERS MAKE A DIFFERENCE

Social psychologists have described the characteristics of three-member groups, or triads (48), and of "primary" small groups, with seven to 12 members (9, 33). The characteristics of social institutions, or large social organizations with a membership numbering in the hundreds, have been a major study area of sociologists. However, there have been limited studies of groups of 30 to 50 members, which is the range of patients and staff participants in therapeutic community meetings on psychiatric wards in mental health institutions.

Regular formal meetings of 30 to 50 inpatients and staff on a hospital ward primarily are influenced by the over-all institutional policies, standards, and regulations that govern the activities of the ward. Hospital-wide medical standards, life-safety codes, dietary and sanitation procedures, and health insurance reimbursement regulations will directly or indirectly impact upon the large group discussions of therapeutic community meetings.

For example, therapeutic community (TC) meetings in psychiatric programs initially are concerned with the quality of the food, the quality of the housekeeping, decisions about overnight passes to leave the hospital, and decisions about length of hospital stay. Although the staff have decision-making authority about these issues, the authority is subject to the sanctions of the policies, standards, and regulations of the hospital administration. The hospital, in turn, is controlled by its external environment.

The initial attention of patient and staff to matters of food, housekeeping, and regulations concerning passes indicates that in group meetings, which are large enough "to be heard," the pressing issues are the strong social controls that highly stratified formal institutions impose upon their members. For this reason, ward governance meetings often have been included within the TC format or are held in concert with the TC meetings in psychiatric programs.[1] On the other hand, the conduct of small groups of seven to 12 patients and staff, within the over-all TC format, can "set aside" issues related to institutional control and focus upon the personal concerns of the group members, except at times of major institutional policy changes.

INTERRELATIONSHIP WITHIN A SOCIAL SYSTEM

The small group and the larger TC group also have a psychosocial interrelationship as subsystems of the social system of the hospital institution within which they function. In this context, there is an ever present interaction between the system and the subsystems involving formal and informal shared values and beliefs. The development of a TC format on the psychiatric wards of a general hospital or on the wards of private or state hospitals cannot be sustained without operating policies based upon the explicit or implicit congruence between the general values and beliefs of the executives of the institutions and the ward directors (2).

However, executive policies are invariably subject to change due to changes in the external policies of the agencies that have control over the financial, regulatory, and monitoring activities of the hospital. Institutional policy changes, whatever the external reality, alter the congruence between its values and beliefs and those of subsystems. For example,

---

[1] In most psychiatric programs today, the TC format tends to be used to refer to regularly scheduled meetings of all patients and staff members. Generally, they are held once or twice weekly, for 1½ hours. The TC format in the residential drug treatment programs, refers to the over-all organization and objectives of the programs. The description by Maxmen et al. (36) of the TC format for a psychiatric hospital unit is more applicable today to the residential drug treatment programs. The marked reduction in the average length of stay of psychiatric inpatients has been a major factor in determining the TC format.

an executive order to discontinue all overnight and weekend passes because of public reaction to the antisocial behavior of some patients will have a negative impact on the total TC setting, including the small groups.

This is not to say that the influence of the policy changes upon the TC or the small group will be acknowledged by the members. The occurrence of disruptive behavior within the program setting by several patients, which not uncommonly follows this type of policy change, often is avoided by "selective inattention." Klein (31), for example, observed the following:

While it seems almost too obvious to mention that the social setting in which a person finds himself has some effect on the way he behaves, mental health professionals who treat hospitalized psychiatric patients often appear to be operating on the assumption that patients and those who treat them are somehow immune from influence by the world around them. It is not unusual to discover that disordered behavior is perceived entirely as the patient's response to his own internal events, as if treatment is provided for behavioral disorders occurring in a social vacuum. Little attention is paid to the role of the hospital environment as a behavioral determinant. (Even) with the development of therapeutic milieus or therapeutic communities . . . the more specific dynamic considerations which characterize the ward are often unexplored and their influence remains somewhat mysterious. It is clear, for example, that to understand the role of a patient or a staff member in a group requires some understanding of their roles as defined more broadly within the social system of the ward.

RATIONALE FOR GROUP APPROACHES IN ADDICTIVE DISORDERS

The rationale for the use of group approaches in the treatment of addictive disorders is based upon the interrelationship of the effects of drug use, the personality of the individual, and the influence of the social environment upon the development and course of the addictive process. Although the prevailing view still is based upon the concept of the "addiction-prone" personality, Zinberg (54) commented about this issue:

The idea that certain personality types seek out drug experience because of specific, early, unresolved developmental conflict, and that such people predominate in the addict group or in the much larger group of controlled users, is based on retrospective falsification. That is, looking at drug users and especially addicts, after they have become preoccupied with their drug experience, authorities assume that these attitudes and this personality state are similar to those the user had before the drug experience, and thus led to it . . . . This is *not* to say that internal factors are not involved in the decision to use drugs, in the effects of the drugs on the individual, on the rapidity and extent of the increase in drug use, and on the addiction itself and its psychological and social concomitants. But it is to say that there are no psychological profiles or consistent patterns of internal conflicts or phase-specific developmental sequences that can be put forward as the determining factor in the history of drug use and addiction.

The Individual and the Social Environment

The role of the social environment, noted early in psychoanalytic theory, has received renewed interest in recent years, following Hartmann's (22) formulation of the autonomous functions of the ego in adaptation to reality. Of particular relevance for the use of group approaches in the treatment of addictive disorders is the essential role of the social environment in the development and maintenance of internalized values and standards. Rapaport (41) presented his views on this relationship:

There is evidence that structures other than defenses are also dependent upon external stimulation for their maintenance. For instance, it has recently been demonstrated [37, 40] that the passive aggressive tendencies of psychiatric patients become exacerbated by hospitalization unless the hospital setting specifically combats these tendencies. The increased corruptibility of the superego of a person who is removed from his usual setting, the mores and standards of which have nourished and supported his superego, seems to be a further example.

The developments surrounding the Vietnam War have provided another, dramatic, example of the effect of the change of environment upon the individual's social adaptation. Many soldiers became addicted to narcotics during the time they served in Vietnam, the majority of whom were no longer addicted after a short period of time when they returned home (42, 53). A converse example is the almost immediate relapse upon returning home of some addicted patients who had no cravings while hospitalized. Some individuals develop spontaneous withdrawal symptoms when they first approach the social environment within which they had been addicted. The occurrence of "conditioned abstinence" (51) in a natural setting lends support to the interrelationship of biological, psychological, and environmental determinants in the development of the addiction process. Among the environmental determinants, peer group relations have a unique role.

Peer Groups and the Social Environment

There has been limited attention to the functions of peer group formations in childhood and adolescent development, despite the literature about the unique attributes of homogeneous small groups in educational and therapeutic settings. Buxbaum (6) cited statistical reports that a large majority of preadolescents and adolescents participate in peer group formations. She concluded that the group situations have a unique developmental function:

Possibly a group offers a greater choice of persons than everyday life does . . . . It appears to be an interstitial group, a manifestation of readjustment between childhood and maturity . . . . *The group has a part to play which cannot be substituted by any other human individual relationship"* (emphasis added).

Erikson (15) attributed to the adolescent peer group, which has become a significant social group for the individual member, an essential role in the consolidation of identity formation:

It is this identity of something in the individual's core with an essential aspect of the group's inner coherence which is under consideration here: for the young individual must learn to be most himself where he means most to others—those others, to be sure, who have come to mean most to him. The term identity expresses such a mutual relation in that it connotes both a persistent sameness within oneself (selfsameness) and a persistent sharing of some kind of essential character with others . . . as a maintenance of an inner solidarity with a group's ideals and identity.

The interrelationship between "ego identity" and "group identity" expressed by Erikson has a similar basis as Rapaport's construct of the essential role of the external environment in the development of ego autonomy. Erikson added to the schema the specific developmental role of the values and beliefs of the adolescent peer group in the maintenance of the member's identity.

Kaplan and Razin (27) postulated a similar interrelationship between the members of a "self-help" group and the over-all belief systems of the self-help group or organization:

In self-help groups, the member's shared beliefs are manifested by a collective idealized symbolism about the values of the groups . . . . The idealization process may be focused on the values of the group (as in AA and residential drug treatment programs); on the omnipotent powers of the leader of the group (as in mystico-religious sects); on the superior virtues of the way of life espoused by the groups (as in communal living arrangements); or on the superiority of the methods of procedures used to cure the members or to achieve other group objectives (as in TOPS or other weight-controlling self-help groups).

Later in this chapter there is a description of the interrelationship of the small "encounter" group and the TC program, in which the primary objective of both the large and small group settings is to instill in addict members the values and belief systems of the over-all organization. We suggest that the retention and stabilization of addicts in residential drug treatment programs is correlated with the degree to which they achieve this objective. In their assessment of outcome evaluations of five programs for alcoholics, in which AA was the only intervention, Emrick and his associates (14) made a similar observation:

Members who internalize AA belief systems, and who more carefully adhere to AA procedures, achieve the most successful results. In general these findings seem to suggest that successful AA members, compared to failures, become more actively involved in the organization, *adopt its beliefs more completely*, and *follow its behavioral guidelines more carefully* (emphasis added).

The use of small and large group meetings (as well as a pairing relationship between an established AA member and a new member) are the major methods used by AA. The therapeutic influence of group formations was noted some years ago by Freud (16):

On the other hand it appears that where a powerful impetus has been given to group formation neuroses may diminish and at all events temporarily disappear. Justifiable attempts have also been made to turn this antagonism between neuroses and group formation to therapeutic account. Even those who do not regret the disap-

pearance of religious illusions from the civilized world of today will admit that so long as they were in force they offered those who were bound by them the most powerful protection against the danger of neurosis. Nor is it hard to discern in all the ties with mystico-religious or philosophico-religious sects and communities the manifestation of distorted cures of all kinds of neuroses.

In a recent study, Galanter (17) reported that new members of a religious cult show a statistically significant reduction in preexisting symptoms. It would seem from the foregoing that there is a basis for the use of group approaches in the treatment of addiction disorders. What remains to be developed are the types of group methods appropriate for specific individuals; the time and setting in which specific group methods should be used; and, not the least, is the need to clarify the treatment and supportive arrangements that will enable the addicted individual to reestablish new social relationships outside of the institutional framework, as well as outside of the social groups within which the addiction process developed.

SOME PRACTICAL CONSIDERATIONS

Length of Stay and the Residential Basis of the TC Format

It will be apparent in the following discussion that the TC format to which we refer is based upon a residential patient population. As described by Jones (24), the TC format requires that the average patient remain in residence for 3 to 6 months, both to provide for a sufficiently large core patient group to maintain the TC "culture" and to have sufficient time for patients to be influenced by the TC "culture."

As a result of recent changes in health insurance policies, the average length of stay of psychiatric patients in general hospitals is 2 to 3 weeks and, therefore, the use of the TC method, or of small group treatment, is not appropriate in most private hospitals. The length of stay for the less severely ill in state mental hospitals also has been significantly reduced, and the long stay patient population (i.e., children, senile elderly) are not appropriate for the TC method.

Short Term and Nonresidential Basis of Encounter Groups

By contrast to the TC format, the T-group or encounter group typically have been held on a short term basis for 10 to 15 meetings. The meetings are arranged in a concentrated schedule of daily meetings for 1 or 2 weeks or on a once a week basis for 10 to 15 weeks. In the latter arrangement, the participants do not maintain a common residence. In the concentrated schedule, the participants often arrange for a temporary residence close to the training site, which may or may not be provided by the program sponsors.

The participants in the typical encounter group, thus, are not embedded in a social subsystem, such as the small group within the social system of a health institution. Although residential drug programs (except for short-stay detoxification) are not located in health institutions, they all have a hierarchical superstructure to which all members of the TC are subordinate.

GROUP APPROACHES IN RESIDENTIAL DRUG TREATMENT PROGRAMS

THE ENCOUNTER GROUP WITHIN THE THERAPEUTIC COMMUNITY (TC)

In this section we will describe the features of the group approaches in four residential drug treatment programs. The use of group approaches in other drug treatment programs, particularly as part of a methadone maintenance program, will be discussed in the following section. The four residential programs, which all strongly adhere to a drug-free treatment approach, are Synanon, Phoenix House, Daytop Village, and Odyssey House (7, 11–13, 19, 21, 34, 38, 39, 44, 45, 50, 52). Because of the close interrelationship between the TC group and the encounter group in these residential programs, we will discuss the features of both group settings and the rationale that has been offered about these features. Tables 36.1 and 36.2 contain a summary of some of the major characteristics of the TCs and encounter groups in each of the residental programs.

THE THERAPEUTIC COMMUNITY (TC) IN RESIDENTIAL DRUG TREATMENT PROGRAMS

1. The TC has been based upon a self-help group format, modified by the programs according to their views about the group methods most effective for their residents, who consist primarily of ex-addicts.[2] The TC format in the Synanon program, which was the first to be established (52), has influenced the use of the TC in Phoenix House, Daytop Village, and Odyssey House, but with Odyssey House showing the greatest difference.

2. The basic framework of TC's is based upon the view that a total 24-hour residential community is needed to resocialize drug addicts (10).

3. The TC is a hierarchical organization with an autocratic leadership.

4. The activities of residents are very structured from morning to night with most of the time being spent in various group situations: work, encounter groups, marathons, a variety of other group meetings, and socializing. Limited opportunities are available for solitary activities, such as reading, listening to music or watching television, with the purpose to prevent the resident's avoidance of contact with his peers (50) as well as to keep his behavior under the constant purview of others.

5. On the other hand, the new resident is isolated from his former life, because friends and family are considered to be part of the addict's problem. A new resident may not have outside contact with family or friends either by receiving or making visits, phone calls, or letters; he may not leave the house or grounds without permission; at Daytop Village, he is strongly discouraged from talking to other new members, lest they reinforce each other's negative attitudes (50). The breaking of any of these rules results in some form of punishment (detailed below). This initial period of isolation coupled with the intense activity schedule and 24-hour-a-day residence is designed to maximize the effect of the TC, imbuing the resident with a new set of values and norms for behavior.

6. Residents are able to work their way up through the organization to staff positions of increasing responsibility. This requires drug abstinence, no violence, industrious working, and indications of personal growth in terms of self-awareness, honesty, and responsibility, as well as indications of adherence to the beliefs exposed by the TC's approach to drug rehabilitation. The senior residents become role models for more junior residents,

---

[2] Although Synanon currently serves nonaddicts as well as addicts, it initially was founded as a residential treatment program for drug and alcohol abusers only.

Table 36.1
Characteristics of Encounter Groups

	Synanon	Phoenix	Daytop	Odyssey
Frequency of meeting	Three times/week	Three times/week	Three times/week	Can be daily
Length of meeting	Unspecified	3–4 hours	1½–2 hours	Unspecified
Size of group	10–15	8–12	8–12	Unspecified
Composition (static or variable)	Variable—selected by "Synamaster" before each Synanon[a]	Variable—director and coordinator ensure that "indicter" and "indicted" are in same group	Two variable groups: "gurus" decide who are placed together based on complaints; one static group	Variable: house supervisor arranges encounter based on complaints
Agenda	Some planned in advance to deal with particular problem	Based on "slips" (complaints) submitted prior to encounter	Variable group: based on "slips" (complaints) submitted prior to encounter	Based on "encounter slips" (complaints) submitted prior to encounter
Group leader Formal/informal	Emergent leadership in each group; use of "Synanist"—Senior member of TC—to spark session and serve as role model	1. Floor encounter—newcomers—No appointed leader 2. Staff tutorial encounter—appointed leader	Formal leader "facilitator"—resident with most status, coordinator or department head	Formal leader
Professional/ex-addicts	Ex-addicts only	Ex-addicts only	Ex-addicts only	One group with ex-addict treatment supervisor or two ex-addict co-leaders; one group with psychiatrist and ex-addict as co-leaders
Type of group process	Confrontation-aggressive verbal attacks	Confrontation-aggressive verbal attacks	Variable group: confrontation-aggressive verbal attacks "patching-up" Static group: more of general introspection and insight and less confrontational	More traditional group therapy with directive leadership; use of confrontation and insight for nonschizophrenics; support therapy only for schizophrenics
After encounter group	Social hour	Coffee and cake	Informal "patching-up"	Unspecified

[a] "Synamaster" or "Guru"—Ex-addict senior members of the TC who select members for encounter group, but are not part of the encounter themselves. "Indicter" and "Indicted"—those who issue and are the object of complaints.

Table 36.2
Salient Aspects of Therapeutic Communities

	Synanon	Phoenix	Daytop	Odyssey
Sponsorship of program	Private donations; fee paid by resident upon entrance	Public funding under New York City	NIMH initially; public funding from New York City and state	Federal grants, public funding from New York City and state; private donations
Referral source	Self-referral	Self-referral; men under criminal certification from court	Self-referral; referral from courts for convicted male addicts on probation or parole	Self-referral; referral from courts for convicted addicts on probation
Use of professional staff	None	MD, RN, research psychologist, social worker, teacher	Use of non-ex-addicts in administrative functions; RN, teacher	Program run by professionals and ex-addicts together; MD, RN, psychiatrists, teachers
Emphasis on reentry	Against reentry	Some emphasis on reentry; has an educational program	Greater emphasis on reentry; educational program	Of the four TCs, greatest emphasis on reentry; has an education and vocational program
Use of individual counseling	None	None	"Gurus" serve as full time counselors to residents	Near time of reentry, resident may have individual therapy in addition to group
Use of other groups	Seminar: discussion of a concept or practice of public speaking; Open house: weekly meeting with community; Public speaking lessons; "Haircut": small group used to verbally discipline a member who has broken the rules	Seminars: Ad lib speeches; Morning meetings; Debates; Mock speaking engagements; Marathons: when house has special problems; "Haircut"	Seminars; Morning meetings; Probe—group session probing into fears and anxieties; 12–18 hours; Copouts—meeting of entire house when there is "slippage"; Motivation group—for residents who do not respond to copouts; Peer group; Open house; Marathons—30-40 hours, several times a year; "Haircut"	Morning meetings; Marathons—extensive use of long group sessions that can become marathons at particular points in resident's stay (e.g., "probe—in," "inquiry—out," "probe—out"), as well as at other times; can last from 24–36 hours; "Haircut"

thereby serving as a focal point for their hope for rehabilitation as well as undermining any tendency for the residents to form a "we-they" philosophy of staff against ex-addicts.

7. The TC's operate under a rigid system of rewards and punishments made explicit to the entering addict and continually reiterated and reinforced through his residency. As a resident demonstrates his maturity according to the values and norms of the TC, he is rewarded in two major ways: (a) promotions and (b) an increase in privileges.

If, on the other hand, he breaks any of the rules, then a variety of punishments can be instituted ranging in severity depending upon the infraction. "Haircuts" or blistering verbal reprimands administered by a group of peers and staff are used in all four TC's under review. Signs or symbols of a resident's problem may have to be worn for a certain period of time. For example, if a person explodes in anger outside of an encounter group, which is the only forum in which he is allowed to vent feelings, he may be required to wear a large sign stating "I am a baby. I cannot control my feelings. Please help me" (50). Job demotion and loss of privileges are both common forms of punishment.

The severest punishment for men is the shaved head or closely cropped hair (11, 38, 50, 52) and for women is wearing a stocking cap covering all of her hair and not being allowed to wear make-up (50). The ultimate punishment is expulsion from the TC and is usually resorted to only when one of the cardinal rules is broken. Other deviations from the requirements of behavior that are not so seriously viewed as to invoke the above are generally handled in the encounter group. In addition, in Daytop Village (50) an even milder sanction known as the "pull-up" can be used, which is having one's peer call attention to the mistake, out loud, giving the resident a chance to correct it. If the resident fails to respond in the appropriate manner and correct the mistake, this could then result in a more serious punishment.

8. The major therapeutic tool of the TC's is considered to be the encounter group, which is discussed in the following section.

THE ENCOUNTER GROUP IN RESIDENTIAL DRUG TREATMENT PROGRAMS

When Synanon was in its formative stages in 1958, prior to its being a residential community, the major structure in the organization was the encounter group with Chuck Dederich as leader (52). Today the TC refers to this over-all program: a 24-hour a-day, 7-days-per-week enterprise, very complex, with many features, as outlined above. However, the encounter group is still viewed by many as the centerpiece of the therapeutic community concept.

The major group method is the use of abrasive, verbal attacks upon an individual in confronting him about his attitudes and behavior. The emphasis upon this method is based upon the TC concept of total honesty as an essential feature of interpersonal behavior. The concept serves as a rationale for the use of very aggressive techniques with the stated purpose of cutting through the layers of lies, manipulation, and the tough-guy posture that characterize the behavior of many addicts (52). The confrontational method also attempts to produce a "gut-level" response rather than intellectual insight. This is the prevailing norm for the interactions in the encounter group as well as the belief in what is considered to be therapeutically effective. Although screaming, yelling, and profanity are prohibited at other times in the TC, the residents are encouraged to do this in the encounter group (45). Yablonsky (52) summarized his theoretical rationale for the encounter group method: "Behavior and thinking are modified by verbal-sledgehammer attacks . . . the individual is blasted, then supported, and he seems to learn to change his behavior as a result of this positive traumatic experience."

The focus is on the "here-and-now" of the addict's world, which is essentially the TC, as opposed to discussions of the influence of childhood development on current problems. Because the TC is a residential community, much of the material brought into the encounter group is based upon how the resident is relating to others, performing his work, and his current feeling states. The sharing of emotional experiences is said to be cathartic as well as encouraging of tolerance and permissiveness among the group members (7).

The support aspect for the individual in the encounter group has varying degrees of emphasis placed on it in the different TC's. The encounter group at Synanon is reported to have "virtually no support, no attempt to draw similarities between members, no gentle invitation to members to engage in the group" (34). Daytop Village seems to emphasize support the most strongly by establishing norms of support during the encounter as well as creating a structure after the encounter in which "human first aid" is administered in order to "patch up" the resident who has been the focus of the encounter.

The encounter group is held to serve two major functions for the TC. First, it is described as a *therapeutic* tool, used for the resocialization of the addict. Secondly, it is an instrument of *social control* needed for the daily functioning of the TC. The encounter group is a major forum for dealing with infractions of the TC's values and norms. In Phoenix House, Daytop Village, and Odyssey House there is a formal structure whereby complaints of one resident against another are compiled from the time of the last group encounter and systematically addressed. Synanon deals with the infractions within the encounter group, too, but without this formal structure.

MEMBERSHIP AND LEADERSHIP CHARACTERISTICS OF THE ENCOUNTER GROUP

In addition to the agendas and after sessions of the encounter group already commented on, there are two other important facets of the encounter group: how the membership composition and the leadership of the group are determined. The members of the group are changed from session to session by a staff person in all four TC's being reviewed. The reason given for this is that with static groups, informal contracts can develop between residents whereby they might agree not to say anything against each other, thus undermining the effectiveness of the group process. The variable group method in Phoenix House, Daytop Village, and Odyssey House also allows the placement of the "indicter" and "indicted" together in the same group, as indicated by the "slips" or complaints the residents reported. Through the variable composition of the groups, the leadership also emphasizes the need for the residents of the house to relate to all members of the house, and not just the same few who would be in a static encounter group. An additional function, which is not always stated, is that it provides a means for the

social control of the organization over the residents' lives.

The use of an appointed or emergent leader also involves the issue of control. A formal leader, such as in Phoenix House, Daytop Village, or Odyssey House indicates that the organization, through the leader, wants the encounter group to be progressing in a certain way. If the group begins to go off on the wrong track, the group leader, well versed in the way of group encounters and the TC will bring it back on track. The use of emergent rather than formal leadership is one of the major differences of the encounter group in the different settings, which influences the conduct of their respective groups.

In particular, if the formal leader is a professional, as in Odyssey House, other treatment approaches can be used besides confrontation. The psychiatrist as a co-leader of the encounter at Odyssey House tends to deemphasize confrontation, is more eclectic in her approach, and is able to provide insight. By having a psychiatrist and ex-addict co-lead half of the encounter groups at Odyssey House, the therapeutic community has come full circle from its initial fanaticism of excluding the professional from any aspect of treatment.

GROUP APPROACHES IN AMBULATORY DRUG TREATMENT PROGRAMS

The small group setting is the major group approach in ambulatory drug treatment, which for the most part is conducted as a component of methadone maintenance treatment programs. There are considerable variations in the type of small group methods employed in the different programs, as well as variations within programs at different stages of treatment, with some programs offering no group sessions at all. The general rationale for the use of group approaches in ambulatory programs, however, is the same as for residential programs: to utilize the constructive influences of positive peer group relations to improve the member's realistic capacity for adaptation. The relatively brief involvement in the small groups in methadone clinic programs is a less intensive experience compared to the 24-hour-a-day environment in residential programs. A less obvious difference is the considerable staff attention in ambulatory programs required for problems of the general health of the addicts, as well as their problems about housing, clothes, and food.

GROUP APPROACHES AND SOCIAL CONTROL OF THE METHADONE CLINIC

All methadone programs share a similar environmental influence. The real and symbolic reactions to the dispensation of the narcotic drug, methadone, influence every aspect of the program. No activity can be assessed apart from this consideration. The concept of "rational authority," about which Brill and Lieberman (5) have written, reflects the realistic problems confronting the staff member in attempting to develop a constructive therapeutic relationship with a patient in the context of a setting that also must enforce legal and social controls over the patient.

The following descriptions of the intake and intermediate group approaches are presented from the viewpoint of the predominant influence of the mandated social controls of the clinic upon the addict during the entry period and the following periods of adjustment.

Intake Groups

The objectives of intake groups relate to the induction of the addict into the regulatory system under which all methadone maintenance clinics operate. Intake groups, which have been used in ambulatory psychiatric services (30), are effective in methadone clinics if there is an initial screening to arrange for a compatible group membership. At this stage, however, a counselor, who may not be the group leader, is assigned to each new patient and has the major role in his adjustment to the clinic setting.

The intake group provides both an orientation to the clinic setting and the group support for their shared reactions to the clinic regulations by which they must abide. The ambivalent feelings are not directly expressed but may be reflected in their responses to prescribed methadone doses. Discussion of realistic problems is encouraged. Lowinson and Millman (35) commented about the interventions during the first weeks in treatment:

In general, efforts should be directed to the development of realistic, rewarding alternatives to drug use. Some discussions of methadone dosage or other drug use may be inevitable; however, practical, realistic discussion of jobs, school, and relationships may often prove more fruitful.

Members may participate in the intake group for as long as 3 months, but the average time will be less, particularly in the instance of patients with long term addiction and prior clinic attendance. The size of the group varies from eight to 10 members, and the duration of the meetings averages 1 to 1½ hours. It is an "open group," that is, new members are added regularly. Professional staff or nonprofessionals (including ex-addicts) with training in conducting groups lead the meetings (26). The effectiveness of an intake group (and most group approaches in the methadone clinic setting) requires communication between the group leader and the member's individual counselor. This requirement and its reasons are discussed at the initial group formation and with each new member.

Intermediate Group

The composition of this group is made up of addicts who have been maintained in the clinic for a period of at least 3 months. They may be selected from the intake groups or referred by their individual counselor. The group is open to new members and has a membership of eight to 10 addicts. Although the underlying theme of their shared reactions to the social controls imposed by the clinic will continue to be present, the overt topics relate to the personal problems of the members about issues such as difficulties in maintaining the methadone drug regimen, problems in personal relationships, as well as the realistic issues concerning their health, living arrangements, work, and financial problems.

The duration of the intermediate group is from 6 to 9 months, although the member's participation varies depending upon alternate program arrangements that the addict's specific circumstance requires. For example, referral to special problem-oriented group is made when abuse of alcohol or other drugs complicates the methadone treatment. Group members who return to the use of injectable narcotics and who require restabilization on methadone are seen together as a subgroup. The onset of pregnancy requires special services that may or may not preclude continued membership in the intermediate group.

GROUP APPROACHES AND INDIVIDUAL SOCIAL CONTROL

In some methadone maintenance treatment programs, members who are stabilized on methadone and whose life circumstances have become more organized are referred to a therapeutic group that is modeled, to an extent, upon formal group therapy methods. The characteristic of this group approach at this more advanced stage is the shift of focus to the member's responses to the "here and now" of the interactions within the group, as well as to similar responses to interactions outside the group setting (25). The members at this time can temporarily "set aside" the influence of the clinic's mandated social controls.

There are similarities to the encounter group, described above, in that members are "confronted" with observations about their behavior at the time it occurs in the group. The group method in ambulatory programs, however, differs in the following aspects. There is a designated group leader, either a professional or highly trained nonprofessional, who has an active role in directing the focus of the group. The group membership is kept relatively stable, with particular attention to the characteristic reactions to the introduction of new members (29).

The behavior with which a member is confronted is for the purpose of identifying how he influences and is influenced by the behavior of other members in the group. The overall objective is to improve the ability of the addict-member to gain control over his social behavior. Although members react to the confrontations as criticisms, regardless of the type of behavior identified, the use of negative observations is seldom needed. In actuality, an innocuous observation, that is timed to the member's readiness to listen can be both more effective and more anxiety provoking than a focused barrage of angry criticism.

It is this latter point that bears comparison to formal group therapy. The group members, particularly the group leader, direct attention to the "way" each member circum-

vents awareness of the effect of his behavior upon others, rather than focus upon value judgments about the behavior. That is, interpretations are directed toward the ego defenses or mechanisms that protect the member from awareness of the effect of his behavior. The "readiness" of a member to listen to interpretation and his ability to contain the resultant anxiety depend in large measure upon the ego support he derives from the positive identifications established between members of a cohesive group (28). This requires a stable group membership over a number of months.

COMBINED GROUP AND FAMILY APPROACHES

In recent years group modalities have been supplemented by programs involving the addict's family members (49). The rationale for this approach is that the family constitutes a significant part of the social environment for those addicts who have maintained family relationships. Kovacs (32) recommended that the addict and the family members should meet together, in order to focus upon the "here and now" interactions. The "readiness" of the addicts *and* the family members for this type of encounter method is an obvious prerequisite.

Another approach is to conduct concurrent but separate groups for addicts and their spouses. This approach was used in the experimental cyclazocine treatment program conducted by Jaffe and Brill (23).[3] An essential aspect of the approach was the coordination of the concurrent group treatment that was achieved by having the same co-leader in each group.

EVALUATION OF GROUP APPROACHES IN DRUG TREATMENT PROGRAMS

EFFECTIVENESS OF THE ENCOUNTER GROUP WITHIN THE TC PROGRAM

There are few data about the effectiveness of the encounter group that is conducted as part of the residential drug treatment pro-

---

[3] This article does not describe the concurrent marital group program, the details of which have not been published. The group treatment of the spouses was supervised by Dr. Seymour Kaplan.

grams. However, because the encounter group in residential programs is closely interrelated with the over-all TC program, the evaluation of the TC program indirectly reflects upon the encounter group. The retention rate for TC's is very low. The median length of time residents spent in a standard TC was 6.6 months (46), with reported annual dropout rates ranging from 60 to 86 per cent (18, 43). In a study of a TC in Philadelphia, Gaudenzia, Inc., over half of the dropouts occurred by the end of the first month, two-thirds by the end of the second month, and three-quarters by the end of the third month (18). At Odyssey House, 45 per cent leave or are expelled in the first week (43).

The percentage of addicts successfully graduating from TC's was found to be only 4.9 per cent in the nation-wide Drug Abuse Reporting Program (DARP) study (46), and reentry continues to be a problem for graduated addicts (see Chapter 22) (4, 8, 38, 43, 44). However, follow-up studies of the TC samples have shown that significant predictors of group outcomes in TC programs regarding drug use, criminality, and employment (47) are correlated with good performance during treatment, graduation, and time in treatment. Thus, for the small select group of addicts who stay in residence, the TC, and perhaps the encounter group, have been effective in important areas of resocializing addicts.

One of the major limitations of the encounter group as conducted within most residential drug programs may be that its primary efforts are directed toward reinforcing the values and behavior of the over-all program. It does not deal with the addict's specific needs, particularly with his individual difficulties in behaving in a socially accepted manner when separated from the influence of the residential setting. This criticism was made by both graduates and dropouts of Daytop Village and is probably a universal problem in TC's (8). With the exception of Odyssey House, this seems to be related to the exclusion of any professional staff in the encounter group. After all, the TC was founded as a self-help group, spurning professionals.

Related to this problem is the use of the same type of group process, the confrontational method in the encounter groups, for the therapeutic plan for all addicts regardless of their special needs and problems. Of the four TC's discussed, only Odyssey House has reported the recognition of this as a significant problem. They reported (11) confrontation was used within the encounter and marathon groups, but psychological insight and interpretation were used as well, along with other methods. In addition, schizophrenic addicts were identified as a special subgroup and given support therapy only. The limited use of individual counseling in the TC is apparent and was cited as a need by over three-fourths of a sample of former residents of Daytop Village (8).

It would seem that the encounter group and the TC as a whole suffer from the same problem: they work for a certain proportion, and the remainder leave. What is indicated is a better tailoring of the use of the small group method to the needs of the patients. This would include a greater selectivity of patients assigned to encounter groups, a greater variety in therapeutic methods, and the inclusion of more trained professional staff. However, in view of explicit or implicit use of the small group as a means of reinforcing the values and beliefs espoused in the over-all TC group, these changes would alter the unitary approach of the TC format in drug problems. In social system terms, such a profound change in the encounter group subsystem would have a significant impact upon the over-all system of beliefs and values.

EFFECTIVENESS OF THE EXTRAMURAL ENCOUNTER GROUP

There is a comparative analysis of the confrontational type of encounter group method, used in residential drug treatment programs, with other encounter group methods in the study by Lieberman et al. (34). They compared 17 encounter groups, all conducted on an extramural basis, with members selected from among Stanford University students. One of the groups in their study was sponsored by Synanon.[4]

Most of the observations that were characteristic of the group conducted by the Synanon ("game") method also were observed about the groups conducted by the Gestalt method and the psychodrama method. The

---

[4] At the time of the study in 1969, Synanon "games" were conducted for 2,000 participants who were not residents in Synanon and who were not addicts.

leaders of these three groups were perceived to be the most charismatic and were labeled "energizers"; their group norms were least supportive of erotic behavior ("expressing sexually toned behavior appears to have been ambiguously received"); they were least oriented to "here and now" topics but rather to outside personal matters; they spent the most time focused upon one person in the group ("putting the game" or the "hotseat"); they had a high level of emotional intensity in the early sessions, which decreased rapidly; peer-oriented norms were not sanctioned.

The Synanon group had the highest dropout rate (28 per cent) and a low "group yield." Lieberman and his associates offered the following explanation for this development:

More generally, all types where the most negative changes occurred did not have norms that supported peer control. . . . There was medium to high acceptance of hostile confrontation. . . . Peer-oriented norms which prohibit manipulation and domination, and discourage withdrawal and indifference may well be needed to protect members against negative outcomes.

Specific group process comments by the observers of the Synanon group also seem relevant to the comparatively negative results of this method:

Observers saw the leaders as high-challenge, low-support, and highly active. They taunted, ridiculed, used a great deal of humor. They would suddenly move off the person they were attacking, and move on to another person. There was virtually no support, no attempt to draw similarities between members. . . . Leaders provided a framework to the members on how to change, or occasionally gave explanatory statements on how to play the game. The leaders generally did not manage the group aside from the meeting. . . . The leaders' statements were generally focused on interpersonal and intrapersonal issues. They almost never made statements about the group, although not infrequently they would make statements about Synanon.

In the discussion of the charismatic leaders (the "energizers"), it is noted that:

Only these leaders were strongly attached to an articulated belief-system, as well as emotionally tied to the founder of their school of thought. . . . Despite examples of other influences in the Synanon format, Synanon leaders perceive the founder of the movement as the originator of all innovations for changing individuals. Synanon

rituals include a formal prayer, suggestive of the heavy religious overtones of the movement. The Gestalt school, founded by Fritz Perls, also has a sectlike flavor. Witness the published posters of Perls' saying which have taken on the character of a Gestalt prayer.

The parallels among these men as encounter leaders and as followers of "religiostic" movements are striking. All these leaders communicate a faith beyond that which characterizes members of the healing professions as a whole. . . . As might be expected, the level of proselytizing behavior was highest for members of groups led by charismatic leaders.

It is apparent, then, that the extramural Synanon group was conducted in a similar manner to the confrontational type of encounter group method used within the residential drug treatment programs. "The shadow of Synanon, the institution, loomed large in the group." The general effect also is similar to the observations noted above about this over-all TC approach. More than any other group, the Synanon group in the study by Lieberman and his associates evoked a bimodal response. There was a high dropout rate, with those who left expressing highly negative reactions toward their experience in the group.

However, among those who remained, there was a highly positive response. Some of these members, "in fact, continued with Synanon long after the end of the project." The abrasive type of confrontational encounter method seems to have a selective appeal among individuals who suffer from addictive disorders as well as among individuals who do not have identifiable mental or addictive disorders.

References

1. American Psychiatric Association Task Force Report. *Encounter Groups and Psychiatry.* Washington, D.C., American Psychiatric Association, 1970.
2. Astrachan, B. M., Harrow, M., and Flynn, H. R. Influence of a value system of a psychiatric setting on behavior in group therapy meetings. Soc. Psychiatry 3:165, 1968.
3. Biase, V. Phoenix Houses: Therapeutic communities for drug addicts: A comparative study of residents in treatment. In *Phoenix House: Studies in a Therapeutic Community (1968–1973),* G. deLeon, editor, pp. 100–105. New York, MSS Information Corporation, 1974.
4. Bockover, J. S. *Moral Treatment in American Psychiatry.* New York, Springer, 1963.
5. Brill, L., and Lieberman, L. *Major Modalities in the Treatment of Drug Abuse.* New York, Behavioral Publications, 1972.

6. Buxbaum, E. Transference and group formation in children and adolescents. Psychoanal. Study Child 1:351, 1945.

7. Casriel, D. *So Fair a House: The Story of Synanon.* Englewood Cliffs, N. J., Prentice Hall, 1963.

8. Collier, W. V., and Hijazi, Y. A. A follow-up study of former residents of a therapeutic community. Int. J. Addict. 9:805, 1974

9. Cooley, C. H. The roots of social knowledge. Am. J. Sociol. 32:59, 1926.

10. deLeon, G., and Rosenthal, M. S. Therapeutic communities. In *Handbook on Drug Abuse*, R. L. Dupont, A. Goldstein, and J. O'Donnell, editors, pp. 39–47. Washington, D.C., National Institute on Drug Abuse, 1979.

11. Densen-Gerber, J. *We Mainline Dreams: The Odyssey House Story.* New York, Doubleday, 1973.

12. Densen-Gerber, J., and Drassner, D. Odyssey House: A structural model for the successful employment and re-entry of the ex-drug abuser. J. Drug Issues 4:414, 1974.

13. Edmonson, W. R. Long term rehabilitation of the drug dependent person: The Odyssey House method. J. Nat. Med. Assoc. 64:502, 1972.

14. Emrick, C. D., Lassen, C. L., and Edwards, M. T. Nonprofessional peers as therapeutic agents. In *Effective Psychotherapy: a Handbook of Research*, A. S. Gurman and A. M. Razin, editors, pp. 120–161. Oxford: Pergamon Press, 1977.

15. Erikson, E. H. *Identity and the Life Cycle: Psychological Issues.* New York, International Universities Press, 1959.

16. Freud, S. Group psychology and the analysis of the ego (1921). In *Standard Edition of the Complete Psychological Works of Sigmund Freud*, J. Strachey, editor, vol 18. London, Hogarth Press, 1955.

17. Galanter M. The "relief effect": A sociobiological model for neurotic distress and large-group therapy. Am. J. Psychiatry 135:588, 1978.

18. Glaser, F. B. Splitting: Attrition from a drug-free therapeutic community. Am. J. Drug Alcohol Abuse 1:329, 1974.

19. Glasscote, R. M., Sussex, J. N., Jaffe, J. H., Ball, J., and Brill, L. *The Treatment of Drug Abuse: Programs, Problems, Prospects.* Washington, D.C., American Psychiatric Association, 1972.

20. Goffman, E. *Asylums: Essays on the Social Situation of Mental Patients and Other Inmates.* Chicago, Aldine, 1961.

21. Gorsica, D. T. Director, Public Information, Odyssey House. Personal communication, 1980.

22. Hartmann, H. *Ego Psychology and the Problems of Adaptation.* New York, International Universities Press, 1939.

23. Jaffe, J. H., and Brill, L. Cyclazocine, a long-acting narcotic antagonist: Its voluntary acceptance as a treatment modality by narcotics abusers. Int. J. Addict. 1:99, 1966.

24. Jones, M. *The Therapeutic Community.* New York, Basic Books, 1953.

25. Kaplan, S. R. Therapy groups and training groups: Similarities and differences. Int. J. Group Psychother. 17:473, 1967.

26. Kaplan, S. R., Boyajian, L. Z., and Meltzer, B. The role of the nonprofessional worker. In *The Practice of Community Mental Health*, H. Grunebaum, editor. Boston, Little, Brown and Company, 1970.

27. Kaplan, S. R. and Razin, A. M. The psychological substrate of self-help groups. J. Operational Psychiatry 9:57, 1978.

28. Kaplan, S. R., and Razin, A. M. The psychodynamics of group cohesion. In *Group Cohesion: Biological, Psychological and Sociological Perspectives*, H. Kellerman, editor. New York, Grune and Stratton, 1980.

29. Kaplan, S. R., and Roman, M. Characteristic responses in adult therapy groups to the introduction of new members: A reflection in group processes. Int. J. Group Psychother. 11:372, 1961.

30. Kaplan, S. R., and Roman, M. *The Organization and Delivery of Mental Health Services in the Ghetto: The Lincoln Hospital Experience.* New York, Praeger, 1973.

31. Klein, R. H. Inpatient group psychotherapy: Practical considerations and special problems. Int. J. Group Psychother. 27:201, 1977.

32. Kovacs, J. An approach to treating adolescent drug abusers. In *Developments in the Field of Drug Abuse*, E. Senay, V. Shorty, and H. Alksne, editors. Cambridge, Mass., Schenkman, 1975.

33. Lewin, K. *Field Theory in Social Science.* New York, Harper, 1951.

34. Lieberman, M. A., Yalom, I. D., and Miles, M. B. *Encounter Groups: First Facts.* New York, Basic Books, 1973.

35. Lowinson, J. H., and Millman, R. B. Clinical aspects of methadone maintenance treatment. In *Handbook on Drug Abuse*, R. L. Dupont, A. Goldstein, J. O'Donnell, editors. Washington, D.C., National Institute of Drug Abuse, 1979.

36. Maxmen, J. S., Tucker, G. J., and Lebow, M. *Rational Hospital Psychiatry.* New York, Brunner/Mazel, 1974.

37. Miller, S. C. Determinants of the role-image of the patient in a psychiatric hospital. In *The Patient and the Mental Hospital*, M. Greenblatt, D. J. Levinson, and R. H. Williams, editors, pp. 380–401. Glencoe, Ill., Free Press, 1957.

38. Nash, G. The sociology of Phoenix House: A therapeutic community for the resocialization of narcotic addicts. In *Phoenix House: Studies in a Therapeutic Community (1968–1973)*, G. deLeon, editor, pp. 42–61. New York, MSS Information Corp., 1974.

39. O'Brien, W. B. Therapeutic community and drug-free approaches to treatment. In *A Multicultural View of Drug Abuse*, Proceedings of the National Drug Abuse Conference, 1977, D. E. Smith et al., editors, pp. 359–368. Cambridge, Mass., Schenkman, 1978.

40. Polansky, N., Miller, S. C., and White, R. B. Some observations regarding group psychotherapy in inpatient psychiatric treatment. Group Psychother. 8:254, 1955.

41. Rapaport, D. On the psychoanalytic theory of motivation. In *Nebraska Symposium on Motivations*, M. R. Jones, editor, pp. 173–247. Lincoln, University of Nebraska Press, 1960.

42. Robins, L. A followup study of Vietnam veterans' drug use. J. Drug Issues 4:62, 1974.

43. Rohrs, C. C., Murphy, J. P., and Densen-Gerber, J. The therapeutic community: The Odyssey House concept. In *Drug Abuse: Proceedings of the International Conference*, C. J. D. Zarafonetis, editor, pp. 571–575. Philadelphia, Lea & Febiger, 1972.

44. Rosenthal, M. S. Phoenix House: A therapeutic com-

munity program for the treatment of drug abusers and drug addicts. In *Yearbook of Drug Abuse*, L. Brill and E. Harms, editors, pp. 83–102. New York, Behavioral Publications, 1973.

45. Rosenthal, M. S. The Phoenix House therapeutic community: An overview. In *Phoenix House: Studies in a Therapeutic Community (1968–1973)*, G. de-Leon, editor, pp. 12–25. New York, MSS Information Corp., 1974.

46. Sells, S. B., editor. *Studies of the Effectiveness of Treatments for Drug Abuse. Vol. I: Evaluation of Treatments*. Cambridge, Mass., Ballinger, 1974.

47. Sells, S. B. Treatment effectiveness. In *Handbook on Drug Abuse*, R. L. Dupont, A. Goldstein, and J. O'Donnell, editors, pp. 105–118. Washington, D.C., National Institute on Drug Abuse, 1979.

48. Simmel, G. The number of members as determining the sociological form of the group. Am. J. Sociol. 8: 1, 158, 1902.

49. Stanton, M. D. Structural family therapy with heroin addicts. In *The Family Therapy of Drug and Alcohol Abusers*, E. Kaufman and P. Kaufmann, editors. New York, Gardner, 1978.

50. Sugarman, B. *Daytop Village: A Therapeutic Community*. New York, Holt, Rinehart & Winston, 1974.

51. Wikler, A. *Opiate Addiction: Psychological and Neurophysiological*. Springfield, Ill., Charles C Thomas, 1952.

52. Yablonsky, L. *The Tunnel Back: Synanon*. New York, Macmillan, 1965.

53. Zinberg, N. E. Heroin use in Vietnam and the United States. Arch. Gen. Psychiatry 26:486, 1972.

53. Zinberg, N. E. Addiction and ego functions. Psychoanal. Study Child 30:567, 1975.

CHAPTER 37

A CONTEMPORARY PSYCHOANALYTIC VIEW OF ADDICTION THEORY AND TREATMENT[1]

Edward J. Khantzian, M.D.

Howard Shaffer, Ph.D.

The addiction literature is in a conflicting and controversial state of affairs; with the notable exception of learning/conditioning theories applied to the problems of substance abuse (7, 13, 46–48), there are few reports in the literature that relate theory to practice. Consequently, there is little agreement as to the etiology of addiction and even less consensus as to the course of proper treatment (11, 42).

The reasons for this situation are complex. However, three factors may be responsible: (a) There is a lack of interface between theory, research, and practice, i.e., a precise method for translating the former two into the latter (see reference 21 for an examination of this problem in the psychoanalytic litera-

ture); (b) a disregard for the functional difference between existing theories of addiction that deal primarily with etiology and the need for new theories that provide effective strategies for the treatment of the problems associated with addiction; and (c) the failure of practitioners to rely upon their own clinical experiences to develop an explicit and viable "theory of practice" for the treatment of addiction (i.e., make explicit the implicit rules that govern therapeutic activities with patients). In fact, Gambino and Shaffer have demonstrated that the field of addictions is preparadigmatic, that is, without an operative paradigm. Consequently, "it is difficult to agree on the important parameters of addiction; furthermore, the evidence intended to support the constructs of abuse, addiction, and drug dependence is often clouded because addiction experts have difficulty agreeing on the important data ... Thus, during a pre-paradigm period, controversy continues without a foreseeable end" (11).

[1] Observations and conclusions in this chapter are based, in part, on work supported by National Institute on Drug Abuse (NIDA) Grant No. 1 RO1 DA 01828-01 and NIDA Contract No. 271-77-3410.

OVERVIEW OF THEORY

When accompanied by guidelines for promising alternatives, scientific progress is achieved by the criticism of contemporary theory (24, 26, 32). Consequently, the purpose of the present chapter is to present a critical review of some contemporary theories of addiction and relate these to current treatment approaches. This review will have an admitted bias, namely, a contemporary psychoanalytic perspective that places an emphasis and importance on understanding the psychodynamics associated with the structural impairments of narcotic addicts.

The influences of early psychoanalytic formulations that emphasized the regressive and pleasurable use of drugs still persist to explain the compelling nature of addiction. In contrast more recent psychoanalytic formulations have placed greater emphasis on understanding how an individual's ego-psychological organization, including drives and affects, interacts with addictive drugs. During this discussion, we will examine how narcotic addicts depend on the effect of opiates to overcome feelings of dysphoria and ego disorganization associated with rage and aggression—affects and drives that have otherwise been overwhelming for these individuals. Because this theme emphasizes the notion of rage and aggression, a short summary of the psychoanalytic view of aggression requires a brief digression. This will be followed by an examination of the psychodynamic/psychoanalytic theories of addiction and the consequent clinical implications.

PSYCHOANALYTIC PERSPECTIVES OF AGGRESSION

Historically, the psychoanalytic literature has debated the question of whether aggressive behavior is a result of an instinctual drive or is an ego-defensive reaction. Hartmann et al. (17) and Anna Freud (9) have taken the instinctual position and considered aggression to have a somatic source. These theorists have postulated that aggressive energy is constantly generated within the body, albeit in an unknown and unspecified manner. Consequently, unless this energy is released in a socially acceptable manner (e.g., physical activity, or transformed to neutralized energy available to the ego), these stored up urges inevitably lead to aggressive behavior directed toward oneself or others. This orthodox psychoanalytic position espoused by Hartmann et al. considers aggressive behavior to be similar to sexual behavior in many respects. Thus, both behaviors are considered to be the product of a "constant driving force." Moreover it was theorized that environmental objects became associated with these drives only as a result of the consequent satisfactions obtained.

An alternative analytic position has stressed the role of aggressive behavior and ego functioning. This position is characterized by the premise that aggression is not an unmodifiable innate destructive driving force. For example, Rank (36) believed "that aggressive behavior means adaptation to the surrounding reality, hence is a part of ego organization." Berkowitz (2) considered both of these conceptions onesided. Undoubtedly, aggressive actions are sometimes carried out to achieve certain purposes—as the ego formulation maintains. However, it is also apparent that the automatic processes, unaffected by ego controls, also occasionally govern the magnitude of aggression displayed in a given situation. These automatic processes do not reflect the operation of an exclusively internally based destructive drive; thus, Berkowitz considered the major flaw in these positions to be the neglect of situationally determined stimulus conditions that provoke aggressive behavior.

PSYCHODYNAMIC/PSYCHOANALYTIC THEORIES OF ADDICTION

Early psychoanalytic theorists stressed the importance of libidinal factors in addiction (1, 10). For example, during his description of the specific effects of alcohol on the removal of repression, Abraham noted that morphine has a similar effect; Abraham suggested that both drugs play a part in overcoming sexual inhibitions, particularly in men. In addition to this emphasis on libido, these early approaches tended to minimize the different effects that various substances produced. For example, in an early paper, Rado (34) minimized the differences between drugs such as alcohol, morphine, and cocaine; moreover, Rado (34) suggested that an understanding of addiction came from the recognition that the impulse to use a substance was more important than the substance used in determining whether or not an individual became an addict. Years later, however, Rado (35) shifted his perspective and acknowledged that, although many drugs share common characteristics, there is a need for "a special theory for each drug or group of drugs."

Although Rado acknowledged the underlying depression and the pain-removing action of narcotics, he and most early theorists consistently stressed the pleasurable aspects of taking drugs as the main factor in causing addiction. Once introduced to narcotics, Rado suggested that the individual continues to seek a "super-pleasure" due to a "corruption" produced by the narcotics. Rado viewed the mechanism of "enlightened hedonic control" as responsible for maintaining a normal individual's behavior. Rado did not support this conclusion with clinical data, however. In his now classic work, "The Problem of Melancholia," Rado commented on the relationship between aggression and depression; however, he did not speculate on the role of aggression in narcotic addiction. Rado's continued emphasis on "hedonic control and super-pleasure" as the main factors responsible for narcotic addiction tends to detract from his sensitive understanding of the underlying nature of depression and its role in producing narcotic addiction.

Like Rado and the early analysts, Wikler's early work (45) emphasized the difficulty addicts had in obtaining satisfaction of their "primary needs." Similarly, Wikler and Rasor (49) argued that neurotics and psychopaths use narcotics differentially; that is, neurotics use narcotics to relieve anxiety or produce "negative euphoria," whereas psychopaths seek only to produce the euphoria associated with narcotics. The clinical evidence offered to support this distinction is not clear. Furthermore, Wikler and Rasor failed to elaborate upon their own observation that narcotics have a stabilizing effect on behavior by influencing the anxieties associated with aggressive and sexual impulses and behavior. Thus, like Rado, and in spite of the fact that they observed a relationship between aggression and narcotics use, Wikler and Rasor focused too narrowly on the pleasure- and satisfaction-producing effects of narcotics. Wikler's later work (47, 48), along with that of Schuster (40) and Lindesmith (27), demonstrated and documented that conditioning factors play a significant role in the development and maintenance of addiction to opiates. Most of this work is based on the premise that opiates act, in two stages, as reinforcers to (a) induce and (b) sustain addiction. First, euphoric experience associated with opiate administration is its own reward and causes the addict repeatedly to seek out the pleasureable experience (opiate use as positive reinforcement). Secondly, once addicted, the self-administration of opiates quickly eliminates the abstinence syndrome (opiate use as negative reinforcement). Goldstein (13) speculated that methadone works as a treatment agent because it raises the tolerance threshold to the euphorogenic effect of heroin; thus, the powerful positive reinforcing effects that result from the euphoria associated with heroin administration are eliminated. Discounting psychopathological factors associated with substance abuse, Goldstein utilized the operant and classical conditioning theories offered by Wikler (47, 48) to support his position that the action of methadone is purely pharmacological.

Wikler's initial formulation of the role that conditioning factors play in opiate addiction and relapse emerged within the zeitgeist of the growing popularity of behavioral models of psychopathology (46). Wikler was the first to consider the roles of instrumental and classical conditioning in addiction; in addition Wikler preceded contemporary cognitive-behavior modification theorists and practitioners by analyzing the relationship between cognitive and behavioral phenomena. Thus, Wikler carefully examined and considered the mediating role of cognition in the acquisition and maintenance of addictive behavior patterns. Consequently, Wikler's view of the addict was one of an active, self-directed individual who is not simply a victim of circumstance or a victim of conditioning. Addicts were human beings who have thoughts, motives, and ideas; all of these factors come into play during the acquisition, maintenance, and extinction of addictive behavior. Specifically, Wikler's position foreshadowed contemporary research by indicating that (a) euphoria and (b) fear of withdrawal were not sufficient to account for heroin addiction. Also, Wikler made the distinction between (a) reinforcement that is a result of reinforcing properties of the drug (pharmacological reinforcement) and (b) reinforcement that is indirect and not contingent upon drug usage (i.e., secondary reinforcement).

Wikler's formulations are supported by data obtained in the animal laboratory. Because the generalization of this type of data to humans at best can be considered equivocal, Wikler's propositions are in need of additional empirical support.

Undoubtedly, conditioning factors are present in narcotic addiction, particularly in relation to the problems of physical dependence and the ability of opiates quickly to relieve symptoms of the abstinence syndrome. However, it seems unwarranted to conclude unequivocally that laboratory animals addict themselves solely because of the euphorogenic actions of opiates. Thus, for example, one can reasonably infer that laboratory animals prefer opiates because they cannot successfully relieve the stress induced by laboratory conditions—a situation with which the animal is instinctively ill equipped to deal (21). In their now classic study on the executive monkey, Brady et al. (3) demonstrated that certain laboratory protocols could induce gastroduodenal ulcers in monkeys. We can only hypothesize how these animals might have reacted if, in addition to the vigilant behavior that they needed to display in order to control their environment, opiates had been available as an alternative source of tension reduction.

The notion that relief of tension and distress may be a motive for taking narcotics was first emphasized in the formulations of Fenichel (8), Savit (38, 39), and Wieder and Kaplan (44). However, Wieder and Kaplan and Savit all considered the induction of a pleasurable regressive state through the use of drugs as the mechanism responsible for the relief of psychic pain associated with addiction. Wieder and Kaplan referred to this as a "narcissistic blissful state." Moreover, Savit speculated that the intravenous use of drugs represents an attempt by the addict to obtain a more primitive state of fusion and regression by achieving a parasitic fetal relationship via the umbilicus—the "vascular channel."

In contrast to the emphasis placed by early psychoanalytic theories on the libidinal and erotic aspects of addiction, Glover (12) focused primarily on aggression and sadism as the causative factors in producing addiction. Similar to Rado, Glover deemphasized the difference between the variety of addicting drugs; he believed that the "pharmaco-toxic effects of drugs" are not very specific. In spite of Glover's reluctance to hypothesize about the pharmacological effects produced by various drugs, he did view the use of drugs as a primitive defense mechanism. To Glover, drugs symbolized an important body part or substance. He believed that, by projecting one's conflicts onto these drugs, one was defending against a regression to a more psychotic state.

Thus, Glover viewed the addictions as a fixation to a transitional system between the more primitive "paranoid-schizoid" state and the more advanced obsessional neurosis. Addiction served a defensive function by controlling against "sadistic charges, which, although less violent than those associated with paranoia, are more severe than the sadistic charges met with in obsessional formations" (12). Consistent with the view that addiction is a coping mechanism and primarily defensive in nature, Glover viewed the addict's obsessional involvement with his drugs and his related unconscious homosexual fantasy systems as a "progressive" and successful defense against paranoid-sadistic tendencies and psychosis. Clearly, Glover's view of addiction as a progressive rather than regressive adaptation marked the onset of a new paradigm in the psychodynamic formulation of addiction. Glover's work marked the first real attempt to look at the unconscious, instrumental use of drugs; nevertheless, as Khantzian noted, Glover "places excessive emphasis on the force and power of the drug's symbolic meaning to the addict, and he makes little distinction between the addicting substances and their pharmacologic action" (21).

Wikler (45) and Westermeyer (43) have considered sociocultural variables in relation to addiction. Specifically, they have contrasted and compared the effects of opiates and alcohol in the different patterns of the use and abuse of these substances in Occidental and Oriental cultures. Both advance the argument that it is not accidental that alcohol is abused more in Western than Eastern cultures. That is, because opium results in the reduction and control of drives and alcohol has the opposite effect and facilitates the expression of internal states, they suggested that alcohol is abused more in Western cultures in which the release and expression of aggression is not only more acceptable but is actually valued and encouraged. In contrast, Eastern cultures value placidity and reduced aggression; among these peoples there is a greater consumption and abuse of opium. Although these formulations seem to have merit, there are little or no scientific data to support them.

Chein et al. (4), in their classic *The Road to H*, examined the sociological, economic, and personality variables associated with narcotic addiction. They argued that narcotic addiction is the result of long lasting severe personality disturbance and maladjustment. More specifically, they provided a rich description of the addict's ego and superego pathology and the concurrent problems associated with the addict's narcissism and sexual identification. Chein et al. (4) stressed the addict's limited ability to interact with his environment in sustained and constructive ways and his general inability to consider the consequences of obviously destructive or careless behavior. As a result of their work, Chein et al. offered the working hypothesis that "the probability of addiction is greater if the person experiences changes in his situation in connection with his use of opiate drugs which may be described as adaptive, functional, or ego-syntonic and which he describes . . . as extremely worthwhile despite, or perhaps especially because of, the inconveniences and difficulties of being an addict in our society." Chein et al. clearly stated that addiction is "adaptive and functional"; that is, in order to help oneself cope and interact with one's emotions and outside world, narcotics are used.

Although the observations of Chein et al. are comprehensive and vivid, their thesis that addiction is adaptive is not fully substantiated. Moreover, these authors described the addictive personality by indicating what the addict "is not." As with the early theorists, Chein et al. also placed undo emphasis on a "nirvana type pleasure associated with heroin."

The adaptive use of narcotics received further support in two papers published in the early 1970's (20, 50) in which the authors almost simultaneously, but independent of each other, came to similar conclusions. The authors stressed how narcotics were used as a means to counteract the disorganizing influences of rage and aggression—affects with which addicts have particular difficulty. In addition, they indicated that methadone is more effective in controlling addiction because of its greater length of action. Both of these works considered "craving" as a desire for relief from threatening and dysphoric feelings associated with unmitigated aggression.

Similarly, Hartmann (16) offered a perspective of adolescent drug use that emphasized a passive tendency in certain adolescents to avoid active mastery of developmental challenges and tasks through the use of narcotics. According to Hartmann, narcotics are used to provide a passive solution to intrapsychic conflicts often associated with the adolescent phase of development (e.g., the prospect of facing adult role expectations with inadequate preparation, models, etc). Wieder and Kaplan (44) developed this perspective further by emphasizing that preadolescent developmental conflicts left certain individuals specifically vulnerable to problems of anxiety, depression, and physical discomfort during adolescence. In these cases, drugs seem to induce a desirable ego regression.

Wieder and Kaplan also identified induced ego states, that is, specific drugs seem to be related to stage-specific developmental conflicts. For example, opiates were considered to produce a state reminiscent of a blissful closeness and union with the mother; consequently, this state avoided the separation anxiety aroused by the adolescent dependency crisis. Despite a superficial resemblance to earlier formulations that stressed regressive pleasurable use of drugs, the work of Wieder and Kaplan represents an important advance and elaboration of trends set in motion during the 1950's. Utilizing recent developments in ego theory, Wieder and Kaplan appreciated that an individual will self-select different drugs as a function of his respective personality organization and ego impairments. Thus, their emphasis on the use of drugs as a "prosthetic" and their focus on developmental considerations, adaptation, and the ego clearly set their work apart from earlier simplistic formulations based on an id psychology (23).

Based on the work of Wieder and Kaplan and the problems associated with adaptation and the ego function of addicts, Milkman and Frosch (29) examined the hypothesis that self-selection of specific drugs is related to preferred defensive style. Using a Bellack and Hurvich interview and rating scale for ego functioning, they compared heroin and amphetamine addicts in drugged and non-drugged conditions. Their preliminary findings supported the hypothesis that heroin addicts prefer the calming and dampening effects of opiates; opiates also seemed to strengthen the addict's tenuous defenses while simultaneously reinforcing their tendency toward withdrawal and isolation. Conversely, amphetamine addicts use the stimulating action of these drugs to induce an inflated sense of self-worth and a defensive style involving active confrontation of their environment. Using psychological tests and interview data, Hendin (18) provided support for the findings of Milkman and Frosch. Hendin concluded that heroin as well as barbiturates assisted the addict in withdrawing and avoiding intimacy and, therefore, served to defend the ego against overwhelming destructive impulses (23).

Alternatively, Wurmser (50, 51) and Khantzian (20–22) suggested that the excessive emphasis on the regressive effects of narcotics in the studies cited above is unwarranted. Wurmser and Khantzian considered the specific pharmacological action of opiates as a progressive effect, whereby regressive states may actually be reversed. Wurmser's work suggests that narcotics are used adaptively by narcotic addicts to compensate for defects in affect defense, particularly against feelings of rage, hurt, shame, and loneliness. Khantzian stressed the use of narcotics as a drive defense. He believes that narcotics act to reverse regressive states by the direct antiaggression action of opiates; opiates serve to counteract the disorganizing influences of rage and aggression on the ego. Both Khantzian and Wurmser suggested that the psychopharmacological effects of drugs can substitute for defective or nonexistent ego mechanisms of defense. In addition, Wurmser and Khantzian also considered developmental impairments, the severe predisposing psychopathology, and problems in adaptation as central issues in understanding the nature of addiction. The interested reader is referred to Radford et al. (33) for detailed case material that supports the formulations of Wurmser and Khantzian.

Despite differences in emphasis, the works of Gerard and Kornetsky, Hartmann, Wieder and Kaplan, Milkman and Frosch, and Hendin share a common stress on opiate use as an attempt to correct impaired or defective ego functions and thereby assist the individual to cope. It is also recurrently evident in the work of these investigators that this attempt is only partially successful at best. Their findings suggest that adopting passive solutions through opiates induces a self-perpetuating tendency for maladaptive and pathological ego and drive regression. The discrepancy between the adaptive and maladaptive effects of opiate use implied in these formulations requires further empirical clarification (23). Although the controversy between the progressive and regressive effects of opiate use on the ego remain, Krystal and Raskin (25) considered that opiates may be used either to permit or prevent ego regression. These authors did not focus on the specific effects of different drugs; however, their work attends more precisely to the relationship between (a) the affects of pain, depression, and anxiety; and (b) drug and placebo effects. Krystal and Raskin clarified the difficulty addicts have in recognizing and tolerating painful affect. For example, they considered that the tendency for the affects of depression and anxiety to remain somatized, unverbalized, and undifferentiated in addicts results in a defective stimulus barrier and thus leaves such individuals illequipped to deal with their feelings, predisposing them to drug use. Krystal and Raskin also examined the major problems addicts experience with the positive and negative feelings about themselves and others. Krystal and Raskin believed that addicts have major difficulties in being good to themselves and in dealing with their positive and negative feelings toward others because of rigid and massive defenses, e.g., splitting and denial. Thus, Krystal and Raskin suggested that addicts prefer and utilize short acting drugs to (a) assist the ego in defending against painful affect and (b) allow them to experience briefly and, therefore, "safely" feelings like fusion ("oneness") with love objects. For addicts, these more positive affects are otherwise suppressed by the defenses that rigidly protect the ego against more painful affect such as rage and aggression (23).

Zinberg (53) has offered a significantly different perspective regarding the question of ego regression among narcotics addicts. Specifically, Zinberg minimized the causal role that psychopathology plays in accounting for the rather uniformly regressed appearance and behavior of narcotics addicts. Central to Zinberg's position is the concept that the ego is relatively autonomous. He suggested that the enforced social isolation and deviant status of illicit narcotics users results in a significant reduction of balanced input from the individual's environment. This deficit undermines the ego's relative autonomy from the id and simultaneously erodes superego structures that are maintained by social support systems. Thus, the perpetual nature of addiction, in which the user continuously cycles from high to low and back again, serves to keep drive tension high, which results in increasing dependence on the environment for obtaining drugs and for whatever is left of coherent social relations, thus weakening relative autonomy from the environment. Under these conditions, the ego could be expected to undergo a regressive process that results in the "typical impulse ridden, psychopathic junkie" who is the subject of most clinical studies (53).

In sum, the present literature review indicates that psychoanalytic theories regarding the use of addicting drugs have progressed from (a) the rather narrow perspective stressing almost exclusively the pleasurable, regressive aspects of opiate use to (b) the viewpoint that narcotic addiction is ego defensive and perhaps progressive.

Because this review has of necessity been selective and representative of the more commonly invoked theories of addiction, the interested reader is referred to more extensive reviews by Rosenfeld (37), Yorke (52), Platt and Labate (31), Khantzian and Treece (23), and Gambino and Shaffer (11).

CLINICAL AND TREATMENT IMPLICATIONS

Early investigators acknowledged the powerful pain-relieving and tension-reducing actions of narcotics. For example Chein et al. (4) referred to opiates as effective "tranquilizing or ataractic drugs." The specific psychopharmacological and psychotropic properties of the opiates were examined by Chein et al. and Jaffe in descriptions of the physiological and clinical aspects of narcotic analgesics. Nevertheless, despite the fact that opiates reduce dysphoric emotional states, the plea-surable aspects of narcotics continue to be stressed to explain the compelling nature of opiate addiction. In spite of the relief obtained from emotional pain and psychological distress through the use of opiates, conditioning theorists still stress the pleasurable experience associated with heroin as the main motive for drug taking. Similarly, analytic theorists focus on the "pleasure principle" in opiate use, that is, many analysts stress the pleasurable regressive states induced by euphoria-producing drugs.

Glover's early contributions are fundamental to a contemporary psychoanalytic understanding of the defensive and adaptive role that drugs may play in an addict's life. Specifically, Glover examined how the sexual and pleasurable aspects of drugs were used defensively against the enormous difficulties that addicted individuals have with aggression. Glover suggested that drugs could be used "progressively" (as opposed to regressively) to defend against regression to psychotic states. This notion remains in direct opposition to the still prevailing view that drugs are used for the associated regressive pleasurable qualities. More recently, the thesis that drugs can be used progressively rather than regressively has been examined in more detail by Khantzian, Wurmser, and others. These authors have proposed that drug habituation and addiction represents a process of self-selection in relation to different drugs—a process that Glover failed to recognize. For example, Chein et al. have noted how narcotics may help an individual function sexually by reducing concurrent anxieties. Also, Khantzian and Wurmser have considered that narcotics specifically attenuate rage and aggression and consequently reverse regressive states.

Close observation of narcotic addicts treated with methadone maintenance has led the present authors to hypothesize that a significant portion of these individuals became addicted to opiates because they discovered that the drug acts specifically to reverse regressive states by attenuating and making more bearable dysphoric feeling involving regression, rage, and related depression. The evidence for this premise has been derived from four major sources: (a) observations of patients in individual psychotherapy; (b) careful drug and psychiatric histories obtained from patients seeking treatment for opiate addiction; (c) observations of a variety of addicts participating in many different groups in a drug abuse program; (d) follow-up evaluations and observations of patients who have been stabilized on methadone maintenance. During interviews, many of our patients report histories of physical violence, accidents, and physical trauma dating back to childhood; in some instances these patients report being physically beaten by cruel, sadistic, and impulsive parents. Similarly, these patients gave histories of impulsive and delinquent behavior in school as well as antisocial and violent behavior that predated their addiction. In many instances, this kind of behavior seemed to be precipitated by major losses and disappointments. In the course of responding to carefully taken drug histories, Khantzian has noted that patients gave ample descriptions of dysphoric states of bodily tensions and restlessness, anger, rage, violent feelings, and depression that were relieved by heroin and other opiates. "With an almost monotonous regularity, the patients used terms such as "relaxed", "mellow", "calming", and emphasized a total body response, to describe the effects of opiates when they *first* began to use such drugs" (21)

While observing patients in groups, particularly at the time of intake into a methadone maintenance program, we were afforded the opportunity to watch some of these problems played out in the patients' group interactions. For example, unmitigated angry verbal attacks on each other were quite common; the regular use of obscenities, especially with reference to genital, fecal, and anal elements, seemed to have an assaultive quality. In group meetings, group leaders and members were often frustrated in their attempts to gather information. This frustration often led to paranoid outbursts and massive projections, with a marked tendency to turn these attacks on the group leader.

As patients become stabilized on methadone, significant behavioral and psychological shifts often occur. Typically, the patient's aggressive, motoric restlessness disappears or becomes more subdued. Patients on methadone maintenance are often quieter in their interactions and show less lability, angry projections, and paranoia than during their intake or pretreatment presentations. Moreover, these patients often demonstrated a greater capacity for sustained constructive behavior in program activities and outside work. Previously, Khantzian (21) reported that "with some exceptions, I generally observed shifts away from regressed states towards less regressed states, from lability towards stability, from egocentricity towards a more concerned interest in others. Conversely, as patients were gradually withdrawn from methadone (for various reasons, but mostly at the patients request), there was a re-emergence of previously observed patterns of aggressive-impulsive outbursts, projections, paranoia, and psychotic patterns of thinking and behavior in a significant percentage of the patients." For example, the following vignette will illustrate the psychotropic, anxiety- and aggression-reducing qualities of methadone maintenance.

Mr. O. is a 29-year-old male of Caucasian descent. Mr. O. has been in treatment at a methadone maintenance program for 14 months. During intake, Mr. O. complained of symptoms that included paranoia, disorientation, somatic complaints, anxiety, depression, and aggressive ideation and behavior. During treatment, this patient was stabilized on a moderately high dose of methadone (60 to 90 mg). At these dosage levels, Mr. O. manifested few symptoms. He was not a management problem and displayed few aggressive behaviors. When Mr. O. began to detoxify at his own request, however, this situation began to change dramatically. At approximately 40 mg of methadone per day, Mr. O. began to display many of the symptoms that originally led him to seek treatment. In addition, he began to report auditory hallucinations as well as experience acute anxiety attacks. In spite of his persistence to continue the detoxification, Mr. O's dosage was increased to a moderately high level. During this time these symptoms once again remitted. A number of months later, this sequence of events repeated itself in a similar fashion. In order to more accurately assess the effects of methadone levels on Mr. O., the third attempt at detoxification was conducted in a single-blind manner. In spite of the fact that Mr. O. was not aware of his dosage level, once again at 40 mg he began to manifest a variety of distressing physical and dysphoric emotional symptoms. Moreover, during detoxification Mr. O. became suicidal and violently aggressive toward objects in his environment. This detoxification procedure was replicated one final time with identical results. Currently, Mr. O. remains in methadone maintenance treatment at a moderately high dosage level. At this level, Mr. O. is capable of maintaining his life in the community and is being treated and supported on an outpatient basis. Although this case was not rigidly controlled in an experimental manner, methadone does seem to have served an adaptive function for Mr. O.

Wurmser has similarly described a pattern of reemergence of "rage, hurt, shame, and narcissistic decompensation" as methadone was withdrawn in a group of patients participating in intensive psychotherapy (50).

In contrast to the short acting opiates such as morphine and heroin, where a constant apprehension and anxiety of withdrawal is ever present, methadone maintenance is effective in controlling addiction because it is slowly metabolized and long acting when taken orally. Because of its longer action, it not only relieves emotional pain and distress, but its sustained activity prevents the stress and frustration of frequent withdrawal and thereby lessens the likelihood of regressive reactions. At the same time, like other narcotics, methadone has a specific psychotropic action that attenuates rage and aggression, counteracting the disorganizing influences of these powerful affects on ego functions (21).

Why some patients fail to respond to methadone maintenance and revert to previous maladaptive behavior patterns remains a question in need of further empirical research. However, clinical experience and careful observation have led the present authors to the hypothesis that the variety of responses to methadone maintenance are related to the problems of narcissism often associated with developmental failures and regressed states. The ability that an individual has to relinquish his narcissistic orientation to life and discover alternative satisfactions and "healthier" patterns of adaptive behavior seems to determine how well one can respond to methadone maintenance. New research should focus on how narcotics and similar substances are used adaptively by individuals to cope with their impulsive, aggressive drives and their environment. As we have seen, much of the theoretical literature has failed to adequately consider the psychopharmacological action of narcotics in aiding

the individual with coping and adapting to his/her environment. This deficit might explain why conventional psychotherapeutic approaches have been so marginally successful in dealing with the addiction. Thus, instead of psychotherapists concerning themselves prematurely with the maladaptive aspects of drugs, they should first engage the patient by trying to understand why the addict so desperately feels s/he needs his/her drug of choice.

The notion that narcotic addicts depend on the effect of opiates to overcome feelings of dysphoria and help regulate the ego-disorganizing influence of unmitigated rage and aggression has important implications for treatment modalities other than methadone maintenance and detoxification. For example, narcotic addicts often obtain relief and help in a variety of self-help and other "drug-free" treatment programs. These programs have a variety of significant features that are relevant to the present discussion.

First, these programs often place heavy emphasis on removing the addict from the street—where heroin is readily available to provide relief from psychic distress. Secondly, these programs place early and consistent emphasis on work, with the concurrent expectation that all work assignments be carefully executed. These features play a critical role in establishing and maintaining a positive attitude toward work as well as a vehicle for the development and reinforcement of self-control and regulation. Similarly, subjecting the addict to the success of forced work and the performance of humiliating tasks and activities is probably due to the effective manipulation of the addicts sadomasochistic tendencies. However, these approaches have tended to produce temporary change, inasmuch as these "treatments" tend to play into the addict's sadomasochism rather than exert therapeutic pressure toward positive change. Thus, there exists the danger that "treatment" may sustain or even become a symptom of the problem.

Many programs employ skilled therapists who provide real opportunities for growth and permanent change. However, drug treatment programs are often inclined to offer interventions that require confrontation and catharsis; these approaches are of questionable value for the narcotic addict. These interventions often succeed in breaking down the massive denial and sense of entitlement that are present in many addicts. This success is often short lived, however, because the improvements are usually the result of (a) compliance rather than change and (b) the sanctioned ventilation of the addicts' rage and aggression in a controlled setting (21). These encounter-oriented treatments grossly underestimate the addict's limited capacity to cope with intense affect and aggressive impulses. Thus, unless an individual is capable of dealing successfully with intense emotional states, a cathartic experience may lead to further narcissistic injury and a sense of failure. For example, in their excellent examination of the use of catharsis as a technique to deal with aggression, Green and Quanty (15) found that catharsis only produces decreased arousal under some conditions. These authors indicated that (15): "At present, therefore, we must conclude that the notion of (the value of) catharsis has not been confirmed . . . ." Thus, individuals who are emotionally unprepared to deal with the forced expression of intense aggressive feelings and affect in the hope that the cathartic experience will reduce their underlying depression, frustration, or anxiety are more likely to experience anxiety and dysphoric affect. In fact, the expression of aggressive affect by an individual with poor impulse control may lead to further aggressive impulses and/or behavior.

SUMMARY

Historically, there has been a surprising paucity of psychoanalytic literature that relates theory to current treatment approaches of narcotic addiction. Most theories account for the anxiety- and tension-relieving action of opiates with considerable emphasis on the pleasurable aspects of opiate use as a causal factor invoked to explain the compelling nature of narcotic addiction. The theme developed in the present chapter suggests that problems with aggression predispose and play a central role in persons becoming addicted to opiates. Individuals dependent on opiates quickly learn that these drugs support their efforts to cope by relieving dysphoric states associated with rage and aggression. This situation is due to the direct muting action of these drugs on these powerful affects. We have presented evidence to suggest

that part of the "success" of methadone maintenance is related to the specific "antiaggression" action of methadone. In addition, we have suggested that before clinical decisions are made about treatment alternatives, treatment providers should consider the major role aggression plays in opiate addiction and the importance of appreciating the influences of this emotion and drive when determining suitable and acceptable therapeutic interventions.

REFERENCES

1. Abraham, K. The psychological relation between sexuality and alcoholism. In *Selected Papers of Karl Abraham*. New York, Basic Books, 1960.
2. Berkowitz, L. The concept of aggressive drive: Some additional considerations. In *Advances in Experimental Social Psychology*, L. Berkowitz, editor, vol. 2. New York, Academic Press, 1965.
3. Brady, J. V., Porter, R. W., Conrad, D. G., and Mason, J. W. Avoidance behavior and the development of gastroduodenal ulcers. J. Exp. Anal. Behav. 1:69, 1958.
4. Chein, I., Gerard, D. L., Lee, R. S., and Rosenfeld, E. *The Road to H.* New York, Basic Books, 1964.
5. Cochin, J. Factors influencing tolerance to and dependence on narcotic analgesics. In *Opiate Addiction: Origins and Treatment*, S. Fisher and A. M. Freedman, editors. Washington, D.C., Winston, 1974.
6. Collier, H. O. J. Drug dependence: A pharmacological analysis. Br. J. Addict. 67:277, 1972.
7. Dole, V. P. Narcotic addiction, physical dependence and relapse. N. Engl. Med. 286:988, 1972.
8. Fenichel, O. *The Psychoanalytic Theory of Neurosis.* New York, W. W. Norton, 1945.
9. Freud, A. Aggression in relation to emotional development. Psychoanal. Study Child 3–4:37, 1949.
10. Freud, S. Three essays on the theory of sexuality (1905). In *Standard Edition of the Complete Psychological Works of Sigmund Freud*, vol. 7. London, Hogarth Press, 1955.
11. Gambino, B., and Shaffer, H. The concept of paradigm and the treatment of addiction. Prof. Psychol. 10:207, 1979.
12. Glover, E. On the etiology of drug addiction. In *On the Early Development of Mind*. New York, International Universities Press, 1956.
13. Goldstein, A. Heroin addiction and the role of methadone in its treatment. Arch. Gen. Psychiatry 26:291, 1972.
14. Goldstein, A., and Goldstein, D. B. Enzyme expansion theory of drug tolerance and physical dependence. In *The Addictive States*, A. Wikler, editor. Baltimore, Williams & Wilkins, 1968.
15. Green, R. G., and Quanty, M. B. The catharsis of aggression: An evaluation of a hypothesis. In *Advances in Experimental Social Psychology*, L. Berkowitz, editor. vol. 10. New York, Academic Press, 1977.
16. Hartmann, D. A study of drug taking adolescents. Psychoanal. Study Child 24:384, 1969.
17. Hartmann, H., Kris, E., and Loewenstein, R. M.

Notes on the theory of aggression. Psychoanal. Study Child 3–4:9, 1949.

18. Hendin, H. Students on heroin. J. Nerv. Ment. Dis. 158:240, 1974.

19. Jaffe, J. H., and Sharpless, S. K. Pharmacological denervation supersensitivity in the central nervous system: A theory of physical dependence. In *The Addictive States*, A. Wikler, editor. Baltimore, Williams & Wilkins, 1968.

20. Khantzian, E. J. A preliminary dynamic formulation of the psychopharmacologic action of methadone. In *Proceedings of the Fourth National Methadone Conference*, San Francisco, January 1972. New York, National Association for the Prevention of Addiction to Narcotics, 1972.

21. Khantzian, E. J. Opiate addiction: A critique of theory and some implications for treatment. A. J. Psychother. 28:59, 1974.

22. Khantzian, E. J. Self selection and progression in drug dependence. *Psychiatry Digest* 36:19, 1975.

23. Khantzian, E. J., and Treece, C. J. Psychodynamics of drug dependence: An overview. In *Psychodynamics of Drug Dependence*, J. D. Blaine and D. A. Julius, editors, NIDA Research Monograph 12, pp. 11–25. Rockville, Md., National Institute on Drug Abuse, 1977.

24. Kruglanski, A. W. On the paradigmatic objections to experimental psychology: A reply to Gadlin and Ingle. Am. Psychol. 31:655, 1976.

25. Krystal, H., and Raskin, H. A. *Drug Dependence Aspects of Ego Function*. Detroit, Wayne State University Press, 1970.

26. Kuhn, T. S. The Structure of Scientific Revolutions, ed. 2. Chicago, University of Chicago Press, 1970.

27. Lindesmith, A. R. Problems in social psychology of addiction. In *Narcotics*, D. M. Wilner and G. G. Kassebaum, editors. New York, McGraw-Hill, 1965.

28. Martin, W. R. A homeostatic and redundancy theory of tolerance to and dependence on narcotic analgesics. In *The Addictive States*, A. Wikler, editor. Baltimore, Williams & Wilkins, 1968.

29. Milkman, H., and Frosch, W. A. On the preferential abuse of heroin and amphetamine. J. Nerv. Ment. Dis. 156:242, 1973.

30. Paton, W. D. A pharmacological approach to drug dependence and drug tolerance. In *Scientific Basis of Drug Dependence*, H. Steinberg, editor. London, Churchill, 1969.

31. Platt, J., and Labate, C. *Heroin Addiction*. New York, John Wiley & Sons, 1976.

32. Popper, K. R. *Objective Knowledge: An Evolutionary Approach*. London, Oxford University Press, 1973.

33. Radford, P., Wiseberg, S., and Yorke, C. A study of "main line" heroin addiction. Psychoanal. Study Child 27:156, 1972.

34. Rado, S. The psychoanalysis of pharmacothymia. Psychoanal. Q. 2:1, 1933.

35. Rado, S. Narcotic bondage: A general theory of the dependence on narcotic drugs. Am. J. Psychiatry 114:165, 1957.

36. Rank, B. Aggression. Psychoanal. Study Child 3–4: 43, 1949.

37. Rosenfeld, H. A. The psychopathology of drug addiction and alcoholism: A critical review of the psychoanalytic literature. In *Psychotic States*. London, Hogarth Press, 1965.

38. Savit, R. A. Extramural psychoanalytic treatment of a case of narcotic addiction. J. Am. Psychoanal. Assoc. 2:494, 1954.

39. Savit, R. A. Psychoanalytic studies on addiction: Ego structure in narcotic addiction. Psychoanal. Q. 32: 43, 1963.

40. Schuster, C. R. Psychological approaches to opiate dependence and self-administration by laboratory animals. Fed. Proc. 29:2, 1970.

41. Seevers, M. H., and Deneau, G. A. A critique of the "dual action" hypothesis of morphine's physical dependence. In *The Addictive States*, A. Wikler, editor. Baltimore, Williams & Wilkins, 1968.

42. Shaffer, H., and Gambino, B. Addiction paradigms. II. Theory, research and practice. J. Psychedelic Drugs, 11: 299, 1979.

43. Westermeyer, J. Use of alcohol and opium by the Mao Laos. Am. J. Psychiatry 127:1019, 1971.

44. Wieder, H., and Kaplan, E. Drug use in adolescents. Psychoanal. Study Child 24:399, 1969.

45. Wikler, A. A psychodynamic study of a patient during experimental self-regulated re-addiction to morphine. Psychiatr. Q. 26:270, 1952.

46. Wikler, A. Conditioning factors in opiate addiction and relapse. In *Narcotics*, D. N. Wilner and G. G. Kassenbaum, editors. New York, McGraw-Hill, 1965.

47. Wikler, A. Interaction of physical dependence and classical and operant conditioning in the genesis of relapse. Res. Publ. Assoc. Nerv. Ment. Dis. 46:280, 1968.

48. Wikler, A. Some implications of conditioning theory for problems of drug abuse. Behav. Sci. 16:92, 1971.

49. Wikler, A., and Rasor, R. W. Psychiatric aspects of drug addiction. Am. J. Med. 14:566, 1953.

50. Wurmser, L. Methadone and the craving for narcotics: Observations of patients on methadone maintenance in psychotherapy. *Proceedings of the Fourth National Conference on Methadone Treatment*, pp. 525–528. New York, National Association for the Prevention of Addiction to Narcotics, 1972.

51. Wurmser, L. Psychoanalytic consideration of the etiology of compulsive drug use. J. Am. Psychoanal. Assoc. 22:820, 1974.

52. Yorke, C. A critical review of some psychoanalytic literature on drug addiction. Br. J. Med. Psychol. 43: 141, 1970.

53. Zinberg, N. E. Addiction and ego function. Psychoanal. Study Child 30:567, 1975.

CHAPTER 38

VOCATIONAL REHABILITATION

Bertram J. Black, M.S.W.

Harold M. Kase, Ed.D.

Celia Benney, M.S.S.

In the mid-1900's the principal author of this chapter (Bertram Black) served as chairman of mental health program grants committees of the National Institute of Mental Health dealing with community services and later with delinquency. Before both review bodies came a number of proposals to demonstrate treatment and/or rehabilitation of alcoholics and drug abusers (14). Because no known form of cure was available for either condition and the experience of the reviewer was in rehabilitation of recurring, exacerbating illnesses, he was frequently consulted as to the merits of the proposed approaches. His warning that "re-abling" of people with such handicaps, to use a more descriptive British term, takes a long time, in years rather than in weeks, generally fell on deaf ears. Only practitioners with a psychoanalytic bent, thinking in terms of restructuring the personality, would contemplate lengthy treatment, and it was quickly recognized that psychoanalysis or lengthy psychotherapy was a lost cause if not altogether contraindicated.

The parallelism with relapsing, exacerbat-ing illness (such as tuberculosis before the advent of chemotherapy, or heart disease, diabetes, epilepsy, mental illness, etc.) had serious limitations. In the first place neither of the major substance abuses was then clearly accepted as illness; secondly, medical resources were not the most likely to which the sufferer would turn. Questions abounded as to whether whatever intervention was used would be more or less successful if provided in the social environment in which the addiction took place. Psychological theories abounded, and still do, as to the causes for deviance from the major culture. Various chapters in this book give evidence to the many approaches developed upon these theories.

What is pertinent to a discussion of rehabilitation is that almost none of the agencies traditionally experienced in dealing with the handicapped were interested in or found it possible to handle rehabilitation of the substance abusers. Alcoholics and heroin users are looked upon as "hard core," as unmotivated, and as poor rehabilitation risks. Years after the passage of the National Addiction Rehabilitation Act of 1966 (PL 89-73) and the subsequent development of specialized programs, vocational rehabilitation counselors were still saying, "Almost every type of client is easier to deal with than the drug-involved individual" (15).

The title of the 1966 federal act is significant. It is rehabilitation "legislation" rather than "treatment." In contrast to the division of labor usually referred to as between treatment and rehabilitation of the physically handicapped, Congress here enunciated a concept that is only now becoming recognized in services to the mentally disabled. Dale Cameron, drawing on ideas developed by the World Health Organization (WHO), stated (5): "It is often difficult and sometimes impossible to separate concepts of treatment from those of rehabilitation. Rehabilitation begins with the first contact between drug users and 'helping personnel' and continues through the aftercare period. The term 'treatment', as used here, includes rehabilitation." He went on to enunciate the WHO concept that treatment and rehabilitation of drug-dependent persons are not different from those involved for individuals suffering from chronic relapsing disorders in which deviant, often socially unacceptable, behavior is present. The reference, of course, must be to mental illness (see for example, 3). Although a good case can be made for similarities from a medical or health viewpoint, the volume of the substances abuse problems quickly overwhelmed any logical health-minded approaches. Most of the programs developed for dealing with substance abusers are quite distinct from traditional health service practices, even where they are under health or medical auspices.

Although there is no one common denominator in characteristics of substance abusers, there are concentrations that have greatly conditioned the kinds of treatment/rehabilitation programs provided. There is a great aggregation of young people among the drug abusers. This has necessitated building remedial education and prevocational services into the programs. There is generally low motivation for treatment by both drug and alcohol abusers (16). This has led to the development of authoritarian and "outreach" approaches and the use of peer pressure and peer support efforts of social motivation.

Serban made reference to underlying depression in hard drug users (16). Similar findings for "soft" drug abusers abound in the Altro experience described later in this chapter. Depression appears as a constant theme in the descriptions of alcohol abusers by Bell (1) in his book about his Donwood Treatment Plan, and the use of the newer lithium treatment for depressives is increasingly appearing as chemotherapy for alcoholism (10). The largest volume of drug abusers occurs among socially and economically disadvantaged populations, and this has shaped both the location of and format of therapeutic community programs as well as methadone clinics and outreach programs for young amphetamine and barbiturate abusers.

No matter what forms the treatment/rehabilitation services take, however, whether institutional or in open community, whether authoritative or peer supportive, whether chemotherapeutic or without medication, there is an emphasis on preparation for return to the world of work, or what the social anthropologist would call "productive participation" in society—what is more commonly referred to in our context as vocational rehabilitation.

In a special article for *Rehabilitation Literature* updating the rehabilitation of heroin addicts, Schoolar and his colleagues (15) stated emphatically that "In discussing the factors important to successful rehabilitation . . . employment adjustment is always a major scheme," and also "Since we believe that vocational adjustment is extremely important in the overall treatment . . . the TRIMS drug program stresses the vocational aspects of our clients' rehabilitation." More recently, after more than a decade of experience, Dole and Nyswander ascribed apparent limitations of methadone therapy to lack of simultaneous psychosocial rehabilitation that would help the addicts reenter productive living (8).

Preparation for employment is not only an end goal in the treatment/rehabilitation of all types of substance abusers. It has been woven into the very therapeutic processes themselves. Almost every program that has survived over the years has built a strong component of vocational rehabilitation into its therapy. In at least one instance a service for hard drug users has been built around job evaluation, training, and paid work trials. Known as "the Wildcat Way," it has received wide publicity (19). Wildcat, supported by Ford Foundation and government grants, employed heroin addicts under methadone treatment on jobs assisting municipal government in cleaning and repairing tasks, in messenger services, and the like. These were all "entry level" occupations, used to gradually develop working skills. In keeping with many addiction service programs, ex-addicts were employed as work foremen and counselors.

It was William Faulkner who said " . . . One of the saddest things that a man can do for eight hours a day, day after day, is work. You can't eat eight hours a day nor drink for eight hours a day nor make love for eight hours—all you can do for eight hours is work" (quoted in 2). Had Faulkner been a substance abuse therapist he would have added also that you cannot run a therapeutic community confrontation for 8 hours nor administer methadone for hours on end. Work provides a structure, as we shall see, a socially acceptable structure in which rehabilitation can take place, and so it can have a "therapy" all its own.

Fundamental questions to the use of vocational rehabilitation procedures are: Can the substance abuser work? Can the abuser or addict be motivated to employment? Does the disability resulting from substance abuse diminish the vocational abilities of the user? If the answers to the first two questions are positive and that to the third question is not too damaging, then: What processes will be most productive in leading to employment?

Over the years we have learned to avoid stereotyping addiction. As Brill stated (4):

It is better understood today that drug users comprise a wide range of individuals from varying class, ethnic, and geographic backgrounds; with varying psychological and social needs; and with different degrees of involvement with different kinds of drugs or the 'addictive system' . . . We are moving away from the former tendency to focus on the 'terminal cases'—the tertiary stage of chronic addiction in the sense of the confirmed street junkie or chronic alcoholic—as if this constituted the entire population.

Schoolar stated (15): "Even for patients who have made a respectable beginning, on whom vocational rehabilitation may make an impact, there is still the possibility that a stereotyped approach may be self-defeating." He and his colleagues pointed out, nevertheless, that of the adult patients treated in their methadone clinic only 20 to 30 per cent could be said to have anything like a vocation or a beginning employment career.

Dole and Wolkstein (9) are emphatic that ". . . most of the patients in the methadone treatment program professed a desire to work, and after a year of treatment the majority had actually obtained employment of some kind without the help of any vocational placement service." The experience of the Wildcat program and of others gives positive answer to the question, Can the addict work? An interesting study of addiction and employment reported (6): "We have seen that fully 61 percent of the working addicts held a full time job by the time they turned 17, and that a majority entered the labor market before they became addicted to drugs."

The question of motivation is a troubling one. Dole and Nyswander (7) pointed out that: "The transition from the status of an addict on the street to that of a respected member of the community with a family, a decent place to live, and a job measuring up to capabilities, is a long, hard course with roadblocks of discrimination, prejudice, fear, ignorance, and scarcity of jobs." They might have added that lack of education and often of any prior association with the normal workaday world directly or through some working member of the family are also roadblocks to rehabilitation. The formal rehabilitation establishment is accustomed to rely on the patient's motivation, a strong indicator for success in dealing with the physically disabled or the mentally retarded. There is generally little motivation toward entering vocational rehabilitation by persons suffering from schizophrenia, but knowledgeable rehabilitation counselors and facilities proceed to develop it in their clients. The special treatment/rehabilitation programs for the addictions, as described in other chapters, have evolved their own approaches to stimulating or developing motivation for remaining with the "long hard course."

The third question posed above is a necessary one in rehabilitation of chronic relapsing, exacerbating illnesses. We are dealing with a younger population generally without manifest permanent physical handicaps and with disabilities that seem mainly to be educational, social, and cultural and that seem as though they might be overcome. The outlook for vocational rehabilitation of substance abusers, therefore, should be optimistic. The procedures of vocational rehabilitation are predicated upon such optimism.

The Accreditation Council for Psychiatric Facilities of the Joint Commission on Accreditation of Hospitals has developed Standards for Drug Abuse Treatment and Rehabilitation Programs (17). Those for vocational rehabilitation cover the following headings, which are consistent with any good rehabilitation approach:

For each applicant/client there shall be an assessment of his or her vocational status.

The vocational assessment be undertaken by a short-term detoxification program. NOTE: This establishes rehabilitation as beginning with recognition of disability.

A program may delegate vocational rehabilitation responsibilities to an outside vocational rehabilitation agency.

Vocational services, whether by the program or delegated as above, shall be provided in a manner consistent with an individualized written plan, developed in partnership with the client and reflecting his or her strengths and weaknesses.

A client shall receive counseling specifically oriented to his or her vocational needs.

The vocational rehabilitation program shall include job development and the client's job readiness.

Referral to an employer shall be made only upon written authorization from the client to do so.

There shall be regular follow-up and review of the client's vocational status.

Possibly the largest number of substance abusers are served in this manner through cooperation or delegated arrangements with the federal-state vocational rehabilitation program. State offices or divisions of vocational rehabilitation have existed under federal law since 1920 (11). It was not until 1943, however, that this cooperative program was expanded to include mental handicaps, and not until revisions in the Act of 1954 that demonstration projects were opened to public and voluntary agencies including services to the alcoholic and drug abusers (12, 13). Further changes in the federal vocational rehabilitation law have occurred in 1965, 1968, 1973, and 1978, each one adding components of service, provision for research, and, most recently, allowing for "independent living" as a goal along with employment and setting

up an Institute for Handicapped Research.

The significance of the federal-state rehabilitation program to services to the substance abuser is 2-fold. First, through the use of federal funds (which reaches 75 per cent of state expenditures even in a state like New York with liberal state participation), counseling staff is provided by local units of the state agency. Clients of substance abuse programs can be referred directly to the rehabilitation counselor, who, in addition to counseling, may authorize "fees for service" to other rehabilitation agencies, including sheltered workshops and halfway houses. The state agency, however, can also support clients in schooling toward a vocational goal, assist in setting a client up in business, and provide specialized tools for vocational training. Special funds through the federal act have been available for developing vocational rehabilitation programs in community agencies and schools. At the federal level this program is under the auspices of the Rehabilitation Services Administration, Office of Special Education and Rehabilitative Services, Department of Education (18).

A more detailed understanding of the processes of vocational rehabilitation can be gained from a description of the Altro program. Altro Health and Rehabilitation Services, Inc. is a New York-based comprehensive rehabilitation center with many years of experience with chronic, relapsing exacerbating illness. It pioneered in rehabilitation of the mentally ill in the 1950's and experimentally added a range of substance abusers in the early 1970's.

Altro Health and Rehabilitation Services, Inc. and Altro Work Shops, Inc., provide a variety of social, psychological, remedial, and vocational skills training and rehabilitation services geared at leading a client toward self-sufficiency, independence, and, eventually, the world of work. These services are provided by a case management team that generally consists of a social case worker, serving as manager, a psychiatrist, a psychologist, a remedial educator, a nurse, and a vocational instructor.

Before entering the vocational rehabilitation program, some of the clients require detoxification. After a medical and chemical determination of severity of habit through examination and urinalysis, the client undergoes detoxification at one of the cooperating medical services, such as Montefiore Hospital and Medical Center, the Bronx Municipal Hospital Center, or Beth Israel Hospital's Bernstein Institute.

The detoxification units at these facilities provide short term and crisis-oriented treatment to assist the drug abuser or addict in the initial withdrawal process and to diagnose and evaluate his needs. Withdrawal treatment will be provided and social history information gathered. Diagnosis and evaluation are carried out by a team that includes the Altro intake social worker. This preliminary evaluation report will then be provided to the Altro intake team for comprehensive evaluation and referral.

Vocational rehabilitation services offered at Altro Work Shops are provided in a "sheltered" work setting enabling the client to gain progress at his own pace and to move toward increased responsibilities in a gradual steady flow. Clients are paid "sheltered workshop" rates, under supervision and certification of the United States Department of Labor. Traditionally, the entering client is begun at a low wage rate and, as progress is made, the wage rate increases proportionately. As the client begins to reach productivity and wage rate approaching normal minimum standard, this is indicative of his nearing completion of the sheltered work program and of his readiness to seek gainful employment in the regular labor market.

While engaged in the rehabilitation program at Altro Work Shops during the day, the client may already be living independently or may still be a resident of a state hospital, group residence, or other institutional or semiinstitutional facility. Traditionally, Altro maintains close liaison with the referral agency and the client's family to ensure coordination of efforts in leading the client to productivity.

Patients are referred to Altro by a number of institutions and facilities throughout the city in a variety of ways. Often, liaison arrangements utilizing an Altro intake social worker stationed in the referring program provide a fast, efficient, and smooth transition in moving the patient from total institutional care to a more advanced program of Altro's vocational rehabilitation facility. The patient is accepted into one of two major tracks. In the usual track, the patient is accepted for an Altro evaluation. This includes

a full battery of psychological tests, psychiatric interview, history taking, and work sampling in each of the Altro program components. The evaluation period ranges from 4 to 8 weeks and provides the referring institution with a comprehensive picture of the patient's social and vocational potential, as well as professional recommendations as to the best course of treatment for the patient. The second track provides immediate acceptance into the full vocational rehabilitation program of Altro Work Shops. This would involve similar testing as in the evaluation track during an intake period and then placement of the patient into one of Altro's work areas, skipping the work sampling. The workshop facility has capacity for about 500 transitional work patients. Work programs are available in the following areas: garment manufacturing, embracing a wide variety of trades from simple finishing, packaging, and warehousing to complex and skilled sewing and cutting; data processing and computer management; clerical trades; machine shop trades; printing and duplicating; packaging and bench assembly.

Sometimes it is necessary for patients to wait for the program of their choice, because data processing and printing generally have waiting lists. During this waiting period, they are indoctrinated to the sheltered workshop by beginning the rehabilitation process in one of the other work units. The Altro program may be best described by listing the following characteristics:

1. A concern for bringing a group of people with chronic illness and handicapping conditions to the highest level of functioning that is possible.

    a. The objective of minimizing the possibility of relapse or exacerbation of illness.

    b. A process to help the individual understand his illness and avoid conditions that lead to regression.

2. The provision of a network of medical, psychological, social, and vocational services to help individuals reach the potential of return to the world of work.

    a. The use of medical services as part of the team approach to ensure that the individual's medical condition has not been violated. To assure competent diagnosis and to supply consultation to referring medical practitioners, clinics, or hospitals that are providing the ongoing medical or psychiatric treatment.

b. The use of psychological testing to assess the ability of the individual to learn and to work, and as a guide in planning his rehabilitation.

c. The use of social services, vocational consultation, and remedial instruction to the client and to his family where this is indicated. The client is helped to deal with economic, social, and psychological conditions that may affect his rehabilitation and is helped to coordinate the network of community resources on his behalf.

3. The sheltered and rehabilitation setting at Altro Work Shops has the following qualities:

a. It provides a full range of work opportunities and skills training from the simplest operation to relatively sophisticated semiskilled levels.

b. It has the look and feel of a normal work setting in that real equipment is used to perform real work tasks similar to those the client will encounter in the regular world of work.

c. The arrangements of work are such as to preserve the therapeutic quality of rehabilitation; for example, the hours of work for an individual are tailored to meet his medical condition, the pressure upon him at work tasks takes into consideration his ability at the time, and he may be shifted from task to task or setting to setting depending upon his individual rehabilitation needs. His vocational instruction is related to real jobs on hand and is performed in small groups. Remedial instruction is provided in reading job specifications, writing as required by the job, and arithmetic as related to the job assignment. This often is conducted in small groups.

d. The client population constitutes a mix in age range, socioeconomic status, intellectual capacities, and handicapping conditions, comparable to what the patient will encounter in the world of work.

e. There are weekly evaluations of the work progress of each client and a semi-monthly review of his earning capacity with appropriate wage adjustments. Each week a utilization review meeting is held at the workshops, including all team participants and the referring institution's representative, in order to best appraise the client's progress and the next steps in the course of his rehabilitation.

f. The workshops are well integrated into the over-all clinical program of the agency. No individual is allowed to remain in the sheltered setting of Altro Work Shops longer than is best for his own rehabilitation interests.

4. Upon completion of the training, Altro's job development staff, incorporating the recommendation of the interdisciplinary team and those of the host referral facility, will be responsible for a suitable job placement.

Substance abusers who find their way into a vocational rehabilitation agency such as Altro Work Shops, Inc., are a somewhat "select" group. This does not imply superiority in relation to prognosis. In fact, for one subgroup the prognosis, at least for vocational achievement, is quite the contrary. These are those who could not "make it" on the street and who, even with methadone maintenance, did not find it possible to enter or reenter the mainstream of the world of work or vocational education.

The Altro programs have served a group of clients who fall into three general categories:

1. The first category are lower income, former heroin addicts being maintained on methadone and referred primarily from one methadone clinic.

2. A second group consisted of heroin addicts who were heroin free at referral but who often continued to abuse alcohol. This group generally had more ego strength than those in the first group and were capable of sustaining themselves in the program and acquiring vocational skills.

3. A third group consisted of middle-class young people who abused drugs in order to cope with impending or florid psychoses. Many of these were involved with a broad spectrum of multiple drugs and, even when referred as "drug free," often continued to abuse marihuana and/or alcohol. Some experimented with heroin, but the group as a whole did not have long histories of heroin addiction—more often it was variations on the theme of lysergic acid diethylamide (LSD), cocaine, amphetamine, and barbiturates.

Within these categories, sight must not be lost of the many individual and unique differences in life style, native intellectual endowment, drug-related organic cerebral damage, concomitant sociopathy, histories of work achievement, marital status, etc.

Although most clients labled "substance abusers" received rehabilitation services concurrently with attendance at Altro Work Shops, most of those referred from the methadone clinic attended an 8-week prevocational (cognitive skill training) program at Altro Health and Rehabilitation Services. This was an experimental venture with a close liaison relationship between staff of the rehabilitation agency and staff of the methadone clinic.

The most germane finding of the experiment was reinforcement of the necessity for comprehensive clinical assessment, including psychological, medical, social, and language and arithmetic evaluation. The conclusion reached was that the goal of service to many of those referred should be a limited one of maintaining contact with a clinic for supervision of medication and for such social contacts as they could tolerate, be these in the form of therapeutic groups, remedial groups, or task-oriented activities. If the core problem is recognized as one of ego deficits stemming from severe deprivation (emotional, biological, and economic), it follows that this group has great difficulty in establishing authentic relationships. They function with other human beings on an "as if" basis. The loose and somewhat distant involvements in a clinic setting offer the necessary human nourishment without demanding much emotional commitment. To set goals toward enhanced vocational competency and reentry or entry to the world of work is not only frustrating for clients and staff but economically wasteful.

An example of such a situation is the following:

Ms. Mary D., a 34-year-old woman referred by a methadone clinic, had a history of drug abuse since the age of 15 and heroin addiction since age 16, a habit she supported by prostitution. She also had a history of barbiturate abuse but was said to be free of this at the point of initial contact. Background data revealed an alcoholic mother with a history of hospitalization for psychiatric reasons, a brother alleged to be a drug pusher, and a deceased father who died of a gunshot wound when she was 22. Subsequent to her father's death, she felt impelled to leave her mother's home, claiming her mother resented her because of the client's strong attachment to her father.

Ms. D. had dropped out of school in the eighth grade and tested in the low dull normal range with a marked perceptual analytic deficit.

She presented as tough and hard and manipulative, a facade for her obvious anxiety and dependence. In the Altro program she showed ability to learn and she continued with remedial reading classes at the clinic. However, her anger, tendency to flee from painful situations, defensiveness, poor impulse control, and excessive clinging demands for staff time interfered greatly with her progress. Although giving verbal acquiescence to continued rehabilitation, she was subsequently unable to maintain contact, and it was felt that she could not cope with the demands of a vocational program. It was recommended that efforts be directed toward maintaining her in the clinic program and that she be given nurturance and support on the one hand and that on the other she be confronted with her anger and manipulations and how these served to alienate people. It was recognized that she was a depressive personality who had coped with this aspect of her problem by buying "Elavil" on the street; recommendation was made that she be offered a medically supervised antidepressant.

In several cases, suicidal depression was a repetitive theme among the methadone clients, who came from severely pathological deprived backgrounds. With limited ego strengths and minimal if any environmental supports, they generally could not be maintained in the vocationally oriented environment where any expectations were perceived as overwhelming.

Of course, there were exceptions, and these represented those who had work histories and some family supports. One man of 38, orphaned at 5, did have an older sister, an aunt, and an uncle who sustained interest in him, and, in spite of his complaints about mistreatment by relatives, there was a continued interest and contact on their part, reducing social isolation. He had been able to achieve marriage, albeit one fraught with serious problems that led to separation, and was the father of four children whom he saw occasionally. Although he had a history of arrests and a history of addiction for 15 years, there was no history of violence, and he was alleged to have held one job for 5 years. He had been sent to several schools for training but had dropped out of all programs. Although he did well in the Altro program and was able to remain for 8 weeks, he defeated attempts to help him vocationally by unrealistic requests for training for which he was not qualified. Again, he was referred back to the clinic for continued work toward taking the high school equivalency test. He was able to achieve this and ultimately did secure employment, which was, however, short lived. His basic dependency needs, however, continued to be met by the clinic.

A second group was similar to the above in socioeconomic cultural deprivation but had greater ego strengths and basic endowment, and with these there was achieved a much higher degree of vocational success.

Ms. Dorothy G. is illustrative. She is a person whose long history of multiple drug abuse, life style in a high crime area, emotionally deprived background, and medical history would augur poorly for successful vocational rehabilitation.

Aged 45, she began to use heroin in 1950 and continued until 1966, using not only heroin, but also cocaine and a variety of other drugs. She supported her addiction by stealing and also to some extent by dealing in drugs. She gave up the heroin "cold turkey" but then turned to alcohol.

Background history reveals that she is one of three siblings whose mother died when she was 12 years old and whose father was unknown to her. Her mother had been ill for some years before her death, and to a great extent the children brought themselves up.

Ms. G. had a relationship for 15 years with a man she met at age 20, a man who was an alcoholic and a drug addict. She had five children with him, all of whom were placed in foster care when she was declared an unfit mother. Shortly before her referral to Altro, this decision was reversed and she began to have some contact with one of her daughters. In addition, she continued contact with one of her siblings.

Medically she had a history of tuberculosis, malnutrition, blackouts, and accidents resulting in facial scars.

On the positive side, she had been able to work for a short period in a clerical capacity. In spite of her long history of drug and alcohol abuse, she still tested psychologically on an above average level and had excellent finger dexterity. It was noted by the Altro psychologist that she had suffered from a lifelong sense of loneliness and depression.

In spite of her history, she appeared as a likeable woman who used her sense of humor to avoid difficult issues. Although she had areas of capability, it was quickly apparent to the counselor that she was quite fragile and had great difficulty trusting people. She was, however, ultimately able to develop a relationship with a counselor who was available to her for ongoing help in developing self-awareness, enhancing impulse control, as well as nonjudgmentally helping her during her periods of relapse from sobriety. These relapses usually occurred during transition points involving greater responsibility vocationally—i.e., when assigned to an agency job site after training in the clerical field, and when outside job placement was imminent, etc. It required 2 1/2 years of intensive psychological, social, and vocational service to enable her to be ready to take a job. She was helped to reestablish a relationship with her children, to move from her extremely deteriorated neighborhood, and to remain connected with a psychological treatment facility.

Her ability to use rehabilitation services toward a vocational goal rested in part upon her residual ego strengths as manifested by her capacity to form sustained relationships, her ability voluntarily to "kick" the heroin addiction, and her capacity to concentrate and learn and to achieve some awareness and insight into her self-destructive behavior.

The rehabilitation components of a nurturing but firm counselor and the availability of a realistic but benign vocational training milieu, plus the integration of community supports over a fairly lengthy period of time, were all essential factors in her progress.

Another young man of 30, with an equally difficult pathological background and even less by way of native endowment and capacity, was also successfully rehabilitated. He, too, had a long history of heroin and cocaine addiction and had been involved in a number of arrests, dealing in arms, drugs, and "hot" merchandise to support his habit. He was the eldest of six children who grew up in a home where the father was an addict and the mother an alcoholic. Yet he had a strong sense of loyalty and devotion to his mother, was able to move into a marriage, albeit short lived because of his addiction, and had a sense of responsibility to his young child currently living with the separated wife. He had a history of 5 years of steady employment on one job (rather low level) even while on drugs.

Apparently, too, in spite of his antisocial behavior, he had considerable remaining superego, leading to guilt and depression. He, too, was able to detoxify from heroin, although he did it in a hospital.

He saw work as a defense against his destructive impulses. He was also motivated by his desire to achieve financial independence.

During the course of his evaluation at the Altro Work Shops, he was given psychological tests that revealed borderline intelligence in the verbal area, and it was found that he functioned on a mentally retarded level in performance. It was noted that he could do practical manual and mechanical activities involving assembly and working with pictorial representation, provided the tasks were simple enough to give him a feeling of personal adequacy.

When tested by an educational therapist, his reading level was 4.7 and arithmetic 3.2. He adapted readily to the workshop setting where he was placed initially in mechanical assembly program. His attendance was near perfect; he became socially involved with his peers, including women, and attended remedial reading and arithmetic classes regularly. Initially discouraged, he made very good progress when assigned to a male teacher who focused on those aspects of arithmetic directly related to his work in the machine shop where he was ultimately placed—such elements as shop measurement and blueprint reading. Although slow, he persevered and learned.

Emotional and concrete supports were provided by a case worker who also served as a role model and whom he gradually came to trust. As he began to move toward employment, his anxiety began to mount and lateness became a problem. In his clinical sessions, separation anxiety was discussed as well as the reality losses of welfare, Medicaid, and the supportive environment that would be attendant upon competitive employment. Nevertheless, with continued help, he was able to move into a machine tool operator job.

The third, and by far the largest group served at Altro, included those who abused drugs in an attempt to ward off or cope with the dangers of impending or florid psychosis. As with other groups, this is not a homogeneous body, but consists of a wide range of persons for whom individual assessment and individual goals must be determined—based on ego assessment, family and community supports, motivation, and degree of pathology.

Mr. D. was a 24-year-old college graduate, personable but unkempt, and intellectually in the very superior range. His parents were professional people, and his background was upper middle class. Referred with a diagnosis of schizoaffective psychosis, he had had four hospitalizations. His substance abuses had consisted of marihuana, hash, peyote, cocaine, heroin, and many LSD trips. When referred for vocational rehabilitation, he was still heavily committed to "pot." Although he claimed to have given up the other drugs, he constantly threatened his counselor that he might return to their use.

Initially he had great difficulty handling problems of daily living—housekeeping, dealing with banks, landlords, managing money, medical care, etc. He had been treated with lithuim, which had reduced some of his manic symptoms and helped his depression somewhat, although he continued to mourn the loss of his father and resorted to marihuana to ease some of the pain of feeling guilty and yet abandoned. His psychiatric problem had become manifest when he was quite young (about 15), and he was probably able to complete his education only because his intellectual capacity made this possible with a minimum of effort. As his symptoms became more invasive, he began to use drugs.

During the course of rehabilitation, he was assigned to a data processing program. He gradually developed a relationship with his counselor, who was supportive and related to his mood changes, so that he could deal with precipitating factors that triggered depressions before they became overwhelming. His experienced counselor also mitigated the pressure of the family's high expectations and provided special support during transition points, such as entering schooling for advanced technical training and ultimately job placement. During the course of his 3-year contact with Altro, he did not resume multiple drug abuse and was ultimately able to function in competitive employment.

Although no single factor can explain

either drug addiction or psychosis, empirical experience leads to the belief that some apparent "drug-induced psychosis" might well be labeled in reverse as "psychosis-induced drug abuse." One wonders whether in another period of history this group might have sought relief from pain in more socially acceptable and more structured outlets, e.g., the army, religious retreats, careers at sea.

Mr. L. T., age 30, is a case in point. Although referred for vocational rehabilitation with the diagnosis of drug-induced psychosis, an intensive clinical study quickly pointed to a preexisting paranoid schizophrenia. Mr. L. T. came with a history of having used cocaine, heroin, and alcohol. He began using the drugs upon completion of high school when he felt his mother was pushing him toward heterosexual activities. Even then, he felt he actually was a woman (a delusion that persisted even through the early months of rehabilitation).

His employment history also revolved around his sexual identity conflict, and he felt he was fired from each job because of his appearance (trying to look like a woman).

On a socioeconomic level, he was one of five siblings born out of wedlock and raised by his mother under economically deprived circumstances. Mr. L. T., although now living apart from his mother, retained close ties to her.

Rehabilitation services included vocational training and counseling directed toward improvement in self-esteem, containment of his delusion, encouragement of artistic vocational interests, and control of his angry impulses. Strongly dependent, he experienced considerable regression upon separation from the workshop but ultimately was able to move into a part time supervised employment program.

In conclusion, vocational rehabilitation for substance abusers rests upon a conceptual framework that has the traditional three-pronged components of the rehabilitation process: medical (includes psychiatric), psychosocial, and vocational. Selected experiences of rehabilitation agencies would seem to indicate that many, if not most, of those abusers who come to their attention will not meet our careful assessment in the above areas.

Services must include psychosocial treatment concomitantly with vocational activities, and goals must be individually tailored both in the interests of the client and in cost to the community.

References

1. Bell, R. G. *Escape from Addiction.* New York, McGraw-Hill, 1970.
2. Black, B. J. *Principles of Industrial Therapy for the Mentally Ill*, p. 2. New York, Grune and Stratton, 1970.
3. Black, B. J. Rehabilitation of long-term mental patients: Where is the asylum? Int. J. Ment. Health 6: 27, 1978.
4. Brill, L. Historical evolution of the current drug treatment perspective. In *Rehabilitation Aspects of Drug Dependence*, A. Schecter, editor, pp. 11–20. Cleveland, Ohio, CRC Press, 1977.
5. Cameron, D. C. Drug dependence: Broad perspectives and international approaches. In *Rehabilitation Aspects of Drug Dependence*, A. Schecter, editor, pp. 82–83, Cleveland, Ohio, CRC Press, 1977.
6. Caplovitz, D. Work history of working addicts. In *The Working Addict*, p. 30. White Plains, N. Y., M. E. Sharpe, 1978.
7. Dole, V. P., and Nyswander, M. Rehabilitation of methadone patients. N. Y. State J. Med. 74:1416, 1974.
8. Dole, V. P., and Nyswander, M. Methadone maintenance treatment: A ten year perspective. J.A.M.A. 235:2117, 1976.
9. Dole, V. P., and Wolkstein, E. C. Vocational rehabilitation of patients on the Beth Israel methadone maintenance program. Mt. Sinai J. Med. 41:267, 1974.
10. Kline, N. S., and Cooper, T. B. Evaluation of lithium therapy in alcoholism in the *Effects of Centrally Active Drugs on Voluntary Alcohol Consumption*, pp. 143–153. Helsinki, The Finnish Foundation for Alcohol Studies, 1975.
11. Public Law 236, 66th Congress, 1920.
12. Public Law 113, 78th Congress, 1943.
13. Public Law 565, 83rd Congress, 1954.
14. Public Law 911, 84th Congress, Title V, 1955.
15. Schoolar, J. C., Winburn, G. M., and Hays, J. R. Rehabilitation of drug abusers: A continuing enigma. Rehabil. Lit. 34:327, 1973.
16. Serban G. New approach to the rehabilitation of the hard core drug addict: A pilot community study. J. Clin. Psychiatry 39:111, 1978.
17. Vocational rehabilitation. In *Standards for Drug Abuse Treatment and Rehabilitation Programs*, chapter 21, pp. 61–63. Chicago, Accreditation Council for Psychiatric Facilities, Joint Commission on Accreditation of Hospitals, 1975.
18. Whitten, E. B. Disability and physical handicap: Vocational rehabilitation. In *Encyclopedia of Social Work*, R. Morris et al., editors, 16th issue, vol. 1, pp. 236–245. New York, National Association of Social Workers, 1971.
19. (The) Wildcat Way. The New York Times Magazine, pp. 56–60, 67–78. April 28, 1974.

CHAPTER 39

THE USE OF BEHAVIOR MODIFICATION TECHNIQUES IN DEVELOPING SOCIALLY APPROPRIATE BEHAVIORS IN SUBSTANCE ABUSERS

Frances E. Cheek, Ph.D.

Marie DiStefano Miller, M.A.

REVIEW OF STUDIES IN THIS AREA TO DATE

Although some investigators have attempted to treat substance abusers by dealing only with their drug-using behaviors, others have noted that almost inevitably the drug-using individual suffers from numerous life problems associated with a complex of inadequate and often self-destructive attitudes and behaviors, often created by his drug use, which must be addressed if he is to develop a drug-free existence. Thus, research has shown addicts to be characterized by a meager affective life, low self-esteem, anxiety, irrational thinking, and inappropriate assertiveness (24) and to be impulsive, undepend-able, self-indulgent, and lacking in the persistence to achieve a goal (36, 38, 45). Indeed, some have felt that the strengthening of socially appropriate behaviors should have priority in the treatment process. This chapter deals with attempts to manipulate this attitudinal and behavioral complex, as an adjunct to treatment of the drug abuse per se, by means of ideas and techniques from the area of behavior modification. Treatment of alcoholism by these methods will not be included because, although use of behavior modification techniques in this area has been extensive, it presents a special problem and has been adequately reviewed elsewhere (49).

A recognition of the learned aspects of drug-using behavior, first proposed by Lindesmith (47) and later put forth by many others (1, 6, 27, 31, 53, 61, 67) has encouraged many investigators to attempt to utilize behavior modification approaches in the treatment of the drug-using behavior itself. In a comprehensive review of the literature on behavioral techniques in the treatment of drug abuse, Gotestam and his associates (39) listed 17 studies in which the drug-using behavior per se was the target. Aversion therapies (faradic, chemical, and imaginal) and extinction (classical and covert) were utilized. In the first case, drug-using behaviors were associated with negative experiences such as electroshock, such drug-induced reactions as vomiting, or undesirable imaged situations. In the second case, detoxification was achieved by gradually conditioning the patient to an alternative stimulus as injection occurred or by having the patient imagine no effect after injection.

However, many investigators recognized a need to build up alternative behaviors to the drug use itself, if not to address additional socially inappropriate attitudes and behaviors, which is the primary focus of this chapter. Thus, 16 studies are also reported in Gotestam's review in which an attempt was made to strengthen alternative behaviors and/or to build up socially appropriate ones by behavior modification techniques, usually in addition to working on the drug-using behavior with these methods or with others. These studies and subsequent work in the field are described below. Five modalities were utilized. Two (desensitization-relaxation and covert conditioning) employed primarily conditioning techniques; two (contingency contracting and token economy) involved a reinforcement paradigm; and the fifth (a broad spectrum approach) combined several techniques, often from both behavioral approaches.

COVERT DESENSITIZATION AND RELAXATION

In covert desensitization, a state of relaxation plus alternative images of increasingly tense scenes followed by a calm scene are utilized to reduce tension in an up-tight situation (69). This approach is of particular interest in the treatment of drug abuse in view of the reported presence of high tension or social anxiety in the heroin addict (16, 21).

Indeed, Kraft (43) suggested that the basic disturbance in drug addiction is frequently one of social anxiety and that when this has been corrected the patient no longer requires drugs for his support. However, most of the reported work of this kind has involved abusers of drugs other than heroin. Thus, Kraft (43) used it to reduce social anxiety in a 20-year-old male addicted to Drinamyl (dexamphetamine plus amylobarbital). Three other papers described its effective use in treating lysergic acid diethylamide (LSD) flashbacks (2, 50, 62), and successful termination of a "bad trip" from LSD use is reported by Suinn and Brittain (64). On the other hand, the practice of meditation and biofeedback training, both much utilized in the area of heroin abuse, also involves states of deep relaxation.

COVERT CONDITIONING

Covert conditioning techniques, including covert sensitization and covert modeling, thought stoppage, and covert control, usually utilize imagery in which the problem behavior is associated with a negative or no consequence and/or the alternative behavior is rewarded. Cautela (8) has been primarily responsible for the development of this area. Flannery (34) reported treatment of a psychedelic user with behavioral rehearsal, thought stopping, covert modeling, and covert control, which was successful in the short run but not at a 6-month follow-up. A self-control model was utilized, with the patient being taught to act as her own therapist. Wisocki (68) reported treating a heroin user with similar methods. Wisocki's aim, in addition to eliminating the drug behavior, was to improve self-concept and to establish prosocial behaviors, and this combination of techniques may acccount for the patient remaining drug free over an 18-month follow-up period. In an interesting use of these procedures in a group setting, Duehn (29) reported treatment of seven male users of amphetamine, LSD, and marihuana with covert sensitization, including self-administration of covert sensitization procedures at home to develop aversions to other drugs. Imagined withdrawal from the scene without drug use was rewarded by positive imagery. Six of seven were drug free at an 18-month follow-up; one was lost to the study.

However, Droppa's (28) study with four heroin users, using desensitization on one and sensitization procedures with the other three, proved unsuccessful, failing to reduce craving in the user treated with desensitization and producing no more than a temporary decrease in drug craving with the sensitization procedures. Interestingly, where an attempt was made to build up alternative behavior to the drug, success was somewhat greater, and Droppa concluded his study with a recommendation that a broad spectrum approach be utilized.

TOKEN ECONOMY

Ideally, token economy involves systematic observation of patient behaviors, designation of desirable behaviors, and designation of reinforcers, tokens, and rules of exchange (44). Although not always meeting all these specifications, it has been utilized in several settings with drug abusers. Glicksman et al. (37) described one of the first attempts in this area, in which addicts were released from the treatment program when a certain number of points were earned by desirable behaviors. The subjects were 32 male heroin abusers. In a follow-up evaluation conducted by Ottomanelli (57), no significant changes could be found in personality as measured by the Minnesota Multiphasic Personality Inventory (MMPI), nor did these clients differ from those treated at the facility by other modalities with regard to aftercare retention rates. However, it was discovered that the token economy was responsible for positive behavioral adjustments to the institutional setting as measured by program participation. Significant changes in institutional adjustment, in terms of reduced client drug use and reduced highly aggressive behavior, were also achieved by using the return of good time as a reinforcer in a study of 16 inmate addicts (44).

Coghlan et al. (26) utilized a token economy within a psychodynamic residential context. The program was structured around four stages with several levels within each stage. New privileges and new responsibilities were introduced to the client in each stage. Points were given daily in the first two stages for improving behavioral problems, as well as work in the cottage, school, etc. Unfortunately, details of the subsequent stages are scant, as are treatment data and results. A similar treatment program, utilizing five instead of four stages, is described by Clayton (25). Here, the token reinforcement was discontinued when the clients, who were adolescents, reached the fourth stage. In addition to the token economy, group therapy, family therapy, and activity therapy were utilized. Hence, any treatment results could not be directly attributable to token economy. Once again, no outcome data were presented.

A very well developed token economy program for 52 addicts was described by Eriksson et al. (32). The drugs abused by these clients were opiates, amphetamine, and hallucinogens. Points were given for 35 desirable target behaviors representing varying levels of difficulty. Ten back-up reinforcers, consisting of privileges and consumables, were obtained when a specific number of points were earned. The investigators found a significantly higher target behavior activity level for the clients during program periods than during nonprogram periods.

In a more recent report MacDonough (48) provided some interesting information on the relative effectiveness of behavioral versus other modalities in a carefully designed evaluation of two kinds of drug and alcohol rehabilitation programs for active military personnel. One was a medically oriented hospitalization program, which treated 260; the other was a short run therapeutic community program structured in terms of a collection of feedback and behavior modification techniques, which treated 252 clients. In the case of the drug abusers, the behavioral approach proved superior, whereas in the case of the alcohol abusers, no significant difference appeared between the two modalities.

CONTINGENCY CONTRACTING

In contingency contracting, contracts are made in which the relationship between the target behavior and positive or negative consequences is specified (63). Boudin (3) was the first to describe the use of this technique in the treatment of drug addiction. In this case, an abuser of amphetamine agreed to a contract in which any drug use or suspected drug use resulted in money being sent to an organization disliked by the patient (the Ku Klux Klan). The contract required a very close 24-hour consultative relationship between therapist and client. The patient remained drug free over a 13-month follow-up. Subsequently, Boudin and Valentine (4) expanded their contingency contracting model by delineating obligations, consequences, privileges, bonuses, and special situations.

Polakow and Doctor (58) described the use of contracting for a married couple in a probationary setting where the performance of one nondrug-related activity per week reduced the total probationary period by 1 week. In a later paper (59) the authors reported that successively more difficult positive behaviors of their probationaries were achieved and maintained on reinforcement through a three-stage process, whereas deviant and drug-related behaviors were diminished through counterconditioning. In comparing the results of this behavior modification approach with traditional probationary contact, the authors maintained that new arrests, probationary violation, work attendance, and duration were significantly altered.

Contingency contracting has also been used in the treatment of heroin addicts in a psychiatric hospital ward. O'Brien et al. (56) described the first ward program of this sort in which various target behaviors—such as getting up in the morning, cleaning, obeying rules, attending meetings, etc.—were rewarded by access to radio and television, access to the recreation room, wearing street clothes, and having visitors and passes. One hundred and fifty patients participated in this study, the majority being males. During the treatment phase, there was a 60 per cent increase of target behaviors performed.

Melin and Gotestam (52) described a similar use of contracting in a program for 16 female amphetamine addicts that included three phases: detoxification, treatment, and rehabilitation. Advancement was achieved by the patients' attaining specified numbers of points for successfully performed target behaviors. The investigators found that some specific behaviors altered positively—there was significantly higher frequency of getting up in the morning, less use of prescribed drugs, and a decrease in the number of phone calls to doctors. A modified form of these procedures is reported in a methadone maintenance program for 25 heroin addicts by Melin et al. (51) that led to greater participation in program activities. Contingency contracting and self-monitoring were utilized

with incarcerated females by Moinat and Snortum (54) over a 9-week period to promote self-control. The targeted behaviors were smoking, food intake, fingernail biting, hair twisting, and telling lies. Improvement in final performance as compared to baseline levels was demonstrated in 16 of 17 projects. Self-praise and social reinforcement proved as effective as material rewards.

In an interesting study, Boudin and his associates (5) utilized contingency contracting with drug abusers in the natural environment. In an attempt to shape goal-directed behavior, the investigators sought to replace behaviors associated with a drug-dependent life style with behaviors associated with functional antagonists such as work/school, project requirements, and proper individual and social behaviors. Case outcome, in terms of adjustment on all four criterion variables during a 15-month follow-up period, was positive for all those who graduated from the program.

BROAD SPECTRUM APPROACHES

As in behavior therapy generally (46), the need for a broader approach, addressing a range of behaviors and attitudes and involving a variety of techniques, was posited in the behavioral treatment of substance abusers. The earliest statement of this appears in the work of Dr. Frances Cheek (10, 19, 23) in which training in relaxation, desensitization, self-image improvement, behavior analysis, behavior management, assertive training, and rational thinking were presented to heroin addicts in a program of methadone build-up with the purpose of fostering self-awareness and self-control. This program will be described in detail later in this chapter.

The second report was the work of O'Brien and Raynes (55), who suggested that comprehensive treatment of drug abuse would involve the building up of suitable alternative drug-free behavior or behaviors. Working with 17 heroin addicts and three barbiturate users, their combination approach included applied relaxation, desensitization, assertive training and aversive therapy, contingency contracting, family contracting, and self-monitoring. On a 2-year (median) follow-up, ratings of improvement were predominantly positive. A study of Callner and Ross (7) drew upon one technique only that has been identified with the broad spectrum approach, namely assertive training, in treating eight drug abusers. Verbal performance, in terms of affect, duration, and fluency in a behavioral performance situation improved, but not questionnaire responses.

SUMMARY

In most cases, as Gotestam and his associates noted, it is difficult to evaluate the effectiveness of the behavioral approaches described above because of inadequacies of population size and description, research design, and short and long-term assessment procedures. However, the work in the field shows a clear movement from simple approaches to eliminating the drug-using behavior itself to a concern for building up alternative behaviors and then to an interest in addressing a broad range of inadequate and inappropriate attitudes and behaviors. The studies also show a shift from working on attitudes and behaviors while the drug user is in an inpatient setting to working in the natural life setting. Finally, the beginnings of a movement from external control to self-control are seen.

In the next section we will describe a program developed by Dr. Cheek in which an attempt was made to build up a variety of strategic socially appropriate attitudes and behaviors in the addict by teaching him a number of modification self-control-enhancing ideas and techniques while in an inpatient setting but aimed at carryover to his natural life setting. This program, which was utilized as an adjunct to a program of methadone maintenance build-up, was the first to employ a broad spectrum approach in the treatment of drug addiction and the first to emphasize the importance of developing self-control in the addict through behavior modification training. In another way it also pioneered, in that it recognized the importance of training other persons associated with the addict—namely inpatient staff, family members, and outpatient staff—in the same techniques so that they might function as appropriate role models and behavior reinforcers for the addict while in the inpatient setting or when returned to the community.

SELF-AWARENESS AND SELF-CONTROL TRAINING FOR ADDICTS AND THE STAFF WORKING WITH THEM

The program was developed by Dr. Cheek during the late 1960's and early 1970's at the New Jersey Neuropsychiatric Institute (19). It originated in attempts to teach behavior modification techniques to parents of convalescent schizophrenics so that they might modify undesirable behaviors of their offspring (18). However, the program moved on to work with alcoholics and their spouses (14), drug addicts (23), staff working with drug addicts (22), mental patients (17), and most recently prison inmates (13) and corrections staff (20).

Thus, two forms of the program for addicts exist, a client program and a staff program. In connection with the behavior modification program for alcoholics at the institute, a family program was also developed. However, although the importance of this type of program for families of addicts was recognized and such a program was planned, it was never carried out at the institute. In both client and staff programs the same techniques and ideas are taught, namely deep relaxation; desensitization; self-image improvement; behavior analysis; behavior management; social skills of complimenting, criticizing, and apologizing; and assertive training and rational thinking. However, the presentation differs in terms of the focus of the program, the number of participants in the training programs, and the kinds of time schedules in which the program is taught.

THE ADDICT PROGRAM

For the addict, the training takes place in eight 2-hour sessions (one per week for 8 weeks). The training groups ideally consist of 10 or 12 participants. Usually, there are two group leaders plus one or two addict group leader aides who assist in translating the material to the life of the addict. The program consists of lectures, explaining the nature of each technique and how it can be useful, group discussions, exercises, and role playing. A training manual is given to each group member in which all the material of the program is presented, including the outline of each meeting, the lectures, techniques, playlets, and role-playing situations, as well as poetry, quotations, and pictures that illustrate the material. The group meetings are supplemented by voluntary private sessions in which the materials are further worked over and their utilization discussed. Diplomas are given for completing at least six of the eight sessions.

The first three meetings of the addict program deal with inner experience and the remainder with outer experience. The training begins with inner experience because it is believed that the addict's heritage of attitudes from the past of hostility, frustration, resentment, insecurity, etc., will dominate his perceptions of himself and of others, his thoughts, his feelings, and his behaviors so that new learning and growth are obstructed. Not this negative heritage from the past, but the individual himself, must be in control.

The content of the eight meetings is as follows.

Meeting 1—Orientation and Relaxation Training

The addict program begins with an orientation in which its basic aim and the nature and purpose of each technique are made clear. Participants are told that, to a very large extent, they themselves shape their own lives. Thus, their lives flow out of, first, their inner experiences, their thoughts, feelings, attitudes, pictures of themselves; and, second, their outer experiences, how they act toward others and how they react to the behaviors and attitudes of others. However, this process is not necessarily a conscious one, so that sometimes past experiences and past learning dominate our lives without our conscious, rational, objective choice. They are told that the program will help them to become more *aware* of how their inner and outer experiences shape their lives and that this awareness is a first step in control. They are also told that they will be taught simple but effective methods of changing their inner and outer experiences, if they wish to do so, to produce consequences in their lives that they really have chosen consciously, rationally, and objectively.

As a first step, to help addicts become free of the past and rationally in control of themselves, methods of deep relaxation are taught,

for attitudes, feelings, and behaviors are bound and defended by tension, hostility, and emotional withdrawal. A variation of Jacobsen's progressive muscle relaxation technique (40) is employed, plus two additional methods involving feelings of "lightness" and "heaviness," as well as a brief form of "self-relaxation." Participants are asked to tighten then relax various muscle groups, beginning with the feet and legs and ending with the face. Deep breathing is included as part of the exercise.

It is pointed out that, in addition to promoting personal growth and self-control, the relaxation techniques can be useful in reducing the anxiety and tension associated with giving up an addiction and the subsequent problems of building a new life and that they may promote good physical and mental health as well as physical, intellectual, and social effectiveness.

Participants then begin to learn the deliberate control of tension through imagery. They are instructed, while they are relaxed, to think of a "calm scene" (lying on the beach, walking in the woods), so that this scene will become "glued" to the state of deep relaxation. When later they bring it to mind, perhaps in a tense situation, the calm scene will trigger a state of relaxation that will give them more control over their own behavior so that they may function more effectively.

Meeting 2—Desensitization

In the second meeting, the work with self-control through relaxation and imagery is continued as participants are taught how to defuse in advance specific situations that would ordinarily make them tense and uptight and reduce self-control. In the case of addicts, these might include being offered a drug by an old friend, meeting with the hostility of family members, or looking for a job after leaving the treatment facility. This is accomplished by the technique of "covert desensitization" (70).

Participants are first taught to rate their own level of tension at any time on a subjective scale from 0 to 100. This is to help them evaluate the effectiveness of the tension-reducing methods they will learn, but it also makes them more aware of the physical and emotional concomitants of tension so they may effectively check acceleration as tension begins to rise. Next, participants learn how to image a tense scene. Now, while relaxed, they will hold the tense scene in mind for 20 seconds, then shift to the calm scene for 20 seconds, alternating three or four times. In the beginning they work with a scene of low tension (60 or so) to master the technique. Later, they may move on to scenes of greater tension. If the scene chosen is one of very high tension, they are taught to use a hierarchy of two or three lower to higher level scenes.

Meeting 3—Self-image Improvement

Self-image is usually a problem for addicts whose past experiences typically leave them feeling guilty, ashamed, resentful, and lacking in self-confidence. Participants are made aware of the inner television set that each has in his head and on which are played over scenes from the past, present, and future. How these visualizations can influence one's life is demonstrated. Thus, thinking of a wrong action in the past, one feels ashamed; this feeling is reflected in one's posture and one's manner of approaching others, and this influences how they respond in return. Participants learn deliberately to put positive images of themselves in their minds to affect their feelings and behavior favorably, utilizing Susskind's "idealized self-image technique" (65).

An important part of the self-image work has to do with handling the past self, in terms of accepting that one has indeed engaged in wrong behaviors; the present self, in terms of really experiencing and living in the present; and the future self, in terms of moving into the future with change and growth rather than drifting. In the work on the future self, the concern is with goal setting, an area in which many addicts have problems. For instance, an addict might say, "I want to change my life in every way," suggesting a shotgun approach that could be of little use to him. He would be taught to select one area of his life to work on at a time and to begin with one on which it was possible to start immediately and observe positive change right away so that he might have immediate and positive feedback. Visualizations of taking the first positive step would be utilized.

To further assist the addict in developing a more positive self-image, two exercises are utilized, the "I am" technique, and the "Trade Last Game." In the "I am" technique, participants are asked to complete 10 "I am" statements so as to present the 10 most important things about them. They are asked not to include too many status statements, like "I am black, married, etc." but rather to express significant things about their personality and situation. They are told they may include, if they wish, both positive and negative statements, as well as past, present, and future references. Each group member is then asked to read his "I am" statements to the group. The exercise has a dual positive aspect in that it gets the individual to look deeply into himself and also helps him to become more aware of and interested in what is going on in others around him. Moreover, it tends to bring the group together.

In the Trade Last Game, each participant is asked to write down what he regards as his three best physical and three best personality characteristics, as well as what he regards as the one best physical and one best personality characteristic of each other member of the group. Then the group leader reads out what each has said about himself and what the others have said about him. His own self-comments are later returned to the participant plus the added positive comments of the others. This, again, has a very positive effect on both the individual and the group. The most sceptical and reluctant are typically most eager to secure the paper with all the positive comments about themselves.

Meeting 4—How Behavior Is Influenced

The transition to work on outer experience now begins. Participants are now shown how people actually influence one another in their interaction together, how sometimes undesirable behavior in one's self is shaped and maintained by others, or how undesirable behavior in others may be shaped and maintained by oneself, often unconsciously. This is called "learning to write one's own script"—not being the bad actor in someone else's play.

Many addicts have not been taught that much of their behavior has been learned. This is pointed out, as are the kinds of settings (family, peer group, etc.) in which this learning takes place and the methods (instruction, modeling, reward and punishment, etc.) that are involved. The kinds of rewards that influence behavior are examined, with descriptions and examples of basic versus secondary rewards; material, social, and inner rewards; and immediate or delayed rewards. The disadvantages of punishment as a way of changing behavior are examined, and the importance of working with delayed rewards and of finding inner rewards is stressed. In the addict population too much and too severe punishment may have been given in early life with consequent learning of escape mechanisms, hostile attitudes, and violent behaviors. Also, in the early years the importance of delayed and inner rewards may not have been taught, with later negative career effects because of overconcern with immediate and material rewards.

To help addicts examine their own value system, they are given a list of eight values (wealth, respect, health, etc.) and asked to rank order them in terms of those that they would least be willing to give up. In taking part in this exercise and then in sharing their rankings with other group members they become more aware of what they really value, as well as their differences and similarities to others.

Finally, in this meeting, several brief playlets that participants act out illustrate how individuals may influence one another in interaction—how undesirable behavior often produces additional undesirable behavior, whereas desirable behavior often promotes desirable behavior.

Meeting 5—How Behavior May Be Changed

In this meeting, the addicts are taught how to change the behavior of others, using ideas and principles from behavior modification. Many times they must deal with the hostility and disrespect of others as a result of their own past behaviors. It is pointed out that the most common ways in which people try to change the negative attitudes and behaviors and/or bad habits of others—namely, by nagging, criticism, hostile attack, etc.—are frequently unsuccessful and, even if successful, often make the attacker a negative stimulus for the other person.

According to behavior modification principles, to change the behavior of others it is first necessary to change one's own behavior and attitudes. If one has, as a consequence of the undesirable behavior of the other person, become tense, angry, and rejecting, these attitudes and the behaviors that go with them will automatically make one a poor behavior modifier. So the first step is to calm down and recognize it is not the total person that one rejects, but rather one or some of his behaviors. To become effective as a behavior modifier it is then necessary to begin to act positively toward the other individual in terms of giving attention, showing sincere interest in him as a person, giving compliments, etc. Nagging and criticism should stop, and when the behavior that is desired happens to occur, it must be reinforced immediately. The other person must be informed that this specific behavior is appreciated and told in what special way it is rewarding. Various examples of successful modification of behavior are given.

Additionally, in this meeting, participants are taught the importance of simple social skills like complimenting, criticizing, and apologizing (and receiving compliments, criticisms, and apologies correctly) and are shown how to carry out these skills properly. Many addicts seem deficient in these simple skills that are crucial for the maintenance of good and harmonious social relations.

For instance, it is pointed out that the husband who never compliments his wife on her cooking, appearance, etc., often has a wife who is angry, resentful, unsure of how he feels about her, unsure of herself, with poor self-image. So the compliment is an important social tool. On the other hand, compliments may be given inappropriately—"That's a lovely dress; too bad it fits you so poorly"—or received badly—"Well, that's the first nice thing you've said in 10 years; what have you been up to?" So specific guidelines for giving and receiving compliments, criticisms, and apologies are offered.

Meeting 6—Assertive Training

This is of great importance for the addict who may have learned only aggressive means of standing up for his rights. Assertive training helps the individual to deal with situations involving tension, such as refusing illegitimate requests, asking for things to which one is legitimately entitled, and expressing both positive and negative attitudes and feelings. To promote awareness, typical underassertive and overassertive behaviors are described, including their nonverbal, verbal, and behavioral characteristics. The consequences of under- and over-assertiveness are examined in terms of how the individual treats and is treated by others, how he feels about himself and others, how others feel about him, what feedback he gets, and why he can or cannot make use of it. Finally, simple guidelines for correct assertiveness (the six C's) are presented, and the reason for each one explained: Correct timing, keeping Cool, Considering the other person's point of view, Communicating your own situation, Clarifying a solution together, and looking at the Consequences of taking this new solution as opposed to continuing as before.

Members of the group are now asked to contribute situations in which they feel they have at present, or have had in the past, problems with assertiveness. Several of these are now acted out by group members to illustrate what over-, under-, and correct assertiveness look like and what their consequences are.

Meeting 7—Rational Thinking

This meeting deals with the thinking process, using ideas and techniques from rational-emotive therapy developed by Ellis and Harper (30). Participants are made aware of how the thoughts one puts into one's head may cause oneself and others trouble. For instance, in what Ellis calls "catastrophizing," a person makes himself miserable and ineffective by the negative thoughts he puts into his own mind about an adverse situation. Or in what Ellis calls "musturbation," he makes himself upset because he puts the irrational thought in his head, for instance, that he "must" be able to cope by himself with all situations or that someone else "must" do something for him or else he will be devastated.

Ellis listed several common errors of thinking—dichotomous thinking, overgeneralization, stereotyped thinking, etc.—that may be causing difficulties in the addict's relations with himself, other addicts, or straight society. For instance, a dangerous over-generalization might be "all treatment personnel in addiction units are cold and inhuman in their treatment of addicts." These errors are described and examples in the addict experience elicited and discussed. Ellis' rational points of emphasis, common irrational ideas that cause trouble, are also discussed in relation to the situation of the addict.

Meeting 8—Review and Future Planning

The basic purpose and content of the program are reviewed. Participants are shown how each meeting builds on those that precede it and how the whole package is interrelated. For instance, assertive training, as taught in the program, involves relaxation, desensitization, self-image work, plus an understanding of behavior influence, behavior management, and rational thinking.

Finally, participants are asked to list three positive aspects of themselves that are helpful in adjusting to their present situation and/or will be helpful when they return to the community. They are also asked to list three negative things about themselves that may be making present adjustment difficult and/or may interfere with their adjustment when they return to the community. They are then asked what they are presently doing or planning to do to overcome these negative features of themselves. It is suggested that they "keep their ammunition dry" by continuing relaxation practice regularly and by rereading their workbooks frequently. Each is asked to plan specifically for his relaxation practice—what days of the week, what times, places, whether a tape will be used, etc.

EVALUATION

To examine the usefulness of this approach with addicts, in November, 1971, an initial demonstration program was conducted at the New Jersey Neuropsychiatric Institute, in which 29 male and 14 female addicts in the inpatient phase of a methadone maintenance program participated (23). To evaluate the effectiveness of the program, preprogram and postprogram measures of anxiety level (Taylor Manifest Anxiety Scale (66)), susceptibility to inner versus outer control (Rotter I-E Scale (60)), self-acceptance (Tennessee Self-concept Scale (33)), and degree of assertiveness (developed from a series of questions regarding assertiveness in behavior therapy techniques by Wolpe and Lazarus (70)) were obtained. Reactions to and evaluations of the program were also elicited immediately after the program and 3 months later by means of questionnaires.

Also, to provide a more objective measure of the effectiveness of the program, it was decided to compare the 6-month outcome of the group taught behavior modification techniques with that of the group of patients immediately preceding them in the drug treatment unit who had received only the regular program.

Accordingly, 6 months after the patients had completed the behavior modification program, the social workers responsible for checking their progress in the various methadone maintenance clinics around the state were contacted by telephone or by a direct visit to the facility and asked to rate the progress of their patients on a three-point scale as follows:

1. "Successful": Those persons who had adjusted well to the requirements of the program and were making good progress on methadone.

2. "Marginal Adjustment": Those who showed only marginal adjustment but were continuing on the programs. This included drinking problems; use of other drugs, such as heroin, barbiturates, and so forth; legal problems; and severe emotional problems.

3. "Failure": Those who had met the program requirements, had been detoxified, and not reinstated in the program.

This information was obtained for 40 of the 43 patients in the program. A similar procedure was carried out with a group of 20 addicts who immediately preceded the treatment group at the drug treatment unit. The outcomes of the treated and untreated groups were compared by chi-square.

Although only a carefully controlled study would provide adequate evaluation, statistically significant changes in the pre- and post-program test data suggested that the experimental behavior modification programs reduced anxiety, improved self-image, and made for more appropriate assertiveness and increased inner control on the part of the addicts treated.

Moreover, 58 per cent of the behavior modification treated group as opposed to 45 per cent of the comparison group were rated successful on follow-up, although this difference was not significant when tested by chi-square. However, it was also noted that the greater the exposure to the program (in terms of number of sessions attended), the greater was the likelihood for successful outcome.

The group data lent further support to these findings. The questionnaire responses of the addicts suggested that they understood the aims of the program and how to carry out the techniques and make use of them in relation to their problems, both before and after leaving the hospital. While the addict program was operative at the New Jersey Neuropsychiatric Institute, from 1971 through 1973, 775 addicts were trained in the program by the behavior modification staff at the institute.

THE STAFF PROGRAM

Originally, the staff training program was initiated so that inpatient staff would understand the ideas and techniques involved in the client behavior modification training program and thus be more helpful to the addicts who were trying to make use of them (intramural programs). Soon, it was extended to outpatient staff and various state-wide clinics and facilities for the same reason (extramural programs). Later, it was recognized that the program could be useful in additional ways. In the first place, as with the addicts, it would help the staff member grow and develop in terms of his own personal and professional performance and make him a more effective model and reinforcer for the addict's own development. Secondly, it was felt that some staff members working with the addicts in individual or group counseling sessions might incorporate one or more of the techniques taught and thus add to their professional armamentarium. Thus, relaxation might be practiced routinely, with the aim of increasing communication. Thirdly, it was felt that some staff members might learn to run similar self-control training programs for clients or staff, either at the institute in the case of the intramural programs, or in their own facilities in the case of the extramural programs.

SCHEDULE

Intramural programs consisted of nine 1½-hour group sessions, one session per day, twice per week over a 5-week period.

Extramural programs consisted of 10 group sessions, two sessions per day, 1 day per week over a 5-week period. Practicums were held for 1 hour at noontime for 3 intermediate days.

PROGRAM CONTENT

The content of the staff program replicated that of the client program, including training in relaxation, desensitization, self-image improvement, behavior analysis, behavior management, social skills of complimenting, criticising and apologizing, assertive training, and rational thinking. However, the staff programs also included an introductory meeting that presented an overview of the development of the area of behavior modification. The extramural sessions included a tenth meeting of discussion, criticism, and evaluation that was not part of the intramural program. As with the addict program, the sessions included lectures, practice of techniques, role playing, and group discussions. A training manual was also presented to each participant, as was a diploma for attendance at eight of 10 sessions. Special Group Leader diplomas were available for those who completed the course and also successfully ran a similar training program in their own facility. An observation visit by behavior modification staff was necessary for the trainee to receive the Group Leader Certificate.

PARTICIPANTS

Intramural Program

During the period of operation of the program for addicts at the institute (1971 to 1973), three intramural programs were conducted training 30 persons, most of whom were nursing personnel and social workers.

Extramural Program

To date 33 state-wide and eight national programs have been conducted training 2,174 persons from New Jersey and 463 persons from facilities in other states. Although the program is geared primarily toward the training of paraprofessionals, many supervisory personnel, nurses, social workers, psychologists, psychiatrists, and parole and probation officers have taken the programs. An earlier survey showed more than half of the participants were college trained, with about 20 per cent having had additional graduate training. Also, although the program was initiated for the training of drug addiction personnel, many staff members from alcoholism centers, corrections, probation and parole facilities, and institutions for the elderly, the mentally ill, and the retarded have participated in the program.

To date 231 Group Leader certificates have been issued to staff members who have suc-

cessfully conducted the program in their own facilities.

EVALUATION

As in the inmate program, level of anxiety, self-acceptance, degree of assertiveness, and degree of inner control were measured pre- and postprogram. Additionally the Custodial Mental Illness Idealogy Scale (35) was used at these times to examine changes in therapeutic attitudes. The first intramural group and two extramural groups (numbers one and five) were studied in this way.

For the *Intramural 1* participants, only the Custodial Mental Illness Ideology Scale changed significantly in a positive direction, toward more therapeutic attitudes.

For the *Extramural 1* participants, self-acceptance rose significantly, as did degree of inner control.

For the *Extramural 5* group, all scores changed significantly in a positive direction, suggesting more effective presentation of the material as time passed.

DISCUSSION

This historical account has indicated that behavior modification approaches that confined themselves to the drug-using behavior per se or even to the build up of alternative behaviors directly related to the drug use have met with little success and have led investigators to move toward a broader approach, dealing with a variety of life problems, emphasizing self-control and relevance of the relearned behaviors to the natural setting.

In the self-control training programs for addicts and staff described above that utilized this broader approach, the behavior modification techniques were not also addressed to the drug-using behavior itself. This was handled by methadone maintenance. In the future it would be of interest to combine behavior modification approaches such as covert sensitization, aimed at the drug-using behavior, with work on the associated complex of social behaviors.

However, in order for such broad based programs to operate successfully, it is important to have good information regarding the kinds of life problems experienced by addicts in reshaping their lives. To provide such information, a recent study by Dr. Cheek (15,

16) has attempted to look at role changes and reinforcement differentials in the movement from heroin to methadone.

Social role functioning at five critical periods in the life of the addict (childhood, preheroin, early heroin, late heroin, and methadone maintenance) was examined, in terms particularly of familial, occupational, and peer group roles. To clarify mechanisms whereby subculture and conventional roles are maintained, the kinds of social, physical, and material reinforcements at the five critical periods were examined in detail. Three outcome groups—"Successful," "Marginally Successful," and "Failure"—in a methadone maintenance program were compared to determine what extent differences in social roles and reinforcement existed among the groups in the movement from heroin to methadone and whether such differences were associated with "success" on the methadone program.

The study suggested that differentials in reinforcement available at various time periods did indeed relate to the outcome of the treated addicts. Thus, the "Successful" group showed a pattern of higher initial negative reinforcement in many areas, followed by higher positive reinforcement on methadone. The "Marginally Successful" group showed also more negative reinforcement prior to treatment but continued to show negative reinforcement afterward. The "Failures" were low in negative reinforcements earlier, whereas after treatment negative reinforcements were high.

The examination of social role changes revealed the meaning of these findings in depth. Thus, in the "Successful" group, unhappy childhood experiences offered good prognosis, particularly when combined with an adolescent pattern of active rebellion from a conventional family background where the drug life style was the major reinforcer. On the other hand, in the "Marginally Successful" group, unstable childhoods associated later with a passive, drifting pattern with feelings of personal inadequacy and with the drug itself as the major reinforcer related to poor prognosis. In the "Failure" group, positive early experience, combined however, with a marginal early environment in which the drug life was a natural career choice and both it and the drug experience itself were highly valued, seemed to be associated with poor prognosis. Also, it seemed that the more

negatively both life style and drug use were seen in late use, the better the prognosis. Finally, the better the past role models that were available and the more positively a conventional life style was reinforced by families and/or peer group, the better the outcome. Similar observations regarding three different life styles of addicts have been offered by Chein et al. (24), although not related to outcome in that case.

What do these feelings suggest with regard to treatment? For addicts like the "Failures" for whom addiction is a natural career choice in terms of their environment and whose life style around drugs is not seen negatively, it is important that they be taught the negative long term *consequences* of that life style and that they be removed from their previous environment, given new role models, and taught the nature and advantages of a different style of life. For drifters, like the "Marginally Successful" group, work on their self-image seems of paramount importance. They, too, badly need good role models; for the male addicts, good male role models seem particularly important in view of a female-dominated past. For addicts like the "Successful" group, who are rebelling from a more conventional past, it seems especially important that they be given reinforcement in the conventional roles they assume in treatment. Thus "Successful" group members report much closeness and support from their families while on methadone. Their previous rebellion has evidently indicated a depth of emotional investment in their families so that support either from their own parents or from parental surrogates is evidently an important matter for them at this time.

Finally, these findings suggest the importance of applying broad spectrum behavior modification approaches, including such techniques as self-image improvement, or manipulation of reinforcement contingencies within the context of an in-depth understanding of the life career of the addict. Additionally, they point up the significance of such auxiliaries as families and inpatient and outpatient staff as role models and reinforcers. If behavior modification techniques are to be successfully utilized in the treatment of drug abuse, it must be within the context of an in-depth approach that encompasses an understanding of the social role changes in the life of the addict moving from addiction to rehabilitation, as well as the associated reinforcement differentials.

References

1. Ausubel, D. P. *Drug Addiction*. New York, Random House, 1958.
2. Boer, A. P., and Sipprelle, C. N. Induced anxiety in the treatment of LSD effects. Psychother. Psychosom. 17:108, 1969.
3. Boudin, H. Contingency contracting as a therapeutic tool in the deceleration of amphetamine use. Behav. Ther. 3:604, 1972.
4. Boudin, H. M., and Valentine, V. E. Behavioral techniques as an alternative to methadone maintenance. Unpublished manuscript, 1973.
5. Boudin, H. M., Valentine, V. E., Inghram, R. D., Brantley, J. M., Ruiz, M. R., Smith, G. G., Catlin, R. P., and Regan, E., Jr. Contingency contracting with drug abusers in the natural environment. Int. J. Addict. 12:1, 1977.
6. Cahoon, D. D., and Crosby, C. C. A learning approach to chronic drug use sources of reinforcement. Behav. Ther. 3:64, 1972.
7. Callner, D. A., and Ross, S. M. The assessment and training of assertive skills with drug addicts: A preliminary study. Int. J. Addict. 13:227, 1978.
8. Cautela, J. R. Covert processes and behavior modification. J. Nerv. Ment. is. 157:27, 1973.
9. Cheek, F. E. Exploratory study of drugs and social interaction. Arch. Gen. Psychiatry 9:566, 1963.
10. Cheek, F. E. Broad-spectrum behavioral training in self-control for drug addicts. Behav. Ther. 3:515, 1972.
11. Cheek, F. E. Behavior modification for addicts on methadone maintenance. Curr. Psychiatr. Ther. 16:223, 1976.
12. Cheek, F. E. Treatment of drug addiction. In *The Group Treatment of Human Problems*, G. H. Harris, editor. New York, Grune and Stratton, 1977.
13. Cheek, F. E., and Baker, J. Training in self-control techniques for inmates. Psychol. Rep. 41:559, 1977.
14. Cheek, F. E., Burtle, V., Laucius, J., Mahnche, M., and Beck, R. A behavior modification training program for alcoholics and their wives. Presented at the American Psychological Association Meeting, Washington, D.C., 1971.
15. Cheek, F. E., Holstein, C., Fullam, F., Arana, G., Tomarchio, T., and Mandell, S. From heroin to methadone: Social role changes and reinforcement differentials in relation to outcome on methadone. Part I. The study of reinforcement differentials. Int. J. Addict. 11:659, 1976.
16. Cheek, F. E., Holstein, C., Fullam, F., Arana, G., Tomarchio, T., and Mandell, S. From heroin to methadone: Social role changes and reinforcement differentials in relation to outcome on methadone. Part II. The study of social role changes. Int. J. Addict. 11:695, 1976.
17. Cheek, F. E., Kline, A., and Sander, C. A behavior modification training program in self-control for hospitalized acutely mentally ill young adults. In *Mental Health in Children*, D. V. Siva Sankar, editor. vol III. New York, P.J.D., 1976.
18. Cheek, F. E., Laucius, J., Mahnche, M., and Beck, R. A behavior modification training program for parents of convalescent schizophrenics. In *Advances in Behavior Therapy, 1969*, Proceedings of the AABT, September, 1969, R. D. Rubin, H. Fensterhein, A. A. Lazarus, and C. M. Franks, editors, pp. 211–231. New York, Academic Press, 1971.
19. Cheek, F. E., and Mendelson, M. Developing behavior modification training programs with emphasis on self-control. Hosp. Community Psychiatry 24:410, 1973.
20. Cheek, F. E., and Miller, M. Stress awareness and coping techniques training for correctional officers. Presented at the American Society of Criminology Meeting, allas, Texas, 1978.
21. Cheek, F. E., Sarett, M., Newell, S., and Osmond, H. A survey of the experience of tension in alcoholics and other diagnostic groups. Int. J. Neuropsychiatry 11:477, 1967.
22. Cheek, F. E., Tomarchio, T., Burtle, V., Moss, H., and McConnell, D. A behavior modification training program for staff working with drug addicts. Int. J. Addict. 10:1073, 1975.
23. Cheek, F. E., Tomarchio, T., Standen, J., and Albahary, R. Methadone plus: A behavior modification training program for male and female addicts on methadone maintenance. Int. J. Addict. 24:969, 1973.
24. Chein, I., Gerald, D. L., Lee, R. S., and Rosenfield, E. *The Road to H*. New York, Basic Books, 1964.
25. Clayton, T. The adolescent and the psychiatric hospital. Hosp. Community Psychiatry 24:398, 1973.
26. Coghlan, A. J., Dohrenwend E. F., Gold, S. R., and Zimmerman, R. S. A psychobehavioral residential drug abuse program: A new adventure in adolescent psychiatry. Int. J. Addict. 8:767, 1973.
27. Crowley, T. J. The reinforcers for drug abuse: Why people take drugs. Compr. Psychiatry 13:51, 1972.
28. Droppa, D. C. The application of covert conditioning procedures to the out-patient treatment of drug addicts: Four case studies. Int. J. Addict. 13:657, 1978.
29. Duehn, W. D. Covert sensitization in group treatment of adolescent drug abusers. Int. J. Addict. 13:485, 1978.
30. Ellis, A., and Harper, R. *A Guide to Rational Living*. Englewood Cliffs, N.J., Prentice Hall, 1961.
31. Epling, W. F., and Bradshaw, P. An experimental analysis of the shaping, maintaining and elimination of drug abuse behavior. Br. J. Med. Psychol. 47:341, 1974.
32. Eriksson, J. H., Gotestam, K. G., Melin, L., and Ost, L. G. A token economy treatment of drug addiction. Behav. Res. Ther. 13:113, 1975.
33. Fitts, W. H. *Tennessee Self-Concept Scale Manual: Counseler Recordings and Tests*. Nashville, Tenn., 1965.
34. Flannery, R. B. Use of covert conditioning in the behavioral treatment of a drug dependent college dropout. J. Counsel. Psychol. 19:547, 1972.
35. Gilbert, D. C., and Levinson, D. J. "Custodialism" and "humanism" in mental hospital structure and staff ideology. In *The Patient and the Mental Hospital*, M. Greenblatt, D. J. Levinson, and R. H. Williams, editors. Glencoe, Ill, Free Press, 1957.
36. Gilbert, J. G., and Lombardi, D. N. Personality characteristics of young male narcotic addicts. J. Consult. Psychol. 31:536, 1967.
37. Glicksman, M., Ottomanelli, G., and Cutler, R. The earn your-way credit system: Use of a token economy in narcotic rehabilitation. Int. J. Addict. 6:525, 1971.
38. Gotestam, K. G., and Melin L., Covert extinction of

amphetamine addiction. Behav. Ther. 5:90, 1974.

39. Gotestam, K. G., Melin, L., and Ost. L. G. Behavioral techniques: The treatment of drug abuse: An evaluation review. Addict. Behav. 1:205, 1976.
40. Jacobsen, E. *Progressive Relaxation*. Chicago, University of Chicago Press, 1938.
41. Keil, T. J., Dickman, F. B., and Rush, T. V. Client demographics and therapeutic approach as predictive factors in the in-treatment outcomes of opiate users. Int. J. Addict. 13:709, 1978.
42. Keltner, A. A., and Gordon, A. Corrective and social psychiatry. J. Behav. Tech. Meth. Ther. 22:42, 1976.
43. Kraft, T. Successful treatment of a case of chronic barbiturate addiction. Br. J. Addict. 64:115, 1969.
44. Krasner, L., and Krasner, M. Token economy and other planned environments. In *Behavior Modification Education*. C. E. Thoresen, editor. Chicago, University of Chicago Press, 1972.
45. Kurtines, W., Hogan, and Weiss, D. Personality dynamics of heroin use. J. Abnorm. Psychol. 84:87, 1975.
46. Lazarus, A. *Behavior Therapy and Beyond*. New York, McGraw-Hill, 1971.
47. Lindesmith, A. R. *Opiate Addiction*. Evanston, Ill, Principea Press, 1947.
48. MacDonough, T. S. The relative effectiveness of a medical hospitalization program vs. a feedback-behavior modification program in treating alcohol and drug abusers. Int. J. Addict. 11:269, 1976.
49. Marlatt, G. A., and Nathan, P. E. *Behavioral Approaches to Alcoholism*. New Brunswick, N.J., Rutgers Center of Alcohol Studies, 1979.
50. Matefy, R. E. Behavior therapy to extinguish spontaneous recurrences of LSD effects: A case study. J. Nerv. Ment. Dis. 156:226, 1973.
51. Melin, L., Anderson, B. E., and Gotestam, K. G. Contingency management in a methadone maintenance treatment program. Addict. Behav. 1:151, 1976.
52. Melin, L., and Gotestam, K. G. A contingency management program on a drug-free unit for intravenous amphetamine addicts. J. Behav. Ther. Exp. Psychiatry 4:331, 1973.
53. Miller, P. M. Behavioral treatment of drug addiction: A review. J. Addict. 8:511, 1973.
54. Moinat, S., and Snortum, J. R. Self-management of personal habits by female drug addicts. Crim. Justice Behav. 3:29, 1976.
55. O'Brien, J. S., and Raynes, A. E. The use of aversion therapy in a combination approach applied to the treatment of heroin addiction. Presented at the Eighth Annual Meeting of the Association for Advancement of Behavior Therapy, Chicago, 1974.
56. O'Brien, J. S., Raynes, A. E., and Patch, V. D. Treatment of heroin addiction with aversion therapy, relaxation training and systematic desensitization. Behav. Res. Ther. 10:77, 1972.
57. Ottomanelli, G. A. Follow-up of a token economy applied to civilly committed narcotic addicts. Int. J. Addict. 11:793, 1976.
58. Polakow, R. L., and Doctor, R. M. Treatment of marijuana and barbiturate dependency by contingency contracting. J. Behav. Ther. Exp. Psychiatry 4: 375, 1973.
59. Polakow, R. J., and Doctor, R. M. Behavioral modification program for adult drug offenders. J. Res. Crime Delinq. 11:63, 1974.
60. Rotter, J. B. Generalized expectancies of internal vs. external control of reinforcement. Psychol. Monogr. 80:609, 1966.
61. Solomon, E., and Marshall, W. L. A comprehensive model for the acquisition, maintenance and treatment of drug-taking behavior. Br. J. Addict. 68:215, 1973.
62. Sepvack, M., Pihl, R., and Rowan, T. Behavior therapies in the treatment of drug abuse: Some case studies. Psychol. Rec. 23:179, 1973.
63. Stuart, R. B. A three-dimensional program for the treatment of obesity. Behav. Res. Ther. 9:177, 1971.
64. Suinn, M., and Brittain, J. The termination of an LSD "freak-out" through the use of relaxation. J. Clin. Psychol. 26:127, 1970.
65. Susskind, D. The idealized self-image (ISI): A new technique in confidence training. Behav. Ther. 1:538, 1970.
66. Taylor, J. A. A personality scale of manifest anxiety. J. Abnorm. Soc. Psychol. 28:285, 1953.
67. Wikler, A. On the nature of addiction and habituation. B. J. Addict. 57:73, 1961.
68. Wisocki, P. A. The successful treatment of a heroin addict by covert conditioning techniques. J. Behav. Ther. Exp. Psychiatry 4:55, 1973.
69. Wolpe, J. *The Practice of Behavior Therapy*. New York, Pergamon Press, 1969.
70. Wolpe, J., and Lazarus, A. *Behavior Therapy Techniques*. Oxford, Pergamon Press, 1966.

CHAPTER 40

THE TRANSCENDENTAL MEDITATION PROGRAM AND THE TREATMENT OF DRUG ABUSE

Larry M. Siegel, M.S.W., M.P.H.

The Transcendental Meditation (TM) program has been used as a treatment modality in drug abuse prevention programs and in community-based treatment programs. Several encouraging studies have been completed in both of these areas, and they will be briefly summarized in this chapter. However, my major focus will be the rapidly growing use of the TM program by drug treatment units in state and federal prisons. I will review a number of these prison studies and include descriptive comments from institutional staff. The program seems to be proving itself an effective adjunct to traditional inmate drug rehabilitation efforts. However, before reviewing these programs, it is necessary first to describe the TM technique and outline the method by which it is learned.

WHAT IS THE TRANSCENDENTAL MEDITATION TECHNIQUE?

The Transcendental Meditation technique is a simple, natural, effortless, mental procedure practiced 15 to 20 minutes in the morning and evening while one sits comfortably

with the eyes closed and mentally repeats a sound known as a mantra. During the process of meditation there is a spontaneous reduction of mental activity as the mind experiences progressively quieter or "less excited" levels of thinking. As the thinking process settles down, thoughts are appreciated at more and more refined levels, until a "least excited" state of consciousness is reached. This least excited state is one in which the mind is in a state of restfulness with inner wakefulness or awareness but without an object of awareness. This experience is known as "transcending." Due to the natural coordination between mind and body, this lessened mental activity gives rise to a state of profound rest at the same time.

The research findings on the effects of the TM technique have shown that the subjective state of least excitation of consciousness is accompanied by an objectively measurable, extremely high degree of orderliness of brain functioning and of the physiology as a whole (12, 17, 24). Investigation has also demonstrated that during the practice of the technique, oxygen consumption, heart rate, and respiratory rate significantly decrease. Cardiac output is also reduced, while over-all cardiovascular efficiency increases. Measurements of skin resistance and blood chemistry also verify that during meditation an individual gains a profoundly deep state of rest, deeper than deep sleep, yet brain wave patterns indicate that during this deep rest the individual remains alert and able to respond to stimuli (6, 9, 11, 12, 14, 18, 19, 24, 38–40).

These natural effects are reported to distinguish the TM technique from hypnosis, autosuggestion, and other methods that involve even the slightest mental effort. Researchers have described the period of the TM technique as a state of "restful alertness" indicative of a fourth major state of consciousness as natural as the other three physiologically defined states—wakefulness, dreaming, and deep sleep (38–40).

Those practicing the TM technique report that this state of restful alertness is both physically and mentally refreshing. In addition to self-reports of increased energy, TM participants have been reported to experience improved mind-body coordination, more developed creative intelligence, more inner stability, and improved clarity of perception (27, 28, 32, 34, 41). More than 400 studies to date on the TM technique have documented effects in these and many other areas of life, many of them employing experimental designs that render unlikely alternative explanations such as placebo or experimenter effects (4, 20).

The TM technique is a process of direct experience rather than one of intellectual analysis. The technique is easily learned regardless of educational or cultural background.

According to the TM teaching organization, by 1979 more than 2 million people world-wide had learned the TM technique, and now there are more than 7,000 teachers of the TM program in the United States alone. Each teacher has been personally qualified by Maharishi Mahesh Yogi, the founder of the TM program. In the United States more than 300 TM centers have been established to provide instruction and follow-up programs.

RESEARCH ON THE TM PROGRAM AND DRUG ABUSE

Several studies have focused on the effect of the TM program on drug abuse. These studies have consistently reported substantial decreases of drug use among those practicing the TM technique.

SURVEY RESEARCH STUDIES

One of the first studies, published by Benson and Wallace in 1972 (7), used questionnaires that were given to 1,950 subjects who were attending a month-long TM teacher training course. There were 1,862 completed responses. Most of the subjects were college students and had been practicing the technique for an average of 20 months. Drug use was categorized as follows: For marihuana, narcotics, amphetamine, barbiturates, hard liquor, and cigarettes, the researchers defined light use as less than three times a month, medium use as one to six times a week, and heavy use as once a day or more. For hallucinogens, light use was less than once a month, medium use was one to three times a month, and heavy use was more than once a week.

The researchers reported that practice of the Transcendental Meditation technique decreased the number of drug abusers in all categories studied. The longer the TM practice continued over time, the greater the subjects had decreased their abuse, until after 21 months of meditation most subjects had stopped abusing drugs. In the 6-month period before starting meditation, about 80 per cent of the subjects used marihuana and of those about 28 per cent were heavy users. After practicing the TM technique for 6 months, 37 per cent continued to use marihuana and of those 6.5 per cent reported heavy use. After 21 months of the practice, only 12 per cent continued to use marihuana and of those most were light users; only one individual was a heavy user. Before starting the TM technique, almost half of the subjects had used lysergic acid diethylamide (LSD), with about 14 per cent reporting heavy use. Within 3 months of TM instruction 11 per cent of the subjects used LSD, whereas after 21 months only 3 per cent used LSD. The increase in the number of nonusers after starting the TM technique was similar for the other drugs. Nonusers of the other hallucinogens after 21 months of the practice rose from 61 to 96 per cent; for the narcotics from 83 to 99 per cent; for amphetamines from 70 to 99 per cent; and for the barbiturates from 83 to 99 per cent.

Leon Otis (31) of Stanford Research Institute (SRI) conducted a questionnaire study and found similar results. The SRI study had 620 respondents, of whom 396 reported that they had used drugs. Eighty-four per cent of these reported stopping all drug use after starting the TM program. Forty-nine people in the study had used opiates; 42 stopped after beginning the TM program. Otis also found a decreased use of prescribed psychoactive drugs in the meditator group.

The methodologies of these first studies were subject to some serious criticisms, which Marcus (25) has previously summarized. They are as follows: (a) All subjects were currently practicing the TM technique. It is not known how many people may have started the technique and later stopped and returned to drug use. In the Benson and Wallace study, subjects were attending an advanced TM course and cannot be considered representative of the average meditator population. (b) The subjects had a higher than average educational level and may have been highly motivated to improve themselves. (c) Prospective TM participants are required to abstain from recreational drug use for 15 days prior to instruction. Thus, seriously drug-dependent people may have been prevented from beginning the program. Furthermore, these early studies were not longitudinal and they did not use control groups for comparison.

Another questionnaire study was conducted by Shafii and his colleagues (36) at the University of Michigan in 1972. This study was more sophisticated than the previous studies because it used a control group. Seventy-six per cent of the study participants were under age 30, and 67 per cent were college graduates or college students. Each participant provided the researchers with the names of two friends who were similar to themselves in age, sex, and educational level but who were not practicing the TM technique. Respondents included 126 TM participants and 90 control subjects.

The researchers reported that almost half of those who had practiced the TM technique for a period of 1 to 3 months decreased or stopped their use of marihuana. Again it was found that the longer a person had practiced meditation, the higher was the probability that marihuana use would be discontinued. Of those who had practiced the TM technique for more than 2 years, 92 per cent had significantly decreased their use of marihuana and 77 per cent had totally stopped. Shafii et al. (37) subsequently reported dramatic reductions in alcohol use among TM participants.

Monahan (27) sent drug use surveys to all TM participants he was able to locate in the Philadelphia area. They were asked to report their own drug use over the past several years. For comparison purposes, the TM participants were asked to identify a nonmeditating friend to complete and return a similar survey. Monahan reported consistent significant decreases in drug use for TM participants across all categories of substances studied with no consistent change for controls. The drugs included "hard" and "soft" illegal drugs, prescription and over-the-counter medications, alcohol, tobacco, and caffeine.

Lazar et al. (23) studied self-reported marihuana, alcohol, and tobacco use in college students and adults just prior to TM instruction and at either 4-, 8-, or 12-week intervals postinstruction. Findings indicated sharp declines across the three categories as well as significant reductions in anxiety. Decreased anxiety was found to be correlated with decreased use of drugs.

In a prospective questionnaire study of high school and college students in which there were data for 150 TM subjects and 110 controls, Katz (21) also reported a significant decrease in the use of marihuana and other drugs and concluded that students who are not using marihuana and start the TM technique are less likely to begin to use it than are students who do not start the TM technique.

RESIDENTIAL TREATMENT PROGRAM STUDIES

The TM program has been taught in perhaps a dozen drug treatment programs in the United States, including Soul Site in Berkeley, California, Walden House in San Francisco, the Addiction Treatment Research Corporation in New York City, and the methadone maintenance program of the West Philadelphia Community Mental Health Consortium. These were pilot programs, and, although there were numerous subjective reports of positive benefits, no formal evaluations were conducted.

Two studies, however, have been done in European drug abuse treatment programs, one in Germany and one in Sweden. The German research conducted by Schenkluhn and Geisler (35) studied 76 patients at a drug rehabilitation center in Arbeiterswohljahrt in Mulheim/Ruhr. The results were very significant drops in the use of all drugs, including amphetamine, barbiturates, and opiates after 12 months of TM practice. The researchers reported the following:

TM was the primary therapy. The subjects were generally drug dependent and a few were "addicts." Two months prior to beginning TM, the number of drug users and the categories of drugs used were as follows: 42 of the subjects used marihuana and hashish (17 heavy users, 21 medium users and 4 light users); 11 used LSD and other hallucinogens (4 heavy users and 7 medium users); 10 used amphetamines and barbiturates (4 heavy users, 4 medium users and 2 light users); and 5 used opiates (4 heavy users and 1 light user).

After twelve months of TM only 18 used marihuana and hashish (4 heavy, 10 medium and 4 light users); only 2 still used LSD and other hallucinogens (1 medium and 1 light user); none used amphetamines and barbiturates; and only 1 used opiates. The study found no significant trends to give up drugs before starting TM except for LSD and other hallucinogens.

The Swedish study (8) lasted 6 months. It included 20 subjects, 12 who primarily used hashish and eight subjects who had used "hard" drugs (defined as LSD, amphetamine, and opiates) more than 10 times in the previous 6 months. About half of the subjects had been injecting drugs intravenously. The subjects were stratified into two categories of hashish and "hard" drugs. Each category was then randomly split into a control and experimental group of equal size. No attempt was made to influence the subjects not to use drugs during the study, except for the standard 15 days prior to TM instruction.

To summarize the results, it can be said that the Transcendental Meditation program had an immediate short-term effect on hashish and "hard" drug usage and also had an effect over a longer period of time . . .

During the two years that have passed since the closing of the experiment there have been relapses in about 80% of the subjects, whether sporadically or for longer periods of time. The tendency has been, however, to return to Transcendental Meditation, because it seems to have provided the

subjects with a way to increase their well-being without the use of drugs.

PRISON DRUG PROGRAM STUDIES

The TM program has been used as a treatment modality in more than 30 state and federal prisons in the United States. A number of the programs have specifically involved inmates in prison drug abuse programs, whereas others have been used with general inmate populations.

The measurement of any voluntary program's effects on drug abuse in prison settings is a difficult task. Drug abuse in prisons, especially in drug treatment units, influences one's chances of parole and carries other penalties as well. Under such circumstances inmates are understandably reluctant to self-report their involvement with drugs despite any assurances of confidentiality that may be offered, and those who are using drugs almost unanimously refuse to volunteer for any program that includes more direct screening for drug usage such as urinalysis. As a result other variables are often studied not so much as proxy measures of drug use, but rather because they are thought to be influences on drug use. Because of these measurement difficulties, I have supplemented some of the research reports presented below with staff impressions of the TM program's impact on drug abuse in the institutions studied.

The first study of the TM program on incarcerated drug users was conducted at the Federal Correctional Institution at La Tuna, Texas (30). Twelve prisoners addicted to heroin who were in the prison drug program participated in the TM program. They were compared to seven control subjects.

Orme-Johnson observed that prior to TM instruction the TM group had more spontaneous galvanic skin responses (GSR) per subject than the control group. After 2 months the regular meditators reduced their level of spontaneous GSR's significantly more than irregular meditators and control subjects. GSR is an accepted physiological measure of anxiety. Fewer GSR's are associated with greater nervous system stability (28). In this study the regular meditators also had significantly lower scores on the Minnesota Multiphasic Personality Inventory (MMPI) psychasthenia and social introversion scales than the comparison group.

At Stillwater State Prison in Minnesota, Ballou (5) studied 46 meditating prisoners from August, 1972, to August, 1973, in a study using a random assignment to groups design. The meditating subjects dropped from what was an abnormally high average level of anxiety prior to instruction to a low normal level within the first 2 weeks after instruction. This lower level of anxiety persisted throughout the experiment, whereas anxiety levels of the control subjects remained unchanged.

Ballou also assessed behavioral change. The number of disciplinary write-ups of a subgroup of 24 meditating inmates decreased by two-thirds (67.5 per cent). No significant change was observed among the 24-member control group. This decrease is significant because it is believed that a reduction in disciplinary infractions may be directly related to a decrease in recidivism. Of 16 meditating inmates who were subsequently paroled (and had been on parole for an average of 6 months), only one had violated parole. In addition to standard psychological inventories, 23 inmates completed written self-reports. Although the exact level of drug usage could not be ascertained, 14 reported the TM program to be the reason for their decline or cessation of drug abuse. One felt some temporary change, and eight did not respond.

In addition, the inmates in the TM program participated in a greater variety of constructive activities, such as educational and vocational training programs and clubs, than before the program. The amount of time they spent in such activities tripled.

Three recent programs have reported substantial decreases in hostile and aggressive behavior among TM practitioners in prison settings. Ramirez (33) conducted a 9-week evaluation of the TM program at the Milan Federal Correctional Institution in Michigan. Of 100 volunteers from the institution's two federally funded drug treatment programs for heroin addicts, 80 subjects were randomly selected for the study. Forty were then randomly assigned to the TM group and 40 to the control group. The researcher was blind to group assignment.

Ramirez reported that self-esteem, emotional stability, ego strength, and maturity were significantly enhanced by the practice of the TM technique according to the MMPI and the neuroticism subscales of the Eysenck Personality Inventory. Aggressiveness was significantly reduced among regular meditators. Regular meditators were reported to have decreased their tendency to experience aggressive or hostile impulses and simultaneously increased their ability to control these tendencies, as indicated by the MMPI and Buss-Durkee Hostility Inventory. There were no differences between groups detected on the Ravens Progressive Matrices, the Rotter Locus of Control, the Finger Tapping Test, or the Hooper Visual Organization Test. The meditators had fewer behavior incidents. Personality changes were found to exceed cognitive changes. Regular meditators showed greater progress than less regular meditators.

Douglas Lansing (22), unit management coordinator at Milan, commented on the effect of the program for staff as well as inmates:

A correctional institution is a very stress-producing environment for both staff and residents. Our staff has found that by practicing TM, our ability to cope with the stress is greatly enhanced and that our productivity increased. Nearly 50 of our residents are meditating and the response is equally favorable. Several residents who have had behavior problems have claimed that TM has been responsible for them being more relaxed, able to think more clearly and gain self-control.

And Clarence Guienze (15), associate warden of the same institution, stated in a letter:

... it is clear that the men who meditated regularly and properly definitely benefited. Not only have they noted changes among themselves, but each person sees himself as a considerably better individual. Others who had contact with them noted significant changes.

This project is considered to have been a highly successful one and it is certainly a basis for the introduction of TM to this institution on a large scale. It also clearly suggests that TM has a place in other correctional settings as an important "new" tool for providing an opportunity for growth and change in a simple, but profound and lasing way.

The largest program to date is in progress at the California State Prison at Folsom (1). As of September, 1979, 300 inmates had been instructed in the TM technique. Although selection criteria did not require a previous drug history, many of the participants had long histories of drug abuse both in and out of the institution. In fact, a number of the first participants in the program were thought to have controlled much of the drug traffic within the institution.

An extensive cross-validation study design was employed to measure the impact of the program at Folsom. Two separate studies measured essentially the same variables. Each study included approximately 30 experimental and 30 waiting control subjects. Each study lasted 3 months.

Although experimental and control subjects were quite similar across the variables at pretest, there were a number of significant differences at posttest. Both TM groups were significantly lower than controls on state and trait anxiety and neuroticism. Both TM groups were significantly lower than controls over-all on the Buss-Durkee Hostility Inventory. In addition, the first TM group was significantly lower on two of seven subscales of the inventory—negativism and suspicion—and the second TM group showed significant effects on five subscales—reduced assault, irritability, negativism, resentment, and verbal hostility. There were also significant improvements in sleep patterns. Cigarette smoking did not change.

More recent data were reported by the authors concerning recidivism rates (2). Fifty-six of the 122 participants in the TM program at Folsom (at the time of the report) had been released on parole and/or discharged over the preceding 21 months. Three of these men have been returned to custody (5.4 per cent) on parole violations and only one of these with a new term. Of the 17 men who were released for a period of 1 year or longer, only one has returned to complete his term (5.9 per cent) due to a parole violation. In contrast, the California state average is 12.9 per cent returns 1 year after release. The return for former Folsom inmates after 1 year is 15.2 per cent.

The State of Massachusetts, Division of Drug Rehabilitation, funded a program for 66 inmates at Massachusetts Correctional Institution—Walpole, another maximum security institution. Again, inmate reluctance to admit drug abuse prevented direct investigation of this area. A study similar to the one conducted at Folsom was implemented, and there were similar results (13).

Despite the lack of proper experimental control and some difficulty in collection of posttest data, the author reported consistent reductions in anxiety and hostility, improvement in sleep, and reduction of behavior infractions among the meditating inmates. The report stated (13):

The TM technique and its after effects provided a new dimension of experience for inmates, which in many cases replaced the need for a drug-induced high. Collection of quantitative data on actual reduction in drug abuse was beyond the scope of this program, but confidential reports to counselors and the program's teaching staff helped verify the great value of the technique for many individuals in their struggle against drug habits. *Some individuals who had no intention nor desire to stop using drugs found to their surprise that after practicing the technique for a short time they became disinterested in drug use* (italics added).

William Clark (10), staff psychologist at Walpole, lends additional corroboration as to the program's effect on drug use:

In several confidential interviews, individual meditators have described to me how they felt freed from their long-standing drug addiction and immensely reassured in their belief in themselves. Others told of a significant drop in their previous tendency to succumb to stressful situations with depression or with impulsive acting out. I have sensed a general increase in a kind of quiet pride and self-confidence among the meditators.

Finally, Frank Hall (16), commissioner of corrections for the state of Massachusetts, wrote:

It would appear that the stress levels of the inmates who are meditating have decreased significantly, and our institutional records indicate a notable decrease in disciplinary reports among the inmates who have learned the TM technique. I am pleased by the positive comments I hear from correctional officers, administrative staff members and inmates about the TM program and its effects on the men at MCI-Walpole.

A THEORETICAL CONTEXT

In a recent article, Aron and Aron (4) presented a theoretical discussion of the TM program's effects in the reduction of drug abuse as well as other addictive behaviors. Following Miller (26), they presented five categories of variables affecting addictive behaviors: situations, social influences, emotions, cognitions, and physiology. Each category is then examined in terms of its purported influence on addictive behavior. Finally, citing a wide body of research findings on the TM technique, the authors attempted to demonstrate how the technique reduces the influence on addictive behaviors of each category of variables. Their presentation posits a number of possible, although not contradictory, explanations for findings to date on the TM programs's positive effects on the reduction of drug abuse, each one seemingly worthy of further investigation.

The Arons note that very few TM participants who were initially using drugs began the program with the intent of reducing or ceasing their use. In time they noticed that drug use prior to meditation interfered with their experiences during it, whereas drug use afterward clouded the sense of mental clarity and increased energy that are generally found to follow the practice. What followed for many of these people was a short or very long experimental period of little or no use of drugs. The length of this experimental period depended on many factors, including the variables cited above and their experiences during and following meditation.

There would often be a return to the addictive behavior at least once as part of this experimentation. The change appeared to be very gradual, spontaneously and internally motivated. Later individuals seemed to feel that rather than having broken a "bad" habit, they simply moved with time toward what were more satisfying experiences.

PROGRAM FOR AGENCY CLIENTS

An extensive follow-up program after instruction in the TM technique has been found to be essential in rehabilitation settings. The follow-up program establishes an understanding of the practice, guides the client in a regular meditation schedule, and provides continued verification of the correct practice. In addition, it provides the opportunity for clients to discuss their experiences and understand the positive changes that occur as the practice continues. Varying degrees of follow-up are recommended depending upon the nature of the rehabilitation environment, but the minimum client program lasts 12 weeks.

PROGRAM FOR AGENCY STAFF

It has been found that staff members who practice the TM technique have an increased understanding of the clients' experiences in the TM program because of their increased knowledge of the nature of the practice and the benefits it provides. Client programs have been most effective when they have been preceded by staff programs because of the greater acceptance and support of the client program by a staff familiar with the TM technique. Staff programs typically last from 5 to 12 weeks and consist of weekly meetings and personal checking sessions following instruction in the TM technique.

IMPLEMENTATION

The Institute for Social Rehabilitation (ISR) which is contacted through local TM Centers, contracts services to the institution or agency that has responsibility for the planned program. All teaching in rehabilitation settings is done by certified teachers of the TM program as employees of ISR.

CONCLUSION

The positive findings among TM participants in these studies seem to be of sufficient magnitude to consider seriously the implementation of the TM program as a major treatment modality in both community and institutional drug treatment programs. The TM program is simple to administer, inexpensive, easily integrated into existing programs, and does not disrupt program or institutional routines. Results of work to date indicate the effectiveness of the TM program in reducing many problems in the drug abuser's life, while simultaneously improving the capacity to live a more fully developed, useful, and enjoyable life.

References

1. Abrams, A. I., and Siegel, L. M. The Transcendental Meditation program and rehabilitation at Folsom State Prison: A cross-validation study. Crim. Justice Behav. , 5:3, 1978.
2. Abrams, A. I., and Siegel, L. M. Transcendental Meditation and rehabilitation at Folsom State Prison: Response to a critique. Crim. Justice Behav., 6:13, 1979.
3. Aron, A., and Aron, E. The Transcendental Meditation program, higher states of consciousness, and supernormal abilities. Presented at the 86th Annual

Meeting of the American Psychological Association, Toronto, August, 1978; revised February, 1979.

4. Aron, A., and Aron, E. The Transcendental Meditation program's effect on addictive behavior. Addict. Behav., 53: 1980, In press.

5. Ballou, D. The Transcendental Meditation program at Stillwater Prison. In *Scientific Research on the Transcendental Meditation Program: Collected Papers*, D. W. Orme-Johnson and J. T. Farrow, editors, pp. 569–576. Livingston Manor, N. Y., MIU Press, 1976.

6. Banquet, J. P. Spectral analysis of the EEG in meditation. Electroencephalogr. Clin Neurophysiol. 35: 143, 1973.

7. Benson, H., and Wallace, R. K. Decreased drug abuse with Transcendental Meditation: A study of 1,862 subjects. In *Drug Abuse: Proceedings of the International Conference*, C. J. D. Zarafonetis, editor, pp. 369–376. Philadelphia, Lea and Febiger, 1972.

8. Brautigam, E. Effects of the Transcendental Meditation program on drug abusers: A prospective study. In *Scientific Research on the Transcendental Meditation Program: Collected Papers*, D. W. Orme-Johnson and J. T. Farrow, editors, pp. 506–514. Livingston Manor, N. Y., MIU Press, 1976.

9. Bujatti, M., and Riederer, P. Serotonin, noradrenaline, dopamine metabolites in Transcendental Meditation technique. J. Neural Transm. 39:257, 1976.

10. Clark, W. Private communication, 1977.

11. Dhanaraj, H. V., and Singh, M. Reduction in metabolic rate during the practice of the Transcendental Meditation technique. In *Scientific Research on the Transcendental Meditation Program: Collected Papers*, D. W. Orme-Johnson and J. T. Farrow, editors, pp. 137–139. Livingston Manor, N. Y., MIU Press, 1976.

12. Farrow, J. T. Physiological changes associated with transcendental consciousness: The least excitation of consciousness. In *Scientific Research on the Transcendental Meditation Program: Collected Papers*, D. W. Orme-Johnson and J. T. Farrow, editors, pp. 108–133. Livingston Manor, N. Y., MIU Press, 1976.

13. Ferguson, R. E. The Transcendental Meditation program at MCI-Walpole: An evaluation report. Unpublished paper, 1976. (Institute for Social Rehabilitation, 17310 Sunset Blvd., Pacific Palisades, California 90272.)

14. Glueck, B. C., and Stroebel, C. F. Biofeedback and meditation in the treatment of psychiatric illness. Compr. Psychiatry 16:303, 1975.

15. Guienze, C. Private communication, 1975.

16. Hall, F. Private communication, 1977.

17. Haynes, C. T., Hebert, J. R., Reber, W., and Orme-Johnson, D. W. The psychophysiology of advanced participants in the Transcendental Meditation program: Correlations of EEG coherence, creativity, H-reflex recovery and experience of transcendental consciousness. In *Scientific Research on the Transcendental Meditation Program: Collected Papers*, D. W. Orme-Johnson and J. T. Farrow, editors, pp. 208–212. Livingston Manor, N. Y., MIU Press, 1976.

18. Jevning, R., and Wilson, A. F. Altered red cell metabolism in Transcendental Meditation (abstract). Psychophysiology 14:94, 1977.

19. Jevning, R., Wilson, A. F., and Davidson, J. M. Adrenocortical activity during meditation. Horm.

Behav. 10:54, 1978.

20. Kannelakos, D. P. Transcendental consciousness: Expanded awareness as a means of preventing and eliminating the effects of stress. Stress Anxiety 5: 262, 1978.

21. Katz, D. Decreased drug abuse and prevention of drug abuse through the Transcendental Meditation program. In *Scientific Research on the Transcendental Meditation Program: Collected Papers*, D. W. Orme-Johnson and J. T. Farrow, editors, pp. 536–543. Livingston Manor, N. Y., MIU Press, 1976.

22. Lansing, D. Private communication, 1975.

23. Lazar, A., Farwell, L., and Farrow, J. T. The effects of the Transcendental Meditation program on anxiety, drug abuse, cigarette smoking, and alcohol consumption. In *Scientific Research on the Transcendental Meditation Program: Collected Papers*, D. W. Orme-Johnson and J. T. Farrow, editors, pp. 524–535. Livingston Manor, N. Y., MIU Press, 1976.

24. Levine, P., Hebert, J. R., Haynes, C., and Strobel, H. EEG coherence during the Transcendental Meditation technique. In *Scientific Research on the Transcendental Meditation Program: Collected Papers*, D. W. Orme-Johnson and J. T. Farrow, editors, pp. 187–207. Livingston Manor, N. Y., MIU Press, 1976.

25. Marcus, J. B. The Transcendental Meditation technique: Consciousness expansion as a rehabilitation technique. J. Psychedelic Drugs 7:169, 1976.

26. Miller, P. M. The addictive behavior: Common ground. Presented at Taos International Conference on Treatment of Addictive Behavior, 1979.

27. Monahan, R. H. Secondary prevention of drug dependence through the Transcendental Meditation program in metropolitan Philadelphia. Int. J. Addict. 12:629, 1977.

28. Orme-Johnson, D. W. Autonomic stability and Transcendental Meditation. Psychosom. Med. 35: 341, 1973.

29. Orme-Johnson, D. W., and Farrow, J. T., editors. *Scientific Research on the Transcendental Meditation Program; Collected Papers*, vol. 1. Livingston Manor, N. Y., MIU Press, 1976.

30. Orme-Johnson, D. W., Kiehlbauch, J., Moore, R., and Bristol, J. Personality and autonomic changes in meditating prisoners. In *Scientific Research on the Transcendental Meditation Program: Collected Papers*, D. W. Orme-Johnson and J. T. Farrow, editors, pp. 556–561. Livingston Manor, N. Y., MIU Press, 1976.

31. Otis, L. S. Changes in drug usage patterns of practitioners of Transcendental Meditation. Unpublished report, 1972. (Stanford Research Institute, Menlo Park, California.)

32. Pelletier, K. Influence of Transcendental Meditation upon autokinetic perception. Percep. Mot. Skills 39: 1031, 1974.

33. Ramirez, J. Transcendental Meditation as a possible treatment modality for drug offenders: Evaluation of a pilot project at Milan FCI. Unpublished report. (Institute for Social Rehabilitation, 17310 Sunset Blvd., Pacific Palisades, California 90272.)

34. Reddy, M. K. The effects of the Transcendental Meditation program on athletic performance. Unpublished master thesis, Maharishi European Research University, 1976.

35. Schenkluhn, H., and Geisler, M. A longitudinal

study of the influence of the Transcendental Meditation program on drug abuse. In *Scientific Research on the Transcendental Meditation Program: Collected Papers*, D. W. Orme-Johnson and J. T. Farrow, editors, pp. 544–555. Livingston Manor, N. Y., MIU Press, 1976.

36. Shafii, M., Lavely, R., and Jaffe, R. Meditation and marijuana. Am. J. Psychiatry 131:60, 1974.

37. Shafii, M., Lavely, R., and Jaffe, R. Meditation and the prevention of alcohol abuse. Am. J. Psychiatry 132:942, 1975.

38. Wallace, R. K. Physiological effects of Transcendental Meditation. Science 167:1751, 1970.

39. Wallace, R. K., and Benson, H. The physiology of meditation. Sci. Am. 226:84, 1972.

40. Wallace, R. K., Benson, H., and Wilson, A. F. A wakeful hypometabolic physiological state. Am. J. Physiol. 221:795, 1971.

41. Wilcox, G. Autonomic functioning in subjects practicing the Transcendental Meditation technique. In *Scientific Research on the Transcendental Meditation Program: Collected Papers*, D. W. Orme-Johnson and J. T. Farrow, editors, pp. 239–242. Livingston Manor, N. Y., MIU Press, 1976.

CHAPTER 41

ACUPUNCTURE IN SUBSTANCE ABUSE

Lorenz K. Y. Ng, M.D.

Hsiang-Lai Wen, M.D.

Acupuncture (derived from the words "acus," meaning a sharp point, and "punctura," meaning puncturing), as its name implies, consists of stimulating certain points on or near the surface of the body by insertion of needles. As an ancient Oriental therapeutic art, it has been practiced in China for more than 5,000 years. The wide publicity given the successful use of acupuncture as a method of anesthesia in surgery in the People's Republic of China, after President Nixon's trip to that country in 1972, generated considerable interest in the layman as well as in the medical profession in this particular modality.

ACUPUNCTURE IN DRUG ADDICTION

Besides its reported effectiveness in the production of analgesia, acupuncture seems to have other potentially useful clinical and research applications (17, 23). Its use in the treatment of drug addiction represents a rather recent application of a very old treatment technique. There are a number of practical and theoretical considerations that prompt a closer look at the use of acupuncture in the treatment of drug-dependent in-

dividuals. Available evidence (27, 46) indicates that there may be a close relationship in terms of neurochemical mechanisms between analgesia and the development of tolerance and physical dependence. Attempts to dissociate the analgesic effects of narcotics and opiates from their addictive liability have been rather unsuccessful, despite several decades of intensive research efforts. This and the recent findings from research on endorphins suggest that the neuropsychobiological factors involved in the development of narcotic dependence may be intimately related to the processes involved in the production of analgesia. Thus, a modality that can produce analgesia may have potential value for modifying the processes involved in narcotic dependence. A nonchemical modality such as acupuncture seems particularly intriguing, especially because it is relatively easy to use, safe, and would appeal to individuals who are trying to rid themselves of chemical dependency.

In practice, the application of acupuncture in the treatment of narcotic addiction derives from a rather serendipitous observation made by Dr. H. L. Wen of Hong Kong in 1972. Here is a brief description by Dr. Wen of how this incident came about:

In early November 1972, a 50-year old man was admitted to the Neurosurgical Unit of the Kwong Wah Hospital, Tung Wah Group of Hospitals, Kowloon, in Hong Kong, because of cerebral concussion. He was a known opium addict of five years' duration. While in the ward, he was given tincture of opium to relieve his withdrawal syndrome. After the cerebral concussion had improved, the patient was asked whether he would agree to cingulumotomy (11) to relieve his drug abuse problem. He agreed. He was scheduled for surgery on the 9th of November, 1972. During the operation for surgery, instead of local anesthesia being injected under the scalp (where the incisions were to be made), acupuncture anesthesia (analgesia) was used.

Four needles were inserted into the right hand, using the following acupuncture points: Hoku = LI − 4: Houshi = SI − 3, and in the arm at Hsimen = EH − 4; Szutu = TB − 9. Another two needles were inserted into the right ear at the "brain-stem" and "god's door" points. Stimulation with an electrical stimulator, BT − 701 (made in China) was carried out for ½ hour. At that time, our interest was in discovering whether the patient obtained analgesia in the scalp prior to surgery. During stimulation, 15 to 30 minutes later, the patient voluntarily stated that his withdrawal symptoms had completely cleared up. We examined him and found that he was free of withdrawal symptoms. The operation was cancelled and the patient returned to the ward with advice to the nursing staff that the doctor should be informed if the patient showed withdrawal symptoms again. At 9:00 p.m. that night, I (HLW) was informed that the patient had had another withdrawal syndrome. Again, acupuncture and electrical stimulation was carried out in a similar manner to the method earlier in the day. After half an hour of acupuncture and electrical stimulation (AES), the withdrawal symptoms again disappeared. Encouraged by this, the next day we saw two other patients from the orthopedic wards of the same hospital, who were both opium abusers. One was suffering from a chronic leg ulcer and the other, from a fracture of the head of the femur. When we explained how we wanted to treat their withdrawal symptoms, both agreed to the procedure. Both responded well to the half hour of AES, and their withdrawal symptoms stopped.

After the above observations, Dr. Wen and his colleague, Dr. Cheung, of the Kwong Wah Hospital, subsequently reported on a series of 40 heroin and opium addicts that acupuncture, combined with electrical stimulation, was effective in relieving the symptoms of narcotic withdrawal (53).

ELECTROACUPUNCTURE: TREATMENT METHODS

Acupuncture with electrical stimulation is used as a method of intervention to reduce the symptoms of withdrawal. The patient receives needling in the concha of both ears. The needle used is about ½-inch long and 32 gauge. After the ears have been cleansed with alcohol swab, a sterile needle is inserted into each concha subcutaneously at the "lung" point for about 0.5 cm. The needles are then connected to a constant current electrical stimulator that has a total voltage of 12 volts and a built-in frequency of 1 to 125 cycles per second. It is difficult to predict the voltage or amperage that will suit a particular patient. The patient is asked to control the stimulus parameters as determined by his or her level of comfort and preference. The average voltage used is usually between 4 and 5 volts and about 3 milliamperes. If the patient has pain in the back and abdomen, extra needles can be inserted, using the same frequency. For backache, bladder points B-24 to B-54, B-57, and B-60 can be utilized. For anxiety and insomnia, large intestine—LI-4, heart—H-5 or H-6, or the ear points Shen-Men are used.

EFFECTS OF ELECTROACUPUNCTURE STIMULATION

It has been observed that symptoms presented by the patients gradually improve after about 15 minutes' treatment and usually disappear after 30 minutes. Signs and symptoms of lacrimation, runny nose, aching bones, wheezing, cramps in the stomach, cold feeling, and irritability usually disappear after 10 to 15 minutes of stimulation. Often it has been noted that patients have a desire to urinate and also that they feel thirsty and ask for water. After treatment, patients often seem less drowsy, are more talkative, and involve themselves more with their surroundings, beginning to do more for themselves in the wards. Also during stimulation, the patient's craving for the narcotic drug seems to diminish. The observed improvement in withdrawal signs and symptoms often lasts in the order of several hours (25, 50, 53). However, no systematic studies have yet been done to compare the effects of different acupuncture treatment techniques with that of placebo controls in the same setting.

Side Effects. It goes without saying that sterile techniques must be employed. In qualified hands, this procedure is remarkably free of side effects. It should be carried out cautiously in pregnant female patients because of the possibility of inducing premature labor. Some patients may complain of dizziness and headaches when the current is increased greatly beyond limits of comfort. These can be prevented by limiting the amount of current used. Syncope may occur when and if the needles are wrongly placed in the concha and also in anxious or nervous patients, but this can be avoided if patients are treated lying down in bed during the initial stages. Acute gastric distention may occur if prolonged and continuous stimulation is given. However, the symptom usually subsides once the stimulation is stopped, and this complication has been observed only rarely.

Advantages. One advantage of electrical acupuncture is that it is easy to administer. Also it is inexpensive and economical in terms of the technique itself and in terms of expenses for drugs such as methadone, which can be quite costly in developing countries. Another advantage is that this is a nonchemical technique that may appeal to certain individuals who are trying to rid themselves of a chemical dependency, and there is no danger of addiction.

SOME SEQUELS TO THE INITIAL OBSERVATIONS

Since the initial report of Wen and Cheung, a number of investigators, both in this country and abroad, employing variations of this basic acupuncture paradigm, have reported beneficial effects on the narcotic withdrawal syndrome and on the clinical opiate detoxification process. However, the various acupuncture procedures that have been used are quite varied and diverse. Variations of this basic paradigm employ varying numbers of acupuncture points and various stimulation techniques. These include the use of needles with manual or electrical stimulation (4, 5, 7, 16, 41–43, 45, 48), use of staple puncture with electrical stimulation (40, 47), as well as the stimulation of "acupuncture points" with surface electrodes without needles (30, 31, 33). These techniques have also been used in the treatment of alcoholism

(22, 32, 45, 52), obesity (19), and cigarette smoking (8, 19, 21, 22, 29).

DETOXIFICATION USING ACUPUNCTURE

Inpatient. Treatment of the abstinence syndrome of drug addiction by acupuncture and electrical stimulation in an inpatient setting was first reported in 1973 (53). In the inpatient setting, treatment can be carried out two or three times or more a day for optimum effect. The periods of hospitalization vary in individuals but, on average, last about 7 days. This method is somewhat cumbersome, treatments have to be given frequently, and it takes an average of 7 to 8 days to detoxify the patients.

Outpatient. The technique of acupuncture and electrical stimulation has also been used on an outpatient basis in detoxification programs. Of the 300 cases reported by Wen (49), it was observed that a total of 10 per cent of the patients can be detoxified during a 14-day program. Another program where outpatient acupuncture treatment has been available is the detoxification project of the Haight-Ashbury Free Medical Clinic in San Francisco (4). Clients could choose between the acupuncture modality and the project's traditional medication modality on a voluntary basis. Although client retention in the acupuncture modality tended to be poor, it was found that about 37 per cent of those clients who began the acupuncture modality persisted long enough to derive real benefits from the program. Small though this proportion is, it seems to compare respectably with the proportion of drug-dependent clients judged clean at the time of termination from the project's conventional detoxification modality. This portion has averaged about 17 per cent over the 1975 to 1977 period.

Rapid Detoxification Using Naloxone and Electrical Acupuncture. The successful use of naloxone as a means of rapid detoxification of addicts from narcotic drugs has previously been reported by Resnick (38, 39) and Blachly (2, 3). These investigators have shown that naloxone-precipitated withdrawal, administered under proper supervision, is neither physically nor psychologically harmful to medically healthy individuals who elect this method of detoxification.

More recently, this rapid detoxification technique has been used combining naloxone with acupuncture and electrical stimulation (AES) (51). With this particular technique, the patient is first primed for ½ hour with AES, before naloxone hydrochloride is injected in increasing doses until 0.8 mg (2 ml) is administered. Of the 50 cases that have been treated with this technique, 41 were detoxified. The patients stated that the symptoms produced by naloxone could be better tolerated when AES was given but not when the current was decreased or stopped. It was also noted that patients seemed to suffer more if the current of the stimulator was not maintained. Symptoms tended to decrease when the current was increased slightly after a short interval. It was reported that the patients were detoxified within 3 hours and that the abstinence syndrome produced by naloxone was much milder and tolerable, and the time and dosage schedule was also well tolerated by the patients. Unfortunately, no controls were included in this study to compare the relative efficacy of electrical acupuncture on the naloxone-induced withdrawal syndrome. Because the naloxone-induced withdrawal symptoms are essentially self-limiting and manageable by conservative methods, the relative usefulness or efficacy of electrical acupuncture in attenuating withdrawal or in affecting the outcome of detoxification remains to be tested.

CRITIQUE

Although the array of favorable reports that have been published are quite impressive, the claims of the effectiveness of acupuncture on withdrawal symptoms or detoxification outcome seem to be based upon clinical observations that lack adequate controls and standardized procedures, thus making comparisons of techniques and results of outcome difficult. In none of these studies reported to date has there been an attempt to determine whether the observed effectiveness of the acupuncture treatment derives from "placebo" (i.e., nonspecific) factors or from certain specific stimulus components of the treatment procedure that make up the acupuncture treatment paradigm. For example, because so many seemingly different techniques seem to be effective, what are the basic elements that may be responsible for

therapeutic efficacy? How crucial is the role of expectation that the therapist and the patient bring to the treatment process? Is the ritual (i.e., the administering of a reputedly potent treatment modality) a critical part of the paradigm? Can one isolate different components in the ritual itself that are responsible for particular biological effects? Is the needle insertion a critical component or is the stimulation itself the important component? Is the combination of needle with electrical stimulation more effective than use of either stimulation alone without needles or needles alone? How critical and specific are the so-called "acupuncture" points? Is specific localization of these points vital, or is the sensory modulation produced by stimulation of particular sensory distributions the critical variable? Obviously, these questions will require much intensive research conducted through properly controlled studies before they can be adequately answered.

IMPLICATIONS FOR RESEARCH

At the present time, the possible mechanisms by which electrical acupuncture produces alleviation of the narcotic withdrawal syndrome are highly conjectural. In animal studies utilizing an experimental model for auricular electroacupuncture, Ng et al. (26, 28) found that electrical stimulation of the conchae of morphine-dependent rats produced significant attenuation of the naloxone-precipitated withdrawal syndrome, as manifested by diminished hyperactivity in the electrical acupuncture-treated rats, coupled with lower "wet dog" and teeth chattering scores, as well as a diminished rise in plasma catecholamines compared with untreated abstinent rats. More recently, auricular electroacupuncture in mice has also been found to be successful in reducing the naloxone-precipitated withdrawal symptoms of morphine-addicted mice, accompanied by a diminished rise in plasma adrenocorticotropin (10) and an elevation of brain "opiate-like activity" (15). These findings suggest that electroacupuncture stimulation may cause the release of a substance with morphine-like properties and are consistent with observations in humans (24) and in animals (36) that show that naloxone injection can abolish the analgesia produced by acupuncture stimulation (manual as well as electrical). Hypophysectomy has also been found to abolish most of the acupuncture-induced analgesic effects (35). The somewhat slow induction period and the long lasting effects of acupuncture implicate a neurohumoral mechanism. These observations have led to the hypothesis that needling in appropriate points can stimulate sensory nerves to activate the pituitary or brain stem to release endorphin, which may at least in part mediate some of the acupuncture-induced effects (34, 44).

It should be pointed out that, although there is preliminary evidence to suggest that manual or electrical stimulation may activate certain somatosensory pathways (9, 37), including perhaps certain central neurohumoral mechanisms (1, 14) and possibly the endorphin system (10, 15, 24, 26, 28, 34, 35, 36, 44), it is still far from clear whether any or all or which of the components embodied in the acupuncture paradigm are causally responsible for initiating such responses. It is premature to attribute a causal relationship between the observed improvement in subjective symptoms in addicts undergoing withdrawal to a particular treatment technique utilized or to a specific neurochemical effect observed. However, in a treatment modality as complex as that inherent in the acupuncture paradigm, the difficulty encountered in trying to isolate causal factors in such a complex set of relationships should not detract from the possible therapeutic uses of such a modality. There is clearly a great need for better controlled studies to help us develop our understanding of the mechanisms of action of acupuncture.

Although we may not understand how acupuncture works, it would be erroneous to equate acupuncture with hypnosis or placebo or conditioning as though these are all one homogeneous or unitary phenomenon (18). It is quite possible, and perhaps even likely, that the extremely complex phenomena of hypnosis, placebo response, the bedside manner of the attending physician and the autogenic suggestion of the patient are but some of the pieces in the jigsaw puzzle of acupuncture. It would be far too simplistic to label all acupuncture-induced phenomena as hypnosis or conditioning or placebo or autosuggestion, because in fact we know little of how these various modalities work. By equating acupuncture as hypnosis or placebo or conditioning or autosuggestion, we are

labeling, in effect, X with Y, when we do not really know what X or Y is. From a research standpoint, it would be far more helpful to try to determine the commonalities and differences that may exist among these various modalities and to try to ask questions of manageable proportions, such as: What specifiable processes underlie acupuncture? Just as, what specifiable processes underlie hypnosis or placebo or conditioning? What are their similarities and what are their differences? What clinical states can be induced with acupuncture? With hypnosis? With placebo? What are the optimal stimulus parameters? And how do these vary with and interact with the intervening variables and with the psychobiological program of the organism?

Because these various modalities in a clinical context are all complex, it may be more useful to shift from single cause to multifactorial models and to focus attention on the nature of *interactions* that can produce sufficient conditions for effective outcomes rather than to confine ourselves to the search for single causal effects. It would seem that an interactive conceptual model would be more appropriate and applicable to our understanding of complex and multifactorial modalities such as acupuncture, hypnosis, placebo, etc., in which therapeutic outcomes are understandably the result of interaction of many factors. A conceptual scheme for such an interactive model for acupuncture and other multifactorial phenomena is presented in Figure 41.1.

At one end, we can specify the input (independent) variables, as shown in *Box I* ("Stimulus"). These may be pharmacological (drugs) or nonpharmacological. The latter includes modalities utilizing one or more sensory inputs—e.g., somatosensory (acupuncture, transcutaneous nerve stimulation), propriokinesthetic (biofeedback, massage), audiovisual (hypnosis). At the other end, we can look at the output (dependent) variables (*Box V*—"Identifiable Response"). These may include induced effects such as alterations in autonomic function, motor function, sensory perception, emotions, consciousness, cognition, or behavior. It is clear that the input can interact with many possible intervening variables to result in a particular observed effect (output). These intervening variables include the psychobiological pro-

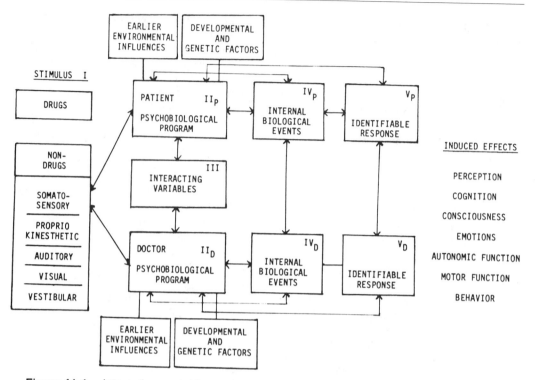

Figure 41.1. Interaction model for acupuncture and related sensory-induced phenomena.

gram of the patient (genetic/learning/environmental factors—*Box II*), the motivation and expectation of the patient (*Box III*—"Interacting Variables"), and the interoceptive factors (*Box IV*—"Internal Biological Events"). These all may interact with each other and with the stimulus input (*Box I*) to produce a particular end effect (*Box V*). Even in the case of pharmacological agents with known specific effects, the end effects, also, can vary depending on the set and setting under which the agent is administered. Similarly, different individuals may respond to the same agent differently on the basis of certain genetic predisposition ("pharmacogenetic") or because of different learning/conditioning/motivational factors. Also, the doctor-patient interaction may be critically important in determining the final outcome or induced effects, as shown in Figure 41.1.

This interaction model is presented as a framework that can be used to analyze and understand the multifactorial nature of complex modalities, such as acupuncture, hypnosis, biofeedback, etc., as applied in a treatment setting, in which the therapeutic outcome is the result of interaction of many factors. The needle in the acupuncture para-

digm may be a necessary condition (if one defines acupuncture as "puncturing with a sharp instrument") but not in and of itself a sufficient condition for successful therapeutic effects. If it is the sensory stimulation that should prove to be the critical variable in producing a desired effect, then the needle in the acupuncture paradigm would merely serve as a vehicle for sensory modulation, using manual or electrical stimulation.

There is increasing evidence to suggest that, in fact, acupuncture shares many similarities with transcutaneous electrical nerve stimulation (TENS) (6, 12, 20) and that it is the stimulation that is the important or critical variable. In this perspective, electrical acupuncture should be described more appropriately as "percutaneous electrical nerve stimulation" (PENS), and the so-called "acupuncture points" should be viewed in a relative sense as providing clues for sites of stimulation, rather than in absolute terms as requiring specific localization, because with electrical stimulation one would obviously be stimulating a field or a particular segmental distribution rather than a unique point. It should be pointed out that acupuncture stimulation (i.e., stimulation delivered through the skin with a needle) does offer certain advantages under certain situations. It allows for a more localized delivery of the stimulus to a greater depth than would be possible with surface (or transcutaneous) stimulation; also, by piercing the skin with a needle, the large resistance of the skin is overcome so that a much smaller amount of current is needed for stimulation.

It is our view that electrical acupuncture is a form of percutaneous nerve stimulation similar to the transcutaneous electrical stimulation that is gaining increasing acceptance in the West. As such, electrical acupuncture provides a simple, nonchemical means of stimulating or modulating certain neural pathways, and the needle merely provides a useful vehicle for sensory modulation using electrical current. Obviously, further research will be needed to allow us to determine the extent to which the physical stimulus components of the treatment paradigm contribute to the biological effects and to the clinical outcome. From the standpoint of an interactive model, it is understandable that sufficient conditions for effective outcome may be achieved from permutations derived from one or more of the different categories shown in Figure 41.1. The hierarchy of effects that can be produced by these permutations under appropriately controlled conditions remains a challenging area for further investigation. Much remains to be learned, and much careful research will be required before proper conclusions can be reached in regard to the many important questions that are being raised.

References

1. Acupuncture Anesthesia Research Group, Hunan Medical College, Changsha, China. Relation between acupuncture analgesia and neurotransmitters in rabbit brain. Chinese Med. J. 8:478, 1975.
2. Blachly, P. Naloxone in opiate addiction. In *Current Psychiatric Therapies*, J. Masserman, editor, vol. 16. New York, Grune and Stratton, 1976.
3. Blachly, P., et al. Rapid detoxification from heroin and methadone using naloxone. In *Developments in the Field of Drug Abuse*, E. C. Senay et al., editors, pp. 327–335. Cambridge, Mass., Schenkman, 1975.
4. Blum, K., Newmeyer, J. A., and Whitehead, C. Acupuncture as a common mode of treatment for drug dependence: Possible neurochemical mechanisms. J. Psychedelic Drugs 10:105, 1978.
5. Bradshaw, J. The use of acupuncture in the treatment of heroin addicts. Presented at the 31st International Congress on Alcoholism and Drug Dependence, February 23–28, 1975, Bangkok, Thailand.
6. Chapman, C. R., et al. Comparative effects of acu-

puncture and transcutaneous stimulation on the perception of painful dental stimuli. Pain 2:265, 1976.
7. Chen, C. S., Hung, L. F., Su, C. Y., Lin, C. S., Lin, B. S., and Wa, Y. M. Preliminary clinical report on the treatment of narcotic addiction by using acupuncture and electrical stimulation. Presented at the International Congress on Acupuncture, 1976, Taipei, Taiwan.
8. Chen, J. Y. P. Treatment of cigarette smoking by auricular acupuncture: A report of 184 cases. Presented at the National Symposia of Acupuncture and Moxibustion and Acupuncture Anesthesia at Beijing, China, January 1–5, 1979.
9. Chiang, C. Y., Chang, C. T., Chud, H. L., and Yang, L. F. Peripheral afferent pathway for acupuncture analgesia. Sci. Sin. 16:210, 1975.
10. Choy, Y. M., Tso, W. W., Fung, K. P., Leung, K. C., Tsang, Y. F., Lee, C. Y., Tsang, D., and Wen, H. L. Suppression of narcotic withdrawals and plasma ACTH by auricular electro-acupuncture. Biochem. Biophys. Res. Commun. 82:305, 1978.
11. Foltz, E. L., and White, L. E., Jr. Experimental cingulumotomy and modification of morphine withdrawal. J. Neurosurg. 14:655, 1957.
12. Fox, E. J., and Melzack, R. Comparison of transcutaneous electrical stimulation and acupuncture in the treatment of chronic pain. In *Advances in Pain Research and Therapy*, J. J. Bonica and D. Albe-Fessard, editors, vol. 1. New York, Raven Press, 1976.
13. Han, C. S., Chou, P. H., Lu, C. C., Lu, L. H., Yang, T. H., and Jen, M. F. (Research Group of Acupuncture Anesthesia, Peking Medical College). The role of central 5-hydroxytryptamine in acupuncture analgesia. Sci. Sin. 22:91, 1979.
14. Han, C. S., Tang, J., Jen, M. F., Zhou, Z. F., Fan, S. G., and Qui, X. C. (Research Group Acupuncture Anesthesia, Peking Medical College). The role of central neurotransmitters in acupuncture analgesia. In Press.
15. Ho, W. K. K., Wen, H. L., Lam, S., and Ma, L. The influence of electro-acupuncture on naloxone-induced morphine withdrawal in mice: Elevation of brain opiate-like activity. Eur. J. Pharmacol. 49:197, 1978.
16. Kao, A. H., and Lu, Y. C. Acupuncture procedure for treating drug addiction. Am. J. Acupuncture 2:201, 1974.
17. Kao, F. *Acupuncture Therapeutics*. New Haven, Conn., Eastern Press, 1973.
18. Kroger, W. S. Acupunctural analgesia: Its explanation by conditioning theory, autogenic training, and hypnosis. Am. J. Psychiatry 130:855, 1973.
19. Lau, M. P. Acupuncture and addiction: An overview. Addict. Dis. 2:449, 1976.
20. Loeser, J. D. Nonpharmacologic approaches to pain relief. In *Proceedings of Conference on Pain, Discomfort, and Humanitarian Care*, held at the National Institutes of Health, February 15–16, 1979, L. K. Y. Ng and J. J. Bonica, editors, *Developments in Neurology*, vol. 4, pp. 275–292. New York, Elsevier-North Holland, 1980.
21. Low, S. A. Acupuncture and nicotine withdrawal. Med. J. Aust. 2:687, 1977.
22. Malizia, E., Andreucci, G., Cerbo, R., and Colombo, G. Riv. Tossicol. Sper. Clin., In press.
23. Mann, F. *The Treatment of Disease by Acupuncture*. London, Heinemann Medical Books, 1972.

24. Mayer, D. J., Price, D. D., Barber, J., and Rafii, A. Acupuncture analgesia: Evidence for activation of a pain inhibitory system as a mechanism of action. In *Advancement in Pain Research and Therapy*, J. J. Bonica and D. Albe-Fessard, editors, pp. 751–754. New York, Raven Press, 1976.

25. Ng, L. K. Y. Unpublished observations.

26. Ng, L. K. Y., Douthitt, T. C., Thoa, N. B., and Albert, C. A. Modification of morphine-withdrawal syndrome in rats following transauricular electro-stimulation: An experimental paradigm for auricular electro-acupuncture. Biol. Psychiatry 10:575, 1975.

27. Ng, L. K. Y., Szara, S., and Bunney, W. E., Jr. On understanding and treating narcotic dependence: A neuropsychopharmacological perspective. Br. J. Addict. 70:311, 1975.

28. Ng, L. K. Y., Thoa, N. B., Douthitt, T. C., and Albert, C. A. Experimental "auricular electro-acupuncture" in morphine-dependent rats. I. Behavioral and biochemical observations. Am. J. Chin. Med. 3:335, 1975.

29. Parker, L. N., and Mole, M. S. The use of acupuncture for smoking withdrawal. Am. J. Acupuncture 5: 363, 1977.

30. Patterson, M. A. Electro-acupuncture in alcohol and drug addiction. Clin. Med. 81:9, 1974.

31. Patterson, M. A. Acupuncture and neuro-electric therapy in treatment of drug and alcohol addictions. Aust. J. Alcoholism Drug Dependence 2:90, 1975.

32. Patterson, M. A. *Addiction Can be Cured*. Berkhamsted, England, Lion Publishing, 1975.

33. Patterson, M. A. Effects of neuro-electric therapy (N.E.T.) in drug addiction: Interim report. Bull. Narc. 28:55, 1976.

34. Pomeranz, B. Do endorphins mediate acupuncture analgesia? Adv. Biochem. Psychopharmacol. 18:351, 1978.

35. Pomeranz, B., Cheng, R., and Law, P. Acupuncture reduces electrophysiological and behavioral responses to noxious stimuli: Pituitary is implicated. Exp. Neurol. 54:172, 1977.

36. Pomeranz, B., and Chiu, D. Naloxone blockade of acupuncture analgesia: Endorphin implicated. Life Sci. 19:1757, 1976.

37. Pomeranz, B., and Paley, D. Electro-acupuncture hypalgesia is mediated by afferent nerve impulses: An electrophysiological study in mice. Exp. Neurol. 66:398, 1979.

38. Resnick, R. B., Kastenbaum, R., Gaztanaga, P., Volavka, J., and Freedman, A. The problem of detoxification. In *Developments in the Field of Drug Abuse*, E.C. Senay et al., editors, pp. 321–326. Cambridge, Mass., Schenkman, 1975.

39. Resnick, R. B., Volavka, J., Kastenbaum, R. S., and Freedman, A. M. A new method of opiate detoxification and naloxone induction. In *Neuropsychopharmacology*, P. Deniker, C. Radouco-Thomas, and A. Villeneuve, editors. Oxford, Pergamon Press, 1978.

40. Sacks, L. L. Drug addiction, alcoholism, smoking, obesity treated by auricular staplepuncture. Am. J. Acupuncture 3:147, 1975.

41. Sainbury, M. J. Acupuncture in heroin withdrawal. Med. J. Aust. 2:102, 1975.

42. Schnaib, M. Acupuncture treatment of drug dependence in Pakistan. Am. J. Chin. Med. 4:403, 1976.

43. Severson, L., Markoff, R. A., and Chun-Hoon, A. Heroin detoxification with acupuncture and electrical stimulation. Int. J. Addict. 12:911, 1977.

44. Sjolund, B., Terenius, L., and Eriksson, M. Increased cerebrospinal fluid levels of endorphins after electroacupuncture. Acta Physiol. Scand. 100:382, 1977.

45. Smith, M. O. Acupuncture and natural healing in drug detoxification. Am. J. Acupuncture 7:97, 1979.

46. Synder, S. Opioid peptides in the brain. In *The Neurosciences: Fourth Study Program*, F. O. Schmidt and F. G. Worden, editors. Cambridge, Mass., MIT Press, 1978.

47. Tennant, F. S. Outpatient heroin detoxification with acupuncture and staplepuncture. West. J. Med. 125: 191, 1976.

48. Tseung, Y. K. Acupuncture for drug addicts. Lancet 2:839, 1974.

49. Wen, H. L. Acupuncture and electrical stimulation (AES) outpatient detoxification. Mod. Med. Asia 15: 39, 1979.

50. Wen, H. L. Treatment of drug addiction by electroacupuncture: Report of one hundred cases. In *Basic Acupuncture: A Scientific Interpretation and Application*, pp. 199–212. Taipei, Taiwan, Acupuncture Research and Training Center, 1977.

51. Wen, H. L. Fast detoxification of heroin addicts by acupuncture and electrical stimulation (AES) in combination with naloxone. Comp. Med. East West 5: 257, 1978.

52. Wen, H. L., and Cheung, S. Y. C. How acupuncture can help addicts. Drugs Society 2:18, 1973.

53. Wen, H. L., and Cheung, S. Y. C. Treatment of drug addiction by acupuncture and electrical stimulation. Asian J. Med. 9:138, 1973.

CHAPTER 42

RATIONAL AUTHORITY: AN EXAMINATION OF THE USE OF COERCION IN TREATMENT

Leon Brill, M.S.S.

This chapter comprises a retrospective examination of our country's use of authority in relation to its drug problem(s) since passage of the Harrison Narcotics Act in 1914. We shall be examining the various elements that constituted our efforts at management and social control; among them, our criminal definition of the problem, which generated a self-fulfilling or self-defeating prophecy for our society (2–4, 30, 39). Concern was focused almost exclusively on the villain drug, heroin, and relatedly, if not serendipitously, on marihuana and cocaine because of their presumed association with heroin. A further anomaly to be noted was our indifference to other more pervasive and insidious drugs such as alcohol, barbiturates, amphetamine, and tobacco, the first three of which were finally brought under regulation by the Federal Drug Abuse Control Acts of 1965 and 1970. Many "state of the art" misunderstandings were endemic as well, such as the belief that there is a uniform narcotic addict with similar social and psychological characteristics, an unvarying diagnosis of character disorder, and uniform family constellation (3, 4,

28). It was only in the past 20 years that we began to distinguish between different kinds of users and develop a typology encompassing a spectrum of experimenters, social-recreational users, "seekers" becoming more involved with drugs, medical users, and the tertiary or chronic cases, characterized by a compulsive craving for drugs (3, 4).

Before proceeding with our main discussion, it would be well to pause to consider whether such long term, chronic relapsing conditions as described in the 1950's still exist today. The issue is important because it touches on the question of goals and success in treatment and control efforts (3, 4, 28). Although the existence of such addictions was not questioned previously, the pendulum seems to have swung in the opposite direction, toward the belief that *no* heroin addiction is chronic. This feeling was heavily buttressed by the Vietnam experience, during which at least 20 per cent of the soldiers became heavily addicted to heroin with most not becoming fully readdicted after returning to the United States: 56 per cent abstained from heroin entirely, 32 per cent relapsed without becoming readdicted, and only 12 per cent became readdicted (36–38).[1] Robins' studies nevertheless confirmed what many practitioners had known all along: that there are different kinds of heroin users—large numbers of "chippiers" who use irregularly but do not become addicted, others who become addicted but do not become chronic users, and still others who become addicted but are never caught up in the full unconventional behavior of the street addict (3, 6, 8). The author treated a number of middle-class methadone and cyclazocine patients of the South Bronx in the 1960's, many of them "hidden addicts" conventional in every area of living but their drug use. They came from conventional middle-class families, established middle-class families of their own, enjoyed lucrative licit occupations, and had never been arrested, hospitalized for their addiction, or otherwise detected (3, 4).

Regarding the diversity of heroin users, Chein, in the 1950's, first differentiated between addicts driven by craving, which he viewed as the hallmark of compulsive addiction, and "situational users" who might behave in all external respects like the confirmed users yet never developed the characteristic craving themselves (11). Starting in 1951, the author followed some 2,000 dischargees from the Public Health Service Hospital at Lexington, Kentucky, for a period of 10 years. Among them were numbers of old-time users in their fifties and sixties and a few in their seventies still actively pursuing heroin or other opiates after a lifetime of use (13). Stephens and Weppner, in several papers, described the "street addict" as a distinct category, with homogeneous characteristics, values, pursuits, and life styles (46, 49). In the early 1970's, Sheppard et al. at the Haight-Ashbury Clinic in San Francisco reported on three discrete types of heroin users: the "old junkies" (OJ's) who had used heroin before 1969 and seemed to resemble the confirmed cases described in the literature; the

"transitional junkies" (TJ's) addicted between January 1969 and January 1971: and the "Watergate-era junkies" (WJ's) after 1971 (41). Each group had varied beginnings and careers, some emanating from the flower children of the later 1960's.

A question regarding the existence of confirmed older addicts was crystallized by the early paper of Winick, who postulated a "maturing out process" based on an examination of Federal Bureau of Narcotics (FBN) files. The addiction ceased spontaneously due either to the duration of the addiction or the actual chronological age of the addict. Winick felt that most people, by their late thirties, reached a state of "emotional homeostasis" as the stresses of the younger years subsided; other addicts simply "burned out" by becoming so debilitated that they could no longer maintain the habit of their youth (50). Although Winick's conclusion seemed to be valid for certain addicts, there was evidence that he did not speak for all. O'Donnell, in his Lexington follow-up study of 288 dischargees, demonstrated that most had never found their way to the FBN files (33). Ball and Lau's study of a group of Chinese addicts discharged from Lexington between 1957 and 1962 revealed that 88.4 per cent were over 40 and most were long term addicts (cited in 34). Other studies related to some 60 elderly Chinese addicts registered in the methadone maintenance program of the Lower Eastside Multi-Service Center in New York City (34). Another study by Capel et al. in New Orleans in 1972 comprised 38 elderly street addicts between the ages of 48 and 73 not enrolled in any treatment program. They confirmed that many addicts do not burn out or mature out but succeed in escaping official attention and detection. Many had switched from heroin to Dilaudid—because it was cheaper, easier to obtain, and more dependable—and had also decreased their daily dosage of drugs or adjusted to occasional substitutions of other drugs such as alcohol or barbiturates (9, 10). A recent follow-up of these addicts noted that they were using drugs in about the same dosage and frequency as in 1969 (10). In an update of a 1972 study, Capel et al. specifically focused on age distributions in the New Orleans methadone maintenance population between 1969 and 1976. A steady increase in the number of older addicts between 45 and 59 was noted,

---

[1] The Vietnam situation nevertheless seems to be a special case. Robins explored the question of maturing out (38) and postulated a possible addiction career of approximately 9 years. This is based in part on a special study of the author's (2) that gave a mean of 9 years but a range of from 4 to 21 years; and on Winick's "maturing out" paper (50), which estimated 8.6 years. It would be helpful to clarify what is meant by "chronic" in defining an addiction.

along with a decline in the under-37 group, with the intervening age group remaining stable. Capel concluded (10):

If the present holding rate of the clinics continues, it can be expected that within the next 10 years, the number over 60 will have tripled or quadrupled its present size. If this prediction is replicated for the approximately 800 clinics across the country, even without including addicts living on the streets without treatment, one can anticipate a national geriatric drug abuse problem of significant proportions.

The point we have been attempting to underline in this discussion is the need to keep stressing the factor of diversity among heroin users, including also the chronic cases as with other addictions. How these patterns continue in the future will require further study. For the moment, it is crucial that we understand the chronic nature of many addictions—as in schizophrenia—with the need for long term support systems in the community and an acceptance of the concept of limited goals in treatment.

In returning to the evolution of our current management perspective, we need to consider the punitive approaches that prevailed from 1914 to about 1961 and more recent efforts to develop more rational strategies comprising such elements as the change from criminal to civil commitment and court diversion, viewing drug use as an "illness" or "disease" to be treated, and reliance on a medical model of care rather than legal coercions alone (3, 5, 22, 28, 29, 44). Until the late 1960's and 1970's, it often proved impossible to distinguish between law enforcement and therapeutic interventions, because both relied on long term institutionalization as their primary modality (17, 28, 35). That the issue is far from resolved is evidenced by the continuing struggle to rescind the famous landmark Miranda Decision of the 1960's, to maintain search-and-seizure procedures, wiretapping without prior court authorization, invasion of the home, and other violations of individual privacy without prior warrant as well as the strong move to reinstitute the death penalty. In treatment, although it seemed that we had finally learned the importance of pursuing a comprehensive multimodality approach, there has been increasing animosity toward methadone maintenance as a viable modality even though it has served some 90,000 pa-

tients nation-wide and 40,000 in the New York City area alone. Part of our problem is the conflict between civil rights and management, treatment versus custodial issues. On the one hand, we find a growing emphasis on "consumers' rights" and the "treatment contract" concept of Karl Menninger, in which clients have the right to help determine the conditions of their treatment, and a movement away from what the author has termed the institutional-aftercare or parole model of treatment (3, 28, 29). For both prisons and therapy, the gravamen of effort coincides with the idea of "deinstitutionalization", i.e., treatment of the client in the community to the extent possible (1, 3, 14, 28). Clients and patients are increasingly questioning the right of authorities to impose treatment in closed settings or, indeed, in any form, whether traditional or new, including treatments that have at times been the subject of fierce debate, such as psychosurgery or extreme forms of aversive therapy entailing the use of such negative reinforcements as chemicals that may literally paralyze the inmate or client if he is not conforming to treatment.

The other side of the coin relates to the rights of society vis-à-vis individuals who are behaving antisocially or, in any case, illegally; who may be confirmed criminals or otherwise constitute a continuing problem for themselves and society (17, 20, 35). Many have been classified as "unmotivated" or "recalcitrant" and seem to be untreatable or unchangeable by any known methods. Still others are psychotic, violent, suicidal, homicidal, or perennially acting out in dangerous ways and need to be protected from themselves. Our society is greatly perturbed about "crime on the streets" and "law and order" issues, which often turn out to be euphemisms for discriminatory or racist attitudes in the opinion of some. This was evident in the tough Rockefeller legislation enacted in New York in 1973 (16). Although some of our citizen concerns have a realistic basis, we tend to seek simplistic solutions. Other concerns still emanate from our "Protestant ethic" or "Puritan temper," with their insistence on the work ethic and avoidance or delayed gratification of the pleasure principle. Regarding drug use, it was early decided that drugs were to be used only as medication and as prescribed by medical doctors. An associated issue has been that of "crimes without victims" in the cases of drug use, gambling, prostitution, homosexuality, and abortion (39). It is argued that society has no right to "legislate morality," and efforts to do so will inevitably backfire as they did with Prohibition and, more recently, marihuana. Furthermore, the issue of involuntary commitment is still being debated. Goffman has well described the "degradation rituals" for persons coming into mental hospitals, who have their ability to assume responsibility reduced, perhaps forever, once they come into the "total institution" (19). The institution operates like a prison to control all aspects of their lives in an authoritarian manner. Yet some individuals clearly cannot remain in the community and need to be removed for shorter or longer periods (24–26, 29, 35).

The social theorist, Michel Foucault, has described the evolution of Western penal methods since the 17th century. Initially, the emphasis was on inflicting the most barbarous physical cruelties. In the last two centuries, concern gradually shifted to dealing with the inner man, with the soul or mind; to viewing trespasses as an "illness" and using psychological measures to cure and reform (17). Offenders could now be coerced into treatment that might have all the earmarks of ordinary punishment inasmuch as they were incarcerated and subjected to punishing techniques for prolonged periods. Still, Justice Hugo Black could declare in 1949 that "Retribution is no longer the dominant objective of criminal law. The reformation and rehabilitation of offenders have become the important goals of criminal jurisprudence" (cited in 42). The question of authority must obviously be examined within the context of our society's larger concerns: how we came to establish our values and standards of behavior; what constitutes deviance; and what coercions and punishments need to be applied to discourage such deviance (30). In our society, strange differentiations in attitude prevail for different drugs, with far greater penalties imposed for some that are more innocuous, and, until recently, an indifference to others that are a cause for concern. As to our criminal justice system, Silberman believes that, given the impact of racism, poverty, and community disorganization in promoting crime, we can expect little reduction in crime from changes in this system.

Nothing seems to be working, and increased levels of punishment will not reduce crime. Attacking the root causes is his answer (42). But to eliminate crime by eliminating its ultimate causes, as Silberman recommends, seems an impossible task if only because these causes are so deeply embedded in our cultural system, family structure, and (if we accept Silberman) in the historical legacy of violence among certain segments of our population. Regarding the value of rehabilitation, Martinson (cited in 42), a criminologist, concluded pessimistically, after evaluating some 231 research studies in 1974: "With few and isolated exceptions, the rehabilitation efforts that have been reported so far have had no appreciable effect on recidivism. Whether incarcerated or placed on probation, whether given psychotherapy, group counseling, job training or no assistance at all, the proportion of offenders who return to crime seem to be about the same—roughly one in three". Although this is indeed discouraging, I do not believe it represents the whole truth or even an adequate understanding of what is involved. As may be seen in the following sections of this chapter, a number of approaches have been effective. Much depends on an adequate comprehension of what constitutes suitable goals in the treatment of such chronic, long term conditions as addictions, confirmed criminality, and some schizophrenias for which long term support systems and relatively limited goals are appropriate. Our understanding would also need to encompass the real place of civil commitment, court diversion, and the use of "rational authority" within this context (5–7, 29).

THE ISSUE OF DRUGS AND CRIME

For many years, it was believed that crime derived from drug use and that drugs were the sole cause of crime in our larger cities—a belief that helped harden attitudes about heroin use. Another view propounded by sociologists and psychologists was that, for certain individuals, both crime and drug abuse represented ways of "acting out" emotional needs for danger and engaging in self-destructive behavior to gain secondary rewards in terms of the subculture's restricted opportunities for legitimate achievement. Criminality, drug use, and drug selling were known to constitute high status forms of behavior in these subcultures of the inner city. Although both views have validity, the actual links between crime and drugs are, in fact, too complex to be explained by simple formulas. For one thing, because heroin had been outlawed, it could only be obtained illicitly; the exorbitant amounts of money required to support a habit generally entailed around-the-clock activity of the sort described as the "hustling syndrome" (46, 49). Still, as indicated earlier, some users managed to avoid illegal activity, a fact that underlines the idea that criminal activity depends on the person, the extent to which he is involved in the addiction system, and the general context of his use (3, 8, 46, 49). There is evidence from such studies as those of black male addicts in St. Louis, from the Lexington Public Health Service Hospital, and from the New York State Office of Drug Abuse Services that many addicts pursued criminal life styles prior to their drug use. Many grew up in an inner-city subculture where both criminal and addict life styles were common. Crime and addiction, therefore, seemed to be two sides of the same coin for them: the crime may have antedated the addiction or the addiction the crime (37, 35). Virtually all pre- and postaddiction studies show substantial increases in arrests and self-reported crimes after the onset of addiction. The findings regarding pre- and posttreatment criminality are not as consistent, but these conclusions resulted more from deficiencies in the research methodology than from the existence of definitive negative findings (27). One of the problems is that addiction typically begins during a high risk age for criminality, and crime may thus have increased without addiction. Nevertheless, according to McGlothlin et al., virtually all the pre- and postaddiction studies have shown an increase in crime after addiction. The large majority of methadone maintenance studies have also found that crime decreases during treatment. Crimes that increase with addiction include selling drugs, forgery, conning, sex crimes, and theft—mostly offenses that are small income-generating crimes. The results are unequivocal in confirming that, during the periods of addiction, individuals are more likely to be arrested for property crimes and more likely to report that they are engaged in criminal behavior, commit more crimes, and acquire more money from crimes than when

they are not using narcotics daily (27). The rate of crime may actually fluctuate with the amount of heroin being used. Women addicts steal less than men because they can acquire money more easily through prostitution.

EFFORTS TO APPLY RATIONAL AUTHORITY

The following section will describe some recent experiences with rational authority, civil commitment, and court diversion approaches. Included are descriptions of the Washington Heights Rehabilitation Center conducted by the author in New York City between 1962 and 1967; federal and state efforts to apply civil commitment in California and New York; the Narcotic Addict Rehabilitation Act (NARA) and Treatment Alternatives to Street Crime programs (TASC). Mention will also be made of the retrogressive Rockefeller legislation of 1973.

WASHINGTON HEIGHTS REHABILITATION CENTER

Cues from the earlier New York Demonstration Center directed by the author between 1952 and 1962 (7, 13) were developed further in the Washington Heights Rehabilitation Center. As a result of the New York Demonstration Center experience, there had been question regarding the feasibility of helping most addicts on a voluntary basis and emphasis on the need for some form of authority as a structuring device in treatment (7). At the Washington Heights Center, it was planned to use "rational authority" as described by Max Weber and Erich Fromm. The authority to be used was visualized as the use of controls, coercion, and limit setting through a series of deterrents that would minimize the acting-out behavior of clients and help retain them in treatment. The relationship established between the two main cooperating agencies—the center and the New York City Department of Probation—differed from the traditional collaboration in that the use of authority was placed in the very forefront of the program, with full sharing of information between the two agencies. Clients were informed in advance that there would be no confidentiality between the two and that the decision making and planning would be shared jointly. They were, therefore, less able to manipulate one agency against the other as they had done with other agencies and in relation to their parents in the service of their own impulsive needs. In all, approximately 100 clients were seen at the center and 100 comparable clients by the Department of Probation (5).

The evaluation questions posed proved difficult because there were serious misconceptions at that time regarding the nature of addiction and the goals to be sought as well as a definition of what constitutes success. Because the key characteristic of narcotics addiction is the use of drugs, almost all programs had hitherto been oriented exclusively toward keeping addicts totally drug free. When they relapsed to drugs, they were considered failures. The center's approach was novel in that a confirmed addiction was viewed, at least for the population being served, as a chronic illness, with relapse to be expected as an inevitable part of the rehabilitation process. It was postulated that there are different stages in the movement toward abstinence and theoretical and practical reasons why most addicts cannot become immediately abstinent. Therefore, the objective was to get clients moving toward abstinence by cutting down on the frequency, duration, and amount of drug use and increasing the periods of abstinence between relapses. The primary focus was on improved social functioning, regardless of the achievement of immediate, total abstinence, an approach that was subsequently bolstered by the advent of the chemical modalities, most notably methadone maintenance. To obtain better measures of client adjustment, staff secured data regarding their patterns of use before they came to the center and at specified intervals thereafter. There was continual check on the "vicissitudes" of clients in their move toward abstinence by counting the number of "clean man months" of abstinence when clients were in the community and observation of patterns of increasing intervals of abstinence between relapses. These data were then combined into an index of "extent of heroin use" that gave a before and after picture and indicated whether there was movement in the desired direction.

Using this index, improvement was noted in almost half (48 per cent) of the clients. Although there was no improvement in an additional 14 per cent these were individuals who came to the center with only a moderate

history of drug use but with every indication of increasing involvement with the drug culture. Their drug use was thus checked in the early stages so that no further deterioration occurred. In effect, then, 62 per cent of the clients represented "success," although some had used drugs while in the program. Indices were also created to measure improvement in other areas considered important, such as criminality, work and conventional social adaptation. For the index of criminality, 72 per cent improved and an additional 8 per cent stayed well, for a total of 80 per cent. For work, 37 per cent improved and 15 per cent stayed well, for a 52 per cent improvement. And for conventional social adaptation—i.e., sexual and marital adjustment, support of family, conventional use of leisure-time activities, and ability to associate with nonaddict friends— 41 per cent improved and 30 per cent stayed well, for a total of 71 per cent. For the most part, rational authority seemed to have the greatest impact in the area of criminality, which seems understandable in view of the very close supervision maintained by both the center and probation staffs. The Washington Heights Rehabilitation Center was useful as a forerunner of the many diversion programs started later and as a prototype for efforts to effect better linkages with the criminal justice system (5).

CALIFORNIA CIVIL COMMITMENT PROGRAM

The President's Commission on Law Enforcement in 1967 described the term "civil commitment" as misleading since this type of commitment usually takes place at some point during criminal proceedings. They were termed "civil" because they suspended the criminal proceedings and did not result in a penal confinement. Civil commitment subsequently came to be understood as a court-ordered confinement in a special treatment facility followed by discharge to outpatient status under supervision in the community, with provision for final release of the patient if he/she abstained from drugs or return to confinement if there was a relapse. The total commitment was for an indeterminate period, not to exceed the prescribed maximum term. One question to be raised here relates to the objectives: the individual's own good versus that of society. Is it treatment if it is not for the individual's good but only for society's?

The California "Civil Addict Program" was established in 1961 under the Department of Correction to "treat, rehabilitate and control, not punish." Commitment occurred in three ways. First, for persons convicted of a felony or misdemeanor who were also adjudged to be addicted or "in imminent danger of becoming addicted" to narcotics, the courts could suspend the criminal proceedings and, after a hearing, commit to the program. Second, a person not convicted of, or even charged with, a crime might be involuntarily committed after a judicial hearing after a report by any person to the district attorney that he was believed to be addicted or in imminent danger of becoming addicted. Third, an individual who believed himself addicted or about to become addicted could apply for voluntary commitment, in which case the term was 2½ years. The two involuntary procedures called for a 7-year commitment. The median length of stay initially proved to be about 14 months; users were then placed on outpatient service for a statutory limit of 7 years. They reported regularly to supervisors, were tested for drug use, and could be compelled to attend group therapy sessions. According to Kramer, statistics for the first admission revealed that only 35 per cent of the 1,209 outpatients released between June 1962 and 1964 remained in good standing for 1 year and only 16 per cent for 3 years, with most of the failures a consequence of relapse to drug use (22). The rate of failure was found to be essentially the same as for other programs for addicts conducted under correctional auspices. In an article entitled "The State vs. the Addict: Uncivil Commitment," Kramer concluded (22):

Commitment for a treatment which is not proven effective is cruel and unusual punishment... The trouble with the California... program, and perhaps with the New York and Federal Civil Commitment Programs as well, is not merely that it violates the spirit, if not the letter of the Supreme Court Decision in Robinson vs. California, but also that it does not work.

For a number of years, Kramer's conclusions tended to discourage belief in civil commitment. Yet they were based on a very small sample and included nonheroin cases, so that the criticisms seemed not valid. More recent studies by McGlothlin throw a different light on the program. According to McGlothlin, most of Kramer's earlier criticisms were answered at least partially by changes in commitment procedures and program policies and by reliance on methadone maintenance. In 1970, the number of consecutive drug-free years required for early release was reduced to 2, except for methadone patients, for whom the period remained 3 years. At the beginning of the program, about 40 per cent of male and 50 per cent of female commitments either followed misdemeanor convictions or were made under the no-criminal-charge provisions. By 1974, 92 per cent of the total commitments followed a felony conviction, and only five of some 2,100 commitments were in the no-criminal-charge category. Current civil commitment proceedings are largely pro forma, because individuals are rarely committed where the likely alternative sentencing disposition is less severe than the civil commitment. Therefore, civil commitment is currently a misnomer. Commitment would be more accurately described as an alternative sentencing disposition. Of equal interest is the fact that, during the same period that Kramer studied, those who continued in the program fared better than those who obtained a writ for discharge. The group continuing in the program reported less daily narcotic use, less criminal activity, and less time incarcerated, with more employment and being alive at the time of the interview. It was also clear that the outpatient services portion of the program was relatively effective (22). To a lesser extent, the program also seemed to have lasting benefits subsequent to discharge. The supervision and testing for narcotic use tended to have a moderating effect even where they could not always prevent narcotic use. Evidence was also provided regarding the effectiveness of methadone maintenance in reducing daily narcotic use and criminal behavior. Of 212 patients enrolled in methadone programs, for the 42 per cent of time enrolled, the reported daily narcotic use averaged 6 per cent compared with 48 per cent when not enrolled; and self-reported criminality during methadone treatment was about one-fourth of that when not enrolled (22).

In a larger summary study that included earlier surveys, McGlothlin examined four samples of male admissions. The total sample included 292 admissions during 1962 and 1963 who were discharged by writ prior to first release to outpatient services; 289 admissions of 1964; 282 admissions of 1970; and 153 admissions of 1964 discharged as successes. The main comparison was between the 1964 sample, which continued in the normal 7-year commitment, and a matched sample of 1962 and 1963 admissions discharged by writ. A second comparison was between the 1964 and 1970 admissions, i.e., a comparison of behavior during periods of strict and relatively more lenient control policies enacted in 1970. It was found that the program significantly reduced daily narcotic use and associated behavior among the 1964 sample during the period of commitment. For the 7 years after admission, the mean percentage of nonincarcerated time using narcotics daily was 13 for the 1964 sample versus 48 for the 1962 and 1963 group. The 1964 sample also had a significantly higher rate of employment and lower rates of nondrug arrests and self-reported criminal activity than did the 1962 and 1963 comparison group. Other positive results were as described previously (25). McGlothlin et al.'s conclusion seems to jibe with the author's emphasis on chronicity of addiction and the need for limited goals (25): "A policy of containment aimed at limiting the extremes of narcotic usage and its associated criminal behavior can be successful in minimizing the social costs of addiction although perhaps not achieving the traditional goal of abstinence." One of the main factors contributing to the favorable performance during civil commitment was the ability of the outpatient supervision (OPS) supervisors to limit the length of daily narcotic use runs. Even with the current relatively lenient policies in which 48 per cent of those on OPS gave positive urine specimens, the ability to prevent prolonged daily use runs produced relatively favorable results. The availability of methadone maintenance also seemed to be an important component in this approach. With the rapid decline in admissions over the past 2 years, the Civil Addict Program is nearing an end, at least in the form in which it has existed for the past 18 years. Civil commitment, as indicated, has become essentially a sentencing alternative for felony convictions and is rarely used when the individual prefers the

normal criminal justice disposition. It can be argued that the issue is not whether addicts fare equally well under civil commitment as opposed to other criminal justice dispositions, but whether or not coercion should be used at all for simple use of narcotics. However, the question is also becoming largely irrelevant for civil commitments, because by 1978 only 15 per cent of male and 21 per cent of female commitments were for user offenses; the remainder followed convictions for drug sales or nondrug crimes. In general, the California program was relatively successful in reducing addiction and associated social costs during the period of commitment, and this rate is not adequately measured by the rate of successful discharges. The results of McGlothlin's current follow-up show that, during the 7 years after commitment, the rates of addiction and criminal behavior were significantly lower than for the comparison group. They also had a significantly lower rate of nondrug arrests and a higher rate of employment. The costs of the program were less than those of New York and NARA: $7,000 for inpatient and $2,000 for outpatient treatment.

NEW YORK STATE DIVISION OF DRUG ABUSE SERVICES

This Division, first known as the Narcotic Addiction Control Commission (NACC), then Drug Abuse Control Commission (DACC), then the Office of Drug Abuse Services (ODAS), before it was combined with the alcoholism services, and currently as DSAS, was first proposed by Governor Rockefeller in 1966 as a massive attempt to deal with the state's drug problem from a rehabilitation standpoint after a public outcry about "crime on the street." Reinforced by the Supreme Court Decision of 1962, which held valid California's involuntary treatment of narcotic addicts, the New York Legislature passed a comprehensive bill to deal with the "disease" of narcotic addiction. It created the Narcotic Addiction Control Commission to treat, on an inpatient basis, individuals referred to it by the courts. The statute had a 2-fold aspect in that it covered both noncriminals as well as criminals who were also addicts. The court could order a physical examination to ascertain the fact of addiction; the accused was provided with counsel and other safeguards. After the trial, whether jury or nonjury, a finding of addiction could result in a conviction of a felony for an indeterminate period up to 5 years (a misdemeanor was up to 3 years) in a state rehabilitation center. The second section of the bill contained a procedure under the general power of the state very much akin to the involuntary commitment of the mentally ill—to treat those who were not accused of a crime, even against their will. This procedure was called "certification" to NACC. There were amplifications of the program in succeeding years, with greater emphasis on other drugs than heroin (hence the change to DACC) and on the treatment of younger users as well as on prevention. In the author's own experience with the program, a sharp reduction in referrals occurred by 1974 so that clients needed to be found through other sources. This was accomplished primarily through the creation of centralized screening and referral centers called "Multi-Purpose Outreach Units" in different parts of the state. Efforts were made to move away from the institutional-aftercare model, with some success. The state finally removed itself from providing direct services and turned over all treatment to the community voluntary programs. The program was terminated in 1978–1979 with only 180 persons in the state program. Five hundred million dollars had been spent between 1966 and 1978. As in the case of California, New York needs to think through where it wishes to go from here and whether any provision should be made for the use of civil commitment in some new form in future.

FEDERAL NARA PROGRAM

Prior to enactment of the Narcotic Addict Rehabilitation Act of 1966, the efforts of the federal government were centered on the two Public Health Service Hospitals in Lexington, Kentucky, and Fort Worth, Texas, for the treatment of both prisoner and nonprisoner patients. There was no means of providing aftercare services. Passage of the NARA act introduced a new civil commitment procedure that changed the legal criteria of eligibility for treatment at the federal level: narcotic addicts could now petition a United States District Court for commitment to treatment, thus coming under the custody of the court and the Office of the Surgeon-General

(23). The NARA act had three basic provisions known as Titles I, II, and III, which covered the three processes by which a patient could enter the program. Titles I and III created access to treatment for both those charged with an offense and those not charged (Title III was for voluntary commitments). Title I authorized the federal courts to commit for treatment any narcotic addict charged with certain federal offenses in lieu of trial. The addict was ineligible if he had committed a crime of violence or had three previous civil commitments as a narcotic addict. Under Title II, addicts already convicted of a crime were committed to the custody of the Attorney General for treatment for a maximum of 10 years. They were treated in institutions, mostly selected prisons, for a minimum of 6 months and could then be paroled to outpatient aftercare in the community. Under Title III, civil commitment was provided for addicts not charged with a federal offense. The procedure could be initiated only by petition by the addict or a relative. As to the number of admissions, in fiscal year 1969, it was almost 3,500; admissions reached a peak of 5,500 by 1970. The number declined thereafter: there were 2,100 in the program in 1971, 1,500 in 1973, and 295 by May 1975. For several years, the National Institute of Mental Health (NIMH) attempted to phase out the program, but Congress delayed following through. According to Karst Besteman, former Acting Director of the National Institute on Drug Abuse, because of the "institutional prejudices" of the NIMH against methadone maintenance, drug-free outpatient treatment was stressed.

In a careful study conducted by Mandell for the NIMH in 1973, a population of 7,353 was looked at, of some 10,000 in all who applied for the program between July, 1967 and June 30, 1971. Different categories of the attempted admissions were then interviewed to learn their characteristics and gauge the effectiveness of the NARA program (23). The study entailed comparison of the different subgroups: those considered not suitable for treatment (NST) (roughly 50 per cent of those considered for admission were found to be NST); patients who experienced examination and evaluation only; those found not suitable for aftercare (NSA); those who escaped (ESC); patients who left against medical advice; patients who completed the inpatient phase up to a maximum of 36 months and were discharged to aftercare (DCA); and "successful completions" who were released if they had completed 12 consecutive drug-free months, were "independent of the drug-seeking community," and had "socially acceptable behavior." Among the significant findings was the fact that of the 51 per cent admitted for treatment (N = 3,774), 68 per cent were discharged to aftercare, 14 per cent were considered not suitable for aftercare, and 18 per cent left against medical advice. Thus, 35 per cent of those attempting to enter the NARA system never reached aftercare. Almost one-half of the persons admitted to the program were designated not suitable for treatment. The percentage of persons applying for NARA treatment who were discharged to aftercare increased significantly by 1971. A higher percentage of blacks was designated "not suitable for treatment" than whites (54 per cent and 45 per cent, respectively). The inpatient system was able to complete treatment to the point of discharge for only about one-third of all applicants. Of those considered suitable for treatment, 70 per cent of the whites and 63 per cent of the blacks were discharged to aftercare. Applicants in the oldest group (35 and over) were more often considered not suitable for treatment (55 per cent) compared to the younger groups (45 per cent). A higher percentage of younger patients (15 to 24) absconded (20 per cent) than in either of the other groups (17 per cent and 13 per cent). Twenty-five per cent of the applicants completed the inpatient treatment and 1 year's aftercare. A comparison of the variables that differentiated between "successes" and "failures" revealed that "successes" were more often males; were older, with a mean age of 30 compared to 26 for the "failures"; were more highly educated and trained; began using narcotics later (mean age 23 against mean age of 19 for "failures"); and got into trouble less in school. As regards life styles, both were quite different prior to application to NARA, including differences in employment, drug use, alcohol use, health, criminality, and interpersonal relations (23). It was found generally that, to a great extent, pretreatment experiences were important indicators of posttreatment behavior. A strong association was found between success and time in treatment, although the more subtle ramifications proved difficult to tease out.

Regarding the NARA program as a whole, many provisions made it unwieldy and difficult of access so that, although it was expanded after several years to include alcoholics, it never had any appreciable impact on the community or the addict population. Its major thrust was toward tightly controlled confinement or close supervision in the community; and it was largely administered under public auspices so that the private sector never had much of a chance to become involved. NARA did succeed, however, in focusing attention on the need to provide treatment rather than punishment for individuals primarily addicts rather than criminals.

The NARA program would seem to be best described as a quasivoluntary operation, according to Mandell, in spite of its designation as a civil commitment program. There was no real use of the authority inherent in the program, and it was all too easy for patients to drop out of the treatment system. Remaining in treatment and being discharged to aftercare were clearly related to racial and age characteristics. The system was particularly unacceptable and probably inappropriate for young, black, inner-city men. As a group, addicts in NARA between 1969 and 1971 were improving their life styles, however, and reducing their drug use patterns. These results proved relatively stable between 1972 and 1973, but this was probably also happening to clients in all types of programs in those years. Those addicts motivated to stay in the NARA program did significantly better than those who were not. Educational and vocational training, employment, later start in drug use, noninvolvement with a criminal life style before treatment, the possession of friends, and nonuse of nonnarcotic drugs favored a reduction in addiction. NARA can perhaps best be described as a program of transition from one period of history to another—and a program full of compromises. It was expensive and never could make the compulsory parts of its program work.

TREATMENT ALTERNATIVES TO STREET CRIME (TASC)

The federal government, through the Special Action Office for Drug Abuse Prevention (SAODAP), espoused the TASC approach, which entailed the "diversion" and referral of addict-defendants to community-based treatment in lieu of prosecution. TASC thus used the lever of criminal justice to bring addicts into treatment and hold them there. At the same time, it reduced processing, custodial, and other burdens on the police, courts, and penal institutions. Arrested persons could be evaluated by a diagnostic unit and sent to a holding facility, pending their transfer to a community treatment program. If an individual dropped out of treatment or did not comply with the other conditions of release, he/she was treated by the court as if he/she had violated the conditions of release. TASC was initially focused on pretrial intervention, a concept that was resisted by prosecutors in many areas. It was subsequently broadened to reflect local preferences. The 1974 strategy was to have each locality determine such issues as mandatory versus voluntary screening procedures, eligibility standards, points of referral, choice of treatment modality, and definition of success (44, 48). There have been many criticisms of the program to the effect that such diversion procedures impeded necessary law reform, that reliance on court referrals often altered the basic role of the treatment program vis-à-vis the community, that treatment programs sometimes became formal extensions of the court and agents of social control, that there might be a shifting of responsibility by the treatment agency from the patient to the courts, and that treatment goals might be altered to fit the needs of the court rather than of clients (44, 48).

Data regarding the over-all impact of TASC and other diversion programs are generally still not available. Evaluation has generally been limited to study of program procedures: it has apparently been successful as a treatment outreach function, with about 50 per cent of referrals entering treatment for the first time. About 10 per cent are rearrested on a new charge while in the program, and 30 per cent are classified as dropouts and/or failures. By providing an alternative to criminal justice dispositions, they have protem resolved the dilemma of how to deal with the heroin addict who is chronically involved in minor property crimes (51).

OTHER PRETRIAL DIVERSION EFFORTS

The diversion programs, particularly those in which pretrial referral to treatment re-

placed criminal prosecution, developed as a result of a crisis in criminal justice. After the initiation of TASC, there followed a bewildering array of schemes for diversion in almost every jurisdiction where drug use was a problem. In their second report, the Presidential Commission on Marijuana and Drug Abuse tallied the following possible points of diversion that had been noted in different states: prearrest diversion for detoxification or withdrawal; postarrest diversion for detoxification; treatment as a condition of pretrial release; emergency treatment while awaiting trial; treatment in lieu of prosecution; treatment as a condition of deferred entry of a judgment of guilt and conditional discharge or as a condition of suspension of sentence or probation; treatment as a condition of parole; commitment for treatment in lieu of other sentence or while serving sentence in a correctional facility (44). Several states now legislatively authorize diversion, in certain cases, for drug-dependent persons into treatment programs. Other jurisdictions have established diversion programs by court rule or by operational understandings without formal authorization. Participation in most diversion programs has been voluntary or semivoluntary because most individuals regard referral to treatment as a preferable alternative to continuation of the criminal proceedings. There has been a growing trend to use diversion for first offenders and other categories of defendants in which the interests of rehabilitation and public safety are best served by treatment rather than conviction.

ROCKEFELLER LEGISLATION OF 1973

The 1973 Rockefeller legislation represented a throwback from the move to develop more treatment-oriented approaches rather than punitive methods for dealing with drug-dependent individuals. It was enacted over the opposition of such groups as the State and City Bar Associations, the Judicial Conference, the Drug Abuse Council, and the American Civil Liberties Union, not to mention most therapeutic programs. It proceeded as if the work of NACC-DACC had been a total failure, although the effectiveness of that agency had never been evaluated adequately. What the legislation established was a classification of crimes into felony classes listed as A I, A II, A III; B Felony; C Felony; and A

Misdemeanor. These categories were significant because they had a bearing on the lifetime sentences to be imposed in Classes A I, A II, and A III. Unlike nondrug felonies, felons needed to remain on parole for their entire lifetime (this was altered in 1977). A I entailed the sale of 1 ounce of any narcotic or possession of 2 ounces of a substance containing a narcotic; A II a sale, ranging from 1 ounce of a narcotic to 5 mg of lysergic acid diethylamide (LSD) or possession of any amount of a narcotic; A III the sale of 1/8 ounce of any narcotic or possession of 5.25 mg of LSD or other substances.

Many problems followed upon enactment of this legislation. Defendants facing a life sentence naturally resorted to all sorts of maneuvering troublesome to the courts. Jurors were understandably reluctant to convict individuals to life sentences for what they considered minor infractions. There were limited opportunities for plea bargaining, a traditional way out of difficult court situations. The stringent law applied to marihuana needed to be revised in light of the better understanding of the effects of its use, and this was done in 1977. The law was increasingly criticized by civil libertarians for its severity and by corrections officials because it dislocated the prison system. A *New York Times* article of February 13, 1979, indicated that the governor was planning to cut mandatory terms for illegal possession of "modest amounts of narcotics and dangerous drugs." It was reported that some 3,800 persons had received maximum life sentences since the law took effect. It could not be determined how many of these sentences were for sale and how many for possession. Two cases described involved women: one sentenced to from 4 years to life for selling a single dose of cocaine to an undercover agent; the other to 5 years to life for possession of more than an ounce of cocaine found in her apartment.

A *New York Times* article of May 14, 1979, reported that the New York City Bar Association in a special report remarked that "The key lesson to be drawn from the experience with the 1973 drug law is that passing a new law is not enough." The following statement by the special narcotics prosecutor is also cited: "Enforcement alone is not the answer. You need rehabilitation, education, prevention."

DISCUSSION: THE USE OF CIVIL COMMITMENT AS RATIONAL AUTHORITY

It is apparent that the criminal justice system has not been well related to the needs of troubled people and that "correction does not always correct." Although some 70 per cent of inmates may have a history of drug involvement or drug dependency, there has been no concerted effort to track them or others for special attention. Apart from the usual problems of the court system, there has been a dearth of skilled staff on hand to perform diagnostic, screening, referral, or treatment services or to serve as professional advisors to judges and other court personnel who make the determinations in very complex situations. There has been much misunderstanding of what is involved in drug dependency—as well as mental health problems generally—and of how the court system can be used for different kinds of offenders, if only by sorting out their needs and distinguishing between minor (one, two, or three) offenders and confirmed criminals (20, 42). The civil commitment approach presupposes a therapeutic direction because offenders are turned over to a body of behavioral specialists for help. In an earlier paper, the author reviewed the concept of civil and criminal commitment, indicating that it had been misunderstood, insofar as it was generally equated with the institutional-aftercare or parole model of treatment. It was suggested that it should rather be viewed as a multiform approach that provides a range of options for the diversity of users we now understand is involved. Treatment need not invariably begin in an institutional or inpatient setting, but rather in the community in most cases. Selected individuals might indeed need a period of care in a residential setting, but this would be determined, not routinely and on the basis of a careful "differential diagnosis." Civil commitment was, therefore, best thought of not as a treatment modality in itself but as a structuring device for engaging often recalcitrant individuals and retaining them in treatment (29). It should be added that the use of various forms of rational authority in treatment can be extended not only to offenders but more generally to all kinds of acting-out persons. While the authority we have discussed here is court derived, other forms could emanate from the personal and professional authority of the therapist, the nature of the agency represented, the involvement of the family as additional supports, and the use of ancillary helpers or "aids," as Schilder and Simmel suggested many years ago and as the author undertook at the Lincoln Hospital in the South Bronx by drawing upon indigenous paraprofessionals, medical students, and ex-addicts to reinforce the group therapy and general treatment program.

Although it is important to remain open and fluid in our thinking, the present climate of our country has unfortunately made this far more difficult. As an example, we might cite the powerful new force termed "neoconservatism" that is offering intellectual reinforcement for the swing to the right, using such former liberals as Nathan Glazer, Patrick Moynihan, Daniel Bell, Bayard Rustin, and others. The goal is to uphold corporate America and undermine the "welfare state." Our culture is described as having become slack and corrupt so that there is need to ameliorate the "crisis of authority"—not in our economic institutions but in our cultural outlook. This group believes that previous governments overextended themselves in social programs for our underclass, a large, uneducable, unemployable element of the urban population alien to middle-class norms of behavior. The presence of this class is the primary obstacle to success in the government's poverty, housing, and unemployment programs. Liberals who press for "justice" and "equality" sap the government's legitimate authority. Therefore, we must avoid new government initiatives that "feed the fires of egalitarianism," urge the public to lower its expectation, and tame the liberals. Our society needs a strong Establishment (45). In such a climate, it becomes more important than before to hold onto what we have learned over the years and not let the pendulum swing back so that we are doomed to repeat our mistakes and rediscover the wheel "recidivistically."

SUMMARY AND PROSPECTUS

In this chapter, the author undertook a retrospective study of the use of authority in relation to drug use. In looking back, we needed to sort out the various elements that helped confound our efforts to deal rationally with the problem. Among them were our criminal definition of the drug problem; the complex of questions emanating from issues having to do with characteristics of addicts, problems of psychoanalysis, and therapy and "state of the art" misunderstandings," primarily the excessive preoccupation with heroin and lack of concern about such other drugs as the barbiturates, amphetamine, alcohol, and tobacco; use of a uniform model of treatment—the institutional-aftercare model; our misunderstanding of what constitutes adequate goals in treatment and of the chronic relapsing nature of many confirmed addictions; as well as the confusion between control and treatment issues and the proper role of civil commitment, rational authority, and court diversion techniques. Although many questions still require resolution, we do understand better today the factor of diversity of use and the need for a typology that comprises a spectrum of users: controlled and uncontrolled as well as "adaptive" use—or use that helps individuals function better (3, 4). We are beginning to understand better the need to decentralize our services and meld them better with mental health services, to involve clients more meaningfully in treatment. The author expressed his belief that we must learn to use whatever authority comes to hand to help persons who are not in control and are caught up in recidivistic patterns of asocial behavior. A large part of the problem derives from the fact that so much of the behavior is deeply rooted in family and community systems and in characteristics that are chronic and resistant to change. As indicated earlier, some schizophrenias require a lifetime of community support, and this is also true for some addictions. We have learned much over the years about the criminal justice system and also about the use of civil commitment. The long experience with civil commitment includes 18 years of the California program and some 13 years with the New York and NARA programs. It is imperative that the experiences of these programs and those of such others as TASC, court diversion, and deferred prosecution programs be evaluated carefully so that we may learn what they truly have to offer and how we are to proceed in future with the use of coercion and civil commitment. The author is collaborating in an intensive study sponsored by the National Institute on Drug Abuse utilizing the research of McGlothlin, Mandell, and others to evaluate the experiences of the California, New York, and federal civil commitment programs as well as others—such as the programs in British Columbia and Southeast Asia. The study is timely since the various civil commitment programs in this country have slowed down to a halt, with only two patients remaining in NARA and about 178 in New York. Where do we go from here?

One thing is clear: civil commitment is a costly and cumbersome system and, if it is set up at all, it must be used firmly and consistently. It will not do to invest so much funding and energy in a system that turns out to be voluntary or quasivoluntary (as in the case of NARA) or to use the civil commitment poorly (as in the case of New York). California seems to have been the only program that used its civil commitment machinery effectively, and this seems to be true also of the new British Columbia program and the program in Singapore. The other point relates to the older multimodality concept: there are programs that can receive clients or patients who come in "voluntarily," although admittedly under some kind of pressure, still free from the use of legal coercion. However, over the years, there has been much concern about the "recalcitrants" who are a problem for themselves and the community, who do not come into treatment of their own accord, who are heavily engaged in criminal behavior, and need the lever of coercion or compulsion before they are brought into treatment through the criminal justice system with which they have become involved. These issues have been spelled out by the author in a series of papers (3, 5–7, 28, 29). We are in a period of transition and need to review our experiences with the use of authority, coercion, and civil commitment so that we can gauge better how they can best be applied in the coming years.

References

1. Bachrach, L. *Deinstitutionalization: An Analytical Review and Sociological Perspective*, NIMH Series D, Number 14 (DHEW Publication # ADM 76-351).
Washington, D.C., Department of Health, Education and Welfare, 1976.
2. Brill, L. *The De-Addiction Process.* Springfield, Ill., Charles C Thomas, 1972.
3. Brill, L. Drug abuse. In *Encyclopedia of Social Work.* Washington, D.C., National Association of Social Work, 1977.
4. Brill, L. Historical evolution of the current drug treatment perspective. In *Rehabilitation Aspects of Drug Dependence*, editor A. Schecter, Cleveland, Ohio, CRC Press, 1977.
5. Brill, L., and Lieberman, L. *Authority and Addiction.* Boston, Little, Brown and Company, 1969.
6. Brill, L., and Lieberman, L. *Major Modalities in the Treatment of Drug Abuse.* New York, Behavioral Publications, 1972.
7. Brill, L., et al. *Rehabilitation in Drug Addiction: Report of a Five-year Community Experiment of the New York Demonstration Center*, Mental Health Monograph # 3. Washington, D.C., Public Health Service, 1963.
8. Brotman, R., and Freedman, A. *A Community Mental Health Approach to Drug Addiction*, (JD Publication No. 9005). Washington, D.C., Department of Health, Education and Welfare, Social and Rehabilitation Service, Office of Juvenile Delinquency and Youth Development, 1969.
9. Capel, W. C., Goldsmith, B. M., Waddell, K. J., and Stewart, G. T. The aging narcotic addict: An increasing problem for the next decades. J. Gerontol. 27: 102, 1972.
10. Capel, W. C., and Peppers, L. G. The aging addict: A longitudinal study of known abusers. Addict. Dis. Int. J. 3:389, 1973.
11. Chein, I., Gerard, D. I., et al. *The Road to H: Narcotics Delinquency and Social Policy.* New York, Basic Books, 1964.
12. Drug Abuse Council. *A Perspective on "Get Tough" Drug Laws.* Washington, D.C., Drug Abuse Council, 1973.
13. Duvall, H. J., Locke, B. J., and Brill, L. Follow-up study of narcotic drug addicts five years after hospitalization. Public Health Rep. 73:185, 1963.
14. Ennis, B. J., and Emery, R. D. *The Rights of Mental Patients.* New York, Avon Books, 1978.
15. Fenichel, O. *The Psychoanalytic Theory of Neurosis.* New York, W. W. Norton, 1945.
16. *Final Report of the Joint Committee on New York Drug Law Evaluation.* Washington, D. C., The Association of the Bar of the City of New York and Drug Abuse Council, 1977.
17. Foucault, M. *Discipline and Punish: The Birth of the Prison.* New York, Pantheon Books, 1977.
18. Fromm, E. *Escape from Freedom.* New York, Farrar and Rinehart, 1941.
19. Goffman, E. *Stigma: Notes on the Might of Spoiled Identity.* Englewood Cliffs, N. J., Prentice-Hall, 1967.
20. Gross, H. *A Theory of Criminal Justice.* London, Oxford University Press, 1978.
21. Kaufman, I., and Reiner, B. S. *Character Disorders in Parents of Delinquents.* New York, Family Service Association of America, 1959.
22. Kramer, J. The state vs. the addict: Uncivil commitment. In *Drug Use and Social Policy*, J. Sussman, editor, vol. 2. Beverly Hills, Calif., Sage Publications, 1974.

23. Mandell, W., and Amsel, Z. *Status of Addicts Treated under the NARA Program* (HSM-142-72-37). Baltimore, Department of Mental Hygiene, School of Hygiene and Public Health, The Johns Hopkins University (special report for the National Institute of Mental Health), 1973.

24. McGlothlin, W. H. California civil commitment: A decade later. J. Drug Issues 6:369, 1976.

25. McGlothlin, W. H., Anglin, M. D., and Wilson, B. D. *An Evaluation of the California Civil Addict Program*, Services Research Monograph Series (HEW Publication No. ADM 78-558). Washington, D.C., Department of Health, Education and Welfare, 1977.

26. McGlothlin, W. H., Anglin, M. D., and Wilson, B. D. A follow-up of admissions to the California civil addict program. Am. J. Drug Alcohol Abuse 4:179, 1977.

27. McGlothlin, W. H., Anglin, M. D., and Wilson, B. D. Narcotic addiction and crime. Criminology 16: 293, 1978.

28. Meiselas, H., and Brill, L. The treatment of drug abuse. In *The Yearbook of Drug Abuse, L. Brill and E. Harms, editors. New York, Behavioral Publications, 1973.*

29. Meiselas, H., and Brill, L. The role of civil commitment in multimodality programming. In *Drugs and the Criminal Justice System*, J. Inciardi and C. D. Chambers, editors, vol. 2. Beverly Hills, Calif., Sage Publications, 1974.

30. Musto, D. F. *The American Disease*. New Haven, Conn., Yale University Press, 1973.

31. *New York State Drug Abuse Program: 1974–1975: State Plan Update*. New York, New York State Office of Drug Abuse Services, 1975.

32. Nimmer, R. T. *Diversion: The Search for Alternative Forms of Prosecution*. Chicago, American Bar Association, 1974.

33. O'Donnell, J. A. *Narcotic Addicts in Kentucky*, Public Health Services Publication (No. 1881). Bethesda, Md., United States Public Health Service, 1969.

34. Petersen, D. M., Whittington, F. J., and Beer, E. T. Drug use among the elderly. J. Drug Issues 9:5, 1979.

35. Program for drug abuse treatment and prevention. In *Community Crime Prevention*, a volume of the National Advisory Commission on Criminal Justice Standards and Goals, chapter 4. Washington, D. C., 1973.

36. Robins, L. N. *The Vietnam Drug User Returns*, Special Action Office Monograph Series A, No. 2. Washington, D.C., United States Government Printing Office, 1974.

37. Robins, L. N. *Veterans' Drug Use Three Years after Vietnam*. St. Louis, Department of Psychology, Washington University School of Medicine, 1975.

38. Robins, L. N. Addict careers. In *Handbook on Drug Abuse*, R. L. Dupont, A. Goldstein, and J. A. O'Donnell, editors. Rockville, Md., National Institute on Drug Abuse, 1979.

39. Schur, E. *Crimes without Victims*. Englewood Cliffs, N. J., Prentice-Hall, 1965.

40. Senay, E., Shorty, V., and Alksne, H. *Developments in the Field of Drug Abuse*. Cambridge Mass., Schenkman, 1975.

41. Sheppard, C. W., Smith, D. E., and Gay, G. R. The changing face of heroin addiction in the Haight-Ashbury. Int. J. Addict. 7:109, 1972.

42. Silberman, C. F. *Criminal Violence, Criminal Justice*. New York, Random House, 1978.

43. Simmel, E. Alcoholism and addiction. Psychoanal. Q. 17:6, 1948.

44. Smith, R. C. Addiction, coercion and treatment: Reflections on the debate. In *Developments in the Field of Drug Abuse*, E. Senay, et al., editors. Cambridge, Mass., Schenkman, 1975.

45. Steinfels, P. The reasonable right. Esquire 24, February 13, 1979.

46. Stephens, R. C., and McBride, D. C. Becoming a street addict. Hum. Organiz. 35:87, 1976.

47. Terry, C. E., and Pellens, M. *The Opium Question* (1928), Publication 115, reprint series. Montclair, N. J., Patterson Smith, 1970.

48. *Treatment Alternatives to Street Crime*. Washington, D.C., Special Action Office for Drug Abuse Prevention, 1972.

49. Weppner, R. S. An anthropological view of the street addict's values. Hum. Organiz. 32:111, 1973.

50. Winick, C. Maturing out of addiction. Bull. Narc. 14: 1, 1962.

51. Winick, C. Personal communication, May 1979.

PART 6

SPECIAL TREATMENT PROBLEMS

CHAPTER 43

SUBSTANCE ABUSE PROGRAMS AND "THE COMMUNITY": AN OVERVIEW

Pedro Ruiz, M.D.

It was during the decade of the 1960's, when the federal government embarked on a series of categorical programs aimed primarily at assisting the socially disadvantaged, that the notion of direct "community participation" in human service programs was broached as government policy. Lacking a precise definition of either word, the phrase remained an objective to be variously interpreted and implemented by program sponsors as they saw fit, while policy directives continued to find euphemisms for "community control." Nonetheless, the period marks a watershed in the social history of the United States and, for better or worse, was profoundly to affect the public delivery of human services, including programs that dealt with treatment for substance abuse. This chapter will focus on the experience of urban communities as they came to grips with this new formulation of the social scene.

LEGISLATIVE HISTORY

In 1961 the Juvenile Delinquency Act required that neighborhood service centers "must meaningfully involve neighborhood residents" (44). The Economic Opportunity Act of 1964 gave us the phrase "maximum feasible participation" of residents of the areas and members of the groups served (26)—in other words, the poor. The Demonstration Cities and Metropolitan Development Act of 1966 established a Model Cities Administration whose policy statement called for "the constructive involvement of citizens in the model neighborhood area" (18). In 1967 amendments to the Economic Opportunity Act put more teeth into "maximum feasible participation" by requiring that at least half of the governing boards of local agencies must be residents of the area and members of the groups served. The amendments also required that community residents be employed by Office of Economic Opportunity agencies and given opportunities for training and career advancement (14, 27).

In virtually all programs, however, community boards served in advisory capacities with little control over program priorities and goals. Particularly in urban areas, the vague definition of functions, methods of selection of board members, intergovernmental administrative tangles, and other well documented problems plagued efforts to effectively include community residents in decision making (41). By 1970 sociologists studying urban renewal and the community action programs found that "among academic analysts of social policy, civic leaders, and new left critics, the conclusion is now abroad that citizen participation has failed" (59).

But in the long history of volunteerism in America, prominent and middle-class citizens have always participated in decision making—on boards of hospitals, settlement houses, and a variety of health-promoting, social welfare, and charitable organizations (48, 55). They served in part because of their ability to raise money for operations, in part because of religious or ethical principles, and in part because of a sense of "noblesse oblige" embraced by the privileged as a basic aspect of liberal democracy.

The new element in "citizen participation" came with the human service programs of the turbulent 1960's, sparked by the civil rights movement and funded by taxpayers. The poor, or otherwise disadvantaged, *themselves* were to be included in decision making at the community level where services were consumed (58, 62). This represented an ideological shift toward a more egalitarian society, and there would be no turning back, in spite of confusing directives, agency vacillation as to means and ends, provider/consumer confrontation, and a body of serious criticism from political and social scientists (7, 29, 63, 64).

The die was cast. As summed up by Bolman in 1972 (10): "New groups with different perspectives are demanding a say about services that are provided for them by others."

RATIONALE FOR CITIZEN PARTICIPATION AT THE COMMUNITY LEVEL

Noting that the concept of citizen participation has been credited with duping the poor, fostering scandal, and encouraging riot, the Cahns (15) believe that, with all of its faults, it is indispensable to any real effort to eliminate poverty in America, and its values fall into three broad categories.

It provides: 1. a means of mobilizing unutilized resources—a source of productivity and labor not otherwise tapped; 2. a source of knowledge—both corrective and creative—a means of securing feedback regarding policy and programs, and also a source of new, inventive and innovative approaches, and 3. an end in itself—an affirmation of democracy and the elimination of alienation and withdrawal, of destructiveness, hostility and lack of faith in relying on the people.

It has been exhaustively documented (4, 6, 19, 21, 60) that the poor have always been dependent for survival on events and decisions over which they have little or no control, leading to psychological impoverishment and a sense of worthlessness. Another argument for community participation is seen in the possibility of a viable power base for the poor in serving on boards. Despite the widely held assumption that the causes of poverty lie within an individual's inabilities (45), there are those who believe that the causes of poverty lie in the institutional structure of society. Participation of the poor can be a means of building up a new political force to bring about significant social change (24).

Participation in the form of employment of community residents as nonprofessional "helpers," had more than an economic value. Such a policy served to develop needed manpower resources in the health and welfare field, and nonprofessionals coming out of the same cultural, ethnic, or socioeconomic background as clients were quite able to interpret their needs and problems to professionals (34). The helper therapy principle—that people with a special problem or handicap can help others with the same problem—was seen as particularly workable with the poor (46).

Against these reasoned high hopes, it cannot be denied that valid community participation had only spotty success in urban areas. Predominant patterns of participation, for example in the Community Action Programs (CAPS), rarely show any increased power on the part of the poor. Three modes of involvement were found to be predominant: *containment*, in which token representatives on boards were politically appointed; *cooptation*, where middle-class, rather than poor, minority members were appointed; and *co-determination*, where elected spokesmen for the genuine poor work with welfare professionals to some effect (57).

A good deal of the literature concerned with effective community participation places stress on the importance of community organization (12, 25, 32, 38). The question of who represents the community has been a thorny problem throughout the movement toward local control, particularly in disadvantaged areas. And yet, in almost all communities, including the most unstable, there are indigenous organizations—fraternal, ethnic, church based, social—that can be approached once they are identified. But somebody has to do it, and funds for community organizers and training in leadership techniques are not readily forthcoming from sponsoring agencies (31).

A danger is that self-appointed representatives will surface to fill the vacuum and proceed to use advisory boards as a base for personal political power or other self-serving ends. Beyond venality, Hersch, although not rejecting the community control principle, observed that (31) "in community control settings, with a certain regularity, there appear leaders who, by objective and clear-cut criteria, show evidence of formal thought disorder and psychiatric disability." However, an informed public, given the franchise and a system of checks and balances, finds ways to deal with such situations. At the urban community level, plagued with problems of economic survival, residents have had little experience of participation in the middle-class mainstream. It is hardly surprising that they did not always behave in an orderly and polite manner. Direct expression of aggressive feelings, regardless of disapproval, is more characteristic of a lower class norm; cooperative group behavior and repression of hostility are middle-class norms. But the middle class has no need for militancy and hostility in making their needs known. In many poverty areas, these were postures that contributed to the functional effectiveness and cohesiveness of local advisory groups (39). The interface between ghetto communities and middle-class managers of human service programs was bound to be abrasive, given their widely differing value systems and modes of communication. Bolman reported that in case after case where there were conflicts between the community and professionals, the community had valid reasons to

differ, but professionals found it difficult to hear what turned out to be constructive and informed (11).

CITIZEN PARTICIPATION FROM MIDDLE-CLASS AND GHETTO PERSPECTIVES

Two case histories graphically portray the difference between the development and scope of community involvement in programs in a middle-class area, predominantly white, and those in an inner-city ghetto, predominantly Hispanic and black. Bertelsen and Harris (8) gave a glowing description of the orderly and active cooperation between professionals and citizens in planning and operating a community mental health center in San Francisco, a collaborative effort of city and county delivering services from several bases. Starting in 1968, with an interim advisory board selected from a well attended first meeting in the community, citizen task forces were organized to make a needs assessment for the entire area and to prepare for the selection of a permanent board that would be geographically and ethnically representative. Once a 28-member permanent board was elected, they put in 4 hard working years preparing grant applications, working with legislators, advocating for more and better mental health services. In 1972, six past and present board members and six staff members who had worked closely with the board were interviewed on the pros and cons of citizen participation as presented in the literature. Neither board nor staff agreed with the negative views encountered in the literature. On the contrary, staff felt that the board successfully carried out its liaison role between the center and the community, and board members did not believe that staff had misinformed or manipulated them. There was general agreement about the board's accomplishments from all respondents, with evident mutual respect. In this middle-class area, board members viewed staff primarily as clinicians and tended to disregard their limitations in administrative matters.

In sharp contrast is the story of the Lincoln Community Mental Health Center in the Bronx (51), which received the Silver Achievement Award for its "imaginative and innovative services for a deprived urban population" from the American Psychiatric Association in 1968 and was forced to shut down services completely in 1969 as a result of a painful community confrontation. In this case many issues were relevant, but what stands out was the enormous gap between what professionals saw as an imaginative and innovative program for a deprived area and what the community, comprised largely of blacks and Hispanics, saw as an imposition of well paid outsiders on their territory, without prior consultation with or accountability to indigenous groups in the community on matters of administration and programming. The center was salvaged when a new director, endorsed by several community organizations, was appointed, high level staff were recruited reflecting the ethnic composition of the area, and all aspects of the center's programs—including staff recruitment, budget review, and recommendations for program changes—were scrutinized and agreed to by a central board made up of representatives from three local neighborhood organizations. Once these steps were taken, services were resumed and a more tranquil atmosphere prevailed. However, the crisis shook up the Establishment as the program successfully moved from the vague concept of "community participation" to the very real one of "community control."

THE MOVEMENT FROM "PARTICIPATION" TO "CONTROL"

Clearly, there is a dynamic relationship between the human service field and the social context of the times (56). And in the 1960's, particularly in large cities riding the tide of social reform, direct and active citizen participation became transformed into a movement toward citizen control of all community institutions. Proponents in the literature presented a number of advantages, both theoretically and arrived at empirically, in support of community control (16, 22). In theory, programs should be not only acceptable but accountable to the community served, and this can only come about when community representatives have significant power to make decisions about policy. Furthermore, in the judgment of many community organization practitioners, until the funds for community programs were controlled by the prospective beneficiaries, "welfare colonialism" would continue to reinforce the structured dependency historically experienced by the poor. On a pragmatic note, and importantly from the standpoint of staff and program administrators, community control is frankly recognized as insurance against violent civil disorder.

Although not disagreeing with the community control principle, critics (33) have pointed out its limitations, focusing on its use as a diversionary tactic; that is, it can be used to divert the attention of the poor from the need for institutional changes in the over-all power structure. Examined in its broad social context, "community control" as defined by its advocates does not exist. In the United States, control of the three basic building blocks of a health services institution—its capital budget, its expense budget, and its supply of staff—does not lie with its administrators. Control lies with the state, that is the President and the Congress, the governors and the state legislatures, the mayors and the city councils, and the people with whom they have the most contact and to whom they appear to be most responsive—industrial leaders, bankers, heads of major universities and foundations, and the like. They determine national priorities and national attitudes—no matter who does what to whom on a local, day-to-day level.

When the community control concept is applied to schools, we are reminded that many of the decisions in complex organizations are no longer in the hands of any one group. Superintendent contracts, teacher tenure, legal sanctions for union negotiations—all remove large numbers of decisions from everybody's review. "The point is that, in many organizations, the issues of importance to the poor are no longer truly controlled by the bureaucrats either" (55). Put in another way, decisions at the local level involve the implementation of national and regional policies rather than the creation of policies that affect major resource allocation (9).

Conceding that one of the strengths of the movement for popular power has been its revival of the concept of community, against the alienation of mass society, Aronowitz (3) pointed out that the community control movement failed to forge broad alliances to achieve the united goal of specific institutions. Groups within the same neighborhood fighting for local control of different institutions are isolated from one another, and this failure to coalesce around national socioeconomic issues, concentrating instead on the struggle for community control, is viewed as a step backward.

In these kinds of struggles, working and welfare class people find themselves fighting administrators whose powers are circumscribed. According to Jonas (33): "when a community group wins, they are led to believe that they have really won something, when in fact they have won little. When they lose, energies have been wastefully dissipated, and perhaps more importantly, adversaries have been incorrectly identified. Thus, people become disillusioned and unnecessarily worn out."

It is against this heightened awareness of the issues of community participation/control that a new social pressure came to the forefront in the mid-1960's. A startling increase of illegal drug use was affecting the middle-class young along with the ghetto users, and society was forced to relate to the whole racial and socioeconomic spectrum at once (23). The "war on poverty" was now joined by a "war on drugs" as a major part of domestic programs, and treatment was to be provided in community settings.

SUBSTANCE ABUSE PROGRAMS AND THE "COMMUNITY NEIGHBORHOOD MODEL"

To a substantial degree, the narcotics policy in the United States had from the beginning been identified with underprivileged minorities, criminals, and social outsiders in general, and for over half a century popular literature tended to take an attitude of moral chastisement and therapeutic hopelessness toward all forms of drug dependence (13). But in a landmark case, the Supreme Court in 1962 decided that drug "addiction" was an illness, and held that a state could not make this status a crime (47). Civil committment (involuntary) was to be only for purposes of treatment. As the wave of drug taking reached its crest in the 1960's, perhaps 2,000 additional treatment facilities appeared, most of them nonresidential and voluntary (61). At the same time, hundreds of self-help therapeutic communities, established on the pattern of Synanon, sprang up around the country. Although most of these programs reject the medical model of drug dependence as an

illness, methods of milieu control, rehabilitation through work, and group therapy featuring confrontation do have their antecedents in the history of psychiatric facilities. This type of treatment, usually located some distance from the community of origin, has received a considerable amount of publicity about success in rehabilitation of addicts; but it has been authoritatively pointed out that this method—emphasis on self-discipline and vertical mobility, the use of the guilt concept in encounter therapy, etc.—reflects dramatized versions of middle-class values. With ethnic groups and subcultures that do not share these norms, such methods have proved to be inappropriate (42).

From the standpoint of the urban community, public policy decreed the "deinstitutionalization" of both mental patients and drug abusers; treatment and rehabilitation programs shifted from large institutions to neighborhood settings. The Community Mental Health Centers Amendments of 1970 directed community centers receiving federal money to extend services to "persons with drug abuse and drug dependence problems." The Drug Abuse Office and Treatment Act of 1972 further conditions federal assistance to state community mental health programs on developing treatment facilities that provide voluntary and emergency care to all "drug abusers." The shift to community treatment from isolated institutions reflected a need for more flexibility in treatment approaches to include prevention of relapse by dealing with social and economic problems surrounding opiate dependence; furthermore, it moved the dominance of drug and narcotic policies from the criminal justice system to the health system.

When we consider treatment programs for substance abuse in communities, we face a paradox: the much vaunted ideal of community autonomy can militate against a needed service if the local neighborhood is parochial or conservative. The same can be said of ghetto communities where substance abusers are integrated into the social and economic mores and life style, which they feel may be threatened by outside interference. Added to this, classical psychiatry and other mental health disciplines have been slow to arrive at successful treatment modalities and rehabilitation for substance abusers. Bolman (11) recounted his experience as director of a community mental health center, when an advisory board member suggested that he "do something about this terrible drug problem we have in our community." He replied in a vaguely affirmative tone, "but in fact I didn't know much about drugs, the extent of the problem, or what type of programs were already in existence in my catchment area." Later, at a monthly meeting of the center's board, a group in Afro-style clothes took the floor to demand their inclusion in the center so they could receive funding for their treatment programs for heroin addiction. Says Bolman, "I attempted to point out that our present structure and funding was basically oriented toward mental illness and not toward heroin addiction;" but "they knew that heroin addiction was a major community mental health problem." Ex-addict street professionals from several groups, with the help of the center, were able to develop a comprehensive drug treatment program for the catchment area, and original misconceptions were largely worked through. "By the time the center received a large federal treatment grant, the program structure, fiscal management, and policy control were worked out sufficiently to allow for rapid implementation . . . this would have been impossible without continuously active and expert community and street professional help."

Many communities were aware of the need for services, and indeed fought for them. In response to a public questionnaire designed to assess major mental health needs in a San Francisco community mental health center, citizens rated drug abuse and undiagnosed alcoholism as the first two priorities (8). The demand for treatment is dramatically demonstrated in the methadone maintenance program of the Albert Einstein College of Medicine in the Bronx, which began in 1968. By 1970, long waiting lists for treatment prompted an expansion grant from the New York State Addiction Control Commission that allowed for the opening of nine new clinics. On August 31, 1970, the day before the expansion grant went into effect, there were 350 patients on the census. On July 14, 1972, there were 2,125 (54). All across the country, there was a sharp increase in the levels of addiction (30), possibly accelerated by the Korean and Vietnam Wars (49). Still

many communities resisted efforts to establish programs in their midst for a variety of reasons. That substance abuse was a national problem requiring treatment was not at issue. What apparently is at issue is where treatment should take place.

As pointed out earlier, prior to 1958 the treatment of addiction was centered outside of the community in two federally sponsored facilities, the United States Public Health Service Hospitals at Lexington, Kentucky, and Fort Worth, Texas, both isolated and self-contained and offering little opportunity for the rehabilitation of addicts and their reentrance into community life (36). An important breakaway occurred when a group of ex-addicts founded Synanon, a drug-free therapeutic community operating in residential neighborhoods. The problems this group faced in acquiring residential properties where addicts could be treated outside of institutions set a pattern for community resistance that has not changed appreciably today (17,65). But there is a difference in reasons for opposition between middle-class and disadvantaged areas. In middle-class communities, the situation is reminiscent of the civil rights movement for desegregation and equality for blacks: northern liberals were all for it—until it became a matter of blacks moving next door or being bused to schools in white neighborhoods. Opposition in middle-class areas tends to be outspoken, better organized, and somewhat more violent than in lower class communities, where opposition is characterized by a passive undercurrent of suspicion and resentment (52).

Although substance abuse is no longer confined to the ghetto communities, it is still concentrated there, and this fact enables middle-class communities to deny the need for treatment among their own (37). Particularly in areas in the process of social and economic transition, homeowners and businessmen fear a rise in crime and vandalism, with subsequent devaluation of property and disruption of business. This fear is enhanced by the kind of publicity that attributes muggings and other street crimes to the drug addict's need for a "fix" but fails to note that the objective of a methadone maintenance program is to remove the craving for a "fix." Nevertheless, it is not uncommon for landlords to refuse to rent appropriate space and provide adequate maintenance services in this type of community or for residents to seek court injunctions to block the opening and/or continuation of a treatment center and to put pressure on community boards and politicians. All these methods and others have been used in order to have the addiction program go somewhere else. The same methods have been used to resist other services, such as alcoholism programs (43) and mental health services (28).

There is no way for poverty areas to ignore the drug problem; many have learned to live with it. Undeniably, a complex social and economic system exists that is often at cross purposes with the objectives of treatment programs. There is an important sense in which addicts are significant members of their communities, and every effort is made by local residents to protect them when they are faced with something strange or foreign—even a new program or treatment modality. Particularly in methadone maintenance programs, communities have reacted with charges that they are being used as guinea pigs or that they are being "enslaved"—in short, that they are victims of social control.

In addiction treatment, as in areas of health, education, family planning, and housing, there has been little attempt to involve local residents in early planning stages. Too frequently, the emphasis is placed on a one-way flow of information—from officials to citizens—with no channel provided for feedback and no power for negotiations. Under these conditions, particularly when information is provided at a late stage in planning, observes Arnstein (2), "people have little opportunity to influence the program designed 'for their benefit.'" To avoid conflict later, it is recommended that all interested groups, and especially consumers, should be involved in planning and evaluation from the start. If this is not done, it is possible that such plans will be vulnerable to charges of continued "colonialism" (48).

Two types of outsiders contribute to resistance to programs (particularly methadone maintenance programs) in urban poor communities. Professionals, such as nurses, doctors and other staff, arrive from outside the neighborhood, usually from ethnic backgrounds different from those being served, creating suspicion that this is one more means

of social control by the white majority. This feeling is exploited by drug traffickers who live outside the community and see their market in danger. They create resistance in various ways, even to the extent of hiring provocateurs—and this agitation can be mistaken for genuine hostility on the part of the neighborhood. Another strategem employed by professionals in overcoming opposition to clinic sites in commercial areas is reported by Lowinson and Langrod. (36). They found this was best handled by informing political and community leaders of their plans and calming their fears.

In the planning phase for substance abuse programs, community leaders and organizations should be consulted, keeping in mind that different communities may have different cultural value systems. On the operational level, to the extent possible, personnel should be recruited from the community itself, reflecting its ethnic composition in both direct service and administrative jobs. Linkages to all social services, such as access to welfare and problems faced by families, should be built into the program, with the cooperation of local government authorities, and staff training should incorporate all aspects of community life. To defend the rights of the rehabilitated addict and guarantee the availability of appropriate treatment services, voter registration projects should be mounted among staff, patients, their families, and friends. This is seen as part of a comprehensive community education plan that would allow for an effective impact on government bodies. Ambulatory treatment sites are best situated in commercial rather than residential areas of the community, and services should be limited to patients living or working in the area. In order to strengthen effective programs and to eliminate those that are not, community leaders and local organizations should be involved in ongoing program evaluation (53).

It is recommended that, before a program opens in middle-class communities, homeowners and businessmen should know that the possibility of property devaluation and business disruption is for the most part mythical, especially if the program opens away from strictly residential areas and is affiliated with a recognized medical or health facility. Moreover, it should be made clear that the goal is not only the treatment of the addict population but a resolution of the addiction problem as well.

SUBSTANCE ABUSE AND COMMUNITY EDUCATION

It has been remarked that treatment of drug abuse can relieve suffering and improve an individual's social and vocational functioning but does nothing to prevent other people from developing the same problem and subsequently requiring treatment (35). A strong case can be made for recruiting community residents into educational programs. A World Health Organization report (40) suggested that "community attitudes to problems of alcohol and drug dependence may be most effectively changed when representative groups of the community are themselves involved in developing a program to deal with these problems."

Certainly, drug education in the schools has been heavily criticized as counterproductive; information is exaggerated and inaccurate and very often designed only to justify preconceived personal biases. Scare and fear tactics have certainly not worked. In a drug-oriented culture, where legal drugs are advertised and ingested on a mass basis every day of the year, it is not surprising that youngsters are unimpressed with school drug education programs.

A more realistic approach might be to recognize the existence of various patterns of illicit drug use and provide young people who are using drugs occasionally with information on the variations in quality of available street drugs or to provide prophylactic information to the young street addict—who cannot be reached for treatment—that will enable him to avoid serious medical problems or death from an overdose. From a medical-sociological point of view, according to Balter (5), the critical distinctions between use and abuse come down to the following questions: "In what manner is the drug being used, in what situations, for what purposes, and with what consequences?" Who can answer these questions better than citizens of an urban ghetto where the drama is openly played in the streets? And where else can we gain information regarding social factors that can explain why some individuals cease using heroin after an early juvenile involvement while others pursue a career of addiction?

After an exhaustive 2-year investigation of the drug problem in the United States, the National Commission on Marihuana and Drug Abuse in its final report had this to say about communities (42): "At the community level, objective analysis of the problem must be tempered by an intimate appreciation of local needs and idiosyncracies, and for this reason it is important that community institutions do not surrender all initiative to state and federal government." The commission also emphasized the need for local planning and local programs that are run by and are responsive to the community.

CONCLUSION

From time immemorial substance abuse has existed in one form or another in most cultures and at all levels of society. Addiction has resulted in incarceration, death, crippling side effects, and wasted lives. What we have now is a heightened awareness of the proliferation of both harmful substances and of the numbers of people who abuse them, to the point of unacceptable social cost. Because no "magic bullet" of immunization against substance abuse has been found, treatment has focused on the casualties, and mental health workers found themselves embarked on a salvage operation. But psychiatry has moved toward a general systems theory of character disorder and mental illness; that is, the genesis of a problem of mental disability may lie outside intrapsychic or biological factors. It may be a result of environmental influences—such as family dynamics, intercultural stress, institutional racism, and the powerlessness of poverty in an affluent society (1). Although not exactly revolutionary, the theory was to have substantial impact on communities.

What was more progressive was the involvement of the poor in the war on poverty programs of the 1960's. Never before had the poor been given credit for much expertise regarding the area of their own experience (59). The community mental health movement followed the principle of consumer participation and undertook to prevent the onset of illness as well as the treatment and rehabilitation of formerly institutionalized citizens in their community of origin. The treatment of substance abusers also moved from centralized and remote institutions to centers located in the neighborhood itself, and services shifted from punitive approaches to more humane rehabilitative efforts. Those professionals who derogate the community mental health movement have clearly given up too soon. In spite of critics who disparage or deny the ability of communities to organize, understand, and articulate their needs and how to fulfill them, the 1975 Congress underscored the importance of the community control concept in amendments to the Community Mental Health Act of 1963 (20). The amendments give specific powers to governing boards of Community Mental Health Centers to (a) schedule hours for service, (b) approve the center's annual budget, and (c) approve the selection of a director for the center. Furthermore, the governing board is to be "composed, where practicable of individuals who reside in the center's catchment area and who, as a group, represent the residents of that area taking into consideration their employment, age, sex and place of residence, and other demographic characteristics of the area."

Those treatment programs for substance abuse (particularly methadone maintenance) that are affiliated with community mental health centers are also under the purview of local citizens. However, substance abuse programs have been significantly influenced by the social movement of the 1960's and more specifically by the community mental health ideology.

It must be acknowledged that the progress gained has been gradual, and the process has been often painful and frustrating. However, we are now prepared to utilize those experiences and move forward to offer more meaningful services to those afflicted, many of whom are members of ethnic minorities. If relevant services are not provided and community members are not allowed to participate in those services, the end result will be the aggravation of the problem rather than its solution.

References

1. Alvarez, A., Batson, R., Carr, A., Parks, P., Peck, H., Shervington, W., Tyler, F., and Zwerling, I. *Racism, Elitism, Professionalism: Barriers to Community Mental Health*, p. 26. New York, Jason Aronson, 1976.
2. Arnstein, S. R. Eight rungs on the ladder. In *Citizen Participation: A Case Book in Democracy*, E. S. Cahn and B. A. Passett, editors, p. 343. Trenton, New Jersey Community Action Training Institute, 1969.
3. Aronowitz, S. The dialectics of community control.

4. Baldwin, J. *The Fire Next Time*. New York, Dial Press, 1963.
5. Balter, M. B. Drug abuse: A conceptual analysis and overview of the current situation. In *Drug Use: Epidemiological and Social Approaches*, E. Josephson and E. E. Carroll, editors, pp. 3–21. New York, John Wiley & Sons, 1974.
6. Banfield, E. C. *Political Influence*. New York, Free Press of Glencoe, 1961.
7. Bellush, J., and Hausknecht, M. Urban renewal and the reformer. In *Urban Renewal: People, Politics and Planning*, J. Bellush and M. Hausknecht, editors. Garden City, N.Y., Anchor Books, 1967.
8. Bertelsen, K., and Harris, M. Citizen participation in the development of a community mental health center. Hosp. Community Psychiatry 24:553, 1973.
9. Blum, A., Miranda, M., and Meyer, M. Goals and means for social change. In *Neighborhood Organization for Community Action*, J. B. Turner, editor, p. 114. New York, National Association of Social Workers, 1968.
10. Bolman, W. M. Community control of the community mental health center. I. Introduction. Am. J. Psychiatry 129:175, 1972.
11. Bolman, W. M. Community control of the community mental health center. II. Case examples. Am. J. Psychiatry 129:181, 1972.
12. Brager, G., and Specht, H. *Community Organizing*. New York, Columbia University Press, 1973.
13. Brill, H. The treatment of drug dependence: A brief history. In *Drug Use in America: Problem in Perspective*. Appendix: Second Report of the National Commission on Marihuana and Drug Use, vol. 4, pp. 109–126. Washington, D.C., United States Government Printing Office, 1973.
14. Brody, S. J. Maximum participation of the poor: Another Holy Grail? Soc. Work 15:68, 1970.
15. Cahn, E. S., and Cahn, J. C. Maximum feasible participation. In *Citizen Participation: A Case Book in Democracy*, E. S. Cahn and B. A. Passett, editors, p. 14. Trenton, New Jersey Community Action Training Institute, 1969.
16. Campbell, J. Working relationships between providers and consumers in a neighborhood health center. Am. J. Public Health 61:97, 1971.
17. Casriel, D. *So Fair a House: Story of Synanon*, p. 38. Englewood Cliffs, N.J., Prentice Hall, 1963.
18. City Demonstration Agency Letter No. 3, United States Department of Housing and Urban Development, October 30, 1967.
19. Clark, K. B. *Dark Ghetto: Dilemmas of Social Power*, pp. 11–12. New York, Harper & Row, 1965.
20. Community Mental Health Centers Amendments of 1975, Public Law 94-63. Section 201(c) (1)(A).
21. Dahl, R. A. The analysis of influence in a local community. In *Social Science and Community Action*, C. Adrian, editor, pp. 24–42. East Lansing, Michigan State University Press, 1960.
22. Darley, P. J. Who shall hold the conch: Some thoughts on community control of mental health programs. Community Ment. Health J. 10:185, 1974.
23. Deitch, D. A. Treatment of drug abuse in the therapeutic community: Historical influences, current considerations and future outlook. In *Drug Use in America: Problem in Perspective*. Appendix: Second Report of the National Commission on Marihuana and Drug Use, vol. 4, pp. 158–175. Washington,

Soc. Policy 47, 1970.

D.C., United States Government Printing Office, 1973.

24. Dubey, S. N. Community action programs and citizen participation issues and confusions. Soc. Work 15:76, 1970.

25. Dudley, J. R. Citizens' boards for Philadelphia community mental health centers. Community Ment. Health J. 11:410, 1975.

26. Economic Opportunity Act of 1964, Section 202(a) Subsection (3).

27. Economic Opportunity Amendments of 1967, Senate Report No. 563, p. 45. Senate Committee on Labor and Public Welfare, 90th Congress, 19th Session.

28. Flatbush rejects a psychiatric facility. New York Times 36, October 9, 1971.

29. Glazer, N. Blacks, Jews and the intellectuals. Commentary 47:33, 1969.

30. Greene, M. H., Nightingale, S. L., and Dupont, R. L. Evolving patterns of drug abuse. Ann. Intern. Med. 83:402, 1975.

31. Hersch, C. Social history, mental health, and community control. Am. Psychol. 27:753, 1972.

32. Holton, W. E., New, P. K., and Hessler, R. M. Citizen participation and conflict. Administration Ment. Health 96, 1973.

33. Jonas, S. A theoretical approach to the question of "community control" of health service facilities. Am. J. Public Health 61:916, 1971.

34. Katz, A. H. Application of self-help concepts in current social welfare. Soc. Work 10:68, 1965.

35. Levy, M. R. Community-wide prevention strategies. In *Drug Abuse: Modern Trends, Issues and Perspectives*, Proceedings of the Second National Drug Abuse Conference, New Orleans, La., 1975, pp. 1003–1011. New York, Marcel Dekker, 1978.

36. Lowinson, J., and Langrod, J. Neighborhood drug treatment centers: Opposition to establishment: Problem in community medicine. N. Y. State J. Med. 75:766, 1975.

37. Lukoff, I. F. Issues in the evaluation of heroin treatment. In *Drug Use: Epidemiological and Sociological Approaches*, E. Josephson and E. Carroll, editors, pp. 129–157. New York, John Wiley & Sons, 1974.

38. Mogulof, M. B. Advocates for themselves: Citizen participation in federally supported community organizations. Community Ment. Health J. 10:66, 1974.

39. Moore, M. L. The role of hostility and militancy in indigenous community health advisory groups. Am. J. Public Health 61:922, 1971.

40. Moser, J. *Problems and Programs Related to Alcohol and Drug Dependence in 33 Countries*, p. 5. Geneva, World Health Organization, 1974.

41. Moynihan, D. P. *Maximum Feasible Misunderstanding: Community Action in the War on Poverty*. New York, Free Press, 1969.

42. National Commission on Marijuana and Drug Abuse. *Drug Use in America: Problem in Perspective*. Second Report of the National Commission on Marihuana and Drug Abuse, Appendix, vol. 4, p. 319. Washington, D.C., United States Government Printing Office, 1973.

43. Neighborhood groups oppose alcoholic center on 14th Street. New York Times 41, February 22, 1976.

44. O'Donnell, E. J. The neighborhood service center.

Welfare Rev. 6:12, 1968.

45. Report of the Committee on Education and Labor, p. 2. 88th Congress, 2nd Session, June 3, 1964.

46. Riessman, F. "The helper" therapy principle. Soc. Work 10:27, 1965.

47. Robinson versus California, 370 United States Supreme Court 660, 1962.

48. Roman, M., and Schmais, A. Consumer participation and control: A conceptual overview. In *Progress in Community Mental Health*, H. H. Barten and L. Bellak, editors, vol. 2, pp. 63–84. New York, Grune & Stratton, 1972.

49. Ruiz, P. Community approach to addiction problems. N. Y. State J. Med. 72:970, 1972.

50. Ruiz, P. Consumer participation in mental health programs. Hosp. Community Psychiatry 24:38, 1973.

51. Ruiz, P., and Behrens, M. Community control in mental health: How far can it go? Psychiatr. Q. 47: 317, 1973.

52. Ruiz, P., Langrod, J., and Lowinson, J. Resistance to the opening of drug treatment centers: A problem in community psychiatry. Int. J. Addict. 10:149, 1975.

53. Ruiz, P., Langrod, J., and Lowinson, J. Community acceptance of addiction treatment programs: A contemporary perspective. In *Critical Concerns in the Field of Drug Abuse*, Proceedings of the Third Annual Drug Abuse Conference, New York, 1976, pp. 1030–1035. New York, Marcel Dekker, 1978.

54. Ruiz, P., Lowinson, J., Marcus, N., and Langrod, J. Treatment of drug addiction in two different communities. N. Y. State J. Med. 73:2244, 1973.

55. Saliterman, G. Schools: A Washington case. In *Citizen Participation: A Case Book in Democracy*, E. S. Cahn and B. A. Passett, editors, pp. 150–175. Trenton, New Jersey Community Action Training Institute, 1969.

56. Saranson, S. B. Foreward. In *A Social History of Helping Services: Clinic, Court, School and Community*, M. Levine and A. Levine, editors. New York, Appleton-Century-Crofts, 1970.

57. Shostak, A. B. Containment, co-optation or co-determination. Am. Child 44:15, 1965.

58. Tischler, G. L. The effects of consumer control on the delivery of services. Am. J. Orthopsychiatry 41: 501, 1971.

59. Van Til, J., and Van Til, S. Citizen participation in social policy: The end of the cycle? Soc. Probl. 17: 313, 1970.

60. Waterman, K. S. Local issues in the urban war on poverty. Soc. Work 11:57, 1966.

61. Watson, D. D. *National Directory of Drug Abuse Treatment Programs*. Washington, D.C., United States Government Printing Office, 1972.

62. Whitaker, L. Social reform and the comprehensive community mental health center: The model cities experiment. Am. J. Public Health 62:216, 1972.

63. Wilson, J. Q. Citizen participation in urban renewal. In *Urban Renewal: The Record and the Controversy*, J. Wilson, editor, pp. 407–421. Cambridge, Mass., M.I.T. Press, 1966.

64. Wilson, J. Q., and Banfield, E. Public-regardingness as a value premise in voting behavior. Am. Polit. Sci. Rev. 58:876, 1964.

65. Yablonsky, L. *The Tunnel Back: Synanon*, p. 26. New York, Macmillan, 1965.

CHAPTER 44

MATERNAL AND NEONATAL EFFECTS OF DRUG DEPENDENCE IN PREGNANCY

Loretta P. Finnegan, M.D.

Despite the increasing use of psychoactive agents, licit and illicit, by women in our country, the exact magnitude of drug dependency in pregnant women has been difficult to determine. During the past decade, though, increasing numbers of pregnant drug-dependent women have been presenting themselves to medical facilities, some only to deliver their infants and others to receive ongoing prenatal care. Unfortunately, in the past, these women did not wish to risk confrontations with legal authorities, and, therefore, did not seek medical care. In general, the pregnant addict has a low standard of self-care, and prior to this decade nearly three-quarters of these women never saw a physician once during their pregnancies. Therefore, addiction in pregnancy became an important health problem due to the increased incidence of morbidity and mortality in the mother and the infant.

This chapter will review the current literature, as well as the experiences of the author in regard to the sociomedical characteristics of pregnant drug-dependent women and their effect upon pregnancy, the fetus, and the newborn with respect to immediate and long term morbidity and mortality. Recommendations for management of both the pregnant drug-dependent women and her infant/child, based on the clinical research of others as well as the author, will be presented.

SOCIAL AND MEDICAL CHARACTERISTICS OF THE PREGNANT DRUG-DEPENDENT WOMAN INFLUENCING THE INTRAUTERINE MILIEU

The narcotic-dependent woman frequently suffers from chronic anxiety and depression. She lacks confidence and hope for the future and has extreme difficulty with interpersonal relationships, especially heterosexual relationships. The resolution and treatment of the superimposed addiction are complicated and require understanding and patience. These problems have taken a long time to develop, and one cannot expect a rapid recovery. Despite the need for psychosocial and medical treatment, the life style of the pregnant addict has an influence upon her psychological, social, and physiological processes. In addition, her life style is also detrimental to society. To meet the high cost of maintaining a heroin habit, the pregnant drug-dependent woman must often indulge in robbery, forgery, the sale of drugs, and prostitution. Because most of her day is engulfed between the two activities of either obtaining drugs or being overcome by drugs, she spends most of her time unable to function in the usual activities of daily living. She will have intermittent periods of normal alertness and well-being, but for most of the day she will either be "high" or "sick." The "high" or euphoric state will keep her sedated or tranquilized, absorbed in herself, and lost to all responsibility. The "sick" stage, or the state during which she is going through abstinence symptoms, is generally characterized by craving for narcotics with malaise, nausea, lacrimation, perspiration, tremors, vomiting, diarrhea, and cramps. Because of the way that her day is characterized, and also because she fears calling attention to her drug habit, she does not seek prenatal care. In the past, women were convinced through their past experiences that their fears and mistrust were a realistic reflection of their worth in society.

Therefore, in the past, it was characteristic for the pregnant heroin addict to arrive in the hospital during the first stage of labor. The physician or nurse could easily define that the woman was heroin addicted, for frequently there was no history of any prenatal care, either in a hospital setting or in a private physician's office. The woman was frequently unmarried and had venereal disease. Tattoos or self-scarring of the forearm to disguise needle marks were frequently evident. Due to the diminished pain perception when smoking while "high," burns of the fingertips and cigarette burns of the clothes were frequently found. The use of poorly cleaned needles or shared needles predisposed these women to serum hepatitis; therefore, they sometimes had jaundiced skin or sclera. Other signs of infectious processes due to unclean needles were also evident (34).

Additional history taking revealed several other aspects of the pregnant heroin addict's life. She may have had several other children who are currently not with her, but instead with a relative or in placement. These women are generally intelligent, although in our series the mean grade of high school attendance was the tenth. Housing situations are frequently chaotic, and plans for the impending birth of the child have not been considered.

Opiate dependence in the pregnant woman is not only overwhelming to her own physical condition but also to that of the fetus and eventually to the newborn infant. The vast majority of these women neglect health care in general. Therefore, these women are predisposed to a host of obstetrical and medical care complications during pregnancy that affect their well-being as well as that of the unborn fetus. Obstetrical complications that are associated with heroin addiction include: abortion, abruptio placenta, amnionitis, breech presentation, increased need for cesarean section, chorioamnionitis, eclampsia, intrauterine death, gestational diabetes, placental insufficiency, postpartum hemorrhage, preeclampsia, premature labor, premature rupture of membranes, and septic thrombophlebitis (Table 44.1). About 10 to 15 per cent of drug-dependent women have toxemia of pregnancy, and nearly 50 per cent of women who are heroin dependent and have no prenatal care deliver prematurely. The resultant infant born to the drug-dependent mother is not only born early but also weighs less than normal infants at the same gestational age (19).

Because of the obvious lack of quality control seen in street drugs, the pregnant woman frequently experiences repeated episodes of withdrawal and overdose. Maternal narcotic withdrawal has been associated with the occurrence of stillbirth. Severe withdrawal is associated with increased muscular activity, thereby increasing the metabolic rate and oxygen consumption in the pregnant woman. During maternal withdrawal, fetal activity also increases, and the oxygen needs of the

Table 44.1
Obstetrical Complications Associated with Heroin Addiction (29)

Abortion	Intrauterine death
Abruptio placenta	Intrauterine growth retardation
Amnionitis	Placental insufficiency
Breech presentation	Postpartum hemorrhage
Previous cesarean section	Preeclampsia
Chorioamnionitis	Premature labor
Eclampsia	Premature rupture of membranes
Gestational diabetes	Septic thrombophlebitis

fetus can be assumed to increase. The oxygen reserve in the intervillous space of the placenta may not be able to supply the extra oxygen needed by the fetus. During labor, contractions compromise the blood flow through the uterus, which consequently has an effect on the oxygen reserve in the intervillous space. The longer and stronger the contractions, the more compromised the circulation through the uterus. If labor coincides with abstinence symptoms in the mother, the increased oxygen needs of the withdrawing fetus would coincide with a period of variable uterine blood flow. Hypoxia and possibly death may occur in the fetus if it is exposed to an environment of insufficient oxygen for any length of time. As the fetus grows older, the metabolic rate and oxygen consumption are greater; therefore, a pregnant woman undergoing severe abstinence symptoms during the latter part of pregnancy would be less likely to supply the withdrawing fetus with the oxygen it needs than would an addict in the first trimester of pregnancy (98).

Naeye (81) has studied other fetal complications of maternal heroin addiction and found that nearly 60 per cent of the mothers or their newborn infants showed evidence of acute infection. Most of the infected mothers delivered prematurely, whereas those not affected delivered at term. The placentas of the heroin-exposed infants commonly revealed meconium histiocytosis, suggesting that they had experienced episodes of distress during fetal life. The infants born to these heroin addicts were, as a group, small for gestational age, with all of their organs affected. An explanation for the retardation of fetal growth could not be found in regard to maternal undernutrition. This investigator has suggested the possibility that periodic episodes of heroin withdrawal during pregnancy might restrict fetal growth by reducing uterine or placental blood flow. However, it is unlikely that a uterine or placental disorder was responsible for their growth retardation because the organ and cellular growth pattern associated with fetal growth retardation in uteroplacental disorders is quite different from that observed in the offspring of heroin addicts. The high incidence of meconium histiocytosis in the placentas of heroin-exposed infants suggests that they experience episodes of hypoxia or some other form of distress during fetal life, perhaps related to episodes of heroin withdrawal. In nonad-

dicted women, undernutrition restricts both size and the number of cells in many organs during the last trimester. The adrenal glands, liver, and adipose tissue are affected more than other organs. By contrast, the smallness of many of these organs in infants exposed to heroin in the third trimester was due mainly to a subnormal number of cells. Growth retardation of the addicted fetuses was still apparent after cases had been placed in appropriate maternal nutritional categories, suggesting that maternal undernutrition was not the only factor responsible for growth restriction. It seems likely that heroin has a direct effect on antenatal growth (51, 81).

Various other parameters have been studied in the drug-abusing pregnant woman; content of amniotic fluid, prostaglandins, corticosteroid production, estriol excretion, heat-stable alkaline phosphatase, liver function studies, serum immunoglobulin M (IgM), and lecithin/sphingomyelin ratios in amniotic fluid have been studied. In comparing the content of amniotic fluid prostaglandin to normal, diabetic, and drug abuse human pregnancy, Singh and Zuspan (107) did not find any significant differences.

Glass et al. (44) assessed the effects of heroin on fetal and maternal adrenocortical function. Serum cortisol levels were comparable in both study and control infants, but addicted mothers had significantly lower concentrations than nonaddicted mothers. Heroin decreases cortisol production in adults by inhibiting secretion of adrenocorticotropic hormone (ACTH). Decreased levels were found in pregnant addicts at the time of delivery, and values were similar in infants of addicted and nonaddicted mothers. The reason for these differences has not been explained. The authors stated that the findings may reflect a decreased responsiveness of the fetal pituitary to heroin or a relative insensitivity of the fetal adrenal cortex to fluctuations in ACTH secretion.

Northrop et al. (85) studied the esteriol excretion profiles in narcotic-maintained pregnant women during their last trimester. In these women the concentration of estriol in their urine remained low. Their urinary estriol concentrations rapidly increased toward or exceeded the average values expected for their gestational time after withdrawal. Neither ACTH nor metyrapone (Metopirone) stimulated estriol excretion, although a daily dose of 4 mg of dexamethasone decreased urinary estriol excretion. The authors concluded that careful consideration must be given to drugs a patient may be taking when fetal well-being is monitored with urinary estriol excretion.

Harper et al. (54) studied heat-stable alkaline phosphatase in methadone-maintained pregnancies. Placental heat-stable alkaline phosphatase (HSAP) has been reported to be of value as an indicator of placental function. It is elevated in maternal serum in normal pregnancy in progressively increasing amounts and falls after delivery. Because rising values might reflect subtle placental damage, the authors elected to study this enzyme in methadone-maintained addicts throughout pregnancy. High concentrations of HSAP were found in 80 per cent of addicted women who were maintained on greater than 60 mg of methadone. In women who were maintained on 60 mg per day or less, 20 per cent had high concentrations of HSAP. The higher levels of HSAP in women receiving higher doses of methadone during pregnancy suggested that methadone may affect the maternal-placental-fetal unit in more subtle ways than have previously been considered.

Lecithin/sphingomyelin (L/S) ratios have been studied in the amniotic fluid in normal and abnormal pregnancy by Gluck and Kulovich (46). Only in normal pregnancy does the L/S ratio correlate with gestational age. The authors found that abnormalities of pregnancy, including maternal, fetal, and placental conditions, may markedly affect the maturation of the fetal lung. Certain conditions associated with maternal hypertension and severe placental problems, including retroplacental bleeding and ruptured membranes, accelerate the L/S ratio maturation, and other conditions (such as diabetes) delay maturation of the L/S ratio. In 10 narcotic-addicted patients, it was noted that all had accelerated L/S ratios. The studies of these individuals suggest that an association exists between fetal major organ system maturation and the L/S ratio, independent of gestational age or birth weight.

Laboratory and animal studies have shown that narcotics may have an inhibitory effect on enzymes of oxidative metabolism and oxygen-carrying cytochromes. They alter fetal placental perfusion by constricting the umbilical vessels and decrease fetal brain oxygenation. These metabolic side effects may cause a decrease in oxygen availability to and utilization by the fetus, resulting in fetal hypoxia or acidosis. Chang et al. (13) reported two randomized control trials on the effects of nalorphine, pethidine, morphine, and heroin on fetal and maternal acid-base status. The effects of the four narcotic agents studied form a pattern of change in maternal and fetal acid-base status. The narcotic agents caused a decrease in pH and an increase in pCO_2 in the maternal blood and a decrease in pH and base excess in the fetal scalp blood. The fetal changes were independent of changes in the maternal blood. When given alone and in equivalent dosages, nalorphine caused a decrease in pH and an increase in pCO_2 in the mother to a greater extent than those caused by pethidine and morphine. This was thought to be due to the drug having a considerable respiratory depressant effect.

The data of Chang et al. (13) indicate that narcotic agents may cause an accumulation of nonvolatile acids in the fetus and that this effect seems independent of changes in maternal blood. This supports the suggestion that narcotic agents may have adverse metabolic side effects on the fetus. The effects of all the drugs other than heroin were small.

Zuspan et al. (136) studied the effects of detoxification of a pregnant methadone-maintained woman. In the mid-trimester of pregnancy, the patient was begun on a methadone detoxification program. The fetal neurobiological response was monitored by serial amniotic fluid amines (epinephrine and norepinephrine). The detoxification program showed a marked fetal response of the adrenal gland (increase in epinephrine) and sympathetic nervous system (increase in norepinephrine) that was blunted when the methadone dose was increased. These investigators concluded that detoxification during pregnancy was not recommended unless the fetus could be biochemically monitored. Unfortunately, in practice, many women try to detoxify themselves during pregnancy, or, on some occasions, physicians feel that a drug-free status is best and will attempt detoxification without appropriate monitoring.

The decrease in birth weight in infants born to heroin-addicted mothers has been reported by many investigators (32, 41, 84, 121, 134). Although earlier reports did not differentiate between term infants who were small for gestational age and premature infants, it is evident that many of these low birth weight infants were, in fact, small for gestational age. It was long suspected that low birth weights were related to poor maternal nutrition and health. Although these factors may be important, there is laboratory evidence that heroin itself may be a factor in growth retardation (57, 110, 122, 132). However, the mechanism for inhibition of growth by heroin is not known. Several investigators have noted that infants born to women who have used methadone have somewhat higher birth weights than infants born to women using heroin (18, 63, 133).

The effect of chronic maternal methadone exposure on perinatal development has been studied by Zagon and McLaughlin (132). Perinatal exposure to methadone and effects on body growth and brain development were studied in the rat. Body weights were reduced in drug-treated mothers during gestation and the first 2 weeks of lactation. No differences in gestation time, litter size, or infant mortality were recorded. However, methadone-treated offspring grew more slowly than controls. From birth to day 21, brain weight and length, cerebral width, and cerebellar weight and width were generally smaller in methadone-exposed rats. It seemed from these results that maternal methadone treatment retards the growth of young rats and affects brain development. Studies by Smith et al. (110) in salamanders have shown that methadone prevents regeneration of the limb and can cause taste bud degeneration.

Hutchings et al. (57) administered methadone hydrochloride orally to four groups of pregnant rats on days 8 through 22 of gestation. Methadone, particularly at higher dose levels, reduced maternal weight gain during pregnancy and increased both maternal mortality and total mortality among the young (resorptions plus stillbirths). Birth weight covaried with dose level and litter size: the 5-, 10-, and 15-mg/kg dosage yielded litter sizes comparable to, or somewhat smaller than, controls but with lower birth weights; the 20-mg dosage yielded the smallest litter sizes but with birth weights greater than any other treated or control group. Blood levels were dose related and corresponded to those found in human subjects receiving daily maintenance doses of approximately 30, 60, and 100 mg, respectively.

Raye et al. (9ˈ) studied the effects of maternal morphine administration on maternal nutrition and on fetal growth in a rabbit model. They found that fetal narcotic exposure results in a significant inhibition of fetal growth in the rabbit. This growth inhibition was not thought to be a result of alterations in maternal food intake but seemed to be morphine dose dependent. Weight growth seemed to be most severely affected with relative sparing of brain growth. They were not able to determine whether the growth inhibition resulted from a diminution in cell number, in cell size, or both. Therefore, they felt that the implications of the effects of these fetal growth restrictions on long term growth and development remain unclear. Additionally, they felt that narcotic-associated fetal growth inhibition in the fetal rabbit does not prove that a similar mechanism is responsible for the observed growth restrictions noted in human offspring born to drug-addicted mothers, because fetal narcotic metabolism and the effects of drugs or their metabolites on end organs might be markedly different in various species.

An analysis of birth weights of 338 neonates in relation to history of maternal narcotic usage was undertaken by Kandall et al. (63). Mean birth weight of infants born to mothers abusing heroin during the pregnancy was 2,490 g, an effect primarily of intrauterine growth retardation. Low mean birth weight (2,615 g) was also seen in infants born to mothers who had abused heroin only prior to this pregnancy and mothers who had used both heroin and methadone during the pregnancy (2,535 g). Infants born to mothers on methadone maintenance during the pregnancy had significantly higher mean birth weights (2,961 g), but they were lower than the control group (3,176 g). A highly significant relationship was observed between maternal methadone dosage in the first trimester and birth weight; for example, the higher the dosage, the larger the infant. In contrast to the fact that heroin has been found to cause fetal growth retardation that may persist beyond the period of addiction, this study has shown that methadone may promote fetal growth in a dose-related fashion after maternal use of heroin.

In addition to the numerous obstetrical complications seen in pregnant drug-dependent women, medical complications abound. The following are those frequently encountered: anemia, cardiac disease (frequently secondary to subacute bacterial endocarditis), cellulitis, poor dental hygiene, diabetes mellitus, edema, hepatitis, hypertension, phlebitis, pneumonia, and tuberculosis. Urinary tract infection is common, including cystitis, urethritis, and pyelonephritis. Due to the fact that a considerable number of women use prostitution as a means of supporting their drug habit, venereal disease is common. This includes condyloma acuminatum, gonorrhea, herpes simplex, and syphilis (Table 44.2). Therefore, medical complications in the drug-dependent woman can be seen in nearly 40 to 50 per cent of those observed in the prenatal period (19).

The drug-dependent pregnant woman more often develops anemia due to iron and folic acid deficiency. Nutritional deficiencies in drug addiction are due largely to the lack of proper food intake because of inhibition of the central mechanism that controls appetite and hunger. Furthermore, toxic responses to narcotics may contribute to malnutrition by interfering with the absorption or utilization of ingested nutrients. Absorption abnormalities are common in drug addicts because of the high incidence of lesions of the intestine, liver, and pancreas, and malnutrition is common because of the frequent presence of liver disease. Sometimes in the chronic drug addict peripheral neuritis is seen. This is usually due to thiamine depletion, although a deficiency of vitamin B_6, pathothenic acid, or nicotinic acid may produce identical signs. Hypoglycemia, vitamin B_6 deficiency, thiamine depletion, or magnesium deficiency may cause seizures in both

Table 44.2
Medical Complications Encountered in Pregnant Addicts (29)

Anemia	Tetanus
Bacteremia	Tuberculosis
Cardiac disease, especially endocarditis	Urinary tract infections
Cellulitis	Cystitis
Poor dental hygiene	Urethritis
Diabetes mellitus	Pyelonephritis
Edema	Venereal disease
Hepatitis—acute and chronic	Condyloma acuminatum
Hypertension	Gonorrhea
Phlebitis	Herpes
Pneumonia	Syphilis
Septicemia	

alcoholics and drug addicts. Hepatitis, a frequent complication of abuse of injectable drugs, is nutritionally depleting because it causes a loss of protein, vitamins, minerals, and trace elements. Intensive diet therapy is desirable in drug and alcohol addiction, and parenteral therapy may be necessary to correct fluid, mineral, and vitamin deficits in acutely ill patients (58).

STUDIES OF CHROMOSOMES IN INFANTS BORN TO NARCOTIC-DEPENDENT MOTHERS

Abrams (1) studied the cytogenetic risks to the offspring of pregnant addicts. He studied peripheral blood chromosomes in 34 newborn infants who had been exposed to heroin and methadone in utero and 22 newborn controls. He concluded from his study that infants exposed predominantly to heroin in utero showed a significant increase in the frequency of chromosomal aberrations in their peripheral blood compared with controls, whereas infants exposed predominantly to methadone in utero did not. Adverse environmental factors that may have contributed to the abnormal cytogenetic findings in the heroin-exposed infants were less prominent in the methadone-exposed infants. The presence of chromosomal rearrangements in both groups of drug-exposed infants led this author to suspect that heroin and methadone can induce chromosome damage in vivo and permits one to infer that these drugs are potentially harmful to the fetus from the cytogenetic point of view. The chromosomal rearrangements that Abrams found in both drug-exposed groups included dicentrics and rings.

Amarose and Norusis (2) studied the cytogenetics of methadone-managed and heroin-addicted pregnant women and their newborn infants. They assessed chromosomal damage prenatally and at delivery from 99 addicted pregnant women (80 from a methadone maintenance program and 19 heroin addicts) and their 101 offspring at delivery. About 10 per cent of the 27,907 cells scored showed chromosomal aberration. Chromosome damage was random, affected all chromosomes, and was mainly of the acentric fragment type. The percentage of hypodiploidy was significantly higher than the percentage of hyperdiploidy. In the mothers, no significant differences were found with respect to dosage and duration of methadone treatment and years of heroin abuse. No significant association was found between maternal variables and infant chromosome damage. Many have been concerned that drug abuse may possibly produce irreversible chromosome damage that could be deleterious. Although chromosomal changes in general are not pathognomonic of narcotic abuse, the increased incidence of chromosomal abnormalities in the lymphocytes from these narcotic abusers when compared to nondrug users strengthens the possibility of a causal relationship. A review of the life styles of the 99 subjects did not demonstrate a single instance of aseptic administration of drugs, and there is no way that one can prove the purity of the preparations. In these patients, the drug addiction was compounded by the presence of poor nutrition, lack of rest, stress, increased incidence of tuberculosis, hepatitis, syphilis, and a lack of early and consistent prenatal care. Consequently, for the above reasons as well as simultaneous polydrug abuse, it is impossible to isolate either methadone or heroin as causative agents. Any of the above factors could have damaged the detoxifying potential of the liver to such an extent that the small lymphocytes became fragile, infected, or primed so that in vitro stimulation into mitosis either elicited existing residual chromosomal damage or engendered chromosome damage in these weakened cells within the in vitro milieu. These investigators concluded that the biological implications of chromosome damage, observed in their study, cannot be completely understood until it can be ascertained how the human subject reacts to chromosome damage when there is no evidence of clinical or pathological syndromes.

MORBIDITY IN THE INFANT BORN TO THE NARCOTIC-DEPENDENT WOMAN

Because of the extremely high risk situation in which the pregnant drug-dependent woman is placed, she consequently predisposes her infant to a host of neonatal problems. In heroin-dependent women, the majority of the medical complications seen in their neonates reflects the fact that they are prematurely born, and, therefore, such conditions as asphyxia neonatorum, intracranial hemorrhage, hyaline membrane disease, intrauterine growth retardation, hypoglycemia, hypocalcemia, septicemia, and hyperbilirubinemia are commonly seen in more than 80 per cent of infants. Inasmuch as infants born to women who receive methadone maintenance are more apt to have higher birth weights and a decreased incidence of premature birth, medical complications generally reflect: (a) the amount of prenatal care that the mother has had; (b) whether she has suffered any particular obstetrical or medical complications, including toxemia of pregnancy, Rh hemolytic disease, hypertension, or infection; and, most importantly, (c) multiple drug use that may have permitted an unstable intrauterine milieu complicated by withdrawal and overdose. The latter situation for the newborn infant is extremely hazardous in that it predisposes the infant to meconium staining and subsequent aspiration pneumonia, which in itself causes a marked morbidity and increased mortality (19).

Connaughton et al. (19) also found that morbidity in infants born to drug-dependent women was dependent upon the amount of prenatal care as well as the kind of dependence (heroin or methadone). Over three-quarters of infants born to heroin addicts without prenatal care, as well as those born to methadone-dependent women with insignificant prenatal care, suffered neonatal morbidity. This morbidity was somewhat decreased in infants born to methadone-dependent women who had adequate prenatal care. Mean duration of hospitalization was 17 days for infants of methadone-maintained mothers and 27 days for infants of heroin-addicted mothers. The majority of these drug-dependent women were in Family Center Program, currently located at Thomas Jefferson University in Philadelphia, which is a comprehensive program providing obstetrical, medical, and psychosocial care and methadone maintenance for pregnant women.

Dar et al. (20) analyzed palmar crease variants in a group of at risk newborns without any evidence of congenital anomalies. In this study there were 108 prematures, 74 small for gestational age infants, 62 infants with a history of gestational complications, and 46 newborns with a history of intrauterine methadone exposure. The investigators developed a system of classification based on observations of 500 normal newborns as control subjects, 466 normal mothers, and 200 normal children. The palmar crease variants were divided into four main groups, schematically presented as normal variants, simian crease and its variants, Sydney line and its variants, and another group of unusual variants that do not fit into the other groups. A study of these various groups revealed that familial components, race, sex, and age are factors that can influence the expression of palmar crease patterns. There also was an increased frequency of abnormal creases in each of the groups of "at risk" newborns; moreover, there was an apparent association of interrupted transverse creases in infants who had intrauterine methadone exposure.

Rementeria et al. (97) reported that multiple births occur in drug-addicted women at a greater rate than that seen in the general population. Of 126 pregnant drug addicts, two sets of twins and two sets of triplets were delivered. The over-all multiple birth incidence of one to 32 is three times more prevalent than that found in the general population. Three of the four multiple births were dizygotic. The mothers with the dizygotic multiple births were on moderate to elevated levels of heroin or methadone at the time of conception. The authors postulated that the pharmacological action of methadone and heroin may be a direct one (on the ovary) to stimulate the release of an extra follicle or two. Milstein et al. (79) have reported that drug addicts using heroin for more than 2 years have increased mitotic indices and chromosomal replications in their peripheral lymphocytes. Heroin may act in a similar manner on the ovaries. The pharmacological effect of these narcotics may be an indirect one—stimulation of the pituitary by way of the hypothalamus—to release gonadotrophins (as in the case of clomiphene), which in turn will effect the release of multiple ova. Another factor to consider is whether there may be a direct relationship between the dosage of the narcotic and superovulation.

Nathanson et al. (83) found a lack of significant jaundice among infants of heroin-addicted mothers. Further investigation found increased bilirubin glucuronide transferase activity in morphine-addicted mice and the morphological demonstration of an increase in the smooth endoplasmic reticulum of their liver cells as seen by electron microscopy. The authors reported that the significance of increased hepatic bilirubin glucuronide transferase activity by opiates established in mice and suggested in infants of heroin-addicted mothers may extend beyond the metabolism of bilirubin to enhance excretion of other biological substances requiring glucuronidation or to induction of other enzyme systems within and beyond the liver.

The majority of infants born to drug-dependent women undergo abstinence symptoms of varying degree and duration. With the increased use of numerous psychoactive drugs by pregnant women over the past decade, more than the narcotic analgesics have been found to produce abstinence symptoms in newborns. The description of the neonatal abstinence syndrome, as well as the drugs involved in producing this syndrome, will be provided later in this chapter.

MORTALITY IN THE INFANT BORN TO THE NARCOTIC-DEPENDENT WOMAN

With the increase in obstetrical and medical complications, the lack of prenatal care, and the increase in low birth weight infants, it is not unusual to find that mortality statistics in infants born to drug-dependent women are markedly increased. Twenty years ago, when neonatologists lacked the techniques to care for the very low birth weight infant, the majority of infants born to drug-dependent women were reported not to survive. With the advent of newer techniques for the care of sick newborn infants, mortality rates in the 1970's have markedly decreased, to about 3 to 4.5 per cent (36, 133).

GENERAL MORTALITY

Available data on 278 infants born to drug-dependent women and 1,586 control infants from the general population delivering at the same hospital as the drug-dependent women revealed an increased incidence of low birth weight and neonatal mortality in the infants of drug-dependent women (36). The incidence of mortality in the drug-dependent population composed of heroin- and methadone-dependent mothers (the latter a stratified group of women having inadequate and adequate prenatal care) revealed an over-all mortality incidence of 5.4 per cent in contrast to controls in which it was 1.6 per cent. In low birth weight infants mortality in the drug-dependent population was 13.3 per cent and in the controls, 10.0 per cent. There was a marked difference between the methadone-dependent group with inadequate prenatal care and those with adequate prenatal care, revealing that methadone maintenance with inadequate prenatal care may contribute to a significant mortality in newborn infants. Over-all mortality in the methadone/inadequate care group was 10 per cent, in contrast to 3 per cent in the methadone-dependent/adequate prenatal care group and 4.8 per cent in the heroin-dependent group. The same trend was found in the mortality rates seen in the low birth weight infants. In general, the causes of neonatal mortality can be ascribed to the over-all lack of health care that the pregnant drug-dependent woman undergoes, with the subsequent onset of premature labor resulting in the birth of a low weight infant and all of the initial sequelae secondary to premature birth. In this study, causes of mortality included those that were seen in low birth weight infants as well as those that were seen when perinatal asphyxia occurs. These data revealed that comprehensive care for pregnant drug-dependent women significantly reduced the morbidity and mortality in both the mother and the infant.

NEUROPATHOLOGICAL FINDINGS

Specific neuropathological studies were done on 10 of the infants in the previous study (100). Detailed neuropathological examination revealed eight categories of lesions, three of which were thought to bear some relationship to the maternal drug dependence. (These latter lesions have not been seen in severely ill infants of similar gestational ages.) These included: gliosis (five of 10), foci of old infarction (four of 10), and developmental retardation of brain (three of 10). Only minor microscopic brain malformations were found in three cases. Other lesions identified included those common to high risk neonates: germinal plate hemorrhage (seven of 10), acute brain necrosis with and without hemorrhage (five of 10), germinal plate cysts (four of 10), and focal subarachnoid hemorrhages (three of 10). Two

isolated examples of unique lesions consisting of vascular proliferation and arachnoidal proliferation (one of 10) and a posterior poliomyelitis (one of 10) completed the spectrum of abnormalities in these infants. The evidence reported in this study suggests that the majority of the adverse effects resulting from addictive drugs may be due to nonspecific secondary gestational complications. Nevertheless, several aspects of neuropathological findings suggest that there are, in addition, primary and specific effects of the addictive drugs on the developing nervous system. Further studies, including those that utilize an animal model, are necessary to define further the role of maternal addiction on the nervous system of the neonate.

NARCOTICS AND SUDDEN INFANT DEATH SYNDROME

Sudden unexpected death in infancy, otherwise known as crib death, has been defined as "the sudden death of an infant or a young child unexpected by history in which a thorough postmortem examination fails to demonstrate an adequate cause for death" (125). From a review of the literature (15, 52, 87, 92), as well as a review of our own data (36), there seems to be an association between the use of methadone (as well as other psychoactive drugs, alcohol, and smoking) and sudden infant death syndrome. However, whether the effect is direct or indirect has not yet been delineated. Several recurrent themes, though, seem to be operational in infants born to smoking, alcoholic, and drug-dependent women and include: prenatal and postnatal growth deficiency, vascular changes, and hypoxic episodes, either caused by interference with oxygen-carrying capacity (i.e., by nicotine), episodes of depression (overdose), or withdrawal (i.e., by alcohol and opiates). Hypotheses suggesting the effect of the automatic nervous system of the neonatal abstinence syndrome and its subsequent treatment, chronic fetal hypoxia, and infection seem to be highly suggestive in the cases reported herein.

The incidence of sudden infant death syndrome in infants of opiate-dependent women is further listed in Table 44.3. In addition to the methadone-dependent mothers' infants, Kahn et al. (59) reported one infant in 38 infants born to heroin-dependent mothers.

Table 44.3
Incidence of Sudden Infant Death Syndrome (SIDS) in Infants of Opiate-dependent Women (30)

Investigator	Total Infants (N)	SIDS (N)	Incidence of SIDS (%)
Kahn et al. (1969) New York (59)	38	1	2.6
Pierson et al. (1972) New Haven (87)	14	3	21.4
Harper et al. (1973) New York (52)	244	4	1.6
Rajegowda et al. (1976) New York (92)	383	8	2.1
Chavez et al. (1978) Detroit (15)	688	14	2.0
Finnegan (1978) Philadelphia (30)	389	5	1.3
Total	1,756	35	2.0

Only by more careful study of the previous cases, as well as future cases, will we be able to clarify the role of opiate use in pregnancy as a causative or contributory factor in the sudden infant death syndrome (30).

NEONATAL NARCOTIC ABSTINENCE SYNDROME

DESCRIPTION OF SYMPTOMATOLOGY

During the 1950's and 1960's, numerous reports in the medical literature described the symptoms of narcotic abstinence in the newborn (16, 49, 56, 72, 73, 80, 106, 109, 115). Various therapeutic approaches were recommended by these authors in order to reduce the morbidity and mortality in this infant population. Heroin was the major drug of abuse at that time, but over the past 5 years, increasing numbers of reports have described the neonatal abstinence syndrome as a result of combinations of heroin and methadone dependence seen in pregnant addicts (25, 42, 82, 86, 102, 133).

Recently, additional nonnarcotic drugs of addiction have been identified as also precipitating the neonatal abstinence syndrome. In addition to the barbiturates, certain nonbarbiturate sedatives and minor tranquilizers

have been incriminated, including bromide, chlordiazepoxide (Librium), diazepam (Valium), ethchlorvynol (Placidyl), diphenhydramine hydrochloride (Benadryl), pentazocine (Talwin), imipramine (Pertofran), and propoxyphene hydrochloride (Darvon). Alcohol and amphetamine have also been reported to produce withdrawal symptomatology (Table 44.4) (3, 7, 12, 24, 48, 89, 90, 93, 103, 124, 128). When any of these pharmacological agents is used in combination with narcotics, the neonatal effects are likely to be exaggerated.

To assess effects of changing drug abuse patterns in pregnant drug-dependent women on neonatal abstinence, 60 infants were randomly chosen from 275 consecutive births to drug-dependent women enrolled in our comprehensive care-methadone maintenance program during the last 4½ years. A comparison was made between 30 infants (Group A) born in the first 32 months of this period and 30 infants (Group B) born in the latter 25 months. Maternal heroin histories were similar in both groups. Striking differences existed as to use of other drugs (depressants, stimulants, tranquilizers) concomitantly with methadone maintenance: Group A, 37 per cent; Group B, 90 per cent (especially prevalent was excessive use of benzodiazepines, 53 per cent). Duration of methadone maintenance during pregnancy was similar in both groups, but daily dose needed for maternal comfort was significantly higher (p < .05) in Group B ($\bar{x}$: B = 28 mg; A = 16 mg). Birth weights, gestational ages, and 1-minute and 5-minute Apgar scores were similar in both groups. Our previously reported system for assessment and pharmacotherapy of neonatal abstinence using paregoric or phenobarbital (33) showed: Group A, 77 per cent of the

Table 44.4
Pharmacological Agents That May Cause Abstinence Symptoms in the Neonate (31)

Heroin	Diazepam (Valium)
Morphine	Ethchlorvynol (Placidyl)
Alcohol	Pentazocine (Talwin)
Barbiturates	Imipramine (Pertofran)
Amphetamine	Propoxyphene hydrochloride (Darvon)
Bromides (Relaxa tablets)	Diphenhydramine hydrochloride (Benadryl)
Chlordiazepoxide (Librium)	

infants required pharmacotherapy for 10 days (range 2 to 34 days); Group B, 86 per cent required pharmacotherapy for 23 days (range 2 to 62 days). Neither pharmacological agent nor dosing regimen used significantly affected the number of days of pharmacotherapy required to control neonatal abstinence. These data indicate that changing patterns of simultaneous drug abuse where narcotics have been combined with the use of other psychoactive drugs, especially benzodiazepines, markedly increase duration of pharmacotherapy for control of neonatal abstinence seen in infants born to methadone-maintained women (35).

Neonatal abstinence syndrome is described as a generalized disorder characterized by signs and symptoms of central nervous system hyperirritability, gastrointestinal dysfunction, respiratory distress, and vague autonomic symptoms that include yawning, sneezing, mottling, and fever (Table 44.5). Infants who are afflicted generally develop tremors that are initially mild and occur only when the infants are disturbed but that progress to the point where they occur spontaneously without any stimulation of the infant. High pitched cry, increased muscle tone, and irritability develop. The infants tend to have increased deep tendon reflexes and an exaggerated Moro reflex. The rooting reflex is increased, and the infants are frequently seen sucking their fists or thumbs, yet when feedings are administered they have extreme difficulty and regurgitate frequently. The feeding difficulty occurs because of an uncoordinated and ineffectual sucking reflex. The infants may develop loose stools and, therefore, are susceptible to dehydration and electrolyte imbalance (29).

The origin of the neonatal abstinence syndrome seems to lie in the abnormal intrauterine environment. A series of steps seems to be necessary for its genesis and for the infant's recovery. Growth and survival of the fetus in an intrauterine environment are endangered by the continuing or episodic transfer of drugs of addictive potential from the maternal to the fetal circulations. The fetus undergoes a biochemical adaptation to the presence of the abnormal agent in its tissues. Abrupt removal of this source of the drug at delivery precipitates the onset of symptoms. The newborn infant continues to metabolize and excrete the drug, and withdrawal or abstinence signs occur when critically low tissue levels have been reached. Recovery from the abstinence syndrome is gradual and occurs as the infant's metabolism is reprogrammed to adjust to the absence of the dependence-producing agent (25)

At birth, most passively dependent infants, whether born to heroin- or methadone-addicted mothers, seem physically and behaviorly normal. The time of onset of withdrawal varies from shortly after birth to 2 weeks of age, but the majority appear within 72 hours

Table 44.5
Abstinence Symptoms in the Neonatal Period (31): Frequency Seen in 138 Newborns at Family Center Program in Philadelphia

Symptoms	Frequency
	%
Common symptoms	
Tremors	
Mild/disturbed	96
Mild/undisturbed	95
Marked/disturbed	77
Marked/undisturbed	67
High pitched cry	95
Continuous high pitched cry	54
Sneezing	83
Increased muscle tone	82
Frantic sucking of fists	79
Regurgitation	74
Sleeps less than 3 hours after feeding	65
Sleeps less than 2 hours after feeding	66
Sleeps less than 1 hour after feeding	58
Respiratory rate greater than 60/minute	66
Poor feeding	65
Hyperactive Moro reflex	62
Loose stools	51
Less common symptoms	
Sweating	49
Excoriation	43
Mottling	33
Nasal stuffiness	33
Frequent yawning	30
Fever less than 101° F	29
Respiratory rate greater than 60/minute and retractions	28
Markedly hyperactive Moro reflex	15
Projectile vomiting	12
Watery stools	12
Fever higher than 101° F	3
Dehydration	1
Generalized convulsions	1

of birth. If the mother has been on heroin alone, the majority (80 per cent) of infants will develop clinical signs of withdrawal between 4 and 24 hours of age. If she has been on methadone alone, the baby's symptoms may not appear until the end of the first day, and several methadone babies have had their onset of withdrawal after the first or second week of life. The type of drug or drugs utilized by the mother, her dosage, timing of the dose before delivery, the character of labor, the type and amount of anesthesia and analgesic given during labor, the maturity, nutrition, and presence or absence of intrinsic disease in the infant may all play a role in determining the time of onset in the individual infant (25).

Because of the variation in time of onset and variation in degrees of severity, a range of types of clinical courses may be delineated. Withdrawal may be mild and transient, delayed in onset, have a stepwise increase in severity, be intermittently present, or have a biphasic course that includes acute neonatal withdrawal followed by improvement and then the onset of acute withdrawal (25).

More severe withdrawal seems to occur in infants whose mothers have taken large amounts of drugs for a long time. Usually, the closer to delivery a mother takes heroin, the greater the delay in the onset of withdrawal and the more severe the symptoms in her baby. The maturity of the infant's own metabolic and excretory mechanisms plays an important role after delivery. According to the severity of the withdrawal, the duration of symptoms is anywhere from 6 days to 8 weeks. Although the infants are discharged from the hospital after drug therapy is stopped, their symptoms of irritability may persist for 3 to 4 months or more.

Fortunately, not all infants born to drug-dependent mothers undergo withdrawal symptomatology. Several investigators have reported that between 60 and 90 per cent of infants show symptoms (16, 56, 134). Although this syndrome is widespread, it is unfortunate that our knowledge is still quite limited. The biochemical and physiological processes of withdrawal in the neonate are still poorly understood. The neonate has been exposed in utero to multiple drugs in nonreproducible amounts on irregular schedules. Maternal histories are vague, distorted, or

withheld. It is not surprising then to find so many different descriptions and experiences in reports from different centers (102).

Further elaboration of the most common symptoms of withdrawal is necessary in order to more fully understand the difficulties in identifying and treating the passively dependent infant. Central nervous system hyperirritability and gastrointestinal disturbances are commonly seen, although most body systems may be involved. The degree of irritability can be gauged from the number of hours the infant sleeps after feeding. The frequency of withdrawal signs in 85 symptomatic infants born to drug-dependent mothers at Philadelphia General Hospital was described by Finnegan and Mac New (34). Over 50 per cent of these symptomatic infants born to drug-dependent mothers showed central nervous system hyperirritability evidenced by tremors, restlessness, and hyperactive reflexes. More than a third of the infants had high pitched cries, increased muscle tone, and regurgitation.

During withdrawal, the newborn's rooting reflex is extremely exaggerated, but his sucking and swallowing reflexes seem uncoordinated and ineffectual. A nurse is prompted to feed him, but he feeds so poorly that she must "milk" the formula into him as one does with a sick or premature infant. When he is returned to his bassinet, he promptly regurgitates a good portion of the feeding. Projectile vomiting may occur, as well as loose stools, which may complicate the illness further. Dehydration, due to the poor intake, coupled with excessive losses from the gastrointestinal tract, may occur. Malnutrition and weight loss can follow, with subsequent electrolyte imbalance, shock, coma, and death.

The infant's respiratory system is also affected during the withdrawal syndrome, causing excessively nasal secretions, stuffy nose, and rapid respirations, sometimes accompanied by retractions, intermittent cyanosis, and apnea. Severe respiratory embarrassment occurs most often when the infant regurgitates, aspirates, and develops aspiration pneumonia.

The effect of heroin withdrawal on respiratory rate and acid-base status has been studied (42). Infants with acute heroin withdrawal have shown increased respiratory rates associated with hypocapnia and an increase in blood pH during the first week of life. The observed respiratory alkalosis was thought to have a beneficial role in the binding of indirect serum bilirubin to albumin and possibly in the prevention of the respiratory distress syndrome, which is rarely observed in infants of addicted mothers. On the other hand, alkalosis can decrease the levels of ionized calcium and lead to tetany.

Although the frequency of respiratory distress syndrome increases progressively with decreasing gestational age in premature infants whose mothers are not addicted to heroin, no respiratory distress syndrome was noted among 33 premature infants born to heroin-addicted mothers at the Harlem Hospital Center, by Glass and associates (43). This study compared addicted infants to nonaddicted premature infants with gestational ages of 32 to 37 weeks.

Taeusch and others (122) concluded from studies on pregnant does and fetal rabbits that accelerated lung maturation may explain why infants born to heroin-addicted mothers have less than the expected incidence of hyaline membrane disease. Although these investigators concluded that heroin increases lung maturation in animals, they also have demonstrated that heroin decreases fetal body weight. They cautioned that their results in no way sanction the use of opiates in treating or preventing respiratory distress syndrome in human infants.

Roloff and others (99) injected morphine subcutaneously in doses of 2.5 to 10 mg/kg every 6 hours into pregnant rabbits from the end of the first week of pregnancy until delivery by hysterotomy on the twenty-seventh, twenty-eighth, or twenty-ninth day. In their attempts to study the effect of morphine administration on fetal growth and lung development, they found no differences in fetal lung maturity between the fetuses of treated and control animals. They found that the lecithin/sphingomyelin ratio in the amniotic fluid of rabbits did not correlate with lung maturity. There were no differences between fetuses and control animals. They concluded that morphine, when administered to pregnant rabbits, does not accelerate fetal lung development. Therefore, the observed reduction in the incidence of respiratory distress syndrome in infants of heroin-addicted

mothers had no direct equivalent in this animal model.

Newborn infants have decreased levels of 2,3-diphosphoglycerate (DPG) and, therefore, cannot unload oxygen effectively at the tissue level. At Philadelphia General Hospital, studies were carried out to investigate the status of this enzyme in infants of drug-dependent mothers in an effort to determine whether a maturing effect occurred subsequent to prenatal usage of the drugs of abuse. Cord blood and maternal venous blood were obtained, and the p_{50} (partial pressure of oxygen at which hemoglobin is 50 per cent saturated), hematocrit, and red cell, 2,3-DPG were measured (40). All the infants monitored for signs and symptoms of hyaline membrane disease showed no evidence of the disease. Mean values of p_{50} in the cord blood and total 2,3-DPG in muM/ml of red blood cells were increased in the opiate-addicted infants in comparison to normal controls. Maternal values were slightly elevated for both, as compared to normal controls. Such a shift of the oxygen hemoglobin equilibrium curve to the right is achieved in term infants by the sixth to the ninth week of life under normal conditions. It seemed from these studies that newborn infants of opiate-dependent mothers achieve tissue oxygen unloading comparable to that of a 6-week-old term infant, suggesting that opiates may function as enzyme inducers, resulting in increased blood levels of 2,3-DPG and a decrease in oxygen affinity.

Blinick (8) has reported on variations in the birth cries of newborn infants from narcotic-addicted and normal mothers. Sound spectrograms of the birth cries of 369 newborns demonstrated a significant increase in abnormal voice changes among the 31 babies of addicted mothers.

At the Philadelphia General Hospital it was clinically documented by the nursing staff that passively drug-dependent infants have difficulty with the sucking reflex. In addition, by means of a precise instrument, Kron et al. (67) studied their sucking rate, pressure, and the organization of their sucking, as well as the amount of nutrient consumed. These findings have been compared to normal controls and to infants born to toxemic mothers who have received such drugs as magnesium sulfate. The infants of both heroin and methadone mothers show reduction in sucking rates, pressures, and amounts consumed, and the organization of their sucking ability is distinctly abnormal in comparison to the control infants.

Because newborn infants undergoing narcotic withdrawal have seriously disturbed sleep, Sisson et al. (108) studied electroencephalographic tracings and electromyographic recordings of eye and mouth movement simultaneously before, during and after treatment of heroin and methadone withdrawal in 10 infants. Rapid eye movement (REM) and non-REM sleep patterns were correlated with muscular and respiratory activity. These studies concluded that narcotics will obliterate REM sleep in the neonate, that withdrawal will prevent normal adequate periods of deep sleep in such infants, that proper therapy will cause the return of REM and deep sleep cycles, and that the maintenance of therapy can be best regulated by interpretation of such polygraphic recordings as in this study, rather than the reliance upon the observed absence of more gross signs and symptoms of withdrawal. Schulman (105) reported the absence of quiet sleep and a significant decrease in REM sleep in eight full-term infants whose mothers used heroin until delivery. Heroin-affected infants had evidence of mild withdrawal but did not require medication.

In evaluating the sweating deficit of premature infants, Behrendt and Green (5) noted that 30 of 131 healthy full size babies and two of 108 healthy low birth weight babies demonstrated spontaneous generalized sweating under standardized conditions. In contrast, eight of 20 low birth weight infants of heroin-addicted mothers had spontaneous generalized sweating. In addition, the pharmacological threshold for sweating was decreased in low birth weights infants of addicted mothers as compared to healthy low birth weight controls. The authors suggested that this paradox may result from the predominantly central-neurogenic stimulation of sweat glands induced by heroin withdrawal.

LATE PRESENTATION OF NEONATAL ABSTINENCE SYNDROME SYMPTOMS

Late presentation of neonatal abstinence syndrome symptoms in newborns has been observed by Kandall and Gartner (64). Sig-

nificant symptoms of neonatal drug abstinence first occurred between 2 and 4 weeks of age. In seven infants, irritability and tremulousness were the major late symptoms. Seizures occurred in one infant who had progression of symptoms and who expired at 3 weeks of age. Although patterns of drug taking varied, methadone hydrochloride was taken in all cases. In two women, urine test findings confirmed methadone to be the only drug of abuse. Fetal accumulation and delayed excretion of the drugs may account for delayed onset of symptoms.

It has been noted that in adults the withdrawal syndrome develops and lasts much longer when methadone usage rather than heroin is discontinued (96). The delayed onset of symptoms is poorly understood. Goodman and Gilman (50) reported that methadone leaves the blood rapidly and accumulates in the lung, liver, kidney, and spleen. They postulate gradual accumulation and slow excretion of the drug to explain the more prolonged symptoms. Dole and Kreek (26) offered excellent evidence in adults that tissue binding of methadone may explain the prolongation of its pharmacological action.

PERSISTENT SYMPTOMS OF ABSTINENCE

The neonatal abstinence syndrome seems to persist in some infants for weeks and in others for months (25, 77, 129). Various investigators have found these infants to have hyperphagia, increased oral drive, sweating, hyperacusis, irregular sleep patterns, poor tolerance to holding or to abrupt changes of position in space, and loose stools (25).

EFFECTS OF MATERNAL METHADONE MAINTENANCE ON NEONATAL OUTCOME

With the changing character of narcotic addiction, moving from heroin to methadone usage, a new set of unsuspected difficulties has arisen in regard to the effects in newborns (83, 96, 133). In 1974, it has been estimated that 75 to 80 per cent of pregnant addicts in New York City were using methadone alone or in combination with heroin. Experience at the Philadelphia General Hospital was similar, in that 80 per cent of drug-dependent women who delivered at this hospital were on methadone or combinations of methadone and heroin. With this large shift from heroin dependence to methadone dependence in pregnant women, neonatologists have had to deal with the methadone abstinence syndrome. Various reports in the literature show marked disagreement in the response of infants to methadone abstinence. Behavioral differences have been observed between infants passively addicted to heroin or methadone (67, 68). Also, investigators disagree about the severity of the withdrawal syndrome in heroin- and methadone-addicted babies. Blatman (6) proposed that methadone babies are "better off" due to the superior pre- and postnatal care available to women treated in methadone maintenance programs. Blinick (8) reported observing mild to moderate withdrawal symptoms in approximately half of 19 infants addicted to methadone; none of them developed severe symptoms. Rajegowda et al. (91) found a higher incidence and more prolonged duration of withdrawal symptoms among methadone-addicted infants than among those addicted to heroin. However, mothers in Rajegowda's study were on higher doses of methadone (80 to 160 mg/day) than Blinick's patients (60 to 120 mg/day).

Zelson et al. (134) studied 34 infants born to mothers who had used methadone alone or in combination with heroin and 24 mothers who used heroin only. A comparison of the two groups showed the following: (a) The incidence of low birth weight infants was similar. (b) Among infants born to mothers on methadone, weight and gestational age were more frequently concordant than for infants born to heroin-addicted mothers. (c) Methadone infants had higher birth weights. (d) Apgar scores were lower in infants exposed to methadone. (e) The severity of withdrawal and number of signs were greater in methadone babies. (f) Seizures were also more frequent in methadone babies. (g) Severe hyperbilirubinemia was more frequent in the methadone infants. (h) Hyaline membrane disease occurred in methadone infants but had not been seen in heroin infants. Drug doses for methadone and heroin were not comparable in this study.

Davis et al. (23) have found that 80 per cent of infants born to addicts maintained on low doses of methadone (mean 45 mg/day) had evidence of withdrawal, but fewer than one-third showed signs that were severe enough to require therapy. Such results probably reflect the relative potency and length of action of each drug and the doses available to addicts. Methadone programs supply mother (and infant) continuously with this long acting pure narcotic, but street addicts encounter unpredictable changes in availability and purity of the shorter acting heroin.

Methadone assays in pregnant women and progeny were done by Blinick et al. (9) in an effort to delineate factors that may influence the severity of withdrawal signs in the neonate. These investigators presented data on the concentration of methadone in maternal plasma and urine of pregnant women on methadone in relationship to levels of amniotic fluid, cord blood, fetal urines, and breast milk. Their findings did not demonstrate a simple relationship between methadone levels in the neonate and the intensity of the withdrawal syndrome. They postulated that the effects of multiple drug abuse and other, perhaps unknown, factors may influence the severity of withdrawal signs in the neonate.

In Detroit at Hutzel Hospital, Ostrea et al. (86) carried on a prospective study of 196 drug-addicted mothers and their infants to determine the maternal, fetal, or environmental factors that may affect the severity of narcotic withdrawal in newborn infants. They found that the severity of neonatal withdrawal did not correlate with the infant's gestational age, sex, race, or Apgar score, nor maternal age, parity, duration of heroin intake, or the level of morphine measured in the infant's urine or blood. Reduction in the amount of illumination and noise in a study nursery also did not lower the incidence of severe withdrawal in their infants. There was, however, a significant correlation between the severity of withdrawal in the infant and the maternal methadone dose. These individuals, therefore, recommended that mothers on methadone treatment should be put on a low dose of drug (less than 20 mg per day) as soon as it is safely possible to prevent serious withdrawal in their infants. Similar conclusions were reached by Madden et al. (76). Because of a significant reduction in the frequency of withdrawal symptoms among infants born to mothers whose methadone dose at the time of delivery was less than 20 mg, these authors suggested a reduction of methadone in late pregnancy.

In New York City, Rosen and Pippenger (101) studied the relationship between the maternal dose of methadone and the incidence and severity of neonatal signs of withdrawal, placental transfer of drug, and the relationship between maternal and neonatal plasma levels of methadone. These investigators studied 30 mothers and their infants and analyzed plasma levels of methadone by using a gas chromatographic method. Their studies demonstrated that the relationship between maternal dose of methadone and the incidence of neonatal withdrawal symptoms was unpredictable. The time and onset of withdrawal symptoms was closely related to the last maternal dose of methadone. The ratio of neonatal to maternal plasma concentrations of methadone was 2.2:1. They concluded that neonatal withdrawal symptoms were related to individual variations in maternal metabolism of the drug, placental transfer of methadone, and individual variations in the rate of excretion of methadone as reflected in the neonatal plasma half-life. At plasma levels of methadone greater than or equal to 0.06 µg/ml, the symptomatic patients seemed to be protected from withdrawal, but when plasma concentrations fell below this level, withdrawal symptoms began within 24 hours.

In yet another study by Harper et al. (53), in which the relationship between maternal methadone dosage and severity of subsequent neonatal methadone withdrawal was studied, the severity of the abstinence was found to be positively correlated with the total amount of methadone ingested by the mother during the last 12 weeks of pregnancy, the maternal dose of methadone at the time of delivery, and the intrapartum maternal serum methadone level. These authors suggested that adequate prenatal care coupled with a decrease in methadone dosage during pregnancy provide optimal management of the pregnant methadone-maintained woman and her neonate.

Comparisons at Philadelphia General Hospital of pregnant addicts treated with methadone and street addicts on heroin show an improved fetal outcome in the methadone-treated group. Table 44.6 describes the withdrawal symptomatology in three groups of infants (N = 260) from drug-dependent mothers. The majority of the mothers received low dose methadone maintenance,

Table 44.6
Withdrawal Symptomatology in 260 Infants of Drug-dependent Mothers (19)

	Group 1[a] (N = 60)	Group 2[b] (N = 72)	Group 3[c] (N = 128)
	%	%	%
No withdrawal	5.0	6.9	9.4
Mild withdrawal	36.7	38.9	24.2
Moderate withdrawal	33.3	41.7	53.9
Severe withdrawal	25.0	12.5	12.5
Total withdrawal	94.9	93.1	90.6

[a] Heroin dependent; no prenatal care (average dose six bags/day).
[b] Methadone dependent; average daily dose 32 mg; average prenatal visits 1.8.
[c] Methadone dependent; average daily dose 38 mg; average prenatal visits 8.2.

and the incidence of severe withdrawal was 12.5 per cent in comparison to 25 per cent among infants of mothers on heroin only (19).

Preliminary studies on high versus low dose methadone and its effects on neonatal outcome are currently underway at our program here in Philadelphia. In this study of the effect of average maternal daily dose of methadone during pregnancy on two groups of infants, mothers in one group (N = 106) had inadequate prenatal care, and mothers in the other group (N = 186) had adequate prenatal care. The average maternal daily dose of methadone was divided into three intervals: less than or equal to 35 mg, 36 to 70 mg, and greater than 70 mg. When the two groups were compared, the results to date revealed: (a) The average daily dose of methadone was similar in both groups, 27 and 30 mg. (b) The average birth weight was significantly higher in the group of infants whose mothers had adequate prenatal care. (c) The incidence of prematurity was significantly lower in infants whose mothers received adequate prenatal care and also lower for all dose intervals in that group. (d) With all infants pooled, the average maternal daily dose of methadone and duration of maintenance during pregnancy increased as the severity of the withdrawal syndrome increased. A mild or moderate syndrome was associated with an average daily methadone dose of equal to or less than 35 mg. (e) There were no statistically significant differences in withdrawal syndrome severity within each group when the infants were defined as term appropriate for gestational age, premature, or intrauterine growth retarded. Because the average daily dose of methadone was very similar for the two groups discussed, it would seem that the average dose alone did not contribute to the different infant outcomes. Amount of prenatal care also seemed to play a significant role. Our data probably suggest that adequate prenatal care in combination with low dose methadone maintenance produces the most optimal infant outcome.

One can conclude from the recent data that has been presented that once again the recommendation for comprehensive prenatal care for the pregnant drug-dependent woman as well as an attempt to provide as low a dose of methadone as possible, preferably less than 30 mg, should put the infant at the best advantage for a mild to moderate abstinence syndrome.

SEIZURES IN INFANTS UNDERGOING NARCOTIC ABSTINENCE

Of great concern is the difference in reporting in regard to neonatal seizures associated with narcotic withdrawal in the newborn. In the early reports, Zelson et al. (134) found that seizures were more frequent in infants of methadone-dependent mothers. In our own program, we have found that 1 per cent of infants who have withdrawn from heroin and/or methadone have had generalized seizures. Goddard and Wilson (47) reported that of more than 150 infants, they have only seen one seizure they could attribute to abstinence symptoms in their neonates born to heroin- or methadone-addicted mothers.

The most extensive report and one that implicates seizures in infants born to narcotic-addicted mothers is that by Herzlinger et al. (55). These investigators reported that among 302 neonates passively exposed to narcotics during pregnancy, 18 (5.9 per cent) had seizures that were attributed to withdrawal. Of these 18 infants, 10 were among the 127 infants (7.8 per cent) exposed to methadone, four were among the 78 (5.1 per cent) exposed to methadone and heroin, and three were among the 14 (21.4 per cent) exposed to "other" drugs taken during pregnancy. Methadone dosages in those mothers on known treatment regimens were variable,

ranging from 10 to 100 mg/day. There was no apparent relationship between maternal dosage and frequency or severity of seizures, and no significant differences were found between neonates with seizures and those without, in birth weight, gestational age, occurrence of other withdrawal symptoms, day of onset of withdrawal symptoms, or the need for specific pharmacological treatment. All infants with seizures manifested other withdrawal symptoms prior to the initial seizure. Only two of 48 infants initially treated for withdrawal with paregoric subsequently developed seizures, compared to five of the 12 infants initially treated with diazepam, a statistically significant difference. The mean day of seizure onset was 10.1 ± 8.0 days with a range of 3 to 34 days. Generalized motor seizures or rhythmic myoclonic jerks, each of which occurred in seven infants, were the principal seizure manifestations. In some, however, seizure manifestations were complex. Three of the 18 had refractory seizure activity, and paregoric was more effective than diazepam in controlling both initial and subsequent seizure episodes. Seizure activity in three of five infants treated with phenobarbital alone and in two of eight treated with paregoric and phenobarbital failed to respond. Seizure activity in none of 10 patients treated with diazepam alone responded.

Electroencephalograms (EEG's) were recorded in 13 of the 18 patients with seizures in the Herzlinger study (55). Five of the initial infants had no EEG's performed; six others had normal tracings after clinical seizures had ceased. In seven patients, EEG's were obtained during the acute withdrawal stage. One had a normal record, during which no clinical seizures were observed. Two had clinical seizures associated with extensive movement artifacts; interictal activity was within normal limits. Three infants showed either unifocal or multifocal discharges preceding and accompanying clinical seizures. In two of these infants, myoclonic jerks were noted; in the third infant, staring episodes and chewing movements predominated. In these infants interictal records showed no definite abnormalities. In another infant who had refractory clonic focal seizures, several EEG's showed a persistent right central sharp wave focus associated with a bifrontal slow dysrhythmia, and they returned to normal after cessation of clinical seizures. Thus, the study suggests that abnormal EEG activity occurs only during the active seizure phenomenon with normal interictal tracings. However, movement artifact interferes with obtaining technically satisfactory tracings for detailed analysis of EEG recordings obtained during the acute abstinence syndrome. Although some reports have indicated uncertainty in regard to the mechanism of neonatal myoclonic jerks in the neonatal abstinence syndrome (54, 59, 74), the report by Herzlinger et al. (55) suggests but does not prove that such movements are true seizures. Neither seizure occurrence nor myoclonic activity was related to maternal dosage of methadone, and no blood levels of methadone were obtained in that study.

In our experience since 1969 with almost 400 infants born to women maintained on methadone and dependent on opiates or nonnarcotic psychotropic agents (studied in conjunction with grants from the National Institute on Drug Abuse that began in 1972 and continued to the present), there have been five cases of confirmed seizure activity (clinical and EEG seizure activity). Furthermore, in more than 200 EEG's completed at the time of the infants' discharge from the nursery, there was a 19 per cent incidence of abnormal EEG's. Of these passively dependent infants, approximately: (a) 5 percent did not demonstrate abstinence symptomatology; (b) 38 per cent demonstrated abstinence symptomatology that did not require pharmacotherapeutic intervention for treatment ("control"); (c) 57 per cent demonstrated abstinence symptomatology requiring pharmacotherapeutic intervention for treatment ("control").

Thus, there remain many unanswered questions related to seizure, EEG activity, and myoclonic movements in the neonatal withdrawal syndrome.

ASSESSMENT AND MANAGEMENT OF NEONATAL NARCOTIC ABSTINENCE

The neonate's prognosis for recovery from withdrawal is good because he/she is only physically dependent. Because not all infants of addicts have withdrawal symptomatology, prophylactic drug therapy is not recommended. The narcotic-exposed infant should be observed in the hospital for at least 5 days. Even if he/she is still symptom free at that time and evaluation of home and mothering capability have been adequate to permit discharge, observation at close intervals should be continued. If there has been polydrug abuse, a longer period of observation (7 to 10 days) in the hospital is advisable. In any case, a home visit or return appointment should be made within a few days after discharge and the mother alerted to the possibility of late onset of withdrawal signs (29).

If symptoms do appear, simple, nonspecific measures should be instituted, such as gentle infrequent handling, swaddling, and demand feeding. If symptoms progress, a decision must be made concerning drug therapy and readmission (29).

Indications for treatment, dosage schedules, and duration of treatment courses have varied widely in different hands, with some of this variation undoubtedly due to observer difference in judging severity of symptoms. To improve the objectivity of these judgments, some clinicians have devised neonatal abstinence scoring systems. Our symptom-rating scale has been found very useful as a research tool and treatment guide. This system is comprised of 21 of the most commonly seen symptoms in the passively addicted neonate born to the drug-dependent mother. Signs are recorded as single entities or in several categories if they occur in varying degrees of severity (Fig. 44.1 and 44.2).

Each symptom and each degree of severity of each symptom have been assigned a score. The higher scores were given to signs and symptoms that were found in infants with more severe abstinence syndromes. The total score for the interval of measured behavior is added and listed at the bottom of the scoring sheet.

It should be emphasized that the scoring system is dynamic rather than static, that is, all of the signs and symptoms observed during the 2- or 4-hour intervals in which infant symptomatology is monitored are point totaled for that interval.

All infants born to drug-dependent mothers are assessed for withdrawal symptomatology by using the Neonatal Abstinence Score at 2-hour intervals for the first 48 hours of life (Fig. 44.1), then every 4 hours thereafter (Fig. 44.2). If at any point the infant's score is 8 or greater (regardless of age), every 2-hour scoring is initiated and continued for 24 hours from the last total score of 8 or greater. If the 2-hour scores continue to be 7

NAME:_____

DATE:_____

NEONATAL ABSTINENCE SCORE

(First 48 Hours of Life or Every 2 Hour Scoring)

SYSTEM	SIGNS AND SYMPTOMS	score	AM 2	4	6	8	10	12	PM 2	4	6	8	10	12
CENTRAL NERVOUS SYSTEM DISTURBANCES	High Pitched Cry	2												
	Continuous High Pitched Cry	3												
	Sleeps < 1 Hour After Feeding	3												
	Sleeps < 2 Hours After Feeding	2												
	Hyperactive Moro Reflex	2												
	Markedly Hyperactive Moro Reflex	3												
	Mild Tremors Disturbed	1												
	Moderate-Severe Tremors Disturbed	2												
	Mild Tremors Undisturbed	3												
	Moderate-Severe Tremors Undisturbed	4												
	Increased Muscle Tone	2												
	Excoriation (specify area):_____	1												
	Myoclonic Jerks	3												
	Generalized Convulsions	5												
METABOLIC/VASOMOTOR/RESPIRATORY DISTURBANCES	Sweating	1												
	Fever < 101 (99-100.8 F./37.2-38.2 C.) . . .	1												
	Fever > 101 (38.4 C. and higher)	2												
	Frequent Yawning (> 3-4 times/interval)	1												
	Mottling	1												
	Nasal Stuffiness	1												
	Sneezing (> 3-4 times/interval)	1												
	Nasal Flaring	2												
	Respiratory Rate > 60/Min.	1												
	Respiratory Rate > 60/Min. with Retractions.	2												
GASTROINTESTINAL DISTURBANCES	Excessive Sucking	1												
	Poor Feeding	2												
	Regurgitation.	2												
	Projectile Vomiting	3												
	Loose Stools	2												
	Watery Stools	3												
SUMMARY	TOTAL SCORE													
	SCORER'S INITIALS													
	INITIATION OF THERAPY: (+)													
	INCREASE IN THERAPY: (↑)													
	DECREASE IN THERAPY: (↓)													
	DISCONTINUE THERAPY: (−)													

Figure 44.1. Neonatal Abstinence Score sheet used at Thomas Jefferson University Hospital for 48 hours after birth.

NAME:_____

NEONATAL ABSTINENCE SCORE
(Daily Score After 48 Hours)

SYSTEM	SIGNS AND SYMPTOMS	score	Date: AM 2	6	10	PM 2	6	10	Date: AM 2	6	10	PM 2	6	10
CENTRAL NERVOUS SYSTEM DISTURBANCES	High Pitched Cry	2												
	Continuous High Pitched Cry	3												
	Sleeps < 1 Hour After Feeding	3												
	Sleeps < 2 Hours After Feeding	2												
	Sleeps < 3 Hours After Feeding	1												
	Hyperactive Moro Reflex	2												
	Markedly Hyperactive Moro Reflex	3												
	Mild Tremors Disturbed	1												
	Moderate-Severe Tremors Disturbed	2												
	Mild Tremors Undisturbed	3												
	Moderate-Severe Tremors Undisturbed	4												
	Increased Muscle Tone	2												
	Excoriation (specify area): _____	1												
	Myoclonic Jerks	3												
	Generalized Convulsions	5												
METABOLIC/VASOMOTOR/RESPIRATORY DISTURBANCES	Sweating	1												
	Fever < 101 (99-100.8 F./37.2-38.2 C.) . . .	1												
	Fever > 101 (38.4 C. and higher)	2												
	Frequent Yawning (> 3-4 times/interval)	1												
	Mottling	1												
	Nasal Stuffiness	1												
	Sneezing (> 3-4 times/interval)	1												
	Nasal Flaring	2												
	Respiratory Rate >60/Min.	1												
	Respiratory Rate >60/Min. with Retractions .	2												
GASTROINTESTINAL DISTURBANCES	Excessive Sucking	1												
	Poor Feeding	2												
	Regurgitation	2												
	Projectile Vomiting	3												
	Loose Stools	2												
	Watery Stools	3												
SUMMARY	TOTAL SCORE													
	SCORER'S INITIALS													
	INITIATION OF THERAPY: (+)													
	INCREASE IN THERAPY: (↑)													
	DECREASE IN THERAPY: (↓)													
	DISCONTINUE THERAPY: (—)													

Figure 44.2. Neonatal Abstinence Score sheet used at Thomas Jefferson University Hospital after neonate is more than 48 hours old.

or less for 24 hours, then 4-hour scoring intervals are resumed.

The need for pharmacological intervention is indicated when the total abstinence score is 8 or greater for three consecutive scorings (e.g., 9–8–10) or when the average of any three consecutive scores is 8 or greater (e.g., 9–7–9). The total abstinence score also dictates the dose of the pharmacotherapeutic agent (i.e., the dose is titrated against the total abstinence score).

The total abstinence score has been categorized into ranges of scores indicating the severity of the withdrawal syndrome; i.e., the higher the score, the more severe the syndrome; therefore, the greater the dose of detoxicant needed to control the symptomatology.

If a hospital has sufficient nursing staff who can be trained to use this method of recording symptoms, the observation of the course and response to treatment can be facilitated greatly. As a general guide, if, in spite of nonspecific measures, babies have difficulty feeding, diarrhea, marked tremors, irritability even when undisturbed, or cry continuously, they should be given medication to relieve discomfort and prevent dehydration and other complications. Dosage must be regulated so that symptoms are minimized without excessive sedation.

Several drugs have been used in the treatment of neonatal narcotic withdrawal, that seem to be effective in relieving symptoms, but there has been little controlled comparison of their safety and effectiveness. The agents most commonly employed have been camphorated tincture of opium, U.S.P. (paregoric), phenobarbital, chlorpromazine, and diazepam. Methadone has been used very little, because its pharmacology in the human neonate has not been studied.

Using our scoring system at Thomas Jefferson University Hospital, we have studied the relationship between dosage and serum concentration using a high oral loading dose (16 mg/kg) of phenobarbital followed by maintenance dosing for treatment of neonatal abstinence syndrome. This method has provided therapeutic serum levels more rapidly and has controlled the neonatal abstinence syndrome more easily than previously accepted dosing regimens. With a 16 mg/kg oral loading dose of phenobarbital, a level of

18 μg/ml was the minimum effective serum level to achieve control. Although most infants treated with a 16 mg/kg oral loading dose were effectively controlled, because a small number remained difficult to stabilize, we have begun to study the relationship between dosage and serum concentration using 16 mg/kg (Group I) and 20 mg/kg (Group II) oral loading doses. The oral loading doses and maintenance doses administered were:

	Group I (N = 18)	Group II (N = 15)
Day 1	16 mg/kg	20 mg/kg
Day 2	x̄ 8.4 mg/kg	x̄ 7.1 mg/kg
Day 3	x̄ 6.3 mg/kg	x̄ 6.6 mg/kg

The serum levels (EMIT technique) at various hours after the oral loading doses and maintenance doses were ($\bar{x} \pm$ standard deviation):

	Group I	Group II
3 hours	16.0 ± 2.6	17.8 ± 7.3
12 hours	18.9 ± 3.0	18.1 ± 5.6
24 hours	18.6 ± 3.4	20.3 ± 5.5
48 hours	20.6 ± 4.0	22.4 ± 5.7
72 hours	23.9 ± 5.9	29.8 ± 7.8

The use of the larger loading dose has produced the expected higher phenobarbital level but not noticeably until day 3. The observed greater interpatient variability of serum levels and delayed increase in serum levels probably reflect a phenobarbital effect on drug absorption. Additional data are necessary prior to recommending this method to clinicians for general use in the neonatal abstinence syndrome (37).

BEHAVIORAL STUDIES IN THE NEONATAL PERIOD

Several studies have delineated the behavioral effects upon rats exposed to narcotics in utero (45, 78, 111). Sonderegger (111) investigated the developmental, neuroendocrine, and behavioral effects of early morphine addiction in female rat pups in a series of studies in which treatment agents were varied. When compared with controls, body weights of morphine-injected animals, regardless of treatment age, were depressed during treatment and remained depressed for periods of up to 105 days. Delayed eye opening and early vaginal openings occurred in some of the animals administered morphine before day 14. Behaviorally, animals treated with the narcotic from days 3 to 12 showed impaired ability to learn a condition suppression response; all animals in any early morphine treatment group showed a reduced analgesic response to morphine, some even when 156 days old. Neonatally narcotic-treated rats also showed a decreased steroid rise in response to morphine challenges in adulthood. The author (111) felt that the persistence of these effects suggests that exposure of the immature female rat to morphine results in prolonged, possibly permanent, morphine-specific alteration of brain mechanisms concerned with behavioral and neuroendocrine phenomena and supports the feasibility of using a rat model to study long term effects of neonatal narcotic addiction.

The effects of maternal morphine or methadone intake on the growth, reflex development, and maze behavior of rat offspring were studied by McGinty and Ford (78). Information derived from this pilot study indicates that there are real differences between the experimental treatment groups and the normal control group with respect to birth, growth, and brain weights, histological analysis of brain tissue, and reflex development. If a nutritional deficiency alone were responsible for the deficits in the drug-treated animals, one would expect to find no differences between the morphine-treated litters and the litters pair fed against the morphine litters. However, differences between these two groups are suggested, particularly in body weights and in cerebrocortical thicknesses at birth. The authors felt that the data on the methadone-treated animals were more difficult to interpret in the absence of an adequate pair fed control group. They felt that their data suggested an independent effect of methadone if one considers the histological analysis of the cerebral cortex. Although differences in cortical thickness may be nutritionally derived, the disruption of the columnar organization of the cells in the cortices of the methadone-treated animals alone did not seem to be a nutritionally related phenomenon. The authors felt that further investigation of these variables in a larger sample of rats would be worthwhile.

Zimmerberg et al. (135) studied the behavioral effects of in utero administration of morphine. When the litters were 2 weeks old, the morphine was withdrawn and the offspring weaned, assuring that they would have had no exposure to morphine except through the maternal placenta or mammary glands. When they were 2½ months old, the mice born to both the control and drug groups were tested for shock-elicited escape behavior on day 1 and for morphine sensitivity on day 2. The results of the day 1 experiment suggest that litters exposed to morphine in utero may exhibit an altered response to stress. The authors felt that this alteration may occur as a consequence of an increase in pain sensitivity or hyperreactivity to the same degree of pain. They felt that this finding would be relevant to a hypothetical role of stress in human drug addiction. The day 2 test for the morphine sensitivity revealed tolerance to the drug. Tolerance to morphine has been observed a year after administration of a single dose to rats. This study indicates that tolerance can occur in mature mice if the drug is administered through the mother during gestation and lactation. The personal "morphine experience" with long term consequences can, therefore, be similarly acquired by placental, lacteal, and other routes of administration. Because passive administration of morphine in adult animals can increase the probability of subsequent addiction, the fact that the placental route of administration of morphine is similar to other routes seems a critical issue in opiate addiction during pregnancy.

It is particularly important to determine whether in utero exposure to opiates alters the probability that the progeny will become "addicts" as adults. Because morphine is readily transferred across placental and lacteal barriers, Glick et al. (45) studied the development of self-administration behavior in rats receiving the drug during gestation and lactation. They concluded that, although sensitivity to morphine was not altered, in utero exposure facilitated the rate at which self-administration behavior was learned. It was suggested that, if applicable to humans, clinicians should be cautioned when making therapeutic decisions regarding opiate addiction during pregnancy.

Human infants born to narcotic-dependent mothers have been studied in the neonatal period by several investigators (69, 75, 112, 119).

The Brazelton Neonatal Assessment Scale

has been used extensively for evaluating newborn behavior. This instrument assesses habituation to stimuli such as the light and bell, responsivity to animate and inanimate stimuli (face, voice, bell, rattle), state (sleep to alertness to crying) and the requirements of state change (such as irritability and consolability), and neurological and motor development. Soule et al. (113) studied the clinical usefulness of the Brazelton Scale in control infants and those born to heroin-addicted mothers who were on methadone maintenance. Nineteen methadone babies who had received no pharmacological treatment prior to the first exam were compared to 41 babies who were subjects of an unrelated developmental study. Infants were tested at 48 and 72 hours of age. Group differences on the Brazelton Scale scores clearly indicate the methadone babies' state of narcotic withdrawal. Typically, the infants were restive and tended to be in a neurologically irritable condition. They cried more often and were state labile. They were more tremulous, and hypertonic and manifested less motor maturity than the normal group. A striking pattern of differences in responsiveness to the visual and auditory stimuli was also present. Although quite available and responsive auditorially, the methadone subjects responded poorly to visual stimuli. The babies seemed to be uncomfortable when opening their eyes and attempting to focus (pupil size was within normal limits). Although score differences suggested drug withdrawal, other characteristics of these methadone babies must be related to the findings. These factors include parity, socioeconomic conditions, race, birth weight, and prenatal care.

Strauss et al. (118) also studied the behavior of newborns passively dependent on narcotics and non-drug-dependent newborns in the first 2 days of life by way of the Brazelton Neonatal Behavioral Assessment Scale. In addition to the classic signs of narcotic abstinence, the addicted infants were less able to be maintained in an alert state and less able to orient to auditory and visual stimuli. These deficits were especially pronounced at 48 hours of age. Addicted infants were as capable of self-quieting and responding to soothing intervention as normal neonates, although they were substantially more irritable. These findings have substantial impact on caregivers' perceptions of infants and, depending on their extent and the duration of manifestation, may have long term consequences for the development of infant-caregiver interaction patterns.

Lodge et al. (75) studied the behavioral and electrophysiological characteristics of infants born to narcotic-addicted mothers. They compared the neonatal characteristics of 29 infants born to heroin-addicted mothers who were receiving varying degrees of methadone treatment during pregnancy with those of a control group of 10 normal infants. Their findings included the fact that the neonatal withdrawal period was characterized by heightened auditory responsiveness and orientation, lowered over-all alertness, and poor attentiveness to and following a visual stimulus. Electroencephalographic recordings revealed high frequency dyssynchronous activity suggestive of central nervous system irritability. Analysis of evoked response data further corroborated the behavioral findings with evidence for low arousal value of visual stimulation in the vertex frequency characteristics and poorly defined occipital responses. Auditory evoked responses seemed better integrated. The long range developmental significance of these findings needs to be further evaluated.

Infants undergoing neonatal narcotic abstinence have an uncoordinated and ineffectual sucking reflex as a major manifestation. Neonatal nurses who have been caring for such infants have long since clinically documented the poor sucking patterns seen in passively drug-dependent infants. Kron (65, 66) developed a precise instrument that was capable of studying the sucking rate, pressure, and organization of sucking as well as the amount of nutrients consumed. Measures of nutritive sucking were used to monitor the severity of the neonatal narcotic abstinence syndrome in a series of infants born to narcotic-dependent mothers who were either attending the methadone clinic or street addicts. These findings have been compared to normal controls and to infants born to toxemic mothers who have received such drugs as magnesium sulfate. Fifty subjects born to known addicts were studied on an as-you-come basis in the high risk nursery. Infants were tested on the sucking instrument twice daily just prior to the 10 a.m. and 2 p.m. routine nursery feedings according to standard procedures. Thirty-two of the subjects were born to mothers receiving low dosage methadone maintenance therapy with a mean dose of 42 mg/day and who attended our prenatal care program with the opportunity for frequent examinations by an obstetrician experienced in the care of pregnant addicts. Eighteen babies were born to street addicts taking heroin, most of whom did not come for hospitalization until the onset of labor; thus these women rarely had any prenatal care. All of the 50 infants studied underwent some degree of withdrawal reaction during the first 24 hours after delivery. However, not all were deemed to require specific treatment. Those who did were treated with a variety of agents. Twenty-eight received sedation with phenobarbital. Of the remaining infants, five were treated with paregoric, six with diazepam (Valium), and three with chlorpromazine (Thorazine). Withdrawal symptoms in the remaining eight babies were not considered severe enough to require drug treatment, and this group received no sedation or narcotic drugs whatsoever during the testing period. One control group consisted of 10 infants born to mothers who received magnesium sulfate and various amounts of barbiturates for treatment of toxemia of pregnancy. These infants were chosen because, like the addicted infants, they received special care in the high risk nursery and, therefore, experienced a neonatal environment similar to that of the newborn addicts. In addition, a second control group of 10 normal full term infants was studied, randomly drawn from the apparently healthy populations in the normal nursery and whose mothers had received no general analgesic or sedative drugs during labor. The results for sucking rates in the addictive and control groups are shown in Table 44.7. Of the several sucking parameters, rates seem to be most sensitive in distinguishing among all four subjects, although the pressure parameters also indicated significant differences between the control and the addict population. It had been previously found that pressure-dependent sucking parameters were consistent attributes of the individual infant and were relatively insensitive to environmental influences. For example, if the infant sucked at all, it tended to generate a characteristic range of sucking pressure. However, the present data showed that one effect of drug addiction is to depress pressures as well as sucking rates. Average values for the toxemic babies seem to fall between the normal and heroin groups, but this is due to the fact that the measures in Table 44.7 are means over six trials. On the first two trials the toxemic babies had scores for sucking rates similar to those of the addicts, but on subsequent trials they rapidly recovered and their scores approached those of the normals. Drug-addicted babies remained depressed throughout. Because these trials were done over the first 3 to 4 days of life, one cannot be sure of how rapidly the methadone-dependent infants would recover. It is postulated that, because of the longer action of methadone, the effects may have been more prolonged (70).

The dependence of sucking behavior upon the type of detoxicant treatment is analyzed in Table 44.8. Paregoric-treated infants tend to suck more vigorously than infants treated with sedatives such as phenobarbital and were even superior to those who received no therapy at all. The paregoric group approached control levels on most of the parameters. The averages for the no-treatment group were consistently lower than those for the paregoric babies, despite the fact that their withdrawal symptoms were judged to be quite mild and did not indicate the need for drug therapy. Diazepam-treated infants were greatly depressed in feeding behavior.

Table 44.7
Sucking Measures for Addicted and Control Groups (27)

	Addicts		Controls	
	Methadone (N = 32)	Heroin (N = 18)	Toxemia (N = 10)	Normal (N = 10)
Sucking rate (sucks per minute)	18.3 ± 2.1^a	26.2 ± 3.2	32.2 ± 3.9	39.6 ± 4.6

[a] Mean over six trial feedings ± SE, two 10-minute trials per day for 3 days performed just prior to the 10 a.m. and 2 p.m. routine nursery feedings beginning at 24 to 36 hours of age.

Table 44.8
Effect of Different Detoxicants on Sucking Behavior (27)

	Paregoric (N = 5)	Phenobarbital (N = 28)	Diazepam (N = 6)	Nothing (N = 8)
Sucking rate (sucks/minute)	30.5 ± 3.0[a]	19.4 ± 2.3	13.4 ± 7.2	23.2 ± 4.3

[a] Mean over six trial feedings ± SD.

Of the six diazepam subjects, five hardly sucked at all (however, the high sucking scores of the sixth subject brought up the group mean) (70).

These results raise questions about a number of a priori assumptions regarding the safety and efficacy of current treatment methods for maternal drug dependence and neonatal abstinence. Continuing studies in our nursery are involved in further delineating the behavioral effects of the drugs of abuse on the neonate as well as the efficacy of currently recommended detoxicant drugs used for neonatal abstinence.

LONG TERM OUTCOME OF CHILDREN WHO HAVE UNDERGONE IN UTERO EXPOSURE TO NARCOTIC AGENTS

Despite the fact that a newborn may be free of physical, behavioral, or neurological deficits at the time of birth after intrauterine exposure to pharmacological agents, one cannot assume that no effect has occurred. It has been known for many years that the effects of pharmacological agents may not become apparent for many months or years. Therefore, the follow-up of infants prenatally exposed to pharmacological agents is extremely important. Evaluations of infants born to women who have taken licit drugs are somewhat easier than those involving the use of illicit drugs. Therefore, few studies in regard to maternal drug addiction are available, and the numbers of patients involved are small.

The easiest part of caring for the neonate is over when drug therapy has been discontinued and he is physically well. Now there is the rest of his life to consider. How does one prepare for the discharge of this infant? Prior to the use of methadone, there was almost no follow-up of infants born to heroin-addicted mothers. Until 1970, only four infants born to heroin addicts had been followed for more than 6 months (49, 56). Because there is no universal method by which

decisions are made as to the disposition of these infants after discharge from the hospital, some may be found with mothers, some with relatives, and others placed in custody of a state agency or voluntarily released by the mother to private agencies for temporary or permanent placement.

Some individuals recommend separation of the infants from the addicted mothers. This solution may not be practical in cities where social services and courts are already understaffed and overworked. Foster care is expensive and hard to find. Pediatricians basically feel that the mother-infant association should not be dissolved except in extreme situations. If we are dictatorial about birth control devices for addict mothers, we are open to charges of racism and genocide. If we insist on a protected environment for the mother and her infant, such as a therapeutic community, we are urging a service that is very expensive and difficult to organize for large numbers of patients (34).

In our program at Thomas Jefferson University Hospital in Philadelphia, all addict mothers are given their infants when they are ready for discharge unless a team—consisting of a nursery nurse, pediatrician, psychiatric social worker, obstetrician, and public health nurse—has shown that the mother cannot care for her infant adequately with the supportive services available to her. With strong support from this team and with intensive psychosocial services during her pregnancy and immediately after delivery, she usually is prepared to cope more realistically with motherhood. However, if the team believes that she neither wishes nor is able to assume this responsibility, arrangements are made for temporary foster placement or for another relative to accept the major caretaking duties.

In 1973, Wilson et al. (130) reported on the course of growth and development of 30 infants of heroin addicts who were observed from 3 to 34 months. Eighty per cent had signs of neonatal withdrawal, and 60 per cent continued with subacute withdrawal signs for

3 to 6 months. Behavioral disturbances, predominantly hyperactivity, brief attention span, and temper outbursts, were identified in seven of 14 infants observed for 1 year or longer, and two had neurological abnormalities. Growth impairment was associated with behavioral disturbances in four of the seven infants. These disturbances seemed to be unrelated to subsequent environmental factors. Infants performed at age-appropriate levels on behavioral testing that was accomplished by the Gesell schedule. Factors that adversely influence the results of this study are that the majority of the infants were either in foster homes or were being raised by family or friends. Furthermore, the sample size is extremely small for drawing strong conclusions.

Ramer and Lodge (94) studied 35 infants who were born to 32 mothers registered in a San Francisco city-operated methadone maintenance treatment program. The infants were studied by the Bayley Scales of Infant Mental and Motor Development that were given at 3-month intervals during the first year and at 6-month intervals during the second and third years. Sixty per cent of the infants demonstrated mild or no symptoms, and 40 per cent developed moderate or severe symptoms of withdrawal. The infants whose symptoms were most severe were born to mothers who had documented histories of polydrug abuse. Many infants were slow to gain weight in the neonatal period. Thereafter, growth and development remained generally within the normal range. The results of these studies revealed that the older infants showed age-appropriate development in the area of vocalization and language. Their performance on perceptual motor tasks was somewhat less adequate. The authors cautioned that it has not been possible to assess the relative impact of genetic, prenatal, and subsequent environmental factors upon the over-all developmental picture. Furthermore, the developmental quotients during these early years, although useful in identifying areas of strength and weakness, may not predict subsequent intelligence quotients. Despite this, their results lend encouragement to the possibility that the provision of a modified methadone maintenance program that includes good prenatal care and nutrition, neonatal care, and continued support and encouragement to the mother after the birth of the child may offset the detrimental effects of the neonatal withdrawal experience for the infant and foster an environment that may facilitate development within the normal range.

In 1976, Sardemann et al. (104) evaluated the prognosis of 19 children who were born to drug-addicted women, a majority of whom were addicted to narcotics. During the neonatal period, 16 of the infants had withdrawal symptoms, and 11 required medical treatment. One infant died of congenital malformations. Of the surviving 18 infants, 14 were discharged to their mothers and four went to a children's home. During follow-up, which varied from 2 months to 2 years and 8 months of age, 10 of the children had to be placed in a children's home for a period. No physical abnormalities were found in the children. Motor and perceptual development were normal in 12, but in three speech development was delayed. Again, this sample seems to be too small to draw specific conclusions. Moreover, the lack of a control group further decreases its validity.

In 1976, Strauss et al. (119) reported evaluations on 60 infants born to women addicted to narcotics and enrolled in the Hutzel Hospital's methadone treatment perinatal care program. These infants were compared with 53 infants who were born to mothers who were not addicted. The psychological development of the infants was evaluated with the Bayley Scales of Infant Development at 3, 6, and 12 months of age. Anthropometric measurements were obtained at 12 months of age for 21 addicted and 24 nonaddicted infants. These studies conclude that the average course of infants born to addicted mothers is well within the normal range throughout the first year of life. Their data do show that the level of psychomotor development of these children is not consistent through the first year, but declines. Examination of the particular items that addicted infants passed less frequently at 1 year of age than their nonaddicted counterparts indicated that the motor development difference between these groups at 12 months was primarily in the area of locomotion. Addicted infants were significantly less likely to be walking unaided at this age. The decline does not seem to be a statistical artifact, because in a sample from another addicted cohort that is currently being followed, a similar decline between 3 months and 1 year of age was found. The authors have not been able to determine whether this finding reflects some endogenous process or the influences of the caregiving environment. The authors suggested that repeated evaluations of the behavioral development of "congenitally" addicted infants during infancy and early childhood, as well as assessments of their environment, are necessary to specify more clearly the degree and determinants of risk for developmental dysfunction in this population.

In Philadelphia, in our specially designed comprehensive program for pregnant drug-dependent women (Family Center), a follow-up study in infants born to methadone-maintained women has been in progress. In this program, as in many in the United States, there has been great concern about the use of methadone maintenance in pregnant women in regard to its effect on the fetus and neonate. The initial outcome for the neonate seems to be somewhat favorable in regard to a better physical condition, although concern exists about the severity of the abstinence syndrome. It was unknown until recently what possible effects or irreversible damage methadone might cause in the future for these newborns. Current literature (94, 117) has indicated that as early as 3 months of age and throughout the first year of life infants born to methadone-dependent women do function within the normal range in their mental and motor development. It is encouraging to find that these studies, as well as ours, support similar findings.

Follow-up studies in Family Center included 59 infants, born to women maintained on methadone during pregnancy, who were evaluated periodically in regard to development and physical growth and compared with a control group of 42 infants. Controls were randomly selected from the same socioeconomic class delivering at the hospital. No drug use was evident in the control group. All were evaluated by the Gesell Developmental Schedule. The data indicated that children of mothers maintained on methadone during pregnancy were lighter in weight and shorter in stature from birth through 89 weeks of age when compared to a control group. Statistical analysis of measurements from birth through 38 weeks showed that,

although the study group was consistently below the fiftieth percentile for weight and height, they did not demonstrate growth lag in comparison to the control group. Furthermore, the study group did not have any unusual or significant health problems as compared to the control group, and there were no abnormal neurological findings. There was no correlation between maternal drug intake, degree of neonatal withdrawal, or Gesell behavioral profiles (developmental schedules were accomplished through 24 months of age) (38).

As part of our ongoing research in Family Center, an additional 45 infants (27 1-year-olds and 18 2-year-olds) exposed to methadone in utero and 33 control infants (16 1-year-olds and 17 2-year-olds) randomly selected from a population of comparable socioeconomic, racial, and medical backgrounds were assessed with the Bayley Mental Scale of Infant Development. No differences were found between infants exposed to methadone at birth and control infants at 1 and 2 years of age (mean ± S.E.):

	Family Center	Control
1-year-olds	102.74 ± 10.21	108.00 ± 9.16
	(N = 27)	(N = 16)
2-year-olds	92.11 ± 9.29	91.94 ± 9.52
	(N = 18)	(N = 17)

These data support previous findings that in utero methadone exposure does not seem to have an adverse effect on mental development in infancy. However, the decrement in scores between the 1- and 2-year-olds for both groups was significant (t = 5.56, p < .05) and suggest that environment may confound long term infant outcome (61).

Although our data and those of others suggest that infants born to women maintained on methadone are within the normal range of mental development at 1 and 2 years of age, these data are limited and require further replication before conclusive statements can be made regarding the effect of in utero methadone exposure.

The methods of treatment for the neonatal abstinence syndrome have long been of concern to clinicians in the field. Therefore, in Philadelphia, we have been evaluating the effects of our oral phenobarbital loading dose regimen for management of the neonatal abstinence syndrome on early infant development of fetuses exposed to therapeutically administered methadone. The assessment, pharmacotherapy, and control of neonatal abstinence syndrome are based upon our previously reported comprehensive scoring system (33). As part of an ongoing study, a cross-sectional sample of 27 1-year-old infants born to mothers who received therapeutically administered methadone during pregnancy has been evaluated using the Bayley Mental Scale of Infant Development. Seven infants in the sample were born during the past 1.5 years and treated by phenobarbital loading (Group 1). Twenty infants were managed by a phenobarbital or paregoric dosing method (33), and six of these (Group 2) were compared to Group 1 because they were born during the same period. Mean birth weight, gestational age, maternal therapeutically administered methadone dose, and duration were similar in both Groups 1 and 2. The mean Bayley Scale of Infant Development score for Group 1 was 102 ± 7.85 and 105 ± 11.55 for Group 2; there was no significant difference between group mean Bayley Scale of Infant Development. Furthermore, there seems to be no difference between mean Bayley Scale of Infant Development for Group 1 and the 20 infants managed by phenobarbital and paregoric dosing methods (102 ± 10.21). These preliminary data suggest that the phenobarbital loading method of controlling neonatal abstinence syndrome has not adversely affected development of these infants at 1 year of age (37).

Additional studies in progress in Philadelphia include assessments of a present total of 50 4-year-old children. Twenty-five study children were born to women who received methadone maintenance during pregnancy as well as prenatal care while enrolled in the Family Center Program. The 25 control children were randomly selected from a stratified population of comparable socioeconomic, race, and medical background from a pediatric outpatient clinic. In the preliminary evaluations 22 children, 10 males and 12 females, have been studied. The mean age of the methadone-exposed group is 4 years 4 months, and the mean age of the control group is 4 years 4.5 months. Children are assessed by way of a neurological examination, the Weschler Preschool and Primary Scale of Intelligence, the Test of Language Development, Imitation of Gestures, and the Motor-Free Visual Perception Test. Table 44.9 describes the group means and standard deviations for the Wechsler Preschool and Primary Scale of Intelligence. The differences between children born to women maintained on methadone and the controls are very small and not statistically significant for both subscales and the full scale I.Q.'s. Both groups performed better on the verbal scale than on the performance scale. Table 44.10 describes the group means and standard deviations for the Imitation of Gestures, the Test of Language Development, and the Motor-Free Visual Perception Test. The data also show no differences between the groups. All neurological findings were within the normal range, and there was no relationship between severity of neonatal withdrawal and the I.Q. scores (60).

These data suggest that, at 4 years of age, children born to women maintained on methadone who underwent neonatal abstinence are functioning within the normal range in their mental development, and there do not seem to be any differences in language and perceptual skills between these children and those of comparable backgrounds whose mothers were not involved with drugs. However, the question of differences in behavioral patterns still requires extensive investigation, as does the question of the possible existence of learning disability.

Illicit drugs taken individually, as well as

Table 44.9
Results of Wechsler Preschool and Primary Scale of Intelligence (60)

	Children of Methadone-dependent Women (N = 10)		Control Children (N = 12)	
	Mean	Standard Deviation	Mean	Standard Deviation
Verbal scale	94.44	11.32	97.75	20.78
Performance scale	86.11	12.81	88.25	13.76
Full scale I.Q.	89.33	12.97	92.66	18.05

Table 44.10
Results of Perception and Language Assessment (60)

	Children of Methadone-dependent Women			Control Children		
	N	Mean	Standard Deviation	N	Mean	Standard Deviation
Imitation of Gestures	9	13.77	2.48	13	12.76	4.14
Test of Language Development	7	81.00	6.16	11	81.81	6.96
Motor-Free Visual Perception Test	6	83.33	11.23	10	82.50	10.55

in combination, are being excessively used by women in general, as well as those that are pregnant. In this situation, the potential hazard to the fetus, neonate, and child is overwhelming, not only due to the fact that the fetus has been exposed to an adverse physical and social milieu, but also because of the vast combinations of drugs that may interact, compounding the total effect upon the fetus. Additional studies are still necessary to define further the physical, developmental, and social effects of these illicit drugs upon the neonate, infant, and older child.

EFFORTS TO "NORMALIZE" THE INTRAUTERINE MILIEU OF THE PREGNANT DRUG-DEPENDENT WOMAN TO PREVENT ADVERSE FETAL, NEONATAL, AND LONG TERM OUTCOME

It is evident from the many observations of clinicians who have cared for pregnant drug-abusing women that these women are afflicted with numerous problems, all of which must be dealt with in order to decrease the morbidity and mortality of both mother and infant. It is essential, therefore, to provide a comprehensive approach that will specifically meet the needs of pregnant women who have been involved with the drugs of abuse. Although multiple drug use is seen in a considerable number of pregnant women, the majority abuse opiates as the primary drug.

The specific areas that must be met in the schema for comprehensive care for the pregnant drug abuser are obstetrical, psychosocial, addictive, and long term planning for the mother and her newborn infant. Before in-depth treatment can begin in the area of obstetrics or psychosocial counseling, the addict's physical dependence on opiate drugs must be dealt with. In 1972, the American Medical Association's Council on Mental Health and the Committee on Alcoholism and Drug Dependence provided recommendations for the treatment of morphine-type dependence by withdrawal methods. They recommended that a pregnant drug-dependent woman should undergo withdrawal prior to delivery. If there was insufficient time to accomplish withdrawal before delivery, the woman could be maintained during labor and then withdrawn after the delivery process (123). Chappel (14) and others (18) strongly disagree and would emphasize the referral of pregnant addicts to addiction treatment programs because they feel that withdrawal from opiates is not indicated in the third trimester. Late in pregnancy, withdrawal carries the dual danger of inducing early labor and fetal withdrawal. Several investigators have observed episodes of neonatal death due to meconium aspiration resulting from opiate withdrawal prior to labor (19, 98, 123).

Powell and Chen (88) studied the action of dolophine on the animal uterus. Preparations of isolated uteri from nonpregnant rabbits, rats, golden hamsters, cats, and guinea pigs, as well as uterine horns of rabbits and cats, were exposed to varying concentrations of methadone. The action of methadone was found to depend on the initial uterine activity. It was found to inhibit uterine activity that is in rhythmic movements, but it stimulated stationary uteri. The authors concluded that the action of methadone is probably not on the autonomic nervous system of the uterus, but that the drug is endowed with a direct muscular action capable of relaxing an active, but stimulating an inactive, uterus. In relating this to human experiences, one may expect that methadone should diminish the activity of the uterus during labor and stimulate the uterus not in active labor, therefore enhancing the chance of premature onset of labor. This has not been documented by various investigators who have studied the use of methadone in pregnant drug-dependent women (10, 14, 18).

Chronic opiate addicts have been said to have frequent endocrine aberrations including amenorrhea, anovulation, and infertility. Their severe dysmenorrhea is most likely due to pelvic inflammatory disease. The women themselves believe that amenorrhea and infertility always occur when they are using substantial amounts of heroin. Morphine may interfere with ovulation. Under experimental conditions, morphine has been shown to depress adrenocorticotrophic hormone release and adrenal function. Observed pregnancies, however, as well as case reports of pregnancy among women with chronic addiction, cast doubt on the concept that narcotic use suppresses reproductive function (11). Wallach et al. (127) have found that women maintained on methadone have regular menstruation, ovulation, conception, and apparently normal pregnancies. Other investigators also support the use of methadone in the treatment of the pregnant opiate addict (17–19, 21–23, 32, 39, 54, 62, 84, 113, 116, 117, 120, 126, 131).

Blinick et al. (10) found methadone maintenance to be successful in their observation of 105 pregnancies in narcotic-addicted women in the methadone maintenance treatment program of the Beth Israel Medical Center. They found that there was no maternal mortality, and that complications of pregnancy and fetal wastage were unremarkable. One-third of the infants were premature by weight. Methadone hydrochloride was used in the management of labor in this series. No serious effects attributable to methadone were seen in the neonatal period. Follow-up of a small number of the newborn infants revealed normal growth and development.

Although methadone maintenance has been beneficial in the treatment of addiction during pregnancy, several investigators caution that the use of methadone alone without psychosocial support is less helpful (14, 17, 18, 23, 32, 54, 84, 113).

In 1972, Statzer and Wardell (114) recognized the need for additional psychological support for the pregnant drug-dependent woman. A specialized program of prenatal care for the high risk mother was developed at the Hutzel Hospital Project of the Detroit Maternal and Infant Care Program. Each patient was seen by a nutritionist, social worker, and public health nurse, as well as receiving the usual prenatal care. Additional personnel with specialized training in the psychological requirements of the heroin user were needed. Increasing numbers of patients remained in this program postpartum.

Newman (84) has reported findings from the New York City methadone maintenance treatment program that agree with others in the successful use of methadone. There has been a high incidence of neonatal withdrawal symptoms reported by the mothers with no consistent dose relationship but no evidence to date of sequelae from the use of methadone during pregnancy. He also reported an extraordinarily high retention rate in the treatment program among women after delivery, with over 95 per cent remaining in treatment.

Harper et al. (54) organized Family and Maternity Care Program for pregnant addicts, their spouses, and the newborn infants at the State University of New York Downstate Medical Center. Low dose methadone maintenance coupled with intense psychosocial support seemed to alleviate many of the common problems associated with addiction in pregnancy, although it failed to prevent withdrawal in the newborn infant. The infant withdrawal, though, was unassociated with an increase in mortality or known prolonged morbidity.

Kandall et al. (62) studied 230 infants born to drug-dependent women and 33 infants born to ex-addicts between the years 1971 and 1974. They found that heroin abuse declined while methadone usage increased during those years. When comparing heroin abuse to methadone maintenance treatment during pregnancy, they found that the latter was associated with more consistent prenatal care, more normal fetal growth, and reduced fetal mortality. Meconium staining of amniotic fluid was increased in heroin and heroin-methadone groups, but this was not associated with an increase in meconium aspiration or a reduction in Apgar scores. Infants born to former heroin addicts who were free of narcotic use during pregnancy also showed severe intrauterine growth retardation. In this program, neonatal withdrawal from methadone seemed to be more severe than that of heroin, but severity of the withdrawal did not correlate with late pregnancy maternal methadone dosage. Of particular interest in the study was that neonatal seizures occurred in 1.5 per cent of the heroin group and 10 per cent of the methadone group.

Strauss et al. (117), in their comparison of 72 pregnant methadone-maintained women and 72 nonaddicted women, all of whom received prenatal care, concluded that low dose methadone maintenance in conjunction with comprehensive prenatal care seems to reduce obstetrical risk to a level comparable with that of nonaddicted women of similar socioeconomic circumstances.

In Philadelphia, Connaughton et al. (19) recommended a comprehensive approach that has been used to care for nearly 300 pregnant addicts. The method of patient management in the Family Center Program includes consultations with obstetricians and medical consultants, psychiatric social workers, public health nurses, community workers, and psychiatrists, along with maintenance care. These health workers conduct the addict's obstetrical, psychosocial, and addictive intensive prenatal care. Addictive care is arranged according to the patient's needs. Some will be able to be managed drug free, whereas others will choose methadone detoxification (if this is possible at the particular state of pregnancy that the patient is enrolled). Most of the patients choose methadone maintenance and can thereby be managed most successfully. The patient is started on 10 mg of methadone daily, which is increased only if she requires a higher dosage to prevent withdrawal symptomatology. Methadone is kept, if possible, below 35 mg per day. Other drugs, such as tranquilizers, are strictly avoided unless the patient is addicted to these medications. In case of such addiction, the patient is transferred to a special detoxification ward where she can safely be weaned from drugs potentially more dangerous than opiates.

Generally, the methadone-using patient is admitted for a 4-day hospital stay. An initial evaluation consists of a detailed medical and drug history, complete physical evaluation, and chest x-ray. Various laboratory tests (urinalysis, complete blood count, Venereal Disease Research Laboratory test, blood type, Rh factor, SMA 12, and thin layer chromatography) are performed, and her opiate addiction is substantiated. She has the opportunity to meet with other professionals involved in the program including the neonatologist, public health nurse, and community worker. The obstetrician and social worker have the opportunity to develop a rapport with the patient during the hospital stay (18).

During labor, the patient is managed like any other parturient. Physicians in charge of the labor floor are aware of her drug usage, and an effort is made to start conduction anesthesia as early as possible to avoid the use of narcotic analgesics. On admission to the labor floor, a urine specimen is sent to the toxicology laboratory for verification of the presence of methadone and to rule out the presence of other drugs. A record is made of when the last dose of methadone was taken, and, if necessary, methadone is given to the patient for analgesia and prevention of withdrawal symptoms. The approach has significantly reduced maternal and infant morbidity that heretofore have been associated with pregnancies complicated by opiate addiction.

Table 44.11 lists the percentage of obstetrical complications seen in three groups of addicted patients and two nonaddicted populations who delivered at Philadelphia General Hospital. Group A are patients who received no counseling and delivered while still actively using heroin. Group B are patients who were admitted to the Family Center Program for drug-dependent mothers but received minimal (less than four clinic visits) prenatal care and counseling for this addiction. Group C are patients who were admitted to the Family Center Program and received intensive psychosocial counseling with methadone maintenance or detoxification, as well as adequate prenatal care (four or more visits to prenatal clinic). Over three-quarters of the patients receiving methadone took less than 50 mg per day. In general, most received an average dose of 35 mg per day. Also included for comparison are two groups labled D and E. These are randomly selected non-drug-dependent pregnant patients who delivered at Philadelphia General Hospital between 1969 and 1974. Group D patients had no prenatal care, and Group E had more than four prenatal visits. Maternal statistics are of interest, in that obstetrical complications show a definite downward trend in Groups B and C compared to Group A. The incidence of low birth weight infants is remarkable and

Table 44.11
Obstetrical Complications by Groups: 261 Family Center Patients and 150 Controls,
Philadelphia General Hospital, 1969 to 1974 (28)

	Group A	Group B	Group C	Group D[a]	Group E[b]
Number of patients	62	77	122	75	75
Average number of prenatal visits	0	2	8	0	9
Obstetrical complications (%)	34	20	24	28	25
Incidence of low birth weight (%)	47	39	21	20	16

[a] Nonclinic control.
[b] Clinic control.

extremely significant. In Group A, 49 per cent of patients delivered infants weighing less that 5½ pounds, whereas in Group C the incidence was 21 per cent. The fact that nonclinic, nonaddicted patients (Group D) had only a 20 per cent incidence of low birth weight infants is most impressive, inasmuch as this is the first time that it has been possible to implicate narcotics per se for obstetrical complications rather than the lack of prenatal care. With additional patients by 1978, Family Center has seen nearly 500 women. The results seen in 1975 by Connaughton et al. (18) continue in regard to improved morbidity and mortality rates for mothers and infants who are provided with the comprehensive approach designed earlier in the 1970's at this Philadelphia program (28).

CONCLUSIONS AND RECOMMENDATIONS

As the epidemic of drug abuse has increased over the past decade, bringing with it numerous complex problems, a significant health dilemma has occurred in the United States and many countries of the world for which solutions must be found. Despite the accepted belief that opiate dependency suppresses hypothalamic function and fertility is affected, the ratio of addicted women to men has increased rapidly and helps to account for the steady rise in addict births during the 1960's and 1970's. Numerous investigators have reported the extremely high incidence of obstetrical and medical complications among addicts and the morbidity and mortality among passively addicted newborn infants that far exceed those found in any other high risk maternal and infant population. There still are insufficient data on the long term effects of maternal drug usage. Controversy exists on how best to prevent and treat the adverse sequelae of addiction. However, initial data in programs providing comprehensive care for addicts have shown a significant reduction in morbidity and mortality to both mothers and infants. Further studies are needed to test whether it is possible to assist the mothers through education, counseling, and early diagnosis and treatment of mental disorders.

Based on the successes of various approaches in the literature, as well as the paucity of specific conclusions in regard to prevention, treatment, and long term outcome from reported data, the following recommendations for treatment and further research for drug-dependent women are listed.

1. The pregnant woman who abuses drugs must be designated as "high risk" and warrants specialized care in a perinatal center where she should be provided with comprehensive addictive and obstetrical care and psychosocial counseling.

a. Addictive care may involve voluntary drug-free therapeutic communities, methadone detoxification (depending on the time in pregnancy that it is requested), or methadone maintenance.

b. The pregnant drug-dependent woman should be evaluated in a hospital setting where a complete history and physical examination may be accomplished and certain laboratory tests carried out to evaluate her over-all health status. When appropriate, low dose methadone maintenance with substantial medical and paramedical support should be instituted. Detoxification, if requested or necessary, should preferably take place between the sixteenth and the thirty-second week of gestation and be extremely slow (5 mg reduction every 2 weeks). The pregnant woman addicted to barbiturates or major tranquilizers along with opiates should be detoxified during her second trimester in a very specialized detoxification center.

c. Psychosocial counseling should be given by experienced social workers who are aware of the medical needs, as well as the social and psychological needs, of this population.

d. Encourage maternal-infant attachment prenatally and postpartum. Special emphasis should be on enhancing parenting skills of these women in an effort to decrease the expected increase in child neglect in this population.

e. Social and medical support should not end in the hospital setting; an outreach program, incorporating public health nurses and community workers, should be established.

f. Assess ability of mother to care for the infant after discharge from the hospital by frequent observations in the home and clinic settings.

g. Assure mechanisms by which to follow and supervise the infant's course after discharge from the hospital.

2. Future *research* should encompass the following:

a. Study the effects of heroin and methadone use on the pregnant addict's life style and collect socially and medically relevant data.

b. Investigate newer treatment modalities for the drug-dependent mother to include the safety of various methadone maintenance dosage regimens for the fetus.

c. Study the dietary habits and nutritional status of the pregnant addict and compare results with control groups of nonaddicted patients.

d. Evaluate mothering practices of women who have abused drugs during pregnancy to assess their ability to carry on a child-rearing role.

e. Develop "outreach" mechanisms so that more mothers and infants may be assessed in follow-up. This should provide a large enough experimental population for appropriate statistical analysis, as well as comparable control populations.

The major impact of comprehensive care coupled with methadone maintenance for narcotic-dependent women has been the reduction of low birth weight infants, including those prematurely born and appropriate for gestational age as well as those born near term but inappropriate for gestational age, in whom mortality rates are the highest. This, in itself, has dramatically changed the incidence of morbidity and mortality for infants and children born to these women who have nearly a 50 per cent incidence of low birth weight. The death rate of the low birth weight neonate is 40 times that of term infants of normal weight.

Moreover, it is known that the low birth weight infants born to heroin-addicted women will contribute heavily to the population of infants who will eventually be mentally retarded (I.Q. of 70 or below), as well as those who will have great difficulty in school because they are "poor learners." These handicapped individuals will be unable to compete fully in our increasingly complex society. In addition, there is a high incidence of prematurity and undersized term infants among untreated pregnant drug-dependent women. The majority of deaths among newborn infants are associated with low birth weight. Moreover, the incidence of cerebral palsy, associated with the prematurity, may be as high as 10 times; mental deficiency, five times; and lethal malformations in the undersized infants, seven times that in the full size infant. Emotional disturbances, social maladjustments, and visual and hearing deficits are also multiplied. If we do not begin to cope with this population in terms of prevention as well as treatment, with the increasing number of female addicts we can expect an increasing need for custodial facilities for their mentally and neurologically deficient infants. The medical and custodial costs for these individuals are incalculable (4).

However, if pregnant drug-dependent women are maintained with low dosages of methadone and are given adequate prenatal care, the complications of pregnancy can be readily diagnosed and treatment administered, and the morbidity and mortality during pregnancy, the neonatal period, and in childhood can be markedly reduced.

Clinicians in the field must continue to strive for excellence in the care of pregnant drug-dependent women and their children. Government agencies must realize the responsibility to these women and children and to society and provide adequate funding for comprehensive services. Only if clinicians and government funding officials consider the appropriate care for pregnant drug-dependent women and their children as priorities will the human race be able to cope with the potential pathophysiological and behavioral effects of the transplacental transfer of narcotic drugs to the fetuses and newborns of these narcotic-dependent women.

Acknowledgements. The author wishes to acknowledge the ongoing efforts of the clinical and research staff of Family Center Program without whom the many experiences with pregnant drug-dependent women described in this manuscript could not have been made possible. Special gratitude is expressed to Dian S. Reeser, B.A., for her untiring efforts in editing and reference search, and to Kathleen Gibbons for her patience and diligence in the preparation of the manuscript.

References

1. Abrams, C. A. L. Cytogenic risks to the offspring of pregnant addicts. Addict. Dis. 2:63, 1975.
2. Amarose, A. P., and Norusis, M. J. Cytogenetics of methadone managed and heroin addicted pregnant women and their newborn infants. Am. J. Obstet. Gynecol. 124:635, 1976.
3. Athinarayanan, P. Chlordiazepoxide withdrawal in the neonate. Am. J. Obstet. Gynecol. 124:212, 1976.
4. Babson, S. G., Benson, R. C., Pernoll, M. L., and Benda, G. I. *Management of High Risk Pregnancy and Intensive Care of the Neonate*. St. Louis, C. V. Mosby, 1975.
5. Behrendt, H., and Green, M. Nature of the sweating deficit of prematurely born neonates. N. Engl. J. Med. 286:1376, 1972.
6. Blatman, S. Methadone and children. Pediatrics 48:173, 1971.
7. Bleyer, W. A., and Marshall, R. E. Barbiturate withdrawal syndrome in a passively addicted infant. J.A.M.A. 221:185, 1972.
8. Blinick, G. Fertility of narcotic addicts and effects of addiction on the offspring. Soc. Biol. 18 (Suppl.): 34, 1971.
9. Blinick, G., Inturrisi, C. E., Jerez, E., and Wallach, R. C. Methadone assays in pregnant women and progeny. Am. J. Obstet. Gynecol. 121:617, 1975.
10. Blinick, G., Jerez, E., and Wallach, R. C. Methadone maintenance, pregnancy and progeny. J.A.M.A. 225:477, 1973.
11. Blinick, G., Wallach, R. C., and Jerez, E. Pregnancy in narcotic addicts treated by medical withdrawal. Am. J. Obstet. Gynecol. 105:997, 1969.
12. Blumenthal, I., and Lindsay, S. Neonatal barbiturate withdrawal. Postgrad. Med. J. 53:157, 1977.
13. Chang, A., Wood, C., Humphrey, M., Gilbert, M., and Wagstaff, C. The effects of narcotics on fetal acid base status. Br. J. Obstet. Gynaecol. 83:56, 1976.
14. Chappel, J. N. Treatment of morphine-type dependence (Letters). J.A.M.A 221:1516, 1972.
15. Chavez, C. J., Ostrea, E. M., and Stryker, J. C. Sudden infant death sydrome among infants of drug dependent mothers. Presented at the National Drug Abuse Conference, Seattle, Washington, April 3–8, 1978.
16. Cobrinik, R. W., Hood, T. R., and Chusid, E. The effect of maternal narcotic addiction on the newborn infant: Review of the literature and report of 22 cases. Pediatrics 24:288, 1959.
17. Cohen, S. N., and Neumann, L. L. Methadone maintenance during pregnancy. Am. J. Dis. Child. 126:445, 1973.
18. Connaughton, J. F., Finnegan, L. P., Schut, J., and Emich, J. P. Current concepts in the management of the pregnant opiate addict. Addict.Dis 2:21, 1975.
19. Connaughton, J. F., Reeser, D., Schut, J., and Finnegan, L. P. Perinatal addiction: Outcome and management. Am. J. Obstet. Gynecol. 129:679, 1977.
20. Dar, H., Schmidt, R., and Nitowsky, H. M. Palmar creases and their clinical significance: A study of newborns at risk. Pediatr. Res. 11:103, 1977.
21. Davis, R. C. Psychosocial care of the pregnant narcotic addict. J. Reprod. Med. 20:316, 1978.
22. Davis, R. C., and Chappel, J. N. Pregnancy in the context of addiction and methadone maintenance. In *Proceedings of the Fifth National Conference on Methadone Treatment*, vol. 2, p. 1146. New York, National Association for the Prevention of Addiction to Narcotics, 1973.
23. Davis, R. C., Chappel, J. N., Mejia-Zelaya, A., and Madden, J. Clinical observations on methadone-maintained pregnancies. In *Perinatal Addiction*, R. D. Harbison, editor, pp. 101–112. New York, Spectrum, 1975.
24. Desmond, M. M., Schwanecke, R. P., Wilson, G. S., Yasunaga, S., and Burgdorff, I. Maternal barbiturate utilization and neonatal withdrawal symptomatology. J. Pediatr. 80:190, 1972.
25. Desmond, M. M., and Wilson, G. S. Neonatal abstinence syndrome: Recognition and diagnosis. Addict. Dis. 2:113, 1975.
26. Dole, V. P., and Kreek, M. J. Methadone plasma level: Sustained by a reservoir of drug in tissue. Proc. Natl. Acad. Sci. 70:10, 1973.
27. Finnegan, L. Clinical effects of pharmacologic agents on pregnancy, the fetus, and the neonate. Ann. N. Y. Acad. Sci. 281:74, 1976.
28. Finnegan, L. P. Narcotic dependence in pregnancy. J. Psychedelic Drugs 7:299, 1975.
29. Finnegan, L. P., editor. *Drug Dependence in Pregnancy: Clinical Management of Mother and Child*. A manual for medical professionals and paraprofessionals prepared for the National Institute on Drug Abuse, Services Research Branch, Rockville, Md. Washington, D.C., United States Government Printing Office, 1978.
30. Finnegan, L. P. In utero opiate dependence and sudden infant death syndrome. Clin. Perinatol. 6: 163, 1979.
31. Finnegan, L. P. The effects of psychoactive drugs (including opiates) on the fetus and newborn. In *Research Advances*, O. Kalant, editor, vol. 5. New York, Plenum Press, 1979.
32. Finnegan, L. P., Connaughton, J. F., Emich, J. P., and Wieland, W. F. Comprehensive care of the

pregnant addict and its effect on maternal and infant outcome. Contemp. Drug Probl. 1:795, 1972.

33. Finnegan, L. P., Emich, J. P., and Connaughton, J. F. Abstinence score in the treatment of the infants of drug dependent mothers. Pediatr. Res. 7:319, 1973.

34. Finnegan, L. P., and Mac New, B. A. Care of the addicted infant. Am. J. Nurs. 74:685, 1974.

35. Finnegan, L. P., and Reeser, D. S. Maternal drug abuse patterns: Effect upon the duration of neonatal abstinence. Pediatr. Res. 13:368, 1979.

36. Finnegan, L. P., Reeser, D. S., and Connaughton, J. F. The effects of maternal drug dependence on neonatal mortality. Drug Alcohol Depend. 2:131, 1977.

37. Finnegan, L. P., Reeser, D. S., Kaltenbach, K., and Mac New, B. A. Phenobarbital loading dose method for treatment of neonatal abstinence: Effect upon infant development. Pediatr. Res. 13:331, 1979.

38. Finnegan, L. P., Reeser, D. S., and Ting, R. Y. Methadone use during pregnancy: Effects on growth and development. Pediatr. Res. 11:377, 1977.

39. Finnegan, L. P., Schut, J., Flor, J., and Connaughton, J. F. Methadone maintenance and detoxification programs for the opiate dependent woman during pregnancy: A comparison. In *Drug Abuse in Pregnancy and the Neonate*, J. L. Rementeria, editor, pp. 40–62. St. Louis, C. V. Mosby, 1977.

40. Finnegan, L. P., Shouraie, Z., Emich, J. P., Connaughton, J. F., Schut, J., and Delivoria-Papadopoulos, M. Alterations of the oxygen hemoglobin equilibrium curve and red cell 2,3-diphosphoglycerate (2,3-DPG) in cord blood of infants born to narcotic addicted mothers. Pediatr. Res. 8:344, 1974.

41. Glass, L. Narcotic withdrawal in the newborn. J. Natl. Med. Assoc. 66:117, 1974.

42. Glass, L., and Evans, H. E. Narcotic withdrawal in the newborn. Am. Fam. Phys. 6:75, 1972.

43. Glass, L., Rajegowda, B. K., and Evans, H. E. Absence of respiratory distress syndrome in premature infants of heroin addicted mothers. Lancet 2:685, 1971.

44. Glass, L., Rajegowda, B. K., Mukherjee, T. K., Roth, M. M., and Evans, H. E. Effect of heroin on cortisol production in pregnant addicts and their fetuses. Pediatr. Res. 7:320, 1973.

45. Glick, S. D., Strumpf, A. J., and Zimmerberg, B. Effect of in utero adminstration of morphine on the subsequent development of self-administration behavior. Brain Res. 132:194, 1977.

46. Gluck, L., and Kulovich, M. V. Lecithin/sphingomyelin ratios in amniotic fluid in normal and abnormal pregnancy. Am. J. Obstet. Gynecol. 115:539, 1973.

47. Goddard, J., and Wilson, G. Management of neonatal drug withdrawal. J. Pediatr. 91:638, 1977.

48. Goetz, R. L., and Bain, R. V. Neonatal withdrawal symptoms associated with maternal use of pentazocine. J. Pediatr. 84:887, 1974.

49. Goodfriend, M. J., Shey, I. A., and Klein, M. D. The effects of maternal narcotic addiction on the newborn. Am. J. Obstet. Gynecol. 71:29, 1956.

50. Goodman, L. S., and Gilman, A., editors. Narcotic analgesics. In *The Pharmacological Basis of Therapeutics*, ed. 4. New York, Macmillan, 1970.

51. Gruenwald, P. Chronic fetal distress and placental deficiency. Biol. Neonate 5:215, 1963.

52. Harper, R., Concepcion, G. S., and Blenman, S. Observations on the sudden death of infants born to addicted mothers. In *Proceedings of the Fifth National Conference on Methadone Treatment*, p. 1122. New York, National Association for the Prevention of Addiction to Narcotics, 1973.

53. Harper, R. G., Solish, G., Feingold, E., Gersten-Woolf, N. A., and Sokal, M. M. Maternal ingested methadone, body fluid methadone and the neonatal withdrawal syndrome. Am. J. Obstet. Gynecol. 129:417, 1977.

54. Harper, R. G., Solish, G. I., Purow, H. M., Sang, E., and Panepinto, W. C. The effect of a methadone treatment program upon pregnant heroin addicts and their newborn infants. Pediatrics 54:300, 1974.

55. Herzlinger, R. A., Kandall, S. R., and Vaughan, H. G. Neonatal seizures associated with narcotic withdrawal. J. Pediatr. 91:638, 1977.

56. Hill, R. M., and Desmond, M. M. Management of the narcotic withdrawal syndrome in the neonate. Pediatr. Clin. North Am. 10:67, 1963.

57. Hutchings, D. E., Hunt, H. F., Towey, J. P., Rosen, T. S., and Gorinson, H. S. Methadone during pregnancy in the rat: Dose level effects on maternal and perinatal mortality and growth in the offspring. J. Pharmacol. Exp. Ther. 197:171, 1976.

58. Jones, J. Nutrition, drugs and their interrelations. Pa. Health 35:3, 1974.

59. Kahn, E. J., Neumann, L. L., and Polk, G. The course of the heroin withdrawal syndrome in newborn infants treated with phenobarbital or chlorpromazine. J. Pediatr. 75:495, 1969.

60. Kaltenbach, K., Graziani, L. J., and Finnegan, L. P. Development of children born to women who received methadone during pregnancy. Pediatr. Res. 12:372, 1978.

61. Kaltenbach, K., Graziani, L. J., and Finnegan, L. P. Methadone exposure in utero: Effects upon developmental status at 1 and 2 years of age. Pediatr. Res. 13:332, 1979.

62. Kandall, S. R., Albin, S., Gartner, L. M., Lee, K., Eidelman, A., and Lowinson, J. The narcotic dependent mother: Fetal and neonatal consequences. Early Hum. Dev. 1:159, 1977.

63. Kandall, S. R., Albin, S., Lowinson, J., Berle, B., Eidelman, A. I., and Gartner, L. M. Differential effects of maternal heroin and methadone use on birth weight. Pediatrics 58:681, 1976.

64. Kandall, S. R., and Gartner, L. M. Late presentation of drug withdrawal symptoms in newborns. Am. J. Dis. Child. 127:58, 1972.

65. Kron, R. E. Instrumental conditioning of nutritive sucking behavior in the newborn. Recent Adv. Biol. Psychiatry 9:295, 1967.

66. Kron, R. E. The effect of arousal and learning upon sucking behavior in the newborn. Recent Adv. Biol. Psychiatry 10:302, 1968.

67. Kron, R. E., Litt, M., and Finnegan, L. P. Behavior of infants born to narcotic addicted mothers. Pediatr. Res. 7:292, 1973.

68. Kron, R. E., Litt, M., and Finnegan, L. P. Effect of maternal narcotic addiction on sucking behavior of neonates. Pediatr. Res. 8:346, 1974.

69. Kron, R. E., Litt, M., Phoenix, M. D., and Finnegan, L. P. Neonatal narcotic abstinence: Effects of pharmacotherapeutic agents and maternal drug usage

on nutritive sucking behavior. J. Pediatr. 88:637, 1976.

70. Kron, R. E., Kaplan, S. L., Finnegan, L. P., and Litt, M. The assessment of behavioral change in infants undergoing narcotic withdrawal: Comparative data from clinical and objective methods. Addict. Dis. 2:257, 1975.

71. Kron, R. E., Stein, M., and Goddard, K. E. Newborn sucking behavior affected by obstetric sedation. Pediatrics 37:1012, 1966.

72. Kunstadter, R. H. Narcotic withdrawal symptoms in newborn infants. Bull. Narc. 11:15, 1959.

73. Kunstadter, R. H., Klein, R. I., Lundeen, E. C., Witz, W., and Morrison, M. Narcotic withdrawal symptoms in newborn infants. J.A.M.A. 168:1008, 1958.

74. Lipsitz, P. F., and Blatman, S. Newborn infants of mothers on methadone maintenance. N. Y. State J. Med. 74:994, 1974.

75. Lodge, A., Marcus, M. M., and Ramer, C. M. Neonatal addiction: A two-year-study. Part II. Behavioral and electrophysiological characteristics of the addicted neonate. Addict. Dis. 2:235, 1975.

76. Madden, J. D., Chappel, J. N., Zuspan, F., Gumpel, J., Mejia, A., and Davis, R. Observation and treatment of neonatal narcotic withdrawal. Am. J. Obstet. Gynecol. 127:199, 1977.

77. Deleted in proof.

78. McGinty, J. F., and Ford, D. H. The effects of maternal morphine or methadone intake on the growth, reflex development and maze behavior of rat offspring. In *Tissue Responses to Addictive Drugs*, C. H. Ford and D. H. Clouet, editors, pp. 611–629. New York, Spectrum, 1976.

79. Milstein, M., Morishima, A., Cohen, M. I., and Litt, I. F. Effects of opium alkaloids on mitosis and DNA synthesis. Pediatr. Res. 8:392, 1974.

80. Mims, L. C., and Riley, H. D., Jr. The narcotic withdrawal syndrome in the newborn infant. J. Okla. State Med. Assoc. 62:411, 1969.

81. Naeye, R. L. Malnutrition, a probable cause of fetal growth retardation. Arch. Pathol. 79:284, 1965.

82. Nathenson, G. Neonatal addiction in 1973. J. Natl. Med. Assoc. 66:19, 1973.

83. Nathenson, G., Cohen, M. I., Litt, I. F., and McNamara, H. The effect of maternal heroin addiction on neonatal jaundice. J. Pediatr. 81:899, 1972.

84. Newman, R. G. Pregnancies of methadone patients. N. Y. State J. Med. 1:52, 1974.

85. Northrop, G., Ditzler, J., Ryan, W. G., and Wilbanks, G. O. Estriol excretion profiles in narcotic addicted women. Am. J. Obstet. Gynecol. 112:704, 1972.

86. Ostrea, E. M., Chavez, C. J., and Strauss, M. E. A study of factors that influence the severity of neonatal narcotic withdrawal. J. Pediatr. 88:642, 1976.

87. Pierson, P. S., Howard, P., and Kleber, H. D. Sudden deaths in infants born to methadone maintained addicts. J.A.M.A. 220:1733, 1972.

88. Powell, C. E., and Chen, K. K. Action of dolophine on the animal uterus. J. Am. Pharm. Assoc. 37:516, 1948.

89. Preis, O., Choi, S. J., and Rudolph, N. Pentazocine withdrawal syndrome in the newborn infant. Am. J. Obstet. Gynecol. 127:205, 1977.

90. Quillian, W. W., II, and Dunn, C. A. Neonatal drug withdrawal from propoxyphene. J.A.M.A. 235:2128, 1976.

91. Rajegowda, B. K., Glass, L., Evans, H. E., Maso, G., Swartz, D. P., and Leblanc, W. Methadone withdrawal in newborn infants. J. Pediatr. 81:532, 1972.

92. Rajegowda, B. K., Kandall, S. R., and Falciglia, H. Sudden infant death (SIDS) in infants of narcotic addicted mothers. Pediatr. Res. 10:199, 1976.

93. Ramer, C. M. The case history of an infant born to an amphetamine addicted mother. Clin. Pediatr. 13:596, 1974.

94. Ramer, C. M., and Lodge, A. Neonatal addiction: A two-year study. Part I. Clinical and developmental characteristics of infants of mothers on methadone maintenance. Addict. Dis. 2:227, 1975.

95. Raye, J. R., Dubin, J. W., and Blechner, J. N. Fetal growth retardation following maternal morphine administration: Nutritional or drug effect. Biol Neonate 32:222, 1977.

96. Reddy, A. M., Harper, R. G., and Stern, G. Observation on heroin and methadone withdrawal in the newborn. Pediatrics 48:353, 1971.

97. Rementeria, J. L., Janakammal, S., and Hollander, M. Multiple births in drug-addicted women. Am. J. Obstet. Gynecol. 122:958, 1975.

98. Rementeria, J. L., and Nunag, N. N. Narcotic withdrawal in pregnancy: Stillbirth incidence with a case report. Am. J. Obstet. Gynecol. 116:1152, 1973.

99. Roloff, D. W., Howatt, W. F., Kanto, W. P., Jr., and Borer, R. L., Jr. The effect of long-term maternal morphine administration on the growth and lung development of fetal rabbits. In *Basic and Therapeutic Aspects of Perinatal Pharmacology*, P. L. Morselli, S. Garattini, and F. Serini, editors. New York, Raven Press, 1975.

100. Rorke, L. B., Reeser, D. S., and Finnegan, L. P. Nervous system lesions in infants of opiate dependent mothers. Pediatr. Res. 11:565, 1977.

101. Rosen, T. S., and Pippenger, C. E. Pharmacologic observations on the neonatal withdrawal syndrome. J. Pediatr. 88:1044, 1976.

102. Rothstein, P., and Gould, J. B. Born with a habit: Infants of drug addicted mothers. Pediatr. Clin. North Am. 21:307, 1974.

103. Rumack, B. H. Neonatal withdrawal following maternal ingestion of ethchlorvynol (Placidyl). Pediatrics 52:714, 1973.

104. Sardemann, H., Madsen, K. S., and Friis-Hansen, B. Follow-up of children of drug-addicted mothers. Arch. Dis. Child. 51:131, 1976.

105. Schulman, L. Alterations of the sleep cycle in heroin addicted and "suspected" newborns. Neuropadiatrie 1:89, 1969.

106. Semoff, M. C. Narcotic addiction of the newborn. Ariz. Med. 24:933, 1967.

107. Singh, E. J., and Zuspan, F. P. Content of amniotic fluid prostaglandins in normal, diabetic and drug-abuse human pregnancy. Am. J. Obstet. Gynecol. 118:385, 1974.

108. Sisson, T. R. C., Wickler, M., Tsai, P., and Rao, I. P. Effect of narcotic withdrawal on neonatal sleep patterns. Pediatr. Res. 8:451, 1974.

109. Slobody, L. B., and Cobrinick, R. Neonatal narcotic addiction. Q. Rev. Pediatr. 14:169, 1959.

110. Smith, A. A., Hui, F. W., and Crofford, M. Retardation of growth by opioids. In *Perinatal Pharmacology: Problems and Priorities*, J. Dancis and J. C. Hwang, editors, pp. 195–201. New York, Raven Press, 1974.

111. Sonderegger, T. Persistent effects of neonatal narcotic addiction in the rat. In *Tissue Responses to Addictive Drugs*, D. H. Ford and D. H. Clouet, editors, pp. 589–609. New York, Spectrum, 1976.

112. Soule, A. B., III, Standley, K., Copans, S. A., and Davis, M. Clinical uses of the Brazelton Neonatal Scale. Pediatrics 54:583, 1974.

113. Statzer, D. E., and Wardell, J. N. Heroin addiction during pregnancy. Am. J. Obstet. Gynecol. 94:253, 1966.

114. Statzer, D. E., and Wardell, J. N. Heroin addiction during pregnancy. Am. J. Obstet. Gynecol. 113:273, 1972.

115. Steg, N. Narcotic withdrawal reactions in the newborn. Am. J. Dis. Child. 94:286, 1957.

116. Stimmel, B., and Adamsons, K. Narcotic dependency in pregnancy: Methadone maintenance compared to use of street drugs. J.A.M.A. 235:1121, 1976.

117. Strauss, M. E., Andresko, M. A., Stryker, J. C., Wardell, J. N., and Dunkel, C. A. Methadone maintenance during pregnancy: Pregnancy, birth, and neonate characteristics. Am. J. Obstet. Gynecol. 120:895, 1974.

118. Strauss, M. E., Lessen-Firestone, J. K., Starr, R. H., Jr., and Ostrea, E. M. Behavior of narcotics addicted newborns. Child Dev. 46:887, 1975.

119. Strauss, M. E., Starr, R. H., Ostrea, E. M., Chavez, C. J., and Stryker, J. C. Behavioral concomitants of prenatal addiction to narcotics. J. Pediatr. 89:842, 1976.

120. Sullivan, H. R., and Blake, D. A. Quantitative determination of methadone concentration in human blood, plasma, and urine by gas chromatography. Res. Commun. Chem. Pathol. Pharmacol. 3:467, 1972.

121. Sussman, S. Narcotic and methamphetamine use during pregnancy: Effect on newborn infants. Am. J. Dis. Child. 106:325, 1963.

122. Taeusch, H. W., Jr., Carson, S. H., Wang, N. S., and Avery, M. E. Heroin induction of lung maturation and growth retardation in fetal rabbits. J. Pediatr. 82:869, 1973.

123. Treatment of morphine-type dependence by withdrawal methods (Editorial). J.A.M.A. 219:1611, 1972.

124. Tyson, H. K. Neonatal withdrawal symptoms associated with maternal use of propoxyphene hydrochloride (Darvon). J. Pediatr. 85:684, 1974.

125. Valdes-Dapena, M. A., Greene, M., Basavanand, N., and Catherman, R. The myocardial conduction system in sudden death in infancy. N. Engl. J. Med. 289:1195, 1973.

126. Waldeman, H. Psychiatric emergencies during pregnancy and in the puerperium. Munch. Med. Wochenschr. 115:1039, 1973.

127. Wallach, R. C., Jerez, E., and Blinick, G. Pregnancy and menstrual function in narcotic addicts treated with methadone. Am. J. Obstet. Gynecol. 105:1226, 1969.

128. Webster, P. A. C. Withdrawal symptoms in neonates associated with maternal antidepressant therapy. Lancet 2:318, 1973.

129. Wilson, G. S. Somatic growth effects of perinatal addiction. Addict. Dis. 2:333, 1975.

130. Wilson, G. S., Desmond, M. M., and Verniaud, W. M. Early development of infants of heroin addicted mothers. Am. J. Dis. Child. 126:457, 1973.

131. Yacavone, D., Scher, J., Kim, Y. R., Schwitz, B., and O'Connor, H. Heroin addiction, methadone maintenance, and pregnancy. J. Am. Osteopath. Assoc. 75:826, 1976.

132. Zagon, I. S., and McLaughlin, P. J. Effect of chronic maternal methadone exposure on perinatal development. Biol. Neonate 31:271, 1977.

133. Zelson, C. Infant of the addicted mother. N. Engl. J. Med. 288:1393, 1973.

134. Zelson, C., Rubio, E., and Wasserman, E. Neonatal narcotic addiction: 10-year observation. Pediatrics 48:179, 1971.

135. Zimmerberg, B., Charap, A. D., and Glick, S. D. Behavioral effects of in utero administration of morphine. Nature 247:376, 1974.

136. Zuspan, F. P., Gumpel, J. A., Mejia-Zelaya, A., Madden, J., and Davis, R. Fetal stress from methadone withdrawal. Am. J. Obstet. Gynecol. 122:43, 1975.

CHAPTER 45

SUBSTANCES OF ABUSE AND SEXUAL BEHAVIOR

Charles Winick, Ph.D.

Substances of abuse may have a substantial range of effects on their users' sexuality and sexual behavior. Much of what is known about this subject derives from anecdotal or other nonsystematic sources, because of ethical and other difficulties in collecting data.

Patients who have been dependent on drugs can recall how different substances affected their sexuality. Their psychotherapists hear about different aspects of the patients' sexuality. Patients in sex therapy provide information on the substances that they have been taking. Animal studies' findings may be analogized to humans. But direct observations on how a substance affects sexual behavior are difficult to make. During the 1960's and early 1970's, the existence of a drug subculture, many members of which were believed to be sexually active, provided unusual opportunities for studying a special group, but there is no way of knowing how representative the members of the drug subculture may have been.

This chapter will present an overview of current knowledge on sexuality and substances of abuse, in terms of substance effects on sex. The substances of interest include the range of psychoactive and mood-modifying drugs. They may be licit or illicit, and some licit drugs may be taken outside of a treatment setting. The substances considered are aphrodisiacs, opiates, barbiturates, tranquil-

izers, lysergic acid diethylamide (LSD), cocaine, amphetamine, amyl nitrate, marihuana, and alcohol.

Frequency of use, dosage, and chronicity of use are important in the effects of a drug on sexuality. A depressant might facilitate a sexual response at a low dose and inhibit it at a high dose (7). Situational dimensions, basic personality structure, and relationship with the partner also contribute to drug effects. A drug may have little effect in one setting but substantial impact in another context. In the case of any substance on which a user is dependent, the compulsion or activities required to obtain it may obliterate or mask sexual interest.

Whether a person has had little or much sexual experience, his usual degree of sexual effectiveness, established patterns of sexual behavior, mood, age, physiological condition, previous drug history, the partner and situation, and related factors all contribute to the effect of drugs on sexual activity and responsiveness. The user's expectations will contribute very substantially to a drug's effect on sex.

Our ability to generalize about drugs and sex is complicated by the fact that most contemporary drug abusers are polydependent. The realities of the drug marketplace make it difficult for a user to get a drug of choice on any regular basis. As a result, at any given time, he may be under the influence of more than one substance. The several substances being taken may or may not have compatible effects.

Most studies of the effects of drugs on sexual behavior are conducted by interviewing users or former users and are limited by the users' memories and the nature of the interview situation. The interviewees are seldom able to identify the dose and purity of the substance they took, to distinguish drug effects from the nature of the sexual opportunity or situation, and to be precise about preingestion mood. Even in a more controlled experimental situation, because nondrug-related sexual behavior is so variable and because there is an enormous range of response to mood-modifying substances, it is extremely difficult to make firm generalizations about how drugs influence sexual behavior. The kind of dose-response effect data we expect in other kinds of drug studies are seldom available.

For many psychoactive drug users, intravenous ingestion is heavily sexualized. The needle may be symbolically analogous to a penis, and some users experience a "flash" response to the injection situation itself, regardless of the substance being ingested. Many users enjoy letting the blood in and out of the needle ("boosting") in a masturbatory manner, before finally plunging in the drug.

Drugs of abuse are often taken by young adults, who represent the age group most likely to be sexually active. It is certainly possible that for some young people, becoming a regular drug user is one way of dealing with the social pressures and biological urgencies related to sex. For such persons, a career as a serious drug user could be a technique for avoiding sexual activity. It is easier to deal with chemicals than with a person, and chemicals are not generally believed to have gender.

APHRODISIACS

An aphrodisiac agent must be able to affect a person whose neuro-vascular-endocrine system is able to respond to sexual stimulation (2). Aphrodisiac qualities have been attributed to a large number of substances, but there is no drug that can be ingested orally that has an effective and consistent aphrodisiac action.

Intravenous administration of some substances has been said to lead to an orgasm-like sensation, which may result from a pharmacological effect or from diffuse cerebral stimulation. These substances include d-amphetamine (Dexedrine), methylepinephrine (Methedrine), methylphenidate (Ritalin), and phenmetrazine (Preludin).

Cantharides ("Spanish fly"), deriving from a beetle, is thought by many men to be an aphrodisiac, partly because of its citation in the writings of the Marquis de Sade. It is actually toxic for both sexes and does not directly affect the genitalia. By irritating the bladder and urethra, it can cause the man to feel pseudosexual excitement. It is believed to have caused impotence and death in some users.

OPIATES

Most of our impressions of opiates' effects on sexuality come from street heroin users. As a result, the information could be reflecting life style, e.g., poor nutrition or lack of sleep, rather than drug effects.

Sandor Rado's concept of an alimentary orgasm that is experienced by the opiate addict has been reformulated by Chessick as the pharmacogenic orgasm (4). This euphoric sensation involves a slowing down of time, a reduction in aggression, a desire to sleep, fantasies and dreams, a feeling of warmth, and a sense of fullness, primarily in the stomach. It is possible that the drug leads to a neurological effect in the alimentary area, with a seizure-like phenomenon involving discharge of tension.

The total pharmacogenic orgasm that a heroin addict may experience is so satisfying that he is unlikely to seek out coitus. Opiate users with little interest in sexual behavior may nonetheless have dreams about it. The user's libido varies substantially with his physical condition, diet, and the degree to which he has opiates in his body.

Being "on the nod" often means that the user has scant concern for any human interaction, much less for sexual activity. The "hustle" and activities involved in getting drugs may be so demanding, time consuming, and satisfying that a user may have little energy for or interest in sex.

During periods of heroin taking, there is usually a decline in masturbation, nocturnal emissions, and intercourse (5). The time required to achieve ejaculation increases, and the orgasm quality is poor. The drug could interfere with arousal and permit a user to engage in sexual behavior without experiencing strong feelings. Frequency of sexual activity usually declines as the size of an opiate habit increases and also reflects the availability of a sexual partner.

An addict in withdrawal is likely to divert his attention and libido to getting drugs. An addict can become more libidinally responsive as the drug wears off. During periods of abstinence, as in jail, libido is likely to return. Any generalizations on sexuality of opiate users must, of course, reflect their degree of use, the purity of the drug, whether they are taking the drug by injection or ingesting it in some other way, the extent to which they are functioning effectively in the larger society, and similar factors. Interview data from physician and nurse addicts, who usually take meperidine (Demerol) and continue to function professionally, suggest that their sex lives are more likely to resemble those of nonaddict physicians and nurses than they resemble street addicts' sex lives (23).

In perhaps half of female heroin addicts, there is amenorrhea or irregular menstruation, suggesting that the drug affects hormonal balance. Lesbianism among heroin users is not uncommon; in institutional samples of female heroin users, from 25 to 35 per cent seem to be homosexual or bisexual.

A substantial number of women addicts become prostitutes in order to raise the very substantial amounts of money needed in order to buy heroin regularly (24). When they drift out of drug use, often in their thirties, they may also no longer continue working as prostitutes. Among prostitutes' motivations for taking heroin may be a desire to deaden themselves to their work. Prostitutes who have taken heroin generally try to conceal this from their client, who may feel that such a woman is "no good for me."

Whether prostitution precedes heroin use or vice versa is difficult to determine, because information on the subject derives from interviews conducted under circumstances in which valid recall may be difficult. Some women may come from a subculture in which heroin use and sexual activity for pay are both likely. Others might start as prostitutes and then begin taking heroin. Still others were heroin users who became prostitutes.

A number of pimps maintain control of their prostitutes by the heroin they supply to the women. Some pimps are themselves addicted and use their prostitutes' earnings for drugs. Another factor is that the same people who control prostitution may also control heroin sales in a particular community.

A number of therapeutic communities that treat heroin addicts have found that their female residents' sense of femininity and sexuality is very underdeveloped. Some facilities deal with this area quite directly in the course of the treatment process, by control over dating and clothing, formal lectures, and other instruction.

Methadone patients report that they typically increase sexual desire and capacity after replacing their heroin use with methadone, although some of the change could result from the less stressful aspects of the patients' lives once they enter treatment. Heroin addicts who have been taking other blocking drugs, like cyclazocine, often say that their sexual awareness, which had been at a low level when they were on heroin, reasserted itself after they entered treatment.

BARBITURATES

Barbiturates typically contribute to a decline in libido, especially in high dosages, that leads to a generalized sedative-hypnotic effect. In moderate doses, there may be cerebral disinhibition of behavioral and sexual excitement. Barbiturates have no specific effect on the genitals but act on the central nervous system.

Barbiturates may permit a user to function more effectively in a sexual situation by regularizing the sleep cycle and thus making the user less likely to be anxious at night, when most sexual activity occurs. The decline in anxiety can improve sexual satisfaction.

TRANQUILIZERS

Although most tranquilizers are prescribed by a physician for relief of anxiety or depression, a substantial number of persons take them outside of medical supervision or at a higher dose level than is recommended. These substances include chlordiazepoxides (Librium, Valium), meprobamate (Miltown), antidepressants (Elavil), and lithium.

It is likely that none of these substances has a direct impact on sexual behavior. However, as the user becomes less anxious and depressed, there may be an improvement in sexual awareness and effectiveness. The user's better interpersonal relations may extend into enhanced sexual relations.

LSD

LSD is a hallucinogen that seems to be related to suggestibility and altered sensory perception. It disrupts the ordinary cognitive process of the brain and produces extreme variations in sexual sensations and images. Sexual interaction seems much more complex, and orgasm often is deeper, occurring on a kind of parallel basis to a user's reaction to the drug. The social and personality context of use are central to any sexual reaction.

A "bad trip" will overshadow any sexual dimension of the response to the drug. Even a "good trip" might involve difficulties in coordination and concentration, both of which are necessary for effective sexual functioning. The distortion in perception and cognition that the drug induces tends to make a sexual situation more narcissistic than interactive.

COCAINE

Cocaine is a potent central nervous system stimulant that is usually sniffed and can heighten libido and may improve sexual performance. The cocaine "flash" or "rush" is maximized by intravenous ingestion, but the pleasure lasts for only 5 to 10 minutes. Cocaine sometimes leads to multiple orgasm, which may be related to its street name of "girl." Cocaine is occasionally rubbed on the head of the penis to facilitate the male's ability to engage in extended thrusting. It is also occasionally used in a douche to enhance sexual pleasure.

Cocaine's aphrodisiac qualities are so much a part of the drug's folklore that some users reserve it for sexual situations. The cocaine "rush" is quite similar to the orgastic response. The substance often leads to an increase in intensity of sexual drive and to prolongation of the length of sexual interaction.

Heavy users may report a decline of sexual interest. For some, the drug is so satisfying that sex becomes less interesting. For other users, cocaine leads to a kind of undifferentiated sexual urgency. Loss of control and motor restlessness, which may be stressful and exhausting, sometimes result from cocaine use and are nonerotic.

AMPHETAMINE

Amphetamine is a stimulant that acts directly on the brain. Effects of chronic amphetamine use on sexual behavior are quite variable, reflecting the user's personality, dose, circumstances of use, and gender. Women seem to be more directly influenced than men. In many men, erection occurs simultaneously with injection.

Of those users who experience more sexual desire after amphetamine ingestion, there is often an increase in polymorphous activities and more self-confidence and interest in trying new activities. The amphetamine "rush" is very powerful and involves the whole body. Intravenous amphetamine injection typically leads to a desire for sex, sexual fantasies, and greater sexual aggressiveness.

However, a "speed freak" may be uninterested in sex and so out of touch with reality that sexual activity is irrelevant. Chronic users frequently report diminished libido and sexual difficulties. Intravenous amphetamine has been known to lead to psychotic episodes involving sexual urgency. The negative features of amphetamine use are so well known that prominent counterculture figures like poet Allen Ginsberg have denounced it, and the Food and Drug Administration (FDA) in 1979 recommended, following the lead of Canada and England, that its use for purposes of treating obesity be prohibited. The FDA would still permit amphetamine to be prescribed for treatment of narcolepsy and hyperactivity in children, but its elimination in obesity treatment would cut the number of pills manufactured each year from 290 million to 35 million.

AMYL NITRATE

Amyl nitrate is a vasodilator that is used to treat angina pectoris. It is a volatile aromatic compound that is generally ingested by breaking the small vial in which it is contained. The drug is inhaled and enters the lungs and blood stream, causing vasodilation of coronary blood vessels. These "poppers" (named after the prescription form, which had a popping sound when the vial was broken) are primarily used for sexual purposes by heterosexual men just before orgasm, in order to increase awareness and response. Amyl nitrate delays ejaculation and extends the duration of orgasm.

During the 1960's, among some users of psychedelics, amyl nitrate was taken in conjunction with LSD in order to enhance a sexual experience. LSD leads to perceptual changes and color patterns that reach a peak, at which time coitus occurs, when the amyl nitrate is popped. Amyl nitrate is sometimes taken in conjunction with marihuana, especially at orgies (8). Homosexual men may use "poppers" in conjunction with sadomasochistic activities involving pain and fear.

MARIHUANA

Marihuana has been said to make orgasm more pleasurable, to heighten sexual feeling, awareness, and appetite. In general, however, there is no clear evidence for any physical aphrodisiac effect of the drug. In fact, there may possibly be a role for marihuana in the origin of some forms of impotence (9).

Young people who experiment with marihuana may do so in a social setting that involves the presence of the opposite sex. Such a context can contribute to an atmosphere in which sexual perception and activity are facilitated. Because of distortion of the sense of time, sexual activity under marihuana may seem to last longer. Marihuana users tend to believe that the drug enhances their responsiveness to sound, color, and texture, which can contribute to a better sexual interaction. Because marihuana is smoked, it lends itself to kinds of intimacy that may enhance sexual interaction. Thus, a couple smoking the same "joint" may blow the smoke into the partner's mouth, kiss, and continue the sequence of inhaling, blowing the smoke into the partner's mouth, and kissing.

In a study of young members of the San Francisco drug culture, marihuana was cited by 80 per cent as the drug that most improved their sexual pleasure (11). The effect seems to be a reflection of the drug's disinhibitory qualities, time distortion, and heightening of sensory awareness, all of which may contribute to empathy in a sexual situation.

Among college students, Goode found that the greater the amount of marihuana used, the greater the likelihood of premarital sexual activity, the more sexual partners, and the more intercourse the smoker had (13). Positive correlations were found between all measures of sexual activity and all measures of drug use. There was no way of determining whether sex led to drug use or vice versa. It is plausible to speculate that there may be an underlying factor, such as a generalized liberal ideology, that leads both to sexual permissiveness and marihuana use.

Females probably experience more of a sexual spur from marihuana than do males, and young users cite more impact than do older persons. Frequent users report more sexual effects from marihuana than do infrequent users. Sexually experienced users tend to have greater arousal than less experienced ones. In a national survey, one-half the adults who had ever tried marihuana felt that the drug increased sexual pleasure (19). Such a finding could, of course, reflect the expectation that marihuana would have such an effect.

Marihuana is believed to heighten whatever a person is experiencing, so that a sexual situation may seem more satisfying and a sexual partner more attractive. It is likely that marihuana, although not an aphrodisiac, serves to ease inhibitions, so that the user is better able to be responsive to a sexual situation. Because of the drug's reputation for enhancing sensory experiences, the user may be more aware of the partner. There seems little reason to believe that marihuana sharpens predatory sexuality, alters established behavior patterns, or advances promiscuity.

ALCOHOL

How alcohol affects sexual behavior reflects the user's personality, expectations, readiness state, age, amount of the drug, the social context, and the user's relationship with the partner. Such a statement, which would be relevant for any drug, is less poetic and generalizable than the conventional wisdom about alcohol expressed in Macbeth (Act 2, Scene 3): "It provokes and unprovokes: it provokes the desire but it takes away the performance."

Alcohol's depressive effect on the brain first exerts itself on the areas regulating fear and anxiety, so that there is a disinhibition effect that may manifest itself in heightened sexual awareness. However, cross-cultural studies have concluded that alcohol does not necessarily lead to disinhibition (17).

Beyond some levels of alcohol in the blood, sexual performance is probably impaired but at moderate levels of ingestion, social learning factors are more likely to influenece sexual behavior (21). Alcohol may be believed to be an aphrodisiac because of the way it can reduce anxiety about sexual behavior and contribute to muscle relaxation, which could prolong sexual interaction.

In a number of "uncivilized" cultures, such as the Central African Lepcha and Azandi, alcohol consumption has sexual overtones such as lewd jokes and fondling of breasts. On another level, cocktail parties in our own society may have an analogous atmosphere of heightened sexual awareness. The Mardi Gras in New Orleans is another contemporary example of the interaction between alcohol use and public acceptance of sexuality, even in a culture that is usually more inhibited. Horton concluded that there is a substantial correlation between sexually permissive attitudes in a society and the incidence of insobriety (14).

Several careful experimental studies have concluded that the user's beliefs have a greater impact on alcohol's effects on sexual behavior than does any physiological mechanism that is activated by the alcohol (15, 22).

In an experimental study with 48 male undergraduates divided into groups receiving four varying levels of alcohol and two different sets of expectancies about the effects of alcohol on sexual arousal, there was a significant negative linear relation between penile tumescence and amount of alcohol consumed (3). Different levels of alcohol consumption did not differentially affect sexual content on the Thematic Apperception Test. Wilson and Lawson, using the vaginal photoplethysmograph, found a negative linear relation between alcohol doses and vaginal pressure pulse (22). There was no significant correlation between vaginal pressure pulse scores and self-report of sexual arousal.

A number of clinicians have noted that sexual tension is seldom found in alcoholics, perhaps because of some combination of minimal interest in sex, lack of time to pursue sex, and difficulties in arousal. An alcoholic who feels sick is relatively unlikely to be interested in sexual activity. Long term drinking could also lead to neurological damage and a generalized decline in health, which can depress the level of sexual functioning and interest. Acute intoxication can contribute to a range of symptoms, including delayed ejaculation.

Alcohol is sometimes used by women as an excuse for various kinds of sexual behavior: "I found myself in bed with a man and haven't any idea of how I got there". Similarly, many men who frequent prostitutes are only able to do so when drunk. This may reflect a convenient excuse for the man to justify what is otherwise socially unacceptable behavior, the extent to which drinking permits a temporary suspension of inhibition, a social situation in which several men who have been drinking can shed responsibility for their behavior via a shared experience, or a situation in which the circumstances of drinking are related to easy access to prostitutes. "I only did that because I was drunk" is an alibi that permits disclaiming responsibility for a variety of other sexual episodes.

ALCOHOL AND SEXUAL PROBLEMS

If someone is able to engage in successful sexual activity after drinking, he or she may tend to believe that alcohol is necessary to achieve similar results. Substantial increase in alcohol use could lead to subsequent sexual failure and impotence.

Masters and Johnson have observed that excessive alcohol consumption is the largest single cause of secondary impotence in men in their late forties and early fifties (18). However, Lemere and Smith found impotence in only 8 per cent of 17,000 alcoholic patients (16). Women alcoholics seldom complain of sexual difficulties, so that the problem could be directly related to damage to the penile erection process.

Some women begin drinking to improve their sexual functioning and then drift into heavy drinking, as a result of which their sexual functioning is likely to decline. It is also possible that some women may drink to mask sexual difficulties or to conceal from themselves that they have such difficulties.

However, many women alcoholics may experience difficulties with desire, orgasm, and lack of vaginal lubrication but not discuss such symptoms because of cultural conditioning. An impotent man can quickly become aware of his symptom, but women may have more difficulty in becoming aware of symptoms and especially in discussing them. In the later stages of alcoholism, both men and women lose sexual desire, as the drinker's major relationship becomes "just me and my bottle."

Secondary psychological impotence probably increases along with the length and intensity of alcoholism. As the alcoholic becomes less sexually adequate, he may experience guilt and anxiety and avoid sexual activity, which could lead to more anxiety about masculinity, which in turn could contribute to more alcohol consumption (10). The impotence would thus be reinforced, and the continued drinking could be contributing to long term vascular changes and peripheral neuropathy.

A man who is impotent with his wife when he has been drinking might find another sexual partner. If he were successful with the nonmarital partner, he might only be able to have intercourse with a person other than his wife and further reinforce the impotence with the wife.

ALCOHOL AND SEXUAL VIOLENCE

Forcible rape is the most rapidly increasing violent crime in the country. Reports on the proportion of rapists who have been drinking have been inconsistent, ranging from 0 to 50 per cent. In one study, alcohol was present in 27 per cent of the offenders (1). In 63 per cent of the cases involving alcohol, both offender and victim had been drinking.

A nonalcoholic rapist may drink to overcome timidity with the opposite sex, so that the alcohol acts secondarily to reinforce rape behavior. In one study of rapists, the alcoholism rate was 35 per cent (20). The alcoholic rapists were likely to have previously used drugs other than alcohol, to have used them at the time of the rape, and to have used them in conjunction with alcohol at the time of the rape.

Another possible category is rape that is triggered by alcohol in persons for whom alcohol may set in motion some fantasies and sensations that do not otherwise occur and that may lead to an interaction between sexual and aggressive drives.

Several theories have been proposed to explain the rape-alcohol connection. One theory is that alcohol, for some rapists, provides a stimulus for the man who needs a spur to engage in a difficult situation that requires a sense of mastery. Alcohol may also have a direct impact on the sexual and/or aggressive centers in the brain. Another possibility is that chronic alcohol use may modify the male's testosterone level, which in turn could affect violence or aggression.

Of 1,356 white male convicted sex offenders, two-thirds of the pedophiles were drunk at the time that they committed the offense (12). One-half of those convicted for heterosexual assault were either drunk or somewhat intoxicated.

Even a nonrape sex situation may have a dimension of violence with an alcoholic. One woman observed, "I may not want to have sex with a drinker but if he threatens me with violence, I have no choice."

SEXUAL PROBLEMS IN THE TREATMENT OF THE ALCOHOLIC

When the alcoholic is in treatment, and especially in early stages of sobriety, a considerable range of problems related to sexual functioning may emerge. Generalized sexual dysfunction and depression are common complaints.

Sexual feelings can be frightening to persons who may have used alcohol to dull sensations and have learned to drink to deal with various conflicts, including sexual conflicts. A recovering alcoholic's marriage is likely to be in difficulty, which often expresses itself sexually. The spouse of an alcoholic, who has seen him or her drunk for an extended period, may have problems in experiencing romantic feelings. One wife asked, "If I have sex with my husband while he is drinking, am I giving him a license to keep on drinking?"

Another wife asked, "How can I have sex with my husband when I get so turned off because he smells of booze and acts drunk?" The reverse of this situation is represented by the woman who complained that ". . . my husband is a dry alcoholic who thinks that his sobriety is his ticket to make love to me whenever he wants." A man in treatment complained that " . . . the aura of sexual excitement that I got from drink is missing now that I am sober. Drink used to relieve some of my guilt. Now a lot of the guilt is gone but so is the intense excitement."

A former drinker who attempts and fails in a sexual situation may be more likely to return to drinking. A person could have been able to engage in some kinds of sex while drinking but find it impossible later: "My husband wants oral sex, which was okay when I was drunk, but I don't like it now that I'm sober." Someone else may find sexual relations impossible without liquor, after having formerly associated them with drinking.

The recovering alcoholic's problems may be compounded because Alcoholics Anonymous (AA) meetings are generally not likely to deal with sexual matters. A recovering female alcoholic's going to an AA meeting may lead to unanticipated difficulties: "My husband thinks that I'm looking for another man at AA meetings." Some women will only go to women's AA meetings because they want to avoid relationships with men. Other women will seek male AA sponsors or attend mixed meetings because they want to feel valued by men.

A special problem may arise in the case of a homosexual alcoholic who has previously spent much of his social life in bars but is unable to do so after he becomes abstinent. Such a person must learn new forms of socializing.

Sex therapy with a couple, one of whom has an alcoholism problem, usually starts with a history of the couple's sexual relationship. Any sex problem can reflect the alcohol, the previous relationship of the couple, or larger characterological dimensions.

Recovering female alcoholics often experience general sexual dysfunction, which could reflect their feelings of depression. One form of treatment involves modification of the interaction that the patient has with her partner, via structured sensate focused on pleasuring exercises that ultimately lead to coitus. Recovering male alcoholics, who may be impotent, are often treated by graded sexual tasks to ease their anxiety. A similar approach is used in the treatment of premature or retarded ejaculation.

For both men and women recovering alcoholics, dealing with sexuality can contribute to the development of a more confident and effective person who is able to function in a manner that is less dependent on chemicals. In the Donwood Institute's alcoholism treatment, sex therapy is introduced 3 months after the patient has completed the 1-month program, because the patient has so many other physical and emotional adaptations to make during this period (6).

In couples groups for alcoholics, who are being treated on an outpatient basis, the discussion of sexual difficulties is often similarly deferred until a later phase of treatment. One therapist leaves such material for the middle phase of treatment, around the fifteenth session (10). If a couple has an acute sexual problem before then, the therapist sees them privately.

The kinds of sex-related problems noted in the treatment of the alcoholic have emerged over several decades of providing treatment for alcoholics. We have much less experience in the treatment of other kinds of drug-dependent people. As therapy of drug-dependent persons becomes more established, it is probable that new strategies and approaches to their sexual difficulties will emerge.

One plausible generalization is that psychoactive drugs have a tendency to reinforce a user's underlying personality characteristics. As we learn more about whatever personality characteristics may be related to drug use and as we increase our knowledge about sexual behavior and the contexts in which it occurs, our ability to integrate these data from different sources into the establishment of an accepted and valid body of knowledge on the relationships between sexuality and drug use should improve substantially.

References

1. Amir, M. *Patterns in Forcible Rape.* Chicago, University of Chicago Press, 1971.
2. Benedek, T. G. Aphrodisiacs: Fact and fable. Med. Asp. Hum. Sex. 5:42, 1971.
3. Briddell, D. W., and Wilson, G. T. The effects of alcohol and expectancy set on male sexual arousal. J. Abnorm. Psychol. 85:225, 1976.
4. Chessick, R. D. The "pharmacogenic orgasm" in the drug addict. Arch. Gen. Psychiatry 3:545, 1960.
5. De Leon, G., and Wexler, H. K. Heroin addiction: Its relation to sexual behavior and sexual experience. J. Abnorm. Psychol. 81:36, 1973.
6. Dowsling, J. L. Sex therapy for recovering alcoholics. Presented to National Council on Alcoholism, April 28, 1978.
7. Ellinwood, E. H., Jr., and Rockwell, W. J. K. Effect of drug use on sexual behavior. Med. Asp. Hum. Sex. 9:10, 1975.
8. Everett, G. M. Effects of amyl nitrate ("poppers") on sexual experience. Med. Asp. Hum. Sex. 9:146, 1972.
9. Ewing, J. A., et al. Roundtable: Alcohol, drugs, and sex. Med. Asp. Hum. Sex. 4:18, 1970.
10. Gallant, D. M. The effect of alcohol and drug abuse on sexual behavior. Med. Asp. Hum. Sex. 2:30, 1968.
11. Gay, G. R., and Sheppard, C. W. Sex in the "drug culture." Med. Asp. Hum. Sex. 6:28, 1972.
12. Gebhard, P. H., et al. *Sex Offenders.* New York, Harper and Row, 1965.

13. Goode, E. Drug use and sexual activity on a college campus. Am. J. Psychiatry 10:1272, 1972.

14. Horton, D. The function of alcohol in primitive societies: A cross cultural study. Q. J. Stud. Alcohol 4:199, 1943.

15. Lang, A. R., et al. Effects of alcohol on aggression in male social drinkers. J. Abnorm. Psychol. 34:508, 1975.

16. Lemere, F., and Smith, J. W. Alcohol-induced sexual impotence. Am. J. Psychiatry 130:212, 1973.

17. MacAndrew, C., and Edgerton, R. B. *Drunken Comportment.* Chicago, Aldine, 1969.

18. Masters, W. H., and Johnson, V. E. *Human Sexual Response.* Boston, Little, Brown and Company, 1966.

19. National Commission on Marihuana and Drug Abuse. *Marihuana: A Signal of Misunderstanding,* pp. 434–439. Washington, D.C., United States Government Printing Office, 1972.

20. Rada, R. T. Alcohol and rape. Med. Asp. Hum. Sex. 9:48, 1975.

21. Wilson, G. T. Alcohol and human sexual behavior. Behav. Res. Ther. 15:239, 1977.

22. Wilson, G. T., and Lawson, D. M. Expectancies, alcohol, and sexual arousal in male social drinkers. J. Abnorm. Psychol. 85:587, 1976.

23. Winick, C. Drug dependence among nurses. In *Sociological Aspects of Drug Dependence*, C. Winick, editor, pp. 155–168. Cleveland, CRC Press, 1974.

24. Winick, C., and Kinsie, P. M. *The Lively Commerce.* New York, New American Library, 1969.

PART 7

SPECIAL PROBLEMS IN SUBSTANCE ABUSE

CHAPTER 46

INTERNATIONAL NARCOTIC DRUG TRAFFICKING: THE IMPACT OF LAW ENFORCEMENT

Peter B. Bensinger

Donald E. Miller, J.D.

Availability of illicit drugs here or anywhere else is a result of supply and demand. If we are to reduce availability, both sides of the equation must be addressed—and they must be addressed simultaneously. The Drug Enforcement Administration (DEA) must utilize its resources so as to apply maximum efforts at the national and international level against the illicit drug traffic.

The problem of drug abuse, with its individual and social costs, results from an extensive illicit drug traffic involving tens of thousands of individuals participating at various levels of criminal activity all over the world. It would be difficult to describe adequately the complexity of this criminal enterprise in an entire book, much less in a single chapter. We have, therefore, confined ourselves to a discussion of the general nature of this activity, the assumptions on which law enforcement efforts to combat it are based, and relevant historical examples that indicate both problems and progress. It is appropriate

to state the general themes of the illicit drug traffic and the people who control it.

As other chapters of this volume point out, the individual motivation for the abuse of drugs varies considerably and, in many cases, is poorly understood. With some people, it seems to be a matter of psychological necessity; with others, perhaps, it may be merely a desire to remain fashionable in the eyes of a group of associates. Alternately, it may be a result of curiosity stimulated by provocative literature, or it may be simply the accidental by-product of legitimate but loosely supervised medical treatment.

All these and many other possibilities make the grist of learned discussions about human motivation and drug intoxication largely irrelevant when it comes to analyzing the mechanism that makes the drugs available. On the supply side, the primary motivation is simply and easily understood by everyone. The traffic in illicit drugs is sustained by the desire for enormous profit.

Seldom are drugs smuggled or diverted, except in the smallest of quantities, for any other purpose than to make money. And the profits are significant, representing a return on investment in excess of almost any other form of legitimate or criminal commerce. For example, the value of a kilogram of heroin purchased in Mexico and smuggled into the United States may increase by 667 per cent before it is even further diluted and retailed to other distributors. The price of a kilogram of marihuana in Colombia increases from approximately $8.80 at the source to roughly $1,500 once it is sold on the street in the United States. In Afghanistan, a kilogram of crude opium may be sold by a native grower for an equivalent of $71.00, which will ultimately be converted and diluted into a quantity of street-level heroin worth $223,000. The individuals who involve themselves in this chain of commerce reap varying degrees of this profit. In any case, whether it is the farmer, the smuggler, the wholesaler, or the street dealer, the sum is always significantly above that which they could obtain in any legal form of activity in which they could hope to engage.

Another important fact about the drug traffic is that it must be conducted in an organized fashion if the profits are to be consistently reaped. The big profit depends on the consumer, and, for the consumer to have access to the goods, various harvesting, processing, and shipping arrangements must be made to create and deliver the product. The commerce in these substances is truly a classic form of negotiation relying on extensive national and international financing and communications capabilities.

These principal characteristics of the drug traffic constitute the weak points through which it can be successfully attacked. Trafficking in drugs is not a crime of passion that cannot be deterred. It is a premeditated crime of reason for the sake of money. If the risk of engaging in it can be raised to unacceptable dimensions, many persons will abandon it for some other less dangerous sources of income. Obviously, the degree of risk that is acceptable will vary from individual to individual and, more specifically, from nation to nation and culture to culture, depending upon the other legal and illegal economic opportunities available.

The risks of engaging in the illicit drug trade are almost exclusively those relating to apprehensions by law enforcement authorities and punishment through the penal system. Criminal enterprise is otherwise sufficiently reliable to guarantee deliveries and safeguard investments in most cases. When a trafficker thinks in terms of risks as they measure up against potential profits, he is usually attempting to gauge the likelihood of his apprehension and the consequences to him should he be convicted. It is obvious that this also varies radically from nation to nation and from culture to culture.

Law enforcement efforts, if vigorously pursued, can take the profit out of drug trafficking; but, in addition, they can also reduce the volume of traffic by disrupting the organization of this commerce at any of its crucial points. If a group of smugglers can be identified and apprehended, the entire line of supply supporting them will collapse until replacements are found. The fact that this traffic must be organized, and all of it can be considered outside of the law, provides numerous opportunities for attack and harassment. If investigative effort is successful at any given point, it is possible for a whole pattern of illicit trade to be immobilized.

For example, several years ago, it was common knowledge that diversion of large quantities of licit opium production in Turkey and the clandestine production of heroin in France were responsible for nearly all of the supply of heroin in Europe and the Americas. Beginning with the French efforts against the clandestine laboratories, with Turkey's decision to ban all opium production, and with stronger, more aggressive law enforcement efforts in Turkey, France, Canada, and the United States, the Turkish-French opium-heroin trafficking organizations were smashed. This was one of the first real signs that vigorous, substained law enforcement programs can be highly successful.

The successful breakup of the "French Connection" in the early 1970's left a temporary void in the world heroin marketplace that was soon filled by a steadily increasing flow of Mexican heroin. By 1975, Mexican brown heroin accounted for 87 per cent of all heroin imported into the United States (6.5 of 7.5 metric tons). At that time, the remaining 13 per cent, or 1.5 metric tons, was Southeast Asian heroin. National retail purity of all heroin reached a high of 6.6 per cent in early

1976, and the corresponding price per milligram pure was $1.26. The effectiveness of the Mexican government's opium poppy eradication program, in which the United States State Department and DEA played important roles, coupled with an intensified enforcement program were responsible for the ensuing significant decrease in the amount of Mexican heroin available. In 1979 the nationwide heroin purity reached its lowest point— 3.5 per cent—since the beginning of the 1970's. Mexican brown heroin was substantially lower at 2.0 per cent and represented about 30 per cent of the reduced heroin flow reaching the United States in 1979.

THE PROBLEM

The foundation of our international program rests on one fact: all of the heroin and cocaine and 90 per cent of the marihuana in the United States' illicit market emanates from foreign countries. We know that supply reduction efforts are most effective at the point closest to the source. Simply, the drug control problem becomes increasingly less manageable the further the drugs move from the growing stages in foreign countries to the importing and distribution networks here in the United States. It is, therefore, useful to consider the different circumstances with which law enforcement must deal.

OPIUM

The uncontrolled or illicit opium production still exists primarily in Southeast Asia (The Golden Triangle), Southwest Asia (Afghanistan, Pakistan, and Iran), and Mexico.

In Burma, the Government's measures to reduce the extent of illicit opium production may impact on that country's position as a major source of opiates for the international illicit traffic. In Thailand, the commitment of the Thai government to reduce drug trafficking continues to be borne out by its actions. But, as it is with Burma, this general progress has been and will continue to be enormously difficult and will require dedicated efforts for a long time to come.

In Southwest Asia, Afghanistan and Iran stand out as particularly difficult problems. There is illicit cultivation in about one-half of the provinces, many poor farmers are involved, there has been only limited success

of law enforcement in restricting the outflow of opium from the country, and it is clear that the governments face many problems in achieving meaningful results in the near future. Pakistan also has many problems in bringing about reversal of the spiraling international trafficking in opium and its derivatives originating in the Middle East. Although the Pakistan government has been attempting to reform the existing system of opium distribution for quasimedical use through licensed "vends," and although it was required by treaty obligations to abolish the quasimedical use of opium by mid-December, 1979, the complex problems mitigate against Pakistan gaining early and effective control of illicit production, distribution, and manufacture of narcotic drugs.

In Mexico, the momentum in the campaign against illicit production of opium continues to be maintained. World-wide recognition must be given to the government of Mexico for its commitment to destroy narcotics at the source. An organized program of large scale eradication of poppy fields has been highly successful, particularly in diminishing the supply of heroin reaching the United States.

COCAINE

The cocaine available in the United States emanates from South American countries. The coca plant, from which cocaine is derived, grows easily and with little required care. It fares best at altitudes of 1,500 to 7,100 feet and can be grown in poor soil. The leaves are first harvested when the plant is 2 to 3 years old and can continue to be harvested from two to six times annually for a period of 20 to 40 years. Coca is normally grown in vertical terraces. The Andes mountains provide the moderate temperatures and good rainfall that enable the coca bush to survive. Although there is sporadic wild or semiorganized growth in many countries in South America, Peru and Bolivia are the principal and only legal producers, with approximately 25,000 and 20,000 hectares under cultivation, respectively. The countries of Peru, Bolivia, Colombia, and Ecuador are the principal sources for the growing of coca or processing of paste, base, or cocaine. Peru is considered the world's largest coca cultivator and is one of two licit producers of coca. Increasingly, cocaine in final form is produced here; however, most illicit activities center on the production of coca base and paste, which are then smuggled north to Ecuador or Colombia for further processing.

Bolivia is the other South American country where coca production is legal. Here, however, there is a long history of transporting the finished product, cocaine hydrochloride, out of the country. Ecuador, at times, serves as an alternative staging point for the conversion of Bolivian and Peruvian paste into base and cocaine hydrochloride. Strict enforcement of coca-growing laws in Peru and Bolivia is hampered by the Andean peoples' deep rooted traditions and economic dependence on the coca bush. The Peruvian and Bolivian governments are faced squarely with the dilemma of balancing, on the one hand, the sensitivity of socioeconomic-political issues surrounding consumption and cultivation of coca by their people and, on the other, their international agreements with respect to coca control.

In Colombia, coca cultivation is also traditional in the Andean region. Recently received intelligence indicates that cultivation of coca may be spreading to other nontraditional sections of the country. Throughout Colombia, there are a large number of clandestine laboratories that are capable of processing paste or base into a final product. The criminal elements in Colombia are the most sophisticated and organized of any in South America. They have the necessary international contacts and expertise needed to move significant quantities of cocaine to the world market and have access to large amounts of cash.

MARIHUANA

At present, about 75 per cent of all marihuana entering the United States is of Colombian origin. The government of Mexico, responding to the belief that marihuana has been the primary drug problem in their country, accelerated its marihuana eradication program using the herbicide paraquat. The demand for Mexican marihuana dropped dramatically, and marihuana from Colombia soon filled the void in the market. The economic implications for Colombia are staggering. It is alleged that marihuana has surpassed coffee as the primary cash crop. Drug trafficking proceeds entering the Colombian

economy range from upward of $1 billion annually. Cocaine alone may account for most of this amount of cash. The drug-fueled inflation rate has most recently been placed at 25 per cent.

The government of Colombia, under the direction of President Turbay, has undertaken very commendable initiatives to interdict illicit drugs leaving the country. Their campaign, a military effort to interdict the drugs as they leave the principal staging area in that country, is having discernible results. There are indications that the traffickers are shifting some of their plantations and are altering their methods of operation. The Guajira campaign has been a deterrent to the small unorganized trafficker; however, far too much marihuana is still available for the major trafficking networks. Long term initiatives inevitably must include crop destruction combined with interdiction.

SUPPLY REDUCTION: HOW IS IT ACHIEVED?

Assuming the validity of the foregoing assumptions as to the potential of law enforcement efforts to disrupt the drug traffic, let us next look at the manner in which these efforts are to be achieved. First, experience has shown that to be truly successful in reducing the supply of drugs, law enforcement must be international in scope. Strong enforcement programs in source countries—and swift and meaningful judicial deterrents for drug traffickers—are proving to be the only means by which we can curb the *supply* of illicit drugs. If this flow of drugs can be attacked at its foreign sources, before distribution has occurred in the United States, major and immediate impacts on domestic availability can be achieved.

An important consideration in developing international supply reduction programs is flexibility. The requirements of our programs vary according to the country and drugs involved, global and political issues, and user-demand requirements. Consequently, international programs are based on interrelated diplomatic, enforcement, and intelligence objectives and then are tailored to the specific needs of the area involved.

The goals of the ongoing United States programs are realistic in terms of furthering international cooperation and disrupting illegal manufacturing and trafficking networks. These programs emphasize the importance of the team approach in contending with the drug trafficking problem. DEA's place is at the forefront of the development of enforcement and intelligence cooperative efforts to document the activities of international trafficking organizations to lead to their arrests and subsequent immobilization. The diplomatic initiatives of the State Department and the Department of Justice in advancing bilateral agreements to enhance the capability of governments to trace and document the international flow of illegal narcotic-related financial transactions, mutual assistance treaties, and extradition treaties are significant. Accomplishments of this sort will aid all governments in source and consumer markets in their efforts and will further ensure that there will be limited havens left for the drug traffickers. Mindful of the speed with which Mexican brown heroin replaced the French-produced product and cognizant of the growing successes of the Mexican opium poppy eradication effort, DEA managers developed a strategy to place the agency in a posture to combat an *anticipated* threat of the next likely heroin source—Southeast Asia. Consequently, in June, 1977, the Special Action Office/Southeast Asia (SAO/SEA) was created within DEA. All the disciplines and specialties within DEA were tasked to implement a 20-point action program directed at three broad initiatives: diplomatic, intelligence, and enforcement. As part of the SAO/SEA operation, DEA Special Agents in 30 domestic offices and 20 overseas offices initiated and developed criminal investigations directed at the highest levels of the traffic. As a result, eight of the 20 different suspects identified in the DEA Top Ten Southeast Asian Heroin Violator program were arrested.

A fundamental enforcement objective of SAO/SEA was to develop a program to upgrade the interdiction of Asian heroin at airports from source to destination. Ultimately, the "Integrated Airport Drug Enforcement Program" was conceived to combine the vital function of investigative effort and Customs control into a total, effective program.

In Western Europe, where substantial numbers of seizures are made at airports, programs of this type are proving most beneficial. For example, as a result of using the airport trafficker information in Madrid and Barcelona and the intelligence derived from seizures, we are now learning that there is far more traffic in Southeast Asian heroin through Spain than was ever imagined.

In addition to anticipating and consequently watching the changes in the trafficking of Southeast Asian heroin, we have been carefully monitoring the reemergence of Southwest Asian heroin. In this country, there were negligible amounts of Southwest Asian heroin in 1975; by 1976 it represented about 2 per cent (0.1 metric ton) of the heroin in this country; and in 1977, Southwest Asia was the source for approximately 8 per cent (0.4 metric ton) of the heroin imported into the United States. By 1979 heroin from Southwest Asia had captured over one-third of the United States market, and special action efforts involving diplomatic, enforcement, interdiction, and financial interests are now underway.

Modeled on SAO/SEA, in 1979 DEA set up the Special Action Office for Southwest Asian heroin (SAO/SWA). Intelligence programs were instituted to determine international trafficking routes and key target cities in the United States. Many special agents were reassigned, some temporarily, to the Northeast corridor and to Europe to increase investigations of major heroin traffickers. Some initial enforcement successes have been achieved by immobilizing heroin laboratories in Europe and the Middle East. The reestablishment of heroin trafficking routes through Europe into the United States remains an ominous threat.

Although the United States has not yet been deluged with Southwest Asian heroin, the reemergence of Southwest Asian heroin has had a far greater impact on the countries of Western Europe. Whereas 2 years ago in West Germany Southwest Asian heroin represented 20 to 30 per cent of the heroin available, it now represents approximately 70 per cent. Formerly, West German addicts had to travel to the Netherlands for their heroin supplies; now, Turkish nationals are bringing heroin directly to Berlin. And the street purity there is a startling 35 per cent. The traffickers have turned to the West European market, in part, because the United States' coordinated law enforcement program meant too many risks and because the United States market required at least one additional route of entry.

In addition to working closely with host country law enforcement, DEA maintains close relations with United States military authorities to monitor the impact of trafficker activity on United States citizens stationed overseas.

Because of the real threat that the Middle Eastern heroin represents world-wide, DEA is again looking to programs that curtail the drug at the source. Middle Eastern heroin is processed in laboratories located in Iran, Pakistan, Turkey, and Afghanistan from opium poppies grown in Afghanistan, Iran, and Pakistan. The forced closing of the DEA office in Tehran has created an intelligence gap. Nonetheless, we know that the problems and instabilities within all three governments create difficulties in establishing and maintaining viable narcotics programs. For example, the family ties of the Kurds on both sides of the Turkey/Iran border are far stronger bonds than those of nationalism.

Our programs in Pakistan have met with considerably more success. A DEA/Pakistani Customs interdiction effort in Karachi, which has been actively supported by the United States Department of State and United States Customs Service, has been relatively successful in increasing the effectiveness of enforcement operations by Pakistani authorities. Although not all the seizures have been large, this program is building Pakistani confidence regarding their ability to control the movement of drugs.

The official *Federal Strategy* document, endorsed by the President, highlights the important role DEA and Customs have with respect to providing technical and management training to foreign enforcement officials. The Department of State sponsors and DEA conducts a variety of programs, including In-Country Training Schools, Advanced International Schools, and Executive Observation Programs, that upgrade the capability of foreign law enforcement officers. Significantly, many of the students are drug enforcement instructors in their own countries and apply their new knowledge in their own programs. These programs are yet another example of how DEA and the State Department work in harmony to realize particular goals. An important by-product of these international enforcement training programs is the development and strengthening of ties between United States personnel and their foreign counterparts.

In spite of our cooperative enforcement and training programs, there have been far too many instances where major violators have remained virtually undisrupted by taking advantage of the absence of bilateral and multilateral agreements for prosecution and extradition. To reach and immobilize traffickers who did not enter the United States, but were directly responsible for drug law violations here, the United States and Mexico developed a prosecutorial procedure known as Operation JANUS. This is a continuing arrangement by which the United States certifies documentary evidence that is used by the Mexican government to prosecute Mexican citizens and third-country nationals in Mexico. Operation JANUS was initiated by DEA and the Mexican Attorney General's Office by Executive Memorandum in April, 1975. JANUS is not limited to federal investigations; state and local cases are eligible for JANUS consideration.

For the first several years, the JANUS program met with limited success. I believe, however, that since the United States Department of Justice has become more involved in Operation JANUS and because the program will become more formalized through bilateral agreements, we will see greater results. Furthermore, we hope to expand this type of program to include other source countries.

From the law enforcement perspective, in order to immobilize major international trafficking networks, extradition and mutual assistance treaties are of enormous value. Far too many upper level Colombian narcotics traffickers have been "untouchable" for far too long. I am optimistic that the recent signing of these treaties in 1980 will have a significant impact on traffickers in both the United States and Colombia. Dismantling and immobilizing major trafficking organizations means hitting them where it hurts most—in their pocketbooks. By using the laws available to us—the Controlled Substances Act, the conspiracy laws, the continuing Criminal Enterprise statutes, and the Internal Revenue Service Statutes—we can become and, in fact, are becoming increasingly more proficient at disrupting trafficking groups.

SUPPLY REDUCTION: WHAT ARE THE EFFECTS?

With this background as to what law enforcement can achieve, we shall next turn our attention to the basic purpose that we hope to serve. As has been documented elsewhere in this volume, the costs of drug abuse are staggering in terms of lost opportunities, disruption of family relations, psychiatric and medical expenses, accidents, and civil and criminal justice system costs. To the extent that drug abuse can be reduced either in terms of frequency of abuse, numbers of abusers, or potency of the material abused, these associated costs to society and the individual will also be reduced. Effective law enforcement can achieve major reductions in the following ways. First, it has been shown that law enforcement can reduce the over-all availability and purity of specific drugs, thereby resulting in a net reduction of all of the above factors. Because of the enforcement efforts in Mexico, Europe, and Southeast Asia, the average purity of available heroin has dropped from 6.6 per cent in 1976 to a current level of 3.8 per cent, while at the same time, the price has increased from approximately $1.26 per milligram to $2.14.

The result of this decrease in heroin availability is difficult to completely establish. However, the evidence suggests that it has resulted in: (a) a net decrease in the number of persons who really are narcotic addicts; (b) consumption of a lower purity and, therefore, less dangerous and addictive quantities of heroin by the remaining addict population; (c) a decline in the exposure of and experimentation by the nonaddict population, and (d) a sharp decrease in heroin-related overdose deaths and injuries. This represents a significant achievement directly attributable to law enforcement efforts.

Another manner in which drug abuse damage can be reduced is by creating inconvenience to consumption, disrupting supplies, driving up prices, and otherwise evidencing society's strong disapproval. Consumption of drugs can be made costly, inconvenient, and hazardous. All of these are facts that tend to inhibit the size and growth of the drug-abusing population.

Finally, reducing supply can actually reduce demand. The legitimate advertising industry has long been aware of the principle that product visibility in and of itself increases product demand. Conversely, if a product remains unavailable for a sufficient period of time, many actual and potential consumers will lose interest in it and demand will sharply decrease. In the case of drugs of abuse, there persists a hard core of addicts and habitues whose demand for certain drugs will persist in spite of shortages, but these persons actually represent the smallest percentage of the total drug-abusing population. Therefore, there is strong reason to believe that, if law enforcement can produce continuing shortages of major drugs of abuse, the actual demand for these substances will sharply decline.

SUPPLY REDUCTION: PERMANENT SUCCESSES

Given the enormity of the task that we have outlined, it is fair to consider the most important question of all: that is, can we succeed? Is it feasible to expect that so many factors can be successfully organized, that drug supplies can be sharply reduced, and that demand, in turn will finally subside to some less damaging level? There have been major successes that would suggest that this can be achieved. In particular, the sharp decline in heroin availability and purity that has persisted for a few years must be regarded as significant beyond previous experience. On the other hand, major problems still threaten and persist. The Southwest Asian potential for the supply of heroin is known to be enormous, and illicit trade routes between these sources and Western Europe are becoming firmly established. Thus far, most of this heroin is being consumed in Western Europe, with little of it reaching the United States. In contrast, the situation in the Caribbean has progressively deteriorated in the last several years. Enormous quantities of cocaine and marihuana and appreciable amounts of dangerous drugs are being smuggled by sea and air into the Southeastern United States. The value of the marihuana trafficking alone is estimated from $15 to $22 billion annually. Thousands of square miles of Colombia are exclusively devoted to cultivation of the illegal marihuana crop.

Finally, in spite of the gains made in eliminating diversion of legitimately produced drugs at the wholesale level, large quantities are still diverted from the retail and practitioner level. There are more than 600,000 individuals and businesses registered in this category, and the very small percentage who are willing to engage in criminal behavior still constitutes a significant problem. The drugs that are most commonly diverted include narcotics, barbiturates, amphetamine, and major tranquilizers. These legitimate controlled substances can become stronger and more addicting than the street level heroin that is now available. Abuse of these licit pills produces severe health symptoms as well as overdose deaths.

The foregoing are all specific drug trafficking and abuse problems to which we must successfully respond. At present, they constitute the negative side of the ledger that balances the significant gains previously mentioned. Nevertheless, plans exist for combating these situations, and success is feasible. Past successes in the three strategic areas previously mentioned—i.e., international policy initiatives at the source, special enforcement operations, and high level investigative efforts—show that we do have the ability to succeed through law enforcement. The larger question is whether we are able as a nation to sustain our will to succeed and to create the degree of organization among various inter- and intragovernmental units necessary to this end. These represent significant questions to which the answer is yet to be given. The measures we must take can be easily identified.

First, the various source countries where illicit drugs are produced must vigorously support enforcement efforts in their separate sovereign areas.

Second, enforcement pressure must be sustained at a constant level. In the past, gains have been sometimes jeopardized because of rapid shifts in policy, organization, or leadership and, in some cases, reduction of presence overseas. To discourage both drug traffickers and drug abusers, they must be convinced that enforcement pressure and short supply are not transient phenomena but will persist.

Third, we must anticipate threats and shifts in the drug traffic before they occur. For example, the advantage gained from the success in breaking the "French Connection" in the early 1970's was largely lost through a failure to anticipate the rapid growth of Mexico as a source of heroin supply. There was, in fact, evidence of this shift known to law enforcement officers, but, to be effective, early warnings must be heeded by undertaking preventive actions. This was not adequately done in the case of Mexico in the early 1970's.

Finally, we must unravel the confusion that has become the essence of our own criminal justice system. Justice is both uneven and slow and, in the case of drug trafficking, lacks deterrence because of an unrealistic and much abused bail system.

Drug traffickers learn that millions of dollars can be made at the risk of perhaps no confinement. There is no bail too large for many of them to make and often this will give many additional months of freedom during which to pursue their illicit activity. Thus far, except in the case of heroin trafficking, our criminal justice system has not had successes in producing the kind of deterrent necessary to convince calculating criminals that the risks and consequences outweigh the potential profit.

To have any chance of long term successes, the efforts of the Drug Enforcement Administration must continue to be aimed at enhancing the interest and capability of foreign drug law enforcement officials by providing training to foreign police officers, by distributing to foreign law enforcement agencies the greatest amount of intelligence possible, and in working directly with foreign police officers in the initiation of effective programs to immobilize key violators, international trafficking organizations, and destruction of illicit narcotics at the source.

CHAPTER 47

FEDERAL INVOLVEMENT IN SUBSTANCE ABUSE POLICY

Michael R. Sonnenreich, J.D.

Robin Import, J.D.

This chapter will discuss the elements of the federal system that create substance abuse policy, their statutory and judicial evolution, and actions and deliberations on current issues. Especially vital to understanding federal policy making is the increased role of the administrative agencies. These agencies have often taken the lead away from Congress and, rather than await specific legislative direction, guided federal policy through new interpretations and extensions of existing law. Current issues involving "prescription drug abuse" have provided a fertile area for such administrative initiatives, which may eventually lead to additional federal regulation of the medical profession.

Included in this review of the policy-making elements in the federal system is a discussion of those basic threshold inquiries on which policy development relies. The present inability to develop sound and generally accepted definitions and the related failure to generate a useful information base have made the creation of a unified substance abuse policy unattainable for today's legislators and administrators.

SOURCES OF PUBLIC POLICY IN THE UNITED STATES

BACKGROUND

"Federal legislation" is a term that describes the laws passed by Congress, but the laws are ineffective without the regulatory details provided by the federal administrative agencies that implement the programs created by a new law.

The decade of the 1970's brought with it a dramatic expansion of the role of the regulatory agencies.[1] In a period called different from all previous regulatory history for reasons such as the extraordinary surge of rule making, increased concern about informal

---

[1] The growth of agency power was not taken lightly by the Nixon Administration, which established the President's Advisory Council on Executive Organization, known as the Ash Council, after its chairman, Roy L. Ash. Despite a finding that the agencies were not sufficiently accountable for their actions to either Congress or the President, the Council's report received little support, and the issue has not been seriously explored since.

and unreviewed discretionary action, and the effects of the Freedom of Information Act (4), regulatory activity affecting drug enforcement has not differed from this general trend.

Regulatory Agencies

The traditional balance of powers established in the Constitution between the legislative, executive and judicial branches of government has been modified over time to include a somewhat amorphous group of administrative experts known as administrative or regulatory agencies. These agencies, which technically derive their power from the President, routinely act independent of the President's supervision as they regulate, implement, and enforce statutory or executive programs within their particular expertise.

This independence of agency initiative causes and encourages a source of federal policy independent of the Congress. Because the agencies exist to develop experience in and expertise over specific areas, great deference is given to the acts of these agencies in implementing the laws of the United States. This is especially true as a matter of precedent within the judicial system:

[I]t is established that the Court should show great deference to the interpretation given a statute by the officers or agency charged with its interpretation (28).

Once proposed legislation becomes law, the administrative agencies are guided by that legislation's history but expand and interpret it as the legislation is incorporated into an agency's general mandate and regulations are written. Once this independent rule-writing process is begun, the end product, as created by interpretive rule making, many times differs dramatically from the original intent of the legislators.

Law Enforcement

The Drug Enforcement Administration (DEA) is charged with management of American drug enforcement initiatives. Under Reorganization Plan Number Two of 1973 (21), DEA was created within the Department of Justice to coordinate and carry out functions transferred from other agencies including the functions of the well known Bureau of Nar-

cotics and Dangerous Drugs (BNDD),[2] the Bureau of Custom's functions pertaining to drug investigations and intelligence, the Office for Drug Abuse Law Enforcement (ODALE), and the Office of National Narcotics Intelligence (ONNI).[3] The research function was also transferred from the Law Enforcement Assistance Administration (LEAA) to DEA.

DEA was to assume several major responsibilities, including: development of an overall strategy; investigation of violations of drug trafficking laws; communication with drug law enforcement officials of foreign governments; communication with state and local enforcement; and regulation of the legal manufacture of pharmaceuticals and other controlled substances under federal jurisdiction.

DEA's scope of review overlaps to a certain extent with that of the Food and Drug Administration (FDA), which regulates the manufacture and distribution of prescription and nonprescription drug products. It might be broadly stated that FDA regulates who manufactures what product and DEA regulates how the manufactured product is used. Substance abuse policy is, therefore, being formulated by at least these two agencies, whose actions significantly affect new developments in medical therapy.

FDA has no statutory authority.[4] The Bu-

---

[2] In 1920, the Prohibition Unit of the Treasury Department became responsible for narcotics enforcement. Then the Narcotic Drugs Import and Export Act enlarged the administrative role in the Federal Narcotics Control Board in 1922. In 1930, Congress abolished the Federal Narcotics Control Board and established the Federal Bureau of Narcotics (FBN). In 1968, FBN was combined with the Bureau of Drug Abuse Control within the Department of Health, Education, and Welfare to form the Bureau of Narcotics and Dangerous Drugs (BNDD) in the Department of Justice. Finally, in Reorganization Plan No. Two of 1973, the Drug Enforcement Administration (DEA) was created combining ten federal agencies in five Cabinet departments performing drug enforcement functions.

[3] ODALE and ONNI were abolished with the creation of DEA.

[4] Under Reorganization Plan No. One of 1953, the Department of Health, Education, and Welfare was created. Part of HEW's authority was derived from the functions it inherited from the Federal Security Agency, including the authority over food and drugs. The HEW Secretary then delegated that authority over food and drugs to the Commissioner of Food and Drugs under HEW. There is

reau of Narcotics and Dangerous Drugs, and later DEA, was given broad powers to control and regulate drugs and substances covered by the statute.[5] In fact, regulations allow DEA to add new drugs that it can control (22).

PRESCRIPTION DRUG ABUSE: CONGRESS' TOP PRIORITY AMONG SUBSTANCE ABUSE ISSUES

Substance abuse is a broad term, originally encompassing substances without medically recognized value and only more recently expanding to incorporate substances developed for their medicinal properties but subsequently abused or diverted to illicit markets. The abuse of prescription drugs is the most significant and publicized substance abuse issue today, and it is also an area of intense debate and disagreement.[6] It seems that, despite the trend to deregulate in other areas of government involvement in the private sector, the controls over substance abuse are likely to involve increased supervision of physicians and patients through regulation, as well as increased attacks on traffickers through prosecution.

The problem with immediate implementation of such a regulatory response is that little is really known about the extent of prescription drug abuse or its social significance. Compare this lack of information with the volumes of studies done on the social role of alcohol or smoking in American culture. The first and most basic policy question to be answered is: Is this really something to worry about? Unfortunately, in the area of

drug policy making, lack of information has never seemed to be a meaningful impediment to political calls for action. In the second report of the National Commission on Marihuana and Drug Abuse, it was noted that (13):

The Commission's recommendations repeatedly stress the need for well-conceived research to fill gaps in present knowledge about drug use. Some of this research should be directed toward the problems posed by policy questions. Additional data are needed, for example, on the incidence of drug use, and the frequency of drug use patterns. Even more critical, however, is the need for evaluative research of present treatment and prevention programs. Current knowledge in this area is inadequate and has created a major difficulty in the Commission's work. In short, it is now impossible to tell whether current treatment and prevention programs are producing their intended consequences.

Medication or Abuse: The Need for Definitions

The Comprehensive Drug Abuse and Control Act of 1970 focused on two areas: the legitimate distribution system of manufacturer-distributor-pharmacist-physician-patient; and the illegal traffic in abusable substances. The law addresses both substance use and substance abuse in its two policy objectives: the discouragement of drug abuse itself (a term that today encompasses alcohol abuse) and the reduction of the consequence of abuse. Stated differently, there are two concurrent policy goals under the Comprehensive Act: to reduce the supply of abusable substances, and to provide treatment and rehabilitation as well as to focus prevention efforts on the abusing populations (27). Since the passage of the law in 1970, this dual treatment and deterrent approach to the management of drug abuse has been generally accepted. However, there is still no definition of "drug abuse" that has general and common acceptance. (See reference 6 for a discussion of the problems of definition of events of alleged drug abuse.) Use and abuse are relative terms and, as value judgments, are applied differently depending on who defines the terms for purposes of enforcement or nonenforcement.

no direct statutory aproval of a Food and Drug Administration under the Federal Food, Drug, and Cosmetic Act. HEW became the Department of Health and Human Services on May 4, 1980, when a separate Department of Education was created.

[5] The powers to enforce and implement the Comprehensive Act were given to the United States Attorney General (Sec. 201) and the Attorney General was specifically given the authority to delegate those functions and issue regulations deemed necessary to enforce the Act. (Sec. 501) The Bureau of Narcotics and Dangerous Drugs (BNDD), the predecessor agency of the Drug Enforcement Administration, was given powers later transferred to DEA.

[6] This is not to imply that heroin abuse and other non-medically approved drugs are not serious social problems, only that the current policy (as opposed to enforcement) focus is on prescription drug abuse.

MEASURING THE PROBLEM

DAWN: The Difficulty of Gathering Meaningful Statistics

One of the most widely quoted of the measuring devices for ascertaining substance abuse is the Drug Abuse Warning Network (DAWN).[7] DAWN is a rather large data collection system, jointly operated by the National Institute on Drug Abuse and DEA since 1972, funded annually at approximately $1.5 million to gather reports from 24 large cities and surrounding counties known as Standard Metropolitan Statistical Areas (SMSA's) and a random sampling of 200 emergency rooms outside metropolitan areas.

The system was developed specifically to measure drug abuse cases appearing in emergency rooms, crisis centers, and coroners' or medical examiners' offices. Under the Controlled Substances Act, a system was required to consider eight criteria for the control or decontrol of a drug. Four of these are measured by the DAWN system: (a) actual or relative potential for abuse; (b) historic and current pattern of abuse; (c) scope, duration, and significance of abuse; and (d) risk a drug presents to the public health.

The single most significant handicap of DAWN and similar data collection systems is that, without a consensus definition of "drug abuse," the data base is subjective and, therefore, limited. Despite the existence of the DAWN system and the federal funds it receives, a true understanding of present patterns of abuse may elude the system for at least two reasons: (a) The system is an observation measure and is not designed to distinguish types of drug abusers. (b) None of the circumstances surrounding a reported incident are reported or analyzed. (Consider diazepam (Valium): DAWN gives a large number of emergency room "mentions" for diazepam, but because of the widespread prescribing of the drug, it is a question of interpretation as to whether a given occurrence constitutes abuse (5).

Policy makers must balance the desire to use data such as the DAWN system produces with the understanding that such data are presently incomplete and ambiguous. Expanding on the diazepam example, it is accurate to note that diazepam is associated with a high frequency of DAWN-reported drug "events." However, because it is used by a cross-section of the population, because it is prescribed by so many medical specialties, and because of the way the DAWN data are coded, it is impossible to tell how many of the diazepam reports were caused by deliberate abuse and how many were accidental combinations of the drug with alcohol, other pharmaceuticals, or illicit substances.

In acknowledging the need for information, the Select Committee on Narcotics Abuse and Control of the House of Representatives held a hearing in 1978 on psychotropics. In September, 1979, the Senate Health Subcommittee of the Labor and Human Resources Committee held an "oversight" hearing on diazepam. Both hearings focused on anecdotal reports of abuse but no clear evidence as to the scope of the problem or how and whether the government should intervene was brought forward. Those hearings have contributed, however, to the growing sentiment that in some way the manufacturers of mind-altering drugs and the physicians who prescribe them are not performing properly under the present system.

Therapeutic Benefit versus Abuse

The vagueness of the understanding of drug events recorded makes the formulation of a program to separate therapeutic benefit from problems of abuse with prescription drugs a Procrustean task. This is where the presently inadequate definitional and data base for drug abuse is the most evident. Despite the stories of abuse recounted at Congressional hearings, these same Congressional committees were presented with substantial evidence of the effectiveness and utility of the accused prescription drugs. In the Report of the Special Populations Subpanel on Mental Health of Women submitted to the President's Commission on Mental Health in February, 1978, the panel recognized the unsettled nature of the issue (14):

There seems to be a growing acceptance of the use of psychoactive drugs . . . Opinions differ as to whether or not this rate of use is desirable.

---

[7]DAWN I   September 1972 –March 1973
DAWN II   April 1973   –March 1974
DAWN III   April 1974   –April 1975
DAWN IV   May 1975   –April 1976
DAWN V   May 1976   –April 1977
DAWN VI   May 1977   –April 1978

Some have argued that the minor tranquilizers (e.g., Valium, Librium, Miltown) which are currently the world's most commonly prescribed drugs, are harmless and are, if anything, underutilized (Balter, 1974). Other researchers have questioned the safety and effectiveness of the minor tranquilizers and other psychoactive drugs on both physiological and psychological grounds . . .

POTENTIAL RESPONSES

The often unstated but nonetheless recognized issue is how can prescription drug abuse be controlled without preventing patients from receiving prescription drug benefits? Presently this balancing process is in the hands of the physician. There loom on the legislative and regulatory horizon, however, several potential regulatory controls on the physician.

Drug Regulation Reform

As part of the comprehensive review of the Federal Food, Drug, and Cosmetic Act generally referred to as Drug Regulation Reform proposals, Congress has been considering proposals to extend the regulatory theories of the Controlled Substances Act to include additional controls on the distribution of non-covered drugs.[8] Such proposals would permit the Food and Drug Administration to examine who writes a prescription, for whom it is prescribed, how it is filled, and what the physicians prescribe. Under this proposed revision of federal law, Section 506 provides for limiting a product's distribution for post-marketing surveillance and for batch-by-batch inspection by the manufacturer as alternatives for controlling the distribution and dispensing of prescription drugs used in this country. This "limited distribution" system would, at its narrowest (and most optimistic), permit some new drugs to reach the market before they would under orthodox FDA approval procedures. Their use, however, would by definition be restricted to certain patient populations or to certain medical specialties or to certain medical facilities, all raising questions about the potential inequality of patient care that would be created.

More broadly construed, this proposed policy of controlled distribution would permit the federal government to control exactly which products were on the market and who would have access to them. Some physicians, some patients, and some hospitals would have newer and better medication than others, raising issues of Constitutional dimension, such as discrimination by state action and the absence of equal protection, surely to be strenuously argued in court.

Professional Standards Review Organizations: Peer Review

Another potential avenue of control of the physician may come by way of extended peer review through the professional standards review organizations (PSRO's) that now oversee the practices of physicians who receive federal reimbursement for the treatment of Medicare and Medicaid patients.[9] By simply enlarging the scope of PSRO review to include the nonfederally supported patients in a physician's practice, the federal government, through its PSRO structure, would have complete control over how a physician treats patients.

Public Necessity

There is also a third possible method of addressing drug abuse control, a method more dramatic and public. In 1978, the substance that won the attention of Congress, the public, and the President was phencyclidine, commonly known as PCP, a chemical approved only as a veterinary anesthetic that was and continues to be abused as a hallucinogenic. The House Select Committee on Narcotics Abuse and Control held a hearing and prepared a report that helped create and shape public policy with respect to PCP. The report stated (9):

PCP is the most life and health threatening drug to hit the streets in some time. Its abuse resulted in more than 4,000 hospital room emergency visits

---

[8] S.1075, the Drug Regulation Reform Act of 1979, was passed by the Senate on September 18, 1979. The Section referred to is Sec. 506. The House bill never reached a vote, and Congress adjourned without passing legislation reforming the Federal Food, Drug, and Cosmetic Act.

[9] PSRO's, Professional Standards Review Organizations, were established by the Social Security Amendments of 1972, Public Law 92-603. That law required the development of a PSRO network of regional review to promote effective and efficient health care service delivery. The PSRO's were mandated to assure that medical treatment paid for under government programs was of the proper quality and, at the same time, to attempt to reduce expenditures.

and more than 100 deaths during the last year. Because of the danger which PCP abuse presents to society the Select Committee has sought to publicize the horrors associated with PCP abuse.

After the hearing, the Select Committee on Narcotics Abuse and Control met with members of the House and Senate committees with responsibility in the drug area and then met with White House staff. The result was a program called "The Federal Response to the PCP Problem." The White House established a PCP Action Coordinating Committee, chaired by the White House Drug Policy Office with members from DEA, the National Institute on Drug Abuse (NIDA), the National Institute on Mental Health (NIMH), and the FDA. NIDA established a special program on PCP to collect and disseminate information. In 1978, DEA included PCP on its list of priority drugs and expanded enforcement efforts. DEA, FDA, and NIDA successfully worked toward getting PCP moved from Schedule III to Schedule II of the Controlled Substances Act, the schedule including the most dangerous of the legitimate drugs.

Although this is a laborious and costly way to respond to spontaneous drug fads, it may be the most feasible way to generate enough bipartisan support to create action programs that impact on the various aspects of the problem. During 1978 and 1979, there was a groundswell of activity with respect to diazepam (Valium), pentazocine (Talwin), propoxyphene (Darvon), and methaqualone (Quaaludes).[10] An examination of the uses and abuses of those drugs is underway to determine whether efforts to tighten controls on any of them—which may include rescheduling them under the Controlled Substances Act—are justified.

The three methods mentioned for implementing policy changes at the federal level—legislative reform, professional peer review, and crisis-oriented programs—illustrate the breadth of federal reach into routine medical practice and also the limited role of traditional legislative change. The Marihuana Commission summed it up:

Patterns of drug-using behavior have been ignored except as an afterthought of intervention.

When increases in prohibited drug use continue to escalate, policy makers respond, not by reassessing the problem from different perspectives, but rather by pressing forever-more costly mechanisms of control; costly both in terms of resources and important social values. Drug policy can be thus summed up: increased use of disapproved drugs precipitates more spending, more programs, more arrests and more penalties, all with little positive effect in reducing use of these drugs (13).

A look at historical developments leading up to modern statutes, the statutes themselves, and the American role in international drug policy follows as a necessary complement to the discussion of current events.

TOWARD A PUBLIC POLICY ON DRUG ABUSE CONTROL

THE HISTORICAL PREDICATE

The fundament of federal legislation is public policy. Acts passed by the legislature both make and justify public perceptions. The Harrison Narcotic Act in 1914 first established a national policy of restricting availability of dependence-producing substances of that era—specifically, opium, cocaine and morphine. Succeeding generations of lawmakers at both the state and federal levels have reaffirmed the basic policy. Rigid controls were extended by legislation to heroin, marihuana, and other psychoactive drugs. For more than six decades, a consistent pattern has been followed.[11] This firm decision restricting availability of dependence-producing substances contrasts with a continuing ambivalence about the appropriate public posture toward individuals who, despite society's efforts, have become dependent on prohibited or restricted substances (2).

The policy the United States follows today took form at the beginning of this century when federal legislators decided to regulate the purity of food and drugs (6) and began the crusade against the general distribution of narcotic substances (1). The right and power of Congress to pass such laws was immediately challenged and was ultimately upheld by the Supreme Court, which stated that Congress had the right not only to pass laws that regulated commerce among the

---

[10] Cocaine, already a Schedule II drug, was also a topic for Congressional oversight hearings.

[11] This pattern was followed with a single, albeit significant, exception: alcohol.

states and with foreign countries but also to keep the channels of commerce free from illicit or harmful products that might be injurious to the public (11). Subsequent Supreme Court decisions cautioned that they would not extend the scope of the law beyond the point where Congress indicated it would go because of "a regard for purpose to touch phases of the lives and health of people which in circumstances of modern industrialism are largely beyond self-protection..." (3).

Penalties were secondary, and the protection of the public health primary, under the Food and Drug Act. Under the Opium Act, the concern focused on the control of drug traffic and the prevention of abuse. These two rationales, prevention and enforcement, are the same rationales that today complement and compete for federal attention and funding.

Every Presidential administration since the turn of the century has acknowledged the antinarcotic consensus in this country and has furthered the goal of attempting to exclude harmful products from the flow of American commerce. The system has never been perfect or wholly effective, being limited by technical knowledge on the one hand and political and economic pressures on the other.

AN OUTLINE OF CONTEMPORARY STATUTES

The basic legislative statement of current policy on reducing use of illicit drugs is found in the Comprehensive Drug Abuse Prevention and Control Act of 1970 (the Comprehensive Act) (15), and the legal basis for current strategy of control and enforcement is found in the Controlled Substances Act (16). The Comprehensive Act has recently been extended to include the Forfeiture Act (25) and the Psychotropic Substances Act (26).

1. The Controlled Substances Act (Public Law 91-513): (a) stated, in the opinion of Congress, the reason for the legislation; (b) defined certain operative terms such as "addict" and "controlled substances"; (c) established the Commission on Marihuana and Drug Abuse[12]; (d) increased the number of

enforcement personnel (now employed by the Drug Enforcement Administration); (e) created a list of products classified under each "schedule" of controlled substances, I, II, III, IV, or V; (f) provided rules for registration, denial, and suspension of registration of manufacturers, distributors, and dispensers; (g) established labeling and packaging requirements; (h) set quotas and means for adjustment of quotas; and, (i) defined offenses and set penalties.

2. The Psychotropic Substances Act (Public Law 95-633) (effective November 10, 1978): (a) stated, in the opinion of Congress, the reason for the legislation; (b) provided a procedure for amending the Controlled Substances Act to include a new or transferred substance consistent with the actions of the United Nations Commission on Narcotic Drugs; and (c) amended the law to avoid conflict with United States obligations under the International Convention of Psychotropic Substances.

3. The Forfeiture Act, Title III of the Psychotropic Substances Act of 1978 (effective November 10, 1978): (a) subjected the profits of illegal drug transactions to forfeiture; and, (b) extended forfeiture features of the Controlled Substances Act to include anything of value furnished or intended to be furnished illegally in exchange for controlled substances.

The prevention and rehabilitation aspects of drug policy were codified into law 2 years after the passage of the Comprehensive Act. The law was the Drug Abuse Office and Treatment Act of 1972 (17), which created the Special Action Office for Drug Abuse Prevention (18), the National Advisory Council for Drug Abuse Prevention (19), and the National Institute on Drug Abuse (20).

4. The Drug Abuse Office and Treatment Act of 1972, (Public Law 92–255) (effective March 21, 1972): (a) stated in the opinion of Congress, the reason for the legislation; (b) created the Special Action Office for Drug

---

[12] The commission was mandated to conduct a study of marihuana use; sources of arrests and convictions; users and nature of use; an evaluation of existing marihuana

laws; a study of the pharmacology of marihuana; the relationship of marihuana use to behavior and crime, and to other drugs; and the international control of marihuana. After 1 year, the commission was obligated to report to the President and to Congress on recommendations and proposals for legislation and administrative action. The first report of the National Commission was entitled *Marihuana: A Signal of Misunderstanding*, and the second report was *Drug Use In America: Problem in Perspective*.

Abuse Prevention[13]; (c) created the National Advisory Council for Drug Abuse Prevention; (d) set out National Drug Abuse Strategy and created a Strategy Council; (e) provided grants to states for drug abuse prevention and control; (f) created the National Drug Abuse Training Center; and (g) created the National Institute on Drug Abuse (NIDA).[14]

THE EDUCATIONAL VEHICLE: NATIONAL INSTITUTE ON DRUG ABUSE (NIDA)

The National Institute on Drug Abuse was established for a specific educational purpose described in its implementing legislation (20):

There is established the National Institute on Drug Abuse . . . to administer the programs . . . of the Secretary of Health, Education, and Welfare . . . with respect to drug abuse prevention functions . . . develop and conduct comprehensive health, education, training, research, and planning programs for the prevention and treatment of drug abuse and for the rehabilitation of drug abusers.

NIDA does not function in isolation. It coordinates its efforts with the other two institutes that are part of the Alcohol, Drug Abuse and Mental Health Administration (ADAMHA), the National Institute on Alcohol Abuse and Alcoholism and the National Institute on Mental Health. NIDA activities are reviewed annually by Congress when its funding is renewed. The Senate Committee on Labor and Human Resources, which oversees the NIDA budget, has said:

Ordinarily for programs of such imperative importance serving a compelling need (especially since these programs have been under a one year extension for fiscal year 1979), the Committee would recommend a longer extension to insure program continuity and to foster long range planning at the Federal, State and local levels.

---

[13] The Special Action Office was phased out and its functions taken over by the Office of Drug Abuse Policy (ODAP) under Public Law 94-237, March 19, 1976. Under the Reorganization Act of 1977, 91 Stat. 1633, ODAP was abolished and its over-all functions assigned directly to the Executive Office of the President, Domestic Policy Staff.

[14] NIDA now exists as part of the Alcohol, Drug Abuse and Mental Health Administration (ADAMHA) since the passage of Public Law 93-282, the Comprehensive Alcohol Abuse and Alcoholism Prevention, Treatment and Rehabilitation Act Amendments of 1974.

The Committee has determined not to follow this pattern in this situation because of serious concern in both Houses of Congress concerning potential modifications of NIDA funding and management techniques, and *because of the need for continued oversight and possibly legislative changes to assist NIDA and the Domestic Policy Staff in adjusting to meet changing patterns of drug abuse in this country* (emphasis added) (27).

FEDERAL POLICY IS SOLIDIFIED THROUGH INTERAGENCY COOPERATION

Federal strategy for drug abuse and drug traffic prevention is assessed annually by the Strategy Council on Drug Abuse, first created by the Drug Abuse Office and Treatment Act of 1972 (23). The Strategy Council represents the agencies involved with drug abuse control: the Department of Justice; the Department of Health and Human Services; the Department of the Treasury; the Department of State; the Department of Defense; the Veterans Administration; and the Office of Management and Budget. There are also six members from outside the government on the council.

There are working groups within the Strategy Council that include representatives of other agencies of the federal government: The Drug Enforcement Administration and the Criminal Division of the Department of Justice, the United States Customs Service, the Federal Bureau of Investigation and Internal Revenue Service of the Treasury.

The Council also has contact with the American Medical Association and the National Board of Medical Examiners as well as specialty boards for improving drug and alcohol abuse education.

In 1979, the goals of the Strategy Council were expressed by reinvoking the words of President Carter's August 1977 Message to Congress on Drug Abuse (7):

We must set realistic objectives, giving our foremost attention domestically to those drugs that pose the greatest threat to health and to our ability to reduce crime.

My goals are to discourage all drug abuse in America—and also discourage the excessive use of alcohol and tobacco—and to reduce to a minimum the harm drug abuse causes when it does occur.

No government can completely protect its citizens from all harm—not by legislation, or by medicine, or by advice. Drugs cannot be forced out of existence . . . But the harm caused by drug abuse can be reduced. We cannot talk in absolutes—that drug abuse will cease . . . we know that is beyond our power.

CONGRESSIONAL SOURCES FOR PUBLIC POLICY ON SUBSTANCE ABUSE

The Budget

One good indication of current policy trends is an examination of what Congress is willing to fund. When a bill is passed by Congress, it contains an authorized funding amount, a dollar figure Congress deems adequate to implement the new law. The new program is written into the proper agency's budget for the following fiscal year, and it receives its actual appropriation from that budget process.

The budget of the United States is an annual road map of priorities. In the President's yearly budget proposal, priorities are set out, and then Congress uses the President's proposal as a guideline in its hearings and debates. The budget relates two important elements: economic policy and priorities, and the relationship between the public sector and private institutions and citizenry.[15]

An example of the budget process' effect on drug abuse strategy may be seen in funding for NIDA. The Administration recommended for fiscal year 1980 that NIDA grants be consolidated with those under the Comprehensive Alcohol legislation and some other federal programs. The Senate Committee on Labor and Human Resources disagreed and opted to protect the independence of NIDA and to avoid a possible reduction in the money available for drug abuse preven-

tion and treatment.[16] The recommendation accompanied the report of the Committee on its authorization for funding. The "power of the purse" was, therefore, used to effect substantive policy.

Congressional Perceptions

The Senate committee also shapes policy with respect to particular types of drugs. It can create or dissipate a "problem." This can be seen with respect to heroin. The Committee wrote, in 1979 (27):

The heroin epidemic of the late 1960's, which originally focused federal attention on the widespread abuse of narcotics and other drugs, has passed crisis stage.

Heroin, a narcotic synthesized from morphine, was widely accepted at the turn of the century for relief of pain and was not recognized as an addictive substance for several years. The Harrison Narcotic Act of 1914 was the first comprehensive effort to control the use of heroin in the United States. Concurrently, the international community was devoting increased attention to the control of heroin use through treaties and domestic legislation. At the present time, no one can really say whether the heroin problem has ended or to what extent the "crisis" has passed. Perhaps one could question whether heroin was really ever a "crisis" given the lack of verifiable statistical information concerning "the problem." Public policy has determined the level of concern, primarily on a nonstatistical, emotional basis.

The general response to the management of abuse is still crisis oriented.

Committee Action

On July 29, 1976, the House of Representatives voted overwhelmingly to create the Select Committee on Narcotics Abuse and Control,[17] an entity within Congress with jurisdiction to oversee all facets of the federal

---

[15] Congress follows budget procedures set out in the Congressional Budget and Impoundment Act of 1974 (Public Law 93-344). Requests for appropriations are first considered by the House Appropriations Committee through its specialized subcommittees. The Ways and Means Committee reviews proposed revenue measures, and the two committees then recommend action to be taken by the full House. As they are approved, the bills are forwarded to the Senate, where a similar procedure is carried out. In case of disagreement, a conference committee is established with members of both the House and the Senate. The conference report is sent to both Houses for approval, and, when agreed to, the budget is sent to the President for his approval or veto. Once this process is complete, the budget becomes the basis for agency operations for the next fiscal year.

[16] The President's budget proposed to transmit at a later date a request for an additional $99 million for a consolidated mental health, alcoholism and drug abuse formula grant. The committee wanted the funds allocated during the regular budget process without consolidating that part of the ADAMHA budget.

[17] The vote to create the Select Committee lead to House Resolution 77, which was unanimously passed on January 11, 1977.

narcotics effort (9) and coordinate the response of the seven legislative committees in the House each with jurisdiction over narcotics.[18] The House Select Committee is rather unique. Unlike a standing committee such as Labor and Human Resources in the Senate, it was established with investigative and fact-finding jurisdiction only (10), which means it cannot authorize funding and may only act in a supportive capacity to the seven standing committees that have jurisdiction to legislate in the narcotics area.[19] The Select Committee, instructed to conduct a continuing and comprehensive study and review of the problems of narcotics abuse and control, has stated that there is a serious lack of reliable information about the extent of drug use and users (9):

We are still suffering from the paucity of reliable information about the extent of drug use, the number of addicts and users, and the amount of drugs being smuggled into the United States. The total absence of reliable statistics and abuse patterns, incidence and prevalence of drug abuse, the lack of available information on the supply of drugs in either host or victim nations makes intelligent assessment of the problems extremely difficult. Congress cannot legislate effectively or provide resources that would better combat the problem without reliable data on these topics.

ROLE OF THE WHITE HOUSE IN SUBSTANCE ABUSE POLICY

The White House plays a major role in drug abuse public policy in two ways. It supports the Domestic Policy Staff Drug Policy Office that leads the Executive Branch drug efforts, and it creates policy by entering into Executive Agreements and Treaties with other countries for drug abuse control.[20] The activities of the White House may not be immediately noticeable insofar as they tend to guide policy rather than implement it. At the President's urging, the Drug Policy Office may lobby Congress to pass certain antiabuse legislation or appropriate funds for a particular antiabuse program. The President may also convene meetings and press conferences and call attention to issues, and the agencies may be requested to spend some of their discretionary funds in a remedial way. Depending upon the issue and the President, the Drug Policy Office will be more or less successful in leading substance abuse prevention, treatment, or control policy.

EFFECT OF INTERNATIONAL PROGRAMS ON NATIONAL EFFORTS

The United States has treaty obligations under the Single Convention on Narcotic Drugs of 1961.[21] Those treaty obligations are as binding on the United States as laws passed by Congress.

The Economic and Social Council (ECO-SOC) of the United Nations, in July 1958, decided to convene a conference for the adoption of a unified convention on narcotic drugs to replace with one document the existing multilateral treaties in the field and to make provision for the control of the production of raw materials. The treaty was designed to impact on the agricultural countries of the world involved in production of narcotic drugs.

Seventy-three nations were represented at the conference, as were many international

---

[18] The seven committees are: The Committee on Armed Services, the Committee on Government Operations, the Committee on International Relations, the Committee on Interstate and Foreign Commerce, the Committee on the Judiciary, the Committee on Merchant Marine and Fisheries, and the Committee on Ways and Means.

[19] The Senate, observing the specialized functioning of the House Select Committee, considered creating its own Select Committee on Narcotics Abuse and Control during the 96th Congress, under Senate Resolution 207. The resolution, however, was not brought to a vote.

[20] Executive Agreements do not require consent of the Senate and may, therefore, go further in conforming to international rather than solely national approaches to abuse problems.

[21] As of September 1978, the following 108 countries were parties to the 1961 Convention: Afghanistan; Algeria; Argentina; Australia; Bahamas; Bangladesh; Barbados; Belgium; Benin; Brazil; Bulgaria; Burma; Byeloruseian SSR; Canada; Chad; Chile; Colombia; Costa Rica; Cuba; Cyprus; Czechoslovakia; Denmark; Dominican Republic; Ecuador; Egypt; Ethiopia; Fiji; Finland; France; Gabon; German Democratic Republic; German Federal Republic; Ghana; Greece; Guatemala; Guinea; Haiti; Holy See; Honduras; Hungary; Iceland; India; Indonesia; Iran; Iraq; Israel; Italy; Ivory Coast; Jamaica; Japan; Jordan; Kenya; Kuwait; Lao People's Democratic Republic; Lebanon; Lesotho; Luxembourg; Madagascar; Malawi; Mali; Malaysia; Mauritius; Mexico; Monaco; Morocco; Netherlands; New Zealand; Nicaragua; Niger; Nigeria; Norway; Pakistan; Panama; Paraguay; Peru; Philippines; Poland; Portugal; Republic of Korea; Romania; Saudi Arabia; Senegal; Singapore; Socialist Republic of Viet-Nam; South Africa; Spain; Sri Lanka; Sudan; Sweden; Switzerland; Syrian Arab Republic; Thailand; Togo; Tongo; Trinidad and Tobago; Tunisia; Turkey; Ukrainian SSR; USSR; United Kingdom; United Republic of Camaroon; United States of America; Upper Volta; Uraguay; Venezuela; Yugoslavia; Zaire; and Zambia.

organizations. The United States ratified the treaty and formally became a participant in 1967. Despite the level of international cooperation and enthusiasm behind the Single Convention, it is now clear that neither this treaty nor any other will be able to stop illicit heroin traffic.

There are other treaties that look to different objectives, however, such as the Psychotropic Substances Convention, which was the product of the United Nations Conference for the Adoption of a Protocol on Psychotropic Substances, held in Vienna in 1971. The convention is the first international instrument adopted for the purpose of addressing the abuse of psychotropic substances and the illicit traffic that is created by such abuse. The convention defined the area of psychotropics to include hallucinogens, amphetamine, barbiturates, and tranquilizers.

The most significant difference between the Single Convention and the Psychotropic Substances Convention is not the substances they address but the nations focused upon in the control effort. The latter treaty requires the cooperation of the governments of the most advanced countries in the world, the countries producing the psychotropics, whether or not they are in agreement with the treaty or even are members of the United Nations. As international law is established, it becomes the law for all nations.

The United States is not currently a party to the psychotropic treaty, which became effective in 1976 upon the ratification of the required number of nations.[22] The United States was a leading advocate of the convention during its drafting stages, seeing it as a major effort toward the international control of drugs that, although having legitimate medical uses, were sold in an illicit market for nonmedical purposes. It was anticipated that the treaty's requirement that nations adhere to the decisions of the Commission on Narcotic Drugs rather than follow their own

laws would delay or even preclude participation of most of the technologically advanced nations. At one time, the United States was in a position to affect the success of the treaty because many Western European nations had agreed to participate in the convention once the United States agreed to its terms. However, as time passed, France, both Germanys, Spain, and Greece ratified the treaty, as did the Scandinavian nations and several members of the Soviet bloc. American participation would probably trigger entry of the United Kingdom but would not otherwise significantly affect participation in the international community.

The Psychotropic Substances Convention has been endorsed by the Department of State (8), the Office of Management and Budget (29), the Office of Drug Abuse Policy (8), the Department of Justice (29), the Department of Health and Human Services (29), and others.

It is possible for this country to enter into the treaty agreement "with reservation" so that the fully participating nations would be aware of United States objections and limitations. It is likely that the Senate will consent to the treaty with reservation and that the United States will more formally participate in convention goals. Should the treaty ultimately be rejected by the Senate, the United States would continue cooperating informally as it does now.

The treaty is not self-implementing in the United States, which means that, in addition to the Senate giving its advice on and consent to participation in this international agreement, both houses of Congress must agree to make the appropriate changes in existing United States laws to meet the requirements of the convention. Such legislative approval to amend United States laws was given in 1978 (24), after several years of debate.

However, another roadblock is hindering the actual participation of the United States in the Psychotropic Substances Convention: the Senate has not been able to schedule debate to give its advice and consent, as required by the United States Constitution for all treaties in which the United States takes part. Until such time, the United States will continue to cooperate informally with international drug traffic control efforts in substances covered by this convention and other earlier multilateral and bilateral treaties.

---

[22] Nations participating in the Convention on Psychotropic Substances, September, 1978: Algeria; Argentina; Barbados; Benin; Brazil; Bulgaria; Chile; Costa Rica; Cuba; Cyprus; Denmark; Dominican Republic; Ecuador; Egypt; Finland; France; German Democratic Republic; German Federal Republic; Greece; Guyana; Holy See; Iceland; India; Iraq; Jordan; Lesotho; Madagascar; Mauritius; Mexico; Monaco; Nicaragua; Norway; Pakistan; Paraguay; Phillipines; Poland; Republic of Korea; Saudi Arabia; Senegal; South Africa; Spain; Sweden; Syrian Arab Republic; Thailand; Togo; Tonga; Uruguay; Venezuela; Yugoslavia; Zaire.

Some of the arguments the Senate will hear against ratification will be the same as those heard when the issue of whether or not to amend American law was debated. For example, the convention requires that controls be initiated on four schedules of drugs, schedules very similar to those in the Controlled Substances Act. Drugs and substances can be added to the schedules after full examination by the international Commission on Narcotic Drugs. But just how drugs would be added is unresolved, as is the method for review of the commission's decision. Who shall be heard and whether such a "hearing" will be meaningful are questions that go to the essence of American law making and Constitutional due process protections. The issue of a right to a hearing is important, because the convention will not only curb the illicit use of controlled substances but create a concurrent limitation on the availability of these drugs for medical research.

The National Commission on Marihuana and Drug Abuse discussed the deficiencies in the convention (13):

It is particularly important that international controls not interfere with legitimate scientific and medical research. Certain drugs, for example, have become difficult to obtain for research purposes ... The Commission urges that the international system of controls promote needed research and establish an environment in which the responsible researcher can function unimpaired by needless restrictions.

[T]he Convention would interfere improperly with United States domestic law, imposing record-keeping requirements contrary to those in the Comprehensive Drug Abuse Prevention and Control Act of 1970 and possibly placing drugs under domestic control without the approval of the Secretary of Health, Education, and Welfare.

Despite such problems, it seems that Congressional and Executive sentiment presently favors formal adoption of the convention.

CONCLUSION

Federal policy on substance abuse is increasingly originating from administrative initiative rather than new legislation. With perhaps the most controversial new area in substance abuse, prescription drug abuse, there has been Congressional concern expressed but no mandate to change the present system.

It seems that the administrative agencies may attempt to place new controls on prescription distribution through application of existing legislative authority. Such attempts have the potential to increase considerably the role of the federal government in the physician's practice in addition to that presently existing under the Controlled Substances Act.

Perhaps the most crucial issue facing policy makers, both in Congress and the federal agencies, is the lack of reliable data on which to base changes of the existing system for the better. Until such data are available, along with the definitional basics needed to collect these data, it is unlikely that a coherent policy on prescription drug abuse will arise from legislative activity.

References

1. Act to Prohibit Importation and Use of Opium, 1909.
2. Bonnie, R. J., and Sonnenreich, M. R. *Legal Aspects of Drug Dependence*, p. 3. Cleveland, Ohio, CRC Press, 1975.
3. 62 Cases, More or Less, Each Containing Six Jars of Jam versus U.S., 71 S.Ct. 515, 340 U.S. 593, 95 L.Ed. 566, 1951.
4. Davis, K. C. 1 Administrative Law Treatise §1:9.
5. *Drug Abuse, Data Systems, and Regulatory Decisions*. Medicine in the Public Interest, 1978.
6. Federal Food and Drugs Act of 1906, Ch. 3915, 34 Stat. 768, 1906.
7. *Federal Strategy for Drug Abuse and Drug Traffic Prevention*, (No. 052-003-00640-5), p. 2. Washington, D.C., United States Government Printing Office, 1979.
8. Hearing before the House Subcommittee on Health and the Environment of the Committee on Interstate and Foreign Commerce, House of Representatives, 95th Congress, 2d Session, on H.R. 9796, No. 95–99, February 17, 1978.
9. House of Representatives, Select Committee on Narcotics Abuse and Control. *Annual Report for the Year 1978*. House Report 95-1832, p. vii. 95th Congress, 2d Session, p. 50, 1978.
10. House Resolution 77, 95th Congress, 1st Session, January 11, 1977.
11. McDermott versus Wisconsin, 33 S.Ct. 431, 228 U.S. 115, 57 L.Ed. 754, 1913.
12. National Commission on Marihuana and Drug Abuse. *Marihuana: A Signal of Misunderstanding*. Washington, D.C., United States Government Printing Office, 1972.
13. National Commission on Marihuana and Drug Abuse. *Drug Use in America: Problem in Perspective*. Washington, D.C., United States Government Printing Office, 1973.
14. President's Commission on Mental Health. *Report*

of the President's Commission on Mental Health, vol. 3. Appendix, *Task Panel Reports*, pp. 1048–1049. Washington, D.C., United States Government Printing Office, 1978.

15. Public Law 91-513, October 27, 1970, 84 Stat. 1242; 21 U.S.C.A. Sections 801 et. seq.

16. Public Law 91-513. 21 U.S.C.A. Sections 812 et. seq.

17. Public Law 92-255, March 21, 1972, 86 Stat. 66; 21 U.S.C.A. Sections 1101 et seq.

18. Public Law 92-255. 21 U.S.C.A. Sections 1111 through 1123.

19. Public Law 92-255. 21 U.S.C.A. Sections 1151 through 1155.

20. Public Law 92-255. 21 U.S.C.A. Sections 1191 through 1193.

21. Public Law 93-253, Section 1, 88 Stat. 50. 38 F.R. 15932, 87 Stat. 1091, as amended, March 16, 1974.

22. Public Law 93-253. Section 201(a)(1).

23. Public Law 94-237, 90 Stat. 241.

24. Public Law 95-633, 95th Congress, 2d Session, 1978.

25. Public Law 95-633. 21 U.S.C.A. Section 881.

26. Public Law 95-633. 21 U.S.C.A. Section 811(d).

27. Senate Report 96-104 to accompany S.525, 96th Congress, 1st. Session, April 30, 1979, p. 7.

28. Udall versus Tallman, 380 U.S. 1, 1964.

29. *United States Code Congressional and Administrative News*, 95th Congress, 2d Session, vol. 7, pp. 9507–9511, 1978.

CHAPTER 48

WHY DO WE HAVE DRUG ABUSE?—ECONOMIC AND POLITICAL BASIS

Paul Lowinger, M.D.

The underlying causes of substance abuse in the United States today are social, economic, and political and are deeply rooted in American history. It is interesting to note that China, also the victim of a historic and monumental drug problem, was able to overcome its narcotic addiction in only 3 years, between 1949 and 1953. I will discuss how they did this later in this chapter.

In the United States, unemployment, poverty, racism, sexism, feelings of powerlessness, and alienation leading to breakdown of family and community life are the underlying causes of drug abuse. Many victims of these conditions are drawn into the drug culture to escape their painful reality. The constant media campaign of drug and liquor advertising creates a climate in which people feel that taking drugs is good for them. The advertising of legal drugs makes illegal drugs more attractive also. If legal drugs make you feel so good, think what illegal drugs might do for you!

Why is it so easy for Americans to become drug addicts: Partly because the United States government has passed laws that have made the narcotic business very profitable for police and officials (corrupt and otherwise) and, of course, for the powerful crime syndicate.

As Rufus King says in *The Drug Hang-up* (13): "...cops and pushers found themselves identically interested in squeezing the addict by cutting him off from possible help as a patient and have maintained a de facto partnership...."

Drug abuse became noticeable in the 19th century and is as American as apple pie according to recent Yale University reports (20, 21). In the early 19th century, transporting opium on American clipper ships from Turkey to China was big business (5, 6, 8, 33, 35). The first identifiable group of people to become addicted in the United States were Civil War soldiers who were given opium preparations when they were wounded, ill, or shell shocked (30).

Opium tinctures for medical purposes were widely sold to the public through drug and general stores after the Civil War. By 1878 a survey of opium use in Michigan recorded 7,763 "opium eaters," or one in every 200 people in the state (18). Strangely enough, this is close to the ratio of narcotic addicts in the population of Michigan in a 1971 survey (1). By the turn of the century a white housewife living in a small town had taken the place of the Civil War veteran as the average addict (30). Opium was used for common complaints like insomnia and menstrual cramps. By 1935, there had been another change. Heroin had taken over as the main drug of addiction. It was mostly injected by white males in their thirties living in medium size cities (3). After World War II, the typical addict was a poor black or Latino male in his teens or early twenties living in the ghetto of a large city. During the 1960's and 1970's the black addicts were joined by many young white males in flight from suburbia (15).

From 1914, the drug problem had been exacerbated by actions of the United States government, beginning with the Harrison Act. This act was the first attempt at opium prohibition. It required registration and record keeping by distributors of opium, including physicians and pharmacists, and provided for a small tax on opium sales. Beginning in 1915, the Treasury Department, which was charged with the enforcement of the Harrison Act, used this mild regulatory act to make criminals of narcotic addicts (14). By obtaining Supreme Court decisions, they made it virtually illegal for doctors to prescribe narcotics for addicts (20). Many physicians were arrested and some served penitentiary sentences because of enforcement of the Harrison Act. A new police force was created inside the Treasury Department to enforce the narcotics laws and also to enforce the new national prohibition of alcohol, the Volstead Act, passed in 1919. Although a criminal label had been placed on addicts by the Harrison Act, the United States Public Health Service opened 40 clinics across the country to treat them in 1919. These were medical clinics that offered maintenance on narcotics or gradual withdrawal programs for addicts. Immediately these clinics came under heavy attack by the Treasury Department, and all were closed by 1923 (20).

The main leader in the police activity against addicts, fanning the flames of hysteria and fear, was Harry Anslinger, who worked his way up to become the first Commissioner of Narcotics in 1930. Under Anslinger's regime, federal penalties and enforcement powers were increased in 1951 and again in 1956 and 1965. Anslinger was also determined to stamp out marihuana, claiming that marihuana use was the direct by-product of Mexican immigration. Anslinger managed to make marihuana illegal through legislation

on both the federal and state level in the 1930's (2).

The major beneficiary of government efforts to stop drug traffic was the creation of a very profitable illegal narcotic syndicate (Table 48.1) that boomed after World War II when Americans were suffering from the postwar problems in society (32, 34). Police and officials were often paid directly by the Mafia or syndicate (4, 9, 11, 17, 31, 36). It was easy to get illegal drugs if one could pay the price. Well publicized drug busts only led to more crime by addicts so they could pay the higher prices because of temporary scarcity (11). Narcotic addiction reached epidemic proportions in the 1960's as a part of the political and social unrest of that time. This is the epidemic that was still with us through the 1970's, with 640,000 using heroin (7).

Legal drugs currently are also overused and abused. One reason for this is the tremendous advertising campaign of drug companies to sell these drugs. They spend $4,000 to $5,000 on each of the 200,000 doctors, using direct sales by detail persons and other forms of advertising (24–26). Many of the legal drugs are over-the-counter drugs. A recent survey found that in a typical week of commercial television on one network, there were 152 messages encouraging the use of specific drugs (28). As a result, doctors overprescribe

Table 48.1
Revenues from the Rackets[a]

	Estimates in billions of dollars[b]	
	Gross	Net
Gambling	$38.0	$ 7.6
Loan sharking	[c]	10.0
Narcotics	5.0	4.0
Hijacking	1.5	1.2
Pornography and prostitution	2.0	1.7
Cigarette bootlegging	1.5	.8
Total	$48.0	$25.3

[a] Reprinted by permission from *Time*, The Weekly Newsmagazine; Copyright Time, Inc., 1977.
[b] Calculations based on data from the National Gambling Commission, the Drug Enforcement Administration, the Tobacco Tax Council, the Senate Small Business Committee, the New York State Commission of Investigation, and various law enforcement agencies.
[c] $2.5 to $3.5 billion loaned out at any given time.

because of patient demand. Drug company profits certainly are one powerful reason for drug abuse. Also, about one-half of the 12 billion amphetamine pills produced in the United States find their way to the illegal drug market (10). Other prescription drugs—like barbiturates, tranquilizers, and methaqualone—are also sold on the street illegally.

As I remarked before, China had an addiction problem—one that lasted for almost 200 years and involved an incredible 7 million to 80 million people, 2 to 20 per cent of the population. Today China is virtually drug free (16), and there are some things we might learn from the Chinese experience.

In the 19th century, China was forced into addiction by the Opium Wars. Contrary to popular belief, these wars—from 1839 to 1842—did not originate because China wanted to export opium. They began when China resisted England's demand to import opium in exchange for Chinese products—mostly tea, silk, and porcelain. China lost these wars, and among other indignities was forced to exchange its goods for opium.

As a result it became a highly narcotized country, a victim of ruthless Western economic and political policy. By 1850 an entire fifth of the revenue of the British government of India—the source of opium—came from Chinese consumption of this drug. By the 20th century, China produced its own opium to the profit of urban gangsters, regional warlords, and officials in the government of Chiang Kai-Shek. Punishment for addicts was severe, but opium remained ubiquitous and profitable despite prison sentences and executions of addicts.

In October of 1949, the People's Republic of China was proclaimed. Within a year the Communist Government instituted a comprehensive program designed to eliminate this threat to the nation. All evidence indicates that by 1953 the problem of narcotic drug abuse was practically eliminated.

One important factor was the changed ideology of the young people—no new supply of addicts was forthcoming. The changes in outlook included a redefinition of the nation and its youth, of their worth and role. Women were given the same rights as men. In rural areas this new definition was based on land distribution; collective farming; new educational, social, and vocational opportunities; and the election of local councils. In the cities it took the form of nationalization of commerce and industry, full employment, worker control, and the end of foreign domination. This total ideological transformation of the younger generation was accompanied by the reintegration of Chinese society through small street committees that offered political leadership.

Equally significant in the Chinese drive to eliminate narcotic addiction were its methods of plugging the source. China is 85 per cent rural, and an unknown but significant part of the land had been turned into poppy cultivation. The first major economic and political mass campaign of the government was land reform, and this aim was coordinated with elimination of poppy growth. Distribution of land from large landholders to landless peasants was accompanied by the need to convert the opium cash crops to badly needed food crops. Today China produces enough opium to meet its medical needs, but no more.

The borders were closed, but smuggled opium was still a source of the drug. China acted to stop this supply with a policy of "carrot and stick." Leniency was recommended for employees and workers of opium traffickers, but heavy penalties existed for those controlling the traffic, manufacture, or growth of opium. Twenty or 30 of the gang leaders who continued the opium traffic in Shanghai and other large cities were executed (12, 19, 22, 23, 29).

China's attitude toward the individual reformed addict was one of goodwilled congratulations; this represents another important reason why the narcotic probem was overcome. The rehabilitation of opium addicts began with their registration. Arrangements by city-wide antiopium committees for addict rehabilitation included treatment to break the habit at home, in clinics, and in hospitals.

At every stage of personal rehabilitation, the ideological motivation was stressed. Given China's attitudes, this ideology was strong on political, social, and economic information. China's policy was not simply to deprive a person of drugs, but to replace the need for narcotics with a forceful, national commitment. Equally significant, the former addict was fully accepted back into Chinese life without official stigma or prejudice.

Naturally, some questions have to be answered about the Chinese experiences, but the fact is that the Chinese have eliminated their narcotic addiction problem, in contrast to Chinese populations outside the People's Republic of China. For example, Hong Kong, with a population of 4 million, still has a severe narcotics problem, with 80,000 to 100,000 addicts (27). For us, the message of this Chinese solution of drug addiction is that the problem requires political and economic answers, but our solution has to be different. The Chinese experience cannot be used as an exact model for America in dealing with the drug problem. We cannot close our borders, plow under other countries' poppy crops, or control the habits of our people. Our individualistic society is less unified and more competitive and profit oriented than that of China.

An attack on drug abuse in the United States is futile unless the laws are changed to free drug addicts from criminal prosecution. Penalties must be removed from drug use, possession, and the transfer of personal amounts of all drugs, including narcotics. With the profit motive gone, the crime syndicate will have no incentive to push drugs and create new addicts. As for solving the problem of legal drug abuse, the prime action would be to ban all drug advertising in both professional and public media. Doctors and pharmacists should be well enough informed through their journals, meetings, and continuing education without the advertising directed at them. The public should learn about the role of drugs through community health education. But, most of all, the real issues that must be dealt with are the unemployment, poverty, racism, sexism, feelings of powerlessness, and alienation in our society.

References

1. An estimate of the narcotic population of Detroit. *FYI*. Lansing, Michigan Office of Drug Abuse, 1971.
2. Anslinger, H., Burroughs, W., Coburn, J., Dass, B., Fiedler, L., Finlator, J., Fort, J., Oteri, J., and Watts, A. Playboy panel: The drug revolution. Playboy 17: 53, February 1970.
3. Ball, J., and Chambers, C. D. *The Epidemiology of Opiate Addiction in the United States*. Springfield, Ill., Charles C Thomas, 1970.
4. Brecher, E. *Licit and Illicit Drugs*. New York, Consumers Union, 1973.
5. Collis, M. *Foreign Mind*. New York, W. W. Norton, 1946.
6. Dennett, T. *Americans in Eastern Asia*. New York, Macmillan, 1922.
7. Dupont, R., Goldstein, A., and O'Donnell, J. *Handbook on Drug Abuse*, National Institute on Drug Abuse, Monograph. Washington, D.C., United States Government Printing Office, 1979.
8. Fairbank, J. *Trade and Diplomacy on the China Coast*. Stanford, Calif., Stanford University Press, 1953.
9. Ginsberg, A. Documents on police bureaucracy's conspiracy against human rights of opiate addicts and Constitutional rights of medical profession causing mass breakdown of urban law and order. J. Psychedelic Drugs 4:104, 1971.
10. Grinspoon, L., and Hedbloom, P. *The Speed Culture*. Cambridge, Mass., Harvard University Press, 1975.
11. Holahan, J., and Henningsen, P. The economics of heroin. In *Dealing with Drug Abuse*, P. Wald, editor. New York, Praeger, 1972.
12. Kaplan, I., and Cole, M. How China got rid of drug addiction. In *China and Us*, vol. 3, p. 1. New York, United States-China Peoples Friendship Association, 1979.
13. King, R. *The Drug Hang-up*. New York, W. W. Norton, 1972.
14. Kramer, J. Introduction to the problem of heroin addiction in America. J. Psychedelic Drugs 4:15, 1971.
15. Levengoo, R., Lowinger, P., and Schooff, K. Heroin addiction in suburbs. Am. J. Public Health 63:209, 1973.
16. Lowinger, P. The solution to narcotic addiction in the People's Republic of China. Am. J. Drug Alcohol Abuse 4:165, 1977.
17. Maas, P. *The Valachi Papers*. New York, Bantam Books, 1968.
18. Marshall, O. The opium habit in Michigan. In *Narcotic Addiction*, J. O'Donnell and J. Ball, editors, pp. 45–54. New York, Harper & Row, 1966.
19. Mirsky, J. Heroin and China. New York Times, July 27, 1973.
20. Musto, D. *The American Disease*. New Haven, Conn., Yale University Press, 1973.
21. Musto, D., and Trachtenberg, A. As American as apple pie. Yale Alumni Magazine, 16, January, 1972.
22. Opium and China: New China kicked the habit. New York, United-States-China Peoples Friendship Association, 1974.
23. Rubenstein, A. How China got rid of opium. Monthly Rev. 58, October 1973.
24. Select Committee on Small Business, United States Senate, 92nd Congress, 1st Session, Part 2, July 21–23 and September 22, 1971. *Advertising of Proprietary Medicines Hearings*. Washington, D.C., United States Government Printing Office, 1971.
25. Select Committee on Small Business, United States Senate, 92nd Congress, 2nd Session, November 2, 1972. *Competitive Problems in the Drug Industry: Summary and Analysis*. Washington D.C., United States Government Printing Office, 1971.
26. Select Committee on Small Business, United States Senate, 96th Congress, 1st Session, September 20, 1979. *Competitive Problems in the Drug Industry: Psychotropic Drugs Summary and Analysis*. Washington, D.C., United States Government Printing Office, 1979.
27. Singer, K. *The Prognosis of Narcotic Addiction*. Boston, Butterworth, 1975.

28. Smith, F., Trivax, G., Zuehlke, D., Lowinger, P., and Nghiem, T. Health information during a week of television. N. Engl. J. Med. 286:516, 1972.
29. Southwell, N. Kicking the habit. New China 1:24, 1975.
30. Terry, C., and Pellens, M. *The Opium Problem.* Montclair, N. J., Patterson Smith 1970.
31. *The Knapp Commission Report on Police Corruption.* New York, George Braziller, 1972.
32. The Mafia: Big, bad and booming. Time 32, May 16, 1977.
33. *The Opium Trail.* Boston, New England Free Press, 1972.
34. There are people who say, "Well, business is business." Forbes 19, April 1, 1970.
35. Waley, A. *The Opium War through Chinese Eyes.* Stanford, Calif., Stanford University Press, 1958.
36. Walinsky, A. The Knapp connection. Village Voice, March 1, 1973.

CHAPTER 49

THE CRIMINAL JUSTICE SYSTEM AND THE USER[1]

Peter K. Manning, Ph.D.

Approaches to the control of the use of substances with remarkable effects on human consciousness or behavior are culturally, societally, and historically variable. Cultures, over time, have altered their approaches to control, as can be seen in the changing use of Kava among Polynesians (13). Societies develop quite different formal control strategies, as can be seen by observing the quite striking cyclical attempts by the British government to control the production and use of gin in the 18th and 19th centuries. Some societies and cultures possess relatively stable, semipermanent modes of substance control, but they are, in Levi-Strauss' terms, "frozen" or "cold" societies resistant to social change. As a general rule, however, one can argue that all societies make some effort to control the degree of access to, use of, and forms and amounts of available "feel good substances" (2). In relatively sacred societies, taboos, ceremonies, rituals, and holy offices may control the consumption of these substances, whereas in industrializing societies, where sacredness is diminished, more secular controls are developed. These controls may be of the same *form* as those found in sacred societies, but the content differs. Whereas priests and ruling classes controlled access to coca in Inca society, modern-day Peru controlled by analogously powerful class and status groups regulates access to coca by law. In industrializing and industrialized societies, the law serves the semisacred function of prohibition and control. It marks the attempt of industrial societies to circumscribe use.

The law in industrialized societies is a reflection of class interests working in some complex fashion through interest groups, elections, corruption, and media filtration. The law in practice contains a historical archaeology of competing, conflicting, disparate laws and regulations, reflections of historical interests and needs. Law, although seen from the outside as a sacred practice, is more and more a complex formulation of particular interests, in particular those of the government and the largest corporations. (This is not to argue that the interests of these corporations or of "government" are themselves coherent and consistent. They are not.) The application of various laws is *problematic*, in part because of the large number of laws involved. In the drug control field with respect to controlled substances, there are

[1] The research reported here was supported by the Law Enforcement Assistance Administration in the form of a Visiting Fellowship (NILECJ Grant #N1-74-99-029) to Dr. Manning in 1974–75 and a grant to the Research Triangle Institute, Jay R. Williams, Principal Investigator (NILECJ Grant #N1-76-99-109, 1976–78). Lawrence J. Redlinger, Manning, and Williams were responsible for the conduct of the Research Triangle Institute grant and were authors of the final report (28).

some 900 federal statutes bearing on control. The number of state laws is unknown and perhaps unknowable. The number of agencies of various kinds involved (federal, state, county, municipal, and ad hoc task forces at various levels) exceeds 17,000, and the *mandate* of each agency implicated in the enforcement of these laws is negotiable.

Social control in mass industrialized societies does not emerge in the context of traditional mores and folkways that guide the application of sanctions. Rather, it takes the form of negotiation between the agents of control, their significant supporting audiences, and their target groups. Negotiation implies a selective, active discretionary choosing of targets, levels of enforcement, expenditures, and desired outcomes. Lemert (13) captured the implications of this notion of "active social control" for the phenomenon being controlled:

> The implications of active social control for deviation are not easily stated in systematic form, but they can be made apparent by applying an ends-means, schema, qualified by costs and other factors, to the agencies and agents of social control. Agencies of social control . . . when operating in areas of value conflict and in situations complicated by technological change . . . select from and implement values in variable ways. The norms that individual agents of social control within are called upon to enforce or follow frequently become functional alternatives to ends. Such individuals seek to gain conformity to norms they do not share, or ignore those they do not share, depending upon the availability of means of control, the costs of action, and the competition of values within and outside the control agency. Unless such factors are known in particular situations, it is impossible to determine what norms will be invoked to define a given behavior, or class of behavior, as deviant and to attach the behavior to persons.

Shifts in political pressures, in community structure, and in the agencies themselves produce changes in the level and kind of enforcement of drug laws (3, 29). More importantly, the *degree* of discretion left to individual agents is very wide. In one sense, the sacralization of the law and of administrative agency structures has concealed the wide variation in practices within agencies and between agents in the same agencies. The reification of social control reveals and conceals, but on the whole the social science investigation of the police enforcement of drug laws has only begun to reveal the patterning of enforcement and the impacts of enforcement upon the user.

This chapter is a preliminary overview of local drug enforcement based upon several years' study of some eight units in the United States, encompassing several types of data, and focused on the impact of police strategies and tactics upon drug markets.[2] Although the field work undertaken in connection with this grant was aimed at an understanding of the patterns of reaction of control agencies, primarily the municipal police, it included data on special task forces, other locally based agencies and prosecutor's offices, and data on the interconnection of use and distribution of drugs and the control system.

It is clear that in some subtle way the market effects the control system and that the control system effects the market (24, 25). In an important fashion the constraints of the law, of information, of the market, and of the organizational structure of local police departments would seem multiply to determine the arena in which the narcotic officer ("the narc") operates. He is reduced to operating in microarenas of interaction characterized by duplicity, lying, fraud, misrepresentation, and extortion. These little patterns of interpersonal conduct are referred to here as the narcs' game. The user participates and shares in the pleasures of the narcs' game and, indeed, is the necessary condition for the game itself.

---

[2] The following discussion of the impact of narcotics police enforcement strategies on the market and use of drugs is based on our work in eight narcotics units in six metropolitan areas in the United States in 1976 to 1978. Five of the units were studied intensively for 6 weeks to 6 months; three were studied from periods of 1 week to a month. All were located in metropolitan areas of more than 500,000 persons with major self-defined drug problems, and the units ranged in size from 13 to 61 members at the time of the research. The data gathered included *interviews* ranging from 20 minutes to 3 hours with officers and supervisory personnel in each of the units. The interviews covered career lines, past and present investigations, objectives, strategies and tactics of the officer and of the unit as a whole, priorities in drugs considered as problematic, and levels and kinds of cases and informants worked and being worked at present. *Field work* involved observations and detailed note taking focused on *key episodes*: interrogation of suspects and informants, search and arrest warrant serving ("raids"), squad and unit meetings, and informal socialization on and off the job. *Official records* were obtained from each department, although the number and kinds of records gathered and used are variable.

THE LAW AND THE POLICE MANDATE

Since the early 20th century, American law has been aimed at criminalization of the process of use, distribution, and manufacture of selected drugs in an attempt to make illicit narcotics unavailable (the eradication approach) or to make them available only at severely inflated prices to a vastly restricted clientele (the containment approach) (7, 9, 14, 22). Although attempts were made recently by federal agencies, such as Office of Drug Abuse Law Enforcement (ODALE), Narcotics Treatment Administration (NTA), Special Action Office for Drug Abuse Prevention (SAODAP), National Institute on Drug Abuse, among others, to reduce demand (principally through methadone maintenance programs), narcotics control has aimed in the most general terms to immobilize dealers and/or to intervene in the distribution process either to inflate costs or to disrupt or interdict supply.

In the past, the assumption has been that the corrective control model of substance control adequately captured the dynamics of the law enforcement approach to control. In simplest terms, it was assumed that the actions of the control agencies were a direct reflection of some legally stated legislative intent, that this intent was translated as "policy" or operating procedures in law enforcement agencies, and that these policies when implemented served to control the law violating behavior at issue. At very least, it did not *amplify* or increase the behavior targeted, and enforcement worked in at least three ways: to deter the potential violator, to control the actual violator by increasing the difficulty or operational costs associated with carrying out the crime, and to punish those captured. In a further extension of this model, violators were to be adjudged, and, where appropriate, punishment or retribution would be demanded. It has been frequently noted that in the case of economic or transactional crimes, those where a market provides satisfactions for participants, "profits" in a more precise sense, and affirms certain life style preferences, values, and culturally affirmed norms, legal controls tend to be limited in effect. A number of scholars analyzing the effects of legal control of drugs, especially the opiates in North America, argue that this corrective control model is very misleading. They have identified a few of the consequences of adopting the corrective control model and the legal-prohibition approach to suppressing the use of selected drugs: (a) A black market is created with higher prices, illegal practices, and low quality goods. (b) Legal markets in analogous substances are protected. (c) The user is stigmatized and barred from legitimate kinds of work and opportunities. (d) A corrupt enforcement structure is made more likely. (e) Conflicting paradigms of treatment, education, and punishment are established. (f) Legal protection and many other social services are denied users. (g) Courts are clogged with minor offenders, costs of processing and prosecution are escalated, and courts become more likely to deal with cases in "batches" through plea bargaining and to make other "efficient" adjustments.

These negative consequences of the prohibition model—so well documented by the works of Lindesmith (14), Blumberg (1), Kaplan (12), Skolnick (27), Musto (22), and Helmer (9)—are well known. The creation and amplification of police power and discretion have not been equally well illuminated. However, the suggestive works of Skolnick (27), Wilson (31), DeFleur (3), Gould et al. (6), and Johnson and Bogomolny (11) describe in detail how the police *work* within the legal prohibition mandate, the structure of departmental rules and procedures, and occupational norms and understandings to maximize their own advantage. This playing for one's advantage is called the narcs' game (17, 28).

The self-serving aspects of the narcs' game take place within a structural context that must be outlined before we can examine the consequences, structural and social-psychological, that are associated with the narcs' game. The context has conveniently six main aspects: the market as an economic, political and cultural system; the law guiding drug law enforcement; the strategies and tactics of enforcement; and the organizational rewards, justifications, and ends. These are each *constraints* upon the enforcement of drug laws, and they produce the agent-centered police work that has been frequently observed. Although there are exceptions to this generalization, the controlling decisions of the agent shape fatefully the risks to the user. It is these risks that are described by example in the final section of this chapter.

A CHARACTERIZATION OF THE CONTEXT OF THE NARCS' GAME[3]

Narcotics are traded like other commodities, and, like other illicit products, its markets share several structural properties in common with markets for licit commodities. Both involve willing buyers and sellers; the buyers make demands for goods and services and the sellers provide them in exchange for reimbursement. In both illicit and licit markets, the sellers attempt to make a profit and ideally to maximize that profit. Both types of market are regulated by agencies whose mission it is to do so, and both types of markets have sellers within them who seek effective control over the manner and type of regulations that will be applied to them. However, on the other hand, the *moral intent* of regulation of illicit markets is to *eradicate* or suppress them rather than merely to regulate them. The personnel involved in the regulation of legitimate markets owe *loyalty* to the market process itself and are, therefore, interchangeable between regulatory agencies and the regulated. This credibility is denied dealers in illicit markets. Rather than guiding the market, the intent of the application of sanctions to illicit markets is to accomplish virtual *cessation*; the process of sanctioning tends to move in the direction of absolute sanctions and punishment and the villification of enforcement targets (18, 19, 25).

Unlike other crimes that involve a complainant, narcotics is a transactional offense with implicit agreement between the parties involved (at least a priori). Enforcement depends on information concerning the transactions. Analogously, information about information (meta-information)—where to fall on possible users and thus to threaten them with a charge unless they inform, where prostitutes work who are known users or who associate with known users, information on feuds that might trigger revenge against a dealer—must be attended to. Informants, often users or dealers themselves (some with charges pending for narcotics offenses) and others involved in or on the fringes of the drug world (prostitutes and small time property criminals), are essential to enforcement.[4]

---

[3] The term "narc" apparently is derived in some way from the old English expression, "Nark," which referred to a spy employed by the police. The term now refers primarily to drug police, although it is not in national use. In the Western United States (especially in California), such police units are called "narco units," but officers nowhere in the country refer to themselves as "narcs." I was not aware of this when I began the study, and even through the early weeks of the study I continued to use the term to refer to my study and to the officers I interviewed and observed. Drug users, on the other hand, do refer to police drug officers as "narcs" (although, of course, there are local variants such as a "roller," the expression in Washington, D.C., for a police officer). The term has negative connotations to users and is not used by officers. It has a nice ring to it, so I continue to use it (17). The irony of its use here is intended, for I am looking at the work as it is seen from the user's perspective.

[4] The term informant is broadly used in narcotics units. It can refer to some or specifically one of the following: (a) anyone who calls in information to a unit; (b) anyone who has in the past called in information to the unit; (c) someone who has worked in another unit, or the district vice units in Metro, for an officer. There are funds to pay informants in burglary and robbery as well as in district vice units around Metro City. Suburban detectives also have some funds to pay informants, but they are thought to be more limited than those of the vice unit; (d) a person working off a charge, either a drug charge or another type of charge; (e) a person who is working for payment, for information received, either by task or on salary; (f) a person who has worked for pay in the past; (g) a person who is working for pay and has been approved by the sergeant, has been written up and played in the department's informant files, and has had his activities written up in these files some or all of the times that he has worked for an officer in the unit; (h) a person who is reliable in legal terms, which is variable on the two units. It can be broadly defined as a person who gave information that was corroborated by other independent sources and shown to be correct and has proven through deeds that his information is valid, for example, has claimed to have seen drugs in a place where they were in fact found upon the serving of a search warrant. Often in drug units, having made a controlled buy (where the informant is stripped-searched, found to have no drugs or money or the serial numbers of the money given him as recorded precisely to identify his money, and instructed to make a buy of drugs of a certain amount from a certain person, if possible, and in a designated location) is crucial for establishing reliability.

The term "informant" is not a restrictive one and covers a variety of meanings. When combined with such adjectives as "good," "my," or "reliable," the range of possible meanings increases. I have purposively avoided citing or detailing the elaborate, legalistic debates about informants, their control and protection, and issues of Fourth Amendment freedoms that the use of informants raises. From the officer's point of view they are ex post facto legalisms of only marginal interest. It has been fairly convincingly argued by Oaks (23) that the exclusionary rule has minimal impact on everyday police practices. This position is consistent with my observations.

This reliance on informants is bedeviled because many informants are unwilling to inform and must be persuaded, threatened, or coerced to serve the interest of law enforcement. Thus, the actions of agents to obtain information and informants (and to reward them, often by reducing charges against them) ineluctably patterns the very market they work to suppress.

In Table 49.1, the *strategies* of enforcement employed by seven units studied are used as an example of the range of strategies. Note that Strategies 1, 3, 4, and 7 rely less on informants than do the remaining approaches. Frequently, the *source* of the initial clue that precipitates an investigation is an informant of some sort, but the relative dependence of the success of the investigation upon the informant varies with the strategy and over time with any given strategy. If an informant is recruited to make a buy and then introduces or "walks in" an undercover officer to make additional buys, his role in the final outcome of the case diminishes as additional buys are made. On the other hand, hassling or "falling on" street dealers requires only knowledge of places, times, and people to watch and "fall on" as they make sales. Finally, at the other end of the spectrum, the testifying informant strategy is fully reliant on an informant who will make buys and appear in court to testify. The point of this table, other than illustrating diversity across units and the temporal aspects of the role of the informant, is to show why the informant is the figure around which the efforts of

agents revolve. The greater the role of the informant in the enforcement strategy complement, the greater the significance of the manipulation and use of the informant in the success of the unit and of the individual officer (for details of this argument, see Reference 17, Chapters 6 to 8). In addition, the larger the dealing-using "scene" or the ecological places in which dealing goes on, the easier it is for low level focused enforcement to continue. Visibility is a central feature of the enforcement pattern. Because the most visible scenes are in lower class urban areas in large cities, the more there are minorities involved in these areas, the more enforcement will be racist.

The *means* or tactics in the game are those conducive to prying out information and include conventional stop-frisk-search techniques; warrants (both personal arrest and search), both held for potential execution and possible; the arrest itself, which is conducive, after charge and release on bail, to informing; and alterations in charges. In addition, there are quasilegal or illegal means of generating information: the use or threat of violence, flaking (placing evidence on a suspect during the course of a search), padding (adding to the quality or amount of seized drugs to increase the charge), extortion by the threat of violence, and the arrogation of seized property (drugs, money, and goods received by dealers, for example). (For a more detailed description of these means, see Reference 19.)

Rewards for playing the narcs' game from the perspective of the agent can be seen to

Table 49.1
Patterns of Strategy Employed in 1975 to 1977 by Seven Local Police Drug Units[a]

Strategy	Unit						
	S.E. City	Centro	Columbia	Metro	Mohawk	S.W. City	Suburban
1. Undercover buys and buy-bust	Yes	Yes	Yes	Yes	Yes	Yes	Yes
2. Informant and search warrant-raid	Yes	Yes	Yes	Yes	Yes	Yes	Yes
3. Falling on street dealers	Yes	b	No	Yes	a	No	No
4. Wire-tap-pen register used for surveillance	Yes	No	No	Yes	No	Yes	No
5. Diversion	No	Yes	Yes	Yes	No	No	No
6. Conspiracy cases worked in last year	Yes	No	No	Yes	No	Yes	Yes
7. Arrest warrant, e.g., uniform unit makes arrest	Yes	Yes	Rare	No	Rare	b	No
8. Testifying informant used.	No	No	Yes	No	No	b	Yes

[a] Based primarily on interviews and observation, not on the inspection of arrest or case records.
[b] Empty cells represent missing information.

vary. For, although on the one hand there are rewards within the legitimate organizational sphere, there are also additional and complementary rewards available in the illegitimate sphere. The illegitimate rewards ("corruption") are great precisely because the aim of regulation is to suppress and to deny all credibility and legitimate influence to dealers, thus limiting the scope of their pressure to the agents with whom they must deal as businessmen (19). Legitimate rewards come in several forms, depending on the department and unit. There are a variety of informal and formal "perks" for investigators in drug units. They are allowed to dress as they like (one unit prohibited specific clothes, such as combat jackets, T-shirts, and tennis shoes, but then this unit also refused to permit drinking on the job), associate with people in places at times that are denied other officers, work a variety of hours, and have great flexibility about where and when they work. They set their own cases for the most part (some squads control assignments more than others), and they are paid overtime or given "comp" time off. They do not have to wear a uniform, follow "uniformed discipline," deal with unexciting "dirty work" and non-crime work that plagues uniformed officers, and are involved in exciting, varied, interesting cases. Where court appearances or overtime are paid (this was true in five of the units), it is quite profitable to be a drug officer. Drug work is considered good training for other investigative work within the department and is given prestige by other officers. There is much freedom, excitement, and intrinsic satisfaction in the work. Because the reasons for joining drug units vary, and formal statements of requirements, purposes, or over-all aims were found to be operational in only two of the units, justifications for the work vary.

The *justifications* for the game itself are critical. Although human action is largely coordinated by assumptions unrevealed in everyday conduct, when called to account for the reasons they acted as they did, people can either produce *justifications* (assertion of the moral rectitude of conduct) or *denial* (abdication of the moral responsibility for the consequences of the act) (14). The justifications for the narcs' game provide definitions of the parameters of the game. Some justifications (derived from field notes and 6) are:

1. Heroin causes and increases crime (i.e., because addicts must meet their daily needs and in this view do not or cannot work, they turn to crime to support their habits. The more heroin, the more addicts; the more addicts, the more crime).

2. What to do about "junkies" is not my concern. We do not make the laws, we only enforce them; our only job is to arrest junkies.

3. Heroin addicts are chronic criminals; arresting them on drug charges reduces the opportunity for committing other crimes. We prevent crime by arresting people on drug charges.

4. We do not bother anyone who is not breaking the law. Round-up arrests—all the persons on the premises—searches, and arrests of occupants of a vehicle with drugs, are not "bothering anyone" because, if those arrested are innocent, they will be freed by the courts.

5. Junkies are so degenerate ... it seems as if drug users have no morals left after awhile (by implication they are not entitled to procedural or civil safeguards; they are morally compromised).

6. Once a "junkie," always a "junkie." When you "bust" them they may not have junk on them, but that is only a technicality. I will book addicts on anything I can.

7. If they do not play the game by the legal rules, why should they expect us to?

The problem of *evaluation* is made complex by the fact that the indices of activity and success are multiple and crude. Investigators are likely to reject the principal modes of formal gathering of data. Activity sheets totaling their arrests, court appearances, and the like are called "lie sheets." Lieutenants and sergeants likewise view them as misleading, and one lieutenant told me that he "rarely read them." Furthermore, there is a problem obtaining information on the activities of a given investigator other than from his reputation for general skill. Investigators do not as a rule talk about their cases with anyone except their partners. They may not actually do that. The information they provide to sergeants is sporadic and truncated, often something as elliptical as, "I'm going out to check on that business with Slick." Therefore, investigators are unaware, except on occasion when a raid goes down or persons are arrested and brought into the squad room, of precisely what other investigators are working on, if at all, how they have resolved various cases, and what the disposition of a particular case is. There is much small talk about what happened to people who were locked up. However, investigators rarely keep track of cases other than their own, and information of their own cases, if they are not called to testify, is often highly variable and inexact.

Although the Metro Department, for example, is authorized to make arrests, they do not make the charge against the accused; this is the domain of the United States Attorney's office. Although by the presentation of evidence and negotiation with representatives of that office the police can have an important effect on the resultant charge, there is a constant exchange and negotiation of cases between the narcotics branch and the United States Attorney's office. If an arrest is rejected, or "no-papered," it will not be sent forward for prosecution. A further complication is introduced by the fact that drug offenders can be charged under either federal or local law; violations of federal laws carry felony penalties, whereas local laws treat most drug offenses as misdemeanors. The investigators view the federal court as more problematic, even though they would prefer to prosecute under federal laws. Most charges are reduced to lesser charges and are tried in local courts. As a result of the ambiguity of charge and legal systems in which it will be adjudicated—that is, what is acceptable to the courts and prosecutor's office—arrest, charge, and conviction are seen as almost independent phenomena. Any one can be used as evidence of "success" or "failure"; however, compare the strategy of defining success in terms of "making cases."

Several "characteristic" attitudes of narcotics policemen result. They tend to view the narcs' game as being one of building up convictions against a person, even on lesser drug offenses, thus discrediting his testimony in court, increasing his "back-up time" (the time left to serve that must be done on parole and that, if he is convicted again, will more likely result in a prison sentence), and, conversely, raising the credibility and authority of the officer, both in court and with the defendant. Whether the person pleads guilty and serves time or "works off the beef," additional charges against him are always welcomed by officers.

Given this characterization of the narcs' game, it is perhaps quite easy to see that there is an ineluctable ambiguity about the *ends* of the game. The following ends have been reported in interviews and in secondary sources:

1. Immobilizing the trafficker, and thereby reducing the amount and kind of drugs available to the user.
2. Arresting the user-dealer-trafficker.
3. Bringing in the dope—making seizures of drugs.
4. Reducing crime by locking up "junkies." The number of users on the streets seeking money through criminal means to support their habit is thus reduced.
5. Increasing convictions—on dealers especially.
6. Harassing users to keep up the pressure on them and to create respect for drug officers.
7. Getting "junkies" off "dope."
8. Making arrests in order to get arrestees to inform on those who deal.
9. Protecting society, making sure young kids do not start using.

Much has been written about the *constraints* on police drug control. Within the prohibition model, established legal rules and procedural protections have variable salience for the working police officer. Works of Skolnick (27), Oaks (23), McDonald (16), DeFleur (3), and Manning (17) suggest that the effects of legal constraints on officers increase as the case becomes more "complicated," i.e., when it requires the use of a search warrant, large amounts of money, and/or legal a priori approval (as in the case of a communications intercept—"wire tap"). Inasmuch as the vast majority of drug cases are short term, involve small amounts of drugs, and do not require warrants or large amounts of money, the impact of the law is primarily to focus action on the small, vulnerable, and easily arrested user, rather than to protect the citizen from violation of legal protections of various kinds. It should be further emphasized that these external constraints are only made significant because of the legalistic ideology of the police themselves when attempting to rationalize their own failures or failures ascribed to them by the public. They are quite willing to seize on the law as the principal constraint on their actions because this has credibility with the public and because it avoids attention being focused on other, unmodifiable constraints, both externally and internally. The international flow of opiates is beyond the control of any single nation and certainly is entirely beyond the control of police agencies whose only concern is with interdiction of already extant supply, or in shaping demand. The dynamics of interagency cooperation (actually, the rather complete failure of this at the federal and local level) and of the markets themselves exert more control than the law in maintaining the level and type of demand. Information is not shared among agencies; quite the contrary. Agencies do not possess systematic information on the drug markets they are mandated to control; they lack the capacity to guide and evaluate the validity of their guidance to targets, markets, or groups, and supervision is after the fact and largely irrelevant to the prospective choices of agents. Skills are minimal and learned, if at all, through apprenticeship-type training (17).

Limitations on equipment, personnel, and monetary resources are, of course, considerable, but the most obvious constraints are not the most obvious ones at all. More money, resources, personnel, and equipment will have little appreciable effect on the impact of the narcs on the market given the organizational structure of local policing and the external constraints described above. Whatever the rhetoric, public justifications, and formulations of the game, it is mostly boring, unsystematic, catch as catch can, and focused on obtaining immediate rewards of arrest and charge and hassling low level users of non-narcotic drugs, primarily marihuana. It should be emphasized in the following discussion of the narcs' game that the primary function of municipal police units is hassling users of small quantities of marihuana; that most arrests are not made by narcotic or drug officers, but by patrol officers; that the arrests made by drug units are not for "dealing" or distribution charges but, overwhelmingly, for possession; that a very small part of all arrests are for opiates, and these are mostly possession charges. Finally, somewhere around 50 per cent of all arrests are dropped prior to court, either for violations of legal procedures, lack of evidence, or to get informants to work in exchange for dropped charges. What this means, in turn, as Skolnick has shown, is that the hierarchy of punishment is reversed, reversing the common-sense role of legal constraints. That is to say, the larger dealers are most frequently the ones on whom charges are dropped. In turn, the con-

straints of the law work not to "frustrate" narcs but to abet them in threatening users extralegally and using the avoidance of charging with a crime as a work tool.

Finally, what must be emphasized in the study of all attempts to control drug use of various sorts is that agencies themselves have an independent, autonomous capacity to carve out a negotiated domain or mandate that separates the agency from its environment and internally permits agents to shape their own choices, work the cases they determine they will work, in the fashion they determine they will work them, and to the conclusions they wish to seek. Whether or not these outcomes are theirs to determine is, as has been argued above, less in their hands than in the forces of the market, international economics, and extraorganizational factors. In the end, *the agent determines the predominate tactic of the agency*, where it will intervene, if at all, the extensiveness of the work invested in any given case, and the over-all patterning of investigation. It is this reason then that the narcs' game, more than any other single thing, shapes what contingencies or risks are faced by the user. Reification of the "criminal justice system," the "law," or the nature of the "market" does little good unless one understands the proximal controls exercised by the agent.

The argument explaining the actions of the agent can be briefly summarized in terms of several general principles derived from field work in eight agencies:

1. General strategies and tactics, unless they are short term "campaigns" or organizationally rooted allocations of personnel—e.g., specialized pharmacy, undercover, or school squads—are insufficiently supervised to constrain agents' choices of cases.

2. Payoff and rewards shift in importance over the course of a case, period of the month, and public emphases on types of drugs of interest—e.g., when a phencyclidine campaign is mounted.

3. Good cases, good seizures, and good informants shift in meaning.

4. Definitions of success vary and pattern the direction of effort of the agent.

5. Levels of skill and types of skill vary, and one adjusts one's cases to fit one's skills rather than the opposite.

It is not insignificant that from the legal perspective previous arrests and convictions constitute prima facie evidence that the person who has been arrested for a subsequent crime could have been "predisposed" to have committed it. In other words, the defense of entrapment, an important legal weapon for those arrested on drug charges, is mitigated by prior arrests, especially for drug charges. The present status of the entrapment defense makes it virtually impossible for entrapment to be proved if the defendant is seen as having been "predisposed" to a criminal activity (8). The reasoning is, of course, circular, because the defendant is charged with having committed the crime and is, therefore, from the police perspective, already both predisposed and guilty.

THE USER AND THE NARCS' GAME

There are two general types of consequences of the narcs' game. The first is structural and economic, and the second is social-psychological and personal. Many of the economistic consequences of the game have been noted in previous publications (7, 8, 10, 12, 18–21, 24, 25). Each of these reveals the poverty of the corrective control model of police action and documents the structural effects on the market, on the number of users and the subculture, and on crime. Enforcement personnel argue that arrests reduce the availability of drugs. Because virtually all arrests above the level of street dealing (and most of those not made by patrol) involve buys of drugs by informants or undercover officers and any attempt to "move up" the dealing "pyramid" will involve making larger buys, sometimes involving payments or "front money" for drugs that "walk" (are stolen and no drugs are delivered), enforcement directly infuses money into the drug culture, therefore stimulating demand. Arrests produce more informants, who are in turn paid either in money or drugs for their work. They are paid for the buys; they are paid rewards in some departments and by federal agencies in the range of 10 per cent of the worth of the seizures or a flat sum for an arrest, guns, or information leading to an arrest; and they are paid miscellaneous amounts for other expenses (a six-pack of beer, taxi fare, a telephone bill). Money "fronted" is often lost, and at the federal level most of the money is not recovered. These amounts infused into the market have not

only risen in absolute amounts but in percentage of the money lost from year to year, according to Senate investigators and a government audit.

It has also been claimed that enforcement reduces the numbers of persons involved in the addict subculture and its viability. It is to the advantage of narcotics policemen to have their informants on the street, rather than in jail; they *require* an active body of informants (Metro Department has files on some 145 informants, some of them with previous criminal records, virtually all of whom are users-dealers in narcotics). These informants, as explained above, are protected under certain conditions from criminal charges. In Metro Department some $200,000 a year is paid into the market by narcotics agents. In a suburban department we studied, nearly $24,000 was expended in buys, and in 1974–1975 some $1,713 in bonuses for seizures was paid. For the six departments from which we have data, we can estimate that around $500,000 is infused into the heroin market yearly by *local police.*

If one were to total for the nation all monies expended for purchases of evidence, i.e., spent in the market by local, state, and federal law enforcement, the figure would probably exceed several million dollars. Perhaps the most revealing facts were stated in a report to the Senate committee inquiring into federal drug enforcement in 1975–1976 (26), in which the costs of enforcement were revealed and the amount which goes directly into the market in futile attempts to "buy up" was presented to the committee: a General Accounting Office report summarizes their findings with respect to the amount and uses of monies:

In addition to being used to purchase evidence and information, these funds are being used by DEA to pay rewards and flash rolls; that is, large sums of money are shown to drug traffickers as proof that DEA undercover agents can purchase large quantities of illicit drugs.

The budget for purchase of evidence and payments to informants has increased from $775,000 in fiscal 1969 for BNDD (DEA's forerunner) to an estimated $9 million in fiscal 1976 for DEA.

A relatively small amount of money used for purchase of evidence is recognized by DEA. For example, in fiscal 1974, only about $160,000 in purchase of evidence money was recovered by DEA compared to about $4 million used for the purchase of evidence in that year. Approximately 95% of the funds (spent) on purchasing evidence in fiscal 1974 was lost in the illicit market for the purpose of buying to apprehend upper level dealers...(26).

It was also documented in the testimony that money spent on lower level dealers (Drug Enforcement Administration (DEA) classifications III and IV) did not result in the arrest of higher dealers. For the first 6 months of fiscal 1975 in the domestic regions of DEA, "82 percent of the money expended for the purchase of evidence and 44 percent of the money expended for the purchase of information was on class III and IV cases" (26). Thus, it could be generalized that, although the more money an agency has, the more probability that the agency can move up the dealing structure, it is also true that, in absolute terms, this means that more money will be poured into the market, especially at the lowest levels.

It is assumed by narcotics agents that most of this money returns to the market, directly through buys and indirectly through informants who are paid for buys and then subsequently use the fees to support their habits. To the extent that informants are involved in the heroin scene, they are useful to police; ipso facto it is in the interest of the police to maintain a viable, and even in some cases a visible, addict street culture.[5] Through payments, protection, and working informants, policemen help maintain the addict subculture.[6]

In addition, three other effects occur. The first is the increasing "hardening" or *vertical differentiation* of the market structure and reduced competition that occurs as a result of the arresting of street users (most arrests are of small users, involve little investigation, and produce no seizures (11)), associated increased costs to protect against arrest, and withdrawal of smaller dealers. Police involvement in regulating the drug world creates a premium for betrayal, induces users to remain in the world as informants working off charges, and infuses money into the dealing system through payments to informants for controlled buys, seizures, and information. The economics of the drug world are influenced in some *indeterminant* fashion by enforcement payments and buys. The market reflects both the legitimate costs of doing business (supply and operating costs, including profit) and security costs, including those costs of operating that cannot be eliminated by security and remain as the costs of the risk and consequences of being caught and punished (10). The primary effect of enforcement is to produce a "risk cost" (7), the cost of protection against police raids and seizures, and thus to raise the sellers' prices and the consumers' costs of using. It has the effect, then, of raising the *profits* for the higher level dealers, increasing risk costs at the small wholesaler and retailer levels, and producing higher costs to the user. If he maintains the same level of use, he suffers higher risks of being caught, and greater pressures to steal to support his/her habit and/or to raise money to make bond.[7]

A second effect is that enforcement makes users distrustful, thus indicating violence (see above), and renders them more resistant to enforcement tactics. (This has occurred in Lansing, Michigan, where newly formed regional drug squads, operating with high pressure to produce adequate monies for payments, and closely supervised undercovermen have begun to impact strongly on a new and naive addict population. Enforcement may be producing a set of more sophisticated, hardened users who will be more wary "next time.")

Finally, undercover work involves the officer directly in buying drugs and may require him to use or feign use of drugs, arrange

---

[5] For example, in one city fines from drug possession cases go into the city treasury and are credited in the budget to the Vice Control Unit. In another city we studied vice fines were used to pay overtime (indirectly only, because the money went into the general operating fund, which was in turn used to pay court-generated overtime). In this indirect fashion, arrests serve to a point to maintain revenue. Conversely, it is in the interest of the police to maintain the capacity to arrest small time pimps, whores, and drug users in order to get court time, generate fines for the city, and show that they are active.

[6] The *Detroit Free Press* (4a) reported that the Detroit police were *developing* guidelines for payments to informants, especially use of payments in drugs. Attorney General Levi announced similar policy for the Justice Department. It is unlikely that such rules would be required were frequent violations not already known.

[7] A recent study showed that the majority of drug users on bail were dealing again to raise bail, to pay their lawyers, or to recoup losses occasioned by their arrest (26).

buys, serve as a middleman between persons wishing to transact business, infuse money in the form of front money and buys, and take on the life style, argot, and culture of the addict.[8]

The social-psychological consequences of the impact of the police enforcement effort are insufficiently appreciated. From the police point of view, these consequences are simply "costs" of being an addict or breaking the law, rather than an *essential* feature of the enterprise. When reading stories of police "successes" in the newspaper, one is presented with a single-dimensional vision of the work. Failures, tragedies, violence, terror, and destruction of property and intimate relations are but a set of associated "by-products" or, as the more fashionable systems language would have it, "trade-offs" for the "higher good" of control of crime. It is impossible on the basis of limited field work to provide a "representative" sample of critical incidents or episodes that illustrate the impact of the enforcement enterprise on the life worlds of users. Instead, what follows are some examples of the chaos produced by the pursuit of lawbreakers. The structure of the markets and internal pressures to produce mean that officers act out powerfully in their areas of discretion in order to "succeed." Many of the delicts that have been explained are direct functions of pressures to succeed and attempts by agents to make sense of the problematic situations they frequently face. There are, in addition, instances of gratuitous violence, terror, the animation of personalized violence, revenge, and hatred that are only minimally explained by sociological analyses of organizational action and economic, political, and legal constraints. Some of these examples fill in the blind spots of newspaper coverage of dramatic raids and seizures, police public relations releases, and the everyday assumptions of the person in the street concerning the legitimacy and utility of drug law enforcement. The flavor here is terror, the targets vulnerable, and the results execrable.

Episode 1. It was Thanksgiving Eve. A sister seeking revenge on her brother informed narcs that on this evening her brother would be holding a party at home for a large number of friends and their families. She stated that her brother would have some hash and marihuana in the house for the Thanksgiving dinner. The brother had been known to them as a "dope dealer" (marihuana), and they planned, on the basis of her information, to raid the house with a search warrant. Narcs hit the house as the turkey was cooking in the oven, and the smell of the sweet potatoes, homemade breads, and pumpkin pies was mingling with happy voices in the rooms where people were gathered. Narcs secured the house, assembled the crowd of people under custody in the living room where they could view the officers, sat down at the table, and ate the festive Thanksgiving dinner with gusto. They left the house with the prisoners, and the women were alone to clean the table, throw out the greasy bones of the now stripped carcass, and comfort the crying children.

Episode 2. The Drug Enforcement Agency, the Desert County Sheriff's Department, and Desert City Police Department received information that heroin was being transported across the border from Mexico by an illegal Mexican immigrant. They assembled noisily and jubilantly in the parking lot behind the modern white police station. They were driving (motors were raced to assure each other) seized four-wheel-drive vehicles; large, colorful, heavily chromed late model machines; and "flash cars" (powerful "muscle cars" used to impress dealers). The sun glared off the pavement and the shiny cars on the drive south. The small motel in which the "dealer" was staying was a remnant of a 1940's Raymond Chandler story: shabby, with peeling paint, broken screens, and tired cars collapsed in the faintly marked slots in front of the units. A dry swimming pool, full of dirt, leaves, and debris, mirrored the hopes of the occupants of the motel. As a mass assembled, the door was hit; three children wandered out of the room blinking into the parking lot. Dirty T-shirts were set off by sugar-stained faces, their eyes deep brown and frightened. Inside the hot little room on the bed sat a small tired women, her round face yellow and filled by large eyes heavy with sadness. The compact man, powerful and dark, had concealed several bags of

---

[8] These activities are not more rhetoric; case law affirms the legality of these practices, as well as establishing the right of the agent to use guile and deception. A useful, albeit shocking review of practices that have been subject to court test is found in Reference 7.

heroin in a bureau drawer. They were quickly found, even as the room began to clear. The children and the women were jaundiced, that is, they had hepatitis. The narcs' anger suffused the room: the dealer had not told them his family was sick; he had not taken his wife and children to a doctor; he had exposed all of them to a serious disease. A DEA agent, staring at his polished white shoes over his slight paunch and white belt, stuck his .38 into a discrete holster inside his green pants and kicked a stone toward the dilapidated Oldsmobile that had brought him all this trouble up from Mexico.

Episode 3. They could not raise a black and white car on the radio, so they decided to drive the "hippie van" they used for such operations directly to the park to seek the assistance of the mounted unit. The horses, huge, restless, and wide eyed, kicked the stalls and snorted, almost as if they knew what was needed. The horse officers, tall, muscular, and leathery, were unavailable at the moment. The raid proceeded as planned. After the marihuana had been purchased in the house by an undercover officer, he flashed his car lights as he drove away. Two detectives rushed out of the van and stormed into the house and down the hall. They collided with the dealer as he slipped out of his room along the wall and into the hall. He hardly felt the first few of a rain of blows struck against his head from the truncheon; soon he could not see at all, for the blood well obscured his view of the officer who threw him back into the room. He fell strewn among the chaos of his lodgings, soon escalated by the officers who dumped the contents of each of his drawers, going from left to right around each room, onto the floor. When the horse officers arrived, all more than 6 feet tall and equipped with the usual complement of weapons, they heavily and intentionally marched through, over, and on the now considerable mess, sought out the bathroom, and went in and urinated, ceremonially, one at a time, in the villain's toilet. The blood ran down his face and onto his T-shirt; he was told he had earned this beating because, according to the officer, he was a "pimp," a "drug dealer," and a "con-man." The several battered, messy joints found in a paper bag were proudly seized and listed as evidence. He was taken in to be charged with his friend, whose car was impounded as

evidence (not before the wires to both speakers were ripped out). It sat in front of the house as they rushed in and was believed to play a part in the arrested man's crimes.

Episode 4. DEA called for assistance from the local department: they needed drivers and cars to follow a car (driven by the informant in the case) transporting dealer and dope from some point to a motel at the airport where a deal (buy-bust) was to take place. It was dark as a narc and his partner pulled around the edge of the motel building in their car, but they saw the person under surveillance throw something in his mouth and swallow it. The police believed it was bulk heroin, not packaged in a balloon, that had been seen to have been swallowed. They seized 1½ pounds of heroin and arrested three prisoners. Being federal agents, they wanted to make a "tighter case" on the man who was seen to have swallowed the bulk dope. The swallower was made comfortable manacled to his bed in a jail cell and, upon defecation, was requested to retain the warm specimen in a small, white porcelain bowl until the federal agents could systematically conduct a careful fecal scrutiny to obtain the essential evidence of the crime. According to an officer: "Every time he took a shit they were up there (in the jail) pawing through it. They never found anything. . . . The guy sued us all; I think it was dropped. I don't know why they did it in the first place because they had a good case, but they cluttered it up." The diligence did not pay off. "The guy they had up there pawing through his shit . . . he was the big man. He was *the* man. They had it down so good; I don't know whether we could tie things tighter (with the hoped-for evidence) or something."

Episode 5. The narcs sent the door sailing into the room and followed it, only to encounter a huge dog, up on his hind legs, threatening them. They brushed past him, searching furtively for the elusive dope prize. It could not be found. A small child was in the living room watching as his father dove for the gun he kept on the table beside the couch in the living room of the apartment. He could not reach it in time. After a futile search of an hour or so, one of the officers sat down with the child, made small talk, and asked him where his daddy hid the dope. The child pointed under the bed in the other room. They crawled through the dust, pushed aside the shoes, and found a small bag of heroin. The little boy smiled and was pleased because he had been so helpful.

Episode 6. The apartment was in a comfortable lower middle class area on the north side of town. It was a long ride there, and the driver of one car drove rather more carefully than usual. He and his passengers had had a collision at 60 miles an hour earlier in the evening. As they accelerated to 60, up a bridge ramp, a camper entered on their right, rolling innocently out into their path. Spinning and swerving first to the wall and out into the lane, they stopped short of the guard rail protecting them from a 30-yard drop to a road below. They had taken their time driving to this raid because both were still shaking. Even the most competent driver in the unit, at the wheel, felt unnerved and uncertain of his driving skills. When they charged and hit the door, the ram, smashing the knob, ripping the door, crashed into the foot of the officer in the second rank behind the rammers. He jumped and howled as the others surged upstairs, only to find a man and a women in flagrante delicto. Somewhat hampered by his concurrent task, the man had been unable to reach the .357 magnum Colt he had carefully placed under the bed. She screamed as she rolled away across the red silk bed sheets, whether from anger, frustration, or fear it was not known. The television built in above their heads was an unseeing eye. The house was searched; in the kitchen were found balloons (used to package heroin), a coffee grinder (used to cut opiates and to blend in various substances to cut the heroin), and a beautifully laid table set for a fine Sunday breakfast. She sat on the edge of the sofa surrounded by large incurious men clutching to herself a too small robe and rocking back and forth. The subdued light of the apartment illuminated no evidence. The raid came up "dry."

Episode 7. It was believed, if an informant was to be believed, that he had bought and was holding several bags of heroin. He was invited out in front of the house where he was living by two uniformed officers. He was told that a van fitting the description of his had been involved in a hit and run accident. He came out to answer some questions about his van, was read the warrant, and was held while the narcs tumbled from the car, sprinted into his parents' house, and began unsystematically to "turn it over." He was threatened with further destruction of the order of the house unless he told them where the dope was secreted. He refused; they began in his parents' room and overturned the bed, heaped the contents of the drawers on the mattress, layered the clothes from the closets on top and on the floor, and swirled around the room peering here and there. In the basement, they ripped open drawers, shoe boxes, and cardboard cartons, sending letters, diaries, little mementos of trips to the shore, souvenirs, torn ticket stubs, love notes, and cards spinning aimlessly and erratically from one side of the room to the other. Chaos reigned. The frightened young woman who also lived in the basement was left to crouch on the floor without relief. She was finally allowed to use the toilet. She squeezed into the room with a young and embarrassed officer whose eyes played on the leaves of the trees outside the window; he tried not to watch or listen. A small gram of powder assumed to be dope was found (subsequent laboratory analysis showed that it was not heroin). The house was left. The mother and father soon came home from work.

The picture of the world of drug enforcement is one of *cryptic* romanticism. What is described almost in code are the "conditions" of the life that are said to cause use: the threat to the young, the dramatic success of the officers. Yet, from time to time, newspapers inadvertently conspire to show the ineffectual, offensive, and repressive nature of the enforcement game. Instead of the ostensibly informed buy-bust strategy or the informant-dominant strategy, stories can illustrate the more common strategy of "street-hassling," falling on street dealers, or simply searching and interrogating people in locales where dealing and using are known to take place. A *Detroit Free Press* article (5) described what one of their reporters saw. This scene was a part of a larger "heroin hunt" or "dope drive" round-up of an alleged ring.

We'll hit that apartment house. Sergeant Dave Simmons pulls the unmarked Plymouth into a parking lot behind a high school. "You want me to call them in boss?" "Yes, bring everybody in, and we'll hit that apartment house on Collingwood," answers Inspector Isalah McKinnon. While Simmons makes the radio call ordering the youth crime officers to rendezvous in the parking lot, McKinnon turns to the undercover policeman in the back seat ... "Okay, you've been here almost two weeks," says McKinnon, "So if you see a single one of those kids who've been selling the dope, I want 'em pointed out." Before he finishes the sentence, the alley is filling with unmarked cars. McKinnon slides his 6-foot-4 frame out of the car and walks over to Sgts. Bill Hubbard and Herb Simmons, who are co-ordinating the arrest sweeps against the teenage pushers. "What've we got Herb?" "We've been hurting 'em, no doubt about that, but we've still seen 'em working near that apartment house ... " "The place on Collingwood?" "Yeah, and down by the park, too. Rube's sitting on that." "Okay, we're gonna hit the apartment house and the park at the same time," says McKinnon. "Get everybody together." In 30 seconds, the lot is empty, and cars are converging on the vacant apartment building. "Not again! What the hell's the problem with you guys?" screams a man wearing a motorcycle jacket and a shabby pair of jeans. He and a dozen other people are spread-eagled against the front wall of the building at the corner of Twelfth and Collingwood. "Hey, brother, as long as the dope's in town, we're gonna be around," answers Officer Fred Davis as he pats the man down. "Hey boss, come up here! You've gotta see this!" yells Trice, hanging out of a second-floor window. McKinnon walks into the building. He's met by a family of cockroaches running down the hall. The floor's littered with hundreds of torn heroin packets, once used, now discarded. Hypodermic needles crunch under his feet. As he walks back out a few moments later, McKinnon slowly shakes his head. As his unit finishes up the search, neighbors are gathering on the corner. "I'm telling you, it's him," says a woman. "Hey, are you in charge here?" asks a man who walks up to the car. "Sure am. Can I help you?" "Yeah, well, I'm the manager of this place, and I'd like to know what's going on." "Well, sir, we've received a number of citizen complaints about narcotics dealing at this address," says McKinnon patiently. "Isn't this place vacant and condemned?" "Yeah, well, I'm the manager until they tear it down," he answers, edging away from the car. It's about 3:30 p.m. and McKinnon is back in his office housed in the castle-like structure on Grand River. He listens to a report from Officers Frank Scott Fowler and Clinton Kirkwood, leaders of two intelligence crews. "We've got 'em running and we're staying right on their tails," says Fowler. "When they move, we're right with 'em." McKinnon smiles. "Keep squeezing them, Frank," he says, "keep squeezing them." "Right now, that's the only thing they understand," says Kirkwood. About an hour later, Deputy Chief Gerald Hale is on the phone in his downtown office. "Okay, like that's what I like to hear. Let's stay right on top of them." Hale hangs up the phone and swings around in his chair. "It's a damn shame. Kids who should be the hopes of our future out on street corners selling drugs. But we're destroying their operation. We're tearing it apart at the bottom. And you know what happens after that don't you? The top falls." (Reprinted with the permission of the *Detroit Free Press*.)

The story about this operation does not describe any seizures, arrests, informants acquired, any evidence of their guilt, or any connection of persons searched to the "ring." In short, as described, it was intrusive terrorizing. Note also that the police conclude that it was a good operation because they were hassling street dealers and that this, ultimately, would produce a caving in at the top. This is empirically untrue, because the most replaceable level in the market is the user-dealer, the pathetic powerless street user willing to fill a working role in exchange for access to dope (6, 7).

CONCLUDING STATEMENT

The evidence presented here has the character of a miscellany. From the field work evidence, the official records, evidence and testimony before the Senate, as well as the works of scholars and other writers, one can see that the narcs' game is a result of unanticipated consequences of the prohibition approach to drug control and the obdurate constraints that remain, regardless of the legal "tools" that are said to be produced for law enforcement agencies. Once the work becomes game-like, such basic human protective devices as deception, lying, manipulation, and self-deception become central. In the episodes presented here, the personal minichaos is emphasized, because these consequences are rarely seen as direct results of the drug enforcement mandate and, indeed, are seen by officers as mere penalties and added costs associated with using illegal drugs. What consequence can they be shown to have on subsequent behavior with respect to drug use? As the tone of any close and sympathetic description of police work will reveal—e.g., Wambaugh's *Choirboys*; Higgins' *Diggers' Game* or *Coogans' Trade*; the recent work on the Washington, D.C., fencing operation, *Surprise, Surprise*—revenge, retribution, and personalized hatred are underlying motives in much enforcement. Drug enforcement, whatever else it does, produces terror among users, revenges for life style delicts, assesses a cost to those whose drugs of preference differ from the middle and lower middle classes, whose life chances are meager, and whose ability to retaliate legally or nonlegally is low. Public support of drug enforcement is based on a mystified and inaccurate view of the enterprise and fundamentally is rooted in misplaced moral revulsion and resentment.

Acknowledgment. The author acknowledges the assistance of E. Sitwell in preparing for the writing of this chapter.

References

1. Blumberg, A. *Criminal Justice.* Chicago, Quadrangle, 1967.
2. Brown, R. Alcohol, oligopoly and crime. Washington, D.C., National Center for Alcohol Education. Unpublished manuscript, 1974.
3. DeFleur, L. Biasing influences on drug arrest records: Implications for deviance research. Am. Sociol. Rev. 40:88, 1975.
4. Dix, G. Undercover investigations and police rule-making. Texas Law Rev. 53:202, 1975.
4a. Detroit Free Press, December 11, 1976.
5. Flanigan, B. We'll hit that apartment house. Detroit Free Press. August 19, 1979.
6. Gould, L., et al. *Connections: Notes from the Heroin World.* New Haven, Conn., Yale University Press, 1974.
7. Heller, J. The attempt to control illicit drug supply. In *Drug Use In America: Problem in Perspective.* Appendix, vol. III: *Technical Papers of the Second Report of the National Commission on Marijuana and Drug Abuse,* pp. 383–407. Washington, D.C., United States Government Printing Office, 1973.
8. Hellman, A. *Laws against Marijuana.* Urbana, University of Illinois Press, 1975.
9. Helmer, J. *Drugs and Minority Repression.* New York, Seabury Press, 1974.
10. Holahan, J. The economics of heroin. In *Dealing with Drug Abuse,* P. Wald, editor, pp. 255–299. New York, Praeger, 1972.
11. Johnson, W., and Bogomolny, R. Selective justice: Drug law enforcement in six American cities. In *Drug Use in America: Problem in Perspective.* Appendix, vol. III: *Technical Papers of the Second Report of the National Commission on Marijuana and Drug Abuse,* pp. 498–650. Washington, D.C., United States Government Printing Office, 1973.
12. Kaplan, J. *Marijuana: The New Prohibition.* New York, Pocket Books, 1970.
13. Lemert, E. *Human Deviance, Social Problems and Social Control.* Englewood Cliffs, N.J., Prentice-Hall, 1972.
14. Lindesmith, A. *The Addict and the Law.* Bloomington, University of Indiana Press, 1965.
15. Lyman, S., and Scott, M. *Sociology of the Absurd.*

New York, Appleton-Century-Crofts, 1970.
16. McDonald, W. F. Enforcement of narcotics laws in the District of Columbia. In *Drug Use in America: Problem in Perspective.* Appendix, vol. III: *Technical Papers of the Second Report of the National Commission on Marijuana and Drug Abuse,* pp. 651–685. Washington, D.C., United States Government Printing Office, 1973.
17. Manning, P. K. *The Narcs' Game: Informational and Organizational Constraints on Drug Law Enforcement.* Cambridge, Mass., Massachusetts Institute of Technology Press, 1980.
18. Manning, P. K., and Redlinger, L. J. Invitational edges of corruption: Some consequences of narcotic law enforcement. In *Drugs,* P. Rock, editor, pp. 279–310. Rutgers, N.J., Society Books, 1977.
19. Manning, P. K., and Redlinger, L. J. Working bases for corruption: Some consequences of narcotic law enforcement. In *Drugs, Crime and Public Policy,* A. Trebach, editor, pp. 60–89. New York, Praeger, 1978.
20. Manning, P. K., and Redlinger, L. J. Observations on the impact of police strategies upon the trade in opiates. In *IROS: The International Review of Opium Studies.* Philadelphia, Institute for the Study of Human Issues, In press.
21. Moore, M. *Buy and Bust.* Lexington, Mass., Lexington Books, 1977.
22. Musto, D. *The American Disease: Origins of Narcotics Control.* New Haven, Conn., Yale University Press, 1972.
23. Oaks, D. Studying the exclusionary rule in search and seizure. Univ. Chicago Law Rev. 37:665, 1970.
24. Redlinger, L. Dealing in dope: Market mechanisms and distribution patterns of illicit narcotics. Department of Sociology, Northwestern University, Unpublished Ph.D. Dissertation, 1969.
25. Redlinger, L. Marketing and distributing heroin: Some sociological observations. J. Psychedelic Drugs 7:331, 1975.
26. Senate Testimony. Federal Drug Enforcement. Hearings before the Permanent Subcommittee on Investigations of the Committee on Government Operations. United States Senate, Ninety-fourth Congress, First Session. June 9, 10, and 11, 1975, Part 1, pp. 100–112. Washington, D.C., United States Government Printing Office, 1975.
27. Skolnick, J. *Justice without Trial,* ed. 2. New York, John Wiley & Sons, 1975.
27a. Washington Post, January 16, 1977.
28. Webster, J. Drug enforcement: Have the police gone into business for themselves? In *The Police in Society,* E. Viano and J. Reiman, editors, pp. 189–204. Lexington, Mass., D. C. Health, 1975.
29. Wells, L. E., Johnson, W. T., and Peterson, R. E. Arrest probabilities for marijuana users as indicators of selective law enforcement. Am. J. Sociol. 83:681, 1977.
30. Williams, J. R., Redlinger, L. J., and Manning, P. K. *Police Narcotics Control: Patterns and Strategies.* Final Report Submitted to National Institute of Law Enforcement and Criminal Justice, Law Enforcement Assistance Administration (Grant #76-N1-49-0109), June, 1979.
31. Wilson, J. *The Investigators.* New York, Basic Books, 1978.

CHAPTER 50

EMPLOYMENT

Father John McVernon

H. Daniel Carpenter

For those of us who grew up before the 1960's, the possibility of becoming a drug addict was almost beyond our imagining. We knew there were men like the boxer Barney Ross who returned from the war addicted to morphine, and the older generation told stories of the coked-up hop-heads of the 1920's and before. We heard of musicians who smoked what they then called gage or tea, and, in some neighborhoods, people were concerned about the young men who lived off capsules of heroin. Still it was easier to imagine oneself ending life strapped to the electric chair in Sing-Sing than wracked by withdrawal like "The Man with the Golden Arm."

In the last 20 years all that has changed. Numbers of young people from every sector of society have initiated their adult years with a prolonged foray into the drug experience. Leon Hunt, a mathematician and epidemiologist, says that "drug use has grown so and become so popular in the last decade that it's virtually endemic" and that is so at every age level. Hunt continues, "Like drinking, it's everywhere" (2).

Unlike drinking, much drug use is illegal. Unlike deep involvement with drink, the heavy use of street drugs has been socially unacceptable. Most Americans use alcohol and understand that controlled use of the beverage is manageable and is the most frequent style of use. People do not have that kind of confidence about street drugs even if they themselves are regular users of more powerful prescription medications. Many imagine that every user of substances like heroin or lysergic acid diethylamide (LSD) is a problem user.

A second distinction is that people are not so sure that the regular user of those drugs can leave them behind. Almost everyone has a friend or relative who has succeeded in recovering from heavy alcohol use either through Alcoholics Anonymous, hospitalization, or on their own. Few have the confidence that the hold street drugs have on the dependent person can be broken readily or permanently.

Finally, alcohol problems are seen more in their true proportions rather than in a framework of myths and fears. Alcohol use, for all its problems, is rather well integrated in our society. The substance is part of our religious ritual and social behavior. A whole variety of taboos have developed around its use and limit its power to do harm. We are expected not to drink in the morning, not to drink alone, and not to drink and drive. Although there is a subculture of drug use that sets out norms for socially appropriate and physically safe adventures of the mind, not everyone is aware of, or confident in, those rules and their power to control.

The person who has been deeply involved with illegal drugs, and to a lesser extent the person who has been involved with legal medicines so heavily as to require treatment, is looked upon as a strange case. How can one be sure the drugs have been left behind? Can we trust they will avoid such behavior in the future?

1. The first obstacle to employment that the recovered drug dependent must contend with is the label society lays upon them.

2. The second obstacle is the label they lay upon themselves.

3. The third obstacle is the individual's social disadvantage. Many compulsive drug users come from a background of nutritional deficiency, disrupted family situations, inadequate educational experiences, negative community environments and estrangement from the larger society. These are obstacles to employment that have to be overcome with or without the history of drug use.

4. Finally there are the needs beyond good health, adequate education, and appropriate work skills. The need for the social skills that make obtaining and holding a job possible.

THE LABEL SOCIETY IMPOSES

Fitting people into categories allows for a simpler social life. The mind, by nature, slots individuals into already determined types so that we do not have to start from scratch in understanding each new event. Categorization is a habit of the mind that applies to more than our understanding of people. Although not all Edsels were lemons and not all Pekinese are ill tempered, still in these cases generalizations are fair enough. The categorizing of human beings, although it does make social functioning easier, is never either accurate or fair.

People shape their lives and themselves by their own choices. Heredity, environment, and experience are influences in human life but not determinants.

Drug dependents have been grouped and stigmatized in American society. When opium and cocaine first appeared in America, their use was thought of as foreign and threatening. Opium was considered part of the world of the Chinese, and its use was linked with the menace of this inscrutable

wave of humanity. Cocaine was linked with the young black male and feared as part of the obscure threat posed by this unassimilated population in the gut of America. Marihuana was alien on two counts. Springing from the Mexican population in the Southwest, its use was accepted by the "beatnik" population of the North. LSD became visible in America among the hippies who in the late 1960's were as bizarre a presence as Martians might be. The bad feelings Americans had toward these aliens in their midst were translated into bad feelings about the drugs they used. It seemed that the drugs were what made them alien and strange.

The societal impression has been that by becoming involved with these substances the users—more so the addicts—set themselves apart from the American mainstream (4).

Even now, when much of the fear and antipathy toward such groups has abated, a residue remains . . . strong negative feelings about dependence on chemicals, far out of proportion to their pharmacological potential for harm. When it comes to employment, these anxieties are translated into a reluctance to hire the former drug-dependent individual.

On top of that foundation, treatment programs have raised more barriers. To justify the monies committed to drug rehabilitation, the argument has been that the investment in treatment is more effective than the dollars spent on incarceration. The figures on drug-related crime were dramatically charted. The fear of the drug-deprived addict became a motivation for funding. Prevention and treatment programs profiled the drug-using youngster as incredibly manipulative and unredeemably untruthful, with a libido that just would not quit. The public bought the message and drew unexpected conclusions. If people who get involved with drugs are such freaks, who needs them?

Under the influence of structural, cultural, and legal changes, the stigma of addiction is fading. There has been a revision in the concept of addiction. Rather than thinking of that phenomenon as an entity, it is now seen as a process. Although the medical profession has its definition of addiction (in fact more than one definition), the terms "user," "abuser," and "addict" are popularly used almost interchangeably.

That bespeaks a certain wisdom. A person

does not become an addict once and for all any more than a person becomes tubercular or syphilitic for keeps. Addiction is a condition that a person moves into and out of. People who are in the drug scene speak of how many times they have had a habit. Now using, now doing without the drug, now compulsively involved in full blown use, now occasionally involved . . . addiction is more a state of mind than a state of being.

The stigma on the drug user is lessened too by the fact that many people today know someone who has been "into drugs." If we have been close to such a person we know the label does not tell the whole story about them. To call someone "addict" or "abuser" is to describe only a small part of their being and their life. The label chooses an area of their behavior where they are different and ignores the vast reality of their lives and themselves where they are very much more like, than unlike, the rest of humankind.

Large corporations now realize that their prospering depends on the flourishing of the society in which they exist. Good citizenship, for a business as much as for an individual, means contributing to the well-being of your community. Those firms that have committed themselves to operating in the urban environment are especially sensitive to the social problems that impact on the corporation's life—problems like drug use, abuse, and addiction. •

In law, the Rehabilitation Act of 1973 (6) has been extended to include alcoholics and drug abusers among those protected by its provisions. The text forbids government contractors from discriminating against the handicapped, and, in keeping with the legislation, the Department of Labor calls for large firms to install affirmative action efforts to include such persons in the work force. In every instance, the expectation is that the person hired is truly qualified.

Much negative editorial comment followed Assistant Secretary Elisberg's statement in July, 1977, that called for affirmative action hiring programs for alcoholics and drug abusers on a par with those directed toward minority groups and females. Fortune magazine headlined one article "Leave No Stoned Worker Unturned" (3), and Victor Riesel asked, "If they can fulfill the work, why call them . . . drug abusers . . . and why handicapped?"

The answer to Riesel's latter question is that the mentally or physically impaired are not the only class of handicapped persons. Those who have a record of such impairment—for example, the mentally restored and recovered victims of heart disease—are handicapped by those histories. Also handicapped are those who simply are thought of as having such an impairment. Thus the appropriately medicated person with epilepsy or the person who uses drugs recreationally or once used drugs destructively qualify as handicapped people because others treat them as such.

Resistance to the inclusion of alcoholics and drug abusers among those protected by the law was strong enough to cause amendments to be introduced that would single out this population. The Rehabilitation Act was in the midst of revision during the 96th Congress. In its version, the House of Representatives went so far as to exclude, for the purpose of Sections 503 and 504, "any person who is an alcoholic, or who is a drug abuser *in need of rehabilitation*" (emphasis added) (6).

The Senate—thanks to better information from members well acquainted with Alcoholics Anonymous, concerned workers in the field of drug treatment, and the experts of the Legal Action Center in New York—did not incorporate that language in its version. The text that passed and was signed into law by President Carter in November, 1978, excludes from Sections 503 and 504 of the Rehabilitation Act "any individual whose current use of alcohol or drugs prevents such individual from performing the duties of the job in question or whose employment, by reason of such current alcohol or drug abuse, would constitute a direct threat to property or the safety of others" (6).

It may seem unnecessary to specify that any person who cannot do the job or whose presence would be so serious a problem need not be hired. To that extent the wording may be unwelcome, because it sets these people apart as particularly troublesome.

The text is a plus in so far as alcoholics and drug abusers are the only groups specifically named in the law. The mention resolves any discussion about the legislators' intent in protecting them. Alcoholics and drug abusers are in. In on what?

1. Section 501, which requires every

agency of the Executive Branch to hire, place, and promote the handicapped.

2. *Section 502,* which calls for architectural accommodations and provisions in transportation for the needs of the handicapped.

3. *Section 503,* forbidding discrimination against the handicapped by government contractors and subcontractors.

4. *Section 504,* which forbids the exclusion of the handicapped from employment or provision of services by facilities, agencies, and governmental units that receive federal aid (6).

Recovered substance abusers, handicapped as they are by the fears and myths that are associated with drug use, ought to be aware of the protection the law provides for them. We all should be mindful of the fact that the law does not mean they must be hired. "Qualified" is always the norm.

What has been created is an atmosphere where an individual can reasonably ask a potential employer whether an affirmative action program for hiring the handicapped exists in an organization. If one does exist, the former drug abuser can ask to take advantage of the program.

Whereas all firms that have government contracts in excess of $2,500 are required to abide by Section 503, those that have contracts of $50,000 or more and employ 50 persons or more must have Affirmative Action Programs for handicapped workers. The Department of Labor, which administers compliance with Section 503, calls for such affirmative action efforts to include the establishing of contacts with treatment programs and organizations of and for handicapped persons, initiating active enlistment efforts, training supervisors to adapt to the presence of handicapped workers, publicizing the existence of the program, and providing every employee and applicant with an invitation to take advantage of the program.

That invitation has to be phrased carefully so as to encourage involvement in the program by explaining the advantages to be gained by applying while making clear the protected nature of the information given. The Department of Labor restricts how that data can be shared (with supervisors who may have to make accommodations, with first aid and safety personnel who may have need to know, and with government officials reviewing compliance). The application must inform workers that they are free to ask for inclusion at a later date and that their choice will in no way be used to their harm.

Many firms have found the compliance review a helpful experience since the Department of Labor officers are able to provide them with useful techniques and sources for recruiting qualified handicapped workers.

In March, 1979, the Supreme Court reversed a previous decision of a lower court and allowed that the Transit Authority of the City of New York was justified in excluding methadone patients from employment. The general Transit Authority policy excludes persons who use narcotics, and methadone is a narcotic. The final decision suggested that the best plan would be to judge each case singly, taking into consideration the sensitivity of the position in question and the status of each applicant. Nonetheless, the policy of the employer was seen as rational and licit, because any rule that might be adopted would be less precise and more costly for a system as large as the Transit Authority (5).

The proportion of high risk jobs in the Transit Authority is so great and the total number of employees so large that the situation is almost unique and cannot lead to the conclusion that affirmative action for recovered substance abusers is a dead issue.

THE STIGMA WITHIN

The labels we pin on ourselves are even more difficult to deal with than those that others place on us. Our knowledge of who and what we are is both direct and indirect. The way we interpret the information we acquire about ourselves is influenced in general by how we feel about life and in particular by how we have experienced ourselves in the past. The variety of terms by which we describe our perception of self hints at the richness of our whole experience and the partial nature of each individual glimpse. Body image, self-image, self-concept, self-esteem, self-awareness all describe something of our knowledge of self. To understand ourselves and how we fit into life around us, each of us tends to assume a role and then act as befits that status.

We may act out many roles in a variety of settings. It happens that, for some, one role comes to the fore and dominates a large part of their actions, feelings, and thoughts. So the person styles himself/herself as "Born Again" or "Don Juan" or as "The Boss." There is a role, too, called "The Addict." The addict serves a function in society by presenting a model of a life style beyond the borders of acceptability. The addict knows the part expected and lives it out. "Once an addict always an addict" is part of the game.

Those who have allowed that addict role to penetrate their inner life and color all perception of self find it difficult to know themselves as other than addicts.

The role makes it hard to imagine being drug free, succeeding in love, or achieving success on a job. For those people, doing well at work is more difficult to take than failure, because failure corresponds better to what they know of themselves. For the "addict," success forces a whole new evaluation of who and what he or she is.

The treatment program that uses the admission of being a "dope fiend" as an initial therapeutic tool eventually has to replace that identity with a more positive perception of the self as the client moves away from the treatment experience and into the larger society.

In conducting an employment project for recovered drug dependents, the National Association on Drug Abuse Problems' experience has been that almost 50 per cent of those who have appointments for job screening fail to appear for those meetings. Of those who are referred out for job interviews, 25 per cent are "no-shows." When they are successfully screened, interviewed, and hired, 10 per cent fail to report for the first day of work.

In following the early work experiences of former drug abusers the "walkaway" is seen as a common phenomenon. The newly placed person leaves the workplace unannounced or just stops showing up at the job. Upon inquiry the experience has been that the workers felt everyone was aware of their drug history; they did not think they were performing satisfactorily and wanted to leave before they were fired; or the tension of being on "display" was too great for them.

Various programs have attempted to forestall these events. One effort keeps very close contact with the newly placed recovered drug abuser. A counselor meets with each client upon placement and offers practical counseling on job problems, referral for personal difficulties, and the opportunity for group involvement with other working persons in settings where experiences can be shared and compared (7).

The Wildcat Project used the strategy of having the newly employed recovered drug dependents work together in teams so that the comradeship which had been developed in the street could be put to positive use as an enforcement of the commitment to work and a support against early disabling anxiety (1).

The investment of staff time at the point of reentry into the workforce is well worthwhile since newly employed persons who have succeeded in treatment need all the help available to sustain them in the formulation of an image of self more positive than that of "ex-dope-fiend."

SPECIFIC SOCIAL NEEDS

For some who have been on drugs, the possibility of long term upwardly mobile employment is farfetched. We cannot expect of recovered drug dependents a kind of behavior we do not demand of the average person.

Some people are neither cut out for, nor interested in work. Reentry for them may mean no more than constructive insertion in the life of their block, their family, or a neighborhood social center. Perhaps as many as a third of those with drug problems are in that situation . . . a reinforcement of our position that most of the impediments to work have nothing to do with drugs.

There are nutritional deficiencies in prenatal and infant life that undermine the natural process of maturing. Child abuse and nonsupportive family settings create problems with self-image that program a person for defeat. Shortcomings in the educational experience contribute antagonism toward schooling in general or leave voids in basic skills that are difficult to supply in later life. Maturing in a community that devalues work accomplishment and extols the "hustle" as a style of survival militates against commitment to the more conventional styles of functioning in society. Identifying the business community with the oppressing class or buying into the welfare way of life stands firmly between program participants and doing their bit in the world of work.

Counselors need not feel that they have sold out to the Establishment to do a good job of counseling. Reality dictates that, in aiding recovered drug dependents in creating new identities that will support them in their resolve to get by without addiction, integration into the world of work has to be one of the possibilities.

Legal difficulties block former drug users in their employment efforts. Drug use and criminal records often go together. It is not so much that the drug use causes the crime as that drugs and crime are rooted in the same causes, often enough simply a marginal style of life or the educational, familial, and societal problems we have described.

Some legal problems are direct obstacles to employment, for example, outstanding warrants, convictions for crimes of dishonesty, and licensing regulations that exclude persons with convictions. Every effort should be made to determine just what the history of arrests and convictions contains. Problems cannot be dealt with until it is known what they are. The process for the resolution of warrants ought to be well known by all program personnel. The fact that court officers are very eager to have old warrants cleared and are inclined to believe that the active participant in a drug treatment program has made an honest attempt to set things right is an encouragement. Participants who have been arrested but not convicted ought to be encouraged to explore the possibility of recovering photographs and fingerprints that were taken and try to have their records removed from local, state, and federal files. Each site where such a memento of one's brush with the law remains is a potential problem source.

Those who are convicted should appeal to a magistrate for a certificate for the relief of civil disabilities where available. That document removes from the convicted person the limits on their voting rights and any denial of license privileges.

Those who have served time should be encouraged to apply for a certificate of good behavior that documents that the person made the period of incarceration work for him or her.

Where convictions are for crimes of dishonesty or breach of trust, difficulties arise in the areas of bonding and the regulations of the Federal Deposit Insurance Corporation (FDIC), which monitors banking operations. Many corporations find that they can press

bonding agents to cover any individual. Banks variously interpret the FDIC's regulation that excludes from employment persons convicted of "crimes of dishonesty or breach of trust." The regulation itself excepts from the exclusion felons who have been rehabilitated. Some banking executives make the judgment regarding an applicant's rehabilitation on their own and wait for the FDIC monitor to complain. Others, in the same situation, await the approval of the monitor; a procedure that takes so long that the applicant loses interest or the position is otherwise filled.

Legal problems that pose an indirect obstacle to employment are those that so occupy a person's time or attention as to distract him/her from concentrating on the task of preparing for and obtaining employment. Debt, housing problems, and marital difficulties festering for years have a way of hitting just as one is ready to embark on a job. Long standing anxiety surrounding anything concerning the law causes many to avoid appearances in court and ignore summonses. Such failure puts the person in the wrong, right from the start.

Program personnel must work to allay that fear and encourage the participant to see such a difficulty as one more problem that must be dealt with. Avoidance here is slipping back into the same old patterns that made the problems for the person in the first place.

Counselors respond very positively when they see that the court system is negotiable. The same insight and skills that make those persons competent to understand and respond to the program participants' clinical needs can help in defining legal difficulties and determining the strategy that will solve them.

THE WORK CULTURE

To some degree a real deficit lies in the nature of the classic drug treatment program. Vocational rehabilitation has not regularly been a high priority item. The emphasis on clinical needs has been so stressed that other aspects of the client's need have often been misdiagnosed or simply missed.

In society's response to the newly visible drug abuse problems of the 1960's, the contribution on the part of men and women without professional training was very significant. Programs like Synanon and Odyssey, although they had professionals as mentors and sources of inspiration, put the individual gifts and skills of a whole variety of persons to greater use.

Specific expertise was less important than one's charisma and dedication. Even in the chemotherapeutic programs, the personality of each staff member was of primary importance. It has been said that the early success of methadone maintenance may have been due in large part to the dynamism of Dr. Marie Nyswander, that technique's co-developer.

Being "good people" and having "rapport," laying down a great "rap," and "respecting yourself" do count in providing a model of self-actualized living appropriate to the need of the compulsive drug user. Still, getting one's head together is not a sufficient goal; you also have to get your act together.

Many of the staff members in drug treatment programs come from backgrounds in education and social work. Some come from work in community development or out of the life themselves. Many others are former members of the clergy. Few have had much contact with the world of work as most people know it. Factory work, office work, and manual labor are alien to the experience of many drug workers. The expectations and behavioral styles of that workaday world are as foreign to the counselors as they are to the clients.

Vocational rehabilitation has to start on the first day of treatment. More than any other achievement—cutting free of the drugs, changing one's circle of friends, reestablishing broken family ties, accepting control and responsibility over one's own behavior—vocational accomplishment is a sign of success to the former drug abuser and to society at large. The drug treatment process has not really begun until the vocational rehabilitation process has started. "How is this person, once recovered, going to fit into the larger society?" That question must begin to be explored on day 1.

As displeased as critics of our culture may be, the world out there is the only one we have. Regardless of the specific process by which an individual may develop drug problems, the intensive and compulsive use of those substances soon leaves many estranged from that real world. Helping drug-de-

pendent individuals turn their lives around involves helping them to insert themselves in the culture. Keeping control over our own lives is the first step in asserting our influence over what goes on in the world around us. Accomplishing something is a certain antidote to alienation.

From the start, an assessment ought to be made of the possible avenues this participant might follow. Vocational rehabilitation does not mean getting a job.

The art of rehabilitation has its history in the effort to help veterans of the First World War who returned from Europe injured in such a way as to forbid them taking up their former employment. The field developed as more states became aware of the numbers of persons disabled by industrial accidents and the needs of the physically and mentally handicapped in general. With time, the studies came to reveal persons who were blocked from involvement in the active world around them by learning difficulties, educational deficits, emotional burdens, and the insults to incentive that poverty, discrimination, and the lack of opportunity inflict.

Vocational rehabilitation now embraces the whole array of needs that describe the shortfall between an individual's skills, knowledge, and social adjustment and what is expected by the world around that person: educational experience; one's readiness and capacity to be involved in common tasks with others, either in a paid or voluntary relationship; the ability to set goals and structure behavior toward the achievement of those goals; familiarity with the jargon and unspoken cues that mark a person as a worker.

The world of the drug dependent is a subculture with its own style of interaction. Even the solitary dependent knows what is expected of one in that way of life. Just as the solitary drinker knows you hide bottles in the light fixtures, your desk, and the garage, so the middle-class person feeding on amphetamine and barbiturates knows the games one plays with physicians and the way you call your friends late at night to appeal for help. The subculture of the street drug user is an even more complete environment. Its argot is as refined as any, its value system very demanding, its taboos explicit, and a whole framework of myths provides a background for the addict's sense of self.

Remarkably enough, that life calls for skills

that can be readily applied to the demands of the larger society. To survive in the hustle, a man or woman must know a great deal about human nature (who can be trusted, who to avoid), how to organize the obtaining of a supply of drugs, how to distribute the same, how to form bonds with the competition and keep the fuzz away from your door—a demanding job description that calls for real competence and provides experience that, applied to the world of licit enterprise, could pay off handsomely. Turning the participant around ought to involve helping him/her to see that not all the time spent "chasing the bag" was wasted.

There was a time when any honest attempt to help drug dependents could get funding, provided the program had community acceptance. Governmental agencies and the public were so concerned about drug problems and felt so ill equipped to deal with them that they were reluctant to refuse any reasonable offer. Now, that period of panic has passed. Drug abuse is no more a hot issue. Acceptance of recreational involvement is more and more widespread, as is a tolerance for the fact that some of those who fool with drugs will be fooled by drugs. Budget cutbacks have fallen where the fat seemed to be. Vocational components, where they existed, were often the first to go, because that effort was not seen as of primary importance. Where vocational staff were lost to programs, line counselors had to pick up the effort and become newly aware of how tragic it was for a participant to do well in a program and go nowhere with his or her life because of vocational deficits.

Even before acquiring the specific skills to contribute to the vocational readiness of program participants, counselors must familiarize themselves with the business milieu, deal with their own pessimism about the marketability of former drug abusers, and accept some share of responsibility in this issue.

The business community is not a monolith. There are people in responsible positions in management who want no part of former drug users. There are others at the same level whose only questions have to do with job performance. What a worker is or was is of no concern to them. Their only question is, "Will they do the job?" Others in corporate life are particularly sensitive to recovered drug dependents because someone close to

them had a drug habit or they themselves have had to deal with a chemical problem. Others are simply sensitive, helpful types. There are even some characters at that level of employment who are getting high themselves. The world of commerce is as heterogenous as any other slice of American life.

In every firm, an internal conversation is taking place as to what the policy and practice should be regarding drug users, current and former. Men and women who have struggled to free themselves from drug problems have their advocates behind the paneled doors of business and industry. What those decision makers need is good information on the capability and reliability of the former drug user. Counselors have to equip themselves with and make known the best information on the marketability of recovered drug dependents.

Companies that have hired people successful in treatment find them performing on a par with other workers, similarly employed, who have no history of drug use. Initially they may make more frequent trips to the corporate medical department and have problems budgeting. Those are consequences of their return to functioning where they assume responsibility over their physical and financial well-being. As for lateness, absences, following orders, and getting along with co-workers, their problems are no more numerous than those of other newly employed persons. In entry level positions, these four failings are the most frequent causes for dismissal. Counselors must invest a good deal of effort prior to placement and, in the early months of employment, help program participants avoid that fate. People who have been deeply into drugs can well do without one more experience of failure.

Very few recovered drug abusers are fired for return to drug use or even suspected drug use. At most, 2 per cent lose their jobs for those reasons. Criminal behavior is an even less frequent cause of termination.

Contrary to the popular myth, most people in drug treatment have held jobs, possess skills, and, upon recovery, find work on their own, although often at levels beneath their capacity.

Those who are hardest to place are those who are at either end of the spectrum, those who are suffering from multiple impediments to employment and those who have education beyond the 4 years of college. The individual who has gone to graduate school is looking for a level of employment that involves a corresponding degree of responsibility. Even very cooperative firms are reluctant initially to place a recovered drug dependent at that level.

One fact counselors and participants alike should be sure of is the eagerness of the personnel officer to hire qualified people. When you go for a job interview the individual who meets with you is always anxious that you *will* be hired. Their task is not to ferret out reasons to reject you but to hire. They have pressures on them to fill the empty positions and would like to accomplish that goal with the least investment of time and energy. If you fit the need, their task is completed. The general rule is the interviewer is on your side.

Finding work is part of reentry. The counselor's task is not finished until the first steps of reentry have been taken. The counselor has to open the minds of the participants to an appreciation of work. The various types of employment should be explained and each individual's gifts and interests explored. Appropriate dress and grooming for work and what to expect on the job should be outlined. How to summarize your work history and present it in a resume should be covered, as well as filling out a job application and preparing for the job interview.

The person looking for work ought to be helped to see that a certain style of dress, speech, and behavior is expected, especially upon interview, where that first impression is made.

The interview will have an informal introduction, the purpose of which is to put the applicant at ease. The bulk of the interview will explore the work history and interests of the applicant and describe something about the firm's operation. In the normal course, some feedback will be given to the applicant about the possibility of his or her skill and the employer's job openings matching. Finally the interviewer will ask the applicant whether he or she has any questions, and honest inquiries are welcome.

No interview is a failure. From each such exchange something can be learned. Counselors should go over the interview experience with the person to maximize their learning.

If the participant is hired, the counselor should walk beside him/her in his/her first few months of employment to help them deal with this new and sometimes frightening experience. Just because the former drug abuser has a job we cannot think his/her file is closed. Times of change are times of stress for all of us. Our needs are high in such a transition, and a reliable supportive counselor can greatly enhance the chance of seeing participants succeed in this period of adjustment.

References

1. Freidman, L. N. *The Wildcat Experiment: An Early Test of Supported Work in Drug Abuse Rehabilitation.* Rockville, Md., National Institute on Drug Abuse, 1978.
2. Hunt, L. Counting heads. Washington Drug Rev., 4: 3, 1979.
3. Leave no stoned worker unturned. Fortune Magazine, August 1977.
4. Musto, D. F. *The American Disease: Origins of Narcotic Control.* New Haven, Conn., Yale University Press, 1973.
5. New York Transit Authority versus Beazer, March 21, 1979. United States Supreme Court No. 77-1427.
6. 96th United States Congress. Rehabilitation Act, 1973.
7. Winick, C. and Lloyd, J. *The First 90 Days.* New York, The National Association on Drug Abuse Problems, 1978.

CHAPTER 51

DRUGS IN INDUSTRY

Robert S. Graham, M.D.

Whereas alcohol abuse has been regarded by many in management and labor as a problem in industry since the 1940's and 1950's, abuse of other substances generally was not recognized until the mid to late 1960's and the 1970's. Unfortunately, even now many leaders in business feel that, although a few employees of some organizations other than their own may have these problems, certainly their own do not. Generally, if they have a business employing more than a few people the problems are there—unrecognized and unmanaged.

NATURE OF THE PROBLEM

We are a drug-oriented society and unfortunately the use of substances to alter moods may get out of control, whether the person is employed or not. Usually, regardless of the substance used, attendance, performance, and on-the-job behavior are not impaired until control is lost. Some abusers may go into and out of periods of loss of control, varying widely in duration and frequency, whereas others may never lose control.

The drug most frequently abused by the employed is alcohol. Marihuana ranks next. Tranquilizers, barbiturates, and other prescription drugs follow in frequency of abuse and often are used in association with alcohol. Hard drugs are used by relatively few. Use is not uncommonly associated with alcohol abuse and that of other drugs. For this reason, it is not realistic to approach drug abuse prevention and treatment through programs purely oriented to only one substance. Polydrug use necessitates a broader approach. This is particularly true when dealing with the problems of younger employees.

Business people usually think that substance abuse among employees will result in loss of productivity, poor quality of work produced, absenteeism, adverse effects on the morale of fellow workers, disruption of the work group, theft, increased benefits costs, decreased employee retention with increased costs for orientation and training, increased accidents, and loss of personnel time used to handle these problems. How many of these problems are actually drug related and how many are due to other changes in the social and educational backgrounds of employee populations and other factors cannot be determined. Management journals now frequently cite these same problems as present among higher graded white collar workers and upper management people where drug habits (except for alcoholism) are not commonly thought to exist.

EXTENT OF PROBLEM AMONG THE EMPLOYED AND THE COST

No one knows the extent of the problem of substance abuse including alcohol among the employed. Figures regarding problem drinking have been published widely by government and private agencies. They are alarming. Some estimates are as high as 10 per cent. Although the incidence of alcoholism is known to be greater in some industries than others, I know of no personnel or medical officer of any large corporation, including those in industries thought to be of greater risk, who believes that the incidence of alcoholism in his or her organization is that high. However, because many alcoholics can function adequately on the job (at least for a period of time) and there is a tendency for fellow workers and supervisors to "cover up," no organization actually ever learns the extent of the problem among its own people.

With substance abuse other than alcoholism, because of the way society views it, employees usually keep their problems to themselves. No cover-up by supervisors or fellow employees generally occurs. Assistance programs for employees with such problems are rare, and dismissal is the usual rule. This generally occurs because of attendance or performance problems. Management and labor usually are not aware of the true cause of the employee's work failure. Therefore, they cannot estimate the amount of drug abuse among employees.

In 1970, the then New York State Narcotic Addiction Control Commission did a study of drug use among employed workers in various occupation groups (5). This revealed that some ½ per cent of employed people regularly (six or more times per month) used heroin and that some 1.3 per cent of employed people had at some time used it. Those using barbiturates, tranquilizers, and other sedatives ranged from 1 to 3 per cent who regularly used such drugs to 8.6 to 19.5 per cent who used them at some time or another. From 4 to 12 per cent used marihuana and from 3/10 to 2.6 per cent used lysergic acid diethylamide (LSD). Most agree that these figures represent only the tip of the iceberg. Substance abuse by the employed is undoubtedly considerable. However, it must be emphasized again that a person can be an alcoholic and/or abusing other substances including multiple drugs at the same time and yet may be able to perform satisfactorily on the job, behave normally at work, and maintain acceptable attendance.

Because no accurate estimate can be made of the extent of drug abuse among the employed or of its effect on the national product, no valid estimate can be made of the total cost to industry.

INDUSTRY'S CONCERN

Gradually many in management and labor have come to realize that substance abuse, including alcoholism, out of control does affect production costs. Furthermore, whether or not it is recognized by a particular industry, substance abuse undoubtedly does exist and, therefore, should be a proper concern to it as a producing and profit-making business and a good corporate citizen. Many of our more progressive companies are facing up to the realities of the times and their corporate responsibilities by developing appropriate policy and implementing it with effective programs. They are working through and with community agencies to prevent drug abuse and alcoholism and to assure good treatment facilities and are becoming directly involved with vocational rehabilitation and employment.

POLICY MAKING

Many companies have gone through several changes of attitude to arrive at a meaningful policy regarding substance abuse among employees. Some two or three decades ago it was recognized that alcoholism was a treatable disease rather than a character flaw, and policy began to be developed that was consistent with that concept. As experience was gained, it was found that such policy must originate with the chief executive officer, be written, widely publicized, and be properly understood down through the ranks. To be effective, policy must be nonpunitive, constructive, and provide for treatment, rehabilitation, and follow-up. Confidentiality is essential. It must contain provision for self-referral to a company program as well as for referrals by family members, supervisors, and friends. The policy has to be reaffirmed on a regular basis. This is usually done through company publications.

Policy regarding substance abuse other than alcohol is more difficult to develop. Many people in management and labor at the time drug abuse among the employed began to become apparent found it hard to understand. First, it was thought by them to be associated with the young and with "anti-Establishment" people to whom it was hard for them to relate. Young drug abusers were quite a contrast to the older, established, and usually personally known person with an alcohol problem to whom they could relate frequently as "old drinking buddies." Later, they were shocked to learn that all kinds of people at many levels of management could be involved.

The greatest problem was created by the concept of the drug abuser as a drug fiend or addict. Few business managers realized that most drugs are consumed in moderation and/or sporadically (weekends, holidays, parties, etc.), not unlike alcohol. Scare tactics and propaganda produced by some government and private agencies created an unrealistic fear of drugs. Only in the last few years has more accurate information been generally available through the media. Now many business people have had children, friends, or employees who use drugs. The emotional impact has lessened sufficiently to allow policy development. Generally this occurs in stages as knowledge increases. The stages frequently are as follows:

1. No company policy is believed necessary because management thinks that people abusing drugs do not want to work (it does not permit sufficient time for stealing to support the habit); or if work is wanted they are incapable of it because of their habit.

2. An unwritten company policy generally develops after it is learned that some drug abusers actually do work. This generally is directed toward protection of other young employees from drug users; it is believed that the users will spread the habit rapidly among other employees to support their own habit. Also, this is directed toward protection of the company from theft, etc. This type of policy generally encourages all supervisors to be alert for any signs of drug abuse among employees. This is the "seek out and dismiss" policy. Urine testing of suspect employees and of all prospective employees has generally been done by companies with such policies.

3. The next stage of policy development usually is still unwritten but provides that all employees known to be using drugs be dismissed. However, when this is done they are referred to a community drug treatment and rehabilitation center for *addicts*. At this stage, nonaddictive or social use of drugs is still not recognized.

4. As more is learned of drug abuse by the employed, policy may be written or unwrit-

ten but usually provides for dismissal with referral to a center that handles drug abuse problems, not just hard core addicts. Also, there may be a provision for rehiring the employee after a stated period of successful treatment and rehabilitation (usually 1 year).

5. As understanding and experience progress, companies are likely to develop a written policy. This usually provides that employees using drugs and not involved with selling or passing drugs are not fired providing they undergo indicated treatment and rehabilitation. If this can be done without interfering with work, they may remain on the job. If it cannot, then the problem is regarded as any other illness and they are returned to work when they have recovered.

6. The next advancement in written policy provides that drug abuse becomes the concern of the company only when it interferes with attendance or performance or behavior. Behavior includes that which off the job reflects unfavorably on the company and on the job is inappropriate or involves use of drugs at work or passing or selling of drugs on the premises. It is treated as any other medical problem. Confidentiality is regarded as essential.

The policy must originate with the chief executive officer, be completely understood as a company policy by all ranks of management, published in a clear and understandable fashion, distributed to all employees, publicized, and periodically reaffirmed. Policy should be nonpunitive, constructive, provide for treatment, rehabilitation, follow-up, and, most certainly, confidentiality.

Many companies now combine alcoholism and other substance abuse into a single policy statement. Still others include alcoholism and all substance abuse in an umbrella policy dealing with the "troubled employee."

POLICY IMPLEMENTATION

Policy regarding substance abuse, including alcohol, among employees is most successfully implemented when the emotional responses to it have been considered and appropriately managed. Many companies have used small group orientation meetings with no more than 15 to 20 supervisors per group. During these, common fears, anger, and prejudices are faced frankly. It is emphasized that people from any background can have substance abuse problems. Participants are encouraged to recall people they have known or have direct knowledge of with substance abuse problems. This helps them to relate better to the problem and to relieve some of their anxiety. Discussion should be organized to assure full understanding of the policy, its purpose, and how it will work to benefit the troubled person, his/her family, and the company. It is essential that it be understood that the policy will be administered in a nonpunitive fashion and with complete confidentiality. A free discussion should be permitted with just enough direction to assure that comments and questions are to the point. The leader should be aware of the emotions of participants in a group.

At the same time the policy is made known, implementation procedures should be explained in detail.

OCCUPATIONAL PROGRAMS FOR PREVENTION AND CONTROL OF SUBSTANCE ABUSE

Occupational programs for substance abuse must have the complete support of the chief executive officer and of all levels of management and labor right down the line. Those companies with both a personnel department (or person) and a medical department (or person) must assure that both work together in developing and carrying out the program.

All records pertaining to individuals in the program must be kept in one place. They must be completely confidential and available only to those people who have the direct responsibility for carrying out the program. No reference to participation should be made in personnel files. Where there is a medical department and the medical records are completely confidential, it is good to make program records a part of that file. However, it must be understood by those in personnel that only medical department staff members have access to medical records.

ALCOHOLISM PROGRAMS

Many progressive companies, large and small, have alcoholism programs. Few provide other than counseling services in-house. Generally, this is offered to both the patient and his or her family. The employee is then referred to a community resource for complete physical and emotional evaluation, detoxification, and the initiation of any therapy required for physical problems. Following this the individual is transferred to a rehabilitation center.

The family may be referred for appropriate counseling.

It is essential that a company person responsible for carrying out the program have a good relationship with the people providing this care.

The local affiliate of the National Counsel on Alcoholism is a good resource for finding out where in the community good detoxification, treatment, and rehabilitation services are available.

After completion of rehabilitation, the individual generally is referred to an appropriate Alcoholics Anonymous (AA) group or a similiar program in his/her community. When emotional health problems are present, referral is then made to a psychologist or psychiatrist. When able, the employee is returned to work. Once returned, the employee is expected to maintain the same level of attendance and performance as any other employee.

After return, company counseling may be necessary in a number of areas, such as debt consolidation, tax problems, etc. If this type of counseling is not available within the company, referral should be made to specific community resources.

Appointments for follow-up discussions of problems and in-house counseling should be given. Generally, an employee will not voluntarily request a counseling appointment for fear of being a "bother" or because of reluctance to admit that after all the attention he/she has received a problem does still exist.

ROLE OF THE SUPERVISOR

The supervisor must realize his/her essential role in the program. Support should be given, as should instructions as to how to carry out his/her part.

To help the supervisor understand the program, he/she must be assured of the following:

1. Referral of an employee to the program is an act of friendship and support. It is in no way an expression of disloyalty or an act of a "squealer."

2. Job conservation generally will result from the referral. There is expectation that the individual will return to being a satisfactory employee.

3. Treatment and rehabilitation may preserve the family unit. Family members as well as the employee may benefit emotionally and physically by the process.

4. To the individual being helped, it may mean the actual saving or prolongation of life.

5. A likely outcome is restoration to a life style of dignity and to being a contributing member of society.

6. Most occupational alcoholism programs have a success rate of between 60 and 80 per cent.

At first some supervisors are reluctant to confront employees with drinking problems for fear of a mistake. This need not be a concern if they discuss with the employee actual job problems such as attendance, performance, on-the-job behavior, etc. After this they may comment that it seems there may be a drinking problem and why. All such observations should be documented, indicating exactly what occurred, when, and where. An accusation of alcoholism ordinarily should not be made by the supervisor.

Generally the employee will deny any problem with alcohol or readily admit that he/she did have a problem but claim that now it is over. The supervisor should state that he/she is not in a position to evaluate the employee's problems other than by attendance, performance, behavior, etc., but that there is concern; therefore he/she is being referred for help. If no drinking problem exists, this will be determined by the program staff, and appropriate referral for other evaluations will be made.

If the employee does not choose to take advantage of the referral offer, then administrative action should be taken on the basis of the current work record. It is the threat of job loss that makes occupational alcoholism programs more effective than most others.

A supervisor who can be genuinely concerned for his/her troubled employee and yet be firm and hard in insisting on corrective action is most effective. With experience and success, many supervisors become expert in handling such problems and develop great pride and satisfaction from it.

DRUG ABUSE PROGRAMS

Drug abuse programs in industry are relatively new and comparatively few in number. Few if any exist in the absence of some kind of alcoholism program. The same staff members generally carry out both programs.

Generally programs consist of detection, evaluation, counseling, and referral to community resources for more definitive action. This consists of evaluation of extent of the habit, substances abused, physical and emotional problems present, detoxification, treatment, and rehabilitation.

ROLE OF THE SUPERVISOR

As is true with alcoholism programs, the role of the supervisor is vital. To review:

1. Supervisors must be aware of his/her importance in any employee program for drug abuse.

2. Each must recognize that early detection through alertness to change in an employee and prompt referral for intervention is an act of concern, friendship, and responsibility directed toward the well-being of the employee. It is not to be regarded as an unfriendly or hostile act.

3. Intervention may result in job retention and restoration to productive employment. Successful rehabilitation generally occurs in 50 to 70 per cent of cases (very close to that for alcoholism). The most important result may be emotional health and the strengthening of the economic and social resources of the employee.

4. Improvement may occur in family relationships.

5. The expectation is for restoration of the employee's personal dignity and self-respect.

Work problems should be documented and discussed with the employee. The supervisor should be frank and accurate about his/her observations. It should be emphasized that the discussion is occurring because of the desire to help and that a referral is being made in the interest of providing assistance. Accusation of drug abuse should not be made. Regardless of what excuse is made if the problem has been severe enough to effect his/her work, then help is required. Referral should be made to the counselor or medical person used by the company. If the employee does not accept the offer for referral, then appropriate administrative action should be taken on the basis of attendance, performance, and on-the-job behavior.

DETECTION

This was the most frequently employed drug abuse prevention and control activity carried out by companies during the late 1960's and early 1970's. Generally this consisted of the physical examination of prospective employees for evidence of drug abuse, particularly puncture wounds and analysis of urine for evidence of drugs. A few companies rejected people because of dress, appearance, and particularly speech patterns that suggested "street knowledge," assuming that all such people were drug addicts. Some employed lie detector tests. Such tests generally were used to weed out not only drug users but homosexuals and others management felt would not make desirable employees. Some ran similiar examinations on all employees at intervals to "seek out" and get rid of drug abusers.

Most companies who did urinalysis for evidence of drug abuse have given it up. The tests were expensive, frequently inaccurate, and generally not productive. Many considered it an invasion of privacy and a violation of civil rights. It seems more reasonable to spend the money used for such testing on positive actions for enhancement of employee health and morale.

There is no need to discuss lie detection techniques used for drug detection. This type of activity resulted from fear and ignorance.

A drug abuser out of control usually very quickly will come to the attention of the alert supervisor because of problems in one or more of the following areas: attendance, frequent absences from his or her immediate work area, frequent visits to the company medical facility, performance, appearance, on-the-job behavior. The good supervisor need only carry out his/her normal alertness for change in an employee to detect drug abuse out of control.

Company medical service providers are the most frequent detectors of drug abuse other than supervisors.

Security staff personnel also are charged with detection. A decade or so ago they were primarily involved in the program with seeking out drug abusers. Now they are concerned more with illegal activities such as drug pushing or passing on the premises, taking of drugs while at work, theft, etc.

Detection is contributed to by self-referrals and referrals by family members, friends, and fellow workers. But this does not become a viable source until a nonpunitive policy is established and an effective program is in place that protects the rights of the employee, maintains confidentiality, and the company and the program earn the trust and confidence of employees.

COUNSELING SERVICES

Drug abuse programs (as well as those for alcoholism and the troubled employee) require that experienced, well trained counselors be available. Those companies that provide the services themselves usually do so through the employee health department, personnel department, or a special department for counseling. Counselors are rarely used only for counseling as a part of a particular employee program such as drug abuse or alcoholism but rather are a part of an emotional health program directed toward a wide range of services. Some of the recent publications of Dr. James S. J. Manuso (2, 3) may be of help in establishing such a program or enhancing or evaluating one already in existence.

Some companies share counseling services. Still others rely on those available in the community. Wherever the services are obtained, counselors must have special expertise and experience in dealing with people and drug problems if a program is to be successful. The drug abuser generally is a master in deceiving, lying, manipulation, denial, and self-delusion. He or she cannot be properly evaluated much less counseled except by a person skilled in handling this type of behavior.

REFERRAL FOR TREATMENT AND REHABILITATION

Community resources ordinarily are used for determination of what drugs are being used, whether or not alcohol is also a problem, the degree of substance abuse, the extent of the physical and psychological dependence, general physical and emotional health, detoxification, treatment, rehabilitation, and follow-up.

Determination of exactly which community treatment and rehabilitation centers are to be used must be a part of the initial organization of the program. Such facilities vary widely in quality, in the type of drug problems treated, kind of treatment offered, and in the backgrounds of clients. For instance, some are primarily for the hard core street addict. In such a place those with enough conventionality to be employed may be given a very hard time and end up worse off for the experience.

Help in selecting the facility may be obtained from the department of psychiatry of a local medical school or teaching hospital or state, county, or community mental health service departments. Local physicians, particularly psychiatrists and psychologists, may be of help.

The company medical staff person or, if none, the personnel staff member concerned should maintain contact with the treatment-rehabilitation program and if possible with the employee to provide as much support as possible during this period. After return to the job, the company representative and the treatment-rehabilitation program staff member should continue the relationship. This allows progress to be noted and problems to be resolved before they develop into real trouble.

After the employee has returned to the job, he/she should be seen by program staff members on a regular basis with decreasing frequency if progress is good. Employees, if told to return only if they have a problem, generally will not do so until the problem has progressed too far. It is well to provide continuing support particularly for the first 6 months to a year.

"TROUBLED EMPLOYEE" PROGRAMS

Supervisors generally cannot and should not diagnose the condition causing changes in an employee. Therefore, a problem may arise as to which program or service a person should be referred. This is particularly true when services are fragmented into separate sections for alcoholism, drug abuse, physical health problem, emotional health, etc. Rather than risk an error, supervisors may simply resort to administrative action and terminate the services of the person.

A helpful way of organizing services is the "troubled employee" approach. Such programs provide the same drug abuse and alcoholism services to employees as specific special programs but in addition handle all other physical and emotional conditions that may impair employee productivity as a part of an over-all employee health or emotional health unit. This has the added advantage that all of the diverse and multiple problems of a troubled employee can be addressed. Employees are treated as whole people and not as individual problems, e.g., the "alcohol case" or "drug abuse case", etc.

EDUCATIONAL PROGRAMS

Most school children and young adults today know a great deal about alcohol and the various drugs in popular use and their effects. It is doubtful that educational programs that consist of printed materials, movies, or lectures on the actions of drugs will have any significant impact on this group. In fact, there is some evidence that such materials may actually encourage experimentation. Such educational programs may be of help to older employees who wish to become familiar with drug names and how they act. However, such material must be chosen for accuracy and presentation to avoid producing fear and undesirable emotional responses.

Educational materials are helpful when designed to help management and labor develop policy and programs and to assist supervisors in understanding their role and employees to know what services are available and how to obtain them.

INSURANCE

A number of company group benefit plans now include coverage for alcohol rehabilitation. Some states have mandated that all group plans must include this feature. Acute care and detoxification, when done in an accredited hospital, are covered by most group health plans.

Generally the cost of adding coverage for rehabilitation for alcoholism and drug abuse to a group plan is modest.

Group life insurance is issued to all employees of larger companies who provide it regardless of the past health history of those covered.

Individual health insurance is ordinarily not issued to active alcoholics and drug abusers. However, after a period of abstinence, the duration of which varies with the underwriting standards of the company, it can be purchased. Premiums vary, depending on the period of abstinence and the current life style of the individual. Most companies will not issue to people maintained on methadone.

Individual life insurance is available on about the same basis as health insurance. That is, coverage and level of premium depend on the period of abstinence, on whether or not the person is gainfully employed, and on the life style of the individual.

EMPLOYMENT OF THE REHABILITATED EX-DRUG ADDICT

In the previous chapter, the problems of the rehabilitated ex-addict in obtaining employment were considered.

Management and labor generally must depend on treatment and rehabilitation facilities in the community to carry out that part of their drug abuse programs. It then becomes an obligation to help these facilities place rehabilitated ex-addicts who are job ready. Furthermore, as good corporate citizens, industries are needed to restore those who are ready to return to work to useful employment. This also helps the company comply with Section 503 of the Rehabilitation Act.

A number of companies have found that job-ready rehabilitated ex-addicts make good employees. Among them Equitable Life in New York City now has a 10-year experience with hiring ex-addicts. When this program was started, it was decided to run an ongoing study of the rehabilitated ex-addict as an employee compared with other similar employees without known histories of addiction. This was done by machine matching the ex-addict at employment with another person employed on or about the same day, of the same age and sex, same educational background, entering at the same level, at the same type job. This 10-year study has recently been written up by Graham and Gottcent (1). It was found that:

1. Job retention rate was similar in the two groups. Age, sex, education, or job entry level did not significantly affect it.

2. Job progress as measured by promotions, punctuality, and performance was essentially the same.

3. Of those whose employment had terminated, there was no significant difference between the two groups in the length of time worked before termination or in the number dismissed and those who resigned.

The conclusion of the study is that rehabilitated ex-addicts, if carefully selected for skills and job readiness, are no different from other similiar employees who have no known history of drug abuse. A much larger study composed of the experience of several companies has been done by the National Association of Drug Abuse Problems (6). The conclusions essentially are the same.

The key to hiring ex-addicts who will be good employees is to know the quality of the program from which they received their vocational rehabilitation. Many treatment programs have no vocational rehabilitation. They take the word of the patient as to his skills and job readiness. Few if any of their staff members have actually worked in industry. Even in some programs with vocational rehabilitation, it is not uncommon for counselors never to have held a job. Of course, this makes it difficult for them adequately to judge a client's readiness for employment. Also, many counselors are not aware of the skills needed by industry. If they have not worked in industry, it is unlikely that they can prepare clients for the work environment. Sometimes there is bias against business.

A good way of evaluating a program is to visit and talk with the vocational rehabilitation counselor.

A few management and labor people have donated their time to work with vocation rehabilitation programs. Some of the areas in which they have assisted counselors are: in the overcoming of fear and prejudice toward business, orientation of clients to the meaning of work, determination of skills needed by industry in the areas, support of training to develop those skills, and helping patients and counselors in understanding "job readiness." This term is defined as having a marketable skill, a willingness to be employed, the capacity for accepting supervision, a reasonable appearance while at work, acceptable productivity, attendance, and promptness in reporting to the job. In the process of helping the programs, most of those participating from management and labor have learned much from the people they have helped, regarded it as time well spent, found that it was an appropriate business activity, and enjoyed doing it.

WORKING TOGETHER FOR MUTUAL BENEFIT

If ex-addicts are to be restored to productive employment and become contributing citizens of their communities, good treatment and vocational rehabilitation programs are needed and jobs are essential. Treatment-rehabilitation programs need business, and business needs them. It is logical for management and labor to join against drug abuse in their community by forming a working coalition with good treatment-rehabilitation programs. The National Association for Drug Abuse Problems (NADAP) in New York City[1] is now the only such organization. It is private and nonprofit, created in 1972 by people from business and labor. One of its primary purposes is to locate jobs for rehabilitated ex-addicts. It conducts programs for program counselors preparing ex-addicts for employment. It has assisted programs with skills development, cooperated in the development of a computerized job skills bank, assisted industry in obtaining job-ready people who are properly skilled for the job, followed them on the job to evaluate progress and provide assistance if problems develop. It has developed a transition program to help those who are prospective employees and counselors learn what the business place, business people, working, and benefits are all about. Meanwhile people from management and labor are learning about ex-addicts as prospective employees and the programs from which they have come.

NADAP assists management and labor by consulting on drug abuse problems in industry and helps in the development of policy and in creating substance abuse and troubled employee programs.

It is a unique model. It could be duplicated to help management and labor in other areas deal with the problem of drugs in industry, develop troubled employee programs, and assist community substance abuse prevention efforts as good corporate citizens.

The reader is encouraged to supplement the information provided in this chapter by a report prepared by the National Institute On Drug Abuse on occupational drug abuse programs (4) based on information obtained from a review of the literature and site visits. It includes an excellent bibliography.

References

1. Graham, R., and Gottcent, R. Restoration of Drug abusers to useful employment. In *A Multicultural View of Drug Abuse,* D. Smith, S. Anderson, M. Buxton, N. Gottlieb, W. Harvey, and T. Chung, editors. G. K. Hall/Schenkman, 1978.
2. Manuso, J. Corporate mental health programs and policies. In *Strategies for Public Health,* L. Ng and D. Davis, editors. New York, Van Nostrand Reinhold, 1979.
3. Manuso, J. Staffing a corporate emotional health program. In *Employee Mental Wellness Programs,* Boston University-Washington Business Group on Health, editors. New York, Springer Verlag, 1979.
4. National Institute on Drug Abuse. *Services Research Administrative Report on Occupational Drug Abuse Problems* (NIDA IQC Contract #271-75-1140). Washington, D. C., United States Department of Health, Education and Welfare, Public Health Service, Alcohol, Drug Abuse and Mental Health Administration, 1976-1979.
5. New York State Narcotics Addiction Control Commission. *Reported Drug Use by Employed Workers in New York State,* 8/1970. Highlights of the Study, July, 1971.
6. Wijting, J. P. *Relationship of Background, Work-Experience and Drug History Variables to the Employability of Recovered and Recovering Drug Abusers.* New York, National Association of Drug Abuse Problems, in press.

[1] National Association on Drug Abuse Problems, Inc., 355 Lexington Ave., New York, New York 10017 (212) 986-1170.

CHAPTER 52

DRUGS AND THE MILITARY

Arnold Sterne Leff, M.D.

Joan L. Donley, M.S.W.

Although drug abuse in the United States military is not new, the experience of the last decade made the search for clearer understanding of the drug abuse phenomenon a serious effort. Reports of morphine use by Civil War soldiers (10), anecdotal reports of marihuana use by American soldiers in Panama in the 1920's (16), and marihuana's use by principally black soldiers in the 1940's (8) existed, but only in the Vietnam War era and beyond did the use of drugs by the United States military reach proportions described by the United States Congress as a "drug plague" having substantial national security implications (32).

The changing sociopolitical environment in the United States during the Vietnam and post-Vietnam era could not help but impact on the American military social system. This occurred principally as a result of the rather rigid military class structure being unable to relate to the short term (usually 2 years) enlistee who brought the changes occurring in the civilian environment to an ill prepared military. The military responded in an exaggerated manner, generally denying the social upheaval that was occurring until its recognition was undeniable and its serious implications reached monumental proportions.

During the Vietnam War era, there was a clear change in the principal substances of abuse among the lower echelons of the military. Alcohol has been known to be the principal drug of abuse since wars have been fought, but the military has never been preoccupied with its alcohol problem, generally relegating it to a minor "in house" difficulty. However, as the Vietnam War progressed, the American military leadership became aware that young soldiers, sailors, and airmen were using "socially unacceptable" drugs (defined as drugs other than alcohol) in ever increasing numbers. Although the existence of drug abuse (principally marihuana) was known to be occurring in the Vietnam era military earlier than 1971 (1, 5, 18, 29), it was not until that time that the extent and seriousness of nonalcohol drug use, and the consequence of multiple drug use (especially opium and heroin), became known. In fact, the widespread use of heroin by the American military in Vietnam went virtually unrecognized by the American public until June, 1971, when President Nixon's appointment of Jerome Jaffe as his Special Assistant on Drug Abuse resulted in a high priority effort directed toward military drug abuse. This public recognition occurred some 6 to 7 years after the build-up of troops in Vietnam, and some 3 to 4 years after widespread drug use was known to be occurring among United States military forces in Southeast Asia. During this later period, the troop strength was being decreased in Vietnam, making the implications of drug use among Vietnam veterans a more direct and serious problem with respect to its possible spread to the continental United States. In hindsight, the public panic regarding military drug abuse in Vietnam (and later Thailand and Germany) served the purpose of assuring a more rational approach by the military to the problem, if only by forcing the recognition that the causes and solutions were not short term and that the traditional punitive approach would not help the military accomplish its mission (27).

INCIDENCE DATA

Numerous studies (1, 11, 18, 24, 29) purport to claim varying amounts of drug abuse among American military members in various parts of the world, including the United States, at differing times. Most of these sources indicate that at least a majority of servicemen between the ages of 18 and 25 tried marihuana, and probably as many as 44 per cent of enlisted Army men in Vietnam tried narcotics (22). In Germany, as late as 1978, unsubstantiated figures as high as 40 per cent were being given for the incidence of heroin use among some units stationed in Berlin (3). All of the military services have abundant data on various aspects of drug use among the military populations. These data include voluntary referrals, individuals identified through a urinalysis testing program, those identified as incident to medical care, as well as those drug users identified through investigations, apprehensions, and arrests. These are broken out by major geographic areas, major commands, primary subtances involved, dispositions of central treatment centers, numbers in rehabilitation, average ages, race, education of users, category of abuse (experimenter, user, addict, supplier, possessor), and occupational distribution. A similar data array exists for alcohol abuse. In the United States Air Force's statistical summary on drug abuse and alcohol abuse control, even such things as "drug trends around the world" are catalogued. All these data are collected on a world-wide basis and allow military leaders to analyze trends and follow patterns of drug use from country to country

and from command to command. Although the authenticity of these data is sometimes questionable, it is generally the only available tool by which the leadership can determine the prevalence of various drug use throughout its world-wide system. The questions facing the leadership, however, are not those of which drugs are being used by which people in which countries at what time, but, more importantly, are questions relating to the impact of drug use on military readiness, job performance, and the ever elusive "national security."

ETIOLOGY AND IMPACT

The soldier coming to Southeast Asia in the 1960's and early 1970's was there for a 1-year tour of duty in an often ill defined, boring war. Minorities, often poorly educated[1] and unable quickly to adapt to the military social structure, were disproportionately represented. Many of these young draftees eventually saw themselves as fighting an unpopular war far from home with supervisors who did not understand their needs. As mentioned above, this paralleled the changing social order occurring in the United States at the time and became severely exaggerated in the remote military environment overseas. Adding the isolated tour of duty to the cultural strain of fighting an unpopular war in a remote country to the ready availability of drugs, it should surprise no one that these forces interacted to produce the so-called Vietnam drug abuse epidemic.

No one factor can be clearly blamed for the drug abuse problem in Southeast Asia, although some emphasize the widespread availability of drugs as the proximate cause. They even go so far as to associate this availability to a conspiratorial effort on the part of the United States' enemies to subvert the war effort by implication of American soldiers in heroin use (32).

There is no question that widespread availability of drugs existed in the extreme during this period. In fact, drugs of all kinds were even available over the counter from phar-

---

[1] It is worth mentioning that, although minimum education requirements were imposed before allowing enlistment, recruiters were under tremendous quota pressures and many enlistees did not meet educational requirements.

macies in Bangkok and Saigon (where no prescription laws existed). They were also easily available in great quantities from any corner vendor in upcountry Vietnam or Thailand, thereby supporting availability as a major factor.

There is support, however, for the alternate theory that the widespread and ever increasing availability of drugs in Southeast Asia was a *result* of the need expressed for them by the American soldier rather than their use being a result of their availability. Studies (14, 22) indicating the large numbers of enlistees using drugs prior to coming to Southeast Asia support this contention.

To some extent, the military's lack of understanding of the drug abuse problem led to even greater abuse. In the early years in Vietnam, marihuana was the principal nonalcoholic drug used by the American military. Its widespread use at the time was not well understood by American military leaders, and the punitive approach taken against those caught possessing or smoking marihuana may have contributed to the later widespread use of heroin by the American military. This early approach included use of informants, dogs trained to identify the smell of marihuana being brought in during unannounced barrack inspections, and many punitive discharges as a result of personal possession. Although efforts also occurred to decrease trafficking in marihuana, Southeast Asia has high potency marihuana growing wild and no reasonable person believed that one could substantially decrease the availability of marihuana during this period. As marihuana has quite a distinctive odor and is used in a greater bulk when compared to heroin, it was not too long before the American military soldier recognized that this new white powder could be smoked without emitting an odor and could easily be concealed, thereby setting the stage for the change from marihuana use to widespread heroin use. At the same time that heroin was being used by the American soldier in Southeast Asia, the use of other drugs was becoming evident in United States Forces in Europe (30). In this case, heroin was not the available drug it was in Vietnam, but drugs such as amphetamine, barbiturates, hashish, lysergic acid diethylamide (LSD), and methaqualone were being widely used by American soldiers stationed in Germany (23, 31).

In the post-Vietnam era, heroin use by the American military in Germany (3, 7) became quite prominent, but it is quite apparent that drug abuse in the United States Armed Forces persists throughout the world. More importantly one must recognize that even with the experience of the late 1960's and early 1970's, an annual Department of Defense drug abuse budget that reached $82.1 million in 1972, nothing prevented the heroin use situation that ultimately existed in Germany in 1978.

Besides the specific drug factors that relate to the causes of military drug abuse, certain policy factors significantly influence its incidence. Military policies assure a turnover of leadership, as well as the lower echelon enlistees, as often as every 1 to 2 years. In addition, because of pressure from labor union groups, the military, for the most part, is forbidden from doing public service jobs, thereby setting the stage for the boredom and feeling of uselessness found among American military enlistees as well as others in the military social system. Often the military member has little to do but such "make work" efforts as cleaning barracks. To the extent that these conditions occur in the civilian sector, drug use will also tend to occur, but in the military circumstance, these problems are endemic to a peacetime military and, under certain conditions, a military at war. Abundant models are used to describe the conditions that predispose people to widespread drug use. The communicable disease model defines epidemics of illicit drug use (15), whereas the sociological models (12, 19, 35) seek better to understand the conditions surrounding drug use. All indicate that factors such as availability, peer group pressure, and personal and environmental stress contribute to the drug abuse phenomenon. In the military, especially during wartime, many of these things are exaggerated. Nevertheless, it became apparent as early as 1972 (25) that the military drug abuser in Vietnam (even though using heroin) was different from the nonmilitary user, in that the use was primarily situational. This was later confirmed in the well known study of Robins (22), although one study believes there are more similarities than differences (9).

It finally becomes apparent that drug use (even heroin addiction) can be situational in origin and that by changing the situation one can change the characteristic of the addiction, the drugs used, and possibly (15) whether any drugs at all will be used. Although somewhat simplistic, drug users can be divided into two distinct populations: those whose drug use is associated with underlying social deviancy and those whose drug use is situational. In dealing with military drug abuse problems, it is essential that we clearly define the population with which we are dealing. The military drug abuser was (and is) more often than not in the situational group, although there is a small but significant percentage of military drug abusers in the deviant group (14).

It is now a well accepted fact that those American military members who were addicted to heroin under the situation of a Vietnam in the late 1960's and early 1970's for the most part did not return to the United States to continue their addiction or spread it throughout the civilian sector (22, 29). Interestingly, anecdotes are reported (21) where heroin was thought to be therapeutic in that small numbers of American enlistees are described who became psychotic after withdrawal of their heroin and were later diagnosed as overt schizophrenics, the heroin having abated the symptoms during battle. Some studies (2, 17), point toward the potential therapeutic role of marihuana use in the military environment. None of this is to minimize the very tragic circumstances that can surround the drug culture, especially the use of some very dangerous drugs in unknown quantities and of unknown type. Needless to say, a young death as a result of heroin overdose or a psychosis or suicide as a result of LSD use are consequences of drug use that American society (whether civilian or military) will never tolerate and will always feel some responsibility to prevent.

Nevertheless, in the last decade we have begun to understand (partially as a result of the military experience) that we cannot decrease the use of all drugs by decreasing the availability of the one currently being used. We have learned that if one decreases the availability of one drug, another will often take its place if the social conditions continue. We have learned that all drugs have the potential for destruction, but that heroin is not more dangerous by virtue of its high risk of physical dependence than many other drugs with less potential for addition. We have learned that one cannot just inform a

given population of the dangers of drug use and expect that they will heed the realistic dangers when faced with a peer system that encourages drug use. And, last but not least, we have learned that a large majority of a population can in fact use a drug with substantially potent mind-altering effects without a noticeable decrease in job performance. This is surely true of the situational military drug user to which many reports attest (1, 7, 12, 17, 19).

THE MILITARY METHOD

The approach to drug abuse in the military includes continued law enforcement activities, use of urinalysis testing under some conditions, and the provision of treatment for those identified through urinalysis or those volunteering for treatment via amnesty-type programs.

One cannot discuss drug abuse in the military without some discussion of drug urinalysis and its association with the military approach to the drug abuse problem. Using principally gas or paper strip chromatographic procedures (more technical aspects of urinalysis for drugs of abuse have been well described elsewhere (6, 13)), the military started wide use of urinalysis for drugs in the early 1970's. Faced with the possibility of a serious heroin epidemic that potentially could spread drug addiction to the United States (it was not known until later that the vast majority of Vietnam drug users would not bring their "addiction" back to the United States), the immediate approach was to require urinalysis on all returning Vietnam military members on or near their date of departure to the continental United States. Later, in an effort to (a) identify current drug users, and (b) *prevent* further addiction, the mandatory random urinalysis system was instituted. This system required the wide scale use of urinalysis testing among American military members using random numbers and requiring those called on to submit a urine (the collection of which was observed) for analysis. Originally the system included the requirement that all "from Private to General" be included in the random testing, but this was later limited to those under age 25, because the amount of heroin use in other than that age group (by virtue of data received in the early days of random urinalysis testing) was quite low. Unfortunately, this change in policy, although decreasing the cost of the testing, served to heighten the separation between the career and noncareer military.

In addition to the random technique, unit commanders had the authority to order ("Command Direct") any one individual or group of individuals (even a whole unit) to submit their urine for collection and analysis. The urinalysis system, being random, was supposed psychologically to discourage use, inasmuch as one could be called *at any time* to submit his or her urine. All people with a laboratory positive urinalysis were required to see a physician who would "medically" confirm or deny the fact of drug abuse. If confirmed, the individual was normally, not to be disciplined but, instead, referred for treatment.

The random urinalysis approach was a massive undertaking. Although fraught with many difficulties, it did identify large numbers of military drug users in Vietnam and Thailand, as well as other stations around the world. Its actual impact on prevention and abatement of use, however, is to this day unknown. Serious problems—such as untrained physicians being responsible for medical confirmation, the collection process not being controlled enough to avoid switching "clean" urine for "dirty" urine, a technology that was not quite sophisticated enough fo be used on such a large scale, and real concerns about the protection of the civil liberties of servicemen—all combined to cause Congress to limit the *random* urinalysis system in 1976. Command directed urinalysis was not prohibited and is still widely used in the military. Department of Defense and White House policy as late as 1977 (33) still favored urinalysis as a tool to combat drug abuse in the military. Its widespread use as a deterrent and identification tool is an essential difference between how the military and civilian sectors handle the drug abuse problem, in that the civilian sector only rarely uses urinalysis (generally limiting its use to law enforcement-correction programs) as a means of controlling drug abuse.

Current advocates for reinstating a mandatory random urinalysis system point to the need to identify "hot spots" in the military in order to begin intervention. Those against urinalysis point to its adverse impact on morale and call for its curtailment. Because man-

datory random urinalysis can no longer be used and its current disadvantages seem to outweigh potential benefits, some need still exists objectively to predict or determine when any given unit or area of the world is having, or is about to have, a serious drug abuse problem. A recently described *anonymous* epidemiologically guided random urinalysis approach (7) may in fact help objectively to confirm problem areas, without the attendant disadvantages of large scale urinalysis programs.

PROBLEMS AND PERSPECTIVES

To deal adequately with drug abuse in the military, one must return to the basic assumptions underlying the need for action. It is not the kind of drugs used nor the incidence of use that is of utmost importance to the military (and the nation): it is the impact of the drugs on performance of the mission. Major approaches to the problem should be performance related rather than drug related. In addition, in order for the military to respond adequately to its drug abuse problem in a way that optimizes resource allocation, while simultaneously containing the drug use that has the potential for truly impairing national security, certain specific policy changes as well as changes in identification programs must be made.

The current military approach to drug abuse starts at the time of enlistment, when questions about past drug use behavior have the potential for eliminating as many as 32 per cent (4) of otherwise acceptable candidates. Such drug use identification techniques as arbitrary command directed urinalysis and use of informants tend rarely to be objectively performance related. After identification of the user, treatment programs of variable quality attempt to rehabilitate drug users and return them to the unit (26). If treatment is unsuccessful, the individual may be discharged and referred to a Veterans Administration Drug Program. Even those soldiers whose job performance is not affected by the drugs they use and who may be using drugs only in a social context are sometimes put through this system. All of this assumes ongoing law enforcement efforts aimed at decreasing supply.

The policy that encourages continued reassignments should be changed balancing the military's need to assure a breadth of experiences with the need to improve unit management. The military should increase efforts that would allow some units to take on meaningful public service jobs, thereby decreasing the boredom and feeling of uselessness often evident in enlistees and contributing to drug use. More importantly, the military must strengthen its management capability at the company or squadron level. This may require the provision of organizational development consultation at the unit level but must result in a renewed emphasis on clear job expectations and the monitoring of objective performance indicators.

For the military to improve its program against the use of drugs, it must have a better *performance-based* surveillance and treatment program, similar to the industrial alcoholism models that have been credited with substantial success (20). Military supervisors must be held accountable for objectively evaluating individual performance and referring poor performers to a diagnostic and screening unit for evaluation. Drug abuse (and alcoholism) per se should not be overemphasized, relegating the reasons for poor performance or behavior problems to the experienced diagnosticians in the screening unit. Manned by experienced personnel, this unit would then either (a) refer to appropriate treatment resources, monitoring the care given in conjunction with the individual's supervisor, or (b) refer back to the unit for disposition if the poor performance or poor behavior is unrelated to a treatable problem (e.g., "social" deviancy).

It is essential that any treatment referrals be associated with a good supervisor/screening unit/treatment monitoring system; all must evaluate progress on a continuous basis. If progress is poor, either the treatment modality must be changed (a mutual decision between the poor performer, the screening unit, and the supervisor) or the individual referred back to the supervisor for disposition.

This method can be used for any military members who are performing poorly, irrespective of the cause. Such things as financial or family problems, general mental illness, and alcoholism often decrease performance. In the vast majority of cases, where adequate programs exist, these problems can be corrected and the individual returned back to the unit, becoming a healthy and productive part of it. On the other hand, pure criminal activity, poor performance, or behavior that is unrelated to a correctable problem should (and under this system can) be dealt with swiftly and decisively.

The military, in actuality, is quite experienced in using this method of detecting and correcting problems, in that their nuclear reliability program (currently reserved for those units involved in extremely sensitive areas) is very similar to this system. Expanding a modified nuclear reliability program throughout the military can be accomplished by diverting some current drug enforcement and education activities to setting up diagnostic and screening units and additional general mental health treatment capability.

Reemphasizing a performance-based management system that is associated with a feedback-based treatment or correction system, rather than the continual emphasis on the specific drugs of abuse, will have the dual advantage of improving general military management at the supervisor level as well as containing the drug and alcohol abuse that adversely affects performance. Continued over-all monitoring by means of anonymous epidemiological methods will direct the leadership to those areas where supervision is weak and the system failing. Increased supervisory training to those areas of weakness will normally counter perceived difficulties.

DEPENDENT DRUG ABUSE

No discussion of military drug abuse can occur without some mention of the rather unique circumstances surrounding the adolescent military dependent, especially those stationed overseas and having to cope with the well described (34) cultural isolation. Military drug abuse seems no different than dependent drug abuse in American families assigned to posts overseas. The drug-using behavior of the teenage dependent being in close age proximity to the military enlistee is often influenced by (or influences) the drug-using behavior occurring among military enlistees. No amount of official discouragement can prevent this often significant interaction between these two groups, and no understanding of drugs in the military can occur without recognizing the interaction.

The often widespread availability of drugs

of all kinds, combined with the expected adolescent adjustment reaction, sometimes produces an explosive drug-related situation resulting in serious morbidity and mortality. Previously unpublished data (28) based on the experience of a United States government team brought into focus a significant problem in the American dependent population in Bangkok, Thailand. It was evident to that Special Action Office for Drug Abuse Prevention team in 1972 that there were families in severe crisis and that the approach designed for the military may not be either appropriate or successful if used for dependents. However, at that time the same approach was being used. Faced with a "heroin epidemic" in the military in Thailand as well as the American dependent population, several things occurred:

1. A survey of adolescents in Bangkok performed by the Southeast Asian Treaty Organization Laboratory Affiliate of Walter Reed Army Research Institute in 1971, indicated that 15 per cent of youths in the local junior and senior high school had used heroin (mainly smoking) and that 9 per cent were then currently using the drug.

2. A drug abuse review board was set up by the American authorities to deal with the increasing number of drug-related incidents among American youths that included, during the period of September, 1971 through January, 1973 (of a total of approximately 1,500 adolescents), 21 hospital admissions due to drug abuse, five deaths (four of which were directly related to heroin use), and 115 confirmed (by urinalysis) opiate users. The Drug Abuse Review Board (which included the military, State Department, other United States government workers and members of the American business community) approach was to order urinalysis on teenagers in the school system and to order early departures from Thailand. During the period July, 1971, through December, 1972, 58 families with 72 drug-using youths departed early, at significant cost to both the families involved and the United States government.

In early 1973, a team of adolescent and drug abuse treatment professionals arrived in Bangkok and set up a youth treatment center under the auspices of the American embassy. That team trained a number of Americans (wives of those stationed there and former schoolteachers) to set up and operate the residential and outpatient treatment program for families and adolescents that the team initiated. Although there were massive administrative and technical problems (e.g., the Thais do not recognize the confidentiality of drug abuse records), the results—which included a complete abatement of drug overdose deaths over the next year, decreased hospital admissions for overdose, and a substantial decrease in the number of families ordered to return to the continental United States—clearly validated the approach taken.

It seems clear from this first experiment designed to treat American dependents overseas that there needed to be a comprehensive approach to adolescents and their families, one that recognized the complex military, family, and community systems within which the adolescent existed.

It is also evident from the experience in Thailand that the normally high risk nature of families with adolescents is further increased if the family is overseas and that this is especially true when the family or marital couple has had previous interpersonal difficulties. A rather direct relationship between alcoholism in the family and drug abuse in the adolescent dependent was also noted.

Although one cannot "scientifically" attribute the decrease in significant drug abuse morbidity to the government treatment team sent to Thailand, it is believed that providing a caring crisis intervention program that focuses on the system identified as "at risk" can successfully intervene in what often becomes a self-perpetuating community problem.

EPILOGUE

Toward the beginning of the end of the Vietnam War era, many in and out of the military were sounding the alarm about drug abuse. Many of those who were in Southeast Asia during the late 1960's fully believed that the military leadership at the time was making serious errors in their approach to the drug problem. Later difficulties, especially the infusion of large amounts of heroin into the area and subsequent increased treatment efforts, proved those outspoken people correct in their assessment.

It is hoped that all now recognize that new approaches must exist for the United States reasonably to assure itself that it is making the correct decisions with respect to drug abuse in the Armed Forces. May our nation never have to fight a war for survival that depends upon an Army of Americans who use, on a continuous basis, a whole array of mind-altering drugs. If we do, however, may our decisions with regard to this problem be the right ones.

References

1. Baker, S. L. Drug abuse in the U.S. Army. Bull. N.Y. Acad. Med. 47:541, 1971.
2. Bey, D. R., and Zecchinelli, V. A. Marihuana as a coping device in Vietnam. Milit. Med. 136:448, 1971.
3. Bourne, P. G. White House Communication to the Secretary of Defense. March 1, 1978.
4. Callan, J. P., and Patterson, C. D. Patterns of drug abuse among military inductees. Am. J. Psychiatry 130:260, 1973.
5. Colbach, E. Marihuana use by G.I.'s in Vietnam. Am. J. Psychiatry 128:96, 1971.
6. De Angelis, G. G. Testing for drugs: Advantages and disadvantages. Int. J. Addict. 7:365, 1972.
7. Duncan, C. W. Testimony on drug abuse in the military before Select Committee on Narcotics Abuse and Control, House of Representatives. July 27, 1978.
8. Freedman, H. L., and Rockmore, M. J. Marihuana: A factor in personality evaluation and Army maladjustment. J. Clin. Psychopathol. 7:765, 1946.
9. Frenkel, S. I., Morgan, D. W., and Greden, J. F. Heroin use among soldiers in the United States and Vietnam: A comparison in retrospect. Int. J. Addict. 12:1143, 1977.
10. Glaser, F. B. Drug use in the military. N. Engl. J. Med. 286:609, 1972.
11. Greden, J. F., and Morgan, D. W. Patterns of drug use and attitudes toward treatment in a military population. Arch. Gen. Psychiatry 26:113, 1972.
12. Ingraham, L. H. The boys in the barracks. Unpublished manuscript, Walter Reed Army Institute of Research, Washington, D. C., 1978.
13. Kaistha, K. K., and Jaffe, J. H. Reliability of identification techniques for drugs of abuse in a urine screening program and drug excretion data. J. Pharm. Sci. 61:305, 1972.
14. Kolb, D., Nail, R. L., and Gunderson, E. K. E. Preservice drug abuse as a predictor of in-service drug abuse and military performance. Milit. Med. 140:104, 1975.
15. Levengood, R., Lowinger, P., and Schooff, K. Heroin addiction in the suburbs: An epidemiologic study. Am. J. Public Health 63:209, 1973.
16. Marcovitz, E., and Myers, H. J. The marihuana addict in the Army. War Med. 6:382, 1944.
17. Mirin, S. M., and Mc Kenna, G. J. Combat zone adjustment: The role of marihuana use. Milit. Med. 140:482, 1975.
18. Nail, R. L., and Gunderson, E. K. Characteristics of hospitalized drug abuse cases in the naval service. J. Nerv. Ment. Dis. 155:91, 1972.
19. Newby, J. H. Small group dynamics and drug abuse in an Army setting: A case study. Int. J. Addict. 12: 287, 1977.
20. Norris, J. L. A program for alcoholics in a company. Int. Psychiatry Clin. 6:287, 1969.
21. Personal communications with various physicians in Southeast Asia, 1972.
22. Robins, L. N. The Vietnam Drug User Returns: Final Report. Contract No. HSM-42-72-75 SAODAP. Washington, D.C., United States Government Printing Office, 1973.
23. Rock, N. L., and Silsby, M. D. Methaqualone abuse among U.S. Army troops stationed in Europe. Int. J. Addict. 13:327, 1978.
24. Roffman, R. A., and Sapol, E. Marihuana in Vietnam: A survey of use among enlisted men in the two southern corps. Int. J. Addict. 5:1, 1970.
25. Sarg, M. J. Heroin use in the Navy. N. Engl. J. Med. 286:111, 1972.
26. Schwam, J. S., Stein, J. I., and Winn, F. J. A drug-abuse program at a U.S. Army post. Compr. Psychiatry 17:125, 1976.
27. Silsby, H. D., Lawson, T. L., and Hazlehurst, C. D. Drug abuse prevention in the military: A punitive/administrative action approach. Milit. Med. 140:486, 1975.
28. Special Action Office Drug Abuse Prevention. Unpublished data, 1973.
29. Stanton, M. D. Drugs, Vietnam, and the Vietnam veteran: An overview. Am. J. Drug Alcohol Abuse 3:557, 1976.
30. Tennant, F. S. Drug abuse in the U.S. Army, Europe. J. A. M. A. 221:1146, 1972.
31. Tennant, F. S., Preble, M. R., Groesbeck, C. J., and Banks, N. J. Drug abuse among American soldiers in West Germany. Milit. Med. 137:381, 1972.
32. United States Senate. Hearings before Subcommittee on Alcoholism and Narcotics of the Committee on Labor and Public Welfare. First Session on Military Drug Abuse. June 9 and 22, 1971.
33. White House Office of Drug Abuse Policy. Drug abuse assessment in the Department of Defense: A policy review. November 1977.
34. Workman, S. Hazards of rearing children in foreign countries. Am. J. Psychiatry 128:8, 1972.
35. Zinberg, N. E. Heroin use in Vietnam and the United States: A contrast and critique. Arch. Gen. Psychiatry 26:486, 1972.

CHAPTER 53

MEDICAL MANAGEMENT OF METHADONE-MAINTAINED PATIENTS[1]

Mary Jeanne Kreek, M.D.

The management of specific medical and surgical problems in methadone-maintained patients should be the same, for the most part, as in the general population. Usually the same medications and dosage schedules can be used and the same general treatment regimens followed. There are a few exceptions, however, where alternative medications must be selected or different dosages or regimens followed, because of the pharmacological effects of methadone or because of known (or hypothetical) interactions between methadone and some other drugs; these exceptions will be detailed below (44, 52). As in the general population, a large percentage of methadone-maintained patients use excessive amounts of alcohol (45, 49). The management of medical problems related to al-

cohol abuse including alcoholism itself will be discussed. Management of problems related to polysubstance abuse will be considered. Most medical problems occurring in methadone-maintained patients are similar to the problems experienced by the general population. However, some disorders are found in large numbers of maintenance patients and are related, directly or indirectly, to the chronic unsterile self-administration of narcotics along with many unidentified substances found in illicit drugs (45, 48, 49). These chronic medical problems, which are prevalent in methadone-maintained patients, will also be discussed.

MEDICAL MANAGEMENT OF PROBLEMS RELATED TO THE PHARMACOLOGICAL AND PHYSIOLOGICAL EFFECTS OF METHADONE

MANAGEMENT OF METHADONE-RELATED PROBLEMS DURING INITIATION OF MAINTENANCE TREATMENT

When methadone maintenance treatment is first initiated and the patient has come into

[1]This study was supported in part by Grant DA-01138 from the National Institute on Drug Abuse, Grant C-147605 from the New York State Division of Substance Abuse Services to The Rockefeller University through New York Hospital, and General Clinical Research Center Grant RR-00102 from the National Institutes of Health.

This investigation was supported in part by a Research Scientist Development Award, DA-00049, from the Alcohol, Drug Abuse, and Mental Health Administration awarding National Institute on Drug Abuse.

treatment directly from ongoing use of heroin, the patient may experience mild signs and symptoms of narcotic withdrawal. These may occur both during the first 1 to 2 hours after the daily oral methadone dose is given, thus before maximum plasma levels of methadone are achieved (peak levels usually 2 to 4 hours after an oral dose), and also 12 to 16 hours after the oral dose, if a once daily dosage regimen is followed (35, 46). Although methadone is a long acting narcotic, with a duration of action of 24 to 36 hours in most individuals receiving the drug on a daily basis (as opposed to heroin or morphine, which are short acting narcotics with durations of action of only 4 to 8 hours), its long acting properties are in part dependent upon slow release from nonspecific (or specific) reservoirs after chronic administration; repeated dosing is apparently essential before such reservoir storage is adequate to give a sustained effect (34, 54). The problems of mild withdrawal during the first few days of methadone treatment usually can be managed by the use of divided doses of methadone, approximately 12 hours apart. Sometimes administration of appropriate doses of short acting narcotics between methadone doses may be desirable clinically, yet it is rarely feasible in outpatient settings.

MANAGEMENT OF METHADONE-RELATED PROBLEMS DURING EARLY AND CHRONIC PHASES OF MAINTENANCE TREATMENT

Both short and long acting narcotics have multiple physiological and pharmacological effects in addition to the desired effects of analgesia and euphoria when used on an acute or intermittent basis. As tolerance develops, most of these effects disappear, although at different rates. Many of the so-called "side effects" of methadone observed mostly in the early phases of maintenance treatment, while doses are gradually being increased or stabilized, are in fact simply well described acute narcotic effects to which tolerance has not yet developed, and most of these signs and symptoms disappear with time on steady daily doses of methadone (31, 45, 48, 101). Signs and symptoms observed during the first 6 months of treatment include primary narcotic effects of euphoria (or "high"), drowsiness, somnolence ("nodding"), and also bradycardia and hypoten-

sion, nausea and vomiting, edema of the lower extremities, difficulty in urination, menstrual irregularities, problems with sexual function, insomnia, constipation, and excessive sweating (31). After 6 months or more of treatment, most of these signs and symptoms disappear; only between 20 and 30 per cent of patients in one study continued to complain of problems of sleep and sexual function abnormalities, whereas over 40 per cent of patients experienced persistent constipation requiring laxative use and also had persistent increased sweating (101). In another prospective study of patients in high dose treatment with methadone (80 to 120 mg per day) for more than 3 years, only 10 to 20 per cent of patients continued to experience any abnormalities in sleep, libido, sexual performance, or constipation. However, around half of all patients continued to experience excessive sweating, although this caused no medical problems or other symptoms even during vigorous exercise in heat or sun. Thus tolerance seems to develop with time to most of the narcotic effects observed during the early phase of methadone treatment. However, tolerance does not seem to develop to the two desired effects of methadone as used in maintenance treatment, that is, prevention of narcotic abstinence symptoms and prevention of "drug hunger." When these undesired "side effects," or actual narcotic effects, occur during the early phases of treatment, prior to the development of tolerance to each, the problems can be managed either by lowering the daily dose of methadone to a level where minimal to no undesired effects occur or simply by holding the daily dose at a steady level until tolerance develops and the signs and symptoms disappear.

Constipation does persist as a medical complication of methadone maintenance treatment in around 15 to 20 per cent of patients in chronic treatment and should be managed aggressively. The only reported death due to metadone itself in a methadone-maintained patient was due to severe constipation that led to ileus and eventually to death (78). The patient had suffered from chronic constipation followed by total obstipation and had refused medical treatment for this problem; he eventually died of complication related to prolonged complete obstipation. A postmortem examination confirmed that this was the cause of death. In most cases, the chronic constipation observed in methadone-maintained patients can be managed effectively by use of either stool softeners or by mild laxative use, such as milk of magnesia or mineral oil. In most patients, regular use of laxatives will not be necessary after the first 6 to 12 months of treatment, because tolerance to the constipating effects of methadone does develop.

Tolerance develops rapidly to all analgesic effects of methadone during moderate to high dose methadone maintenance treatment for narcotic addiction. Of course, this is fortunate, for otherwise patients in maintenance treatment would not be able to recognize acute or chronic pain, which is often a critically important sign of injury or disease. Methadone-maintained patients seem both to perceive and experience with suffering pain, just as do persons not on chronic long acting narcotic treatment. On a hypothetical basis, the maintained patient might experience even more pain than unmedicated patients, if exogenous opioid such as methadone should suppress binding or responsiveness of endogenous opioids, such as the endorphins. However, no documentation of such increased sensitivity to pain has been reported, and analytical techniques have not been refined sufficiently to make biochemical determinations to test such a hypothesis.

In the management of pain, short acting narcotics such as meperidine or morphine are effective in methadone-maintained patients, just as in patients not on methadone treatment. The doses of the short acting narcotics needed to relieve pain may be slightly larger and also may need to be given more frequently because of narcotic cross-tolerance. It should be stressed, however, that in maintenance patients analgesia cannot be achieved by simply increasing the dose of methadone, because methadone is a long acting narcotic with minimal peak effect (and minimal peak elevations in plasma levels over the maintained steady state plasma levels). Also, it should be emphasized that use of pentazocine (Talwin) is contraindicated in methadone maintenance patients, because this drug is a mixed narcotic agonist and antagonist and will precipitate narcotic abstinence symptoms in a narcotic-tolerant and -dependent individual.

When methadone-maintained patients must undergo diagnostic or surgical procedures requiring local or general anesthesia, questions may be raised concerning the appropriate dose and route of administration of methadone and also the type of anesthetic agent to be used. The daily methadone dose definitely should not be simply withheld for extended periods of time in this setting, as this will only result in the unnecessary precipitation of narcotic abstinence symptoms that will complicate the medical or surgical problem. When a patient must have oral fluids withheld, the daily dose of methadone should be given parenterally. In some hospitals with considerable experience in managing methadone-maintained patients in a variety of clinical settings, it is standard practice on the day of a procedure to give the daily methadone dose in two divided doses (77). Anesthetic agents in general usage can be used effectively in methadone-maintained patients. Clinical anecdotes have suggested that some methadone-maintained patients may require increased amounts of anesthetic agents, although there is no documentation of such a need.

Although it has been suggested that methadone may enhance hepatic microsomal drug-metabolizing enzyme activities, there has been no clear-cut documentation of this in humans. However, substantial numbers of methadone-maintained patients are chronic heavy users of ethanol (see below), and they may use barbiturates. Both of these types of agents may accelerate the metabolism of some drugs and chemicals, and it has been observed that alcohol-abusing patients and those using barbiturates may require increased amounts of many drugs, including anesthetic agents, to achieve desired results because of this enhanced drug-metabolizing capacity. Thus, of the clinical anecdotes concerning the need of some methadone-maintained patients for increased amounts of methadone, these patients with the need may also be using large amounts of alcohol or other drugs. There have been concerns that methadone may accumulate in the central nervous system, thus creating a potential hazardous situation when central nervous system depressants such as anesthetic agents must be used. An initial study of cerebral spinal fluid concentrations of methadone in patients undergoing spinal anesthesia has been carried out, and it has been shown that, at all time points after an oral or parenteral dose of methadone, the spinal fluid concentrations of methadone are less than those in simultaneously obtained plasma (76).

METHADONE-RELATED BIOCHEMICAL AND PHYSIOLOGICAL ALTERATIONS DURING EARLY AND CHRONIC PHASES OF METHADONE TREATMENT WITH AND WITHOUT CLINICAL MANIFESTATIONS

Several biochemical and physiological abnormalities have been observed during the early phases of methadone treatment that also are, for the most part, well established acute narcotic effects to which tolerance develops during chronic narcotic administration. Most of these observed biochemical abnormalities have no documented clinical manifestations. There are abnormalities that have been observed during the first 2 to 12 months of treatment including: decreased levels of the reproduction-related peptide hormones and follicle-stimulating hormone (FSH) and luteinizing hormone (LH); abnormal metapyrone tests of hypothalamic reserve, indicating a reduced capacity to release additional amounts of adrenocorticotropic hormone (ACTH) in the setting of relative glucocorticosteroid deficiency; and also abnormalities in respiratory function, including decreased sensitivity of the central nervous system chemoreceptors to carbon dioxide, alveolar hypoventilation, and arteriolar hypercapnia (28, 44, 61, 63, 71, 78, 81, 82). It has been shown that each of these abnormalities returns to normal during several months of chronic methadone treatment (27, 28, 48, 80–82). Abnormalities in metapyrone test results return to normal after 2 months of methadone maintenance treatment, as observed in one study, when steady state treatment dose levels were reached and tolerance to most easily observed narcotic effects was achieved. This finding is of special interest, because it suggests that control of release of ACTH becomes normal, along with the development of tolerance to many other acute narcotic effects. Recent laboratory studies of several groups have suggested that ACTH and beta-lipotropin (LPH), the parent peptide hormone of beta-endorphin, an endogenous peptide documented to exert some narcotic-like effects in vivo and to bind to the specific opiate receptors in vitro, both come from the same large peptide precursor. It has also been shown that ACTH and LPH are simultaneously released in equal amounts from the parent peptide, thus suggesting that release of beta-endorphin may parallel release of ACTH (56). It is of considerable interest that ACTH release, which may be abnormal during the early months of methadone maintenance treatment and which is known to be abnormal after acute administration of a narcotic to animals or to humans, seems to become normal during chronic methadone treatment. This suggests that release of the endogenous opiate-like peptide, beta-endorphin, may also become normal during chronic methadone maintenance treatment. Appropriate studies to further investigate this possibility must await the development of more sensitive as well as highly specific assay techniques for measurement of beta-endorphin and other opioids in human peripheral plasma and other body fluids.

There are other biochemical and physiological alterations that have been observed to persist in some methadone-maintained patients during long term methadone maintenance treatment but that also have no related clinical problems or abnormalities yet identified. A lowered serum level of testosterone has been observed in some male patients (15 to 50 per cent of patients studied), but without any correlation to the presence of subjective symptoms of abnormal libido or sexual performance. Similarly, decreased seminal fluid volume and reduced sperm motility have been observed in one study of volunteer methadone-maintained patients, although in that study, patients who were using alcohol on a chronic basis were not excluded and the abnormalities observed could have been due either to alcohol or to the methadone treatment (2, 20, 27, 28, 64, 65). In one study, patients who have had lowered levels of testosterone have normal levels of both FSH and LH (27, 28). Because no correlation has been found between the presence of biochemical abnormalities and subjective complaints of sexual dysfunction, and because men with either subjective complaints or objective findings of abnormal tests have fathered children while in chronic methadone treatment, it is not clear whether or not either of these types of abnormalities is directly related to methadone treatment. No medical management has been developed or should be initiated on the basis of findings of biochemical abnormalities alone. In one recent study in which conditions of time of day, time of methadone dose, documentation of lack of use or abuse of other medications or alcohol, along with selection of patients with no evidence of liver disease, or factors that could alter endocrine function, it has been shown that plasma levels of prolactin are highest around the time of peak plasma level of methadone (at midday, approximately 4 hours after the oral dose of methadone), rather than in the early morning as usually observed in normal subjects. This finding suggests that the well documented effect of narcotics administered on an acute basis causing prolactin release may be preserved even during chronic methadone maintenance treatment (53). To date, this is the only neuroendocrine abnormality identified in patients who are tolerant to and dependent on the long acting narcotic methadone, as used in maintenance treatment, and it may provide some insight into the mechanisms underlying maintenance of the tolerant and dependent states, inasmuch as prolactin release is normally under inhibitory control by dopamine or dopamine-like substances (88). However, elevated levels of prolactin are seen only in some patients who show this abnormal variation of prolactin release. It is not known whether·these alterations in prolactin release have any clinical implications (35, 53).

Several abnormalities in tests of thyroid have been observed in patients during chronic methadone treatment. These include increased levels of thyroxine-binding globulin and both thyroxine and triiodotyronine levels. These latter two abnormalities are probably related to increased levels of binding globulins that, in turn, are due to the same unknown mechanisms that cause elevations in all types of serum proteins in street heroin addicts and in methadone-maintained patients. Patients with these abnormalities do not have abnormal results in dynamic tests of thyroid function, nor are they clinically hyperthyroid (3, 53, 81, 88, 97).

One abnormality of normal physiological control of respiration has been observed to persist in otherwise tolerant methadone maintenance patients—that is, a reduced sensitivity of the central nervous system receptors to hypoxia. However, no clinical problems have been described relating to this alteration in normal respiratory function.

A wide variety of serum protein and immunological abnormalities have been observed in methadone-maintained patients that persist in a high percentage of patients during years of chronic treatment (44, 45, 48, 49). Most of these abnormalities are probably related to the long period, prior to entry into methadone maintenance treatment, of repeated unsterile injections of drugs and also of the various unknown substances added to illicit drugs (45, 48, 49). Other factors that may contribute to these abnormalities are the high prevalence of chronic liver diseases in methadone-maintained patients, as well as in street heroin addicts, both sequelae of viral hepatitis and also alcohol-related liver disease, which can cause some protein and immunological abnormalities similar to those observed. However, these abnormalities are also observed in maintenance patients with no evidence of chronic liver disease. Some of the alterations observed may be due, in part, to the narcotic drug itself, heroin or other illicit narcotics, and during treatment, methadone, as has been demonstrated in one instance (elevated levels of serum albumin in methadone-maintained patients at time of entry into and during chronic methadone treatment). Total serum proteins and elevations in levels of total serum globulins have been observed in over 30 per cent of patients in prospective and retrospective studies. In some studies, elevations of gamma-globulins and alpha$_2$-globulins have been observed in more than 50 per cent of patients (1, 44, 49). Persistent elevation in two immunoglobulins (Ig), IgG and IgM levels, have been observed in more than 30 per cent of methadone-maintained patients in different studies (21, 25, 45, 48, 49). Biological positive tests for syphilis are frequently observed and may be related to persistent elevation in IgM levels (30). Relative and absolute lymphocytosis have been observed in more than 20 per cent of methadone-maintained patients in one prospective study (45). It has been reported from in vitro studies using blood from methadone-maintained patients that the percentage of B-cells and also T-cell rosette formation is abnormal (26).

One extremely interesting clinical observation has been made and confirmed concerning serum albumin levels in methadone-maintained subjects. In the population of patients with a very high prevalence of liver disease of various types of degrees and severity (more than 60 per cent of all patients in methadone treatment), generally poor nutrition, prevalent alcohol abuse, and often other chronic diseases, all of which may lead to decreased synthesis and thus decreased serum levels of albumin, most patients were observed to have normal and some even elevated levels of serum albumin (7, 44, 45, 48, 49).

Laboratory studies have been performed to explore this clinical observation, and it has been shown in the rabbit that chronic methadone administration causes an increased total body amount of albumin, coupled with increased serum albumin levels and an increase in albumin degradation weight, all suggesting a sustained increase of albumin synthesis (75). Whereas lowered levels of serum albumin may result in multiple clinical problems, including edema and ascites, normal serum albumin levels are usually equated with normal hepatic function as well as overall normal protein synthesis and normal health. There is no precedent for the finding of sustained elevated levels of serum albumin, and no clinical abnormalities have been detected in methadone maintenance patients with this finding.

No abnormalities of blood cells (total red blood cell count, hematocrit, or hemoglobin) or white blood cells have been observed in methadone-maintained patients (44, 45). However, it has been recently reported that thrombocytosis may occur and persist for several weeks in babies born of methadone-maintained mothers (4). In this clinical report, it was not known whether or not the mothers were using or abusing other drugs or alcohol. Thus, the thrombocytosis observed could be due to methadone or to other drugs or alcohol. Also, it could be due to the stress of narcotic withdrawal experienced by all infants after birth, and possibly also to relative narcotic abstinence experienced by the fetus in utero.

MANAGEMENT OF METHADONE-RELATED PROBLEMS DURING DETOXIFICATION FROM MAINTENANCE TREATMENT

During significant dose reduction or detoxification from methadone, signs and symptoms of narcotic abstinence may appear. These symptoms seem to be clinically less severe during slow detoxification from methadone maintenance, yet still are experienced by most patients undergoing detoxification. The most striking of these signs and symptoms are sleep disorders (especially insomnia), irritability, restlessness, and often depression. Based on observations carried out on a single-blind basis (the patient not aware of rate or specific timing of dose reductions), it has been noted anecdotally that many patients experience the most significant symptoms of narcotic withdrawal during the final phases of detoxification. Thus in many clinics, it has become the practice to reduce doses of methadone relatively rapidly during the initial stages of detoxification (down to around 15 to 25 mg/day), but then to proceed very slowly with the final stages. These anecdotal observations, coupled with other observations that well rehabilitated, long term methadone maintenance patients may be satisfactorily treated with low doses of methadone, suggest that possibly a relative "deficiency syndrome," intrinsic or induced, is present in the narcotic addict or methadone-maintained patient that may be satisfactorily managed by chronic treatment with low doses of a long acting narcotic after initial moderate to high dose treatment to assist in early management (elimination of illicit narcotic use and initiation of rehabilitation). Such an induced deficiency syndrome might be similar to that observed (and biochemically well documented) during and after chronic adrenocorticosteroid treatment for a variety of medical indications.

After full detoxification from methadone, many (or possibly most) patients continue to experience some persistent signs and symptoms of narcotic abstinence. Certain physiological features of the protracted narcotic abstinence syndrome have been well described by Martin et al. (62). Other signs and symptoms are less easily described and cannot be measured satisfactorily at this time. However, the constellation of signs and symptoms, coupled with so-called "drug hunger" (in part, a recognition by the individual that readministration of narcotics will alleviate the undesired signs and symptoms), may well constitute the major reason for return of most heroin addicts to narcotic use after detoxification (69). Many former methadone maintenance patients also return to heroin use or, more often, to use or abuse of a "legitimate" drug such as diazepam or alcohol (24, 33, 90).

To date, there is no known effective therapeutic approach to minimize or prevent the signs and symptoms of protracted abstinence other than the reinstitution of treatment with a narcotic drug, preferably a long acting narcotic. In many drug-free individuals, the problem seems to persist for extended, indefinite periods of time. At this point in our medical knowledge, it may be far preferable to resume methadone maintenance treatment in patients with significant symptoms than to allow them to develop new substance abuse patterns (e.g., alcoholism or other types of drug abuse that are potentially much more harmful to specific organs and over-all body functioning). Procedures for facilitating reentry of such patients into maintenance treatment need to be developed.

Recently, a new approach for the acute management of narcotic withdrawal symptoms during slow or abrupt detoxification from heroin or methadone has been introduced and is currently undergoing extensive clinical trials. Gold, Kleber, and colleagues first introduced the use of the antihypertensive drug, clonidine, for the rapid detoxification of narcotic-dependent individuals after observations that both clonidine and morphine blocked the effects of electrical and pharmacological activation of the major noradrenergic nucleus of the brain, the locus coeruleus (38, 39). It has also been observed that clonidine and opiate withdrawal signs and symptoms are similar with respect to changes in vital signs and mood. In early studies conducted to date, it seems that clonidine causes a prompt and significant decrease in opiate withdrawal signs and symptoms during gradual detoxification from methadone maintenance treatment or heroin addiction (38–40). In a recently reported trial of use of clonidine after the abrupt cessation of chronic methadone treatment, again it was shown that clonidine suppressed many signs and symptoms of narcotic withdrawal, with the exception of insomnia, bone pain, and a few other symptoms. Some patients in the trial experienced a precipitous fall in blood pressure, necessitating either reduced dose or cessation of clonidine (37). Further clinical trials are in progress to determine the safety and efficacy of clonidine management for the

acute narcotic abstinence syndrome. No studies have yet been reported of patients followed for more than 21 days after clonidine-assisted narcotic withdrawal. Thus, the long term outcome of clonidine-detoxified patients has yet to be determined. From a theoretical standpoint, it is unlikely that the acute use of clonidine during narcotic withdrawal will have any effects on the protracted narcotic abstinence syndrome nor the related persistent "drug hunger" that has been commonly observed in drug-free former narcotic-dependent individuals. Although clonidine may prove to be a very effective agent for use both in the detoxification of methadone-maintained patients and also may replace methadone as the drug of choice for the short term detoxification of heroin addicts, there are no studies to date suggesting that its use will reduce the postdetoxification recidivism (return to narcotic use or to use of other drugs, especially the benzodiazepines or alcohol) observed in former narcotic-dependent individuals. Also, there are no studies to date to suggest that clonidine would be a safe, as well as effective, drug for the long term maintenance treatment of narcotic addiction.

MANAGEMENT OF METHADONE-RELATED PROBLEMS AFTER INTAKE OF METHADONE BY NONTOLERANT INDIVIDUALS

Serious fatal complications directly due to methadone effects will occur after accidental or purposeful ingestion of a large maintenance dose of methadone by a naive or weakly tolerant person, if treatment is not initiated promptly. However, such complications can be prevented or effectively managed if treatment is started soon after ingestion. Because profound respiratory depression may ensue, an airway should be established first and respiration supported as needed, and the narcotic antagonist naloxone administered intravenously (0.01 mg/k). Naloxone must be readministered every 2 to 3 hours as needed for up to 72 hours, because methadone has a duration of action of 24 up to 72 hours after ingestion of a large dose by a naive person, whereas naloxone has a duration of action of only 2 to 3 hours. Even if a patient, when first seen, is in a semicomatose or comatose state and narcotic ingestion has not been established, rather only suspected, naloxone may be administered with safety, because it is a pure narcotic antagonist with no agonist properties. A patient who has ingested a large dose of methadone should be observed in the hospital for 48 to 96 hours after the ingestion.

MEDICAL MANAGEMENT OF PROBLEMS RELATIVE TO INTERACTIONS OF OTHER DRUGS OR ETHANOL WITH METHADONE AS USED IN CHRONIC MAINTENANCE TREATMENT

INTERACTIONS BETWEEN RIFAMPIN AND METHADONE

A clinically significant drug interaction between the antituberculosis drug, rifampin, and methadone has been observed and documented in methadone maintenance patients with tuberculosis (50). In a special methadone maintenance program for patients with pulmonary disease, it was observed that several patients developed signs and symptoms of narcotic withdrawal when rifampin was added to the antituberculosis treatment regimen. In all, 21 of 30 patients receiving rifampin developed withdrawal symptoms, which would begin around 6 to 8 hours after the daily dose of methadone and persist until 1 to 2 hours after the subsequent dose of methadone was given. Six of seven patients experiencing severe narcotic withdrawal symptoms were studied to determine whether rifampin alters methadone disposition (50). Each of these six patients was studied both while receiving methadone alone and methadone plus rifampin. Plasma levels of methadone were consistently and significantly lower (33 to 68 per cent) at each time point after oral methadone administration during concomitant rifampin treatment, as compared with during methadone treatment alone. The mean 24-hour urinary excretion of the major N-demethylated pyrrolidine metabolite increased during rifampin treatment, and fecal excretion of the pyrrolidine metabolite was even more significantly increased during rifampin treatment (50–52). Inconsistent changes in plasma disappearance rates of methadone were observed. These findings suggest that the rifampin may affect methadone disposition, both by enhancement of

hepatic microsomal drug-metabolizing enzyme activities by rifampin and also by alterations in methadone distribution and excretion. The narcotic withdrawal symptoms observed during rifampin treatment are probably due to the abrupt and highly significant lowering of plasma levels of methadone. When rifampin treatment is indicated in methadone-maintained patients, it is essential that narcotic withdrawal symptoms be anticipated and that increased doses and/or divided doses of methadone be administered as necessary to prevent or alleviate such undesirable symptoms. At this time, special dispensation from the Food and Drug Administration may be needed for such changes in methadone administration in some patients.

POSSIBLE INTERACTIONS BETWEEN PHENYTOIN AND METHADONE

Several clinicians and investigators have made clinical observations of apparent narcotic abstinence symptoms when treatment with the anticonvulsant, phenytoin, is added to the regimen of methadone maintenance patients. One such clinical observation was reported several years ago (36). Collaborative studies are now in progress at The Rockefeller University and the University of California at San Francisco to determine whether or not significant drug dispositional interactions between methadone and phenytoin occur during concomitant treatment with these two agents.[2] If significant interactions do occur between these two agents, the management required would be similar to that for the interaction between rifampin and methadone; that is, the daily dose of methadone might need to be increased and/or divided.

POSSIBLE INTERACTIONS OF OTHER DRUGS WITH METHADONE

No other definite dispositional interactions with methadone have been documented in humans. However, in animal models it has been shown that concomitant administration of barbiturates, diazepam or desipramine, with methadone causes significant dispositional drug interactions (47, 58, 89). Studies

---

[2]Dr. M. J. Kreek at The Rockefeller University; Dr. N. Jaffery at the All India Institute of Medical Sciences (AIIMS); Dr. T. Tong, Dr. S. Pond, and Dr. N. Benowitz at the University of California at San Francisco.

to determine whether such interactions occur in humans are now in progress.

INTERACTIONS BETWEEN ETHANOL AND METHADONE

A single study has been carried out to determine whether acute use of moderate ("social") amounts of ethanol alter methadone disposition (29). A group of five methadone-maintained patients who were not alcohol abusers and who had no evidence of liver disease were studied. Plasma levels of methadone after the usual daily dose of methadone were determined while receiving methadone alone and after administration of 90 ml of a 50 per cent solution of ethanol 1 hour after the oral methadone dose. No significant differences in plasma levels were noted. Ethanol disappearance rates were also determined and were found to be similar to those reported in control subjects (0.23 ± 11 mg/dl/minute). Studies of the effects of chronic alcohol abuse on methadone disposition have not yet been reported. However, studies in rats suggest that after chronic concomitant administration of ethanol and methadone and then withdrawal from ethanol, plasma levels of methadone are lowered (47). Similarly, Borowsky and Lieber have reported significant effects of chronic ethanol treatment on the disposition of a single dose of methadone in rats (10). In another recently reported study carried out in rats, it has been suggested that chronic administration of methadone may accelerate the blood disappearance rate of ethanol (99).

MEDICAL MANAGEMENT OF COMMONLY ENCOUNTERED MEDICAL PROBLEMS IN METHADONE-MAINTAINED PATIENTS

Many of the medical problems encountered in methadone maintenance patients are due to preexistent chronic disease, present at time of entry into methadone treatment and related directly or indirectly to chronic self-administration of a variety of substances including drugs, often by the parenteral route using unsterile techniques. The most common problems of this type include various chronic sequelae of viral hepatitis (affecting more than 60 per cent of methadone maintenance patients) and also a variety of types

of renal disease. Other medical problems commonly encountered in methadone maintenance patients are related to chronic abuse of ethanol (a continuing problem in 20 to 50 per cent of methadone-maintained patients), which usually began prior to methadone treatment and often prior to heroin addiction, and also to abuse of other substances. Otherwise, most medical problems in the methadone-maintained patient are similar to those encountered in the general population.

MANAGEMENT OF CHRONIC LIVER DISEASE IN METHADONE MAINTENANCE PATIENTS

Chronic liver disease of a variety of types and degrees of severity has been documented repeatedly to be the most common medical problem encountered in heroin addicts, methadone-maintained patients and drug-free former addicts (15, 17–19, 43–45, 48, 49, 59, 83, 84, 91–93, 98), occurring in 60 per cent of all subjects in these groups. Probably the most commonly found lesion is that of chronic persistent hepatitis, a relatively benign problem that can result from viral hepatitis. Other postviral lesions seen less commonly include chronic active hepatitis and postnecrotic cirrhosis. In prospective and retrospective studies of more than 1,600 patients, it has been shown that methadone itself is not hepatotoxic (that liver abnormalities do not appear in patients with normal liver function at time of entry into methadone treatment) unless acute viral or alcoholic disease occurs during treatment (44, 45, 48, 49). In one prospective study, it was shown that 12 per cent of patients in chronic methadone treatment for more than 3 years were carriers (mostly silent carriers) of the hepatitis B (surface) antigen, and 46 per cent had hepatitis B (surface) antibody, indicating prior infection with that virus. Approximately 0.2 per cent of the general population of New York City are carriers of hepatitis B (surface) antigen (16).

Although no studies of the prevalence of non A-non B hepatitis antigen and antibodies in methadone maintenance patients have been reported yet, recent studies of this type of hepatitis virus suggest that it may frequently lead to mild chronic sequelae of the type seen in many methadone-maintained subjects (6).

The other very common types of liver dis-

ease found in methadone-maintained patients are related to chronic alcohol abuse.
These include acute fatty infiltration of the
liver, alcoholic hepatitis, and alcoholic cirrhosis.

Management of all types of liver disease in
methadone maintenance patients should be
similar to that carried out in the general
population.

MANAGEMENT OF CHRONIC RENAL DISEASE IN METHADONE-MAINTAINED PATIENTS

Chronic renal disease is much less commonly observed than chronic liver disease in
methadone maintenance patients, occurring
in around 5 to 10 per cent of patients (45, 98).
Several different types of renal disease have
been described in this patient population,
and it has been suggested that at least some
types observed may be directly or indirectly
related to the chronic injection of drugs or
other foreign substances or to infections resulting from unsterile parenteral drug abuse
by patients prior to entry into methadone
maintenance treatment (12, 22, 42, 66, 79, 85,
94, 96, 100). To date, there is no well documented evidence that the so-called "heroin
nephropathy" is related to the drug heroin
per se. Of interest are the recent reports of
renal amyloidosis in heroin addicts and
methadone-maintained patients (42, 66, 85).
Although it has been suggested that this disorder might be related to some aspect of the
as yet unexplained immunological abnormalities observed both in heroin addicts and in
methadone-maintained patients long after
cessation of parenteral drug abuse, most of
the reports of renal amyloidosis in this population have concluded that the amyloid was
probably related to chronic slow suppuration,
a common result of parenteral drug abuse.

Management of renal disease in methadone maintenance patients is similar to that
in the general population. There has been
some concern that possibly methadone might
be accumulated in patients with significant
chronic renal disease, because in otherwise
healthy patients up to 50 per cent of the daily
dose of methadone is excreted in urine as
unchanged methadone or the major pyrrolidine metabolite (52). However, in preliminary
studies of three methadone-maintained patients with severe chronic renal disease, no
such accumulation of methadone in plasma

was observed; in one patient who was anuric
and undergoing chronic hemodialysis, it was
shown that, although very small amounts of
methadone were removed in the dialysate,
almost the entire daily dose of methadone
could be accounted for in feces, primarily as
the major pyrrolidine metabolite. Thus, in
the setting of chronic renal disease, it seems
that the fecal route of excretion of methadone
and its metabolites, which usually accounts
for 15 to 45 per cent of a daily dose, can
become essentially the sole route of excretion
(55).

MANAGEMENT OF CHRONIC ALCOHOL ABUSE IN METHADONE-MAINTAINED PATIENTS

Chronic alcohol abuse is a common problem in heroin addicts and in methadone-
maintained patients, just as it is probably the
major medical problem in our society today.
In each of these groups, medical problems
associated with alcohol abuse include alcoholism per se and a wide variety of medical
complications of the toxic effect of alcohol on
the hepatobiliary, pancreatic, gastrointestinal,
endocrine, neurological, cardiovascular, and
other organ systems.

In various prospective, retrospective, and
special studies of methadone-maintained patients, it has been shown that 20 to 50 per
cent of patients are chronic abusers of alcohol
(8, 9, 11, 13, 14, 41, 44, 45, 49, 52, 57, 60, 67,
68, 70, 72, 74, 86, 87). Chronic alcohol abuse
may be the leading over-all cause of medical
complications appearing during methadone
treatment and also may be, directly and indirectly, the primary factor leading up to
involuntary discharge of patients from treatment.

Significant occurrence of alcohol abuse is
apparently an even greater problem in methadone-maintained patients during and after
detoxification from methadone (23, 32, 73).
Alcohol abuse in this setting may be due, in
part, to the nonspecific symptoms of narcotic
abstinence and "drug hunger," coupled with
an unwillingness on the part of many rehabilitated patients to ever return to illicit narcotic abuse.

The medical complications related to alcohol abuse may be treated in methadone
maintenance patients in similar ways to their
management in the general population. It has
been suggested that alcoholic liver disease

may progress more rapidly in the methadone-maintained patient. To date, there are no data to substantiate this suggestion based on clinical observations (7).

Alcoholism or alcoholic abuse is in some respects similar to narcotic addiction, and yet, unlike narcotic addiction, one for which no definite or specific pharmacological approaches to treatment are available. Disulfiram is the only pharmacological tool that has been shown to be helpful in the management of former alcoholics, and its action is simply one of producing highly noxious symptoms when alcohol is used. Preliminary studies carried out in methadone maintenance patients suggest that there are no clinically significant dispositional interactions between disulfiram and methadone (95). Also, the medical safety and efficacy of disulfiram in methadone maintenance patients has been reported (14, 70).

There has been (and still is) much pessimism regarding the efficacy of methadone maintenance treatment for narcotic addiction for individuals who are also alcoholics. However, in a recent prospective study of this subgroup of "problem patients," it was shown that 41 per cent of adult alcoholic methadone-maintained patients remained in methadone treatment for more than 2 years and, during that time, were successfully treated for narcotic addiction, even though alcohol abuse continued on a chronic basis (7). It has never been claimed or shown that methadone is an effective treatment for alcoholism. This documented retention in treatment and efficacy of methadone treatment in this large subgroup of alcohol-abusing patients suggests that alcoholic heroin addicts should be offered methadone maintenance treatment. However, more innovative and effective approaches to the difficult problem of management of these combined addictive diseases need to be developed.

Acknowledgment. The author would like to acknowledge the assistance of Mr. Jay G. Ruckel for preparation of this manuscript, as well as the many workers in this laboratory and colleagues, both at this institution and elsewhere, who have assisted in many different ways in the work in this area.

References

1. Adham, N. F., Soon, M. K., and Erg, B. F. Hyperalpha-2-macroglobulinemia in narcotic addicts. Ann. Intern. Med. 88:793, 1978.

2. Azizi, F., Apostolos, G. V., Longscope, C., et al. Decreased serum testosterone concentration in male heroin and methadone addicts. Steroids 22:467, 1973.

3. Azizi, F., Vagenakis, A. G., Portnay, G. I., et al. Thyroxine transport and metabolism in methadone and heroin addicts. Ann. Intern. Med. 80:194, 1974.

4. Barstein, Y., Giardina, P. J. V., Rausen, A. R., et al. Thrombocytosis and increased circulating platelet aggregates in newborn infants of poly drug users. J. Pediatr. 94:895, 1979.

5. Bastomsky, C. H., and Dent, R. R. M. Elevated serum concentrations of thyroxine-binding globulin and ceruloplasmin in methadone-maintained patients. Clin. Res. 24:655A, 1976.

6. Berman, M., Alter, H. J., Ishak, K. G., et al. The chronic sequelae of non-A non-B hepatitis. Ann. Intern. Med. 91:1, 1979.

7. Beverley, C. L., Kreek, M. J., Wells, A. O., et al. Effects of alcohol abuse on progression of liver disease in methadone-maintained patients. In *Proceedings, 41st Annual Scientific Meeting of the Committee on Problems of Drug Dependence*, R. C. Petersen and L. S. Harris, editors, NIDA Research Monograph, pp. 399–401. Rockville, Md., National Institute on Drug Abuse, 1980.

8. Bihari, B. Alcoholism and methadone maintenance. Am. J. Drug Alcohol Abuse 1:79, 1974.

9. Bihari, B. Alcoholism in M.M.T. patients: Etiological factors and treatment approaches. In *Proceedings, Fifth National Conference on Methadone Treatment*, Vol. 1, pp. 288–295. 1973.

10. Borowsky, S. A., and Lieber, C. S. Interaction of methadone and ethanol metabolism. J. Pharmacol. Exp. Ther. 207:123, 1978.

11. Brown, B. S., Kozel, N. J., Meyers, M. B., et al. Use of alcohol by addict and nonaddict populations. Am. J. Psychiatry 130:599, 1973.

12. Brown, S. M., Stimmel, B., Taub, R. N., et al. Immunologic dysfunction in heroin addicts. Arch. Intern. Med. 134:1001, 1974.

13. Chambers, C. D., Babst, D. V., and Warner, A. Characteristics predicting long-term retention in a methadone maintenance program. In *Proceedings, Third National Conference on Methadone Treatment*, pp. 140–143. Washington, D.C., United States Government Printing Office, 1970.

14. Charuvastra, C. V., Panell, J., Hopper, M., et al. The medical safety of the combined usage of disulfiram and methadone. Arch. Gen. Psychiatry 33:391, 1976.

15. Cherubin, C. E. The medical sequelae of narcotic addiction. Ann. Intern. Med. 67:23, 1967.

16. Cherubin, C. E., Hargrove, R. L., and Prince, A. M. The serum hepatitis related antigen (SH) in illicit drug users. Am. J. Epidemiol. 91:510, 1970.

17. Cherubin, C. E., Kane, S., Weinberger, D. R., et al. Persistence of transaminase abnormalities in former drug addicts. Ann. Intern. Med. 76:385, 1972.

18. Cherubin, C. E., Rosenthal, W. S., Stenger, R. E., et al. Chronic liver disease in asymptomatic narcotic addicts. Ann. Intern. Med. 76:391, 1972.

19. Cherubin, C. E., Schaefer, R. A., Rosenthal, W. S., et al. The natural history of liver disease in former drug users. Am. J. Med. Sci. 272:244, 1976.

20. Cicero, T. J., Bell, R. D., Wiest, W. G., et al. Function of the male sex organs in heroin and methadone users. N. Engl. J. Med. 292:822, 1975.

21. Cushman, P., Jr. Persistent increased immunoglob-

ulin M in treated narcotic addiction: Association with liver disease and continuing heroin use. J. Allergy Clin. Immunol. 52:122, 1973.

22. Cushman, P., Jr. Hyperimmunoglobulinemia in heroin addiction: Some epidemiologic observations including some possible effects of route of administration and multiple drug abuse. Am. J. Epidemiol. 99:218, 1974.

23. Cushman, P., Jr. Detoxification from methadone maintenance. J.A.M.A. 235:2604, 1976.

24. Cushman, P., Jr., and Dole, V. P. Detoxification of rehabilitated methadone-maintained patients. J.A.M.A. 226:747, 1973.

25. Cushman, P., Jr., and Grieco, M. H. Hyperimmunoglobulinemia associated with narcotic addiction: Effects of methadone maintenance treatment. Am. J. Med. 54:320, 1973.

26. Cushman, P., Jr., Gupta, S., and Grieco, M. H. Immunological studies in methadone maintained patients. Int. J. Addict. 12:241, 1977.

27. Cushman, P., Jr., and Kreek, M. J. Methadone-maintained patients: Effects of methadone on plasma testosterone, FSH, LH, and prolactin. N. Y. State J. Med. 74:1970, 1974.

28. Cushman, P., Jr., and Kreek, M. J. Some endocrinologic observations in narcotic addicts. In Narcotics and the Hypothalamus, E. Zimmermann and R. George, editors, pp. 161–173. New York, Raven Press, 1974.

29. Cushman, P., Jr., Kreek, M. J., and Gordis, E. Ethanol and methadone in man: A possible drug interaction. Drug Alcohol Depend. 3:35, 1978.

30. Cushman, P., Jr., and Sherman, C. Biologic false-positive reactions in serologic tests for syphilis in narcotic addiction. Am. J. Clin. Pathol. 61:346, 1974.

31. Dobbs, W. H. Methadone treatment of heroin addicts. J.A.M.A. 218:1536, 1971.

32. Dole, V. P., and Joseph, H. Where do the old addicts go? (Abstract). Clin. Res. 25:513A, 1977.

33. Dole, V. P., and Joseph, H. Long-term outcome of patients treated with methadone maintenance. Ann. N. Y. Acad. Sci. 311:181, 1978.

34. Dole, V. P., and Kreek, M. J. Methadone plasma level: Sustained by a reservoir of drug in tissue. Proc. Natl. Acad. Sci. USA 70:10, 1973.

35. Dole, V. P., Nyswander, M. E., and Kreek, M. J. Narcotic blockade. Arch. Intern. Med. 118:304, 1966.

36. Finelli, P. F. Phenytoin and methadone tolerance. N. Engl. J. Med. 294:227, 1976.

37. Gold, M. S., Pottash, A. L., Sweeney, D. R. et al. Clonidine detoxification: A 14-day protocol for rapid opiate withdrawal. In Proceedings, 41st Annual Scientific Meeting of the Committee on Problems of Drug Dependence, R. C. Petersen and L. S. Harris, editors, NIDA Research Monograph Series, p. 226. Rockville, Md., National Institute on Drug Abuse, 1979.

38. Gold, M. S., Redmond, D. E., Jr., and Kleber, H. D. Clonidine blocks acute opiate withdrawal symptoms. Lancet 2:599, 1978.

39. Gold, M. S., Redmond, D. E., Jr., and Kleber, H. D. Clonidine in opiate withdrawal. Lancet 1:929, 1978.

40. Gold, M. S., Redmond, D. E., Jr., and Kleber, H. D. Noradrenergic hyperactivity in opiate withdrawal supported by clonidine reversal of opiate withdrawal. Am. J. Psychiatry 136:100, 1979.

41. Jackson, G. W., and Richman, A. Alcohol use among narcotic addicts. Alcohol Health Res. World 1:25, 1973.

42. Jacob, H., Charytan, C., Rascoff, J. M., et al. Amyloidosis secondary to drug abuse and chronic skin suppuration. Arch. Intern. Med. 138:1150, 1978.

43. Jersild, T., Johansen, C., Balslov, J. T., et al. Hepatitis in young drug users. Scand. J. Gastroenterol. (Suppl.) 7:79, 1970.

44. Kreek, M. J. Medical safety, side effects and toxicity of methadone. In Proceedings, Fourth National Conference on Methadone Treatment, pp. 171–174. New York, National Association for the Prevention of Addiction to Narcotics, 1972.

45. Kreek, M. J. Medical safety and side effects of methadone in tolerant individuals. J.A.M.A. 223: 655, 1973.

46. Kreek, M. J. Plasma and urine levels of methadone. N. Y. State J. Med. 23:2773, 1973.

47. Kreek, M. J. Effects of drugs and alcohol on opiate disposition and actions. In Factors Affecting the Action of Narcotics, M. W. Adler, L. Manara, and R. Saminin, editors, pp. 717–740. New York, Raven Press, 1978.

48. Kreek, M. J. Medical complications in methadone patients. Ann. N. Y. Acad. Sci. 311:110, 1978.

49. Kreek, M. J., Dodes, L., Kane, S., et al. Long-term methadone maintenance therapy: Effects on liver function. Ann. Intern. Med. 77:598, 1972.

50. Kreek, M. J., Garfield, J. W., Gutjahr, C. L., et al. Rifampin-induced methadone withdrawal. N. Engl. J. Med. 294:1104, 1976.

51. Kreek, M. J., Gutjahr, C. L., Bowen, D. V., et al. Fecal excretion of methadone and its metabolities: a major pathway of elimination in man. In Critical Concerns in the Field of Drug Abuse: Proceedings of the Third National Drug Abuse Conference, Inc., New York, 1976, J. H. Lowinson, conference chairperson, pp. 1206–1210. New York, Marcel Dekker, 1978.

52. Kreek, M. J., Gutjahr, C. L., Garfield, J. W., et al. Drug interactions with methadone. Ann. N. Y. Acad. Sci. 281:350, 1976.

53. Kreek, M. J., and Khuri, E. Effects of methadone maintenance on prolactin release. Abstracts of The Endocrine Society Annual Meeting, Anaheim, Calif., 1979. Endocrinology, p. 289.

54. Kreek, M. J., Oratz, M., and Rothschild, M. A. Hepatic extraction of long-and short-acting narcotics in the isolated perfused rabbit liver. Gastroenterology 75:88, 1978.

55. Kreek, M. J., Schecter, A. J., Gutjahr, C. L., et al. Methadone use in patients with chronic renal disease. Drug Alcohol Depend. 5:197, 1980.

56. Krieger, D. T., and Liotta, A. S. Pituitary hormones in the brain: Where, how, and why? Science 205: 366, 1979.

57. Liebson, I., and Bigelow, G. A behavioural-pharmacological treatment of dually addicted patients. Behav. Res. Ther. 10:403, 1972.

58. Liu, S.-J., and Wang, R. I. H. Increased analgesia and alterations in distribution and metabolism of methadone by desipramine in the rat. J. Pharmacol. Exp. Ther. 195:94, 1975.

59. Louria, D. B., Hensle, T., and Rose, J. The major medical complications of heroin addiction. Ann. Intern. Med. 67:1, 1967.

60. Maddux, J. F., and Elliott, B. Problem drinkers among patients on methadone. Am. J. Drug Alcohol

Abuse 2:245, 1975.

61. Marks, C., and Goldring, R. Chronic hypercapnia during methadone maintenance. Ann. Rev. Respir. Dis. 108:1088, 1973.

62. Martin, W. R., and Jasinski, D. R. Physiological parameters of morphine dependence in man—tolerance, early abstinence, protracted abstinence. J. Psychiatr. Res. 7:9, 1969.

63. Martin, W. R., Jasinski, D. R., Haertzen, C. A., et al. Methadone—a reevaluation. Arch. Gen. Psychiatry 28:286, 1976.

64. Mendelson, J. H., Mendelson, J. E., and Patch, V. D. Plasma testosterone levels in heroin addiction and during methadone maintenance. J. Pharmacol. Exp. Ther. 192:211, 1975.

65. Mendelson, J. H., Meyer, R. E., Ellingboe, J., et al. Effects of heroin and methadone on plasma cortisol and testosterone. J. Pharmacol. Exp. Ther. 195:296, 1975.

66. Novick, D. M., Yancowitz, S. R., and Weinberg, P. G. Amyloidosis in parenteral drug abusers. Mt. Sinai J. Med. 46:163, 1979.

67. Pascarelli, E. F., and Eaton, C. Disulfiram (Antabuse[R]) in the treatment of methadone maintenance alcoholics. In *Proceedings, Fifth National Conference on Methadone Treatment*, Vol. 1, pp. 316-322. New York, National Association for the Prevention of Addiction to Narcotics, 1973.

68. Perkins, M. E. and Bloch, H. I. A study of some failures in methadone treatment. Am. J. Psychiatry 128:47, 1971.

69. Pescor, M. J. Follow-up study of treated narcotic drug addicts. Public Health Rep. (Suppl.) 170:1, 1943.

70. Publiese, A., Martinez, M., Maselli, A., et al. Treatment of alcoholic methadone-maintenance patients with disulfiram. J. Stud. Alcohol 36:1584, 1975.

71. Renault, P. F., Schuster, C. R., Heinrich, R. I., et al. Altered plasma cortisol response in patients on methadone maintenance. Clin. Pharmacol. Ther. 18:269, 1972.

72. Richman, A., Jackson, G., and Trigg, H. Follow-up of methadone maintenance patients hospitalized for abuse of alcohol and barbiturates. In *Proceedings, Fifth National Conference on Methadone Treatment* Vol. 2, pp. 1484-1493. New York, National Association for the Prevention of Addiction to Narcotics, 1973.

73. Riordan, C. E., Mezritz, M., Slobetz, F., et al. Successful detoxification from methadone maintenance: Follow-up of 38 patients. J.A.M.A. 235:2604, 1976.

74. Rosen, A., Ottenberg, D. J., and Barr, H. L. Patterns of previous abuse of alcohol in a group of hospitalized drug addicts. In *Proceedings, Fifth National Conference on Methadone Treatment*, Vol. 1, pp. 306-315. New York, National Association for the Prevention of Addiction to Narcotics, 1973.

75. Rothschild, M. A., Kreek, M. J., Oratz, M., et al. The stimulation of albumin synthesis by methadone. Gastroenterology 71:214, 1976.

76. Rubenstein, R. B., Kreek, M. K., Mbawa, N., et al. Human spinal fluid methadone levels. Drug Alcohol Depend. 3:103, 1978.

77. Rubenstein, R. B., Spira, I., and Wolff, W. I. Management of surgical problems in patients on methadone maintenance. Am. J. Surgery 131:566, 1976.

78. Rubenstein, R. B., and Wolff, W. I. Methadone ileus syndrome: Report of a fatal case. Dis. Colon Rectum 19:357, 1976.

79. Salomon, M. I., Poon, T. P., Goldblatt, M., et al. Renal lesions in heroin addicts: A study based on kidney biopsies. Nephron 9:356, 1972.

80. Santen, R. J. How narcotics addiction affects reproductive function in women. Contemp. Obstet. Gynecol. 3:93, 1974.

81. Santen, R. J., Sofsky, J., Bilic, N., et al. Mechanism of action of narcotics in the production of menstrual dysfunction in women. Fertil. Steril. 26:538, 1975.

82. Santiago, T. V., Pugliese, A. C., and Edelman, N. H. Control of breathing during methadone addiction. Am. J. Med. 62:347, 1977.

83. Sapira, J. D. The narcotic addict as a medical patient. Am. J. Med. 45:555, 1968.

84. Sapira, J. D., Jasinski, D. R., and Gorodetzky, C. W. Liver disease in narcotic addicts. II. The role of the needle. Clin. Pharmacol. Ther. 9:725, 1968.

85. Scholes, J., Derosena, R., Appel, G. B., et al. Amyloidosis in chronic heroin addicts with the nephrotic syndrome. Ann. Intern. Med. 91:26, 1979.

86. Schut, J., File, K., and Wohlmuth, T. Alcohol use by narcotic addicts in methadone maintenance treatment. Q. J. Stud. Alcohol 34:1356, 1973.

87. Scott, N. R., Winslow, W. W., and Gorman, D. G. Epidemiology of alcoholism in a methadone maintenance program. In *Proceedings, Fifth National Conference on Methadone Treatment*, Vol. 1, pp. 284-287. New York, National Association for the Prevention of Addiction to Narcotics, 1973.

88. Shenkman, L., Massie, B., Mitsuma, T., et al. Effects of chronic methadone administration on the hypothalamic-pituitary-thyroid axis. J. Clin. Endocrinol. Metab. 35:169, 1972.

89. Spaulding, T. C., Minium, L., Kotake, A. N., et al. The effect of diazepam on the metabolism of methadone by the liver of methadone-dependent rats. Drug Metab. Dispos. 2:458, 1974.

90. Stimmel, B., Goldberg, J., Cohen, M., et al. Detoxification from methadone maintenance: Risk factors associated with relapse to narcotic use. Ann. N. Y. Acad. Sci. 311:173, 1978.

91. Stimmel, B., Vernace, S., Heller, E., et al. Hepatitis B antigen and antibody in former heroin addicts on methadone maintenance: Correlation with clinical and histological findings. In *Proceedings, Fifth National Conference on Methadone Treatment*, Vol. 1, pp. 501-506. New York, National Association for the Prevention of Addiction to Narcotics, 1973.

92. Stimmel, B., Vernace, S., and Tobias, H. Hepatic dysfunction in heroin addicts: The role of alcohol. J.A.M.A. 222:811, 1972.

93. Stimmel, B., Vernace, S., and Tobias, H. Hepatic function in patients on methadone maintenance therapy. In *Proceedings, Fourth National Conference on Methadone Treatment*, pp. 419-420. New York, National Association for the Prevention of Addiction to Narcotics, 1972.

94. Streepada, R. T. K., Nicastri, A. D., and Friedman, E. A. Renal consequences of narcotic abuse. Adv. Nephrol. 7:261, 1978.

95. Tong, T. G., Benowitz, N. L., and Kreek, M. J. Methadone disulfiram interaction during methadone maintenance. (Abstract). Clin. Pharmacol. Ther. 23:132, 1978.

96. Treser, G., Cherubin, C., Lonergan, E. T., et al. Renal lesions in narcotic addicts. Am. J. Med. 57: 687, 1974.

97. Webster, J. B., Coupal, J. J., and Cushman, P., Jr. Increased serum thyroxine levels in euthyroid narcotic addicts. J. Clin. Endocrinol. Metab. 37:928, 1973.

98. Webster, I. W., Waddy, N., Jenkins, L. V., et al. Health status of a group of narcotic addicts in a methadone treatment programme. Med. J. Aust. 2: 485, 1977.

99. Wendell, G. D., and Kreek, M. J. Effects of chronic methadone treatment on rate of ethanol elimination in the rat *in vivo*. Abstracts of the Tenth Annual NCA/AMSA/RSA Medical-Scientific Conference of the National Alcoholism Forum, Washington, D.C. Alcoholism 3:200, 1979.

100. White, A. G. Medical disorders in drug addicts: 200 consecutive admissions. J.A.M.A. 223:1469, 1973.

101. Yaffe, G. J., Strelinger, R. W., and Parwatikar, S. Physical symptom complaints of patients on methadone maintenance. In *Proceedings, Fifth National Conference on Methadone Treatment*, Vol. 1, pp. 507–514. New York, National Association for the Prevention of Addiction to Narcotics, 1973.

CHAPTER 54

LEGAL ASPECTS OF CONFIDENTIALITY IN SUBSTANCE ABUSE TREATMENT[1]

Patrick R. Cowlishaw, J.D.

Given the stigma associated with the labels "addict" and "alcoholic," the confidentiality of patient records must be scrupulously protected if individuals are to seek substance abuse treatment voluntarily. That commonplace observation, whatever its empirical underpinnings, has had enough force to result in a comprehensive set of federal statutes and regulations of importance to everyone involved in the field of substance abuse—as clinicians, researchers, or administrators. This chapter provides an introduction to the legal matrix and to selected problems that arise within it.

Two statutes passed by Congress in the early 1970's narrowly define the circumstances in which the records of patients in federally assisted or regulated substance abuse treatment may be disclosed.[2] Both statutes delegated substantial rule-making responsibility to the Department of Health, Education, and Welfare (HEW), and in 1975 HEW issued an exhaustive set of regulations under the heading "Confidentiality of Alcohol and Drug Abuse Patient Records" (hereinafter "the regulations").[3] These regulations fill many gaps in the authorizing legislation and supersede any state or local law less protective of the confidentiality of patient records. For all practical purposes these regulations constitute the universe of legal requirements in this area.

Familiarity with the confidentiality regulations is essential to anyone directly or in-

---

[1] This chapter is intended to provide an introduction to the legal requirements surrounding the confidentiality of patient records in substance abuse treatment. Those requirements are subject to change. In fact, changes in the governing federal regulations are currently under consideration. (See footnote 8). An understanding of legal requirements in this area must be periodically updated. Moreover, although the chapter suggests methods for complying with the requirements in a variety of recurring problem areas, the chapter cannot be relied upon for a definitive answer in any particular situation, which may present its own unique circumstances. Anyone who desires legal advice should consult an attorney individually.

[2] Drug Abuse Office and Treatment Act of 1972, §408, 21 U.S.C. §1175; Comprehensive Alcohol Abuse and Alcoholism Prevention, Treatment and Rehabilitation Act of 1970, §333, 42 U.S.C. §4582.

[3] 42 C.F.R. Part 2; 40 Federal Register 27802 (July 1, 1975).

directly involved with substance abuse treatment, for the unknowing proceed at peril of criminal liability. Violating the regulations is punishable by a fine of up to $500 for a first offense or up to $5,000 for each subsequent offense (§2.14[4]). Moreover, the National Institute on Drug Abuse (NIDA) and the National Institute on Alcoholism and Alcohol Abuse (NIAAA) may require compliance with the regulations as a condition of grants to treatment programs. Violation in such circumstances risks termination of funding.

Equally important, many of the nettlesome problems that may arise under the regulations can be avoided through foresight. Some basic familiarity with the regulations' requirements will facilitate communication and reduce the confidentiality-related conflicts among program, patient, and outside agency to a few relatively rare situations.

One may not assume that an understanding of the general ethical and legal standards that protect patient confidences in the field of medicine will suffice to ensure compliance with the confidentiality regulations pertaining to substance abuse treatment. On the contrary, these regulations are more restrictive of communications in many instances than the physician-patient privilege itself. For example, unlike many formulations of the privilege, the confidentiality regulations protect more than the information that a physician must obtain in order to provide treatment to a patient.[5] In contrast to the privilege, a patient's waiver does not by itself remove the protection of the regulations.[6] Indeed, the confidence most jealously guarded by the regulations—a patient's identity as a patient—is generally not protected by the physician-patient privilege at all.[7]

What follows is an elementary map through the regulations. After examining the breadth of the regulations' applicability and defining the terms of the general prohibition on disclosure, the discussion will touch upon the various conditions that permit disclosure with patient consent and the few that allow for unconsented disclosures to third parties. In the process, the effect of the regulations on such topics as the following will be highlighted: communications with third-party payees and funding sources; access to patient records for research purposes and restraints on follow-up studies; medical records containing secondary diagnoses of drug or alcohol abuse; and crime and child abuse reporting.[8]

THE GENERAL RULE AGAINST DISCLOSURE: ITS BREADTH AND TERMS

Except under certain specified conditions, the regulations prohibit the disclosure of the records of any patient that are maintained in connection with the performance of any alcohol or drug abuse prevention function supported or licensed by the federal government (§§2.12, 2.13). This general rule is indeed broad in scope, as the definitions of its various terms will make clear.

ACTIVITIES AND ORGANIZATIONS SUBJECT TO THE REGULATIONS

The confidentiality regulations apply to records maintained in connection with "any alcohol abuse or drug abuse prevention function." That term includes all activities relating to substance abuse education, training, rehabilitation, or research (§2.11(k)).[9] The regulations reach those activities even when they are conducted by an organization that is not primarily concerned with drug abuse, as in

---

[4] Citations in the form "§2.___" refer to specific sections of the confidentiality regulations, codified at 42 C.F.R. §2.1 through 2.67.1.
[5] On the scope of the privilege, see, e.g., New York C.P.L.R. §4504(a). On the scope of the regulations, see "Patient Records; Secondary Diagnoses of Drug Abuse."
[6] A patient may waive the privilege; see, e.g., New York C.P.L.R. §4504(a). On the prerequisites to disclosures with patient consent under the confidentiality regulations, see below.
[7] See, e.g., People versus Newman, 40 A.D.2d 633, 336 N.Y.S. 2d 127 (1972), *reversed on other grounds*, 32 N.Y.2d 379, 345 N.Y.S.2d 502 (1973), *cert. denied*, 414 U.S. 1163 (1974).

[8] On January 2, 1980, HEW issued a notice that it intends to make changes in the confidentiality regulations (45 Federal Register 53 (1980)). HEW solicited comments on the need for changes in several specific contexts, but did not announce the nature of any proposed changes. When specific changes are proposed, they will be announced in the Federal Register.
[9] The regulations define alcohol abuse prevention function and drug abuse prevention function with equal breadth. The same set of regulations governs the records of both alcohol and drug abuse patients, and the restrictions are in all respects the same. For convenience the remainder of this chapter will refer only to drug abuse or substance abuse; the discussion, however, is equally applicable to alcoholism and alcohol abuse treatment.

the case of a diversion program conducted by a law enforcement agency.

Although the regulations cover only those drug abuse prevention functions authorized or supported by the federal government, the federal tie is defined to reach many, if not most, programs. If any form of federal licensing or approval is necessary to operate a program, such as a methadone maintenance treatment program, the program is subject to the general rule against disclosure of patient records. And federal support, which also triggers the general rule, is not limited to federal funds that may reach a program directly or indirectly. A program that is exempt from federal income taxes or whose donors receive federal income tax deductions for their charitable contributions is also subject to the confidentiality regulations (§2.12).

PATIENT RECORDS; SECONDARY DIAGNOSES OF DRUG ABUSE

Throughout this wide range of activities, the general rule prohibits disclosures of patient records, which are defined with similar breadth. For purposes of the regulations, the term "patient" means anyone who has applied for or received diagnosis or treatment for drug abuse (§2.11(i)). Applicants are included, whether or not they were admitted to treatment. The term covers former patients and deceased patients. It includes a person who upon arrest is interviewed or diagnosed regarding drug abuse to determine eligibility for a treatment or rehabilitation program.

The definition of "patient" does imply one important limit on the scope of the regulations. The regulations define drug abuse prevention so broadly as to include general education programs and, at first glance, might be thought to apply to records of anyone who received drug abuse education. The definition of "patient," however, clarifies that the regulations pertain only to records of persons who have been individually diagnosed or treated for drug abuse. Thus, a drug abuse education program that admits students on the basis of involvement or suspected involvement in drug abuse would be covered by the regulation; a course in drug abuse taught to all students at a junior high school would not.

The general rule prohibits disclosure of the "records" of any of these patients. Records

include any information acquired about a patient in the course of drug abuse treatment, research, or education (§2.11(o)). The term is not limited to medical information, but includes such items as the patient's identity and address, as well as communications by the patient that may not be related to drug abuse. The rule covers all this information, whether or not it is in writing. The general rule applies to all who have access to these records—treatment program personnel, researchers, auditors, or others. It applies to them whether or not they are compensated for their activity, and it continues to apply to them after they have terminated their employment or relationship with the program (§2.22).

Hospital records that contain a secondary diagnosis of drug abuse present a special problem. The regulations only apply to records maintained in connection with a drug abuse prevention function. Thus a hospital record in which the primary diagnosis is unrelated to drug abuse but which contains a secondary diagnosis of the patient as a drug abuser is subject to the regulations only if the record is prepared or used in connection with the treatment of the patient's drug abuse.

An example will explain the distinction. Take two individuals admitted to a hospital, one for a broken leg and one for a condition requiring long term hospitalization. Both are methadone maintenance patients, and the hospital records note that fact. The first individual has his leg set and leaves the hospital without receiving methadone or any other drug abuse treatment. The hospital maintains the second individual during his stay, and his records reflect that fact. Because this second set of records was used in providing drug abuse treatment—even though that treatment was not the primary purpose for the patient's admission—it is subject to the regulations. The first is not (8).[10]

PROHIBITED DISCLOSURES

Having some understanding of what the regulations mean by "patient" and "records,"

---

[10] The letter cited here and others referenced throughout this chapter are opinions prepared through the Office of the Assistant General Counsel for Public Health, part of HEW's Office of General Counsel. They state the official HEW understanding of the regulations, binding on NIDA and NIAAA. Although not binding on a court of law, the opinions are an important guidepost as the expression of the agency that drafted the regulations.

one must finally consider what constitutes a "disclosure" and therefore violates the general rule. A disclosure is simply any type of communication of a patient's records. Implicit, as well as explicit, disclosures are included (§2.13(e)). Thus one may not disclose that a particular individual is not attending a program. Such a disclosure could reveal that a program knows the individual, implying a connection with drug abuse treatment, although he or she is not in attendance. Moreover, a pattern could develop from which the inquirer understands that "No, he is not here" means just that, but "that information is confidential" means the individual attends the program. Accordingly, all requests for unauthorized disclosures should be met with a noncommittal response, e.g., "federal law prohibits the release of that information." Specific reference to the confidentiality regulations, however, should be avoided if the reference might identify the subject of the inquiry as a substance abuse patient. Such inadvertent identification could occur, for example, if a visitor at a hospital's general reception area is denied access to a patient because of regulations governing "drug abuse treatment."

The regulations specify three types of communications that are not considered disclosures and so are not prohibited by the general rule. Sensibly, the regulations do not apply to internal program communications that are necessary for personnel to carry out their duties. Similarly, the regulations recognize that a program may need to procure the services of outside agencies—to perform vocational counseling or urinalysis, for example. To facilitate necessary communication, a program may enter a "qualified service organization agreement" with the outside agency. Under this simple arrangement, the outside organization agrees that it will comply with the confidentiality regulations in handling all information about patients that it receives from the program and that it will contest any attempt to obtain such information that is not permitted by the regulations. Once the program and the outside agency have entered an agreement of this kind, the program may freely communicate information from patient records to the "qualified service organization," but only that information needed by the organization in order to provide services to the program.

Finally, a communication is not a "disclosure" if it contains no "patient-identifying information" (§2.11(p) (3)). "Patient-identifying information" includes an individual's name, address, and any other information from which a patient's identity can be determined, either directly or by reference to other public information.

It is the rare communication that will contain no "patient-identifying information" but still prove useful. Reports of aggregate data about a program's treatment population provide one significant example. Despite the fact the data are drawn from patient records, they may be reported so long as they cannot be used to identify particular individual patients. Similarly, one may report an individual case history, provided the reader cannot piece together the subject's identity from the reported facts and other information.

Less clear is whether program personnel may identify an individual in a communication to outside parties, as long as they do not disclose the individual's status as a patient or reveal their own connection with drug abuse treatment (which would disclose that status implicitly). The more prudent course in this context is to assume that any communication, anonymous or otherwise, of such specific information as an individual's name constitutes a "disclosure" and is permissible only under one of the conditions described below under "Disclosures with Patient Consent" and "Disclosures without Patient Consent." The "anonymous communication" question arises in an important, controversial way with respect to reporting patient crimes, which is specifically discussed under "Disclosing Criminal Activity by Patients."

REPRISE: THE GENERAL RULE

It is now time to return to the general rule. Except for intraprogram communications, communications with qualified service organizations, and communications that contain no patient-identifying information, patient records simply may not be disclosed. Well, of course, not so simply. The regulations do provide for certain types of disclosures with patient consent and, far more rarely, without consent. To avoid getting lost in the exceptions, however, one does well to keep the general rule uppermost in mind and to operate on the following principle: do not disclose anything about a patient, at least without being able to state why the regulations permit the particular disclosure.

EXCEPTIONS TO THE GENERAL PROHIBITION: A RULE OF THUMB

The regulations set out a host of conditions permitting limited disclosures of records upon patient consent and a very few conditions in which disclosures may—or, even more rarely, must—be made whether or not the patient consents. Each condition permitting disclosure has its own peculiar requirements and limitations, all of practical significance. The welter of detail can pose a significant obstacle to one who, contemplating whether a particular inquiry into patient records is permissible, must locate and understand the regulations' answer.

However, four simple questions will carry one a long way toward overcoming this hurdle. To determine whether a particular request for information about a patient falls within an exception to the general prohibition on disclosure, one should ask the following: (a) Is the proposed communication related to a medical emergency? (b) Is the proposed communication for purposes of research or part of an audit or an examination of a program's compliance with government standards? (c) Is the proposed communication the subject of a court order? (d) Does the proposed communication concern a crime or a threatened crime on the premises of a program or against program personnel?

If the answer to all the above questions is no, then the proposed communication cannot be made without patient consent. Even with consent, there may be further preconditions to disclosure. Moreover, the regulations specify the form the consent must take. These additional requirements are discussed under "Disclosures with Patient Consent." Nevertheless, a negative answer to the above questions unequivocally indicates that patient consent is a necessary prerequisite to disclosure.

If the answer to one of the above questions is yes, the situation may permit or even require disclosure whether or not the patient consents. These situations pose relatively complicated questions under the regulations, less subject to generalized answers. "Disclosures without Patient Consent" discusses the

regulations' approach toward these issues in more detail. One practical initial step toward minimizing confidentiality problems, however, is to inform program personnel that, in any of these situations, only the program director or some designated individual versed in the confidentiality regulations may authorize disclosures. Even then, certain situations, particularly those involving court orders, may require the advice of counsel.

DISCLOSURES WITH PATIENT CONSENT

As seen above, with very few exceptions the regulations permit disclosures of patient records only upon the consent of the patient. There are two prerequisites to a legal consented disclosure: (a) the patient's consent must meet certain formal requirements; and (b) the disclosure must be for a purpose recognized by the regulations as permissible.

In this latter regard, it is important to understand that the regulations do not set up the patient as the final arbiter of disclosures. Based on an assumption that substance abuse treatment patients will frequently be vulnerable to outside pressures and manipulation, the regulations generally require the program to make an independent judgment that the proposed communication is in the patient's best interests. This independent judgment requirement will be more fully explored below in the discussion of situations in which a consented disclosure is permissible. Before turning to those situations, however, one should become familiar with the formal requirements that apply to virtually all consented disclosures.

FORMAL PREREQUISITES TO CONSENT

Under the regulations, a consent to disclose must be in writing and must contain the following eight items of information: (a) the name of the program making the disclosure; (b) the name of the individual or organization that will receive the disclosure; (c) the name of the patient who is the subject of the disclosure; (d) the purpose or need for the disclosure; (e) the extent or nature of the information to be disclosed; (f) a statement that the patient may revoke the consent at any time; (g) the date or condition upon which the consent expires if not previously revoked; and (h) the signature of the patient, with the date on which the consent is signed (§2.31(a)).

Understanding these requirements is important not only for those administering treatment programs, but also for anyone who would communicate with a program. The latter may wish to facilitate those communications by developing his or her own consent forms. Any form furnished to a program must meet the requirements listed above, however, or the program will be forbidden by the regulations to make the proposed disclosure (§2.31(c)). Moreover, it is a violation of the regulations for anyone knowingly to furnish to a program a consent form that is false with respect to any of these required items of information (§2.31(d)).

The requirements obviously preclude use of any general release of medical records. They contemplate a separate consent form for each type of disclosure and each different recipient. A single form may suffice for a series of disclosures of the same type to the same recipient, such as verifying to a particular funding source the occasions on which treatment was provided during the period of a patient's attendance at the program. But a disclosure of a different nature to the same organization or of the same nature to a different organization would require a new consent.

Statements of the Purpose and the Nature of the Disclosure

Several of the items that must be included in a consent form merit further explanation. Each consent form must contain *both* a statement of the need or purpose for the disclosure *and* a description of the nature or extent of information to be disclosed. A frequently occurring error is to omit one of these statements. Both statements are necessary to ensure that the consent meets the rule that applies to all disclosures under the regulations, with or without consent: one may disclose only the information that is necessary in light of the need or purpose for the disclosure (§2.18). The fact that the patient has consented to a disclosure in the proper form and for a permissible purpose does not permit unrestricted communication. Only that which is necessary to the moment may be disclosed.

Duration and Revocability of Consent

A similar principle governs the duration of consent under the regulations. Each consent must, first, state that it is revocable at the patient's will at any time. Of course, disclosures cannot be taken back, and no one will be penalized for acting upon the basis of a disclosure made prior to revocation.

In addition to the fact that a consent must be revocable, however, the form must state a date, event, or condition on which it will expire if not previously revoked. This requirement stems from the general rule under the regulations that a consent shall be limited in duration to the period necessary to carry out the purpose for the disclosure (§2.31(b)). Thus a consent for disclosures to a funding source to verify drug abuse treatment for purposes of reimbursement might properly be set to last throughout the patient's treatment at the program. Consent for disclosure of a methadone maintenance patient's dosage level to a physician treating the patient for an unrelated condition, on the other hand, could not be tied to the length of time the person is in methadone treatment. Rather, it should extend only through the period that the patient receives treatment for the other condition. Once that treatment ceases, further disclosures to the physician concerning the patient's methadone treatment would be unnecessary and violate the regulations.

As with the required statements of the need for disclosure and the nature of the information, the requirement that a consent form state when it expires rests on a simple rule for maintaining confidentiality: disclose only what is necessary and only for so long as it is necessary.

Minor Patients

Obtaining consent from patients who are minors presents a special problem. In most states a minor is a person under 18 years of age. Some states permit a minor to seek substance abuse treatment without consent or notification of parent or guardian; others do not. This distinction plays a significant role in the confidentiality regulations.

If a program is in a state that permits minors to seek treatment without parental consent, then the program need obtain only the minor's consent in making disclosures (§2.15(c)). Obtaining parental consent to a disclosure in these circumstances is not only unnecessary but would itself constitute an unauthorized disclosure. Indeed, a program in such a state may not directly or indirectly request payment for the minor's treatment from his parents or guardian without the patient's consent. On the other hand, in states that require parental consent for drug abuse treatment of minors, consent of both the minor patient and parent or guardian must be obtained prior to disclosures from the patient's records (§2.15(b)).

The regulations attempt to smooth one additional wrinkle presented by minors. As seen above, applicants for treatment are considered "patients" whose records are protected by the confidentiality regulations. What then to do with a minor applicant who does not want his or her parents notified in a state where parental consent is required for admission to treatment? The regulations' answer is that the program cannot notify the applicant's parents without the minor's approval. Of course the program should explain to the applicant that it cannot provide treatment without contacting his or her parents, but the choice is left to the minor. If the individual refuses, the program cannot notify his or her parents of the application for treatment without violating the regulations (§2.15(d)).

The only exception to this rule is the case of an applicant who in the program director's judgment is so young or suffers from a mental or physical condition to such an extreme that the child cannot make a rational decision about notifying his or her parents. In those circumstances, if the applicant's situation poses a serious threat to his or her physical well-being or to that of other persons, a threat the program director feels would be reduced by communicating with the child's parents or guardian, the program may do so (§2.15(e)).

Incompetent and Deceased Patients

Incompetent and deceased patients require brief mention. In the case of a patient who has been adjudicated incompetent to manage his or her affairs, consent to disclosures of drug abuse treatment records may be made by the individual's guardian or other person authorized by the state to act in his or her behalf.

Similarly, consent to the disclosure of records of deceased patients may be made by the personal representative of the deceased's estate. If no personal representative was appointed, the patient's spouse or, if none, any responsible family member may give the required consent. Even without consent, a program may make disclosures required by federal and state laws involving the collection of vital statistics.[11]

Written Prohibition of Redisclosure

Once the consent form has been properly completed, there remains one formal prerequisite to a valid disclosure. The regulations require that any disclosure pursuant to written patient consent be accompanied by a written statement that the information disclosed is protected by federal law and that the recipient cannot make any further disclosure of it unless permitted by the regulations (§2.32(a)). This statement, not the consent form itself, should be delivered and explained to the recipient at the time of disclosure or earlier. The regulations themselves provide a model statement for this purpose.[12] A program need not make this statement to a recipient of information whose records are independently subject to the confidentiality regulations, such as another substance abuse treatment program.

Routinizing Compliance with the Formal Requirement

The formal requirements for a valid consent may seem onerous or complicated at first blush. For the most part, however, they

---

[11] As mentioned at the outset, the federal regulations supersede state laws that are less protective of confidentiality. The regulations specifically state that vital statistics information required under state law may be disclosed without consent. Absent that specific reference, the regulations would have superseded state vital statistics reporting laws. Consequently, the fact that vital statistics laws may be followed has no bearing on other state law reporting requirements, such as crime reporting, that are not acknowledged by the regulations. "Disclosing Criminal Activity by Patients."

[12] The written statement must read substantially as follows (§2.32(a)):

This information has been disclosed to you from records whose confidentiality is protected by Federal law. Federal regulations (42 CFR Part 2) prohibit you from making any further disclosure of it without the specific written consent of the person to whom it pertains, or as otherwise permitted by such regulations. A general authorization for the release of medical or other information is NOT sufficient for this purpose.

are easily met. One important step is the development of forms that eliminate the need to recall the formal requirements. Standard forms should be developed for disclosures that must be made for the same purpose to the same recipient for many patients, such as disclosures to funding sources or central registries. For less frequently recurring situations, programs should use a form with appropriately labeled blanks ("purpose or need for disclosure," "nature or extent of information to be disclosed") that will guide the individual filling out the forms toward meeting the various requirements. The use of such forms, accompanied by a meaningful explanation of their terms to the patient, will not only satisfy the regulations, but also, more importantly, lay the groundwork for a truly understanding consent.

SITUATIONS IN WHICH CONSENTED DISCLOSURE IS PERMISSIBLE

The regulations define seven situations in which a program may disclose patient records upon obtaining consent in a form that meets the requirements discussed immediately above. A catch-all provision governs any other situation that might arise.

As a general proposition, a program or person may keep in line with the regulations on consented disclosures by adhering to this rule: disclose only what is necessary, for only as long as necessary, in light of the purpose of the communication, and do so only upon making an independent judgment that disclosure is in the patient's best interests.

Each situation specified by the regulations, however, has its own peculiarities—some, for example, permit disclosures of only a particular scope or duration. To ensure full compliance with the regulations, a program has no alternative but to familiarize itself with the requirements surrounding each situation and to develop consent forms and procedures that will accommodate them.

The situations permitting consented disclosures break down into two types. The first consists of disclosures that may be prerequisites to treatment. These include disclosures to funding sources and third-party payers, central registry disclosures to prevent multiple enrollment, and, in cases of referral to treatment from the criminal justice system, disclosures to the referring or supervisory

agency. In these situations, providing treatment may be contingent upon making or promising the disclosures and, correspondingly, upon obtaining the individual's consent. Assuming the individual wants and needs treatment, an independent judgment of the appropriateness of the disclosure would be irrelevent, and the regulations do not require one. Although consent in these circumstances inevitably contains an element of involuntariness, the requirements of the regulations serve to assure that the "consent" is an informed one.

The second set of situations is not inherently connected to eligibility for substance abuse treatment. These include the following: disclosures necessary to procure diagnosis, treatment, or rehabilitation services not provided by the program itself; disclosures to a patient's family; disclosures to employers and employment agencies; disclosures to a patient's lawyer; and disclosures for all situations not otherwise provided for under the regulations. In these situations, the proposed disclosure will not generally be indispensable to a patient's admission to or continuation in treatment. Correspondingly, these are the situations in which, with one exception, the regulations require a program to make an independent determination whether disclosure would serve the patient's best interests.

Organizing the situations permitting consented disclosure into these two groups may help one remember the specific situations and understand the regulations' approach to them. Full compliance, however, requires a more detailed examination of each situation.

Third-party Payers and Funding Sources

Upon consent, the regulations permit disclosures of patient records to third-party payers and funding sources (§2.37).[13] Given the variety of contractual and funding arrangements, the regulations could not lay down specific limits on the scope of such disclosures. Rather, they set the general rule that disclosures must be limited to the informa-

---

[13] Under the regulations, a third-party payer is an organization that pays for diagnostic or treatment services on the basis of a contractual or other individual relationship between the payer and the patient (§2.11(s)). A funding source, on the other hand, is a public or private entity that makes payments directly in support of a program (§2.11(t)).

tion that is "reasonably necessary" for the payer or funding source to meet its legal obligations.

This restriction on the scope of disclosure, although couched in general terms,[14] does have practical significance. Disclosures to third-party payers and funding sources generally serve to document that the patient is someone whose treatment is reimbursable (i.e., that the patient meets the eligibility criteria set by a funding source, such as Medicaid, or that he or she is covered by an insurer for the treatment services in question).[15] These eligibility determinations can generally be made without disclosure of clinical records. Restricting disclosure to "reasonably necessary" information, therefore, requires omitting such clinical information.

The provision on third-party payers and funding sources has several other noteworthy consequences. First, a payer or funding source that maintains records identifying individuals as recipients of treatment or rehabilitation services for substance abuse becomes subject to the confidentiality regulations itself. In other words, once the state agency administering Medicaid, for example, receives patient-identifying information on individuals in drug abuse treatment, its records of those individuals become subject to the regulations and can only be redisclosed under the conditions explained throughout this chapter. The same would be true for third-party payers.

The patient who refuses to consent poses a particular problem. If reporting eligibility data is a prerequisite to the treatment program's receiving reimbursement or funding for its services, a refusal to consent to disclo-

sure sets up a conflict that can only be resolved by denying treatment.[16]

The problem becomes more difficult when a refusal to consent to this type of disclosure occurs after treatment has commenced. Here the patient's refusal means the program or hospital cannot disclose patient-identifying information to the payer or funding source to obtain payment for the services already provided.

The regulations offer no easy route to collecting payment of the patient's bill. The program or hospital may enter a qualified service organization agreement with a collection agency. (See the discussion of the definition of and restrictions on qualified service organizations under "Prohibited Disclosures," above.) The collection agency, however, may only communicate with the patient; as a qualified service organization it could not disclose patient-identifying information to third parties, as a lawsuit to collect payment would require.[17] If communications be-

---

[14] Even without the limitation in the provision on third-part payers and funding sources to "reasonably necessary" disclosures (§2.37), that restriction would have been implicit under the general rule limiting disclosures to the information necessary in light of the purpose for the communication (§2.18). See "Formal Prerequisites to Consent."

[15] Access to patient records to verify that reimbursed services have actually been provided is treated by the regulations as access for audit purposes. Although theoretically a consent could cover payer or funding source disclosures of this nature, audits in fact proceed under a special provision allowing access for these purposes without patient consent. This provision and the conditions and safeguards accompanying it are discussed under "Disclosures for Audit or Evaluation Purposes."

---

[16] In the case of a funding source such as Medicare, patient-identifying information may not be necessary to ascertain eligibility for reimbursement. A program could inform the funding source that an individual with a particular income, etc., had applied for treatment. HEW's Office of General Counsel has advised that the program could assign a number to each such communication (other than the number that may be used by the program to identify a patient for more general purposes) that would permit the funding source to make reference to particular cases that might pose eligibility problems. Because neither the eligibility information nor this number would allow the funding source to identify an individual as a patient, the Office of General Counsel concluded that such communications would not constitute disclosures and could be made without consent. See reference 3 and "Prohibited Disclosures" above, discussing the definition of "disclosure."

This approach has problems. First, it will only work if such anonymous disclosures are acceptable to the funding source. Second, it is unclear why the assigned number is not a "patient-identifying number," which under the definition of disclosure cannot be disclosed without consent. Proceeding by way of consent eliminates any uncertainties about the opinion from the Office of General Counsel and, by its straightforwardness, accords the individual patient greater respect.

[17] Communications to patients of their own records are generally treated as disclosures that can only be made in accordance with the regulations, e.g., when the patient consents and disclosure would serve his or her best interests. See "Situations Not Otherwise Provided for; Patient Access to Records" below. HEW's Office of General Counsel, however, has determined that a collection agency's communication to a patient of information he or she already knows (that he or she received certain

tween the collection agency and the patient fail to produce payment, the hospital's only alternative would be to seek a court order authorizing further disclosures that might bring about payment, for example, the disclosures necessary to pursue collection by a lawsuit. (See "Court-ordered Disclosures.")

Central Registry Disclosures

Central registries that collect patient data from narcotic maintenance treatment or detoxification treatment programs to enable the programs to prevent multiple patient enrollment present a second situation in which consent to disclosure may be required at the outset of treatment (§2.34).[18]

The confidentiality regulations restrict the scope of permissible communications between a central registry and its member programs. In the first place, the registry must enter into a qualified service organization agreement with its member programs, delineating the scope of anticipated communications, agreeing that the registry itself will abide by the regulations, and promising to protect the information received from the member programs against unauthorized inquiry. (See discussion of qualified service organizations under "Prohibited Disclosures.")

Upon entry into such an agreement, a member program may make the following types of disclosures to a central registry. When an individual applies to a member program for treatment, the program, with consent, may contact the registry and ask whether the individual is currently enrolled in another maintenance or detoxification program.[19] When the patient is accepted for treatment, when the program changes the type of drug or dosage that the patient re-

ceives, or when treatment is interrupted, resumed, or terminated, the program, again assuming consent has been obtained, may communicate those facts to the registry.

Disclosures by the registry to its member programs are even more limited. If an applicant for treatment is currently enrolled in another program, the registry may inform the inquiring program of the name, address, and phone number of the program where the applicant is enrolled. Alternatively, the registry may contact the latter program and inform it of the particular patient and the program to which he or she has applied. The two programs involved should then communicate with one another to verify the multiple enrollment and to resolve the situation in accordance with sound clinical practice.

The procedures detailed above warrant two comments. First, the limited disclosures to prevent multiple enrollment are the only disclosures of patient-identifying information that a central registry may make. Central registries cannot make other disclosures, even under circumstances that would allow a program to disclose patient records, e.g., for research purposes (5). (Disclosures by a program for research purposes are discussed under "Situations in Which Consented Disclosure Is Permissible.") Absent a qualified service organization agreement to provide some other services, a registry may communicate patient data only to programs, and only as described above.

Second, although the disclosures by programs to a registry require written patient consent, that consent must be obtained before accepting a patient for treatment.[20] Moreover, the consent form must list all programs and registries to which this type of disclosure will be made, and it must state that the patient's consent covers all programs subsequently established within 200 miles and any registry serving them. Finally, patient consent to central registry disclosures remains effective as long as the patient is enrolled at the program obtaining the consent, and the consent form should state as much.

Criminal Justice System Referrals

Perhaps the most complicated rules surrounding disclosures with consent concern

---

treatment services) is not a disclosure subject to the regulations (9).

[18] The provision of the regulations that describes the conditions permitting central registry disclosures applies only to registries serving narcotic maintenance and detoxification treatment programs (§2.38). HEW has advised, however, that disclosures to central registries serving other types of programs, e.g., alcoholism treatment, would be permissible with patient consent if they would serve the patient's best interests. See reference 7 and discussion of "Situations Not Otherwise Provided for; Patient Access to Records" below.

[19] A program may make a similar inquiry to any other program within 200 miles that is not a member of a registry in common with the inquiring program.

[20] There is an exception for detoxification treatment.

patients referred to treatment from the criminal justice system (§2.39). This chapter will only touch upon these rules, which have been thoroughly discussed elsewhere (10).

These special disclosure rules apply to individuals referred to substance abuse treatment as a condition of release from confinement, the disposition of criminal proceedings, or the execution or suspension of a criminal sentence. The rules are unusual in three respects: they permit unrestricted communication about the patient; they do not permit the patient to revoke his or her consent; and they explicitly set the duration of this type of consent.

Under the regulations, a patient may consent to unrestricted communication about himself or herself between the program and the agency or individual in the criminal justice system that is responsible for the referral or for supervising the individual, e.g., the court granting pretrial conditional release or a probation or parole officer. The program and the criminal justice system agency may agree to restrict the type of disclosures that will be made, but the regulations permit a broader communication that in practice may be required by the agencies of the criminal justice system. The recipients of criminal justice system disclosures, it should be noted, may use the information only in connection with the subject patient and the criminal proceedings from which he or she was referred.

An individual whose release from confinement or whose probation or parole is conditioned upon treatment may not revoke his or her consent to disclosures to the referral or supervisory agency. This is the only situation in which the regulations permit a program to require an irrevocable consent. Only upon termination of the patient's release, probation, or parole may he or she revoke the consent.

Finally, the regulations specify the duration of criminal justice system referral consents. Such a consent expires 60 days after it is given or whenever there is a substantial change of the individual's status within the criminal justice system, *whichever is later*. The regulations define "substantial change in status" in detail. Basically, the change occurs when an individual moves from one stage of the criminal justice process to another. For example, an individual who, upon arrest, had been referred to treatment and consented to disclosures of this type would undergo a substantial change in status when the arrest resulted in either formal criminal charges or unconditional release. If more than 60 days had passed since that individual signed his or her consent, the consent would expire with the change in status. If not, the consent would remain effective until the end of the 60-day period.

Disclosures for Diagnosis, Treatment, and Rehabilitation

In the remaining situations in which the regulations permit consented disclosures of patient data, the relationship between the disclosure and the patient's admission to or retention in treatment is less direct than in those discussed above, if it exists at all. In these situations, the patient wishes the program to communicate about him or her to some outside agency. The communication may serve the patient's treatment or rehabilitation, or it may be completely unrelated to them.

Presuming the vulnerability of drug abuse treatment patients to outside coercion and manipulation, the regulations do not require, or even permit, a program to defer unquestioningly to a patient's wishes regarding disclosures. In each of the situations described below, save one, the regulations require some independent program judgment that the communication will serve the patient's interests. Compliance with the regulations in these situations, then, requires the following elements: a written consent in the appropriate form; a program determination that disclosure is in the patient's best interests; and a disclosure limited in content and duration to what is necessary in light of its purpose. Even then, disclosure is discretionary with the program. Here as in most places, the regulations set only the minimum requirements of confidentiality. If a program's clinical judgment in these circumstances leads it to impose stricter requirements, it is free to do so. Against this background, the individual situations contemplated by the regulations require but brief comment.

With patient consent, a program may disclose information to someone from whom the patient is seeking diagnostic, treatment, or rehabilitation services (§2.33). The recipients of the information need not be medical personnel; the regulation covers nonmedical counseling and rehabilitation services as well. To make a consented disclosure of this type, the program need only ascertain that the information will aid the recipient in providing its services to the patient.

In a related vein, the regulations permit special disclosures for patients on medication who become separated from their programs by travel, incarceration, or hospitalization. In those circumstances, or if for some other reason such a patient is unable to deliver a written consent, the program may communicate the patient's status and the information necessary to provide him or her with appropriate medication. The program may make such a disclosure only to medical personnel who can provide the needed medical services and only upon their oral representation that the patient has requested medication and consented to the disclosure. The program making the disclosure must record it in a written memorandum. It bears repeating that this disclosure based on oral consent applies only to patients on medication who are unable for some reason to deliver a written consent.

Disclosures to Patient's Family and Others

Upon appropriate written consent, a program may provide an evaluation of a patient's current or past treatment to anyone with whom the patient has a personal relationship (§2.36). The relationship need not be one of blood or marriage. However, consent notwithstanding, the regulations prohibit any communication that, in the judgment of the person responsible for the individual's treatment, would be harmful to the patient.

Disclosure to Employers and Employment Agencies

The regulations permit limited disclosures of patient information to employers and employment agencies that meet certain criteria (§2.38). Prior to such a disclosure, the program director—or someone appointed by the director to manage confidentiality problems—must have reason to believe that the employer or agency will not use the information to deny the patient employment because of his or her drug abuse history. In other words, a program may disclose patient information only to an employer that—by past performance, written assurance, or other means—has demonstrated that it will use the information as part of a good faith, nondiscriminatory evaluation of the patient's fitness for a particular job. In addition, the program must determine that the proposed disclosure is reasonably necessary in light of the type of job in question.

The regulations limit employment disclosures to a verification of treatment status or a general progress evaluation. The program may disclose more detail only if the information is directly related to the particular employment situation involved.

Restricting disclosures to employers and agencies who will not discriminate does not mean a program can never release adverse information, even with potentially adverse consequences. For example, a program might provide periodic progress reports to an employer. Those reports could contain negative information, so long as the program knows the employer will use that data to assist in the patient's rehabilitation. Although this is a matter for the program's clinical judgment, the regulations would permit disclosure of a negative evaluation to an employer it knew would attempt to help the patient with his or her drug abuse problem and would consider disciplinary steps only when an individual's drug abuse reduced job performance to an unacceptable level. Of course, all these disclosures require patient consent that, under the formal rules discussed above, remains revocable throughout its duration. (See "Formal Prerequisites to Consent.")

Disclosure to Patient's Legal Counsel

The regulations make special provision for disclosures to a patient's attorney (§2.35). First, the program need not make any independent judgment whether disclosures to a patient's attorney are in the patient's best interests. Once the program determines that the attorney actually represents the patient, it may, upon consent, turn over the patient's records. Although a program retains discretion to limit its response, it should recognize that the purpose of this provision is to ensure that, assuming consent, the attorney receives all information he or she needs to advise the patient (§2.35-1).

Second, the usual rule restricting disclosures to necessary information does not apply; a program may disclose any information in the patient's records to his or her attorney.

(Recall the broad definition of "records" discussed under "Patient Records; Secondary Diagnosis of Drug Abuse," above.) The attorney, however, may not redisclose any information received from the program's records by this means, even if the client consents.

Finally, there is some uncertainty about the formal requirements for consent in this context. On one reading, the regulations do not require consent forms for disclosures to attorneys to contain the eight items discussed under "Formal Prerequisites to Consent," above. The patient's written request for disclosure, endorsed by the attorney, seems sufficient. The regulations are very vague in this regard, however. To avoid this uncertainty, a program may quite properly use a consent form that contains the eight items required for all other purposes and obtain the attorney's endorsement on that form.

Situations Not Otherwise Provided for; Patient Access to Records

Of course the regulations could not anticipate the myriad situations in which communication of patient data might be beneficial to the patient. To provide for such contingencies, the regulations permit disclosures with proper written consent in situations other than those discussed above, provided two conditions exist (§2.40). First, the patient's consent must be voluntary. Second, the program director or his or her authorized representative must determine that the disclosure will not harm the patient, the patient's relationship with the program, or the program's capacity to provide services in general.

Disclosures to patients of their own records must meet these criteria. This chapter cannot explore the various state laws governing patient access to medical records. However, the federal confidentiality regulations do supersede state law. Under those regulations, a patient who wishes to see his or her records may do so only if the disclosure will not harm the patient or the program's capacity to provide services, under the criteria stated above.

DISCLOSURES WITHOUT PATIENT CONSENT

Unlike the situations discussed above, the relatively few circumstances in which the regulations permit disclosures regardless of patient consent do not easily submit to generalization or routinized administration. For the most part, these situations call for a thorough understanding of the regulations, the exercise of discretion, and the assumption of substantial responsibility. Accordingly, authority to make disclosures without consent should be confined to the program director or delegated to a single individual well versed in the regulations. Other personnel should be aware of the circumstances that may call for such disclosures; their response should be to bring such circumstances to the director's attention. (To identify situations that may call for disclosures without consent, see "Exceptions to the General Prohibition: A Rule of Thumb.")

This chapter will conclude with an introduction to the rules surrounding disclosures without consent, broken into the following categories: medical emergencies; research, program audits and examinations; court orders; and crime reporting. The multitude and variety of issues that may arise under these categories defy anticipation. All that can be done is to acquaint the reader with the approach the regulations take in each category and to point out the situations in which counsel should be sought. The rest depends upon the judgment of directors of substance abuse treatment programs and, importantly, upon the cooperation of the researchers, auditors, government authorities, and law enforcement agencies that seek information from them.

MEDICAL EMERGENCIES

The regulations permit disclosures to public or private medical personnel to the extent necessary to meet a bona fide medical emergency (§2.51). The contemplated disclosures include drug abuse treatment information, e.g., type of medication and dosage, that others may need to determine the proper treatment of an emergency medical condition. They also include disclosures to the Food and Drug Administration (FDA) when the FDA determines that an error in packaging or manufacturing a drug that is used in substance abuse treatment may endanger the health of patients.

The regulations do not permit a broad definition of "medical emergency" to open a loophole for disclosures. The situation must be one requiring immediate medical attention. For example, drug treatment programs may not report a positive venereal disease test to public health authorities as a medical emergency (6). Such a report requires patient consent; without consent, a program wishing to make such a report would have to seek a court order. (See "Court-ordered Disclosures," below.)

The regulations permit one additional type of medical emergency disclosure. In the case of an individual suffering from a serious medical condition as a result of drug or alcohol abuse, the treating physician may disclose the patient's condition to anyone with whom the patient has a personal relationship. The physician may give such a notification without consent only when the patient is incapable of rational communication.

DISCLOSURES FOR RESEARCH PURPOSES

A topic of importance throughout the substance abuse treatment field is the accessibility of patient data for research purposes. The confidentiality regulations permit a program to disclose patient-identifying information to researchers without patient consent, providing certain safeguards are met (§2.52).[21]

A program may only release data to researchers who are qualified, both in terms of the ability to carry out the nature of the research in question and the administrative capacity to conduct research without making unauthorized disclosures of patient data. Most importantly, the regulations restrict the conduct of the researchers who receive such disclosures. They are strictly forbidden from redisclosing any patient-identifying information. Research reports may not identify a patient, directly or indirectly. No patient-identifying information obtained by a researcher may be used in any legal, administrative, or other action involving the subject patient. Indeed, the regulations prohibit a researcher from redisclosing such information even in response to a federal or state court order, and they provide that those

courts have no power to compel disclosures from the records of those who have received patient data for research purposes (§§2.56, 2.62).[22]

The regulations provide only two exceptions to the prohibition on redisclosure by researchers. First, the researcher may communicate with the program that provided the data. Additionally, in a medical emergency that cannot be resolved by communication with that program, the custodian of records for research purposes may make disclosures under the conditions described under "Medical Emergencies," above.

It bears emphasizing that the research provisions discussed thus far only *permit* unconsented disclosures to qualified researchers; they do not compel them. Absent special conditions described below, a treatment program's participation in such a venture is voluntary, and it may condition its participation on the creation of further safeguards it may find desirable.

Whenever research is conducted by or on behalf of a federal or state agency, the regulations authorize that agency to set the minimum qualifications of the personnel involved. The program whose records are sought may not second guess those qualifications (§2.53). Without more, however, participation in such research remains voluntary with the program. No state or any of its branches, by contract or otherwise, may require a program to provide access to patient data for research purposes unless the following conditions are met: the recipient of the information must be legally prohibited from disclosing any patient-identifying information and from using such information as the basis of any administrative or other action involving the patient; and the chief legal officer of the state must furnish the program an opinion that verifies the existence of these legal prohibitions and that describes the security measures that will be used to protect the data.[23]

Follow-up evaluations of former patients present a particular problem under the con-

---

[21]The confidentiality regulations are concerned only with the release of patient data. Although they do not require patient consent for disclosures for research purposes, the regulations do not diminish the force of other laws that may require the informed consent of research subjects. When informed consent is required in human experimentation is beyond the scope of this chapter. See HEW Protection of Human Subjects Regulations 45 C.F.R. Part 46. The confidentiality regulations neither add to nor subtract from any such requirements.

[22] The courts' resort, if any, is to the program in custody of the original records. See "Court-ordered Disclosures," below.

[23] No federal agency may require a program to provide access to data for research purposes unless these conditions are met, except that the Attorney General's opinion need not verify the legal prohibition on disclosures by recipients (§2.53(e)).

fidentiality regulations. A program—or a researcher to whom it has disclosed patient data—may only attempt to contact a patient if it can do so without disclosing the patient's relationship with the treatment program to third persons. Accidental disclosure to a third person would not constitute disclosure to a qualified researcher; unless authorized by a provision of the regulations discussed elsewhere in this chapter, it would be illegal. Accordingly, no inquiries—whether to relatives, friends, law enforcement agencies, or anyone else—designed to locate a former patient for evaluation purposes may be conducted unless they can be carried out in a way that will not reveal, even indirectly, the individual's prior status as a substance abuse treatment patient.[24]

DISCLOSURES FOR AUDIT OR EVALUATION PURPOSES

The regulations treat disclosures of patient data for purposes of management audits, financial audits, or program evaluation in much the same manner as research disclosures. A program may make such disclosures, without patient consent, to qualified personnel; recipients may not disclose any patient-identifying information in an audit report or otherwise, and any information the program discloses may not be used in any action involving the patient (§2.53).[25]

As in dealing with researchers, a program ordinarily must decide itself whether auditors are qualified, both in terms of conducting the audit or evaluation and in terms of safeguarding confidentiality. A state or federal agency, however, may determine the qualifications of personnel conducting audits or evaluations on its behalf; the program subject to such an examination must accept this determination.

However, the regulations do not give the agency free reign in selecting its examiners and auditors. It must restrict them to tasks for which they are qualified. Individuals who lack the training or responsibility to evaluate quality of treatment must confine their activities to administrative and financial records as far as possible (§2.53(b)). The corollary of this requirement is that programs must organize their records so that the data needed for administrative or financial reviews may be disclosed without revealing clinical information.

These conditions determine when a program *may* disclose patient data for audit or evaluation purposes and set the minimum requirements an individual or agency must meet to conduct such an audit or evaluation. A program may be *required* to disclose patient data for these purposes only if additional safeguards are met.

A program may be required to make this type of disclosure as part of what the regulations broadly define as an "examination" (§2.54). An examination includes any scrutiny of program records to determine the accuracy or adequacy of any of these records, the quality or performance of program management, or program adherence to administrative, financial, medical, legal or other standards. In short, almost anything that might be labeled an audit or evaluation falls under the regulations' definition of "examination."

To require a program to disclose patient data, an examiner—public or private, individual or organization—must meet several conditions. First, of course, the examiner may not disclose any patient-identifying information to anyone, voluntarily or in response to a court order (§2.56).[26] Second, the examiner must notify the program of the location and custodian of all records of patient-identifying information that are retained, and it

---

[24] In addition to the confidentiality obligations of researchers who receive information under the regulations discussed in the paragraphs above, the Attorney General and Secretary of Health, Education, and Welfare have the power to authorize persons engaged in research involving controlled substances, alcohol, or psychoactive drugs to withhold the identities of their research subjects. Researchers with this authorization may not be compelled to divulge their subjects' identities in any proceeding whatsoever (Controlled Substances Act of 1970, §502(c), 21 U.S.C. §872(C); Public Health Service Act of 1970, §303(a), 42 U.S.C. §242(a)). Where granted, these authorizations largely overlap with the confidentiality regulations. The important point for present purposes is that, whether or not a researcher has one of these authorizations, he or she must comply with the prohibition on redisclosure discussed above if he or she has been granted access to records of patients in federally assisted or regulated substance abuse treatment.

[25] See "Disclosures for Research Purposes," above. As in the case of a researcher, a recipient of information for audit or evaluation purposes may communicate with the program providing the information and may make limited disclosures outside the program where necessary to respond to a medical emergency.

---

[26] This requirement applies to all recipients of patient data for research, audit, or evaluation purposes, even if the information was volunteered to them by the program.

must disclose the purpose of retaining such records (§2.54(c)). Third, the examiner may retain such records only as long as they are needed or for 2 years, whichever comes first. If during that time a formal legal proceeding has been commenced against the *program*—it must be repeated that no records disclosed to an examiner may be used in any type of proceeding against a patient—the records may be retained until the termination of the proceeding (§2.54(e)).

At the end of the permissible time period, the examiner must destroy all records, including copies, of patient-identifying information that it has possessed or return them to the program (§2.54(d)). Upon disposing of the records, the examiner must give the program a written statement either claiming compliance with all the requirements described above or detailing any noncompliance with those requirements (§2.54(f)).[27]

The regulations set out special examination rules for programs that dispense narcotic drugs as part of maintenance or detoxification treatment (§2.55).[28] These rules require such a program to permit the Drug Enforcement Administration and parallel state drug law enforcement agencies access to its premises to determine whether the program meets legal requirements on the security of its stock of narcotic drugs as well as record-keeping requirements on such drugs. The regulations strictly limit the use of information obtained in this manner and prohibit any use against individual patients. Similarly, the regulations require narcotic maintenance and detoxification programs to permit access by the Food

and Drug Administration and comparable state health agencies to determine compliance with treatment standards. These agencies, too, must operate under strict confidentiality safeguards and cannot use information obtained in this manner against a patient.

COURT-ORDERED DISCLOSURES

A program confronted with a subpoena or court order directing it to produce patient records or testimony about patient records cannot respond safely without the advice of legal counsel. More than any other situation contemplated by the confidentiality regulations, those involving subpoenas and court orders require counsel. The regulations limit the grounds upon which a court may authorize or order a program to make disclosures, and they set out strict guidelines on the scope of such disclosures. However, courts on occasion have issued orders that go beyond the limits set by the regulations. Although such court orders may be erroneous, the consequences of disobeying them may be severe, possibly including imprisonment for contempt. In view of these consequences and the variety and complexity of situations and proceedings in which some type of judicially compelled disclosure may arise, resort to counsel is imperative.

Subject to this caveat on the advice of counsel, the regulations' approach to court orders may be briefly sketched. Under the regulations, a court may authorize a program to make disclosures of patient data that would otherwise be prohibited (§2.61). A court may issue one of these authorizing orders, however, only after it follows certain procedures and makes particular determinations specified by the regulations (§§2.63–2.66).

Accordingly, a subpoena directed to a program's patient records or a court order issued without adherence to the prerequisites set by the regulations does not validly authorize a program to make disclosure.[29] A program served with a subpoena alone or with a defective court order should—if possible—appear in court to explain that the prerequisites

---

[27] There are two additional situations, similar to an examination, in which a governmental unit may require a program to provide access to patient records. First, access may be required for a long term evaluation study. The government unit requiring access, however, must meet the same standards set by the regulations for mandatory disclosures for research purposes (§2.53(c)). (See footnote 23 and accompanying text.) Second, when a government agency funds treatment, it may insist on access to such data as are necessary to determine that individual patients and the treatment they receive meet funding eligibility criteria. Although the funding source may condition reimbursement on access to such data, a program may only disclose patient-identifying data to a funding source with the patient's consent. (See "Third-party Payers and Funding Sources," above.)

[28] Section 2.55 of the regulations, discussed in the accompanying text, applies to all persons registered to dispense narcotic drugs under §303(g) of the Controlled Substances Act, 21 U.S.C. §823(g), and all applicants for such registration.

[29] A subpoena is not a court order, but a mechanism by which litigants invoke the power of a court to compel an individual to testify or to produce documents. Failure to respond to a subpoena—whether by complying with its terms or by appearing in court to object to it (moving to "quash" the subpoena)—may constitute contempt.

set by the regulations must be met before the program may be authorized to make the disclosure in question. Again, distinguishing subpoenas and court orders and determining the adequacy of court orders call for the advice of counsel.

What are the prerequisites to a court order authorizing disclosure? In general, the program and any patient whose records are sought must be given notice of an application for the order and some opportunity to make an oral or written statement to the court. The application and any court order must use fictitious names for any known patient, and all court proceedings in connection with the application must be confidential unless the patient requests otherwise (§2.64).

Before authorizing a particular disclosure, a court must find that there is "good cause" for it. The court must find that the public interest and the need for disclosure outweigh any adverse effect that the disclosure will have on the patient, the doctor-patient relationship, and the effectiveness of the program's treatment services with the patient and in general. If the information sought is available elsewhere, the court ordinarily should deny the application (§2.64).[30]

Finally, there are general limits on the scope of disclosure that a court may authorize, even when good cause is present. Disclosure must be limited to the information essential to fulfill the purpose of the order; it must be restricted to those persons who need the information for that purpose (§2.64). A court may only authorize disclosure of *objective* information, such as dates of attendance and urinalysis results. The regulations do not permit any court order to authorize disclosure of communications by a patient to program personnel (§2.63).[31]

An investigative, law enforcement, or prosecutorial agency seeking an order to authorize disclosures for purposes of investigating or prosecuting a patient for a crime must meet additional prerequisites (§2.65). Before issuing such an order, a court must find that several criteria are met. First, the crime involved must be extremely serious, such as an act causing or threatening to cause death or serious injury, or it must have occurred on program premises or against program personnel. Second, the records sought must be likely to contain information of significance to the investigation or prosecution. Third, there must be no other practical way to obtain the information. Fourth, the public interest in disclosure must outweigh any actual or potential harm to the doctor-patient relationship in the program involved and in similar programs, as well as to those programs' ability to attract patients. Orders authorizing disclosure for purposes of investigating or prosecuting patients are subject to the same limitations of scope and nature that apply to court-ordered disclosures generally. According to the regulations, a court may under no circumstances authorize a program to turn over patient records in general to a law envorcement, investigative, or prosecutorial agency.[32]

It bears repeating that the court orders contemplated by the regulations simply authorize a program to make a disclosure that would otherwise be prohibited. The regulations themselves do not give a court authority to compel disclosure. If, however, a court issues an order compelling disclosure under another source of judicial power *and* issues an order authorizing disclosure under the regulations, or if an order authorizing disclosure is accompanied by a valid subpoena, the program is legally bound to make the disclosure that has been authorized. The variety of forms that these orders and processes may take reinforces the need for counsel in this area.

A final word about a positive use programs may make of court orders. On rare occasions

---

[30] Note, however, that the regulations do not permit courts to order disclosure of patient records held by researchers, auditors, or evaluators who have received them from a program under the provisions discussed under "Disclosures for Research Purposes" and "Disclosures for Audit or Evaluation Purposes," above (§2.62). Court orders under the regulations are to be directed to the programs that have custody of the original records.

[31] The only exception to the prohibition on court orders authorizing disclosure of patient communications arises during litigation when a patient introduces evidence about such a communication (§2.63).

[32] The regulations also contain special provisions regarding court orders authorizing disclosures for purposes of investigating or prosecuting a program or its employees and court orders authorizing a government agency to place an undercover agent or informant in a program to gather evidence of serious criminal conduct by the program or its employees (§2.66–2.67). The regulations set strict prerequisites for obtaining such orders and prohibit the use of information obtained through these means against patients.

a program may feel constrained to disclose information over a patient's objection or to make a disclosure that will in some sense be against a patient's interests. Evidence of child abuse by a patient may in some circumstances provide an example.

A program faced with such a situation may decide that it wishes to make a disclosure, for example, to a child welfare agency. Following the procedures discussed above, the program could place the problem before a court and allow it to resolve the competing claims of program, patient, and public.

DISCLOSING CRIMINAL ACTIVITY BY PATIENTS

A patient reveals to a counselor that he or she plans to commit a serious crime. A patient assaults a program nurse. A police officer arrives at the program door with an arrest warrant for a patient. In all these situations, the confidentiality regulations restrict the communications the program or its personnel may make to a law enforcement agency or a court. All these situations raise serious questions of treatment philosophy, community relations, and ethics as well. All tend to arouse strong emotions that may cloud decision making.

This chapter cannot solve those deeper questions or paint a bright line toward correct decisions. It can, however, describe the regulatory context in which these questions must be resolved and the limits on decision making imposed by those regulations. Concluding the chapter with the issue of disclosures of patient criminal activity will also serve as a reprise to all the previous discussion. The issue requires an understanding of the general prohibition on disclosures and the limits of disclosure with patient consent, and it introduces a final type of disclosure without consent.

Consider a hypothetical patient who reveals an intent to commit a robbery. May the patient's counselor, consistent with the confidentiality regulations, seek the assistance of the police if there seems no other way to prevent the crime?[33]

As an initial proposition, of course, the general prohibition on disclosure would prevent any communication of a patient's records, including his or her identity, to an outside party. (See "The General Rule against Disclosure: Its Breadth and Terms," above.) Would disclosure become permissible if the patient consented or, a more practical possibility, if the patient's consent to such disclosures had been required prior to admission to treatment?

Not otherwise provided for by the regulations, a consented disclosure in this situation would only be permissible if the program determined that the disclosure would not be harmful to the patient or to the program's capacity to provide service (§2.40). (See "Situations Not Otherwise Provided for; Patient Access to Records," above.) Because reporting a crime or the threat of a crime could lead to the apprehension and prosecution of the patient, the program will be unable to make the former determination and, quite possibly, the latter. Consent does not provide a basis for disclosure in these circumstances.[34]

Is there any basis, then, for disclosing patient criminal activity without consent? The answer is a qualified "yes." If the patient has committed or threatened a crime on program premises or against program personnel, the

---

[33] To repeat, this chapter is solely intended to explain what types of disclosures the regulations permit and what types they forbid. Deciding whether to make a permissible disclosure of patient criminal activity raises separate ethical, political, and clinical questions beyond

the scope of this chapter. The hypothetical question discussed in the text above is simply whether the proposed communication *may* be made, not whether it *should* be made.

[34] In a slightly different situation, consent might be effective. Consider an adolescent who runs away from a residential treatment program. In many states running away renders minors liable to prosecution and incarceration for a status offense. Given that possibility, a treatment program ordinarily could not report to the police that a child had run away, even if consent to such disclosures had been obtained. However, if the program were to receive assurances that the police would take no action against the child other than to return him or her to the program, it might be in a position to determine that reporting to the police would not harm the child. If the individual's consent to such disclosures had been properly obtained, such a report would in these circumstances be permissible.

Consent can also provide the basis for disclosing patient criminal activity in the case of a patient referred from the criminal justice system who has properly consented to unrestricted communication between the program and probation or parole office or other authority responsible for the individual's supervision (§2.39). (See "Criminal Justice System Referrals," above). Information disclosed under these circumstances can only be used in connection with the criminal proceedings that formed the basis for the referral or in related proceedings.

regulations permit program personnel to report the crime to a law enforcement agency or to seek its assistance (§2.13(d)). The report may identify the suspect but may not disclose that he or she is a substance abuse treatment patient. The fact that an individual's patient status may be obvious from the context or source of the report does not seem to preclude reporting a crime on premises or against program personnel, as long as patient status is not directly disclosed. Thus a program employee may report that he or she was the victim of a robbery and identify a suspect, and a program may call the police to control a patient holding another patient at knife point on program premises. Program personnel may not, however, reveal patient status or provide details beyond those necessary to report the crime or secure the program's premises unless authorized to make such disclosures by a court order.[35]

If the crime or threatened crime is not on program premises or against program personnel, the special provision does not apply. Is there any basis for disclosure in these circumstances?

Recall that the regulations' definition of "disclosure" excludes communications that contain no patient-identifying information (§2.11(p) (3)). (See "Prohibited Disclosures," above.) Patient-identifying information includes a name, address, or similar information from which the identity of a patient can be determined (§2.11(j)). From these definitions, it follows that a very limited type of communication may be made concerning patient crimes that are not committed against program personnel or on program premises. Consistent with these definitions, a program may report a patient crime or the threat of one, so long as it neither identifies the individual suspect nor the source of the report (disclosing the source, that is, the program, would lead directly to the conclusion that the suspect is a patient in substance abuse treat-

ment).[36] This very limited type of communication may be of little practical value. Any greater disclosure of patient crime off premises and not against program personnel, however, requires a court order.

Related to disclosures of patient criminal activity are the problems that arise when law enforcement officers seek access to program premises to search for someone suspected of a crime or for evidence of a crime. The most important measures to be taken in this area are preventive. Programs should establish relationships with local law enforcement officials, discuss the confidentiality regulations and their underlying rationale, and try to achieve an understanding of the limits on permissible disclosures that will keep law enforcement inquiries within proper bounds when the heat of pursuit or investigation rises.

Granting physical access to a program constitutes a disclosure of patient records if the visitor will see either patients or any records identifying them. Permitting law enforcement officers to enter program premises in such circumstances is, in the first analysis, forbidden by the regulations. If the officers are in search of a particular patient who committed or threatened a crime on the premises or against program personnel, the program may produce the individual without identifying him or her as a patient, minimizing disclosure of other patients as far as possible. Otherwise, however, the program may not permit officers access absent a court order authorizing such a disclosure.

Neither an arrest warrant nor a search warrant constitutes the type of court order that authorizes a program to permit law enforcement officers into its premises with resultant disclosure of patient data. Rather, the order must be one that meets the requirements described earlier in the chapter.[37]

A program confronted by a law enforcement officer with an arrest or search warrant

---

[35] The procedures and conditions under which a law enforcement agency or the program itself may obtain a court order authorizing disclosures of patient data for purposes of investigating or prosecuting a patient are set out at §2.65 and discussed under "Court-ordered Disclosures."

[36] Along these lines, the National Institute on Drug Abuse has advised that a program concerned about child abuse by a patient could make arrangements with a

social service agency for care of the child, if this could be done without identifying the program or the parent (1). The advice of HEW Office of General Counsel on crime reporting is consistent with this approach and the text above (4).

[37] See §2.65 and "Court-ordered Disclosures," above, discussing the procedures and standards for entry of a court order authorizing disclosures for purposes of investigating or prosecuting patients.

should take the following steps. Produce a copy of the regulations and explain that under them the program cannot grant him or her physical access without an appropriate court order. Seek time to notify counsel and let counsel attempt to resolve the situation with the officer or a superior. Finally, if the officer insists on entry, do not forcibly resist. Refusing to obey the orders of a law enforcement officer may constitute a crime, even though the officer's orders are later shown to be erroneous or illegal. By contrast, no one should be held liable under the regulations for obeying an officer's order to allow entry although a prohibited disclosure ensues. Anyone contemplating resistance should seek the advice of counsel as to the consequences.

If law enforcement officers are in "hot pursuit" of someone who is a patient and is present at the program facility, the program may have discretion under the regulations to grant the officers access to the suspect. In such circumstances, the individual's flight may itself constitute a crime, committed on the program premises by the individual's very presence. Under the regulations, the program could seek police assistance concerning this on-premises crime (2). Caution is warranted in invoking this interpretation; if possible, counsel should be consulted to determine whether the patient's presence constitutes a crime in the particular circumstances.

CONCLUSION

At first blush, the federal confidentiality regulations may seem to be an indecipherable maze of legalese that diverts program resources from treatment to paperwork and that blocks people from communicating with programs on frequently important matters. A basic understanding of the regulations, however, is not difficult to achieve. With it, compliance may be routinized with little drain on resources. But compliance is not an end in itself. Rather, it is hoped, compliance will further the more important ends the regulations are designed to serve—encouraging those in need to seek alcohol and drug abuse treatment while protecting their privacy, consistent with the needs of the greater community.

References

1. Besteman, K. (Deputy Director, NIDA). Letter to Edward Brown (prepared in consultation with HEW Office of General Counsel). April 27, 1976.
2. Dormer, R. (Legal Assistant, HEW Public Health Service). Letter to Robert Gardner. May 10, 1976.
3. Edelman, S. (HEW Assistant General Counsel for Public Health). Memorandum to Borge Varmer. August 16, 1976.
4. Edelman, S. (HEW Assistant General Counsel for Public Health). Letter to Arthur L. Burnett. June 15, 1977.
5. Greene, S. N. (HEW Office of General Counsel, Public Health Division). Letter to Jeremiah Gutman. January 21, 1976.
6. Greene, S. N. (HEW Office of General Counsel, Public Health Division). Letter to Victoria Young. July 18, 1977.
7. Lanman, R. (HEW Office of General Counsel, Public Health Division). Letter to William E. Ford. September 16, 1976.
8. Lanman, R. (HEW Office of General Counsel, Public Health Division). Letter to Martin Keeley. October 21, 1976.
9. Lanman, R. (HEW Office of General Counsel, Public Health Division). Letter to Richard M. Clark. June 7, 1977.
10. Weissman, and Berns, Patient confidentiality and the criminal justice system: A critical examination of the new federal confidentiality regulations. Contemp. Drug Prob. 5:531, 1976.

CHAPTER 55

POLYDRUG ABUSE: A REVIEW OF TREATMENT APPROACHES

David E. Smith, M.D., Ph.D.

Donald R. Wesson, M.D.

The term *polydrug abuse* was popularized by a federally implemented polydrug research and demonstration project developed in 1973 to study the nature and extent of nonopiate abuse. In 1973, the National Institute on Alcoholism and Alcohol Abuse was funding treatment for alcohol-related problems, and the federal focus on drug abuse treatment was for the study and treatment of heroin. Thus, "polydrug abuse" became the abuse of drugs other than alcohol or heroin. According to this definition, abuse of a single drug, such as a barbiturate, would be classified as polydrug abuse (8).

With the exception of the Polydrug Project efforts, polydrug abuse is commonly defined as simultaneous or sequential use of more than one psychoactive drug for nonmedical purposes (7). Some authors include alcohol; others do not. Multiple drug abuse and mixed addictions are used more or less synonymously with polydrug abuse. This use of "polydrug" parallels the concept of "polypharmacy" used in medical therapeutics. In this chapter, polydrug abuse applies to the simultaneous use of different psychoactive drugs including alcohol.

Polydrug abusers may present for treatment in a bewildering array of medical complications, psychiatric syndromes, and drug-induced reactions (or interactions). Although there is a vast literature that emphasizes differential features that distinguish psychiatric syndromes from toxic reactions produced by psychedelic drugs, sympathomimetics, or drug withdrawal states, Sapira and Cherubin (5) presented a review that raises considerable question as to the extent to which this is possible on initial assessment.

The polydrug-using population is very diverse in terms of age, socioeconomic status, and reason for using drugs. Polydrug abusers whose primary motives for consuming drugs are social-recreational must be treated differently from individuals who are abusing drugs in an effort to self-medicate pain, anxiety, or other psychic discomfort. Youthful drug users who are using drugs in a social-recreational manner find store-front clinics acceptable as places to obtain treatment, whereas many individuals prefer treatment in a more traditional or psychiatric setting (9).

TREATMENT CONCEPTS

Drug abuse treatment is frequently conceptualized in terms of a specific treatment modality based upon the drug of abuse; for example, methadone maintenance used for the treatment of heroin dependency. Although drug-specific treatment has some clinical utility in the sense that it specifies the type of drug problem suitable for treatment (e.g., methadone maintenance may be an appropriate treatment for heroin dependency, but not for barbiturate dependency), such drug-specific treatment concepts have little utility in working with polydrug abuse.

Because of the heterogeneity of the polydrug-using population and the wide range of treatment settings, we prefer to conceptualize treatment of the polydrug abuser as a series of strategic interventions that can be adapted to various individuals and settings using rational guidelines. The timing of interventions is critical, and a treatment intervention that may be highly effective at one time in an individual's efforts to move away from the destructive use of drugs may be contraindicated at another time.

Crisis intervention plays an important role in the delivery of drug abuse treatment services. The crisis situation is frequently the drug abuser's entry into treatment, and the skill with which crisis services are provided is often pivotal regarding the individual's decision to remain in treatment after the crisis is resolved.

The goals of crisis intervention are 2-fold: to resolve the presenting complaint and to foster entry into more definitive therapy.

Staffing patterns of drug abuse treatment facilities frequently place their more junior members or even trainees in the crisis intervention role. Diagnostic assessment and appropriate intervention in the crisis situation require the utmost skill and should generally be done by the most knowledgeable, experienced members of the treatment team.

Individual psychotherapy—the process of meeting with the patient on a one-to-one basis for the purpose of discussing problems, offering advice, examining relationships, and trying to understand the reasons for an individual's behavior—is likely to be called psychotherapy when done by a psychologist, or clinical social worker and counseling when done by others. Individual psychotherapy alone is not a highly regarded treatment modality in the drug abuse field.

In the early stages of treatment, psychotherapy concerns itself primarily with issues of (a) maintaining the individual in treatment, (b) orienting the individual toward long term psychotherapeutic work, and (c) helping the individual cope with stresses of withdrawal and the disruption of what may be a long established pattern of self-prescribing. This phase of work may frequently occur during the period of detoxification and typically requires an active stance on the part of the psychotherapist. Rarely are classical psychoanalytic techniques helpful and, precisely to the extent that they are effective in mobilizing affect, may be counterproductive. A preferred psychotherapeutic stance in most instances in early treatment is strong orientation toward problem solving, support, and analysis of resistances that tend to undermine the treatment process. During detoxification, individual psychotherapy can be supportive of the detoxification process by allowing the patient a framework for discussing the emotions that emerge as the patient's drug use is reduced. In addition, regular psychotherapeutic sessions serve to establish rapport and trust and assist in keeping the individual in treatment. After the psychotherapist-client relationship becomes established, the relationship can be a powerful influence over the patient's behavior. Psychotherapy sessions are used for identification and assessment of new problem areas and definitions of goals and offer the opportunity to assess the need and impact of other treatment interventions. Psychotherapy during the early phases of treatment probably exerts much of its therapeutic effect by identification with the therapist and through modeling of the therapist's problem-solving skills.

For patients whose drug use was motivated in an attempt to self-medicate neurotic conflict or affective disturbance or to defend against emergence of psychotic process, long term individual psychotherapy may be indicated. Psychotherapy at this phase can be more psychodynamically or "insight oriented" and nondirective. The transition to this phase of psychotherapy is frequently problematic. The psychotherapeutic style helpful during the earlier phases of treatment may become a liability, and the psychotherapist may have difficulty making the transition. At times, it may be appropriate to use the initial psychotherapeutic relationship to assist the individual into a long term psychotherapeutic relationship with a different therapist. With drug abusers, a psychotherapist-medical manager split is frequently helpful in preventing psychotherapy from becoming focused on medication schedules, dosages, side effects, etc.

If the patient is in such a role with his psychotherapist that he has to convince the psychotherapist of the need for certain medications, he may become obsessively involved with manipulations and the psychotherapist runs the risk of becoming effectively incapacitated as a psychotherapist. This is a compelling reason to split the psychotherapist-prescriber role, a maneuver of general usefulness in dealing with the addictions.

Group therapy is used to refer to a wide range of activities that take place during treatment of the drug abusers. Like individual psychotherapy, group therapy cannot be considered a unitary modality because of the diversity of therapist styles and orientation. Group activities can be confrontive, supportive, analytical, growth oriented, or task or educationally oriented. Groups conducted by Alcoholics Anonymous or Narcotics Anonymous are structured and conducted very differently from traditional psychotherapy groups. Although all types of group activities have a place in comprehensive treatment intervention programs, patients should be carefully selected for each group, and attention to the timing of introduction is important. Initially, groups should be supportive and educationally or task oriented. Confrontive or self-help groups are generally more helpful later, especially with the recreational drug abuser. Psychotic individuals may further decompensate during group confrontation and prove frustrating to self-help groups when they interject inappropriate or tangential remarks. Traditional psychoanalytic psychotherapy led by an experienced professional is suitable for individuals who have the capacity for introspection and the ability to form empathetic relationships. Individuals who are psychotic are best treated in a supportive group setting or individual psychotherapy, and individuals who are not psychotic but who have personality disorders are best treated in a confrontive group setting, preferably as part of a residential drug treatment program.

PHARMACOTHERAPY INTERVENTIONS

The judicious use of psychotropic medication can be an effective intervention at any stage of treatment (e.g., naloxone (Narcan) to reverse the effects of opiate overdose; phenobarbital for sedative-hypnotic detoxification). Pharmacotherapy can be considered under four nonmutually exclusive categories whose therapeutic rationales are sufficiently diverse such that each is discussed separately.

Detoxification is the process of safely withdrawing the individual from his or her drug of abuse. Techniques are described in detail in other chapters and will not be discussed further here.

Drug maintenance involves the use of *prescribed* amounts of the drug of abuse or a drug with similar properties. In the treatment of heroin dependence, for example, methadone develops in the individual tolerance to the narcotic effects that are cross-tolerant with heroin. Because this tolerance blocks the effects of heroin, the individual's incentive for using heroin is greatly reduced. No comparable tolerance-producing agents exist to block the effects of sedative-hypnotics or stimulant drugs. Because of a tendency for polydrug users to escalate dosages as tolerance develops, maintenance on the drug of abuse is generally not feasible, although there are cases in which the carefully controlled *prescription* of the drug of abuse can be used advantageously.

Treatment of the individual with drugs that block the desired effects of the drug of abuse is called *antagonist therapy*. Cyclazocine (2) and naltrexone (3) have been used experimentally to block narcotic effects, and a variant of antagonist therapy is the use of disulfiram (Antabuse) in the treatment of alcoholism. Ingestion of alcohol after ingesting disulfiram results in nausea, vomiting, and other unpleasant, and sometimes dangerous, signs and symptoms. No true antagonist exists for the effects of sedative-hypnotics.

In *psychotropic drug therapy*, the goal is

treatment of underlying psychopathology that may be contributing to the individual's drug-abusing behavior. Generally, this is best initiated after detoxification. Many patients experience transient disturbances in mood and sleep, increased anxiety, and decreased pain threshold during the withdrawal period, which should be handled nonpharmacologically if possible. Assessment of the feasibility of psychopharmacological treatment should take into consideration the patient's past response and experience with medications, the patient's attitude toward medications, and the patient's reliability in taking medications as prescribed. Unfortunately, psychopharmacological treatment of many drug abusers— even when clear-cut indications exist—is not feasible because of their intermittent use of illicitly obtained drugs. Although the use of certain psychotropic medications may be clearly indicated from a psychological diagnostic perspective, the hazards of such therapy may contraindicate its use. Sometimes, with careful administration of the drug at a halfway house, the drug abuse treatment staff can circumvent the problem of inconsistent or unreliable drug usage, although concurrent abuse of illicitly obtained drugs may still expose the individual to the risk of adverse drug interactions. The following are some of our observations on the use of psychotropic medications in the treatment of drug abusers.

Tricyclic antidepressants, for relief of depression and such associated symptoms as insomnia, are frequently useful. Pharmacotherapy with tricyclics may be of value in treating the rebound depression amphetamine abusers experience after detoxification. Progress is enhanced by a balanced approach using a tricyclic antidepressant for relief of depression while involving the client in such other forms of treatment as psychotherapy and residential treatment. Woody et al. (10) have reported the combined use of doxepin (Sinequan) with methadone maintenance clients and observed decreased depression and improved participation in rehabilitation. Amitriptyline hydrochloride (Elavil) and imipramine hydrochloride (Tofranil), 100 to 200 mg at bedtime for a period of 3 to 6 months, with careful monitoring of any side effects, may be effective. Although tricyclics are not generally considered to be drugs of abuse, self-administration of amitriptyline has achieved some popularity among methadone maintenance clients in New York and is now on the black market.

Clients with suicidal depression should be prescribed tricyclics in no more than a 7-day quantity because tricyclics, if used in an overdose, may result in seizures, cardiac arrhythmias, or death.

Lithium carbonate has been particularly effective as a treatment modality for individuals with affective disorders, including manic-depressive illness, unipolar mania, and some unipolar endogenous depression. Insomnia associated with underlying mood disorders resolves as the mood disturbance is brought under control. To benefit from lithium therapy, the individual must be reliable in taking the daily dosage; lithium blood levels must be monitored and are titrated to levels of 0.5 to 1.0 meq/L by careful adjustment of the daily dosage. Clients with suicidal depression should be given the medication in no more than weekly quantities because of its high toxicity when taken in overdose quantities. As with the use of tricyclic antidepressants, lithium is most effective when used in conjunction with psychotherapy and, if needed, residential placement.

ANTIPSYCHOTICS

The phenothiazines, chlorpromazine (Thorazine), trifluoperazine hydrochloride (Stelazine), fluphenazine hydrochloride (Prolixin), and haloperidol (Haldol), as well as other antipsychotics, are sometimes effective in treating thought disorders that are either precipitated by drug use or masked by heavy drug abuse. Antipsychotics should generally not be used in the crisis intervention phase because of the possibility of idiosyncratic reactions and additive effects with the drugs the client may have taken. Phenothiazines should not be used where sedative-hypnotic withdrawal is suspected to be the precipitant of psychosis, as they lower the seizure threshold. If preexisting psychopathology of a psychotic variety must be managed in individuals withdrawing from sedative-hypnotics, haloperidol can be used for management of psychosis, and the sedative-hypnotic withdrawal should proceed at half the usual rate. Finally, antipsychotic medication is rarely necessary in the treatment of amphetamine-induced psychosis, as the thought disorder clears quickly upon cessation of amphetamine use, and the premature usage may obscure the diagnosis of psychiatric disturbances not related to amphetamine usage. For psychotic-like symptoms that emerge with the ingestion of hallucinogenic substances, excessive doses of amphetamine, or phencyclidine, the best therapy is nonpharmacological, supportive, custodial care and removal of the individual from an overstimulating environment.

For clients who manifest thought disorders in the postdetoxification period, antipsychotic medication is generally effective in both eliminating the psychotic symptoms and in alleviating the anxiety the client was attempting to medicate. Again, drug maintenance on phenothiazines is effective only insofar as it is supported by other treatment modalities. If residential placement is required, the policy and attitude of the program toward antipsychotic medication should be explored, as many drug abuse treatment residential programs will not allow psychoactive drug use of any kind. Similarly, it is important that therapy be provided by a professional who supports the use of the medication. Finally, it is often helpful to have the drug administered on a daily basis during periods of crisis for clients who have difficulty taking the medication as directed.

BIOFEEDBACK

Biofeedback has received much attention as a therapeutic modality for anxiety, and the medical literature abounds with reports attesting to the utility of biofeedback for treatment of anxiety and stress-related symptoms. Most studies, however, are not controlled. The newness of the procedure and the impressive equipment may serve to mobilize hope and may exert prominent placebo effects (6). Positive results have been substantiated with tension headaches (1).

With biofeedback, physiological functions such as electrical activity of muscles, hand temperature, or brain waves are electronically measured and electrically processed to convert the measured signal to an auditory or visual signal that can be perceived by the patient. The most widely known form of biofeedback is the electroencephalogram (EEG) in which the frequency and amplitude of brain waves are processed electronically to detect frequencies in the range of 8 to 13 Hz,

commonly known as alpha waves. Electromyography (EMG) converts muscle electrical activity to a tone that is proportional to the amount of muscle electrical activity. The individual attempts to reduce muscle activity by altering the tone. With temperature biofeedback, the individual's temperature (usually measured by a thermistor on the fingers) is made proportional to a tone. As anxiety and unpleasant emotions activate the limbic system of the brain, with consequent vascular constriction, teaching the individual to warm his hands is a method of teaching control of anxiety. In addition, temperature biofeedback is used for treatment of migraine headaches. Galvanic skin resistance, heart rate, and gastrointestinal motility also have been utilized for biofeedback and may be useful in symptomatic treatment of some patients with anxiety. Temperature and EMG biofeedback seem to hold the most promise for symptomatic treatment of anxiety.

To achieve maximum therapeutic benefit, biofeedback sessions should be given daily for 30 to 50 minutes each. The patient may acquire physiological control with a few sessions, however additional practice and the use of other feedback modalities can be helpful. Patients should be encouraged during biofeedback sessions to express their feelings about the various sensations that they experience while learning control. Patients with chronic anxiety may initially equate anxiety with alertness and have no experiential concept of being alert and relaxed.

Although biofeedback alone is insufficient therapy for many patients, the modality may have some utility in the therapy of most patients with anxiety. As symptoms are brought under control, the individual has less need for sedatives. Biofeedback training also has nonspecific effects as well as placebo effects (4). The knowledge that the individual is able to acquire control over his or her physiological processes is frequently of importance in increasing the individual's self-esteem and feelings of mastery over his environment. The goal of biofeedback is the acquisition of physiological control, and its utilization has been successful when the patient acquires control. Psychotherapy and biofeedback are frequently complementary. Biofeedback serves to build self-esteem, a feeling of mastery, and the acquisition of nondrug control of feeling states. Psychotherapy, on the other hand, can serve to modify human interactions—a change that cannot be acquired through biofeedback.

CONCLUSIONS

Comprehensive treatment of the polydrug abuser generally requires the strategic use of a variety of treatment modalities and techniques. The use of a particular modality is most effective when consideration is given to the needs of a particular client and to the appropriate timing of a given intervention. We have presented a range of possible treatment interventive techniques that need to be adapted to the client's needs. Perhaps the biggest obstacle to successful treatment is our own need to produce a "quick cure" and thereby allow ourselves to be seduced into the short term gratification model shared by all drug abusers.

References

1. Blanchard, E. B., and Young, L. D. Clinical applications of biofeedback training. Arch. Gen. Psychiatry 30:573, 1974.
2. Freedman, A., Fink, M., Sharoff, R., and Zaks, A. Cyclazocine and methadone in narcotic addiction. J.A.M.A. 202:191, 1967.
3. Martin, W. R., Jasinski, D. R., and Mansky, P. A. Naltrexone, an antagonist for the treatment of heroin dependence. Arch. Gen. Psychiatry 28:784, 1973.
4. Miller, N., and Dworkin, B. Critical issues in therapeutic applications of biofeedback. In *Biofeedback: Theory and Research*, G. Schwartz and J. Beatty, editors. New York, Academic Press, 1977.
5. Sapira, J. D., and Cherubin, C. E. *Drug Abuse: A Guide for the Clinician.* Amsterdam, Excerpta Medica, 1975.
6. Shapiro, A. K. Placebo effects in medicine, psychotherapy, and psychoanalysis. In *Handbook of Psychotherapy and Behavioral Change: Empirical Analysis*, A. E. Bergin and S. L. Garfield, editors. New York, John Wiley & Sons, 1971.
7. Tinklenberg, J. R., and Berger, P. A. Treatment of abusers of nonaddictive drugs. In *Psychopharmacology: From Theory to Practice*, J. D. Barchas, P. A. Berger, R. Ciarenello, and G. R. Elliott, editors. New York, Oxford University Press, 1977.
8. Wesson, D. R., Carlin, A. S., Adams, K. M., and Beschner, G. *Polydrug Abuse: Results of a National Collaborative Study.* New York, Academic Press, 1978.
9. Wesson, D. R., Smith, D. S., and Lerner, S. E. Streetwise and nonstreetwise polydrug typology: Myth or reality. J. Psychedelic Drugs 7:121, 1975.
10. Woody, G., O'Brien, C., and Rickels, K. Depression and anxiety in heroin addicts: A placebo-controlled study of doxepin in combination with methadone. Am. J. Psychiatry 132:447, 1975.

PART **8**

TARGET GROUPS

CHAPTER 56

THE PROBLEM OF ADDICTION IN THE BLACK COMMUNITY

Beny J. Primm, M.D.

Daniel R. Cook

Joseph Drew, Ph.D.

But to come very near to a true theory, and to grasp its precise application, are two very different things, as the history of science teaches us. Everything of importance has been said before by somebody who did not discover it.

Alfred North Whitehead

The generation of a meaningful interpretation about drug abuse among black Americans is a function of time and the comprehensiveness of data. In the past "factors explaining why drug abuse in black communities has been so common have been cited so often that they have become cliches" (31). The list of such factors would be incomplete if the following, at a minimum, are not included: (a) the history of racism in the United States, and the black Americans' slave history and forced exile from Africa; (b) poverty, unemployment, lack of job and career opportunities; (c) failure of police to rid community of drug pushers, hence easy availability of drugs in black communities; (d) disproportionate attention of law enforcement agencies in making arrests of blacks on drug charges; (e) drug abuse politics and get-tough laws; (f) economics of drugs as alternative careers; (g) hopelessness of ghetto life; (h) life styles that reject menial or subsistence jobs in favor of hustling and the drama of dope dealing; (i) peer pressures; (j) cultural and class conflicts; (k) inadequate educational preparation and the dropout syndrome; (l) rising material, social, and success expectation and aspirations; (m) breakdown of family life and welfare policies that encourage single-parent households; (n) frustration from continuing discrimination and rejection; (o) responsiveness to the dominant culture's media imperative for instant gratification (31).

In addition, it must be noted that many authors have claimed to identify economics, alone, as the key factor in drug abuse among blacks in America. Furthermore, a significant number of the studies that have outlined these "causative" factors among blacks have been based on samples that are unrepresentative of the entire black American community in one or more dimensions. Thus, many of the studies have focused on black prisoners, the poorest of rural or urban black Americans, residents of therapeutic communities, or ex-offenders. This fact has not gone unnoticed by theorists of drug abuse or by their critics.

Our aim in this chapter, however, is decidedly not to deny any of these factors as significant, nor is it to offer a substitute for any one, for a combination, or for all of them another equally one-sided or limited causal theory of black drug abuse in America. Our goal, rather, is to seek a medical intermediary that might be viewed as a resultant of most, if not all, of the forces noted in the literature summarized above and that may offer a physiological translation for cultural phenomena, thus providing the physician with an available point of intervention in the process.

Although the scientific method finds as a starting point clear definitions, we would like to note that a lack of agreement plagues those seeking suitable definitions in this field. This is especially unfortunate in an object of investigation that necessarily impinges upon a wide variety of fields, because as one author noted in the 17th century (30), "in the Solution of Questions, the Maine Matter was the well-stating of them, which requires motherwitt and Logick, for let the question be but well-stated, it will worke almost of itself." Nonetheless, at least three definitions of drug dependence have attained credence in the medical community at the time of this writing and ought to be recognized here. Perhaps the most widely respected definition was written by the late head of the Committee on Problems of Drug Dependency of the National Academy of Science, Maurice Seevers. Seevers began by observing that the term "drug dependence" denotes predictable and reproducible individual drug interactions that can be described precisely in medical, psychological, and pharmacological terms. "Drug abuse, on the other hand, represents a value judgment of society. It may refer to any type of drug or chemical without regard to its

pharmacological actions... The term is used to imply either individual injury or social harm, without regard to the nature of the injury or the organ systems involved... The term 'drug abuse' has only one uniform connotation, the disapproval of society" (43).

Two other important definitions are those developed by A. L. Tatum (46) and by the World Health Organization (49). Definitions are particularly central to our understanding of drug dependence among black Americans, because the question all authors seek to address is, what exacerbates or makes the problem different among this population when compared to other communities? Clearly, the mechanism of physiological dependence should be the same for all persons, no matter what their racial, ethnic, linguistic, national, or other category within the over-all population. Within the framework outlined below, those definitions that encompass the sociological orientation are the most appropriate to the medical care of the black community, whereas those that emphasize physical dependence, psychological predisposition, or behavioral dependence are less so. For the purposes of this chapter, and because our knowledge of drug dependence varies continuously, we propose the following: Drug dependence is the state produced by repeated administration of a drug such that the drug user will engage in substantive and replicable behavior patterns over an extended period of time with such behavior leading specifically to further administrations of the drug (47).

Our readers, in applying the definition we have offered, will note readily that the multiple "causative" factors leading to drug dependence listed at the outset can all be related to the behavior described to some extent. They are all in fact basic to the substantiation of the argument we wish to present here. Few active in this field of medicine today can deny that claims of causation can be advanced with reason for most, if not all, of them. The question, of course, to which we must turn, logically, is as noted above: Have the studies that have heretofore generated statements about these issues been so limited in population sample as to sacrifice claims of universal validity? If we are to understand the underlying causes of drug abuse among black Americans, ought we not, as author Messolonghites suggests (31), study "typical members of the communities?" Indeed, it is to meet this criterion of study that we have chosen to examine a single community of black Americans. In so doing, we will delimit such variables as geography, climate, social history, economic stability, population movements, and so forth that may, in fact, have cast serious doubt on the validity of studies in the past. The community we have chosen is homogeneous. It is situated in a specified, clearly demarcated zone, can be defined without much dispute, and is the home of an overwhelmingly black American population. Further, it is the community of American blacks par excellence, the focal point or capital of both American blacks and much of the world African diaspora. It is the single setting conjured up in the minds of millions, if not billions, of residents of this planet when blacks are mentioned. It is, of course, Harlem, the undisputed and quintessentially black capital of America.

Using this community, one that has been examined before by students of social and medical science and for which a solid bank of data is now available, we will attempt to demonstrate and support a revised analytical approach to drug dependence among black Americans.

Let us first, however, approach the subject by arguing for the exogenous sociological basis for drug dependence; in so doing, we may free the physician of the restraints to medical treatment that might be engendered by a limited understanding of the external forces central to the nature of a "social disease." An examination of the literature indicates that too often professionals, "experts," and administrators, as well as physicians, have overlooked basic theoretical assumptions of the social sciences while undertaking their own analyses of the problem. They have thus failed to point to the most profitable treatment approaches. We believe that central elements of the nature of drug dependence, a social problem par excellence, have been explained already through the explorations of many illustrious thinkers. These scholars have simply been overlooked by "experts" in the field of drug abuse who, operating within a relatively restricted frame of reference, have not referred to this literature.

In his epic work *Suicide*, Emile Durkheim

(8), the preeminent French social scientist and the father of much of contemporary American sociology, argued convincingly that the apparently most intimate and personal of actions, suicide, is not at all personal. Actually, he shows, suicide is essentially social in its nature. Social factors determine the rate of suicide, the types of settings more or less conducive to this condition, and the social basis for individual surrender to a "suicidogenic" impulse. Durkheim further argued, in many of his works but especially in his *The Rules of the Sociological Method* (10), that social facts exist sui generis, without regard to individual psychological states. This perception is central to our understanding of drug addiction, for it raises the understanding of the behavior pattern to a point above and beyond the individual level. Finally, Durkheim argued in his famous essay, "On The Duality of Human Nature" (9), that the personality itself is actually as much a social product as it is an individual one. In this assertion he is not far from the mark set by the master of the role of the individual personality, Sigmund Freud. Freud, in his outstanding and oft-cited work, *Civilization and Its Discontents* (14), wrote, like Durkheim, that both social and individual (or "instinctual") generation undergirds the personality.

Similarly, Franz Fanon, the eminent black Caribbean psychiatrist and philosopher of culture, pointed out in both *The Wretched of the Earth* (11) and *Black Skin, White Masks* (12) that the social dislocations to the personality engendered by European domination of most of the world wrought sometimes irreversible, often deep individual psychiatric adjustments to the colonized. Two black American psychiatrists, Dr. William Grier and Dr. Price Cobbs, in their well received work, *Black Rage* (19), argued similarly, extending the exposition to American minority populations, that blacks in this country have been methodically, if individually, driven to disturbance by the world around them.

Twentieth-century social theorists, including the existentialist movement, the absurdist movement, the labeling sociologists, the social interactionist perspective, and the dramaturgical school, all have presented impressive arguments for the assertion that individual behavior, especially individual behavior that is "deviant" and destructive to the practical life one must lead, is thoroughly grounded in social forces beyond the control of individuals. Indeed, from the great Italian Vilfredo Pareto to the prominent American Talcott Parsons, from Karl Marx to Soren Kierkegaard, from Frederick Nietzsche to George H. Mead, from Jean Piaget to Thomas and Znaniecki, from Park to Malinowski, the list is almost endless: many scholars have agreed that personality and society are inextricably intertwined. In fact, this is a point Western scholars have been making since Aristotle's day (39).

In spite of these schools of thought, much of the medical analyses of drug dependence during this century focused on theories of individual weakness, maintaining, for example, that drug addicts are fundamentally emotionally immature, childlike persons and that the drug addict is a problem of personality structure, a point which must be kept in mind when it comes to his treatment. Others have written in this same vein. "There is a threatened or actual loss of primal love." And, "The damaged ego of the drug addict reacts to this with panic and regresses to the oral stage... The urge for passive object love, i.e., to have a nipple in the mouth, is felt as a physical craving for a "fix"... The process of injecting the drug is equivalent to the introduction of the ambivalently loved mother, and results in the satisfaction of a love aim, where the breast is placed in the mouth and satiation after feeding occurs" (1).

Dollard et al. writing in 1939, proposed that some individuals are easily frustrated and deal with their frustration by becoming aggressive. Heroin dampens or sedates their feelings of both frustration and aggression. "In short, heroin use has provided an escape from their inability to cope with intense feelings of anger" (7).

These strictly psychological theories may be more or less accurate as individual analyses of patients; they overlook the underlying social causative factors, however. Closer to the mark, in our opinion, have been those genuinely social psychological explanations offered by scholars such as Merton, who postulated that society does not always provide a sufficiency of legitimate means for people to realize normatively prescribed goals. Thus, he said, many addicts reject the legitimate means that exist for attaining these goals. They substitute illegitimate goals, as

well. When either the means or the goals are not accepted, conformity no longer exists. A substitution of goals may be termed "retreatism"; a substitution of means, "innovation"; and a rejection of both, either "retreatism" or "rebellion" (29).

Furthermore, a major set of social factors related to drug dependence behavior may be grouped under the rubric "economic." It may be clearly shown, for example, that the statistics of drug dependency vary in correlation to the availability of employment in American history. This argument has been amply set forth in a major work on drug abuse entitled *Drug Use, The Labor Market, and Class Conflict* (22). The authors maintained that "not only is the socioeconomic pattern of narcotics use the same as it was a century ago, but... the problem of widespread addiction is a recurrent and cyclical one (and) we are forced to examine the social constants which have operated in each case or episode in the cycle" (22).

Drug abuse, patently a widespread problem, is grounded in the very nature of our society. In societies that predispose individuals to the drug abuse impulse, the incidence of drug abuse will rise correspondingly as the causative reasons mount. In societies for which such an outlet does not exist, or where drug abuse is not a part of what might be called the social vocabulary, or in places where no exposure to chemical adjustments akin to drug abuse has yet occurred, drug abuse will be minimal or nonexistent. Increasingly, however, the planet is becoming a global village; distant villages are growing interconnected with metropolitan centers. Increasingly, therefore, societies around the world are developing what might be termed a "tolerance" for drug abuse, to borrow a not so surrendipitous word from the study of addiction.

If we assume that history has shown that American society has developed this tolerance and that black Americans have a special predisposition for drug abuse given their historical experience, then we can posit that major drug abuse problems among this population will persist until social earthquakes, either induced or natural, occur. And because it is not ethical or moral backsliding but a complex of social forces that brings a minority group or a nation to drug abuse, so drug abuse is not a condition requiring ministers as principals, just as it calls for neither doctors nor chemists alone. It does require the concerted efforts of all these professionals. They can be most effective by recognizing that drug abuse is primarily a social phenomenon. Thus, the social group of preeminence to individuals in America, the ethnic or "minority" group, assumes the key role in the determination of drug abuse behavior—we believe—its treatment.

Although there are additional theories and further statistics available for numerous communities substantiating these contentions, we wish to turn now to the study of our quintessentially "normal" black community, Harlem, for a closer examination of some of the social indicators related to drug dependency. We are convinced that any fair reading will reveal unequivocally the close relationship between social environment and drug dependence. Therefore, we shall only briefly discuss the relationship found in our case study of Harlem and we will then procede to our principal theoretical formulation.

Geographically, Harlem is typically described as that section of northern Manhattan Island in the City of New York that is bounded on the south by 110th Street, on the north by the Harlem River, on the east by Fifth Avenue, and on the west by the Morningside Avenue-St. Nicholas Avenue continuum. Various agencies of the New York City government today affix a wide range of similar if somewhat varying boundaries to this area, and it is also known as "central Harlem," "uptown," and "Northern Manhattan." The Department of Planning designates an almost identical area to the location we have described above and identifies it as Community Planning District 10 (36). The Health Department of New York City adds census tracts 196, 198, 204, 206, and 210 to the east and calls the area the Central Harlem Health District, and the Health Services Agency adds three blocks to the western sector and labels the area Health Planning District "F." In addition, the Human Resources Administration designates Harlem as "Community District 28." For all practical purposes, however, these agencies are describing the same area geographically. We may summarize Harlem's location by listing its census tracts, according to the United States Bureau of the Census, as follows: 186, 190, 197.02, 200, 201.02, 207.02, 208, 209.02, 212, 213.02, 214, 216, 217.02,

218, 220, 221.02, 222, 224, 226, 227.02, 228, 230, 231.02, 232, 234, 235.02, 236, and 243.02.

Spiritually, Harlem, the center of the famed "Harlem Renaissance" of the 1920's, served for most of the early part of this century as the "Mecca of the 'New Negro' and the center of the Negro Renaissance," as sociologist E. Franklin Frazier (13) wrote. Although black Americans have lived in Harlem for nearly a century in large numbers, it was the mass migration of blacks to the North after the First World War that really brought Harlem its world-wide fame as center of the black universe. It was in Harlem that the famed Marcus Garvey led his movement for a return to Africa; it was in Harlem that black theatre, art and music found their most vibrant expression; and, of course, it was to Harlem that all looked for the political and social leadership of black America.

Surprising events have been shaking Harlem ever since its rise to fame, and not all of them have been noticed by observers outside the district. One of the most important of these changes has been in the area of population statistics. Blacks moved into Harlem in the 1920's in wake of an exodus of roughly 100,000 whites. Although in 1920 blacks comprised but 35.9 per cent of the Harlem population, by 1930 the figure was 81 per cent. And, by 1920 blacks living in Harlem comprised 48 per cent of all blacks living in New York City.

What is surprising is that between 1950 and 1970 Harlem lost more than 70,000 people. The estimated population of Harlem in 1975 was only 141,578. And although black Harlem represents only 7.7 per cent of all blacks living in New York City today, it clearly is the most homogeneous black community in New York, if not the nation, because blacks make up 94.6 per cent of that population.

Who has left Harlem, and why? Studies show that most of those leaving from 1950 to 1970 were in the 25 to 44 age group, the working-earning population with greatest economic potential. Harlem has become skewed in population, with peaks on the graph for youngsters and for the elderly. It is apparent that as housing opportunities arose elsewhere in the post-World War II era, successful blacks moved out. Harlem today is but a way station to better times, not unlike Chinatown or Little Italy; and, like those communities, Harlem may serve as an emotional "capital" for black America, a center of various activities. It is no longer the population center (25); however, let us look at the other social indicators.

Education. Although the median level of education for New York City is 12.19 years, for blacks in Harlem the level is 10.04. Although for the city as a whole 20.7 per cent of the residents are college graduates, for Harlem blacks the rate is 2.8 per cent. Although city-wide, 45 per cent of all students fail to graduate, in Harlem the figure exceeds half of the total student body. Moreover grade levels of the students fall by every year in school; by the sixth grade, students are academically 3 years below their counterparts from elsewhere in the city, and the levels fall continuously after that. Moreover, an untold number of Harlem residents are functional illiterates (33).

Unemployment. The erosion of the manufacturing base of New York City and the addition of numerous migrants from other lands, especially those south of the American border, have wiped out the relatively improving situation that was found at the time of World War II. More than 600,000 manufacturing jobs have been lost to New York over the past few years, with a disproportionate effect upon the blacks of Harlem. Thus, in 1978, with national unemployment at 6 per cent, New York City reported 8.9 per cent. In that year, 12.1 per cent of black male adults in Harlem were unemployed, as were fully 47.8 per cent of Harlem's black teenagers (20, 26).

Income. Although in 1970 the median family income for residents of the island of Manhattan was $8,983, for Harlem the figure was $6,137. At that time only 6.58 per cent of the residents of Harlem had family incomes in excess of $15,000. As of 1970, almost 23 per cent of all Harlem families were below the poverty level. As late as 1971, the Health Systems Agency estimated that there were 48,757 public assistance recipients in Harlem, that the public assistance rate in Harlem was at 30.6 per cent, and that countless thousands of Harlem residents were subsisting just slightly above the official poverty level and thus shut off from income or medical assistance. The allotment for a family of four on public assistance in Harlem equals just 47 per cent of what the federal government says is a minimum subsistence level for a family of four in New York (36).

Housing. In 1932, Nathan wrote about the impact of the poor housing conditions in the health status of residents of Harlem in the years after World War I (32):

> In the six years 1919–1924 the total deaths per 1,000 apartments in Manhattan averaged 44 for those built under the old law and 29 for those built under the new law. The number of tuberculosis cases per 1,000 apartments averaged 10.3 for the old law and 6.5 for the new law.

Not surprisingly, most of the residents of black Harlem still live in substandard housing, with the City of New York perhaps becoming the largest slumlord in the nation, as public housing buildings slide downward. The list of atrocities occurring in these buildings (nonfunctioning furnaces in winter, no garbage collection, etc.) is known widely. Furthermore, although in New York City as a whole 22.9 per cent of all residential housing is owner occupied, in Harlem the figure is but 4.02. There may be some hope for improved housing in some parts of the area, but one can safely predict continued deterioration of Harlem's housing into the beginning of the next century.

For this chapter we have compared the total number of liquor stores, restaurants, and taverns in New York. In Queens and Richmond there exists one such establishment for each 5,000 to 6,000 residents and in Brooklyn and the Bronx for each 4,500 residents, but in Harlem there is one for each 2,870 residents (32).

What are the medical indicators for Harlem? From the beginning of life, Harlem residents suffer. Infant mortality rates in Harlem are exceedingly high (Fig. 56.1). At the present time, 42.8 black babies perish per 1,000 live births, compared to a figure of 13.6 for New York City whites. In his classic study of the impact of unemployment upon infant mortality, Harvey Brenner concluded (3):

> "There is an inverse relationship between national economic changes and infant mortality under 1 year in each of the major age categories.
>
> This relationship occurs at even the smallest interval calculated (i.e. annually): however, the larger the change in the economic indicator, the stronger is the relationship."

The seven leading causes of death in New York City (and Harlem) are (35): (a) cardiovascular and renal disease; (b) malignant neoplasms; (c) cirrhosis of the liver; (d) pneumonia and influenza; (e) diabetes; (f) homicide; (g) accidents. The mortality rates for these diseases in New York City as a whole and in Harlem, their progressions, and trends since 1960 provide a grim picture of the course of health status in Harlem (35) (Table 56.1).

From the figures in Table 56.1 we can see that the major causes of death in New York City are generally declining, whereas in Harlem they are going up and off the scale. Between 1970 and 1975, the New York City age-adjusted death rate fell from 10.49 to 9.51. In Harlem, it rose from 15.74 to 16.05 (34). It will be observed that blacks are five times more likely to be a victim of homicide.

The incidence of tuberculosis in Harlem is 137.6 per 100,000 population; the city rate is 32.8 (21). This high discrepancy, more than four times the city rate, indicates a health constituency whose status is compromised by squalid, unwholesome living conditions.

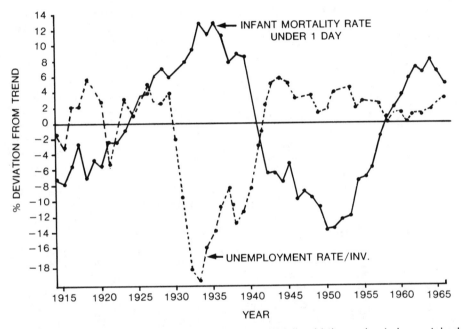

Figure 56.1. Fluctuations in infant mortality rate per 1,000 live births under 1 day matched with those in rate of unemployment index/inverted for the United States, 1915 to 1967. *Top,* data with trend included. *Bottom,* detrended data. Infant mortality rate moved forward 1 year to show relationship at 1-year lag. (Reprinted by permission from Brenner, M. H. Fetal, infant, and maternal mortality during periods of economic instability. Int. J. Health Serv. 3:149, 1973.)

Table 56.1
Leading Causes of Death in New York City and Harlem[a]

Cause of Death	New York City			Harlem		
	1960	1970	1975	1960	1970	1975
Cardiovascular-renal disease	418.4	543.8	485.1	421.9	610.2	630.8
Malignant neoplasms	220.5	207.2	204.8	208.2	232.5	255.0
Cirrhosis		34.1	29.5		117.1	126.3
Pneumonia-influenza	46.2	42.2	36.5	71.2	44.9	44.8
Diabetes	21.7	24.0	22.0	32.2	47.1	44.8
Homicide		13.2	19.9		71.1	92.1
Accidents	34.2	22.7	17.4	49.4	35.6	23.6

[a] Rates per 100,000 population.

The incidence of hepatitis in Harlem is 117.6 per 100,000 population (21); the city rate is 56.9. Much of the hepatitis in Harlem is a reflection of high patterns of narcotic addiction.

The age-specific death rate for adolescents-young adults (15 to 24) in Harlem is an astonishing 403.0, as opposed to 127.8 per 100,000 for New York City (21).

The crude death rate for genital cancer in Harlem is more than two and a half times higher than the city rate (47.15 versus 18.21). The crude death rate for tuberculosis in Harlem, 22.51 per 100,000 population, is five times the city rate of 4.62 (21).

The multiplier factor found in the comparative health indices in Harlem against other areas is not a statistical artifact that can easily be dismissed. These figures indicate thousands of unwarranted deaths and human suffering of intolerable proportions. Within the statistics we can gather more clues; for example: Harlemites have tuberculosis more than four times as often as other city residents, but *die* from it more than *five* times as often (21). Living conditions are poor, health care is poor, and medical care is poor.

MORTALITY OF NARCOTICS ADDICTS

Although narcotic-associated deaths in New York City have remained low since 1972, blacks are disproportionately represented in the mortality rate (55 per cent versus 30 per cent for whites) (35). The most common causes of death in narcotic-related deaths are (42): respiratory depression, pulmonary edema and complications, liver damage, secondary infections, and trauma.

Researchers have engaged in heated controversy as to whether the deaths that had been labeled as "overdoses" were actually acute reactions to the narcotics and their dilutants inasmuch as the doses involved were not at great variance with usual and accustomed doses (5). Baden noted a sharp increase in violent deaths of addicts. Others have noted that this trend continues even for addicts in treatment, particularly those in methadone maintenance treatment programs.

Although Harlem had 2.3 per cent of the city's population in 1970, it had 9.6 per cent of the city's narcotic-related deaths (113 of 1,173) (34). Harlem had the highest mortality

rate for drug dependence of any area in New York City (1970)—51.4 per 100,000 against 8.91 for the city as a whole (34).

A 1972 study of homicide and suicide found that addicts were at high risk for both of these categories (44). The national rate for homicide was 7.2 per 100,000 and for suicide it was 10.9 per 100,000. The comparable figures for addicts were 395 and 122, respectively.

INCIDENCE AND PREVALENCE OF NARCOTIC ADDICTION

In December of 1978 the New York State Division of Substance Abuse Services published a report on drug use trends (37). The report said:

It should be noted, however, that the people found in this household survey are additional heroin users and do not include addicts on the street, in prison, or in hospitals and treatment centers. Our survey did not include institutions or transient quarters where addicts are likely to live....

Despite these limitations the survey found:

1. Black teenagers in New York State were twice as likely to begin using heroin in 1975 than white teenagers.

2. Of 7,000 teenagers who began using heroin in New York State in 1975, 3,000 were black.

3. Incidence of blacks all ages (heroin) was 237 per 100,000 against 142 per 100,000 for entire all age population.

4. Black incidence *increased* with income and increased education in heroin use.

a. Of blacks with household income less than $5,000, incidence of lifetime use is 3 per cent (8,000 persons); more than $30,000, incidence is 14 per cent (3,000 persons).

b. Of blacks with less than high school education, 1 per cent have used heroin; with some high school, 2 per cent; but blacks with some college have prevalence of 5 per cent; black college graduates, 3 per cent.

For the year 1971, the Narcotics Registry reported that there were 17,641 addicts registered from the Central Harlem Health District (2). Based on that district's population, this represents 9.65 per cent of the citizenry. There remains in effect a registry of addicts who have participated in methadone-dispensing programs over the past few years in the city of New York (38). Based on postal zip codes of reported addicts, there are at least 13,000 such addicts in Harlem. Of course, these are addicts who have actually sought treatment. The New York State Division of Substance Abuse Services estimates that only 17 per cent of the state's black narcotic addicts are in treatment (37).

Other social indicators are relevant to this medical analysis of Harlem. Crime, for example, is higher in Harlem than in other areas of the city; indeed, to many outsiders and to some residents, the name Harlem is synonymous with crime.

Notwithstanding some declines, the rate of crime in Harlem remains very high today. The 1970 homicide rate in Harlem was 72.8 per 100,000 population (34) versus 13.2 for the city and 10.9 for the nation. There were 115 homicides in Harlem in 1970 and 118 in 1978, so this has not abated. From 1968 to 1973, the first and second leading causes of death for New York City's 15 to 24 age group were drug dependence and homicide. This is still the case for Harlem (35). (See Table 56.2 for crime statistics.)

It is clear that drug dependency is a response to a variety of "causative" social indicators, and it is equally clear that drug dependency may be viewed as a sociological phenomenon having its origin in forces outside the individual but manifested in the victim ultimately. We have further attempted to present a brief medical and social biography of black America's premier location, Harlem, and to offer readers a short introduction to recent advances in the psychopharmacology of drug dependency.

Let us now introduce a factor that we believe finds its natural position midway between the accepted causative social features noted at the onset of this chapter and drug dependency. To date it has been curiously absent from much of the literature. This mediating element is stress. Stress is the resultant of a multiplicity of exogenous impulses—social, economic, or cultural in nature—but it produces clear physical responses in individuals. For years, physicians have noted the role of stress in the health of patients.

Rahe et al. (40) have demonstrated a link between "stressful life events" and the incidence of illness. George Vaillant (48) has reported on a 40-year study of the relationship between mental health and the development of physical disease. Vaillant's work noted that mental health status was an accurate indicator of subsequent illness. Khantzian et al. (27) found that addicts' failure to develop adaptive solutions to stress is a major contributor to addiction.

Thus it is possible for seemingly innocuous items to become noxious stimuli for people who have experienced patterns of failure and frustration. School buildings, nice cars, pretty couples, fine houses, prosperous businessmen, etc., can send some people into fits of distemper, jealousy, frustration, and depression.

Beset by omnipresent depressing stimuli and persistent self-doubt, some victims of stress are in a state of chronic, psychic pain. Using the Beck Depression Inventory, Inwang et al. (24) have hypothesized that depression of this sort seems to be a primary psychological issue in narcotic addiction. Zimmerman et al. (50) characterized the main element of the Heroin Behavior Syndrome as an underlying depression. Cowan et al. (6) wrote:

> ...psychoactive drugs (e.g. alcohol, opioids) may be used to relieve persistent or episodic feelings of defeat.
> Drugs that counteract feelings of defeat need not do so by producing feelings of success; producing amnesia for defeated feelings may be sufficient.

Zimmerman et al. (50) cited drug use as a learned response to stress. Eric Gnepp (15) perceived drug use as operant conditioning to cultural obstacles and frustrations. From Berlin, Lurssen (28) wrote that drugs are taken not to achieve gratification but to reduce intolerable intrapsychic tension, an escape to nothingness. From Edinburgh, Carstairs (4) reported that American heroin addicts exhibited feelings of worthlessness, anxiety, and depression.

Black Americans in Harlem live with morbidity and mortality rates far higher than those of whites and suffer disproportionately on every social indicator available for study. Given, especially, racial prejudice, continuing high unemployment, and crime in the black population districts, it is unquestionable that black Americans suffer an inordinate amount of stress. We can readily speculate that the reason blacks are represented so dispropor-

Table 56.2
Crime Comparison Statistics

Classification	1969	1970	1971	1972	1973	1974	1975	1976	1977	1978
For 28th precinct										
Homicide	71	57	105	117	123	95	96	80	88	49
Forcible rape	51	49	64	99	82	84	95	78	69	73
Robbery	2,380	2,488	3,198	3,576	2,647	2,238	2,434	2,062	1,389	1,093
Felonious assault	844	848	993	1,090	967	1,031	1,026	944	858	735
Burglary	2,571	2,355	2,395	2,051	1,502	1,382	1,626	1,624	1,146	846
Grand larceny	1,348	1,517	1,519	1,257	900	835	824	801	548	573
Narcotic felonies	1,171	2,037	1,712	941	1,303	1,153	1,257			
Total felonies	9,276	10,141	10,987	10,043	8,359	7,714	8,210	8,082	6,730	5,679
For 32nd precinct										
Homicide	62	58	79	107	97	78	88	74	62	69
Forcible rape	64	82	97	150	149	154	137	92	105	102
Robbery	3,018	3,087	3,261	2,825	2,688	2,669	2,625	2,284	1,563	1,179
Felonious assault	711	755	830	934	937	919	999	825	800	787
Burglary	3,129	3,293	3,430	2,366	1,965	2,369	2,374	2,058	1,315	1,195
Grand larceny	1,468	1,151	1,329	670	592	701	938	1,076	818	643
Narcotic felonies	536	1,282	1,151	627	820	889				
Total felonies	10,038	10,853	11,344	8,820	8,414	8,838	8,607	8,066	6,707	5,375
For New York City										
Homicide	1,049	1,118	1,466	1,680	1,691	1,554	1,645	1,622	1,557	1,518
Forcible rape	2,120	2,141	2,415	3,735	3,271	4,054	3,866	3,400	3,899	3,882
Robbery	59,151	74,102	88,994	72,750	78,202	77,940	83,190	86,183	74,408	74,029
Felonious assault	17,552	18,410	20,460	24,469	23,357	26,084	27,712	27,456	27,217	27,234
Burglary	171,393	181,694	181,331	148,846	148,311	158,321	177,032	195,243	178,888	164,447
Grand larceny	73,851	78,276	79,369	50,197	53,337	64,915	80,738	105,803	104,752	104,787
Narcotic felonies	15,507	28,428	25,703	22,843	17,804	19,205				
Total felonies	434,091	489,138	510,048	419,477	417,169	440,919	492,486	552,696	517,554	491,896

tionately among drug-dependent cohorts is the existence of unbearable high stress, the need to ameliorate its incapacitating effects by self-administration of dependence-producing drugs, and the absence of body defenses against these drugs as a preexisting result of stress itself. Stress can hardly be expected to diminish for the black resident of Harlem. Short of a massive social change in America, therefore, drug dependency will no doubt continue as a physical resultant of stress, itself the creation of a host of unfavorable social indicators, for black Americans today.

The physician treating patients who are drug dependent must realize that only a relatively broad scale and all-encompassing social-medical orientation will enable him to remedy the ills to which society has given birth.

We conclude this review of the social indicators in Harlem by asking the impartial observer, is it not a small wonder that all residents of Harlem are not using drugs to alleviate the stress that is inevitably to be encountered in association with daily life there?

Obviously, the social indicators present in Harlem to such an unusual extent portend a great deal for those concerned with drug dependency in black America. To complete our view of the problem, however, it is important to present some basic scientific facts uncovered within the past few years and directly relevant to the topic at hand.

There are many conclusions that can be drawn from all of the aforementioned. Certainly, many age-old hypotheses, suggestions, nuances, and speculative innuendos have subtly been interjected so that the reader would be ever mindful that, whatever the predisposing factors, causes, and results of drug abuse in the black community, stress is the response and bottom line, common to every aspect of this perplexing phenomenon.

The word stress, in the sense of its usage here, designates the aggregate of all the nonspecific effects of factors (normal activity, environment, economy, housing, drug availability, employment, etc.) and those specific factors such as drug pharmacology, inter- and intracellular response.

Twenty-four centuries ago, Hippocrates, the Father of Medicine, told his disciples in Greece that disease is not only suffering (Pathos) but also toil (Ponos), that is, the fight of

the body to restore itself toward normal. There is a vis medicatrix naturae, a healing force of nature, that cures from within. The great French physiologist Claude Bernard taught that one of the most characteristic features of all living beings is their ability to maintain the constancy of their internal milieu despite the changes in the surroundings. The physical properties and the chemical composition of our body tissues and fluids tend to remain remarkably constant despite all the changes about us.

Walter B. Cannon, the famous Harvard physiologist, subsequently called this power to maintain constancy in living beings *homeostasis* (from Greek homoios, like, similar plus statis, position, standing) (45). Claude Bernard and Cannon emphasized that the constancy of the organism is to a large extent controlled by the vegetative, or autonomic, nervous system. The specific action of this system is mediated by chemical substances with a sterospecificity for intra- and extracellular receptor sites. This complex chemical neurohumoral transmitter (norepinephrine, epinephrine, acetylcholine, and many others of recent discovery) and receptor system is responsible for our specific responses to all internal and external stimuli.

Neuropharmacologists have understood for many years the theory of neurohumoral transmission, that is, that nerves transmit their impulses across most synapses and neuroeffector junctions.

The identity of the pituitary hormone beta-lipotropin (C. H. Li B-LPH 61-91 1974), an inactive presursor of beta-endorphin (16), methionine and leucine enkephalin (23), and dynorphin (17) extended the pharmacologist's knowledge of neurohumoral transmitters and the role they play in a plethora of the body's functions and responses. The starting point for these remarkable discoveries was a search for receptors in the human body utilized by exogenous drugs of the morphine type that relieve pain and anxiety. Stereospecific receptor sites for opiates were identified in the brain, the pituitary gland, the medial pain pathways in the spinal cord, the intestinal tract, and the reproductive organs. Their specific neuroeffectors (endorphin, dynorphin, enkephalins) have been demonstrated to have the same precursor peptides as adrenocorticotropin (ACTH) and melanocyte-stimulating hormone (MSH) and to be intimately associated with the release of prolactin, the lactogenic hormone, and the growth hormone, all of which play major and minor roles in the body's defense mechanism to acute and chronic stress.

The opioid characteristics of dynorphin, beta-endorphin, and enkephalins have triggered intense curiosity and speculation about the possible physiological and pathophysiological roles they may play in the human body's response to mental and emotional disorders, pain, and most of all stress. There is an overwhelming body of evidence that the endogenous opioids act precisely as morphine does. Morphine combats the effect of stress, releases some pituitary hormones, and suppresses others; it has been found that endorphins have a similar action in humans. Chronically administered morphine has been reported to depress adrenocortical function in humans and to inhibit the glands' response to stress, suggesting that chronically opiate-addicted individuals could possibly have reduced natural body response to stress of which the adrenocortical role is so important.

Avram Goldstein, M.D., had the foresight to say after great caution (16):

In 1973, even before the endogenous opiates were actually discovered (although their existence seemed almost certain), we suggested that a defect in a system that regulated mood, pain, and anxiety responses would almost inevitably result in behavioral disorders. We postulated such a defect could make one subject prone to addiction, to which another, whose endorphins were working normally, might prove invulnerable. I do not mean to suggest that addiction is simply a matter of genetics, which may account for some inborn predisposition. Obviously addiction is a complex social phenomenon in which, I am sure, economics and life-styles are more significant factors than the effectiveness of endorphins in any given population. However, the endorphin system may explain why it is that, given the same drug availability, some individuals will become addicted and others will not. It may elucidate the vulnerability factor in addiction.

Still another possibility is that addiction might be produced not by a constitutional defect in the endogenous system but by its suppression or severe impairment as a result of habitual use of exogenous opiates (16).

Recently it was reported that there were 15 documented cases of congenital insensitivity to pain, and that these subjects responded to pain only after having been given the narcotic antagonist naloxone that selectively blocks the endogenous opioid neurotransmitters (dynorphin, beta-endorphin, enkephalins). When the effects of naloxone waned, the inability to perceive pain returned. Clearly this finding suggests that there are individuals who may have an overproductive or faulty neurotransmission system that is always activated. Why then could there not be individuals exhibiting the opposite conditions, an underproductive faulty neurohumoral transmission or some mutation as was cautiously suggested by Goldstein and his colleagues that simply led to the production of defective endogenous peptides that would not activate the stereospecific receptor sites? Morphine's ability to relieve pain, anxiety, and stress is enhanced by the simultaneous administration of amphetamine, suggesting an additive role for norepinephrine or dopamine (central noradrenergic mechanisms) (18).

Addicts have been practicing this pharmacological feat since time immemorial by mixing heroin and cocaine, giving it the appropriate name "speedball." It is reported to be a "great high" and is considered a delight by most addicts.

During the Korean War, paratroopers and members of the Green Berets were issued amphetamine specifically because of this action when involved in stressful hazardous duty or where there may have been injury requiring morphine. The Viet Nam experience taught us that men serving their country in a place where drug availability and stress were high were more prone to addictive behavior and that when they returned to less stressful conditions for the most part there was a cessation of opiate addiction behavior (41).

Much has been presented in this chapter to indicate more than a casual relationship between those stressful conditions existing in a homogeneous black community, the availability of exogenous opiates and other substances of abuse, and their use. The inordinately high incidence and prevalence of narcotic addiction and substance use in that community could possibly be explained as an attempt by that population to self-medicate in order to cope with those seemingly unalterable conditions of our society.

References

1. Abrams, A., Gagnon, J. H., and Levin, J. Psychosocial aspects of addiction. Am. J. Public Health 58:2142, 1968.
2. Andima, H., Krug, D., Bergnor, L., Patrick, S., and Whitman, S. An initial estimate of narcotic abuse prevalence in N.Y.C. Contemp. Drug Prob. 1:727, 1972.
3. Brenner, M. H. Fetal, infant, and maternal mortality during periods of economic instability. Int. J. Health Serv. 3:149, 1973.
4. Carstairs, G. M. Personality and social factors in drug addiction. J. Med. Liban 25:409, 1972.
5. Cherubin, C., McCusker, J., Baden, M., Karvoler, F., and Amsel, Z. The epidemiology of death in narcotic addicts. Am. J. Epidemiol. 96:11, 1972.
6. Cowan, J., Kay, D. C., Ross, F., Neidert, G., and Belmore, S. Defeated and joyless. Unpublished report.
7. Dollard, J., Doob, L. W., Miller, N. E., Mowrer, O. H., Sears, R. R., Ford, C. S., Hovland, C. I., and Sollenberger, R. T. Frustration and Aggression. New Haven, Conn., Yale University Press, 1939.
8. Durkheim, E. Suicide. New York, The Free Press, 1951.
9. Durkheim, E. On the duality of human nature. In Essays on Sociology and Philosophy, K. H. Wolff, editor, New York, Harper and Row, 1964.
10. Durkheim, E. The Rules of the Sociological Method. New York, The Free Press, 1964.
11. Fanon, F. The Wretched of the Earth. New York, Grove Press, 1965.
12. Fanon, F. Black Skin, White Masks. New York, Grove Press, 1967.
13. Frazier, E. F. Black Bourgeosie. New York, The Free Press, 1957.
14. Freud, S. Civilization and Its Discontents. London, Hogarth Press, 1933.
15. Gnepp, E. A causal theory of addiction. Psychology 13:13, 1976.
16. Goldstein, A. Endorphins: Their physiological and pathological potentials: Current concepts in postoperative pain. A Special Report Prepared for Pfizer Laboratories by Hospital Practice, January, 1978.
17. Goldstein, A. Therapy: Principles and use of drugs. Lecture, Stanford University School of Medicine, San Francisco, California, 1979.
18. Goodman, L. S., and Gilman, A. The Pharmacological Basis of Therapeutics, ed. 5. New York, Macmillan, 1975.
19. Grier, W., and Cobbs, P. Black Rage. New York, Basic Books, 1968.
20. HarYou Act. Youth in the Ghetto. New York, 1964.
21. Health Systems Agency. Health Care Needs Profile, Northwest Manhattan Health Care Study. Draft, June 16, 1975.
22. Helmer, J., and Vietorisz, T. Drug Use, the Labor Market and Class Conflict. Washington, D.C., Drug Abuse Council, Monograph Series #22, 1974.
23. Hughes, J., Smith, T. W., Kosterlitz, H., Fothergill, L. A., Morgan, B. A., and Morris, H. R. Identification of two related pentapeptides from the brain with potent opiate agonist activity. Nature 258:577, 1975.
24. Inwang, E. E., Primm, B. J., and Jones, F. L. Metabolic disposition of 2-phenyl-ethylamine and the role of

25. Katz, W. L. Eyewitness: The Negro in American History. New York, Pitman, 1968.
26. Kempton, M. Welfare job program: A cure no better than the disease. The New York Post 27, December 17, 1979.
27. Khantzian, E. J., Mack, J. E., and Schatzberg, A. F. Heroin use as an attempt to cope: Clinical observations. Am. J. Psychiatry 131:160, 1974.
28. Lurssen, E. Psychoanalytic theories of addiction structures. Suchtgefahren, 20:141, 1974.
29. Merton, R. K. Social Theory and Social Structure. New York, The Free Press, 1968.
30. Merton, R. K., Broom, L., and Cottrell, L. S., editors. Sociology Today: Problems and Prospects. New York, Harper Torchbooks, 1965.
31. Messolonghites, L. Multicultural Perspectives on Drug Abuse and Its Prevention. Washington, D.C., National Institute on Drug Abuse, 1979.
32. Nathan, W. B. Health Conditions in North Harlem. Social Research Series #2, M. Dempsey, editor. New York, National Tuberculosis Association, 1932.
33. New York City Board of Education. Community and High Schools Profile, 1974–75. New York, New York City Board of Education, 1976.
34. New York City Department of Health. Vital Statistics by Health Areas and Health Center Districts. New York, New York City Department of Health, 1970.
35. New York City Department of Health. Summary of Vital Statistics, 1960–1978. New York, New York City Department of Health, 1979.
36. New York City Department of Planning. Community Portfolio Fact Book, Manhattan District 10. New York, New York City Department of Planning, 1977.
37. New York State Division of Substance Abuse Services. Fact Sheet: Trends in Drug Abuse. New York, New York State Division of Substance Abuse Services, 1978.
38. New York State Division of Substance Abuse Services. (A) Report on the Non-Medical Use of Drugs among the New York State Household Population. December, 1978. New York, New York State Division of Substance Abuse Services, 1978.
39. Parson, T., Shils, E., Naegele, K., and Pitts, J. R., editors. Theories of Society: Foundations of Modern Sociological Theory. New York, The Free Press, 1965.
40. Rahe, R. H., McKean, J. D., and Arthur, B. J. A longitudinal study of life change and illness patterns. J. Psychosom. Res. 10:355, 1967.
41. Robins, L. N., Helzer, J. E., and Davis, D. H. Narcotic use in Southeast Asia and afterward: Interview study of 898 Vietnam returnees. Arch. Gen. Psychiatry 32: 955, 1975.
42. Roizin, L., Halpern, M., Baden, M., Kaufman, M., Hashimoto, S., Liu, J. C., and Eisenberg, B. Methadone fatalities in heroin addicts. Psychiatr. Q. 46: 393, 1973.
43. Seevers, M. Drug dependence vis-a-vis drug abuse. In Drug Abuse: Proceedings of the International Conference, C. Zarafonetis, editor, pp. 9–16. Philadelphia, Lea and Febiger.
44. Sells, S. B., Chatham, L. R., and Retka, R. A study of differential rates and causes of death among 9,276

depression in methadone dependent and detoxified patients. Drug Alcohol Depend. 1:295, 1975–6.

opiate addicts during 1970–71. Texas Christian University, Institute of Behavioral Research. Research Report for NIMH—TC Drug Abuse Reporting Program, Contract #HSM 42-69-6, 1972.

45. Selye, H. *The Stress of Life*. New York, McGraw Hill, 1956.

46. Tatum, A. L., Seevers, M. H., and Collins, K. H. Morphine addiction and its physiological interpretation based on experimental evidence. J. Pharmacol. Exp. Ther. 36:447, 1929.

47. Thompson, T., and Unna, K., editors. *Predicting Dependence Liability of Stimulants and Depressant Drugs*. Baltimore, University Park Press, 1977.

48. Vaillant, G. Natural history of male psychologic health: Effects of mental health on physical disease. N. Engl. J. Med. 301:1249, 1979.

49. World Health Organization. *Evaluation of Dependence Liability and Dependence Potential of Drugs*, WHO Scientific Committee Technical Report, Series 577. Geneva, World Health Organization, 1975.

50. Zimmerman, R. S., Pixley, L., and Coghlan, A. J. Psychological Substrata of addiction: Implications for therapy. In *Proceedings of the 30th International Congress of Alcoholism and Drug Dependence*, vol. 1. Lausanne, Switzerland, International Congress of Alcoholism and Drug Dependence, 1972.

CHAPTER 57

THE HISPANIC ADDICT[1]

Angel Gregorio Gómez, M.D.

Donald M. Vega, S.J., M.A.

HISTORICAL BACKGROUND: MYTH VERSUS REALITY

In the United States the term "Hispanic" defines the ethnic origin of an important and growing segment of the nation's population. It includes people of Hispanic and Latin ancestry who migrated to or were born in the United States, such as the Mexican-Americans (some prefer to be called Spanish-Americans), Puerto Ricans, Cubans, and others.

The vast majority of Hispanics speak both English and Spanish. Their bilingualism depends on such variables as age, generation, geographical location, socioeconomic status, educational opportunities, group insulation versus transcultural socialization, and others. The language factor is of utmost importance because it may describe or give us an idea of the kind of Hispanic we are dealing with or talking about. Although some of them may speak only English, frequently the nonverbal ways of communicating among themselves are Hispanic, even in the second or third generations, as is the case with Puerto Ricans in the United States. Inasmuch as verbal and nonverbal communication are deeply rooted

in the cultural background of a person, Hispanic psychiatrists have recently been pointing out elements of history to facilitate the understanding of behavior expressed by Hispanics in this country. In this regard special notice should be taken of Bernal y del Río (6, 7), Cohen (9), Gómez (14, 15, 18), Rumbaut (34), Canino and Canino-Stolberg (8), Ruiz (33), Martínez (28), Arce (2), Jiménez (24), and others.

Those acquainted with the history of the United States know, as Jiménez (24) indicated, that a substantial portion of the country, particularly large sections of the South and the Southwest, had been under Spanish rule for more than 200 years "before so-called Americans arrived" and that "Hispanic culture has been part and parcel of this country's development since before the Mayflower landed at Plymouth Rock." Jiménez emphasized that it would be an injustice to see the Hispanics simply as a people who migrated to this country prior to and after World War II. Said Jiménez: "Although it's true that the largest portion of Hispanics did come here in the last three decades, in fact we've been here for a long, long time."

Rumbaut (34) pointed out:

With the Spaniards came commerce and trade on an international scale, industry, mining, technology, banking, architecture; the fine arts, the basic and the applied sciences and the learned professions; the alphabet, the printing press,

[1] The opinions expressed in this chapter reflect the opinions solely of the authors and do not represent any official position of the Department of Addiction Services of the Commonwealth of Puerto Rico. However, the authors are grateful to the department for its cooperation in the preparation of this chapter.

schools and universities. Spaniards introduced Spanish, the first European language to be spoken in this part of the earth and, almost simultaneously with it, Latin. They brought books by the hundreds, and then printed the first books this side of the Atlantic. Finally, with them came the immense Greek-Roman-Judeo-Christian tradition and accumulation of knowledge and wisdom.

Hispanics are one of the four main minority ethnic populations in the United States. In terms of skin color they are found within an ample spectrum that ranges from the lily-white, Nordic, blue-eyed blonde to the dark-violet African black. However, the stereotypic view of the Hispanic in this country is that of a person with dark (or olive) skin, dark brown eyes, and straight black hair. The men, of course, wear moustaches. This stereotype has been reinforced by the mass media, particularly the motion picture industry, which have portrayed the "Latin" as Mediterranean lover or "sociological lady killer"; as the loud-mouthed "bandido" or the sloppily dressed, undernourished, passive, submissive, lazy peasant enjoying his siesta; as the assertive, articulate drug smuggler ghettoized in huge metropolitan cities. The movie image of the Hispanic female challenges the wildest imagination. What is true is that the darker the skin the more minority the Hispanic is. For example, in the case of a black Hispanic female, she is three times minority. According to the stereotype, all Hispanics, regardless of sex, should speak with a heavy "south-of-the-border" Spanish accent. Some of them should show evidence of below normal intelligence. Both male and female should be ardently seductive.

The aforementioned image should not be taken lightly as an exaggerated reaction to what has been a consistent subliminal stimulus projected for decades into the brain of the general population. This constant audio-visual image of the Hispanic could account for the reinforcement of racial prejudice in some non-Hispanics and also could help to impoverish the self-image of some Hispanics in certain situations. This is of paramount importance for both caregivers and caretakers in the field of human services.

In spite of its traditional inability adequately to identify Hispanics, the United States Census Bureau projects that by the 1980's the Hispanic populations in this country will have reached 20 million (not including the 3 million Puerto Ricans living in Puerto Rico), and by the 1990's Hispanics will constitute the nation's largest minority group. Furthermore, the United States Immigration Service estimates that a million illegal aliens enter the United States per year, and that about 85 to 90 per cent of these are Hispanics. The illegal immigrants are believed to enter mainly through the Mexican border and Puerto Rico, which serve as a bridge for people from the Caribbean and Latin American countries.

Hispanics are to be found in the four cardinal points of the United States, with the Mexican-Americans being the major group. Eighty per cent of these are located in Texas, California, Arizona, and New Mexico. Puerto Ricans live on the northeastern seaboard: New York, New Jersey, New England. Large populations live in Boston, Philadelphia, and other cities. The majority of Cubans live in Florida. According to Arce (2), the geographical migration follows the traffic lanes, for "there has always been heavy traffic between San Juan and New York and between Havana and Key West; obviously, the Mexican-Americans come across the border overland." According to Gómez (15), Puerto Ricans tend to avoid the South because of its historically consistent racial prejudice and prefer the northern states where, they believe, they are less likely to become victims.

However, the impact of prejudice can be diminished by another social phenomenon: population growth of the minority. When it occurs, it tends to balance political forces because of new voting strength. In its October 18, 1978, issue, *Time* magazine startled millions of citizens across the United States, particularly politicians, with a feature article entitled: "U. S. Hispanics: An Awakening Minority." *Time* called attention to the slow growth of Hispanic affluence and educational attainment as mirrored in politics and in government bureaucracies and pointed out:

The problems, and promise, of the Hispanic-American experience in the U. S. may be best illustrated, however, by what is happening in three other cities: metropolitan Miami, whose Cuban population (430,000) is exceeded only by Havana's; metropolitan Los Angeles, whose 1.6 million Hispanic population, which is overwhelmingly Chicano, makes it the world's second largest Mexican agglomeration after Mexico City; and New York, which surpasses San Juan in Puerto

Rican population (1.3 million). There is a fourth community that also demands study: that furtive, elusive subculture-within-a-subculture, the illegal aliens.

The growing political power of the Hispanics, according to *Time*, was illustrated in Sacramento, California, when Governor Jerry Brown appeared at a Mexican-American convention. "You're the leading minority in the Southwest," Brown was quoted as telling the crowd. "It's your turn in the sun and I want to be part of it."

With this brief resume, we have summarized the historical background of Hispanics in the United States and have taken a glimpse into future perspectives. This is essential for assessing the present existential condition in which the Hispanic, according to *Time*, is involved in a "grinding struggle for survival," because " . . . for them (life) experience today is all too often one of blighted hopes. . . . "

Let us now see this situation as related to substance abuse and drug addiction.

HISPANICS AND THE DRUG SCENE

Evidently, it is traumatic that, as a minority population (sometimes a many-fold minority), Hispanics are forced to deal with the inequities of a polarized social system in pluralistic America. In addition to the language barrier in many cases, group insulation of Hispanic people is due mainly to historically rooted sociocultural factors, to economic status, and to the Darwinian social stratification evident in the traditional American ethnic totem pole. Because of their daily group struggle for social survival, it sometimes seems as though Hispanics are living in a foreign country; and this produces an unbearable problem of national identity.

If external reality for the Hispanic is so tragic, and if most of the time he feels powerless to change it, why not resort to an internal, autoplastic change through chemistry? Why not take the pleasurable route of escapism through mind-changing drugs? After all, other minorities use drugs; whites also use drugs; and humans have been using drugs since the stone age whenever faced by an external unpleasurable reality.

What is the real situation of the use and abuse of, or addiction to, controlled substances by Hispanics in the United States? On this subject, the literature is abundant,

but, upon review, the authors found that conclusions are not definite and that research findings are quite often paradoxical and contradictory.

The problem one faces in discovering a direct (cause-effect) relationship between ethnicity and drug abuse can best be illustrated by an examination of two important reports published by the National Institute on Drug Abuse (NIDA).

First, we will refer to the NIDA Statistical Series (Annual Data 1977, Series E, No. 7) from the Client Oriented Data Acquisition Process (CODAP). This report is of great importance for the Hispanic because it presents data collected by NIDA on clients of different ethnic backgrounds who were admitted to or discharged from federally funded drug abuse treatment centers during 1977. Therefore, it permits a comparative analysis of the relationship between ethnicity and drug use.

The purpose of this report was to provide ample information on drug abuse and its treatment to a wide public. The range and depth of this information were designed to appeal to the needs of professionals working in drug abuse treatment and research, as well as to the general public. The report presents data based on such variables as race-ethnicity, age, and sex at admission by primary drug.

At first view, the data seem to indicate that Hispanics as a group, as well as subdivided by ethnic origin, use more heroin as primary drug than whites at admission. However, upon analyzing samples of the total number of cases reported as active by CODAP, it is clear that Hispanics, in this particular, do not differ significantly from other ethnic groups. The same result was obtained when we revised the variable of client age by primary drug at admission. In this regard NIDA's report calls attention to the complexity and difficulty in collecting the data.

This analysis should not surprise anyone. In its Research Issue No. 21 (29) entitled *Drugs and Minorities*, NIDA gave a note of caution in the preface stating that " . . . there is a considerable disagreement in the interpretation of available data and there is a need for additional research. . . . "

For a relatively unprejudiced observer, it is interesting to note that the publication makes a remark about "designations based on skin color." This is an honest indication of what has been a basic rule in American literature for describing and defining an American's origin and probably for making inferences as to his/her quality of life, goals, and social opportunities. American citizens either as individuals or a group are constrained to a very narrow and simplistic spectrum based on skin color: white or black; the in-between is known as "nonwhite" (there is no such thing as "nonblack"). Ethnicity is something else. Generally speaking, the Hispanic, although ethnically a nonblack, is found on the other side of the white fence.

This is an important observation when determining the Hispanic's place in the American drug scene. In the introduction to the above mentioned report, B. D. Johnson gave a final warning:

It has been contended that prior to the 1950's, narcotic use was essentially a problem of whites. During the 1950's the trend reversed (as measured by drug arrest statistics) and narcotic use became a problem of the black community. Finally the 1960's and 1970's have seen the trend reverse again, and whites comprised the bulk of the drug arrests. The work of Johnson and Nishi (25), De Fleur (11), and Helmer and Vietorisz (22) suggests that drug arrests may be more a reflection of political pressures and enforcement policies, than a true indication of the white and black narcotic using population.

On this black and white sociocultural checkerboard, where is the Hispanic and what is his place in the drug scene? Is there such a thing as "Chicano addiction," as some have proposed? "Puerto Rican addiction"? "Cuban addiction"? Or just an addiction or dependency disorder shown by Mexican-Americans, Puerto Ricans, or Cubans?

Ethnic background, skin color, and geographical area have been used as main variables in exploratory surveys and special research programs across the country to assess the prevalence, incidence, frequency, and situational content of all types of drug use within the general population. These explorations have taken place in the most contrasting settings: the individual versus the family, the urban versus the rural, the civilian versus the military, the free community versus the prison, and so forth. It seems that drug use, abuse, and addiction are not necessarily linked to or associated with ethnicity per se,

but rather with the existential condition or life situation in which a given ethnic individual or group is likely to be found at any given historical moment.

In a 1976 review of the literature on minority drug abuse, Johnson and Nishi (25) focused on such specific topics as methodological biases in studying minority drug abuse, the social history of opiates and minorities, models of addiction, research findings, and treatment programs. In regard to estimating minority drug abuse, the authors pointed out:

Even though the estimates of addiction to narcotics by minorities in the United States vary considerably, there appears to be little doubt that blacks, Puerto Ricans, and Mexican-Americans are overrepresented in the population of known addicts. However, prevalence and trend estimates of drug addiction as an illegal activity, particularly as they relate to racial-ethnic minorities, are fraught with difficulties. For instance, Drug Enforcement Administration statistics include only addicts who have come to the attention of law enforcement agencies, primarily for narcotics law violations and secondarily for loitering or other criminal acts. Virtually excluded are those illegal drug users who have not become involved with the police, those who obtain legal drugs from doctors, and those who are in prison. . . .

The heavy use of minor charges and a "revolving door policy" kept drug arrest for nonwhites very high. . . .

In regard to research findings, Johnson and Nishi stated that:

Regardless of how addiction is defined, most research studies have shown evidence demonstrating that blacks, Puerto Ricans, and Mexican-Americans are overrepresented in the institutionalized addict populations in comparison with their proportions in the total population, while whites and Asian-Americans are underrepresented. This idea that minorities are particularly susceptible to heroin addiction is contradicted when international and historical comparisons are made, and where careful distinctions between use, regular use, and addiction are made in general or special surveys of noninstitutional populations.

Finally, Johnson and Nishi concluded:

Although addiction among minorities is perceived by the public as a serious social problem, many facts indicate that the extent of the problem does not warrant the amount of public concern and attention given. The moral filter through which addiction is perceived grossly distorts and magnifies the issue. Because of the often racist attitude of government officials, drug treatment personnel, and social scientists, minorities continue to be the focus of blame for drug addiction as well as the object of social control efforts. The "problem" of drug abuse has remained virtually stalled at the same place it was in the 1950's. While the substantive issues around which the debates revolve have shifted, the symbolic role of drug abuse remains unchanged. For many whites, it symbolizes their fears of the mythic violent black. To many blacks, it symbolizes their hatred for their white oppressors.

Could this be the case concerning Hispanics in the United States?

One way of understanding Hispanic involvement in the American drug scene could be through the utilization of the conceptual scheme proposed by Gómez (16) on the multicausality shown by Puerto Ricans in both addictive and criminal behavior. This theoretical construct could serve as a rational hypothetical point of departure.

In Gómez's conceptualization, the Hispanic addict is seen as being affected by three different converging forces: (a) the biological, as expressed by a possible genetic vulnerability in terms of predisposing neurophysiological and biochemical constitutional factors; (b) the psychogenic, as represented by a lacunar character structure, which is also part of the predispositional base; and (c) the sociocultural, as a constant, dynamic element emerging from political and social changes, which also generate a nonanticipatory change in traditional, deeply rooted, intrapsychic values. The unanticipated change comes from lateral or horizontal mobility (foreign or domestic migration) and/or vertical mobility (an upward or downward stress-producing move on the socioeconomic totem pole). Essential areas that account for a person's quality of life, such as health, education, housing, etc., are affected. This social whirlpool provokes a continuous, accumulative stress that is both precipitating and perpetuating. The most vulnerable individual very soon finds himself struggling with the pain/anxiety versus relief/pleasure dilemma. The pervasive and accumulative effect of stress overcomes the biological and psychological hedonistic quality of the individual now dealing with a feeling of either helplessness or powerlessness. Gómez, influenced by Halleck's (20)

concept of behavioral adaptation, believes that helplessness and powerlessness could lead the person to either conformism, activism, or "deviant behavior": mental illness, dependency disorder, or crime, as adaptational alternatives (Figs. 57.1 and 57.2).

If the struggle for an adaptive behavior becomes a source of more, detrimental stress, then escapism takes place through drug use (autoplastic quality) or criminal behavior (halloplastic quality). Of course, we know that people involved in drug use quite often are also involved in drug-related crimes.

The sociocultural force with its constant external change also demands a constant, quick, biopsychological change in the human body to maintain the biosocial equilibrium. At present, the external demand is directed by an accelerated force governing our technological and technocratic society, in such a way that the individual is unable to keep pace with the outward demanding force. Thus, he is in constant, anxious movement as though walking over burning coals. This could explain his recourse to the primitive tendency for migration as a survival mechanism.

It has been a persistent sociological thesis in both European and American studies of deviant behavior that crime is associated with urbanization, migration, and residential mobility (5). Migration also introduces particular stresses that increase the disparity between generations (27). This was the conclusion of Canino and Canino-Stolberg (8) and of Arce and Torres-Matrullo (3) with regard to the intergenerational conflict among Puerto Rican migrants, and of other authors concerning Hispanic domestic migration.

In regard to escapism, it has been said that the individual addict is overwhelmed by the necessity to "shut out" certain aspects of reality that are intolerable (1). A direct reference to the escape character of narcotic use as a motivating factor was made by Crowther (10) when he stated of one Hispanic group that " ... it is possible that the lower class Mexican-American sees heroin as a means of escaping responsibility with the difficult life cycle that envelopes him. . . . " As a matter of fact, escapism through drug chemistry started when prehistoric humans realized their limitations as mortal beings. Therefore, it should be of no surprise that the stressful, and sometimes paradoxically strange, social milieu with which the Hispanic is forced to

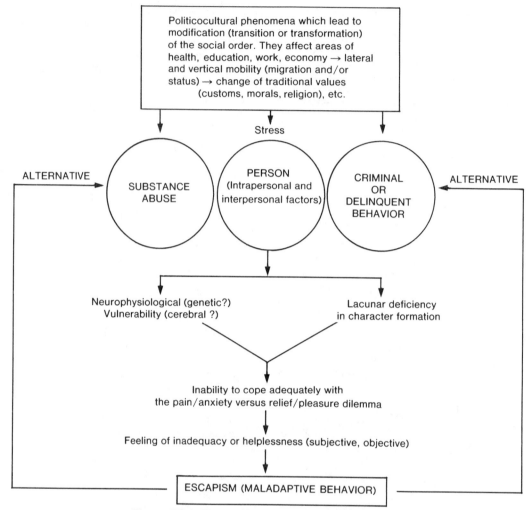

Figure 57.1. The multicausality of addiction–crime.

deal in the United States could account for addiction escapism in the biopsychologically predisposed.

THE SITUATION IN PUERTO RICO

At this point the authors would like to shift their attention to a special Hispanic population, the Puerto Rican living in Puerto Rico. Because Puerto Rican society is a more homogenous ethnic group and is relatively free of overt racial prejudice, our analysis of drug use in Puerto Rico will serve not only as a transcultural frame of reference, but will also give an idea of the side effects of dependency disorders that result from rapid social change.

Due to its geographic location in the Caribbean, the Commonwealth of Puerto Rico is considered to be "at the crossroads of the Americas" for all kinds of cultural and commercial interchange. On the one hand, our Spanish ancestry and cultural heritage give us a Latin American profile in terms of language, tradition, folklore, and life style; on the other hand, due to our political bonds with the United States, we share with that nation a common citizenship, advantages, and misfortunes. Drug addiction, within its universal scope, is one of the latter.

According to a 1977 census, the population of Puerto Rico was approximately 3,320,000 living in an area of 3,421 square miles, giving us a population density of 970 persons per square mile.[2] It is also estimated that between 1½ and 2 million Puerto Ricans live in the

---

[2] Division of Human Resources, Puerto Rico Planning Board, February, 1978.

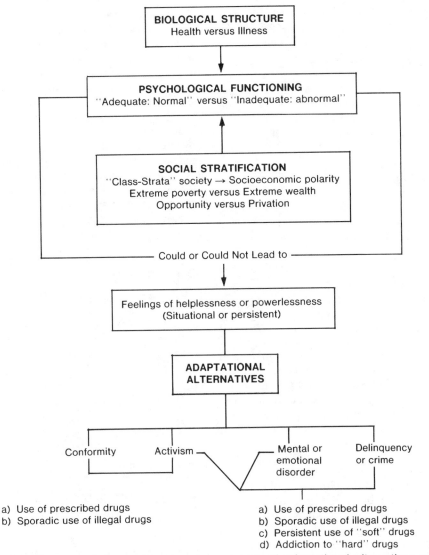

Figure 57.2. The use of drugs viewed as an outcome of adaptational alternatives within an individual's historical context.

continental United States, creating a kind of migratory revolving door.

Drug addiction in Puerto Rico has become a social problem of epidemic proportions within the last 15 years. According to one survey (4), 242 addict residents of Puerto Rico were admitted to and discharged from the United States Public Health Service Hospital in Lexington, Kentucky, between 1935 and 1962. Of these, 122 were located and interviewed during a 1962 to 1964 follow-up field study in Puerto Rico. Of the 122 former Lexington patients interviewed, three who were found to be marihuana users without a

history of opiate addiction were excluded from the study. Of the 119 opiate addicts, 107 were male and 12 were female. At the time of the interview, the mean age of the males was 30.8 years; of the females, 36.2. Comparison with the 1960 census data revealed that the addicts came from families that were generally representative of the Puerto Rican population in regard to socioeconomic status. The median years of schooling completed by male subjects was 10.0; by females, 9.0. Eleven of the subjects had attended or completed college.

Ball (4) concluded:

The onset of heroin use among Puerto Rican youth of this study is similar to the onset of juvenile delinquency in metropolitan areas of the United States. In both instances, there is the dominant influence of deviant peer associations. Members of this deviant group are perceived as friends, and the deviant behavior is carried out in a neighborhood street setting. To what extent the beginning opiate user or delinquent is aware of the dangers and probable consequences of the illicit act is unknown; it seems likely that an overly rationalistic conception of the phenomenon of onset has been projected upon the young boy or girl. . . .

And he adds:

It is pertinent to note that the interpersonal and situational factors associated with the onset of marihuana smoking and opiate use among Puerto Rican addicts of this study have not changed during the past 40 years. The evidence suggests that the peer group behavior leading to the onset of drug addiction has remained unchanged during this period.

During the 1962 to 1964 period in which the data were collected, there were an estimated 5,000 heroin addicts in Puerto Rico. By 1967 when the report was published, the number of Puerto Rican addicts on the island and/or going through the New York—San Juan revolving door was thought to be close to 10,000. In 1971 García and Roselló (13) estimated 13,600 addicts on the island, and a year later, based on the Hunt formula, it was believed the number of addicts to be about 36,000 (30). That figure doubled in 5 years when, according to the Hunt formula, it was estimated that there was a total of 72,920 addicts in Puerto Rico for the period 1976 to 1977.

During the past several years there has been growing dissatisfaction with the use of the Hunt and other formulas for estimating the number of addicts in Puerto Rico. For this reason the Department of Addiction Services, of which we will speak further on, designed its own methodology and has embarked on an ambitious "Study of the Magnitude of the Drug Problem in Puerto Rico."[3]

---

[3] Preliminary analysis of the data collected to date based on known addicts in public and private treatment programs indicates that the prototype is a 25-year-old male who lives in a metropolitan area and has completed ninth grade.

When Puerto Rico officially awoke to the drug problem, it found itself in the middle of the heroin epidemic of the late 1960's and early 1970's. The average citizen had the impression that there was a heroin addict on every street corner, especially in the San Juan metropolitan area. This impression was due to the high visibility and easy identification of the heroin addict.

From 1966 to 1972, Puerto Rico's major drug problem was definitely heroin addiction. However, from 1972 to the present, with slight variations, there has been a noticeable reduction in the use of heroin and a dramatic increase in polydrug abuse, with a special preference for marihuana.

This upsurge in the use of marihuana has forced treatment and prevention people to question their options and strategies as well as given rise to the questioning of Puerto Rican drug laws that, at present, make no distinction between hard and soft drugs nor in the legal consequences of their possession, transportation, and sale.

Although most direct and indirect indicators point to the widespread use of marihuana cutting through all age, social, and economic brackets, with special concentration among the youth and school population, Puerto Rico has yet to rethink effectively its public policy and readjust its social response to the present patterns and nature of substance abuse.

THE DEPARTMENT OF ADDICTION SERVICES

The drug epidemic of the 1960's caught Puerto Rico by surprise. Neither resources nor personnel nor know-how were immediately available to respond to the clamor of the community for help. Isolated efforts by the Health Department were buttressed by stronger efforts of the newly elected government in 1968 that created treatment programs in the fledgling Department of Social Services and prevention programs in the Department of Education. Ex-addict-run programs began to appear with economic assistance from a desperate community.

Although some of the efforts were excellent and recognized as such by the National Institute of Mental Health (NIMH)—especially those of the Department of Social Services—they were scattered, fragmented, and poorly coordinated; there was duplicity and poor use of existing resources, as well as the marked absence of a clear, coherent, and integrated public policy. Drug addiction, as well as alcoholism, were just not among the top priorities of existing agencies, when it came to alloting economic and human resources for programs. Medical, paramedical, and mental health personnel showed a marked resistance to becoming involved with drug addicts and alcoholics. And yet, something had to be done. Addiction and alcohol services, interagency coordination, and the allotment of resources could not continue to be left to the discretion of individual agencies.

In May of 1973, in a far reaching, far sighted, and courageous decision, which anticipated later developments in the United States, the Puerto Rican legislature created the cabinet-level Department of Addiction Services (DAS).

In its Statement of Motives, Public Law 60, which created the Department, reads as follows:

The Puerto Rican community is aware of the compelling need to face this evil (i.e. addiction). Notwithstanding, the addiction problem has spread in such a way that it has rendered ineffective existing structures which are scattered and uncoordinated. There is a need for an integrated central vision with which to face this problem in all its aspects. This integral view must be based on a thorough study of the problem and on the development of prevention and treatment mechanisms, conscious of the fact that there is no single ideal method with which to cope with this problem.

Law 60, known as the Organic Act of the Department of Addiction Services, empowers the Department to develop and implement a comprehensive, unified, and integrated public policy for dealing with the problem of drug addiction and alcoholism with their different ramifications and consequences. The law also authorizes the department to group into a single state agency all government programs, centers, and instrumentalities dedicated to "the prevention, care, relief and solution of the problems of addiction to narcotic drugs, dependence on depressant and stimulant drugs, and alcoholism, aimed at the promotion, conservation, and restoration of the psychosocial health of the Puerto Ricans."

The department also has the responsibility for co-ordinating, channeling, and properly utilizing all economic resources available, both state and federal, for the purpose of establishing necessary prevention and treatment programs, research, training, and community education and orientation.

In 6 years and despite chronic budgetary problems, DAS has implemented multimodality treatment and prevention programs throughout the island. Its Research Institute is conducting what promises to be the only valid scientific study on the magnitude and nature of the problem of substance abuse in Puerto Rico. The DAS Training Institute, while training service deliverers for both public and private programs in Puerto Rico, has become an international training center for the Caribbean, Central America, and South America.

Due to the fact that approximately 62.4 per cent of all addicts in treatment have some form of legal constraints as well as the fact that 60 per cent of all convicts confined in penal institutions have some type of substance abuse problem, DAS has established special treatment programs at each point of the treatment—criminal and juvenile justice interface including pretrial diversion programs, treatment programs within the penal institutions and comprehensive counseling, training and employment services for convicts prior to and after release.

Although DAS has the major responsibility for developing and implementing Puerto Rico's response to the substance abuse problem, its efforts are complemented by a variety of community-based programs. Although most of these are religiously oriented, the largest is an ex-addict-run, therapeutic community program known in Puerto Rico as Hogares CREA, Inc. (Homes for the Re-education of Addicts), with 60 centers scattered throughout the island.

Because of the migratory revolving door between the island of Puerto Rico and the United States mainland, DAS also has the responsibility for delivering services to the Puerto Rican—or any other United States citizen—who initiates drug abuse treatment in any of the states and then goes back to Puerto Rico for a prolonged visit or permanent residency. Continuation of treatment for these persons, particularly if they are on methadone maintenance or attending drug-free programs under a court order, is of utmost importance. There have been some problems due to faulty communications between the mainland agency and the corresponding DAS program.

Quite often the Puerto Rican client living in the United States claims a lack of understanding of "his problem," meaning that the non-Puerto Rican service deliverer lacks sufficient knowledge about the client's culture and ethnic background and, therefore, does not know how to deal with the client's problem in a culturally oriented way.

The cultural gap between the caregiver and the caretaker is not particularly limited to Puerto Ricans, for there are other Hispanics equally affected. For example, attention has been called to the necessity of understanding the history and the culture of the tecato (Chicano junkie) in order to develop adequate and effective prevention and treatment programs for an important segment of the Mexican American population.[4]

THE RELEVANCY OF TRAINING

Following the above observations, the authors would like to call attention to a problem frequently faced by the Hispanic drug user in the United States: the inability of non-Hispanic service deliverers to understand him. In April of 1978, at the National Drug Abuse Conference held in Seattle, Washington, the senior author stressed the relevancy of ethnicity and transculturality in training personnel to work with clients with dependency disorders.

We have already mentioned that, from the point of view of causation, dependency disorders are confined to three broad etiological categories: the biochemical-neurophysiological, the psychogenic, and the social-environmental.

Although psychogenic and social-environmental factors are less concrete, more subjective etiological elements of the addiction problem, they are more attractive to and more readily understood by the majority of those who work with addicts, because caregivers are trained principally in the social sciences.

The abundant literature on the psychogenic and social-environmental factors of ad-

diction reveals a common denominator: the role of the family.[5] Theoretical overviews and research findings seem to substantiate the conclusion that, the more cohesive the family group and the more acute the sense of human solidarity and belonging, proportionately less is the risk of becoming a delinquent drug user. However, it is surprising to find that little importance is given to ethnicity and transculturality in the effort to preserve family cohesiveness.

Very few medical schools or departments of behavioral sciences have introduced course material on the cultural aspects of substance abuse. In this regard, a review of the literature reveals the still embryonic state of course content and class hours. One medical school offers only 1 hour on the "cultural aspects of addiction." In psychiatry—the most sophisticated and integrated offspring of medicine and the behavioral sciences—the study of culture has not yet come into its own, according to Favazza and Oman (12), in spite of the fact that most social change is accompanied by an intensification of social and cultural sources of psychological conflict (26).

We believe that efforts to include subject matter on ethnicity and transculturality in the curricula of training programs on dependency disorders are far from adequate. We would like to state clearly our opinion that such academic apathy, not to say ignorance, is truly regrettable.

In all training programs for personnel working with clients with dependency disorders, the same basic questions must be asked: who is training whom, how, and for what? Due to issues related to civil rights and the constitution, federal agencies have recently released specific policy guidelines for federally funded training programs.

The draft "Report of the Workgroup of Manpower Training—Research and Development" of the National Institute of Mental Health (December 1976) clearly states that "particular attention in the R and D training efforts would be given to training approaches that would seek to heighten the awareness and sensitivity of the trainees to the life

---

[4] More information can be obtained from the Spanish Speaking Mental Health Center, University of California, Los Angeles.

[5] A good review of the literature can be found in the annotated bibliography drawn from sociology, psychology, psychiatry, and social work that appears in a Research Issues Series Monograph edited by NIDA in November, 1974.

styles, culture, and language of the various ethnic minority groups and their implication for effective service." In its guidelines on training (February 21, 1978), NIDA advised that "in order to operate valid training systems, states must be aware of staffing patterns within service delivery programs in order to establish and maintain adequate training support for all workers with special emphasis on the unmet needs of special populations in the state (racial and ethnic minorities, as well as women)." In its 1978 report the President's Commission on Mental Health recommends that the President also direct ". . . The Department of Health, Education, and Welfare to give further priority to (a) minority mental health workers (b) researchers from minority groups and (c) persons serving bicultural and bilingual groups."

If training is geared to serve the Hispanic minorities in the United States, we must be careful of our definition of "minority groups," because this is a loose phrase that can mean different things to different people (21).

We also believe that, for training to be relevant, it should serve the needs of the client and not the needs of the caregiver.

In delivering services to clients with dependency disorders, "therapy" is still the key word used to label the emotional transaction between parties. Everyone seems to have a therapeutic (magical?) solution for the non-biological treatment of these clients regardless of their ethnic background. Today the alternatives range anywhere from the mysticotranscendent to therapeutic communities, from behavior modification to relationship enhancement programs, from rigid discipline to folkloric rites.

As we have said elsewhere (18), we insist that whatever the particular therapeutic approach to be employed, ethnic and transcultural factors should always be present in the mind of the caregiver. Rogers pointed out (32) that communication and empathic understanding, or "understanding *with* a person, not *about* him," are clues to successful therapy and can bring about major changes in personality.

With regard to the delivery of human services to the Hispanics we repeat Maurice Nicoll's wise observation (31): "A man is his understanding. If you wish to see what a man *is*, and not what he is *like*, look at the level of his understanding. . . . "

SUMMARY

In the United States Hispanics suffer from a stereotyped image reinforced by mass media and bearing most of the stigma traditionally inflicted upon minority groups by majority prejudice. Hispanics, who include Mexican-Americans, Puerto Ricans, Cubans, and others, are one of the four main minority ethnic populations in the United States and by the 1990's will constitute the nation's largest minority group.

With regard to the use and abuse of, or addiction to, controlled substances by Hispanics in the United States, the authors found that conclusions are not definite and that research findings are often quite paradoxical and contradictory. The Hispanic addict does not differ from addicts of other ethnic backgrounds in terms of predisposing neurophysiological and biochemical factors, nor in terms of the psychogenic factors, such as lacunar character structure, that could possibly be part of a predisposition base. The difference between Hispanic addicts and non-Hispanic addicts obviously rests on sociocultural factors in which horizontal mobility (foreign or domestic migration) and/or vertical mobility (an upward or downward stress-producing move on the socioeconomic totem pole) play an important role. Added to acculturation, or a forced change of cultural values, this impinges upon the Hispanic's quality of life and affects essential areas such as health, education, housing, etc. This social whirlpool provokes a continuous, cumulative stress that is both precipitating and perpetuating, leading sometimes to escapism through the use and abuse of, or addiction to, controlled substances.

A view of one segment of the population of Hispanics, the Puerto Rican, is presented. Information about the efforts of a government agency to deal with substance abuse and addiction in Puerto Rico is offered.

The authors emphasize the relevancy of training in ethnicity and transculturality for non-Hispanic service deliverers who work with Hispanic clients, in order to make prevention and treatment programs more pragmatic, effective, and relevant.

References

1. Abrams, A., Gagnon, J. T., and Levin, J. J. Psychosocial aspects of addiction. Am. J. Public Health 58: 2142, 1968.
2. Arce, A. The Hispanic American. In *Cultural Issues*

in Contemporary Psychiatry (tape). Smith, Kline & French, 1978.

3. Arce, A. A., and Torres-Matrullo, C. Acculturation: Its impact on treatment strategies. Presented at special session "The Hispanic-American Family: Stress and Strengths", 131st American Psychiatric Association Annual Meeting, Atlanta, Georgia, May, 1978.

4. Ball, J. C. Onset of marijuana and heroin use among Puerto Rican addicts. Br. J. Criminol. 7:408, 1967.

5. Ball, J. C., and Bates, W. M. Migration and residential mobility of narcotic drug addicts. Soc. Prob. 14: 56, 1966.

6. Bernal y del Río, V. Imitation, identification, and identity (remarks on transcultural observations). The Herman Goldman International Lecture Series, New York Medical College, May 14, 1971.

7. Bernal y del Río, V. Ethnophobia and socio-cultural detoxification. Special lecture delivered at the Harvard School of Medicine, March, 1977.

8. Canino, I. A., and Canino-Stolberg, G. J. Impact of stress on the Puerto Rican family: Treatment considerations. Presented at special session "The Hispanic-American Family: Stress and Strengths." 131st American Psychiatric Association Annual Meeting, Atlanta, Georgia, May, 1978.

9. Cohen, R. Preventive mental health programs for ethnic minority populations: A case in point. Presented at the XXXIX Congreso Internacional de Americanistas, Lima, Perú. (Available from the Laboratory of Community Psychiatry, Harvard Medical School) August, 1970.

10. Crowther, B. Patterns of drug abuse among Mexican-Americans. Int. J. Addict. 7:633, 1972.

11. De Fleur, F. B. Biasing influences on drug arrest records: Implications for deviance research. Am. Sociol. Rev. 40:88, 1978.

12. Favazza, A. R., and Oman, M. Overview: Foundations of cultural psychiatry. Am. J. Psychiatry 135: 293, 1978.

13. García, C. S., and Roselló, J. *Estudios de la Magnitud del Problema de Drogas en Puerto Rico*. University of Puerto Rico School of Medicine, 1971.

14. Gómez, A. G. Service delivery in the Spanish-speaking community. Presented at Session VIII—Forum on "Delivery of Services to Minority Groups" at the Annual Meeting of the American Psychiatric Association, Anaheim, California, May, 1975.

15. Gómez, A. G. Some considerations in structuring human services for the Spanish speaking populations of the U. S. Int. J. Ment. Health 5:60, 1976.

16. Gómez, A. G. Sobre la multicausalidad del problema addicción-criminalidad. Lecture Series, Puerto Rico Department of Addiction Services, San Juan, 1977.

17. Gómez, A. G. Ethnicity and transculturality: Its relevancy in training personnel to work with clients with dependency disorders. Presented at the National Drug Abuse Conference, Seattle, Washington, April, 1978.

18. Gómez, A. G. Cultural aspects of the mental health care for Puerto Rican Americans. Workshop on Cultural Issues in Psychiatric Training, Boston University School of Medicine, Division of Psychiatry, Boston, April 18–19, 1979. To be published by the National Institute of Mental Health.

19. Gómez, A. G., and Silva, J. T. Mental health services to addict offenders in Puerto Rico. Presented at Session II, 130th Annual Meeting of the American Psychiatric Association, Toronto, Canada, May, 1977.

20. Halleck, S. *Psychiatry and the Dilemma of Crime*, pp. 51–83. Berkeley, University of California Press, 1971.

21. Heck, E. T., Gómez, A. G., and Adams, G. L. *A Guide to Mental Health Service*. Pittsburgh, University of Pittsburgh Press, 1973.

22. Helmer, J., and Vietorisz, T. *Drug Use, the Labor Market, and Class Conflict*. Washington, D. C., Drug Abuse Council, 1974.

23. Hunt, L. G. *Heroin Epidemics: A Quantitative Study: Current Empirical Data*. Washington, D. C., Drug Abuse Council, 1973.

24. Jiménez, R. The Hispanic American. In *Cultural Issues in Contemporary Psychiatry* (tape). Smith, Kline & French, 1978.

25. Johnson, B., and Nishi, S. M. Myths and realities of drug use by minorities. In *Drug Use and Abuse among U. S. Minorities*, P. Iiyama, S. M. Nishi, and B. Johnson, editors, pp. 3–68. New York, Praeger, 1976.

26. Kiev, A. Cultural perspectives on the range of normal behavior. In *Social Psychiatry*, vol. II: *The Range of Normal in Human Behavior*, J. M. Masserman, editor, pp. 37–41. New York, Grune & Stratton, 1976.

27. Lukoff, I., and Brook, J. A sociocultural exploration of reported heroin use. In *Sociological Aspects of Drug Dependence*, C. Winick, editor, pp. 35–56. Cleveland, Ohio, CRC Press, 1974.

28. Martínez, C. The Hispanic American. In *Cultural Issues in Contemporary Psychiatry* (tape). Smith, Kline & French, 1978.

29. National Institute on Drug Abuse. *Drugs and Minorities*. Research Issue #21. Washington, D. C., National Institute on Drug Abuse, 1978.

30. Negrón de Martin, I. *La Magnitud del Problema de la Addicción a Drogas en Puerto Rico*. San Juan, Comisión Permanente para el Control de la Narcomanía, 1972.

31. Nicoll, M. *The New Man*, part II. Baltimore, Penguin Books, 1973.

32. Rogers, C. R. *On Becoming a Person: A Therapist View of Psychotherapy*. Boston, Houghton Mifflin, 1961.

33. Ruiz, P. The Hispanic American. In *Cultural Issues in Contemporary Psychiatry* (tape). Smith, Kline & French, 1978.

34. Rumbaut, R. D. The Hispanic prologue. In *A Hispanic Look at the Bicentennial*, D. Cordus, editor, pp. 5–22. Houston, Institute of Hispanic Culture of Houston, 1978.

CHAPTER 58

WOMEN'S USE OF LICIT AND ILLICIT DRUGS

Jane E. Prather, Ph.D.

Women, unlike men, use and potentially abuse more legally available drugs than illegal drugs (17, 55, 58). The distinctions between legitimate and illegitimate drug use based upon source (prescription, forgery, street purchase) or upon purpose (medical or recreational) are not particularly useful when studying women's drug use. Anyone may misuse or abuse a prescription drug regardless of source or purpose. Such other factors as dosage, quantity, frequency, and interaction with other drugs become more important than source or purpose for studying drug problems. The difference between using a legally available drug for a medical or for a nonmedical purpose is also nondescriptive when applied to women. For example, to take a tranquilizer or a stimulant to "feel better" may incorporate medical as well as recreational use. Even the use of illegal drugs may have some medical or psychological overtones, as illustrated by female heroin users who stated that their first use of heroin was seeking "relief of personal disturbance" (10).

Men and women acquire different patterns of drug use. Men use heroin, lysergic acid diethylamide (LSD), and cocaine more than women and claim more recreational use of sedatives, stimulants, and tranquilizers than women. Marihuana use is higher among men than women, although the sex difference declines among youth (76). Women use more prescription and other over-the-counter analgesics and psychotropics than men (58, 73). Even though more men are involved in illicit drug use than women, this does not mean that women have fewer drug problems. The percentage of women using licit drugs is higher than the percentage of men using illicit drugs.

Hence, the "at risk population" susceptible to drug problems is much higher among women than men. In addition, the number of victims reporting to emergency rooms for drug problems is higher among women than men (59).

As will be discussed, the problems and issues women encounter with licit and illicit drugs are quite different; consequently, this chapter will be divided into two sections—licit and illicit drugs.

LICIT DRUGS

Licit drugs in this discussion refer to any drug that is legally available either by prescription or over-the-counter purchase. This section includes all licit drugs, although the discussion will focus on psychotropic drugs because of their high potential for abuse, dependency, and harmful effects.

During the past decade the use of prescription psychotropics (sedative-hypnotics, stimulants, antidepressants, and minor tranquilizers) by Americans has increased. The use of stimulants and sedatives for the past 5 years seems to have stabilized and slightly decreased, whereas the number of Americans (adults 18 and over) reporting ever having used minor tranquilizers for medical purposes increased from 24 per cent in 1972 to 35 per cent in 1977 (58). The use of one kind of minor tranquilizer, diazepam (Valium), is so popular that this drug has become the most widely prescribed drug in the United States (4, 11). Twice as many women as men use psychotropic medications. For example, 42 per cent of women in the national survey reported having ever used prescription tranquilizers, contrasted with 27 per cent of the men (58). More than one in every five women in the United States stated they had used a prescription tranquilizer in the past year, as contrasted to one in 10 American men (58). Twice as many women as men have been found to be frequent users of psychotropics (taking a psychotropic drug daily for at least 2 months) (51).

Teenagers seem to model adult drug behavior. More teenage girls than teenage boys state they have used sedatives and tranquilizers (79). If mothers used psychotropics, they increased the probability of their daughters using psychotropics (13). Even aspirin usage is higher among young women than men (44).

Scientists (17, 25, 62, 71) differ in their interpretation of psychotropic drug use as being cause for concern. One group views American society as "overmedicated," whereas the other argues that it is "undermedicated." Scientists taking the overmedicated position point to such factors as: amount of drugs being manufactured versus the number being prescribed, the intense market competition among pharmaceutical companies, the large amount of money spent on advertising psychotropic drugs, and the increase in adverse drug reactions. Other scientists raise questions about the use of psychotropics for relief of everyday stress symptoms (45). Even though psychotropics can provide temporary relief of these symptoms, the drugs may actually hinder the user's exploration of effective solutions to prevent stress-provoking situations.

Scientists assuming the undermedicated position emphasize that few Americans use psychotropics frequently. They refer to evidence that only 5 per cent of the men and 10 per cent of the women use psychotropics on a daily basis for at least 2 months (55). These scientists also argue that the American public holds stoic attitudes toward psychotropic drug usage. For example, in a national survey 85 per cent of the respondents thought will power was a better way of solving problems than tranquilizers (50).

Why women use more psychotropics and analgesics than men or why physicians prescribe more of these drugs to women than men remains speculative. One theory suggests that psychotropic drugs are labeled as feminine because women's assumed emotional make-up is more susceptible to problems that psychotropics can allieviate. Admitting one has such symptoms as nervousness, insomnia, or despair becomes associated with weakness, hence, matching society's stereotype that women are physically and emotionally weaker than men. Women more often than men describe their health in emotional or psychological terms and admit experiencing various psychological symptoms (55). Women also describe more painful conditions than men (16). In American culture women are allowed—if not encouraged—to complain about being under mild psychic distress, whereas men are strongly sanctioned for disclosing any such emotional symptoms (17). Men learn to avoid revealing signs of nervousness, anxiety, or depression. During states of pregnancy, childbirth, menstruation, and menopause women are presumed to suffer psychological as well as physical symptoms. Over-the-counter medications have been specially created and advertised to aid women during these periods (56).

Another explanation for the sex difference in psychotropic usage relates to changes in women's roles. According to this perspective, women may be experiencing stress (8, 33, 48) as they move away from traditional roles. Although men may be suffering poor health because of the demands of their traditional male role (26, 30, 36), the feminine label attached to psychotropic drugs indicates women would be attracted to their use, whereas men would avoid these medications.

Still another interpretation of women's greater use of psychotropics is that these drugs provide relief for symptoms caused by the unequal social status of the sexes (79).

Drug taking, according to this theory, represents a political act. The drugs suppress the symptoms caused by the unequal status but do not alleviate the underlying causes; thus, the drugs help perpetuate the unequal sex roles (79).

Finally, there are theories that women receive more prescriptions for psychotropics because of physicians' attitudes toward female patients. In one study (19) physicians' perceptions of male and female patients' symptoms influenced their prescribing behavior. Even though women made more physician visits than men, the significant variable for explaining sex differences in prescriptions was the physicians' perceptions of patients' symptoms. There is also evidence that physicians are more likely to ignore women's symptoms and consider them as complaints rather than legitimate symptoms (2). Similarly, physicians often label female patients as hypochondriacs or hysterical (69) or have stereotypes that housewives are bored and frustrated (9, 78). All such cases might encourage the physician to write a psychotropic prescription (25).

SOURCE OF LICIT DRUGS

Regardless of the reasons women give for using licit drugs (even for recreational purposes), most women rely upon a physician as their drug source (14, 54). Even though the prescription psychotropics are listed as Controlled Substances according to the Drug Control Act of 1970 (most stimulants and sedatives are Schedule II; minor tranquilizers are Schedule IV), most drug users report little difficulty in obtaining prescriptions for psychotropics. The majority of users report the general practitioner as their initial source for licit drugs (18, 51), even if the user develops additional sources for psychotropics as dependency increases (14).

The significance of obtaining a psychotropic drug via a prescription is 2-fold. First, prescription psychotropic users tend to use psychotropics for a longer period of time, more consistently, and more frequently than users who had to resort to other sources (54). Second, the use of psychotropic drugs obtained from a physician's prescription is likely to be perceived by the user and her family and friends as legitimate and, therefore, necessary.

Physicians unwittingly contribute to women's drug problems because of their limited information about licit drugs; their use of prescription writing as a means of coping with patients; and their perpetuation of drug dependency through multiple and refill prescribing practices. Each of these areas will be discussed.

Although psychotropic medications have been on the market for approximately 20 years, physicians may have limited knowledge about these drugs (32, 81). New drugs appear each year. Medical schools rarely provide extensive training in psychopharmacology (7), with some medical students receiving less than 6 hours' training in psychopharmacology (64). General practitioners, the specialists who write the most prescriptions for psychotropic drugs, report their major source of drug information comes from pharmaceutical company detailmen (40, 68). Detailmen spend more time with general practitioners than any other specialists (61). The amount of time all physicians spend per week discussing drugs with detailmen has been steadily increasing (7). Most physicians claim the *Physicians Desk Reference* (PDR) is their most valuable source of drug information (64). Drug advertisements in medical journals comprise another important source of drug information (68). These advertisements have been strongly criticized for their encouragement of psychotropic use for relieving tension of everyday life (45) and for their stereotypical portrayal of women needing psychotropic medications to relieve nervous tension (56, 67, 70, 71). All these sources—PDR, ads, detailmen—are sponsored by pharmaceutical companies.

Research indicates that physicians write prescriptions for drugs when they have difficulty relating to a patient (12), when they are pessimistic about other treatment (72), or when they perceive the patient described only vague symptoms (12). Physicians who tend *not* to write prescriptions for psychotropics are those with advanced medical training and those who perceive the patient as a whole entity (41). Physicians claim it is easier to prescribe a psychotropic than to explain why they will not write the prescription (64). Writing the prescription can also be a means of terminating an office visit—a tangible act satisfying both physician and patient that some service was performed (57).

Lastly, the physician can contribute to the potential for psychotropic misuse-abuse through multiple prescribing, prescribing excessive dosages, or continuously refilling prescriptions (52, 53). Multiple prescribing occurs when a patient receives a variety of psychotropic prescriptions from one or several physicians. The situation is compounded if the various involved physicians fail to verify whether or not the patient has received other prescriptions for psychotropics or if the patient conceals such information from the physicians. The potential for overuse, drug dependence, or drug interactions increases with multiple prescribing.

Prescribing excessive dosages occurs when the physician orders a prescription larger in quantity or dosage than what might ordinarily be considered safe or than what might be required for the patient. This practice is not uncommon among physicians and occurs most frequently with psychotropic drugs (52).

Repeat or refill prescriptions have the potential for drug dependency if the patient continues to seek and the physician continues to grant a refill without verification that the medication is indeed still required. Psychotropic refills represent a special problem, because the possibility of dependency occurring increases as the need for stronger dosages increases with continuous and prolonged usage. The physician feels he or she cannot refuse the request without offering the patient some other viable alternative (6).

SPECIAL ISSUE: DRUG SAFETY

The safety of licit drugs is often difficult to ascertain. Drugs placed on the market as innocuous may later prove to have serious side effects or difficulties that only emerge after prolonged usage or after a history of use with a variety of individuals. Newly introduced psychotropics and analgesics are continually subject to this "safety" problem.

Drug safety is first ascertained through controlled experiments involving animals and/or humans. Controlled experiments can measure physiological tolerance of drugs and measure "safety margins"; however, experiments do not take into account the behavioristic or human factors that affect usage. The patient ingesting a psychotropic drug rarely uses it as precisely or methodically as the subject in the controlled experiment. Other factors may affect the "safety" of the drug, such as the patient's health, nutritional patterns, fatigue level, use of other medications, consumption of alcohol, etc. Thus, to assert a drug as "safe" based upon controlled experiments can be misleading.

Of all the psychotropics, the minor tranquilizers have the reputation of being the safest or least harmful of these drugs. One minor tranquilizer, diazepam (Valium), in particular has been labeled as safe by the general public as well as the medical community (49). Even the American Medical Association (AMA) (in its publication *Drug Evaluations*) refers to the safety of diazepam and concludes (1): "Indeed the wide margin of safety of benzodiazepines virtually precludes their successful use for suicidal purposes."

In spite of the AMA's conclusion, diazepam was the drug most frequently mentioned by individuals reporting to emergency rooms for drug problems in the United States, with women constituting 67 per cent of the victims (59, 60).

In summary, to understand women's use of licit drugs, especially the psychotropics, involves comprehending women's beliefs in their own weakness or nervousness and comprehending physicians' stereotypes about emotionally distressed female patients. In addition, studying licit drug use in this society encompasses an investigation of the extensive influence of pharmaceutical companies upon physicians through such means as medical advertisements, detailmen, and the *Physician's Desk Reference* (64). Finally, examining licit drug problems entails describing the processes of establishing drug safety.

The victim in licit drug use is most often a woman. The woman who abuses legal drugs poses a difficult problem for treatment centers. Neither she nor her family usually defines her problems as drug abuse. Most likely to be Caucasian and middle class, she does not find traditional treatment programs appealing. Her first attempt for treatment may be directed toward her personal physician, who may have been the original source of her drugs. Just as he may not have sufficient expertise in recognizing drug problems, he is rarely trained to treat these problems. Not infrequently, the woman continues her drug use for years before obtaining treatment.

ILLICIT DRUGS[1]

Statistics on the number of illicit drug users identified by sex and drug category are almost nonexistent. Most research on illicit drug use focuses only upon men, and funds for research or treatment for women have been limited (28, 80). What data are available on female use of illicit drugs usually concern only heroin users. Consequently, most of the information in this section is derived from studies of women using heroin; however, the data can be generalized to women who use other illicit drugs because most drug users are poly users.

Information about users of illicit drugs usually comes from two sources—research from treatment centers or surveys of drug prevalence among various populations. Both sources offer limited information. Data from treatment populations are subject to bias according to the kinds of users attracted to each treatment center. Survey data often do not capture sufficient female drug users in all demographic categories to provide relevant data.

In recent years there has been an increased concern about the lack of drug treatment facilities for women and the lack of research on women and drugs (28, 79). Two factors have stimulated this interest. One factor is evidence that opiate use has increased among women at a greater rate than among men (37). Second, research now indicates that among teens and young adults sex differences in illicit drug use seem to be diminishing (76). For example, among youth sampled in a national survey women were just as likely to have used phencyclidine as men (65). In a New York survey of state treatment centers, boys and girls did not significantly differ in use of inhalants (77).

Sex differences are most pronounced among heroin and cocaine users, although the number of female users of these drugs is also increasing. Among heroin users one-fourth of the users are women, and women comprise 20 to 25 per cent (28) of all users in treatment programs. Similarly, estimates of cocaine abuse derived from the National In-stitute on Drug Abuse Client Oriented Data Acquisition Process (CODAP) data suggest that approximately one-fourth of all cocaine users in treatment are women (75).

Even though the numbers of women using illicit drugs seem small in contrast to men, there are indications that, as women continue to gain social equality with men, women will adopt independent if not rebellious life styles that would include recreational use of illicit drugs (74).

Women using illicit drugs come from different backgrounds than licit drug users. Illicit drug users have a high probability of being from a working class or lower class background (15, 24), whereas licit users represent the middle class with middle incomes (47). Although female illicit users are usually Caucasian, there are larger percentages of minority women among illicit drug than licit drug users (23). The woman using illicit drugs usually has less education than the woman using licit drugs. Not infrequently, the illicit drug user has dropped out of high school, (15, 24), whereas the licit drug user has attended some college (66). A typical woman using licit drugs is in her thirties (66); the illicit drug user is in her twenties (24). Whereas licit drug users obtain economic support for their drug use through legitimate jobs or through their husband's income; users of illicit drugs rely upon prostitution and such criminal activities as shoplifting, forgery, and drug sales (20, 39).

Women who use illicit drugs often use licit drugs, too, but the reverse does not usually occur. Illicit drug users begin drug use with licit or quasilicit drugs. Black women, for example, reported using marihuana as their first drug, whereas Caucasian women selected legally available psychotropic drugs (15).

In contrast to women using licit drugs, women involved with illicit drugs have very traditional and conservative attitudes toward women's roles, political issues, abortion, and sexual behavior (5).

DRUG SOURCES

The relationships of men and women using illicit drugs are complex and interdependent. Men usually initiate women into illicit drug use, but the reverse situation rarely occurs (23, 43). Women take drugs in settings where

---

[1] Marihuana is not included as an illicit drug in this chapter because this author perceives the increased social acceptance of marihuana as placing it in the same category as tobacco and alcohol.

both men and women are present, whereas men use drugs most often in male-only settings. Among needle freaks, women usually receive injections from a man, whereas men inject themselves (38).

Women, in contrast to men, frequently receive their drugs as gifts from a male companion rather than having to purchase them (23, 43). Similarly, women will receive money from a spouse to support their drug habit, whereas men most often resort to pushing, dealing, or stealing drugs (23). Engaging in criminal activities to support a drug habit is common for both men and women, with some research indicating that there is no significant sex difference in the tendency to turn to crime to provide money for drugs (23).

Research on the relationship between prostitution and drugs indicates that approximately 40 per cent of all female users support their drug habit through prostitution (15) (with some estimates also ranging as high as 70 per cent) (20). Most illicit users who use prostitution for drug support claim they only turned to prostitution after becoming addicted (23). Minority women are much more likely to participate in illegal activities, particularly prostitution, to support their drug habits than Caucasian users (83). Perhaps white women (particularly young and attractive ones) are more likely to have high status in both black, Caucasian, or mixed racial groups and, hence, can rely upon others—such as male companions—for their drugs rather than hustling to support their habit.

Men and women develop interdependent relationships in the drug subculture. The women who hustle frequently have to depend upon men for protection from other men and gangs. The man may serve as her pimp or the seller of her stolen goods. Women protect men by assisting them hustling by being a decoy, lookout, or driver. Women are able to serve as accomplices in these situations because police are reluctant to search a female suspect for drugs or stolen items (27, 83).

The drug subculture provides women with male companionship and acceptance that may have been absent in their lives. Women involved in illicit drug subcultures report very low self-esteem (31), low impressions of their sexual attractiveness (21), and a high rate of incest and sexual abuse as girls (39). Women, in contrast to men, are more likely

to be married and, hence, supported by a spouse who is also an addict (28).

An ethnographic study (27) revealed that in the drug subculture women emulate roles played by men. Women who achieve the highest status, like the high status men, sell or deal in drugs. Although there are a few independent female dealers and lesbian dealerships, most women attach themselves to a male dealer. Next in prestige is the role of bag follower. Usually an attractive, Caucasian woman, the bag follower transports drugs from the dealer to the customer. The bag follower, like a rock star groupie, has high status among both males and females as long as she maintains her favored position with the male dealer. The most common role for women using illicit drugs is the hustler, who engages in prostitution or such criminal activities as shoplifting or burglary. Hustlers have less status than dealers or bag followers but have more status than workers or dependents, who maintain a marginal status to the drug culture. Among hustlers are those who only engage in prostitution, others who only participate in criminal activities, and still others who take part in prostitution and criminal activities. Women, however, do not permanently occupy any of these roles, but instead flow in and out of them.

SPECIAL ISSUES: PREGNANCY AND TREATMENT

Women who use any kind of drugs during pregnancy may encounter drug problems. A recent survey found that pregnant women used an average of 4.5 drugs during their pregnancy, 80 per cent of which were self-prescribed. In these women drug intake correlated with congenital abnormalities (34).

Women using illicit drugs face even more difficulties during pregnancy than women using licit drugs. The illicit drug user is less likely to be in the care of a physician than the licit drug user and more likely to be having a pregnancy that is unplanned and perhaps undesired. Illicit drug users often neglect their general health care and avoid seeking early prenatal care (28). In addition to poor maternal nutrition, illicit users abuse or overuse tobacco and alcohol (29). Infants born from illicit drug users show body growth retardation—small body weight, short length, and small head circumference

(84). Infants of drug-dependent mothers show a higher rate of mortality (29) and increased probability of being born prematurely (29) and are more likely to be multiple births (42). Use of methadone to control heroin addiction reduces problems in pregnancy as well as increases the mother's interest in her health (84).

Drug-dependent women seeking treatment encounter enumerable problems, because most treatment centers do not have the services, counselors, or knowledge for handling female clients (22, 28, 46). For example, women in one treatment center stated they did not want to have any more children, yet they were not currently using effective contraceptive techniques, even though the women knew birth control services were available (23). The importance of motherhood for women with poor self-concepts cannot be underestimated. Children provide a stable influence upon a woman in treatment, at the same time creating a source of anxiety about their adequate care (23). Few treatment centers have provisions for child care, leaving the mother the option of relinquishing custody of her children to agencies or relatives.

Treatment centers either ignore women's needs for job training and placement or else provide a highly stereotyped training for jobs such as domestic or laundry workers (46). The women least responsive to treatment have intensive involvements in criminal activities (82) or live with and, hence, are supported by male addicts (23). The most successful women in treatment have strong self-concepts (3). These findings suggest women need job training, assertion skills, and general coping skills. Perhaps most importantly, drug-dependent women need skills in dealing with men in their lives (28), particularly if they have been subjected to physical or sexual abuse and have developed partnerships with men in the drug subculture.

Considering the multitude of problems women in treatment face—including sexual abuse by the male staff (63)—it is not surprising that fewer women than men enter treatment and that women have a lower retention rate and a lower success rate than men (46).

In conclusion, women taking licit drugs and women using illicit drugs represent different social classes, different familial backgrounds, different ages, and frequently different racial or ethnic heritages. Nevertheless, they face similar drug problems. An analysis of these similarities reveals three crucial issues that merit continued discussion and investigation.

First, there is a need for awareness that women, like men, are victims of drug abuse. The common stereotype of a typical drug abuser is that of a lower class, minority male youth. Most scientific research and drug treatment programs focus on this model. There is, however, a critical need for research on female drug abusers and treatment modalities for women. Although fewer women than men are involved in illicit drug use, the sex differences are declining among younger populations. Of special importance is the large number of women who use licit psychotropic drugs or use these drugs in combination with alcohol. The percentage of women using licit drugs far exceeds the number of men using illicit drugs, indicating the potential for drug problems among women is very high. To illustrate, the number of times women mentioned two popular tranquilizers (Valium and Librium) as causing an emergency room crisis was three times greater than the number of times men mentioned heroin as causing emergency treatment (59).

Second, drug use among women, whether licit or illicit, is related to women's relationships with men. (Note, the converse is not necessarily true: men's drug problems are not usually associated with their relationships with women.) Both licit and illicit drug users usually receive initiation into drug use and receive reinforcement for continual drug dependency from men. The licit drug user obtains prescriptions for drugs from physicians (the majority of whom are male in the United States), and the illicit drug users identify male partners as their major suppliers. Both licit and illicit female users have accepted characteristics of feminine stereotypes. The illicit user exhibits low self-esteem and admits poor relationships with men. Using drugs for her becomes a means of gaining approval of others and affection from men. The licit user identifies with the stereotype that women are nervous, emotional, and suffer from diffuse symptoms that psychotropics can relieve. In both cases, gender role expectations reinforce drug use.

Third, drug treatment programs for women

encompass different treatment tasks than for men. To enter treatment, women using illicit drugs may have to break off two important relationships—a relationship with an addict husband or boyfriend and a relationship with her child, whose custody she may lose. To obtain treatment, the female licit drug user has to recognize that she has a drug problem, which may include confronting her physician concerning her drug or her drug and alcohol use. In either case, successful drug treatment focuses on issues that at first glance seem indirectly related to drug abuse, such as birth control, child care, financial independence, sexual abuse, self-assertion, health, and perhaps even beauty care, and consumer protection. Treating a woman often means the agency is involved with treating others—her children, her husband or lover, her physician, and even future generations.

References

1. American Medical Association. *Drug Evaluations.* Chicago, American Medical Association, 1977.
2. Armitage, K. J., Schneiderman, L. J., and Bass, R. A. Response of physicians to medical complaints in men and women. J.A.M.A. 241:2186, 1979.
3. Aron, W. S., and Daily, D. W. Graduates and splitees from therapeutic community treatment programs: A comparison. Int. J. Addict. 11:1, 1976.
4. Backenheimer, M. Valium and Librium: Use and risk. Presented at the Drugs, Alcohol and Women Conference, Miami Beach, 1975.
5. Baldinger, R., Capel, W. C., Goldsmith, B. M., and Stewart, G. T. Pot smokers, junkies and squares: A comparative study of female values. Int. J. Addict. 7: 153, 1972.
6. Baliant, M. Conclusions: What can be done? In *Treatment of Diagnosis: A Study of Repeat Prescriptions in General Practice*, M. Balint, J. Hunt, D. Joyce, M. Marinker, and J. Woodcock, editors. London, Tavistock, 1970.
7. Bauer, R. A., and Wortzel, L. H. Doctor's choice: The physician and his sources of information about drugs. J. Marketing Res. 3:40, 1966.
8. Bernard, J. *The Future of Marriage.* New York, World Press, 1975.
9. Brahen, L. Housewife drug abuse. J. Drug Educ. 3: 13, 1973.
10. Brown, B. S., Gauvey, S. K., Meyers, M. B., and Stark, S. D. In their own words: Addicts' reasons for initiating and withdrawing from heroin. Int. J. Addict. 6:635, 1971.
11. Cant, G. Valiumania. The New York Times Magazine 33, February 1, 1976.
12. Cartwright, A. Prescribing and the relationship between patients and doctors. In *Social Aspects of the Medical Use of Psychotropic Drugs*, R. Cooperstock, editor. Toronto, Addiction Research Foundation, 1974.
13. Chambers, C. P. The use and abuse of licit drugs in rural families. Addict. Dis., In press.
14. Chambers, C., Brill, L., and Inciardi, J. A. Barbiturate use, misuse and abuse. J. Drug Issues 2:15, 1972.
15. Chambers, C., Hinesley, R. K., and Moldestad, M. Narcotic addiction in females: A race comparison. Int. J. Addict. 5:257, 1970.
16. Christie, D. The analgesic abuse syndrome. Int. J. Epidemiol. 7:139, 1978.
17. Cooperstock, R. Sex differences in the use of mood-modifying drugs: An explanatory model. J. Health Soc. Behav. 12:238, 1971.
18. Cooperstock, R. Some factors involved in the increased prescribing of psychotropic drugs. In *Social Aspects of the Medical Use of Psychotropic Drugs.* R. Cooperstock, editor. Toronto, Addiction Research Foundation, 1974.
19. Cooperstock, R. Psychotropic drug use among women. Can. Med. Assoc. J. 115:760, 1976.
20. Cushman, P. Methadone maintenance treatment of narcotic addiction: Analysis of police records of arrest before and after treatment. N. Y. State J. Med. 72:1752, 1972.
21. Densen-Gerber, J., Wiener, M. and Hockstedler, R. Sexual behavior, abortion and birth control in heroin addicts: Legal and psychiatric considerations. Contemp. Drug Prob. 1:783, 1972.
22. Doyle, K. M., Quinones, M. A., Tracy, G., Young, D., and Hughes, J. Restructuring rehabilitation for women: Programs for the female drug addict. Am. J. Psychiatry 134:1395, 1977.
23. Eldred, C., and Washington, M. Interpersonal relationships in heroin use by men and women and their role in treatment outcome. Int. J. Addict. 11:117, 1976.
24. Ellinwood, E. H., Smith, W. G., and Vaillant, G. E. Narcotic addition in males and females: A comparison. Int. J. Addict. 1:33, 1966.
25. Enelow, A. *The Two-edged Sword of Psychotropic Drugs.* Medical Insight Reprint. New York, Insight Publishing Company, 1970.
26. Fasteau, M. *The Male Machine.* New York, Dell, 1975.
27. File, K. H. Sex roles and street roles. Int. J. Addict. 11:263, 1976.
28. Finnegan, L. P. Women in treatment. In *Handbook of Drug Abuse*, R. I. Dupont, A. Goldstein, and J. O'Donnell, editors. Rockville, National Institute on Drug Abuse, 1979.
29. Fricker, H. S., and Segal, S. Narcotic addiction, pregnancy and the newborn. Am. J. Dis. Child. 132: 360, 1978.
30. Goldberg, H. *The Hazards of Being Male.* New York, Nash, 1976.
31. Gossop, M. Drug dependence and self esteem. Int. J. Addict. 11:741, 1976.
32. Gottlieb, R., Nappi, T., and Strain, J. The physician's knowledge of psychotropic drugs: Preliminary results. Am. J. Psychiatry 135:29, 1978.
33. Gove, W., and Tudor, J. F. Adult sex roles and mental illness. Am. J. Sociol. 78:812, 1973.
34. Guillozet, N. Drug risks in pregnancy revisited. J. Fam. Pract. 4:1043, 1977.
35. Hargraves, R. Introduction. J. Drug Issues 6:1, 1976.
36. Harrison, J. Warning: The male sex role may be

dangerous to your health. J. Soc. Issues 34:65, 1978.

37. Hoover, J. E. *Crime in the United States.* Uniform Crime Reports. Washington, D. C., United States Government Printing Office, 1973.

38. Howard, J., and Borges, P. Needle sharing in the Haight: Some social and psychological functions. J. Health Soc. Behav. 11:220, 1970.

39. James, J., Gosho, C., and Wohl, R. The relationship between female criminality and drug use. Int. J. Addict. 14:215, 1979.

40. Johnson, D. A. W. The psychiatric side effects of drugs. Practitioner 209:320, 1972.

41. Joyce, C. R., Lost, B., and Weatherall, M. Personal factors as a cause of differences in prescribing general practitioners. Br. J. Prevent. Soc. Med. 21:170, 1967.

42. Kementeria, J. L., Janakammal, S., and Hollander, M. Multiple births in drug addicted women. Am. J. Obstet. Gynecol. 122:958, 1975.

43. Klinge, V., Vaziri, J., and Lennox, K. Comparison of psychiatric inpatient male and female adolescent drug abusers. Int. J. Addict. 11:309, 1976.

44. Krupka, L. R., et al. Patterns of aspirin use among American youth. Int. J. Addict. 13:911, 1978.

45. Lennard, H. L., Epstein, L. J., Bernstein, A., and Ransom, D. C. *Mystification and Drug Misuse.* San Francisco, Jossey-Bass, 1971.

46. Levy, S., and Doyle, K. Attitudes towards women in a drug abuse treatment program. J. Drug Issues 4: 428, 1974.

47. Linn, L. S., and Davis, M. S. The use of psychotherapeutic drugs by middle aged women. J. Health Soc. Behav. 12:331, 1971.

48. Lipman-Blumen, J. Changing social conditions with implications for researchable problems in women's health. Presented at Conference on Women and Health, University of California Medical Center, San Francisco, 1975.

49. Maletzky, B., and Klotter, J. Addiction to diazepam. Int. J. Addict. 11:95, 1976.

50. Manheimer, D., et al. Popular attitudes and beliefs about tranquilizers. Am. J. Psychiatry 130:1246, 1973.

51. Manheimer, D., Mellinger, G., and Balter, M. Psychotherapeutic drugs. Calif. Med. 109:445, 1968.

52. Maronde, R., Lee, P. V., McCarron, M., and Seibert, S. A study of prescribing patterns. Med. Care 9:383, 1971.

53. Maronde, R., Seibert, S., Katzoff, J., and Silverman, M. Prescription data processing—its role in the control of drug abuse. Calif. Med. 117:22, 1972.

54. Mellinger, G. D., Balter, M. B., and Manheimer, D. I. Patterns of psychotherapeutic drug use among adults in San Francisco. Arch. Gen. Psychiatry 25: 385, 1971.

55. Mellinger, G. D., Balter, M. B., Parry, J., Manheimer, D., and Cisin, I. An overview of psychotherapeutic drug use in the United States. In *Drug Use: Epidemiological and Sociological Approaches,* E. Josephson and E. Carroll, editors. New York, Hemisphere Publishers, 1974.

56. Mosher, E. H. Portrayal of women in drug advertising: A medical betrayal. J. Drug Issues 6:72, 1976.

57. Muller, C. The overmedicated society: Forces in the marketplace for medical care. Science 16:488, 1972.

58. National Institute on Drug Abuse. *National Survey on Drug Abuse.* Rockville, Md., National Institute on Drug Abuse, 1977.

59. National Institute on Drug Abuse. *Drug Abuse Warning Network.* Prepared by IMS America. Rockville, Md., National Institute on Drug Abuse, 1978.

60. National Institute on Drug Abuse. Top 26 problem drugs in the United States. In *Capsules.* Rockville, Md., National Institute on Drug Abuse, May, 1978.

61. Nelson, G. Advertising and the national health. J. Drug Issues 6:28, 1976.

62. Parish, P. Drug prescribing—the concern of all. R. Soc. Health J. 4:213, 1973.

63. Peak, J. The female patient as booty. In *Developments in the Field of Drug Abuse,* E. Senay, V. Shorty, and H. Alksne, editors. Cambridge, Mass., Schenkman, 1975.

64. Pekkanen, J. The impact of promotion on physicians: Prescribing patterns. J. Drug Issues 6:13, 1976.

65. Petersen, R. C., and Stillman, R. C. Phencyclidine: An overview. In *Phencyclidine Abuse: An Appraisal,* R. C. Petersen and R. C. Stillman, editors. Rockville, Md., National Institute on Drug Abuse, 1978.

66. Prather, J. Socio-psychological characteristics of minor tranquilizers users. Presented at the Pacific Sociological Association Annual Meeting, Sacramento, 1977.

67. Prather, J., and Fidell, L. Sex differences in the content and style of medical advertisements. Soc. Sci. Med. 9:23, 1975.

68. Reinstein, P. A regulator's perception of drug advertising. J. Drug Issues 6:60, 1976.

69. Schmidt, D. D., and Messner, E. The female hysterical personality disorder. J. Fam. Pract. 4:573, 1977.

70. Seidenberg, R. Advertising and abuse of drugs. N. Engl. J. Med. 284:789, 1971.

71. Seidenberg, R. Images of health, illness and women in drug advertising. J. Drug Issues 264, 1974.

72. Shader, R. I., Binstock, W. A., and Scott, D. Subjective determinants of drug prescription: A study of therapists' attitudes. Hosp. Community Psychiatry 19:384, 1968.

73. Shapiro, S., and Baron, S. Prescriptions for psychotropic drugs in a noninstitutional population. Public Health Rep. 76:481, 1961.

74. Sheffet, A., Hickey, R. F., Duval, H., Millman, S., and Louria, D. A model for drug abuse treatment program evaluation. Prev. Med. 2:510, 1973.

75. Siguel, E. Characteristics of clients admitted to treatment for cocaine abuse. In *Cocaine: 1977,* R. C. Petersen and R. C. Stillman, editors, NIDA Research Monograph 13. Rockville, Md., National Institute on Drug Abuse, 1977.

76. Smith, B. D., and Nacev, V. Drug usage as determined under conditions of anonymity and high questionnaire return rate. Int. J. Addict. 13:725, 1978.

77. Stephens, R. C., et al. Sniffing from Suffolk to Syracuse: Report of youthful solvent use in New York State. In *Voluntary Inhalation of Industrial Solvents,* C. W. Sharp and L. T. Carroll, editors. Rockville, Md., National Institute on Drug Abuse, 1978.

78. Stimson, G. Women in a doctored world. New Soc. 32:265, 1975.

79. Suffet, F., and Brotman, R. Female drug use: Some

observations. Int. J. Addict. 11:19, 1976.

80. Valentine, N. M. Women and drug abuse: A bibliography. Nurs. Clin. North Am. 11:559, 1976.

81. Weiner, J., and Schumacher, G. D. Psychotropic drug therapy knowledge of health care practitioners. Am. J. Hosp. Pharmacol. 33:237, 1976.

82. Weipert, G. D., D'Orban, P. T., and Bewley, T. H. Delinquency by opiate addicts treated at two London clinics. Br. J. Psychiatry 134:14, 1979.

83. Weissman, J. C., and File, F. Criminal behavior patterns of female addicts: A comparison of findings in two cities. Int. J. Addict. 11:1063, 1976.

84. Wilson, G. S. Somatic growth effects of perinatal addiction. Addict. Dis. 2:333, 1975.

85. Woody, G. E., O'Brien, C. P., and Greenstein, R. Misuse and abuse of diazepam: An increasingly common medical problem. Int. J. Addict. 10:843, 1975.

CHAPTER 59

ADOLESCENCE AND SUBSTANCE ABUSE

Robert B. Millman, M.D.

Elizabeth T. Khuri, M.D.

Adolescence is a time of intense change and turmoil that occurs incident to unique psychobiological, cultural, and economic realities. Individuals progress from the safety and insularity of childhood to an appreciation of their relationship to an adult world, with its responsibilities, pleasures, and pain. It is during these years that most people begin to use psychoactive substances (1).

Few adolescents believe that they will measure up to the demands of society; they lack an adult identity and often feel powerless. They are told that this is a critical period of preparation and not to be lived for its own sake, but they have a realistic and pervasive dread of the future. Testing and experimentation are an integral part of the young person's search to discover himself and his society and to progress from the dependence of childhood to the independence of maturity. At the same time, the rules of behavior remain those of the adult world, with curiosity, spontaneity, enthusiasm, and initiative frequently mistaken for impulsiveness or aggressiveness. The societal institutions the adolescent must relate to, including the family and particularly the educational system, are often unresponsive or hostile. Given these pressures, the inability of some adolescents

to focus on long range goals, their desire for immediate gratification, and their lack of appreciation for the consequences of behavior are not surprising (7, 17, 44).

It is a period of emotional upheaval marked by intense yearnings for praise and approval and a wish for an idealized supportive relationship. Narcissistic crises—in which self-esteem is severely impaired, with resultant shame, rage, and despair—are common (41, 64). Peer affiliation and acceptance are crucial for the adolescents' sense of self. They need to compare what they feel they are to what they seem to be in the eyes of others, although many of them do not have the necessary confidence or experience to develop productive relationships (17). In addition to drugs, early sexual activity is considered to be a source of pride and pleasure. Yet many of these ill prepared young people find these experiences to be unsatisfactory and a source of intense anxiety and further demoralization (46).

Poverty, minority group status, or physical, psychological, or intellectual disability compound the problems of being young and further reduce the enjoyment, sense of dignity, uniqueness, and power of the adolescent in the "straight" world. Familial supports are critical to these deprived young people, yet families are often in disarray. Successful role models in adult legitimate society are often unknown or distant. Many of these youngsters, particularly those who live in inner-city ghettos, acquire an enormous and sophisticated range of survival skills on the street. They may be intelligent and highly perceptive judges of people and situations (52). Yet they are often unprepared for the educational system and find classes boring, irrelevant, and frequently demeaning. A sense of hopelessness, resentment, and inevitable failure may frequently result from these conditions (7, 44). In this context, the self-administration of psychoactive substances remains one of the few pleasurable options for many adolescents; it may be a predictable, reliable method by which to punctuate an otherwise unrewarding life. The youthful drug taker may obtain peer acceptance and a pharmacological effect that enhances self-esteem and relieves tension and anxiety (46, 62, 63).

PATTERNS OF USE AND ABUSE

Young people are most often introduced or "turned on" to the various drugs by a close friend or, in the case of alcohol, by a relative (6, 25). Initial intentions may be to share an exciting or pleasurable experience or diffuse some of the shame or guilt associated with drug taking. The behaviors may then become a focus for group interaction and identity (30). Most of these youngsters believe themselves able to control their drug taking so that it will not be personally destructive, despite the warnings of parents, media, and school authorities as to the dangers of drug use. In fact, they are often personally familiar with victims of this behavior. In most cases they are right; the drugs are less destructive to them than they have been led to believe (46, 55, 66).

Early drug experiences primarily reflect social and cultural factors, including the availability of particular psychoactive substances, media emphasis, and legal sanctions (6, 8, 30, 61). Subsequent patterns become more dependent on psychobiological and pharmacological factors (42, 50). Teenagers typically begin psychoactive drug use at age 13 or 14 with beer and wine and occasionally hard liquor. They drink in association with friends at social functions or often with par-

ents or other family members. During this initial period, the use of nicotine and, somewhat later, marihuana may begin. Use of depressants, excitants, or hallucinogens may then occur, in large part depending on sociocultural factors; opiates are often the last drug in this decidedly nonlinear, complex progression. In certain urban areas, however, opiates may be used early, just after the initial alcohol exposures (23, 33).

Many adolescents stop at particular points in this sequence; the drug effects may be perceived as unpleasant or dangerous. Some young people will use only one drug or group of drugs during a particular period. More often, a variety of drugs will be used, depending on the availability of the drugs, their assessment of the situation, and their needs. This so-called *polydrug abuse pattern* is more prevalent than exclusive use of a single substance or class and varies in severity from the intermittent use of drugs on special occasions to the disorganized, dangerous, multiple-drug abuse patterns of severely disturbed young people. It is not unusual for well adjusted teenagers to take marihuana, methaqualone, and cocaine in preparation for a concert. They consider themselves to be sophisticated drug takers and disdain those who cannot handle their drugs. The compulsive abuser of depressants and heroin who is unable to function in school or relate meaningfully to his peers is so considered (31, 46). It is interesting and somewhat reassuring to note that as young people give up more dangerous abuse patterns, they often return to the drugs they had used earlier (23). Some theorists suggest that the progression from experimental to heavier use is a function of social learning. The future drug abuser first learns about the drug and the manner of administration from friends. This process of anticipatory socialization includes orientation into the pleasurable effects of drugs and a drug-dominated society. The adolescent then learns to associate drug administration with psychoactive and physiological effects that he learns to identify as pleasurable. The experience is then repeated (2). Physiological and/or behaviorally induced withdrawal symptoms and craving may then supervene, resulting in a compulsive abuse syndrome (15, 42, 45). These views do not depend on premorbid psychopathology in the future abuser. At the same time, it is likely that personality patterns importantly influence this sequence (46, 65).

The question of whether marihuana use leads to other drug use is controversial (22). Although much of the enlightened literature denounces this belief as retrospective falsification, it deserves further examination. If one took no drugs, including alcohol, nicotine, and coffee, obviously there could be no progression to harder drugs (8, 23). Many people who derive enjoyment or relief from the use of cannabis do, in fact, then experiment with other drugs. The experience of altering or controlling consciousness or mood with a psychoactive substance often prompts users to attempt other manipulations. Whereas the marihuana use may have been benign, the subsequent experimentation with heroin or depressants may facilitate the development of severe drug problems in some youngsters. It is clear, however, that the psychological and social predisposition of individual adolescents is more important in the development of these problems than whether he or she has ever used marihuana or nicotine (46).

PHENCYCLIDINE

Phencyclidine abuse has received a remarkable amount of attention in the media, in schools, and in treatment programs. It is considered in detail in Chapter 18. In many ways, however, it is a phenomenon distinct to adolescents and young adults and should be considered in this discussion. It is generally used in addition to a variety of other drugs, as part of a polydrug abuse syndrome. Popular knowledge suggests that the drug is so powerful or unpleasant that most people who take this drug are severely disturbed and that most of the drug-taking episodes are marked by dysphoric and often violent effects. In fact, according to reliable surveys and some clinical impressions, the people who intermittently use phencyclidine are often in no way different from other polydrug abusers; they run the gamut from normal through all the diagnostic categories of psychopathology. They also generally say that they enjoy the drug experience; the disorientation, numbness, and other perceptual aberrations are considered a good "high" or "trip." Interestingly, they also generally acknowledge that the drug is quite dangerous (31).

There is no doubt that, during the late 1970's, the incidence of use of this drug and similar others, such as ketamine, increased significantly. This is based on survey reports of use, but also on the significant incidence of untoward reactions, particularly acute and prolonged psychotic episodes, that were reported by emergency rooms, psychiatric hospitals, and other treatment programs.

A number of deaths have also been reported as occurring incident to phencyclidine use. These have been due to its behavioral effects as well as its pharmacological effects, because the drug is distinct from most of the other psychedelics in that at high doses it produces profound physiological effects that may culminate in seizures or coma. There is no question that the drug is prevalent and dangerous, but it is possible that the incidence of phencyclidine use and its associated untoward reactions have been overestimated. This may be due in part to the excitement generated by this drug in the media and in the field of substance abuse and is reminiscent of the situation in the 1960's, when the impact of glue sniffing was grossly overestimated (9).

There has also been a tendency to attribute psychotic episodes of diverse etiologies to phencyclidine. Psychotic episodes that were precipitated by marihuana, hallucinogen, or stimulant abuse have been related to possible phencyclidine contamination of the other drug, as have purely functional psychoses. It is as if it is more acceptable to patients as well as their families and friends to consider a psychotic episode as due to a toxic chemical rather than a constitutional predisposition. It is probable, moreover, that, as with all other psychoactive substances, a significant proportion of the adverse psychological or behavioral reactions that were clearly incident to phencyclidine use occurred in predisposed individuals (46, 66). There has been inadequate documentation of the role of phencyclidine in many of these psychotic reactions; toxicological and additional psychological information should be obtained in these episodes.

EPIDEMIOLOGY

Accurate assessments of the incidence and prevalence of drug abuse patterns are difficult given the rapidity of change of these patterns, great cultural and geographical variation, and the illegal or otherwise stigmatized nature of the phenomena (26, 53). Surveys of adolescents are often done in schools. Those students who do not attend school regularly, often for drug-related reasons, will not be represented (49, 56). Then, too, the responses of those who do respond may be biased by the fact that the surveys are school sponsored. An additional technical problem is that the age range of adolescents surveyed varies considerably in different studies; it is difficult to define adolescence (7). Some surveys include only young people between the ages of 14 and 18 years; others include all who fall into the 12- to 20-year range. A critical issue is that surveys do not sufficiently distinguish between the intermittent, controlled use of psychoactive substances and more compulsive abuse syndromes (27, 66). It is also likely that some surveys exaggerate the prevalence or severity of the problem to demonstrate or dramatize the need for public funding and expansion of research and treatment programs. Despite these limitations of data, it is, nevertheless, possible to outline some of the broad trends in adolescent substance abuse.

ALCOHOL

Just as their parents do, adolescents have long used and/or abused alcohol more than any other psychoactive drug (6, 33). Perceptions of the extent and patterns of use have often been based more on media focus, legislative concerns, or emotionality rather than on data. During the 1960's and early 1970's little attention was paid to adolescent alcohol use, because the use of the illicit drugs represented a new and frightening epidemic and captured public interest (9). Recently, there has been public and professional concern that drinking and alcohol problems have been assuming epidemic proportions among the young.

It is clear that the prevalence of alcohol use in adolescents increased significantly from World War II to the mid-1960's. There is little evidence that the proportion of young drinkers has increased since then. Although older adolescents are more likely to drink than are younger ones, and males more than females, recent data suggests that alcohol use is increasing in the younger adolescent pop-

ulations and in women. Approximately 70 per cent of today's teenagers have had alcohol experiences (1, 6, 31).

According to several surveys, drinking to intoxication increased from approximately 15 to 20 per cent of teenagers studied prior to 1966, to 45 to 70 per cent in the 1970's. The proportion of adolescents who reported being intoxicated at least once a month rose from 10 per cent before 1966 to 19 per cent between 1966 and 1975. The prevalence of problem drinking has varied from 19 per cent to 28 per cent in different surveys (1, 6, 31).

According to a study of 7,000 students at 34 New England colleges, more than 90 per cent of undergraduates reported at least occasional drinking. Twenty per cent of the men and 10 per cent of the women said getting drunk was important to them. Heavy drinkers included 29 per cent of the men and 11 per cent of the women (21).

It should be appreciated that it is often difficult to distinguish between *"normal"* or *"social"* drinking and *"problem"* drinking in the young. In some social or cultural situations, relatively heavy drinking to intoxication is the norm. Young people drink less regularly than older people but tend to consume a larger amount on a drinking occasion (6). It is not clear whether this behavior has recently increased or whether it will lead to problem drinking in the adult years. According to one study, those who were abstinent in college were most likely to be abstinent and least likely to be problem drinkers 25 years later. Similarly, those who were problem drinkers in college were most likely to be problem drinkers and least likely to be abstinent 25 years later. At the same time, the predictability of later drinking patterns from earlier drinking patterns was found to be slight (19).

In the late adolescent and early adult years, the percentage of problem drinkers increases rapidly and there is a higher risk than at any other time of life for incurring the negative consequences associated with the acute effects of alcohol. These include deterioration in school and work performance, violent behavior, including suicides and homicides, and automobile accidents. Young people tend to be impulsive and may have acquired little tolerance or other adaptive responses to the effects of alcohol. Lowering the legal drinking age to 18 years has apparently led to an increase in the number of fatal automobile accidents (6).

Certain subsets of young people do experience more excessive drinking. Studies indicate that delinquent adolescents drink more and develop more pathological symptoms (5). Children of alcoholic parents, particularly of an alcoholic father, are more likely to exhibit deviant drinking behavior (57). A high incidence of problem drinking has also been shown to occur in American Indian children. It is difficult to evaluate the data on alcohol use patterns in black and Hispanic youths. Whereas, surveys show that black and Hispanic adolescents use alcohol less than whites, it is possible that there are more problem drinkers in these populations (6).

DRUGS

During the decade from 1965 to 1975, there was an explosive increase in the use and abuse of all drugs. This was associated with the development of a media-popularized counterculture that rejected conventional values and sought to find truth and meaning in pharmacologically altered states of consciousness. A complex series of social, metaphysical, and religious beliefs supported this search and provided a focus for group identification and pride. Marihuana use increased initially during the period 1962 to 1967, particularly in males and those living in metropolitan areas. Use of stronger drugs remained at low levels during this period. During the period 1967 to 1977, a substantial increase in use of marihuana occurred in the young, associated with a significant, although less profound, increase in use of stronger drugs, including psychedelics, cocaine, heroin, and other opiates. By 1977, more than one-half of young adults between the ages of 18 and 25 reported having used marihuana at least once, as did more than one-fourth of all youth 12 to 17 years old. Use of stronger drugs similarly increased to approximately 5 to 10 per cent of samples studied. There is some evidence among several large subgroups of youth that approximately 60 per cent of those who had ever used marihuana reported using the drug in the prior month. About one-third of the youth and one-fifth of the young adults who have ever had one of the stronger drugs may be considered current users. About one-fifth of young adults who have ever used cocaine reported current use. Current use of inhalants is rare (1, 31).

During the years between 1974 and 1978, surveys indicate a slight leveling off of the current use of all drugs with some exceptions (1, 31). Whereas the use of psychedelics may have declined, the lifetime experience with phencyclidine probably increased to approximately 6 per cent of some samples. More recent reports indicate that there may also be a leveling off of phencyclidine use. It is always difficult to analyze the causes of these trends, the data are so imprecise and the determinants so complex. It is possible that the decline in phencyclidine use occurred incident to the growing barrage of media and street intelligence attesting to the dangers of this drug (66). Increased heroin use is also being reported currently, as measured by applications for treatment programs and overdoses, and may be a function of increased heroin availability, presumably from Iran and Southwest Asia. Cocaine use is also increasing, particularly among the middle class and affluent.

Certain points deserve note. Illicit drug use is strongly related to age and, in general, seems to be much less likely to occur on a regular and continuing basis. In general, current use rates are higher for young adults from 18 to 25 years than for the younger people. At the same time, it seems as if use is moving downward to the younger age groups, and from groups in which drug use increases were initially seen, to groups that demonstrated low use rates in the 1960's. Thus, drug use has spread from urban, minority groups to rural areas and middle-class whites. Then too, the initial preponderance of drug use in males versus females has decreased considerably (1, 8, 31).

Adolescent drug use may be conceptualized as having gone from an epidemic situation, where use increased precipitously and involved young people across all social and psychological lines, to an endemic situation, where use has become an integral part of the "coming of age" in America for many young people (16). As with alcohol, the various drugs are well known, and patterns of abuse and adverse consequences have become part of popular culture. Where, previously, a significant proportion of the drug use led to adverse consequences, it is probable that the preponderance of current adolescent drug use is more sophisticated and controlled and will often not result in severe disability. It is the psychologically or socially disabled youngsters who are most at risk of becoming compulsive abusers and suffering adverse consequences (46, 66).

DETERMINANTS OF DRUG ABUSE BEHAVIOR

Multiple determinants of drug abuse behavior in the young have been cited in the literature; these include sociological, parental, psychobiological, genetic, and pharmacological factors (4, 6, 8, 18, 32, 42, 60). These are covered in detail elsewhere in this volume. It should be recognized that an association between these characteristics and the abuse of psychoactive substances does not necessarily represent a causal relationship. In fact, none of these characteristics and no psychological or other sorts of examinations has been shown to be predictive for the development of drug abuse behavior or which people will use which drug (15, 42, 46, 66). It is also important to note that these oft-quoted determinants are frequently associated with drug use of any kind or severity. Few attempts have been made to characterize the transition from experimentation to compulsive use.

SOCIOCULTURAL

As noted earlier, in some communities at certain periods, adolescence itself may be considered a risk factor in the incidence of drug use and abuse. Other frequently described determinants include inadequate parental control and support, more delinquency, lower school achievement, and less religiosity (6, 10, 23, 32, 51, 58). Several studies have suggested that, not surprisingly, high school dropouts from inner-city communities are at high risk for initiating and continuing in drug abuse careers (8, 24, 34, 44, 54).

Some parents violently condemn the controlled and occasional use of marihuana when they themselves abuse alcohol. Children may be made to feel that they have severe psychological or social problems and that they are morally inadequate. They often feel that they might just as well identify strongly with the "sick" group and take more drugs. Alterna-

tively and probably more frequently, adolescents have been convinced that alcohol is the drug of choice for mature, ambitious adults (46, 66). Some have been weaned off cannabis and onto alcohol after much anger, cajoling, and prayer.

Sexual experiences in the adolescent sector are frequently unsatisfactory due to the lack of experience and feelings of anxiety and inadequacy. Many young people find that low doses of sedatives, opiates, or alcohol increase desire, relieve inhibitions, and improve performance. Some males are able to sustain an erection only when they are "stoned." The great vogue methaqualone has had in recent years relates to this phenomenon. The development of tolerance necessitates increasing dosages, resulting in decreased ability, and recurrence of the anxious, depressed feelings. Some youngsters may continue to use, effectively decreasing their sexual interest and the associated conflicts. Cannabis in its various forms has increased sexual desire and sensitivity in some people; in others, it is associated with a marked disinterest in sex. Stimulants also have a markedly variable influence on sexual interest and performance. It should be emphasized that the compulsive use of most drugs is generally associated with decreased sexual interest and performance (45, 46).

PSYCHOLOGICAL

Controversy still exists as to whether compulsive drug abuse implies a personality disturbance that antedates the drug use and, also, whether specific patterns of abuse may be associated with certain personality types (4, 34, 35, 46, 64, 65). Youthful drug users are described as more interested in sensation seeking, being low in self-esteem or coping abilities, being more rebellious, untrustworthy, impulsive, and less ambitious (6, 8, 32). Other workers see the drug use in more functional terms as self-treatment of painful affects of shame, rage, loneliness, guilt, and depression (36, 37). A so-called "masked depression" is considered by some workers to be etiological in drug and alcohol use. The boredom, restlessness, apathy in school, wanderlust, philosophizing, sexual promiscuity, and frantic seeking of new activities may represent depressive states in young people (20). Some young people may be seeking to satisfy or control unacceptable drives, particularly sexual longings, security needs, or primitive sadistic and aggressive impulses (18). It has been postulated that there may be an impairment in affect or drive defense in some young people such that these feelings and desires are experienced as overwhelming. Narcissistic or borderline personality disturbances have also been implicated in compulsive drug use (35, 64).

The problem is that much of these data are based on retrospective formulations, after people have already become compulsive drug users. The psychopathology noted may well be a reaction to the drug or its pattern of use in a society that condemns the drug-dependent life. There are no data from prospective studies that have defined specific psychodynamic constellations of adolescents at greatest risk; there is no good evidence for the existence of a well defined "addictive" or "alcoholic personality" type (15, 42, 46, 65).

Recent studies suggest that adolescent drug and alcohol abusers run the gamut from normal to a variety of neurotic, personality, and psychotic disorders (34, 46, 59, 65). It is necessary to define the meaning of the drug use in each youngster. In fact, the choice of drugs may reflect psychodynamic patterns (43). A borderline or psychotic adolescent may use heroin and other drugs in an attempt to control unwelcome thoughts and feelings (37). Compulsive alcohol use may facilitate the denial of feelings of vulnerability and loneliness and allow the expression of long suppressed anger. Many severely disturbed young people will use only opiates or depressants and will not use marihuana, hallucinogens, or stimulants, because these drugs further weaken their hold on reality and enhance anxious or paranoid feelings. At the same time, there are psychologically disabled people who preferentially abuse these drugs. There is some evidence to suggest that the intense psychoactive effects, however unpleasant, may insulate them from their own thoughts or feelings or perhaps facilitate attempts to rationalize their "craziness" (46). The evidence that the pharmacological actions of the various drugs may be important in the development of psychopathology is preliminary, although quite suggestive. It is not difficult to accept the possibility that chronic use of euphoriants, such as the opioids or benzodiazepines, may result in chronic depressive or anxiety states. This is particularly provocative in light of the recent work on endogenous morphine-like substances or the discovery of high affinity binding sites for benzodiazepines in the brain (42).

Not only does the choice of drugs reflect personality characteristics (as it does various social factors), so also do abuse patterns reflect ego structure pathology (65). A depressed obsessive character may use heroin compulsively, but in a structured, organized fashion. Psychotic or borderline youngsters may take large quantities of a wide variety of drugs in a disorganized, chaotic manner, such that they suffer frequent adverse reactions or overdoses. Interestingly, some of these people take great pride in calling themselves "garbage heads" who will take anything in any quantity, regardless of the dangers. They may have little else of which to be proud (46). In Erikson's terms, they may depend on a "negative identity" for a measure of self-esteem and self-definition (17).

PREVENTION AND TREATMENT

PREVENTION

The provision of appropriate prevention and treatment measures, as with adult patients, depends upon the accurate characterization of the adolescent, including his personality characteristics, psychopathology, social and familial milieu, as well as the pattern and type of alcohol and drug use. Treatments must be individualized in recognition of the markedly differing needs of each adolescent. Whereas treatments may be provided by a wide variety of personnel and programs, to be effective these must be prepared to handle the multiple problems of adolescence in addition to drugs. Many of the treatment issues will be covered elsewhere in this volume. This discussion seeks to focus on the particular problems raised by adolescent patients (8, 46).

Prevention programs and early treatment efforts must be available before drug abuse patterns have become well established and before the adverse sequelae of these behaviors become manifest. Because the causes of drug abuse are complex and varied, approaches to prevention should not be oversimplified. High pressure educational campaigns focused on the community or the schools that have stressed, and sometimes exaggerated, the dangers of drug use have not proven to be particularly effective. Often, those youngsters with some drug experience dismiss these efforts as scare tactics, and more naive adolescents may even be prompted to begin experimenting. Carefully planned, organized programs that require participation and discussion on the part of the young have shown promise. The provision of reasonable, rewarding, emotional, educational, vocational, and recreational alternatives to drug abuse should probably be of prime concern. Attempts should be made to stress the pleasurable and rewarding aspects of life without drugs, rather than focusing on the possible dangers (29, 44).

The stringency of legal sanctions is controversial, particularly in the young. It is clear that the users of these drugs who have not been major dealers are victims and have committed only victimless crimes. Every attempt should be made to treat these people and not subject them to the criminal justice system prematurely. Programs that seek to divert so-called "juvenile offenders" into treatment systems have met with limited success. It is likely that systems of this sort would be more effective if the treatment options are better defined and treatment programs are able to remain independent of the criminal justice system, a difficult and delicate task (40).

There is no need to belabor the obvious role of the family in drug and alcohol abuse prevention in the young. Families must well recognize the influence of their own drug-taking practices on their children. Finally, physicians must be extremely prudent in their prescribing practices. Every effort should be made to help adolescents cope with stress and/or psychopathology without medication when this is possible.

GENERAL TREATMENT CONSIDERATIONS

Adolescent drug abusers commonly do not come in contact with treatment personnel until their behavior has progressed to the point that it is recognized by family, school, or legal authorities or they suffer a complication of the drug taking (28, 39). They often perceive their drug-taking behavior as enjoyable, safe, and under control. The drug taking is likely to be sufficiently short term and free of adverse consequences such that they may not appreciate the implications of their drug use. It is often not until the adult years that the behavior will be seen as self-destructive. They are also wary of seeking help from conventional authorities. They are uncomfortable revealing themselves to people with whom they believe they have no rapport. They consider the doctor, teacher, even parent, as alien and somewhat hostile presences. They believe that they will not be understood or appreciated, even by well meaning authorities. They are also intensely concerned with confidentiality (3, 38).

This reluctance to seek treatment is particularly poignant in young people, because it is during these years that the adolescent changes markedly in relation to his society. His self-image may improve given appropriate opportunities to demonstrate quality or ability. His sense of power and dignity may increase given adequate support. In contrast to adult patients, the youthful are more likely to develop the necessary skills and tastes to live reasonably contentedly with themselves and without drugs. The drug use may significantly influence these changes. Then, too, behavior patterns and psychobiological sequelae of the drug use may be sufficiently short term as to render this population likely to do better in treatment than adults. Interestingly, there are few data supporting this idea that the provision of early treatment to drug abusers, particularly during the adolescent years, will ensure better results. At the same time, the data are suggestive, and clinical impressions are strongly supportive of this premise (44).

It is often difficult to engage adolescents in regularly scheduled formal therapy or counseling sessions. They may be uncomfortable in one-on-one encounters with a therapist, and they are often loath to discuss the intimate details of their lives, particularly their failures. This difficulty is compounded if the therapist assumes the traditional stance of neutrality and reserve. It is often necessary, particularly at the outset of treatment, to schedule short informal sessions, with the therapist actively discussing practical issues of survival. Often discussions of music, sports, or clothing will be valuable in establishing a therapeutic alliance. Issues of drug use must, of course, be discussed, but the therapist should exercise care that he does not assume a critical parental role of exhortation and threats. Most of these kids have heard it all before; they will benefit most from a dignified, supportive relationship with an accepting, interested, knowledgeable adult. Optimally, they will come to appreciate their worth and potential in this relationship (46).

Adolescent patients will often minimize or exaggerate the extent of their drug use or in other ways distort historical data so as to create a desired effect. Direct confrontation of these failures to tell the truth, particularly at the outset of treatment, may lead to increased resistance or power struggles. At the same time, if the therapist accepts the information without reservation, he may undermine the sense of trust and respect that is the basis of the therapeutic alliance. This may also increase the patient's already intense guilt feelings. If possible, the therapist must act as an ally, such that the responsibility for behavior and improvement rests on the patient. An attitude of gentle but persistent curiosity is more effective than approach as an adversary. It may be necessary to listen carefully but neutrally and gloss over questionable issues at different stages. Confirmed problems and behaviors may be considered in more depth with a view to returning to the possible inaccuracies at a later treatment stage (11, 46).

When appropriate, patients should be treated within the family group. This is a controversial issue, because it is often more useful to see the youngster separately and allow him to feel that the therapist is his advocate and worthy of trust. In these situations, the therapist should see the parents only when the patient is present and should apprise the patient as to the nature of any contacts, including telephone conversations, held with the parents alone. Patterns of familial interaction that provoke drug abuse behavior should be identified and altered. Families must sometimes be advised to protect themselves from the abuses of a drug-using adolescent who steals to support his habit or engages in other disruptive acts. It is sometimes necessary to suggest that a family turn a compulsive drug user out so that he will be forced to seek treatment. On other occasions it is necessary to encourage the separation of the patient from a family situation that is destructive, particularly one in which there are other compulsive drug abusers present (46).

Caring for impoverished youngsters from the inner city, particularly members of ethnic minority groups, or the rural poor, where the determinants of the drug and alcohol abuse are primarily social, the focus should be on providing realistic, attractive alternatives to drug abuse (44). Some need a place to live or legal representation. Many need help in returning to school or preparing for their high school equivalency diplomas. They may have lost considerable time and confidence during their drug-taking careers and require encouragement to return to an academic milieu. Others need practical vocational training and job placement so that they can be self-sufficient. Introducing some of these deprived youngsters to such pleasurable options as sporting or cultural events and hobbies may be beneficial. Group or milieu therapy is particularly useful with this group of adolescents, particularly when supervised by therapists who have shared similar cultural experiences. The general focus should be on common problems, methods of coping, the establishment of trusting relationships with each other, and sexual problems (8, 46, 48).

Treatment of the psychopathology that led to or resulted from the drug abuse behavior will obviously depend on the individual personality patterns. This is discussed in detail elsewhere in this volume. Certain general considerations deserve emphasis. These people have often been unable to get adequate satisfaction from any phase of their lives save the intermittent drug "high" and perhaps the attendant life style. Drug usage has substituted for defenses, relationships, and other satisfactions. Many of these young men and women are disappointed in themselves; they feel helpless and inadequate in the face of the real problems of living. The treatment team must be sensitive to this profound lack of self-esteem as well as to the various modes of denial they employ. Patients should be taught to identify the extremes of emotion, particularly anxiety and depression, that they have been unable to recognize. Their inability to assess adequately the risks of particular behaviors requires careful work and often firm intervention. The overwhelming guilt that many of these youngsters feel should be recognized and, to some degree, assuaged (38, 46).

PHARMACOTHERAPY

Most adolescent drug abusers should be treated without medication, particularly those agents that are liable to abuse. At the same time, many compulsive drug abusers are medicating themselves in order to function, and it may not be possible to attempt to treat some of this significant pathology through talking therapies alone (37). In these cases, despite the risk of abuse or noncompliance, carefully administered psychotropic drugs should be considered an integral part of therapeutic regimens. Antipsychotics, antidepressants, and lithium may be indicated in the treatment of some disturbed youngsters. On rare occasions, with intensely anxious patients, benzodiazepines might be administered in low doses for short periods (46).

Detoxification from sedative-hypnotics, alcohol, or opiates should be approached, as with adults, utilizing appropriate medications. Clonidine has shown promise in the detoxification of some youthful opiate addicts. Methadone maintenance has been used with good result in certain populations of adolescent opiate addicts. In general, youthful patients should not be maintained on methadone unless their addiction is demonstrated to be long term and they have experienced failures on other treatment programs. A useful model utilizes low dose methadone maintenance for relatively short periods of time, followed by slow detoxification. Naltrexone may also have a place in the treatment of some well motivated, carefully selected patients (46, 48).

TREATMENT PROGRAMS

School-based programs are critical for prevention, case finding, evaluation, and early treatment in some young people. Teachers may be the first to recognize a drug abuse problem through direct observation or indirectly because of frequent absences or decreasing involvement with school. A variety of programs of differing, but undocumented, effectiveness exist in this country to serve these functions. In general, there is an educational-preventative component that teaches about the dangers of drugs. These are sometimes run according to a peer-group format, supervised by counselors with some knowledge of drugs or alcohol (8). A major problem with some of these programs is that they take an unrealistically hard line, e.g., "All drug and alcohol use represents weakness and is dangerous." This may discourage troubled youngsters from seeking early help. Interestingly, some prevention and early treatment efforts serve to encourage continued use. There continues to be a vogue for inviting well rehabilitated ex-addicts to address student audiences on the dangers of drugs. They often look and speak so elegantly that frightened and insecure adolescents are encouraged to continue these behaviors so they can be as "cool" as the speaker.

It is controversial as to whether schools should provide treatment for adolescents with severe drug abuse problems. Minimally, if the school does not provide treatments, it should attempt to refer appropriate students for intensive care and provide adequate follow-up. It is not useful merely to remove these kids from the school; they may well continue to have relationships with other less drug-involved students, perhaps as dealers and, in essence, spread the disease (25). Every effort should be made to keep these young people in school and ensure that they are receiving adequate treatment (44).

Individual therapists, including family physicians, psychiatrists, and other psychotherapists, have a place in the treatment of adolescent substance abuse. They may be the only resource available in certain locations. Then, too, the youngster's drug abuse behavior may still be sufficiently benign such that admission to a drug treatment program is not warranted. Unfortunately, therapists all too often do not know as much about the drug use as do some of their young patients. Also, to be effective, they must be sensitive to the value systems of the adolescent, particularly as they are determined by association with a subculture that rejects conventional values and orientation. They must also be prepared to provide educational, legal, or medical assistance or at least be familiar with the resources that are available for this. Given the economics of private practice, this is often not an easy task (46).

The use of age-oriented treatment programs focused on the adolescent population seems to be the most effective and efficient means of providing care and preventive services to troubled youngsters whose drug use has not yet become the primary focus of living. Some innovative programs, such as "The Door" in New York, are cultural-recreational centers for adolescents and provide extensive medical and rehabilitative services as part of the package. Educational and psychosexual counseling are critical elements in these programs. The adolescents are encouraged to identify with the center or the program, to attend programs daily and in the evenings, and to utilize it as a significant life resource. Community groups, such as the Boys' Clubs of America, or religious groups may be valuable resources as well, although they are often unable to provide the extensive multidisciplinary support required by disabled youngsters, and they are often not sufficiently knowledgeable about alcohol and drug abuse (28, 38).

Programs based on the therapeutic community model are widely used in the treatment of adolescent drug abusers. A well organized, structured program is essential to facilitate the development of the residents. The sense of isolation that many young people feel may be reduced through this experience. Role models for responsible behavior are provided by staff and graduates. A major problem with some of these has been an undue emphasis on confrontation and breaking down of unhealthy behavior patterns. Young people are often loath to enter these facilities; they do not want to leave family and friends to enter an unpleasant and repressive milieu. They also frequently leave precipitously. In recognition of these factors, many programs are providing warm encouragement and access to pleasurable alternatives in addition to the necessary structure. A related problem is that few of the therapeutic communities are prepared to handle adolescents with significant psychopathology. It is likely that the professional component of some of these programs should be enhanced to serve this population (38, 46).

A model that provides the diverse treatment capability necessary for adolescent drug abusers combines an inpatient and outpatient therapeutic community (or milieu therapy) structure with extensive medical and psychiatric backup. Clients may enter the system at any point, depending on their needs, and move through it at their individual rates. They may enter in the inpatient phase, move to an intensive outpatient or day care center phase, and progress to a more limited clinic phase as they develop ties to the larger society and have less need for program support. If difficulties arise with any patient on any level, more supportive care is available. Some workers believe that the elements of this coordinated program should be separate, so that more naive users are not exposed to more compulsive, more "street-wise" patients.

Hospitalization of youthful drug abusers is often necessary. In general, this may be useful to provide detoxification services or other acute care, although long term stays have proven to be less effective. Liaison should be established between these traditional medical facilities and more appropriate programs that are prepared to handle these troubled adolescents.

As with adult patients, the lack of good data makes it difficult to evaluate the efficacy of various treatment approaches. This is due to the paucity of follow-up studies on adolescents who have been in treatment. Certainly, it is essential that every treatment program provide regular follow-up of those who have completed treatment or dropped out prematurely. Adolescents are often too proud to admit slippage or failures. A primary goal is to facilitate the readmission of these young people to treatment when this is necessary. Continued contact, however infrequent, may also be necessary as a source of support, relationships, and validation. Follow-up is also essential to determine which people do well in which programs. Although it is a quite expensive undertaking, optimally a counselor or other skilled professional should be responsible for the follow-up. Home visits or, in the inner city, extensive tracking may be necessary to secure the requisite contacts (46, 48).

A related issue is the tendency on the part of governmental and treatment agencies to seek technological or procedural solutions to complex biopsychosocial phenomena. Various treatment approaches are contrasted in regard to efficacy or efficiency, as if particular modalities were all similar and interchangeable. Methadone programs, therapeutic communities, and school-based programs are not easily compared with each other, because within each modality the character and quality of the program and the staff vary so widely. Certain youngsters may do well in a particular therapeutic community, although they do not find others as attractive or useful. It may, therefore, be necessary to try several modalities, either individually or often in appropriate combination.

Many of the adolescents who are referred to therapists, treatment programs, or psychiatric facilities are not in need of intensive treatment. Although their drug or alcohol use may seem incomprehensible to their parents or other authorities, it may be reasonably normal within their social milieu. It may, in fact, represent benign and even healthy experimentation. There is a real danger of precipitous action or overtreatment here. The disruption of the lives of some of these young people may be far worse than the consequences of their drug use. They have serious concerns about their abilities, potential, and even sanity, and inappropriate interventions may confirm their worst fears. Their primary need may be for reassurance, support, and some validation of their own experience (46, 56). After a thorough evaluation has determined that the youngster is progressing reasonably well in his development and the drug use does not represent a serious danger, it may be useful to reassure him as to his sanity and his prospects for the future. It is not easy to be young, and, on occasion, warm support and encouragement in a few informal sessions, with provision for follow-up care, may be appropriate treatment (46).

References

1. Abelson, H. I., Fishburne, P. M., and Cisin, I. *National Survey on Drug Abuse: 1977*. Rockville, Md., National Institute on Drug Abuse, 1977.
2. Becker, H. S. History, culture and subjective experience: An exploration of the social basis of drug-induced experiences. J. Health Soc. Behav. 8:163, 1967.
3. Bernstein, B., and Shkuda, A. N. *The Young Drug User: Attitudes and Obstacles to Treatment*. New York, Center for New York City Affairs, New School for Social Research, 1974.
4. Bihari, B. Drug dependency: Some etiological considerations. Am. J. Drug Alcohol Abuse 3:409, 1976.
5. Blacker, E., Demone, H. W., Jr., and Freeman, H. E. Drinking behavior of delinquent boys. Q. J. Stud. Alcohol 26:223, 1965.
6. Blane, H. T., and Hewitt, L. E. Alcohol and youth: An analysis of the literature 1960–75. Final report prepared for National Institute on Alcohol Abuse and Alcoholism under Contract No ADM 281-75-0026. March, 1977.
7. Blos, P. *On Adolescence*. Glencoe, Ill., The Free Press, 1962.
8. Blum, R., and Richards, L. Youthful drug use. In *Handbook on Drug Abuse*, R. I. Dupont, A. Gold-

stein, and J. O'Donnell, editors, pp. 257–267. Rockville, Md., National Institute on Drug Abuse, 1979.
9. Brecher, E. M., and Editors of Consumer Reports. *Licit and Illicit Drugs: The Consumers Union Report on Narcotics, Stimulants, Depressants, Inhalants, Hallucinogens, and Marijuana, Including Caffeine, Nicotine, and Alcohol.* Mount Vernon, N. Y., Consumers Union, 1972.
10. Burkett, S. R. Religion, parental influence and adolescent alcohol and marijuana use. J. Drug Issues 7: 263, 1977.
11. Chappel, J. N., and Schnoll, S. H. Physician attitudes: Effect on the treatment of chemically dependent patients. J.A.M.A. 237:2318, 1977.
12. Cherubin, C. E. A review of the medical complications of narcotic addiction. Int. J. Addict. 3:167, 1968.
13. Cohen, A. Y. The journey beyond trips. J. Psychedelic Drugs 3:16, 1971.
14. Dishotsky, N. I., Loughman, W. D., Mogar, R. E., and Lipscomb, W. R. LSD and genetic damage. Science 172:431, 1971.
15. Dole, V. P. Narcotic addiction, physical dependence and relapse. N. Engl. J. Med. 206:998, 1972.
16. DuPont, R. L., and Greene, M. H. The dynamics of a heroin addiction epidemic. Science 181:716, 1973.
17. Erikson, E. H. *Childhood and Society*, 2nd ed. New York, W. W. Norton, 1963.
18. Fenichel, O. *The Psychoanalytic Theory of Neurosis.* New York, W. W. Norton, 1945.
19. Fillmore, K. M., Bacon, S. D., and Hyman, M. *Alcohol Drinking Behavior and Attitudes*, Rutgers Panel Study Report prepared for National Institute on Alcohol Abuse and Alcoholism. New Brunswick, N. J., Rutgers Center of Alcohol Studies, 1977.
20. Gallemore, J. L., and Wilson, W. P. Adolescent maladjustment or affective disorder? Am. J. Psychiatry 129:608, 1972.
21. Getting back to the booze. Time Magazine, November 5, 1979.
22. Goode, E. Marijuana use and the progression to dangerous drugs. In *Effects on Human Behavior*, L. L. Miller, editor, pp. 303–338. New York, Academic Press, 1974.
23. Hamburg, B. A., Kraemer, H. C., and Jahnke, W. A. Hierarchy of drug use of adolescence: Behavioral and attitudinal correlates of substantial drug use. Am. J. Psychiatry 132:1155, 1975.
24. Hein, K., Cohen, M. I., and Litt, J. F. Illicit drug use among urban adolescents: A decade in retrospect. Am. J. Dis. Child. 133:38, 1979.
25. Hughes, P. H., and Crawford, G. A. A contagious disease model for researching and intervening in heroin epidemics. Arch. Gen. Psychiatry 27:149, 1972.
26. Hunt, L. G. Incidence and prevalence of drug use and abuse. In *Handbook on Drug Abuse*, R. I. DuPont, A. Goldstein, and J. O'Donnell, editors, Rockville, Md., National Institute on Drug Abuse, 1979. pp. 395–403.
27. Hunt, L. G., and Zinberg, N. E. *Heroin Use: A New Look*. Washington, D.C., Drug Abuse Council, 1976.
28. Institute of Medicine. *A Conference Summary: Adolescent Behavior and Health*. Washington, D.C., National Academy of Sciences, 1978.
29. Jacobson, R., and Zinberg, N. E. *Social Basis of Drug Abuse Prevention*. Washington, D.C., Drug Abuse Council, 1975.

30. Jessor, R. Predicting time of onset of marijuana use: A developmental study of high school youth. In *Predicting Adolescent Drug Abuse: A Review of Issues, Methods and Correlates,* D. J. Lettieri editor, Research Issues 11. Rockville, Md., National Institute on Drug Abuse, 1975.

31. Johnston, L. D., Bachman, J. G., and O'Malley, P. M. *1979 Highlights: Drugs and the Nation's High School Students, Five-Year National Trends.* Washington, D.C., United States Department of Health Education, and Welfare, Public Health Service, Alcohol, Drug Abuse and Mental Health Administration, 1979.

32. Kamali, K., and Steer, R. A. Polydrug use by high school students: Involvement and correlates. Int. J. Addict. 11:337, 1976.

33. Kandel, D., Single, E., and Kessler, R. C. The epidemiology of drug use among New York State high school students: Distribution, trends, and change in rates of use. Am. J. Public Health 66:43, 1976.

34. Kaufman, E. The Psychodynamics of opiate dependence: A new look. Am. J. Drug Alcohol Abuse 1: 349, 1974.

35. Kernberg, O. F. *Borderline Conditions and Pathological Narcissism.* New York, Jason Aronson, 1975.

36. Khantzian, E. J. Opiate addition: A critique to theory and some implications for treatment. Am. J. Psychother. 28:59, 1974.

37. Khantzian, E. J., Mack, J. E., and Schatzberg, A. F. Heroin use as an attempt to cope: Clinical observations. Am. J. Psychiatry 131:160, 1974.

38. Lecker, S., Hendricks, L., and Turanski, J. New dimensions in adolescent psychotherapy: A therapeutic system approach. Pediatr. Clin. North Am. 20:883, 1973.

39. Litt, I. F., and Cohen, M. I. The drug-using adolescent as a pediatric patient. J. Pediatr. 77:195, 1970.

40. Litt, I. F., and Cohen, M. I. Prisons, adolescents, and the right to quality medical care: The time is now Am. J. Public Health 64:894, 1974.

41. Mechanic, D. Development of psychological distress among young adults. Arch. Gen. Psychiatry 36:1233, 1979.

42. Meyer, R. E., and Mirin, S. M. *The Heroin Stimulus: Implications for a Theory of Addiction.* New York, Plenum, 1979.

43. Milkman, H., and Frosch, W. A. On the preferential abuse of heroin and amphetamine. J Nerv. Ment. Dis. 156:242, 1973.

44. Millman, R. B. Drug abuse in adolescence: Current issues. In *Developments in the Field of Drug Abuse: Proceedings of the First National Drug Abuse Conference, 1974,* E. Senay, V. Shorty, and H. Alksne, editors. New York, National Association for the Prevention of Addiction to Narcotics, 1975.

45. Millman, R. B. Drug abuse, addiction and intoxication. In *Textbook of Medicine,* P. B. Beeson and W. McDermott editors, pp. 585–597. Philadelphia, W. B. Saunders, 1975.

46. Millman, R. B. Drug and alcohol abuse. In *Handbook of Mental Disorders in Childhood and Adolescence,* B. B. Wollman, J. Egan, and A. C. Ross, editors, pp. 238–267. Englewood Cliffs, N. J., Prentice-Hall, 1978.

47. Millman, R. B., and Khuri, E. T. Drug abuse and the need for alternatives. In *Current Issues in Adolescent Psychiatry,* J. Scholar, editor, pp. 148–157. New York, Brunner/Mazel, 1973.

48. Millman, R. B., Khuri, E. T., and Nyswander, M. E. Therapeutic detoxification of adolescent heroin addicts. Ann. 311:153, 1978.

49. New York State Office of Drug Abuse Services. *A Survey of Substance Use among Junior and Senior High School Students in New York State.* Report No. 1: *Prevalence of Drug and Alcohol Use, Winter 1974/75.* New York, New York State Office of Drug Abuse Services, 1975.

50. Oakley, S. R. *Drugs, Society and Human Behavior.* St. Louis, C. V. Mosby, 1972.

51. O'Donnell, J. A., Voss, H. L., Clayton, R. R., et al. *Young Men and Drugs: A Nationwide Survey,* NIDA Research Monograph 5. Rockville, Md., National Institute on Drug Abuse, 1976.

52. Preble, E., and Casey, J. J., Jr. Taking care of business: The heroin user's life on the street. Int. J. Addict. 4:1, 1969.

53. Project DAWN V. *Phase Five Report of the Drug Abuse Warning Network, May 1976–April 1977* (DHEW Publ No (ADM) 78–618). IMS America, 1977.

54. Robins, L. N., and Murphy, G. E. Drug use in a normal population of young Negro men. Am. J. Public Health 57:1580, 1967.

55. Rubin, V., and Comitas, L. *Ganja in Jamaica.* The Hague, Mouton, 1975.

56. Schnoll, S. H. Alcohol and other substance abuse in adolescents. In *Addiction Research and Treatment: Converging Trends,* pp. 40–45. New York, Pergamon, 1979.

57. Schukitt, M. A., Goodwin, D. A., and Winokur, G. A study of alcoholism in half-siblings. Am. J. Psychiatry 128:1132, 1972.

58. Simonds, J. F., and Kashani, J. Drug abuse and criminal behavior in delinquent boys committed to a training school. Am. J. Psychiatry 136:1444, 1979.

59. Steer, R. A., and Schut, J. Types of psychopathology displayed by heroin addicts. Am. J. Psychiatry 136: 1463, 1979.

60. Tennant, F. S., Detels, R., and Clark, V. Some childhood antecedents of drug and alcohol abuse. Am. J. Epidemiol. 102:377.

61. Wechsler, H. Alcohol intoxication and drug use among teen-agers. Q. J. Stud. Alcohol 37:1672, 1976.

62. Weil, A. *The Natural Mind.* Boston, Houghton Mifflin, 1972.

63. Wider, H., and Kaplan, E. H. Drug use in adolescents. Psychoanal. Study Child 24:399, 1969.

64. Wurmser, L. Psychoanalytic considerations of the etiology of compulsive drug use. J. Am. Psychoanal. Assoc. 22:820, 1974.

65. Zinberg, N. E. Addiction and ego function. Psychoanal. Study Child 1975.

66. Zinberg, N. E., Jacobson, R. C., and Harding, W. M. Social sanctions and rituals as a basis for drug abuse prevention. Am. J. Drug Alcohol Abuse 2:165, 1975.

CHAPTER 60

DRUG ABUSE AND THE ELDERLY

Emil F. Pascarelli, M.D.

Significant advances in our knowledge of psychotropic drug dependence and alcoholism coupled with an increasing interest in gerontology have added new dimensions to our perspective of drug use in the elderly. Psychic suffering, physical disabilities, isolation, poverty, and other factors predispose the elderly to the jeopardies of inappropriate drug use. Furthermore, elderly persons are more susceptible to the actions, interactions, and side effects of many pharmaceuticals. Aging is accompanied by a decreasing ability to metabolize medications, yet the elderly are the largest consumers of legal drugs (17). Most medical professionals have had little training in gerontology. This has led to profligate, often inappropriate, prescribing, particularly of psychoactive substances, in an attempt to deal with problems that are frequently complex and baffling. Iatrogenic overmedicating in institutions to render a patient docile in the interests of administrative efficiency is an example of this phenomenon.

Other realities must also be taken into account. Depression and its sequelae increase substantially with aging. Twenty-five per cent of all suicides occur in persons over 65 years of age. Problems relating to alcohol use alone or in combination with other drugs have been underestimated. In the aged, it seems as though we have misunderstood many of the issues relating to use, misuse, and abuse of drugs and the ensuing problems

of dependence, overdose, and their medical and psychiatric concomitants. There exists a responsibility to study available information about the emotional needs of the elderly and how they lead to the use of alcohol and drugs as a solution to the stresses caused by psychic pain and physical disability.

There is no clear definition of the elderly. Aging is a dynamic physiological and social process we know relatively little about. By 65 years of age most persons have acquired at least one medical, emotional, or social ailment, consistent with being considered old (18). Obviously some suffer these consequences earlier than others. Sixty-five years has been the stereotypical retirement age; however, attitudes about retirement are rapidly changing. These are some of the factors that make it difficult to obtain and interpret meaningful data relating to the phenomenon of aging. It is equally difficult to define drug abuse in terms of the elderly. In attempting to gain a clear perspective, we must consider not only the phenomenon of abuse, but use and misuse as well (13). The purpose of this chapter is to explore these issues.

USE OF LEGAL DRUGS BY THE ELDERLY

Presently in the United States, persons over 65 number about 23 million, constitute about 10 per cent of the total population, and are increasing in number by approximately 1,600 daily. Five per cent of these elderly persons are in long term care institutions, 15 per cent live in the community with their children, 25 per cent live alone, and 50 per cent live with spouses (8). Seventy-five per cent of persons over 65 use some kind of medication, at least a third of which is obtained over the counter. Twenty-five per cent of all legal prescriptions are for persons in this population.

A number of researchers have examined patterns of prescribed drug use in subsegments of this population (5,7,14,16). Results of these studies are remarkably consistent for the types of drugs used. Differences in patterns of use seem to reflect the life style, social circumstances, and degree of infirmity of the different groups.

In the institutionalized elderly, women generally outnumber men by about two to one. In one study 22,897 elderly persons were surveyed. About 38 per cent of these people received one or more cardiovascular drugs (including digitalis and diuretics), about 14 per cent received analgesics (including propoxyphene), and 9 per cent received a tranquilizer or hypnotic (16). In fact, the elderly are more likely to use depressant drugs than any other age group. A survey of institutionalized elderly with mental disorders revealed that 60 per cent of the residents received at least one psychoactive drug, and about 50 per cent received at least three (14).

In a study of 5,600 noninstitutionalized persons over 65, about 60 per cent reported the use of prescription drugs (7). The three drug classes most frequently cited were cardiovascular (39 per cent), tranquilizers or hypnotics (14 per cent), and analgesics (9 per cent). One-third reported using between two and four prescription drugs.

Another study of 242 community elderly showed that about 40 per cent of the medications used were of the over-the-counter variety (5). This group reported a high use of analgesics (67 per cent), as well as cardiovascular drugs (34 per cent), laxatives (31 per cent), vitamins (29 per cent), and tranquilizers (22 per cent). Studies such as these give us some perspective of drug consumption by the elderly. Attention should also be focused on how these legal drugs can be misused.

MISUSE OF LEGAL DRUGS BY THE ELDERLY

Properly dispensed pharmaceuticals are vital to the practice of modern medicine, yet we are aware that frequently drugs are improperly prescribed, administered, or taken. The ancient medical dictum "primum non nocere" suggests that there are benefits to be derived from a conservative approach to prescribing. Misuse of drugs can involve not only overuse but underuse, erratic use, or use in contraindicated circumstances. The fault may lie with the physician or health worker as well as the patient, especially when the latter is elderly and living with the stresses of poverty, isolation, or illness.

Many professionals continue to harbor society's negative stereotypes of the elderly or are poorly trained in gerontology as well as substance abuse. Failure to recognize the complex nature of the aging process often leads to medical solutions for essentially nonmedical problems. Iatrogenic mishaps can occur through lack of understanding of drug effects, side effects, adverse reactions, or interactions. Poor physician-patient communication can lead to medication error or poor compliance. Compliance diminishes with increasing age and can be worsened by lack of education, low income, being unmarried, and a regimen of multiple medications or doses (3).

The problem of underuse of legal drugs also exists, but there seems to be a greater risk of overuse, particularly when psychoactive drugs are involved. Under certain circumstances this can lead to acute drug reactions that constitute a medical emergency.

Acute drug reactions among persons over 50 years of age occur in about 5 to 6 per cent of all reported incidents (6). The reasons for this unexpectedly low figure are not entirely clear. More than 80 per cent of acute drug reactions in the elderly stem from the misuse of psychotropic drugs, such as barbiturates or benzodiazepines. An additional 10 per cent involve the abuse of propoxyphene. Almost all acute drug reactions reported in the elderly relate to the use of prescribed drugs. Attention has been given to some other characteristics of acute drug reactions among the elderly. In a study involving 60 persons (12), acute reaction occurred more commonly among white females. Blacks of both sexes, were overrepresented in relation to population. In almost one-third of the cases, two or more substances were used. One-third of the elderly admitted that they were consciously attempting suicide. The most commonly misused drugs were diazepam, Tuinal, phenobarbital, and propoxyphene. Similar results are found in the nation-wide Drug Abuse Warning Network (DAWN) reports (6).

Misuse of drugs can accompany or lead to abuse of various substances. The phenomenon of legal drug abuse will be discussed in the ensuing text.

ABUSE OF LEGAL DRUGS BY THE ELDERLY

We are presently aware that, over-all, many more elderly persons are dependent upon depressants than on opiates (10). Depressants are usually legally prescribed by physicians or purchased by the consumer as alcoholic beverages. They include barbiturates, benzodiazepines, and other nonbarbiturate tranquilizers and hypnotics as well as alcohol used alone or in combination with other drugs. By far the single biggest abuse problem is alcoholism. Depressants of the central nervous system carry with them a grave potential threat to health because of adverse effects on organ systems as well as life-threatening withdrawal reactions. Patterns of abuse reflect the complex dynamic interactions of medical, psychiatric, environmental, and socioeconomic factors. The stress associated with these factors can enhance the likelihood of abusing the very substances prescribed or self-administered to cope with these problems.

TRANQUILIZER AND HYPNOTIC ABUSE

Large numbers of elderly persons receive a variety of legally prescribed psychoactive substances. These include barbiturates, nonbarbiturate tranquilizers and hypnotics, benzodiazepines, and a number of over-the-counter sleeping medications. In many parts of the country, particularly cities, older persons receiving Medicare or Medicaid have relatively easy access to primary care sources and can "shop around" to obtain multiple prescriptions from different sources (1). How many actually become addicted to depressant medications is difficult to determine. Numerous drug surveys (5, 7, 14, 16) correlated with studies on acute reactions (13) suggest that depressant abuse, including alcohol, is a serious health problem for the elderly. Patterns of abuse of these substances are similar to those described in other chapters of this

book. The clinician treating these problems must be aware of the caveats relating to the special effects of these substances on the aging body and mind.

ALCOHOL ABUSE

The true prevalence of alcoholism among the elderly has not been documented, although it is undoubtedly the major substance of abuse (19). Because increasing amounts of alcohol are being consumed per capita and because more persons are living longer, it has been inferred that the number of elderly alcoholics will increase. It has been estimated that alcoholism affects between 2 and 10 per cent of the general aged population (15).

At least two types of elderly alcoholics have been identified. One-third of elderly alcoholics develop a drinking problem in later life, whereas two-thirds seem to be long standing alcoholics who drank heavily into old age (19). In contrast to younger alcoholics, there are more women elderly alcoholics. In both types of elderly alcoholics it is generally felt that drinking persists because of continuing stress. Once sober and medically stabilized, older alcoholics tend to respond rapidly, even dramatically, to purposeful rehabilitation in the company of contemporaries, in marked contrast to younger counterparts. These observations can also lead to an effective preventive approach.

It is useful to remember that, even in the elderly, use of alcohol can accompany other forms of drug abuse. The combined effects of these drugs on the central nervous system can be additive or synergistic and lead to inordinate difficulties in treatment (9).

PROPOXYPHENE ABUSE

Propoxyphene is worthy of special mention because it is one of the most frequently prescribed drugs for the elderly. It is generally given for arthritis-related pain in combination with aspirin or acetaminophen (Darvon compound, Darvocet) and is classified as a nonnarcotic analgesic. Actually it is a mild narcotic with a molecular structure related to methadone. The drug has been used as an alternative to methadone maintenance in opiate addicts, and overdose symptoms are reversed by naloxone, a narcotic antagonist. A substantial number of elderly persons are treated for acute reaction to propoxyphene, which presently constitutes about 10 per cent of all drug overdoses reported in this group (6, 13). In view of the large number of elderly using this medication, it is reasonable to assume that many have developed a mild dependency state. In the case of propoxyphene, it is often difficult to distinguish between misuse and abuse.

OTHER LEGAL DRUGS

Antidepressants should be recognized as potential drugs of abuse. The most commonly prescribed substances are amitriptyline (Elavil) and perphenazine and amitriptyline in combination (Triavil). Because they seem to cause euphoria and produce withdrawal symptoms upon abrupt cessation, abuse is a possibility and has been encountered in two elderly persons by the author (11).

Stimulants such as methylphenidate (Ritalin) are occasionally prescribed for elderly persons, but misuse and abuse of stimulants are primarily a youth phenomenon and tend to diminish by 30 years of age. The same also is true for cocaine.

ABUSE OF ILLEGAL DRUGS BY THE ELDERLY

OPIATES

Opiate abuse continues to exist among a group of predominantly urban elderly who are in the twilight years of a lifetime drug habit. Relatively little is known about this group. Certain among them enter methadone treatment programs, but a substantial number remain hidden in the community, using either heroin or legally manufactured substances like hydromorphone (Dilaudid) that are usually obtained through street sources (4). Economic necessity fostered by inability to compete in the frantic street life force compromises that result in assuming a low profile and using less opiate. The largest single ethnic concentration of elderly addicts is found among the Chinese, who use their opiates in a socially tolerant environment, avoiding many of the medical complications by oral or pulmonary ingestion of their drugs (2). Physician opiate addicts as a group also tend to be older.

In recent years many elderly addicts have joined methadone treatment programs. It is by far the most common facility used by the opiate addict (10). In 1976, data obtained from the Community Treatment Foundation Methadone Information Center indicated that 0.7 per cent of 35,000 persons on methadone maintenance were over 60 years of age, up from 0.5 per cent in 1974. In 1979 that figure rose to 1.1 per cent, indicating that the number of elderly in methadone treatment is slowly but steadily increasing as the population in treatment ages. Characteristically, the elderly person in treatment is doubly disenfranchised because of age and ex-addict status and finds it difficult to enter the mainstream of supportive services, such as placement in nursing homes. Furthermore, there is ample evidence that present treatment programs are falling far short of meeting the needs of elderly abusers.

OTHER ILLEGAL DRUGS

Neither stimulants nor hallucinogens seem to be abused to any great degree by elderly persons.

The situation with marihuana is not so clear cut. The author's experience with older methadone patients suggests that marihuana use continues in a significant number of persons just as regular cigarette smoking does. It is interesting to speculate on the likelihood of even larger numbers of older marihuana users as the present population ages. Perhaps at that time the line between use and abuse of marihuana will be less distinct.

ISSUES IN PERSPECTIVE

Drug use patterns in elderly persons are beginning to come into perspective. In the past, considerable emphasis has focused on areas where data were most readily available and where societal attitudes about drug use were most emphatic, as in the case of opiate abuse. Only recently have we come to understand the nature and dimensions of the more widespread problems, such as alcoholism and depressant abuse. Placed in its proper perspective, alcoholism is by far the most serious drug problem in elderly persons. We have come to recognize various abuse patterns that relate to a variety of factors. On the one hand, some elderly drinkers are simply continuing a lifelong pattern of drinking that has not tapered off appreciably but has been sustained by the stresses generated by factors accompanying aging. On the other hand, many elderly persons turn to alcohol and become problem drinkers as a direct reaction to catastrophic events in their lives. In either case, workers have been impressed by the relative ease with which clinical improvement can occur once the problem is recognized and dealt with in a positive manner, using such therapeutic tools as group discussions, recreational activities, physiotherapy, occupational therapy, and appropriate medications, such as antidepressant drugs (19). Some confusion has also been generated as a result of our inability to recognize these problems for what they are, as well as an unwarranted fear of creating new problems. Thus, the beneficial therapeutic effects of alcohol use by elderly persons are lost by not recognizing its potential positive value or not allowing its recreational use in certain settings, such as nursing homes, on moral grounds.

This is also true in the prescribing of tranquilizers, hypnotics, and antidepressants that, under proper circumstances, can provide relief and stabilization during times of severe stress. The beneficial use of drugs and their abuse are separated by a fine line in the elderly because of their diminished tolerance to most drugs, because they receive greater absolute quantities of prescribed drugs, and because they have more reasons for taking these medications. The medical profession is often more profligate in administering depressants to elderly persons than it ought to be. Reasons for this range from ignorance to the application of these substances to pharmacologically subdue persons with difficult medical psychological or social problems. In addition, health care workers often fail to recognize problems relating to side effects of drugs, drug interactions, and self-medication problems in the elderly. These issues present an ever increasing challenge to the profession as more persons grow older and more drugs are made available.

Through the years, the study of narcotic abuse in elderly persons has been obscured by a lack of knowledge as well as unfortunate stereotyping based on the small amount of existing data available. With the advent of methadone treatment programs, the subject has become easier to define. We now know that many elderly narcotic users have not actually "burned out" but have continued to use narcotics by adapting to their circumstances. Thus a switch is often made from heroin to hydromorphone, and dosage is adjusted down to meet the economic restrictions imposed by physical limitations. The drug habit usually persists, except for occasions on which methadone maintenance is sought. Another phenomenon we are beginning to recognize is the aging of persons within the confines of methadone programs. In 1974 (11) we noted that there were 171 clients over 60 years of age out of a total of over 34,000 (0.5 per cent) in New York City methadone programs. Five years later the total number has dropped to 30,000 but the number of persons over 60 has increased to 340 (1.1 per cent). Furthermore, the number of frail elderly is increasing: 53 of these 340 persons are over 70, five are over 80, and the oldest is 84 years of age. Of the 30,000 persons in methadone treatment, 346 are presently between 55 and 59 years of age, which suggests that the aging of this population will continue.

Long term care placement has also become a more severe problem, with agencies still reluctant to admit elderly patients from these programs and provide them with maintenance medication. In 1979 in New York City, the methadone program at Mount Sinai Hospital reported that six of its patients are in nursing homes, and The Roosevelt Hospital program reported two. Staffs of both programs continue to lament the difficulty of placement. Thus the dilemma of these doubly disenfranchised persons persists years after attention was called to it (1).

Although much has been learned, particularly in the past 5 years, much remains to be learned, particularly in relation to effects of drugs in the aging. New interest in gerontology should provide us with much additional clinical and statistical information. Burgeoning interest in the physiology of pain is enhancing our skills in the control of pain while lessening the risks of addiction. But the problem goes beyond the study of drugs and their actions. Until we begin to deal with the complex relationships of such factors as life style, nutrition, poor or inadequate medical care, housing, economic difficulties, and societal attitudes, we cannot conquer the stresses that will continue to foster drug misuse and abuse in elderly persons.

References

1. Alcohol and Drug Abuse among the Elderly; Proceedings of the Senate Committee on Labor Public Welfare, Subcommittee on Alcohol and Narcotics and Subcommittee on the Elderly. Washington, D.C., June 7, 1976.
2. Ball, J. C., and Lau, M. P. The Chinese narcotic addict in the United States. Soc. Forces 45:68, 1966.
3. Brand, F. N., Smith, R. T., and Brand, P. A. Effect of economic barriers in medical care as a factor in patient's noncompliance. Public Health Rep. 91:72, 1977.
4. Capel, W. C., Goldsmith, B. M., Waddell, K. J., et al. The aging narcotic addict: An increasing problem for the next decades. J. Gerontol. 27:102, 1972.
5. Chien, C. P., Townsend, E. J., and Townsend, A. R. Substance use and abuse among the community elderly: The medical aspect. Addict. Dis. 3:357, 1978.
6. Drug Abuse Warning Network. *Phase VI Report, May 1977–April 1978*. Ambler, Pa., I.M.S. America.
7. Guttman, D. Patterns of legal drug use by older Americans. Addict. Dis. 3:337, 1978.
8. Knapp, R. J., and Capel, W. C. Drug use among the elderly: Introduction. J. Drug Issues 9:1, 1979.
9. Mendelson, J. H. Biologic concomitants of alcoholism. N. Engl. J. Med. 283:24, 71, 1970.
10. Pascarelli, E. F. An update on drug dependence in the elderly. J. Drug Issues 9:47, 1979.
11. Pascarelli, E. F., and Fischer, W. Drug dependence in the elderly. Int. J. Aging Hum. Dev. 5:347, 1974.
12. Petersen, D. M., and Thomas, C. W. Acute drug reactions among the elderly. J. Gerontol. 30:552, 1975.
13. Petersen, D. M., Whittington, F. J., and Beer, E. T. Drug use and misuse among the elderly. J. Drug Issues 9:5, 1979.
14. Prien, R. F., Haber, P. A., and Caffey, E. M. The use of psychoactive drugs in elderly patients with psychiatric disorders: Survey conducted in twelve Veterans Administration hospitals. J. Am. Geriatr. Soc. 13:104, 1975.
15. Shuckit, M. A., and Miller, P. L. Alcoholism in elderly men: A survey of a general medical ward. Ann. N. Y. Acad. Sci. 273:558, 1975.
16. Snider, D. A., Pascarelli, D., and Howard, M. *Survey of the Needs and Problems of Adult Home Residents in New York State*. New York, Welfare Research, Inc., New York State Department of Social Services, 1979.
17. Task Force on Prescription Drugs: *The Drug Users*. Washington, D.C., United States Government Printing Office, 1968.
18. United States Public Health Service. *Working with Older People: A Guide to Practice*. Vol. II: *Biological, Psychological and Sociological Aspects of Aging*. Washington, D.C., United States Department of Health, Education and Welfare, 1970.
19. Zimberg, S. Alcohol and the elderly. In *Drugs and the Elderly*, D. M. Petersen, F. J. Whittington, and B. P. Payne, editors, pp. 28–40. Springfield, Ill., Charles C Thomas, 1979.

CHAPTER 61

SUBSTANCE ABUSERS WITH PSYCHIATRIC PROBLEMS

Bernard Salzman, M.D.

The severely disturbed drug abuser represents a covert subpopulation that profoundly challenges our diagnostic and therapeutic acumen. It can be reasonably said that all drug abusers are mentally disturbed; however, our attention will be directed to individuals with psychosis who abuse drugs. For the purposes of this chapter, the term "drug abuser" will be used in its most generic sense, including both the addicted and nonaddicted individual. The role of various drugs in psychosis is extremely complex. Abused drugs may cause, attempt to cure, or uncover psychosis in vulnerable individuals.

In this chapter, I will discuss the factors that contribute to the difficulties in diagnosing psychosis in drug abusers. These factors involve our way of thinking about and describing the drug abuser.

In most individuals, psychosis is a symptomatic product of the interaction between the susceptible individual and specific drug effects. The effect of drugs will be discussed in terms of various diagnostic categories of patients. In the final portion of the chapter, the interaction of the disturbed drug abuser and various treatment modalities will be discussed.

Historically, there has been considerable difficulty in separating the relative roles of drug effect (toxic) and predisposition as causative agents of psychosis. The example of the debate surrounding morphine would be illustrative. Crothers (8) defined morphinism as a psychosis, "much like borderland insanities, paranoiacs and dipsomaniacs." He described morphine addicts as having "delusions of will power," when in fact they were suffering from paralysis of will. A later author (60) stated that addicts are often insane and would have developed psychoses independently of their drug habit. The same author went on to say: "In some cases it appears that the psychosis itself is responsible for the addiction." In their encyclopedic study of drug addiction, Terry and Pellens (55) presented the views of a variety of physicians on the relationship of morphine to psychosis. Erlenmeyer (16) stated that chronic morphinism gives rise to psychosis, whereas Schneider (47) argued against a specific morphine psychosis and for concomitant dementia precox. A third author, Legeive (33) saw the psychosis as part of an abstinence syndrome. So accepted was this idea of the relationship between morphine and psychosis that it entered the standard nomenclature in the form of "psychosis due to opium or its derivatives (24)." In 1948, Pfeffer and Ruble, in a study of morphine addicts, found psychotic symptoms were due to a preexisting schizophrenia or organic condition and reiterated the idea that there is no characteristic morphine psychosis (38). The issue of the drug (toxic) effect and premorbid personality is part of a continuous debate. The drugs in question have changed from opiates to marihuana, stimulants, and hallucinogens. The primacy given the toxic effects of the drug or its abstinence syndrome has diverted our attention away from the role played by abused drugs on the schizophrenic or vulnerable personality.

The diagnosis of severe mental disorder in a drug-abusing population requires careful analysis. Often these patients remain undetected until, in a seemingly unpredictable manner, the severity of their illness becomes manifest. A major pitfall in establishing the diagnosis of severe disturbance is the tendency to view the drug-addicted population as homogeneous. The addicted individual suffers from a clearly defined set of symptoms. They are often thought to look and act the same. This idea is further reified by the attempts to establish a unified theory of addiction without regard to antecedent personality structure (1, 14, 59). Moreover, treatment programs such as methadone maintenance and therapeutic communities are based theoretically on the homogeneity of their populations. It is within the framework of homogeneity that undiagnosed disturbed addicts find their way into various treatment programs. Most programs are not capable of handling disturbed patients, which often causes a disruptive interaction and premature discharge.

A second difficulty arises out of the limitation of our current psychiatric nomenclature. The interaction of vulnerable individuals, external stress, and particular drug effect may cause dramatic symptoms. Often these symptoms represent schizophreniform decompensations and are extremely transitory. Recovery to characterological levels is equally dramatic, and symptoms are mistakenly attributed to the toxic effects of the drug. This transitory symptomatology, functional in origin, falls into the diagnostic cracks. It is neither toxic nor a fixed functional category such as schizophrenia. The term "borderline personality," in the revised nomenclature, may take into account such phenomena.

TOXIC PSYCHOSIS

There are a considerable number of exogenous substances reported to induce psychosis. A partial listing is cited by Davison and includes many drugs not commonly abused (10). Phenomenologically, the acute psychotic reaction resembles those of schizophrenia, without the genetic loading of premorbid personality. These symptoms include changes in personality, withdrawal, thought disorder, blunted or inappropriate affect, hallucinations, and delusions. Davison classified drug-induced psychosis into four types, based on symptoms. The commonest of these is acute drug reaction, transitory in nature, self-limiting, and schizophreniform in appearance (10). This type of reaction is seen after the use of such hallucinogens as lysergic acid diethylamide (LSD) and phencyclidine. They represent an acute stress reaction without premorbid pathology. A typical scenario would involve an early adolescent knowingly or unknowingly ingesting a hallucinogen for the first time at a noisy rock concert. Paranoid preoccupations and hallucinations are a common concomitant of abrupt, unexpected ego disorganization. The feature of novelty, external stress, and drug effect are similarly operative in acute psychotic phenomena associated with cannabis (32, 51). The acute unmasking of borderline schizophrenia, or the deterioration of preexisting schizophrenia, is a phenomenon associated with marihuana, hallucinogens, or disinhibiting drugs of the alcohol-barbiturate family (3). In this subpopulation, psychotic reactions are often protracted, chronic in nature, and more like the nuclear illness.

Chronic psychosis associated with drugs has been related to LSD, marihuana, and amphetamine. Authors vary in emphasis, however, on the role of the drug as a contributing or causal factor to the psychosis. Using the example of marihuana, a toxic psychosis has been described, including symptoms of paranoia, temporal disorientation, and confusion (7, 54). Descriptions of chronic psychosis associated with marihuana have been quite variable, including schizophreniform psychosis and manic and confusional states (2, 56). The relationship between marihuana and premorbid personality was described by Keup (29). Like previous authors, he separated drug effects into toxic, the uncovering of preexisting pathology, and the aggravating effects of the drug. Glass (20) distinguished three psychiatric syndromes—an acute drug reaction in an already compromised ego, a shift toward more primitive defenses such as projection, and denial in experienced users during stress and drug use in schizophrenia.

An attempt to separate endogenous from exogenous factors in drug-related psychosis would include a careful history of genetic loading, premorbid personality, and the mode of onset of the psychosis. The temporal relationship between the onset of psychiatric symptoms and drug ingestion and the chronicity of the symptoms is often misleading, particularly in the absence of antecedent history.

Another set of circumstances creating difficult diagnostic problems is the psychotic reaction accompanying withdrawal from various abused drugs. Withdrawal psychosis associated with drugs of the alcohol-barbiturate family has been described (17). The psychosis is of the acute delirium type. It occurs between the fourth and fourteenth day of withdrawal, and in benzodiazopines may be seen even at therapeutic dosage levels (17). However, precipitation or uncovering of a schizophrenic process may occur during or after detoxification from an abused drug. In schizophrenic and borderline patients, the abused drug acts as psychological cement or surrogate ego, and withdrawal leads to profound disorganization. The process often unmasks heretofore latent processes. Wurmser, referring to opiate addiction, felt the use of the abused drug becomes an attempt at self-treatment and a bona fide psychotropic agent (62). The central role of the drug loss is illustrated in the precipitous decompensation seen during detoxification from methadone. This phenomenon is relatively uncommon, considering the number of individuals who detoxify. The presence of signs of altered consciousness and clinical response to the originally addicting drug would be helpful in delineating the abstinence syndrome from decompensation. The discussion further emphasizes the psychological significance of the drug and the complexity of its role.

SCHIZOPHRENIA

The relationship between drug abuse and schizophrenia is complex and confusing. There is, for instance, considerable variability in the incidence of schizophrenia among heroin addicts. In various studies of schizophrenia in heroin addicts, the incidence was found to be 20 per cent (6), 19 per cent (57), and 7 per cent (19). Even greater variance was found in adult studies. One study described the incidence as being 2 per cent, about equal to

that of the general population (38). Another study—20 years later—from a psychiatric inpatient service, found the incidence of schizophrenia in drug abusers to be 50 per cent (23). In assessing these studies, a number of factors must be taken into consideration. All the studies quoted were done prior to 1970, a major heroin epidemic year. The addict populations described in these studies were both smaller and more homogeneous than our contemporary populations. Many of the studies were from the United States Public Health Service Hospital, and a more representative population than that from a psychiatric inpatient service (19, 38, 57). The study by Vaillant pointed out that the diagnosis of schizophrenia was not stable and diminished in incidence in follow-up studies (57). A number of the studies used terms such as "incipient schizophrenia" and "schizoid personality," implying a propensity, under stress, to become schizophrenic. The issue of propensity or vulnerability toward schizophrenia creates unstable diagnostic categories. This further complicates determinations of the incidence of schizophrenia among drug abusers.

External stress in drug abusers may precipitate schizophreniform symptoms. Stress, in the form of fear of arrest, loss, or separation from an important person or drug supply, may precipitate a decompensation. Accompanying and often accelerating the deterioration is an increased use of an already abused drug or the introduction of a secondary drug. The resultant ego disorganization often leads to psychotic symptoms in many individuals that disappear dramatically after short term hospitalization.

Another issue that adds to the diagnostic dilemma is related to the psychotropic action of chronically abused or addicting drugs. The drug effect plays many intrapsychic roles in the schizophrenic patient. The drug serves as a surrogate ego and produces a homogeneous, albeit artificial, affect. In some patients, the drug effect becomes an externalized object, literally an alter ego. The structural and functional import of the drug becomes so vital that its relative or absolute absence leads to precipitous decompensation.

The most difficult diagnostic problems arise as a corollary to the stress of addiction. Addicted patients represent a heterogeneous population in terms of genetic loading, early development, and socioeconomic background. As the individual enters the drug environment, there is a progressive narrowing and reduction of his adaptive repertoire. This reductive process is centered on the acquisition and use of a particular drug. Consequently, this ubiquitous reduction creates the appearance of homogeneity in the addict population, including schizophrenics. In an unpublished study of schizophrenic addicts, I attempted to separate schizophrenic from characterological addicts by studying their history antedating their drug use. In a population of 110 addicts, I could find no significant difference in genetic loading, parental separation or drug use, or aberrant childhood behavior between the two groups. This study raised the issue of the accuracy of the initial diagnosis or any single diagnostic impression and the homogeneous appearance of the study population.

A form of behavior indicative of this reductive process is the development of a pseudopsychopathic adaptation. Purposeful, manipulative, and antisocial behavior is an adaptive part of an addict's repertoire. As studied by Géller, schizophrenic patients have drawn their psychotic symptoms into the service of adaptation to their environment (18). Often in a psychotic manner they have learned to be deceptive, prevaricative, and elusive. They seem on the surface like all other addicts, and thereby draw attention away from their nuclear illness. In attempting to carry off a con job, they are grossly inept because of their errors in their appreciation of reality. This form of adaptation is seen in the relationship of the schizophrenic addict to such institutions as hospitals, prisons, and drug therapy programs.

In the preceding text, I have discussed the difficulties in finding and diagnosing this elusive subpopulation. The adaptive reduction, the effect of the drugs themselves, and the transitory nature of symptoms seem to confuse issues. Many severely disturbed drug abusers feed into various categories of vulnerability. These include latent or borderline schizophrenia, schizoid and other primitive personality types. This vulnerability takes the form of genetic loading, environmental and psychological deprivation (19), and organic impairment (5, 21). Drug abuse becomes an attempted solution to a reduced and compromised adaptive repertoire. Under stress, this brittle adaptive shell shatters, and the schizophrenic process emerges.

AFFECTIVE DISORDERS

Depressive mood is a common concomitant of drug abuse (37). The difficulty arises as to whether the affective state is primary or secondary to drug use. In a study of women admitted to an alcohol detoxification center, Schuckit and Morrissey (48) noted that 53 per cent of the women met the criteria for primary alcoholism and 14 per cent for primary affective disorder. These separate subpopulations had similar drinking patterns and were differentiated by genetic loading and non-drug-related period of depressive symptoms (48). A study of depression in methadone maintenance patients found a familial incidence of 14 per cent in depressed addicts (58). Approximately 30 per cent of the methadone patients were depressed, using multiple psychodiagnostic criteria. The authors, however, felt that the majority of their patients were secondarily depressed.

The problem of determining the nature of the depression in drug addicts is compounded by the fact that chronic use of certain drugs causes a biologically determined dysphoria. A classic example is seen in the long term use of opiates (35). The chronic state of illness or calamitous life style may cause a reactive depression. Depressive states are also seen during the withdrawal states of certain drugs, such as opiates, alcohol, and stimulants.

A number of studies have reiterated the sizable incidence of depression in methadone maintenance patients (39, 49). Treatment, however, is based to some degree on differentiating primary from secondary affective states. Certain agents, such as tricyclic antidepressants, are thought to be effective only in primary depressive illness and are of questionable use in secondary depression. Certain tricyclics are abusable, and the drug-abusing population as a whole has an extremely high incidence of suicide (39).

Case evaluation of the patient should include family history of affective disorder and a history of depression, with symptoms, prior to the use of drugs or during periods of sobriety.

An unusual, but probably underdiagnosed, relationship exists between mania and drug abuse. Two recent reports link symptomatic mania due to phencyclidine abuse (42, 50). In the original report, the manic episode occurred in a clear sensorium with classical symptoms of mania. There was neither a family history of affective disorder nor previous psychiatric hospitalization. The psychotic episode was prolonged beyond the half-life of the drug and responded only to lithium. The drug acted as a nonspecific precipitant of a functional psychosis.

The diagnosis of mania is made infrequently. The picture of paranoid symptoms and self-destructive behavior in the presence of drugs is often attributed to a toxic state or paranoid schizophrenia. This is particularly true if the diagnosis of mania is based on the presence of elation and grandiosity. In a sense, the underdiagnosis is due more to diagnostic prejudice than to a confusing clinical picture (15).

The most dangerous aspect associated with severe mental disturbance is suicide. Opiate addicts and the drug-abusing population in general represent a serious suicide risk (36, 45, 46). Self-destructive behavior is an intrinsic aspect of drug abuse that behaviorally seems ·very similar to suicidal behavior in non-drug abusers. In one study of ambulatory drug abusers, 19 per cent of the patients made suicide attempts (45). This produces a rate of suicide attempts as much as 150 times greater than that of the general population. Frequently the drug of primary abuse is not used in the suicide attempt, and the behavior may not be recognized against the background of self-destructive activities. There is frequently a fine line between attempts to reach increased levels of intoxication and taking a fatal overdose. The suicide attempt is often related to loss of a need-fulfilling person, in which drugs act as vehicle for the patient's rage, turned ultimately against himself. This separation of what might be termed drug greed from the violent form of acting out is difficult. Furthermore, the suicidal behavior may exist without any outward signs of depression. In a general sense, every drug abuser is a potential suicide victim and requires careful vigilance and evaluation.

TREATMENT

The disturbed drug abuser is not only a diagnostic dilemma but also a difficult problem in treatment. Treatment begins only after the state of intoxication or addiction is interrupted and a firm diagnostic evaluation can be done. This frequently entails detoxification and short term hospitalization. Subsequent treatment is contingent upon maintaining sobriety, at least during the actual therapy sessions. Similar conditions exist in drug-assisted programs after dosage stabilization. Therapy while the patient is intoxicated is futile.

The most difficult problem arises in converting the patient's drug-related or induced symptoms into intrapsychic or interpersonal terms. The disturbed drug abuser, like his more normative counterpart, externalizes his problems. This technique forms a first line of psychological defense, as the abuser is always abused. The view that the world, not he, must change perpetuates denial of the addict's provocative role and his intrapsychic conflicts. Reduction is another prominent line of defense used by both the patient and his family. It takes the form of reducing the patient's problem to drug taking. A complex intra- and extrapsychic problem is reduced to a bad habit. This form of reduction serves not only denial and repression but becomes a formidable form of treatment resistance.

A second difficulty in establishing treatment is the social stigma given to mental illness in the drug-abusing population. It reflects, albeit in an exaggerated manner, similar attitudes in the general population. The "crazy" drug abuser is thought to be unpredictable and, therefore, not dependable in a mutually dependent subsociety. The overtly disturbed drug abuser is treated like a pariah and socially isolated. Denial of mental illness, in these terms, can become a necessary form of adaptation.

The basis of treatment is the translation of drug-abusing behavior into a broader basis of understanding. The basis may be biological determinism, intrapsychic conflict, or learned maladaptation, but the roots of treatment are in the translation process.

Wurmser discussed the following ingredients of treatment (63). The therapeutic environment must be nurturing and accepting.

Limit setting, in the form of external structure, is necessary to protect both the patient against himself and the therapeutic setting. This external structure also facilitates internalization of controls, an essential part of the therapeutic process. The relationship between the individual patient and the therapeutic institution is often provocative and stormy. Dangerous and antisocial behavior often leads to harsh punitive countermeasures and premature discharge. Any therapeutic setting requires recognition of special patient problems, as well as flexibility and tolerance. Wurmser made the specific recommendation that the intense dyadic therapeutic relationship be diluted or be split up, utilizing a variety of therapeutic approaches and multiple therapeutic relationships to salvage treatment (63). In the next section I will discuss the disturbed drug abuser in a variety of treatment settings. The discussion will point out the theoretical and practical limitations of these settings to this patient population.

INDIVIDUAL PSYCHOTHERAPY

Individual psychotherapy with a disturbed drug abuser is an extraordinarily difficult task. The drug-abusing population seen in private practice is predominantly middle and upper middle class. According to one study, this class has greater psychopathology than their lower class cohorts (27). Although this is a somewhat questionable generalization, it seems true if seen in the light of deviation from class expectation and alternative adaptive opportunities.

The majority of patients seen fall into the categories of borderline personality and schizophrenia. They invariably enter treatment on the urging of important others who, like themselves, reduce their problems to drug usage. The psychodynamics of addiction and clinical course are described elsewhere in the text, so this discussion will be limited to a few observations.

The initial phase of therapy begins by setting the conditions of treatment. This initial contract, which includes the necessity of sobriety during the sessions, is the prologue to treatment. Generally the initial phase centers around the environment of drug use and the repeated inability to remain abstinent. This

central preoccupation becomes the core of the patient's resistance, precluding progress. At times one must impose a moratorium on drug discussion to break through this resistant shell. This phase of discussion does serve an important function. It details the strategic use of the drugs both intrapsychically and as a tactic in defining the patient's relationship to others.

The second phase of treatment involves intense vacillation in the transference, extending from overcompliance to sudden bursts of anger to dangerous acting out. During these acting-out episodes, the patient may go on a drug binge, take a serious overdose, or get himself arrested. The patient's anger is frequently directed at the frustrating therapist or another individual on whom he feels dependent. Ultimately he is the victim of his own behavior. These outbursts create a temporary estrangement from therapy and provide the patient with the necessary distance from the intense transference. Short term hospitalization is often effective and necessary at this stage to interrupt the self-destructive behavior. Not infrequently, the patient will undergo a number of these episodes, and the therapist's availability must be assured.

It is often important to maintain contact with a patient's family, if available, on both a formal and informal basis. The family adds a dimensionality to the treatment, frequently mirroring the transference relationship. The patient's family may take an active role in reinforcing the patient's pathology by reduction, scapegoating, or sabotaging the treatment. Frequently the patient's pathology is part of a more pervasive family pathology, and other members may be invested in maintaining the patient in a "sick role" (53). The patient's family is also a valuable ally and important in reinforcing the behavioral gains of therapy. They are also a most important link in the social network supporting the patient.

The third phase of treatment, and the most protracted, involves the replacement of the patient's drug-related adaptation by an adaptive repertoire that is not only less painful but more flexible and productive. Frequently, at this stage, the patient feels himself bereft of assets and ambition, experiencing volitional paralysis and depression. He has in fact given up a 100 per cent solution. Ancillary forms of treatment, such as psychotropic agents or multidimensional forms of therapy, are often helpful at this stage.

HOSPITALIZATION

One of the most effective and strategic forms of treatment for the disturbed drug abuser is short term hospitalization. The most subtle form of deterioration of mental states appears as change of behavior. This deterioration of behavior precedes or accompanies a change in the drug abuse pattern. This may take the form of increased or idiosyncratic use of an already abused drug or the introduction of secondary or tertiary drugs. Other manifestations of deterioration are changes in the patient's attitude to the therapist or drug rehabilitation program. The change may take the form of withdrawal or avoidance or the assumption of a provocative, litigious stance.

The behavioral manifestations are frequently triggered by an external stress—loss of person, job, or support. The stress triggers ego disorganization, in which the use of the drug serves both to relieve the distress and signal for help.

Short term hospitalization interrupts drug taking or secondary manifestations of the ego disorganization. It allows separation of the drug effects from the underlying mental state, providing a clearer diagnostic picture. The hospital also provides a socially accepted withdrawal from the external stress situation by allowing a medically sanctioned and controlled regression.

Short term results with hospitalized methadone patients have been excellent. The recovery period is rapid. Many of the more florid psychotic symptoms disappear with a return of the more superficial characterological features, seen during the interictal period. The use of low dose neuroleptics is helpful during this period. The use of neuroleptics serves a 2-fold purpose. The drug provides an alternative form of symptom relief and redefines the patient's symptoms in psychological terms. Follow-up of these within the therapeutic program is an important adjuvant to psychiatric care.

Drug abusers who are not part of any therapeutic program also benefit from short term hospitalization. They present with similar symptoms of drug-related decompensa-

tion. They lack, however, the psychotropic effects of methadone or the social network of a therapeutic community. They frequently fall into the borderline diagnostic categories, having led a fragmented and chaotic life. The goals of hospitalization for this group are more complex. The role of drugs in this group is intricate and pervasive, and giving up the abused drug strips the patient of a major defensive and adaptive tool. The patients experience tremendous feelings of emptiness and depression. Hospitalization is a period in which the nature and extent of the disability are revealed. Low dose neuroleptics—such as thorazine, 25 to 75 mg four times a day—are similarly effective. Generally, the period of hospitalization for this group is longer (up to 3 months) and more multidimensional. The treatment program would include milieu, vocational, and family therapy and for this group of patients serves as a prelude to more dimensional forms of therapy or as a new beginning for individual therapy.

PSYCHOTROPIC DRUGS

The use of psychotropic drugs is an important part of treatment of the disturbed drug addict. These patients, however, present a number of difficult problems. One, previously discussed, is establishing an accurate diagnosis. Although patients may manifest similar symptoms, the origins of these symptoms may be functional, toxic, or part of an abstinence syndrome. Frequently, symptoms are transitory and do not fulfill research diagnostic criteria.

There are more intrinsic qualities of the disturbed population that pose difficulties for using psychotropic drugs. There is the generalized stigma against the mentally disturbed. The use of psychotropic drugs becomes the reification of this stigma and, therefore, is frequently unacceptable to patients.

Another issue is related to the psychopathology of the drug abuser. The drug abuser needs to control the drug he ingests, the amount taken, and the circumstances under which it is taken. The passivity intrinsic to medical supervision triggers a defensive posture and frequent noncompliance. Occasionally, the disturbed drug abuser will use the psychotropic drug in idiosyncratic ways, such as storing or taking large overdoses.

A further difficulty arises out of the patient's primitive somatic preoccupations that sensitize him to the frequently occurring side effects of psychoactive drugs. Even trivial side effects, such as dryness of the mouth, may trigger a sudden cessation of medication. More profound side effects, such as dyskinesia or akathesia, precipitate feelings of depersonalization and aggravate an underlying psychosis.

Some psychoactive drugs are sold illicitly. The abuse pattern is a function of its availability and its alleged ability to alter consciousness. Among the drugs most commonly abused are the benzodiazepines and certain tricyclic antidepressants, such as amitriptyline and doxepin. Frequently these drugs are requested by the patient, but their use should be discouraged.

Based on these caveats, the following guidelines would be helpful in using psychoactive drugs with disturbed patients:

1. The patient should play an active role in the decision to use the drugs, determine the target symptoms, and, where possible, when the drug should be taken.

2. Drug-taking-schedules should be simple, with priority given to night-loading to minimize the impact of side effects and aid in sleep.

3. During the initial or induction phase, minimal doses should be used, with upward titration as needed.

4. Preference should be given to drugs with low incidence of side effects, and patients should be informed of these side effects.

5. Patients should be seen at short intervals, weekly or biweekly, and alterations of medication made promptly.

6. Prescriptions should be small and for a designated period of time.

7. Sedatives qua sedatives should rarely be given. Most sedatives are ineffective or abused. The cause of the insomnia must be explored, and the use of a specific psychotropic agent may be helpful.

ANTIPSYCHOTIC MEDICATION

The most commonly used classes of antipsychotic drugs are the phenothiazines and butyrophenones. One group of disturbed drug abusers, on methadone maintenance, does not seem to need large doses of antipsychotic medication (30). Kleber and Gold posit an antipsychotic role for opiate agonist, although the mechanism of this action is unknown. A corrollary to the possible synergistic action of opiate agonist and psychotropic medications may, however, cause considerable difficulty. It is my clinical impression that methadone-maintained patients show a high incidence of side effects at relatively low therapeutic doses. This observation has not been replicated and requires further research.

Major target symptoms in this population include anxiety, disorganization, and such secondary symptoms as delusions and hallucinations. Certain antipsychotic drugs seem to be very effective during the initial or induction phase of treatment because of their low incidence of side effects. Although preferences may differ, low dose thioridazine and chlorpromazine are effective for this purpose. These drugs are both effective and well tolerated. At higher doses, the neuroendocrine side effects of thioridazine and the sedation of chlorpromazine cause greater noncompliance. A known side effect of thioridazine, retrograde ejaculation, is particularly troublesome for this already sexually compromised population.

High potency antipsychotic drugs, such as trifluoperazine and perphenazine, seem less effective with methadone patients. The patients develop side effects at low doses, and it is difficult to maintain them on these medications. Haloperidol has been found to be an effective adjuvant during methadone detoxification but is less effective as a maintenance drug.

ANTIDEPRESSANTS

Depression is a common concomitant, although its etiology is frequently unclear. As many as one-third of the population of methadone patients may be depressed, using a battery of psychodiagnostic tests (58). A frequent accompanying symptom, possibly related to the depression, is difficulty falling or staying asleep. A number of tricyclic antidepressants have been found to be effective with this population. Doxepin is a commonly used antidepressant with anxiolytic properties. It has been found to be effective in a number of studies of depressed methadone patients (52, 61). One author suggested the use of doxepin for anxiety, mild depression, and insomnia (52). Doxepin, however, has recently been reported to be abused and has the same danger as amitriptyline. Another less publicized problem with doxepin and other tricyclics used for insomnia is the precipitation of nightmares and frequent awakenings about 2 hours after the onset of sleep. Recurrence occurs even after changing to another tricyclic, and compliance is difficult to maintain. It seems that tricyclics are effective only for short periods of time. Amitriptyline is an effective but abused drug. Kleber and Gold suggested a form of the drug combined with perphenazine to diminish the abuse potential (30).

This is not an exhaustive discussion of psychoactive drugs that are useful. Many other potential drugs have been found to be abusable or to interact deleteriously with such maintenance drugs as methadone. Considerable research is necessary for new psychotropic agents applicable to this population.

AMBULATORY TREATMENT

Ambulatory care of disturbed drug abusers in conventional mental hygiene facilities has been a major problem. A general distrust has arisen between the clinic and the drug abuser. Many clinics will not serve known drug abusers, forcing many disturbed patients to hide their drug use. In one study, 13.3 per cent of the patients in a mental health facility had urinalyses positive for abused drugs (22). Covert drug abusers were frequently misdiagnosed, were management problems, and had an increased incidence of adverse drug reactions. Mental health facilities that accept drug abusers and have staffs appropriately trained seem to have greater success than standard mental hygiene facilities. Other forms of ambulatory treatment, such as crisis intervention and family and group therapy, add further dimensions to the treatment of the disturbed drug abuser.

The largest ambulatory system for treating disturbed drug abusers is within the methadone maintenance system. This system, based on the theory of the biological origins of addiction, contains a sizable, albeit often covert, number of disturbed individuals. There is no reliable estimate of the number of severely disturbed patients within these programs. A conservative estimate would be around 20 per cent of the total population.

The psychotropic effects of methadone, the homogeneity of the technique, and the reductionistic nature of the illness make diagnostic determinations difficult. Psychopathology is often manifest in the stormy transference between the patient and the clinic (9). For the disturbed patients whose pathology is manifest behaviorally, there is a disproportionately high rate of discharge (31). A particular scenario is played out by the pathologically paranoid patient with the methadone maintenance program (44). This patient manifests extreme vacillation in attitude toward the staff, ranging from pseudocompliance to extremely provocative behavior. This rage is frequently directed at the nurse, who in his mind has placed him in a passive position. The passive role of the patient, because of the highly controlled manner in which methadone is administered, often leads to a higher incidence of administrative discharge and voluntary detoxification by the more paranoid patients.

The staff of methadone maintenance programs is made up of undertrained counselors who are frequently overwhelmed or frightened by the disturbed patient. The interaction leads to considerable intraclinic tension and premature discharge. A second type of disturbed patient, whose pathology is predominantly verbal-cognitive, is not only tolerated but coddled and remains in the program for long periods of time. The clinic becomes for this group an acceptable long term aftercare facility.

Methadone maintenance has been combined with more conventional forms of therapy to retain the disturbed patient. One attempt was to combine methadone and a psychiatric day care program (43). The staff was made up of predominantly mental health professionals who utilized milieu, individual, and group therapies (13). The patients were addicts from the psychiatric inpatient service and from other methadone programs. Patients from other programs were generally severe behavior problems, on the brink of discharge. The majority of patients were retained for longer than 18 months, with the dropouts usually leaving within 3 months. About one-half the population was diagnosed as schizophrenic by prior or clinical histories;

the other half had a variety of characterological disorders. About 10 per cent of the population voluntarily detoxified and remained drug free. The remainder of the population transferred to more conventional methadone or drug-free programs. The most sobering statistic from this group was that 15 of the 110 patients died, either while on the program or within a year of discharge.

The program was necessarily small and, therefore, costly. A fundamental difficulty arose in combining two treatment philosophies, psychiatric and addiction. At certain interfaces, such as evaluating patients' aberrant behavior, the two philosophies clashed. The issue of defining the behavior as "sick" versus "antisocial" created continuous intrastaff conflict and confusion. This is an example of a major drawback in attempting to develop a hybrid program with differing treatment philosophies.

A second variation is the establishment of a miniclinic consisting of psychiatrist and social worker working within a standard methadone maintenance program. The social worker screens disturbed patients on referral from the counselors. The patients are seen on a weekly or biweekly basis and given psychotropic medication if needed and short term psychotherapy. The patient maintains his relationship with his counselor and is subject to the same regulations as other patients. This system is acceptable to the patient, reduces stigmatization, and economically extends the therapeutic repertoire of the standard clinic.

Methadone treatment and long term detoxification are also being combined with therapeutic community in an attempt to capitalize on the advantages of each treatment.

THERAPEUTIC COMMUNITY

The therapeutic community is a residential self-help program. Its goals are the maintenance of drug abstinence and the restructuring of character during treatment (40). The major treatment modalities include modeling, peer pressure, and various forms of group therapy. Group therapy often takes the form of prolonged and caustic encounters among the residents. As the original philosophy was of self-help, there is frequently a strong bias against professional mental health workers.

Therapeutic communities in general have been criticized for their parochialism, rigidity, and resistance to change in step with a changing addict population. There are no clear estimates of the number of drug abusers in therapeutic communities, and there are many difficulties in accumulating this kind of data. A number of communities exclude patients with a history of mental illness (26). In a community where residents are seen as homogeneous, this statistic is often not kept. However, one therapeutic community reported that 40 to 50 per cent of its residents were borderline schizophrenic (4). In a series of studies from one community, the author found that program dropouts exhibited significantly greater psychopathology (11). Using a standard psychodiagnostic battery, the community as a whole resembled a psychiatric population.

In many ways, the high rate of dropping out by drug abusers is not surprising. Disturbed patients are often overwhelmed by the defense-stripping confrontational techniques. The psychologically unsophisticated staff is often perplexed and overwhelmed by the disturbed and bizarre patient. The staff member sees the disturbed patient as a treatment failure and may covertly encourage his elopement. The most difficult problem is the philosophically negative attitude toward any drug taking, including psychotropic drugs. The drugs are perceived as a crutch, and the taker is stigmatized within the community.

The therapeutic community is a potentially ideal vehicle for the treatment of the disturbed drug abuser. The treatment is multidimensional, utilizing many techniques and therapists over a 24-hour period. Formal and informal types of therapy, including modeling, peer pressure, and psychotropic drugs, could be combined, maximizing the effects of each technique. The community could minimize the passive and regressive elements intrinsic to the drug-assisted programs. Recent developments provide reason for optimism. There seems to be increasing recognition of special subgroups within the communities. Some communities have broadened their scope to include disturbed individuals, and professional mental health workers have been added to their staffs. Reliance on the caustic form of group therapy has diminished, and more sophisticated techniques, such as behavior modification, have been added. Finally, in some communities, the use of psychotropic drugs, in selected situations, has been permitted (41).

Another recent development has been the combination of drug-assisted programs with therapeutic communities. For the disturbed addict, this would combine the psychotropic qualities of methadone and the residential and drug prevention aspects of the therapeutic community. Examples of this combination offer many therapeutic modalities and utilize methadone as an adjunct or transitional stage toward abstinence (12, 28).

References

1. Bejerot, N. A theory of addiction as an artificially induced drive. Am. J. Psychiatry 128:842, 1972.
2. Bernhardson, G., and Gunne, L.-M. Forty-six cases of psychosis in cannabis abusers. Int. J. Addict. 7:9, 1972.
3. Breakey, W. R., Goodell, H., Lorenz, P. C., and McHugh, P. R. Hallucinogenic drugs as precipitants of schizophrenia. Psychol. Med. 4:255, 1974.
4. Callum, J. M. The dynamics of change in a therapeutic community. In Drug Abuse: Modern Trends, Issues, and Perspectives, A. Schecter, H. Alksne, and E. Kaufman, editors, pp. 169–175. New York, Marcel Dekker, 1978.
5. Carlin, A. S., Stauss, F. F., Adams, K. M., and Grant, I. The prediction of neuropsychological impairment in polydrug abusers. Addict. Behav. 3:5, 1978.
6. Chein, I., Gerard, D. L., Lee, S. R., and Rosenfeld, E. The Road to H, p. 482. New York, Basic Books, 1964.
7. Colbach, E. M., and Crowe, R. R. Marihauna associated with psychosis in Vietnam. Milit. Med. 135:571, 1970.
8. Crothers, T. D. Morphinism and Narcomania from Other Drugs, p. 66. Philadelphia, W. B. Saunders, 1902.
9. Davidson, V. Love and hate in methadone maintenance. Am. J. Psychoanal. 37:163, 1977.
10. Davison, K. Drug-induced psychoses and their relationship to schizophrenia. In Schizophrenia Today, D. Kemali et al., editors, pp. 105–133. Oxford, Pergamon, 1976.
11. De Leon, G. Phoenix House: Psychopathological signs among male and female drug-free residents. Addict. Dis. 1:135, 1974.
12. Del Rey, A. J., Kirby, J., Langrod, J., Lowinson, J., and Alksne, L. The therapeutic community as adjunct to methadone maintenance. In Drug Abuse: Modern Trends, Issues, and Perspectives, A. Schecter, H. Alksne, and E. Kaufman, editors, pp. 191–199. New York, Marcel Dekker, 1978.
13. Demirjian, A., and Dowell, S. Resocialization: A treatment modality for heroin addicts with severe psychiatric disorder. In Proceedings of the 4th National Conference on Methadone Maintenance, pp. 521–525. New York, National Association for the Prevention of Addiction to Narcotics, 1972.
14. Dole, V. P., and Nyswander, M. E. Heroin addiction: A metabolic disease. Arch. Intern. Med. 120:19, 1967.
15. El-Guebaly, N. Manic-depressive psychosis and drug abuse. J. Can. Psychiatr. Assoc. 20:595, 1975.
16. Erlenmeyer, A. Zur Theorie und Therapie des Morphinismus. Neurol. Psychiatr. 103:705, 1926.
17. Fruensgaard, K. Withdrawal psychosis: A study of 30 consecutive cases. Acta Psychiatr. Scand. 53:105, 1976.
18. Geller, M. Sociopathic adaptation in psychiatric patients. Hosp. Community Psychiatr, In press.
19. Gerard, D. L., and Kornetsky, C. Adolescent opiate addiction: A study of control and addict subjects. Psychiatr. Q. 29:457, 1955.
20. Glass, G. S. Psychedelic drugs, stress and the ego: The differential diagnosis of psychosis associated with psychotomimetic drug use. J. Nerv. Ment. Dis. 156:232, 1973.
21. Grant, I., Adams, K. M., Carlin, A. S., Rennick, P. M., Judd, L. L., Schooff, K., and Reed, R. Organic impairment in polydrug users: Risk factors. J. Am. Psychiatr. Assoc. 135:178, 1978.
22. Hall, C. W. R., Popkin, M., Stickney, S. K., and Gardner, R. E. Covert outpatient drug abuse. J. Nerv. Ment. Dis. 166:343, 1978.
23. Hekimian, L. J., and Gershon, S. Characteristics of drug abusers admitted to a psychiatric hospital. J.A.M.A. 205:125, 1968.
24. Jordan, E. P., editor. Standard Nomenclature of Disease, p. 100. Chicago, American Medical Association, 1942.
25. Karkalas, J., and Lal, H. A comparison of haloperidol with methadone in blocking heroin withdrawal symptoms. Int. Pharmacopsychiatry 8:248, 1973.
26. Kaufman, E. A psychiatrist views an addict self-help program. Am. J. Psychiatry 128:846, 1972.
27. Kaufman, E. The relationship of social class and ethnicity to drug abuse. In A Multicultural View of Drug Abuse, D. Smith et al. editors, pp. 158–163. Cambridge, Mass., G. K. Hall/Schenkman, 1978.
28. Kaufman, E., Williams, R., and Braudy, M. Su Casa: A methadone to abstinence therapeutic community. In Drug Abuse: Modern Trends, Issues, and Perspectives, A. Schecter, H. Alksne, and E. Kaufman, editors, pp. 200–206. New York, Marcel Dekker, 1978.
29. Keup, W. Psychotic symptoms due to cannabis abuse: A survey of newly admitted mental patients. Dis. Nerv. Syst. 31:119, 1970.
30. Kleber, H. D., and Gold, M. S. Use of psychotropic drugs in treatment of methadone maintained narcotic addicts. Ann. N. Y. Acad. Sci. 311:81, 1978.
31. Krakowski, M., and Smart, R. G. Social and psychological characteristics of heroin addicts dropping out of methadone treatment. J. Can. Psychiatr. Assoc. 19:41, 1974.
32. Kroll, P. Psychoses associated with marijuana use in Thailand. J. Nerv. Ment. Dis. 161:149, 1975.
33. Legeive, B. Delirium beim Morphinismus. Z. Gesamte Neurol. Psychiatr. 89:558, 1924.
34. McKenna, G. J., Fisch, A., Levine, M., Patch, V. D., and Raynes, A. The use of methadone as a psychotropic agent. In Proceedings of the 5th National Conference on Methadone Maintenance, pp. 1317–1325. New York, National Association for the Prevention of Addiction to Narcotics, 1973.
35. Mirin, S. M., Meyer, R. E., and McNamee, H. G.

Psychopathology and mood during heroin use: Acute vs. chronic effects. Arch. Gen. Psychiatry 33:1503, 1976.

36. Moore, J. T., Judd, L. L., Zung, W., and Alexander, G. R. Opiate addiction and suicidal behaviors. Am. J. Psychiatry 136:1187, 1979.

37. Paton, S., Kessler, R., and Kandel, D. Depressive mood and adolescent illicit drug use: A longitudinal analysis. J. Genet. Psychol. 131:267, 1977.

38. Pfeffer, A. Z., and Ruble, D. C. Chronic psychoses and addiction to morphine. Arch. Neurol. Psychiatry 56:665, 1948.

39. Prussoff, B., Thompson, W. D., Sholomskas, D., and Riordan, C. Psychosocial stressors and depression among former heroin-dependent patients maintained on methadone. J. Nerv. Ment. Dis. 165:57, 1977.

40. Rockman, A. W., and Heller, M. S. Anti-therapeutic factors in therapeutic communities for drug rehabilitation. J. Drug Issues 4:393, 1974.

41. Rohrs, C. (Psychiatric Consultant, Project Return). Personal communication, 1979.

42. Rosen, A. Case report: Symptomatic mania and phencyclidine abuse. Am. J. Psychiatry 136:118, 1979.

43. Salzman, B., and Frosch, W. Methadone maintenance for the psychiatrically disturbed. In *Proceedings of the 4th National Conference on Methadone Maintenance*, pp. 117–119. New York, National Association for the Prevention of Addiction to Narcotics, 1972.

44. Salzman, B., Kurian, M., Demirjian, A., Morant, C., Dowell, S., Miller, I., and Royo, W. The paranoid schizophrenic in methadone maintenance programs. In *Proceedings of the 5th National Conference on Methadone Maintenance*, pp. 1304–1308. New York, National Association for the Prevention of Addiction to Narcotics, 1973.

45. Saxon, S. Drug abuse and suicide. In *A Multicultural View of Drug Abuse*, D. Smith et al., editors, pp. 165–170. Cambridge, Mass., G. K. Hall/Schenkman, 1978.

46. Saxon, S., Kunsel, E., and Aldrich, S. Drug abuse and suicide. Am. J. Drug Alcohol Abuse 5:485, 1978.

47. Schneider, K. Zur frage der chronische Morphinpsychose und des Zussammenhangs von Sinnestausehungen und Wahrideen. Z. Gesamte Neurol. Psychiatr. 19:25, 1913.

48. Schuckit, M. A., and Morrissey, E. R. Psychiatric problems in women admitted to an alcoholic detoxification center. Am. J. Psychiatry 136:607, 1979.

49. Senay, E. C., Dorus, W., and Yufit, R. I. Prevalence of depression in drug abusers. Unpublished manuscript.

50. Slavney, P. R., Rich, G. B., Pearlson, G. D., and McHugh, P. R. Phencyclidine abuse and symptomatic mania. Biol. Psychiatry 12:697, 1977.

51. Spencer, D. J. Cannabis induced psychosis. Br. J. Addict. 65:369, 1970.

52. Spensley, J. Doxepin: A useful adjunct in the treatment of heroin addicts in a methadone program. Int. J. Addict. 11:191, 1976.

53. Stanton, M. D., Todd, T. C., Heard, D. B., Kirschner, S., Kleiman, J. I., Mowatt, T. D., Riley, P., Scott, S. M., and Van Deusen, J. M. Heroin addiction as a family phenomenon: A new conceptual model. Am. J. Drug Alcohol Abuse 5:125, 1978.

54. Talbott, J. A., and Teague, J. W. Marihuana psychosis: Acute toxic psychosis associated with the use of cannabis derivatives. J.A.M.A. 210:299, 1969.

55. Terry, C. E., and Pellens, M. *The Opium Problem.* New York, Committee on Opiate Addiction, Bureau of Social Hygiene, 1928.

56. Thacore, V. R., and Shukla, S. R. P. Cannabis psychosis and paranoid schizophrenia. Arch. Gen. Psychiatry 33:383, 1976.

57. Vaillant, G. E. A 12-year follow-up of New York narcotic addicts. Arch. Gen. Psychiatry 15:599, 1966.

58. Weissman, M. M., Pottenger, M., Kleber, H., Ruben, H. L., Williams, D., and Thompson, W. D. Symptom patterns in primary and secondary depression: A comparison of primary depressives with depressed opiate addicts, alcoholics, and schizophrenics. Arch. Gen. Psychiatry 34:854, 1977.

59. Wikler, A. Dynamics of drug dependence. Arch. Gen. Psychiatry 28:611, 1973.

60. Williams, E. H. *Opiate Addiction*, p.11. New York, Macmillan, 1922.

61. Woody, G. E., O'Brien, C. P., and Rickels, K. Depression and anxiety in heroin addicts: A placebo-controlled study of doxepin in combination with methadone. Am. J. Psychiatry 132:447, 1975.

62. Wurmser, L. Methadone and the craving for narcotics: Observation of patients on methadone maintenance in psychotherapy. In *Proceedings of the 4th National Conference on Methadone Treatment*, pp. 525–528. New York, National Association for the Prevention of Addiction to Narcotics, 1972.

63. Wurmser, L. Mr. Pecksniff's horse? In *Psychodynamics of Drug Dependence*, J. Blaine et al., editors, NIDA Research Monograph #12, pp. 36–73. Rockville, Md., National Institute on Drug Abuse, 1977.

CHAPTER 62

DRUG-RELATED CHILD ABUSE AND OTHER ANTISOCIAL BEHAVIOR

Judianne Densen-Gerber, M.D., J.D.

In 1969, Odyssey Institute, a not-for-profit corporation whose mandate is the delivery of health care to the socially disadvantaged and which provides services to eight of the American states and two in Australia, began to see a change in drug addiction at Odyssey House, its drug abuse rehabilitation division (5). Persons seeking care were younger, from a wider range of social and economic classes, and, most important, were no longer so predominantly male. The ratio of females seeking admission for treatment had shifted from one out of eight to one out of three, and in some locations were at parity.

Furthermore, these addicts used a pharmacopoeia of drugs rather than simply using opiates. Even those on hard drugs such as heroin were showing a high incidence of pregnancy. For several reasons this incidence was in marked contrast to the years from 1920 to 1965. First, in the early years of the 1920's and 1930's, there were fewer women involved in opiate addiction. Second, women as a group tended to show less social deviancy than men. Third, women usually shied away from using drugs that rely on the needle as they have a more ego-integrated body image and, therefore, are more sensitive to committing acts that permanently disfigure them. Fourth, there was a glamour and machismo attached to drug use that surrounded male

addiction and its crimes of dealing, burglary, and violence but that did not extend to the world of female addiction with its attendant prostitution and degradation. Fifth, prior to the development of effective treatment for venereal diseases, women hooked into a life of drug addiction and prostitution contracted such diseases; they were frequently sterilized as a result (the closure of the fallopian tubes due to gonorrhea) or they aborted or produced nonsurviving babies (as with syphilis). Penicillin and other such medical advances changed this as well. Sixth, and last, in the years prior to the 1960's, with the upsurge in the numbers of people using drugs, heroin passed through fewer hands between the supplier and actual user. This meant that it was diluted fewer times and was much stronger, the average bag being 75 to 95 per cent pure versus that on today's market, which is 1 to 5 per cent heroin and the rest various sugars, diluents, etc. Pure heroin is an anovulatory agent; nature had provided a protection against children being born into drug-addicted, nonnurturing, high risk, abusive environments.

Often I am asked, "How do you know the drug addict is not an adequate parent and what does your research show on this subject, Dr. Densen-Gerber?" Although I could easily answer this with tables and statistics, for purposes of this chapter I would like to remain in the realm of common sense. I ask the reader this simple question: "Would you hire a using addict nodding on heroin, or one in an agitated stupor from barbiturates or actively hallucinating from lysergic acid diethylamide or phencyclidine to babysit your 6-month-old child or grandchild?" If your answer is "Of course not," or even if you only hesitate with doubt but are afraid to commit yourself, then you must question yourself as to why you would permit another 6-month-old child, who simply through accident of birth was not protected as a member of your family, to face such hazards. Children cannot fend for themselves or cope with the addiction of their parents, even including the mind-altering states of heavy alcohol or marihuana use. Particularly in the early heavily dependent years of a child's life, he or she needs the consistent attention and nurturing of reasonably healthy persons.

By 1971, Odyssey Institute confronted the problem of the pregnant addict and the mother with her newborn child. The staff quickly realized that there were no places to refer these patients and their children and, even more important, no one looking for answers to the obvious questions as to what was happening to the children born into drug-addicted homes and what remedial steps could be developed and undertaken to correct or ameliorate the situation so that we did not have second, third, and fourth generation personal and family disruption, if, as could be anticipated, the home environments were negative or harmful.

By the end of that year, 1971, we opened the first, and to this day the only, psychiatric residential center in the United States for the treatment of addicted women, both pregnant and with children under the age of 5—the Odyssey Parents' Program. The entire family is considered the patient unit. Husbands and fathers are admitted as well, although less than 2 per cent of our families had males present. In 1 per cent of the units, single males were the sole parenting figure.

We have learned much about the entity of drug-related child abuse and its related problems of familial violence and disruption, sexual abuse and incest, child pornography and prostitution, and parental alcoholism and addiction in the years 1971 to the present. We have also learned of society's indifference and ignorance, denial and apathy.

In October, 1972, the Select Committee on Child Abuse of the New York State Assembly released its first report entitled *The Children of Addicts: Unrecognized and Unprotected* (12). This document recorded, one after another, the countless atrocities experienced by the unwilling victims of drug abuse: the fetus in utero without prenatal care; the premature, low birth weight newborn in withdrawal; the helpless neonate released unsupervised to the home of an irresponsible, inadequate, often hostile parent; the infant and preschooler, abused and neglected not only by his parents but by a multitude of services and social agencies. If they live, these unfortunate youngsters, as shown by the precedent-setting studies of the Gluecks, are inevitably destined to become the "problemed individuals" of the next generation—the drug addicts, criminals, psychopaths, failures of the 1980's (7).

No one specific or unique set of psychiatric characteristics dictates that drug addicts are always unfit parents, but the generally accepted description of Noyes and Kolb suffices (10):

> . . . for the most part antisocial . . . the majority of the addicts are those with arrests in ego and super ego development and, for the most part, fixed to an ambivalent maternal figure . . . both possessive and rejecting . . . there has been an absence of a strong and consistent father figure. The addict fails to develop internal controls, hopes for immediate gratification of his needs, and yet is continuously frustrated due to his exaggerated demands, his psychosexual immaturity, and his lack of ego capacity that might bring satisfaction by delay and insistent efforts towards his goals.

It is interesting to note at the time that Noyes and Kolb wrote their classic text on psychiatric disorders (1963) addicts were almost exclusively considered to be male. (Consequently, please add or substitute the female pronoun in the above reference.) Sadly, in this, too, the female has come into her own, dragging her child with her. Her pregnancy, although generally unplanned, is not unwanted for two basic reasons: first, most addict women are themselves poorly nurtured, often receiving minimal love and attention. Therefore, they fantasize that their child will provide them with the affection missed during their own unhappy, frequently abusive, lonely, and deprived childhood. The addict mother desires her child as her child would desire a doll for play therapy. Second, the life of a drug addict is guilt ridden and ugly. Understandably, such women suffer from low self-esteem and feelings of worthlessness; little in the relationship of a prostitute-trick or prostitute-pimp is restitutive. However, in our American society the status of motherhood cleanses—to be a mother is to be valued, particularly in the nonliberated concepts of the drug addict subculture. Therefore, her pregnancy is viewed by her as a redemptive phenomenon—she is Madonna-like, free from all sin, purged. Because of these unconscious dynamics and sometimes conscious factors, birth control or abortion play no role in the prevention or understanding of drug-related child abuse. Indeed, Odyssey demonstrated in one study (6) that the more a girl knew about birth control and contraceptive methods the more likely she was to become pregnant. This was an obviously intentional statistical distortion based on the associated fact that more sexually active and sophisticated women usually know more about birth control, and the more sexually active a woman is, the more opportunity for pregnancy.

Unfortunately, these basic expectations of the drug-addicted mother cannot be met by the newborn. The situation is fraught from the onset with failure; child abuse and neglect as a reaction to disappointment are to be anticipated. The newborn or young child (even through adolescence) must take love, not give it, and the parents must be able through their own sense of self-worth to feel gratified with the terms of that relationship. This is not the reality for the drug addict, who often interprets the colicky baby's crying as a rejection of her or a statement as to her inadequacy as a mother. Television commercials have taught us to expect 24-hour happy, cooing babies and have not prepared the new mother—whether healthy, addicted, or teenage—for the other maternal experiences.

Furthermore, small families have not provided many of our youngsters with an "apprenticeship for living" in which they work alongside their mothers and older siblings caring for the young. The Parents' Program at Odyssey Institute has shown us that parenting is a learned experience, not an instinctual one, and many young people are not learning basic parenting skills either within their own family constellations or at school.

It is our firm belief that we must add a fourth "R" to the traditional three—reading, 'riting, and 'rithmatic—that of human relatedness, through which good interpersonal skills, including parenting ones, will be taught. Parenting is one of the most, if not the most, difficult of human tasks, and many of today's young people are so bewildered and frightened at the magnitude of the responsibilities that they are choosing nonparenthood. Unfortunately for our nation, many who so elect are the healthier and stronger young people, whereas the addicted, in their narcotized fantasy world with few, if any, controls, bear young without any consequential thinking or thought for the future.

It is important to have a good conceptual framework that incorporates the elements of adequate parenting and nurturing that a child needs to develop into a full functioning, interdependent adult. Such an adult must be capable of caring for himself or herself; of making meaningful, interpersonal, mutually reciprocal peer relationships; and of rearing another generation of young.

Parenting, for me, has three essential elements. First, the parent must be able to provide on a constant basis a minimum amount of love and security. Of course, more than a minimum is to be desired and to be strived toward, but it is not essential. This gives the child a foundation from which to venture forth into the turbulent world beyond the home and also gives the child the basic inner resources of self-confidence to face the future unafraid. Second, the parents must be able to negotiate the system on behalf of the child. For example, although many parents deeply love their children, parental inadequacies, fears, or handicaps prevent them from adequately caring for the health or educational needs of their young. In such instances, it is important for the community to aid and assist the parents with a multitude of supportive services. An example of this might be the aid given to a middle-class family with a severely deformed child. Third, the parents must be role models for their children. The essence of childhood is to imitate and copy; children learn, primarily through identification and admiration of the parenting figures. If the parent is an alcoholic, a drug addict, sexually promiscuous, lying, stealing, or without values of one kind or another, so usually will be the child. Even during the rebellion of adolescence, the child needs a backboard of parental values and traditions against which to define self. It is better for the parent to be wrong but firm than uncommitted and permissive.

In all these elements—providing a minimum of love and security, being able to negotiate the system, and being an adequate role model—the addict is found wanting; therefore, society must develop alternatives for her children, if disruption is not to pass from generation to generation, "worsening" with each generational passage.

Observations of the addicted parent-child relationship indicate that: (a) addicts do not alter their life style to accomodate a new child, (b) they fail to make responsible decisions concerning their children, and (c) they are incapable of acting in the best interests of their children, and of meeting a child's needs at the denial of their own.

With these facts as our frame of reference, it is now necessary to consider the extent of the problem. Dr. Walter Cuskey, in his independent evaluative study of the Odyssey House Parents' Program for The Department of Health, Education and Welfare, stated (3):

We are, in short, dealing with a very large population-at-risk indeed. If concern has been expressed about 1.2% of the population who make up the children of opiate-addicted mothers, what about the 10.4% of the total population who make up the children of soft drug using mothers? Their risk may not be as great, but it is still very substantial. The drugs may not be—or may not seem to be—as dangerous but the environments the infants endure—and the psychological problems of the mothers, which affect the child—are at least analogous. All of these figures underscore the vital necessity of proper analysis of female addicts and their children, and the influences that create and mold them and their pathologies. To date, information is insufficient and unreliable.

The illegal opiate population is a small part of the whole story of the drug-using population at risk, particularly as far as children born and unborn are concerned. The other significant groups of drug-using mothers who endanger their young include those on the so-called soft drugs (particularly barbiturates, amphetamine, and "mind-altering" drugs) and those on methadone maintenance. This last group is important to consider because there are clear indications of malformation dangers and birth defects to unborn fetuses

from large doses of narcotics, as well as developmental lags in the early formative years of the children born of such pregnancies. The growing embryo cannot distinguish between legal and illegal methadone. At birth he/she will undergo the rigors of withdrawal regardless of whether the mother's drug dispenser is a clinic doctor or the backroom dealer. One study (9) has shown that babies born to addicted mothers, particularly those methadone maintained, have smaller head circumferences (lessened brain development), lower Apgar scores (poor response to the extrauterine neonatal environment), and lower birth weights (signs of prematurity) than normals. Additional studies on rats have shown that rats addicted in utero have a more rapid addiction rate than those born of a pregnancy noncomplicated by opiates. Certainly, because the fetus does not consent to his/her addiction, no question of freedom of choice can be raised here. The real issue is: does a woman have the right to act during her pregnancy in such a way that she damages her young? Or does society have the responsibility to protect the infant? At Odyssey, we believe a child has the right to be well born. This right comes into being as soon as a woman makes the existential choice that she will bear her child. By making that existential choice, she abrogates certain of her own civil rights during gestation on behalf of the greater rights of her child. We believe society has the responsibility to limit her conduct whenever it is reasonable to anticipate that such conduct will be destructive to the development of another surviving human being (1).

For purposes of this argument, let us not consider the woman involved in the negative life style of illicit drug addiction, but rather the hypothetical Medea-like woman who so hates her husband or the man who fathered her child that she wishes to strike out at him by taking thalidomide during her first trimester. Should her need for revenge and should her basic civil rights exceed the right of the child to be born with arms and/or legs? I hope that you, as I, would answer in a resounding "of course not!" But such is not the law anywhere in our land. The embryo has no advocate; its totally dependent parasitic position renders it totally at the mercy of its mother's mental and physical health. Protective legislation to safeguard the fetus is mandatory, because drug-related child abuse begins in utero.

Even though the main thrust of this chapter is drugs other than alcohol, alcohol must be mentioned at this juncture. Recent work at Boston City Hospital (11) has shown that 69 per cent of the babies born to chronically drinking women have one or more severe deformities that will necessitate lifetime support systems paid for by the tax dollar. This disease entity, known as neonatal alcoholic distress syndrome, has only recently begun to receive the attention that its incidence and devastation deserve.

Opponents of this moral position have questioned me as follows: "Dr. Densen-Gerber, is it not better for a pregnant woman to be receiving maintenance drugs from a clinic and, therefore, be away from the street lifestyle? Furthermore, won't she receive good prenatal supportive services and adequate diet only if she is enrolled in such a medical clinic?" The answers to these objections are 2-fold. First, when a woman is on street heroin, its quantity and quality are erratic, therefore the opiate assault upon the fetus is not constant. Consequently, there is more opportunity for the embryonic cells to escape the trauma. Furthermore, because the nature of heroin is short acting, heroin withdrawal is easier than methadone, the latter being long acting and well stored within body tissues. Neonatal withdrawal from heroin usually takes less than 8 days, but methadone withdrawal symptoms have been reported as long as 3 weeks after birth. Also, there is a much higher rate of sudden infant death (crib deaths) in babies born of methadone-maintained mothers than of normal or heroin-addicted women. The mechanism of death is not understood, but it is theorized to be connected to respiratory abnormalities. Opiates cross the placental membrane with ease, and such babies are frequently born addicted. The neonate withdrawing from heroin has a far easier time than his/her brother or sister undergoing methadone detoxification.

Second, to let the women "do their own thing" is not the only alternative to giving methadone. There are other possibilities, such as protective legislation for the right to be well born, mentioned previously, that would enable communities to detain a woman in protective custody under the present law for the duration of gestation to ensure the well-being of her child. An addicted pregnant woman could also be detained under the common law concept of the public health right to incarcerate anyone who presents a danger to him- or herself or others. Clearly, the pregnant addict is a danger to the fetus as well as to herself. Also, she could be detained under a civil commitment statute such as exists in New York; this statute has been found constitutional under the right of the legislature to use its police power in matters of public health and welfare. The New York law permits civil commitment for a maximum of 3 years of anyone who is addicted to opiates or potentially in danger of becoming addicted (Mama would be put in the first category, and baby within the second). The baby in utero should be detained to prevent addiction as well as malformation from occurring. Protective detention is preferable to both licit and illicit drug use.

A word of clarification is in order here. The right to be well born is readily distinguishable from the right to life. The right to be well born comes into existence only after the mother makes the existential choice to bear a child who has the potential of 70-plus years, a potential that can be adversely affected by the actions of his/her mother during a brief 9 months' time span. It is the weighing of these priorities and concerns that is required.

When a drug is legal, women have tended to greater use than men. When opiates were legal, female addicts outnumbered men two to one (4). Therefore, nonopiate drug abuse is of particular significance to any discussion of female addiction, especially because new research material indicates that these drugs, primarily amphetamine and barbiturates, can be extremely dangerous to the developing fetus. Cuskey and Odyssey Institute estimate that a minimum of 10 per cent of the nation's 66 million children under the age of 18 are in homes compromised by substance abuse (including alcohol). Of this number, roughly 2.4 million children are at risk from parental hard drug involvement. Against this background, the urgency to meet the needs and problems of female addicts and their children is obvious. Not only must the entity of drug-related child abuse be identified, but programs to stop this disruption of the family—with its attendant multigenerational passage of addiction, violence, antisocial behavior, and mental illness—must be designed immediately.

In the foregoing I have discussed drug abuse-related child abuse. However, its mirror image disease should be mentioned as well—child abuse-related drug abuse.

One of the first findings when drug-addicted children were admitted to the Odyssey facilities across the United States (some as young as 7, but most 13 to 17 years of age) was that most of these children were victims of child abuse, usually physical for the boys and sexual for the girls, although emotional and physical neglect also played a significant role. We soon realized that adolescent addicts were made—they did not just happen. For instance, in a mind-boggling monumental study on domestic violence, Straus (13) reported that, in 1976, 3.2 per cent of America's children were threatened by a knife or gun held in the hands of a parent. Will this example of home life lead to happy, healthy, full functioning adults, or will it lead to people who use drugs to seal over their pain and who, as parents, repeat the cycle by brutalizing their own children?

The rights of parents are often discussed in this country. I do not believe that parents have any rights vis-à-vis the rights of their children. I believe children have all the rights and parents all the responsibilities, particularly when the child is very young. There is a basic confusion that beclouds the issues. Although parents have no rights vis-à-vis their children, parents have rights vis-à-vis the government or state. Such a right is that of parents to rear their children according to their religious beliefs without governmental interference but not the right to follow a religious practice that is life threatening to their child (e.g., the court's ordering blood transfusions of the Jehovah's Witnesses over their objection). Another clarifying example of this distinction is that, although parents have the right to decide on the type of education their children will receive, the state guarantees the child's right to an education and will proceed against parents who do not properly educate their children.

Another attitudinal change essential to the betterment of the position of children throughout the United States, particularly in circumstances of drug-related child abuse, is the need for Americans to begin to conceptualize their relationship with their children

in terms of a sacred trust rather than property rights. Deeply embedded in the common law Anglo-Saxon tradition is the idea that children are the chattel of their parents—possessions much as their mothers were of their fathers only a short generation ago. As a sacred trust rather than as property, these young lives would be safeguarded as we safeguard our money deposited in a bank or trust. Under a sacred trust formulation, parents would be perceived as trustees or fiduciaries and would be held accountable to a strict code of conduct. If this code were violated, society and the community would be expected and mandated to relieve them of their responsibility, thereby conserving the young. The present epidemic of child abuse is manifesting itself mainly in countries where children are considered property rather than belonging to the entire community as an investment in the future. Adult consciousness must be raised, because adults must accomplish this for children everywhere. Children, differing from all other groups needing rights, cannot battle for their own, because (a) they possess neither economic nor voting power—both powers essential to the democratic process of change; and (b) they suffer the impediment of their age, being able neither to abstract the issues nor speak the concepts. Some, often the most battered and abused, are so young they cannot yet talk.

Most hampering to their struggle for rights and basic safety is the ironic fact that children desperately need family and nurturing more than life itself. So desperate is their need that they will protect the parents by lying about the cause of their injury or by denying sexual traumas completely. As young as 3 or 4, children have been observed to be protecting their own parents in situations of sickness or deprivation. There is nothing a child fears more than the breakup of his/her home, no matter how life threatening or brutal such a home may be. This expression of the need for consistency (probably on an instinctual basis) is clearly revealed through the experiments of Harlow and Harlow (8). Most workers in the field are familiar with their initial studies of maternally and socially deprived monkeys, much of which is directly applicable to our drug-addicted women and their offspring, particularly those of the second and third generations. These monkeys had great difficulty in making lasting relationships with the opposite sex peer, relationships necessary for successful joint rearing of their young. Furthermore, many had difficulty even in the mating process itself. Also analogous to maternally and socially deprived humans, many monkeys compensated for the missing affection by early and frequent promiscuity but without the ability to establish the family roots essential to the rearing of healthy young. Still others did not know how to nurse their offspring, refusing to hold their young close to the breast. Sadly, this is similar to drug-addicted mothers, many of whom hold their babies at arm's length, as far away as possible from body contact. The child's head is held in the hand lower than its feet, which rest on the mother's arm, thus forcing the baby to suck against gravity and to nurse without the comforting reassurance of the long familiar maternal heartbeat. Such a feeding is devoid of all maternal body warmth now accepted to be as essential to healthy development as milk itself.

Harlow and Harlow (8) did additional experiments, whose findings are highly applicable to drug-related child abuse, indeed to the field of child abuse and neglect generally. Their research taught us that baby monkeys preferred to cling and nestle in the arms of a soft terry cloth mother, even if her paps were dry, than remain in the lap of a hard wire feeding monkey. The babies spent as many hours as possible clinging to the softer monkey, and their visits to the wire monkey mother were as brief as caloric intake required. Nurturance clearly makes more time demands than nutrition (an extremely significant finding considering the practice of so many drug-addicted women as well as others to bottle prop). Nature designed nursing to take the time necessary to meet varied needs of the young. As scientists, Harlow and Harlow wanted to learn what level of negative reinforcement was necessary to drive the baby monkeys from the terry cloth monkey's laps to the wire mothers. First, they fitted the terry cloth mothers with electric shock; they found to their amazement that the more the babies experienced pain the more they clung to the terry mothers. As children have been noted to do, probably on an instinctual basis, the baby monkey had globalized mothering, identifying her with safety and security, and

was unable to distinguish that it was mother herself inflicting pain. Additional experiments were done culminating in fitting the terry mothers with breast plates of retractable knives—the baby monkeys clung until they were literally shredded to death. The analogy is overpoweringly obvious to all of us working in the child abuse and neglect field: No matter how much pain the parent inflicts upon the child, he or she is the only parent the child has known and the child will instinctively cling, seeking comfort in the face of pain and fear. Indeed, one of the hallmarks of an abused child is clinging behavior and a desperate need for affection at any price. Therefore, to ask the child to testify in court against the parent is but another example of society's abuse and lack of understanding of the basic dynamics at work. Nowhere is this truer than if the child perceives the parent as sick (often the case with addiction) or when in instances of sexual abuse of the child, she/he has been violated by one parental figure and usually warned by that same figure that the knowledge of the assault will kill or harm the other parent, driving away whatever little love the child may have been receiving from that parent.

Observations at the Odyssey Parents' Program indicate that there is a statistical correlation between sexual abuse experienced as a child and an adult's subsequent substance abuse. In a 1974 study (2) of the Odyssey House female population, women from 26 different states indicated that 44 per cent had been involved in at least one incestuous experience. Most of these experiences represented cross-generational incest with a parental figure such as a father, stepfather, paramour of mother, uncle, grandfather, or, rarely, a mother herself. It was these cross-generational incestuous contacts rather than those representing peer generational relationships (brother, cousin, etc.,) that were most damaging and yielded the sequela of child abuse-related drug abuse. Cross-generational incest frequently involved force and fear; peer generational incest did not. These two types of incest should not be confused nor discussed under the same dynamic. It was only cross-generational incest that produced intense feelings of being trapped and suffocated, often due merely to the body size discrepancy. During psychoanalysis, one patient asked me to imagine what it was like to be a 60-pound 9-year-old girl child and have your 200-pound father lie on top of you during both genital and oral intercourse. It is cross-generational incest alone that produces the feelings of having cheated and hurt the mother (and subsequent fears of abandonment by her) because of the incest. It is cross-generational incest that also produces the most marked feelings of low self-esteem, worthlessness, and guilt, all of which are classic dynamics in the production of addiction and other antisocial self-destructive deviant behavior.

This study's phenomenal, unexpected frequency of incest experiences led us to conclude that incest formed both a major category of child abuse and a predisposition to female drug abuse not as yet fully appreciated by either field. Seventy-five per cent of the incest situations occurred before the female children were 12 years of age and 45 per cent before they were 9. It must be emphasized that incest did not occur because girls were addicts, who were known to indulge in deviant behavior. Each girl is a child first; next she is violated; and last, she turns to drugs, usually in adolescence, with its increase in psychosexual anxiety and conflict and with the development of her ability to say "No" to Daddy by running away from home. Often, as a runaway, she joins a negative street culture using drugs; she begins to use them as a form of rebellion and as a relief from her inner pain. It is relatively easy for her to enter a life of prostitution, for she is already sexualized-sexually experienced, having sometimes begun sexual activity as young as 3. Not infrequently, she has been paid either in money or goods, such as a new dress or coat, by the older man in exchange for her cooperation sexually and/or her silence. She no longer, if she ever did, perceives her body and its inner territory as belonging to herself to be given in love and mutuality, but rather as a means to an end to be manipulated and to manipulate. In the area of learned behavior and pattern setting, there is no better illustration of child abuse, for here we clearly see the development of sociopathic behavior patterns whereby subjective relationships are destroyed and replaced by ones in which people, even oneself, are perceived as objects.

It is this girl, frequently no more than 14 or 15 years of age, lonely, isolated, alienated, and hungry for concern and caring, who finds herself pregnant and who carries within her body the victim of these multigenerational disruptive diseases: drug abuse-related child abuse and child abuse-related drug abuse.

What ramifications do these issues create for our way of life in America? I will show you using a very simple example. There is an entire subculture in the United States that believes that it is perfectly correct to toilet train a 2- to 3-year-old child by washing the excrement off in very hot water. They feel that the child will not only be cleansed and disinfected by this procedure but also that he/she will learn a lesson that will not soon be forgotten. Unfortunately, in many instances, the water is too hot, the immersion too vigorous, or follow-up care too inadequate for the child to survive or to be left without permanent motor handicaps and extensive scarring. This type of toilet training contrasts with a method frequently employed in Communist China. There, in many of the day care centers, children between 14 and 18 months of age are trained by being placed, immediately after eating, when the gastrocolic reflex is maximum, on a row of potty seats known as "Tinkle Toilets" because these toilets tinkle or play music whenever a child produces anything into the bowl. At the sound of music, all the adults present clap for the first child, then the second, and so on. It frightens me as an American to compare the destiny and future of a nation that toilet trains to boiling water with another that socializes its children to music. Sadly, unless there is a change, I have no doubts which will endure.

Of course, most people would react by saying that it is the exception, not the rule, in the United States to toilet train by burning. I agree; but it is the rule not the exception in our country for both the child and the parents to perceive "housebreaking" the young as the second battle for control, the first having been getting the baby to sleep through the night. Toilet training in the Western world is further complicated by our association of elimination with sexual taboos, our feelings that waste products are "dirty," and by our profound ignorance and inability to train present and future parents in the maturational developmental milestones of babies so that parental expectations can be within reason. Recently, a well known private Park

Avenue pediatrician shared the following with me: A mother who was Phi Beta Kappa from Radcliffe came with her child, a first-born son, for a routine visit. She complained bitterly about the unpleasantness of the soiled diapers. She was quite obsessive and compulsive about cleanliness and paid meticulous attention to detail. The baby was beautifully attended to and cared for. She asked the doctor to refer her to a toilet training manual so she could be done with the mess. Her baby was 3 weeks old!

So far I have confined this discussion primarily to issues of drug abuse and child abuse as they relate to the individual, but what of our social agencies and health care support systems? Ninety per cent of the child abuse and neglect deaths autopsied in New York City are known to one or more social institutions before the child dies. It is obvious from the very fact of the autopsy that these institutions did not make the necessary decisions or act in such a way as to safeguard the life of the child. Odyssey Institute has developed a tool, the "Sociological Autopsy" (14), to study retrospectively the problem solving of social institutions charged with protecting the lives of our children; to identify prospectively intermediate danger points; and to demonstrate where timely intervention and decision making would save the child's life. The Sociological Autopsy is an important adjunct to the clinical anatomical autopsy and the psychological autopsy. It should be employed in the analyses of all child abuse and neglect deaths if we want to increase our understanding and knowledge, so that eventually we may reduce and perhaps eliminate this fatal disease.

Workers in child protective services must have a clear understanding of their goals and the order of priorities when approaching each case. The first priority must always be the preservation of the life and safety of the child, and only second the maintenance of the family. Too frequently, the second goal becomes the primary operating priority, yielding a result that sadly finds its way to the autopsy table or to the jails, after years of torture, fear, and suffering.

It cannot be too strongly emphasized that, whenever confronted by circumstances predictive of child abuse and/or neglect, it is mandatory to err on the side of protecting the child; the worker cannot afford to take a wait-and-see attitude.

Known to many as basically conservative in my approach to the solution of social problems, I have been questioned by many people since I began my campaign for the establishment of Cabinet posts for the concerns of children at federal, state, and local levels of government as to how I reconcile this concept with my idea that minimum effective government is the best government and that our present system of welfare is a prime example of a socially encouraged and condoned dependency disease. To me, there is no contradiction in terms: a single unified government coordinator of services equals minimum effective government, for it implies only one unit to turn to for help rather than, say, the 73 present federal divisions that deal with education. Not only would duplication be markedly reduced and efficiency increased, but the present game of avoiding responsibility would be eliminated. At long last, thank heavens, and for the first time in a long time, the grassroots would know at whom to point the finger and say "The buck stops with you." Such an assumption of responsibility and undertaking of the burden of decision making on the part of bureaucrats and the ability of the constituency to relate appropriate demands and register legitimate complaints are essential to the proper functioning of the democratic process. Our present system is markedly compromised by nameless, faceless civil servants, most of whom shift paper and wallow in self-sustained depression as to the futility of their jobs while so many American children are denied a life style commensurate with "The American Dream."

We need more generalists who are concerned about people—especially little people—than we need technical specialists. A department for the Concerns of Children would be organized on the basis of an interpersonal relationship—the "I and thou" of Buber. In other words, the provider of services to children would relate to the whole child (indeed, this is the true nature of parent-child interaction) rather than in terms of a functional relationship, which is now the case, wherein the child is divided into segmentalized areas of concern such as health, or education, or welfare. The first type of organization is based upon considerations of being; the second is doing. In actual practice, the second structure, which is the present one, leads to competition among providers, a fight over what is perceived as a limited financial pie, and destructive "turfdom paranoia"; all of which adversely affect America's future citizens. The first structure, while relating to the entire needs of the child, would still have access to the specialists, for they would be held in resource pools to be drawn on when the specialized needs arose. In fact, this is the nature of present-day good family organization, in which the parent equals the generalist who cares and is responsible for the totality of the developing child and who draws upon the specialist, i.e., the doctor and/or teacher, whenever appropriate. Indeed, modern banking has for the most part shifted to the essential (essence-being) relationship form rather than the existential (existence-doing) one. No longer do the customers enter their local bank having to know what service best meets their needs. For example, no longer do they have to know a priori the exquisite differences between the personal loan and mortgage departments, but, rather, they are greeted by personal service customer representatives who relate to the entire problems at hand, give advice, and draw upon the resources within the banking and other systems that would best meet the customer's needs. This is a much more productive system, because it is safe to assume that customer service people working within the field are much more practiced and are, therefore, aware of a multitude of alternatives, more so than a customer who is facing the problem for a first or second time. All benefit: the customer from the greater familiarity and experience of the customer service person; the customer service person from the broader base of choices; the specialists from their frame of knowledge and less hassle with over-all detail; and the bank from speed and efficiency. Most important, the experience is warmer, more total, more personal, more satisfying. Once again, we learn from the banking industry, as we did in the instance of changing our attitude toward children from that of chattel within the property laws to a sacred trust, a fiduciary relationship within traditional banking concepts.

However, I do not envision a Cabinet post

for the Concerns of Children only handling at risk, in crisis, battered, neglected, or otherwise brutalized children. I see such a governmental branch helping all parents in this most difficult of human endeavors—nurturing the young. The loving good parent with the gifted, exceptional, handicapped, learning disabled, or simply ordinary child in the increasingly technologically sophisticated and more complex and difficult society needs services and support as well. Certainly, it is foolish, illogical, and doomed to failure to demand that even the best, most capable families develop independent solutions and handle on their own situations such as a teenage epidemic of drug abuse or the development and use of polio vaccine. We all, as parents, need help and guidance, and the self-assured capable family welcomes—no, demands—it!

I expect the able-bodied adult to be full functioning and self-sufficient; but it is irrational to make such a demand on an adult who has been crippled in childhood. Society must consider solutions to its problems in the long range. The proper formulation of the issues facing the successful rearing of our young is a broad one: How do we move the fetus through a maturational process that will render that individual at the age of 18 capable of entering the American mainstream and able to care for him or herself without being a burden or parasite upon his or her peers and society at large, except in extraordinary crisis situations? Unfortunately, the tendency today is to formulate our questions and hence our answers in discrete parts, such as what do we do for New Jersey migrant children, or New York drug abuse-child abuse victims, or California's unimmunized. The finger-in-the-dike approach will never build a high enough dam nor will it result in meaningful solutions, because the real issues are not perceived. I believe that maximum service to children is an excellent investment in the future—nowhere is the following statement more applicable than here: "If you give a man a fish he eats for a day; but if you teach him to fish he eats for a lifetime."

References

1. Ament, M. The right to be well born. In *Lawyers Communications.* Salt Lake City, University of Utah College of Law, May 2, 1973.

2. Benward, J., and Densen-Gerber, J. *Incest as a Causative Factor in Anti-Social Behavior: An Exploratory Study.* New York, Odyssey Institute, Inc., 1975.

3. Cuskey, W. R. An assessment of the clinical efficacy of the Mabon parents demonstration. Unpublished report, November, 1977.

4. Cuskey, W. R., Premkumar, T., and Segal, L. Survey of opiate addiction among females in the United States between 1850–1970. Public Health Rev. 1:6, 1972.

5. Densen-Gerber, J. and Rohrs, C. C. Adolescent drug abuse. Prepared for presentation in the Scientific Program of the American Psychiatric Association Annual Meeting, Washington, D.C., May 3–7, 1971.

6. Densen-Gerber, J., Wiener, M., and Hochstedler, R. Sexual behavior, abortion and birth control in heroin addicts: Legal and psychiatric considerations. Contemp. Drug Probl. 1:783, 1972.

7. Fontana, V. The maltreated child. In *Drug Addicted Parents and Child Abuse*, J. Densen-Gerber and C. C. Rohrs, editors. New York, Odyssey House, 1973.

8. Harlow, H. F., and Harlow, M. K. Psychopathology in monkeys. In *Experimental Psychopathology—Recent Research and Theory*, H. D. Kimmel, editor, pp. 203–229. New York, Academic Press, 1971.

9. Mahender, R. A., Harper, R. G., and Stern, B. Observations on heroin and methadone withdrawal in newborn. Pediatrics, 48:353, 1971.

10. Noyes, A., and Kolb, L. *Modern Clinical Psychiatry*, p. 474. Philadelphia, W. B. Saunders, 1963.

11. Ouelette, E., Rosett, H. L., Rosman, N. P., and Weiner, L. Adverse effects on offspring of maternal alcohol abuse during pregnancy. N. Engl. J. Med. 297:528, 1977.

12. Select Committee on Child Abuse, New York State Assembly. *The Children of Addicts: Unrecognized and Unprotected*, Study Report No. 3. Albany, New York State Assembly, October, 1972.

13. Straus, M. A. Societal morphogenesis and intrafamily violence in cross-cultural perspective. Ann. N. Y. Acad. Sci. 285:717, 1977.

14. Wathey, R., and Densen-Gerber, J. Preliminary report on the sociological autopsy in child abuse deaths. Presented at the 27th Meeting of the American Academy of Forensic Sciences, Chicago, February 20, 1975.

PART 9

EVALUATION

CHAPTER 63

FOLLOW-UP AND TREATMENT OUTCOME

Saul B. Sells, Ph.D.

This chapter focuses on the results of a major, long term, large scale study of the effectiveness of drug abuse treatment in terms of client outcomes during and subsequent to participation in specified treatments. The emphasis is on client outcomes in relation to treatment goals implied in various treatment paradigms, as distinguished from evaluation of a single agency or program or evaluation from the viewpoint of cost effectiveness, accountability, community impact, or other considerations that have been subsumed under the general term "evaluation." These distinctions have been elaborated elsewhere (20).

The concept of treatment effectiveness is complex and is not captured fully by any single strategy. The questions raised by clinicians, administrators, and investigators on various occasions have reflected somewhat different concerns—for example, with different criteria of effective outcome, with client characteristics associated with effectiveness of different treatments, with program characteristics and process variables related to effectiveness of particular treatments, with comparison of the over-all effectiveness of different treatments, with the over-all effectiveness of a system or network of treatments, and with the impact of programs on drug use and other factors in communities, in addition to the assessment of treatment effectiveness in terms of selected client outcomes. Although related, these different types of questions require somewhat different methodologies and data and may not all be addressed in any single study.

Studies concerned with the assessment of drug treatment effectiveness in terms of client outcomes have been conceptualized in terms of two contrasting methodological approaches, one borrowed from medical and pharmacological research and the other from survey research in the social sciences. The former, usually referred to as *clinical trials* (15), essentially involves laboratory experimental design with (a) random assignment of subjects to treatment and control groups and (b) "blind" procedures with respect to identification of subjects to investigators. Because of the rigorous controls implied, this approach seeks to avoid important sources of variance believed to affect results that are commonly confounded in the field situation. In addition, by employing objective measurement of relevant dependent variables (e.g., urinalysis to determine drug use), it is argued that the results are not subject to errors of underreporting and distortion characteristic of self-report, which is commonly used in field studies. The information gained from this methodology is important in the assessment of the *potentiality* of particular procedures but is limited in respect to generalization to field operating situations, where clients (as opposed to volunteers for clinical trials) are subject to the day-to-day regulations, frustrations, and red tape characteristic of operational clinics. In addition, in the drug abuse field, in which drug-free as well as chemotherapy treatments are employed, and in which effectiveness depends heavily on posttreatment adjustment after return to a period of unsupervised community living, it must be noted (a) that the clinical trials methodology has not been extended to the evaluation of drug-free treatments and (b) that clinical trials studies of chemotherapy treatments have not included posttreatment follow-up phases. To summarize, clinical trials research on drug treatment effectiveness can be said to answer questions concerning the potential effectiveness of defined treatments but not concerning their field performance under actual operational conditions.

The second approach—field operational, quasiexperimental, evaluation research under representative operational conditions—is actually complementary to field trials, not an alternative. Regrettably, the two have not been undertaken jointly, and there is no literature that can be cited linking the two approaches to evaluation of any particular treatment. Under field conditions, random assignment (and control groups) are usually not appropriate and are frequently impossible to obtain. As a result, clients do not have equal opportunities for inclusion in comparison groups, and distributions of clients with respect to variables believed to influence outcomes tend to be biased, sometimes significantly. Field studies are thus able to attempt to take account of relevant operational biases and constraints but are vulnerable to the confounding effects of uncontrolled factors, particularly in the area of client assignment to treatment. As indicated below, field investigators have been innovative in the development of statistical methods to adjust for sample bias, by means of multivariate analytic methods, and have employed multiple procedures and replication over independent samples to verify results (23, 25, 40), and these have frequently produced convergent results. Nevertheless, in some circles, field research carries the stigma of lack of control, and critics have repeatedly called for random assignment in field studies. In addition, because field studies have attempted to collect data on criminal behavior, employment, and aspects of life style that are proscribed by

regulations concerning confidentiality, in addition to drug use, they have generally relied on self-report data. Obviously, the burden of proof concerning reliability and validity of data and adequacy of analytic methods must be assumed by the field investigator, but the decision should be based on empirical evidence rather than preconception.

The evidence concerning treatment effectiveness presented here is based on a large scale field study of federally supported drug abuse treatment that was initiated in 1968 and is still in progress. This programmatic study, sponsored by the National Institute on Drug Abuse (NIDA) (and its predecessor organizations within the National Institute of Mental Health (NIMH)) has become identified as the DARP research program, the acronym for the initial letters of the Drug Abuse Reporting Program, in which the data were collected.

The DARP data base includes records on approximately 44,000 clients who were admitted to treatment at 52 federally supported treatment centers located throughout the United States and in Puerto Rico between June 1, 1969, and March 31, 1973. For purposes of analysis, they were divided into three cohorts, admitted to treatment in 1969 to 1971, 1971 to 1972, and 1972 to 1973.

Extensive reports have been published on evaluation during the periods that clients were in treatment for all three cohorts and on posttreatment follow-up of samples of the first two cohorts. The during-treatment reports are included in five volumes (18, 19, 26–28). The posttreatment follow-up research has been published in technical reports and scientific journals (16, 17, 23, 24, 29–32, 34, 37, 38, 40, 41). Field work on the Cohort 3 sample was completed in July, 1979, and results for this cohort are not yet available. The results and conclusions presented are based principally on the reports cited above.

DESCRIPTION OF THE DARP RESEARCH PROGRAM

The DARP was initiated in 1969 to provide a data base for longitudinal, prospective research on the evaluation of drug abuse treatment in federally supported programs. Initially, six agencies reported and others were added by the federal sponsors, until in the fourth year there were 52. In the early years the DARP population approximated the universe of programs and clients in the NIMH-NIDA community treatment programs, and even in the final year it represented a substantial majority, although selection of programs to report was based on administrative considerations. A comprehensive description of the goals, scope, design, problems, advantages, and limitations of the program was presented by Sells (21).

CLIENT REPORTS

The agencies reporting in DARP submitted Admissions Reports (on client background and baseline levels on outcome measures) and bimonthly Status Evaluation Reports throughout the period in treatment, covering treatment received and client performance on selected outcomes, including: illicit drugs used (both opioid and nonopioid), alcohol consumption, work on legitimate jobs, school attendance, sources of income (including illegal sources), family and living arrangements, and criminality (arrests and time in jail). These reports were completed for every client admitted at each treatment agency by interviewers (usually counselors) trained in the system and were forwarded to the Institute of Behavioral Research (IBR) identified only by agency code numbers. Strict rules for confidentiality of the data were observed. IBR staff members reviewed and edited the reports, obtained missing data and corrections from the reporting agencies as required, and entered the data into the computer master file that comprised the data base for the research. Most of the information reported was obtained from clients by interview. Data have been presented in support of the reliability of this self-report procedure by Simpson, Lloyd, and Gent (36). Reporting of new admissions was discontinued on March 31, 1973, but Status Evaluation Reports were obtained on all clients then in treatment for a full year thereafter.

CLIENT SAMPLE

Although the total number of admissions reported by the 52 DARP agencies included 43,943 individuals, the final count of the actual number available for the evaluation research was 35,179. The balance were excluded in the process of data management for a variety of reasons: 1,388 from four

agencies whose data were rejected in quality control, 475 nonusers of illicit drugs, 6,708 not at risk during the 2 months preceding admission (mainly because they were in jail or other drug treatments), and 193 with excessive missing data. Of the reduced total, 1,645 were in treatments that could not be classified or that were considered experimental and were excluded from the major analyses; 6,074, who completed intake but did not enter treatment, were excluded from the during-treatment studies but included in the population from which follow-up samples were drawn. A full account of the data management dispositions was presented by Simpson et al. (39) and of the sampling design and procedures by Simpson and Joe (33).

Table 63.1 based on 27,460 clients who entered DARP treatment in one of the four major modalities included in the present study, shows the composition of the sample by year of admission. During the first 2 years (Cohort 1) the DARP population was composed principally of daily opioid users, who were predominantly male, older (over 25), and black. Beginning in the third year (Cohort 2), under new legislation that allowed treatment of other than narcotic addicts, the admissions reflect increased numbers of females, younger clients, and whites. The trend in Cohorts 2 and 3 involved a shift in the population, characterized by increased proportions of clients with later onset of drug use, low pretreatment criminality, fewer dependents, less pretreatment employment, higher socioeconomic status of parents, less legal involvement at admission, and lower educational level. Although most of these factors are a function of the lower age of clients admitted, age at onset and socioeconomic status are not, and these factors were indicative of the entry of white, middle-class, polydrug users into the treatment population, particularly in Cohort 3. This is important to keep in mind, because the follow-up data presented below are based on the first two cohorts and analyses of Cohort 3 are presently in process.

DRUG TREATMENTS IN THE DARP

The major treatment modalities in the DARP were methadone maintenance (MM), therapeutic community (TC), outpatient drug free (DF), and detoxification (DT), both inpatient (DTIP) and ambulatory (DTOP).

Table 63.1
Sex, Age, and Ethnic Group of DARP Clients by Year of Admission

	Percentage of Clients by Year of Admission			
	Cohort 1 (1969–1970)	Cohort 1 (1970–1971)	Cohort 2 (1971–1972)	Cohort 3 (1972–1973)
Sex				
Male	80	80	75	71
Female	20	20	25	29
Age				
Under 18	6	6	9	19
18–22	25	33	37	32
23–30	30	36	35	32
31–40	28	18	14	12
Over 40	11	7	5	5
Ethnic group				
Black	55	49	47	41
Puerto Rican	6	15	12	5
Mexican-American	8	8	8	9
White	30	27	32	44
Other	1	1	1	1
No. clients	1,940	5,719	9,911	9,890

These accounted for almost 95 per cent of all DARP admissions; the remainder involved clients assigned to experimental studies (e.g., of antagonists) and combinations of procedures that could not be classified into any of the four predominant modalities.

Because the DARP research design for evaluation of treatment involved pooling of data from different treatment programs into groups reflecting common treatment paradigms, considerable effort was invested in research on the description and classification of treatment (1, 7–9). Multiple discriminant analyses of an extensive series of descriptors of treatment goals, process, counseling techniques, ancillary and aftercare services, medication, control and sanction procedures, and operational philosophy and values indicated that the four modalities could be considered separate and distinct (7). For a number of reasons, but particularly in order to utilize categories with widely accepted definitions and to maximize sample size in treatment groups, the major analyses have been based on treatment modalities. A taxonomy of treatment types within modalities was developed by Cole and Watterson (1) and received support in a subsequent study by James et al. (9), but this has thus far been utilized only in exploratory studies.

SYSTEM DISTRIBUTION OF CLIENTS BY TREATMENT

The assignment of clients to treatments was the responsibility of the participating agencies, subject to federal guidelines, such as age, drug use history, and prior treatment restrictions for admission to methadone maintenance, boundaries of catchment areas, treatment alternatives available, and treatment "slots" available. Some of the agencies utilized central intake units in which prospective clients were evaluated clinically and others allowed individual units to process admissions. In many cases client preference was respected, but data on this point were not collected. Selectivity in admissions varied among programs from high to low.

As expected, the client composition of the four modalities differed considerably; this is shown in Table 63.2. MM, the largest group (40 per cent), was predominantly male, older, black, and composed of opioid addicts. DT, the next largest group (22 per cent), was very similar in composition to MM. The third largest group, DF (21 per cent), was most dissimilar to MM, having the highest percentage of females, youth, whites, and users of nonopioids only. The smallest group, TC (16 per cent), was in between MM and DF, closer to DF in age and percentage of whites but closer to MM in percentage of addicts (daily opioid users).

Because the variables summarized in Table 63.2 and others correlated with them are associated with treatment prognosis, comparison of outcomes across treatments was not warranted unless adequate adjustments could be made for the population differences. As noted earlier, statistical adjustments have

Table 63.2
Sex, Age, Ethnic Group, and Pre-DARP Drug Use Patterns of Clients in DARP MM, TC, DF, and DT Treatments

	Percentage of Clients by Treatment Modality				
	MM	TC	DF	DT	Total
Sex					
Male	79	74	69	76	75
Female	22	26	31	24	25
Age					
Under 18	1	15	37	4	12
18–22	28	45	34	35	34
23–30	41	28	20	39	34
31–40	22	9	6	17	15
Over 40	8	3	3	5	5
Ethnic group					
Black	58	34	26	50	45
Puerto Rican	15	11	5	6	10
Mexican-American	10	3	5	12	9
White	16	51	63	31	35
Other	1	1	1	1	1
Pre-DARP drug use pattern					
Daily opioids only	45	23	17	48	36
Daily opioids and nonopioids	49	40	18	40	39
Less than daily opioids and nonopioids	5	20	17	5	10
Nonopioids only	1	17	48	7	15
No. clients	11,023	4,505	5,785	6,147	27,460

been developed, and these have been utilized in the DARP studies reported below.

GENERAL ANALYTIC STRATEGY

It has been assumed that a treatment episode is only an interval in the life of a client and that behaviors employed as outcomes may be caused by numerous factors in addition to treatment. Factors that were recorded and analyzed in the DARP in this regard include (a) demographic classification variables, e.g., sex, age, ethnic group; (b) developmental background, e.g., family socioeconomic status, family structure, education, employment history, drug use history, criminal history; (c) prior treatment for drug use; (d) baseline levels on the outcome measures, in most cases for the 2-month period preceding admission; and (e) community context factors that might have direct or indirect influence on client outcomes (13, 25).

The outcome indicators recorded at bimonthly intervals from baseline to termination of treatment (and retrospectively by monthly intervals from termination to post-DARP interview for the follow-up samples) were restricted to behavioral indicators of conformity to societal norms, including use of illicit drugs and alcohol, work on legitimate jobs or time involved in schooling or homemaking, and involvement in criminal activities. Because of limited resources and reservations concerning the validity of available measures, systematic measurement of motivation for treatment, adjustment, personality, value orientations, and other intrapsychic measures was not attempted. Data management procedures were followed that enabled adjustments for time at risk and comparability of measures across time.

Clients were classified by treatment modality and treatment type in DARP, based on information in their Status Evaluation Reports and in treatment classification checklists completed on all treatment programs, following standard procedures. No measure of treatment intensity (or dosage) was available. Time in treatment, which is highly correlated with favorableness of outcomes, was considered, but it is confounded with motivation. The general practice, followed in DARP, has been to regard time in treatment as a dependent variable reflecting the holding power of a program.

Three studies, one on each DARP cohort, have been published that addressed treatment effectiveness based on during-treatment behavioral outcomes (3, 5, 42). Three additional evaluation studies addressed retention of clients in treatment for each of the three cohorts (10–12). In each case the research design emphasized evaluation of each modality separately, and comparison across modalities was mainly a matter of inference based on the results of the within-modality studies. A similar design was employed, in part, by Simpson et al. (41) in a follow-up study of Cohort 1 and 2 samples, based on outcomes for the first year after DARP termination. These authors also addressed the issue of comparison across modalities, as did Sells et al. (23) using outcomes for the first 3 years after DARP termination, based on a different analytic method.

DURING-TREATMENT OUTCOME RESULTS

The during-treatment results have been widely reported and need not be repeated here. In general, they indicated significant improvements on most outcomes in the outpatient treatments; because residential and inpatient clients were only minimally at risk during treatment, comparable data were not computed for them. Of particular interest was the consistent finding that the major change during treatment occurred early, on the first status report for most outcomes, suggesting a *compliance factor* of adjustment to the treatment environment. For many clients additional favorable changes were observed over time in treatment, suggesting a *therapeutic change factor* as well. Length of time in treatment was positively associated with completion as opposed to unfavorable termination (quitting and expulsion) and with favorable scores on the behavioral outcomes. Average time in treatment was longest in MM programs (more than 1 year) and considerably shorter in TC and DF (in the range of 3 to 6 months). Over the period of DARP data collection, there was a general trend toward shorter time in treatment.

EVALUATION DESIGNS WITHIN MODALITIES

Studies within each modality, such as those cited above, have involved two stages. In the first stage, gross differences from baseline to end of treatment (3, 4, 42) or to a posttreatment time, such as the first year post-DARP

(41), were measured for each outcome variable. The second stage involved linear model analyses of variance and co-variance or hierarchical multiple regression analyses for each outcome measure, using the pre-DARP demographic, background, prior treatment, and baseline measures (and, in the Simpson et al. study (41), during-DARP measures as well) as independent measures to identify factors other than treatment that predicted outcomes significantly. Assuming that the gross differences represent the mean for all clients in a treatment, the significant predictors could be used to identify subgroups of clients that had differential outcomes.

This type of two-stage design can answer two important questions. The first stage determines whether or not any significant change occurred for a client cohort and, if so, the magnitude of change on each outcome measure. The second stage is relevant to the question of whether or not such change (even if not significant for the total cohort) differs between subgroups of clients. Demographic, background, baseline, and prior treatment variables (and during-treatment outcomes predictive of posttreatment outcomes) are viewed as definers of meaningful subgroups that have differential outcomes, but not as causal factors. They may indeed have causal significance, but causality involves additional considerations and cannot be addressed in this analytic model.

Evaluation Designs for Comparison of Treatments. Because of differences in the populations served, treatment environments, and approaches, comparison of the effectiveness of treatment modalities in the DARP is admittedly a very difficult problem. In terms of the distributions in Table 63.2, MM and DT seem to have been the most popular treatments for addicts, but there were substantial numbers of addicts in TC (63 per cent) and DF (35 per cent). DF, which has been regarded as the treatment of choice for youthful polydrug and nonopioid users, had 65 per cent of its population in these categories in the total DARP population, but their percentage in Cohorts 1 and 2, for which follow-up data are presently available, was much lower. As noted earlier, a substantial percentage of TC clients were nonaddicts (37 per cent). The different percentages of addicts and nonaddicts in the four modalities have implications for the appropriateness of different outcome measures, as well as for adjustments to control for differential baseline status.

In addition, the treatments are quite different in respect to certain norms and attitudes toward expected client behavior. Without necessarily being moralistic, the drug-free treatments have generally taken a harder line in relation to drug use than MM, although there seems to have been a general tolerance of alcohol and marihuana use in most treatment programs. Many MM programs have also advocated indefinite maintenance or return to maintenance treatment, whereas TC and DF programs have not. These differences imply that occasional drug use is not incompatible with favorable outcome as defined in many MM programs, but that abstinence is generally associated with "success" in the drug-free programs.

They also reflect opposite positions with respect to return to treatment. In relation to outcomes, the client differences between treatments imply that outcomes should probably be weighted differentially for addicts and nonaddicts. Reduction of opioid use and criminality is most relevant for addicts, who have predominated in DARP MM and DT and, to a lesser extent, in TC. However, for the younger and less criminal polydrug users, more typical of DF, these are not the most focal outcomes; nonopioid use is more important, along with general improvement on the other measures. The major studies have combined these groups in order to obtain system data by cohort, but separate studies of addict and nonaddict samples have been completed, and these have been illuminating.

There are, therefore, ideological and client differences between treatments. In the present research it was decided to address the client differences by statistical methods and to deal with the ideological differences in the interpretation of results. The study by Simpson et al. (41) compared MM, TC, DF, DT, and IO (intake only) follow-up samples on individual outcomes and also on a composite measure developed by Hornick et al. (6) for the first year post-DARP. To compare treatment groups, they adjusted the follow-up measures for pre-DARP population differences by means of analysis of co-variance. Client characteristics and performance during DARP treatment were also examined in this study as predictors of post-DARP out-

comes by means of hierarchical stepdown regression analysis.

The study by Sells et al. (23) employed behaviorally defined outcome groups for the first 3 years after DARP, based on distinctive profiles of post-DARP scores for six outcomes, as explained below (6). In a companion study, Neman et al. (14) identified pre-DARP factors that discriminated outcome groups by means of multiple discriminant analysis. Computations were made of both the percentages of each treatment sample in each outcome group and also the percentages expected, based on the significant variables defining the first discriminant function. Examination of two ratios—including (a) actual percentages for each treatment group to the total for all treatments combined and (b) actual to expected percentages (by outcome group)—enabled comparative judgments of treatment effectiveness.

SUMMARY OF FOLLOW-UP STUDY RESULTS

The two DARP follow-up studies by Simpson et al. (41) and Sells et al. (23) were based on the same samples drawn from Cohorts 1 and 2, but they utilized different outcome measures and different methods of analysis. The results were highly consistent and together provide important evidence concerning both the effectiveness of the federally supported treatment system monitored by the DARP and the comparative effectiveness of the four modalities of treatment included in this system. The data presented are taken mainly from Sells et al. (23), representing composite outcome profiles for the sample of approximtely 2,000 black and white males, computed for the first 3 years after DARP termination.

The profiles were based on six outcome variables that could be scored according to the definitions listed in Table 63.3 for any designated time period. In the Sells et al. (23) study, the six elements were scored separately for each of the first 3 years after each client's DARP termination and then averaged (Table 63.3).

Cluster analyses of the individual profiles for random samples of clients from the five treatment groups (6) resulted in 11 outcome groups with distinct profiles. These were arrayed on a scale of favorableness of outcome,

Table 63.3
Definitions of Outcome Measures

E	(employment)	0	Employed more than 67% of time at risk
		1	Employed 1 to 67% of time at risk
		2	Employed 0% of time at risk
O	(opioid use)	0	No use over time at risk
		1	Mean use from less than weekly to 4 days per week
		2	Mean use 5 days per week or greater
N	(nonopioid use, but not including marihuana)	0	No use over time at risk
		1	Mean use from less than weekly to 4 days per week
		2	Mean use 5 days per week or greater
A	(alcohol use)	0	Mean daily intake of 8 ounces of 80-proof liquor equivalent or less
		1	Mean daily intake of more than 8 ounces of 80-proof liquor equivalent
C	(criminality)	0	No arrests and no time in jail
		1	Not more than one arrest and not more than 30 days in jail
		2	More than one arrest or more than 30 days in jail
T	(return to treatment)	0	No treatment after DARP
		1	Any treatment after DARP

from the most favorable, with zero or approximately zero on all six outcome elements, to the least favorable, with maximum scores of 2 on E, O, N, and C and of 1 on A and T. The 11 outcome groups, with their defining profiles, are listed in Table 63.4 in order of over-all favorableness of outcome. In the present discussion, as in some of the analyses reported, the 11 outcome groups were combined into four *outcome levels*, as indicated in Table 63.4.

The composition of the five treatment follow-up subsamples is shown in Table 63.5. Although 87 per cent of the total Cohort 1–2 follow-up sample was located by the field staff approximately 5 years after DARP admission, and interviews were completed on 76 per cent (3,131), the analyses reported here were restricted to black and white males who were represented in all five treatment groups. The differences between treatment groups in these samples are generally consistent with those for the treatment population shown in Table 63.2.

The over-all results, consisting of actual and expected percentages of each treatment group at each outcome level, are shown in Table 63.6. The *actual percentages* were computed based on the number of clients in each treatment group whose profiles were classified in outcome groups within the respective levels. The *expected percentages* were calcu-

lated on the basis of classification predicted by the pre-DARP variables weighted by their discriminant weights in the discriminant function.

The data in Table 63.6 enable assessment of system outcomes for the total sample as well as comparative statements concerning the treatment modalities. The system outcomes are based on actual percentages for the total sample, regardless of treatment group. The comparative statements are based on actual percentages for each treatment group in relation to the corresponding expected percentages.

SYSTEM OUTCOMES

The actual percentages, in the Total column at the right of the upper panel of Table 63.6, indicate that 31.1 per cent of all clients in the follow-up sample had highly favorable outcomes (Level I) as defined above, over the first 3 years after DARP termination. This was almost twice as many as those with highly unfavorable outcomes (Level IV) and is a noteworthy accomplishment. In addition, 20.3 per cent of the total sample had moderately favorable (Level II) outcomes with low (or no) criminality, abstinence or moderate drug use, and about half (mainly in MM) returning to treatment. Combining the percentages for Level II with Level I to estimate

Table 63.4
Outcome Groups Listed in Order of Over-all Favorableness of Outcome

Level	Group No.	Percentage in Group	Profile Description
I	1	15.0	Drug abstinence and favorable on all elements
(Highly favorable outcomes)	3	11.3	Drug abstinence and favorable except for E (mean = 1.4)
	2	5.4	Drug abstinence and favorable except for T (mean = 1.0)
II	8	9.5	Opioid abstinence but moderate nonopioid use, moderate unemployment
(Moderately favorable outcomes)	4	12.2	Moderate opioid but no nonopioid use, no criminality, and 100% returned to treatment (mean T = 1.0)
III	5	9.5	Not heavy opioid use, no nonopioid use, moderate-high criminality
(Moderately unfavorable outcomes)	6	8.0	Moderate-heavy opioid use, no nonopioid use, moderate unemployment
	9	14.0	Moderate drug use, unemployment, return to treatment, and criminality
IV	11	5.8	Moderate-heavy drug use, unemployment, and return to treatment
(Highly unfavorable outcomes)	10	4.2	Moderate-heavy drug use and unemployment, high criminality
	7	5.3	Heavy opioid use, high unemployment and criminality, and 100% returned to treatment

favorable outcomes of the treatment system, the percentage is 51.4 per cent. In view of the skepticism that has often been expressed concerning the effectiveness of drug abuse treatment, these system data from the DARP, based on behavioral indicators over a 3-year period after leaving treatment, stand as impressive positive evidence that over half of the clients followed have carried on at a favorable level in the community.

The total results, representing the entire sample and all five treatment groups combined, require no adjustment for population factors; they reflect the status of the sample followed for the time period represented. However, among the five treatment groups, three represent major treatment modalities (MM, TC, and DF) and the other two, very short term treatment (DT) or no treatment (IO). The differences between the first three and the other two groups in respect to actual and expected outcomes, as shown below, add further force to the implication that valid and meaningful treatment results were produced in the federal treatment system monitored by DARP.

From Table 63.6, the following actual and expected percentages, for Levels I and II com-

bined, were obtained:

	MM	TC	DF	DT	IO
Actual	55.1	52.8	54.3	35.2	37.1
Expected	43.6	54.2	63.5	56.3	56.7

Looking at the actual percentages, there was little variation among the three major modalities, and also little variation between DT and IO, but a large difference of 15 to 20 per cent between the two groupings. At the same time, except for DF, the variations on expected percentages were smaller in magnitude. Finally, the percentages of actual favorable outcomes for DT and IO were about 20 per cent below expectation, whereas those for MM and TC were above (MM + 11.5 per cent) or approximately equal to (TC − 1.4 per cent) expectation. For DF the percentage of actual favorable outcomes was 9.2 per cent below expectation, but this was considerably less than for DT and IO.

Further discussion of the results for DF is presented below. The focal point in this section is that a major difference occurred between at least two of the modalities, MM and TC, which represent well documented treatment approaches, and the two groups that

Table 63.5
Comparison of MM, TC, DF, DT, and IO Follow-up Subsamples on Age, Ethnic Group, and Pre-DARP Levels on Nine Outcome Measures[a]

Comparison Variable	DARP Treatment Group				
	MM	TC	DF	DT	IO
Mean age	27	24	23	26	24
Per cent black	53%	47%	45%	50%	51%
Per cent daily opioid users[b]	84%	61%	48%	80%	70%
Per cent not daily opioid users[c]	16%	39%	52%	20%	30%
Per cent using nonopioids only[c]	3%	11%	25%	7%	9%
Mean opioid use[d]	3.69	3.26	2.64	3.63	3.44
Mean nonopioid use[d]	1.91	2.23	2.13	2.04	2.04
Mean marihuana use[d]	1.77	2.16	2.33	1.89	2.12
Mean alcohol use[e]	1.34	1.37	1.43	1.37	1.25
Per cent employed—2 months pre-DARP	46%	34%	40%	46%	37%
Months employed—12 months pre-DARP	4.8	3.8	4.2	4.9	3.8
Per cent arrested per year—lifetime pre-DARP	21%	24%	15%	17%	19%
Per cent with jail time—lifetime pre-DARP	75%	79%	63%	59%	70%
Per cent with prior drug treatment—lifetime pre-DARP	54%	56%	40%	45%	53%
Number of black and white males in follow-up sample	921	735	289	174	159

[a] Based on Simpson, D. D., Savage, L. J., Lloyd, M. R., and Sells, S. B. *Evaluation of Drug Abuse Treatments Based on First Year Followup.* National Institute on Drug Abuse, Services Research Monograph Series. Rockville, Md., National Institute on Drug Abuse, 1978.
[b] Includes users of daily opioids only and daily opioids plus other drugs during the 2-month period preceding DARP admission.
[c] Based on the 2-month period preceding DARP admission.
[d] Scored for the 2-month period preceding DARP admission: 1, never; 2, less than weekly; 3, weekly; 4, daily.
[e] Scored for the 2-month period preceding DARP admission: 1, no use; 2, 0.1 to 4.0 ounces per day; 3, 4.1 to 8.0 ounces per day; 4, more than 8.0 ounces per day.

Table 63.6
Actual and Expected Percentages for the Five Treatment Groups (MM, TC, DF, DT, and IO) and the Total Black and White Male Follow-up Sample

	Outcome Level	Percentages for Treatment Groups					
		MM	TC	DF	DT	IO	Total
Actual percentages	I	29.5	36.9	34.4	19.6	21.0	31.1
	II	25.6	15.9	19.9	15.6	16.1	20.3
	III	30.8	31.1	31.1	39.3	38.4	32.2
	IV	14.1	16.1	14.6	25.5	24.5	16.4
Expected percentages	I	26.6	34.4	33.7	34.7	32.9	
	II	17.0	19.8	29.8	21.6	23.8	
	III	37.6	29.4	27.8	31.4	22.4	
	IV	19.0	16.5	8.7	12.4	21.0	

received short term detoxification or no treatment, when adjustment was made for pre-DARP population differences. Together with the over-all results, these data support the impression that "treatment works." However, it is reasonable to assume that the four treatments included in DARP did not "work" equally well and also that each may have been more effective for some groups of clients than for others. The first of these points, involving indications of comparative effectiveness, is addressed next. Some additional information concerning client-treatment fit is presented subsequently.

COMPARATIVE EFFECTIVENESS OF TREATMENTS

Looking at Table 63.6, it can be seen that if all five treatment groups had had the same actual percentages at Outcome Level I, this would have been 31.1 per cent (shown in the Total column), which can be regarded as par for Level I in the present sample. However, the TC and DF actual percentages were noticeably higher than par, whereas MM was slightly below par and DT and IO were considerably below par. Taking these at face value, it seems that TC and DF had a surplus of highly favorable outcomes, whereas MM was about average and DT and IO were greatly underrepresented at this highly favorable level. But these *actual* percentages were based on treatment samples that differed considerably in background and status at admission and were not adjusted for expectation based on these population differences. The expected percentages enabled such adjustments, and when these were taken into account a different picture emerged, as shown by the values for the two sets of ratios, summarized in Table 63.7.

The first ratio, A/T, is the *actual* percentage for a treatment at a given level divided by the *total* percentage for that level; for this ratio, par is 1.0. The second ratio, (A - E)/T, is obtained by subtracting the expected (E) percentage from its paired actual (A) percentage and dividing the difference by the corresponding total (T) percentage; for this ratio, which indicates the presence of a treatment effect in proportion to the A - E difference, par is zero. For A/T, par (1.0) indicates that the actual frequency of a treatment group is the same as that for the total sample. For (A - E)/T, par (zero) indicates that there was no additional treatment effect above the frequency expected on the basis of prediction by nontreatment population variables.

The A/T ratio indicates the relative favorableness of outcomes (greater than 1.00 for Levels I and II and less than 1.00 for Levels III and IV) or unfavorableness (less than 1.00 for Levels I and II and greater than 1.00 for Levels III and IV) as they actually occurred. The (A - E)/T ratio assists in the interpretation of A/T, inasmuch as it can be interpreted as an *index of treatment effectiveness*. When (A - E)/T is greater than zero (par) it indicates that the actual percentage exceeded the expected and, for the favorable levels (I and II), that a positive treatment effect occurred. When it is less than zero, it indicates that the actual percentage fell short of expectation and, for the favorable levels, that a positive effect did not occur. For the unfavorable levels, the interpretation is reversed. No appropriate test of significance has been developed for these ratios, and they must be interpreted cautiously. The interpretations offered here are conservative and take into account the entire pattern of ratios for each treatment group as well as their relations to those of the other treatments.

The paired ratios for each of the five treatment groups at each of the four outcome

Table 63.7
Paired A/T and (A−E)/T Ratios for Treatment Groups at Each Outcome Level: Black and White Male Follow-up Sample

Outcome Level	Ratio	Ratios by Treatment Groups				
		MM	TC	DF	DT	IO
I	A/T	.95	1.19	1.11	.63	.68
	(A−E)/T	+.09	+.08	+.02	−.49	−.36
II	A/T	1.26	.78	.98	.77	.79
	(A−E)/T	+.42	−.19	−.49	−.30	−.38
III	A/T	.96	.97	.97	1.22	1.19
	(A−E)/T	−.21	+.05	+.10	+.25	+.50
IV	A/T	.86	.98	.89	1.55	1.49
	(A−E)/T	−.30	−.02	+.36	+.80	+.21

levels are shown in Table 63.7. These have been enclosed in a box for each treatment group-outcome level set for which a positive treatment effect of any magnitude was indicated. It should be noted that in two cases (TC, Level IV and DF, Level I) the (A - E)/T ratio was close to zero. The results for the five treatment groups were as follows.

MM. This was the only treatment group for which a positive treatment effect was found consistently at every level. The A/T ratio (.95) was slightly below par at Level I, reflecting the "hard core addict" character of this group; but even so, the 29.5 per cent of MM clients at this level was greater than expected (26.6 per cent). At Level II, the actual percentage of MM clients was substantially above par (whereas this percentage was well below par for all other groups), and the treatment effect index was +.42 (compared to negative values for the other groups).

It should be noted that Outcome Level II is considered by many to represent a reasonable outcome for MM, and the interpretation of these results is, therefore, critical. Level II is composed of two groups, Group 8—characterized by opioid abstinence and moderate to high nonopioid use and generally low scores on the other outcome measures—and Group 4—with moderate opioid and no nonopioid use, no criminality, and 100 per cent return to treatment. The interpretation of these outcome patterns as *moderately favorable*, particularly for MM, is consistent with the views of many clinicians, and certainly they are discriminably more favorable than the remaining profiles labeled moderately unfavorable (Level III, Groups 5, 6, and 9) and unfavorable (Level IV, Groups 11, 10, and 7). At Levels III and IV, the (A - E)/T ratios for MM were substantially negative.

In summary, it seems that 29.5 per cent of the MM sample had highly favorable outcomes for the first 3 years after DARP and that an additional 25.6 per cent had moderately favorable outcomes. These results exceeded expectation as calculated from pre-DARP client characteristics. The 30.8 per cent with moderately unfavorable outcomes and 14.1 per cent with unfavorable outcomes were both below par and well below expectation. Taking into account the interpretation given above of the Level II results, 55.1 per cent of the MM sample can be said to have had favorable outcomes; these represent

Levels I and II combined, for which A/T was 1.07 and (A - E)/T was +.22.

TC. This group had the highest actual percentage at Level I, 36.9 per cent, with A/T of 1.19 and (A - E)/T of +.08. At the same time, only 15.9 per cent of TC clients (A/T of .78 and (A - E)/T of −.19) were at Level II. This is reasonable, knowing the drug-free ideology of TC programs. At Levels III and IV, the results were essentially at par. Thus TC produced a substantial surplus, compared to par, of highly favorable outcomes. For Levels I and II combined, the TC percentage was 52.8 per cent (very close to MM), but, because Level II reflects outcomes contradictory to TC goals, the most distinctive results for TC must be the very high percentage at Level I.

DF. The DF sample was composed of the highest proportion of younger, noncriminal, polydrug and nonopioid users, compared to the other treatment groups, and had the highest expected percentage for Level II (as well as for Levels I and II combined), reflecting these and related client characteristics. It was not surprising, therefore, to find (a) that 34.4 per cent of the DF sample were at Level I (A/T of 1.11), almost as many as of TC; but (b) that the treatment effect was not discriminably greater than zero, (A - E)/T of +.02. At the other three levels the DF results were very disappointing, and the percentages at the two unfavorable levels (III and IV) were considerably higher than expected. The combined actual percentage of DF at Levels I and II was 54.3 per cent, comparable with MM and TC; but, although this reflected an A/T ratio of 1.06, the corresponding (A - E)/T ratio was −.18. Thus the "favorable" DF results seem to reflect a less deviant client population rather than an effective treatment outcome.

DT and IO. The results for these two groups were similar and consistently negative. Because the DT sample was drawn from outpatient detoxification programs of short tenure and the results were essentially the same as for IO, which consisted of clients who completed intake but did not participate in treatment in DARP, several explanations are possible. There is no reliable information to explain why the 10 clients failed to enter the treatments in which they were enrolled. However, the explanation favored to account for the poor results in these two groups is mainly low (or zero) treatment time, although it can also be argued that the level of intervention in DT was very low compared to that in the other treatments, even DF. In this connection, a study by Simpson (32) is particularly relevant. Simpson compared clients in MM, TC, and DF who had remained in DARP treatment less than 3 months with those in the DT and IO samples and found no differences in post-DARP outcomes. Clients who received no treatment (IO) and those who remained in treatment less than 3 months, regardless of modality, had the poorest over-all outcomes after DARP, whereas those in MM, TC, and DF who remained in treatment more than 3 months did well in proportion to their length of stay in treatment.

SUMMARY

Over-all, the differential results separated the short term DT and zero time (no treatment) IO groups from MM, TC, and DF by considerable differences. The adjusted results for DT and IO can be interpreted as very poor by comparison with the other three groups, which represent the major modalities in which substantial treatment effects should be expected. The results for MM showed favorable differences between actual and expected frequencies at all four outcome levels. Further, if the Level II outcomes are interpreted as· strongly as some MM clinicians advocate, then the case for the effectiveness of MM would be exceptional. However, even the 29.5 per cent at Level I can be regarded as impressive. The results for TC were distinctively favorable only at Level I, with 36.9 per cent of TC clients in this category, compared to 34.4 per cent expected. At Level II, the TC results were predictably poor, and at Levels III and IV they were about par. The results for DF were disappointing, although clearly not at the low level of DT and IO.

If these analyses had gone no further, positive indications would have been justified only for MM and TC. However, Sells et al. (23) carried out an additional analysis in which addicts (defined as daily opioid users) and nonaddicts (all other clients) were considered separately. The results for the addict groups in MM and TC were approximately the same as for the total sample. In contrast to their favorable results in MM and TC, however, addicts had distinctly unfavorable

results in DF. On the other hand, the TC results for nonaddicts were also poor, but the DF results for nonaddicts were relatively good, at least with respect to Level I. Unfortunately, the nonaddict group in DF (and also in TC) was small, and only tentative conclusions could be drawn.

DIFFERENTIAL OUTCOMES FOR CLIENT SUBGROUPS

In general, background status on most outcome measures was correlated with post-DARP status on the corresponding variables (14, 41). This was most dramatically demonstrated in the case of criminality, which was associated with arrests and time in jail, as well as opioid use, after DARP in all treatment groups. However, it was also found that clients with favorable pre-DARP work histories were most likely to be employed after DARP and that heavy substance users pre-DARP, of both drugs and alcohol, were most likely to continue use after leaving DARP.

This does not conflict with the statements earlier concerning over-all treatment effectiveness, but rather it indicates that long established habits tend to persist even after treatment, although sometimes at a lower level, reflecting positive therapeutic effects. In the case of employment, the principle implied tends to enhance the appearance of treatment effectiveness, whereas in the case of opioid use and criminality it helps to identify the most difficult clients.

In the total follow-up sample, no outcome differences related to sex were found for any treatment group. In relation to ethnic group, only one relationship was found with return to treatment; whites tended significantly to enter post-DARP treatment more frequently than blacks or members of other ethnic groups. Age was a differential predictor of outcome only in MM, where clients over age 27 at admission had more favorable outcomes than younger clients (16).

Although several of the relationships mentioned are important, it is not surprising that so few significant predictors of outcome were found. This is consistent with the conclusion that treatment was generally effective and, the more effective the treatment, the less likely it is that outcomes will be predictable. If effectiveness were maximum (say at 100 per cent), then the correlations of all predictors with outcomes would be zero. In general the most promising development related to differential outcomes for subgroups of clients seems to be the results for addicts and non-addicts reported by Sells et al. (23). These will be examined further in Cohort 3 and, if replicated, will have important implications for the matching of clients with treatments.

RELATED DARP FOLLOW-UP RESEARCH

This section summarizes some additional results of the DARP follow-up studies that have been addressed in separate reports. These include (a) research bearing on the interpretation of return to treatment, (b) treatment outcomes measured 1 month after DARP termination, (c) community factors that affect treatment outcomes, and (d) the relation of client evaluation of treatment to treatment outcomes.

Research Bearing on the Interpretation of Return to Treatment after DARP. Logically, the necessity to reenter treatment after a treatment episode would imply that the treatment had not prepared the client to function effectively on his or her own in the community. However, there has been not only a bias in favor of prolonged maintenance in MM programs (2), but also evidence that substantial numbers of MM clients are unable to detoxify and return to community living on a narcotic-abstinent basis (22). This would imply that in some cases, particularly when detoxification is unsuccessful, return to maintenance treatment might be a preferable alternative compared to return to the "street" while dependent on narcotics.

In the selection of outcomes as criteria in the DARP research, the continued "street" use of illicit drugs after treatment was regarded as unfavorable and as a negative indicator of treatment effectiveness. Because continued drug use is a precondition to reentry into treatment, such reentry was also scored negatively. However, because of the position taken by Dole and others, as explained above, it was thought desirable to obtain empirical data on the significance of return to treatment.

Such a study was completed by Simpson and Savage (38) who examined patterns of post-DARP reentry to treatment among the sample of black and white males in the fol-low-up study. They found that 51 per cent of the sample had further treatment lasting 1 month or longer during the first 3 years after DARP, although the percentage in treatment during any single year remained almost constant at around 35 per cent. In the order of popularity, MM was first (48 per cent), followed by TC (31 per cent); DF and DT were around 10 per cent, and 8 per cent were classified as IO.

The 49 per cent who remained out of treatment all 3 years had more favorable outcomes on opioid use, nonopioid use, employment, and time in jail than the 51 per cent who had some further treatment. (It is of interest that 29.5 per cent of MM clients were in the no further treatment category.) Among those who reentered treatment it was found further that (a) reentry was preceded by elevated drug use and criminality and (b) the further treatment had incremental favorable effects on client behaviors. As a result, clients who reentered treatment early (in the first year) and were not in treatment in the third year had more favorable 3-year outcomes than those who remained out of treatment for 1 or 2 years and then returned to treatment. Nineteen per cent were in treatment during at least 1 month in each of the 3 years, and their performance levels were poorest of all, measured during those periods that they were at risk (not in jail or otherwise confined).

These results support the position taken in DARP that return to treatment should be considered as an unfavorable outcome of treatment. However, this position does assume that there are no clients who cannot be detoxified and returned to the community in an abstinent state and, as mentioned, this assumption may not be warranted. It is believed that the question is not yet resolved, although there were substantial numbers of clients in the DARP follow-up sample who scored favorably on criminality and employment but did return to treatment (Outcome Level II). These were labeled "moderately favorable." A decision on this issue at this time must reflect philosophy and value orientation as well as interpretation of data, and the DARP investigators have chosen to point out the problem rather than take what would necessarily be an arbitrary position.

Treatment Outcomes 1 Month after DARP. On most outcome variables, the levels reported for the first year after leaving

DARP were somewhat less favorable than those that prevailed during DARP but considerably more favorable than the baseline, pre-DARP levels. Further favorable change was generally observed up to 3 or 4 years in the DARP follow-up protocols, and the levels reported at the time of interview were frequently more favorable than those during DARP. In relation to the time trends after termination of treatment, there has been much interest in the question of how early the differences between treatment groups, observed after 1 year by Simpson et al. (41) and after 3 years by Sells et al. (24), would appear. This was investigated in a study by Simpson et al. (37). What they found was that the treatment group differences observed in the other studies were generally detectable in the first month after termination. There was only one outcome measure on which these differences failed to appear; this was the percentage of group with time in jail, which had a low over-all prevalence rate of 6 per cent during the month. On the other measures, representing the percentages of each group employed, using opioids daily, using any opioids, and using any nonopioids, the differences between MM, TC, and DF, on one hand, and DT and IO, on the other, were significant. As might be expected, the percentage that returned to treatment in the first month was higher for MM than any other group and slightly higher in DT and IO than in TC or DF. Marihuana and alcohol use, which increased in all groups, followed a different pattern; marihuana use was highest in DF, and alcohol use was lowest in DF.

This study also investigated type of termination (completed, referred, quit, expelled, etc.) and confirmed the relations of this variable to amount of drug use, incarceration in jail, employment, and return to treatment, observed in other DARP studies. Clients who were expelled or quit usually had remained in treatment for shorter periods than those who completed treatment, and they had higher rates of drug use and incarceration in jail than did the completers, who had higher employment rates. These data add support to the credibility of staff judgments of clients in the clinical process.

Community Factors That Affect Treatment Outcomes. At one point in the DARP program, the hypothesis was raised that the race-ethnic composition of the population of a treatment program, as represented by ethnic mix and majority-minority status, might significantly affect client outcomes. Related issues involved the relation of the numeric majority and minority statuses within a program to those of the community at large and variations in proportions of majority and minority clients within programs. Joe et al. (13) carried out a study based on during-treatment data of samples from DARP Cohorts 2 and 3 involving black and white clients from MM and DF programs. In addition to demographic, background, and baseline measures included in the DARP evaluation studies, this study utilized a series of community descriptions from the 1970 Census reports, such as the ratio of female youth to aged, the per cent Spanish, per cent Puerto Rican, male unemployment rate, per cent of black families in poverty, per cent of Spanish families in poverty, and property crime rates. It was not possible to update these 1970 statistics, but they were utilized in this exploratory study with the expectation that, despite community changes over time for the 15 cities in which the MM programs were located and the 15 DF cities, the rank order would not be too distorted. It was found that these community variables were significant predictors of outcomes and that they represent sources of variance in treatment effectiveness not covered by the client variables that have been used. The regression analyses in this study suggested that a race-ethnic factor is important to the understanding of outcomes during treatment that is strongly rooted in the population structure of the community environment.

Relation of Client Evaluation of Treatment to Treatment Outcomes. Subjective evaluations of treatment received and of treatment programs and staff were included in the follow-up interviews, and these were analyzed in a study by Simpson and Lloyd (35). In general, a surprisingly high level of satisfaction with program performance was found. TC programs received the best over-all ratings, but ratings were also high for MM programs; for example, 81 to 82 per cent of the clients in each of these treatment groups indicated that they would recommend their program to others. The satisfaction ratings were not so high for DF and DT (69 and 71 per cent) and were lowest for the IO group, as expected. These favorable client assessments were consistent with the outcome results reported earlier.

SUMMARY AND CONCLUSIONS

The research reported in this chapter is based on data collected in the Drug Abuse Reporting Program (DARP) and represents a large scale treatment evaluation study focused on the effectiveness of four treatment modalities—methadone maintenance (MM), therapeutic community (TC), outpatient drug free (DF), and outpatient detoxification (DT)—for three cohorts of clients admitted to 52 treatment centers located throughout the United States and in Puerto Rico between June, 1969, and March, 1973. The background, during-DARP, and sample follow-up data were confined to behavioral indicators and were obtained mainly by client interview. Issues of sampling, random assignment of clients to treatments, reliability and validity of self-report data, and research design were discussed. Major points addressed are summarized as follows.

1. Although the DARP population was not based on a randomly drawn probability sample of drug users in the United States, it nevertheless includes a large percentage of the treatment population in federally sponsored treatment for the years covered. Also, it includes types of clients by age, race, sex, drug use pattern, type of treatment, region of the country, and major cities in proportions similar to those prevailing during the years after DARP. Therefore, it is believed that the studies based on the DARP data are generalizable to contemporary issues of treatment effectiveness.

2. The DARP research involves field studies in the real world, based on operational program conditions; random experimental designs were considered infeasible in this environment, and control groups were not possible. As a result, analytic designs appropriate to the prevailing conditions were required.

3. The reliability and validity of the self-report data obtained by interview were examined and were considered acceptable.

4. For studies within treatment modalities, a two-stage design was employed. Stage 1 involved assessment of gross change from baseline to end of treatment or posttreatment on designated criteria, and Stage 2 involved

identification of significant predictors of the criteria; the latter could be used as definers of favorable and unfavorable outcome subgroups. For studies across treatment modalities, adjustments were made for population differences between modalities by analysis of co-variance and discriminant function analysis. Although not accounting totally for the variance attributed to the nontreatment variables included, the adjustments obtained independently by different methods have indicated high agreement and lend credibility to the conclusions drawn. Ideological and population differences between treatments also suggested differences in emphasis on several criteria; however, these could not be addressed statistically and were taken into account in the interpretation of results.

5. The data showed that three treatments, MM, TC, and DF, led to favorable results— MM and TC for heroin and other opioid addicts, and DF for nonaddict users of opioids less than daily, usually in conjunction with other nonopioid drugs, and users of nonopioids only. The results for outpatient detoxification (DT) were regarded as unsatisfactory and were attributed both to the short time involved and the low level of intervention observed. Clients who remained in the other modalities (MM, TC, and DF) for comparably short time (less than 3 months) did as poorly as those in DT.

6. In general, time in treatment, favorable (completed) versus unfavorable (quit or expelled) termination from treatment, and during-treatment performance, as reported on the bimonthly DARP Status Evaluation Reports, were significantly correlated with post-DARP performance outcomes.

7. Despite the large size and scope of the DARP data base, the follow-up studies were conducted on samples that, when partitioned by modality and subjected to rigorous data management procedures, were in some cases quite small. Much interest, therefore, attaches to the Cohort 3 data, currently being analyzed, for replication of results (based on Cohorts 1 and 2) that were presented as tentative in the present context.

8. During the period of data collection, average time in treatment in the four modalities studied declined, and changes in the composition of the client population were observed in the direction of increased proportions of females, youth, whites, and drug

users other than daily opioid users (addicts). It is necessary to monitor such change and to study the impact of the several factors involved on treatment effectiveness.

9. The DARP research is based on gross behavioral measures and did not include more detailed, intrapsychic assessment of clients, studies of client-staff interaction, and numerous other facets of the treatment process that have implications for clinical and policy decisions. At the same time, the DARP represents the only large scale research program that has addressed significant issues of treatment effectiveness in a systematic and sophisticated scientific frame.

References

1. Cole, S. G., and Watterson, O. A treatment typology for drug abuse in the DARP: 1971–1972 admissions. In *Effectiveness of Drug Abuse Treatment. Vol. 3: Further Studies of Drug Users, Treatment Typologies, and Assessment of Outcomes during Treatment in the DARP*, S. B. Sells and D. D. Simpson, editors. Cambridge, Mass., Ballinger, 1976.
2. Dole, V. P., and Joseph, H. Long-term outcome of patients treated with methadone maintenance. Ann. N. Y. Acad. Sci. *311*:181, 1978.
3. Gorsuch, R. L., Abbamonte, M., and Sells, S. B. Evaluation of treatments for drug users in the DARP: 1971–1972 admissions. In *Effectiveness of Drug Abuse Treatment. Vol. 4: Evaluation of Treatment Outcomes for the 1971–1972 Admission Cohort*, S. B. Sells and D. D. Simpson, editors. Cambridge, Mass., Ballinger, 1976.
4. Gorsuch, R. L., and Butler, M. C. Toward developmental models of non-medical drug use. In *Effectiveness of Drug Abuse Treatment. Vol. 3: Further Studies of Drug Users, Treatment Typologies, and Assessment of Outcomes during Treatment in the DARP*, S. B. Sells and D. D. Simpson, editors. Cambridge, Mass., Ballinger, 1976. (Reprinted in part in Psychol. Bull. 83:120, 1976.)
5. Gorsuch, R. L., Butler, M. C., and Sells, S. B. Evaluation of treatments for drug users in the DARP: 1972–1973 admissions. In *The Effectiveness of Drug Abuse Treatment. Vol. 5: Evaluation of Treatment Outcomes for the 1972–1973 Admission Cohort*, S. B. Sells and D. D. Simpson, editors. Cambridge, Mass., Ballinger, 1976.
6. Hornick, C. W., Demaree, R. G., Sells, S. B., and Neman, J. F. *Measurement of Post-DARP Outcomes: The Definition of a Composite and Differential Outcome Groups. National Followup Study of Admissions to Drug Abuse Treatments in the DARP during 1969–1972* (IBR Report No. 77-17). Ft. Worth, Institute of Behavioral Research, Texas Christian University, 1977.
7. James, L. R., Hammond, T. J., Hartman, E. A., and Sells, S. B. Treatment process associated with drug treatment modalities. An application of multiple discriminant analyses. In *Effectiveness of Drug Abuse Treatment. Vol. 3: Further Studies of Drug Users, Treatment Typologies, and Assessment of Out-comes during Treatment in the DARP*, S. B. Sells and D. D. Simpson, editors. Cambridge, Mass., Ballinger, 1976.
8. James, L. R., Hammond, T. J., Hartman, E. A., and Sells, S. B. A typology of treatment process for drug abuse. In *Effectiveness of Drug Abuse Treatment. Vol. 3: Further Studies of Drug Users, Treatment Typologies, and Assessment of Outcomes during Treatment in the DARP*, S. B. Sells and D. D. Simpson, editors. Cambridge, Mass., Ballinger, 1976.
9. James, L. R., Watterson, O., Bruni, J. R., and Cole, S. G. Validation of drug abuse treatment classification check lists. In *Effectiveness of Drug Abuse Treatment. Vol. 5: Evaluation of Treatment Outcomes for the 1972–1973 Admission Cohort*, S. B. Sells and D. D. Simpson, editors. Cambridge, Mass., Ballinger, 1976.
10. Joe, G. W. Retention in treatment of drug users in the DARP: 1969–1971 admissions. In *Effectiveness of Drug Abuse Treatment. Vol. 1: Evaluation of Treatments*, S. B. Sells, editor. Cambridge, Mass., Ballinger, 1974.
11. Joe, G. W., and Simpson, D. D. Retention in treatment of drug users admitted to treatment during 1971–1972. In *Effectiveness of Drug Abuse Treatment. Vol. 4: Evaluation of Treatment Outcomes for the 1971–1972 Admission Cohort*, S. B. Sells and D. D. Simpson, editors. Cambridge, Mass., Ballinger, 1976.
12. Joe, G. W., and Simpson, D. D. Treatment retention for drug users: 1972–1973 DARP admissions. In *Effectiveness of Drug Abuse Treatment. Vol. 5: Evaluation of Treatment Outcomes for the 1972–1973 Admissions Cohort*, S. B. Sells and D. D. Simpson, editors. Cambridge, Mass., Ballinger, 1976.
13. Joe, G. W., Singh, B. K., Finklea, D., Hudiburg, R., and Sells, S. B. *Community factors, Racial Composition of Treatment Programs, and Outcomes*. National Institute on Drug Abuse, Services Research Report (DHEW Publication No. (ADM) 78-573). Rockville, Md., National Institute on Drug Abuse, 1977.
14. Neman, J. F., Demaree, R. G., Hornick, C. W., and Sells, S. B. *Client Characteristics and Other Variables Associated with Differential Post DARP Outcome Groups* (IBR Report No. 77-16). Ft. Worth, Institute of Behavioral Research, Texas Christian University, 1977.
15. Renault, P. Clinical trials in drug dependence. Presented at meeting on research and reporting programme in the epidemiology of drug dependence. World Health Organization, Geneva, September, 1976.
16. Savage, L. J., and Simpson, D. D. Posttreatment outcomes of sex and ethnic groups treated in methadone maintenance during 1969–1972. J. Psychedelic Drugs 12:55, 1980.
17. Savage, L. J., and Simpson, D. D. Illicit drug use and return to treatment: Followup study of treatment admissions to DARP during 1969–1971. Am. J. Drug Alcohol Abuse 5:23, 1978.
18. Sells, S. B., editor. *Studies of the Effectiveness of Treatment for Drug Abuse. Vol. 1: Evaluation of Treatments*. Cambridge, Mass., Ballinger, 1974.
19. Sells, S. B., editor. *Studies of the Effectiveness of Treatment for Drug Abuse. Vol. 2: Research on Patients, Treatments, and Outcomes*. Cambridge,

Mass., Ballinger, 1974.

20. Sells, S. B. Techniques of outcome evaluation in alcohol, drug abuse, and mental health programs. In *Program Evaluation: Alcohol, Drug Abuse, and Mental Health Services*, J. Zusman and C. R. Wurster, editors, pp. 61–78. Lexington, Mass., Lexington Books, 1975.

21. Sells, S. B. Problems of conceptualization and design in research on the evaluation of treatment for drug abuse. In *The Origins and Course of Psychopathology: Methods of Longitudinal Research*, J. S. Strauss, H. Babigian, and M. Roff, editors, pp. 407–438. New York, Plenum Press, 1977.

22. Sells, S. B. Treatment effectiveness. In *Handbook on Drug Abuse*, R. L. DuPont, A. Goldstein, and J. O'Donnell, editors. Washington, D.C., United States Government Printing Office, 1979.

23. Sells, S. B., Demaree, R. G., and Hornick, C. W. *The Comparative Effectiveness of Methadone Maintenance, Therapeutic Community, Outpatient Drug-free, and Outpatient Detoxification Treatments for Drug Users in the DARP: Cohort 1–2 Followup Study*. National Institute on Drug Abuse Services Research Administrative Report. Rockville, Md., National Institute on Drug Abuse, 1979.

24. Sells, S. B., Demaree, R. G., Simpson, D. D., and Joe, G. W. Evaluation of present treatment modalities: Research with DARP admissions 1969–1973. Ann. N. Y. Acad. Sci., 311:270, 1978.

25. Sells, S. B., Demaree, R. G., Simpson, D. D., Joe, G. W., and Gorsuch, R. L. Issues in evaluation of drug abuse treatment. Professional Psychol. 8:609, 1977.

26. Sells, S. B., and Simpson, D. D., editors. *Effectiveness of Drug Abuse Treatment*. Vol. 3: *Further Studies of Drug Users, Treatment Typologies, and Assessment of Outcome during Treatment in the DARP*. Cambridge, Mass., Ballinger, 1976.

27. Sells, S. B., and Simpson, D. D., editors. *Effectiveness of Drug Abuse Treatment*. Vol. 4: *Evaluation of Treatment Outcomes for the 1971–1972 Admission Cohort*. Cambridge, Mass., Ballinger, 1976.

28. Sells, S. B., and Simpson, D. D., editors. *Effectiveness of Drug Abuse Treatment*. Vol. 5: *Evaluation of Treatment Outcomes for the 1972–1973 Admission Cohort*. Cambridge, Mass., Ballinger, 1976.

29. Sells, S. B., and Simpson, D. D. The case for drug abuse treatment effectiveness. Br. J. Addict. 75:117, 1980.

30. Sells, S. B., and Simpson, D. D. On the effectiveness of treatment for drug abuse: Evidence from the DARP research programme in the United States. Bull. Narc. 31:1, 1979.

31. Sells, S. B., and Simpson, D. D. Evaluation of treatment outcome for youths in the Drug Abuse Reporting Program (DARP): A followup study. In

Youth Drug Abuse: Problems, Issues, and Treatment, G. M. Beschner and A. S. Friedman, editors, pp. 571–628. Lexington, Mass., Lexington Books, 1979.

32. Simpson, D. D. The relation of time in drug abuse treatment to post treatment outcomes. Am. J. Psychiatry 136:1449, 1979.

33. Simpson, D. D., and Joe, G. W. *Sample Design and Data Collection: National Followup Study of Admissions to Drug Abuse Treatment in the DARP during 1969–1972* (IBR Report No. 77-8). Ft. Worth, Institute of Behavioral Research, Texas Christian University, 1977.

34. Simpson, D. D., and Lloyd, M. R. Alcohol and illicit drug use: Followup study of treatment admissions to DARP during 1969–1971. Am. J. Drug Alcohol Abuse 5:1, 1978.

35. Simpson, D. D. and Lloyd, M. R. Client evaluations of drug abuse treatment in relation to followup outcomes. Am. J. Drug Alcohol Abuse 6:397, 1979.

36. Simpson, D. D., Lloyd, M. R., and Gent, M. J. *Reliability and Validity of Data: National Followup Study of Admissions to Drug Abuse Treatments in the DARP during 1969–1971*. (IBR Report No. 76-18). Ft. Worth, Institute of Behavioral Research, Texas Christian University, 1976.

37. Simpson, D. D., Lloyd, M. R., and Savage, L. J. *Followup Outcomes in the First Month after Drug Abuse Treatment*. (IBR Report No. 79-2). Ft. Worth, Institute of Behavioral Research, Texas Christian University, 1979.

38. Simpson, D. D., and Savage, L. J. Drug abuse treatment readmissions and outcomes. Arch. Gen. Psychiatry 37:896, 1980.

39. Simpson, D. D., Savage, L. J., Joe, G. W., Demaree, R. G., and Sells, S. B. *DARP Data Book: Statistics on Characteristics of Drug Users in Treatment during 1969–1974* (IBR Report No. 76-4). Ft. Worth, Institute of Behavioral Research, Texas Christian University, 1976.

40. Simpson, D. D., Savage, L. G., and Lloyd, M. R. Followup evaluation of drug abuse treatment in the DARP during 1969–1972. Arch. Gen. Psychiatry 36:772, 1979.

41. Simpson, D. D., Savage, L. J., Lloyd, M. R., and Sells, S. B. *Evaluation of Drug Abuse Treatments Based on First Year Followup*. National Institute on Drug Abuse, Services Research Monograph Series (DHEW Publication No. (ADM) 78-701). Rockville, Md., National Institute on Drug Abuse, 1978.

42. Spiegel, D. K., and Sells, S. B. Evaluation of treatments for drug users in the DARP: 1969–1971 admissions. In *Effectiveness of Drug Abuse Treatment*. Vol. 1: *Evaluation of Treatments*, S. B. Sells, editor. Cambridge, Mass., Ballinger, 1974.

CHAPTER 64

EVALUATION

Frances R. Gearing, M.D., M.P.H.

Evaluation has come into prominence during the past 15 years for all health service delivery programs, including the treatment programs that have been devoted to users of illicit drugs, whether these efforts were supported by public or private funds. Until recently much of the evaluation of drug treatment programs has been equated with accountability.

Evaluation is defined as an ascertainment of a numerical value or as a careful appraisal. *Value* is defined as worth, merit, usefulness, esteem, or regard. *Accountability*, on the other hand, is defined as the state of being answerable, liable, or responsible (17).

These definitions place emphasis on cost accounting and time-motion type studies that measure such events as number of patient visits and time spent with various staff members. These studies attempted to answer questions such as: "How many people have received what services by whom and for what?" This type of evaluation is useful and has its place in making the delivery of treatment services more efficient and in eliminating wasted efforts. The missing element has been the effect of treatment on the individual who seeks help for his drug abuse problem. To evaluate drug treatment programs from the patient's standpoint, the kinds of questions that need to be addressed are: What proportion of the patients have been benefited by the treatment or services received, and in what ways? And further: Do those who drop out or who have interruptions in their contact with a treatment program dem-

onstrate a measurable difference in their long term rehabilitation? It has been said that "evaluation research has spawned a voluminous and varied literature" and that the treatment system that serves users of illicit drugs, and especially heroin, has contributed its share to the bulky literature on evaluation research (14). Despite this fact, there has been little agreement on a model for evaluation of treatment effectiveness. Part of the reason for this disagreement results from the fact that the various programs being evaluated have different goals; in addition, each group of evaluators is firm in the belief that they have not only the best but the only model for evaluating treatment effectiveness. It is my belief that most of these efforts by individuals from a wide assortment of backgrounds have been useful and have led to clarification of a number of issues that will be discussed in this chapter.

GOALS AND CRITERIA MEASURES

It is important that both the criteria for admission and the goals of each treatment program be clearly specified, as well as variables relating to which segment of the addict population each program is designed to serve. For instance, criteria for admission to a methadone maintenance treatment program include a history of at least 2 years of heroin use and heroin as the major drug of abuse, whereas the therapeutic communities and other residential treatment programs deal with polydrug users, as well as those whose primary drug of abuse may not be heroin. Furthermore, the residential programs deal primarily with the younger addict (under 25), whereas methadone programs deal with the older, "hard core" addict. In addition, some programs are geared to handle the problems of the addicted woman, with particular reference to pregnancy, delivery, and the neonate (8).

It is clear that each of these programs must be evaluated in the light of the specific population served, and each part of the program needs to be appraised in each specific setting as to what it contributes to the total treatment process and whether or not the program has resulted in a desirable effect in a reasonable proportion of patients served, in the absence of undesirable effects.

OUTCOME VARIABLES

Despite differences in goals and criteria of different program modalities, they have several aims in common. These include reduction in criminal or antisocial behavior associated with drug taking and increase in social productivity as measured by employment, school attendance, or homemaking. The differences in outcome criteria involve mainly the relative importance of abstinence. These differences reflect varying concepts of the purpose of treatment. On the issue of abstinence there is divided opinion concerning whether abstinence is a feasible goal for all narcotic addicts. Dole and Nyswander (6) have based their advocacy of indefinite maintenance for some on the belief that many long term narcotic addicts are physiologically unable to function in a drug-free state. Recent research in areas such as the endorphins (10) has given additional credence to this concept.

Some investigators have employed personality and other psychological measures in addition to the previously mentioned behavioral variables (5). These seem to be of particular interest in therapeutic communities, as opposed to outpatient programs, because residents are usually not comparably at risk with respect to some behavioral measures, such as criminal activity, while in treatment (16).

A review of the abundant literature attempting to do program evaluation using behavioral measurements makes it clear that patients who voluntarily enter any of the major treatment modalities and who stay under observation for a reasonable period will show a decrease in criminal activity. The majority will become socially productive, and most of them will either discontinue or decrease their drug-taking behavior. The references cited are only a small segment of the total literature but are hopefully representative of the various efforts in this area (2–4, 7, 9, 12, 13, 16, 18).

None of these studies are the classic case control or clinical trial type, and most are based on relatively crude data. This has led to skepticism and occasional severe criticism from some of the more sophisticated research-oriented individuals in the field (14). Despite these admitted limitations, all of these research efforts have been useful and have become the basis for the guidelines for Evaluation of Drug Abuse Treatment Programs released by the National Institute on Drug Abuse in 1978.

REACTION TO EVALUATION EFFORTS

Each segment of the general population, when looking at the results of evaluation of the effectiveness of drug abuse treatment on the rehabilitation of their patients, reacts from a different point of view. Often, this reflects a combination of their lack of basic information and their "vested interests," as will be illustrated below.

EVALUATION BY LEGISLATORS AND FUNDING AGENCIES

The major push for funding of drug treatment programs in New York and elsewhere in 1968 was an effort to reduce "crime in the streets." Therefore, the legislators' major interest were the data on the effect of drug treatment on the reduction in criminal activity. Most drug treatment programs, including both abstinence and maintenance programs, have demonstrated this reduction for those who remain under care for a meaningful length of time (4, 7, 9), but "crime in the streets" has not diminished or disappeared. This is understandable, inasmuch as the major area of criminal activity of the heroin addict involves either drug-related crimes or burglary, larceny, and forgery—not primarily the violent "street crimes" of major concern to legislators. In fact, some data indicate that the drug addict is more often a "victim" of violent crime rather than the perpetrator. However, the stereotyped image of the drug addict as a violent individual, which is ingrained in the minds of legislators, has not been changed by any data made available to them to date.

Only within the past 2 years, as a result of the budget crunch and the emphasis on the economic recession, have legislators become interested in indicators of increased social productivity among former drug addicts who have become employable and employed while in treatment. They have become impressed with the fact that a large proportion of these treated addicts are now taxpayers and voters.

Their current emphasis is on getting the former addicts "graduated" from treatment. The notion of long term treatment and provision for "aftercare" for this chronic, relapsing disease has very little support from budget-minded legislators. In addition, the general impression created at the federal level that "the heroin epidemic" is over and, therefore, funds for treatment of addicts can be markedly curtailed, leaves some 65,000 addicts in treatment in the New York area, as well as vast numbers in treatment elsewhere throughout the country, in danger of having their treatment curtailed whether or not they are ready or able to remain drug free.

EVALUATION BY THE MEDICAL PROFESSION

The historic polarization of the medical profession on the issue of whether drug addiction is a treatable disease seems to persist. Musto (15) continually refers to this polarization in his development of the history of narcotics use, legislation, and control. Members of the medical profession have traditionally been ill equipped by their training to deal with the problems related to drug abuse and addiction, even in areas such as emergency treatment of drug overdose, despite the fact that there is currently a considerable body of literature in this area (1).

Since Medicaid payment has been approved for drug abuse treatment (1972), several private physicians have become involved in chemotherapy (methadone, l-alpha-acetylmethadol, and naltrexone) in the New York City area. Some of these physicians seem to be doing a good job, but many have been unable to supply the necessary supportive services. Several of these clinics have been closed, and others are under pressure from the state and the federal governments to improve their service delivery practices.

EVALUATION BY THE JUDICIARY

The criminal justice system has been involved with the drug-abusing population for many years. It was of some interest that, from a list of more than 1,000 requests for copies of reports and publications from an evaluation unit with which I was involved for 12 years, more than one-third were from the criminal justice system, including primarily district attorneys and judges.

This interest was highlighted in 1975 by the ruling by United States District Judge Thomas P. Griesa in a widely publicized case in which a former methadone patient sued the New York Transit Authority for barring him from employment because of his former methadone use. The ruling stated (11):

Plaintiffs have more than sustained their burden of proving that there are substantial numbers of persons on methadone maintenance who are as fit for employment as other comparable persons. . . .

But the crucial point made so strongly by plaintiffs' witnesses was never convincingly challenged—that methadone as administered in the maintenance programs can successfully erase the physical effects of heroin addiction and permit a former heroin addict to function normally both mentally and physically. It is further proved beyond any real dispute that among the 40,000 persons in New York City on methadone maintenance (as in any comparable group of 40,000 New Yorkers), there are substantial numbers who are free of anti-social behavior and free of the abuse of alcohol or illicit drugs; that such persons are capable of employment and many are indeed employed. It is further clear that the employable can be identified by a prospective employer by essentially the same type of procedures used to identify other persons who would make good and reliable employees. Finally, it has been demonstrated that the New York City Transit Authority has ways of monitoring employees after they have been hired, which can be used for persons on methadone maintenance just as they are used for other persons employed by the TA.

All of those working in the field of drug abuse treatment took considerable satisfaction that we had supplied most of the data cited by Judge Griesa in this historic ruling. Unfortunately, the Supreme Court of the United States, in its infinite wisdom, saw fit to reverse this decision in 1979. This is a step backward for all former addicts who are attempting to rehabilitate themselves and become self-supporting citizens. It is fortunate that the Legal Action Council of New York is challenging both the constitutionality of an employment policy that excludes former addicts who are drug free, as well as the legality of exclusionary policies in general under the Rehabilitation Act of 1973.

EVALUATION BY PROGRAM DIRECTORS

Program directors react very positively to evaluation data as long as they are favorable to their program. When comparative data are presented that are more favorable to another program or treatment modality, their reaction becomes very defensive, and they become very critical of the results, even when they were the providers of the basic data.

It is not very useful to present data for any treatment modality that show that those patients entering treatment who have the greatest chance of successful rehabilitation are those who are (a) white, (b) have a high school diploma or better, (c) have a record of fairly consistent gainful employment, and (d) have had little or no previous involvement with the criminal justice system, even though these data seem to be true for most programs.

Data that attempt to point out the differences as well as the strengths and weaknesses of various programs and modalities seem more useful, because no program professes to be perfect, and the various modalities seem to be beneficial for different segments of the addict population.

It has taken more than 10 years in New York City to form a Coalition on Drug Abuse with representation from all treatment modalities focusing on the needs of the addict, rather than on the needs of one program or another. This bodes well for the future if funds for drug treatment programs can be kept from being diverted, once again, to the criminal justice system or elsewhere.

EVALUATION BY PATIENTS AND FORMER PATIENTS

The patients who remain in treatment, whether on methadone or in abstinence programs, are enthusiastic advocates of their par-

ticular treatment modality, and many of them refer to their program as lifesaving. However, when they feel that the rules of the program impinge on their civil rights or that the regulations imposed by either federal or state guidelines are unfair, they become a very vocal and effective group.

One of the issues in which patients have become active is with reference to criteria for discharge. Grievance procedures have been set up by many treatment programs whereby any patient may contest the program's decision to terminate treatment for administrative or behavioral reasons. Patients are involved in this review process.

Among methadone maintenance patients in New York City, a group of patients who were in treatment prior to the issuance of the Federal Methadone Maintenance Guidelines have formed their own coalition. Many of them previously had "take-home" privileges that required them to pick up their medication only once every 2 weeks or once a month. It was their feeling that the new rules on "take-home" medication demonstrated a lack of trust, because they were *not* the source of the diversion that was the major concern of the government in promulgating the guidelines. They also felt that the emphasis on detoxification after 2 years on methadone maintenance was arbitrary and punitive, because all of them had been on methadone maintenance for considerably longer (up to 8 years). In addition, many felt very insecure with the notion of abstinence as a major goal, because all of them had previously tried and failed one or more times as "drug-free" individuals.

Data from interviews with several series of former patients provided additional insight into the strengths and weaknesses of various programs and treatment modalities. The major area of agreement across treatment modalities was the need for additional vocational counseling and job placement, as well as additional group or individual counseling, and the need for provision for "aftercare" and easy readmission to treatment when requested (2, 13, 18).

EVALUATION BY THE COMMUNITY

Most communities or neighborhoods have an inborn fear of having a drug treatment facility in their area. Much of this fear is based on a combination of lack of knowledge and understanding and the influence of the mass media (newspapers, magazines, and television) that have tended to emphasize the negative features of drug treatment efforts. As a result of this continued negative publicity, particularly with reference to methadone clinics, neighborhood groups and zoning boards have made it next to impossible to open a new methadone clinic in New York City today. This is in the face of increased pressure on treatment facilities to decrease the size of their patient load to diminish the problems of "loitering" and "diversion." Most of the treatment programs have made efforts to develop meaningful communications for exchange of information with their local community boards, and the Greater New York Coalition on Drug Abuse and the Urban Coalition Task Force on Drug Abuse are contributing to and supplementing these efforts in order to teach community members that their fears about drug addicts relate to those who are not in treatment rather than those who are.

CONCLUSIONS

After almost 15 years in the field of evaluating drug abuse treatment programs, it is my firm belief that we have come a long way, and that most of the efforts in this area have been useful. No one, to my knowledge, has come up with a model that will predict which patients are best suited to which type of treatment program at which stage in the course of their disease, and neither has anyone come up with a "perfect" answer or a panacea for drug abusers and addicts. Therefore, it seems reasonable to mount efforts to allow the current treatment programs to survive and allow them sufficient flexibility to modify their programs as the pattern of drug abuse changes.

Despite the fact that drug addiction is no longer considered "enemy number one" by either the federal or state governments, we have a responsibility not only to those patients currently in treatment but also to those who will need and will seek help in the future.

References

1. Bourne, P. D. *Acute Drug Abuse Emergencies: A Treatment Manual.* Washington, D.C., Drug Abuse Council, 1976.
2. Cushman, P., and Dole, V. P. Detoxification of methadone maintenance patients. J.A.M.A. 226:747, 1973.
3. DeLeon, G. Phoenix House: Influence of time in program. In *Developments in the Field of Drug Abuse*, E. Senay, V. Shorty, and H. Alksne, editors, sect. II. Cambridge, Mass., Schenkman, 1975.
4. DeLeon, G., Holland, S., and Rosenthal, M. S. Phoenix House: Criminal activity of drop-outs. J.A.M.A. 222:686, 1972.
5. DeLeon, G., Skodol, A., and Rosenthal, M. S. Phoenix House: Changes in psychopathological signs of resident drug addicts. Arch. Gen. Psychiatry 28:131, 1973.
6. Dole, V. P., and Nyswander, M. A. Methadone maintenance treatment: A ten-year perspective. J.A.M.A. 235:2117, 1976.
7. Dupont, R. L. Heroin addiction treatment and crime reduction. Am. J. Psychol. 128:90, 1972.
8. Finnegan, L. P. Women in treatment. In *Handbook on Drug Abuse*, R. L. Dupont, A. Goldstein, and J. O'Donnell, editors, chap. 10. Rockville, Md., National Institute on Drug Abuse, 1979.
9. Gearing, F. R., and Schweitzer, M. D. An epidemiologic evaluation of long-term methadone maintenance treatment for heroin addiction. Am. J. Epidemiol. 100:101, 1974.
10. Goldstein, A. New areas in drug addiction research. In *Handbook on Drug Abuse*, R. L. Dupont, A. Goldstein, and J. O'Donnell, editors, chap. 48. Rockville, Md., National Institute on Drug Abuse, 1979.
11. Griesa, T. P. (Judge) ruling in Beazer vs. N. Y. City Transit Authority 399—F, Suppl. 1032. New York, August 6, 1975.
12. Jaffe, J. H., Zaks, M. S., and Washington, E. N. Experience with the use of methadone in a multimodality program for narcotic users. Int. J. Addict. 4:481, 1969.
13. Lowinson, J., Langrod, J., and Berle, B. Detoxification of long term methadone patients. In *Developments in the Field of Drug Abuse*, E. Senay, V. Shorty, and H. Alksne, editors, sect. V. Cambridge, Mass. Schenkman, 1975.
14. Lukoff, I. F., and Kleinman, P. H. The addict life cycle and problems in treatment evaluation. In *Rehabilitation Aspects of Drug Addiction*, A. Schecter, editor, chap. 10. Cleveland, Ohio, CRC Press, 1977.
15. Musto, D. *The American Disease: Origins of Narcotic Control.* New Haven, Conn., Yale University Press, 1973.
16. Sells, S. B. Treatment effectiveness. In *Handbook on Drug Abuse*, R. L. Dupont, A. Goldstein, and J. O'Donnell, editors, chap. 9. Rockville, Md., National Institute on Drug Abuse, 1979.
17. *The Living Webster Encyclopedia Dictionary of the English Language.* Chicago, The English Language Institute of America, 1971.
18. Trigg, H. L. Clinical problems of selection, prediction and patient failure. In *Proceedings of the Fourth National Conference on Methadone Treatment.* New York, National Association for the Prevention of Addiction to Narcotics, 1972.

CHAPTER 65

COST EFFECTIVENESS STUDIES IN THE EVALUATION OF SUBSTANCE ABUSE TREATMENT

Don C. Des Jarlais, Ph.D.

Sherry Deren, Ph.D.

Douglas S. Lipton, Ph.D.

In the last 15 years there have been substantial advances in the treatment of substance abuse. Methadone maintenance and therapeutic communities have become major treatment modalities, and a wide variety of additional techniques, ranging from antagonists to behavior modification to acupuncture, are currently being used. Parallel to this development of treatment techniques has been the development of methods for evaluating the effectiveness of substance abuse treatment. Cost effectiveness studies are one of the more recent methodologies for evaluating substance abuse treatment.

Cost effectiveness studies may be briefly defined as studies that attempt to determine which course of action will produce the greatest amount of a desired outcome for a given cost. This chapter will first relate cost effectiveness studies to other types of substance abuse treatment evaluation and then present a description of how such cost effectiveness studies are currently conducted and utilized in the New York State Division of Substance Abuse Services.

Throughout the chapter, emphasis will be placed on how the different types of evaluation studies can be or are utilized in decision making. Readers interested in detailed descriptions of how to conduct cost benefit or cost effectiveness analyses should consult references 5, 7, 12, 15, 18, and 19.

COST EFFECTIVENESS STUDIES AND OTHER TYPES OF EVALUATION STUDIES

In discussing evaluation studies in substance abuse treatment, there are three historical trends to keep in mind. First is the knowledge gained from the cumulation of various treatment evaluation studies. Later studies build upon earlier studies in methods for collecting data, in techniques for analyzing data, and in insights for interpreting data. Second, there has been a massive change in the scale of drug abuse treatment efforts within the last 15 years. With a greater amount of public money appropriated for drug abuse treatment, professional administrators have come to manage the treatment effort. This professional administration exists at federal, state, and local levels. Finally, there have been general societal changes in the last 15 years that directly affect the evaluation of drug treatment programs among other public expenditures. A "Great Society-War on Drug Abuse" willingness to commit whatever resources are necessary attitude has been replaced by a "public accountability-maximize the effectiveness of scarce resources" attitude.

TREATMENT FOLLOW-UP STUDIES

Studies that determine the posttreatment outcomes of persons who receive drug abuse treatment constitute the basic type of treatment evaluation study. They provide the foundation upon which other, more economically oriented, studies build. During the 1950's and 1960's, drug abuse treatment outcome studies were usually phrased as answers to the question, "What works?" Treatment effectiveness was primarily measured in terms of the absence of heroin use after treatment. Evaluations tended to answer the question in emphatic terms—this treatment does not work (9), or this treatment does work (2, 3).

In the late 1960's and throughout the 1970's, the basic evaluation question was essentially rephrased to: "Does treatment serve to reduce drug abuse?" This change from an absolutist to a relativist perspective can best be seen in the Drug Abuse Reporting Program, the largest treatment evaluation study

yet conducted (see 19 for a summary). Full recognition was given to various dimensions of posttreatment outcome—drug use, criminal activity, social productivity—to different degrees of achievement on each of these dimensions.

There are two aspects of current treatment follow-up studies that limit their usefulness in decision making. First, follow-up studies are extremely expensive to conduct. They usually require personal interviews with the subjects, and data collection costs alone may run from $200 to $300 per subject. When one also considers the time requirements for a follow-up study (a 1-year posttreatment period is the usual minimum), it becomes impractical to conduct such studies on a routine basis. Follow-up studies are thus usually limited to evaluation of new treatment methods and nation-wide general studies to assess the present state of the art of drug treatment.

The second aspect of follow-up studies that limits their utility in decision making is their complexity. Random assignment of subjects to treatment/no treatment conditions, which greatly simplifies the interpretation of data, is rarely feasible in drug treatment research (4). The great majority of studies do show that drug abuse is reduced after treatment, but there are a variety of factors, such as pretreatment drug history, time in treatment, and circumstances of discharge, that affect the amount of reduction in drug abuse. It thus becomes very difficult to integrate the results of follow-up studies into either policy or management decisions.

One method of increasing the decision-making utility of follow-up studies is to assess the value to society of the reductions in drug abuse. Cost benefit analysis provides a relatively sophisticated framework for doing such assessment.

COST BENEFIT STUDIES

Cost benefit analysis was originally developed by economists, and its first major applications were to flood control and irrigation projects (17). The logic of cost benefit analysis is relatively straightforward:

1. The costs of a particular project are summed, with costs that occur in the future being discounted to reduce them to "present value." Discounting to present value reflects

the idea that a benefit obtained in the present should be worth more than a similar benefit obtained in the future. The presently obtained benefit could be invested and, after n years, would have increased by a factor of (1 + r)^n, where r = the "discount rate." The same factor is used in discounting future costs to a present value (see 15 for a detailed exposition).

Discounting becomes important for decision making when projects involve long time spans, with an uneven distribution of benefits or costs over time. Various discount rates may be used in a single cost benefit analysis to test the sensitivity of the results to different rates. The most commonly used rate in drug abuse treatment studies is 10 per cent.

2. The benefits from a particular project are similarly summed, with benefits occurring in the future also being discounted to arrive at a present value for those benefits.

3. The sum of the benefits is then divided by the sum of the costs to produce a benefit/cost ratio for the project.

4. This benefit/cost ratio is then used in decision making about the project. No projects with a benefit/cost ratio of one or less should be undertaken. Different projects will presumably be undertaken in order of the size of their benefit/cost ratios. Other decision rules, such as annualized rate of return or net present benefits, may be used in cost benefit analyses (15), although the benefit/cost ratio is by far the most popular in drug treatment studies.

The arithmetic operations of summation and division require that all costs and all benefits be valued in the same units of measurement. For a project such as a dam it is relatively easy to use money as this common unit of measurement. The monetary cost of a particular dam can be (relatively) reliably estimated from the known costs of previously built dams. The benefits, such as reduced flood damage and increased agricultural productivity, are also relatively easy to estimate in dollar amounts.

Assessing the value of the "less tangible" benefits, such as the recreational uses of a new lake created by a dam, poses more of a challenge to the cost benefit analyst. Still, the traditional economic method of using market prices can be applied. Thus, the analyst might estimate the number of recreational users over the life of the dam and the amount of money each user would be willing to spend on transportation, food, lodging, and equipment to "use" the new lake in order to arrive at a monetary estimate of the recreational benefit of the new dam.

In performing a cost benefit analysis, it is important to specify the level of analysis for which costs and benefits will be calculated. Cost benefit analyses can be performed with an individual, an organization, or the society as a whole as the level of analysis. For projects involving governmental action, the society as a whole is usually chosen. This does provide the most comprehensive base for both costs and benefits but tends to obscure the fact that the costs and benefits are not likely to be similarly distributed within the society for any given project.

Cost benefit analyses of drug abuse treatment started in the early 1970's, and a literature has developed (5, 6, 10, 13, 14, 16, 19). The actual cost of operating drug treatment programs is the starting point for calculating the "costs" part of the analysis. Additional cost factors that may be included in the analysis include foregone earnings while clients are in residential programs and thus not available for work, and the additional services that clients may receive through association with a treatment program and that do not appear on program budgets. These additional services include health care (through Medicaid), welfare payments, educational and vocational services. (See 1 for a discussion of the various cost factors involved in drug abuse treatment.)

Estimating the benefits from drug abuse treatment is considerably more complicated than estimating costs. There is no market value for reductions in drug abuse that can be used to estimate directly how much a given reduction is worth. In a fundamental sense, all of the benefits must be indirectly estimated. The benefits associated with reductions in drug abuse are derived primarily from the benefits associated with increased employment, decreased criminal activity, and increased general health that occur as a result of successful drug abuse treatment.

Table 65.1 is taken from analysis done by Rufener et al. (19). It shows greater than unity benefit/cost ratios for all treatment modalities, for both unadjusted benefits (assume all modalities produce equal benefits) and for adjusted benefits (different outcomes by modality.) This analysis used the Drug Abuse Reporting Project follow-up data for its esti-

Table 65.1
Cost/Benefit Ratios for Different Treatment Modalities[a]

Treatment Modality	Unadjusted Benefits	Adjusted Benefits
Methadone maintenance	4.42	4.39
Therapeutic community	1.81	2.23
Outpatient drug free	22.50	12.82
Outpatient detoxification	7.48	7.14
Inpatient detoxification	4.40	5.53

[a] From Rufener, B.L., Cruze, A.M., and Rachal, G.V. *Management Effectiveness Measures for NIDA Drug Abuse Treatment Programs*. Vol. I: *Cost Benefit Analysis*. Research Triangle Park, N.C., Research Triangle Institute, 1976.

mates of treatment effects. The authors concluded that the results justify societal investment in drug abuse treatment and suggested that the intermodality differences could be utilized for long range treatment planning. The study used national data, and the authors specifically cautioned against projecting the findings to smaller units of analysis (states or municipalities) because of the imprecision in the estimates.

A second example of a cost benefit analysis is given in Table 65.2. This presents the various "costs to society" for drug abuse in New York State (New York State, 1978). Here the analysis is simplified by considering only the benefits for the during treatment period, primarily in terms of reducing the criminal activity of narcotic addicts. Posttreatment effects are not included in the calculations. These figures are included as part of an annual "Fact Sheet" on drug abuse in the state, which is used for general public information purposes.

Providing data and estimates that demonstrate that society significantly benefits from investing in treatment programs assists in answering the first question about drug abuse treatment—"Should there be such treatment?" Unfortunately, the present level of cost benefit studies in drug abuse treatment provides little assistance for more difficult questions, particularly how to maximize the return from society's investment in drug abuse treatment.

There are three limitations on present cost benefit studies that severely restrict their utility in decision making to maximize returns from investment in treatment programs. First, cost benefit studies require posttreatment outcome data, which are expensive and difficult to collect. The time required to do posttreatment outcome studies also means that the data would often not be available until after a decision needs to be made.

Second, no one has yet been able to make reliable estimates of the "marginal rate of return" for societal investment in drug treatment. The studies that have been conducted have simply averaged the returns across the different programs within the study categories. There are not enough data for making good estimates of changes in the benefit/cost ratio as more treatment programs are added to an existing network of programs. This particularly serves to limit the utility of studies that calculate separate benefit/cost ratios for different modalities. To some extent the different modalities are appropriate for different types of substances abusers. Thus implementing a program that provides an additional modality within a community may be more cost effective than implementing a program that provides a modality already offered within the community, even though previous studies have shown the already provided modality to have a higher "average" benefit/cost ratio than the new modality.

Finally, the valuing of the various effects of drug treatment programs requires numerous assumptions about the values of reduced crime, increased employment, and improved general health. Differences in the assumptions one makes can lead to greatly different results. This is particularly true with respect to assumptions about drug-related crime. For example, some studies (18) treat thefts as "involuntary transfers" of wealth from one segment of society to another, with the result that the only societal benefits from reductions in theft are the reductions in costs for police and criminal justice agencies. Other studies (16) treat all stolen property as "lost to society" and thus include the value of the property not stolen as a major societal benefit from the reduction of drug-related thefts. The disparities that result from making different assumptions in the valuation of the effects of drug abuse treatment tend to reduce the credibility of the method for decision makers.

COST EFFECTIVENESS STUDIES

Cost effectiveness studies are best seen as modified versions of cost benefit analysis. The principal change is that one does not measure the outcomes of the project in the

Table 65.2
Governmental and Social Costs[a] Associated with Narcotic Addiction in New York State in Fiscal Year 1978–1979

Location of Narcotic Addicts	Number of Persons (July 1, 1978)	Expenditures			Cost per Person per Year
		Source of Cost	In Millions of Dollars		
In street (Not in any Program)	168,100	Total	4,000	rounded $	23,795
		Crime	3.458.5		
		Criminal justice system	430.9		
		Welfare	96.0		
		Health re- sources	15.6		
Not under supervision	149,700				
Under supervision: parole, probation	18,400[b]				
In correctional institutions	14,400	Total	$ 212	rounded $	14,722
State prisons	12,100[c]	Program	173.3[g]		14,322
Jails and county penitentaries	2,300[d]	Program	39.1[g]		17,000
In drug treatment programs	36,800[e]	Total	$ 106	rounded $	2,880
Detoxification	800	Total	5.1		6.375
		Program	4.5[h]		
		Welfare	.6		
Public methadone maintenance	27,700	Total	67.6		2,440
		Program	46.6[g]		
		Welfare	21.0		
Private methadone maintenance	2,600[f]	Total	4.7		1,808
		Program	2.7		
		Welfare	2.0		
Residential drug- free programs	1,400	Program	8.4		6,000
Daycare drug-free programs	900	Total	3.1		3,444
		Program	2.4[g]		
		Welfare	.7		
Outpatient drug-free programs	1,900	Total	4.2		2,211
		Program	2.8[g]		
		Welfare	1.4		
State-operated residential and aftercare programs	1,500	Total	13.0		8,667
		Program	12.0[g,h]		
		Welfare	1.0		

[a] Omits cost due to loss of productivity, crimes other than thefts, and the intangible costs associated with effects on family, friends, victims, and self.

[b] Includes an estimated 1,600 persons who are receiving treatment.

[c] Consists of 11,270 addicts not receiving treatment and 830 who are receiving treatment.

[d] Includes approximately 53 addicts who were receiving detoxification in jail.

[e] This total and the census figures below are the estimated number of treated clients whose primary drug of abuse is heroin or illicit methadone.

[f] Excludes private patients not receiving Medicaid.

[g] Includes fringe benefits.

[h] These program costs fund services to addicts (primary clients) plus outreach services, prevention services, and services for secondary clients. Because only addicts (primary clients) are included in the denominator, the annual cost per person is higher than might otherwise be expected.

same units as the costs. Instead one uses whatever unit of measurement is most appropriate (and convenient) for the particular goals of the programs. Cost effectiveness studies were first widely used in the Department of Defense in the 1960's (11). It is very difficult to express the value of the destruction of a military target in terms of present value dollars, but if one adopts "percentage of target destroyed" as the numerator for the benefit/cost ratios, then it is relatively easy to apply the same logic as cost benefit analysis.

This use of nonmonetary objectives, then, has results in two limitations on the uses of cost effectiveness studies. First, it is not possible to use them to justify investment in a particular project. One cannot show that the objectives to be achieved by the project are more valuable than the costs incurred in the project. Second, only projects that produce similar objectives can be compared within a cost effectiveness analysis.

Although there have been few formal studies, cost effectiveness studies are clearly applicable to decisions about drug abuse treatment. Analysis of various objectives—such as months without abusing drugs, clients successfully completing treatment, additional months of employment, or crimes prevented—can be used (19). The National Institute on Drug Abuse (NIDA) has prepared a manual on how to calculate various effectiveness measures at a program level, using Client Oriented Data Acquisition Process data (7). It is a relatively simple matter to add cost data to such indices to then have a variety of cost effectiveness indices. The difficulties in cost effectiveness analyses for drug abuse treatment are more in obtaining reliable and valid data and organizationally integrating the studies into agency decision making. The following section describes how a single state agency has adapted cost effectiveness analysis into the management of its network of drug treatment programs.

COST EFFECTIVENESS STUDIES IN THE NEW YORK STATE DIVISION OF SUBSTANCE ABUSE SERVICES

HISTORICAL BACKGROUND

Since the late 1960's, New York State has developed an extensive network of community-based drug abuse treatment programs (Figure 65.1). There are currently more than 400 separate programs in the state that are monitored by the Division of Substance Abuse Services, the single state agency in New York. The legal arrangement between the state and the programs consists of a contract specifying the services to be provided by the program and that the state reimburse for these services. (Most monies from the National Institute on Drug Abuse to programs in New York State also go through this state-program contract procedure.) Contract managers are assigned to negotiate these contracts, amend them as needed, and generally monitor the performance of the programs.

Cost effectiveness studies were begun shortly after the appointment of a new director for the state agency in 1976. At that time there was a shift toward an accountability orientation in the State Department of the Budget and the State Legislature. The assignment was given to what was then the Bureau of Social Science Research (and is now the Bureau of Cost Effectiveness and Research). Prior to this assignment, the great majority of the work of the bureau had been basic social science research, with little orientation toward decision making within the agency.

Methadone maintenance programs were selected for the first evaluation report, because the most comprehensive data were available for this modality, and there was insufficient time to develop new sources of data. This report comparatively arrayed all methadone maintenance programs in the state on a series of descriptive indices (e.g., percentage of the budget provided by state monies), cost indices (e.g., cost per treatment slot), and effectiveness indices (e.g., utilization of budgeted treatment slots, retention rates). Posttreatment outcome data were not available on a program by program basis. The comparative arrays provided easy identification of atypical programs, which were then investigated more intensively.

This first report was well received and led to a proposed three-phase evaluation model. Phase I involved developing descriptive and cost effectiveness indices for programs in all modalities, with atypical programs identified for further investigation. Phase II included a detailed analysis of service delivery through site visits to individual programs. Phase III consisted of follow-up studies of a sample of clients from programs in order to assess posttreatment outcomes.

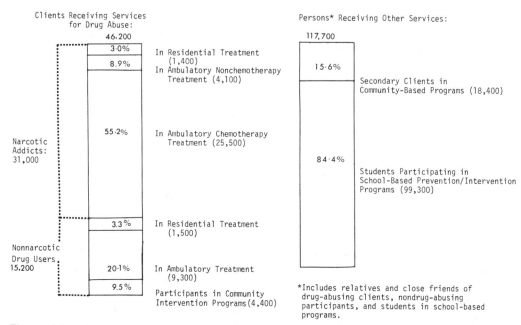

Figure 65.1. Division of Substance Abuse Services: Persons receiving services in treatment programs operated or funded by the Division of Substance Abuse Services of New York State, Spring 1978. The Division of Substance Abuse Services provides services through its treatment programs to 163,900 persons, consisting of: 46,200 clients receiving services for their substance abuse; and 117,700 persons receiving other services. Of the 46,200 clients receiving services for substance abuse, 67 per cent (or 31,000) were narcotic addicts. The vast majority of these clients receive services in ambulatory treatment, especially in ambulatory chemotherapy treatment (25,500 clients). The remaining 33 per cent (or 15,200 clients) were nonnarcotic substance abusers. Despite the smaller number, more nonnarcotic substance-abusing clients are in residential treatment than narcotic-addicted clients: 1,500 versus 1,400. Of the 117,700 persons receiving other services, 84 per cent (99,300) include students participating in school-based prevention/intervention programs. The remaining persons are principally composed of secondary clients who are relatives and close friends of substance-abusing clients.

Given the scope of this evaluation plan, some agency reorganization was necessary. The Phase II site visit responsibilities were later assigned to a new bureau within the agency. Phase III follow-up tasks were limited to programs of special interest. Follow-up studies simply cost too much in time and personnel to be performed for a large number of programs. The Phase I cost effectiveness indices later became formalized as Cost Effectiveness and Evaluation Data (CEED) studies and do not contain any posttreatment outcome data. (In this they are similar to the evaluation studies advocated by Guess and Tuchfeld (7).)

CURRENT EVALUATION STRATEGY AND METHOD

The current CEED studies are organized around three products, all geared toward agency decision making and toward facilitating program comparisons. These are: individual program profiles, modality-wide reports, and summary reports.

1. Individual Program Profiles. These were developed for use by contract managers during contract negotiations. They present selected indices for a particular program, showing its absolute value on each index and its standing relative to other programs with the same modality/environment and in the same area of the state. The number of indices vary by modality, with about 10 to 15 for each modality. Figure 65.2 is a sample format of a program profile form. The particular indices used vary among modalities, depending on the availability of data and relevance to the particular modality.

In addition to the data, two comments sections appear on the profile. The first is used by staff to point out important features

PROGRAM PROFILE FORM
Based on April 1, 1978 - March 31, 1979
(Median and quartiles are based on 31 programs with this modality/environment in Region A and B)

Program Name: Program 123
Modality/Environment   OPDF

Region A   Capacity   100
County   Q   Average Monthly Census 72

Name of Index	1st Quarter		Median		4th Quarter	Program Value	Median Value
Budgeted Cost Per Funded Slot	900	1,100	1,400	1,750	2,000	$1,475	$1,400
Budgeted Personal Services Cost Per Slot	650	800	900	1,100	00	$980	$900
% of Budget Allocated for Personal Services	50	60	80	85	95	88%	80%
% of Budget Expended	78	92	95	99	100	97%	95%
Average Salary Per FTE Staff	8,000	9,000	10,200	11,000	12,500	$10,800	$10,200
Budgeted Clients Per Budgeted FTE Clinical Staff Person	10	13	18	21	30	17	18
Actual Clients Per Actual FTE Clinical Staff Person	7	12	15	18	27	10	15
% of Admissions With Heroin as Primary Drug of Abuse	25	35	40	52	80	28%	40%
% of Admissions With Pills as Primary Drug of Abuse	0	5	20	25	35	33%	20%
% of Admissions With Marijuana as Primary Drug of Abuse	0	4	20	24	34	15%	20%
% of Terminated Clients that Completed Treatment	10	25	40	50	60	35%	40%
% of Terminated Clients That Left Before Completing Treatment	10	15	30	35	40	18%	30%
Utilization Rate	70	80	85	92	105	72%	85%
Turnover Rate	25	50	99	180	250	120%	99%
% of Admissions Retained at least 6 Months	30	40	60	70	100	55%	60%

Note: If the program value falls in the 1st Quarter, this means that the program fell below at least 75% of the other programs on that particular index. If the program value falls in the 4th Quarter, this means that it fell above at least 75% of the other programs in the comparison group.

COMMENTS:

1. While the cost indices (Budgeted cost per slot and budgeted personal services cost per slot) are close to the median, the % of budget allocated for personal services(88%) is higher than in over 75% of the programs in Regions A and B.

2. The ratio of actual number of clients per FTE clinical staff person, 10 to 1, was lower than in over 75% of the programs and substantially lower than the budgeted ratio of 17 to 1. This difference was primarily due to the relatively low utilization rate (72%).

3. 28% of admissions reported heroin as the primary drug of abuse. This program had the 2nd highest rate of admissions with pill abuse (33%). An additional 15% reported marijuana/hashish and the remaining 24% were polydrug abusers.

4. The relatively low utilization rate (72%) may be in part accounted for by the rural location of this program. The current rate is an increase from the previous year, when the utilization was 60%.

CONTRACT MANAGEMENT COMMENTS:

Figure 65.2. Sample format of a program profile form. (Note: The data used in this profile are fictitious and were developed for illustrative purposes only.)

of the profile, to provide additional information that is not available on the profile itself, and to summarize the numerical data. The second section, labeled "contract management comments," is for the contract manager to provide some feedback on the program, in particular any issues or situations that may help explain why a particular program obtained extreme scores on some indices. This feedback mechanism is useful in several ways. It makes evaluation staff aware of issues or data sources that may have been overlooked and should be incorporated in future efforts, and it provides more accurate up-to-date information on the program that is useful for the next level of output, the modality-wide report.

The primary purpose of these profiles is to aid the contract manager in contract negotiations with the program through providing an over-all summary of the program's absolute and relative standing on several key indices. The profiles have also come to serve other functions, including depersonalizing the relationships with agencies they deal with by providing "hard data" for decision making and identifying items that should be more thoroughly investigated by the contract manager on visits to the program.

2. Modality-wide Reports. These combine data across modality/environments and make recommendations on a modality-wide basis. Although the profiles were developed primarily for the contract managers' use (i.e., for the middle level, day to day decision-making process), the modality report is designed primarily for the agency's top management.

The same data compiled for the program profiles are used in these reports, but they are organized for an entire modality and are presented by index with all program values arrayed on one table. These arrays readily permit comparisons by program size. Figure 65.3 contains an example of an index array. This format enables the ready identification of programs that are "outliers," i.e., those that receive extreme scores on an index. In addition to the arrays, tabular data for easy reference are presented as are select comparisons of changes across years on particular indices. Most of the accompanying text serves to aid in interpretation of the data.

After these materials are compiled, recommendations are prepared; they often involve modality-wide recommendations, such as noting that a consistently low utilization of many programs within a particular modality requires further investigation or funding adjustment. Other types of recommendations may be program specific, e.g., if a particular program is an "outlier" on several indices, certain kinds of training or technical assistance may be recommended or a service delivery audit may be indicated. These recommendations are developed in conjunction with contract management personnel.

3. A Summary Report. This integrates data across modalities, makes system-wide recommendations, and is the final step in the process. These recommendations may be substantive, e.g., identifying a possible lack of services in a particular part of the state, or they may be systemic, e.g., identifying the need for additional data elements. After their initial formulation, these recommendations

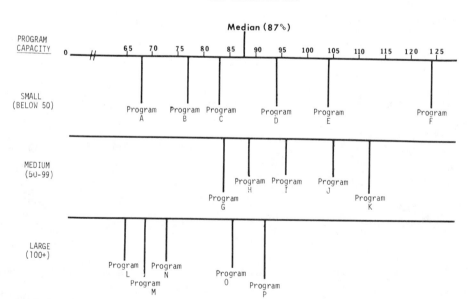

Figure 65.3. Sample format of an index-array. (Note: The data used in this index-array are fictitious and were developed for illustrative purposes only.)

are reviewed with contract managers and jointly presented to top management.

OTHER EFFECTS

Three major by-products emerged during the development of the CEED evaluation studies: (a) The reports have served a catalytic role in fostering accountability throughout the agency. Other bureaus within the agency and funded programs are now aware of the various data and their utility. In addition, a Central Report Bank has been established that is responsible for integrating reports from various bureaus, developing recommendations, and following up on their implementation. (b) Major modifications in the data system in our agency have occurred. A consultant was hired for approximately 1 year to redesign the data system and develop new forms. (c) A restructuring of the agency was made. The initial evaluation plan led to the identification of a need for the assessment of service delivery, and, as noted earlier, a new bureau—Performance Review—was established for that purpose.

The New York State experience illustrates several important aspects of cost effectiveness studies when applied to drug abuse treatment on a routinized basis. This type of study requires extensive cooperation and consultation between the analysts and the persons who will be using the studies in decision making. The decision maker must fully understand the strengths, weaknesses, and meaning of the data; the analyst must understand the context within which the decision is to be made.

Actual posttreatment outcome data are not likely to be available for routine cost effectiveness studies. Such data require too much time and manpower to be collected. Instead, various substitutes—desired outcomes such as retention of clients in treatment, utilization of budgeted treatment slots, and providing treatment to clients with particular characteristics—will have to be used. The cost effectiveness studies will also include other information that is useful for the particular decisions to be made but does not fall within the calculation of desired outcome/cost ratios.

Finally, cost effectiveness studies are a relatively powerful catalyst toward using "objective" data. Once used successfully, they set in motion forces for improving the basic data-gathering systems and toward more extensive program evaluation.

FUTURE OF COST EFFECTIVENESS STUDIES IN DRUG ABUSE TREATMENT

Cost effectiveness studies are a relatively new development in substance abuse treatment. They are the product of (a) a large scale effort toward combatting drug abuse conducted within an environment of limited resources and (b) the rise of professional adminstrators who are trained in working with objective data in decision making. Both of these trends can be expected to continue in the future.

Cost effectiveness studies using posttreatment outcome data are likely to be conducted only when the implementation of new treatment methods are being considered. New treatment methods are being continually developed in drug abuse treatment, and assessing their effectiveness requires posttreatment outcome data. Given a climate of scarce resources available for treatment, it is very unlikely that any new treatment method would be implemented on a large scale without a cost effectiveness analysis of the posttreatment data.

Cost effectiveness studies using substitutes for posttreatment outcomes will probably be conducted with increasing frequency as part of the continuing trend toward professional administration of drug treatment programs. The specific form and content of these studies are likely to vary greatly, however, as they will be tailored to the particular decisions to be made and the data sets available. This will make it very difficult to cumulate findings across studies, and, although cost effectiveness analysis will probably become an increasingly used technique, the building of a body of substantive findings is likely to be rather slow.

References

1. Bjorkland, P. B., Schooley, F. A., Byrd, W., and Borgeson, N. S. *A Survey of Drug Abuse Treatment Costs.* Menlo Park, Calif., Stanford Research Institute, 1975.
2. DeLeon, G., Skodol, A., and Rosenthal, M. S. Phoenix House: Changes in psychopathological signs of resident drug addicts. Arch. Gen. Psychiatry 48:131, 1973.
3. Dole, V. P., Nyswander, M. E., and Warner, A. Successful treatment of 750 criminal addicts.

J.A.M.A. 206:2708, 1968.

4. Dole, V. P., and Singer, B. On the evaluation of treatments for narcotic addiction. J. Drug Issues 9: 205, 1979.

5. Fujii, E. Public investment in the rehabilitation of heroin addicts. Soc. Sci. Q. 55:49, 1974.

6. Goldman, F. *The Relationship between Drug Addiction and Participation in Criminal Activities: An Econometric Analysis.* New York, Center for Policy Research and Columbia University, 1975. Draft copy.

7. Guess, L. L., and Tuchfeld, B. S. *Manual for Drug Abuse Treatment Program Self-evaluation.* Washington, D.C., National Institute on Drug Abuse, Treatment Program Monograph Series, 1977.

8. Hannan, T. H. *The Economics of Methadone Maintenance.* Lexington, Mass., D. C. Heath, 1975.

9. Hunt, G. H., and Odoroff, M. E. Follow-up study of narcotic drug addicts after hospitalization. Public Health Rep. 77:41, 1962.

10. Lemkau, P. V., Amsel, Z., Sanders, B., Amsel, J., and Seif, T. F. *Social and Economic Costs of Drug Abuse.* Baltimore, Department of Mental Hygiene, School of Hygiene and Public Health, The Johns Hopkins University, 1975.

11. Leslie, A. C. *A Benefit/Cost Analysis of New York City's Heroin Addiction Problems and Programs, 1971.* New York, City of New York, Office of Program Analysis, Health Services Administration, 1972.

12. Levin, H. M. Cost effectiveness analysis in evaluation research. In *Handbook of Evaluation Research*, M. Guttentag and E. L. Struening, editors, pp. 89–124. Beverly Hills, Calif., Sage Publications, 1975.

13. Maidlow, S. T., and Berman, H. The economics of heroin treatment. Am. J. Public Health 62:1397, 1972.

14. McGlothlin, W. H., and Tabbush, V. C. Costs, benefits, and potential for alternative approaches to opiate addiction control. In *Drugs and the Criminal Justice System*, J. A. Inciardi and C. D. Chambers, editors, pp. 77–124. Beverly Hills, Calif., Sage Publications, 1974.

15. Mishan, E. J. *Cost-Benefit Analysis.* New York, Praeger, 1976.

16. National Institute on Drug Abuse, Office of Program Development and Analysis; and the Institute of Behavioral Research, Texas Christian University. *Cost Benefit Analysis.* Fort Worth, Texas Christian University, 1975.

17. New York State Division of Substance Abuse Services. *Fact Sheets: Trends in Drug Abuse 1978.* Albany, New York State Division of Substance Abuse Services, 1978.

18. Rothenberg, J. Cost-benefit analysis: A methodological exposition. In *Handbook of Evaluation Research*, M. Guttentag and E. L. Struening, editors, pp. 55–88. Beverly Hills, Calif., Sage Publications, 1975.

19. Rufener, B. L., Cruze, A. M., and Rachal, J. V. *Management Effectiveness Measures for NIDA Drug Abuse Treatment Programs.* Vol. I: *Cost Benefit Analysis.* Research Triangle Park, N. C., Research Triangle Institute, 1976.

20. Simpson, D. D., Savage, L. J., and Sells, S. B. *Data Book on Drug Treatment Outcome*, Report 78-10. Fort Worth, Texas Christian University, Institute of Behavioral Research, 1978.

PART 10

TRAINING

CHAPTER 66

TRAINING AND EDUCATION

Harvey Bluestone, M.D.

Carl Leon McGahee, M.D.

Norman R. Klein, Ph.D.

Although substance abuse has been regarded as largely a medical problem for many years, it has only been within the past decade that systematic efforts toward the formal training of physicians and other health professionals have appeared. In 1971, the National Council on Alcoholism sponsored a conference to review existing medical school teaching programs in substance abuse. The organizers of the conference invited everyone in medical education who they identified as involved at that time in substance abuse. Approximately 130 persons attended, including one of the authors (Dr. Bluestone). The conference impressed how generally inadequate the curricula in medical schools were then. This set the stage for the American Medical Association position paper on the subject, to be discussed below.

This chapter will first examine the training of physicians in substance abuse and follow with a similar review of educational programs for allied professionals and other workers in the field.

TRAINING PHYSICIANS IN SUBSTANCE ABUSE

UNDERGRADUATE MEDICAL EDUCATION

In 1972, the American Medical Association (AMA) Council on Mental Health and its Committee on Drug Dependence published a position statement on medical school education on abuse of alcohol and other psychoactive drugs (1). Their assessment of the educational needs of medical students in the area of substance abuse and their guidelines for curricular development have been generally endorsed by the academic leaders most concerned with such teaching. Therefore, a short summary of the statement is in order.

The council made clear that there had been a long standing need for effective medical school education on substance abuse and that several recent trends had actually intensified that need. The problem of substance abuse had expanded in several ways. The large number of different psychoactive chemical agents of potential abuse had greatly increased, and each one had its own pharmacological and toxicological profile. Moreover, simultaneous use of several drugs had become common. Alcohol and drug abuse had begun to extend alarmingly into younger and younger age groups, reaching down into the early teens and even the preteens. Finally, drug abuse had become more visibly prevalent in middle-class and suburban settings.

As the spotlight of public attention was turned on these developments, physicians were looked to by many for leadership in combatting what seemed to be a growing epidemic. Students entering medical school were particularly receptive to learning about substance abuse. Not only did they view it as an important area for their eventual professional practice, but many had direct, personal exposure to the problem.

Two perhaps obvious facts brought the doctor and substance abuser together: (a) substance abusers have a high rate of morbidity for which medical attention is sought, and (b) physicians are the "gate keepers" for many of the drugs upon which abusers become dependent. It is noteworthy that the council laid great stress on the complexity and multiplicity of factors figuring into the phenomenon of substance abuse—from the biochemical and pharmacological to the social roles and cultural values. Physicians need to be broadly educated in all of these.

The council recognized that schools were experimenting with a variety of curricular formats, particularly in an effort to provide more flexibility and choice for students. Thus, its recommendations were more general and conceptual than had been hoped for by some. They recommended that the acquisition of the body of knowledge be spread throughout the school curriculum and integrated at appropriate levels in the basic scientific and clinical sequences. In the educational process, students should be assisted in differentiating their subjective feelings and objective data. The fact that students themselves very likely have experimented with some types of drugs and that some may be involved with ongoing use must be included in the presentation and assessment of any forthcoming curricula.

The multidimensionality of substance abuse behavior should be confronted early in the students' education. It is important to present a unifying conceptual model to accommodate the complex data. Most schools have appropriate overview courses in the first year, where such material logically could be introduced. Pharmacology courses themselves should go beyond simple therapeutic

uses of medically approved drugs to include pharmacokinetics, pharmacodynamics, toxicology, and behavioral effects of abused substances, such as alcohol and glue, as well as pharmaceuticals that are inappropriately self-administered. In the clinical phase of training, there should be adequate attention paid to the physician's role in the long term management of alcoholics and drug-dependent persons. At the same time, doctors should be knowledgeable about other resources available to these individuals.

Students should have some guidance in critical reading of the scientific literature on substance abuse. In this area, the quality of the vast literature varies greatly. The council went on to assert that it is also important to be aware of public attitudes, mores, local laws, and public policies as they bear upon substance abuse and the abuser. They recommended that societal attitudes and patterns of nonabusive use of various substances, both prescribed and nonprescribed, should be studied as the soil from which abuse takes root. Epidemiological patterns and demographic variables shed light on relevent socioeconomic and cultural factors. Longitudinal patterns require investigation, including substance abuse entry routes, career course, and alternative outcomes. Stereotypic models are clearly inappropriate. For example, entry routes to substance abuse may occur variously via social customs, self-medication, self-expression, criminal exploitation, and faulty prescription practices. The special importance of the latter route to physicians requires particular emphasis. Finally, future physicians must be vigilant to their own risk of abusing drugs from a combination of a potentially high pressured professional life plus their ready access to drugs.

The council's statement concluded by stressing the critical importance of communication skills. The doctor's knowledge is useless if he/she has not been taught the interview skills necessary for the effective exchange of information with the patient.

Toward the end of medical school education, opportunities must be made available to have integrating experiences, bringing together, it is hoped, all that which has gone before.

In the years that have followed this 1972 position statement, how well have medical schools complied with this prescription? In

1976, Pokorny et al. (33) conducted an extensive survey of substance abuse teaching at the medical school level. They obtained completed questionnaires from 105 of 112 medical schools and all nine osteopathic schools. Although no assessment of quality of education was obtained, the investigators measured the amount of required course time in the addictions as well as the availability of related electives. They found that teaching activities during all 4 years of medical school averaged 25.7 hours in the addictions, with a range of 0 to 126 hours. As a proportion of total teaching time, the substance abuse hours represented an average of 0.6 per cent. They found great variability in the number and types of electives and clinical assignments. Size of the school, existence of affiliated alcohol and drug abuse treatment programs, and the presence of a career teacher in the addictions were positively correlated with the number of required hours.

Several single reports have appeared describing either the over-all substance abuse educational program, special courses, electives, or clinical assignments within the medical school curriculum (20, 24, 25, 30, 45, 46). The Mount Sinai School of Medicine in New York City has developed an integrated, interdepartmental curriculum that covers the full 4 years (40). The educational objectives were divided into those that provided the minimum acceptable knowledge for all physicians and those that offered more detailed knowledge in the field. The former would be built into the required curriculum and the latter into elective courses. As a minimum, students were expected to learn about social and motivational determinants of substance abuse, basic clinical and behavioral pharmacology associated with psychotropic agents, medical and social consequences of abuse, and therapeutic alternatives. This body of knowledge would be covered within the first-year courses Introduction to Medicine and Behavioral Science, the second-year courses Community Medicine and Pharmacology, and the third-year clinical clerkships. First- and second-year students are offered electives in a broad range of related topics, such as Aspects of Narcotic Dependency, The Psychopathology and Psychodynamics of Addictive Disease, The Phenomenology of Alcoholism, and Analytic Toxicology. Fifteen per cent of the first-year students chose one of these electives. During the senior year, special clinical electives are available in detoxification units, methadone maintenance treatment clinics, and alcoholism programs.

No matter how sensitive curriculum committees may be to the importance of substance abuse education in medical school, they must not overlook this essential feature of providing experience in an established clinical setting. For example, at the University of Maryland Hospital, teaching is built around a clinical program carried out by professionally supervised alcoholism counselors who are assigned to every major inpatient service (3). Moreover, the University's Institute of Psychiatry and Human Behavior has developed an interdisciplinary program with the joint participation of the Schools of Medicine, Social Work, Nursing, Pharmacy, Law, and Dentistry. Students receive didactic instruction in their respective schools and then spend variable periods of time on field placement in the hospital.

In a 1977 report on a special 1-week course in substance abuse given during the latter half of the second year at the University of Nevada School of Medical Sciences (6), the authors found a heavy clinical emphasis, but the course was primarily didactic in nature. The teaching format varied, including lectures, audiovisual presentations, panel and small group discussions, and on-site field trips. Using instruments to assess attitude change, the investigators found statistically significant shifts toward less negative value judgments regarding abusers. Moreover, they found the students viewed their role as a physician to be more crucial than before the course in the treatment of the substance abuser.

Although it is encouraging that such attitudinal changes may be achieved through concentrated education, it remains to be seen whether statistically significant attitude changes as measured by questionnaires over a 1-week period will translate into practically significant changes in professional practice, withstanding the familiar erosion over the years (16).

At Maryland Medical School, during the first 2 years, students have 4 months in which to choose "mini-mester" electives (31). One very well received elective consists of 12 hours weekly for 4 weeks of supervised experience treating alcoholics and drug addicts.

The patients who participate are mostly volunteers from either an alcoholism halfway house or a methadone maintenance treatment program.

All in all, it is difficult to judge how responsive the medical education establishment as a whole has been to the recommendations of the AMA Council on Mental Health. The consensus is that real progress has been made, but that a generally acceptable level of training across medical schools has not been achieved. Recognition for leadership must be extended to the Career Teacher Training Program in Drug and Alcoholism Abuse (38). Under the joint sponsorship of the National Institute on Drug Abuse and the National Institute on Alcohol Abuse and Alcoholism, two centers have been set up: one at Baylor University School of Medicine and one at State University of New York, Downstate Medical Center. This group has generated a number of curricular guidelines, and, perhaps more importantly, it has sponsored and coordinated the activities of career teachers on the faculties of more than 40 medical schools.

There still remains considerable ambivalence in the medical community about the acceptance of alcohol and drug abuse as "diseases." Doctors have traditionally treated the somatic complications of substance abuse but have tended to view the pathological behavior itself as beyond the scope of their responsibility. Although this has been widely recognized, the focus by most leaders in the field has been on attitudes, biases, value judgments, and emotionally charged personal conflicts. This case has been well stated (27–29).

It seems that there is an important conceptual issue that receives less attention. For the most part, physicians consider *disease* in terms of the traditional biomedical model. So long as the substance abuser is biologically intact—before medical complications set in—the doctor's role in dealing with the problem, if it is acknowledged to exist at all, has been construed to be more as a "friend of the family" or a community authority figure than as a professional practitioner.

Partly in reaction to physicians' general neglect of substance abuse in its earlier phases, but also to reduce social and self-condemnation, leaders in the alcoholism field declared alcoholism a "disease." Definitions of *disease* from the dictionary as well as evidence for genetic factors and enzyme aberrations were cited to make the case.

Despite the worthy objectives of this crusade, the response from physicians has not been altogether favorable and indeed may backfire (22, 35). Bluntly stated, substance abuse, including alcoholism, cannot be adequately subsumed under the traditional biomedical model that is the "folk model" of medicine. In a penetrating analysis of conceptual issues, Bacon (2) wrote: "It is at least possible that much of the confusion and hostility as well as administrative and legal disagreements accompanying the 'disease concept' would be more effectively reduced by developing new classifications of alcoholism; both are probably requisite."

In his classic paper, "The Need for a New Medical Model: A Challenge for Biomedicine," George Engel introduced a modern illness paradigm based on a systems interactional model (14). Until medicine moves beyond linear, cause-effect thinking with automatic priority given to molecular processes, not only the addictions but the established "diseases," in which psychosocial factors almost invariably play important and reciprocal roles with biological factors, will be misunderstood and mishandled.

A final issue has to do, not with conceptual models, but with role models in medical education. The student may hear things in classrooms and have occasion to observe professionals in action on the periphery of medical care, but whether or not such learning—both cognitive and affective—will survive to graduation will depend on the extent to which it is congruent with actual practice as observed in the senior clinicians and faculty on the major medical services. Those who are most respected in the various departments for their clinical skills and professional prestige will constitute the primary role models. How these latter deal with substance abusers will be emulated, for better or worse. A commendable example has been set by a surgeon who operates on many alcoholics for portal hypertension (42). The fact that he has felt and acted on a strong commitment to make postoperative follow-ups and to assist the patients to abstain from alcohol permanently was regarded as exceptional enough to be newsworthy. It seems reasonable to hope that students studying under such a physician would regard it within their purview to identify, evaluate, and, where appropriate, treat alcoholics even before they develop advanced cirrhosis.

POSTGRADUATE TRAINING OF THE PHYSICIAN

THE NONPSYCHIATRIC PHYSICIAN

The high occupancy rate of general hospital beds—ranging between 20 and 50 per cent depending on location—by patients with alcohol and/or drug-related problems is now commonplace knowledge. Medical and surgical consequences of substance abuse, both direct and indirect, have long been well known. The birth of addicted babies and the more recently identified fetal alcohol syndrome (8) should make the issue of substance abuse in pregnant women a critical concern to both obstetricians and pediatricians. Moreover, pediatricians must now be concerned with possible serious substance abuse in preteen children. In the ambulatory setting, primary care physicians are being called on for personal counseling services. According to a survey of the members of the American Academy of Family Physicians, doctors were spending from 17.1 to 27.5 per cent of their practice time in personal counseling; less than 10 per cent of this time was used for problems with substance abuse (39). These facts might be expected to impel intense clinical, teaching, and research efforts in substance abuse during postgraduate medical training. Unfortunately, there is little evidence to bear out this expectation. Some of the barriers to hospitalization for alcoholics and drug abusers have been overcome in the past decade, but there is no question that residents-in-training are still being taught to address, almost exclusively, the somatic complications.

Some innovative efforts are beginning to appear. For example, at the St. Joseph Mercy Hospital in Ann Arbor, Michigan, the director recognized the problems inherent in having internal medicine residents see drug addicts only in an inpatient setting (5). Therefore, he arranged for them to go out once weekly to conduct initial medical examinations on new patients in an ambulatory, hard drug program, directed by ex-addict counselors under a community mental health center. The residents provided follow-up care on the patients they examined and attended monthly seminars led by the clinic staff. Despite a great deal of initial anxiety and hos-

tility on the part of the residents, 1 year and 200 examinations later, the program was regarded a success by all those involved.

The physicians on the front line, the family practitioners, are clearly the ones with the opportunity for the early detection and intervention of substance abuse. Therefore, their training is critical. An encouraging report comes from the Medical University of South Carolina, where a program was introduced to train family practice residents to work with alcoholic patients (17). One-hour sessions were scheduled twice monthly for 7 months. These dealt with problems of diagnosis, confrontation, intervention, and treatment. Pre- and posttesting of the residents demonstrated both cognitive learning and favorable attitudinal change. Most important, evidence of behavioral change was reflected in the increased diagnosis of alcohol abuse among the clinic population. Prior to the course, alcohol abuse was indicated in only 0.85 per cent (!) of outpatients. During the year of the course, the number of diagnosed cases doubled and continued to rise during the year after the course.

Continuing education programs represent another vehicle for teaching physicians about substance abuse, both to remediate deficient basic knowledge and to impart important new information. Physicians are increasingly being required to demonstrate continuing medical education to maintain their credentials. Although no statistics are yet available at this early stage, the preliminary impression is that credit courses in substance abuse are being sought out by many physicians, who are beginning to perceive the value and relevance of skills in this area. At least one suggested curriculum for such a course has been published (13). Although continuing education programs in medicine are still in an early and exploratory phase of their development, they would seem to be a promising means of updating knowledge and skills in treating substance abusers.

PSYCHIATRISTS

Psychiatrists, more than other physicians, have considered the primary behavioral disorder of the substance abuser a proper subject for their clinical attention. Moreover, services for such patients are mandated as part of federally sponsored community mental health centers (34). Nevertheless, substance abuse training in psychiatric residency programs has shown the same variability in the quantity and quality of didactic instruction and clinical supervision that has been evidenced in nonpsychiatric residencies. For the most part, psychiatric residents are taught to be alert to early and covert signs of substance abuse in patients presenting with other complaints; yet, inadequate factual knowledge coupled with negative attitudes often lead to inappropriate treatment, if indeed any treatment is offered at all.

Investigators at Boston City Hospital have contributed some timely and interesting reports on first-year psychiatric residents (15, 19, 32). Using adjective rating instruments, the researchers assessed an entering group of first-year residents for their attitudes toward substance abusers. Not unexpectedly, at the beginning of residency, their attitudes were somewhat negative—more so for drug addicts than for alcoholics. During the first year of training, the residents spent 2 months on an addiction detoxification unit and 10 months on a general psychiatric ward, where they treated a subpopulation of substance abusers. When retested at the end of the year, residents' attitudes had changed as follows: addicts were seen as less in control of their disorder; social factors were seen as proportionately more important; and periodic abuse was more likely to be regarded as pathological. How to interpret these changes is not clear. They may be construed as movement toward a more accurate perception of the problem as a medical one, or attitudes of personal distaste and pessimism over treatability may have become even more entrenched. In any event, the investigators recommend an initial survey as important to pinpoint those attitudes to which educational efforts must be directed.

To summarize, as long as the primary, if not exclusive, exposure of trainees to substance abuse remains on detoxification units, emergency rooms, and wards for acute disease, the likelihood of inculcating therapeutic attitudes seems slow. Such exposure is skewed toward cases that are far advanced in terms of biological, psychological, and social pathology. It is analogous to attending to only advanced cancer patients. The obstacles to effective teaching cannot be overcome by the simple application of vigorous efforts among training staff, as was attempted in one internship program (36). Formal didactic teaching

alone is also insufficient. As Knott (24) expressed it, formal teaching will "make only a transient and generally ineffective impression unless such information is accompanied by some type of structured action-oriented, patient-exposure program." Medical students, residents-in-training, and physicians in practice must be disabused of any single stereotypic model of the alcoholic, e.g., the skid row derelict. The same applies to other substance abusers. Accordingly, contact by medical students and residents with abusers who are acutely ill, out of control, or far advanced in their illness must be balanced with exposure to those others in rehabilitation programs in order to forestall or counteract the pervasive pessimism regarding treatability. As suggested above, even one visit to an Alcoholics Anonymous meeting can serve as some immunization against attitudes of therapeutic nihilism.

TRAINING ALLIED PROFESSIONALS AND OTHERS IN SUBSTANCE ABUSE

Therapeutic intervention for those who abuse drugs and alcohol must extend beyond the sphere of influence of physicians. Paraprofessionals, psychologists, social workers, nurses, teachers, guidance counselors, military personnel, clergy, law enforcers, and industry personnel all deal with the substance abuser, and all make decisions that ultimately play a role in the outcome of any treatment plan. How well prepared are the people in these allied professions to make informed decisions regarding this patient population?

A survey of course catalogues for five major graduate schools of social work[1] in the New York metropolitan area, five major graduate departments of psychology[2] in the same area, and the John Jay College of Criminal Justice in New York City reveals that formal academic training opportunities as they regard the treatment of substance abusers does not go beyond exposure to theory, usually subsumed, if at all, in such elective courses as Policy Issues in Addiction Services; Applied Psychology; Abnormal Psy-

[1] Yeshiva University, Hunter College, Columbia University, New York University, and Fordham University.
[2] Adelphi University, New York University, Teacher's College of Columbia University, Fordham University, and The New York School for Social Research.

chology; Psychosocial Pathology; Counseling Theories in Rehabilitation; Community Health Education; Drug Abuse, Alcoholism and Society—a Survey of Theory, Research, Treatment, and Policy.

Practical training is received typically by way of attending weekend workshops and by electing internships and traineeships on hospital wards and in clinics that serve alcoholics and drug abusers. Such patient populations may be themselves part of a broader psychiatric or forensic medical setting, thereby diluting the specialized training even further. Moreover, these training approaches tend to be situationally specific responses to particular community needs. These agencies represent an unintegrated system of psychiatric ward, state hospital, alcoholism clinic, halfway house, and methadone maintenance (and detoxification) treatment programs.

There seems to be a paucity of graduate training programs and academic courses devoted to the problems of addiction. An exception is Rutgers University, which offers a doctorate in psychology with special concentration in alcoholism. For the most part, however, students who select clinical specialties are not trained in school beyond contemporary psychological theories regarding etiology and treatment—usually covered within some general course in psychopathology—the content of which varies according to the interests and knowledge of individual instructors.

Garvin (18), in his review of social work education in alcoholism, isolates some of the problems that confirm what seems to be a lack of integration and concentration of training for those who wish to do case work within alcoholic populations. Among the problems mentioned are: "1. Students seeking a deeper exploration of alcoholism . . . than that available in general-survey courses do not have such an option. 2. There are no field placements currently being utilized that focus largely or entirely upon alcoholism. 3. There is no information on whether faculty are presenting current material on alcoholism even when they are disposed to deal with the topic. 4. There is no integration among the theory, methods, and resources courses to insure that major gaps do not exist." This situation has been mitigated only slightly in the 10 years since Garvin's report. He goes on to suggest that the implication of his findings is that, although virtually all social work

students go on to deal with substance abuse problems as one of the major issues occurring in almost all social welfare agencies, their education in this topic may be quite limited. Of course, such a system generated pessimism among social workers and may be communicated to their clients, interfering with successful treatment.

This state of affairs seems to be characteristic for graduate training in psychology, and, to a lesser degree, in nursing. Burton (4) discussed nursing education in alcoholism. In her sample survey of nursing schools in the Philadelphia area, she found tremendous variation of focus from school to school. In general, the findings showed that, in terms of credit hours, training in the treatment of the alcoholic patient represents quite a small percentage indeed. Moreover, such exposure was usually poorly coordinated and diffuse. Although orientation included the psychological, sociological, physiological, legal, and medical points of view, these various perspectives were not well integrated. Burton went on to suggest those topics germinal to a well rounded training sequence in alcoholism. They include: operational definitions of the problem, etiology, medical intervention, psychological treatment, social work intervention, spiritual ramifications, counseling techniques, family education, community support services, and clinical experience.

Waring (43) described a successful training program for administrative and management-level social workers and nurses. The program included an 8-week, on-site intensive schedule; with a daily 3-hour seminar/lecture series, visits to alcoholism intervention facilities, field observations of cross-cultural social drinking behavior, and supervised practica both in clinical and community intervention. Content areas focused on strategies for behavior change, politics of planning, resource acquisition, and program evaluation.

Heinemann and Estes (21) outlined a program in alcoholism nursing effectively in force at the University of Washington School of Nursing. This program is separate and distinct from the standard offerings of the University's School of Nursing, with its own admissions policy and with separate faculty. The program was designed as an attempt to answer the need for a comprehensive understanding in the treatment of alcoholism in all its complexities. The program includes three models of study—substantive, integrated, and independent. The first concentrates on physiological and psychological aspects of alcoholism as a disease. Lectures, seminars, workshops, colloquia, and informal discussions are employed with this mode. The second mode, integrated study, deals with the interlocking of alcoholism with other diseases, e.g., cardiac, diabetes. In addition, comprehensive assessment techniques as they regard medical, psychological, and social issues are learned. Independent study, the third mode, involves student-initiated field study. Follow-up studies on 23 graduates of this program showed that the special training had been effective and that the students were using what they had learned (21).

Wehler and Hoffman (44) surveyed 29 paraprofessionals and 21 professionals working in alcoholism and drug treatment programs to determine the training needs therein. The two groups surveyed were (a) psychologists, nurses, social workers, clergymen, rehabilitation counselors; and (b) physicians. They found that the training needs of both groups were highly correlated ($r = +.66$, df = 44, p < .005). They asserted that any in-training program in alcoholism or drug abuse should be planned according to common needs and goals. Moreover, the findings suggest that such a program be interdisciplinary in nature.

Teaching modalities go beyond the traditional lecture/discussion, seminar, or practicum format wherein didactic theory and practice are presented. Innovative alternatives have been employed. Mandel (26) successfully taught health personnel and clinicians in the drug field. Essentially, the training employed simulation techniques involving role playing and psychodrama for those paraprofessionals who work with methadone patients, alcoholics, and other drug abusers. The training included a 5-day simulation period allowing clinicians to become patients, thereby generating experiences that facilitate empathy and insight in their work.

Researchers described a behavior modification training program that emphasizes self-control for staff paraprofessionals working with drug addicts (7). The program took place in ten 1½-hour sessions that included behavior modification theory as well as instruction in techniques of relaxation, desensitization, self-image improvement, behavior analysis, behavior control, assertive training, rational thinking, and how to set up and run similar behavior modification training programs for staff and patients. Since the training began at the New Jersey Neuropsychiatric Institute in November, 1971, a total of 898 staff members—mostly paraprofessionals working with addicts and alcoholics—and 2,021 patients have been trained in similar programs. Preliminary evaluation data have been promising, and participant responses have been enthusiastic (7).

Other investigators studied an attempt to combat the increase in chronic alcohol use among adolescents in a large metropolitan area (41). Community-based paraprofessionals were trained in behavior therapy and treated these adolescents and their families in the home. Preliminary evaluation of the program revealed encouraging results. The training supplied structure for the paraprofessionals' interventions with families and provided them with skills that were of use in ongoing community work. Evolving as one of the few common training emphases is the attention paid to attitude change among those who treat substance abusers. This trend is evidenced in the training of medical (6) and nonmedical personnel across settings and regions. Such changes tend to increase the likelihood that treatment will be more effective.

Kilty (23) analyzed the responses of graduate students, professional social workers, and community residents to scales measuring attitudes and beliefs about alcohol and alcoholism. He found that professionals tend to reflect the opinions and biases of the community within which they work. The thrust of his findings highlights the usefulness of the multidimensional model of attitude structure for comparing attitudes among different groups. The implication is that any training program for the treatment of alcoholics must address and attenuate those specific prejudices particular to a given community.

Curel (9) evaluated the effect of a 3-year specialized training program in alcoholism on opinions and attitude of trainees and faculty members at the University of Washington School of Nursing. He showed that the program influenced the attitudes and subsequent effectiveness of treatment in a positive direction among the trainees. They were found to be more accepting of alcoholism as a "disease," and an increased number of faculty believed alcoholism-related courses should be a part of the curriculum.

A word of caution about generalizing from

these positive findings is in order. Because items on attitude scales rarely meet the criteria for validity and reliability, studies that employ them often give the illusion of representing objective measurement, whereas in fact they remain subjective in nature.

Another caution is suggested by researchers who evaluated a 14-month training program for paraprofessional alcoholism counselors (37). The authors asserted:

A crucial question in education is whether those who are being trained benefit from their experience and become better equipped to take on the tasks for which they have been prepared. . . . Training for clinical tasks should also be measured in terms of its benefits to patients, the treatment agencies and the communities being served . . . (and) the rate of retention in treatment should be a major component in the evaluation of therapists.

In their study, the authors measured the impact of training on 16 paraprofessionals over a 14-month period. They found among them considerable differences in their success in keeping patients in treatment. Moreover, their attitudes did not vary over the course of the training. The implication is that improved clinical skills may be necessary but are not sufficient to ensure patient retention. The authors did not find this surprising, for they concluded that (37):

the counseling process is but one factor among many that determine whether patients drop out or remain in treatment. Other factors that influence the rate of retention include the patient's education and economic level, social stability, and the degree of coercion, and the nature of the treatment offered.

Counselor characteristics also affect outcomes. Age, sex, and interpersonal warmth all interact in accounting for success of treatment.

The most up-to-date and clearly the most comprehensive approach in substance abuse, perhaps in the world, is in force under the auspices of the National Institute on Drug Abuse (NIDA). NIDA was established by an act of Congress in 1972 (Public Law 92-255). The mandate was, in part, to establish a National Drug Abuse Training Center to develop, conduct, and support a full range of training functions for federal, state, and local government agencies. Training materials were to be provided for medical and paramedical personnel, treatment service workers, educators, and for the public at large.

The training was to center on drug abuse prevention, treatment, and rehabilitation methods.

Dendy (10) reported that the 1976 National Drug Abuse Treatment Utilization Survey (NDATUS) identified 60,000 drug abuse treatment workers of which 31,000 were full time paid staff. The number of physicians, including psychiatrists, totaled 4,000—only 600 of whom were full time. There were about 2,500 psychologists, over 3,000 social workers, and nearly 5,000 nurses. Therefore, the remaining workers in drug abuse clinics in the United States in 1976 were paraprofessionals, nearly 20,000 of whom were counselors. Nearly 23,000 more were administrative support personnel and vocational specialists, including clergy, technicians, student trainees, and pharmacists. The thrust of these statistics is that the backbone of drug treatment in this country is the nondegreed professional. Dendy concluded: "The NDATUS data dramatize the need for the training of drug abuse workers in an ongoing and systematic program."

Today, the National Training System (NTS) includes the National Drug Abuse Center for Training and Resource Development, the Career Development Center, five Regional Support Centers, the Medical Career Teachers Program, and the State Training Support Program (10).

According to Robert Detor, Director of Training for the Division of Substance Abuse Services, Bureau of Training and Resource Development (12), the NTS had to reach large numbers of people efficiently. Focus was on two separate and independent systems to answer the demand for comprehensive training. One system addressed the issues of who trains whom, where, when, and under what conditions. The second system addressed the development of course content, preparation, production, and distribution of training materials.

From 1973 to 1978, the NTS had produced more than 20 courses, ranging in duration from 27 to 50 hours. According to Detor, these courses tend to fall into four broad categories: skill development and process training; program development and management skills; technical development; and interpretation of federal regulations. Much time and effort went into the analysis of course development and delivery. This process is ongoing at regional and local levels, and new courses continue to be adopted and delivery techniques refined.

In New York State, the course of offerings includes (11): Adolescent Counseling, Assessment Interviewing for Treatment Planning, Advanced Workshop in Assessment Interviewing, Basic Management Skills, Clinical Supervision, Counselor Training: Short Term Client Systems, Advanced Counselor Training, Family Counseling, Group Therapy, Training of Trainers, Issues in Treatment of Woman Substance Abusers, Overview of Substance Abuse, Puerto Rican History and Culture, and Vocational Rehabilitation.

The course most relevent to our discussion is Training of Trainers, and it is herein presented in detail. The course manual describes 10 modules, each $3\frac{1}{2}$ hours, covering 5 days. The modules are: Introduction to Learning Theory: The Learner, Interpersonal Communication and the Group Process, From Needs Assessment to Behavioral Objectives, Designing Training Activities I, Designing Training Activities II, Small Group Presentations, Individual Presentations, Evaluation Techniques, Trainer Interventions, and Using Trainer Materials. The stated purpose of this course is to provide skill-building activities for beginning trainers in developing training design, delivering of content, and guiding learning in a group setting. The stated behavioral objectives include being able to: Identify four phases of the training process, identify the phases of group delivery, formulate training goals per given need, formulate training objectives per training goal, develop methods to attain behavioral objectives, design a training session with behavioral criteria, show a training technique to encourage participation, and design an evaluation measure.

Robert Detor (12) reported that "business is great!" In fact, courses are so full that student selection priorities had to be established. Those who are trained represent a wide range of medical, nonmedical, degreed, and nondegreed personnel. It seems that the efforts on a national level to train these groups in the treatment of substance abuse are making a difference and are continuing to grow and to meet the ever changing complexities of the problem at hand.

CONCLUSION

In view of the large and ever expanding body of knowledge in the field and the skills required, should there be a separate specialty for a substance abuse expert, call him what you will? In the opinion of the authors, such would actually constitute a retrogressive step. On the contrary, it is precisely the "generalists" in the various disciplines who need most to be sensitive, knowledgeable, and skillful in dealing with the substance abuser. In medicine, primary care physicians occupy a key position, and their effectiveness will depend upon the adequacy of their undergraduate and graduate medical training. The same holds true for the other professional disciplines. Specialization should take place only on the paraprofessional level, and we are speaking here of the alcoholism and drug abuse counselors, who are vital to rehabilitation programs. Although a categorical specialist in substance abuse is not recommended, an interdisciplinary approach is deemed essential to understand and deal with the heterogeneity of critical factors that contribute to the genesis of these disorders, their course, and response to various interventions. Although the start has been late, it is only hoped that the next 10 years will see a continuation and even an acceleration of the efforts that have begun.

References

1. American Medical Association, Council on Mental Health. Medical school education on abuse of alcohol and other psychoactive drugs. J.A.M.A. 219: 1746, 1972.
2. Bacon, S. D. Concepts. In *Alcohol and Alcohol Problems*, W. J. Filstead, editor, pp. 57–134. Cambridge, Mass., Ballinger, 1976.
3. Bosma, W. G. A. Brown University alcoholism conference on undergraduate education: Alcoholism in medical school. R. I. Med. J. 58:391, 1975.
4. Burton, G. Nursing education in alcoholism. Ann. N. Y. Acad. Sci. 178:48, 1971.
5. Carbeck, R. B. Involvement of medicine residents in a drug treatment program: An educational experience. Mich. Med. J. 72:277, 1973.
6. Chappel, J. N., Jordan, R. D., Treadway, B. J., and Miller, P. R. Substance abuse attitude changes in medical students. Am. J. Psychiatry 134:379, 1977.
7. Cheek, F. E., Tomarchio, T., Burtle, V., Moss, H., and McConnell, D. A behavior modification training program for staff working with drug addicts. Int. J. Addict. 10:1073, 1975.
8. Clarren, S. K., and Smith, D. W. The fetal alcohol syndrome. N. Engl. J. Med. 298:1063, 1978.
9. Curel, M. An alcoholism training program: Its effects on trainees and faculty. Nurs. Res. 25:127, 1976.
10. Dendy, R. F. Developments in training. In *Handbook on Drug Abuse*, R. I. Dupont, A. Goldstein, and J. O'Donnell, editors, pp. 415–421. Washington, D.C., National Institute on Drug Abuse, 1978.
11. Department of Health, Education and Welfare. *Na-*

tional Manpower and Training System: Source Book: 1978–1979 (DHEW Publication #(ADM) 78–768). Washington, D.C., Department of Health, Education and Welfare, 1978.

12. Detor, R. E. Personal communication: Taped interview, New York City, May 24, 1979.

13. Einstein, S. Drug abuse training and education: The physician. Int. J. Addict. 9:81, 1974.

14. Engel, G. L. The need for a new medical model: A challenge for biomedicine. Science 196:129, 1977.

15. Ferneau, E., and Gertler, R. Attitudes regarding alcoholism: Effect of the first year of the psychiatric residency. Br. J. Addict. 66:257, 1971.

16. Fisher, J. C., Mason, R. L., Keeley, K. A., and Fisher, J. V. Physicians and alcoholics: The effect of medical training on attitudes. J. Stud. Alcohol 36:949, 1975.

17. Fisher, J. V., Fisher, J. C., and Mason, R. L. Physicians and alcoholics: Modifying behavior and attitudes of family practice residents. J. Stud. Alcohol 37:1686, 1976.

18. Garvin, C. Social work education in alcoholism. Ann. N. Y. Acad. Sci. 178:52, 1971.

19. Gertler, R., and Ferneau, E. W. Attitudes regarding drug abuse and the drug abuser: Effect of first-year of the psychiatry residency. Br. J. Addict. 69:371, 1974.

20. Gross, G. A. Training the medical student in alcoholism therapy. Ann. N. Y. Acad. Sci. 273:433, 1976.

21. Heinemann, M. E., and Estes, N. J. A program in alcoholism nursing. Nurs. Outlook 22:575, 1974.

22. Kaunitz, P. A. On the other hand (editorial). Med. World News 124, November 8, 1974.

23. Kilty, K. M. Attitudes toward alcohol and alcoholism among professionals and nonprofessionals. J. Stud. Alcohol 36:327, 1975.

24. Knott, D. H. The program at the University of Tennessee College of Medicine. Ann. N. Y. Acad. Sci. 178:35, 1971.

25. Kurzman, M. G. First do no harm. Minn. Med. 56:217, 1973.

26. Mandel, H. R. Simulations in drug training. Am. J. Drug Alcohol Abuse 2:215, 1975.

27. Mendelson, J. H., and Hyde, A. P. Alcoholism training in medical schools: Some pedagogical and attitudinal issues. Ann. N. Y. Acad. Sci. 178:66, 1971.

28. Mendelson, J. H., Wexler, D., and Kubzansky, P. E. Physicians' attitudes toward alcoholic patients. Arch. Gen. Psychiatry 11:392, 1964.

29. Mogar, R. E., Helm, S. T., and Snedecker, M. R. Staff attitudes toward the alcoholic patient. Arch. Gen. Psychiatry 21:444, 1969.

30. Morgan, J. P., and Weintraub, M. A course on the social functions of prescription drugs: Seminar syllabus and bibliography. Ann. Int. Med. 77:217, 1972.

31. O'Donnell, J. J. An alcohol and drug abuse minimester model in a medical school. Md. State Med. J. 26:31, 1977.

32. Patch, V., and Ferneau, E. Attitudes regarding alcoholism: The first-year psychiatric resident. Br. J. Addict. 65:195, 1970.

33. Pokorny, A., Putnam, P., and Fryer, J. Drug abuse and alcoholism teaching in U. S. medical and osteopathic schools. J. Med. Educ. 53:816, 824, 1978.

34. Public Law 95-622, 95th Congress. The Community Mental Health Centers Extension Act of 1978.

35. Ragan, C. A., Jr. Alternative approaches to our alcohol problem. Resident Staff Phys. 9:9, 1976.

36. Reynolds, R. E., and Rice, T. W. Attitudes of medical interns toward patients and health professionals. J. Health and Soc. Behav. 12:307, 1971.

37. Rosenberg, C. M., Gerrin, J. R., Manohar, V., and Liftik, J. Evaluation of training alcoholism counselors. J. Stud. Alcohol 37:1236, 1976.

38. Solomon, J., and Davis, D. An update on medical education in alcohol and drug abuse. J. Med. Educ. 53:604, 1978.

39. Stanford, B. J. Counseling: A prime area for family doctors. Am. Fam. Phys. 5:183, 1972.

40. Stimmel, B. The development of a curriculum in drug dependency. J. Med. Educ. 49:158, 1974.

41. Teicher, J. D., Sinay, R. D., and Stumphauzer, J. S. Training community-based paraprofessionals as behavior therapists with families of alcohol-abusing adolescents. Am. J. Psychiatry 133:847, 1976.

42. The surgeon who counsels alcoholics. Med. World News 31, October 20, 1975.

43. Waring, M. L. The impact of specialized training in alcoholism on management-level professionals. J. Stud. Alcohol 36:406, 1975.

44. Wehler, R., and Hoffmann, H. Training needs of paraprofessionals and professionals in the treatment of alcoholism. Psychol. Rep. 41:1093, 1977.

45. Whitfield, C. L. Alcoholism education: Early development and coordination at a new medical school. Md. State Med. J. 24:87, 1975.

46. Willard, W. R. Luncheon address: Medical education and the problem of alcoholism. Ann. N. Y. Acad. Sci. 178:17, 1971.

CHAPTER 67

CREDENTIALING AND CERTIFICATION OF DRUG ABUSE WORKERS: A REVIEW AND STATE OF THE ART REPORT

Lonnie E. Mitchell, Ph.D.

AN OVERVIEW

The subject of credentialing, or the certification of drug abuse workers, is one that has attracted a great deal of attention during the past 6 or 7 years. There are many factors that contribute to this accelerated interest. There are also many factors that tend to make this subject complex. Before we begin to sort out some of the issues, a brief review of the context in which programs and efforts have been developed would be appropriate.

In 1971, the Department of Health, Education, and Welfare (HEW) submitted to Congress its *Report on Licensure and Related Health Personnel Credentialing* (3) with a set of far reaching recommendations for alleviating the critical problems associated with health manpower credentialing. A major recommendation of the report urged the states to observe a 2-year moratorium on the licensure of additional categories of health manpower so that alternative and improved credentialing mechanisms could be explored. In the 1973 follow-up report, *Developments in Health Manpower Licensure* (2), the moratorium recommendation was extended for an additional 2-year period—through 1975—to provide further time for examining options.

These two reports were circulated to the appropriate agencies and institutions, including the states. They received national visibility and generated a number of studies and other activities related to credentialing. Furthermore, the department, since 1971, has become a focal point for credentialing matters, and many national and state organizations have sought the department's consultation in relation to proposed improvements in the credentialing system. These organizations have also expressed much interest in the HEW position on credentialing after termination of the moratorium period. The Manpower and Training Branch, Division of Resource Development, in the National Institute on Drug Abuse (NIDA), has been the initiator of efforts in this area for the drug abuse interest.

To address these issues in a systematic and continuing manner, and to assist in developing a new departmental position in the aftermath of the moratorium, a Subcommittee on Health Manpower Credentialing was established under the aegis of the Public Health

Service (PHS) Health Manpower Coordinating Committee. This subcommittee, chaired by Dr. Harris S. Cohen of the Office of the Assistant Secretary for Health, included representatives of each of the PHS agencies concerned with health manpower. It reviewed the department's numerous credentialing projects conducted since 1971 and considered a broad range of options for future departmental action. Based on this review, as well as an in-depth study and analysis of the appropriate federal role in this area, the subcommittee developed a report that contained a number of proposals with accompanying narrative.

The HEW committee studies indicated that state licensure of the health occupations fostered a patchwork system of varying requirements, responsibilities, and controls that tended to overemphasize formal education and other input measures for entry into a profession at the expense of assuring continued competence throughout one's professional career. In many respects, the licensing boards functioned as formal extensions of state professional associations, bearing little resemblance to regulatory bodies designed to protect vigorously the public health and safety. Other studies confirmed that formal disciplinary procedures available to boards are rarely put to use, and then only in the most exaggerated cases.

According to the HEW report (2):

there is little agreement, at this time, on the best or even appropriate requirements. Thus, the States may very well exacerbate the already serious mobility situation in certain occupations by enacting variable Continuing Education requirements. In addition, there are basic conceptual problems in the area of Continuing Education that will require careful study and analysis. In the absence of this critical examination into the supposed relationship between Continuing Education and continued competence, the States' substantial involvement with mandatory Continuing Education may ultimately prove to be an inappropriate means of assuring professional competence.

Compounding this dilemma in the regulation of health manpower is the rapidly growing number of health occupations seeking and obtaining state licensure. This poses at least two problems: (a) a general proliferation of occupations and roles that can only contribute to inefficiencies in the health system; and (b) the development of arbitrary scopes of practice in fields that will be undergoing

substantial evolution over the next 5 to 10 years. Among the factors contributing to this situation is the assumption on the part of many health occupations that obtaining state licensure is in their best interests, and that only by prosecuting a vigorous political campaign in the state legislatures will they accomplish their objective. Accordingly, legislatures are frequently the setting of intense political battles over the issues of "to license or not to license," with decisions made not on the basis of whether an occupation *required* state licensure but on the basis of the relative political strengths of the actors involved.

In response to this set of findings, HEW, in 1971 and again in 1973, urged the states and health occupations to recognize a *moratorium* on any new legislation that would license a health occupation or role. Each of these moratorium recommendations was for a 2-year period; thus, the moratorium terminated at the end of 1975. The purpose of the moratorium, as spelled out in detail in the 1973 HEW Report (2), was to examine other alternatives for credentialing health manpower and to begin a fundamental reassessment of licensure as a primary method of social control in the field of health manpower.

During this time, the professions, the states, and the federal government initiated a number of critical studies and demonstrations in the general field of health manpower credentialing. Of particular interest are the HEW studies of the feasibility of *national certification* and *institutional licensure* as alternatives to the traditional model of occupational licensure in health. (These studies were specifically called for in the 1971 HEW Report (3).) On the basis of this work, the subcommittee has concluded that the certification alternative should be further developed, whereas the institutional licensure approach—because of the intense controversy that it generated—should not receive further consideration at this time.

EXISTING CREDENTIALING EFFORTS IN DRUG ABUSE: THE NIDA STATUS REPORT

Considerable confusion exists about accreditation, certification, licensure, or registration of staff in drug abuse agencies and about the accreditation of their programs. As the NIDA status report on credentialing will show, confusion exists at every level in all types of agencies, among staff, and does not seem to be improving. This confusion relates not only to accreditation, certification, licensure, and how these relate to each other, but also to the question of whether these traditional processes of identifying competent and qualified personnel can, in fact, improve the delivery of quality drug abuse services.

DEFINITIONS

In preliminary contacts with all levels of drug abuse staff, it quickly became apparent that "credentialing" terminology is used interchangeably and incorrectly. For clarity's sake, we chose generally accepted definitions and applied operational definitions to ensure the reader's understanding of the terminology used in our work.

In the publication, *Study of Accreditation of Selected Health Educational Programs* (SASHEP) (4), the four terms most crucial to an understanding of credentialing are defined as follows.

Accreditation. "The process by which an agency or organization evaluates and recognizes a program of study or an institution as meeting certain predetermined qualifications or standards. It shall apply only to institutions and their program of study or their services" (4).

Certification. "The process by which a nongovernmental agency or association grants recognition to an individual who has met certain predetermined qualifications specified by that agency or association" (4).

Licensure. "The process by which an agency of government grants permission to persons meeting predetermined qualifications to engage in a given occupation and/or use a particular title or grants permission to institutions to perform specified functions" (4).

Registration. "The process by which qualified individuals are listed on an official roster maintained by a governmental or nongovernmental agency" (4).

Our hypothesis assumes that any analysis of credentialing incorporates accreditation, certification and/or licensing, and registration efforts as they affect drug abuse workers, the service area, and service recipients—all of which, conversely, have an effect on credentialing efforts and process.

The credentialing process, then, has several interacting components. Each imposes on drug abuse staff, programs, and facilities various standards, guidelines, criteria, and regulations aimed at improving services to drug abusers. Each represents differing images to staff, usually in relation to their career level. As a result, changes are occurring at all levels. For example, in December, 1974, some 30 therapeutic communities in New York City refused to sign contracts with the Addiction Services Administration because of certain licensing requirements. Another example of the change that occurred is that the Joint Commission on Accreditation of Hospitals' new standards for drug abuse treatment services, for the first time, accredits "nonmedical" services.

Each credentialing mechanism poses both opportunity and potential chaos. As the SASHEP report stated (4):

There is now considerable confusion in the minds of both the professions and the public regarding the proper roles of accreditation, certification, and licensure, and their interrelationships to one another.

Some maintain that certification and licensing boards should demand graduation from an accredited program of study as a precondition for both certification and licensure; others claim that this requirement unduly bars from the health manpower pool.

CERTIFICATION

Certification is designed to recognize and assure the competency of individual practitioners to perform competently in their field of work. The certifying function is performed by professional associations or by agencies set up by the professions. Being certified by a professional group implies that an individual has met qualifying requirements, such as graduating from an accredited school, completing a certain number of years of work in the field, or both.

At present, many groups are searching for alternatives to the traditional method of certification. One such group is the consortium formed by the Office of Child Development to develop a performance-based assessment system to award the credential of Child Development Associate to persons who can competently provide services to children in child development centers. A similar effort is under way to provide credentials for counselors in the field of alcoholism. The National

Institute on Alcohol Abuse and Alcoholism is administering the formation of an advisory board to coordinate efforts to establish certification requirements for workers in the field. Unlike the CEA consortium, the advisory group, following traditional certification practices in establishing requirements for the emerging new profession, certified Alcohol Counselors.

Some fields of work have independent committees or registries that certify workers and maintain, and sometimes publish, lists of personnel who have become certified by passing an examination. Many of the registries were started by persons already working in the occupation who became certified under grandfather clauses. It is being suggested from many quarters that any registry for a new field should require people already working in the field to meet all requirements within specified periods of time.

The need to assure the competence of physicians providing services reimbursed by Medicare and Medicaid has led to a new type of certification process. It is carried out by the Professional Standards Review Organization (PSRO). Ultimately, the program will have a nation-wide network of PSRO's whose physician members will review, as peers, the competence of their colleagues in providing health services to the beneficiaries of HEW's third-party financing programs. Much controversy surrounds the establishment of this peer review program, particularly over the provision that, if the peer review does not proceed satisfactorily, review will be conducted by the Foundation for Medical Care. The PSRO is an experiment designed to determine whether regulatory functions can be passed successfully from publicly accountable government institutions to private organizations.

Several issues must be faced in the consideration of any plans to certify workers in the field of drug abuse. Typical of these are the following:

Who Shall Certify?

There are several different modalities of service in the drug abuse field, and some programs are modeled after and organized in a fashion similar to health facilities, whereas others are operated as part of the criminal justice system. Can the same group provide certification for the many categories of workers employed in these programs? What groups in the drug abuse field might assume the certifying roles traditionally played by professional organizations and associations? The strategy of dropping all credentialing is being advocated by some practitioners. Others are suggesting that certification be provided by employing institutions, rather than professional organizations.

On What Basis Shall Certification Be Granted?

The field of drug abuse treatment lacks consensus on treatment and rehabilitation techniques, a fact that presents an obstacle for any credentialing effort. What standards of performance and methods of performance shall become the standards in the establishment of requirements for certification?

Why Certify?

Much confusion exists in the minds of the professions and the public regarding the roles of accreditation, certification, licensure, and their interrelationships. But certification, with a mechanism built in to involve the public, remains the best way found so far to protect the public interest. Recommendations are currently being made to include the public in certifying processes to ensure that these processes meet the need they were designed to meet.

The acceptance and certification of individuals as professionals remains a predominant issue among workers in the drug abuse field, one that is far from resolution.

LICENSING OF FACILITIES, PROGRAMS, AND PERSONNEL

The process of obtaining licensure of programs and facilities begins prior to a program's operation and continues through a number of steps to recertification. There are credentialing implications for drug abuse treatment and rehabilitation staff all along the way. For example, obtaining approval prior to operation from the state licensing agencies requires an explanation of the categories of staff to be employed and of the functions they will perform.

National policy has been formulated in the Drug Abuse Office and Treatment Act of 1972 to license or accredit drug program facilities and to expand state mental health programs in the area of drug abuse. Regulations for drug facilities receiving grants from the government include requirements for meeting minimum standards for maintenance and operation of facilities and a description of methods for licensing or accrediting the facilities. NIDA has issued guidelines to assist Single State Agencies in helping drug programs become eligible for licensing.

Licensure of personnel in the drug abuse field is well along the way. Because of the rapid proliferation of new job categories in the health field and the confusion and cumbersomeness that has resulted from it, a 2-year moratorium, as noted earlier, on state legislation to establish new categories of professional licensure for the health disciplines was begun in 1971. By the end of the moratorium, the HEW Assistant Secretary for Health noted that more time was needed to assess further the directions in licensure being taken by state legislatures, licensing boards, professional organizations, and the educational community. Some rational policies for licensure are being established. Consensus in this has not yet happened.

Attempts to coordinate state licensing efforts within individual states have met with some success; needs for clarification still exist from one locality to another with respect to job titles and descriptions and licensure procedures.

There are few licensing requirements in the states, the District of Columbia, or the territories for drug abuse or addicting substances staff. NIDA initiated a study of the licensure of drug abuse staff in nine states. It was found at the time that the only mental health/addicting substances-related job titles now licensed in any state are the psychiatric technician in California and the psychiatric attendant in California, Arkansas, and Michigan.

Many issues must be resolved before licensing of workers or programs can become commonplace throughout the country. These include: (a) Should generic or specific job titles be used? (Drug abuse counselor versus counselor?). (b) The need for an over-all policy formulated by the Alcohol, Drug Abuse, and Mental Health Administration concerning the credentialing of drug abuse, alcoholism, and mental health workers. The licensing of workers in the three areas might be easier to achieve if there were over-all coordination of the activities to prevent duplication, confusion, confusion in titles, etc.

In thinking through components of a model credentialing system, two issues must be considered: (a) the licensure and continuation of "elitism" in current licensing practices and (b) whether licensing of drug abuse workers should occur at all. The moratorium on licensure activities in the states that was called by HEW reflected the growing concern about relationships between "pseudogovernmental" credentialing groups and their impact on licensure. Many writers have pointed out the power concentrated in the licensing bodies and the need for the effective public sector counterpart. The government is viewed by many as an enforcer upon the public in behalf of the professions: they urge the involvement of the public sector in credentialing practices.

Many writers are raising the question: Why license at all? They suggest that licensure does not serve as an effective method for assuring high quality health services. Licensed professions have strong, if not absolute, control over the composition of licensure boards that often emphasize keeping outsiders out. And by merely paying a renewal fee, an individual—who may not be a competent practitioner—can maintain his or her licensure for life.

Because of the confusion about licensing and widespread dissatisfaction with current practice, the drug abuse industry faces a crucial question in deciding whether and how to press for licensure of workers in the field.

ACCREDITATION

Accreditation is the voluntary process conducted by an organization, agency, or institution to evaluate a program of services or a program of study and/or the facilities in which the programs operate to determine whether they meet predetermined qualifications or standards.

In health and mental health, the primary accrediting body is the Joint Commission on Accreditation of Hospitals (JCAH) and its affiliate, the Accreditation Council for Psychiatric Facilities (ACPF). Some groups have charged that accrediting bodies such as these are too powerful and actually serve as much to keep some institutions and programs from being accredited as they do to assist in the process. JCAH and ACPF rely primarily on processes of institutional self-study to obtain information about a program's success in meeting of required standards. The Joint Commission has approved standards for components of alcohol and drug programs and is presently working to establish standards for community health centers.

The Bureau of Quality Assurance (BQA) of HEW has basic responsibility for approving health services and facilities for eligibility for Medicare and Medicaid reimbursement for services. BQA provides funds to a Medical Assistance Office in each state to conduct on-site evaluations of programs already approved by the State Medical Assistance Office that apply for eligibility. Program evaluations are conducted by surveyors, usually from the state health department. Once a program has been approved, it is said to have "provider status."

New regulations for intermediate care facilities under Title XIX of the Social Security Act were published in 1974; drug abuse programs can be eligible for payment under these regulations.

Drug programs, like all other types of health care facilities, are preparing for third-party reimbursement under national health insurance. They are beginning to deal with issues such as the following.

1. Types of Services Provided. The JCAH/ACPF "Standards of Providing Drug Abuse Treatment and Rehabilitation Services" provide the possibility for reimbursement to four service areas. Because no third-party insuror will reimburse an unaccredited program, it is extremely important that the JCAH standards be made public and that programs begin the process of becoming accredited.

2. Types of Services That Can Be Reimbursed. Because of the lack of definitive guidelines on what constitutes generally acceptable therapy in drug programs and differing definitions by different insurors of what constitutes therapy, many details will have to be worked out for drug programs to receive reimbursement. Few programs have made an effort to obtain reimbursement (some have resisted such a move), and many, if not most, private insurance companies either prohibit or severely limit availability of coverage for treatment of drug abusers. Furthermore, drug programs provide much chronic care, which is rarely reimbursable,

and the nature of their treatment regimen may exceed time limits of insurance companies.

3. Providers of Service. The potential for accrediting programs that are not directed by physicians or not structured after medical models has not been tested. Who provides services becomes an issue not only from a perspective of competency but from a "who-gets-paid-what?" perspective. Although it may be possible to receive reimbursement for an hour's therapy provided by a psychiatrist, will it be possible to receive coverage for an hour's therapy provided by a well qualified ex-addict? Until agreements can be reached that clearly define roles and functions of different categories of service providers, insurance companies will be understandably resistant to reimbursing drug abuse services.

4. Where Services Are Provided. To qualify for reimbursement, drug programs will have to meet facilities standards. It is unclear whether therapeutic communities, for example, will be able to meet standards that require substantial outlays of money—such as standards governing number, location, and specifications for exits, corridors, and stairs.

Resolution of such issues will not be easily or quickly done. Much effort must be directed toward agreement on standards for accreditation of programs and services within the drug abuse field.

CIVIL SERVICE MERIT SYSTEMS

In effect, the civil service merit systems, operating within state, local, or federal jurisdictions, function as autonomous credentialing systems for civilian employees. Designed to prevent the inequities that can exist in a patronage system, they establish positions in government service and establish qualifications for entry, job specifications, and compensation.

Data were obtained on 39 Single State Agencies (SSA's) pertaining to licensing requirements in the various states. A wide variation was found in the position of the SSA's in the bureaucratic hierarchies. For example, some were created directly from state legislation and granted specific duties; in other states, the SSA was placed within the Department of Health or Department of Mental Health, thus giving the department over-all responsibility for state activities related to drug abuse. Some of the agencies define their purpose as dealing with drugs and alcohol, some with drugs alone, and some with addictive substances in general. Some of the SSA's report directly or indirectly to the governor or are situated within divisions of executive departments, but most are subject to departments that have responsibilities as varied as mental health and public welfare.

In most states, drug program licensing authority lies in the state Department of Health or Department of Mental Health. At the time of our study, 13 of the reporting states indicated that they had no mandatory licensing of drug programs. In many states, all modalities must be licensed, but fewer than half of these have developed regulations or standards for licensing. In most states, a few positions within the drug field—usually at the administrative level—are included within the state civil service merit system, but none has a full scale sequence of jobs in civil service listing.

There is great variation from state to state in job titles and specifications, and no state has a completely developed series covering all positions in drug abuse programs. Many are unclear with respect to experience or education requirements. An examination of job descriptions prepared by the federal government agencies (Veterans Administration, United States Navy, etc.), state governments (36 Single State Agencies), and two local governments revealed the existence of more than 500 titles for jobs that could be performed in drug abuse agencies. In contrast, the Department of Labor's *Occupational Outlook Handbook* provides no descriptions for jobs in drug agencies; in fact, the only job categories in this manual that make any reference to drugs are in the field of pharmacy, even though more than 850 occupational areas and approximately 1,250-positions are described.

There is a total lack of uniformity among Single State Agencies, among the 3,800 civil service merit systems in the country, and among drug programs. Semantic differences complicate the matter—what differentiates a trainee from an aide varies from locality to locality, for example. Attitudes toward the employment of ex-addicts vary from place to place.

The diversity of jobs, on the one hand, and the failure of merit systems or occupational directories to consider the jobs in drug abuse agencies, on the other, points up the overwhelming need for developing standards, defining jobs, and reaching universal agreement on standards and requirements.

ACADEMIC CREDENTIALING

The effect of academic credentials on job entry and career advancement in the allied health fields is substantial. Professional associations traditionally have controlled entry into professions by establishing and regulating training standards, academic training programs, and the numbers of persons trained. Civil service merit systems, moreover, often specify levels of education for job entry.

An examination of responses from 36 state civil service merit systems regarding job requirements for drug workers shows that, although there is considerable variation from state to state, academic credentials provide the most direct access to a job. In general, a person with a bachelor's degree but no experience can start out at a middle-level counselor position, whereas a person without a bachelor's degree must work his or her way up from the bottom, completing several years of work experience for which no academic credit is earned.

In spite of growing public awareness that attainment of an educational degree is not necessarily related to job performance, trends in the organization and control of drug treatment and rehabilitation services will lead to an even greater emphasis on academic credentials in future years. Thus, any new credentialing model for drug workers, instead of ignoring academic credentials, will have to focus on the methods by which these credentials can be obtained. Innovative approaches to academic credentialing that might be considered for a credentialing model can be found in some of the newly developing continuing education programs; some of the features found in various combinations in these programs are off-campus courses, intensive study, open admissions, and credit for work or life experience.

Another trend in education that has particular relevance to a credentialing model for drug workers is the new emphasis on competency-based education. Examples of projects designed to link education/training to treatment requirements are the Middle-level Mental Health Workers project of the Southern Regional Education Board, the Institute on Substance Abuse Staff Training of San Joaquin County, California, and projects in allied health fields funded by HEW.

These alternative approaches fit in with NIDA's plans for a National Training System (NTS). The four principal organizational components of NTS include the National Resource Training Center, Regional Training Resource Centers, the Drug Abuse Career Development Center, and the Medical Education and Training Center. These components will carry out different features of a broad scale plan to develop education/training capability at the state level, through the provision of information and resource support. Specifically, NTS components will assess needs and will design and evaluate programs to meet these needs. The establishment of links between NTS education/training programs and accredited academic institutions is an important consideration.

The achievement of NIDA's academic credentialing objectives will depend on the ability of project personnel to overcome problems relating to linking training with accredited academic programs, ensuring access to academic programs, and linking training with treatment. Some of these problems include the difficulty of reaching consensus on the academic value of course study content and prior learning, possible resistance of drug workers to participation in an academic program, sparse sources for financing tuition, the difficulty of defining training needs, and the problem of balancing job-related instruction with a sufficiently broad educational base to enable upward and outward mobility.

PROFICIENCY TESTING

Proficiency exams are being developed in a growing number of allied health fields, as an alternative credentialing mechanism. Unlike equivalency exams that measure knowledge of a study area, proficiency exams are designed to measure task-related job knowledge.

To date, government agencies have funded projects that may lead to proficiency examination development for 20 or more job titles, but only four examinations are currently completed and in use. Most projects have been funded by agencies of HEW—including the Division of Associated Health Professions (DAHP), the Bureau of Quality Assurance (BQA), and the Bureau of Health Services Research (BHSR). Professional associations and practitioners have played an active role; their participation has been particularly encouraged by agencies hoping that an examination will have long range impact.

Both special purpose and general purpose examination projects have been funded. Most special purpose projects are conducted in response to legislation (Social Security Amendments of 1972, Public Law 92-603) that directs HEW to develop and conduct proficiency examinations for specified health occupations to enable workers not meeting traditional academic and training criteria to qualify for reimbursement of service fee under Medicare. General purpose examination projects are funded with a view to improving the quality of health care by establishing and measuring national standards of job proficiency. In addition, the examinations may be used in evaluating educational and training programs and identifying training needs of individual workers.

The main steps in examination development include task analysis (delineation of roles and functions), test design and validation, and test administration. Two types of validation may be performed: *internal validation*, to ascertain that the instrument measures what it is designed to measure, and *external validation*, to ascertain that what the instrument measures is actually related to job performance. Although professional groups rarely validate their training or certification examinations against job performance, proficiency examinations are not likely to be accepted by practitioners without such validation.

Proficiency testing fits the needs and requirements of a credentialing model for workers in the drug field to the extent that it is the most direct method of assessing job-related knowledge and is particularly appropriate to workers, such as those often found in drug programs, who have acquired job knowledge in nontraditional ways. However, potential problems in incorporating proficiency examinations into a credentialing model need to be considered. These potential problems include lack of consensus on treatment and rehabilitation techniques, diversity of roles and functions of drug workers, aspects of the backgrounds of drug workers, the difficulty of measuring affect, and the possible misuse of objective tests.

SUMMARY AND CONCLUSIONS

To understand more fully the phenomenon of credentialing in the services related to drug abuse, the major impediments to employment, promotion, and certification have to be identified. The former drug user is constrained by many problems, such as the potential effect of disclosure of information about his drug history; the disadvantaged position he is in with regard to educational qualifications; his unfamiliarity with sophisticated testing methods.

This chapter draws attention to the ways in which this situation has been changing recently. Public Law 92-225 establishes some significant safeguards against disclosure of confidential information about prior drug usage. The courts are increasingly eroding the traditional patterns of reliance on arrest records, IQ tests, and evidence of formal training or education (in jobs where these standards are not relevant). These trends are reinforced by the policies promulgated by governmental agencies, e.g., the Civil Service Commission and the Department of Labor. With assistance from such agencies as the Department of Labor, other organizations, e.g., the American Bar Association, have launched efforts to identify artificial or discriminatory impediments and alleviate them. In such endeavors, other groups are providing technical assistance, the American Civil Liberties Union, for instance. Local groups are attacking the problem from other axes, witness the Court Employment Project, providing counseling and vocational services for select defendants in New York City criminal courts.

The process is and must be a continuing one. Laws can be circumvented by administrative regulations. Regulations can be deliberately misinterpreted by personnel. But the impression of substantial progress is a clear one, and the language of the recent statutes should give pause to anyone inclined to violate these laws, especially the references to such consequences as "severe penalties . . . levied on the person making the wrongful disclosure."

The objective of all this effort is simple. It is to determine suitability for a job. In the words of the Civil Service Commission's handbook, it is to judge each rehabilitated applicant "on his own merit."

NIDA'S POSITION: THERE IS NO SINGLE ANSWER

The National Institute on Drug Abuse maintains its concern for the credentialing of drug workers for two reasons. First, persons receiving drug services deserve the highest quality of care. Second, the persons responsible for delivering that care should have the necessary competencies to deliver quality care. If these two concerns are met, then the traditional forms of credentialing, i.e., licensing and certification, become processes for recognition of competency.

All NIDA efforts around the implementation of credentialing efforts have been carried out on a partnership arrangement with states. The NIDA role has been to support the identification of job functions and the skills associated with these functions through a series of efforts involving a number of state-developed task forces. This was done under contract to University Research Corporation (URC) in 1975–1976, during which the functions performed by both drug and/or mental health workers were identified in states (seven states for drugs and six for mental health).

Because of the general nature of job functions, a further effort was necessary to identify the skills and knowledge needed to perform the functions. This activity was carried out under contract to the Medical College of Pennsylvania in 1976–1977. In this effort, six state task forces carried out task analyses of workers to identify skills related to various job functions. Six additional states and a special minority task force reviewed the task analysis data for accuracy and validity.

All task forces included a number of program levels from state employees to direct service deliveries, as well as underserved populations (women and racial/ethnic minorities). The result of this contract effort included: a listing of job functions; task descriptors (skills) related to a large number of the functions identified; and a series of implementation models for using the functional/skill data. These products were immediately distributed to every state agency, and a program for training and technical assistance to states in the use of these materials was established through a work order agreement with Stanford Research International.

It must be stressed at this point that the utilization of the function/skill data involves much more than state establishment of a certification/licensing program.

The models outlined involve: staff development through career ladders and performance evaluation programs; program evaluation procedures through specification of service functions; training and education evaluation through specification of job skills; development of alternative measures/demonstrations of job skills, such as portfolios and simulations; and possibly certification programs that relate more closely to job skills than formal academic preparation. The final users of the function/skill products will depend upon the structure of the state agency. The implementation of these models offer the basis for NIDA's current credentialing priorities.

PRIORITY ISSUES

The National Institute on Drug Abuse efforts in credentialing focus on three priority areas: credentialing models, demonstration of job competencies, and reciprocity among state credentialing efforts. Each of these priorities focuses back to the primary concerns of quality care and worker competence. In its work with state agencies, NIDA serves the role of facilitator and convenor of task forces to deal with the issues of reciprocity, information exchange, development of dem-onstration procedures, and minority concerns.

Credentialing efforts that seek to impact upon the two primary concerns of NIDA will be relatively unique to each state. However, the function/skill data will serve as a common base on which state efforts can build. As has already been seen, even states with existing credentialing programs can make use of the data to improve further the relationship of their credentialing to actual service delivery. The sharing of existing state efforts through the various task forces will minimize duplication of efforts, establish a common data basis for model implementation, and ensure that mechanisms for reciprocity are established. There is no single answer to the delivery of quality care.

There is no single way for individuals to develop and demonstrate their job competence. An ongoing process, including communication, exchange of resources, and refinement of program efforts, is necessary to the operation of the NIDA/state credentialing effort.

References

1. *A Proposal for Credentialing Health Manpower.* Washington, D.C., Department of Health, Education and Welfare, Public Health Service, Health-Services Administration, 1976.
2. *Developments in Health Manpower Licensure* (DHEW Publication No. (HRA) 74-3101). Washington, D.C., Department of Health, Education and Welfare, 1973.
3. *Report on Licensure and Related Health Personnel Credentialing* (DHEW Publication No. (HSM) 72-11). Washington, D.C., Department of Health, Education and Welfare, 1971.
4. Study Commission. *Study of Accreditation of Selected Health Educational Programs* (SASHEP). Atlanta, National Commission on Accrediting, 1972.

PART 11

FUTURE OUTLOOK

CHAPTER 68

FUTURE PATTERNS OF SUBSTANCE ABUSE

Sidney Cohen, M.D.

THE RECENT PRESENT

If nothing else, the drug scene changes. In the past 20 years we have moved from a predominantly psychedelic movement of the early 1960's to the frenzied speed craze of the late 1960's. In retrospect, the 1960's represented the upswing, the stimulant phase of the cycle, to be followed by the downbeat, the sedative period of the 1970's. That decade began an upsurge of heroin usage, and, as that leveled off, a polydrug scene with depressant drugs clearly dominated the stimulants. What has just been said is, of course, a vast generalization, for the abuse of substances is a swirling, faddish panorama with countercurrents of cocaine use surging against the riptide of depressants.

In mid-1979, the following situation seemed to prevail (1). The basic intoxicants, alcohol and marihuana, continued to increase in usage with still younger age groups becoming involved, sometimes overinvolved. Heroin dependence seemed to have plateaued during the preceding few years at about a half million people. Tranquilizer and sleeping pill misuse and abuse remained essentially unchanged, as did the overuse of amphetamine and related compounds, the weight-reducing pills. Lysergic acid diethylamide (LSD) use may have been decreasing, whereas a more dubious hallucinogen, phencyclidine (PCP), was on the rise. The volatile

solvents waxed in popularity among certain juvenile groups and waned in others, not contributing significantly to the over-all national problem.

It was certain drugs, not certain drug classes, that peaked in popularity at that time. Phencyclidine has been mentioned. It has been defined as a dissociative anesthetic with a penchant to induce emergence delirium; alternatively, it has been called a hallucinogen with analgesic, amnesic, and neurological features. Its attractiveness seems to depend upon its easy availability, its reasonable price, and the rather pleasant low dose, disinhibited state. It is hard to believe that anyone is drawn to its ability to evoke intense depersonalization or a paranoid thought disorder at high doses.

Cocaine is another drug that has been coming on strongly. Although expensive and adulterated, its powerful euphoriant properties and hypervigilant state make it an alluring item. The volatile nitrites, amyl and isobutyl nitrites, have been enjoying a brisk popularity in certain circles. Although originally employed as sexual adjuncts, they are now also sniffed during nonsexual intervals for whatever lightheaded mood they induce (4).

So, although our latest cycle of the abuse of chemicals started as a psychedelic revolution that would solve all of our, and the world's, problems, if only we would all turn on, the 1970's degenerated into the decade of the downer. And in other respects the present does not look much prettier. The increasing youthfulness of those who require better living through synthetic chemistry, the growing popularity of the needle, and the intemperate consumption of any or all drugs together or sequentially are all signs of deterioration of the drug abuse story. It all seems to conform to a modification of Gresham's law that could be stated as "Inferior drugs will drive out better ones."

THE FUTURE

What next? What lies in the middle distance? What of the long term? An attempt to prognosticate future events on the basis of the incomplete data at hand and other, even more obscure, imponderables become hazardous and quite uncertain. Some informed guesses are possible for the immediate future simply by extrapolating from current trend lines. Beyond that, so much will depend upon factors outside the substance abuse field (like a major war or an economic collapse), or by unexpected detection or treatment breakthroughs, that considerable speculation will have to be permitted in this chapter.

THE NEAR FUTURE

The Nasal Trip

Although sniffing and snorting are ancient practices that had fallen into disuse, they have been resurrected in recent years. In addition to the venerable snuff insufflation, cocaine and high quality heroin have brought the inhalation of powdery materials back into style. Now a long list of materials are insufflated by recreational drug users. They include amphetamine, pemoline, phencyclidine, ketamine, yohimbine, and ginseng (10). The advantages of nasal absorption consist of rapid entry into the blood stream, no need for syringes, and the bypass of the liver and its detoxifying enzymes. The disadvantage of the nose as a route of absorption is the irritant effect upon the mucous membranes. Sores, ulcers, or, more rarely, septal perforations are possible consequences of intranasal instillation.

Liquids, gases, and smokes are inhaled through the nose or mouth, but most of their absorption takes place in the lung. The volatile solvents and aerosols are prime exam-ples. Amyl nitrite and related compounds should be included in this group. In addition, conventional anesthetics like ether are still occasionally sniffed outside of operating suites. The gases, nitrous oxide and carbon dioxide, are enjoying a relative degree of popularity, too. The number of psychoactive substances that can be effective when smoked is too large to be enumerated. Cannabis, tobacco, dimethyltryptamine, phencyclidine and other hallucinogens, high quality heroin, cocaine paste, and a wide variety of herbs are a few on the long list. Absorption via the lungs has the advantage of rapid onset of action and the evasion of hepatic metabolizing enzymes, at least on the first pass. Its disadvantages lie in the irritant effect of many substances on the bronchial membranes and in the potential for cancer production when coal tar-containing natural products are inhaled over long periods of time.

The increasing popularity of the nose as a transmission and absorption site will not wane. It is safer than the intravenous route and almost as effective. When a psychoactive drug is smoked, the dose can be titrated because the effects come on rapidly, and the desired level of intoxication can be maintained by additional "hits." Whether the nasal pathway is employed because it has symbolic sexual overtones is impossible to say.

The Chemical Transcendental State

The use of certain plants (theobotanicals) to achieve an out-of-the-body religious experience extends far back in human history. It has been suggested that our concept of God may have derived from the experiences of primitive men and women after the accidental or deliberate swallowing of hallucinogenic mushrooms, cacti, beans, roots, or leaves. At present only the peyote cactus and the psilocybe mushroom are used in a religious context in North America, but many other plants, including the fly agaric mushroom and certain varieties of morning glory seeds, have been consumed for sacramental purposes.

Now that synthetic chemists have provided us with long series of hallucinogenic compounds, much more potent and less nauseating than the naturally occurring plant materials, it is obvious that they will be rediscovered by enterprising groups searching for self-transcendence in the years to come. Just as strong efforts were made to establish new religions based on LSD as a sacrament, it is inevitable that the psychedelics of the future will intrigue and entrance some of their takers with similar results. The spontaneous and the chemical transcendental states are fairly similar (3). Differences exist, but both are impressive alterations of consciousness. Usually, the mystique of the new drug is an important feature of the mysticomimetic experience, but ancient nonpsychedelics, like alcohol, nitrous oxide, and opium, have produced similar peak experiences in prepared people. Who can tell whether such a visionary (hallucinatory) religion, chemically initiated, may not one day succeed? God in the test tube? With the right combinations of circumstances and personalities, it could happen here.

Drugs for Pleasure

As the culture goes, so does the drug scene. As we moved from a Puritan ethic to a playboy ethic, the concept of culture-alien, recreational drug use was resurrected (5). As we began discarding notions of delayed gratification, Judeo-Christian morality, and the primacy of the family, hedonic drug taking was not far behind. Unearned pleasure was once a sin; now it is a line of cocaine. Is this freedom or decadence? Perhaps the answer is neurophysiological rather than ethical. Repetitive stimulation of the nonspecific reward centers by a chemical eventually results in a diminution of the pleasurable feeling tone, so that more potent stimuli are needed to augment a waning emotional response. Furthermore, the biphasic quality of emotional response intervenes: for each amphetamine high there is a corresponding postamphetamine depression that requires amphetamine, and so on.

Nevertheless, unless this country becomes authoritarian or bankrupt, the drug problem will remain with us. The technologies to produce and deliver an assortment of chemicals to our urban centers, large and small, exceeds our supply reduction capability by far. Demand reduction, prevention, and treatment have not yet become decisive factors in the equasion.

The eternal search for euphoria continues. Some people believe that what this country needs is a safe, 5-cent euphoriant. Unfortunately, it is not that simple. No drug is without adverse effects. But more important, a consistent preoccupation with drug-induced pleasure states, especially during adolescence, can result in psychological maturation arrest. Techniques for coping with life stresses are not learned. This drawback of reliance on a chemical, however safe physically, is worth considering. Another consideration is the loss of personal freedom that comes with dependence on a substance in order to enjoy.

The societal implications are also worthy of study. The safe euphoriant could become an instrument of repression in a totalitarian society as described by Huxley in his *Brave New World* (7). The daily dose of soma kept the citizenry subdued and content. It was more effective than force in dealing with opposition and dissatisfaction.

Of course, the culturally approved euphoriants will remain with us, and the inherent disadvantages of being a tobacco-alcohol society will be no less burdensome in the future.

Relief from Distress

Perhaps the most common reason for taking mood-altering drugs under medical and nonmedical conditions is to obtain relief from tension, depression, and other noxious feelings. The self-treatment of unpleasures with a variety of mood modifiers will certainly continue for a long time to come. The old-fashioned notion of enduring or toughing out physical or psychological pain is fast becoming outdated.

Future societies do not seem to promise a less stressful existence to their citizens. It can be assumed that anxiety, depression, and their psychosomatic manifestations will continue as today—or even increase. Uncertainty, ambiquity, goallessness, and the failure of nerve will plague our descendants as they do us. Therefore, the acceptable and the unacceptable intoxicants will continue to be sought out.

There is, of course, the possibility that some future society will be designed free of the fears, tumult, and hopelessness of current civilizations. Perhaps, in addition, the education and training of its children will eliminate most of the infantile maladaptive responses that predispose to subsequent personality and affect disorders. If so, the searching out of psychotropic drugs among the emotionally immature and the neurophysiologically vulnerable may diminish. If indeed such a maturation of the human psyche comes to pass, then drug dependence, the ultimate loss of personal freedom, might wither away. But that scenario of the future is based more on hope than on realistic calculations of the way things will be.

A FUTURIST'S VIEW OF ALCOHOL

Although alcohol was originally developed as an agrarian, tribal, social enhancer, intoxicant, analgesic, and tranquilizer, it has succeeded exceedingly well in adapting to modern urban settings. All classes and races (not all religions) are involved, so that it comes close to being the universal solvent for human woes. Neither poverty nor affluence is a bar, in fact, these economic extremes seem to intensify problem drinking. It has, or will, displace the traditional kava in Polynesia and betel nut in the East Indies and is more than holding its own against the upsurge of cannabis use in the developed countries. One of every 10 drinkers is disabled either economically, socially, psychologically, or physically because of his ingestion of ethanol.

Assuming that this civilization continues to become increasingly complex and interlocking, will the use of alcoholic beverages persist? As increasing demands are made upon people for alertness and precision by advanced technologies, will alcohol intoxication become too disruptive to be permitted? Even now the price we pay for overdrinking is more than enough to solve our balance of payments and inflation problems. Nevertheless, there is no reason to believe that beverage alcohol will become obsolete; neither will it be interdicted in the coming centuries. It is not only deeply ingrained in the social matrix, it is a cost effective (although far from ideal) pacifier, relaxant, and disinhibitor. It helps people deal with the harsh scrape of reality, and in the world to come existence may be harsh indeed. It will be used to cope with the increasing impersonal and dehumanizing aspects of high technology societies. Admittedly, the aggressive and destructive aspects of drinking will have to be dealt with better than we have to date, but solutions can be found for these problems. So it would seem that alcohol or something like it will continue to be used into the indefinite future, especially if the trend to increasing time for leisure activities continues.

ANTIANXIETY AND SEDATIVE DRUGS

The tendency to supplant the more dangerous barbiturates and nonbarbiturate sedatives will continue (7). The benzodiazepines will be the preferred class of drugs for the treatment of anxiety and insomnia. It may be that the legitimate manufacture of barbiturates will eventually be discontinued. Street supplies will probably still be available, although in diminished quantity.

It would not be unreasonable to expect the development of new antianxiety compounds with an even more favorable therapeutic index than those in use. Such a development would only partially solve the problem of the abuse of hypnosedatives. Physical and psychological dependence and their combined use with alcohol will still pose problems to the user.

The desire to become sedated or intoxicated will remain, and we can expect continuing involvement with this group of drugs far into the future. Just as the search for a safe euphoriant can hardly succeed, the expectation that nontoxic anxiolytic drugs will be developed is not justified.

STIMULANTS

As indicated, cocaine is increasingly used, increasingly adulterated, and increasingly priced. These trends will continue. A recent development may preempt cocaine snorting, namely coca paste smoking. It has already become popular in some South American cities and has been introduced into the United States with claims that it exceeds alternative methods. Coca paste is the immediate precursor of cocaine and has all its advantages and disadvantages.

Amphetamine and amphetamine-like drugs do not seem to be as popular as in the past. Certainly, their intravenous use has subsided. The tightening of prescribing controls over amphetamine seems to have succeeded in reducing availability, although amphetamine can be readily homemade by mediocre chemists utilizing standard equipment. Methylphenidate (Ritalin) is sporadically being injected, snorted, swallowed, and smoked. Pemoline (Cylert) is infrequently abused. The weight control substances are a negligible problem.

Caffeine, as coffee, is used and overused as much as ever, and the practice is so common that it hardly rates as an abuse problem. This nonproblem will continue. However, increasing attention is being paid to the anxiety-producing effects of large amounts of caffeine or of small amounts in people sensitive to the drug. In summary, the stimulants, except for cocaine, are in a phase of reduced popularity, but it can be anticipated that their use will increase again.

TOBACCO

The actual rewards of the drug tobacco are so minimal that it seems difficult to believe that the smoking of the pyrrolytic products of *Nicotiana tabacum* will continue in coming years. This will be especially true if further proof of its harmfulness when used persistently is uncovered. Increasing population pressures may preempt the land now used for tobacco cultivation for food crops. Less dangerous oral-manual conditioning behaviors (cigarette placebos for example) will be developed for those who require such rewards. The cigarette placebo is almost here, now that nicotine and tars have been reduced to a fraction of their original content. The reinforcing capability of nicotine is undoubtedly making tobacco withdrawal one of the most difficult to accomplish permanently (8).

The remarkable change in attitudes toward public smoking, the effectiveness of many cigarette antipollution efforts, and the reduction of smoking in informed groups (only 20 per cent of doctors smoke, compared to 40 per cent of the adult population) make it possible to predict that it will diminish over the years. The only factor pointing in the opposite direction is the increased number of young women smokers.

HALLUCINOGENS

The ability of the hallucinogenics to evoke a chemical transcendental state has periodically attracted groups of people who wished to explore their inner space. Only a few such clusters need be named here. Le Club des Hachischins gathered in the old Hotel Pimodan in the Latin Quarter of Paris during the mid-19th century. Baudelaire, Dumas, Gautier, Moreau de Tours, and other artists and literati of the date ate hashish to seek their "artificial paradise." Weir Mitchell and Havelock Ellis at the beginning of this century wrote about their peyote adventures in ways that turned on small numbers of their more venturesome friends for a "taste of the infinite."

Our present drug scene may have started with the writings of Aldous Huxley, Gerald Heard, and Allan Watts during the 1950's and the 1960's after mescaline and LSD cleansed their "Doors of Perception" (7). There have been many other such clusters throughout history; many of them became theochemical religions like the Native American Church (peyote) or the psilocybe mushroom quasireligious rituals of the Zapotec Mexican Indians.

So it would be safe to suggest that the transcendental experience achieved with drugs will be rediscovered from time to time and place to place, and that charismatic spokesmen will generate followers who will evaluate the psychedelic state as highly desirable and meaningful.

Phencyclidine (PCP) is a hallucinogen with disturbing psychiatric, neurological, and behavioral features. Although the low dose effects are pleasantly disinhibiting, the multiple problems associated with higher dosages have produced prolonged psychoses, status epilepticus, unrestrained violence, and death. Because it is neither the safest nor the best dissociative agent, one may wonder why it is so popular in many parts of the country at this time. The answer is enlightening if future trends in drug usage are to be understood. PCP is readily available and cost effective. It is not the best, but it is here. The point is that availability is an important element in drug use. It is difficult to visualize a drug-free or a low drug-consuming society if it is flooded with low cost, mind-altering substances.

Phencyclidine has been said to be the first of a series of "pop" drugs that will keep coming forth as legislation tries vainly to catch up with reality. Although the behavioral toxicity generated by PCP is hardly new (remember the speedfreak phenomenon of 10 years ago), the message seems to be that some people will use anything to avoid being themselves. Phencyclidine has about 30 analogues that will make law making and control difficult to accomplish. Beyond these are hundreds of phenethylamine psychedelics still untouched by legislation.

NARCOTICS

Since 1973 the prevalence of heroin dependence has remained essentially unchanged, with only mild upward and downward swings (9). The steep rise that marked the preceding decade was halted partly on the basis of supply reduction and to some extent because many previous consumers left the marketplace after self-treatment or more formal treatment. At present the amount of heroin in the bag is at a low level, and the price per milligram is at its highest on record. Under such conditions some addicts are disinclined to use because the rewards of injecting heroin are not what they used to be. If this situation can be continued over the next few years, we should expect a further reduction in heroinism.

Other scenarios are equally likely. A renewed flow of supplies of heroin could reverse the picture. Synthetic opiates many times more potent than existing narcotics are capable of being synthesized by drug syndicate chemists. Further breakdowns in social and family cohesiveness, increased environmental dissonance, or a deterioration in the quality and quantity of treatment programs can lead to a reversal of the present standoff situation.

It should be recalled that potential worldwide supplies of opium remain very large, more than enough to support a few million heroin addicts in the United States. This is demonstrated by the fact that large numbers of heroin-dependent people now can be counted in countries like Burma, Thailand, and many countries in Western Europe. In these and other lands, the purity of the heroin is better and its cost is much less than in this country. The Southeast Asian countries have been confronted with a recent shift from traditional opium smoking to the intravenous injection of high quality heroin. World-wide, more heroin-dependent people exist than ever before.

So the future of opiate addiction in this country can hardly be predicted because of the multiple, intervening nondrug and drug-related variables that cannot be calculated now.

MARIHUANA

Prognosticating about cannabis is not as simple as it was only a few years ago. At that time state after state had decriminalized the possession of small amounts, and surveys showed an increasing public tolerance for its eventual legalization. More recently, a pause if not a reversal of the trend has occurred. A number of factors have produced this change of direction.

Until recently, the potency of marihuana as smoked in this country has been relatively low with a delta-9-tetrahydrocannabinol content of approximately 1 per cent. With the shift to more potent Colombian varieties, Thai sticks, and hashish, the material smoked is five to 10 times stronger now. In addition, consumers are tending to smoke more frequently, with daily use rising sharply and use throughout the waking hours not uncommon. Preteenagers have become increasingly involved during recent years. All of these factors, in addition to questions raised by researchers about the psychological, pulmonary, and endocrine effects of long term heavy use, will require a reevaluation of the advisability of legalizing cannabis.

With or without legalization, marihuana is now the third most widely used psychoactive substance (1) (omitting caffeine), and it continues on the increase in the age groups under 25. The distribution system is well established, and the trafficking operation has become a burgeoning growth industry. Without question, cannabis use will continue to increase even if certain adverse effects are eventually confirmed. It may achieve a de facto legalization when a sufficient critical mass of the citizenry has become regular users. Laws relating to usage and possession of modest amounts will not be energetically enforced, as is the case in certain areas now. Large scale sale, transportation, or smuggling will continue to be prosecuted. Single seizures of over 100 tons of marihuana have recently been made, indicating that the situation has completely changed from a decade ago when a few kilograms were considered large scale trafficking.

FUTURE PROGRAMS

Recently Dupont has summarized the possible future of drug abuse programs and policies (6). He made the following predictions insofar as treatment is concerned. Self-help groups for the drug abuser will emerge as a key partner in providing services, including those for tobacco. The more traditional health services will increase their involvement in the care of the drug dependent, especially the middle-class person. Family involvement in the treatment of the drug-dependent individual will increase. Prevention strategies will come forth that will have an impact on the situation. Dupont expects a differential attitude to emerge, so that preadolescent and adolescent substance abuse will meet with tougher attitudes than at present. Such sanctions would include the culturally approved recreational drugs, and they may permeate to drug usage by all age groups. In other words, he perceives a partial return to adult authority over children and a linkage of the antipollution trends with dysfunctional drug use prevention.

DISCUSSION

In the foreseeable future, large numbers of people will persist in dysfunctional drug use with a variety of psychochemicals. Patterns will surely change and new products will displace older ones, but the established intoxicants and euphoriants will continue to be in demand. The ability of synthetic chemists to improve on nature will serve to intensify the problem of drug dependence. The fact that they might, one day, supply us with nonaddicting narcotics and sedatives will do little to diminish the over-all problem of the abuse of substances.

We await the results of research with some hope—for example, the identification of receptor sites for opioids and benzodiazepines or the finding that a series of endogenous peptides with narcotic-like actions exist—but whether such research breakthroughs will somehow produce a sober society is quite dubious.

If we were to revert to the analogy of the 1960's, the "war on drugs" will continue with neither victory nor defeat in sight. We will continue to engage in a sort of trench warfare in which hard earned gains in one area will be cancelled out by losses in another sector. The tough, difficult battle will continue, and the final decision will remain in doubt for many years to come. Under the best circumstances, a significant amount of the substance abuse problem will remain with us; illicit drug use will never recede to the levels of 50 years ago.

A definitive return to more acceptable levels of drug abuse will have to be accompanied by improved methods of bringing up children. Parental authority within the context of caring will have to be reinstituted. The quality of life must become more meaningful for the young. Direction will have to be given and limits set without impairing initiative and goal direction. Physical and mental growth, not impairment, should be the goals to be achieved. Such a shift in adolescent values and growth is not impossible. It has happened before, and it is actually happening now, but on all too small a scale. The drug option can be made irrelevant for the young, providing alternative aspirations are learned.

Although much of this chapter has considered the pharmacological side of the equation, the human aspects are at least as important. We must recognize two human predicaments that make this epoch singularly vulnerable to the overuse of consciousness-changing chemicals. The first is the accelerated rate of change through which we are living. Profound revolutions in most aspects of life are occurring at rates never before experienced. There are true revolutions in communications, transportation, energy, sexuality, interpersonal and social relationships, and other facets of existence. Change is stress, and accelerated change produces intensified stress. It is hardly surprising that many people respond to the pressures of attempting to adapt to rapid changes and the consequent loss of roots by seeking chemical relief.

The second predicament confronting us is the loss of goals and values. Moral and ethical codes hardly exist. The established institutions that helped define social and personal behavior—family, church, and nation—no longer command the automatic respect and allegiance that they once did. Citizens seem to be more concerned with pleasure now than with delayed gratification. The work ethic is unraveling, and criminal activities are surely increasing. These tendencies and others provide the basis for a widespread dysphoria. Some call this an age of anxiety, others an age of depression. It is probably both. We have the pervasive feeling that the quality of one's life is not what it should be—or was. We suspect that we are existing in a decadent society. No matter whether this belief is correct or incorrect, the point is that, over-all, the populace is unhappy or, at least, not happy. Noxious feeling tones like anxiety and depression are difficult to endure, and nonmedical relief is sought out.

These two conditions that beset us—multiple revolutions and the loss of direction—are subject to improvement. It is by no means inevitable that the fabric of society will continue to unwind. The process is reversible. If it does, we can expect a reversal of our substance abuse problem.

References

1. Abelson, H. I., Fishburne, P. M., and Cisin, I. *National Survey on Drug Abuse: 1977* (Stock No. 017-024-00707-2), vol. I. Washington, D.C., Superintendent of Documents, United States Government Printing Office, 1977.
2. Blutt, M. J., and Cohen, S. Hypnotic drug therapy. Drug Abuse Alcohol. Rev. 1:1, 1978.
3. Cohen, S. *The Beyond Within: The LSD Story*, ed. 2. New York, Atheneum, 1967.
4. Cohen, S. Inhalant abuse: An overview of the problem. In *Review of Inhalants: From Euphoria to Dysfunction*, C. W. Sharp and M. L. Brehm, editors, NIDA Research Monograph 15, (Stock No. 017-024-00650-5). Washington, D.C., Superintendent of Documents, United States Government Printing Office, 1977.
5. Cohen, S. *Drug Use for Pleasure and Transcendental Experience*. Vol. I of *Encyclopedia of Bioethics*, W. T. Reich, editor. New York, Free Press, 1978.
6. Dupont, R. L. The future of drug abuse prevention. In *Handbook on Drug Abuse*, R. L. Dupont, A. Goldstein, and J. O'Donnell, editors. Washington, D.C., Superintendent of Documents, United States Government Printing Office, 1979.
7. Huxley, A. *Brave New World*. New York, Harper, 1964.
8. Jarvik, M. E. Biological factors underlying the smoking habit. In *Research on Smoking Behavior*, M. E. Jarvik, J. W. Cullen, E. R. Gritz, T. M. Vogt, and L. J. West, editors, NIDA Research Monograph 17 (Stock No. 017-024-00694-7). Washington, D.C., Superintendent of Documents, United States Government Printing Office, 1977.
9. Person, P. H., Retka, R. L., and Woodward, J. A. *A Method for Estimating Heroin Use Prevalence*, NIDA Technical Paper (Stock No. 017-024-00589-4). Washington, D.C., Superintendent of Documents, United States Government Printing Office, 1977.
10. Siegel, R. K. Street drugs 1977: Changing patterns of recreational use. Drug Abuse Alcohol. Rev. 1:1, 1978.

INDEX